France

THE ROUGH GUIDE

Rough Guide Credits

Text Editors:	Richard Trillo with Martin Dunford, Greg Ward and John Fisher
Series editor:	Mark Ellingham
Editorial:	Jonathan Buckley, Jules Brown, Graham Parker
Production:	Susanne Hillen, Andy Hilliard, Gail Jammy, Vivien Antwi, Melissa Flack, Alan Spicer
Finance:	Celia Crowley
Publicity:	Richard Trillo

A big thank you to the many readers of previous editions of this guide and our other France *Rough Guides* (*Paris, Brittany & Normandy, Provence & the Côte d'Azur*) who took the trouble to write in with their comments and suggestions: Mark Aldridge, AJB Allen, Lucy Barker, E. Barlow, Ina Bliss, Bronwyn Brady, Gary L Bratland, Andrea Brusch, Jane Burch, Trillium Burchell, Sarah Bushnell, Francesca Butterworth, Charles Gordan Clark, Jane Clarkson, Paul Commins, Nicola Corbett, Jennifer Dean, Lt. Cdr. CJ Denny, Andrew Dick, Beth and Jim Dooley, Liz Duthie, Charlie Fawell, Margaret Fisher, Sarah Fyfe, Sarah Gardner, Martin Garwood, Brian Gordon, Jonathan Harris, Carol Howarth, Alison Hughes, Clare Hyder, PN Ibberson, Alison Imrie, Alan Jeffreys, Susie Jolly, Susan Jones, Chris and Angela Kenny, Jean Kramer, David Leslie, Leslie Lindsay, Neil Lucock, Billy Macmillan and family, Lee Marshall, J Monnet, Stephen Moore, Andrew Neather, Nigel Newman, Michael Oldcorn, Lucia Osborn, David Parkin, Damien Parsonage, Alan Phipps, Jill Prime, Andrew Prosser, Nancy Reed, John D Renton, Bruce Rogers, Alan Smith, Michael Stafford, Nicholas Stainforth, Nadine Steel, Anne Stevenson, Cindy Taylor, Roberta Taylor, Zoë Thomas, Robbie Thomson, Elizabeth Veitch, Roberta Wedge, Marea Wendt, Marla Wendt, Derek Wilde, Fred van Woerkom, LJ Scott, Tim and Carrie Supple, Gilly Phillips, Anna Crane, RW Coleman, Mr & Mrs Alan Shaw, John Warrick, Judith Ford, M Whittacker, Clare Hayes, Anna Young, Peggy Redmond, Maria Hill, Rita Hughes, J Crockford, Rory Munro, Keith Moor, Fiona Spink, David Hemingway, Tara J Prayag, Tony Stoddart, Michael Feakes, Lynn Pierie, Alistair Martin, Liz Thomas, AF Duncan, CP Abraham, JM Goldbloom, Peter Huxford, Mike Poulard, Marie Bozzetti-Engstrom and Tim Youngs.

Please keep writing! The address is given on p. xi. We also want to thank Florica Kyriacopoulos and Peter Polish, without whose support this book could not have been written in the first place.

This edition originally published by Harrap Columbus 1992.
Reprinted 1992, twice in 1993 and February 1994 by Rough Guides Ltd, 1 Mercer Street, London WC2H 9QJ.

Distributed by the Penguin Group:

Penguin Books Ltd, 27 Wrights Lane, London W8 5TZ
Penguin Books USA Inc., 375 Hudson Street, New York 10014, USA
Penguin Books Australia Ltd, 487 Maroondah Highway, PO Box 257, Ringwood, Victoria 3134, Australia
Penguin Books Canada Ltd, 10 Alcorn Avenue, Toronto, Ontario, Canada M4V 1E4
Penguin Books (NZ) Ltd, 182–190 Wairau Road, Auckland 10, New Zealand

Originally published in the UK by Routledge & Kegan Paul (1986), and Harrap Columbus (1989 & 1992).
Previously published in the United States and Canada as *The Real Guide France*.

Typeset in Linotron Univers and Century Old Style to an original design by Andrew Oliver.
Printed in the United Kingdom by Cox and Wyman Ltd (Reading).
Illustrations in Part One and Part Three by Ed Briant.
Illustration on p.1 by Helen Manning; Illustration on p.772 by Jane Strother.

848p. Includes index.

A catalogue record for this book is available from the British Library.
ISBN 1–85828–050–8 (previously published in the UK by Harrap Columbus under ISBN 0–7471–0273–2).

France

THE ROUGH GUIDE

Written and researched by
Kate Baillie and Tim Salmon

With accounts by
Sharon Clay, Don Grisbrook, Paul Jenner,
Gordon McLachlan, Ann Rook, Robin Salmon,
Christine Smith and Greg Ward

Revised and updated with
Rob Humphreys and Rosie Ayliffe

THE ROUGH GUIDES

CONTENTS

Introduction viii

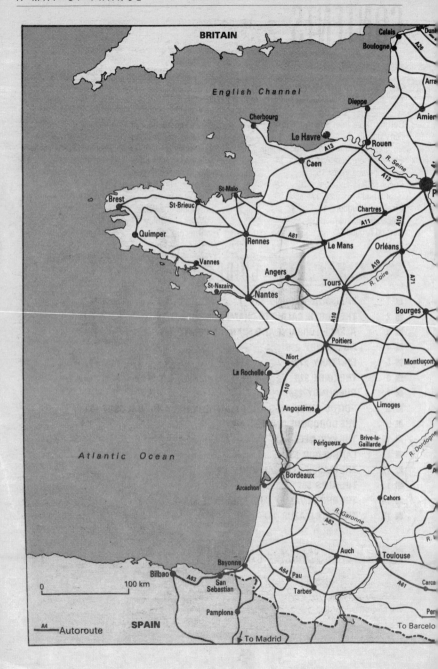

BRITAIN

English Channel

Calais
Dunk
Boulogne
Arra
Amien
Dieppe
Cherbourg
Le Havre
Rouen
Caen
R. Seine
A13
A13
P
St-Malo
Brest
St-Brieuc
Chartres
A11
A10
Quimper
Rennes
A81
Le Mans
Orléans
Vannes
Angers
Tours
A10
R. Loire
A71
St-Nazaire
Nantes
Bourges
A10
Poitiers
Niort
Montluçon
La Rochelle
A10
Angoulême
Limoges
Périgueux
Brive-la-Gaillarde
R. Dordogne
Atlantic Ocean
Bordeaux
Arcachon
Cahors
R. Garonne
A62
R.
Auch
Toulouse
Bayonne
A64
Pau
A61
Carca
Bilbao
A63
San Sebastian
Tarbes
Per
Pamplona
To Barcelo

0   100 km

A4 — Autoroute   SPAIN

To Madrid

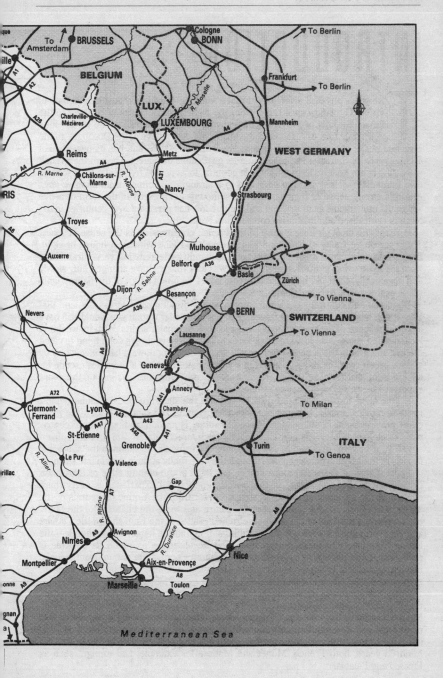

INTRODUCTION

The sheer physical diversity of France would be hard to exhaust in a lifetime of visits. The landscapes range from the fretted rocky coasts of Brittany to the limestone hills of Provence, the canyons of the Pyrenees to the picturesque Germanic hills of Alsace and the lushly wooded valleys of the Dordogne to the glaciated peaks of the Alps. Each **region** looks and feels different, has its own style of architecture, its characteristic food, often its own patois or dialect. Though the French word *pays* is the generic term for a whole country, local people frequently refer to their own immediate vicinity as *mon pays*, and to a stranger as coming from another *pays*. And this strong sense of regional identity, sometimes expressed in the form of active separatist movements as in Brittany and Languedoc, has persisted over centuries in the teeth of centralised administrative control from Paris.

Perhaps the most striking feature of the French **countryside** is the sense of space. There are huge tracts of woodland and undeveloped land without a house in sight. Industrialisation came relatively late, and the countryside remains very rural. Away from the main urban centres, hundreds of towns and villages have changed only slowly and organically, their old houses and streets intact, as much a part of the natural landscape as the rivers, hills and fields.

Historical and cultural associations are so widely disseminated across the land that even if you were to confine your travelling to one particular region you would still have a powerful sense of the past without having to seek out major sights. With its wealth of local detail, France is an ideal country for dawdling; there is always something to catch the eye and gratify the senses, whether you are meandering down a lane, picnicking by a slow, green river, or sipping *Pernod* in a village café. There is also endless scope for all kinds of **outdoor activities**, from walking, canoeing and cycling to the more expensive pleasures of skiing and sailing.

If you need more **urban stimuli** to activate the pleasure buds – clubs, shops, fashion, movies, music, hanging out with the beautiful and famous – then the great cities provide them in abundance. Paris, of course, is an outstanding cultural centre, with its elegant boulevards and atmospheric back streets, its art and its ethnic diversity. If your budget can stand it, you can follow the summer migration to the superchic resorts of the Mediterranean coast – though they are really at their best in late spring.

For a thousand years and more France has been at the cutting edge of **European development**, and the legacy of this wealth, energy and experience is everywhere evident in the astonishing variety of things to see: from the Gothic cathedrals of the north to the Romanesque churches of the centre and west, the châteaux of the Loire, the Roman monuments of the south, the ruined castles of the English and the Cathars and the Dordogne's prehistoric cave-paintings. If not all the legacy is so tangible – the literature, music and ideas of, say, the 1789 Revolution – as much as possible is recuperated and illustrated in museums and galleries across the nation, from colonial history to fishing techniques, aeroplane design to textiles, migrant shepherds to manicure, battlefields and coalmines.

Many of the **museums** are models of clarity and modern design. Among those that the French do best are museums devoted to local arts, crafts and customs like the Musée Basque in Bayonne and the Musée Dauphinois in Grenoble. But inevitably first place must go to the fabulous collections of paintings, many of which are in **Paris**. This is perhaps because the city nurtured so many of the finest creative artists of the last hundred years, both French, Monet and Matisse for example, and foreign, such as Picasso and Picabia.

If you are quite untroubled by a Puritan sense of duty to improve your mind in the contemplation of old stones and works of high art, France is uniquely well endowed to satisfy the much maligned grosser appetites. The French have made a high art of daily life: eating, drinking, dressing, moving, simply being. The **pleasures of the palate** run from the simplest picnic of crusty *baguette*, ham and cheese washed down by an inexpensive red wine through what must be the most elaborate take-away food in the world, available from practically every *charcuterie*; such basic regional dishes as *cassoulet*; the liver-destroying riches of Périgord and Burgundy cuisine; the fruits of the sea; extravagant pastries and ice cream cakes; to the trance-inducing refinements – and prices – of the great chefs. And there are wines to match, at all prices, and not just from the renowned vineyards of Bordeaux, Burgundy and Champagne. If you feel inadequate in the face of all this choice, never be afraid to ask advice, for most French people are true devotees, ever ready to explain the arcane mysteries to the uninitiated.

The people

Visual appearance is important to the French. No effort is too great to make things look good: witness the food shops even in the poorest neighbourhoods of a city, always sparkling clean and beautifully displayed. And it is evident that the people too take pride in looking neat and sharp; they inspect others and expect to be looked at. Life is theatre, lived much more in the public eye – especially in the warm Mediterranean south – than in Anglo-Saxon societies. And for the visitor it's a free and entertaining spectacle.

The French tend to be extremely courteous – it's not unusual for someone entering a restaurant to say "Good evening" to the entire company – and rather formal in their manners. At the same time, if they want something, they may be quite direct. If you are feeling self-conscious about coping with the language, this can seem like rudeness: it isn't. If you observe the formalities and make an effort to communicate, you'll find the French as friendly and interested as anyone else.

As for their reputed arrogance, the French are certainly proud of their culture, something which is reinforced by the education system. Artists and thinkers are held in high esteem in France and their opinions are listened to. Even prime ministers tend to be literate, often accomplished authors in their own right. But in a world dominated by commercial values and, in addition, the English language, the French (not unnaturally, for their language was once the *lingua franca* of the educated) feel this **culture** is under threat. The desire to defend it can sometimes seem like haughtiness.

Where to go and when

France is easy to travel around. Restaurants and hotels proliferate everywhere and the lower-budget ones are much cheaper than in most other developed western European countries. Train services are highly efficient, as is the road network, especially the (toll-paying) autoroutes, and cyclists are much admired and encouraged. Information is highly organised and available from the tourist offices (*syndicats d'initiatives*), a feature of practically every place in the land, as well as from hiking, cycling, camping, hang-gliding and hitchhiking organisations. But although these activities all have their specialist associations, they are not obtrusive; the French will not stand for regimentation, so you're left to your own devices.

There are all kinds of pegs on which to hang a holiday in France: a city, a region, a river or a mountain range, physical activities, cathedrals, châteaux. And in many cases your choice will determine the best time of year to go. Unless you're a skier, for example you wouldn't choose the mountains between November and May; nor at this time would you head for the seaside – though spring on the Mediterranean coast can be very attractive and crowd-free. **Climate**, otherwise, need not be a major consideration in planning when to go. Northern France, like nearby Britain, is wet and unpredictable. Paris perhaps has a marginally better climate than New York, rarely reaching the

THE CLIMATE OF FRANCE

Average Daily Maximum Temperatures

	Jan	Feb	March	April	May	June	July	Aug	Sept	Oct	Nov	Dec
Paris/Ile de France	7.5	7.1	10.2	15.7	16.6	23.4	25.1	25.6	20.9	16.5	11.7	7.8
Alsace	5.5	5.3	9.3	13.7	15.8	23.0	24.1	26.3	21.2	14.9	7.6	4.7
Aquitaine	10.0	9.4	12.2	19.5	18.0	23.7	27.2	25.7	24.2	19.7	15.4	11.0
Auvergne	8.0	6.4	10.1	15.9	17.1	24.2	27.0	24.5	23.3	17.0	11.0	8.3
Brittany	9.3	8.6	11.1	17.1	16.0	22.7	25.1	24.2	21.2	16.5	12.1	9.3
Burgundy	6.1	5.9	10.3	15.3	15.8	23.8	25.8	26.1	21.2	15.5	9.1	6.2
Champagne-Ardenne	6.2	5.6	8.9	13.8	15.1	22.5	23.8	24.9	19.3	15.0	9.6	6.2
Franche-Comté	5.4	4.8	9.8	14.6	15.5	23.0	25.0	26.5	21.8	15.2	9.6	5.8
Languedoc-Roussillon	12.4	11.5	12.5	17.6	20.1	26.5	28.4	28.1	26.1	21.1	15.8	13.5
Limousin	6.1	6.1	9.6	16.1	14.9	22.1	24.8	23.6	21.0	16.2	12.8	8.5
Lorraine	5.5	5.3	9.3	13.7	15.8	23.0	24.1	26.3	21.2	14.9	7.6	4.7
Midi-Pyrénées	10.0	9.0	12.3	18.3	19.1	26.4	27.6	27.2	25.0	19.3	15.5	9.8
Nord/Pas de Calais	6.6	5.6	8.3	13.7	14.9	21.5	22.7	24.0	19.3	15.3	8.3	6.9
Normandy	7.6	6.4	8.4	13.0	14.0	20.0	21.6	22.0	18.2	14.5	10.8	7.9
Picardy	6.6	5.6	8.3	13.7	14.9	21.5	22.7	24.0	19.3	15.3	8.3	6.9
Poitou-Charentes	10.0	8.7	11.7	18.2	16.4	22.4	25.3	24.6	22.0	18.4	14.0	9.8
Provence	12.2	11.9	14.2	18.5	20.8	26.6	28.1	28.4	25.2	22.1	16.8	14.1
Rhône Valley	7.4	6.7	10.8	15.8	17.3	25.6	27.6	27.6	23.5	16.5	10.4	7.8
Riviera/Côte d'Azur	12.2	11.9	14.2	18.5	20.8	26.6	28.1	28.4	25.2	22.2	16.8	14.1
Savoy/ Dauphiny Alps	3.1	3.7	7.9	13.8	15.7	22.4	26.8	25.7	22.7	15.9	10.7	6.3
Val de Loire	7.8	6.8	10.3	16.1	16.4	23.6	25.8	24.5	21.1	16.2	11.2	7.0
Western Loire	9.9	8.6	11.3	17.7	16.7	23.3	25.7	24.6	21.8	16.9	12.4	9.5

Average Sea Temperatures

	May	June	July	Aug	Sept	Oct
Channel						
Calais to Le Havre	10	13	16	17	16	14
Cherbourg to Brest	11	13	15	17	16	14
Atlantic						
Brest to Bordeaux	13	15	17	18	17	15
Bordeaux to St-Jean-de-Luz	14	15	18	19	19	17
Mediterranean						
Montpellier to Toulon	15	19	19	20	20	17
Ile du Levant to Menton	17	19	20	22	22	19

All temperatures are in **Centigrade**: to convert to **Fahrenheit** multiply by 9/5 and add 32.
For a recorded **weather forecast** you can phone the Paris forecasting office at ☎45.55.91.09
(☎45.55.95.02 for specific inquiries).

extremes of heat and cold of that city, but only south of the Loire does the weather become significantly warmer. West coast weather, even in the south, is tempered by the proximity of the Atlantic, subject to violent storms and close thundery days even in summer. The centre and east, as you leave the coasts behind, have a more continental climate, with colder winters and hotter summers. The most reliable weather is along and behind the Mediterranean, where winter is short and summer long and hot.

The single most important factor to take into consideration in deciding when to visit France is tourism itself. As most French people take their holidays in their own country – and what better advertisement could there be than that ? – it's as well to avoid the **main French holiday periods** – mid-July to the end of August, with August being particularly bad. Almost the entire country closes down, except for the tourist industry itself. You can easily walk half a mile and more in Paris, for example, in search of an open *boulangerie*, and the city seems deserted by all except fellow tourists. Prices in the resorts rise to take full advantage and you can't find a room for love nor money, and not even a space in the campsites on the Côte d'Azur. The seaside is worst, but the mountains and popular regions like the Dordogne are not far behind. Easter, too, is a bad time for Paris; half Europe's schoolchildren seem to descend on the city. For the same reasons, ski buffs should keep in mind the February school ski break. And no one who values life, limb, and sanity should ever be caught on the roads the last weekend of July or August, and least of all on the weekend of August 15.

HELP US UPDATE

The authors and researchers have gone to great lengths to ensure that this third edition of **The Rough Guide to France** is as up-to-date and accurate as possible. It's been completely overhauled and expanded with much new background material and a mass of fresh, practical information – 150 extra pages. Credit for this is due not least to the many readers who sent letters, postcards and even dog-eared, annotated copies of the last edition, for which we are always immensely grateful; every contributor is personally acknowledged. But France never stops changing and, if you feel there are places we've under-rated or over-praised, good hotels we've missed or others that have closed – or deteriorated – then please write. The latest details about your favourite restaurant or beach are as useful as route details about mountain walks or altered bus services or route advice; if you want to take us to task on historical and cultural detail we'd be equally pleased to hear from you; and we always aim to improve our maps with each edition. Please locate places as accurately as possible – sketch maps are a help. We've also restructured the book to make it user-friendlier and reduced the type size to keep the weight down: we'd be glad to hear your opinions. We'll send a free copy of the next edition, or any other Rough Guide if you prefer, for the most useful (and legible!) feedback. Please mark letters "Rough Guide France Update" and send to:

Rough Guides, 1 Mercer Street, London WC2H 9QJ, or
Rough Guides, 375 Hudson Street, 4th Floor, New York, NY 10014.

PART ONE

THE
BASICS

GETTING THERE FROM BRITAIN AND IRELAND

The quickest way of reaching France is, of course, by air – at least until the Channel Tunnel opens in 1993 – although it is only from London that you can be reasonably sure of getting any kind of cheap deal. The standard rail or road/sea routes are more affordable, but can be uncomfortable and tiring – and if you're just going for a short break, the journey time can significantly eat into your holiday.

FLIGHTS

Flying to France – particularly to the south – represents a considerable saving in time compared to the ferry and train/car journey: Nice, for example, is just 90 minutes' flying time from London. The main destinations for flights from Britain are Paris, Bordeaux, Toulouse, Montpellier, Marseille, Nice and Lyon: the cheapest, though, are generally those from London to Paris. To find the best you should shop around, ideally a month or so before you plan to leave. **Students** and anyone under 26 can take advantage of a range of special discount fares from London to France. Promising sources for checking the possibilities include the classified travel sections in papers like the Saturday editions of the *Independent* and the *Daily Telegraph* and Sundays like the *Observer, Sunday Times* and *Sunday Independent* and, if you're in London, the back pages of the listings magazine *Time Out* or the *Evening Standard*.

GENERAL DEALS FROM LONDON

The cheaper choices boil down to either a **charter** (*Orion, Air UK* and *British Island Airways* are some of the bigger carriers who sell blocks of seats to tour operators); an Apex or Superpex/Late Saver **scheduled** ticket on *British Airways* or *Air France*; or, often the cheapest, taking the London–Paris leg of a long-haul flight to more distant destinations, like *MAS (Malaysian), PIA (Pakistan International)* or *Kuwait Air.*

Charters are increasingly widely available. *Euro Express* (see box on p.10) offer a good range to the south of France including, in the summer, from British regional airports – Edinburgh, Necastle, Manchester and Bristol – to Nice. Other main destinations are Montpellier, Toulouse, Perpignan and Lourdes. The *Air Europe* Paris charter flights are sold regularly as flight-only deals by *Nouvelles Frontières* (see box on p.10); they offer daily services from London Gatwick to Paris Charles de Gaulle; current prices start at about £69 return, for mid-week flights booked two weeks in advance. Throughout the year, but particularly in summer, *Nouvelles Frontières* operate some daily charter flights from Gatwick to various other French cities.

British Airways, Air France, British Midland and *Dan Air* **Apex tickets** must be reserved two weeks in advance and your stay must include one Saturday night. Your return date must be fixed when purchasing and no subsequent changes are allowed. Current costs start at around £100 return to Paris. **Superpex** or **Pex** tickets from around £140 return to Paris may be booked at any time. *Air France* feature the widest **range of French destinations**, including Biarritz, Bordeaux, Clermont-Ferrand, Lille, Lyon, Marseille, Montpellier, Nantes, Nice, Strasbourg and Toulouse; *British Airways* flies to Bordeaux, Lyon, Marseille, Toulouse and Nice; *Dan Air* offer slightly cheaper deals and their destinations include Montpellier, Perpignan, Toulouse, Nice and Lourdes/Tarbes; *British Midland* fly from East Midlands and London Heathrow to Paris and Nice. *Brit Air* have regular scheduled flights to Brest, Le Havre, Caen and Rennes; they offer special weekend returns, but don't do Apex fares. *Air France* also offer a combined flight and *France Vacances Pass* (see box overleaf); £168 for four days' rail travel and £224 for nine days.

Bargains with **long-haul airlines** are harder to predict. Like charters, availability can be chancy but a good travel agent (*STA Travel* are specialists, see below) should usually find you something to Paris. The drawback is that there is generally only one weekly flight, though there's no maximum stay and you're allowed to make changes if necessary.

Travelling to Paris with a minimum of hassle, flights from **London City Airport** with *Brymon* (☎071/476 5000) feature speedy formalities in a user-friendly airport: riverbuses from Charing Cross or London Bridge leave for the airport every hour, check-in time has been cut to a minimum and tickets (from £188 return) can be collected at the check-in desk.

GENERAL DEALS FROM OUTSIDE LONDON

As often as not, whether you live in Birmingham or Newcastle, Manchester or Aberdeen, you'll find it pays to go to London and fly on to France from there. Scheduled direct flights from British regional airports are very expensive. Charters do exist, though availability is a big problem and prices are unfavourable compared with London flights, even without adding on the additional cost of coach/rail travel to London. What is worth considering, however, are **package deals**, which can often offer exceptional bargain travel – even

if you go it alone on the actual holiday (see box opposite).

RESTRICTED ELIGIBILITY FLIGHTS

Independent travel specialist *STA Travel* (see box) offers special-value flights to various cities for which anyone under 26 and all students under 32 are eligible. Current low-season return prices are: Paris £78; Marseille £108; Nice £99; Toulouse £96; Lyon £96; Bordeaux £108 Perpignan £144. For Paris the cheapest deal is the three-times weekly charter from Gatwick to Beauvais starting at around £55. The drawback is the distance of the airport from the city, although the 70km coach ride to Porte de la Villette in Paris is included in the price.

Another good deal for anyone under 26, and all those working in educational establishments regardless of age, is *Le Fly France* **flexible airpass**. The pass currently costs from £168 for those under 26, and from £217 for the "Academic Pass", and includes the return fare from Gatwick or Stansted to Paris, plus unlimited travel on internal flights, for four days within a calendar month, mostly with *Air Inter*. The calendar month begins on the day that you use your first internal flight, but the pass itself is valid for a year. In order to qualify for the Academic Pass, you must purchase the *STA Academic Card*, currently £6.

◀ AIR AND RAIL ▶

Air France, in conjunction with **SNCF**, the French state railway, offer very good value deals whereby you can **fly direct to Paris** from any one of sixteen UK or Irish airports and then take a **train**. You can buy a return ticket to any specific destination, or get a *France Vacances* pass which entitles you either to four days unlimited train travel within a fifteen-day period, or nine days within one month.

All the prices below include return flights to Paris; the table shows the curent cost of travel to selected French cities, and of *France Vacances* passes, from various UK and Irish airports. All prices are in sterling, and are for second class rail travel. For further details contact any *Air France* or *SNCF* office.

	London	S'thampton	Birmingham	Bristol	Dublin	Glasgow	Manchester
Bordeaux	£136	£150	£170	£167	£231	£213	£183
Brest	£138	£152	£172	£169	£233	£215	£185
Dijon	£119	£133	£153	£150	£214	£196	£166
Lyon	£131	£145	£165	£162	£226	£208	£178
Nice	£166	£180	£200	£197	£261	£243	£213
Orléans	£109	£123	£143	£140	£204	£186	£156
Perpignan	£153	£167	£187	£184	£248	£230	£200
Strasbourg	£126	£140	£160	£157	£221	£203	£173
4-day pass	£168	£182	£202	£199	£263	£245	£182
9-day pass	£224	£238	£258	£255	£319	£301	£271

AIR DEALS FROM IRELAND

If you want to fly directly to France from Dublin or Belfast you'll be limited to the major destinations. *Air France Holidays* (see box below) have package deals including flights from Dublin and Belfast, and *Budget Travel* organise summer charter flights to Paris from IR£129 return. Alternatives via Britain are unlikely to be attractive considering the additional time factor and the cost of a flight from Ireland to Britain. For up-to-date details on the situation, try contacting *USIT*, specialists in student/youth travel (see box).

SPECIAL INTEREST OPERATORS AND ACTIVITY HOLIDAYS

Accents Languages & Leisure, Artemare, 01510 Virieu-le-Grand, France (☎via 061 798 0388). Language course specialists for Francophiles with an emphasis on enjoyment and the "French experience", and highly motivated staff. Centres at Artemare in the Bugey area of the Jura and Forcalquier in Provence.

All for France 6 Turnpin Lane, London SE10 (☎081/853 2706). Impressionist art history breaks in Paris. Also rambling, specific sports events, and cycling in the south for around £300 for five days' unaccompanied tour, flight, HB hotel and luggage transfer included.

Andrew Brock Travel 10 Barley Mow Passage, London W4 4PH (☎081/995 3642). Various specialist deals on offer: art history tours from £660 for six days on the Côte d'Azur, flight and accommodation included; self-drive *pénichette* cruises on the French canals, from £429 for one week and up to five people.

Arblaster & Clarke Wine Tours 104 Church Rd, Steep, Petersfield, Hants GU32 2DD (☎0730/66883). Choice of guided wine tours in all the classsic areas, plus gourmet cooking tours of Normandy and Champagne. Prices from £179 for three days in Champagne.

Belle France, Bayham Abbey, Lamberhurst, Kent TN3 8BG (☎0892/890885). Interesting operator offering bicycle and walking tours of Brittany, Loire et Cher, Solgone, Burgundy, Ardeche, Auvergne and Haut-Provence, with the emphasis on good food and family hotels.

Blakes Boating Abroad Wroxham, Norwich NR12 8DH (☎0603/784131). Wide selection of boats on inland waterways. Prices for a week's hire off season on the Charente: from £215 for up to three people; from £330 for up to six.

Headwater Holidays, 146 London Rd, Northwhich, Cheshire, CW9 5HH (☎0606/48699). Activity holidays specialist with a long list of pursuits including riding, cycling, hiking, canoeing, watersports, bird-watching. Good family and teen-age options.

Holt's Battlefield Tours The Golden Key Building, 15 Market St, Sandwich, Kent CT13 9DA (☎0304 612248). Established leaders in the field with guided coach tours to most of the battlesites of the north. Prices from around £209 for 3 days in the Somme.

Hoseasons, Sunway House, Lowestoft, Suffolk NR32 3LT (☎0502/500 555). The biggest boat hire

company in France. Prices for one week on the Canal du Midi for up to four people range from £287 off season to £584 high season.

Impressions of France, Victoria House, 6 Albion Rd, Twickenham, Middlesex TW2 6QJ (081/898 4849). Upmarket Provence specialists offering escorted 11-day tours for around £1200 including flight. July tour takes in the Aix-en-Provence music festival.

La France des Villages/La France des Activités, Model Farm, Rattlesden, Nr. Bury St Edmunds, Suffolk IP30 0SY (☎0449/737664). Off-the-beaten-track specialists with a variety of villas and farmhouses and some very attractive chambres d'hôte in châteaux and farmhouses. Also arranges golf, horse-riding and boating holidays.

Ramblers Holidays, PO Box 43, Longcroft House, Fretherne Rd, Welwyn Garden City, Herts AL8 6PQ (☎0707/320226). Long-established and reputable walking holiday specialist – good number of trips with a vegetarian special in the Ardèche.

Susi Madron's Cycling for Softies 2–4 Birch Polygon, Rusholme, Manchester M14 5HX (☎061/248 8282). As the name suggests, an easy-going cycle holiday operator to most regions. Seven-day tours, including flight and accommodation, bicycle and back-up (but not luggage transfer) for around £508 per person.

SVP France, The Garden House, Main Rd, Nutbourne, Chichester, W Sussex PO18 8RL (☎0243/377862). Small, helpful company which aims to provide "authentic" holidays in non-touristy areas. Various activities available, including walking, cycling (and off-road mountain-biking) and canoeing.

Velo Vacances ar Dy Feic, Blwch Post 6, Aberteifi, Dyfed SA43 1LN (☎0248/601365). Enthusiastically organised cycle tours in West Brittany, including off-road mountain-bike tours in the Monts d'Arée. Prices vary from £275 for 10 days to a top £520 for 12 days in a luxury hotel, and, as well as travel, include half-board accommodation, courier service and a van for baggage.

Waymark Holidays, 44 Windsor Rd, Slough SL1 2EJ (☎0753/516477). Reliable operator of walking holidays with more than two dozen French routes in the Alps, Pyrenees and other mountain regions (including in the footsteps of Stevenson, *sans* donkey).

BY TRAIN

Until the Channel Tunnel is operational, the only route to France **by train** is via one of the many boat trains from London Victoria which connect with cross-Channel ferries or hovercraft, and with onward services on the other side. The **tunnel** is currently scheduled to come into service in the summer of 1993, and in the short term at any rate will probably use Waterloo as its London terminal.

On the shortest and most economical Channel crossings the choice is between **train and hovercraft** or **train and ferry,** the latter taking from one to three hours longer. Fare options include special deals on *Eurotrain* (for anyone under 26) and senior citizen reductions for those over 65. If you plan to travel a great deal in France you might also consider the *InterRail* or *France Vacances Pass* (see below).

The **hovercraft/catamaran** crossings link Dover (or Folkestone) with Calais or Boulogne. Services are frequent (up to 27 a day from Dover in peak season) and tie in well with the trains. By **train and ferry**, the cheapest crossing is currently Newhaven–Dieppe; the best deals are on the conveniently scheduled (though slightly slower) night trains.

Students and anyone under 26 can buy heavily discounted *BIJ* tickets from *Eurotrain* outlets (see address on p.10) and most student travel agents; a return ticket to Paris is currently priced at £72, or £76 with *Hoverspeed* (1hr 30min faster); an advanced reservation is needed. *British Rail's* cheapest five-day return fare is £61 via Dieppe, and their cheapest two-month adult return is £77 via Dieppe, £67 for under 26s.

RAIL PASSES

If you plan to use the railway network throughout France, you might consider buying a *France Vacances* or *InterRail* pass.

The **France Vacances Pass**, available from most major travel agents, offers unlimited travel throughout France for any four days during a period of fifteen days (£78) or any nine within a month (£134). It also entitles you to reductions on *Hoverspeed* channel crossings.

The **InterRail pass** is available from *British Rail* and many travel agents, and is no longer restricted to young travellers only. The only restriction is that you need to have been resident in Europe for at least six months. One month's unlimited use of all European railways costs £235 or £175 for under-26s; 15 days costs £175 or

£145. **Eurail**, the official rail pass for North American residents, is nowhere near as good a deal, unless you're planning virtually to live on trains for the duration of its validity. Under-26 *Eurail* passes cost US$425/month and US$560/2 months. If you're over 26 the costs become prohibitively high. For details, call STA Travel in North America (see p.13) or contact one of the rail addresses (see below).

> ### USEFUL RAIL ADDRESSES IN THE US AND CANADA
>
> *British Rail International*, 1500 Broadway, New York, NY 10036 (☎212/575-2667); 94 Cumberland St, Toronto, ON M5R 1A3 (☎416/929-3333).
>
> *CIE Tours International*, 108 Ridgedale Ave, Morristown, NJ 07690 (☎201/292-3438 or 800/522-5258). *A prime source for booking rail travel in Europe.*
>
> *Rail Europe*, 226–230 Westchester Ave, White Plains, NY 10604 (☎914/682-2999 or 800/848-7245). *Branches in Santa Monica, San Francisco, Fort Lauderdale, Chicago, Dallas, Vancouver and Montreal. Perhaps the best place to book European rail tickets.*

BY BUS

For the shortest Channel crossing, the choice is again between bus and hovercraft, and bus and ordinary ferry. Prices are very much lower than by train, especially using the hovercraft.

The coach for the **Hoverspeed City Sprint** service leaves from London's Victoria Coach Station, catches the hovercraft from Dover to Calais or Boulogne, and arrives in Paris between eight and nine hours after setting off. There are two coaches per day in winter, four in summer. The regular adult return is £51, and can be purchased through any local agent; for details call *Hoverspeed* on ☎081/554 7061.

The main company for the **bus/ferry** combination is *Eurolines*, 164 Buckingham Palace Rd, London SW1 (☎071/730 0202). They run regular services to over fifty French cities, with regular adult return fares currently at £51 for Paris, £54 for St-Malo (via Portsmouth), £78 for Orléans, £79 for Lyon, £87 for Strasbourg, £99 for Bordeaux, £104 for Perpignan/Montpellier, £115 for Cannes and Nice. Student/youth tickets have a ten percent discount on certain routes.

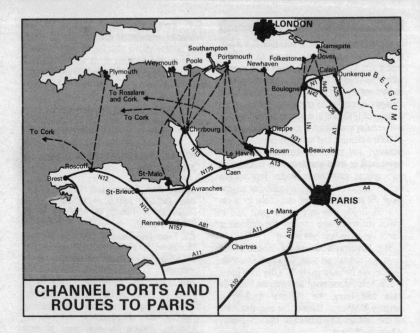

CHANNEL PORTS AND ROUTES TO PARIS

BY FERRY

The cheapest and quickest cross-Channel options for most travellers are the **ferry** or **hovercraft** (or high-speed catamaran) links between **Dover–Calais/Boulogne**, **Folkestone–Boulogne**, and **Ramsgate–Dunkerque**. However, if your starting point is further west than London, it may well be worth heading direct to one of the south coast ports and catching one of the ferries to Normandy or Brittany – **Newhaven–Dieppe**, **Portsmouth/Southampton/Weymouth/Poole–Le Havre/Caen/Cherbourg/St-Malo** and **Plymouth–Roscoff**.

If you're coming from the north of England or Scotland, opting for the **Hull–Zeebrugge** (Belgium) crossing overnight with *North Sea Ferries* (King George Dock, Hedon Rd, Hull HU9 5QA; ☎0482/795141) makes a lot of sense.

Ferry prices are seasonal, and, for motorists, depend on the size of your car; details of routes, companies and current fares are given in the box opposite. You can either contact the companies directly to reserve space in advance (which is essential in peak season if you're intending to drive), or any travel agent in the UK or France can do it for you.

HITCHING

Hitching from Calais or Boulogne to Paris is notoriously difficult, so you'd be well advised to accept through lifts only. The worst black holes – where hitchers become invisible to drivers – are Abbeville and Beauvais. If you can possibly afford one of the cheaper bus or train tickets, you'll save yourself a lot of trouble. If not, get friendly with drivers on the boat over and try to get a promise of a lift before docking. Dieppe is not that much easier to hitch out of. From Caen's port – Ouistreham – you can get a cheap local bus to the city if your thumb fails you. Hitching in Brittany is much more feasible and single passenger fares on *Brittany Ferries* are reasonable.

When hitching, it's worth noting the last two numbers of **car licence plates** which indicate the *département*. 75 is Paris (as you'll soon learn).

Coming back, it may well be worth contacting the ride-share organisation *Allostop*, 84 passage Brady, 75010 Paris, (☎47.70.02.01; Mon–Fri 9am–7.30pm, Sat 9am–1pm & 2–6pm), which matches riders with drivers for 65F for one journey, 200F for eight journeys, plus shared expenses of 16 centimes per kilometre.

1992 FERRY DETAILS

Routes and Prices

	Operator	Crossing time	Frequency	One-way Fares	
				Small car, 2 adults	Foot passenger
BRITTANY					
Portsmouth–St-Malo	*Brittany Ferries*	9hr	Mar–Dec 2 daily	£93–158	£33–40
Plymouth–Roscoff	*Brittany Ferries*	7hr 30min	3–12 weekly	£91–156	£33–40
NORMANDY					
S'thampton–Cherbourg	*Sealink Stena*	6–8 hr	1–2 daily	£86–144	£18–28
Portsmouth–Cherbourg	*P&O*	4hr 45min	1–3 daily	£84–141	£25–30
Poole–Cherbourg	*Brittany Ferries*	4hr 15min	May–Sept 1–4 daily	£78–136	£25–32
Portsmouth–Caen	*Brittany Ferries*	5hr 45min	8–20 weekly	£83–147	£26–33
Portsmouth–Le Havre	*P&O*	5hr 45min	2–3 daily	£84–141	£25–30
Newhaven–Dieppe	*Sealink N/D**	4hr	3–4 daily	£81–148	£26
Newhaven–Dieppe	*Sealink Stena*	4hr	2–4 daily	£92–148	£26
PAS-DE-CALAIS					
Folkestone–Boulogne	*Hoverspeed* ‡	1hr	3–6 daily	£92–134	£22
Dover–Boulogne	*P&O*	1hr 40min	5–6 daily	£65–140	£23
Dover–Calais	*Sealink Stena*	1hr 30min	6–18 daily	£97–142	£23
Dover–Calais	*P&O*	1hr 15min	15 daily	£65–140	£23
Dover–Boulogne/Calais	*Hoverspeed*‡‡	35–40min	6–20 daily	£59–147	£23
Ramsgate–Dunkerque	*Sally Line*	2hr 30min	5 daily all year	£58–127	£15
FROM IRELAND					
Cork–Roscoff	*Brittany Ferries*	13–17hr	1 weekly 15 Mar–Oct 5	£IR173–259	£IR47–67
Cork–Le Havre	*Irish Ferries*	21hr	June–Aug 1 weekly	£IR260–395	£IR67–107
Rosslare–Cherbourg	*Irish Ferries*	18hr	1–3 weekly	£IR260–395	£IR67–107
Rosslare–Le Havre	*Irish Ferries*	22hr	2–6 weekly	£IR260–395	£IR67–107

Special Offers

Brittany Ferries – 3, 5 & 10-day returns, 60-hour returns for foot passengers; discounts for regular users.
Sealink, Sally Line and *P&O* – 60-hour returns for single-fare price, also 5-day returns.
From Ireland: *Irish Ferries* – 13-day Excursion returns (not July & Aug), *Brittany Ferries* 7-day returns.

Addresses in England and Ireland

Brittany Ferries Wharf Rd, Portsmouth PO2 8RU (☎0705/827701); Millbay Docks, Plymouth PL1 3EW (☎0752/221321); Poole (☎0202/666466). In Ireland at 42 Grand Parade, Cork (☎021/277801).

Hoverspeed Maybrook House, Queen's Gardens, Dover CT17 9UQ (☎0304/240101). ‡*Seacat high-speed catamaran*. ‡‡ *Hovercraft and Seacat*.

Irish Ferries 2–4 Merrion Row, Dublin 2 (☎010 610511); Cork (☎021/504333) Rosslare (☎053/33158).

Sally Line Argyle Centre, York St, Ramsgate, Kent CT11 9DS (☎0843/595522); also at 81 Piccadilly, London W1V 9HF (☎081/858 1127).

P&O Channel House, Channel View Rd, Dover CT17 9TJ (☎0304/203388); Continental Ferry Port, Mile End, Portsmouth PO2 8QW (☎0705/827677); also London (☎081/575 8555).

SealinkStena Line Reservations: Charter House, Park St, Ashford, Kent TN24 8EX (☎0233/647047); 24-hour information service for Dover ☎0304/240028; Folkestone ☎0303/42964; Southampton ☎0703/233973; Newhaven 0273/512266.

***Sealink Newhaven/Dieppe** Newhaven Harbour, Newhaven, E Sussex EN9 0BQ (☎0273 512266).

USEFUL ADDRESSES IN BRITAIN & IRELAND

AIRLINES

Air France 177 Piccadilly, London W1V OLX (☎081/742 6600).

Brit Air Room 1028, Northbridge House, Gatwick North Terminal, RH6 0NP (☎0293/502044)

British Airways 156 Regent St, London W1R 5TA (☎081/897 4000).

British Midland Donington Hall, Castle Donington, Derby DE7 2SB (☎071/589 5599).

Dan Air 21–24 Cockspur House, London SW1Y 5BN (☎071/839 1192).

Euro Express, 1 Charlwood Ct, County Oak Way, Crawley, West Sussex (0293/511125).

RAIL AND COACH

British Rail Victoria Station (European Rail Enquiries: ☎071/834 2345).

Eurolines *National Express*, 164 Buckingham Palace Rd, London SW1 (☎071/730 8235).

Eurotrain 52 Grosvenor Gardens SW1 (☎071/730 3402); and regional *Campus Travel* offices.

International Express (coaches): 23 Crawley Rd, Luton, Beds LU1 1HX (☎0582/404511).

SNCF (French Railways), 179 Piccadilly, London W1 (☎071/491 1573).

Thomas Cook 45 Berkeley St, London SW1 (☎071/499 4000); and many regional offices.

Wasteels 121 Wilton Rd, London SW1V 1JZ (☎071/834 7066).

SPECIALIST AGENCIES FOR INDEPENDENT TRAVEL

Campus Travel 52 Grosvenor Gardens, London SW1 (☎071/730 3402); 541 Bristol Rd, Bournbrook, Selly Oak, Birmingham B29 6AU (☎021/414 1848); 39 Queens Rd, Bristol BS8 1QE (☎0272/292494); 5 Emmanuel St, Cambridge CB1 1NE (☎0223/324283); 4 Nicholson Sq, Edinburgh EH8 9BH (☎031/668 3303); 13 High St, Oxford OX1 4DB (☎0865/242067). *Branches at YH Adventure shops and university campuses.*

Council Travel 28a Poland St, London W1V 3DB (☎071/287 3337). *Eight offices in France.*

Eurotrain (see above).

Nouvelles Frontières 11 Blenheim St, London W1Y 5LE (☎071/629 7772). *French agency.*

STA Travel 86 Old Brompton Rd, London SW7 3LH and 117 Euston Rd, London NW1 2SX (tele-sales ☎071/937 9921); 75 Deansgate, Manchester M3 2BW (tele-sales ☎061/834 0668); 88 Vicar Lane, Leeds LS1 7JH; 25 Queens Rd, Bristol BS8 1QE; 38 Sidney St, Cambridge CB2 3HX (tele-sales ☎0223/66966); 36 George St, Oxford OX1 2BJ. *Global independent travel specialist.*

South Coast Student Travel 61 Ditchling Rd, Brighton, E Sussex BN1 4SD (0273/570226). *Plenty to offer non-students as well.*

USEFUL ADDRESSES IN IRELAND

Aer Lingus 42 Grafton St, Dublin(☎01/370 011).

British Airways 60 Dawson St, Dublin 2 (☎01/610 666); 9 Fountain Centre, College St, Belfast (☎0232/245 151).

Budget Travel 134 Lower Baggot St, Dublin 2 (☎01/613 122).

USIT, O'Connell Bridge, 19/21 Aston Quay, Dublin 2 (☎01/778 117); 10–11 Market Parade, Cork (☎021/270 900); Fountain Centre, Belfast BT1 6ET (☎0232/324 073). *Student and youth specialists.*

Note that addresses and telephone numbers may not be in the same location: some airlines and agents use a single telephone-sales number for several offices.

GETTING THERE FROM THE US AND CANADA

Getting to France from the US or Canada is straightforward; there are direct flights from over thirty major US cities to Paris (the only trans-Atlantic gateway), with connections from all over the continent. Nearly a dozen different scheduled airlines operate flights, making Paris one of the cheapest destinations in Europe. In fact, only London can offer more discounted flights; and while a visit to England may appeal, the price difference is rarely sufficient to make a stopover in London a money-saving idea.

FLIGHTS TO PARIS FROM THE US

The most comprehensive range of flights from the US is offered by **Air France**, the French national carrier, which flies non-stop to Charles de Gaulle airport from Anchorage, Boston, Chicago, Houston, Los Angeles, Miami, New York (JFK and Newark) and Washington DC – in most instances daily. *Air France* tends to be expensive, however.

The major American competitors tend to be cheaper, but offer fewer non-stop routes. **American** and **TWA** have the biggest range of "direct" routes. The former flies to Paris Orly non-stop from Chicago, Dallas, New York (JFK and Raleigh-Durham), or with a stop from LA (via Dallas), San Francisco (via Chicago) and San Diego (via JFK) and with good or guaranteed connections from 14 cities in the south and west. *TWA* flies non-stop to Paris Charles de Gaulle from Boston, New York, St Louis and Washington DC, with one-stop flights from Chicago and LA and guaranteed connections (same flight number) from Atlanta, Kansas City, Portland, San Franciso and Seattle.

Delta flies non-stop to Paris Orly from Atlanta and Cincinatti with good or guaranteed connections from over a dozen southern and western cities.

United flies daily non-stop to Paris Charles de Gaulle from Chicago and Washington DC.

Continental flies daily non-stop from New York (Newark) to Paris Orly and also has direct flights (with a stop or same number flight change) from Boston, Denver, Houston, LA and Washington.

Northwest flies daily, direct LA–Detroit–Paris Charles de Gaulle.

The French airline, **UTA** operates three flights a week from San Francisco non-stop to Paris (CDG).

Lastly, there are twice-weekly direct flights (often cheap) with **PIA Pakistan International** from New York to Paris Orly.

The cheapest way to take any of these scheduled flights is with a non-refundable APEX fare, which normally entails booking 21 days in advance of flying, travelling midweek, and staying for at least seven days. Apart from special offers, this is likely to be the best deal you'll get direct from an airline ticket counter.

The best guarantee of a cheap flight, however, is to contact a travel agent specialising in **discounted fares**. The travel sections of the *New York Times*, *Washington Post*, and *Los Angeles Times* advertise them. Restrictions on such tickets are often not all that stringent; you need not assume that youth or student fares are the best bargain, nor worry if you're not eligible for them. The independent travel specialists **STA Travel** and **Council Travel** are two of the most reliable agents, but not suprisingly the French group **Nouvelles Frontières** has some good offers. These firms, together with several of the other larger agents, act as "consolidators" for particular airlines with which they maintain contracts to sell seats on specific terms, invariably below the airlines' own fares, though sometimes less conveniently.

AIRLINES AND TOUR OPERATORS IN THE US AND CANADA

AIRLINE ADDRESSES

Air Canada, 26th Floor, Place Air Canada, 500 Dorchester Blvd W, Montréal, PQ H2Z 1X5 (☎514/879 7000).

Air France, 888 Seventh Ave, New York, NY 10106 (☎212/830-4000 or 800/237-2747); 875 N Michigan Ave, Chicago, IL 60611 (☎312/440-7922); 2000 rue Mansfield, Montréal, PQ H3A 3A3 (☎514/284-2825); 151 Bloor St W, Suite 600, Toronto, ON M5S 1S4 (☎416/922-5024).

American Airlines, PO Box 619616, Dallas/Fort Worth International Airport, Dallas, TX 75261 (☎817/267-1151 or 800/433-7300).

British Airways, 530 Fifth Ave, New York, NY 10017 (☎800/2479297); 1001 bd de Maisonneuve Ouest, Montréal, PQ H3A 3C8 (☎800/668-1059); 112 Kent St, Ottawa, ON K1P 5P2 (☎613/236-0881); 1 Dundas St West, Toronto, ON M5G 2B2 (☎416/250-0880).

Canadian Airlines, 2500 Four Bentall Center, 1055 Dunsmuir St, Box 49370, Vancouver, BC V7X 1R9 (☎604/270 5211)

Continental Airlines, 2929 Allen Parkway, Houston, TX 77019 (☎713/821-2100 or 800/231-0856).

Delta Airlines, Hartsfield Atlanta International Airport, Atlanta, GA 30320 (☎404/765-5000).

Icelandair, 360 W 31st St, New York, NY 10001 (☎212/967-8888 or 800/223-5500).

KLM, 565 Taxter Rd, Elmsford, NY 10523 (☎212/759-3600 or 800/777-5553); 225 N Michigan Ave, Chicago, IL 60601 (☎212/861-9292); 1255 Green Ave, West Mount, Montréal PQ H3Z 2A4 (☎514/933-1314 or 800/361-5073).

Northwest Airlines, Minneapolis-St Paul International Airport, St Paul, MN 55111 (☎612/726-1234 or 800/225-2525).

Sabena, 720 Fifth Ave, New York, NY 100022 (☎800/955-2000); 5959 W. Century Blvd, Los Angeles, CA 90045 (☎213/642-7735); 1001 bd de Maisonneuve Ouest, Montréal, PQ H3A 3C8 (☎514/845-0215).

Swissair, 608 Fifth Ave, New York, NY 10020 (☎718/995-8400 or 800/221-7370); 2 Bloor St W, Suite 502, Toronto, ON M5S 2V1 (☎416/960-4270).

TWA, 100 South Bedford Rd, Mount Kisco, NY 10549 (☎212/290-2141 or 800/892-4141).

United Airlines, PO Box 66100, Chicago, IL 60666 (☎708/952-4000 or 800/241-6522).

US Air, Crystal Park Four, 2345 Crystal Drive, Arlington, VA 22227 (☎703/418-7000 or 800/622-1015).

UTA, 323 Geary St, Suite 401, San Francisco, CA 94102 (☎415/397 84 00)

Virgin Atlantic Airways, 96 Horton St, New York, NY 10014 (☎212/206-6612 or 800/862-8621).

TOUR OPERATORS IN THE US

American Express, World Financial Center, New York, NY 10285 (☎212/640-2000 or 800/800-8891). *Packages, city breaks, etc, all over Europe.*

Contiki Holidays, 1432 Katela Ave, Anaheim, CA 92805 (☎714/937-0611 or 800/626-0611). *Coach tours for under-35s.*

Cosmos/Global Gateway, 92-25 Queens Blvd, Rego Park, NY 11374 (☎800/221-0090). *The leading US budget tour operators to Europe. Bookable through travel agents only.*

Europe Through the Back Door Tours, 109 Fourth Ave N, C-2009, Edmonds, WA 98020 (☎206/771-0833). *Excellent travel club which publishes a regular newsletter packed full of travel tales and advice, sells its own guides and travel accessories, Eurail passes, and runs good-value bus tours taking in the biggest European cities. Worth joining for the newsletter alone.*

Europe Train Tours, 198 Boston Post Rd, Mamaroneck, NY 105431 (☎814/698-9426 or 800/551-2085).

Jet Vacations, 1775 Broadway, New York, NY 10019 (☎212/247-0999 or 800/JET-0999). *French package specialist.*

Mountain Travel, 6420 Fairmont Ave, El Cerrito, CA 94530 (☎800/227-2384). *Hiking specialist.*

Trafalgar Tours, 11 E 26th St, New York, NY 10010 (☎212/689-8977 or 800/854-0103). *Coach tours all over Europe.*

Trophy Tours, 1810 Glenville Drive, Suite 1124, Richardson, TX 75081 (☎800/527-2473). *Good-value coach tours all over Europe.*

DISCOUNT FLIGHT AGENTS AND CONSOLIDATORS IN THE US AND CANADA

Access International, 101 W 31st St, Suite 104, New York, NY 10001 (☎800/TAKE-OFF). *Consolidator with good East Coast and central US deals.*

Airkit, 1125 W 6th St, Los Angeles, CA 90017 (☎213/957-9304). *West Coast consolidator with seats from San Francisco and LA.*

Council Travel, 205 E 42nd St, New York, NY 10017 (☎212/661-1450). 312 Sutter St, Suite 407, San Francisco, CA 94108; (☎415/421-3473); 14515 Ventura Blvd, Suite 250, Sherman Oaks, CA 91403 (☎818/905-5777); 1138 13th St, Boulder, CO 80302 (☎818/905-5777); 1210 Potomac St NW, Washington, DC 20007(☎202/337-6464); 1153 N Dearborn St, Chicago, IL 60610 (☎312/951-0585); 729 Boylston St, Suite 201, Boston, MA 02116 (☎617/266-1926) 1501 University Ave SE, Room 300, Minneapolis, MN 55414 (☎612/379-2323); 2000 Guadalupe St, Suite 6, Austin, TX 78705 (☎512/472-4931); 1314 Northeast 43rd St, Suite 210, Seattle, WA 98105; ☎206/632-2448. *Nationwide US student travel organisation.*

Discount Club of America, 61-33 Woodhaven Blvd, Rego Park, NY 11374 (☎718/335-9612). *East Coast discount travel club.*

Discount Travel International, Ives Bldg, 114 Forrest Ave, Suite 205, Narbeth, PA 19072 (☎215/668-2182 or 800/221-8139). *Good deals from the East Coast*

Encore Short Notice, 4501 Forbes Blvd, Lanham, MD 20706 (☎301/459-8020 or 800/638-0830). *East Coast travel club.*

Interworld, 3400 Coral Way, Miami, FL 33145 (☎305/443-4929). *Southeastern US consolidator.*

Moment's Notice, 425 Madison Ave, New York, NY 10017 (☎212/486-0503). *Travel club that's good for last-minute deals.*

Nouvelles Frontières, 12 E 33rd St, New York, NY 10016 (☎212/779-0600); 800 bd de Maisonneuve Est, Montréal, PQ H2L 4L8 (☎514/288-9942). *French discount travel firm. Other branches in LA, San Francisco and Quebec City.*

STA Travel, ☎800-777-0112 (nationwide); 48 E 11th St, Suite 805, New York, NY 10003 (tele-sales ☎212/986 9470); 7202 Melrose Ave, Los Angeles, CA 90046 (tele-sales ☎213/937 5781); 82 Shattuck Sq, Berkeley, CA 94704 (☎510/841 1037); 166 Geary St, Suite 702, San Francisco, CA 94108 (☎415/391 8407); 273 Newbury St, Boston, MA 02116; (☎617/266-6014). *Worldwide specialist in independent travel.*

Stand Buys, 311 W Superior St, Chicago, IL 60610 (☎800/331-0257). *Good Midwestern travel club.*

Travel Cuts, Head Office: 187 College St, Toronto, ON M5T 1P7 (☎416/979-2406). Others include: MacEwan Hall Student Centre, University of Calgary, Calgary, AL T2N 1N4 (☎403/282-7687); 12304 Jasper Av, Edmonton, AL T5N 3K5 (☎403/488 8487); 6139 South St, Halifax, NS B3H 4J2 (☎902/494-7027); 1613 rue St Denis, Montréal, PQ H2X 3K3; (☎514/843-8511); 1 Stewart St, Ottawa, ON K1N 6H7 (☎613/238 8222); 100–2383 CH St Foy, St Foy, G1V 1T1 (☎418/654 0224); Place Riel Campus Centre, University of Saskatchewan, Saskatoon S7N 0W0 (☎306/975-3722); 501–602 W Hastings, Vancouver V6B 1P2 (☎604/681 9136); University Centre, University of Manitoba, Winnipeg R3T 2N2 (☎204/269-9530). *Canadian student travel organisation.*

Travelers Advantage, 49 Music Sq, Nashville, TN 37203 (☎800/548-1116). *Reliable travel club.*

Travac, 1177 N Warson Rd, St Louis, MO 63132 (☎800/872-8800). *Good central US consolidator.*

Travel Avenue, 130 S Jefferson, Chicago, IL 60606 (☎312/876-1116 or 800/333-3335). *Discount travel agent.*

Unitravel, 1177 N Warson Rd, St Louis, MO 63132 (☎800/325-2222). *Good, reliable consolidator.*

Worldwide Discount Travel Club, 1674 Meridian Ave, Miami Beach, FL 33139 (☎305/534-2082).

Estimating the **cost of round-trip economy class fares** to Paris is tricky, especially as routes, carriers and the state of the market in general are changing all the time. The following ball-park round-trip fares from the discount end of the market (see box overleaf) are a general guide to what you might expect/have expected to pay in 1992 (remember that summer is peak period and note that Friday, Saturday and Sunday travel tends to carry a premium). One-way fares are generally slightly more than half the round-trip.

SAMPLE ROUND-TRIP FARES TO PARIS

Atlanta: $660	**Miami**: $650
Boston: $520	**New York**: $540
Chicago: $610	**Raleigh**: $660
Cincinatti: $660	**St Louis**: $710
Dallas: $730	**San Francisco**: $760
Houston: $690	**Washington DC**: $570
Los Angeles: $760	

Charter flights (a flight chartered by a tour operator from an airline to ferry tourists) can be even cheaper than these prices for scheduled services. But while discounted scheduled services sometimes carry eligibility restrictions, charter flights hedge you in with restricted dates and major financial penalties if you cancel. They're worth considering if you're very organised and know exactly what you plan to do. Most agents sell them.

If you're prepared to travel light at short notice, and for a short duration it might be worth getting a **courier flight**. *Now Voyager* (☎212/431 1616) arranges such flights to Europe from JFK, Newark, and Houston. Flights (from about $400 round trip) are issued on a first-come, first-served, basis, and there's no guarantee that the Paris route will be available at the specific time you want.

FLIGHTS TO PARIS FROM CANADA

The strong links between France and Québec's Francophone community ensure regular air services from Canada to Paris. The main route is Vancouver–Toronto–Montréal–Paris Charles de Gaulle. Most departures orginate in Toronto, however, with **Air France** flying almost daily from Toronto to Charles de Gaulle, either non-stop or via Montréal. **Air Canada** and **Canadian Airlines** fly direct to Paris from Toronto and Montréal, again pretty well daily, and Canadian Airlines flies in from Vancouver twice weekly to guarantee the connection to Paris.

Travel Cuts and **Nouvelles Frontières** are the most likely sources of good-value discounted seats; call for details as flights vary from season to season.

FLYING VIA THE UK

Although **flying to London** is usually the cheapest way of reaching Europe, price differences these days are minimal enough for there to be little point travelling to France via London unless you've specifically chosen to visit the UK as well. Having said that, you may well be able to pick up a flight to London at an advantageous rate.

In recent years, **Virgin Atlantic** has offered some of the best fares from New York, and has now added flights from Los Angeles, Miami, and Boston to its schedules (all into London Gatwick). **British Airways** has entered the fray with a series of rival offers. In summer, the savings are bound to be less, but shop around as there may yet be some European bargains. As well as JFK and Newark, *British Airways* has regular non-stop flights from Philadelphia, Boston, San Francisco, and Los Angeles – and Detroit via Montréal.

For details of European rail passes that can be purchased in North America, see p.7

GETTING THERE FROM AUSTRALASIA

Although there are direct flights from Australia to Paris on *UTA*, **it's generally easier and cheaper to fly to Britain and then make your way to France.** *Qantas* **doesn't fly to France at all, only using its connections with** *Air France* **in London.**

The French international airline, **UTA** (*Union Transports Aériens*) operates three flights a week from Sydney to Paris (CDG) via Jakarta and Singapore which cost the same as flights via London. If you qualify for student or youth discounts, it's better to book through an agent like *STA Travel*, who have over twenty offices in Australia, including 1a Lee St, Railway Sq, Sydney 2000 (☎02/519 9866), and 224 Faraday St, Carlton, Victoria 3053 (☎03/347 4711), and ten in New Zealand (main offices at 147 Cuba St, Palmerston North, Wellington, and 10 High St, Auckland; ☎09/309 9723).

But probably the cheapest way of getting to Paris from either Australia or New Zealand is on the Indonesian airline, **Garuda**, via Jakarta, Bangkok or Singapore and Abu Dhabi. *Garuda's* reputation on international flights is much better than its notorious domestic service would suggest.

RED TAPE AND VISAS

Citizens of EC countries, Japan, Canada and the United States do not need any sort of visa to enter France for a tourist stay for up to ninety days. The British Visitor's Passport and the Excursion Pass (for day trips), both obtainable over the counter at post offices, can be used as well as ordinary passports. Note that black visitors (especially from Britain) have, in the recent past, been targets for obstructive, racist immigration officials.

If you **stay longer than three months** you are officially supposed to apply for a *Carte de Séjour*, for which you'll have to show proof of income at least equal to the minimum wage. However, EC passports are rarely stamped, so there is no evidence of how long you've been in the country. If your passport is stamped, you can legitimately cross the border, to Belgium or Germany for example, and re-enter for another ninety days.

All other passport holders (including Australians and New Zealanders) must obtain a visa **before arrival in France**. Obtaining a visa from your nearest French consulate is fairly automatic, but check their hours before turning up, and leave plenty of time, since there are often queues (particularly in London in the summer).

Three **types of French visas** are currently issued: a transit visa, which is mostly intended for train passengers and valid for three days; a short-stay (*court séjour*) visa, valid for ninety days after date of issue, good for multiple entries; and the most popular multiple-stay *visa de circulation*, which allows for multiple stays of ninety days over three years (maximum of 180 days in any one-year period).

FRENCH CONSULATES ABROAD

AUSTRALIA 303 Angas, Adelaide (☎08/231 8633); 492 St Kilda Rd, Melbourne (☎03/820 0921); 10 Eagle, Brisbane (☎/7/229 8201).

BRITAIN French Consulate General (Visas Section), 6a Cromwell Pl, London SW7 (☎071/823 9555). Also: 7–11 Randolph Crescent, Edinburgh (☎031 225 7954); 523–535 Cunard Building, Pier Head, Liverpool (☎051/ 236 8685).

CANADA Embassy: 42 Promenade Sussex, Ottawa, ON K1M 2C9, (☎613/512-1715). There are consulates in Edmonton, Montréal, Québec, Toronto, and Vancouver.

IRELAND 36 Ailesbury Rd, Dublin 4 (☎01/694 777).

NETHERLANDS Vyzelgr. 2, Amsterdam (☎20/624 8346).

NEW ZEALAND Corner Princes St/Eden Crescent, Auckland (☎09/302 7629); c/o Teachers' College, Christchurch; c/o University of Otago, Dunedin.

USA Embassy: 4101/Reservoir Rd NW, Washington, DC 20007, (☎202/944-6000). Consulates: 934 Fifth Ave, New York, NY 10021, (☎212/535-0100); 540 Bush St, San Francisco, CA 94108, (☎415/397-4893). Consulates in Boston, Chicago, Detroit, Houston, Los Angeles, Miami and New Orleans.

COSTS, MONEY AND BANKS

Because of the relatively low cost of accommodation and eating out, at least by northern European standards, France is not an outrageously expensive place to visit. For a reasonably comfortable existence, including hotel room and restaurant or café stops, you need to allow about 350–400F a day per person. But by counting the pennies, staying at a hostel (between 35F and 75F for bed and breakfast) or camping (around 15F a head in the municipal sites) and being strong-willed about extra cups of coffee and doses of culture, you could manage on 200F or even 150F, including a cheap restaurant meal, and possibly much less if your eating is limited to street snacks or market food.

For two or more people **hotel accommodation** can be almost as cheap as the hostels, though a sensible average estimate for a double room would be around 150F. As for **food**, you can spend as much or as little as you like. There are large numbers of good **restaurants** with three- or four-course menus for between 60F and 85F. **Picnic fare**, obviously, is much less costly, especially when you buy in the markets and cheap supermarket chains. More sophisticated meals – **takeaway** salads and ready-to-heat dishes – can be put together for reasonable prices if you shop at *charcuteries* (delicatessens) and the equivalent counters of many supermarkets.

Transport will inevitably be a large item of expenditure if you move around a lot, which makes the *InterRail* pass an attractive proposition for the restless. The standard tariff for trains is 50 centimes per kilometre (some sample one-way

fares: Paris to Nice 447F, Paris to Bordeaux 269F). Buses are cheaper though prices vary enormously from one operator to another. Bicycles cost about 50F per day to hire. Petrol prices are amongst the highest in Europe, at just over 5F a litre for leaded and just under 5F for unleaded (that's about 25F/imperial gallon, 20F/US gallon). Most motorways have tolls: rates vary, but to give you an idea, Paris to Menton would cost you around 400F just to *use* the *autoroute*.

Museums and monuments are likely to prove another big wallet-eroder. If you're entitled to one, be sure to carry an *ISIC* (International Student Identity Card) – though many museums have reduced admission for all under 26s, and not just students.

Most importantly, if you're on a budget you need to be wary of **nightlife** and **café-lounging**, a major expense being beer and coffee in pubs, bars and clubs.

MONEY

French currency is the *franc* (abbreviated as F or sometimes FF), divided into 100 centimes. Francs come in notes of 500, 100, 50, and 20F, and there are coins of 10, 5, 2, and 1F, and 50, 20, 10 and 5 centimes. With the pound and the franc both fixed into the ERM (Exchange Rate Mechanism), the exchange rate is now always around 9,50F (that's how 9.5F is usually written) to the pound. The dollar rate fluctuates more: at the time of writing it was 5,50F to the dollar.

Standard **banking hours** are 9.30am–noon and 2–4pm; closed Sunday and either Monday or, less usually, Saturday. **Rates of exchange** and **commissions** vary from place to place; the *Banque Nationale de Paris* usually offers the best rates and takes the least commission. There are **money-exchange counters** at airports and the railway stations of all big cities, and usually one or two in the town centre as well; these often keep much longer hours than the high-street banks. However, it would be a sensible precaution to buy some French francs before leaving.

Travellers' cheques, generally considered one of the safest ways of **carrying your money**, are available from almost any major bank (whether you have an account there or not), usually for a service charge of one percent on the amount purchased. Some banks may take 1.25 or even 1.5 percent, and your own bank may offer cheques free of charge provided you meet certain conditions – ask first, as you can easily save £10 to £15. *Thomas Cook, Visa* and *American Express* are the most widely recognised brands. Obtaining **French franc travellers' cheques** can be worthwhile: they can often be used as cash, and French banks are obliged by law to give you the face value of the cheques when you change them, so commission is only paid on purchase.

Alternatively, Europeans can use **Eurocheques**, now offered by most British banks. These can be better value with just one percent commission on each cheque (French banks do occasionally – and wrongly – charge you to cash Eurocheques). You pay an annual fee for the service, and have to apply for a card in advance. However, on the positive side, you can specify the exact amount you want and use the cheques in shops and restaurants, as well as certain cash-

dispensers, and it takes up to six weeks for the money to be deducted from your account. Also worth considering are post office **International Giro Cheques**, which work in a similar way to ordinary bank cheques except that you can cash them at post offices, which are even more widespread and have longer opening hours than banks.

Credit cards are widely accepted; just watch for the window stickers. *Visa/Barclaycard* – known as the *Carte Bleue* – is almost universally recognised, and cash advances can be had at all banks; you can also ask for a PIN number, enabling you to use most cash-dispensing machines in France. *American Express, Access* (*Eurocard/Mastercard* in France) rank considerably lower – only the *Crédit Agricole* and the *Crédit Mutuelle* banks provide facilities for the latter. To report **lost or stolen credit cards** phone one of the following hotlines: *Carte Bleue (VISA)* ☎42.77.11.90; *American Express* ☎47.77.72.00.

HEALTH AND INSURANCE

Under the French Social Security system every hospital visit, doctor's consultation and prescribed medicine is charged (though in an emergency not upfront). Although all employed French people are entitled to a refund of 75–80 percent of their medical expenses, this can still leave a hefty shortfall, especially after a stay in hospital (accident victims have to pay even for the ambulance that takes them there).

To find a **doctor**, stop at any *pharmacie* and ask for an address. Consultation fees for a visit should be from 75–85F and in any case you'll be given a *Feuille de Soins* (Statement of Treatment) for later documentation of insurance claims. Prescriptions should be taken to a *pharmacie* which is also equipped – and obliged – to give first aid (for a fee). The medicines you buy will have little stickers (*vignettes*) attached to them, which you must remove and stick to your *Feuille de Soins* together with the prescription itself. In serious **emergencies** you will always be admitted to the **local hospital** (*Centre Hospitalier*) whether under your own power or by ambulance.

Citizens of all EC countries are entitled to take advantage of each others' health services under the same terms as the residents of the country, if they have the correct documentation. British citizens need form E111. To apply for this, you must first fill in Form SA30, which you can get over the counter at any main post office. They will then issue you an E111 to complete. Only citizens of EC member states are covered under the scheme; others should definitely have travel insurance. France does not require vaccinations. General health care is of the highest standard.

As getting a refund entails a complicated bureaucratic procedure, a better idea is to take out ordinary **travel insurance**, which generally allows full reimbursement, less the first few pounds of every claim.

TRAVEL INSURANCE

In **Britain**, travel insurance schemes to cover medical expenses and theft or loss are sold by all travel agents, from around £30 a month: *ISIS* policies, from *STA Travel* or branches of *Endsleigh Insurance*, are usually good value. Read the small print before signing up to see what is covered, although most are broadly similar. If you have any other insurance policies – house and contents insurance, for example – you'll find some of the optional extra cover in travel insurance only duplicates what you already have at home. Remember that claims can only be dealt with if a report is made to the local police within 24 hours and a copy of the report sent with the claim.

In the **US and Canada**, insurance tends to be much more expensive, and may be medical cover only. Before buying a policy, check that you're not already covered by existing insurance plans. **Canadians** are usually covered by their provincial health plans; holders of **ISIC cards** and some other student/teacher/youth cards are entitled to accident coverage and hospital in-patient benefits for the period during which the card is valid. **Students** will often find that their student health coverage extends during the vacations and for one term beyond the date of last enrollment. Bank and charge **accounts** (particularly *American Express*) often include some insurance cover on items paid for with the card – travel facilties, accommodation, tours. **Homeowners' or renters'** insurance often covers theft or loss of documents, money and vaulables while overseas, though exact conditions vary from company to company.

Only after exhausting the possiblities above might you want to get some specific travel insurance; your travel agent can usually recommend one. Travel insurance offerings are quite comprehensive, anticipating everything from charter companies going bankrupt to delayed or lost baggage, by way of sundry illnesses and accidents. **Premiums** vary widely, from the very reasonable ones offered primarily through student/youth agencies (*STA*'s policies range from about $50–70 for fifteen days, $500–700 for a year, depending on the amount of financial cover), to those so expensive that the cost for anything more than two months of coverage will probably equal the cost of the worst possible combination of disasters. Note that very few insurers will arrange on-the-spot payments in the event of a major expense or loss; you will usually be reimbursed only after going home.

None of these travel insurance policies insure against **theft** of anything while overseas. North American travel policies apply only to items **lost** from, or **damaged** in, the custody of an identifiable, responsible third party – hotel porter, airline, luggage consignment, etc. Even in these cases you'll have to contact the local police immediately to have a complete report made out so that your insurer can process the claim. If you are travelling via London you might be better off taking out a British policy, easily available over the counter (though making the claim may prove more complicated).

DISABLED TRAVELLERS

France has no special reputation for providing facilities for disabled travellers, but at least information is available. In the major cities, and coastal resorts, there are accessible hotels, and ramps or other forms of access are gradually being added to museums and other sites. The French minister appointed to oversee disability issues is himself disabled – a positive move – and there are a number of national organisations which provide a national information network: APF, the Frensh paraplegic organisation, has regional branches in most *départements*.

Public transport is certainly not wheelchair-friendly, and although many train stations now have ramps to enable wheelchair-users to board and descend from carriages, at others it is still up to the guards to carry the chair. At the time of writing, cars with hand controls are simply not available for hire in France.

In Britain, both the *Holiday Care Service* and *RADAR* have lists of accessible **accommodation**; most of the cross-channel ferry companies offer good facilities, though up-to-date information about access is difficult to get hold of. In France, the tourist offices in most big towns have a free booklet *Touristes quand même!*, which though dated (1987), provides useful information on accommodation, transport, accessibility of public places and particular aids such as buzzer signals on pedestrian crossings. The *ATH* hotel reservation service in Paris (☎48.74.88.51) has details of wheelchair access, though only for pricey three- and four-star hotels. As far as **airlines** go, *British Airways* has a better-than-average record for treatment of disabled passengers, and from North America, *Virgin* and *Air*

Canada come out tops in terms of disability awareness (and seating arrangements) and might be worth contacting first for any information they can provide. For more **information** on all this, plus first-hand accounts by disabled travellers to France, see *Nothing Ventured: Disabled People Travel the World*, a *Rough Guide* special (Harrap, 1991), published in America as *Out and About* (Prentice Hall). And contact the organisations below.

TRAVEL WITH A DISABILITY: CONTACTS IN BRITAIN AND THE USA

APF (*Association des Paralysés de France*), 17–21 bd Auguste Blanqui, 75013 Paris (☎45.80.82.40). A national organisation with regional offices all over France which can provide useful inforamtion and lists of new and accessible accommodation.

CNFLRH (*Comité National Française de Liaison pour la Réadaption des Handicapés*), 30–32 quai de la Loire, 75019 Paris (☎45.48.90.13). Information service for disabled travellers, including details of accessible accommodation, holiday centres etc, and distributes various useful guides.

Holiday Care Service, 2 Old Bank Chambers, Station Rd, Horley, Surrey RH6 9HW, England (☎0293/774535). Information on all aspects of travel.

Kéroul, 4545 av Pierre de Coubertin, CP 1000, succ.M Montréal, PQ H1V 3R2, Canada (☎514/

2523104). Specialises in travel for mobility-impaired people.

Mobility International USA, PO Box 3551, Eugene, OR 97403, USA (☎503/343 1248). Information, access guides, tours and exchange programme.

RADAR (*The Royal Association for Disability and Rehabilitation*), 25 Mortimer St, London W1N 8AB (☎071/637 5400; Minicom ☎071/637 5315). Information on all aspects of travel.

Travel Information Center, Moss Rehabilitation Hospital, 1200 W Tabor Rd, Philadelphia, PA 19141 (☎215/329 5715 x2233). Write for access information.

TRIPSCOPE, 63 Esmond Rd, London W4 1JE (☎081/994 9294). Phone-in travel information and advice service.

MAPS AND INFORMATION

The French Government Tourist Office gives away large quantities of maps and glossy brochures for every region of France including lists of hotels and campsites. Some of these, like the maps of the inland waterways, lists of festivals and campsite listings can be quite useful.

In France itself you'll find a tourist information centre – *Syndicat d'Initiative* (**SI**) or *Office du Tourisme* – in practically every town and many villages (SI addresses, and in more important cases their opening hours, are detailed in the guide). From the SIs you can get specific local information, including listings of leisure activities, bike hire, launderettes and countless other things. And always ask for the free town plan.

FRENCH GOVERNMENT TOURIST OFFICES

Australia BWP House, 12 Castlereigh St, Sydney 2000 (☎02/213 5244).

Britain 178 Piccadilly, London W1 (☎ 071/491 7622).

Canada 1 Dundas St, W Suite 2405, PO Box 8, Toronto, ON M5G 1Z3 (☎416/593 4717)

Ireland 35 Lower Abbey St, Dublin 1 (☎01/300 777).

Netherlands Prinsengr. 670, 1017 KX Amsterdam (☎20/24 75 34).

New Zealand 1–3 Willeston House, Wellington (☎720 200).

Norway Handelskammer 0152, Oslo 1, Dronningensgate, 8B (☎2/20 37 29).

Sweden S11146 Stockholm, Normalmstorg 1 Av. (☎8/10 53 32).

USA 610 Fifth Ave, Suite 222, New York, NY 10020-2452 (☎212/757-1125).

Many SIs also publish hotel and restaurant listings, and local car and walking itineraries for their areas. In mountain regions they often share premises with the local hiking and climbing organisers. They are often also willing to give advice about the best places to go in addition to just handing out paper. They may even conduct free town tours. The regional tourist offices are administrative overseers rather than purveyors of useful practical information.

MAPS

In addition to the various free leaflets – and the maps in this guide – the one extra map you'll probably want is a reasonable **road map**. The *Michelin* map no. 989 (1:1M) is the best for the

whole country. A useful free map for car drivers, obtainable from filling stations and traffic information kiosks in France, is the *Bison Futé* map, showing alternative back routes to the congested main roads, clearly signposted on the ground by special green *Bison Futé* road signs.

For more **regional detail** the *Michelin* yellow series (scale 1:200,000) is best for the motorist. You can now get the whole series in one large spiral-bound, *Atlas Routier*. If you're planning to **walk or cycle,** check the *IGN* maps – their green (1:100,000 and 1:50,000) and blue (1:25,000) series. The *IGN* 1:100,000 series is the smallest scale available that has the contours marked – essential for cyclists, who tend to cycle off 1:25,000 maps in a couple of hours.

MAP AND GUIDE SUPPLIERS

BRITAIN

McCarta, 15 Highbury Place, London N5 1QP (☎071/354 1616). Main IGN importer with all 1:25,000 sheets in stock. Mail order only.

The Map Shop 15 High Street, Upton-upon-Severn, Worcs WR8 0HJ (☎06846/31 46). Mail order service.

Nomad Books, 791 Fulham Rd, London SW6 5DH (071/736 4000). Small, friendly travel books specialist.

Stanfords 12–14 Long Acre, London WC2E 9LP (☎071/836 1321); and at *BA*, 156 Regent St, London W1. The world's biggest travel guides and map store with a 7-part French region catalogue of all maps (available on request): carries all IGN 1:100,000 sheets plus selected 1:25,000; selected *Topoguides* (some in English); canal-cruising guides.

USA

The Complete Traveler 199 Madison Ave, New York, NY 10016 (☎212/685 9007).

French and European Publications 115 Fifth Ave, New York, NY10003 (☎212/673 7400).

Latitudes Calhoun Square, 3001 Hennepin Ave S, Minneapolis, MN 55408 (☎612/823 3742)

Map Link 529 State St, Santa Barbara, CA 93101 (☎805/963 4438).

Rand McNally Mapstore 150 E 52nd St, New York, NY 10022 (☎212/758 7488).

GETTING AROUND

With the most extensive railway network in western Europe, France is a country to travel by rail. The mountains are less well-served, but often, where the train stops, a bus, run by *SNCF*, the French rail company, continues the route. The private bus services are confusing and unco-ordinated. Approximate journey times and frequencies can be found in the "Travel Details" at the end of each chapter, and local peculiarities are also pointed out in the text of the guide. For a more private kind of independent transport, by car or bicycle, you'll need to be aware of a number of French road rules and peculiarities. Hitching is less and less popular, but walking, on the extensive network of "GR" footpaths, is recommended, as are the more specialist realms of inland boating and cross-country skiing, both of which have a high profile in France.

TRAINS

SNCF **trains** are, for the most part, clean, fast, and frequent and their staff are courteous and helpful. All but the smallest stations have an information desk and *consignes automatiques* – coin-operated lockers big enough to take a rucksack. Many (indicated in the text of the guide) hire out bicycles, sometimes of rather doubtful reliability. **Fares** are reasonable, at an average – off-peak – of about 50 centimes per kilometre. The ultra-fast *TGV*s (*Trains à Grande Vitesse*) require a supplement at peak times and compulsory reservation costing around 20F. The slowest trains are those marked *Autotrain* in the timetable, stopping at all stations.

While **InterRail, EurRail** and **France Vacances** passes (see p.7) are valid on all trains, and very much worth investigating before you leave home, *SNCF* itself offers a whole range of **discount fares** on *Période Bleue* (blue period) days – in effect, most of the year. A leaflet showing the blue, white (smaller discount) and red (peak) periods is given out at **gares SNCF** (train stations).

Under-26s can buy a *Carrissimo* card allowing travel at half fare on blue period days. It is valid for one year, and is available in Britain at £20 for four journeys, £35 for eight journeys.

The rest of *SNCF*'s cards are available only in France. **Couples** can have a free *Carte Couple*, entitling one of them to a half fare if they travel together and start their journey on a blue period day. **Over 60s** can get the *Carte Vermeille*, which, for 200F, gives you one year's half-price blue period travel. **Families with several children** can use a *Carte Kiwi*, for which one child under 16 is the holder and pays full fare, while the parents, brothers and sisters (four maximum) go half fare. The card costs 350F and entitles all the family to half fares on white or blue period days. And any passenger buying a return ticket for a long-distance journey and willing to travel *en période bleue*, and spend Sunday at their destination, can have a twenty-five percent discount by asking for a *Billet Séjour*.

All **tickets** – but not passes – must be date-stamped in the orange machines at station platform entrances. It is an offence not to "*Compostez votre billet*". Rail journeys may be broken any time, anywhere, but after a break of 24 hours you must "compost" your ticket again when you resume your journey. On night trains an extra 85F or so will buy you a **couchette** – well worth it if you're making a long haul and don't want to waste a day recovering from a sleepless night.

Regional **rail maps** and complete **timetables** are on sale at tobacconist shops. Leaflet timetables for a particular line are available free at stations. *Autocar* at the top of a column means it's an *SNCF* bus service, on which rail tickets and passes are valid.

BUSES

With the exception of *SNCF* services, **buses** play a generally minor role in France's public transport. They can, however, be useful for cross-country journeys. The most frustrating thing about them is that they rarely serve the regions

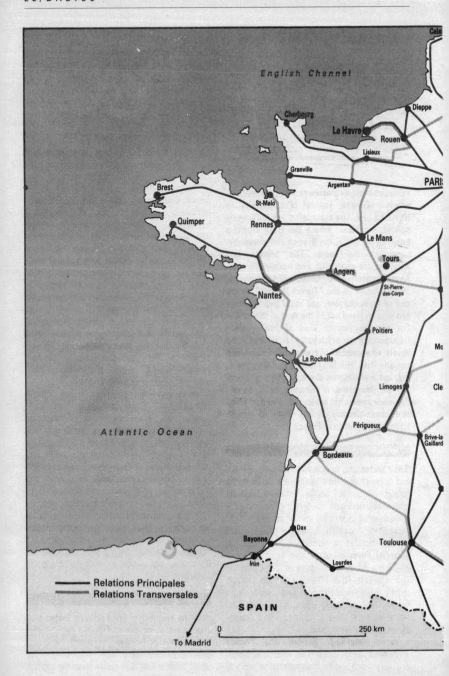

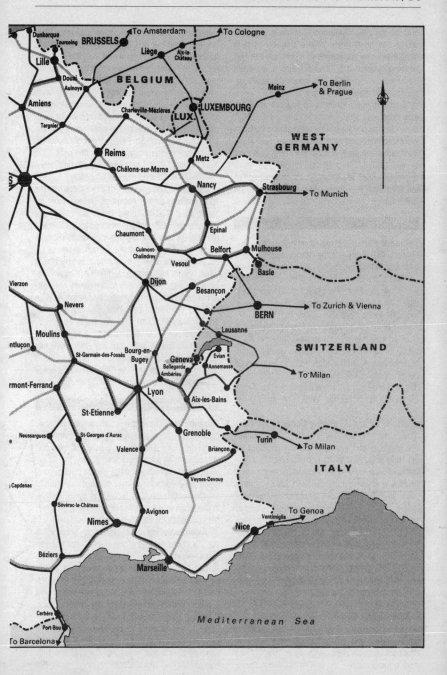

outside the *SNCF* network – which is precisely where you need them. Where they do exist in rural areas, the **timetable** is constructed to suit working, market and school hours – all often dauntingly early. They are, generally speaking, cheaper and slower than trains.

Larger towns usually have a *gare routière* (bus station), often next to the *gare SNCF*. However, the private bus companies don't always work together and you'll frequently find them leaving from an array of different points (the local SI will usually help locate them). The most convenient lines are those run as an extension of rail links by *SNCF*, these always run to/from the *SNCF* station.

DRIVING

Taking a car has its disadvantages: costs and breakdown liability are the most pressing, and if you want to feel the country and its culture around you, also the strong likelihood of reducing your contact with people. However, you do gain freedom of movement and, especially if you're camping, can be a lot more self-sufficient.

Car hire – at upwards of £150/$270 per week – is unlikely to be an economic alternative to taking a car across the channel, unless you're heading for the south of France and pick up a hired car on arrival. Probably the cheapest way to do this is to book through the efficient *Holiday Autos*, 25 Saville Row, London W1X 1AA (☎071 491 1111).

British, EC and US **driving licences** are valid, though an *International Driver's Licence* makes life easier if you get a policeman unwilling to peruse a document in English. The vehicle registration document and the insurance papers must be carried. If your car is right-hand drive, you must have your headlight dip adjusted to the right before you go – it's a legal requirement – and as a courtesy change or paint them to yellow or stick on black glare deflectors. All the major car manufacturers have garage/service stations in France – get their lists of addresses before you go. If you have an accident or break-in, you should make a report to the local police (and keep a copy) in order to make an insurance claim.

RULES OF THE ROAD

A **rule of the road** to remember when driving in France is that you must often give way to traffic coming from your right, even when it is coming from a minor road – the law of *priorité à droite*.

Because it is a major cause of accidents, it is being phased out and it only applies in built up areas, so the old nightmare of the tractor trundling across the country lane without warning is no more. In urban areas, too, many roundabouts no longer operate *priorité à droite*. You still have to be vigilant in towns, keeping a look out along the roadside for the yellow diamond on a white background that gives you right of way – until you see the same sign with an oblique black slash, which indicates vehicles emerging from the right have right of way. "*STOP*" signs mean stop completely: "*CEDEZ LE PASSAGE*" means "Give Way".

Fines for driving violations are exacted on the spot, and only cash is accepted. The minimum for speeding is 1300F. Speed limits are: 130km/hr (80mph) on the tolled *autoroutes*; 110km/hr (68mph) on two-lane highways; 90km/hr (56mph) on other roads; and 60km/hr (37mph) in towns.

Autoroute driving, though fast, is very boring when it's not hair-raising, and tolls are expensive. Nevertheless, it is the only realistic way of covering large distances in a single day. For information on road conditions call *Inter Service Route* on ☎1.48.58.33.33 (24hr). Use the *Bison Futé* map, free from petrol stations, especially to avoid the endless jams that build up over the weekends between July 15 and August 15. For full French driving regulations, see the "AA Traveller's Guide to Europe" (AA Publications £6.95).

HITCHING

Hitching, you'll have to rely almost exclusively on car drivers. Lorries very rarely give lifts. Even so, it won't be easy. Looking as clean, ordinary and respectable as possible makes a very big difference, as conversations with French drivers soon make clear. Experience also suggests that hitching the less frequented D-roads is much quicker. In mountain areas a rucksack and hiking gear will help procure a lift from fellow aficionados.

Autoroutes are a special case; hitching on the *autoroute* itself is strictly illegal, but you can make excellent time going from one service station to another. Remember to get out at the service station before your driver leaves the *autoroute*; the tollbooths are a second best (and legal); ordinary approach roads can be disastrous. If you get stuck at least there's food, drink, shelter and wash facilities at most service stations. It helps to have Michelin's *Guide des Autoroutes*, showing all the rest stops, service stations, tollbooths (*péages*), exits, etc.

For major **long-distance** rides, and for a greater sense of safety, you might consider using the national "hitching" organisation, *Allostop*, with offices in seventeen towns (Strasbourg, Bordeaux, Clermont-Ferrand, Rennes, Montpellier, Marseille, Toulouse, Lille, Angers, Chôlet, Nantes, Angoulême, La Rochelle, Aix-en-Provence, Cannes, Paris, Grenoble, Lyon). You pay to register with them (65F for on trip, 200F for eight journeys, plus 16 centimes per kilometre) and they find a driver who's going to your destination. *Allostop* seems like a desperate measure and lacks spontaneity, but in some circumstances may well be worth considering – sexual harassment can be bad in France (see p.46). Local phone numbers of *Allostop* or of similar organisations are given in the guide.

BICYCLES AND MOPEDS

Bicycles have high status in France. All the car ferries carry them for nothing; *SNCF* makes minimal charges; and the French (Parisians excepted) respect cyclists – both as traffic, and, when you stop off at a restaurant or hotel, as customers. French drivers normally go out of their way to make room for you – it's the great British caravan you might have to watch out for.

These days more and more cyclists are using **mountain bikes**, which the French call *VTTs* (*Vélos Touts Terrains*), even for touring holidays, although if you've ever made a direct comparison you'll soon realise that it's much less effort, and much quicker, to cycle long distances and carry luggage on a traditionally styled touring or racing bike.

Restaurants and hotels along the way are nearly always obliging about looking after your bike, even to the point of allowing it into your room. Most large towns have well-stocked retail and **repair shops**, where parts are normally cheaper than in Britain or the US. However, if you're using a foreign-made bike, it's a good idea to carry spare tyres, as French sizes are different. It's not that easy, either, to find parts for mountain bikes, the French enthusiasm being directed towards highly geared road racers instead. Inner tubes are not a problem, as they adapt to either size, though make sure you get the right valves.

The **railways** run various schemes for cyclists, all of them covered by the free leaflet *Train et Vélo*, available from most stations. *Autotrains* (when marked with a bicycle in the timetable) are usually the only ones on which you can travel with a bike as free accompanied luggage. Otherwise, you have to send your bike as registered luggage, for around 35F. Although it may well arrive in less time, *SNCF* won't guarantee delivery in under five days; and you do hear stories of bicycles disappearing altogether.

You can normally load your bike straight on to the train at the **ferry** port – as on the boat train at Dieppe – but remember that you must first go to the ticket office of the station to register it (there is time). Don't just try to climb on the train with it, as both you and your bike will end up left behind. In addition to the ferries, *British Airways* and *Air France* both take bikes free. You may have to box them though, and you should contact the airlines first.

A CYCLING VOCABULARY					
to adjust	*ajuster*	to deflate	*dégonfler*	rack	*le porte-bagages*
axle	*l'axe*	dérailleur	*le dérailleur*		
ball-bearing	*le roulement à billes*	frame	*le cadre*	to raise	*relever*
		gears	*les vitesses*	to repair	*réparer*
battery	*la pile*	grease	*la graisse*	saddle	*la selle*
bent	*tordu*	handlebars	*le guidon*	to screw	*visser*
bicycle	*le vélo*	to inflate	*gonfler*	spanner	*la clef (mécanique)*
bottom bracket	*le logement du pédalier*	inner tube	*la chambre à air*		
		loose	*dévissé*	spoke	*le rayon*
brake cable	*le cable*	to lower	*baisser*	to straighten	*rédresser*
brakes	*les freins*	mudguard	*le garde-boue*	stuck	*coincé*
broken	*cassé*	pannier	*le pannier*	tight	*serré*
bulb	*l'ampoule*	pedal	*le pédale*	toe clips	*les cale-pieds*
chain	*la chaîne*	pump	*la pompe*	tyre	*le pneu*
cotter pin	*la clavette*	puncture	*la crevaison*	wheel	*la roue*

At most *SNCF* stations bikes are also available for **hire**. At a cost of around 50F per day, you get the use of what is normally a very good condition *Peugeot*, and this you can return to any other station (so long as you specify the place when hiring). *SNCF* do not ask for a deposit, but do need a guarantee and will accept a credit card or cheque card number. You can also hire bikes from some **SI**s (tourist offices) and a fair number of bike shops (which are much more likely to offer you a mountain bike). The bikes are often not insured, however, and you will be presented with the bill for its replacement if it's stolen or damaged. Check whether your travel insurance policy covers you for this if you intend to hire a bike.

MOPEDS AND SCOOTERS

Mopeds and **scooters** are relatively easy to find: everyone in France, from young kids to grandmas, rides one of these, and although they're not built for any kind of long-distance travel, they're ideal for shooting around town and nearby. Places which hire out bicycles will often also hire out mopeds; you can expect to pay at least 150F a day for a moped, 300F a day for a scooter, and 400F a day for a proper motorbike. Crash helmets are compulsory only on machines over 125cc, but you'd be a fool not to wear one even on a moped.

AIDS TO TWO-WHEEL TOURING

For advice on which **maps** to take, see the "Maps" section on p.20. In the UK, the *Cyclists' Touring Club*, Cotterell House, 68 Meadrow, Godalming, Surrey GU7 3HS (☎0483/417217) will suggest routes and supply advice for a small fee, and they run a particularly good insurance scheme. *Cycle Touring in France* by Richard Neillands (Oxford Illustrated Press, £7.95) is a useful handbook for general advice on cycling holidays but extremely sketchy when it comes to actual routes.

The *Youth Hostels Association* also sell combined bike-hire and hostel packages; details from Trevelyan House, St Stephen's Hill, St Albans, Herts (☎0727/55215). And *Vélo Vacances* who run cycling tours of west Brittany, and *Susi Madon's Cycling for Softies* who run tours all over France, are included in the box on p.6. Also contact *Bike Events* (PO Box 75, Bath, Avon BA1 1BX, ☎0225/480130) who run trips every year all over the place.

WALKING

Long-distance walkers are well served in France by a network of over 30,000km of long distance marked **footpaths**, known as *sentiers de grande randonnée* or, more commonly, simply as **GR**s. They're fully signposted and equipped with campsites and rest huts along the way. Some are real marathons, like the GR5 from the coast of Holland to Nice, the trans-Pyrenean GR10 or the *Grande Traversée des Alpes*. The *Chemin de St-Jacques* – GR65 – follows the ancient pilgrim route from Le Puy in the Auvergne to the Spanish border above St-Jean-Pied-de-Port and on to the shrine of Santiago de Compostela, while GR3 traces the Loire from source to sea. There are many more.

Each path is described in a *Topoguide* (available in Britain from *Stanfords*, see p.20), which gives a detailed account of the route (in French), including maps, campsites, refuge huts, sources of provisions, etc. In addition many tourist offices can provide guides to their local footpaths, especially in popular hiking areas, where they often share premises with professional mountain guides and hike leaders. The latter organise climbing and walking expeditions for all levels of experience. The *Topoguides* are produced by the principal French walkers' organisation, the *Comité National des Sentiers de Grande Randonnée*, 8 av Marceau, 75008 Paris (☎47.23.62.32). The main **climbing** organisation is the *Club Alpin Français*, 9 rue de la Boétie, 75008 Paris (☎47.42.38.46).

Maps are listed under the "Information and Maps" section on p.20, but you might like to look at the specialised walking sheets produced by *Didier et Richard* of Grenoble for the Alps. *Walking in France* by Rob Hunter (Oxford Illustrated) gives a general round-up of walking information for the whole country. Other titles worth looking out for (all Cicerone Press) include *Walks and Climbs in the Pyrenees* by Kev Reynolds; *The Tour of Mt Blanc* by Andrew Harper; and *Walking the French Alps: GR5* by Martin Collins.

INLAND WATERWAYS

With some 7500km of navigable rivers and canals, **boating** can be one of the best and most relaxed ways of exploring France. Except on parts of the Moselle, there is no charge for use of the waterways, and you can travel without a permit for up to six months in a year. For information on maximum dimensions, documentation, regulations and so forth, ask at a French Government Tourist Office for their booklet *Boating on the Waterways*. They also have brochures on boating in particular regions and lists of French and British firms that rent out boats. Some are detailed in the box on p.6; for a full list write to the *Syndicat National des Loueurs de Bateaux de Plaisance*, Port de la Bourdonnais, 75007 Paris (☎45.55.10.49).

The principal **areas for boating** are Brittany, Burgundy, Picardy-Flanders, Alsace and Champagne. Brittany's canals join up with the Loire which is only navigable as far as Angers with no links eastwards. But the other waterways permit numerous permutations, including joining up via the Rhône and Saône with the Canal du Midi in Languedoc and then northwestwards to Bordeaux and the Atlantic. The eighteenth-century Canal de Bourgogne and 300-year-old Canal du Midi are fascinating examples of early

canal engineering. The latter completely transformed the fortunes of coastal Languedoc, and in particular Sète, whose attractive harbour dates from that period. Together with its continuation, the Canal du Sète à Rhône, it passes within easy reach of several interesting areas.

The through-journey **from Channel to Mediterranean** requires some planning. The Canal de Bourgogne has an inordinate number of locks, while other waterways demand considerable skill and experience – the Rhône and Saône rivers, for example, have tricky currents. The most direct route is from Le Havre to just beyond Paris, then south either on Canal du Loing et de Briare or Canal du Nivernais to the Canal Latéral de la Loire, which you follow as far as Digoin in southern Burgundy, where it crosses the river Loire and meets the Canal du Centre. You follow the latter as far as Châlon, where you continue south on the Saône and Rhône until you reach the Mediterranean at Port St-Louis in the Camargue.

ACCOMMODATION

At most times of the year, accommodation is plentiful, and you can turn up in any French town and find a room, or a place in a campsite. Booking a couple of nights in advance can be reassuring, however; it saves the effort of trudging round and ensures that you know what you'll be paying. In most towns, you'll be able to get a double for around 130–180F (£13–20/$23–36), a single for around 100–150F (£10–15/$18–27).

We've detailed where to find cheap places to stay in most of the destinations listed in the guide, and given a price range for each (see box), but as a general rule the areas around train stations have the highest density of cheap hotels. Phone numbers as well as addresses are given in the guide, and the "Language" section at the back should help you make the call, though many hoteliers and campsite managers – and almost all youth hostel managers – will speak some English.

Problems arise mainly **between July 15 and August 15**, when the French take their own vacations *en masse*. The first weekend of August is the busiest time of all. During this period, hotel and hostel accommodation can be hard to come by – particularly in the coastal resorts – and you may find yourself falling back on local SIs for help and ideas.

With campsites, you can be more relaxed, unless you're touring with a caravan or camper van. Big cities can be difficult throughout the year: we've given a greater range of possibilities for them in the guide and very detailed accommodation listings for Paris, the worst case of all.

HOTELS

Hotel **recommendations** are given in the text of the guide for almost every town or village mentioned. **Full accommodation lists** for each province are available from any French Government Tourist Office (see p.20) or from local SIs. If you're travelling in peak season, it's worth getting hold of these, together with a handbook for the *Logis et Auberges de France*. The latter are independent hotels, promoted together for their consistently good food and reasonably priced rooms; they're recognisable on the spot by a green and yellow logo of a hearth.

All French hotels are **graded** from zero to three stars. The price more or less corresponds to the number of stars, though the system is a little haphazard, having more to do with ratios of bathrooms-per-guest than genuine quality; ungraded and single-star hotels are often very good. At the cheapest level, what makes a difference in **cost** is whether a room contains a shower: if it does, the bill will be round 30–50F more. **Breakfast**, too, can add 15–30F per person to a bill – though there is no obligation to take it and you will nearly always do better at a café. The cost of eating **dinner** in a hotel's restaurant can be a more important factor to bear in mind when picking a place to stay. Officially it is illegal for hotels to insist on your taking meals – but they often do, and in busy resorts you may not find a room unless you agree to *démi-pension* (half-board). If you are unsure, ask to see the menu before signing in; cheap rooms aren't so cheap if you have to eat a 100F meal. **Single rooms** are only marginally cheaper than doubles so sharing always slashes costs. Most hotels willingly provide rooms with **extra beds**, for three or more people, at good discounts.

Note that many family-run hotels are closed every year for two or three weeks some time between May and September – where possible we've detailed this in the text. In addition, some hotels in smaller towns and villages close for one or two nights a week, usually Sunday or Monday – if in doubt ring first to check.

In country areas, in addition to standard hotels, you will come across *chambres d'hôte*, bed-and-breakfast accommodation in someone's house or farm. These vary in standard but are rarely an especially cheap option – usually costing the equivalent of a two-star hotel. However, if you're lucky, they may be good sources of traditional home-cooking. The brown leaflets available in SIs list most of them.

YOUTH HOSTELS, *FOYERS* AND *GITES D'ÉTAPE*

At between 35F and 60F per night for a dormitory bed, *Auberges de Jeunesse* – youth hostels – are invaluable for single travellers on a budget. For couples, however, and certainly for groups of three or more people (see above), they don't necessarily work out cheaper than hotels – particularly if you've had to pay a bus fare out to the edge of town to reach them. However, many hostels are beautifully sited, and they allow you to cut costs by preparing your own food in their kitchens, or eating in their cheap canteens. To stay at many of the hostels you're meant to be a member of the *International Youth Hostel Federation* (*IYHF*), which currently costs £8.90/$25 for over 21s, £4.70/$10 for under 21s. You can join at the main (British) *YHA* office in the UK at Trevelyan House, St Stephen's Hill, St Albans, Herts (☎0727/55215), or on the spot at most French hostels. A confusion is that there are two rival French youth hostel associations: the *Fédération Unie des Auberges de Jeunesse*, 6 rue Mesnil, 75116 Paris, which has its hostels detailed in the *International Handbook*, and the

Ligue Française pour les Auberges de Jeunesse, 83 rue de Rennes, 75006 Paris. *IYHF* membership covers both organisations – and you'll find all their hostels detailed in the text. A few large towns provide a more luxurious standard of hostel accommodation in **Foyers des Jeunes Travailleurs/euses**. These are residential hostels for young workers and students, in which for round 55F you can usually get a private room. They normally have a good cafeteria or canteen.

At the height of summer (usually July & Aug only), there's also the possibility of staying in **student accommodation** in university towns and cities. The main organisation for this is *CROUS*, 39 av G-Bernados, 75231 Paris (☎40.51.36.00). Prices are similar to the official hostels, at around 50F per person.

A third hostel-type alternative exists in the countryside, especially in hiking or cycling areas, in the **gîtes d'étape**. These are less formal than the youth hostels, often run by the local village or municipality (whose mayor will probably be in charge of the key) and provide bunk beds and primitive kitchen and washing facilities. They are marked on the large-scale *IGN* walkers' maps and listed in the individual GR *Topoguides*. Mountain areas have **mountain refuge huts** on the main GR routes, normally only open in summer. They're extremely basic but invaluable if you get caught by a storm. Costs are round 40F for the night, less if you're a member of a climbing organisation affiliated to the *Club Alpin Français*.

A complete list of all French *gîtes*, *refuges* and hostels is included in the publication *Gîtes et Refuges en France* (65F plus postage from Éditions Créer, rue Jean Amariton, Nonette, 63340 St-Germain Lembron); selections are also included in the French National Tourist Office booklet *Acceuil à la Campagne* (available from most SIs for around 40F).

RENTED ACCOMMODATION: GÎTES DE FRANCE

If you are planning to stay a week or more in any one place it might be worth considering **renting a house**. You can do this by checking adverts from the innumerable **private and foreign owners** in British Sunday newspapers (*The Observer* and *The Sunday Times*, mainly), or trying one of the numerous holiday firms that market accommodation/travel packages (see the box on p.5 for a brief selection of these).

Easiest and most reliable, however, is to use the official French Government service, the **Gîtes de France**. Their base in Britain is at 178 Piccadilly, London W1 (☎071/493 3480). Membership (£3) gets you a copy of their handbook, which contains properties all over France, listed by *département*. The houses vary in size and comfort, but all are basically acceptable holiday homes. There is a photograph and description of each one and the computerised booking service means that you can instantly reserve one for any number of full weeks. The cost varies with the season from around £70–140 per week – and may include concessionary ferry rates.

CAMPING

Practically every village and town in the country has at least one **campsite** to cater to the thousands of French people who spend their holiday under canvas.

The cheapest – at round 10–15F per person per night – is usually the **camping municipal**, run by the local municipality. In season, or when officially open, they are always clean with plenty of hot water and often situated in prime local positions. Out of season, many of them don't even bother to have someone round to collect the overnight charge.

On the coast especially, there are **superior categories** of campsite, where you'll pay prices similar to those of a hotel for the facilities – bars, restaurants, sometimes swimming pools. These have rather more permanent status than the *campings municipals*, with people often spending a whole holiday in the one base. If you plan to do the same and particularly if you have a caravan or camper, or a big tent, it's wise to book ahead.

Inland, **camping à la ferme** – on somebody's farm – is another possibility (generally without facilities). Lists of sites are detailed in the Tourist Board's *Accueil à la Campagne* booklet.

Lastly, a **word of caution**: never camp rough (*camping sauvage*, as the French call it) on anyone's land without first asking permission. If the dogs don't get you, the guns might – farmers have been known to shoot before asking questions. In many parts of France *camping sauvage* on public land isn't tolerated – Brittany being a notable exception. On beaches it's best to camp out only where other people are doing so.

EATING AND DRINKING

French food is as good a reason as any for a visit to France. Cooking has art status, the top chefs are stars, and dining out is a national pastime, whether it's at the bistro on the corner or at a famed house of *haute cuisine*. Eating out doesn't have to cost much, as long as you avoid tourist hotspots and treat the business of choosing a place as an interesting appetiser in itself.

BREAKFAST AND SNACKS

A croissant, *pain au chocolat* (a choc-filled croissant) or a sandwich in a bar or café, with hot chocolate or coffee, is generally the best way to eat **breakfast** – at a fraction of the cost charged by most hotels. (The days when hotels gave you mounds of croissants or *brioches* for breakfast seem to be long gone; now it's virtually always bread, jam and a jug of coffee or tea for about 25F.) *Croissants* and sometimes hard-boiled eggs are displayed on bar counters until around 9.30 or 10am. If you stand – cheaper than sitting down – you just help yourself to these with your coffee, the waiter keeps an eye on how many you've eaten and bills you accordingly.

At **lunchtime** you may find cafés offering a *plat du jour* (chef's daily special) at between 25F and 50F or *formules*, a limited or no-choice menu. The *Croque-Monsieur* or *Madame* (variations on the toasted-cheese sandwich) is on sale at cafés, brasseries and many street stands, along with *frites*, *crêpes*, *galettes* (wholewheat pancakes), *gauffres* (waffles), *glaces* (ice creams) and all kinds of fresh sandwiches. For variety, there are Tunisian snacks like *brik à l'oeuf* (a fried pastry with an egg inside), *merguez* (spicy North African sausage), Greek *souvlaki* (kebabs), Middle Eastern *falafel* (deep-fried chickpea balls with salad) and Japanese tidbits. Wine bars are good for French regional meat and cheese, usually served with brown bread (*pain de campagne*).

Many people also eat **crêpes** for lunch. These filled pancakes, originally from Brittany, are now available all over France. The savoury buckwheat variety (often called *galettes*) are served as a main course; the sweet white-flour ones are dessert. They taste nice enough, but they are usually poor value in comparison with a restaurant meal; you need at least three, normally at over 20F each, to feel even slightly full. That they always excite children shouldn't fool parents into thinking of a *crêperie* as a cheap alternative.

Pizzerias are also common in France. They are somewhat better value than *crêperies*, but quality and quantity vary greatly – look before you leap into the nearest empty seats.

For **picnics**, the local outdoor market or supermarket will provide you with almost everything you need from tomatoes and avocados to cheese and paté. For **takeaway food**, there's nothing to beat the *charcuteries* (delicatessens, mostly pork-based), which you'll find everywhere – even in small villages. These sell cooked meat, prepared snacks such as *bouchées de la reine* (seafood vol-au-vents), ready-made dishes and assorted salads. The cheapest, by far, are the supermarkets' *charcuterie* counters. You purchase by weight, or you can ask for *une tranche* (a slice), *une barquette* (a carton), or *une part* (a portion).

Salons de thé, which open from mid-morning to late evening, serve brunches, salads, quiches, and the like, as well as cake and ice cream and a wide selection of teas. They tend to be a good deal pricier than cafés or brasseries – you're paying for the posh surroundings. *Pâtisseries*, of course, have impressive arrays of cakes and pastries, often using local cream to excess.

FULL SCALE MEALS

There's no difference between **restaurants** (or *auberges* or *relais* as they sometimes call themselves) and **brasseries** in terms of quality or price range. The distinction is that brasseries, which resemble cafés, serve quicker meals at most hours of the day, while restaurants tend to stick to the traditional meal times of noon–2pm and 7–9.30 or 10.30pm. After 9pm or so, restaurants often serve only *à la carte* meals (single dishes chosen from the menu) – invariably more expensive than eating the set *menu fixe*. For the more upmarket places it's wise to make reservations – easily done on the same day. In small towns it may be impossible to get anything other than a bar sandwich after 10pm; in major cities, town centre brasseries will serve until 11pm or midnight and one or two may stay open all night. When hunting, avoid places that are half empty at peak time and treat the business of sizing up different menus as an enjoyable appetiser in itself. Don't forget that hotel restaurants are open to non-residents – and often very good value.

Prices, and what you get for them, are posted outside the restaurant. Normally there's a choice between one or more *menus fixes*, where the number of courses has already been determined and the choice is limited. The *carte* (menu) has everything listed. *Menus fixes* start out as the cheapest option, which revolve round standard dishes such as steak and chips (*steack frites*), chicken and chips (*poulet frites*), or various concoctions involving innards. The *plat du jour*, sometimes a regional dish, is often more appealing. More and more, though, restaurants are offering a variety of *menus fixes*, the most expensive of which offer quite a wide choice for each course, and run to five or more courses – these are always better value than going *à la carte*.

Going *à la carte* does, however, offer greater flexibility and, in the better restaurants, unlimited access to the chef's specialities – though you'll pay for the privilege. A simple and perfectly legitimate tactic is to have just one course instead of the expected three or four. You can share dishes or just have several starters – a useful strategy for vegetarians. There's no minimum charge.

In the French **sequence of courses**, any salad (sometimes vegetables, too) comes separate from the main dish, and cheese precedes a dessert. You will be offered coffee, which is always extra, to finish off the meal.

Service compris or *s.c.* means the **service charge** is included. *Service non compris*, *s.n.c.* or *servis en sus* means that it isn't and you need to calculate an additional fifteen percent. **Wine** (*vin*) or a **drink** (*boisson*) is unlikely to be included, although occasionally thrown in with cheaper menus. When ordering wine, ask for *un quart* (0.25 litre), *un demi-litre* (0.5 litre) or *une carafe* (a litre). You'll normally be given the house wine unless you specify otherwise; if you're worried about the cost ask for *vin ordinaire*.

NOUVELLE CUISINE

Developed in the 1970s, the *nouvelle cuisine* method of cooking turned away from the rich, creamy sauces and bloating portions of traditional cuisine to concentrate instead on the intrinsic flavours of foods and on new combinations in which the mix of colours and textures complements the tastes. Courses are no more than a few mouthfuls, presented with oriental artistry and finely judged to leave you at the end well-fed but not weighed down. At its purest and best, *nouvelle cuisine* can induce gastronomic ecstasy from an ungarnished leek or carrot and elevate the taste sensation of salmon, lobster, or a wild strawberry pastry to the power of sound and vision.

The downside is that it requires absolutely prime, fresh ingredients and precision skills, which means that *nouvelle cuisine* meals are horrendously expensive. Less revolutionary now that it is fairly common, it has had a lasting and healthy effect on the consciousness of all French cooks.

FOODS AND DISHES

Basic terms

Pain	Bread	Poivre	Pepper	Verre	Glass
Beurre	Butter	Sel	Salt	Fourchette	Fork
Oeufs	Eggs	Sucre	Sugar	Couteau	Knife
Lait	Milk	Vinaigre	Vinegar	Cuillère	Spoon
Huile	Oil	Bouteille	Bottle	Table	Table

Snacks

Un sandwich/ une baguette ... **A sandwich**
jambon — with ham
fromage — with cheese
saucisson — with sausage
à l'ail — with garlic
au poivre — with pepper
pâté (de campagne) — with pâté (country-style)
croque-monsieur — Grilled cheese and ham sandwich
croque-madame — Grilled cheese and bacon, sausage, chicken or an egg

Oeufs — **Eggs**
au plat — Fried eggs
à la coque — Boiled eggs
durs — Hard-boiled eggs
brouillés — Scrambled eggs

Omelette ... — **Omelette** ...
nature — plain
aux fines herbes — with herbs
au fromage — with cheese

Salade de ... — **Salad of** ...
tomates — tomatoes
betteraves — beets
concombres — cucumber
carottes rapées — grated carrots

Crêpe — **Pancake**
au sucre — with sugar
au citron — with lemon
au miel — with honey
à la confiture — with jam
aux oeufs — with eggs
à la crème de marrons — with chestnut purée

Other fillings/salads
Anchois — Anchovy
Andouillette — Tripe sausage
Boudin — Black pudding
Coeurs de palmiers — Hearts of palm
Epis de maïs — Corn on the cob
Fonds d'artichauts — Artichoke hearts
Hareng — Herring
Langue — Tongue
Poulet — Chicken
Thon — Tuna fish

And some terms
Chauffé — Heated
Cuit — Cooked
Cru — Raw
Emballé — Wrapped
A emporter — Takeaway
Fumé — Smoked
Salé — Salted/spicy
Sucré — Sweet

Soups (*soupes*) and starters (*hors d'oeuvres*)

Bisque — Shellfish soup
Bouillabaisse — Marseillais fish soup
Bouillon — Broth or stock
Bourride — Thick fish soup
Consommé — Clear soup
Pistou — Parmesan, basil and garlic paste added to soup
Potage — Thick vegetable soup
Rouille — Red pepper, garlic and saffron mayonnaise served with fish soup

Velouté — Thick soup, usually fish or poultry

Starters
Assiette anglaise — Plate of cold meats
Crudités — Raw vegetables with dressings
Hors d'oeuvres variés — Combination of the above plus smoked or marinated fish

Fish (poisson), seafood (fruits de mer) and shellfish (crustaces or coquillages)...

Anchois	Anchovies	*Daurade*	Sea bream
Anguilles	Eels	*Eperlan*	Smelt or whitebait
Barbue	Brill		
Bigourneau	Periwinkle	*Escargots*	Snails
Brème	Bream	*Flétan*	Halibut
Cabillaud	Cod	*Friture*	Assorted fried fish
Calmar	Squid	*Gambas*	King prawns
Carrelet	Plaice	*Hareng*	Herring
Claire	Type of oyster	*Homard*	Lobster
Colin	Hake	*Huîtres*	Oysters
Congre	Conger eel	*Langouste*	Spiny lobster
Coques	Cockles	*Langoustines*	Saltwater crayfish (scampi)
Coquilles St-Jacques	Scallops	*Limande*	Lemon sole
Crabe	Crab	*Lotte*	Burbot
Crevettes grises	Shrimp	*Lotte de mer*	Monkfish
Crevettes roses	Prawns	*Loup de mer*	Sea bass
Louvine, loubine	Similar to sea bass		
Maquereau	Mackerel		
Merlan	Whiting		
Moules (marinière)	Mussels (with shallots in white wine sauce)		
Oursin	Sea urchin		
Palourdes	Clams		
Praires	Small clams		
Raie	Skate		
Rouget	Red mullet		
Saumon	Salmon		
Sole	Sole		
Thon	Tuna		
Truite	Trout		
Turbot	Turbot		

...and fish terms

Aïoli	Garlic mayonnaise served with salt cod and other fish	*Fumé*	Smoked
		Fumet	Fish stock
Béarnaise	Sauce of egg yolks, white wine, shallots and vinegar	*Gigot de Mer*	Large fish baked whole
		Grillé	Grilled
Beignets	Fritters	*Hollandaise*	Butter and vinegar sauce
Darne	Fillet or steak	*A la meunière*	In a butter, lemon and parsley sauce
La douzaine	A dozen		
Frit	Fried	*Mousse/mousseline*	Mousse
Friture	Deep fried small fish	*Quenelles*	Light dumplings

Meat (viande) and poultry (volaille)

Agneau (de pré-salé)	Lamb (grazed on salt marshes)	*Langue*	Tongue
Andouille, andouillette	Tripe sausage	*Lapin, lapereau*	Rabbit, young rabbit
		Lard, lardons	Bacon, diced bacon
		Lièvre	Hare
Boeuf	Beef	*Merguez*	Spicy, red sausage
Bifteck	Steak	*Mouton*	Mutton
Boudin blanc	Sausage of white meats	*Museau de veau*	Calf's muzzle
Boudin noir	Black pudding	*Oie*	Goose
Caille	Quail	*Os*	Bone
Canard	Duck	*Porc*	Pork
Caneton	Duckling	*Poulet*	Chicken
Contrefilet	Sirloin roast	*Poussin*	Baby chicken
Coquelet	Cockerel	*Ris*	Sweetbreads
Dinde, dindon	Turkey	*Rognons*	Kidneys
Entrecôte	Ribsteak	*Rognons blancs*	Testicles
Faux filet	Sirloin steak	*Sanglier*	Wild boar
Foie	Liver	*Steack*	Steak
Foie gras	Fattened (duck/ goose) liver	*Tête de veau*	Calf's head (in jelly)
Gigot (d'agneau)	Leg (of lamb)	*Tournedos*	Thick slices of fillet
Grillade	Grilled meat	*Tripes*	Tripe
Hâchis	Chopped meat or mince hamburger	*Veau*	Veal
		Venaison	Venison

Meat and poultry terms – dishes ...

Boeuf bourguignon	Beef stew with burgundy, onions and mushrooms	*Coq au vin*	Chicken cooked until it falls off the bone with wine, onions, and mushrooms
Canard à l'orange	Roast duck with an orange-and-wine sauce	*Steak au poivre (vert/ rouge)*	Steak in a black (green/red) peppercorn sauce
Cassoulet	A casserole of beans and meat	*Steak tartare*	Raw chopped beef, topped with a raw egg yolk

... and terms

Blanquette, daube, estouffade, hochepôt, navarin and *ragoût*	All are types of stew
Aile	Wing
Carré	Best end of neck, chop or cutlet
Civit	Game stew
Confit	Meat preserve
Côte	Chop, cutlet or rib
Cou	Neck
Cuisse	Thigh or leg
Epaule	Shoulder
Médaillon	Round piece
Pavé	Thick slice
En croûte	In pastry
Farci	Stuffed
Au feu de bois	Cooked over wood fire
Au four	Baked
Garni	With vegetables
Gésier	Gizzard
Grillé	Grilled
Magret de canard	Duck breast
Marmite	Casserole
Mijoté	Stewed
Museau	Muzzle
Rôti	Roast
Sauté	Lightly cooked in butter

For steaks:

Bleu	Almost raw
Saignant	Rare
A point	Medium
Bien cuit	Well done
Très bien cuit	Very well cooked
Brochette	Kebab

Garnishes and sauces:

Beurre blanc	Sauce of white wine and shallots, with butter
Chasseur	White wine, mushrooms and shallots
Diable	Strong mustard seasoning
Forestière	With bacon and mushroom
Fricassée	Rich, creamy sauce
Mornay	Cheese sauce
Pays d'Auge	Cream and cider
Piquante	Gherkins or capers, vinegar and shallots
Provençale	Tomatoes, garlic, olive oil and herbs

Fruit *(fruit)* and nuts *(noix)*

Abricot	Apricot	*Framboises*	Raspberries
Amandes	Almonds	*Fruit de la passion*	Passion fruit
Ananas	Pineapple		
Banane	Banana	*Groseilles*	Redcurrants and gooseberries
Brugnon, nectarine	Nectarine	*Mangue*	Mango
Cacahouète	Peanut	*Marrons*	Chestnuts
Cassis	Blackcurrants	*Melon*	Melon
Cérises	Cherries	*Myrtilles*	Bilberries
Citron	Lemon	*Noisette*	Hazelnut
Citron vert	Lime	*Noix*	Nuts
Figues	Figs	*Orange*	Orange
Fraises (de bois)	Strawberries (wild)	*Pamplemousse*	Grapefruit
		Pêche (blanche)	(White) peach

Pistache	Pistachio
Poire	Pear
Pomme	Apple
Prune	Plum
Pruneau	Prune
Raisins	Grapes

Terms:

Beignets	Fritter
Compôte de ...	Stewed ...
Coulis	Sauce
Flambé	Set aflame in alcohol
Frappé	Iced

Vegetables *(légumes),* herbs *(herbes)* and spices *(épices),* etc

Ail	Garlic	*Endive*	Chicory	*Piment*	Pimento
Algue	Seaweed	*Epinards*	Spinach	*Pois chiche*	Chick peas
Anis	Aniseed	*Estragon*	Tarragon	*Pois mange-*	Snow peas
Artichaut	Artichoke	*Fenouil*	Fennel	*tout*	
Asperges	Asparagus	*Flageolet*	White beans	*Pignons*	Pine nuts
Avocat	Avocado	*Gingembre*	Ginger	*Poireau*	Leek
Basilic	Basil	*Haricots*	Beans	*Poivron*	Sweet pepper
Betterave	Beetroot	*Verts*	String (French)	*(vert, rouge)*	(green, red)
Carotte	Carrot	*Rouges*	Kidney	*Pommes (de*	Potatoes
Céleri	Celery	*Beurres*	Butter	*terre)*	
Champignons,	Mushrooms of	*Laurier*	Bay leaf	*Primeurs*	Spring
cèpes,	various kinds	*Lentilles*	Lentils		vegetables
chanterelles		*Maïs*	Corn	*Radis*	Radishes
Chou (rouge)	(Red) cabbage	*Menthe*	Mint	*Riz*	Rice
Choufleur	Cauliflower	*Moutarde*	Mustard	*Safran*	Saffron
Ciboulettes	Chives	*Oignon*	Onion	*Salade verte*	Green salad
Concombre	Cucumber	*Pâte*	Pasta or pastry	*Sarrasin*	Buckwheat
Cornichon	Gherkin	*Persil*	Parsley	*Tomate*	Tomato
Echalotes	Shallots	*Petits pois*	Peas	*Truffes*	Truffles

Dishes and terms

Beignet	Fritter	*Parmentier*	With potatoes
Farci	Stuffed	*Sauté*	Lightly fried in butter
Gratiné	Browned with cheese or butter	*A la vapeur*	Steamed
Jardinière	With mixed diced vegetables	*Je suis végétarien(ne).*	I'm a vegetarian. Are
A la parisienne	Sautéed in butter (potatoes); with white wine sauce, and shallots	*Il y a quelques plats sans viande?*	there any non-meat dishes?

Desserts *(desserts* or *entremets)* and pastries *(pâtisserie)*

Bombe	A moulded ice cream dessert	*Parfait*	Frozen mousse, some-
Brioche	Sweet, high yeast breakfast roll		times ice cream
Charlotte	Custard and fruit in lining of almond fingers	*Petit Suisse*	A smooth mixture of cream and curds
Crème Chantilly	Vanilla-flavoured and sweet-ened whipped cream	*Petits fours*	Bite-sized cakes/pastries
		Poires Belle Hélène	Pears and ice cream in
Crème fraîche	Sour cream		chocolate sauce
Crème pâtissière	Thick eggy pastry-filling		
Crêpes suzettes	Thin pancakes with orange juice and liqueur	*Yaourt, yogourt*	Yoghurt
Fromage blanc	Cream cheese	**Terms:**	
Glace	Ice cream	*Barquette*	Small boat-shaped flan
Ile flottante/	Soft meringues floating on	*Bavarois*	Refers to the mould, could
oeufs à la neige	custard		be a mousse or custard
Macarons	Macaroons	*Coupe*	A serving of ice cream
Madeleine	Small sponge cake	*Crêpes*	Pancakes
Marrons Mont	Chestnut purée and cream on a	*Galettes*	Buckwheat pancakes
Blanc	rum-soaked sponge cake	*Génoise*	Rich sponge cake
Mousse au	Chocolate mousse	*Sablé*	Shortbread biscuit
chocolat		*Savarin*	A filled, ring-shaped cake
Palmiers	Caramelised puff pastries	*Tarte*	Tart
		Tartelette	Small tart

And one final note: always call the waiter or waitress *Monsieur* or *Madame (Mademoiselle* if a young woman), never *garçon,* no matter what you've been taught in school.

REGIONAL CUISINE

The **geography of France** explains much of the pride of place the country holds in European cuisines. The French can fish and breed seafood in the Channel waters, the Atlantic Ocean and the Mediterranean as well as catching freshwater fish in a thousand lakes and rivers. Mountains, forests, deltas and plains with climates ranging from the aridly sun-soaked to northern cold and wetness allow an extraordinary variety of produce. Added to this is the historical and social factor of a class of *paysans* – small-holders – who have passed down traditional methods from generation to generation. Though it is true that in recent years industrialisation has standardised and sanitised production methods, food imports have greatly increased, and pollution has taken its toll, there remains a strong connection between the countryside and the table, reflected in the different regional cuisines. The gastronomic map of France features certain regions – Alsace, Provence, Brittany and the Pays Basque – in which the preservation of a distinctive cuisine owes much to historical separation. Burgundy, the Auvergne, Normandy and the Dordogne represent classic French cooking from different corners of the country. Lyon has a special position as the meeting place of north and south. Below is a selection of typical dishes and produce from the main gastronomic regions.

Alsace

Game; fruit brandies; cheesecake; braised pork knuckle; *choucroute*, sauerkraut with sausage, bacon and other meats; *baeckeoffe*, pork, beef and lamb stew with onions and potatoes; *tarte flambée* or *flammekueche*, cream, bacon and onion flan with pizza-like pastry; *madeleines*, lemon teacakes beloved of Proust; bilberry tart.

Atlantic Coast

Seafood; ocean fish; eels; snails; *mouclade*, mussel soup with saffron; *chaudrée*, Atlantic fish stew; *mojette*, white beans; *pibales*, baby eels; *bouilliture*, eel stew with red wine and prunes.

Auvergne

Sausages; lentils; bilberries; morel mushrooms; salmon trout; cheeses; rye bread; garlic soup; *aligot*, mashed potato, cheese curds and garlic; *potée auvergnate*, cabbage, pork and bean stew; *tourte au Cantal*, Cantal cheese tart.

Brittany

Oysters, lobster and other seafood; seafish; artichokes; white haricot beans; *crêpes* and *galettes*, wheat and buckwheat flour pancakes, with sweet or savoury fillings; *coquilles St-Jacques*; heavy buttery cakes such as *kouign-amann*; and *far breton*, a prune and custard flan or batter.

Burgundy

Charolais beef; mustard; snails in parsley and garlic; *coq au vin*; *boeuf bourguignon*; *jambon persillé*, ham and parsley in aspic; *pain d'épices*, spiced bread; *pochouse*, freshwater fish stew.

Dordogne

Duck and goose in a myriad of forms including *pâté de foie gras*, preserves, *cou farci du Quercy*, stuffed goose neck marinated in alcohol, and *canard périgourdin*, duck with prunes; truffles;

Languedoc

Rocquefort cheese; anchovies; Bouzigues mussels; *cargolade*, grilled snails and sausages; *boule de Picoulat*, beef, pork, egg and garlic meatball; *crêpes languedociennes*, rum flambéed pancakes filled with vanilla cream.

Lyon

Sausages; smoked meats; tripe; chitterlings; cheeses; *quenelles*; *poulet au vinaigre*, chicken in sour cream and vinegar; *salade Lyonnais*, green salad with croutons, bacon and runny egg; *tarte Lyonnais*, custard flan with kirsch and almonds.

Normandy

Oysters, mussels and other seafood; cheeses; cream; apples and pears; *pain brié*, saltless bread; tripe, in sausages or *à la mode de Caen* (cooked with Calvados and cider or white wine); *sole Normande*, sole with mussels, shrimps and mushrooms; *poulet vallée d'Auge*, Pays d'Auge chicken in cream and cider; *agneau pré-salé*, lamb grazed on salt marshes; *douillon*, pear cooked in pastry.

Pays Basque

Bayonne ham; white tuna; ewe's milk cheese (*brebis*); pimentoes; corn bread; wild pigeon (*palombe*); *gâteau Basque*, black cherry cake; *agneau chilindron*, sautéed lamb with potatoes and garlic; *tourtière landaise*, apple and prune strudel.

Provence

Olive oil; garlic; basil; melons; early fruit and vegetables; citrus fruits; lavender honey; pasta; sea fish soups served with *rouille*, a red pepper and garlic mayonnaise; goat's cheese; fish grilled in fennel or *herbes de Provence*; *aïoli*, salt cod with garlic mayonnaise; *mesclum*, a salad mix of several greens; *estocaficada*, stockfish and tomato stew; *gardiane*, bull meat stew from the Camargue.

The French are much better disposed towards **children** in restaurants than the British, not simply by offering reduced-price children's menus, but in creating an atmosphere, even in otherwise fairly snooty establishments, that positively welcomes kids; some even have in-house games and toys for them to occupy themselves with. It is regarded as self-evident that large family groups should be able to eat out together.

A rather murkier area is that of **dogs** in the dining room; it can be quite a shock in a provincial hotel to realise that the majority of your fellow diners are attempting to keep dogs concealed beneath their tables.

DRINKING

Wherever you can eat you can invariably **drink**, and vice versa. Drinking is done at a leisurely pace whether it's a prelude to food (*apéritif*), a sequel (*digestif*), or the accompaniment, and **cafés** are the standard places to do it. Every bar or café has to display its full **price list** (usually without the fifteen percent service charge added) with the cheapest drinks at the bar (*au comptoir*), and progressively increasing prices for sitting at a table inside (*la salle*), or on the terrace (*la terrasse*). You pay when you leave and it's perfectly acceptable to sit for hours over just one cup of coffee.

Wine – *vin* – is the regular drink. Red is *rouge*, white *blanc*, or there's *rosé*. *Vin de table* – table wine (plonk) – is generally drinkable and always cheap; it may be disguised and priced-up as the house wine, or *cuvée*. Restaurant mark-ups for quality wines can be outrageous, in a country where wine is so cheap in the shops. In bars, you normally buy by the glass, and just ask for *un rouge* or *un blanc*; *un pichet* gets you a quarter-litre jug.

Familiar Belgian and German brands, plus French brands from Alsace, account for most of the **beer** you'll find. Draft (*à la pression*, usually *Kronenbourg*) is the cheapest drink you can have next to coffee and wine – though the smallest glass, *un demi* (0.25l), is rarely less than seven or eight francs. Bottled beer is exceptionally cheap in supermarkets.

British-style ales and stouts are becoming increasingly popular, with a number of special beer-drinking establishments or English-style pubs appearing in the larger cities, and in abundance in the capital. Bear in mind, though, that a small bottle will set you back as much as fifteen francs.

Strong alcohol is consumed from as early as 5am as a pre-work fortifier, and then at any time through the day according to circumstance, though the national reputation for drunkenness has lost much of its truth. Brandies and the dozens of *eaux de vie* (spirits) and liqueurs are always available. Among less familiar names, try *Poire William* (pear brandy), *Marc* (a spirit distilled from grape pulp), or just point to the bottle with the most attractive colour. Measures are generous, but they don't come cheap: the same applies for imported spirits like whisky (*Scotch*). *Pastis* – the generic name of aniseed drinks such as *Pernod* or *Ricard* – is served diluted with water and ice (*glaçons*). It's very refreshing and not expensive. Two drinks designed to stimulate the appetite are *Pineau* (cognac and grape juice) and *Kir* (white wine with a dash of blackcurrant syrup, or champagne for a *Kir Royal*).

On the **soft drink** front, you can now buy cartons of unsweetened fruit juice in supermarkets, although in the cafés the bottled (sweetened) nectars such as apricot (*jus d'abricot*) and blackcurrant (*cassis*) still hold sway. You can also get fresh orange and lemon juice (*orange/citron pressé*), at a price; otherwise it's the standard fizzy cans. Bottles of **mineral water** (*eau minérale*) and spring water (*eau de source*) – either sparkling (*pétillante*) or still (*eau plate*) – abound, from the big brand names to the most obscure spa product. But there's not much wrong with the tap water (*l'eau de robinet*).

Coffee is invariably espresso – small, black and very strong. *Un café* or *un express* is the regular; *un crème* is with milk; *un grand café* or *un grand crème* are large cups. In the morning you could also ask for *un café au lait* – espresso in a large cup or bowl filled up with hot milk. *Un déca* is decaffeinated, now widely available. Ordinary **tea** (*thé*) is *Lipton's* nine times out of ten; to have milk with it, ask for *un peu de lait frais* (some fresh milk).

After overeating, **herb teas** (*infusions* or *tisanes*), served in every café, can be soothing. The more common ones are *verveine* (verbena), *tilleul* (lime blossom), *menthe* (mint) and *camomille* (camomile). *Chocolat chaud* – **hot chocolate** – unlike tea, lives up to the high standards of French food and drink and can be had in any café.

CHEESE

You can unite the French only through fear. You cannot simply
bring together a country that has over 265 kinds of cheese

Charles de Gaulle, in a speech, 1951

For serious cheese-lovers, France is the ultimate paradise. Other countries may produce individual cheeses which are as good as, or even better than, the best of the French, but no country offers a range that comes anywhere near them in terms of sheer inventiveness. In fact, there are officially over 400 types of French cheese (with new ones being created every year), whose recipes are jealously guarded secrets. Many cheesemakers have sucessfully protected their products by *AC* (*appellation d'origine controlée*) laws similar to those for wines, which means that the subtle differences between French local cheese are still not overwhelmed by the industrialised uniformity that has plagued other countries.

Most restaurants keep a well-stocked *plateau de fromages* (cheeseboard), kept at room temperature and served with bread, but not butter. Apart from the ubiquitous Brie, Camembert and goat's cheese (*chèvre*), there will usually be one or two local cheeses on offer – these are the ones to go for. Your best bet for local produce is a *fromagerie*, which often has 200 varieties or more to choose from. Some useful phrases: *une petite tranche de celui-ci* (a small piece of this one); *je peux gouter?* (may I taste?).

The list of cheeses below is just a small selection of some of the most delicious.

Banon
Mild, slightly sour, small cheese from Provence, most commonly made with goat's or ewe's milk, but occasionally from cow's milk. Fermented for at least two months in terracotta jars and wrapped in chestnut leaves soaked in *eau-de-vie*.

Bleu d'Auvergne
One of France's best known blue cheeses, mostly made in the uplands of the Jura and Massif Central from cow's milk. At its best it is sharp, creamy and not over-salty.

Brie
Brie has been around since the 1200s. Originally from the Île de France, the best is generally considered to be *Brie de Meaux*, from Champagne. Don't buy brie with a hard centre as it won't mature.

Cabécou
A tiny, strong, round goat's cheese made in Aquitaine.

Camembert
France's best known cheese, accounting for a quarter of its cheese production. Originally from Normandy, it's now a national product, but the best stuff is still the truly Norman *fermier* variety, hand-made with unpasteurised cow's milk.

Cantal
France's oldest cheese, made in the Massif Central for at least 2000 years. Often described as the "French cheddar", it's a semi-hard, yellowy cheese with a dry, grey rind and a mellow, nutty flavour.

Chaource
A milky white fruity cheese with an unusual dry consistency and high fat content, made in the Champagne region.

Chaumes
A popular pasteurised cheese from the Dordogne with a rich, golden and creamy texture and a tough yellow rind.

Comté
France's best-known version of the hard Swiss cheese *Gruyère*, made in Franche-Comté. A little moisture means it's perfect for eating.

Livarot
Pungent, spicey, thick disc of cow's milk cheese from Normandy, mostly factory-made nowadays, but nevertheless still protected by an *appellation d'origine*.

Munster
Seriously smelly *apellation d'origine* cheese from Alsace, with a distinctive brick-red rind. *Petit Munster* is a common, supermarket variety no less pungent.

Neufchâtel
A very rich, creamy cheese from the Pays de Bray in Normandy, eaten fresh or ripened (*affiné*). It comes in a variety of shapes and sizes.

Pont l'Evêque
Square blocks of tender aromatic *appellation d'origine* cheese, one of the oldest in Normandy, still made from unpasteurised milk for the most part, with a lightly tanned rind.

Port-Salut

The mother of monastery cheeses, semi-soft and extremely popular. The original Port-Salut, from the Abbaye d'Entrammes, is still made and sold under that name. The bland *Saint-Paulin* is its factory-made descendant.

Reblochon

One of France's greatest mountain cheeses from the Haute-Savoie region. It is semi-soft with a fruity flavour and a pinkish-brown rind, and is sold in flat rounds set between two wooden discs.

Roquefort

Quite distinct from every other blue cheese, *Roquefort* is a delicious, soft crumbly cheese, protected by an *appellation d'origine*, which means that it must be ripened for at least three months in the limestone caves of Les Causses in the Massif Central. Far milder than most blue cheeses.

Tomme de Savoie

Strictly speaking a generic term for the family of semi-hard cheeses made in Savoie from skimmed milk, which gives it an unusually low fat content for French cheese. The rind is generally greyish-white in colour, and the flavour mildly nutty and aromatic.

Vignotte

Ridiculously rich and creamy semi-soft cheese, with a mild flavour which belies its above-average pungency.

COMMUNICATIONS: POST, PHONES AND MEDIA

French post offices – *postes* or *PTT*s – are generally open 9am–noon and 2–5pm (Mon–Fri) and 9am–noon on Saturday. However, don't depend on these hours: in larger towns you'll find a main office open throughout the day, while in villages, lunch hours and closing times can vary enormously.

POSTE RESTANTE, MAIL AND PHONES

You can have letters sent to you *poste restante* at any PTT in the country. If you're travelling around, it's simplest to choose towns of some size, though always specify the main post office (*Poste Centrale*) to avoid possible confusion.

To collect your mail you need a passport or other convincing ID and should expect to pay a charge of a couple of francs. If you're expecting mail, it's worth asking the clerk to check under your surname *and* all possible Christian names as well – filing systems tend to be erratic.

Sending letters, the quickest international service is by *aérogramme*, sold at all post offices. Ordinary stamps (*timbres*) you can get at any *tabac* (tobacconist). If you're sending **parcels** abroad, try to check prices in various leaflets available: small *postes* don't often send foreign mail and may need reminding of, for example, the huge reductions for printed papers and books.

You can make domestic and international phone calls from any box (or *cabine*) and can receive calls where there's a blue logo of a ringing bell. Most call boxes only take **phone cards** (*télecartes*), obtainable from post offices, PTT boutiques, train stations and some *tabacs*; the cheapest card is 40F for 50 units. In coin-only boxes, still common in cafés, bars and rural parts, put the money (50 centimes, 1F, 5F, 10F pieces) in after lifting up the receiver and before dialling – you can keep adding more once you are connected. For international calls, dial ☎19, wait for a tone, and then dial the country code (Britain ☎44, Ireland ☎353, USA and Canada ☎1, Australia ☎61, New Zealand ☎64) and the number minus its initial 0. For calls within France – local or long distance – dial all eight digits of the number. The exception is Paris: from Paris to the provinces first dial ☎16, or to call a Paris number from anywhere else, first dial ☎16/1.

An alternative to dialling internationally from *cabines* is to use the numbered **booths at main post offices**. You apply at the counter to be assigned a number and then dial. The disadvantage with these – odd considering the French obsession with technology – is that you can't tell how much you're spending. It's worth counting your units and checking – mistakes are made.

To avoid payment altogether, you can, of course, make a reverse charge or **collect call** – known in French as "*téléphoner en PCV*". You can also do this through the operator in the UK, by dialling ☎19.00.44 and asking for a "reverse charge call". To get an English-speaking AT&T operator for North America, dial ☎19.00.11.

NEWSPAPERS, MAGAZINES AND RADIO

A reasonable selection of **British newspapers**, and the *International Herald Tribune*, are on sale in most large cities and resorts. Elsewhere, it's mostly down to the *Times*, *Daily Mail* or *Sun*.

As for the **French press**, the widest circulation are enjoyed by the **regional dailies**. The most important of these is the Rennes-based *Ouest-France* – though for travellers this, like the rest of the regionals, is mainly of interest for its listings. Of the **national dailies**, *Le Monde* (Tues–Sun) is the most intellectual and

respected, with no concessions to entertainment (such as pictures), but a correctly styled French that is probably the easiest to understand. *Libération* (*Libé* for short; Tues–Sun), is moderately left-wing, independent and colloquial with good, selective, coverage; *L'Humanité* is the waning Communist party newspaper (*L'Humanité Dimanche* is the bulkier Sunday version), with a constantly diminishing readership. All the other nationals are firmly on the right.

Weeklies, on the *Newsweek/Time* model, include the wide-ranging left-leaning *Le Nouvel Observateur*, and its rightist counterweight, *L'Express*. The best, and funniest, investigative journalism is in the satirical *Canard Enchaîné*, unfortunately almost incomprehensible to non-native speakers. There are also the **comics** (*bandes dessinés* – *BD*), which occupy a far more prestigious status in the bookshops and newsstands than they do in Britain or America. *Charlie-Hebdo* is one with political targets; *A Suivre* is a showpiece for amazing graphic talent.

If you've got a **radio**, you can tune into the **BBC World Service** on 463m MW, or between 21m and 31m shortwave. **BBC Radio 4**, too, on 1500m long wave, is usually quite clear in the northern half of the country. **Voice of America** broadcasts regionally on FM: try 102.4, 90.5 or 98.8. **France Inter**, on 1829m long wave, has English-language news bulletins in summer at 9pm and 4pm, Monday to Saturday.

BUSINESS HOURS AND PUBLIC HOLIDAYS

Basic hours of business are 8am–noon and 2–6pm: almost everything in France – shops, museums, tourist offices, most banks – closes for a couple of hours at midday. There's some variation, and the lunch breaks tend to be longer in the south, but the basic working hours are 8–noon and 2–6pm. Food shops often don't reopen till half way through the afternoon, closing around 7.30 or 8pm just before the evening meal. So if you're looking to buy a picnic lunch, you'll need to buy it before you're ready to think about eating.

The standard **closing days** are Sunday and Monday, and in small towns you'll find everything except the odd *boulangerie* (bakery) shut on both days. This includes **banks**. It's all too easy to find

yourself dependent on hotels for money-changing – an alternative that invariably means poor rates and high commission.

Museums are not very generous with their hours, tending to open at around 10am, close for lunch at noon until 2pm or 3pm, and then run through only until 5pm or 6pm. Summer hours may differ from winter; if they do, both are indicated in the listings. Summer hours usually extend from mid-May or early June to mid-September, but sometimes they apply only during July and August, occasionally even from Palm Sunday to All Saints' Day. For museums, the closing days are usually Tuesday or Monday, sometimes both. Admission charges can be very off-putting, though most state-owned museums have one or two days of the week when they're free, and you can get a big reduction at most places by showing a student card (or passport if you're under 26 or over 60). Churches and cathedrals are almost always open all day, with charges only for the crypt, treasuries or cloister and little fuss about how you're dressed. When they are closed you may have to go during Mass to take a look, on Sunday morning or at other times which you'll see posted up on the door. In small towns and villages, however, getting the key is not difficult – ask anyone nearby or seek out the priest, whose house is known as the *presbytère*.

PUBLIC HOLIDAYS

There are thirteen national holidays (*jours fériés*), when most shops and businesses, though not museums or restaurants, are closed. They are:

January 1 New Year's Day
Easter Sunday
Easter Monday
Ascension Day (forty days after Easter)
Pentecost (seventh Sunday after Easter, plus the Monday)
May 1 May Day/Labour Day

May 8 Victory in Europe Day
July 14 Bastille Day
August 15 Assumption of the Virgin Mary
November 1 All Saints' Day
November 11 1918 Armistice Day
December 25 Christmas Day

CULTURAL FESTIVALS

Aside from Bastille Day (July 14) and the Assumption of the Virgin Mary (August 15) annual national events are, for the most part, music- or arts-based occasions, confined to a particular city.

Traditional folk festivals continue to thrive in Brittany and the remote rural regions of the south, though they are these days as much a part of the local tourist industry as they are genuine popular celebrations.

FESTIVALS

Catholicism is deeply ingrained in the culture of French rural areas. As a result, **religious feast days** still bring people out in all their finery, ready to indulge once Mass has been said. These occasions, along with the celebrations around wine and food production, are usually very genuine affairs. Other festivals, based for example on historical events, folklore or literature, are often obviously money-spinners and shows for municipal prestige – not something to go out of your way for.

One **folk festival** that is definitely worth attending is the **Inter-Celtic** event held at **Lorient** in Brittany every August. Another annual event with deep historical roots is the great gypsy gathering at **Les-Saintes-Maries-de-la-Mer** in the Camargue. Though exploited for every last centime and, in recent years, given a heavy police presence, it is a unique and exhilarating spectacle to be part of.

Bonfires are lit and fireworks set off for **Bastille Day** and for the **Fête de St Jean** on June 24, three days from the summer solstice. *Mardi Gras* – the last blow-out before Lent – is far less of an occasion than in other Catholic countries. But the towns on the Côte d'Azur put on a show, at great expense and in questionable taste.

February
The week before Lent – **Nice** *Mardi Gras*

May
Cannes International Film Festival
From Ascension Day to the following Sunday – **Monte Carlo** Formula 1 Grand Prix
24th – **Les-Stes-Maries-de-la-Mer** Gypsy Festival

June
Mid-June – **Le Mans** 24-hour car rally
21st (Summer Solstice) – **Paris** Gay Pride
End June to mid-July – **Douai** Festival of Giants
End June to mid-July – **Montpellier** International Dance Festival

July
First ten days – **Rennes** *Tombées de la Nuit* theatre and music festival
First week for three weeks – **Tour de France**
Second Sunday in July – **Locronan** Breton *Troménie Pardon*
Last two weeks – **Avignon** Dance and Drama Festival
Last two weeks – **Juan-les-Pins** International Jazz Festival
Last ten days – **Gannat, near Vichy** World Folk Festival

Last week – **Quimper** *Festival Cornouaille*
End July to mid-August – **Sarlat** Drama Festival

August
Menton Chamber Music Festival
First full week – **Lorient** InterCeltic Festival
First full week – **Périgueux** International Mime Festival
15th – **all over France** fireworks and *fêtes*

September
First week – **Dijon** International Folk and Wine Festival
Early September – **Paris** *Fête de l'Humanité* cultural festival sponsored by the Communist Party
Mid-September to December **Paris** *Festival d'Automne* International theatre and music
End September to mid-October – **Limoges** International Festival of French-speaking communities
Last ten days – **Charleville-Mézières** Triennial World Fesitval of Puppet Theatre

November
Mid-November – **Metz** International Contemporary Music Festival

December
Second week – **Rennes** *Les Transmusicales* international rock festival

MUSIC, FILM AND THEATRE

The best contemporary music you'll hear in France is likely to be distinctly un-French. Paris is a major centre for African and Latin musicians, many permanent residents, and you'll find everything from Algerian *raï* to Antillean *zouk*. In theatre, directors not playwrights, dominate. Scripts are there, if at all, to be shaken up or scrambled (*Richard II* in Japanese Noh style, for example). But film is taken seriously. The French have treated the cinema as an art form, deserving of state subsidy, ever since its origination with the Lumière brothers in 1895. TV has only just started to threaten, the seat of judgement is still Cannes, and Paris is the cinema capital of the world.

MUSIC

Standard **French rock** largely deserves its miserable reputation. Leaving aside such figures as the 60s rocker, Johnny Halliday (still France's biggest music star, thirty years on), or the execrable electro-pomp composer Jean-Michel Jarre, names like *U2* and *The Cure* are better known to the French than any home-grown artists. The late 1980s saw the phenomenon of **Trashpop** – fun, funky, a bit punky, with splashes of be-bop, heavy metal and even Seventies and Eighties psychedelia. Names to look out for are **Les Rita Mitsouko**, with lead singer Catherine Ringer; **Niagra**, a duo of Muriel Moreno and Daniel Chevenz; and Étienne Daho. More exciting developments have come from large-line-up bands combining West and Central African, Arab or North African and French Caribbean (Antillean) sounds. Catch **Les Négresse Vertes** if you can.

A more archetypically French music survives in the tradition of **popular songs** epitomised by Edith Piaf and Georges Brassens, although the form's greatest exponent – and the most famous post-war singer in the French language – was in fact a Belgian, Jacques Brel. Two of the best contemporary *chansonniers* are Alain Souchon and Serge Lama. Despite the emphasis on poetic lyrics, French folk songs can cross frontiers, as Françoise Hardy proved in the 1960s. British or American audiences, however, permeated by rock, are likely to find most of this form unbearably vapid and wimpish.

Jazz is a different matter, in Paris most of all, where, in the capital's clubs, you could listen to a different band every night for weeks, from trad, through be-bop and free jazz, to highly contemporary experimental. And there are many excellent festivals, particularly in the south (see box). If you hear of **Urban Sax** playing at any of these – or elsewhere – go along, if only for the drama of sixty-plus saxophonists performing together.

If your taste is for **classical music** and its descendants, you're also in for a treat. Pierre Boulez experiments with hi-tech sound beneath Beaubourg. Paris has now got a second opera house and in the provinces there are no less than twelve other companies, of which Strasbourg and Toulouse are said to be the best, and a further dozen orchestras. The places to check out for concerts are the *Maisons de la Culture* (in all the larger cities), churches (where chamber music is as much performed as sacred music, often without charge), and festivals – of which there are hundreds, the most famous being at Aix in July.

CINEMA

While it's true that over sixty percent of films shown in French cinemas are now from the States, there are *ciné-clubs* in almost every city, censorship is very slight, students get discounts, and foreign films are usually shown in their **original language** with subtitles (look for *version originale* or *v.o.* in the listings). Some British movie buffs go to Paris just for English-language films – classics and rarities are always playing.

The **Cannes Film Festival** where the prized *Palme d'Or* is handed out, is not, in any public sense, a festival. Those film fests that are, where anyone can go along and pay to see the movies, take place at **La Rochelle** (*Rencontres Internationales d'Art Contemporain*, June–July), **Sceaux** (festival of women's films); **La Ciotat** (silent films; July); and **Reims** (thrillers: novels and films; Oct–Nov).

THEATRE

The earlier generation of **Genet, Anouilh** and **Camus**, joined by Beckett and Ionesco, hasn't really had successors. In the 1950s **Roger Planchon** set up a company in a suburb of Lyon, determined to play to working-class audiences. It became the *Théâtre Nationale Populaire*, the number two state theatre after the *Comédie Française*, which does the classics with all due decorum. Another interesting group, *Théâtre de l'Action*, tours round the country staying in places before creating a show round local issues; while Ariane Mnouchkine organises militant improvisations with her workers' co-op in the *Cartoucherie* at Vincennes. Other big names come from novels and movies into drama (Marguerite Duras) or involve themselves with opera as well as theatre (Patrice Chéreau). Peter Brook now works almost exclusively in France and Jean-Louis Barrault (of *Baptiste* fame) and Madeleine Renaud (one of the great stage actresses) are still producing theatrical events in huge, bizarre spaces.

In all this, theatrical moments rather than speech, and the theatrical light on the subject rather than realism, are tantamount. If you find one of these shows on, it might be quite an experience even with language difficulties. *Café-Théâtre*, though far from avant-garde, is probably less accessible: satire, chansons and dirty jokes are the standard ingredients. But you might look out for **mime**. New talent keeps appearing from the *Jacques Le Coq* school of mime in Paris and a lot of modern dance incorporates mime.

Finally, there are the **classics and popular favourites**, staple fodder to keep municipal subsidies coming in.

For details of **Paris theatres** see that chapter. In other cities the theatres are often part of the *Maisons de la Culture* or *Centres d'Animation Culturelle*; local SIs usually have schedules. The two major theatre festivals are the *Festival Mondial du Théâtre* in Nancy (June) and the *Festival d'Avignon* (July–Aug).

SPORTS

More than any of the cultural jamborees, it is sporting events that really excite the French – cycling, football, tennis and skiing. At the local level, the gentle sobriety of *boules* is the most obvious manifestation of sporting life.

First and foremost in the French sporting calendar is the *Tour de France* cycle race in July, which takes in most of the country during its three-week run, finishing off with a quick circuit round the Arc de Triomphe in Paris. The race leader traditionally wears a yellow jersey (*maillot jaune*), though the French haven't had a victory since Bernard Hinault in 1985.

The spectator sport most passionately followed is *le foot* – **football**. The best team is *Olympique de Marseille* – *OM* for short – whose top player is star turn **Jean-Pierre Papin**. *OM*'s millionaire manager, Bernard Tapie, is also a household name, not least for his forays into national politics. *Monaco* and *Paris St-Germain* are *OM*'s closest rivals, both in purchasing power and team accolades. Note that France's footballers now take a **break in the season** from Christmas Eve until the end of January – in line with most of Europe.

Tennis is next on the list of popular French sports, given a recent boost in 1991 by the country's first Davis Cup win since 1932, under the flamboyant captaincy of part-time pop star Yannick Noah. The French Open tennis championship, held in early June at Roland Garros in Paris, is part of the illustrious Grand Slam of the four top tournaments.

In every town or village square, particularly in the south, you'll see the older generation playing *boules* or *pétanque*. The principle is the same as bowls but the terrain is always rough (never grass) and the area much smaller. The metal ball is usually thrown upwards from a distance of about 10m, to land and skid towards the wooden marker (*cochonnet*). It's very male dominated and, socially, the equivalent of darts: there are café or village teams and endless championships.

Crowds gather in the Basque country for the national ball game of *pelota*, like a lethally (sometimes literally) fast variety of team squash played in a walled court with a ball of solid wood and whicker slings strapped to the players' arms.

Lastly, in and around the Camargue, the number-one sport is **bull-fighting**. Though not to everyone's taste it is at least a considerably less gruesome variety than that practised by the Spanish – usually bloodless and usually involving variations on the theme of removing cocades from the base of the bull's horns. It's generally the "fighters", rather than the bulls, that get hurt.

SKIING

One sport that millions of visitors come to France to practice rather than watch is **skiing**. And whether downhill, cross-country, or mountaineering it's also enthusiastically pursued by the French. It can be an expensive sport to do independently, however, and the best deals are often to be had from package operators. These you can arrange in France or before you leave (most travel agents sell all-in packages). In France the umbrella organisation is the *Fédération Française de Ski*, 34 rue Eugène-Flachat, 75017 Paris (☎47.64.99.39).

The best skiing is generally to be had in **the Alps**. The higher the resort the longer the season and the fewer the anxieties you'll have about there being enough snow. These resorts are almost all modern, with the very latest in lift technology. They're terrific for full-time skiing, but they lack the cachet, charm or the nightlife of the older resorts such as Megève and Courchevel. The **foothills of the Alps** in Provence have the same mix of old and new on a smaller scale. The clientele are Riviera residents and prices are not cheap, though at least you can nip down to the coast for a quick swim when you're bored of snow. The **Pyrenees** are a friendlier range of mountains, less developed – though that can be a drawback if you want to get in as many different runs as possible per day – and warmer, which means more problems with the snow.

Cross-country skiing (*ski de fond*) is being promoted hard, especially in the smaller ranges of the Jura and Massif Central. It's easier on the joints, but don't be fooled into thinking it's any less athletic a sport. For the really experienced and fit, though, it can be a good means of transport, using snowbound GR routes to discover villages still relatively uncommercialised

Alternatively, if you want to go for the real big time, the Plas y Brenin Centre for Mountain Activities, Capel Curig, Betws-y-Coed, Gwynedd, Wales (☎06904/280), organises summertime **ski-mountaineering** courses in the Alps, including parts of the High Level Route.

TROUBLE AND POLICE

Petty theft is endemic along the Côte d'Azur and pretty bad in the crowded parts of most big cities. Drivers, however, face greater problems, most notoriously break-ins. You're more likely to have dealings with the police, though, if for some reason they ask you for your papers and you don't have any ID.

To safeguard against grab-and-run theft, take normal precautions: keep your wallet in your front pocket and your handbag under your elbow, and you won't have much to worry about. If you should get attacked, hand over the money and start dialling the cancellation numbers for your travellers' cheques and credit cards.

Vehicles are rarely stolen, but tape decks as well as luggage left in cars make tempting targets and foreign number plates are easy to spot. Good insurance is the only answer, but even so try not to leave any valuables in plain sight. If you have an accident while driving, you have officially to fill in and sign a *constat à l'aimable* (jointly agreed statement); car insurers are supposed to give you this with a policy, though in practice few seem to have heard of it.

For non-criminal **driving violations** such as speeding, the police can impose on-the-spot fines. Should you be arrested on any charge, you have the right to contact your consulate (see "Listings" in major cities through the book).

Although the police are not always as cooperative as they might be, it *is* their duty to assist you – as it is in the case of losing your passport or all your money.

People caught smuggling or possessing **drugs**, even a few grammes of marijuana, are liable to find themselves in jail and consulates will not be sympathetic. This is not to say that hard-drug consumption isn't a visible activity: there are scores of kids dealing in *poudre* (heroin) in the big French cities and the authorities are unable to do much about it. As a rule, people are no more nor less paranoid about cannabis busts than they are in the UK or North America.

THE POLICE

There are two main types of French police (popularly known as *les flics*): the *Police Nationale* and the *Gendarmerie Nationale*. For all practical purposes, they are indistinguishable; if you need to report a theft, or other incident, you can go to either.

A different proposition entirely are the *CRS* (*Compagnies Républicaines de Sécurité*), a mobile force of heavies, sporadically dressed in green combats and armed with riot equipment, whose brutality in the May 1968 battles turned public opinion to the side of the students. They still make demonstrations dangerous. Not quite in the same league, but with an ugly recent history, is the separate **Paris police force**. This bunch are prone to pulling up "nonconformists" – often just ordinary teenagers, predominantly from the country's large North African community – for identity checks. You can in fact be stopped anywhere in France and asked to produce ID. If it happens to you, it's not worth being difficult or facetious.

EMERGENCIES
Ambulance ☎18
Police ☎17
Fire Service ☎18

Lastly, in the Alps or Pyrenees, you may come across specialised **mountaineering sections** of the police force. They are unfailingly helpful, friendly and approachable, providing rescue services and guidance.

SEXUAL AND RACIAL HARASSMENT

Women are bound to experience **sexual harassment** in France, where many men make a habit of looking you up and down and, more often than not, passing comment. Generally it is no worse than in the UK or North America, but problems arise in judging men without the familiar linguistic and cultural clues.

A "*Bonjour*" or "*Bonsoir*" on the street is almost always a pick-up line. If you so much as return the greeting, you've left yourself open to a persistent monologue and a difficult brush-off job. On the other hand, it's not unusual to be offered a drink in a bar if you're on your own and not to be pestered even if you accept. This is rarer in big cities than in the countryside, but don't assume that any overture by a Frenchman is a come-on.

Late-night *métros* in the big cities are nowhere near as unnerving as in London or New York, simply because of greater passenger numbers and the fact that people are more inclined to intervene if nasty scenes develop. Hitchhiking is risky – as it is anywhere – and few French women do it except on the Côte d'Azur where public transport is minimal. If you want to hitch it's best to use the agencies and take the same precautions as you would at home.

If you need help, don't go to the police. The *mairie/hôtel de ville* (town hall) will have addresses of women's organisations (*Femmes Battues, Femmes en Détresse* or *SOS Femmes*), though this won't be much help outside business hours. You'll find detailed listings for Paris in *Chapter One*. We've given contacts for other cities where possible, but there are very few permanent centres.

You may, as a woman, be warned about "*les Arabes*" – unexceptional French **racism**. If you are Arab or even just look as if you are, your chances of avoiding unpleasantness are very slim. Empty hotels claiming to be full, police demanding your papers and abusive treatment from ordinary people are all horribly commonplace. Being black, of whatever ethnic origin, can make entering the country difficult and immigration officers can be obstructive and malicious to black holidaymakers.

WORK AND STUDY

Most Britons and North Americans who manage to survive in France do it on luck, brazenness and willingness to live in pretty **basic conditions. In the cities, bar work, club work, freelance translating, data processing and typing are some of the ways people scrape by; in the countryside, the options come down to seasonal fruit- or grape-picking, teaching English, busking or DIY oddjobbing. All these are fine if you're into self-promotion and living hand-to-mouth, but if you're not, it might be wise to think twice.**

Whatever you're looking for, it's important to plan well in advance. The best **general sources** for all jobs in France are the publications *Emplois d'été en France* (£4.95; available in Britain from Vacation Work, 9 Park End St, Oxford; ☎0865/241978) and 1000 Pistes de Jobs (80F; available from *L'Étudiant*, 27 rue du Chemin-Vert, 75011 Paris). *Working Holidays* (£4.80; published by Central Bureau, Seymour Mews House, Seymour Mews, London W1H 9PE) is also useful.

Teaching English is one of the easiest ways of getting a job in France. It's best to apply from Britain; check the ads in the *Guardian's* "Education" section (every Tuesday), or in the weekly *Times Educational Supplement* (*TES*). Late summer is usually the best time. You don't need fluent French to get a post, but a *TEFL* (*Teaching English as a Foreign Language*) qualification may well be required. If you apply from home, most schools will fix up the necessary papers for you. It's also quite feasible to find a teaching job when you're in France but you may have to accept semi-official status and no job security. For the addresses of schools, look under *Écoles de Langues* in the Professions directory of the local phone book. Offering **private lessons** (via university notice boards or classified ads), you'll have lots of competition, and it's hard to reach the people who can afford it, but it's always worth a try.

Au pair work is usually arranged through one of a dozen agencies, all of which are listed in *Working Holidays*. In Britain, *The Lady* is *the* magazine for classified adverts for such jobs, arranged privately. As initial numbers to ring, try *Euroyouth* (☎0702/341434), *Scattergoods* (☎0483/63640) or *Students Abroad* (☎071/428 5823); any of them will fill you in on the general terms and conditions (never very generous), and the state of the market; you shouldn't get paid less than 1000F a month (on top of board and lodging). It is wise to have an escape route (like a ticket home) in case you find the conditions intolerable – many people have had bad experiences.

Temporary jobs in the **travel industry** revolve around courier work – supervising and working on coach tours or summer campsites. You'll need good French (and maybe even another language) and should write to as many tour operators as you can, preferably in early Spring. Ads occasionally appear in the *Guardian's* "Media" section (every Monday). Getting work as a courier on a campsite is slightly easier. It usually takes in putting up tents at the beginning of the season, taking them down again at the end, and general maintenance and trouble-shooting work in the months between. Three companies worth approaching are: *Canvas Holidays* (☎0992/59933); *Eurocamp* (☎0565/50444); and *Sunsites* (☎0306/887733). Competition is fairly intense.

CLAIMING BENEFIT

If you're an EC citizen – and you do the paperwork in advance – you can sign on for **unemployment benefit**. To do so, you must collect form E303 before leaving home, available in Britain from any DSS office. The procedure is first to get registered at an *ANPE* office (*Agence Nationale pour l'Emploi*), then take the form to your local *ASSEDIC* (benefits office) and give them an address, which can be a hostel or a hotel, for the money to be sent. You sign once a month at the *ANPE* and receive the dole a month in arrears – theoretically, at least, payments can be delayed in small towns for up to three months. After three months, you must anyway either leave the country or get a *carte de séjour*.

STUDYING IN FRANCE

It's relatively easy to be a **student** in France. Foreigners pay no more than French nationals (around 400F) to enrol for a course, and the only problem then is to support yourself. Your *carte de séjour* and – if you're an EC citizen – social security will be assured, and you'll be eligible for subsidised accommodation, meals and all the student reductions. In general, French universities are much less formal than British ones and many people perfect their fluency in the language while studying. For full **details and prospectuses**, contact the Cultural Service of any French embassy or consulate – in London at 22 Wilton Crescent, London SW1.

Language schools are offered at a number of establishments in university towns. They are listed in the handout *"Cours de Français pour Étudiants Étrangers"*, also obtainable from embassy or consular cultural sections. Finally, it's worth noting that if you're a full-time student in France, you can get a **work permit** for the following summer as long as your visa is still valid.

DIRECTORY

BEACHES are public property within five metres of the high tide mark, so you can kick sand past private villas and arrive on islands. Under a different law, however, you can't camp.

BRING An alarm clock is very useful for early trains.

BUYING PROPERTY If you're looking to buy a home in France, the best source of information and advice is *Buying Residential Property in France*, available for £5 from *Chambre de Commerce Française de Grande Bretagne*, Knightsbridge House, 197 Knightsbridge, London SW1 (☎071/225 5250). The free monthly *French Property News* (from ☎081 942 0301 or 21 Cromford Way, New Malden, Surrey KT3 3BB) is the main publication for buyers and sellers.

CAMERAS AND FILM Film is considerably cheaper in North America than France or Britain. Stock up if you're coming that way. And if you're bringing a video camcorder, make sure any tapes you puchase in Europe will be compatible. Again, American videotape prices are, in any case, way below French prices.

CHILDREN AND BABIES are generally welcome everywhere, and in most bars and restaurants. **Hotels** charge by the room, with a small supplement for an aditional bed or cot, and family-run places will usually babysit or offer a listening service while you eat or go out. Especially in the seaside towns, most **restau-** rants have children's menus or will cook simpler food on request. You'll have no difficulty finding disposable nappies (*couches à jeter*), but nearly all baby foods have added sugar and salt, and French milk powders are very rich indeed. *SNCF* charge nothing on **trains and buses** for under 4s, and half-fare for 4–12s (see p.21 for other reductions). Most local SIs have details of specific activites for children – in particular, many resorts supervise "clubs" for children on the beach. And almost every town down to small ones has a **children's playground** with a good selection of activities. Something to beware of – not that you can do much about it – is the diffculty of negotiating a child's **buggy** over the large cobbles that cover many of the older streets in town centres.

CONTRACEPTIVES Contraception was only legalised in 1967 but condoms (*préservatifs*) have been available at all pharmacies ever since. You can also get spermicidal cream and jelly (*dose contraceptive*), plus the suppositories (*ovules, suppositoires*) and (with a prescription) the pill (*la pillule*), a diaphragm or IUD (*le sterilet*).

CUSTOMS At least until the end of 1992, if you bring in more than 5000F worth of foreign cash, you need to sign a declaration at customs. There are also restrictions on taking francs out of the country, but the amounts are beyond the concern of most people. Tobacco and alcohol import limits are 400 cigarettes and two litres respectively. What will happen to duty free allowances after January 1 1993 is uncertain at the time of writing – there'll certainly be some increase to the limits and beer and wine are likely to flow freely from France to Britain.

ELECTRICITY is almost always 220V, using plugs with two round pins.

FISHING You get fishing rights by becoming a member of an authorised fishing club – tourist offices have details.

GAY/LESBIAN France is more liberal on homo-sexuality than most other European countries. The legal age of consent is 15 and gay communities thrive especially in Paris and many of the southern towns, though lesbian life is rather less upfront. Addresses are listed in the guide and you'll find details of groups and publications for the whole country in the Paris chapter.

LAUNDRY Launderettes are not common in French towns, although some are listed in the guide – elsewhere look in the phone book under *Laveries Automatiques*. The alternative *blanchis-serie* or *pressing* services are likely to be expensive, and hotels in particular charge very high rates. Your best bet is to wash your own using a travel-soap such as *Dylon Travel-Wash*. If you're staying in hotels, keep quantities small as most forbid doing any laundry in your room.

LEFT LUGGAGE Luggage lockers of various sizes are available at all *SNCF* stations, in addition to *consigne* for larger items or longer periods.

SWIMMING POOLS (*piscines*) are well sign-posted in most French towns and reasonably priced. SIs have addresses.

TIME France is one hour ahead of Britain through-out the year, except for a short period during October, when it's the same. It is six hours ahead of Eastern Standard Time, and nine hours ahead of Pacific Standard Time. This also applies during daylight savings seasons, which are observed in France (as in most of Europe) from the end of March through to the end of September.

TOILETS Usually found downstairs in bars, along with the phone, but still often of the hole-in-the-ground squatting variety, and tending to lack toilet paper.

PART TWO

THE

GUIDE

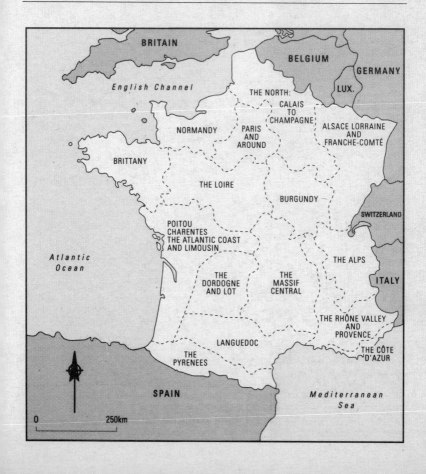

CHAPTER ONE

PARIS AND AROUND

PARIS is the paragon of style – perhaps the most glamorous and the most high-tech city in Europe. And yet it is also deeply traditional, a village-like and in parts dilapidated metropolis whose appeal to outsiders is tempered by the notorious disdain of its inhabitants. While such contradictions and contrasts may be the reality of any city, they are the makings of Paris. Consider the village atmosphere of Montmartre against the cold hard lines of La Défense; the multiplicity of markets and small shops against the giant malls of Montparnasse and Les Halles; or the devotion to *l'informatique* – minitel link-ups for all phone subscribers, touch screen information in shops and métro stations and interactive video in museum displays – while old ladies still iron sheets by hand in the laundries of Auteil.

Paris has long created its own myth. Famous names and events are invested with a peculiar glamour that elevates the city and its people to a legendary realm. It is only in the last couple of decades that Paris has let slip its status as centre of movements in the west: whether artistic (spawning Impressionism and Surrealism), intellectual (Existentialism, Structuralism) or literary (from Sartre and Camus to Joyce and Beckett). Perhaps it is not surprising that, finding themselves at the supposed navel of the world, Parisians have felt that they are superior to ordinary mortals.

Some history ...

The city's history has conspired to create this sense of being apart. From a shaky start the kings of France, whose seat was Paris, gradually extended their control over their feudal rivals, centralising administrative, legal, financial and political power as they did so, until anyone seeking influence, publicity or credibility, in whatever field, had to be in Paris. **Louis XIV** consolidated this process. Supremely autocratic, considering himself the embodiment of the state – "L'état, c'est moi" – he inaugurated the tradition of Paris as symbol: the glorious reflection of the pre-eminence of the State. The Cour Carrée of the Louvre, the Observatoire and Invalides, and the triumphal arches of the Portes St-Martin and St-Denis are his. It is a tradition his successors have been only too happy to follow, whether as king, emperor or president.

Napoléon I added to the Louvre and built the Arc de Triomphe, the Madeleine, and Arc du Carrousel. He instituted the Grandes Écoles, those super-universities for super-competent administrators, engineers and teachers (and totally reorganised the rest of the country, too). **Napoléon III** extended the Louvre even further and had his Baron Haussmann redraw the rest of the city. The **Third Republic** had its World Fairs and bequeathed the Eiffel Tower. **Recent presidents** have initiated the skyscrapers at La Défense, the Tour Montparnasse, Beaubourg and Les Halles shopping precinct. Many of their projects have been completed by **President Mitterrand**: the space age Parc de la Villette complex, the glass pyramid entrance to the Louvre, the Musée d'Orsay, the arch at La Défense, and the new Ministry of Finance quarters, to which Mitterrand himself has added the Bastille opera house and Institut du Monde Arabe. The scale of all this publicly financed construction is extraordinary – so, too, the architecture. The new buildings should, and do, feature as prominently on any visitors' itinerary as the classic city sights.

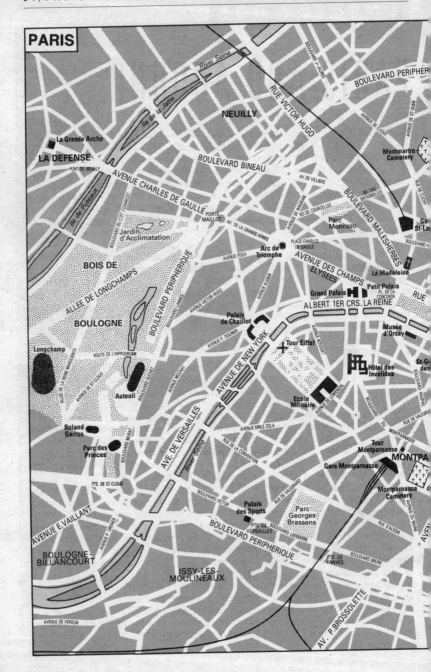

PORTE DE
CLIGNANCOURT
BD. ORNANO
PTE. DE LA
CHAPELLE
BOULEVARD NEY
RUE DE LA CHAPELLE
Canal St-Denis
International
Coach
Station
PTE. DE LA VILLETTE
BOULEVARD MACDONALD
AVENUE DU GÉNÉRAL-LECLERC

MONTMARTRE
Sacré Coeur
RUE DE FLANDRE
Canal de L'Ourcq
PARC DE LA
VILLETTE
AVENUE JEAN LOLIVE

PL. DE CLICHY
PIGALLE
BOULEVARD DE LA CHAPELLE
PORTE DE
PANTIN
AVENUE JEAN JAURES

Gare
du Nord
BOULEVARD DE MAGENTA
Parc des
Buttes-
Chaumont
PTE. DES LILAS

RUE LAFAYETTE
Gare
de l'Est
BOULEVARD DE LA VILLETTE
Canal St-Martin
BELLEVILLE
DE
BELLEVILLE

Opéra
BD STRASBOURG
BELLEVILLE
BOULEVARD PERIPHERIQUE
Bourse
REAUMUR
ST-MARTIN
PLACE
DE LA
REPUBLIQUE
BD. DE BELLEVILLE
RUE
Palais
Royal
SEBASTOPOL
AVENUE DE LA REPUBLIQUE
AVENUE GAMBETTA
BOULEVARD DAVOUT
Forum des
Halles
DE
Louvre
RIVOLI
Beaubourg
Père Lachaise
Cemetery
MENILMONTANT
PTE. DE MONTREUIL
MARAIS
RUE ST-ANTOINE

St-Sulpice
BOULEVARD ST-MICHEL
BD.ST-GERMAIN
Notre Dame
Ile St-Louis
RUE DU FAUBOURG ST-ANTOINE
AVENUE LEDRU
RUE D'AVRON

Sorbonne
Q. ST BERNARD
PL. DE LA BASTILLE
AVENUE PHILIPPE AUGUSTE

Palais du
xembourg
Panthéon
RUE MONGE
Q. HENRI IV
AUSTERLITZ AVENUE
RUE DE LYON
Opéra-
Bastille
COURS DE VINCENNES

Jardin
des Plantes
Q. D'AUSTERLITZ
Gare de Lyon
PLACE
DE LA NATION

ASSE
Mosquée
River Seine
Ministère des
Finances
AVENUE DAUMESNIL

BOULEVARD DE PORT-ROYAL
Q. DE LA RAPÉE
BOULEVARD DE BERCY
BOULEVARD SOULT

LECLERC
Observatoire
BOULEVARD ST-MARCEL
Gare d'
Austerlitz
Parc
Omnisports
de Paris
RUE DE DIJON
RUE DE CHARENTON
BOULEVARD PONIATOWSKI
AVENUE DAUMESNIL

E D'ALESIA
BD. DE L'HOPITAL
AVENUE DES GOBELINS
BOULEVARD VINCENT AURIOL
QUAI DE LA GARE
BOIS DE

PLACE
D'ITALIE
VINCENNES

Parc
Montsouris
RUE DE TOLBIAC
AVENUE D'ITALIE
RUE DE TOLBIAC
BOULEVARD MASSENA
QUAI DE BERCY
RUE DE PARIS

VARD JOURDAN
BOULEVARD KELLERMAN
QUAI M. BOYER
River

JLEVARD PERIPHERIQUE
PTE. D'ITALIE
AVENUE DE FONTAINEBLEAU
RUE LENINE
Seine
River Marne

Yet despite these developments Paris remains compact and remarkably uniform, basically the city that **Haussmann** remodelled in the **mid-nineteenth century**. He laid out those long geometrical boulevards lined with rows of grey bourgeois residences that are the hallmark of Paris. In doing so, he cut great swathes through the stinking wen of medieval slums that housed the city's rebellious poor, already veterans of three revolutionary uprisings in half a century. If urban renewal and modernisation were part of the design, so too was the intention of controlling the masses by opening up more effective fields of fire for artillery and facilitating troop movements. Not that it succeeded in preventing the Commune, the most determined insurrection since 1789.

The traditional barricade-builders have long since been booted into the suburban factory-land, or housed in depressing satellite towns. Corporate business gets its way, the state invests in the monumental building, and the housing shortage remains acute, large areas of the city, especially in the east and north, falling into a state of decay that only the underprivileged immigrant communities are prepared to tolerate, while other working-class bastions are gentrified.

Ethnic diversity is an important, if volatile, element in the weft of the city's life. Long a haven and magnet for foreign refugees and artists, Paris in this century has sheltered Lenin and Ho Chi Minh, White Russians and Iranians (the Ayatollah as well as the Shah's son), dissidents from Eastern Europe, disillusioned writers from America and a host of other assorted expatriates. Since the 1950s immigrants have come from the former French colonies in Southeast Asia, West Africa and North Africa; well-entrenched, if not assimilated, they have their own quarters, shops, cafés and cultures.

. . . and some highlights

The most tangible and immediate pleasures of Paris are to be found in its **streetlife**. Few cities can compete with the thousand-and-one cafés, bars and restaurants that line every street and boulevard. And the city's compactness makes it possible to experience the individual feel of the different **quartiers**. You can move easily, even on foot, from the calm, almost small-town atmosphere of **Montmartre** and parts of the **Latin Quarter** to the busy commercial centres of the **Bourse** and **Opéra** or to the aristocratic mansions of the **Marais**. In **Les Halles** you can shop for every brand-name of note, in the **13e arrondissement** you can discover strange edibles and fiery spirits in the Chinese supermarkets.

The city's lack of open spaces is redeemed by unexpected spots of garden or churchyard like the **Mosque, Arènes de Lutèce** and the courtyard of the **Cluny museum**. The garden of Les Halles has at long last provided greenery in the centre, and there are always the **quais**. And a grand and imposing backdrop to the streetlife is provided by the monumental architecture of the **Arc de Triomphe, Louvre**, the **Eiffel Tower, Hôtel de Ville,** the **bridges** and the institutions of the state. This century's contributions include the **Art Nouveau** and **Cubist** innovations in the **1e and 16e arrondissements,** and more recently **Beaubourg** through to **La Villette**, the **Bastille Opera house** and the **Louvre pyramid**. But these contemporary innovations aside, Paris is most remarkable for its **museums** rather than its buildings: the **d'Orsay, Beaubourg's modern art**, the **Cité des Sciences** at La Villette, the **Palais de Tokyo, Marmottan, Picasso,** the **Orangerie** and **Cluny**.

As for **entertainment**, the city's strong points are in film and music. Paris is a real **cinema** capital, and although French rock is notoriously awful, the best Parisian **music** encompasses jazz, avante-garde, salsa, and, currently, Europe's most vibrant African music scene.

POINTS OF ARRIVAL

By Air

Roissy–Charles de Gaulle Airport (☎48.62.22.80, 24hr)

Roissy, northeast of the city, is connected with the centre by the following:

Roissy–Rail. A combination of airport bus and RER *ligne B* train to Gare du Nord and Châtelet (every 15min from 5am to 11.15pm), where you can transfer to the ordinary métro. Taking about 35 minutes, this is the cheapest and quickest route.

Air France bus. This costs 35F, and departs from door 6 every 15min from 5.45am to 11pm, terminating at the Porte Maillot (métro) on av MacManon, on the northwest edge of the city, a hundred metres from the Arc de Triomphe. There are also *Air France* buses from terminal 2 to Gare Montparnasse.

Taxis into central Paris cost from 150 to 200F, plus a small luggage supplement, and should take between 45 minutes and one hour.

Buses #350 to Gare du Nord and Gare de l'Est, and #351 to place de la Nation.

Orly Airport (☎48.84.52.52, daily 6am–11.30pm).

Orly, south of Paris, also has a bus–rail link. *Orly-Rail*, RER *ligne C* **trains** leave every fifteen minutes from 5.30am to 11.30pm for the Gare d'Austerlitz and other Left Bank stops which connect with the métro. Alternatively there are **Air France buses** to the Gare des Invalides and Montparnasse, or **Orlybus** to Denfert-Rochereau métro in the 14e. Both leave every ten or fifteen minutes from 6am to 11pm. Journey time is about 35 minutes. A **taxi** will take about the same time, costing around 100F.

Other Airports

Paris's third airport, **Le Bourget**, handles internal flights only. *Usit/Campus Travel* (see p.10) operates a charter service to **Beauvais**. This is a 70km bus journey from Paris, but all air tickets should include the price of the coach into the city at the Porte de la Villette international terminal.

By Rail

Paris's **six mainline stations** are equipped with cafés, restaurants, *tabacs*, banks, bureaux de change (long waits in season), and are all connected with the métro system. A central number for all *SNCF* **information** is ☎45.82.50.50.

   The **Gare du Nord** (trains from Boulogne, Calais, the UK, Belgium, Holland and Scandinavia; ☎42.80.03.03 for information, ☎42.06.49.38 for reservations) and **Gare de l'Est** (serving eastern France, Germany, Switzerland and Austria; ☎42.08.49.90 for information, ☎42.06.49.38 for reservations) are next door to each other in the northeast of the city. The **Gare St-Lazare** (serving the UK, Dieppe and the Normandy coast; ☎43.38.52.29 for information, ☎43.87.91.70 reservations) is a little to the west of them. Still on the Right Bank but towards the southwest corner is the **Gare de Lyon**, for trains from the Alps, the South, Italy and Greece (☎43.45.92.22 information; ☎43.45.93.33 reservations). On the opposite side of the river, the **Gare d'Austerlitz** (☎45.84.14.18), is the terminus of trains from southwest France and Spain, while **Gare Montparnasse** serves Versailles, Chartres, Brittany and southern Normandy, and the Atlantic Coast (☎45.38.52.29).

By Bus

Almost all the coaches coming into Paris – international and domestic – use the main **gare routière** at Porte de la Villette; there's a métro station here to get into the centre. *Citysprint* coaches arrive at and depart from rue St-Quentin, around the corner from the Gare du Nord. Check-in takes place at 135 rue Lafayette (☎42.85.44.55).

Driving

If you're driving in yourself, don't try to go straight across the city to your destination. Use the ring road – the *boulevard périphépherique* – to get around to the nearest Porte: it's much quicker, except at rush hour, and easier to find your way.

Information

The **main Paris tourist office is** at 127 av des Champs-Élysées, 8ᵉ (summer Mon–Sat 9am–9pm, Sun 9am–8pm; winter Mon–Sat 9am–9pm, Sun 9am–6pm; ☎47.23.61.72)

There are also offices at the *Gare d'Austerlitz* (summer Mon–Sat 8am–10pm; winter Mon–Sat 8am–3pm; ☎45.84.91.70); *Gare de l'Est,* bd de Strasbourg, 10ᵉ (summer Mon–Sat 8am–10pm; winter Mon–Sat 8am–1pm & 5–8pm; ☎ 46.07.17.73); *Gare de Lyon,* 20 bd Diderot, 12ᵉ (summer Mon–Sat 8am–10pm; winter Mon–Sat 8am–1pm & 5–8pm; ☎43.43.33.24); and *Gare du Nord,* 18 rue de Dunkerque, 10ᵉ (summer Mon–Sat 8am–10pm, Sun 8am–8pm; winter Mon–Sat 8am–8pm; ☎45.26.94.82).

Consider also using the more youth-orientated **Accueil des Jeunes en France** (AJF). They have offices at the *Gare du Nord* suburban station (June–Oct 8am–10pm; ☎42.85.86.19); opposite Centre Beaubourg (Mon–Sat 9.30am–7pm; ☎42.77.87.80), which can also be used as a forwarding address for mail); and at 139 bd St-Michel, 5ᵉ (March–Oct Mon–Fri 9.30am–6.30pm; ☎43.54.95.86).

Getting around the city

Finding your way around is remarkably easy. Paris proper, without its suburbs, is relatively small, with a public transport system that is cheap, fast and meticulously signposted. To help you **get your bearings** above ground, think of the **Louvre** as the centre. The Seine flows east to west, cutting the city in two. The area north of the river is known as the **Right Bank** or *rive droite*; to the south is the **Left Bank** or *rive gauche*. Roughly speaking, west is smart and east is scruffy. The landmarks you most often catch glimpses of as you move about are the **Eiffel Tower**, to the west, and the white pimples of the **Sacré-Coeur** on top of the hill of Montmartre, to the north.

The Metro

The **métro** is the simplest way of moving around. Trains run from 5.30am to 12.30am. Stations (abbreviated: Mº Concorde, etc) are far more frequent than on the London Underground. **Free maps** are available at most stations, and every station has a big plan of the network outside the entrance and several inside. The lines are colour-coded and numbered, although they are signposted within the system with the names of the terminus stations: for example, travelling from Gare-du-Nord to Odéon, you follow the sign *Direction Porte-d'Orléans*; from Gare d'Austerlitz to Grenelle you follow *Direction Pont-de-St-Cloud.* The numerous junctions *(correspondances)* make it possible to travel all over the city in a more or less straight line.

For the latest in subway technology, use the express stations' computerised routefinders, which at a touch of the button give you four alternative routes to your selected destination, on foot or by public transport.

Buses

Don't use the métro to the exclusion of the city's **buses**. They are not difficult to use and of course you see much more. There are **free maps** available at métro stations, bus terminals and the tourist office. Every bus stop displays the numbers of the buses which stop there, a map showing all the stops on the route and the times of the first and last buses. Each bus also has a map of its own route inside and some have a recorded announcement for each approaching stop. Generally speaking, they start around 6.30am and begin their last run around 9pm.

Night buses *(Noctambus)* run on ten routes from place du Châtelet near the Hôtel de Ville every half hour between 1.30am and 5.30am. There is a reduced service on Sunday. Further information is on the *RATP* transport board (53ter quai des Grands-

Augustins, 6ᵉ; ☎43.46.14.14). They also run numerous excursions, including some to quite far-flung places, much cheaper than the commercial operators; their brochure is available at all rail and some métro stations.

Tickets and passes

The **same tickets** are valid for bus, métro and, within the city limits, the RER **express rail lines**, which also extend far out into the suburbs. Long bus journeys can cost two tickets; ask the driver, if in doubt.

For a short stay in the city, **single tickets** can be bought in *carnets* of ten from any station or *tabac* – currently 32.80F, as opposed to around 5F for an individual ticket. Don't buy from the touts who hang round the main stations; you'll pay well over the odds, quite often for a used ticket. There's a flat rate across the city: you need one ticket per journey. Be sure to keep your ticket until the end of the journey; you'll be fined on the spot if you can't produce one. All tickets are available as first or second class, although class distinctions are only in force 9am–5pm.

If you are staying more than a day or two, it's more economical to buy a *Carte Orange*, obtainable at all métro stations and *tabacs* (you need a passport photo). You can get one with either a weekly (*hebdomadaire* or *coupon jaune*; valid Monday morning to Sunday evening; currently 54F for zones 1 and 2, ie within the city proper) or monthly (*mensuel*) coupon. Alternatively there is a one-day coupon at 21F and a 3-or 5-day visitor's coupon (*Paris Visites*) at 75F and 120F respectively, available only for first-class travel. The only advantage of the latter is that, unlike the *hebdomadaire* whose validity runs unalterably from Monday to Sunday, they can begin on any day. All entitle you to unlimited travel on bus or métro.

On the métro you put the coupon through the turnstile slot, but make sure to return it to its plastic folder; it is reusable throughout the period of its validity. On a bus you show the whole *Carte* to the driver as you board – don't put it into the punching machine.

Taxis

If it's late at night or you feel like treating yourself, don't hesitate to use the **taxis**. Their charges are very reasonable. To avoid being ripped off, check the meter shows the appropriate fare rate. Even before you get into the taxi you can check by seeing which of the three small indicator lights on its roof is switched on. *A* (passenger side) indicates the daytime rate for Paris and the *boulevard périphérique*; *B* is the rate for Paris at night, on Sunday and on public holidays, and for the suburbs during the day; *C* (driver's side) is the night rate for the suburbs. You can also expect to pay an additional 10F pick-up charge, a supplement of around 5F at the mainline railway stations, and about the same amount per item of luggage. Tipping is not mandatory, but ten percent will be expected.

Some **numbers to call** are: ☎45.85.85.85; ☎42.70.41.41; ☎42.02.42.02.

Disabled travellers

If you are **handicapped**, taxis are obliged by law to carry you and to help you into the vehicle – also to carry your guide dog if you are blind. Specially-adapted taxis are available on ☎48.37.85.85 or ☎47.08.93.50, but they need to be notified the day before. For **travel on the métro or RER**, the *RATP* offers accompanied journeys for disabled people not in wheelchairs – *Voyage accompagné* – which operates (free) from 8am to 8pm. You have to book your minder on ☎46.70.88.74 a day in advance.

For **wheelchair users** there is an RER access guide obtainable from *RATP* at the address given above, and for blind people a Braille métro map, obtainable from *L'Association Valentin Haüy*, 5 rue Duroc, 7ᵉ (☎47.34.07.90).

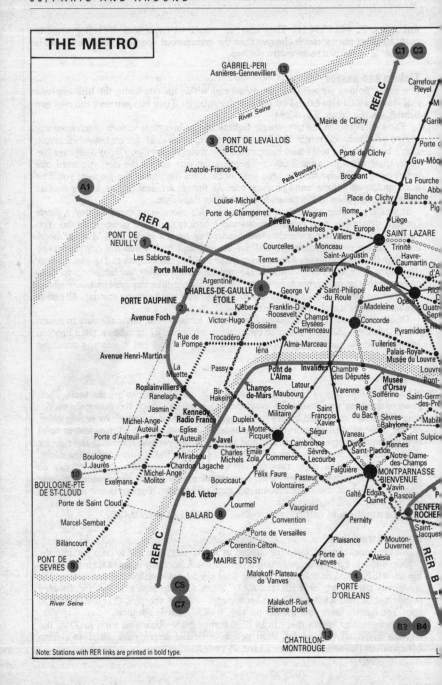

THE METRO

GABRIEL-PERI 13
Asnières-Gennevilliers

C1 C3

River Seine

RER C

Carrefour
Pleyel

Mairie de Clichy

M

PONT DE LEVALLOIS 3
-BECON

Porte de Clichy

Garil

Porte de

Anatole-France

Paris Boundary

Brochant

Guy-Môc

A1

Louise-Michel

Porte de Champerret

Wagram

Péreire

Malesherbes

Villiers

La Fourche
Abb

Place de Clichy

Blanche

Pig

Rome

Liège

SAINT LAZARE

RER A

PONT DE
NEUILLY 1

Les Sablons

Porte Maillot

Argentine

CHARLES-DE-GAULLE
ÉTOILE 6

PORTE DAUPHINE

Avenue Foch

2

Kléber

Courcelles

Ternes

George V

Franklin-D-
Roosevelt

Monceau

Saint-Augustin

Saint-Philippe
-du-Roule

Europe

Trinité

Havre-
Caumartin

Miromesnil

Chambs
Elysées-
Clemenceau

Madeleine

Auber

Opéra

Cha
d'A

Ric

Quatr
Sept

Victor-Hugo

Boissière

Pyramides

Rue de
la Pompe

Trocadéro

Iéna

Alma-Marceau

Concorde

Tuileries

Palais-Royal
Musée du Louvre

Avenue Henri-Martin

La
Muette

Passy

Pont de
L'ALMA

Invalides

Chambre
des Députés

Louvre
Pont-

Musée
d'Orsay

Boulainvilliers

Ranelagh

Bir-
Hakeim

Champs-
de-Mars

Latour
Maubourg

Varenne

Solférino

Saint-Germ
-des-Pré

Jasmin

Kennedy
Radio France

Ecole-
Militaire

Saint
François-
Xavier

Rue
du Bac

Michel-Ange-
Auteuil

Porte d'Auteuil

Eglise
d'Auteuil

Dupleix

La Motte-
Picquet

Ségur

Vaneau

Sèvres-
Babylone

Mabill

Javel

Charles
Michels

Emile
Zola

Cambronne

Sèvres
Lecourbe

Duroc

Saint-Placide

Saint Sulpice

Rennes

Notre-Dame-
des-Champs

Boulogne-
J.Jaurès 10

Mirabeau

Chardon Lagache

Michel-Ange
-Molitor

Commerce

Félix Faure

Boucicaut

Pasteur

Volontaires

Falguière

MONTPARNASSE
BIENVENUE

BOULOGNE-PTE
DE ST-CLOUD

Exelmans

Porte de Saint Cloud

Bd. Victor

Gaîté

Edgar-
Quinet

Vavin

Raspail

P

DENFER
ROCHER

Marcel-Sembat

Lourmel

BALARD 8

Vaugirard

Convention

Pernéty

Plaisance

Saint-
Jacques

Billancourt

Porte de Versailles

PONT DE
SEVRES 9

Corentin-Celton

12 MAIRIE D'ISSY

Porte de
Vanves

Mouton-
Duvernet

Alésia

RER B

River Seine

C5

C7

RER C

Malakoff-Plateau
de Vanves

4

PORTE
D'ORLEANS

Malakoff-Rue
Etienne Dolet

B2 B4

13

CHATILLON-
MONTROUGE

L

Note: Stations with RER links are printed in bold type.

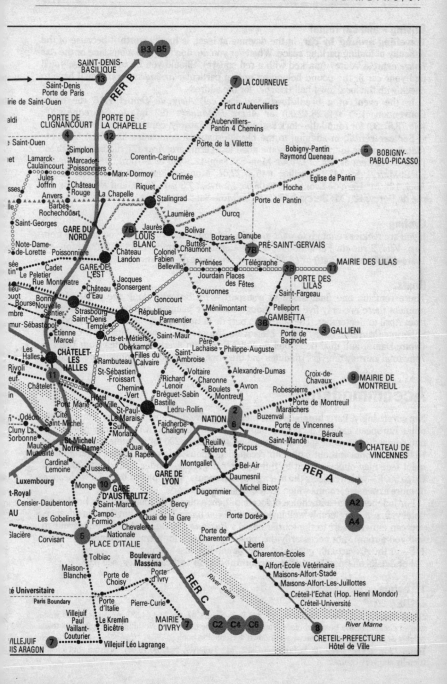

SAINT-DENIS-BASILIQUE

B3 B5

13

Saint-Denis
Porte de Paris

irie de Saint-Ouen

RER B

7 LA COURNEUVE

Fort d'Aubervilliers

PORTE DE
CLIGNANCOURT

PORTE DE
LA CHAPELLE

Aubervilliers–
Pantin 4 Chemins

aldi

e Saint-Ouen

4

12

Porte de la Villette

Bobigny-Pantin
Raymond Queneau

5 BOBIGNY-
PABLO-PICASSO

Simplon

et

Lamarck-
Caulaincourt

Marcadet
Poissonniers

Corentin-Cariou

Jules
Joffrin

Marx-Dormoy

Crimée

Eglise de Pantin

sses

Château
Rouge

Riquet

Hoche

Anvers

La Chapelle

Stalingrad

Porte de Pantin

Barbès-
Rochechouart

Laumière

Ourcq

lle

Saint-Georges

GARE DU
NORD

7B

Jaurès

Bolivar

Botzaris

Danube

Note-Dame-
de-Lorette

Poissonnière

LOUIS
BLANC

Château
Landon

Colonel
Fabien

Buttes-
Chaumont

7B

PRÉ-SAINT-GERVAIS

sée

Cadet

Pyrénées

Télégraphe

3B

11

MAIRIE DES LILAS

tin

Le Peletier

GARE DE
L'EST

Belleville

Jourdain

Places
des Fêtes

PORTE DES
LILAS

Rue Montmartre

Jacques
Bonsergent

Couronnes

Saint-Fargeau

buot

Bonne
Nouvelle

Château
d'Eau

Goncourt

Ménilmontant

Pelleport

Bourse

Sentier

GAMBETTA

mbre

Strasbourg
Saint-Denis
Temple

République

Parmentier

3B

mur-Sébastopol

Etienne
Marcel

Saint-Maur

Père-
Lachaise

Porte de
Bagnolet

3 GALLIENI

Arts-et-Métiers

Les
Halles

CHÂTELET-
LES
HALLES

Oberkampf

Filles du
Calvaire

Saint-
Ambroise

Philippe-Auguste

Rambuteau

Voltaire

Alexandre-Dumas

Croix-de-
Chavaux

9

MAIRIE DE
MONTREUIL

Rivoli

11

St-Sébastien
-Froissart

Richard
-Lenoir

Charonne

Avron

euf

Châtelet

Chemin
Vert

Bréguet-Sabin

Boulets
Montreuil

Robespierre

Porte de Montreuil

in

Pont Marie

Hôtel
de Ville

Bastille

Ledru-Rollin

Maraîchers

Buzenval

n

Odéon

Cité

St-Paul
Le Marais

2

NATION

Porte de Vincennes

Cluny La

Saint-Michel

Sully
Morland

Faidherbe-
Chaligny

6

Bérault

Sorbonne

St-Michel/
Notre-Dame

Saint-Mandé

Mauber
Mutualité

Quai de
la Rapée

Reuilly
-Diderot

Picpus

1

CHATEAU DE
VINCENNES

Cardinal
Lemoine

Jussieu

Montgallet

Bel-Air

RER A

Luxembourg

Monge

10

GARE DE
LYON

Daumesnil

t-Royal

GARE
D'AUSTERLITZ

Dugommier

Michel Bizot

Censier-Daubenton

Saint-Marcel

A2

AU

Les Gobelins

Campo-
Formio

Bercy

Porte Dorée

A4

Glacière

Corvisart

5

Chevaleret
Nationale

Quai de la Gare

Porte de
Charenton

Liberté

Tolbiac

Charenton-Ecoles

Maison-
Blanche

Boulevard
Masséna

Porte
d'Ivry

Alfort-École Vétérinaire

Porte de
Choisy

Maisons-Alfort-Stade

Maisons-Alfort-Les-Juillottes

té Universitaire

RER C

Créteil-l'Echat (Hop. Henri Mondor)

Paris Boundary

Porte
d'Italie

Pierre-Curie

River Seine

Créteil-Université

Villejuif
Paul
Vaillant-
Couturier

Le Kremlin
Bicêtre

MAIRIE
D'IVRY

7

C2

C4

C6

River Marne

ILLEJUIF
IS ARAGON

7

Villejuif Léo Lagrange

8

CRETEIL-PREFECTURE
Hôtel de Ville

Driving – and car rental

Travelling around by car, in the daytime at least, is hardly worth it because of the difficulty of finding parking space. Whatever you do, don't park in a bus lane or the *Axe Rouge* express routes (marked with a red square). Should you be **towed away**, you'll find your car in the pound belonging to that particular *arrondissement*; you'll have to check with the local town hall (*mairie*) for the address.

In the event of a **breakdown** you can call *Aleveque Daniel* (116 rue de la Convention, 15e; ☎48.28.12.00) or *Aligre Dépannage* (92 bd de Charonne, 20e; ☎49.78.87.50) for round-the-clock assistance. Alternatively, contact the police.

For **car rental**, in addition to the big international companies like *Avis*, *Hertz* etc (details from the tourist office), some good local firms are: *Acar* (77 rue Lagny, 20e; Mᵒ Porte-de-Vincennes; ☎43.79.76.48; Mon–Sat 8am–12.30pm & 2–7pm), *Dergi et Cie* (60 bd St-Marcel, 5e; Mᵒ Goberlins; ☎45.87.27.04; Mon–Sat 8am–7pm), *Locabest* (9 rue Abel, 12e; Mᵒ Gare-de-Lyon; ☎43.46.05.05; Mon–Sat 7.30am–7pm), and *Rent a Car* (79 rue de Bercy, 12e; Mᵒ Bercy; ☎45.45.15.15; Mon–Sat 8.30am–7pm).

Cycling

If you are reckless enough to want to **cycle** and don't have your bike, you can hire from *Paris-Vélo*, 2 rue du Fer-à-Moulin, 5e; Mᵒ Censier-Daubenton (☎43.37.59.22; Mon–Sat 10am–12.30pm & 2–7pm) or *La Maison Du Vélo*, 8 rue de Belzunce (☎42.81.24.72).

Boats

There remains one final mode of transport – by *Batobus* along the Seine. At the moment there are only five stops, though more are planned, and the service operates from April to September. The stops are: port de la Bourdonnais (Eiffel Tower), port de Solférino (Musée d'Orsay), quai Malaquais (Musée du Louvre), quai de Montebello (Notre-Dame) and quai de l'Hôtel de Ville. Boats run every 36 minutes from 10am to 7pm: total journey time is 21minutes and the price 20F, or 10F per individual stop.

Accommodation

Not surprisingly, Paris **hotels** are the most expensive in France. However, compared to other European capitals accommodation isn't exorbitant and it is perfectly possible to find somewhere decent and centrally placed for under F200 for a double, even as low as F140, for a room without bath. Our recommendations below are divided by arondissement (see map opposite) and by three price categories – Under 200F, Up to 350F and Up to 500F – which reflects the average cost of rooms. Many places have a few cheaper, or more expensive, rooms which stray outside the category.

For independence and choice of location there's obviously most scope in **booking** a hotel yourself – preferably well in advance. If you haven't booked anything in advance, you can either resort to the tourist board's *Bureaux d'Accueil*, who will endeavour to find you a room (not necessarily the most economical) for a small commission – from 17F – or the *AJF* actually guarantee "decent and low-cost lodging".

For details on **hostels**, **student accommodation** and **campsites**, see p.68.

1ᵉʳ hotels

UNDER 200F

Hôtel Henri IV, 25 place Dauphine, 1ᵉʳ. Mᵒ Pont-Neuf/Cité (☎43.54.44.53). An ancient and well-known cheapie in the beautiful place Dauphine on the Île de la Cité. Nothing more luxurious than *cabinet de toilette* and now somewhat rundown. Essential to book.

Hôtel Lion d'Or, 5 rue de la Sourdière, 1ᵉʳ. Mᵒ Tuileries (☎42.60.79.04). Spartan, but clean, friendly and very central.

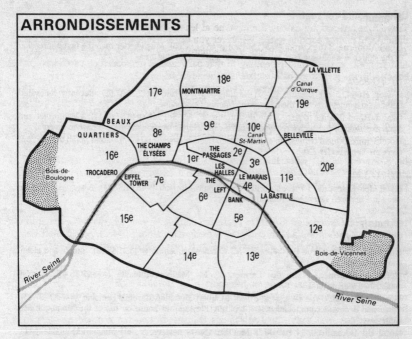

ARRONDISSEMENTS

Hôtel de l'Ouest, 144 rue St-Honoré, 1er. M° Louvre/Palais-Royal (☎42.60.29.89). Rooms rather small and dilapidated. Very close to Louvre and consequently popular. Try and book two weeks ahead.

UP TO 350F

Hôtel Richelieu-Mazarin, 51 rue de Richelieu, 1er. M° Palais-Royal (☎42.97.46.20). Very good for the price, with a laundry. Some much cheaper rooms.

Hôtel Washington Opéra, 50 rue de Richelieu, 1er. M° Palais-Royal (☎42.96.68.06). Pleasant and comfortable.

UP TO 500F

Ducs d'Anjou, 1 rue Ste-Opportune, 1er. M° Châtelet (☎42.36.92.24). A carefully renovated old building overlooking the endlessly crowded place Ste-Opportune in the middle of Les Halles night-life district. A bit posher than our average.

2e hotels

UNDER 200F

Hôtel Tiquetonne, 6 rue Tiquetonne, 2e. M° Étienne-Marcel (☎42.36.94.58). Bargain price in an attractive small street.

Grand Hôtel de Besançon, 56 rue de Montorgueil, 2e. M° Les Halles/Étienne-Marcel (☎42.36.41.08). Only a little over 200F at the top end. A great location in a lively market street.

3e hotels

UNDER 200F

Béranger Hôtel, 23 rue Béranger, 3e. M° République (☎42.78.55.24). A very decent inexpensive place to stay.

4ᵉ hotels

UNDER 200F

Hôtel Moderne, 3 rue Caron, 4ᵉ. Mᵒ St-Paul (☎48.87.97.05). Much better than the first impression of the staircase would suggest, and the price is amazing for this area.

UP TO 350F

Castex Hôtel, 5 rue Castex, 4ᵉ. Mᵒ Bastille/Sully-Morland (☎42.72.31.52). Recently renovated building in a quiet street on the edge of the Marais. Good value.

Grand Hôtel Jeanne d'Arc, 3 rue de Jarente, 4ᵉ. Mᵒ St-Paul (☎48.87.62.11). Clean, quiet and attractive, though – at such a reasonable price – the Marais location means you have to reserve.

Hôtel Pratic, 9 rue d'Ormesson, 4ᵉ. Mᵒ St-Paul/Bastille (☎48.87.80.47). Doubles go up to 320F, but there are some under 200F.

UP TO 500F

Hôtel des Célestins, 1 rue Charles-V, 4ᵉ. Mᵒ Sully-Morland (☎48.87.87.04). A very comfortable sleep in a restored seventeenth-century mansion.

5ᵉ hotels

UNDER 200F

Hôtel des Alliés, 20 rue Berthollet, 5ᵉ. Mᵒ Censier-Daubenton (☎43.31.47.52). Simple and clean, and bargain prices.

Hôtel des Carmes, 5 rue des Carmes, 5ᵉ. Mᵒ Maubert-Mutualité (☎43.29.78.40). A well-established tourist hotel.

Hôtel le Central, 6 rue Descartes, 5ᵉ. Mᵒ Maubert-Mutualité/Cardinal-Lemoine (☎46.33. 57.93). Clean and decent accommodation in a typically Parisian old house on top of the Montagne Ste-Geneviève.

Hôtel du Commerce, 14 rue de la Montagne-Ste-Geneviève, 5ᵉ. Mᵒ Maubert-Mutualité (☎43. 54.89.69). Another renowned if somewhat gloomy cheapie. Communal washing and toilets. No reservations so turn up early.

Hôtel Marignan, 13 rue du Sommerard, 5ᵉ. Mᵒ Maubert-Mutualité (☎43.54.63.81). One of the best bargains in town, and geared to the needs of rucksack-toting foreigners. Try and book a month ahead in summer, five days in winter, though a few rooms are kept free for people who turn up on spec.

UP TO 350F

Grand Hôtel Oriental, 2 rue d'Arras, 5ᵉ. Mᵒ Jussieu/Cardinal-Lemoine, Maubert-Mutualité (☎43.54.38.12). Recently refurbished, but still a pretty good bargain for this locality; nice people.

UP TO 500F

Hôtel Esmeralda, 4 rue St-Julien-le-Pauvre, 5ᵉ. Mᵒ St-Michel/Maubert-Mutualité (☎43.54. 19.20). A discreet and ancient house on square Viviani with a superb view of Notre-Dame, with several much cheaper rooms.

Hôtel de la Sorbonne, 6 rue Victor-Cousin, 5ᵉ. Mᵒ Luxembourg (☎43.54.58.08). An attractive old building, quiet, comfortable and close to the Luxembourg gardens.

6ᵉ hotels

UNDER 200F

Le Petit Trianon, 2 rue de l'Ancienne-Comédie, 6ᵉ. Mᵒ Odéon (☎43.54.94.64). Cheap, basic and right in the heart of things, but tatty and poorly managed. A last resort.

UP TO 350F

Hôtel Alsace-Lorraine, 14 rue des Canettes, 6ᵉ. Mᵒ St-Germain/St-Sulpice (☎43.25.10.14). An old and dingy building in a picturesque lane off place St-Sulpice, in the heart of St-Germain. Rooms clean, quiet and spacious.

Hôtel du Dragon, 36 rue du Dragon, 6ᵉ. Mᵒ St-Germain-des-Prés/Sèvres-Babylone (☎45.48.51.05). Great location and nice people.

Hôtel St-André-des-Arts, 66 rue St-André-des-Arts, 6ᵉ. Mᵒ Odéon (☎43.26.96.16) Reasonable and very central. Some cheaper rooms under 150F but no reservations on these.

UP TO 500F

Hôtel Récamier, 3bis place St-Sulpice, 6ᵉ. Mᵒ St-Sulpice/St-Germain (☎43.26.04.89). Comfortable, superbly sited, with one or two cheaper rooms.

Hôtel des Marronniers, 21 rue Jacob, 6ᵉ. Mᵒ St-Germain-des-Prés (☎43.25.30.60). This is a three-star and a little over the top of our price range, but it is delightful.

7ᵉ hotels

UP TO 350F

Hôtel du Centre, 24bis rue Cler, 7ᵉ. Mᵒ École-Militaire (☎47.05.52.53). An old-fashioned, no-frills establishment in a posh and attractive neighbourhood. Some cheaper rooms.

Grand Hôtel Lévèque, 29 rue Cler, 7ᵉ. Mᵒ École-Militaire/Latour-Maubourg (☎47.05 49.15). Clean and decent; nice people, who speak some English. Book one month ahead.

Hôtel du Palais Bourbon, 49 rue de Bourgogne, 7ᵉ. Mᵒ Varenne. ☎45.51.63.32. A handsome old building in a sunny street by the Musée Rodin. Rooms are spacious and light, and some are still under 200F.

UP TO 500F

Le Pavillon, 54 rue St-Dominique, 7ᵉ. Mᵒ Invalides/Latour-Maubourg (☎45.51.42.87). A tiny former convent in a leafy courtyard. Rather pokey rooms for the price though.

Hôtel de la Tulipe, 33 rue Malar, 7ᵉ. Mᵒ Latour-Maubourg (☎45.51.67.21). Patio for summer breakfast and drinks. Beamy and cottagey.

8ᵉ hotels

UP TO 350F

Hôtel d'Artois, 94 rue la Boétie, 8ᵉ. Mᵒ St-Philippe-du-Roule (☎43.59.84.12). At less than 300F, very cheap for this smartest part of town.

9ᵉ hotels

UP TO 350F

Hôtel des Arts, 7 Cité Bergère, 9ᵉ. Mᵒ Montmartre (☎42.46.73.30). An agreeable and friendly hotel.

Hôtel de Beauharnais, 51 rue de la Victoire, 9ᵉ. Mᵒ Le Peletier/Havre-Caumartin (☎48.74.71.13). Louis Quinze, First Empire . . . every room decorated in a different period style.

Hôtel Chopin, 46 passage Jouffroy, 9ᵉ. Mᵒ Montmartre (☎47.70.58.10). Entrance on bd Montmartre, near corner with rue du Faubourg-Montmartre. A splendid period building right in the old *passage*.

Parrotel Paris-Montholon, 11bis rue Pierre-Sémard, 9ᵉ. Mᵒ Poissonnière (☎48.78.28.94). Not bad at all, though the rooms are a little small and dark.

Victoria Hôtel, 2bis Cité Bergère, 9ᵉ. Mᵒ Montmartre (☎47.70.18.83). Situated in quiet, pleasant courtyard opposite *Chartier's* restaurant, along with several other slightly overpriced touristy hotels.

10ᵉ hotels

UNDER 200F

Hôtel du Centre Est, 4 rue Sibour, 10ᵉ. Mᵒ Gare de l'Est (☎46.07.20.74). An excellent value cheapie, but you'll generally need to book. Some rooms a little over 200F.

Hôtel du Jura, 6 rue de Jarry, 10ᵉ. Mᵒ Gare-de-l'Est, Château-d'Eau (☎47.70.06.66). Primitive, but friendly and decent.

UP TO 350F

Adix Hôtel, 30 rue Lucien-Sampaix, 10ᵉ. Mᵒ Bonsergent (☎42.08.19.74). In a pleasant street close to the St-Martin canal and surprisingly smart for the area.

City Hôtel Gare de l'Est, 5 rue St-Laurent, 10ᵉ. Mᵒ Gare-de-l'Est (☎42.09.83.50). Recently modernised: comfortable enough anchorage close to the stations. Some fine views from the top floor.

11ᵉ hotels

UNDER 200F

Hôtel Central Bastille, 16 rue de la Roquette, 11ᵉ. Mᵒ Bastille (☎47.00.31.51). Basic.

Luna Park Hôtel, 1 rue Jacquard, 11ᵉ. Mᵒ Parmentier (☎48.05.65.50). Good enough for sleeping. The street is quiet, the location interesting.

Hôtel de Vienne, 43 rue de Malte, 11ᵉ. Mᵒ Oberkampf (☎48.05.44.42). A pleasant good-value cheapie.

UP TO 350F

Hôtel Baudin, 113 av Ledru-Rollin, 11ᵉ. Mᵒ Ledru-Rollin (☎47.00.18.91). Clean and pleasant. Traffic noise could be bothersome. Some cheaper rooms.

Hôtel Parmentier, 91 rue Oberkampf, 11ᵉ. Mᵒ Parmentier (☎43.57.02.09). Clean and friendly. Better to get a room on the *cour* if you can.

Plessis-Hôtel, 25 rue du Grand-Prieuré, 11ᵉ. Mᵒ République/Oberkampf (☎47.00.13.38). A friendly, good-value hotel.

Hôtel St-Martin, 12 rue Léon-Frot, 11ᵉ. Mᵒ Boulets-Montreuil (☎43.71.09.14). Rather boring neighbourhood, but the hotel is pleasant enough.

12ᵉ hotels

UNDER 200F

Mistral Hôtel, 3 rue Chaligny, 12ᵉ. Mᵒ Faidherbe-Chaligny (☎46.28.10.20). Cheap and basic.

UP TO 350F

Grand Hôtel de Cognac, 8 cours de Vincennes, 12ᵉ. Mᵒ Nation (☎43.45.13.53). A bit pricey but has charm.

Hôtel des Pyrénées, 204 rue du Faubourg-St-Antoine, 12ᵉ. Mᵒ Faidherbe-Chaligny (☎43.72.07.46). Comfortable and quiet behind its posh reception area.

13ᵉ hotels

UNDER 200F

Victoria Hôtel, 47 rue Bobillot, 13ᵉ. Mᵒ Place-d'Italie (☎45.80.59.88). Basic.

Hôtel de la Place des Alpes, 2 place des Alpes, 13ᵉ. Mᵒ Place-d'Italie (☎45.35.14.14). An agreeable establishment, with some rooms over the 200F mark.

Hôtel de Bourgogne, 15 rue Godefroy, 13ᵉ. Mᵒ Place-d'Italie (☎45.35.37.92). Friendly and adequate. A few doubles over 200F.

14ᵉ hotels

UNDER 200F

Hôtel Clairefontaine, 11 rue Fermat, 14ᵉ. Mᵒ Denfert-Rochereau/Gaîté (☎43.22.05.20). Basic. Just behind Montparnasse cemetery.

UP TO 350F

Hôtel du Parc, 6 rue Jolivet, 14ᵉ. Mᵒ Montparnasse/Edgar-Quinet (☎43.20.95.54). Clean rooms and a very nice *patron*.

15e hotels

UNDER 200F

Mondial Hôtel, 136 bd de Grenelle, 15e. Mo La Motte-Picquet (☎45.79.73.57). Simple lodgings for workers and commercial travellers. Friendly and decent management. Located under the raised métro.

UP TO 350F

Pratic Hôtel, 20 rue de l'Ingénieur-Keller, 15e. Mo Charles-Michels (☎45.77.70.58). Very nice: clean and friendly – with several rooms under 200F. Close to the Eiffel Tower.

Tourisme Hôtel, 66 av de la Motte-Picquet 15e. Mo La Motte-Picquet (☎47.34.28.01). Unprepossessing barrack-like building situated on the corner of bd de Grenelle, but the rooms are fine.

17e hotels

UNDER 200F

Hôtel Avenir-Jonquière, 23 rue de la Jonquière, 17e. Mo Guy-Môquet (☎46.27.83.41). Clean, friendly establishment. Good bargain.

Batignolles Hôtel, 46 rue de la Jonquière, 17e. Mo Guy-Môquet (☎46.27.64.67). Basic and inexpensive.

Hôtel Gauthey, 5 rue Gauthey, 17e. Mo Brochant (☎46.27.15.48). Simple and clean.

UP TO 350F

Hôtel des Batignolles, 26–28 rue des Batignolles, 17e. Mo Rome/Place-Clichy (☎43.87. 70.40). A quiet and very reasonable establishment in a villagey neighbourhood. Some cheaper rooms.

UP TO 500F

Hôtel du Roi René, 72 place Félix-Lobligeois, 17e. Mo Rome/Villiers (☎42.26.72.73). Doubles 420F, singles cheaper. Very nice location by a mini-Greek temple and public garden.

18e hotels

UNDER 200F

Idéal Hôtel, 3 rue des Trois-Frères, 18e. Mo Abbesses (☎46.06.63.63). Marvellous location on the slopes of Montmartre. Cheap and clean. A real bargain.

Hôtel Tholozé, 24 rue Tholozé, 18e. Mo Blanche/Abbesses (☎46.06.74.83). Another real bargain – clean, friendly and quiet, in a steep, quiet street below the Moulin de la Galette.

UP TO 350F

Hôtel André Gill, 4 rue André-Gill, 18e. Mo Pigalle/Abbesses (☎42.62.48.4)8. Prices at bottom of range for very adequate rooms in a great location on the slopes of Montmartre.

Hôtel Regyn's, 18 place des Abbesses, 18e. Mo Abbesses (☎42.54.45.21). Superb site, and lovely views across the city. Comfortable and relaxed.

20e hotels

UNDER 200F

Ermitage Hôtel, 42bis rue de l'Ermitage, 20e. Mo Jourdain (☎46.36.23.44). Clean and close to the leafy, provincial rue des Pyrénées.

Mary's, 118 rue Orfila, 20e. Mo Pelleport (☎43.61.51.68). Simple, clean and friendly. A little far out, at the rue Pelleport end of rue Orfila.

UP TO 350F

Hôtel Nadaud, 8 rue de la Bidassoa, 20e. Mo Gambetta (☎46.36.87.79). Closed in August. A very reasonable hotel, close to the Père-Lachaise cemetery.

Hostels, student accommodation and campsites

There are numerous places offering **hostel** accommodation. In the main you have the choice between three organizations: the official *IYHF* hostels, hostels run by the *Accueil des Jeunes en France (AJF)*, and those run by the *Union des Centres de Rencontres Internationaux de France (UCRIF)*.

IYHF rates in Paris are 90–115F a night and there's normally a maximum stay of three to four days. *AJF* hostels, mostly located in elegant old mansions in the Marais, charge around 90F a night, impose a maximum stay of five days, and won't reserve in advance.There are eleven *UCRIF* hostels in all; we've detailed the most central ones; they charge 85F for dorm beds, rising to 160F for a private room; again no advance bookings accepted. For details of the other *UCRIF* hostels, contact their main office at 4 rue Jean-Jacques-Rousseau, 1er (Mon–Fri 10am–6pm; ☎42.60.42.40).

IYHF hostels

D'Artagnan, 80 rue Vitruve, 20^e (☎43.61.08.75). M^o Porte de Bagnolet. Enormous hostel, with lots of facilities, but a fair way out on the eastern fringes of the city. There's also an annexe at *Hôtel Ste-Marguerite*, 10 rue Trousseau, 11e (☎47.00.62.00) in the Faubourg St-Antoine.

Jules Ferry, 8 bd Jules-Ferry, 11e (☎43.57.55.60). M^o République. Smaller and more central than the other other official *IYHF* hostel, situated in the lively area at the foot of the Belleville hill.

AJF hostels

Le Fauconnier, 11 rue du Fauconnier, 4e (☎42.74.23.45). M^o St-Paul/Pont-Marie.

Le Fourcy, 6 rue de Fourcy, 4e (☎42.74.23.45). M^o St-Paul.

Maubuisson, 12 rue des Barres, 4e (☎42.72.72.09). M^o Pont-Marie/Hôtel-de-Ville.

François Miron, 6 rue François-Miron, 4e. M^o Hôtel-de-Ville. Annexe of above.

Résidence Bastille, 151 av Ledru-Rollin, 11e (☎43.79.53.86). M^o Ledru-Rollin/Bastille/Voltaire.

UCRIF hostels

BVJ Centre International de Paris/Les Halles, 5 rue du Pélican, 1er (☎40.26.92.45). M^o Louvre/Châtelet-Les Halles/Palais-Royal.

BVJ Centre International de Paris/Louvre, 20 rue Jean-Jacques-Rousseau, 1er (☎42.36.88.18). M^o Louvre/Châtelet-Les Halles.

BVJ Centre International de Paris/Opéra, 11 rue Thérèse, 1er (☎42.60.77.23). M^o Pyramides/Palais-Royal.

BVJ Centre International de Paris/Quartier Latin, 44 rue des Bernadins, 5e (☎43.29.34.80). M^o Maubert-Mutualité.

Student accommodation

You can also get **student accomodation** during vacation time. The organisation for this is *CROUS*, Académie de Paris, 39 av Georges-Bernanos, 5e. M^o Port-Royal. ☎40.51.36.00. One last possibility is the *CIDJ*'s information files at their offices at 101 quai Branly, 15e; M^o Bir-Hakeim.

Campsites

There is a **campsite**, usually booked up in summer and in theory reserved for French camping club members, by the Seine in the Bois de Boulogne on allée du Bord-de-l'Eau, 16e. M^o Porte-Maillot (☎45.06.14.98). Three more are further out to the east of the city:

Camping du Tremblay, quai de Polangis, Champigny-sur-Marne. RER Champigny (☎42.83.38.24).

Camping du Camp des Cicognes, bord-de-Marne, Créteil. RER Créteil-l'Echat (☎42.07.06.75).

Camping de Paris-Est, bd des Alliés, Champigny-sur-Marne. M^o Joinville-le-Pont (☎42.83.38.24).

The City

Paris splits into two distinct halves, either side of the Seine. On the north side of the river, the **Right Bank** or *rive droite* is home to the grand boulevards and the most monumental buildings, many dating from the nineteenth-century redevelopment by Haussmann, and is the area that you'll spend most time in, during the day at least. The top museums are here – the Louvre, the Beaubourg, to name just two – as well as the city's widest range of shops around rue de Rivoli and Les Halles; and there are also peaceful quarters like the Marais for idle strolling. The term **Left Bank** (*rive gauche*) connotes Bohemian, dissident, intellectual – the radical student type, whether eighteen years of age or eighty. As a topographical term it refers particularly to their traditional haunts, the warren of medieval lanes round the **boulevards St-Michel** and **St-Germain**, known as the **Quartier Latin** because that was the language of the university sited there right up until 1789. In modern times its reputation for turbulence and innovation has been renewed by the activities of painters and writers like Picasso, Apollinaire, Breton, Henry Miller, Anaïs Nin and Hemingway after the First World War, Camus, Sartre, Juliette Greco and the Existentialists after the Second, and the political turmoil of 1968 which escalated from student demonstrations and barricades to factory occupations, massive strikes and the near-overthrow of de Gaulle's presidency. This is not to say that the whole of Paris south of the Seine is the exclusive territory of revolutionaries and avant-gardists. It does, however, have a different and distinctive feel and appearance, noticeable as soon as you cross the river.

Paris can be explored in any number of ways – you don't have to start with the Eiffel Tower or Champs-Élysées. We've **structured** our account in chunks of territory that do not always correspond exactly to the boundaries of the twenty *arrondissements* but which share a common identity. We start with the monumental axis that runs from the Louvre through the north-west quarter of the city, followed by the centre, first north, then south of the Seine. Then we work outwards in a clockwise direction from the 14ᵉ *arrondissement* through the *Beaux Quartiers* in the west round to the poorer districts of eastern Paris. Apart from the odd suggested walk the descriptions are designed for getting the most out of a neighbourhood, rather than as strict itineraires to be followed. Note that some cafés, markets, shops and museums are mentioned here in passing. For full details or listings see the relevant sections below.

The Voie Triomphale

La Voie Triomphale, or Triumphal Way, stretches in a dead straight line from the eastern end of the Louvre to the modern complex of corporate skyscrapers at La Défense, nine kilometres away. Incorporating some of the city's most famous landmarks – the **Champs-Élysées**, the **Arc de Triomphe**, the **Louvre** and the **Tuileries** – its monumental constructions have been erected over the centuries by kings and emperors, presidents and corporations, to promulgate French power and prestige.

The tradition dies hard. Further self-aggrandisement has recently been given expression in an enormous, marble-clad cubic arch at the head of La Défense, and a **glass pyramid** entrance in the central courtyard of the much-expanded Louvre.

The Arc de Triomphe and Champs-Elysées

The best view of this grandiose and simple geometry of kings to capital is from the top of the **Arc de Triomphe**, Napoléon's homage to the armies of France and himself (10am–5pm; 27F, 15F for under-24s, 5F for under-7s; access from stairs on north corner of av des Champs-Élysées). Your attention, however, is most likely to be caught not by the view but by the mesmerising traffic movements directly below you, around **place de**

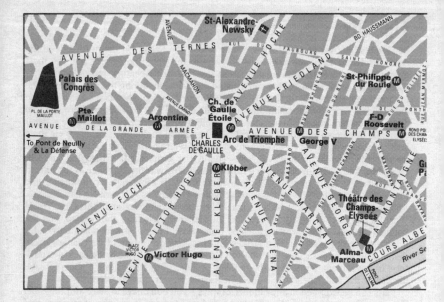

l'Étoile – the world's first organised roundabout. Twelve wide avenues make up the star (*étoile*), of which the busiest is the **Champs-Élysées** – earmarked for a face-lift, although it's doubtful whether anything can bring back glamour to the array of airline offices, car showrooms, hamburger joints and multi-screen cinemas. It only comes to life at Christmas when the fairy lights go on, and on December 31 when it's the equivalent of Trafalgar Square with everyone happily jammed, in their cars, hooting in the New Year. Bastille Day's procession of president, tanks and guns is less appealing.

The best section of the avenue is between place de la Concorde and the Rond-Point roundabout, whose Lalique glass fountains disappeared during the German occupation. It's bordered by chestnut trees and municipal flower beds, pleasant enough to stroll among but not sufficiently dense to muffle the discomfiting squeal of accelerating tyres. The two massive buildings rising above the greenery to the south are the **Grand and Petit Palais**, with their overloaded Neoclassical exteriors, train-station roofs and exuberantly optimistic flying statuary. On the north side, combat police guard the high walls round the presidential **Élysée Palace** and the line of ministries and embassies ending with the US in prime position on the corner of place de la Concorde. On Thursday and at weekends you can see a stranger manifestation of the self-images of states in the postage **stamp market** at the corner of avenues Gabriel and Marigny.

The place de la Concorde, Tuileries and the Louvre

The Champs-Élysées descends to **place de la Concorde**, where crossing over to the middle is again a death-defying task. As it happens, some 1300 people did die here between 1793 and 1795, beneath the Revolutionary guillotine: Louis XVI, Marie-Antoinette, Danton and Robespierre among them. The centrepiece of the *place*, chosen like its name to make no comment on these events, is an **obelisk** from the temple of Luxor, offered as a favour-currying gesture by the viceroy of Egypt in 1829. It serves merely to pivot more geometry: the alignment of the French parliament, the **Assemblée**

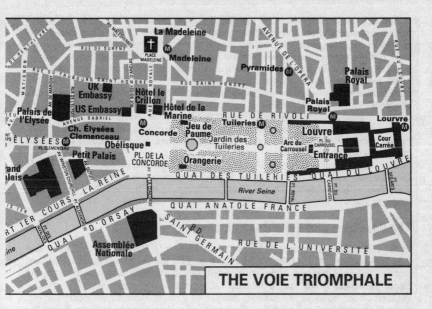

THE VOIE TRIOMPHALE

Nationale, on the far side of the Seine with the church of the Madeleine to the north. Needless to say, it cuts the Voie Triomphale at a precise and predictable right angle.

The symmetry continues beyond place de la Concorde in the formal layout of the **Tuileries gardens**, disrupted only by the bodies lounging on the grass, kids chasing their boats round the ponds, and gays cruising near the **Orangerie** at one end of the western terrace. Since everything on the Voie Triomphale must maintain the myth of Paris as the world's state-of-the-art capital, plans are afoot for major works on the **Tuileries gardens**. The commission is to be given to Ieoh Ming Pei, the architect responsible for the New Age addition to *La Voie Triumphale*, the notorious glass pyramid between the two long arms of the **Louvre**. The Orangerie's twin, the **Jeu de Paume**, ex-royal tennis court and ex-Impressionists museum, has had huge windows cut into its classical temple walls to light the city's newest exhibition space for contemporary art.

La Défense

Angled a few degrees out from the far western end of the Voie Triomphale, **La Grande Arche** has put **La Défense** – one RER stop beyond Charles-de-Gaulle-Étoile – high on the list of places to which visitors to Paris must pay homage, a beautiful and astounding structure, a 112-metre hollow cube, clad in white marble. Suspended within the hollow, which could shelter Notre-Dame with ease, are the open lift shafts and a "cloud" panoply. It houses a government ministry, international businesses and, in the roof section, the *Arche de la Fraternité* foundation who stage exhibitions and conferences on issues related to human rights. You can ride up to the roof (July & Aug Mon & Thurs 9am–7pm, Tues & Wed 9am–5pm, Fri 9am–9pm, Sat 10am–9pm, Sun 10am–7pm; otherwise Mon–Fri 9am–5pm, Sat & Sun 10am–7pm; 30F, 15F for students, pensioners and the unemployed). As well as having access to the *Arche de la Fraternité* exhibitions, you can admire the "Map of the Heavens" marble patios and, on a clear day, scan from the marble path on the *parvis* below you to the Arc de Triomphe and beyond to the Louvre.

Between the Grande Arche and the river is the **business complex** of La Défense, a perfect monument to the horrors of late twentieth-century capitalism. There is no formal pattern to the arrangements of towers. Token apartment blocks, offices of ELF, Esso, IBM, banks and other businesses compete for size, dazzle of surface and ability to make you dizzy. Mercifully, bizarre **artworks** transform the nightmare into comic entertainment. Joan Miró's giant wobbly creatures despair at their misfit status beneath the biting edges and curveless heights of the buildings. Alexander Calder's red iron offering is a *stabile* rather than a mobile and between them a black marble metronome shape without a beat releases a goal-less line across the *parvis*. A nineteenth-century war memorial perches on a concrete plinth in front of a plastic coloured waterfall and, further down, disembodied people clutch each other around endlessly repeated concrete flowerbeds.

You'll find details of all the sculptures in the **Art Défense** exhibition space beside the waterfall, and, if you're desperate to hand over money to the firms surrounding you, there's the enormous *Quatre-Temps* shopping centre to the left of the Grande Arche as you face it.

The Passages and Right Bank commerce

In the narrow streets of the 1er and 2e arrondissements, **between the Louvre and bds Haussmann, Montmartre and Poissonnière**, the grandiose financial, cultural and political state institutions are surrounded by well-established commerce – the rag trade, newspapers, sex and well-heeled shopping. A few years ago, the greatest contrast to the hulks of the Bourse, Banque de France, Bibliothèque Nationale etc, were the crumbling and secretive **Passages**, shopping arcades long predating the concept of pedestrian precincts, with glass roofs, tiled floors and unobtrusive entrances. Almost all have now been rendered as chic and immaculate as they were originally in the nineteenth century, with mega-premiums on their leases.

The Passages

Foremost among the passages is the **Galerie Vivienne** (between rue Vivienne and rue des Petits-Champs), with its flamboyant décor of Grecian and marine motifs enticing you to buy Jean-Paul Gaultier or Yuki Torri gear. The neighbouring **Galerie Colbert**, gorgeously lit by bunches of bulbous lamps, has become a showcase extension for the Bibliothèque Nationale. But the best stylistically are the dilapidated three-storey **passage du Grand-Cerf** (at the bottom of rue St-Denis) and **Galerie Véro-Dodat** (off rue Croix-des-Petits-Champs) named after the two pork butchers who set it up in 1824. This last is the most homogeneous and aristocratic of the Passages, with painted ceilings and panelled shop-fronts divided by black marble columns. At no. 26, Monsieur Capia keeps a collection of antique dolls in a shop piled high with miscellaneous curios.

North of rue St-Marc the grid of arcades round the **passage des Panoramas** are still a touch rough, with no fancy mosaics for your feet. An old brasserie with carved wood panelling has been restored, and new restaurants are moving in, but there are still bric-a-brac shops, bars, stamp dealers, and an upper-crust printshop with its original 1867 fittings. In **passage Jouffroy** across bd Montmartre, a M. Segas sells walking canes and theatrical antiques opposite a carpet emporium while Paul Vulin spreads his secondhand books further down along the passageway.

The garment business

Mass-produced clothes is the business of **place du Caire**, the centre of the rag-trade district. The frenetic trading and deliveries of cloth, the food market on rue des Petits-Carreaux, and general toing and froing make a lively change from the office-bound quarters further west. Beneath an extraordinary pseudo-Egyptian facade of grotesque

Pharaonic heads (a celebration of Napoléon's conquest of Egypt), an archway opens on to a series of arcades, the **Passage du Caire**. These, contrary to any visible evidence, are the oldest of all the *Passages* and entirely monopolised by wholesale clothes shops.

The garment business gets progressively more upmarket west of the trade area. The upper end of **rue Étienne-Marcel**, and Louis XIV's **place des Victoires**, adjoined to the north by the appealingly unsymmetrical **place des Petits-Pères**, are the centre for new-name designer clothes, displayed to deter all those without the necessary funds. The boutiques on **rue St-Honoré** and its Faubourg extension have the established names, paralleled across the Champs-Élysées by **rue François-1er**, where Dior has at least four blocks on the corner with av Montaigne. The autocratic **place Vendôme**, with Napoléon high on a column clad with recycled Austro-Russian cannons, offers all the fashionable accessories for haute couture – jewellery, perfumes, the original Ritz, a Rothschilds office and the Law and Order ministry.

Sex and finance

After clothes, bodies are the most evident commodity on sale in the **1er and 2e arrondissements**, on rue St-Denis above all, where, despite unionisation by the prostitutes, pimps still reign supreme. The pimps get richer towards the Madeleine, while around rue Ste-Anne business is less blatant, being gay, transvestite and underage. For the kids, reaching the age of 13 or 14 means redundancy. Such are the libertarian delights of Paris streetlife.

In the centre of the 2e, the **Bourse** is the scene for dealing in stocks and shares, dollars and gold. The classical order of the facade utterly belies the scene within, which is like an unruly boys' public school, with creaking floors, tottering pigeonholes and people scuttling about with bits of paper. They've only recently latched on to microchips and the real financial sharks go elsewhere for their deals.

Place Madeleine and the Opéra

Another obese Napoleonic structure on the classical temple model is the church of **La Madeleine**, which serves for snob society weddings and for the perspective across place de la Concorde. There's a **flower market** every day except Monday along the east side of the church and a luxurious **Art Nouveau loo** by the métro at the junction of place and bd Madeleine. But the greatest appeal of the square is for rich or window-gazing gourmets. In the northeast corner – at *Fauchon* – are two blocks of the best **food display** in Paris , with a snack bar for gourmet treats.

Bd de la Madeleine, becoming bd des Capucines, leads to the most preposterous building in Paris, the **Opéra de Paris**, whose architect, Charles Garnier, looks suitably foolish in a golden statue on the rue Auber side of his edifice. Excessively ornate and covering three acres in extent, this provided ample space for aristocratic preening, ceremonial pomp and the social intercourse of opera-goers, for whom the performance itself was a very secondary matter. These days, with the new Bastille opera, the Opéra Garnier – as it's now called – is used almost exclusively for ballet. By day you can visit the interior (11am–5pm), including the auditorium, where the ceiling is by Chagall.

Palais Royal

The av de l'Opéra was built at the same time as its namesake – and left deliberately bereft of trees which might mask the vista of the Opéra. It leads down to the **Palais Royal**, originally Richelieu's residence, which now houses various government and constitutional bodies, and the **Comédie Française,** where the classics of French theatre are performed. The palace **gardens** to the north were once a gastronomic, gambling and amusement hot spot overlooked by flats lived in by Cocteau and Colette amongst others. They are now very austere, although new shops have opened in the arcades. But folly has returned in the form of **black and white pillars** in different sizes standing above flowing water in the main courtyard of the palace, the creation of Daniel Buren. Kids use these monochrome Brighton-rock lookalikes as an adventure playground, but for most people the palace grounds are just a useful short cut from the Louvre to rue des Petits-Champs. Beyond this street, just to the left, is the forbidding wall of the **Bibliothèque Nationale**, the French equivalent of the British Museum library. They have a public display of coins and ancient treasures (1–5pm), so you can at least enter the building should you feel so inclined. And if the great French playwright Molière inspires you, you can bow before his statue on the corner of rues Richelieu and Molière.

Les Halles to Beaubourg

In 1969 the main **Les Halles** market was moved to the suburbs after more than eight hundred years in the heart of the city. There was widespread opposition to the destruction of Victor Baltard's nineteenth-century pavilions, and considerable disquiet at what renovation of the area would mean. The authorities' excuse was the RER and métro interchange they had to have below. Digging began in 1971 and the hole was only finally filled at the end of the 1980s. Hardly any trace remains of the working-class quarter, with its night bars and bistros to serve the market traders, and rents now rival the 16e.

The Forum des Halles

From Châtelet-Les Halles RER, you surface only after ascending levels 4 to 0 of the **Forum des Halles** centre, which stretches underground from the Bourse du Commerce rotunda to rue Pierre-Lescot. The overground section comprises aquarium-like arcades of shops enclosed by glass buttocks with white steel creases sliding down to an imprisoned patio. To cover up for all this commerce, poetry, arts and crafts pavilions top two sides in a simple construction – save for the mirrors – that just manages to be out of synch with the curves and hollows below.

From the terrace you can admire the tightly controlled gardens in which shrubs and hedges are caged in wire nets. On the north side a giant head and hand suggest the dislocation of the place, though to be fair it does provide much-needed open space and greenery in the centre of the city. Beneath the garden, amidst the uninspiring shops, there's scope for various diversions such as swimming, watching games of billiards, discovering Paris through videos (see below) and wandering through a tropical garden. Touch-screen computers, with French and English "menus", are on hand to guide you round. After a spate of multi-levels, air conditioning and artificial light, you can seek relief in the water cascading down the perfect Renaissance proportions of the **Fontaine des Innocents**, or in the high Gothic space of **St-Eustache** where a woman preached the abolition of marriage from the pulpit during the Commune.

There are always hundreds of people around the Forum, filling in time, hustling or just loafing about. Pickpocketing and sexual harassment are pretty routine; the law plus canine arm are often in evidence and at night it can be quite tense. The supposedly trendy streets on the eastern side have about as much appeal as contemporary Carnaby Street. The area southwards to **place du Châtelet**, however, teems with jazz bars, nightclubs and restaurants and is far more crowded at 2am than 2pm. Back towards the Louvre streets like **de l'Arbre-Sec**, **Sauval** and **du Roule** revive the gentler attractions of pavement window-shopping, while on the riverfront the three blocks of the **Samaritaine department store** (Mon, Thurs & Sat 9.30am–7pm; Tues & Fri 9.30am–8.30pm; Wed 9.30am–10.30pm) recall the days when art rather than marketing psychology determined the decoration of a store. Built in 1903 in pure Art Nouveau style, its gold, green and glass exteriors and interior ceramic tiles and wrought-iron staircases and balconies have all been restored, though best of all is the view from the roof – the most central high location in the city.

Beaubourg

In the daytime the main flow of feet is from Les Halles to **Beaubourg**, the **Georges Pompidou national art and culture centre** (Mon & Wed–Fri noon–10pm, weekends 10am–10pm; free). This famous building by Renzo Piano and Richard Rogers is showing severe signs of wear and tear, but it remains one of the most popular Parisian buildings, though perhaps more for the plaza's shifting spectacle by buskers of mime, magic, music and fire, than for the more mainstream cultural activities inside.

On the ground floor, the postcard selection and art bookshop betters anything on the streets outside, and there are usually some scattered artworks that you don't have to pay to see. On the second floor, you can consult a wide range of books, tapes, videos and international newspapers for free at the **Bibliothèque Publique d'Information (BPI)**. Whether you want to do this or not, you should ride up the glass intestine of the **escalator** at least once. As the circles of spectators on the plaza recede, a horizontal skyline appears: the Sacré-Coeur, St-Eustache, the Eiffel Tower, Notre-Dame, the Panthéon, the Tour St-Jacques with its solitary gargoyle and La Défense menacing in the distance. From the platform at the top you can look down on the château-style chimneys of the Hôtel de Ville with their flowerpot offspring sprouting all over the lower rooftops.

Back on the ground, **visual entertainments** around Beaubourg don't appeal to every taste. There's the clanking gold *Défenseur du Temps* clock in the Quartier de l'Horloge; a *trompe-l'oeil* as you look along rue Aubry-le-Boucher from Beaubourg; a mural of a monkey eating yoghurt on rue Renard just south of the centre; and sculptures and fountains by Tinguely and Nicky de St-Phalle in the pool in front of Église St-Merri. This waterwork pays homage to Stravinsky and shows scant respect for passers-by, and is the ceiling for IRCAM, the centre for contemporary music. A new, over-ground extension to IRCAM has appeared beside the old public baths on rue St-Merri – a Renzo Piano creation with a facade of stark terracotta marked like graph paper.

Quartier Beaubourg and the Hôtel de Ville

The *quartier Beaubourg* excels in its selection of small **commercial art galleries**, in which you can browse to your heart's content for free. **Rue Quincampoix** and **rue Renard**, the continuation of rue Beaubourg, are particularly promising. Rue Renard runs down to **place de l'Hôtel de Ville**, where the oppressively vertical, gleaming and gargantuan mansion is the seat of the city's government. An illustrated history of the edifice, always a prime target in riots and revolutions, is displayed along the platform of the Châtelet métro on the Neuilly-Vincennes line. After the defeat of the Commune in 1870, the bourgeoisie decided that a Parisian municipal authority worked against the better interests of law and order, property and the suppression of the working class, and for 100 years Paris was ruled directly by the ministry of the interior. The next head of an independent municipality was Jacques Chirac, elected in 1977 and still in control of the city today.

The Marais and the Île St-Louis

Jack Kerouac translates **rue des Francs-Bourgeois** as "street of the outspoken middle classes". The original owners of the mansions lining its length would not have taken kindly to such a slight on their blue-bloodedness. The name's origin is medieval, and it was not until the sixteenth and seventeenth centuries that the **Marais**, as the area between Beaubourg and the Bastille is known, became a fashionable aristocratic district. After the Revolution it was abandoned to the masses who, up until some twenty years ago, were living ten to a room on unserviced, squalid streets. Since then, gentrification has proceeded apace and the middle classes are finally ensconced – mostly media, arty or gay, and definitely outspoken.

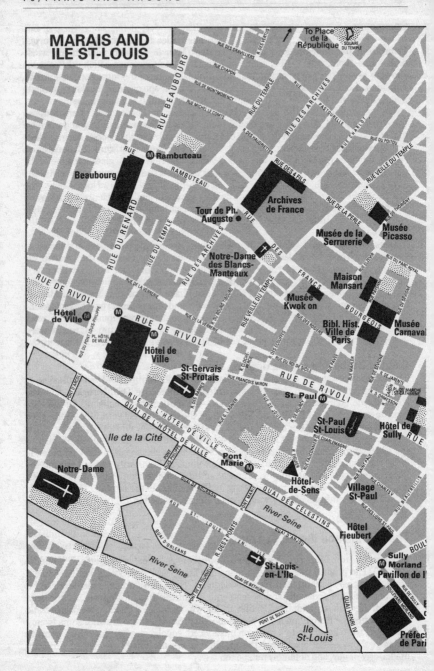

MARAIS AND ILE ST-LOUIS

To Place de la République
SQUARE DU TEMPLE

RUE DES GRAVILLIERS
R. DES VERTUS
RUE CHAPON
RUE DE MONTMORENCY
RUE MICHEL LE COMTE
RUE DU TEMPLE
RUE DES ARCHIVES
RUE PASTOURELLE
RUE CHARLOT
RUE DU POITOU
R. DES HAUDRIETTES
RUE DE BEAUBOURG

Ⓜ Rambuteau
RAMBUTEAU
RUE DES 4 FILS
RUE VIEILLE DU TEMPLE
RUE DE LA PERLE
RUE THORIGNY

Beaubourg

Archives de France

Tour de Ph. Auguste ●

Musée de la Serrurerie
Musée Picasso

RUE DU PARC ROYAL

Notre-Dame des Blancs-Manteaux
RUE DES

Maison Mansart

RUE DE LA VERRERIE
RUE DES ARCHIVES
RUE DU TEMPLE
RUE DU RENARD
RUE DE RIVOLI

Musée Kwok on
FRANCS
BOURGEOIS
Musée Carnaval

Hôtel de Ville Ⓜ
PL. DE L'HÔTEL DE VILLE
RUE DU PONT LOUIS-PHILIPPE
Ⓜ RUE DE RIVOLI
Ⓜ
Bibl. Hist. Ville de Paris

RUE DE LA VERRERIE
RUE DU BOURG TIBOURG
RUE DES ROSIERS
RUE PAVÉE
RUE MALHER
RUE DE SÉVIGNÉ
PL. DU MARCHÉ STE-CATHERINE
R. DE JARENTE
T.D. ORMESSON

Hôtel de Ville
St-Gervais St-Protais
RUE FRANÇOIS MIRON
St. Paul Ⓜ

QUAI DE L'HÔTEL DE VILLE
RUE DE L'HÔTEL DE VILLE
PONT D'ARCOLE
PONT AU DOUBLE

Ile de la Cité

Notre-Dame

Pont Marie Ⓜ
QUAI DE BOURBON
PONT MARIE
QUAI DES CÉLESTINS
River Seine

Hôtel-de-Sens

St-Paul St-Louis
RUE CHARLEMAGNE
RUE ST-PAUL

Hôtel de Sully

Village St-Paul
RUE CHARLES V
RUE DES LIONS ST-PAUL

Hôtel Fieubert

RUE
QUAI D'ORLÉANS
R. ST. LOUIS
R. DES 2 PONTS
QUAI DE BÉTHUNE
River Seine
QUAI D'ANJOU

St-Louis-en-L'Ile

Sully Morland Ⓜ
Pavillon de l'

PONT DE LA TOURNELLE
PONT MARIE
PONT DE SULLY
QUAI HENRI IV
BOULEVARD MORLAND
RUE DE SULLY

Ile St-Louis

Préfecture de Paris

The renovated mansions, their grandeur concealed by the narrow streets, have become museums, libraries, offices and chic apartments, flanked by shops selling designer clothes, house and garden accoutrements, works of art and one-off trinkets. Though cornered by Haussmann's boulevards, the Marais itself was spared the Baron's heavy touch and very little has been pulled down in the recent gentrification. It is Paris at its most seductive – old, secluded, as unthreatening by night as it is by day, and with as many alluring shops, bars and places to eat as you could wish for.

Hôtels and the place des Vosges

Rue des Francs-Bourgeois begins with the eighteenth-century magnificence of the **Palais Soubise**, which houses the *Archives de France*. Further down the street are two of the grandest Marais hôtels, **Carnavalet** and **Lamoignon**, housing respectively the *Musée Carnavalet* and the *Bibliothèque Historique de la Ville de Paris*. Finally you reach the masterpiece of aristocratic urban planning, the **place des Vosges**, vast square of stone and brick symmetry built for the majesty of Henri IV and Louis XIII, whose statue is hidden by trees in the middle of the grass and gravel gardens. Expensive high heels tap through the arcades pausing at art, antique and fashion shops, while toddlers and octogenarians, lunch-break workers and schoolchildren sit or play in the garden, the only green space of any size in the locality.

From the southwest corner of the *place*, a door leads through to the formal château garden, orangerie and exquisite Renaissance facade of the **Hôtel de Sully**. You can visit the temporary exhibitions mounted by the *Caisse Nationale des Monuments Historiques et des Sites* here or just pass through, nodding at the sphinxes on the stairs, to rue St-Antoine.

The Jewish quarter

The area around **rue des Rosiers** is traditionally the Jewish quarter of the city, and remains so, despite incursions by trendy clothes shops. If you sense a certain suspicion of outsiders in this area, the reason is the bomb attacks in recent years on synagogues here and on *Goldenburg's* deli/restaurant. People have died in these assaults, and FN spray cans periodically eject their obscenities on walls and shop-fronts.

Wandering northwards through the 3ᵉ *arrondissement* you're likely to end up at the grimly barren **place de la République**, one of the largest roundabouts in Paris. Dominated on the north side by army barracks, and joining seven major streets all penetrating through the then-surrounding areas of rebellious dissent, this is the most blatant example of Napoléon III's political town planning. In order to build it Haussmann destroyed a number of popular theatres, including the *Funambules* of *Les Enfants du Paradis* fame, and Daguerre's unique diorama.

South: the Pavillon de l'Arsenal

In the southern section of the Marais, **below rue St-Antoine**, the crooked steps and lanterns of rue Cloche-Perce, the tottering timbered houses of rue François-Miron, the medieval *Acceuil de France* buildings behind St-Gervais-et-Protais and the smell of flowers and incense on rue des Barres are all good indulgence in Paris picturesque. But shift eastwards to the next tangle of streets and you'll find the modern, chi-chi flats of the "Village St-Paul" and its expensive clusters of antique shops.

Further east again, at 21 bd Morland, the **Pavillon de l'Arsenal** (Tues–Sat 10.30am–6.30pm, Sun 11am–7pm; free), signalled by a sculpture of Rimbaud, entitled "The man with his souls in front", is an excellent addition to the city's art of self-promotion, its aim to present the city's current architectural projects to the public and show how past and present developments have evolved as part and parcel of Parisian history. To this end they have a permanent exhibition of photographs, plans and models, including a model of the whole city with a laser spotlight to highlight a touch-screen choice of 30,000 images.

The Île St-Louis

Unlike its larger neighbour, the **Île St-Louis** has no monuments or museums, just high houses on single-lane streets, a school, church, restaurants and cafés, and the best sorbets in the world chez *M. Berthillon*. It's also where the likes of the Aga Khan and the Pretender to the throne of France have their Parisian residences. You can find seclusion on the **southern quais**, tightly clutching a triple-sorbet cornet as you descend the various steps or climb over the low gate on the right of the garden across bd Henri-IV to reach the best sunbathing spot in Paris.

Île de la Cité

The **Île de la Cité** is where Paris began. The earliest settlements were sited here, as was the small Gallic town of Lutetia, overrun by Julius Caesar's troops in 52 BC. A natural defensive site commanding a major east–west river trade route, it was an obvious candidate for a bright future. The Romans garrisoned it and laid out one of their standard military town plans, overlapping onto the Left Bank. While it never achieved any great political importance, they endowed it with an administrative centre which became the palace of the Merovingian kings in 508, then of the counts of Paris, who in 987 became kings of France.

Today the lure of the island lies in its tail-end **square du Vert-Galant** and, at the opposite end, the **cathedral of Notre-Dame**. The central section has been dulled by heavy-handed nineteenth-century demolition that displaced 25,000 people and replaced them by four vast edifices largely given over to housing the law. The litter-blown space in front of the cathedral was a by-product, though that at least has the virtue of allowing a full-frontal view.

Pont-Neuf and the quais, Sainte-Chapelle and the Conciergerie

Arriving on the island by the **Pont Neuf**, the city's oldest bridge, steps behind the statue of **Henri IV** (who commissioned the bridge) lead down to the **quais** and the **square du Vert-Galant**, a small tree-lined green enclosed within the triangular stern of the island. The prime spot to occupy is the extreme point beneath a weeping willow – haunt of lovers, sparrows and sunbathers.

On the other side of the bridge, across the street from the king, seventeenth-century houses flank the entrance to the sanded, chestnut-shaded **place Dauphine**, one of the city's most secluded and exclusive squares. The further end is blocked by the dull mass of the **Palais de Justice**, which swallowed up the palace that was home to the French kings until Étienne Marcel's bloody revolt in 1358 frightened them off to the greater security of the Louvre.

The only part of the older complex that remains in its entirety is Louis IX's **Sainte-Chapelle** (entrance from bd du Palais), built to house a collection of holy relics he had bought at extortionate rates from the bankrupt empire of Byzantium. Though much restored, the chapel remains one of the finest achievements of French High Gothic (consecrated in 1248). Very tall in relation to its length, it looks like a cathedral choir lopped off and transformed into an independent building. Its most radical feature is its fragility: the reduction of structural masonry to a minimum to make way for a huge expanse of stunning **stained glass**. The impression inside is of being enclosed within the wings of myriad butterflies – the predominant colours blue and red, and, in the later rose window, grass-green and blue.

It pays to get to Sainte-Chapelle as early as possible (April–Sept 9.30am–6pm, Oct– March 10am–4.30pm; 25F, half price Sun & hols). It attracts hordes of tourists, as does the **Conciergerie** (April–Sept 9.30am–6.30pm; Oct–March 10am–5pm; 25F), Paris's oldest prison, where Marie-Antoinette and, in their turn, the leading figures of the Revolution were incarcerated before execution. The chief interest of the Conciergerie is the enormous late Gothic *Salle des Gens d'Arme*, canteen and recreation room of the royal household staff. You are missing little in not seeing Marie-Antoinette's cell and various other macabre mementoes of the guillotine's victims.

If you keep along the north side of the island from the Conciergerie you come to **place Lépine**, named for the police boss who gave Paris's coppers their white truncheons and whistles. There is an exuberant **flower market** here six days a week, with **birds and pets** – cruelly caged – on Sunday. The police headquarters is right behind.

Notre-Dame

The **Cathédrale de Notre-Dame** (8am–7pm) is so much photographed that even seeing it for the first time the edge of your response is somewhat dulled by familiarity. Yet it is truly impressive, the great west front, with its strong vertical divisions counterbalanced by the horizontal emphasis of gallery and frieze, all centred by the rose window. It demands to be seen as a whole, though that can scarcely have been possible when the medieval houses clustered close about it. It is a solid, no-nonsense design, confessing its Romanesque ancestry. For more fantastical Gothic, look rather at the **north transept facade** with its crocketed gables and huge fretted window-space.

Notre-Dame was begun in 1160 under the auspices of Bishop de Sully and completed around 1245. In the nineteenth century, Viollet-le-Duc carried out extensive renovation work, including remaking most of the statuary – the entire frieze of Old Testament kings, for instance – and adding the steeple and baleful-looking gargoyles, which you can see close-up if you brave the ascent of the towers (April–Sept 10am–5.30pm; Oct–March 10am–4.30pm; 30F). Ravaged by weather and pollution, its beauty will be at least partially masked once again for the next few years, as the scaffolding goes up for further restoration work.

Inside, the immediately striking feature, if you can ignore the noise and movement, is the dramatic contrast between the darkness of the nave and the light falling on the first great clustered pillars of the choir, emphasising the special nature of the sanctuary. It is the end walls of the transepts which admit all this light, nearly two-thirds glass, including two magnificent **rose windows** coloured in imperial purple. These, the vaulting, the soaring shafts reaching to the springs of the vaults, are all definite Gothic elements, yet, inside as out, there remains a strong sense of Romanesque in the stout round pillars of the nave and the general sense of foursquareness.

Before you leave, walk round to the public garden at the east end for a view of the **flying buttresses** supporting the choir, and then along the riverside under the south transept, where you can sit in springtime with the cherry blossom drifting down. Out in front of the cathedral, in the plaza separating it from Haussmann's police HQ, is the unappetising entrance to the **crypte archéologique** (10am–6pm), in which are revealed the remains of the original cathedral, as well as streets and houses of the Cité as far back as the Roman era.

Le Mémorial de la Déportation

At the east tip of the island is the symbolic tomb of the 200,000 French who died in Nazi concentration camps during World War II – Resistance fighters, Jews, forced labourers. The **Mémorial de la Déportation** is scarcely visible above ground; stairs hardly shoulder-wide descend into a space like a prison yard. Within the crypt thousands of points of light represent the dead. Floor and ceiling are black and it ends in a black raw hole, with a single naked bulb hanging in the middle. Either side are empty barred cells. Above the exit are the words "Forgive. Do not forget."

Trocadéro, Eiffel Tower and Les Invalides

The vistas are splendid from the terrace of the **Palais de Chaillot** on place du Trocadéro, across the river to the Tour Eiffel and École Militaire, from the ornate 1900 Pont Alexandre III along the grassy Esplanade to the Hôtel des Invalides. But the scale and the style is despotic. The Palais de Chaillot, like a latterday Pharaoh's mausoleum (1937), is, however, home to several interesting museums (see below) and a theatre used for diverse but usually radical productions.

The Eiffel Tower

Across the river – take the Passerelle Debilly footbridge opposite the Palais de Tokyo – stands the **Tour Eiffel**. When completed in 1889, the tower was the tallest building in the world at 300m. Its 7000 tons of steel, in terms of pressure, sit as lightly on the ground as a child in a chair. Reactions to it were violent. Outraged critics protested "in the name of menaced French art and history" against this "useless and montrous" tower. "Is Paris", they asked, "going to be associated with the grotesque, mercantile imaginings of a constructor of machines?" But it stole the show at the 1889 Exposition, for which it had been constructed. In 1986 the tower was given a new system of illumination from within its superstructure, so that it now looks at its magical best after dark, as light and fanciful as a filigree minaret.

Going to the top (10am–11pm for stages 1 and 2; 10am–10pm for stage 3) costs 49F (17F and 32F respectively for the first two stages) – so it's only really worth the expense on an absolutely clear day.

Around the École Militaire

Stretching back from the legs of the tower, the long rectangular gardens of the **Champs de Mars** lead to the eighteenth-century buildings of the **École Militaire**, now the Staff College, originally founded in 1751 by Louis XV for the training of aristocratic army officers. The surrounding *quartier* is expensive and sought after as an address, but uninteresting to look at, like the **UNESCO building** at the back of the École Militaire. Controversial at the time of its construction in 1958, it looks somewhat pedestrian, and badly weathered, today. It can be visited; there are a number of art works, the most noticeable being an enormous mobile by Alexander Calder, and a quiet Japanese garden. One unexpected corner of this rather austere *quartier*, is the wedge of **early nineteenth-century streets between av Bosquet and the Invalides**. Chief among them is the market street, **rue Cler**, with its cross streets, rue de Grenelle and rue St-Dominique, full of classy little shops, some with their original painted glass panels.

Out on the river bank at quai d'Orsay is the **American Church**, which, together with the American College in nearby av Bosquet (no. 31), is a nodal point in the well-organised life of the large American community. The notice board is usually plastered with job offers and demands. The other quayside attraction is the **sewers**, *les égouts* (entrance at the corner of Pont de l'Alma and Quai d'Orsay; Mon, Wed & the last Sat of each month, 2–5pm). Guidebooks always bill this as an outing for kids, though this is doubtful. The visit consists of an unilluminating film, a small museum and a very brief look at some tunnels with a lot of smelly water swirling about.

Les Invalides

The **Esplanade des Invalides**, striking due south from **Pont Alexandre III**, is a more attractive and uncluttered vista than Chaillot-École Militaire. The wide facade of the **Hôtel des Invalides**, topped by its distinctive dome, resplendent with new gilding to celebrate the bicentenary of the Revolution, fills the whole of the further end of the Esplanade. It was built as a home for invalided soldiers on the orders of Louis XIV. Under the dome are two churches, one for the soldiers, the other intended as a mausoleum for the king but now containing the mortal remains of Napoléon. The Hôtel houses the vast **Musée de l'Armée** (see below).

Both churches are cold and dreary inside. The **Église du Dôme**, in particular, is a supreme example of architectural pomposity, with Corinthian columns and pilasters, and grandiose frescoes in abundance. Napoléon himself lies in a hole in the floor in a cold smooth sarcophagus of red porphyry, enclosed within a gallery decorated with friezes of execrable taste and grovelling piety, captioned with quotations of awesome conceit from the great man: "Cooperate with the plans I have laid for the welfare of peoples"; "By its simplicity my code of law has done more good in France than all the laws which have preceded me"; "Wherever the shadow of my rule has fallen, it has left lasting traces of its value."

Immediately east of the Invalides is the **Musée Rodin**, on the corner of rue de Varenne, housed in a beautiful eighteenth-century mansion which the sculptor leased from the state in return for the gift of all his work at his death (see below). The rest of the street, and the parallel rue de Grenelle, are full of aristocratic mansions, including the **Hôtel Matignon**, the prime minister's residence. At the further end, the **rue du Bac** leads right into rue de Sèvres, cutting across **rue de Babylone**, another of the *quartier*'s livelier streets, with the crazy, rich man's folly, **La Pagode**, now a cinema, down on the left beyond the barracks.

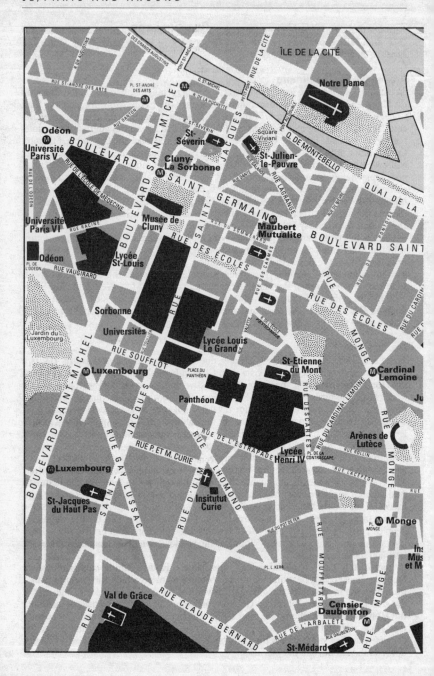

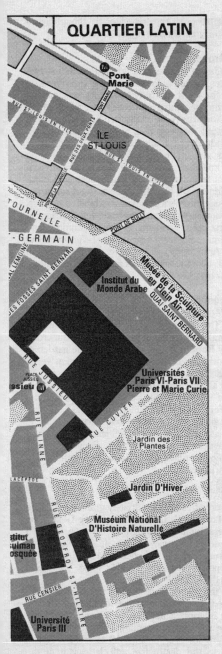

Quartier Latin

The pivotal point of the **Quartier Latin** on the Left Bank of the river is **place St-Michel**, where the treelined **boulevard St-Michel** begins. It has lost its radical penniless chic now, preferring harder commercial values. The cafés and shops are jammed with people, mainly young and, in summer, largely foreign.

Rue de la Huchette, the Mecca of beats and bums in the post-World War II years, with its theatre still showing Ionesco's *Cantatrice Chauve* nearly forty years on, is now given over to indifferent Greek restaurants, as is the adjoining rue Xavier-Privas, with the odd *couscous* joint thrown in. Connecting it to the riverside is the city's narrowest street, the **Chat-qui-Pêche**, alarmingly evocative of what Paris at its medieval worst must have looked like.

Rue St-Jacques

Things improve as you move away from the boulevard. At the end of rue de la Huchette, **rue St-Jacques** is aligned on the main street of Roman Paris, and was in medieval times the road up which millions of pilgrims trudged at the start of their long march to St-Jacques-de-Compostelle in Spain. Just to the right, one block up from rue de la Huchette, the mainly fifteenth-century church of **St-Séverin** (Mon–Thurs 11am–7.30pm, Fri & Sat 9am–10.30pm, Sun 9am–8pm) is one of the city's most elegant with splendidly virtuoso chiselwork in the pillars of the Flamboyant choir, as well as stained glass by the modern French painter Jean Bazaine.

Back towards the river, **square Viviani** with its welcome patch of grass and trees provides the most flattering of all views of Notre-Dame. The mutilated and disfigured church is **St-Julien-le-Pauvre**. The same age as Notre-Dame, it used to be the venue for university assemblies until rumbustious students tore it apart in the 1500s. Round to the left on rue de la Bûcherie, the English bookshop **Shakespeare and Co** is haunted by the shades of James Joyce and other great expatriate literati – though Sylvia Beach, publisher of Joyce's *Ulysses*, had her original shop on rue de l'Odéon.

The river bank and Institut du Monde Arabe

Books, postcards, prints, and assorted goods are on sale from the **bouquinistes**, who display their wares in green padlocked boxes hooked onto the parapet of the **riverside quais**. Continuing upstream, you come to the **Pont de Sully** with a dramatic view of the apse and steeple of Notre-Dame and the beginning of a riverside garden dotted with pieces of modern sculpture, known as the **Musée de Sculpture en Plein Air**.

At the end of the Pont de Sully, in the angle between quai St-Bernard and rue des Fossés-St-Bernard, is the **Institut du Monde Arabe** (daily except Mon 1–8pm; 40F), designed by Jean Nouvel – an elegant glass and aluminium mass, cleft in two, with the riverfront half bowed and tapering to a knife-like prow, while the broad southern facade, comprising thousands of tiny light-sensitive shutters which open and close according to the brightness of the day, mimics with hi-tech ingenuity the *moucharaby* or traditional Arab lattice-work balcony. Inside, there's a permanent exhibition of glass, rugs, ceramics, illuminated manuscripts, wood carving, metalwork and scientific instruments from the Islamic world. On the first floor, contemporary Arab paintings and sculptures are exhibited, while in the basement *Espace Image et Son* (1–7pm) you can watch TV programmes from around the Arab world, and consult a large library of audiovisual material. When you need a rest, take the fastest lifts in Paris up to the café on the ninth floor, which has a brilliant view over the Seine.

Montagne Ste-Geneviève and the Sorbonne

The nearby area around the slopes of the **Montagne Ste-Geneviève**, the hill on which the Panthéon stands, is good for a stroll. The best approach is from **place Maubert** (good **market** Tues, Thurs and Sat morning) or from the St-Michel/St-Germain crossroads, where the walls of the third-century **Roman baths** are visible in the garden of the **Hôtel de Cluny**, a sixteenth-century mansion built by the abbots of the powerful Cluny monastery as their Paris pied-à-terre. It now houses a very beautiful museum of medieval art (see below); entry to the quiet shady courtyard is free.

The grim-looking buildings on the other side of rue des Écoles are the **Sorbonne**, **Collège de France**, and **Lycée Louis-le-Grand**, which numbers Molière, Robespierre, Pompidou and Victor Hugo among its graduates and Sartre among its teachers. All these institutions are major constituents of the brilliant and mandarin world of French intellectual activity. You can put your nose in the Sorbonne courtyard without anyone objecting. Nearby, the traffic-free **place de la Sorbonne**, with its lime trees, cafés and student habitues, is a lovely place to sit.

The Panthéon and St-Étienne-du-Mont

Further up the hill, the broad rue Soufflot provides an appropriately grand perspective on the domed and porticoed **Panthéon**, Louis XIV's thank you to Sainte Geneviève, patron saint of Paris, for curing him of illness. Imposing enough at a distance, it is cold and uninteresting close to – not a friendly detail for the eye to rest on. The Revolution transformed it into a mausoleum for the great, and it is truly deadly inside (April–Sept 10am–6pm; Oct–March 10am–noon & 2–5pm; closed Tues & public hols). There are, however, several good cafés down towards the Luxembourg gardens.

More interesting than the Panthéon is the mainly sixteenth-century church of **St-Étienne-du-Mont** on the corner of rue Clovis, with a facade combining Gothic, Renaissance and Baroque elements. The interior, if not exactly beautiful, is highly unexpected. The space is divided into three aisles by free-standing pillars connected by a narrow catwalk, and flooded with light by an exceptionally tall clerestory. Again, unusually – for they mainly fell victim to the destructive anti-clericalism of the

Revolution – the church still possesses its rood screen, a broad low arch supporting a gallery reached by twining spiral stairs. There is some good seventeenth-century glass in the cloister. Further down rue Clovis, a huge piece of Philippe Auguste's twelfth-century city walls emerges from among the houses.

Just a step **south from the place du Panthéon**, in the quiet rue des Fossés-St-Jacques, the kerbside tables of the *Café de la Nouvelle Mairie* wine bar make an excellent lunch stop, while at the end of the street on rue St-Jacques there are several cheap restaurants, mainly Chinese. There is not much point in going further south on rue St-Jacques: the area is dull and lifeless once you are over the Gay-Lussac intersection, though Baroque enthusiasts might like to take a look at the seventeenth-century church of **Val-de-Grâce**, with its pedimented front and ornate cupola copied from St Peter's in Rome, while round the corner on **bd de Port-Royal** is another big market and several brasseries.

East of the Panthéon

More enticing wandering is to be had in the villagey streets east of the Panthéon. **Rue de la Montagne-Ste-Geneviève** climbs up from place Maubert across rue des Écoles to the gates of the Ministry of Research and Technology. There's a sunny little café outside and several restaurants in rue de l'École-Polytechnique. Rue Descartes runs into the tiny and attractive **place de la Contrescarpe**. Once an arty hangout, where Hemingway wrote – in the café *La Chope* – and Georges Brassens sang, it is now a dossers' rendezvous.

The medieval **rue Mouffetard** begins here, a cobbled lane winding downhill to the church of **St-Médard**, once a country parish beside the now-covered river Bièvre. Most of the upper half of the street is given over to eating places, mainly Greek and little better than those of rue de la Huchette. Like any place wholly devoted to the entertainment of tourists, it has lost its soul. The bottom half, however, with its sumptuous fruit and veg stalls, still maintains an authentic neighbourhood air.

The Paris Mosque and Jardin des Plantes

A little **further east**, across rue Monge, are some of the city's most agreeable surprises. Down rue Daubenton, past a delightful Arab shop selling sweets, spices and gaudy tea-glasses, you come to the crenellated walls of the Paris **mosque**, topped by greenery and a great square minaret. You can walk in the sunken garden and patios with their polychrome tiles and carved ceilings, but not the prayer room (9am–noon & 2–6pm; closed Fri & Muslim hols). There is a **tearoom** too, open to all, and a **hammam** (see p.113).

Opposite the mosque is an entrance to the **Jardin des Plantes** (summer 7.30am–7.45pm; winter 7.30am–5.45pm), with a small, cramped, expensive **zoo** (Mon–Sat summer 9am–6pm, winter 9am–5pm, Sun 9am–6.30pm all year), botanical gardens, hothouses and museums of palaeontology and mineralogy. It's a pleasant space to while away the middle of a day. By the rue Cuvier exit is a fine Cedar of Lebanon planted in 1734, raised from seed sent over from Oxford Botanical Gardens, and a slice of an American sequoia more than 2000 years old. In the nearby physics labs Henri Becquerel discovered radioactivity in 1896, and two years later the Curies discovered radium (Pierre ended his days under the wheels of a brewer's dray on rue Dauphine). The huge edifice by the mosque entrance, in which one of the largest collections of stuffed, dried, pickled and pressed animals have been hidden for years, is being renovated to open as a super-modern gallery of evolution in 1993.

A short distance away, with an entrance in rue de Navarre and another through a passage on rue Monge, is Paris's other Roman remain, the **Arènes de Lutèce**, an unexpected backwater hidden from the street. It is a partly restored amphitheatre, with a *boules* pitch in the centre, benches, gardens and a kids' playground behind.

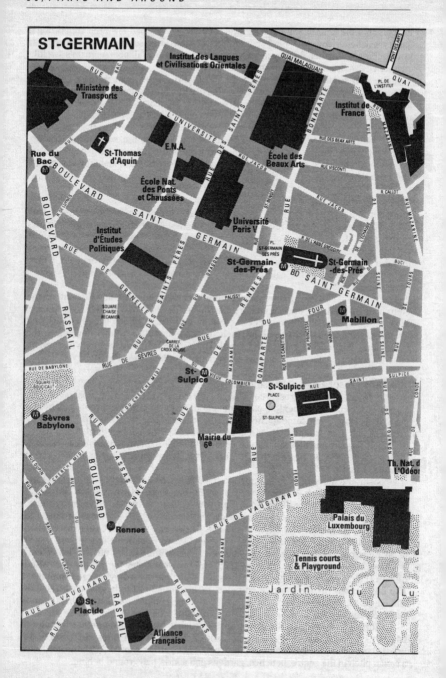

ST-GERMAIN

Institut des Langues
et Civilisations Orientales

QUAI MALAQUAIS

QUAI

PL DE
L'INSTITUT

Ministère des
Transports

RUE DE BAC

DE L'UNIVERSITÉ

RUE DES SAINTS PÈRES

BONAPARTE

Institut de
France

RUE MAZARINE

Rue du
Bac

M

BOULEVARD

St-Thomas
d'Aquin

E.N.A.

RUE DES BEAUX ARTS

RUE JACOB

École des
Beaux Arts

RUE VISCONTI

R. CALLOT

SAINT

École Nat.
des Ponts
et Chaussées

RUE BENOIT

RUE

RUE JACOB

DE

BOULEVARD

RUE

Université
Paris V

R. DE L'ABBÉ GREGOIRE

DE MAZARINE

GERMAIN

PL.
ST-GERMAIN
DES PRÉS

Institut
d'Études
Politiques

RASPAIL

DE GRENELLE DES SAINTS PÈRES

St-Germain-
des-Prés

M

St-Germain
-des-Prés

BD SAINT GERMAIN

BUCI

RUE DE SEINE

RUE DE TOURS

SQUARE
CHAISE
RECAMIER

RUE

RUE DES SAINTS PÈRES

R. DU B PALISSY

DRAGON

RENNES

DU

FOUR

Mabillon

M

RUE PRINCESSE

MABILLON

RUE GUÉNÉGAUD

CARREF
DE LA
CROIX ROUGE

RUE

DE SÈVRES

RUE DES CANETTES

RUE DE BABYLONE

RUE DE SÈVRES

DU VIEUX COLOMBIER

MADAME

BONAPARTE

St-
Sulpice

M

SQUARE
BOUCICAUT

Sèvres
Babylone

M

RUE DU CHERCHE MIDI

RUE D'ASSAS

RUE

St-Sulpice

PLACE

ST-SULPICE

SAINT

SULPICE

RUE DE CONDÉ

RUE DE TOURNON

Mairie du
6e

RUE

Th. Nat. de
L'Odéon

BOULEVARD

RENNES

DU

RUE DE VAUGIRARD

RUE FÉROU

Palais du
Luxembourg

Rennes

M

RUE D'ASSAS

MADAME

RUE GUYNEMER

Tennis courts
& Playground

RUE DE VAUGIRARD

St-
Placide

M

RASPAIL

RUE D'ASSAS

RUE

Jardin

du

Lu

Alliance
Française

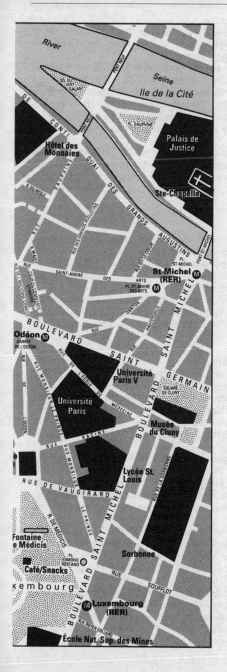

St-Germain

The northern half of the 6ᵉ *arrondisse-ment*, unsymmetrically centred on **place St-Germain-des-Prés**, is the most phys-ically attractive, lively and stimulating square kilometre in the entire city. The most dramatic approach is to cross the river from the Louvre by the **Pont des Arts**, with the classic upstream view of the Île de la Cité, with barges moored at the quai de Conti, and the Tour St-Jacques and Hôtel de Ville breaking the skyline of the Right Bank. The dome and pediment at the end of the bridge belong to the **Institut de France**, seat of the Académie Française, an august body of writers and scholars whose mission is to safeguard the purity of the French language. This is the grandiose bit of the Left Bank riverfront. To the left is the **Hôtel des Monnaies**, redesigned as the Mint in the late eighteenth century. To the right is the **Beaux-Arts**, the school of Fine Art, whose students throng the *quais* on sunny days, sketchpads on knee. Further down is the ornate erst-while railway station now transformed into the **Musée d'Orsay**.

The riverside

The **riverside part of the quarter** is cut lengthwise by **rue St-André-des-Arts** and **rue Jacob**. It is full of bookshops, commercial art galleries, antique shops, cafés and restaurants. Poke your nose into courtyards and sidestreets. The houses are four to six storeys high, seventeenth- and eighteenth-century, some noble, some stiff, some bulging and skew, all painted in infinite gradations of grey, pearl and off-white. Broadly speak-ing, the further west the posher.

Historical associations are legion. Picasso painted *Guernica* in rue des Grands-Augustins. Molière started his career in rue Mazarine. Robespierre and co split ideological hairs at the *Café Procope*, now an expensive restaurant, in rue de l'Ancienne-Comédie. In rue Visconti, Racine died, Delacroix painted and Balzac's printing business went bust. In the parallel rue des Beaux-Arts, Oscar Wilde died, Corot and Ampère, father of amps, lived, and the crazy poet Gérard de Nerval went walking with a lobster on a lead.

If you're looking for lunch, **place** and **rue St-André-des-Arts** offer a tempting concentration of places, from Tunisian sandwich joints to seafood extravagance, and a brilliant food market in rue Buci up towards bd St-Germain. Before you get to Buci, there is an intriguing little passage on the left, **Cour du Commerce,**where Marat had a printing press and Dr Guillotin perfected his notorious machine by lopping off sheep's heads in the loft next door. A couple of smaller courtyards open off it, revealing another stretch of Philippe Auguste's wall.

An alternative corner for midday food or quiet is around rue de l'Abbaye and place Furstemberg, a tiny square where **Delacroix's old studio** overlooking a secret garden has been converted into a museum (at no. 6). This is also the beginning of some very upmarket **shopping territory**, in **rue Jacob**, **rue de Seine** and **rue Bonaparte** in particular.

Place St-Germain-des-Prés

Place St-Germain-des-Prés, the hub of the *quartier*, is only a stone's throw away, with the *Deux Magots* café on the corner and *Flore* just down the street – both renowned for the number of philosophico-politico-poetico-literary backsides that have shined their seats, although nowadays you're more likely to be dragged into some street-clown's act than engaged in high-flown debate.

The tower opposite the *Deux Magots* belongs to the **church of St-Germain**, all that remains of an enormous Benedictine monastery. The interior is its best aspect, with its pure Romanesque lines still clear under the deforming paint of nineteenth-century frescoes.

St-Sulpice and the Jardin du Luxembourg

South of bd St-Germain the streets round St-Sulpice are calm and classy. **Rue Mabillon** is pretty, with a row of old houses set back below the level of the modern street. On the left are the **halles St-Germain**, on the site of a fifteenth-century market. Rue St-Sulpice, with excellent shops for edibles, leads through to the front of the enormous **church of St-Sulpice**, an austerely classical church, erected either side of 1700, with a Doric colonnade surmounted by an Ionic, and Corinthian pilasters in the towers, only one of which is finished.

But the main attraction of **place St-Sulpice** is *Yves Saint Laurent Rive Gauche*, the most elegant fashion boutique on the Left Bank. The least posh bit of the *quartier* is the eastern edge, where the university is firmly implanted, along bd St-Michel, with attendant scientific and medical bookshops, skeletons and instruments of torture as well as a couple of weird and wonderful shops in rue Racine. But there is really no escape from elegance round here.

To the south, rue Férou, where a gentleman called Pottier composed the *Internationale* in 1776, connects with **rue de Vaugirard**, Paris's longest street, and the **Jardin du Luxembourg**, constructed for Marie de Médicis, Henri IV's widow, to remind her of the Palazzo Pitti and Giardino di Boboli of her native Florence. Today it is the seat of the French Senate. The gardens are the chief recreation ground of the Left Bank, with tennis courts, pony rides, children's playground, *boules* pitch, yachts to hire on the pond, and, in the wilder southeast corner, a miniature orchard of elaborately espaliered pear trees. With its strollers and mooners and garish parterres, it has a distinctly Mediterranean air on summer days, when the most contested spot is the shady **Fontaine de Médicis** in the northeast corner. The Luxembourg palace is the seat of the French Senate.

Montparnasse

Like other Left Bank *quartiers* **Montparnasse** still trades on its association with the wild characters of the interwar artistic and literary boom. Many were habitues of the cafés *Select, Coupole, Dôme, Rotonde* and *Closerie des Lilas*, all still going strong on **bd du Montparnasse**. Another major sub-community in the *quartier* in the early years of the century consisted of outlawed Russian revolutionaries. They were so many that the Tsarist police ran a special Paris section to keep tabs on them. **Lenin and Trotsky** both lodged in the area; Trotsky lived in **rue de la Gaîté** near the cemetery, now a seedy street of sex shops and cinemas.

Most of the life of the quarter is concentrated round the station end of bd du Montparnasse, where the colossal **Tour du Montparnasse** has become one of the city's principal landmarks. You can go up on a tour for less than the Eiffel Tower (summer 9.30am–11pm; winter 10am–10pm; 35F), though it makes more sense to spend the money on a drink at the **top-floor bar**. The tower is much reviled as a building because it is totally out of scale with its surroundings. It has bred a rash of workers' barracks in the area behind it and, in front, and beneath it there's an enormous shopping complex. Better to shop on **rue de Rennes** or bd du Montparnasse, at whose animated end at **bd Raspail** Rodin's *Balzac* broods over the traffic.

From Montparnasse cemetery to the Cité Universitaire

Boulevard du Montparnasse marks the boundary between the **6e and 14e arrondissements** and is still a class divide. On the north side the streets are sedate and well heeled, to the south they are working-class and increasingly prey to the developers, especially between av du Maine and the rail tracks, which in years gone by sucked thousands of emigre Bretons into the city.

The change is clear as you soon come to the market in **bd Edgar-Quinet**, where the cafés are full of stall-holders. Just off to one side is the main entrance to the **Montparnasse cemetery**, a gloomy city of the dead, with ranks of miniature temples, dreary and bizarre, and plenty of illustrious names for spotters, from Baudelaire to Sartre and André Citroën to Saint-Saens. In the southwest corner is an old windmill, one of the seventeenth-century taverns frequented by the carousing, versifying students who gave the district its name of Parnassus.

If you are determined to spend your time among the dear departed, you can also get down into the **catacombs** (Tues–Fri 2–4pm, Sat & Sun 9–11am & 2–4pm) in nearby **place Denfert-Rochereau**, formerly place d'Enfer – Hell Square. These are abandoned quarries stacked with millions of bones cleared from the old charnel houses in 1785, claustrophobic in the extreme, and cold.

The Observatoire and Parc Montsouris

Av Denfert-Rochereau and bd Arago lead to the **Observatoire de Paris** where there's a garden open on summer afternoons in which to sit and admire the dome. From the 1660s, when it was constructed, until 1884, all French maps had the zero meridian through the middle of this building. After that date, they reluctantly agreed that 0° longitude should pass through a small village in Normandy that happens to be due south of Greenwich.

If you head south you'll pass Ste-Anne's psychiatric hospital where the great political philosopher, Louis Althusser, died after being committed for murdering his wife. One block further on is **Parc Montsouris**, a tempting place to collapse but you'll be up against more of the city's obsessionally whistling park police the moment you touch the grass. A beautiful reproduction of the Bardo palace in Tunis, built for the 1876 *Exposition Universelle*, is finally being restored. Lenin took strolls here in 1909 when he was living with mum, Krupskaya, and his sisters at **4 rue Marie-Rose** (now a small museum). Later walkers in the park no doubt included Dali, Lurcat, Miller, Durrell and other artists who found homes in the tiny cobbled street of **Villa Seurat** off rue de la Tombe.

The Cité Universitaire

On the other side of bd Jourdan, several thousand students from over 100 different countries live in the curious array of buildings known as the **Cité Universitaire**, a collection of *Maisons* which represent the unobvious selection of nations or peoples willing to subsidise foreign study. Armenia, Cuba, Indo-China and Monaco are neighbours at one end; Kampuchea has been boarded up for years; Switzerland (designed by Le Corbusier in his stilts phase) and the US are the most sought-after for their relatively luxurious rooms; an extradition debate closed Spain; and the Collège Franco-Britannique is a red brick monster. The atmosphere is far from internationalist, but there are films, shows and other events - check the *Maison Internationale*, which is the one resembling Captain Haddock's Marlinspike.

Porte de Vanves and the Parc Georges Brassens

To the south of bd Brune, near Porte de Vanves, one of the city's best **junk markets** takes place on Saturday and Sunday, along av Marc-Sangnier and av Georges-Lafenestre. Book lovers can take a short stroll along bd Lefebvre and down rue Brancion to the old Vaugiraud abbattoir, transformed in the 1980s into the **Parc Georges-Brassens**, where there's an **antiquarian book market** every Saturday and Sunday morning. The park itself is a delight, with ponds and a stream, scented gardens, rocks to climb, and a tiny vineyard. The main entrance, flanked by two bronze bulls, is on rue des Morillons. Just the other side of the park, in **passage Dantzig** off rue Dantzig, stands a curious polygonal building known as **La Rûche** (the beehive), where Modigliani, Léger, and Chagall among others had their studios. It was designed by Eiffel as the wine pavilion for the 1900 trade fair.

The 15ᵉ

The 15ᵉ **arrondissement** lies between the Montparnasse rail tracks and the river. It's big and unfashionable, home of the city's least visible inhabitants. It was in the **rue du Commerce** here that George Orwell worked as a dish-washer, described in his *Down and Out in Paris and London*, these days a lively, old-fashioned high street full of small shops and peeling, shuttered houses. Towards the end of the street, **place du Commerce**, with a Belle Epoque butcher's on the corner and a bandstand in the middle, is a model of old-fashioned petty-bourgeois respectability. It might be a frozen frame from a 1930s movie. The western edge of the *arrondissement* fronts the Seine from the **Porte de Javel** to the Eiffel Tower. Most of the riverbank is marred by a sort of mini-Défense development of half-cocked futuristic towers with pretensious galactic names, rising out of a litter-blown pedestrian platform some ten metres above street level. Far pleasanter riverside strolling is to be had on the narrow midstream island, the **Allée des Cygnes** which you can reach from the Pont de Grenelle. A scaled-down version of the **Statue of Liberty** stands at the downstream end.

The Beaux Quartiers and Bois de Boulogne

The **Beaux Quartiers** are the 16ᵉ and 17ᵉ *arrondissements*. The 16ᵉ is aristocratic and rich; the 17ᵉ, or at least the southern part of it, bourgeois and rich, embodying the cautious values of the nineteenth-century manufacturing and trading classes. The northern half of the 16ᵉ, towards place Victor-Hugo and place de l'Étoile, is leafy and distinctly metropolitan in feel. The southern part, around the old villages of **Auteuil** and **Passy**, has an almost provincial feel, and is full of pleasant surprises for the walker. There are several interesting pieces of **twentieth-century architecture** scattered through the district, especially by Hector Guimard (the designer of the swirly green Art Nouveau métro stations) and by Le Corbusier and Mallet-Stevens, architects of the first "cubist" buildings. Also in the area is the wonderful **Musée Marmottan** (see below).

Auteuil

A good place to start an architectural exploration is the **Église-d'Auteuil** métro station with several **Guimard** buildings in the vicinity for aficionados: 34 rue Boileau, 8 av de la Villa-de-la-Réunion, 41 rue Chardon-Lagache, 192 av de Versailles and 39 bd Exelmans. From the métro exit, **rue d'Auteuil**, with a lingering village high-street air, leads to **place Lorrain** with a Saturday market. There are more Guimard houses at the further end of rue La Fontaine, which begins here; no. 60 is perhaps the best in the city. On rue Poussin, just off the *place*, is the entrance to **Villa Montmorency**, a typical 16^e villa, a sort of private village of leafy lanes and English-style gardens. Gide and the Goncourt brothers of *Prix* fame lived in this one.

Behind it is rue Dr-Blanche where, in a cul-de-sac on the right, are **Le Corbusier's** first private houses (1923), one of them now the *Fondation Le Corbusier* (Mon-Fri 10am–1pm & 2–6pm; closed Aug). Built in strictly cubist style, very plain, with windows in bands, the only extravagance is the raising of one wing on piers and a curved frontage. They look commonplace enough now, but what a contrast to anything that had gone before. Further along rue Dr-Blanche, the tiny rue Mallet-Stevens was built entirely by **Mallet-Stevens** also in cubist style.

Passy

Passy, too, offers scope for a good meandering walk, from place du Trocadéro to Balzac's house and up rue de Passy to the spectacles museum (see below). To the south of Passy métro station, down the back of the ministry of *urbanism* and *logement*, is the cobbled **rue d'Ankara** with the gates of an eighteenth-century château half hidden by greenery and screened by a high wall. This is the Turkish embassy but it was once a clinic where the pioneering Dr Blanche tried to treat the mad Maupassant and Gérard de Nerval, amongst others. From its gates **rue Berton**, a cobbled path with gas lights still in place, follows round the ivy-covered garden wall to an old green-shuttered house with a boundary stone bearing the date 1731. Apart from the embassy security, there is nothing to say that it is not still 1731 in this tiny backwater. The house was **Balzac's** in the 1840s and now contains memorabilia and a library.

Just across the road, **rue de l'Annonciation**, gives more of the flavour of old Passy. You may not want your Bechstein repaired or your furniture lacquered, but as you approach the end of the street there'll be no holding back the salivary glands. At place de Passy you join the old high street, **rue de Passy**, and a parade of eye-catching brand-name boutiques stretching up to métro La Muette.

Bois de Boulogne

The Bois de Boulogne, running all down the west side of the 16e, is supposedly modelled on Hyde Park, though it is a very French interpretation. It offers all sorts of facilities: the **Jardin d'Acclimatation** with lots of attractions for kids (see below); the excellent **Musée National des Arts et Traditions Populaires** (also below); the **Parc de Bagatelle**, with beautiful displays of tulips, hyacinths and daffodils in the first half of April, irises in May, waterlilies and roses at the end of June; a riding school; **bike hire** at the entrance to the Jardin d'Acclimatation; **boating** on the Lac Inférieur; **race courses** at Longchamp and Auteuil. The best, and wildest, part for walking is towards the southwest corner. When it was opened to the public in the eighteenth century, people said of it, *"Les mariages du bois de Boulogne ne se font pas devant Monsieur le Curé"*– "Unions cemented in the Bois de Boulogne do not take place in the presence of a priest." Today's after-dark unions are no less disreputable .

Parc Monceau to Batignolles: the 17e

The 17e *arrondissement* is most interesting in its eastern half. The classier western end is cold and soulless, cut by too many wide and uniform boulevards. A route that takes in the best of it would be from **place des Ternes** with its cafés and flower market, through the stately wrought-iron gates of av Hoche into the small and formal **Parc Monceau**, surrounded by pompous residences. **Rue de Lévis** has one of the city's most strident, colourful and appetising markets every day of the week except Monday, and is also a good restaurant area, particularly up around rue des Dames, rue Cheroy and the bottom-line rue Dulong.

Across the tracks, **rue des Batignolles** is the heart of Batignolles "village", now sufficiently self-conscious to have formed an association for the preservation of its *"caractère villageois"*. At the north end of the street is a semi-circular *place* with cafés and restaurants framing a small colonnaded church that was modelled on the Madeleine. Behind it is the tired and trampled greenery of square Batignolles, with the marshalling yards beyond. The long **rue des Moines** leads northeast towards Guy-Moquet. This is the working-class Paris of the movies, all small, animated, friendly shops, four- to five-story houses in shades of peeling grey, brown-stained bars where men drink standing at the "zinc".

Montmartre cemetery

From Guy-Moquet it's a short walk back along av de St-Ouen to **rue du Capitaine-Madon**, a cobbled alley with washing strung at the windows, leading to the wall of the Montmartre cemetery, where hopefully you will still find the Hôtel Beau-Lieu. Ramshackle, peeling, on a tiny courtyard full of plants, this epitomises the kind-hearted, no-nonsense, sepia Paris that every romantic visitor secretly cherishes. Most of the guests have been there fifteen years or more. Tucked down below street level in the hollow of an old quarry, the **cemetery** itself (Mon-Fri 8am-5.30pm, Sat 8am-8.30pm, Sun 8am-9pm) has its entrance on av Rachel under rue Caulaincourt. A tangle of trees and funereal pomposity, it holds the graves of Zola, Stendhal, Berlioz, Degas, Feydeau, Offenbach, Dalida and François Truffaut among others.

Montmartre and the 9e

Montmartre lies in the middle of the largely petty-bourgeois and working-class 18e *arrondissement*, respectable round the slopes of the *Butte*, distinctly less so towards the **Gare du Nord** and **Gare de l'Est**, where depressing slums crowd along the railway tracks. On its northern edge lies the extensive St-Ouen flea market.The Butte itself has a relaxed, sunny, countrified air; Pigalle at the foot of the hill, is full of sex shops and peep shows interspersed with tired-looking women in shop doorways. It hardly lives up to its romantic, Bohemian screen image, but then it probably never did.

Place des Abbesses and up to the Butte

In spite of being one of the city's chief tourist attractions, the **Butte Montmartre** manages to retain the quiet, almost secretive, air of its rural origins. The **most popular access** route is via the rue de Steinkerque and the steps below the Sacré-Coeur (the funicular railway from place Suzanne-Valadon is covered by the *Carte Orange*). For **a quieter approach**, go up via place des Abbesses or rue Lepic.

Place des Abbesses is postcard-pretty, with one of the few complete surviving **Guimard métro entrances**. East, at the Chapelle des Auxiliatrices in rue Yvonne-Le-

Tac, Ignatius Loyola founded the **Jesuit** movement in 1534. It is also supposed to be the place where **Saint Denis**, the first bishop of Paris, had his head chopped off by the Romans around 250 AD, carrying it until he dropped, where the cathedral of St-Denis now stands, in a traditionally Communist suburb north of the city.

To continue from place des Abbesses to the top of the Butte, two quiet and attractive routes are up **rue de la Vieuville** and the stairs in rue Drevet to the minuscule **place du Calvaire** with a lovely view back over the city, or up **rue Tholozé**, then right below the **Moulin de la Galette** – the last survivor of Montmartre's forty odd windmills, immortalised by Renoir – into rue des Norvins.

Artistic associations abound hereabouts. Zola, Berlioz, Turgenev, Seurat, Degas and Van Gogh lived in the area. Picasso, Braque and Juan Gris invented Cubism in an old piano factory in place Emile-Goudeau, known as the **Bateau-Lavoir**, still serving as artists' studios, though the original building burnt down some years ago. And Toulouse Lautrec's inspiration, the **Moulin Rouge**, survives also, albeit a mere shadow of its former self, on the corner of bd de Clichy and place Blanche.

The **Musée de Montmartre** at 12 rue Cortot (Mon–Sat 2.30–5.30pm; Sun 11am–5.30pm; free), just over the brow of the hill tries to recapture something of the feel of those pioneering days, but the exhibits are a disappointment. The house itself, rented at various times by Renoir, Dufy, Suzanne Valadon, and her alcoholic son Utrillo, is worth visiting for the view over the neat terraces of the tiny **Montmartre vineyard** and the north side of the Butte. The entrance to the vineyard is on the steep rue de Saules.

Place du Tertre to Sacré-Coeur

The **place du Tertre** is the heart of tourist Montmartre, photogenic but totally bogus, jammed with tourists, overpriced restaurants and "artists" doing quick portraits while you wait. Between place du Tertre and the Sacré-Coeur, the old church of **St-Pierre** is all that remains of the Benedictine abbey which occupied the Butte Montmartre from the twelfth century on. Though much altered, it still retains its Romanesque and early Gothic feel. In it are four ancient columns, two by the door, two in the choir, leftovers from a Roman shrine that stood on the hill – *mons mercurii*, Mercury's Hill, the Romans called it. As for the **Sacré-Coeur** itself, graceless and vulgar pastiche though it is, its white pimply domes are an essential part of the Paris skyline. The best thing about it is the **view from the top** (summer 9am–7pm; winter 9am–6pm; 15F), almost as high as the Eiffel Tower, and showing the layout of the whole city. Construction was started in the 1870s on the initiative of the Catholic Church to atone for the "crimes" of the Commune. But **square Willette,** the space at the foot of the monumental staircase, is named after the local artist who turned out on inauguration day to shout, "Long live the devil!"

The Flea Market: les puces de St-Ouen

Officially open 7.30am to 7pm – unofficially, from 5am – the **puces de St-Ouen** claim to be the largest flea market in the world, the name "flea" deriving from the state of the secondhand mattresses, clothes and other junk sold here when the market first operated in the free-fire zone outside the city walls. Nowadays it is predominantly a proper – and very expensive – antique market (mainly furniture, but including old café bar counters, telephones, traffic lights, posters, juke boxes and petrol pumps), with what is left of the rag-and-bone element confined to the further reaches of **rue Fabre and rue Lécuyer**.

Pigalle

From place Clichy in the west to Barbès-Rochechouart in the east, the hill of Montmartre is underlined by the sleazy **boulevards of Clichy and Rochechouart,** the centre of the roadway often occupied by bumper-car pistes and other funfair side-shows. At the Barbès end, where the métro clatters by on iron trestles, the crowds teem round the *Tati* department stores, the city's cheapest, while the pavements are lined with West and North African street vendors offering watches and trinkets. At the place Clichy end, tour buses from all over Europe feed their contents into massive hotels. In the middle, between place Blanche and place Pigalle, sex shows, sex shops, tiny bars where hostesses lurk in complicated tackle, and street prostitutes, both male and female, coexist with one of the city's most elegant private *villas* on av Frochot, and, in the adjacent streets, the best **specialist music shops**.

The Goutte d'Or and the northern stations

Along the north side of bd de la Chapelle, between bd Barbès and the Gare du Nord rail lines, stretches the poetically named quarter of the **Goutte d'Or** – the Drop of Gold: a name that derives from the medieval vineyard that occupied this site. It has gradually become an immigrant ghetto since World War I, when large numbers of North Africans were first imported to replenish the ranks of Frenchmen dying in the trenches. In the late 1950s and early 1960s, during the Algerian war, its reputation struck terror in respectable middle-class hearts, as much for the clandestine political activity and settling of scores as its low dives, brothels and drugs.

It is still a ghetto today, though in the throes of redevelopment which will annihilate its character. It is squalid and overcrowded, but, despite the ever-lurking police vans, it has the ambience of places in hot climates. Old men talk for hours over tea in the numerous tiny cafés; restaurants serve Tunisian delicacies for next to nothing; Raï music resonates from the upper balconies. Understandably, there is a certain suspicion towards outsiders, whether yuppies pondering future property prices or tourists wanting to photograph urban seediness. Wednesday and Saturday, when the **bd de la Chapelle market** attracts large crowds, are perhaps the best days to go. There's a good chance you'll be offered dope if you appear aimless and irresolute on the street – offers best ignored as the quality is notoriously poor and there's almost certainly a plain-clothes *flic* keeping watch nearby.

Canal St-Martin and La Villette

The **Bassin de la Villette** and the **canals** at the northeastern gate of the city were for generations the centre of a densely populated working-class district. The jobs were in the main meat market and abattoirs of Paris or in the many interlinked industries that spread around the waterways. The amusements were skating or swimming, betting on cockfights or eating at the numerous restaurants famed for their fresh meat. Now La Villette is the wonderworld of laser-guided culture, the pride of politicians, and the recipient of over a billion pounds' worth of public spending.

The whole Villette complex stands at the junction of the **Ourcq** and **St-Denis canals**. The first was built by Napoléon to bring fresh water into the city. The second is an extension of the Canal St-Martin built as a shortcut to the great western loop of the Seine around Paris.

Canal St-Martin

The **Canal St-Martin** runs underground at the Bastille to surface again in bd Jules-Ferry by the rue du Faubourg-du-Temple, another key point in the annals of revolutionary street fighting. Barricaded by the *Communards* in 1871 and the *quarante-huitards* in 1848, it is now a peaceable, populous, run-down street of small shops, cafés, Arab sweatshops and crummy passages. Much of it obviously has not changed: the poverty, at least in relative terms, and the physical dilapidation, too. The southern section of the canal is the most attractive. Plane trees line the cobbled *quais* and elegant high-arched footbridges punctuate the spaces between locks. A few momentoes of the area's old identity remain, such as the facade of the **Hôtel du Nord** of Marcel Carné's film, at 102 quai de Jemappes. But grossly bland and strident apartment blocks have elbowed in among the traditional, solid, mid-nineteenth-century bourgeois residences, and north of rue des Recollects redevelopment has mutilated both banks.

Place de Stalingrad

You have to make a brief detour away from the canalside at **place de Stalingrad** (one of many socialist-inspired street names of working-class Paris and suburbs). One benefit at least of the gentrification process has been the tidying up of this square and the restoration of its centrepiece, the Rotonde de la Villette. This was one of Ledoux's **tollhouses** in Louis XVI's tax wall, where taxes were levied on all goods coming into the city – a major bone of contention in the lead-up to the 1789 revolution.

Beyond the *place* is the now defunct **Bassin de la Villette** dock. Re-cobbled, and with its dockside buildings converted into offices for canal boat-trips, the Bassin has lost all vestiges of its former status as France's premier port. At the rue de Crimée, where a unique hydraulic bridge crosses the canal, only one of the facing pair of warehouses, itself now converted into trendy offices, survives. Opposite, even the burrowing slums of the rue de Flandres are succumbing to the bulldozer and the crane. If you keep to the south bank on quai de la Marne, you can cross directly into the Parc de la Villette.

The Parc de la Villette

The major extravagance of La Villette is the **Cité des Sciences et de l'Industrie** built into the concrete hulk of the abandoned abattoirs on the north side of the canal de l'Ourcq. Three times the size of Beaubourg, this is by far the most astounding monument to be added to the capital in the last decade. Giant walls of glass hang beneath a dark blue lattice of steel, with white rod walkways accelerating out of the building across a mock fortress moat. In front of the complex balances the **Géode**, a bubble of reflecting steel dropped from an intergalactic *boules* game into a pool of water that ripples the mirrored image of the Cité. Inside, half the sphere is a projection screen.

South of the canal, past the **dragon slide**, is the largest of the old market halls – an iron-frame structure designed by Baltard, the engineer of the vanished Les Halles pavillions. It is now a vast and brilliant exhibition space, the **Grande Salle**. Between it and the **Zenith** inflatable rock music venue, on the eastern edge of the site, are bizarrely landscaped gardens, with peculiar sculptures such as a half-buried giant bicycle, and bright red "constructivist" follies designed by Bernard Tschumi, housing cafés, crèches, first aid, etc. South of the Grande Salle, is the brand new **Cité de la Musique**, in two complexes to either side of the Porte-de-Pantin entrance. The one to the west houses the national music academy and was designed by Christian de Portzamparc with the worst indulgence to architectural pseudo-intellectualism. It combines waves and funnels, irregular polygons and non-parallel lines, gangways, greenhouses and agressive slit windows. The block opposite, due to be completed during 1992, will have a concert hall, a museum of music, and commercial outlets for everything to do with music-making.

The Parc de la Villette is accessible from Mº Porte-de-la-Villette to the north or Mº Porte-de-Pantin to the south. There are information centres by the northern entrance and by the canal bridge. For details of the Cité des Sciences and the Géode, see below.

Belleville, Ménilmontant and Père-Lachaise

The Eastern districts are no longer revolutionary hotbeds as they were in the nineteenth century, but they are still among the poorest of the city, and opposition to encroaching yuppiedom is visibly expressed in graffiti. Belleville and Ménilmontant have large immigrant populations – Yugoslavs, Greeks, Chinese, Vietnamese, Jews, Arabs, Armenians, Senegalese, Malian – and inevitably a dangerous reputation among western Parisians. The main pleasures of this part of town are the views down onto the city, and discovering the odd corners that have escaped development, though the **Père-Lachaise cemetery** is the obvious focus for a visit.

Parc des Buttes-Chaumont

At the northern end of the Belleville heights, a short walk from La Villette, is the **parc des Buttes-Chaumont** (M° Buttes-Chaumont or Botzaris) constructed by Haussmann in the 1860s to camouflage what until then had been a desolate warren of disused quarries and miserable shacks. The sculpted beak-shaped park stays open all night and, equally rarely for Paris, you're not cautioned off the grass. At its centre is a huge rock upholding a delicate Corinthian temple and surrounded by a lake which you cross via a suspension bridge or the shorter Pont des Suicides. Louis Aragon, the literary grand old man of the French Communist Party, wrote of this bridge that it claimed victims among passers-by who had no intention of dying, but found themselves suddenly tempted by the abyss. Feeble metal grills erected along its sides put an end to such impulses.

Belleville and Ménilmontant

The route from Buttes-Chaumont to Père-Lachaise will take you through the one-time villages of **Belleville** and **Ménilmontant**. Various municipal projects have been introduced to "ameliorate" the area and around every corner the narrow streets are blocked by bulldozers and concrete mixers. Many of the old village lanes disappeared in the 1960s and 1970s tower block mania, and in all probability Belleville and Ménilmontant will end up looking more like the suburbs than Paris proper.

To get an idea of how it all once was, take a look at **Villa Otoz** off rue Piat. The first main street you cross coming down from Buttes-Chaumont, **rue de Belleville**, has become the new Chinatown of Paris. Vietnamese and Chinese shops and restaurants have proliferated over the last few years, adding considerable visual and gastronomic cheer to the area. African and oriental fruits, spices, music and fabrics can be bought at the **bd de Belleville market** on Tuesday and Friday. For French associations, Edith Piaf was dumped, a few hours old, on the steps of no. 72 rue de Belleville. Rue Ramponneau, just southeast of the crossroads with bd de Belleville, was where the last *Communard* on the last barricade held out alone for a final fifteen minutes.

From almost every street you get fantastic views down onto the city, but the best is from **rue de Ménilmontant**, just before it kinks above rue de l'Ermitage – the road appears to target the rooftops of Beaubourg. Just south, at 25 rue Boyer, is a beautiful building, *La Bellevilloise*, built for the *PCF* in the 1920s in Soviet revolutionary style. Further up rue Ménilmontant, at no. 150–154, is one of the best bakers in Paris, *Ganachaud*.

Père-Lachaise Cemetery

The **cimitière Père-Lachaise** – M° Gambetta, Père-Lachaise and Alexandre-Dumas – (daily 7.30am–6pm) is like a miniature city devastated by a neutron bomb: a great number of dead, empty houses and temples of every size and style, and exhausted survivors, some congregating aimlessly, some searching persistently. The first response manifests itself best around Jim Morrison's tomb, where a motley assembly of European hippies roll spliffs against a backdrop of Doors' lyrics and declarations of love and drug consumption graffitied in every Western language on every stone in sight. The alternative response, the searchers, are everywhere, looking for their favourite famous dead in an arrangement of numbered divisions that is neither entirely haphazard nor strictly systematic.

A safe bet for a high score is to head for the southeastern corner (near the rue de la Réunion entrance). There you will find memorials to concentration camp victims and executed Resistance fighters of the last war, Communist Party general-secretaries,

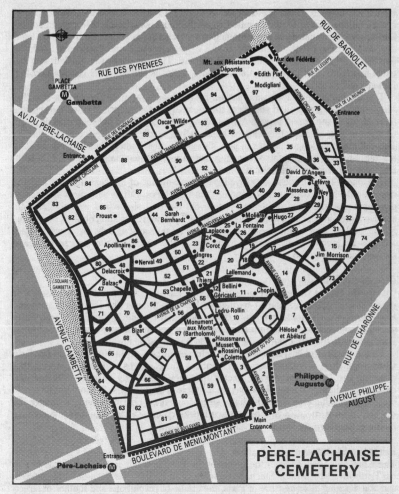

PÈRE-LACHAISE CEMETERY

Laura Marx and the Mur des Fédérés, where troops of the Paris Commune were lined up and shot in the last days of the battle. Defeat is everywhere. The oppressed and their oppressors interred with the same ritual. Abélard and Heloïse side by side in prayer, still chastely separate, the relative riches and fame as unequal among the tombs of the dead as in the lives of the living.

Among other names on the pilgrimage-grave stakes are Oscar Wilde, Edith Piaf, Balzac, and – the latest entry – Yves Montand.

From the Bastille to Vincennes

The column with the "Spirit of Liberty" on **place de la Bastille** was erected not to commemorate the surrender in 1789 of **the prison** – whose only visible remains have been transported to square Henri-Galli at the end of bd Henri-IV – but the July

Revolution of 1830 which replaced the autocratic Charles X with the "Citizen King" Louis-Philippe. When Louis-Philippe fled in the more significant 1848 revolution, his throne was burnt beside the column and a new inscription added. Four months later, the workers again took to the streets. All of eastern Paris was barricaded, with the fiercest fighting on rue du Faubourg-St-Antoine. The rebellion was quelled with the usual massacres and deportation of survivors, and it is still the 1789 Bastille Day that France celebrates.

The Bicentennial in 1989 was marked by the inauguration of the **Opéra-Bastille**, Mitterrand's pet project and subject of the most virulent sequence of rows and resignations of any of the *grands projets*. Almost filling the entire block between rues de Lyon, Charenton and Moreau, this bloated building has totally altered place de la Bastille. The column is no longer pivotal; in fact, it's easy to miss it altogether when dazzled by the night-time glare of lights emanating from this hideous "hippopotamus in a bathtub", as one perceptive critic put it.

The opera's construction destroyed no mean amount of low-rent housing and the **quartier de la Bastille** is now trendier than Les Halles. But as with most speculative developments, the pace of change is uneven: old tool shops and ironmongers still survive alongside cocktail haunts and sushi bars; launderettes and cobblers neighbour Filofax outlets. **Place and rue d'Aligre**, where local protest against the opera centred, still has its raucous daily market, with food in the covered *halles* and second-hand clothes and junk on the *place*.

Around the Bastille

On **rue de Lappe** there are remnants of a very Parisian tradition: the *bals musettes*, or music halls of 1930s "gai Paris", frequented between the wars by Piaf, Jean Gabin and Rita Hayworth. The most famous is *Balajo*, founded by one Jo de France, who introduced glitter and spectacle into what were then seedy gangster dives, and brought Parisians from the other side of the city to the rue de Lappe lowlife.

To the north, and east towards Père-Lachaise, off **rue de la Roquette** and **rue de Charonne**, there's nothing very special about the passages and ragged streets that make up the 11e *arrondissement*, except that they are utterly Parisian, with the odd detail of a building, the display of veg in a simple greengrocer's, the sunlight on a café table or the graffiti on a Second-Empire street fountain to charm an aimless wander. To the south down rue de Lyon, high office blocks conceal a classic nineteenth-century building, the **Gare de Lyon**.

Faubourg St-Antoine

There are quiet havens from the mania of the Bastille traffic in the courtyards of **rue du Faubourg-St-Antoine**. Since the fifteenth century, this has been the principal artisan and working-class *quartier* of Paris, the cradle of revolutions and mother of streetfighters. From its beginnings the principal trade associated with it has been **furniture-making**; the maze of interconnecting yards and passages are still full of the workshops of the related trades: marquetry, stainers, polishers, inlayers etc, many of whom are still producing the classic styles of French furniture.

The 12^e

The 12e *arrondissement* is less appealing than the 11e, and better suited to bus travel. Bus #29 from Bastille takes you down av Daumesnil past the ebullient *mairie* of the 12e, and, almost opposite, the old Reilly freight station, then on to the smug lions of place Félix-Eboué. The disused rail line was earmarked for a green promenade and bicycle track from Bastille to the Bois de Vincennes, but other priorities have had their way.

Between av Daumesnil and the river is yet another area in the throes of major development. The monstrous new **Ministère des Finances** building stretches from the river (where the higher bureaucrats arrive by boat) 400 metres back to rue de Bercy. The best view of the monster is from the Charles-de-Gaulle to Nation métro line as it crosses Pont de Bercy. You can also see, on the other side of bd de Bercy, the **Palais Omnisports de Bercy**, a mega sports and culture venue, with its concrete bunker frame clad with sloping lawns. Yet another project to keep construction companies thriving is a new bridge, the **Pont Charles-de-Gaulle**, alongside the Pont d'Austerlitz, scheduled for completion in 1993.

Vincennes

From Faubourg St-Antoine, various buses head **towards the Bois de Vincennes**. Bus #86 crosses **place de la Nation**, adorned with the Triumph of the Republic bronze, and, at the start of the Cours de Vincennes, the bizarre ensemble of two medieval monarchs, looking sheepish in pens on the top of two high columns. Bus #46, with the same destination, crosses place Félix-Eboué passing the **Musée des Arts Africains et Océaniens** (see below) with its 1930s colonial facade of jungles, hard-working natives and the place names of the French Empire. The bus's next stop is the **Parc Zoologique**.

In the **Bois de Vincennes** itself, you can spend an afternoon **boating** on Lac Daumesnil (by the zoo) or hire a bike from the same place and feed the ducks on Lac des Minimes on the other side of the wood (or bus #112 from Vincennes métro). The fenced enclave on the southern side of Lac Daumesnil is a **Buddhist centre** with a Tibetan temple, Vietnamese chapel and international pagoda, all of which are visitable. As far as real woods go, the *bois* opens out once you're east of av de St-Maurice, but the area is so overrun with roads that countryside sensations don't stand much chance. Nevertheless, a farm with cows and sheep is planned. To the north, near the château, is the **Parc Floral**, with lily ponds and a Four Season Garden for all-year-round displays. To the east of it is the **Cartoucherie de Vincennes**, an old ammunitions factory, now home to four theatre companies including the radical *Théâtre du Soleil*.

On the northern edge of the *bois*, the **Château de Vincennes**, royal medieval residence, then state prison, porcelain factory, weapons dump and military training school, is still undergoing restoration work started by Napoléon III. A real behemoth of a building, it's unlikely to be beautified by the removal of the nineteenth-century gun positions or any amount of stone-scrubbing.

The 13e

The southeast quarter of Paris, **the 13e** was not so long ago a tightly-knit community around rue Nationale living for the most part in slum conditions. Paris was another place, rarely ventured into. But come the 1950s and 1960s, the city planners, here as elsewhere, came up with their sense-defying solution to housing problems.

But it's not all depressing. There are the lively shops in the district's **Chinatown** (now rivalled by Belleville), the odd untouched *quartier* like the Butte aux Cailles, bits and bobs of prewar architecture, the Marguerite Durand library and the admirable *Dunois* jazz venue (see below). It is also the site of yet another *grand projet* that is well on its way to being even more controversial than the Bastille opera house. This is the new **Bibliothèque Nationale**, which is to have four L-shaped transparent towers, 100 metres high, at each corner of a space the size of sixteen football pitches, between rue du Chevaleret and the river. In 1991 the site was squatted by African families evicted from their homes north of the river. Their tent city brought enormous sympathy for the plight of the homeless – and heavy-handed police action. However, of the housing to be built alongside the library, only a third will be municipally owned.

Chinatown

The area between av de Choisy, rue de Tolbiac and bd Masséna, is the **Chinatown** of Paris, with no concessions to organic matter unless it's to be eaten. The *Tang Frères* supermarket and covered market at 48 av d'Ivry is an omnivore's treat. Just down the street, steps lead into an arcade of Chinese businesses which opens onto a tower-block studded concrete platform filled with Far Eastern restaurants. You can exit from the platform onto rue de Tolbiac, where, at no 93, you'll find a municipal library in a steel frame building illuminated by bright blue spotlights. The 3rd floor is the **Bibliothèque Marguerite Durand**, the first official feminist library in France (Tues–Sat 2–6pm; free).

Hôpital de la Salpêtrière

Nearer to the city centre, above bd Vincent-Auriol, the buildings are ornate and bourgeois, dominated by the immense **Hôpital de la Salpêtrière**, built under Louis XIV to dispose of the dispossessed. It later became a psychiatric hospital, fulfilling the same function. Jean Charcot, who believed that susceptibility to hypnosis was proof of hysteria, staged his theatrical demonstrations here, with Freud a captive member of his audiences. If you ask very nicely in the *Bibliothèque Charcot* (block 6, red route), the librarian may show you a book of photographs of the poor female subjects of these experiments. For a more positive statement on women, take a look at the building at 5 rue Jules-Breton which declares in large letters on its facade, "In humanity, woman has the same duties as man. She must have the same rights in the family and in society."

Butte aux Cailles and the Gobelin tapestry workshops

West of av d'Italie small houses with fancy brickwork or decorative timbers have remained intact, and there's a rare taste of pre-high-rise living. On **rue de la Butte aux Cailles** you'll find book and food shops, a community action centre, a worker's co-operative jazz bar (*La Merle Moqueur* at no. 11), and bars and bistros open until midnight. And there's a food market nearby on bd Auguste-Blanqui.

On the other side of the boulevard, rues Berbier-du-Mets and Croulebarbe run over the river Bièvre, covered over in 1910 as a health hazard. The main source of the pollution was the dyes from the **Gobelin tapestry workshops**, 42 av des Gobelins – Mᵒ Gobelins – in operation here for some 400 years. Tapestries are still being made by the same methods on cartoons by contemporary painters – a painfully slow process which you can watch (guided visits Tues, Wed & Thurs 2–3pm).

The Museums

You may find there is sufficient visual stimulation just wandering around Paris streets without exploring what's to be seen in the city's **art galleries and museums**. It's certainly questionable whether the Louvre, for example, can compete in pleasure with the Marais, the *quais* or parts of the Latin quarter. But if established art appeals to you at all, the Paris collections are not to be missed.

The most popular are the various museums of modern art, notably the Beaubourg and Palais de Tokyo, and, the **Musée d'Orsay**, **Orangerie** and **Marmottan**. There are many single artist collections, of which the **Picasso** and **Rodin** museums are best, and **contemporary art** has a new venue for temporary exhibitions in the revamped **Jeu de Paume** in the Tuileries gardens. No less breathtaking, going back to earlier cultural roots, are some of the **medieval works** in the **Musée Cluny**, including the glorious *La Dame à la Licorne* tapestry. Among the city's extraordinary number of technical, historical, social and applied art museums, pride of place goes to the dazzling **Cité des**

Sciences, radical in both concept and architecture – and fun. Entertaining, too, if more conventional, is the **Musée National des Arts et Traditions Populaires**, its equivalent for the past.

We have detailed the **main museums** below, along with a small selection from the rest. You'll find others described in the city sections. A full list can be obtained from the tourist office. Museums that may be closed because of modernisation work include the *Musée de l'Homme* in the Palais de Chaillot and the *Muséum d'Histoire Naturelle* in the Jardin des Plantes.

Admission prices vary. Most of the large museums charge around 30F, and offer reductions to the under-25s and over-60s (ID such as passport required). As for **opening hours**, the Louvre and other state-owned museums close on Tuesday and have half-price admission on Sunday (free days have been abolished); the city-owned museums close on Monday. If you're going to visit a great many museums in a short time, it's worth buying the *Carte Inter-Musées* **museum pass** (50F 1-day; 100F 3-day; 150F 5-day; available from RER stations and museums) – valid for 62 museums in and around Paris, and allows you to bypass the ticket queues. A student card, despite claims to the contrary, is no help in getting reductions unless you're under 25.

Lastly, keep an eye out for **temporary exhibitions**, some of which match any of Paris's regular collections. Beaubourg, the Grand Palais, the Grande Salle at La Villette and the Jeu de Paume host the major ones, well advertised by posters and detailed in *Pariscope* and the other listings magazines. The **commercial galleries** (heavily concentrated in the Beaubourg and St-Germain areas) are always worth a look – which of course you can do without charge.

Beaubourg: Musée National d'Art Moderne

Centre Beaubourg, rue Beaubourg, 4ᵉ. Mᵒ Rambuteau/Hôtel-de-Ville. Mon & Wed–Fri noon–10pm, Sat & Sun 10am–10pm; Musée National d'Art Moderne 23F/17F; Galeries Contemporaines 16F; day pass 50F/45F; free Sun 10am–2pm.

The **Musée National d'Art Moderne** on the fourth floor of Beaubourg is second to none, with a constantly expanding collection of exclusively twentieth-century art. Contemporary movements and works dated the year before last find their place here along with the late-Impressionists, Fauvists, Cubists, Figuratives, Abstractionists and the rest of this century's First World art trends. The lighting and hanging is superb, although only a sixth of the whole collection is exhibited at any one time.

One of the earliest paintings is Henri Rousseau's *La Charmeuse de Serpent* (1907), an extraordinary, idiosyncratic beginning. In a different world, Picasso's *Femme assise* of 1909 brings in the reduced colours and double dimensions of **Cubism**, presented in its fuller development by Braque's *L'Homme à la Guitare* (1914), and, later, in Léger's solid balancing act, *Les Acrobates en gris* (1942–44). Among **Abstracts**, there's the sensuous rhythm of colour in Sonia Delaunay's *Prismes Electriques* (1914) and a good number of Kandinskys at his most harmonious and playful. Dali disturbs, amuses or infuriates with *Six apparitions de Lénine sur un piano* (1931), and there are more surrealist images from Magritte and de Chirico. Moving to the Expressionists, one of the most compulsive pictures – of 1920s female emancipation as viewed by a male contemporary – is the portrait of the journalist Sylvia von Harden by Otto Dix. The gender of the sleeping woman in *Le Rêve* by Matisse has no importance – it is simply a painting of the human body at its most relaxed. Jumping forward, to Francis Bacon, you find the tension and the torment of the human body and mind in the portraits, and – no matter that the figure is minute – in *Van Gogh in Landscape* (1957). Squashed-up cars, lines and squares, wrapped-up grand pianos and Warhol's *Electric chair* (1966) are there to be seen, while for a reminder that **contemporary** art can still hold its roots, there's the classic subject of *Le Peintre et son modèle* by Balthus, painted in 1980–81.

MUSEUMS

1. M. National des Arts et Traditions Populaires
2. M. Arménien & M. d'Ennery
3. M. des Contrefaçons
4. M. Marmottan
5. Atelier d'Henri Bouchard
6. M. des Lunettes
7. M. du Vin
8. Maison de Balzac
9. M. de Radio-France
10. Palais Chaillot
    (M. du Cinema, M. des Monuments Français & M. de l'Homme)
11. M. Guimet
12. M. des Costumes
13. Palais de Tokyo
    (M. d'Art Moderne de la Ville de Paris & Centre National de la Photographie)
14. M. Intercoiffure
15. M. Cernuschi
16. M. de S.E.I.T.A.
17. M. de l'Armée
18. M. d'Orsay
19. M. Rodin
20. M. Valentin-Haûy
21. M. Bourdelle
22. M. de la Poste
23. M. Branly
24. M. Ernest-Hébert
25. M. Zadkine
26. Institut Français de l'Architecture
27. M. Delacroix
28. M. Cluny
29. M. de la Préfecture de Police
30. Institut du Monde Arabe
31. M. Assistance Publique
32. Orangerie
33. Jeu de Paume
34. M. Cognacq-Jay
35. M. de la Parfumerie
36. M. Gustave Moreau
37. M. Renan-Scheffer
38. M. Art Juif
39. M. de Montmartre
40. M. Grévin I
41. M. du Cristal
42. M. des Arts de la Mode (Louvre)
43. M. des Arts Décoratifs (Louvre)
44. M. de la Publicité (Louvre)
45. Centre Culturel des Halles
    (M. Grévin II/M. Holographie)
46. M. National Techniques
47. Beaubourg (M. National d'Art Moderne)
48. M. des Instruments de Musique Mécanique
49. M. de la Serrurerie
50. M. Kwok-on
51. M. Picasso
52. M. Carnavalet
53. M. de l'Histoire de France
54. Maison Victor Hugo
55. M. Adam Mickiewicz
56. Pavillon de l'Arsenal
57. M. Arts Africains et Océaniens
58. M. Edith Piaf
59. Cité de la Musique
60. Cité des Sciences
61. Centre International de l'Automobile

Elsewhere , the Beaubourg has temporary exhibitions of photographs, drawings, collages and prints (**Salle d'Art Graphique and Salon Photo**); **audiovisual presentations and films** on art history, contemporary art and current exhibitions; and the **Galleries Contemporaines** where the overflow of the museum's contemporary collection gets rotated and young artists get a viewing. The **Grande Galerie** right at the top of the building is where the big-time exhibitions are held.

The Louvre

Pyramide, Cour Napoléon, Palais du Louvre, 1er. M° Palais-Royal–Musée du Louvre/ Louvre–Rivoli. Mon 9am–9.45pm (certain galleries only), Wed 9am–9.45pm (all galleries), Thurs–Sun 9am–6pm; temporary exhibitions noon–10pm; Histoire du Louvre rooms, medieval Louvre, auditorium, shops, cafés etc, 9am–10pm; 30F, free for under-18s, reduced price 18–25s and over-60s; half-price Sun (no reductions); closed Tues.

> *"You walked for a quarter of a mile through works of fine art; the very floors echoed the sounds of immortality . . . It was the crowning and consecration of art . . . These works instead of being taken from their respective countries were given to the world and to the mind and heart of man from whence they sprung . . ."*

William Hazlitt, writing of the Louvre in 1802, goes on, in equally florid style, to proclaim this museum as the beginning of a new age, when artistic masterpieces would be the inheritance of all, no longer the preserve of kings and nobility. Novel the Louvre certainly was. The palace, hung with the private collections of monarchs and their ministers, was first opened to the public in 1793, during the Revolution. Within a decade Napoléon had made it the largest art collection on earth with takings from his empire.

However inspiring it might have been then, the Louvre has been a bit of a nightmare over the last few decades, requiring heroic stamina to find one work of art that you want to see amongst the 300,000. The revamped *"Grand Louvre"*, with its startling glass pyramid entrance in the *Cour Napoléon*, was finally inaugurated in 1988, but has failed to solve the problems.

Beneath the pyramid, a subterranean concourse – the *Hall Napoléon* – has lifts and escalators leading into the newly arranged sections of the museum: *Sully* (around the Cour Carrée), *Denon* (the south wing) and *Richelieu* (the north wing), though the last will not open until 1993. These are then divided into numbered rooms, colour-coded for each of the three floors. However, three major divisions for a building this size is not a great deal of help, and the signing system, including the giant electronic billboards in the *Hall Napoléon*, and the arrangement of the works, remains as mysterious and frustrating as it ever was. And when you need a break, you still have to get back down to the ticket concourse to find a cup of coffee. A bonus from the building works, however, has been the opportunity to excavate the remains of the medieval Louvre – Philippe-Auguste's twelfth-century fortress and Charles V's fourteenth-century palace conversion – under the *Cour Carrée*. These are now on display along with a permanent exhibition on the *Histoire du Louvre* from the Middle Ages right up to the current transformations.

The seven basic categories of the museum's collections remain the same: three lots of antiquities, plus sculpture, painting, applied and graphic arts. **Oriental Antiquities** (*Sully* ground floor 1–5) covers the Sumerian, Babylonian, Assyrian and Phoenician civilisations, plus the art of ancient Persia. **Egyptian Antiquities** (*Sully* ground floor 5–7 & 1st floor 6–8) contains jewellery, domestic objects, sandals, sarcophagi and dozens of examples of the delicate naturalism of Egyptian decorative technique, like the wall tiles depicting a piebald calf galloping through fields of papyrus and a duck taking off from a marsh. Some of the major exhibits are: the pink granite *Mastaba Sphinx*, the *Kneeling Scribe* statue (*Sully* ground floor 6), a wooden statue of *chancellor*

Nakhti, the *god Amon*, protector of Tutankhamun, a bust of *Amenophis IV, Sethi I* and the *goddess Hathor*. The **Greek and Roman Antiquities** (*Denon* ground floor 2–4, first floor 3; *Sully* ground floor 7–8, first floor 8) include the *Winged Victory of Samothrace* (*Denon* first floor 3) and the late second century BC *Venus de Milo* (*Sully* ground floor 8) – the biggest crowd-pullers in the museum after the *Mona Lisa*. *Venus*'s antecedents are all on display, too, from the delightful *Dame d'Auxerre* (seventh century BC) and the fifth-century BC bronze *Apollo of Piombino*, still looking straight ahead in the archaic manner, to the classical perfection of the *Athlete of Benevento* and the beautiful *Ephebe of Agde*. In the Roman section are some very attractive mosaics from Asia Minor, and luminous frescoes from Pompeii and Herculaneum which already seem to foreshadow the decorative lightness of touch of the Renaissance.

The **Applied Arts** collection (*Sully* first floor 1–6 & 8; *Denon* first floor 8) is heavily weighted on the side of vulgar imperial opulence and ecologically catastrophic abuses such as the entire doors of tortoiseshell in the work of the renowned cabinet-maker Boulle (active round 1700). There are also several acres of tapestry – all of the very first quality and workmanship, but a chore to look at. Better to seek relief in the smaller, less public items – Marie-Antoinette's travelling case, the carved Parisian ivories of the thirteenth century, and the Limoges enamels and Byzantine ivories.

The **Sculpture** section (*Denon* ground floor 5 & 7–10) covers the entire development of the art in France from Romanesque to Rodin and includes Michelangelo's *Slaves* designed for the tomb of Pope Julius II (*Denon* ground floor 10). But once you have seen the Greeks, you are not likely to want to linger over many of the items here.

The largest and most indigestible section by far is the **paintings** (*Sully* second floor 1–4; *Denon* first floor 1, 2 & 4–10, second floor 9): French from the year dot to mid-nineteenth century, along with Italians, Dutch, Germans, Flemish and Spanish. Among them are many paintings so familiar from reproduction in advertisements and on chocolate boxes that it is a surprise to see them on a wall in a frame. And unless you're an art historian, it is hard to make much sense of the parade of mythological scenes, classical ruins, piety, acrobatic saints and sheer dry academicism. A portrait, a domestic scene, a still life, is a real relief. The early Italians (*Denon* first floor 5 & 7) are perhaps the most interesting part of the collection. All the big names are represented – Giotto, Fra Angelico, Botticelli, Filippo Lippi, Raphael; works to look out for include Uccello's *Battle of San Romano*, a *Crucifixion* by Mantegna, and Paolo Veronese's *Marriage At Cana*, a huge work painted in 1563. If you want to get near the *Mona Lisa* (*Denon* first floor 5), go first or last thing in the day. No one, incidentally, pays the slightest bit of attention to the other Leonardos right alongside, including the *Virgin of the Rocks*. Non-Italian works worth lingering over include Quentin Matsy's moralistic *Moneychanger and his Wife*, Rembrandt's masterful *Supper at Emmaus*, and a number of paintings by Poussin. There are also canvases by the French nineteenth-century artists, David, Ingres and Géricault – whose harrowing *Raft of the Medusa* made his name as an artist. Look out, too, for Courbet's later *Funeral at Ornans*, perhaps the best-know Realist painting of all, its events rendered with dour, passive precision.

Musée d'Orsay

1 rue de Bellechasse/quai Anatole-France (for major exhibitions), 7e. M^o Solférino, RER Musée d'Orsay. Tues, Wed, Fri & Sat 9/10am–6pm, Thurs 9/10am–9.45pm, Sun 10am–6pm; 30F half-price Sun; free guided tours in English by staff lecturer 11am & 2pm.

The conversion of the disused railway station, the Gare d'Orsay, into the spanking new **Musée d'Orsay** marked a major advance in the reorganisation of the capital's art collections. It houses the painting and sculpture of the immediately pre-modern period, 1848–1914, bridging the gap between the Louvre and the Centre Beaubourg. Its focus is the cobweb-clearing, eye-cleansing collection of **Impressionists** rescued from the cramped corridors of the Jeu de Paume, though not – unavoidably – from the coach parties and gangs of brats. Scarcely less electrifying are the works of the **Post-Impressionists** brought in from the Palais de Tokyo.

On the **ground floor**, the mid-nineteenth-century sculptors, including Barye, caster of super-naturalistic bronze animals, occupy the centre gallery. To their right, a few canvases by Ingres and Delacroix (the bulk of whose work is in the Louvre) serve to illustrate the transition from the early nineteenth century. Puvis de Chavannes, Gustave Moreau, the Symbolists and early Degas follow, while in the galleries to the left Daumier, Corot, Millet and the Realist school lead on to the first Impressionist works, including Manet's *Déjeuner sur l'Herbe*, which sent the critics into apoplexies of disgust when it appeared in 1863. *Olympia* is here, too, equally controversial at the time, for the colour contrasts and sensual surfaces, rather than the content, though the black cat was considered peculiar.

To get the chronological continuation you have to go straight up to the top level, where numerous landscapes and outdoor scenes by Renoir, Sisley, Pissarro and Monet owe much of their brilliance to the novel practice of setting up easels in the open to catch a momentary light. Monet's waterlilies are here in abundance, too, along with five of his Rouen cathedral series, each painted in different light conditions. *Le Berceau* (1872), by Morisot, the only woman in the early group of Impressionists, is one of the few to have a complex human emotion as its subject – perfectly synthesised within the classic techniques of the movement. A very different touch, all shimmering light and wide brush strokes, is to be seen in Renoir's depiction of a good time being had by all in *Le Moulin de la Galette* – a favourite Sunday afternoon out on the Butte Montmartre. Cézanne, a step removed from the preoccupations of the mainstream Impressionists, is also wonderfully represented. One of the canvases most revealing of his art is *Still life with apples and oranges* (1895–1900), in which the background abandons perspective while the fruit has an extraordinary reality.

The rest of this level is given over to the various offspring of Impressionism. Among a number of pointilliste works by Seurat and others is Signac's horrible *Entrée du Port de Marseille*. There's Gauguin, post- and pre-Tahiti, as well as some very attractive derivatives like Georges Lacombe's carved wood panels; several superb Bonnards and Vuillards and lots of Toulouse-Lautrec at his caricaturial night-clubbing best – one large canvas including a rear view of Oscar Wilde at his grossest. Plus all the blinding colours and disturbing rhythms of the Van Goghs. The **middle level** takes in Rodin and other late nineteenth-century sculptors, three rooms of superb Art Nouveau furniture and *objets*, and, lastly, some Matisses and Klimts to mark the transition to the moderns in the Beaubourg collection.

As if these exhibition riches weren't enough, **the building** is itself a handsome structure. It was inaugurated in time for the 1900 World Fair and continued to serve the stations of southwest France until 1939. Orson Welles used it as the setting for his film of Kafka's *Trial*, and de Gaulle used it announce his coup d'état of May 19, 1958.

Cité des Sciences et de l'Industrie

Parc de la Villette, 19ᵉ. Mᵒ Corentin-Cariou/Porte de la Villette. Tues–Sun 10am–6pm; 35F, reduced tarif 25F; planétarium 10.30am, 12.30pm, 2pm, 3.30pm & 5pm – 15F extra; Géode Tues–Sun 10am–7pm – 45F/35F, combined ticket with Cité 70F/60F (available from Géode only, see p.140). The entire building is accessible by wheelchair; the médiathèque has a Braille room; and there are signers (in FSL).

This is the science museum to end all science museums, and worth visiting for the interior of the building alone: all glass and stainless steel, crows-nests and cantilevered platforms, bridges and suspended walkways, the different levels linked by lifts and escalators around a huge central space open to the full 40-metre height of the roof. It may be colossal, but you are more likely to lose yourself mentally rather than physically, and come out after several hours reeling with images and ideas, while none the wiser in actual fact about DNA, quasars, bacteria reproduction, rocket launching or whatever.

The **permanent exhibition**, called *Explora*, takes up the top two floors and is divided into thirty units (pick up a detailed plan from the *Accueil Général Explora* on *niveau 1*). These cover different subjects such as microbes, maths, sounds, robots, flying, energy, space, information, language etc. The emphasis, as the name suggests, is on exploring; the means used interactive computers, videos, holograms, animated models and games. Most of the explanations and instructions are in English as well as French; one exception, unfortunately, is the *Jeux de lumière* – "light games", a whole series of experiments to do with colour, optical illusions, refraction etc. In *Mille millards de microbes*, a rabies virus, looking like an evil multi-coloured *Dr Who* dalek, is scaled to the equivalent of you being the height of Everest. A classic example of chaos theory introduces the maths section: a wheel of glasses rotating below a stream of water in which the switch between clockwise and anticlockwise motion is entirely unpredictable. In *Expressions et comportements* you can intervene in stories acted out on videos, changing the behaviour of the characters to engineer a different outcome. Hydroponic plants grow for real in a green bridge across the central space. You can steer robots through mazes; make music by your own movements; try out a flight simulation; watch computer-guided puppet shows and holograms of different periods' visions of the universe; and stare at two slabs of wall parting company at the rate of 2cm a year – enacting the gradual estrangement of Europe and America.

When all this interrogation and stimulation becomes too much, you can relax at the café within *Explora* (*niveau 2* by the planetarium). When you want your head to start reeling again, just join the queue for the **planetarium**. Back on the ground floor there's a **cinema;** a **kids' activity centre**, the *inventorium*; an exhibition of current scientific research; and a whole programme of **temporary exhibitions**. Below ground there are **libraries**, **restaurants** and an **aquarium**. Outside, by the Géode, is a real 1957 French **submarine**, *L'Argonaute*. For details of the Géode, see below under "Cinema".

Musée d'Art Moderne de la Ville de Paris

Palais de Tokyo east wing, 11 av du Président-Wilson, 16ᵉ. Mᵒ Iéna/Alma-Marceau. Tues & Thurs–Sun 10am–5.30pm, Wed 10am–8pm; closed holidays; 30F.

It is difficult to predict which works will be on display and where, for this gallery suffers from seemingly chronic St Vitus' Dance. But you can rest assured that the museum's schools and trends of twentieth-century art will always be richly represented by artists such as Vlaminck, Zadkine, Picasso, Braque, Juan Gris, Valadon, Matisse, Dufy, Utrillo, both Delaunays, Chagall, Modigliani, Léger and many others, as well as by sculpture and painting by contemporary artists.

Among the most spectacular works on permanent show are Robert and Sonia Delaunay's huge whirling wheels and cogs of rainbow colour (now displayed in the ground floor corridor); the pale leaping figures of Matisse's *La Danse*; and Dufy's enormous mural, *La Fée Electricité* (done for the electricity board), illustrating the story of electricity from Aristotle to the then modern power station, in 250 lyrical, colourful panels filling three entire walls. The upper floors of the gallery are reserved for all sorts of contemporary and experimental work, including music and photography.

On sale in the bookshop are a number of artists' designs, among them a set of Sonia Delaunay's playing cards, guaranteed to rejuvenate the most jaded cardsharp. Next to it is an excellent and reasonably priced snack bar.

Musée des Arts Africains et Océaniens

293 av Daumesnil, 12ᵉ. Mᵒ Porte-Dorée. Mon & Wed–Fri 9.45am–noon & 1.30–5.20pm, Sat & Sun 12.30–6pm; 23F/13F; half price Sun.

This strange museum – one of the least crowded in the city – has an African gold brooch of curled-up sleeping crocodiles on one floor and, in the basement, five live crocodiles in a tiny pit surrounded by tanks of tropical fishes. Imperialism is much in evidence in a gathering of culture and creatures from the old French colonies: hardly any of the black African artefacts are dated, as the collection predates European acknowledgement of history on that continent, and the captions are a bit suspicious too. These masks and statues, furniture, adornments and tools should be exhibited with paintings by Expressionists, Cubists and Surrealists to see in which direction inspiration went. Picasso and friends certainly came here often. A treat.

Musée de Cluny

6 place Paul-Painlevé, 5ᵉ (off rue des Écoles). Mᵒ Odéon/St-Michel. Wed–Mon 9.45am–12.30pm & 2–5.15pm; 15F/8F.

If you have always found tapestries boring, this treasure house of medieval art may well provide the flash of enlightenment. The numerous beauties include a marvellous depiction of the grape harvest; a Resurrection embroidered in gold and silver thread, with sleeping guards in medieval armour; and a whole room of sixteenth-century Dutch tapestries, full of flowers and birds, a woman spinning while a cat plays with the end of the thread, a lover making advances, a woman in her bath, overflowing into a duck pond. But the greatest wonder of all is *La Dame à la Licorne. The Lady with the Unicorn:* six enigmatic scenes featuring a beautiful woman flanked by a lion and a unicorn, late fifteenth-century, perhaps made in Brussels. Quite simply, it is the most stunning piece of art you are likely to see in many a long day. The ground of each panel is a delicate red worked with a thousand tiny flowers, birds and animals. In the centre is a green island, equally flowery, framed by stylised trees, and here the scene is enacted. The young woman plays a portable organ, takes a sweet from a proffered box, makes a necklace of carnations while a pet monkey, perched on the rim of a basket of flowers, holds one to his nose . . .

Musée des Arts Décoratifs

107 rue de Rivoli, 1ᵉʳ. Mᵒ Palais-Royale–Musée du Louvre. Wed–Sat 12.30–6pm, Sun 11am–6pm; 20F/15F.

This is an enormous museum, except by the standards of the building housing it – the Louvre – of which it takes up the Tuileries end of the north wing. The contents are the furnishings, fittings and objects of French interiors: beds, blankets, cupboards, tools, stained glass and lampshades, in fact almost anything that illustrates the decorative skills from the Middle Ages to the 1990s.

The meagre contemporary section has been added to recently – works by French, Italian and Japanese designers mainly, including, inevitably, Philippe Starck. The rest of the twentieth century (also on the first floor) is fascinating – a bedroom by Guimard, Jeanne Lanvin's Art Deco apartments and a salon created by Georges Hoentschel for the 1900 Expo Universelle. You can work your way back through the nineteenth century's fascination with the foreign and love of vivid colouring (fourth floor), to the intricate wood-carving of the eighteenth century (third floor), to seventeenth-century marquetry and Renaissance tapestries and ivories (second floor). A section on the third floor is dedicated to toys throughout the ages, with changing exhibitions.

Musée Marmottan

2 rue Louis-Boilly, 16ᵉ (off av. Raphael). Mᵒ Muette. Tues–Sun 10am–5.30pm; 25F/10F.

The star of the show here is the collection of **Monet paintings** bequeathed by the artist's son. Among them is the canvas entitled *Impression, Soleil Levant* (*Impression, Sunrise*), an 1872 rendering of a misty sunrise over Le Havre, whose title the critics usurped to give the Impressionist movement its name. There's a dazzling collection of canvases from Monet's last years at Giverny, including several *Nymphéas* (Water-lilies), *Le Pont Japonais, L'Allée des Rosiers, La Saule Pleureur*, where rich colours are laid on in thick, excited whorls and lines. To all intents and purposes, these are abstractions, much more "advanced" than the work of, say, Renoir, Monet's exact contemporary.

Impression, Soleil Levant was stolen from the gallery in October 1985, along with four other Monets, two Renoirs, a Berthe Morisot and a Naruse. After a police operation lasting five years, and going as far afield as Japan, the paintings were discovered in a villa in southern Corsica, and are back on show – with greatly tightened security measures.

The Orangerie

Place de la Concorde, 1ᵉʳ. Mᵒ Concorde. 9.45am–5.15pm; closed Tues; 23F/12F, half price Sun.

A private collection, inherited by the state with the stipulation that it should always stay together, none of the pictures in the **Orangerie** has been moved to the Musée d'Orsay, with the result that it remains one of the top treats of Paris art museums. Its centrepiece, on the south side of the Tuileries terrace overlooking place de la Concorde, is two oval rooms arranged by **Monet** as panoramas for his largest waterlily paintings. In addition, there are works by no more than a dozen other **Impressionist** artists – Matisse, Cézanne, Utrillo, Modigliani, Renoir, Soutine and Sisley amongst them. Cézanne's southern landscapes, the portraits by Van Dongen, Utrillo and Derain of Paul Guillaume and Jean Walter, whose taste this collection represents, the massive nudes of Picasso, Monet's *Argenteuil* and Sisley's *Le Chemin de Montbuisson*, are the cherries on the cake of this visual feast. What's more, you don't need marathon endurance to cover the lot and get back to your favourites for a second look. The only black mark is the gilt heaviness of the frames.

Musée Picasso

5 rue de Thorigny, 3ᵉ. Mᵒ St-Paul/Filles-du-Calvaire. Wed 9.15am–10pm, Mon & Thurs–Sun 9.15am–5.15pm; 28F/16F.

Housed in the grandiloquent seventeenth-century mansion, the Hôtel Salé, this museum represents the largest collection of Picassos anywhere. A large proportion of the works were personally owned by Picasso at the time of his death, and the state had first option on them in lieu of taxes owed. They include all the different media he used, the paintings he bought or was given by his contemporaries, his African masks and sculptures, photographs, letters and other personal memorabilia.

All of which said, it's a bit disappointing. These are not Picasso's most enjoyable works – the museums of the Côte d'Azur, Barcelona and Madrid are more exciting. But the collection does leave you with a definite sense of the man and his life, partly because these were the works he wanted to keep, and many are accompanied by photographs. The paintings of his wives, lovers and families are some of the gentlest and most endearing here: the portrait of *Marie-Thérèse and Claude dessinant, Françoise et Paloma* for example, painted in 1937, like the portrait of Dora Maar, during the Spanish Civil War when Picasso was going through his worst personal and political crises. This is the period when emotion and passion play hardest on his paintings and they are by far the best. A decade later, Picasso was a member of the Communist Party – his cards are on show along with a drawing entitled *Staline à la Santé* (Here's to Stalin), and his delegate credentials for the 1948 World Congress of Peace. The *Massacre en Corée* (1951) demonstrates the lasting pacifist commitment in his work.

Temporary exhibitions bring to the Hôtel Salé works from the periods least represented: the Pink Period, Cubism (despite some fine examples here, including a large collection of collages), the immediate postwar period and the 1950s and 1960s. There is also a cinema and reference library; and a good, reasonably priced café.

Musée Rodin

77 rue de Varenne, 7ᵉ (just to the east of the Invalides). Mᵒ Varenne. Tues–Sun 10am–5/ 5.45pm; 20F/10F, half price Sun.

This collection represents the whole of Rodin's work. Major projects like *Les Bourgeois de Calais*, *Le Penseur*, *Balzac*, *La Porte de l'Enfer*, *Ugolini et fils*, are exhibited in the garden – the latter forming the centrepiece of the ornamental pond. Indoors (and very crowded) are works in marble like *Le Baiser*, *La Main de Dieu*, *La Cathédrale* – those two perfectly poised, almost sentient, hands. There is something particularly fascinating about the works, like *Romeo and Juliet* and *La Centauresse*, which are only, as it were, half-created, not totally liberated from the raw block of stone.

Other Museums

The full range of the city's museums caters for interests as diverse as sport, the police, literature, freemasonry, fashion, counterfeits, tobacco and ancient scrolls. There are also numerous museums dedicated to individual artists. The selection below includes a number of personal favourites...

Musée National des Arts et Traditions Populaires

6 av du Mahatma Gandhi, Bois de Boulogne, 16ᵉ (beside main entrance to Jardin d'Acclimatation). Mᵒ Les Sablons/Porte-Maillot. 9.45am–5.15pm; closed Tues; 14F/9F.

If you have any interest in the beautiful and highly specialised skills, techniques and artefacts developed in the long ages that preceded industrialisation, standardisation and mass-production, then you should find this museum fascinating. Boat-building, shepherding, farming, weaving, blacksmithing, pottery, stone-cutting, games, clairvoyance . . . all beautifully illustrated and displayed.

Musée de l'Affiche et de la Publicité

107 rue de Rivoli, 1ᵉʳ. Mᵒ Palais-Royal. Mon &Wed–Sat 12.30–6pm, Sun 11am–6pm; 25F/15F.

Publicity posters, adverts and TV and radio commercials are presented in monthly exhibitions, concentrating either on the art, the product or the politics. Usually more entertaining than the *Musée des Arts de la Mode* next door.

Musée des Lunettes et Lorgnettes de Jadis

2 av Mozart, 16ᵉ. Mᵒ La Muette. Tues–Sat 9am–1pm & 2–7pm; closed Aug; free.

Don't look for a museum. This superb collection of focusing aids resides in an ordinary commercial optician's shop. The exhibits span pretty much the whole history of the subject, from the first medieval corrective lenses to modern times, taking in binoculars, microscopes and telescopes on the way. There are lenses set in the hinges of fans and the pommels of gentlemen's canes, and a lorgnette case that pops open to reveal an eighteenth-century dame sitting on a swing above a waterfall. A special collection consists of specs that have rested on the bridges of the famous: Audrey Hepburn, the Dalai Lama, Sophia Loren and ex-President Giscard.

Musée de l'Armée

Hôtel des Invalides, 7ᵉ. Mᵒ Invalides/Latour-Maubourg/École-Militaire. Daily 10am–5pm; 25F/13F.

France's national war museum is enormous. The largest part is devoted to the uniforms and weaponry of Napoléon's armies with numerous personal items of Napoléon's, including his campaign tent and bed, and even his dog – stuffed. Later French wars are illustrated, too, through paintings, maps and engravings. Sections on the two world wars are good, with deportation and resistance covered as well as battles. Some of the oddest exhibits are Secret Service sabotage devices – for instance, a rat and a lump of coal stuffed with explosives.

Musée Carnavalet

23 rue de Sévigné, 3ᵉ. Mᵒ St-Paul. Tues–Sun 10am–5.40pm; closed holidays; 15F/8.50F.

A Renaissance mansion in the Marais presents the history of Paris as viewed and lived in by royalty, aristocrats and the bourgeoisie from François I to 1900. The rooms for 1789–95 are full of sacred mementoes: models of the Bastille, original *Declarations of the Rights of Man and the Citizen*, tricolours and liberty caps, sculpted allegories of Reason, crockery with revolutionary slogans, glorious models of the guillotine and execution orders to make you shed a tear for the royalists as well. In the rest of the gilded rooms, the display of paintings, maps and models of Paris is a bit too exhaustive to give you an overall picture of the city changing.

Musée Kwok-On

41 rue des Francs-Bourgeois, 4ᵉ. Mᵒ St-Paul/Rambuteau. Mon–Fri 10am–5.30pm; 10F/5F.

Changing exhibitions feature the popular arts of southern Asia – the musical instruments, festival decorations, religious objects and, most of all, the costumes, puppets, masks and stage models for theatre, in eleven different countries stretching from Japan to Turkey. The collection includes such things as figures for the Indonesian and Indian Theatres of Shadows, Peking Opera costumes and story-tellers' scrolls from Bengal.

Amusements

When it's cold and wet, and you've peered enough at museums, monuments and the dripping panes of shop fronts and café vistas, don't despair or retreat back to your hotel. There are **Golden Oldie movies** and **videos** to be seen, **music halls** are playing the tango for anyone to dance to, there are **saunas** to soak in, **ice rinks** to fall on, **bowling alleys, boules** and **swimming pools**. And when the weather isn't so bad, you can go for a **ride in a boat**, or even a **helicopter**, after a successful flutter on the **horses** in the Bois de Boulogne. If that doesn't appeal, you could join the Parisian crowds at a **major sporting event**.

Boat trips, balloon and heli rides

Bateaux-Mouches **boat trips** start from the *Embarcadère du Pont de l'Alma* on the right bank in the 8ᵉ, Mᵒ Alma-Marceau; rides (1hr–1hr 15min) every half hour from 10am to noon and 2 to 11pm; winter departures at 11am, 2.30, 4 and 9pm only (30F, under-14s

15F). Make sure you avoid the outrageously priced lunch and dinner trips, for which "correct" dress is mandatory. *Bateaux-Mouches* has other competitors, all much of a muchness and detailed in *Pariscope* under *Promenades*.

Less blatantly tourist fodder are the **canal boat trips** run by *Canauxrama* (reservations ☎42.39.15.00) between the Port de l'Arsenal (opposite 50 bd de la Bastille 12ᵉ; Mᵒ Bastille) and the Bassin de la Villette (13bis quai de la Loire, 19ᵉ; Mᵒ Jaurès) on the Canal St-Martin. The ride lasts three hours – not a bad bargain for 70F (65F weekend afternoons). A more stylish vessel for exploring the canal is the catamaran of *Paris-Canal* with trips between the Musée d'Orsay (quai Anatole-France, 7ᵉ; Mᵒ Solférino) and the Parc de la Villette (11 quai de la Loire, 19ᵉ; Mᵒ Porte-de-Pantin). Details and reservations from ☎42.40.96.97.

A **helicopter** tour above all the city's sights is somewhat prohibitively priced, but if whirly-gig rides turn you on as much or more than a four-star meal or a stalls seat at the theatre, then a quick loop around La Défense is on. The two companies operating are *Héli-France* (9am–7.30pm) and *Hélicap* (8.45am–7.30pm), both at the Héliport de Paris, 4 av de la Porte-de-Sèvres, 15ᵉ (Mᵒ Balard).

Afternoon tangos

One pastime to fill the afternoon hours that might not cross your mind is the **bals musette**. These dance halls were the between-the-wars solution in the down-and-out parts of *Gai Paris* to depression, dole and the demise of the Popular Front. They still attract a mainly working-class clientele, and run both afternoon and evening sessions.

Balajo, 9 rue de Lappe, 11ᵉ. Mᵒ Bastille. The original venue. Music, all recorded, is a mixture of waltz, tango, java, disco and rock. Admission price of around 50F includes a drink. Open 3–6.30pm.

Le Tango, 13 rue au Maire, 3ᵉ. Mᵒ Arts-et-Metiers. One of the oldest dance halls in town. Waltz, tango and chacha; all ages; no chic; and free entry – just cloakroom and drinks to pay for. Open 2.30–6.30pm.

Films and videos

The **Vidéothèque de Paris**, (2 Grande Gallerie, Porte St-Eustache, Forum des Halles, 1ᵉʳ. RER Châtelet-Les Halles) is one of the city's best high-tech treats. Open Tues–Sun 12.30–8.30pm, it screens four films or videos daily but also has a library of 3,500 videos — newsreel footage, film clips, ads, documentaries etc — all with a connection to Paris, that you can access yourself from a computer terminal. You can make your choice via a Paris place-name, an actor, a director, a date and so on, and there are instructions in English at the desk and a friendly "librarian" to help you out. And all it costs is 20F for entry to the complex.

Swimming

For straightforward exercise, for under 20F, you can go swimming in any of the **municipal baths**, but check first in *L'Officiel des Spectacles* for opening times (under *Piscines*) as varying hours are given over to schools and clubs. Private pools are twice as expensive or more, but have their attractions. Three favourites are:

Deligny, 25 quai Anatole-France, 7ᵉ. Mᵒ Chambre-des-Deputés. (Private). Crowded but an amusing, if expensive, spectacle of rich bodies sunning themselves on the vast deck above the Seine.

Jean Taris, 16 rue de Thouin, 5ᵉ. Mᵒ Cardinal-Lemoine. An unchlorinated pool in the centre of the Latin Quarter. A student favourite.

Piscine Susanne Berlioux/Les Halles, 10 place de la Rotonde, niveau 3, Porte du Jour, Forum des Halles, 1ᵉʳ. RER Châtelet-Les Halles. A brand new 50m pool with a vaulted concrete ceiling and a glass wall looking through to the tropical garden.

Hammams

A steam bath and a massage might be just what you need after the Louvre or other sightseeing exertions. The **Hammams**, or Turkish baths, are much more luxurious than the standard Swedish sauna. They are places to linger and chat. The best one of all is the **Hammam de la Mosquée**, 39 rue Geoffroy-St-Hilaire, 5ᵉ. Mᵒ Censier-Daubenton. Here you can order mint tea and honey cakes after your baths, around a fountain in a marble and cedar-wood-covered courtyard. 60F (massage 50F extra). Hours for women are Mon & Wed 11am–7pm, Thurs 11am–9pm, Sat 10am–7pm; for men, Fri 11am–8pm & Sun 10am–7pm; closed August.

Skating, skateboarding and boules

The city's only **ice rink** is the *Patinoire des Buttes-Chaumont*, 30 rue Edouard-Pailleron, 19ᵉ; Mᵒ Bolivar (☎46.03.18.00). This costs 37F including skate hire, and is popular and fun. *L'Officiel des Spectacles* and other such magazines will have details of its seasonally changing hours. **Roller-skating** has a special disco rink at *La Main Jaune* on place de la Porte-de-Champerret, 17ᵉ, Mᵒ Champerret (Wed, Sat & Sun 2.30–7pm, Fri & Sat also 10pm–dawn). Day sessions cost F40. The main outdoor roller-skating and **skateboarding** arena is the concourse of the Palais de Chaillot (Mᵒ Trocadéro). Les Halles (around the Fontaine des Innocents) and the Beaubourg piazza are also popular.

Boules, or *pétanque*, is best performed (or watched) at the Arènes de Lutece and the Bois de Vincennes, but on balmy summer evenings you're likely to see it played in any of the city's parks and gardens.

Mainstream sports

Tennis, squash, golf, skiing on artificial slopes, archery, rock-climbing, canoeing, fishing, windsurfing, water-skiing and parachuting – you name it, you can do it, in or around the city. Whether you'll want to spend the time and money on booking and hiring equipment is another matter. If you're determined, you'll find details in *L'Officiel des Spectacles* (the best of the listings mags for sports facilities) or, for current sporting events, *L'Équipe*, the **daily sports newspaper**. Failing that, ring **Allo Sports** on ☎42.76.54.54 (Mon–Fri 10.30am–5pm) or visit to the **Direction Jeunesse et Sports** (25 bd Bourdon, 4ᵉ, Mᵒ Bastille; Mon–Fri 10am–5.30pm). These are both municipal outfits, so the places they have listed will all be subsidised and cheap.

Paris Marathon
The city's Marathon is held in May over a route from place de la Concorde to Vincennes. Up-to-date information from the runners' shop, *Marathon*, 29 rue de Chazelles, 17ᵉ, Mᵒ Monceau (☎42.27.48.18).

Tour de France
The biggest event of the French sporting year is the grand finale of the **Tour de France**, which arrives in the city through the Arc de Triomphe in the third week of July.

Football and rugby
The *Parc des Princes* (24 rue du Commandant-Guilbaud, 16ᵉ, Mᵒ Porte-de-St-Cloud; ☎40.71.91.91/48.74.84.75) is the capital's main stadium for both **rugby union** and **football** events, and home ground to the first-division Paris football team *Paris-SG* (St-Germain) and the 1990 rugby champions, *Le Racing*.

Tennis

The French Tennis Open takes place in the last week of May and first week of June at *Roland-Garros*, which lies between the *Parc des Princes* and the Bois de Boulogne, with the ace address of 2 av Gordon-Bennett, 16ᵉ, Mᵒ Porte d'Auteuil (☎47.43.00.47). A few tickets are sold each day, but only for unseeded matches; otherwise book four months ahead.

Athletics and other sports

The *Palais des Omnisports Paris-Bercy* (*POPB*) at 8 bd Bercy, 12ᵉ (☎40.02.60.60) hosts all manner of sporting events, including athletics, cycling, show-jumping, ice hockey, ballroom dancing, judo and motocross. Keep an eye on the sports pages of the newspapers.

Horse-racing

Being a spectator at a **horse race** could make a healthy change from looking at art treasures. If you want to fathom the **betting system**, any bar or café with the letters PMU will take your money on a three-horse bet, known as *le tiercé*. The **biggest races** are the *Prix de la République* and the *Grand Prix de L'Arc de Triomphe* on the first and last Sundays in October at Auteuil and Longchamp, both in the Bois de Boulogne. **Trotting races**, with the jockeys in chariots, run from August to September on the *Route de la Ferme* in the Bois de Vincennes. *L'Humanité* and *Paris-Turf* carry details of all races, and admission charges are around 20F.

Kids' Stuff

The latest attraction for **kids** to hit the Paris area is of course European Disneyland (see "Out from the City"), though our advice is to keep quiet about that. There are plenty of possibilities for kids to have fun within the city at far less expense, although keeping teenagers amused in Paris is as hard as it is anywhere.

Many of the **museums** and **amusements** already detailed may appeal; the tours round the **sewers** and the **catacombes** certainly could delight some children; for the smaller ones, look out for *Guignol* (the Punch & Judy equivalent) in the city's parks. A number of museums have activities for children, full details of which are published in *Objectif Musée*, available from the museums or from the *Direction des Musées de France* (34 quai du Louvre, 1ᵉʳ; closed Tues).Otherwise the most useful **sources of information**, for current shows, exhibitions and events, are the special sections in the listings magazines, "*Pour les jeunes*" in *Pariscope*, "*Enfants*" in *7 Jours à Paris* and "*Jeunes*" in *L'Officiel des Spectacles*.

Cité des Sciences et de l'Industrie

Parc de la Villette, 19ᵉ. Mᵒ Corentin-Cariou/Porte-de-la-Villette. Opening times and tarifs are: Tues–Sun 10am–6pm; 35F/25F. **Inventorium** *Mon–Fri 11am, 12.30pm, 2pm & 3.30pm; Sat & Sun noon, 1.30pm, 3pm & 4.30pm; 15F, free for two accompanying adults.* **Cinéma Louis-Lumière** *9am–noon & 2–6pm; 10F extra.* **Planétarium** *10.30am, 12.30pm, 2pm, 3.30pm & 5pm; 15F extra.* **Géode** *Tues–Sun 10am–7pm; 45F/35F, combined ticket with Cité 70F/60F (available from Géode only).*

The **Inventorium**, the Cité's special section for 3- to 6-year-olds and 6- to 12-year-olds is totally engaging. The kids can touch and smell and feel inside things, play about with water, construct buildings on a miniature construction site complete with cranes, hard hats and barrows, experiment with sound and light, and carry out genetic tests with computers. It's beautifully organised and managed, and if you haven't got a child it's worth borrowing one to get in here. The rest of the museum is also pretty good for kids, particularly the planterium and the Omnimax film shows in the Géode.

Jardin d'Acclimatation

In the Bois de Boulogne by Porte des Sablons. Mº Sablons/Porte-Maillot. Daily 10am–6pm; 7.50F, under-16s 3.50F, under-3s free, additional charges for some attractions. Special attractions Wed, Sat and Sun and all week during school hols, including a little train to take you there from Mº Porte-Maillot (behind the L'Orée du Bois restaurant; every 10min, 1.30–6pm; 4F).

The garden is a cross between funfair, zoo and amusement park, with temptations ranging from bumper cars, go-karts, pony and camel rides, to sea lions, birds, bears and monkeys; a magical mini-canal ride (*la rivière enchantée*), distorting mirrors, scaled-down farm buildings, a puppet theatre and a superb collection of antique dolls at the *Grande Maison des Poupées*. There are good animations in the **Musée en Herbe**, and music and movement at the **Théâtre du Jardin pour l'Enfance et la Jeunesse**.

Outside the *jardin*, in the Bois de Boulogne, **older children** can amuse themselves with **mini-golf and bowling**, or **boating** on the *Lac Inférieur*. By the entrance to the *jardin* there's **bike hire** for roaming the wood's cycle trails.

Parc Floral

In the Bois de Vincennes, on rte de la Pyramide. Mº Château-de-Vincennes then bus #112. Summer daily 9.30am–10pm; 8F, 4F for 6–9-year-olds; winter daily 9.30am until 5 or 6pm; 4F, and 2F for the 6–9s; under-6s always free. A little train tours all the gardens (April–Oct Wed–Sun 10.30am–5pm; 4F).

The excellent **playground** in this park has slides, swings, ping-pong and pedal carts; a few paying extras like mini-golf, an electric car circuit, and pony rides (April–Oct daily 2–6pm); and clowns, puppets and magicians on summer weekends. Most of the activities are free and in general you'll be far less out of pocket after an afternoon here than at the Jardin d'Acclimatation. Also in the park a children's theatre, the **Théâtre Astral**, may have mime, clowns and other not-too-verbal shows.

Parc Zoologique

Bois de Vincennes, 53 av de St-Maurice, 12ᵉ; Mº Porte-Dorée. Summer 9am–6pm, winter 9am–5.30pm; 30F/15F.

The top Paris **zoo**, and one of the first in the world to get rid of cages and use landscaping to give the animals more room to exercise.

Beaubourg

Centre Pompidou, rue Beaubourg, 4ᵉ. Mº Rambuteau/Hôtel-de-Ville. Atelier des Enfants Wed & Sat 2–3.30pm & 3.45–5pm; free for visitors to the art museum; some English-speaking animators.

As well as **Beaubourg's** free attractions – the performers on the plaza and the building in itself – you can deposit 6- to 14-year-olds in the *Atelier des Enfants* where they can create their own art and play games.

Jardin des Halles

105 rue Rambuteau. Mº RER Châtelet-Les Halles. 7- to 11-year-olds only; Tues, Thurs & Fri 9am–noon & 2–6pm, Wed & Sat 10am–6pm, Sun 1–6pm; winter closing 4pm; closed in bad weather; 2.20F per hour.

Right in the centre of town at Les Halles, and great if you want to lose your charges for the odd hour. A whole series of fantasy landscapes fill this small but cleverly designed space; on Wednesday animators organise adventure games; and at all times the children are supervised by professional child-carers. You may have to reserve a place an hour or so in advance; on Saturday morning you can go in and play, too.

Dragon Slide

Between the Cité des Sciences and the footbridge over the Canal de l'Ourcq in the Parc de la Villette, 19ᵉ. Mᵒ Corentin-Cariou/Porte-de-la-Villette. Free.

The best slide in Paris, made from recycled cable drums and pipes. Across the Canal de l'Ourcq the park has several curious gardens and sculptures that might entertain climbers and explorers.

Planète Magique

3bis rue Papin, 3ᵉ. Mᵒ Réaumur-Sébastopol. During school holidays the hours are Mon 1–7pm, Tues–Sun 10am–7pm; for the rest of the year Wed, Sat, Sun & holidays 10am–7pm, Thurs & Fri 1–7pm. 10F-30F for each game.

An American-inspired simulation fantasy, with a series of rooms kitted out as different worlds – a space station, an Inca palace, an Arthurian dungeon, a time machine, a Barbie-doll's dressing-room – with video projections and interactive computers for you to work out the riddle, the escape route, the future of the universe and what Barbie's going to wear tonight. All very unoriginal but the kids will probably love it.

Cirque de Paris

On the corner of av Hoche and av de la Commune-de-Paris, Nanterre. RER Nanterre-Ville. ☎47.24.11.70. Nov–June Wed, Sun & school holidays 10am–5pm. 215F+ adults, 175F+ children.

An entire **day at the circus**. In the morning you are initiated into the arts of juggling, walking the tightrope, clowning and make-up. You have lunch in the ring with your artiste tutors, then join the spectators for the show, after which, if you're lucky, the lion-tamer takes you round to meet his cats. You can, if you prefer, just attend the show at 3pm (60–150F/40–95F)

Le Ciel est à Tout le Monde

10 rue Gay-Lussac, 5ᵉ. Mᵒ Luxembourg. Also at 7 av Trudaine, 9ᵉ; Mᵒ Anvers. Mon–Sat 10.30am–7pm; closed Mon in Aug.

The best **kite shop** in Europe. It also sells frisbees, boomerangs, etc, and books and traditional toys.

Shopping

Even if you don't plan – or can't afford – to buy, Parisian **shops and markets** are one of the chief delights of the city. Flair for style and design is as evident here as it is in other aspects of the city's life. Parisians' fierce attachment to their small local traders, especially when it comes to food, has kept alive a wonderful variety of shops, despite the pressures to concentrate consumption in gargantuan underground and multi-storey complexes. Among specific areas, the square kilometre around **place St-Germain-des-Prés** is hard to beat, packed with books, antiques, gorgeous garments, artworks and playthings. But in every *quartier* you'll find enticing displays of all manner of consumeables.

For **essentials**, the cheapest supermarket chains are *Ed Discount* and *Franprix*. **Food** (apart from bread) is best bought from the street markets.

Bookshops

Books are not cheap in France – foreign books least of all. But don't let that stop you browsing. The best areas are the Seine *quais* with their rows of **stalls** perched against the river parapet and the narrow streets of the Quartier Latin, but there are other places where you can sit down with a cup of coffee and a book.

English-language books

Abbey Bookshop/La Librairie Canadienne, 29 rue de la Parcheminerie, 5ᵉ. Mᵒ St-Michel. A Canadian bookshop round the corner from *Shakespeare & Co*, with lots of secondhand British and North American fiction; good social science sections; knowledgeable and helpful staff . . . and free coffee. Mon–Thurs 11am–10pm, Fri & Sat 11am–12pm, Sun noon–10pm.

Shakespeare & Co, 37 rue de la Bûcherie, 5ᵉ. Mᵒ Maubert-Mutualité. A cosy, famous literary haunt, with the biggest selection of secondhand English books in town. Also poetry readings and such. Noon–midnight every day.

Tea and Tattered Pages, 24 rue Mayet, 6ᵉ. Mᵒ Duroc/Falguière. Large collection of good value secondhand books, plus cakes and tea.

Books in French

FNAC, Forum des Halles – level-2, Porte Pierre-Lescot. Mᵒ RER Châtelet-Les Halles. Mon 2–7.30pm, Tues–Sat 10am–7.30pm. Also at 136 rue de Rennes, 6ᵉ (Mᵒ Montparnasse) and 26 av de Wagram, 8ᵉ (Mᵒ Courcelles), both open Mon 2–7pm, Tues–Sat 10am–7pm; and CNIT, 2 place de la Défense (RER La Défense), Mon 2–8pm, Tues–Sat 10am–8pm. Not the most congenial of bookshops but it's the biggest and covers everything.

Clothes

For *haute couture*, the two traditional areas are **av Montaigne, rue François 1ᵉʳ and rue du Faubourg-St-Honoré** in the 8ᵉ, and **av Victor-Hugo** in the 16ᵉ. The fashionable newer designers are to be found around **place des Victoires** in the 1ᵉʳ and 2ᵉ. There's nothing to stop you from trying on the fabulously expensive creations, apart from the intimidating scorn of the assistants and the awesome chill of the marble portals. The current darling of the glitterati is **Azzedine Alaïa** who, in 1991, was prevailed upon to design some gear for the city's **cheapest department store** – *Tati* (main branch at 13 place de la République, 11ᵉ. Mᵒ République). For **clothes to buy** without the fancy labels the best area is **the 6ᵉ**: round rue de Rennes and rue de Sèvres. The **department stores** *Galeries Lafayette* and *Au Printemps* have good selections of designer prêt-à-porter. The **sales** take place in January and July, with up to forty percent reductions on designer clothes. **Ends of lines** and **old stock** of the couturiers are sold all year round in discount shops concentrated in rue d'Alésia in the 14ᵉ and rue St-Placide in the 6ᵉ.

Discount

Azzedine Alaïa, 60 rue de Bellechasse, 7ᵉ. Mᵒ Varenne. His creations at half price. Mon–Sat 10am–6.30pm.

Le Mouton à Cinq Pattes, 8 & 18 rue St-Placide, 6ᵉ, and **L'Annexe** (for men) at no. 48. Mᵒ Sèvres-Babylone. Discounts on a wide range of big names. Mon 2–7pm, Tues–Sat 10am–7pm.

Secondhand and rétro

Rag Time, 23 rue du Roule, 1ᵉʳ. Mᵒ Rivoli. A veritable museum of superb dresses and high fashion articles from the Twenties to the Fifties. Expensive. Mon–Sat 2–7.30pm.

Rétro Activité, 38 rue du Vertbois, 3ᵉ. Mᵒ Temple. Dresses from 1930s to 1960s and men's suits from Fifties and Sixties – unbelievably cheap. Tues–Sat noon–7pm.

Department stores

Au Bon Marché, 38 rue de Sèvres, 7ᵉ. M° Sèvres-Babylone. Paris's oldest department store, founded in 1852. The prices are lower on average than at the chicer *Galeries Lafayette* and *Printemps*. Excellent kids' department and an alluring food hall. Mon–Sat 8.30am–8.30pm.

Au Printemps, 64 bd Haussmann, 9ᵉ. M° Havre-Caumartin. Books, records, a *parfumerie* even bigger than the rival *Galeries Lafayette*, excellent fashion department for women – less so for men. Mon–Sat 9.35am–7pm.

Galeries Lafayette, 40 bd Haussmann, 9ᵉ. M° Havre-Caumartin. The store's forte is, above all, high fashion. Two complete floors are given over to the latest creations by leading designers for men, women and children. Then there's household stuff, tableware, furniture, a huge *parfumerie*, etc – all under a superb 1900 dome. Mon–Sat 9.30am–6.45pm.

La Samaritaine, 75 rue de Rivoli, 1ᵉʳ. M° Rivoli. The biggest of the department stores, spread over three buildings, whose boast is to provide anything anyone could possibly want. It aims down-market of the previous two. Mon, Wed, Thurs & Sat 9.30am–7pm, Tues & Fri 9.30am–8.30pm.

Food

You can of course find sumptuous foodstores all over Paris; the listings below are for the **specialist places**, palaces of gluttony many of them, with prices to match. Buying food with a view to **economic eating**, you will be invariably best off shopping at the **street markets or supermarkets**, though save your bread buying at least for the local *boulangerie*. The cheapest supermarket, although with very limited choice, is *As-Eco* (11 rue Brantôme, 3ᵉ; M° Rambuteau) which stays open till 1am. Food markets are detailed at the end of this section.

The palaces

Fauchon, 26 place de la Madeleine, 8ᵉ. M° Madeleine. Carries an amazing range of super-plus groceries. Just the place for presents of tea, jam, truffles, chocolates, exotic vinegars and mustards, etc. An extensive wine cellar, too, and a self-service. Mon–Sat 9.40am–10pm.

Hédiard, 21 place de la Madeleine, 8ᵉ. M° Madeleine. Since 1850 the aristocrat's grocer. Several other branches throughout the city. Mon–Sat 9.15am–11pm.

Bread

Poilâne, 8 rue du Cherche-Midi, 7ᵉ. M° Sèvres-Babylone. Bakes to ancient and secret family recipes, but there is always a queue. Mon–Sat 7.15am–8.15pm. Also at 49 bd de Grenelle, 7ᵉ (M° Dupleix; Tues–Sun 7.15am–8.15pm).

Charcuterie

Divay, 50 rue du Faubourg-St-Denis, 10ᵉ. M° Château-d'Eau. *Foie gras, choucroute, saucisson* and suchlike. Tues–Sat 7.30am–1pm & 4–7.30pm, Sun 7.30am–1pm.

Goldenberg's, 7 rue des Rosiers, 4ᵉ. M° St-Paul. Superlative Jewish deli and restaurant. Sun–Fri 9am–midnight, Sat 9am–2am.

Cheese

Androuet, 41 rue d'Amsterdam, 8ᵉ. M° Liège. A huge selection, including foreign cheeses. Tues–Sat 10am–7pm.

Barthélémy, 51 rue de Grenelle, 7ᵉ. M° Bac. Purveyors of cheeses to the rich and powerful. Tues–Sat 8.30am–1pm & 4–7.30pm, closed Aug.

Chocolates and pâtisserie

Debauve and Gallais, 30 rue des Saints-Pères, 6ᵉ. M° St-Germain-des-Prés. A beautiful and ancient shop, specialising in chocolate and elaborate sweets. Tues–Sat 10am–7pm; closed Aug.

A la Mère de Famille, 35 rue du Faubourg-Montmartre, 9e. M^o Le Peletier. An eighteenth-century *confiserie* serving marrons glacés, prunes from Agen, dried fruit, sweets, chocolates and even some wines. Mon–Sat 7.30am–1.30pm & 3–7pm.

Salmon, seafood and caviar

Caviar Kaspia, 17 place de la Madeleine, 8e. M^o Madeleine. Blinis, smoked salmon and Beluga caviar. Mon–Sat 9.30am–12.30am.

Snails

La Maison de l'Escargot, 19 rue Fondary, 15e. M^o Dupleix. They even sauce them and re-shell them while you wait. Tues–Sun 8.30am–8pm; closed mid-July to end of Aug.

Vegetarian

Diététique DJ Fayer, 45 rue St-Paul, 4e. M^o St-Paul. Dietary, macrobiotic, vegetarian . . . one of the city's oldest specialists. Tues–Sat 9.30am–1pm & 3–7.30pm.

Wine

Les Caves de la Madeleine, Cité Berryer, 25 rue Royale, 8e. M^o Madeleine. Expensive, but one of the best-stocked cellars in Paris. The proprietor is Steven Spurrier of wine bar fame, and three of his "boys" are English. Mon–Fri 9am–7pm, Sat 9am–1pm.

Michel Renaud, 12 place de la Nation, 12e. M^o Nation. The other end of town and the other end of the scale from the Madeleine *caves* – superb value French and Spanish wines, champagnes and Armagnac. Mon 2–8.30pm, Tues–Sat 9am–1pm & 2–8.30pm, Sun 9am–1pm.

Music

Records, cassettes and CDs are not a particularly cheap buy in Paris, but you may come across selections that are novel enough to tempt you. Like the live music, there are Brazilian, Caribbean, Antillais, African and Arab albums that would be specialist rarities in London, as well as every kind of jazz. Bear in mind that the *Cité de la Musique*, soon to open in La Villette, will have a range of shops devoted to all things musical.

Blue Moon, 7 rue Pierre-Sarrazin, 6e. M^o Odéon. Exclusive imports from Jamaica and Africa: ska and reggae. Mon–Sat 11am–7pm.

Crocodisc, 42 rue des Écoles, 5e. M^o Maubert-Mutualité. Folk, oriental, Afro-Antillais, reggae, soul, country, new and secondhand. Low prices. Tues–Sat 11am–7pm.

Crocojazz, 64 rue de la Montagne-Ste-Geneviève, 5e. M^o Maubert-Mutualité. Jazz, blues and gospel. Tues–Sat 11am–1pm & 2–7pm.

Le Disque Arabe, 116bis bd de la Chapelle, 18e. M^o Porte-de-la-Chapelle. Very good range of Arab music. Mon–Sat 10am–8pm. Also at 125 bd de Ménilmontant (M^o Ménilmontant).

FNAC Musique, 4 pl de la Bastille, 12e. M^o Bastille. Stylish shop with touch-screen computerised catalogues, every variety of music, books, and a concert booking agency. Mon, Tues, Thurs & Sat 10am–8pm, Wed & Fri 10am–10pm. New branch planned for 24 bd des Italiens, 9e, with a greater emphasis on rock and popular music (phone ☎43.42.04.04 to check). The other *FNAC* shops (see above) also sell music and hi-fi.

Virgin Megastore, 56–60 av des Champs-Élysées, 8e. M^o Franklin-Roosevelt. FNAC's new competitor in the mainstream music market.

Sport

Au Vieux Campeur, 2 rue de Latran, 5e. Mon 2–7pm, Tues–Fri 9.30am–8.30pm, Sat 9.30am–8pm. Maps, guides, climbing, hiking, camping, ski gear, plus a kids' climbing wall.

Markets

Markets, like shops, are grand spectacle. Mouthwatering arrays of **food** from half the countries of the globe, intoxicating in their colour, shape and smell, assail the senses in even the drabbest parts of town. Though the food is perhaps the best offering of the Paris markets, there are also street markets dedicated to **secondhand goods** (the *marchés aux puces*), **clothes and textiles**, **flowers**, **birds**, **books and stamps**. Note that several of the markets listed below are described in more detail in the guide.

Flea markets (marchés aux puces)

Porte de Montreuil, 20ᵉ. Mᵒ Porte-de-Montreuil. Best of the flea markets for secondhand clothes – cheapest on Mon when leftovers from the weekend are sold off. Sat, Sun & Mon 7am–7pm.

Porte de Vanves, av Georges-Lafenestre/av Marc-Sangnier, 14ᵉ. Mᵒ Porte-de-Vanves. The obvious choice for bric-a-brac searching. Sat & Sun 7am–7pm.

St-Ouen/Porte de Clignancourt, 18ᵉ. Mᵒ Porte de Clignancourt. The biggest and most touristy, with stalls selling clothes, shoes, records, books and junk of all sorts, as well as expensive antiques. Sat, Sun & Mon 7.30am–7pm.

Flowers and birds

Place Lépine, Île de la Cité, 1ᵉʳ. This flower market transforms into a (rather unappealing) **bird and pet** market every Sunday. Daily 8am–7.30pm.

Place de la Madeleine, 8ᵉ. Flowers and plants. Tues–Sun 8am–7.30pm.

Place des Ternes, 8ᵉ. Flowers and plants. Tues–Sun 8am–7.30pm.

Books and stamps

Marché du Livre Ancien et d'Occasion, Pavillon Baltard, Parc Georges-Brassens, rue Brancion, 15ᵉ. Mᵒ Porte de Vanves. Secondhand and antiquarian books. Sat & Sun 9am onwards.

Marché aux Timbres, junction of avs Marigny and Gabriel, 8ᵉ. Mᵒ Champs-Élysées-Clemenceau. The stamp market. Thurs, Sat, Sun & hols 10am-dusk.

Food markets

Markets usually start between 7am and 8am and tail off mid-afternoon. The covered markets have specific opening hours, which are given below along with details of locations and days of operation.

Place d'Aligre , 12ᵉ. Mᵒ Ledru-Rollin. Tues–Sat.

Belleville, bd de Belleville, 20ᵉ. Mᵒ Belleville/Ménilmontant. Tues & Fri.

Buci, rue de Buci and rue de Seine, 6ᵉ. Mᵒ Mabillon. Tues–Sun.

Carmes, place Maubert, 5ᵉ. Mᵒ Maubert-Murualité. Tues, Thurs & Sat.

Rue Cler, 7ᵉ. Mᵒ École-Militaire. Tues–Sat.

Convention, rue de la Convention, 15ᵉ. Mᵒ Convention. Tues, Thurs & Sun.

Edgar-Quinet, bd Edgar-Quinet, 14ᵉ. Mᵒ Edgar-Quinet. Wed & Sat.

Enfants-Rouges, 39 rue de Bretagne, 3ᵉ. Mᵒ Filles-du-Calvaire. Tues–Sat 8am–1pm & 4–7.30pm, Sun 8am–1pm.

Rue de Lévis, 17ᵉ. Mᵒ Villiers. Tues–Sun.

Monge, place Monge, 5ᵉ. Mᵒ Monge. Wed, Fri & Sun.

Montorgueil, rue Montorgueil and rue Montmartre, 1ᵉʳ. Mᵒ Châtelet-Les Halles/Sentier. Daily.

Mouffetard, rue Mouffetard, 5ᵉ. Mᵒ Censier-Daubenton. Daily.

Porte-St-Martin, rue du Château-d'Eau, 10ᵉ. Mᵒ Château-d'Eau. Tues–Sat 8am–1pm & 4–7.30pm, Sun 8am–1pm.

Port-Royal, bd Port-Royal, near Val-de-Grâce, 5ᵉ. Mᵒ Porte-Royale. Tues, Thurs & Sat.

Raspail, bd Raspail, between rue du Cherche-Midi and rue de Rennes, 6ᵉ. Mᵒ Rennes. Tues & Fri.

Secrétan, av Secrétan/rue Riquet, 19ᵉ. Mᵒ Bolivar. Tues–Sat 8am–1pm & 4–7.30pm, Sun 8am–1pm.

As Eco, 11 rue Brantôme, 3ᵉ. Mᵒ Rambuteau. Supermarket open Mon–Fri 9am–1am, Sat 9am–11pm.

Le Cochon Rose, 44 bd de Clichy, 17ᵉ. Mᵒ Blanche. Groceries, fruit and veg, and *charcuterie*; Fri–Wed 6pm–5am.

La Favourite Bar-Tabac, 3 bd St-Michel, 5ᵉ. Mᵒ St-Michel. *Tabac* open Sun–Thurs 8am–3am, Fri & Sat 24-hr.

Le Terminus Bar Tabac, 10 rue St-Denis, 1ᵉʳ. Mᵒ Châtelet-Les Halles. 24-hr *tabac*.

The three **drugstores** (see p.218–19 for addresses) are open for books, newspapers, tobacco, and all kinds of gift gadgetry until 2am every night.

Saint-Germain, rue Mabillon, 6ᵉ. Mᵒ Mabillon. Tues–Sat 8am–1pm & 4–7.30pm, Sun 8am–1pm.

Tang Frères, 48 av d'Ivry, 13ᵉ. Mᵒ Tolbiac. Not really a market, but a vast emporium of all things Oriental, where speaking French will not help you discover the nature and uses of what you see before you. In the same yard there is also a Far Eastern flower shop. Tues–Sun 9am–7.30pm.

Ternes, rue Lemercier, 17ᵉ. Mᵒ Ternes. Tues–Sat 8am–1pm & 4–7.30pm, Sun 8am–1pm.

Eating and drinking

Eating and drinking is one of the chief delights of Paris. However, it's a sad fact that this most essential element of Parisian life is in decline. Many **cafés** have closed over the last decade, because of changes in lifestyle and rising rents, and neighbourhood brasseries and bistros face competition from the ever-burgeoning fast food outfits. But it's not gone yet, and you'll find you're still spoiled for choice. The different **restaurants and brasseries** are listed here under the same subheadings as are used to divide the city section, in three price categories, and in alphabetical order. You'll also find full lists of **vegetarian** (not Paris's strongest suit) and **late-night** possibilities.

Cafés

Cafés come in all forms: big ones, small ones, scruffy ones, stylish ones, snobby ones, arty ones. Crossroads and intersections are where they chiefly like to congregate, often side by side with the lookalike brasseries. All the main squares and boulevards have cafés spreading out onto the pavements, which are always more expensive than those a little removed from the thoroughfares. Addresses in the smarter or more touristy *arrondissements* set **prices** soaring. The Champs-Élysées and rue de Rivoli, for instance, are best avoided, at double or triple the price of a Belleville, Villette or lower 14ᵉ café. The most enjoyable are often ordinary, local places, but there are particular areas which café-lizards head for, most notably **boulevards Montparnasse** and **St-Germain** on the Left Bank, where you'll find the *Select, Coupole, Deux Magots* and *Flore,* the erstwhile hang-outs of Apollinaire, Picasso, Hemingway, Sartre, de Beauvoir and most other literary-intellectual figures of the last six decades. Most of them are still frequented by the big, though not yet legendary, names in the Parisian world of art and letters, cinema, politics and thought, as well as by their hangers-on and other lesser mortals. The location of other lively **Left Bank café concentrations** is determined by the geography of the university. Science students gravitate towards the cafés in rue Linné by the Jardin des Plantes, humanities in the place de la Sorbonne and rue Soufflot; and all the world – especially non-Parisians – finds its way to the place St-André-des-Arts and the downhill end of bd St-Michel. The **Bastille** is another good area to tour, livelier than ever as the new Opéra and rocketing property values bring headlong development. The same is true of **Les Halles**, though the latter's trade is principally among transient out-of-towners up for the bright lights. The much-publicised *Café Costes* and its rival, the *Café Beaubourg*, are here, Meccas of the self-conscious and committed trendies (*branchés* – plugged in – as they're called in French).

Café Beaubourg, 43 rue St-Merri, 4ᵉ. Mᵒ Rambuteau. Post-modernist clone of the *Café Costes* at 4 rue Berger, 1ᵉʳ. Expensive and sour service, but the location is prime. It shares its rival's loo fetish. Until 2am.

Au Bon Accueil, 15 rue Babylone, 7ᵉ. Mᵒ Sèvres-Babylone. A cosy characterful old-timer right next door to a good lunchtime restaurant, *Au Babylone*.

Le Chien Qui Fume, 19 bd du Montparnasse, 14ᵉ. Mᵒ Duroc/Falguière. Named after a real dog, an old and ordinary café that's a good refuge from its tourist-haunted neighbours.

La Coupole, 102 bd de Montparnasse, 14ᵉ. Mᵒ Montparnasse. Café/restaurant that's still a haunt of the chic and successful. Open until 2am; closed Aug.

Le Cochon à l'Oreille, 15 rue Montmartre, 1ᵉʳ. Mᵒ Châtelet-Les Halles/Étienne-Marcel. Classic little café with raffeta chairs outside and pictures in ceramic tiles inside. Opens at 4am for the local traders. Mon–Sat only.

Café de la Comédie, 153 rue Rivoli, 1ᵉʳ. Mᵒ Palais-Royal–Musée-du-Louvre. Small café opposite the Comédie Française, with a mirror painted with theatrical scenes at the back. Tues–Sun 10am–midnight.

Les Deux Magots, 170 bd St-Germain, 6ᵉ. Mᵒ St-Germain-des-Prés. In summer this picks up a lot of foreigners seeking the exact location of the spirit of French culture. Buskers galore play to the packed terrace. Open until 2am; closed Aug.

Le Flore, 172 bd St-Germain, 6ᵉ. Mᵒ St-Germain-des-Prés. The great rival and immediate neighbour of *Deux Magots*. Open until 2am; closed July.

Le Fouquet's, 99 av des Champs-Élysées, 8ᵉ. Mᵒ George-V. Long-established, expensive watering-hole for ageing stars, rich Lebanese and anyone else who has anything to hide behind dark glasses. 9am–2am.

Le Grand Café, 40 bd des Capucines, 9ᵉ. Mᵒ Opéra. A favourite all-nighter.

Iguana, corner of rue de la Roquette and rue Daval, 11ᵉ. Mᵒ Bastille. Colonial fans and trellises, brushed bronze bar counter and clientele reading récherché art reviews. A place to be seen in. Mon–Sat 10am–midnight.

Café de L'Industrie, 16 rue St-Sébastien, 11ᵉ. Mᵒ Bastille/Bréguet-Sabin. Rugs on the floor around solid old wooden tables and a young unpretentious crowd. Mon–Sat 9am–2am.

Ma Bourgogne, 19 place des Vosges, 3ᵉ. Mᵒ St-Paul. A quiet and agreeable stopover on the corner of the square, with proper meals, too.

Café de la Mairie, place St-Sulpice, 6ᵉ. Mᵒ St-Sulpice. A peaceful, pleasant, youthful café on the sunny north side of the square.

Café Notre-Dame, corner of quai St-Michel and rue St-Jacques, 5ᵉ. Mᵒ St-Michel. With a view right across to the cathedral. Lenin used to drink here.

L'Oiseau Bariolé, 16 rue Ste-Croix-de-la-Bretonnerie, 4ᵉ. Mᵒ Hôtel-de-Ville. Small and friendly, surreal paintings, full of Americans. *Plats du jour,* salads, Breton cider, omelettes. Open until 2am.

Café de la Paix, 12 bd des Capucines, 9ᵉ. Mᵒ Opéra. On place de l'Opéra, this is decorated in the sumptuous, Imperial style of the Opéra. Not the cheapest. Open until 2am.

Au Petit Fer à Cheval, 30 rue Vieille-du-Temple, 4ᵉ. Mᵒ St-Paul. Small classic friendly café with *plats du jour* for 50–65F. Noon–1am.

Le Petit Lappe, 20 rue de Lappe, 11ᵉ. Mᵒ Bastille. A simple café with a beautifully painted exterior, opposite the *Chapelle des Lombards*.

Le Petit Marcel, 63 rue Rambuteau, 3ᵉ. Mᵒ Rambuteau. Speckled tabletops, mirrors and Art Nouveau tiles, cracked and faded ceiling and about eight square metres of drinking space. Friendly barman and "local" atmosphere. Mon–Sat until 2am.

Au Petit Suisse, place Claudel, 6ᵉ. Mᵒ Luxembourg. An attractive small café on the corner of rue de Médicis by some excellent antiquarian bookshops.

La Périgourdine, corner of quai des Grands-Augustins and place St-Michel, 5ᵉ. Mᵒ St-Michel. A classic cane-chaired corner café, big and busy.

Le Pigalle, 22 bd de Clichy, 9ᵉ. Mᵒ Pigalle. 24hr bar, brasserie and *tabac*. A classic, complete with 1950s decor.

Le Select, 99 bd du Montparnasse, 6ᵉ. Mᵒ Vavin. The least spoilt of the Montparnasse cafés, and more of a traditional café than the rest. Open until 3am.

Bars

Though cafés are called *bars* or *cafés* without distinction, some drinking places are definitely more **bar-ish**, with cocktails, music and sometimes a transatlantic, gay or starlet flavour. All of them serve coffee, though, and food.

Broad Café, 13 rue de la Ferronnerie, 1ᵉʳ. Mᵒ Châtelet-Les Halles. Cocktails, snacks; a favourite gay pickup place. 5pm–3am.

La Champsmeslé, 4 rue Chabanais, 2ᵉ. Mᵒ Pyramides. A lesbian bar with some gay men, and a back room reserved for women; not very friendly to outsiders. Cocktails, picture/photo exhibitions and Thurs night cabaret. Mon–Sat 6pm–2am.

La Closerie des Lilas, 171 bd du Montparnasse, 6ᵉ. Mᵒ Port-Royal. A smart, arty, fashionable bar with good cocktails. The tables are name-plated after celebrated habitués, and there's a pianist in residence. Noon–2am.

Conways, 73 rue St-Denis, 10ᵉ. Mᵒ Châtelet-Les Halles. New York-style bar with photos of boxers and gyms on the walls and transatlantic food in the restaurant. Relaxed and friendly without being dull. Open until 1am.

Le Dépanneur, 27 rue Fontaine, 9ᵉ. Mᵒ Pigalle. A fashionable all-night bar in decked out in black and chrome.

L'Endroit, 67 place Félix-Lobligeois, 17ᵉ. Mᵒ Batignolles/Brochant. Smartish late-night bar serving the local trendies. Noon–2am.

La Mouette Rieuse, 66 place de la Réunion, Charonne, 20ᵉ. Mᵒ Alexandre-Dumas/Maraîchers. Co-op with live jazz and *chansons* on Fri and Sat nights. Tues–Sat 7pm–midnight, Sun 11am–2pm.

L'Opus, 167 quai de Valmy, 10ᵉ. Mᵒ Château-Landon. Stylish old warehouse with live classical music (from 10pm) while you sip cocktails. Music costs extra. 7.30pm–2am.

La Perla, 23 rue du Pont-Louis-Philippe, 4ᵉ. Mᵒ St-Paul. Mexican specialities in a spacious trendy corner café. Noon–2am.

Le Piano Vache, 8 rue Laplace, 5ᵉ. Mᵒ Cardinal-Lemoine. Long-established student bar with canned music and a relaxed atmosphere.

Café de la Plage, 59 rue de Charonne, 11ᵉ. Mᵒ Bastille. A multi-racial clientele and as many women as men in this low-ceilinged, youthful bar above a jazz club. Tues–Sun 10am–2pm.

Polly Magoo, 11 rue St-Jacques, 5ᵉ. Mᵒ St-Michel/Maubert-Mutualité. A scruffy all-nighter frequented by chess addicts.

Le Duplex, 25 rue Michel-le-Comte, 3ᵉ. Mᵒ Rambuteau. Young gay bar with an arty atmosphere. 8pm–2am.

Tigh Johnny, 55 rue Montmartre, 2ᵉ. Mᵒ Sentier. Mostly Irish bar that serves a reasonably priced Guinness and has impromptu Celtic bands. Daily 4pm–1.30am, last orders 12.30am.

Wine bars

Revitalised, ironically, by the English, **wine bars** have become an established part of the Paris scene. The attention to wine is serious and scholarly, and the object of the exercise is to make really good or interesting wines available by selling them by the glass. Traditional *bistrots à vin* like *Le Rubis* and *La Tartine* cater to everyone, but the newer generation have a distinctly yuppyish flavour, and are not cheap; nor is the food they serve.

Le Baratin, 3 rue Jouve-Rouve, 20ᵉ. Mᵒ Pyrénées. A good atmosphere and mix of people. Good wines from Cahors and cheap *plats du jour*. Wed 11am–9pm, Thurs–Sat 11am–1.30am, Sun 5pm–1.30am.

Le Baron Rouge, 1 rue Théophile-Roussel, 12ᵉ. Mᵒ Ledru-Rollin. Crowded and popular bar, serving cheese, *charcuterie,* and wines at reasonable prices. Tues–Sat 9.30am–1.30pm & 4.30–7.30pm, Sun 9.30am–1.30pm.

Aux Bons Crus, 7 rue des Petits-Champs, 1er. Mº Palais-Royal. A relaxed workaday place, much cheaper than the neighbours. Closed Sun.

Chez Georges, 11 rue des Canettes, 6e. Mº Mabillon. Attractive place in the spit-on-the-floor mode, with its old shop front still intact. Tues–Sat noon–2am; closed July 14–Aug 15.

L'Écluse, 15 quai des Grands-Augustins, 6e. Mº St-Michel. Forerunner of the new generation of wine bars, with décor in authentic traditional style – an agreeable place to sit and sip. Noon–2am.

Jacques-Mélac, 42 rue Léon-Frot, 11e. Mº Charonne. A highly reputed bar whose *patron* even makes his own wine – the solitary vine winds round the front of the shop. Auvergnat specialities for eats. Mon, Wed & Fri 9am–7.30pm, Tues & Thurs 9am–10pm. ˙

Aux Négociants, 27 rue Lambert, 18e. Mº Château-Rouge. Cheap good wines and snacks. Unsnobby. Mon–Fri 11.30am–9pm, closed July 15–Aug 15.

Café de la Nouvelle Mairie, 19 rue des Fossés-St-Jacques, 5e. Mº Luxembourg. A small, sawdusted bar in a quiet Latin Quarter street, with good wines, *saucisson* and sandwiches. Mon–Fri 10.30am–8.30pm.

Le Rallye, 6 rue Daguerre, 14e. Mº Denfert-Rochereau. The patron offers a bottle for tasting. Good cheese and *saucisson*. Tues–Sat until 8pm; closed Aug.

Le Rouge Gorge, 8 rue St-Paul, 4e. Mº St-Paul. Young clientele sipping familiar wines to the accompaniment of jazz or classical music. Tues–Sun noon–11.30pm.

Le Rubis, 10 rue du Marché-St-Honoré, 1er. Mº Pyramides. One of the oldest wine bars, with a reputation for the best wines, excellent snacks and *plats du jour*. Very crowded. Mon–Fri 7am–10pm; closed three weeks in Aug.

Au Sauvignon, 80 rue des Saints-Pères, 6e. Mº Sèvres-Babylone. Very small, with relaxed, unpretentious feel. Mon–Sat 9am–10pm; closed holidays, and Aug.

La Tartine, 24 rue de Rivoli, 4e. Mº St-Paul. The genuine 1900s article, which still cuts across class boundaries in its clientele. A good selection of affordable wines, plus excellent cheese, and *saucisson*. Wed–Mon until 10pm, closed Aug and Christmas.

Beer cellars and pubs

As their names and décor suggest, **beer-drinking** establishments owe their inspiration chiefly to their cross-Channel cousins and the Belgians. Most stock at least some British draught beers and a host of international bottles.

Académie de la Bière, 88bis bd Port-Royal, 5e. Mº Port-Royal. 120 and more beers from 22 countries. Also food – good mussels and fries, Belgian cheeses and *charcuterie*. Mon–Sat until 2am; closed Aug.

Gambrinus, 62 rue des Lombards, 1er. Mº Châtelet-Les Halles. Installed in the crypt of a thirteenth-century chapel, with thirty ceramic fonts for pulling draught beers.

Au Général La Fayette, 52 rue La Fayette, 9e. Mº Le Peletier. A dozen draughts, including Guinness, and many more bottled. Belle Époque decor, mixed clientele, and very pleasant, quiet atmosphere. Mon–Fri 11am–2am, Sat 3pm–2am.

La Gueuze, 19 rue Soufflot, 5e. Mº Luxembourg. Comfy surroundings: lots of wood and stained glass. Kitchen specials are *pierrades*: dishes cooked on hot stones. Numerous bottles and several draughts, including cherry beer.

Kitty O'Shea's, 10 rue des Capucines, 2e. Mº Opéra. An Irish pub with excellent Guinness and Smithwicks and a favourite haunt of the Irish expats. Noon–1.30am.

La Micro-Brasserie, 106 rue de Richelieu, 2e. Mº Richelieu-Drouot. A fashionable newcomer, brewing its own beer on the spot.

La Pinte, 13 carrefour de l'Odéon, 6e. Mº Odéon. Boozy and crowded, with piano and jazz. 6.30pm–2am; closed Aug.

Pub Saint-Germain, 17 rue de l'Ancienne-Comédie, 6e. Mº Odéon. 24-hr place with 21 draught beers and hundreds of bottles. Huge and crowded. Hot food at mealtimes, otherwise cold snacks.

Le Sous-Bock, 49 rue St-Honoré, 1er. Mº Châtelet-Les Halles. Hundreds of bottled beers and simple, inexpensive food. Frequented by night owls. 11am–5am.

La Taverne de Nesle, 32 rue Dauphine, 6e. Mº Odéon. Vast selection of beers. Full of local nightbirds. 7am–5am.

Le Violon Dingue, 46 rue de la Montagne-Ste-Geneviève, 5ᵉ. Mᵒ Maubert-Mutualité. A long dark student pub, noisy and friendly. Daily 6pm–1am– happy hour 6–9pm daily.

Salons de thé, ice cream and snacks

Snacks and light midday meals can be had in all the places listed below as well as in *brasseries* and most cafés. There are also innumerable **street stands** selling sandwiches, chips, pizzas, kebabs, etc, which are often the best bet of all for a cheap and filling snack. The classier cafés sell confections of cake and **ice cream**, as do the **drugstores** which stay open late and serve proper meals, too. The supreme sorbet experience is *Berthillon* on the Île St-Louis. **Salon de thés** have a chic and refined atmosphere, and don't limit themselves to tea.

Salons de thé and ice cream

Angélina, 226 rue de Rivoli, 1ᵉʳ. Mᵒ Tuileries. A long-established gilded cage for the well coiffed to sip the best hot chocolate in town, plus *pâtisseries* and other desserts of the same high quality. 10am–7pm; closed Aug.

Berthillon, 31 rue St-Louis-en-l'Île, 4ᵉ. Mᵒ Pont-Marie. The very best ice creams and sorbets made and sold here on the Île St-Louis. Also available at *Lady Jane* and *Le Flore-en-l'Île*, both on quai d'Orléans, as well as four other island sites listed on the door. Wed–Sun 10am–8pm.

Le Coquelin Aîné, 67 rue de Passy, 16ᵉ. Mᵒ Muette. Right on place Passy, meeting place of gilded youth and age. Excellent salads, *tartes*, cakes. Not for paupers. Tues–Sat 9am–6.30pm.

A la Cour de Rohan, 59–61 rue St-André-des-Arts, 6ᵉ. Mᵒ Odéon. A genteel drawing-room atmosphere in a picturesque eighteenth-century alley. Tues–Fri noon–7pm, Sat & Sun 3–7pm; closed Aug.

L'Ébouillanté, 6 rue des Barres, 4ᵉ. Mᵒ Hôtel-de-Ville. Very small, with reasonable prices and simple fare: chocolate cakes and *pâtisseries* as well as savoury dishes. Tues–Sun noon–9pm.

Fanny Tea, 20 place Dauphine, 1ᵉʳ. Mᵒ Pont-Neuf. Snacks as well as tea and cakes. Very small. In summer, tables outside in the beautiful seventeenth-century *place*. Tues–Sun 1–7.30pm; closed Aug.

La Fourmi Ailée, 8 rue du Fouarre, 5ᵉ. Mᵒ Maubert-Mutualité. Simple, light fare, including brunch at weekends, in this feminist bookshop-cum-*salon de thé*. Noon–7pm; closed Tues.

JeThéMe, 4 rue d'Alleray, 15ᵉ. Mᵒ Vaugirard. Obnoxious name and nostalgic décor, but sweets, salads and snacks served at reasonable prices and with rare grace. Mon–Sat noon–7pm; closed Aug.

Le Loir dans la Théière, rue des Rosiers, 4ᵉ. Mᵒ St-Paul. "The Dormouse in the teapot" with a mural of the Mad Hatter's tea party. Sunday brunch, midday *tartes* and omelettes, teas of every description and cakes all day. Tues–Sat noon–7pm, Sun 11am–7pm; closed Aug.

Café de la Mosquée, 39 rue Geoffroy-St-Hilaire, 5ᵉ. Mᵒ Monge. In fine weather you can drink mint tea beside a fountain and assorted fig trees in the courtyard of this Paris mosque – a delightful haven of calm. Mon–Thurs, Sat & Sun 10am–9.30pm.

La Pagode, 57bis rue de Babylone, 7ᵉ. Mᵒ François-Xavier/Sèvres-Babylone. A real-life pagoda – one of the most beautiful buildings in Paris in which to have tea. Tables in the Chinese garden in summer. 4–10pm.

La Passion du Fruit, 71 quai de la Tournelle, 5ᵉ. Mᵒ Maubert-Mutualité. An attractive *terrasse* opposite Notre-Dame, serving juice, sorbets, salads, milkshakes and teas – all made with fruit. Mon & Tues 6pm–1.30am, Wed–Sun noon–1.30am.

A Priori Thé, 35–37 galerie Vivienne, 2ᵉ. Mᵒ Bourse. Sip your tea outside but under cover in the watery lighting of a *passage*. Mon–Sat noon–7pm.

Rose Thé, 91 rue St-Honoré, 1ᵉʳ. Mᵒ Louvre-Rivoli. Calm and tranquil, in a courtyard of antique shops and faded bric-a-brac. Teas, milkshakes, *tartes aux fruits*, salads, etc. Reasonable prices. Mon–Fri noon–7pm.

Shake, 16 rue Daval, 11ᵉ. Mᵒ Bastille. Quiches, cakes and Périgourdian *plats du jour* for under 80F in a tiny, stylish salon. Mon–Fri 12.30–5.30pm & 8pm–midnight, Sat 7pm–2am.

Snacks

La Boutique à Sandwiches, 12 rue du Colisée, 8e. M⁰ St-Philippe-du-Roule. The best sandwiches in town, though certainly not the cheapest. Mon–Sat 11.45am–11.30pm; closed Aug.

Drugstore Elysées, 133 av des Champs-Élysées, 8e. M⁰ Étoile. 9am–2am; **Drugstore Matignon**, 1 av Matignon, 8e. M⁰ Franklin-Roosevelt, l0am–2am; **Drugstore Saint-Germain**, 149 bd St-Germain, 6e. M⁰ St-Germain-des-Prés. l0am–2am. All day food including huge, delicious desserts, along with books, newspapers, tobacco, and a multitude of fripperies. Prices are reasonable and the food much better than the decor would suggest.

Fauchon, 24 place de la Madeleine, 8e. M⁰ Madeleine. Narrow counters at which to gobble wonderful *pâtisseries, plats du jour* and sandwiches – at a price. Mon–Sat 9.45am–6.30pm.

Fleur de Lotus, 2 rue du Roi-de-Sicile, 4e. M⁰ St-Paul. Cheap Vietnamese dishes, heated up while you wait, to take away or eat on the premises. 10am–9pm.

Fous du Sandwich, 27 rue St-Louis-en-l'Île, 4e. M⁰ Pont-Marie/Sully-Morland. Soups, sandwiches and desserts on a cheap *menu fixe*. Tues–Fri 11.30am–3pm, Sat & Sun 11am–6pm.

Jarmolinska, 272 rue St-Honoré, 1er. M⁰ Palais-Royal. Polish delicatessen – to eat here or take away: blinis, potato pancakes, herring in dill and cream, borscht. Mon–Sat 9am–7pm.

Lina's Sandwiches, 50 rue Étienne-Marcel, 2e. M⁰ Étienne-Marcel. A spacious, stylish place for your designer shopping break. Mon–Sat 9.30am–5pm.

Monoprix, 23 av de l'Opéra, 1er. M⁰ Pyramides. Top-floor self-service; crowded, but good value. Open evenings as well.

Palais de Tokyo, 13 av du Président-Wilson, 16e. M⁰ Iéna/Alma-Marceau. Good food in the museum snack bar.

Aux Rendez-vous des Amis, 10 av Père-Lachaise, 20e. M⁰ Gambetta. Unprepossessing surroundings for satisfying post-cemetery munchies; around 80F. Mon–Sat noon–2.30pm; closed last two weeks of Aug.

Le Roi Falafel, 34 rue des Rosiers, 4e. M⁰ St-Paul. Take-out Egyptian. Dead cheap.

Self-Service de la Samaritaine, 2 quai du Louvre, 1er. M⁰ Pont-Neuf. In the number two *magasin*. More for the view over the Seine than the food. Mon–Sat 11.30am–6pm.

Sacha Finkelsztajn and **Florence Finkelsztajn**, 27 rue des Rosiers, 4e (Wed–Sun 9.30am–1.30pm & 3–7.30pm) and 24 rue des Écouffes, 4e (Mon & Thurs–Sun 9.30am–1.30pm & 3–7.30pm). Both M⁰ St-Paul. Gorgeous East European breads, cakes, gefilte fish, aubergine purée, tarama, blinis and borscht to take away.

La Table d'Italie, 69 rue de Seine, 6e. M⁰ Mabillon/St-Germain-des-Prés. Italian pasta, snacks, etc, at the counter, plus a grocery selling pasta and Italian delicatessen products.

Restaurants and brasseries

Contrary to what you might expect, **eating out** in Paris need not be an enormous extravagance. There are numerous decent fixed price **menus** for under 80F, and paying a little more than this gives you the chance to try out a greater range of dishes. Once over 150F mark, you should be getting some gourmet satisfaction. Our classification into these three main categories are based on the cheapest fixed-price menu available, and doesn't include drink. If you choose from the *carte*, bear in mind that you may well boost the bill into the next price category. Bear in mind also that this is the one part of France where you're not restricted to French food: the city's **ethnic restaurants** are not necessarily the cheapest, but the range is enormous. In fact the only rarity is food from the Indian sub-continent.

Student restaurants

Anyone in possession of an International Student Card or *Carte Jeune* (for the under 26s) is eligible to apply for tickets for the **university restaurants** under the direction of *CROUS de Paris* (39 av Georges-Bernanos, 5e; M⁰ Port-Royal). They will provide a list of addresses; tickets come in packs of ten and cost 21F each.

Champs Élysées

UNDER 80F

Bistro de la Gare, 73 av des Champs-Élysées, 8ᵉ (☎43.59.67.83). Mᵒ Franklin-Roosevelt. The food is okay, if somewhat plastic. Good for a quick and convenient meal, not for quiet intimacy. Daily noon–3pm & 6pm–1am.

Chez Mélanie, 27 rue du Colisée, 8ᵉ (☎43.59.42.76). Mᵒ Franklin-Roosevelt. Mon–Fri 11.30am–3pm. Simple French classic details in a tiny restaurant on the third floor.

UNDER 150F

Le Daru, 19 rue Daru, 8ᵉ (☎42.27.23.60). Mᵒ Courcelles. Where aged aristocratic Russian exiles come after services at the Orthodox Russian church opposite. Beef Stroganoff, borscht, pickled herring, shashliks, etc. Mon–Fri noon–11pm.

La Fermette Marbeuf, 5 rue Marbeuf, 8ᵉ (☎47.20.63.53). Mᵒ Franklin-Roosevelt. Original Art Nouveau décor in the tiled inner room. A well-heeled, bourgeois clientele. Daily until 11.30pm.

OVER 150F

Fouquet's, 99 av des Champs-Élysées, 8ᵉ (☎47.23.70.60). Mᵒ George-V. A classic name, like *Maxim's,* and outrageous for the price, but you can amuse yourself guessing who are literati and who's a gangster. Daily until midnight.

The Passages and Right Bank Commerce

UNDER 80F

Drouot, 103 rue de Richelieu, 2ᵉ (☎42.96.68.23). Mᵒ Richelieu-Drouot. Admirably cheap and good food, served at a frantic pace, in an Art Nouveau décor. Daily noon–3pm & 6.30–10pm.

Foujita, 45 rue St-Roch, 1ᵉʳ (☎42.61.42.93). Mᵒ Palais-Royal–Musée-du-Louvre. One of the cheaper but best Japanese restaurants. Quick and crowded. Mon–Sat noon–10pm.

L'Incroyable, 26 rue de Richelieu, 1ᵉʳ (☎42.96.24.64). Mᵒ Palais-Royal. Hidden in a tiny *passage*, this tiny restaurant serves decent and very cheap meals. Tues–Thurs lunchtime & 6.30–8.30pm, Sat & Mon lunchtime only; closed Sun & two weeks at Christmas.

UNDER 150F

Aux Crus de Bourgogne, 2 rue Bachaumont, 2ᵉ (☎42.33.48.24). Mᵒ Sentier. Good Burgundy *cuisine*, including lobster at reasonable prices.

Le Vaudeville, 29 rue Vivienne, 2ᵉ (☎42.33.39.31). Mᵒ Bourse. A lively late-night *brasserie* – where it's often necessary to queue – with good food and an attractive interior. Until 2am.

OVER 150F

Le Grand Véfour, 17 rue de Beaujolais, 1ᵉʳ (☎42.96.56.27). Mᵒ Pyramides. The carved wooden ceilings, frescoes, velvet hangings and late eighteenth-century chairs haven't changed since Napoléon brought Josephine here. Luxury cuisine. Mon–Fri 12.30–2pm & 7.30–10pm, Sat 7.30–10pm.

Les Halles to Beaubourg

UNDER 80F

Bistro de la Gare, 30 rue St-Denis, 1ᵉʳ (☎45.48.38.01). Mᵒ Châtelet-Les Halles. Daily noon–3pm & 6pm–1am. See under "Champs Élysées".

Aux Deux Saules, 91 rue St-Denis, 1ᵉʳ (☎42.36.46.57). Mᵒ Châtelet-Les Halles. Cheap if unexciting fare. Daily until 1am.

Le Petit Ramoneur, 74 rue St-Denis, 1ᵉʳ (☎42.36.39.24). Mᵒ Châtelet-Les Halles. Elbow-rubbing cheapie in good bistro tradition; always crowded. Mon–Fri until 9.30pm.

OVER 150F

Au Pied de Cochon, 6 rue Coquillière, 1ᵉʳ (☎42.36.11.75). Mᵒ Châtelet-Les Halles. For extravagant middle-of-the-night pork chops and oysters. Top of the price range. Open 24hr.

The Marais and Île St-Louis

UNDER 80F

Bistro du Marais, 15 rue Ste-Croix-de-la-Bretonnerie, 3ᵉ. Mᵒ St-Paul. A pleasant and inexpensive local.

Le St-Regis, 92 rue St-Louis-en-l'Île, 4ᵉ. Mᵒ Pont-Marie. The one unpretentious brasserie on the Île St-Louis.

UNDER 150F

Goldenburg's, 7 rue des Rosiers, 4ᵉ (☎48.87.20.16). Mᵒ St-Paul. The best-known Jewish restaurant in the capital; its borscht, blinis, potato strudels, *zakovski,* and other central European dishes are a treat. Daily until 11pm.

Auberge de Jarente, 7 rue Jarente, 4ᵉ (☎42.77.49.35). Mᵒ St-Paul. Hospitable Basque restaurant, serving excellent cassoulet, hare stew and *magret de canard.* Tues–Sat noon–2.30pm & 6.30–10.30pm.

OVER 150F

Au Franc Pinot, 1 quai de Bourbon, 4ᵉ (☎43.29.46.98). Mᵒ Pont-Marie. Tues–Sat until 11pm. *Nouvelle cuisine* and high-class wines at high prices, but still a bargain for this kind of cooking and for the seventeenth-century surroundings. Book well in advance.

La Petite Chaumière, 41 rue des Blancs-Manteaux, 4ᵉ (☎42.72.13.90). Mᵒ Rambuteau. Wonderful seafood dishes and other original recipes based on classic sauces, cooked by one of the best women chefs in Paris. Mon–Sat until l0pm, Sun evenings only; closed Aug.

Trocadéro to Les Invalides

UNDER 80F

Au Babylone, 13 rue de Babylone, 7ᵉ (☎45.48.72.13). Mᵒ Sèvres-Babylone. Lots of old-fashioned charm and good value. Mon–Sat lunchtime only; closed Aug.

Germaine, 30 rue Pierre-Leroux, 7ᵉ (☎42.73.28.34). Mᵒ Vaneau. Cheap and good, consequently very crowded. Mon–Fri lunchtime & 6.30–9pm, Sat lunchtime only; closed Aug.

UNDER 150F

L'Ami Jean, 27 rue Malar, 7ᵉ (☎47.05.86.89). Mᵒ Latour-Maubourg. Nice ambience and good Basque food. Mon–Sat lunchtime & 7–10.30pm.

Escale de Saigon, 24 rue Bosquet, 7ᵉ (☎45.51.60.14). Mᵒ École-Militaire. A small and inexpensive Vietnamese.

Au Pied de Fouet, 45 rue de Babylone, 7ᵉ. Good food in a tiny place: there are just four tables and no reservations. Mon–Fri 2–4pm & 7–8.50pm, Sat 2–4pm; closed Aug.

Thoumieux, 79 rue St-Dominique, 7ᵉ (☎47.05.49.75). Mᵒ Latour-Maubourg. A large and popular establishment in this rather smart district. Lunchtime & 7–11.30pm.

Quartier Latin

UNDER 80F

Le Baptiste, 11 rue des Boulangers, 5ᵉ (☎43.25.57.24). Mᵒ Jussieu. Noisy, friendly and full of students. Mon–Fri lunchtime & 7.30–10.30pm, Sat 7.30–10.30pm; closed last week in Dec.

Aux Savoyards, 14 rue des Boulangers, 5ᵉ (☎46.33.53.78). Mᵒ Jussieu. A delightfully friendly place, but likely to be packed. Mon–Fri until 10.30pm, Sat lunchtime only; closed holidays and Aug.

Bistro de la Sorbonne, 4 rue Toullier, 5ᵉ (☎43.54.41.49). Mᵒ Luxembourg. Help-yourself starters and salads, good ices and *crêpes flambées.* Copious portions. More expensive in the evening. Mon–Sat until 11pm.

La Vallée des Bambous, 35 rue Gay-Lussac, 5ᵉ (☎43.54.99.47). Mᵒ Luxembourg. You usually have to wait in line for this popular Chinese restaurant. The cheapest menu is excellent value. Open until 10.30pm; closed Tues & Aug.

UNDER 150F

Le Jardin des Pâtes, 4 rue Lacépède, 5ᵉ (☎43.31.50.71). Mᵒ Monge. A fresh and attractive pasta specialist – all homemade. Tues–Sun lunchtime & 7–10.30pm.

Le Liban à la Mouff, 18 rue Mouffetard, 5ᵉ (☎47.07.30.72). Mᵒ Monge. A pleasant and unusually cheap Lebanese restaurant.

Perraudin, 157 rue St-Jacques, 5ᵉ (☎46.33.15.75). Mᵒ Luxembourg. A well-known traditional bistro. Mon 7.30–10.15pm, Tues–Fri lunchtime & 7.30–10.15pm, Sun lunchtime only.

Le Petit Prince, 12 rue Lanneau, 5ᵉ (☎43.54.77.26). Mᵒ Maubert-Mutualité. Good food in a restaurant full of Latin Quarter charm in one of the *quartier's* oldest lanes. Evenings only, until 12.30am.

OVER 150F

Sud-Ouest, 40 rue de la Montagne-Ste-Geneviève, 5ᵉ (☎46.33.30.46). Mᵒ Maubert-Mutualité. Serious heavy eating: specialises in cassoulet and the cuisine of the southwest. Mon–Sat until 10.30pm; closed Aug.

St-Germain

UNDER 80F

Restaurant des Arts, 73 rue de Seine, 6ᵉ. Mᵒ St-Germain-des-Prés. A small, often crowded, friendly restaurant that serves simple, homely fare. Mon–Thurs all day, Fri lunchtime only; closed Aug.

Restaurant des Beaux-Arts, 11 rue Bonaparte, 6ᵉ (☎43.26.92.64). Mᵒ St-Germain-des-Prés. Daily lunchtime and evening until 11pm. The traditional hang-out of the art students from the Beaux-Arts across the way. The choice of food is wide, the portions generous, and the queues long in high season.

Orestias, 4 rue Grégoire-de-Tours, 6ᵉ (☎43.54.62.01). Mᵒ Odéon. Menu comprising Greek and French cuisine. Generous helpings and reasonably priced. Mon–Sat lunchtime & evening until 11.30pm.

Le Petit Mabillon, 6 rue Mabillon, 6ᵉ (☎43.54.08.41). Mᵒ Mabillon. Decent and straightforward Italian menu. Mon evening until 11.30pm, Tues–Sat lunchtime & evening until 11.30pm; closed mid-Dec to mid-Jan.

UNDER 150F

L'Alsace à Paris, 9 place St-André-des-Arts, 6ᵉ (☎43.26.21.48). Mᵒ St-Michel. A very busy *brasserie* right on the *place*.

Le Muniche, 27 rue de Buci, 6ᵉ (☎46.33.62.09). Mᵒ Mabillon. A crowded old-style *brasserie* specialising in seafood, smack in the middle of the St-Germain night scene. Noon–3am.

Le Petit Saint-Benoît, 4 rue Saint-Benoît, 6ᵉ (☎42.60.27.92). Mᵒ St-Germain-des-Prés. A simple, genuine and appealing local for the neighbourhood's chattering classes. Solid traditional fare. Mon–Fri lunchtime & 7–l0pm.

Le Petit Zinc, 25 rue de Buci, 6ᵉ (☎43.54.79.34). Mᵒ Mabillon. Excellent traditional food, especially seafood, in the middle of the Buci street market. Noon–3am.

Polidor, 41 rue Monsieur-le-Prince, 6ᵉ (☎43.26.95.34). Mᵒ Odéon. A traditional bistro, but not as cheap as it was when James Joyce used to eat here. Good food and great atmosphere. Mon–Sat until 1am; Sun until 11pm.

OVER 150F

Aux Charpentiers, 10 rue Mabillon, 6ᵉ (☎43.26.30.05). Mᵒ Mabillon. A friendly, old-fashioned place belonging to the Carpenters' Guild. Traditional *plats du jour* are their forte. Mon–Sat until 11.30pm, closed holidays.

Lipp, 151 bd St-Germain, 6ᵉ (☎45.48.53.91). Mᵒ St-Germain-des-Prés. A l900s *brasserie,* one of the best-known establishments on the Left Bank, haunt of the successful and famous. Until 2am; closed mid-July to mid-Aug.

Montparnasse to the Cité Universitaire

UNDER 80F

Aux Artistes, 63 rue Falguière, 15ᵉ (☎43.22.05.39). Mᵒ Pasteur. An old-time cheapie that has seen many a poor artist in its time. Still crowded and popular. Mon–Fri lunchtime & 7.15pm–12.30am, Sat 7.15pm–12.30am only.

Le Berbère, 50 rue de Gergovie, 14ᵉ (☎45.42.10.29). Mᵒ Pernety. Unattractive décor, but serves unfussy and cheap North African fare. Daily, lunchtime & evenings until 10pm.

Le Biniou, 3 av du Général-Leclerc, 14ᵉ (☎43.27.20.40). Mᵒ Denfert-Rochereau. A large variety of delicious *crêpes*. Lunchtime & 6.45–10pm.

La Criée, 54 bd Montparnasse, 15ᵉ (☎42.22.01.81). Mᵒ Montparnasse. Part of a good seafood and fish chain.

Au Rendez-vous des Camioneurs, 34 rue des Plantes, 14ᵉ (☎45.40.43.36). Mᵒ Alésia. No lorry drivers any more, but good food. Advisable to book ahead. Mon–Fri lunchtime & 7–9.30pm; closed Aug.

UNDER 150F

Bergamote, 1 rue Niepce, 14ᵉ (☎43.22.79.47). Mᵒ Pernety. A small and *sympa* bistro-style restaurant, in a quiet ungentrified street off rue de l'Ouest. You need to book at weekends. Tues–Sat lunchtime & evenings until 11pm; closed Aug.

Chez Maria, 16 rue du Maine, 14ᵉ (☎43.20.84.61). Mᵒ Montparnasse. *Zinc* bar, candlelight, posters, paper tablecloths – very pleasant. Evenings only, 8.30pm–1am.

N'Zadette M'Foua, 152 rue du Château, 14ᵉ (☎43.22.00.16). Mᵒ Pernety. A small and tasty Congolese – *manioc*, *maboké*, etc. Reservations required weekends. Mon–Sat evenings, until midnight.

OVER 150F

La Coupole, 102 bd du Montparnasse, 14ᵉ (☎43.20.14.20). Mᵒ Vavin. One of the best *brasserie* menus in perhaps the most famous and enduring hangout. Breakfast 7.30–10.30am, lunch noon–2am.

The 15ᵉ

UNDER 80F

Le Commerce, 51 rue du Commerce, 15ᵉ (☎45.75.03.27). Mᵒ Émile-Zola. A long-established restaurant catering for ordinary folk. Still varied, nourishing and cheap. Daily 11am–3pm & 6.30–10pm.

Auteuil and Passy

OVER 150F

Le Mouton Blanc, 40 rue d'Auteuil, 16ᵉ (☎42.88.02.21). Mᵒ Église d'Auteuil. Good traditional food in an establishment once patronised by Molière, Racine, La Fontaine and other literary aces of the time.

Bois de Boulogne

OVER 150F

Café de la Jatte, 67 bd de Levallois, Île de la Jatte (☎47.45.04.20). Mᵒ Pont-de-Levallois. The locale is unbeatable; the clientele is rich and elegant; the food excellent.

Parc Monceau to Batignolles

UNDER 80F

Port de Pidjiguiti, 28 rue Etex, 18ᵉ (☎42.26.71.77). Mᵒ Guy-Môquet. Very pleasant atmosphere and excellent food. Run by a village in Guinea-Bissau, whose inhabitants take turns in staffing the restaurant; the proceeds go to the village. Good value wine list. Tues–Sun only.

Sangria, 13 bis rue Vernier, 17ᵉ (☎45.74.78.74). Mᵒ Porte-de-Champerret. You can help yourself to starters and wine in addition to enjoying three other courses. Very popular and crowded.

Montmartre and the 9ᵉ

UNDER 80F

Casa Miguel, 48 rue St-Georges, 9ᵉ. Mᵒ St-Georges. A meal with wine for an unbelievable 5F. There's always a queue. Mon–Sat noon–1pm & 7–8pm, Sun noon–1pm.

Chartier, 7 rue du Faubourg-Montmartre, 9ᵉ (☎47.70.86.29). Mᵒ Montmartre. Brown linoleum floor, dark-stained woodwork, brass hat racks, mirrors, waiters in long aprons – the original décor of a turn-of-the-century soup kitchen. Worth seeing and, though crowded and rushed, the food is not bad at all. Until 9.30pm.

Fouta Toro, 3 rue du Nord, 18ᵉ (☎42.55.42.73). Mᵒ Marcadet-Poissonniers. A tiny, crowded Senegalese diner in a very scruffy run-down alley. Queues likely. 8pm–1am; closed Tues.

UNDER 150F

Chez Ginette, 101 rue Caulaincourt, 18ᵉ (☎46.06.01.49). Mᵒ Lamarck-Caulaincourt. Good food in a traditionally "Parisian" environment, with a pianist in the evening. Mon–Sat lunchtime & 7.30–11.30pm; closed Aug.

OVER 150F

Les Chants du Piano, 10 rue Lambert, 18ᵉ (☎46.06.37.05). Mᵒ Château-Rouge. Really good food and beautiful décor. Tues–Sat lunchtimes & evenings until 11pm; Sun lunchtimes only, Mon evenings only; closed last fortnight in Aug.

Flo, 7 cours des Petites-Écuries, 10ᵉ (☎47.70.13.59). Mᵒ Château-d'Eau. A handsome old-time *brasserie*, all dark-stained wood, mirrors and glass partitions, where you eat elbow to elbow at long tables. Excellent food and thoroughly enjoyable atmosphere. Until 1.30am.

À la Pomponnette, 42 rue Lepic, 18ᵉ (☎46.06.08.36). Mᵒ Blanche. A genuine old Montmartre bistro, with posters, drawings, zinc-top bar, nicotine stains etc. Expensive but worth it. Tues–Sat lunchtimes & evenings until 9.30pm, Sun evenings only; closed Aug.

Belleville and Ménilmontant

UNDER 80F

Au Trou Normand, 9 rue Jean-Pierre Timbaud, 11ᵉ (☎48.05.80.23). Mᵒ République. A very pleasant cheap local bistro. Mon–Fri lunchtimes & evenings until 9.30pm, Sat lunchtime only; closed Aug.

UNDER 150F

Égée, 19 rue de Ménilmontant, 20ᵉ (☎43.58.70.26). Mᵒ Ménilmontant. Greek and Turkish specialities served with fresh home-made bread. Noon–2.30pm & 7.30–11.30pm.

Mère-Grand, 20 rue Orfila, 20ᵉ (☎46.36.03.29). Mᵒ Gambetta. Very popular classic bistro offering a limited choice of dependable peasant dishes. Mon–Fri noon–2.30pm & 7–9.30pm; closed July.

Chez Justine, 96 rue Oberkampf, 11ᵉ (☎43.57.44.03). Mᵒ St-Maur. Good traditional cooking at very reasonable prices. Menus at 74F and 118F. Mon lunchtimes only, Tues–Sat lunchtimes and evenings; closed Aug.

Le Royal Belleville, 19 rue Louis-Bonnet, 11ᵉ (☎43.38.22.72) and **Le Président** (☎47.00.17.18; the floor above – entrance on rue-du-Faubourg-du-Temple). Mᵒ Belleville. A dramatic staircase leads up to *Le Président*, the more expensive of these two cavernous Chinese restaurants. You go for the atmosphere and décor rather than the food, though the spring rolls and rum banana fritters are acceptable. 11am–2am.

Aux Tables de la Fontaine, 3 rue des Trois-Bornes (☎43.57.26.00). Mᵒ Parmentier. On the corner of a cobbled shady *place*. Excellent uncomplicated fare at very good prices. Mon–Fri lunchtimes and evenings, Sat evenings only; closed Aug.

PARIS FOR VEGETARIANS

Aquarius, 54 rue Ste-Croix-de-la-Bretonnerie, 4ᵉ.

Country Life, 6 rue Daunou, 2ᵉ.

Au Grain de Folie, 24 rue La Vieuville, 18ᵉ.

La Macrobiothèque, 17 rue de Savoie, 6ᵉ.

Piccolo Teatro, 6 rue des Écouffes, 4ᵉ.

Restaurant Végétarien Lacour, 3 rue Villedo, 1ᵉʳ.

Tripti-Kulaï, 2 place du Marché Ste-Cathérine, 4ᵉ.

OVER 150F

Au Pavillon Puebla, Parc des Buttes-Chaumont, 19ᵉ (☎42.08.92.62). Mᵒ Buttes-Chaumont. Luxury cuisine in an old hunting lodge: poached lobster, stuffed baby calimari, duck with *foie gras*, spicy oyster raviolis etc. Mon–Fri noon–10pm.

Bastille to Vincennes

UNDER 80F

Chez Robert, 80 bd Richard-Lenoir, 11ᵉ (☎48.05.07.73). Mᵒ Richard-Lenoir, St-Ambroise. A leftover from the pre-Opéra days when this was a *quartier populaire*. Simple and satisfying fare. Daily noon–2.15pm & 7–9pm.

UNDER 150F

Chardenoux, 1 rue Jules-Vallès, 11ᵉ (☎43.71.49.52). Mᵒ Charonne. An authentic oldie, with engraved mirrors dating back to 1900, that serves solid meaty fare at a very reasonable price. Mon–Fri noon–2.30pm & 8–11pm, Sat 8–11pm; closed Aug.

La Mansouria, 11 rue Faidherbe-Chaligny, 11ᵉ (☎43.71.00.16). Mᵒ Faidherbe-Chaligny. An excellent Moroccan restaurant. Mon & Thurs–Sun lunchtimes and evenings until 11pm, Tues & Wed evenings only; closed for a fortnight in Aug.

OVER 150F

Bofinger, 3–7 rue de la Bastille, 3ᵉ (☎42.72.87.82). Mᵒ Bastille. A well-established and popular turn-of-the-century *brasserie*, serving the archetypal fare of sauerkraut and seafood. Daily until 1am.

The 13ᵉ

UNDER 150F

Hawaï, 87 av d'Ivry, 13ᵉ (☎45.86.91.90). Mᵒ Tolbiac. Everyday Vietnamese food, well appreciated by the locals. Particularly good Tonkinese soups, dim sum and brochettes. 11am–10pm; closed Thurs.

Thuy Huong, Kiosque de Choisy, 15 av de Choisy, 13ᵉ (☎45.86.87.07). Mᵒ Porte-de-Choisy. Chinese and Cambodian combinations such as fish and coconut cream, crackling salad and pancakes with mysterious spicy fillings. Noon–2.30pm & 7–10.30pm; closed Thurs.

Les Temps des Cérises, 18–20 rue de la Butte-aux-Cailles, 13ᵉ (☎45.89.69.48). Mᵒ Place-d'Italie, Corvisart. A well-established workers' co-op with elbow-to-elbow seating and a different daily choice of imaginative dishes. Mon–Fri noon–2pm & 7–11pm, Sat 7–11pm.

And over the top . . .

If you're feeling slightly crazed – or you happen on a winning lottery ticket – there are, of course, some really **spectacular Parisian restaurants**. For *nouvelle cuisine* at its very best, there's *Robuchon,* 32 rue de Longchamp, 16ᵉ, *Lucas Carton,* 9 place de la Madeleine, 8ᵉ, and *Taillevent*, 15 rue Lamenais, 8ᵉ, said to be the pinnacles of gastronomic experience, and not just for bills that can reach 10,000F for two. Unfortunately, the moment's madness that might inspire you to eat in any of these restaurants would most likely come months too late for you to make reservations.

LATE-NIGHT PARIS

CAFÉS AND SNACKS

Le Cochon à l'Oreille, 15 rue Montmartre, 1er. *Opens* at 4am.

Drugstore Élysées, 133 av des Champs-Élysées, 8e (p.128); **Drugstore Matignon**, 1 av Matignon, 8e (p.128); and **Drugstore Saint-Germain**, 149 bd St-Germain, 6e (p.129). All until 2am.

Le Grand Café, 40 bd des Capucines, 9e. All-nighter.

Le Pigalle, 22 bd de Clichy, 9e. 24-hr.

Polly Magoo, 11 rue St-Jacques, 5e. All-nighter.

Le Select, 99 bd du Montparnasse, 6e. Until 3am.

BARS AND BEER CELLARS

Broad Café, 13 rue de la Ferronnerie, 1er. Until 3am.

Le Dépanneur, 27 rue Fontaine, 9e. All-nighter.

Pub Saint-Germain, 17 rue de l'Ancienne-Comédie, 6e. 24hr.

Le Sous-Rock, 49 rue St-Honoré, 1er. Until 5am.

La Taverne de Nesle, 32 rue Dauphine, 6e. Until 5am.

RESTAURANTS

Aux Artistes, 63 rue Falguière, 15e. Until 12.30am.

Bistro de la Gare, 73 Champs-Élysées, 8e and several other locations. Until 1am.

Bofinger, 3–7 rue de la Bastille, 3e. Until 1am.

Chez Maria, 16 rue du Maine, 14e. Until 1am.

La Coupole, 102 bd du Montparnasse, 14e. Until 2am.

La Criée, 31 bd Bonne-Nouvelle, 2e and 54 bd Montparnasse, 15e. Until 1am.

Aux Deux Saules, 91 rue St-Denis, 1er. Until 1am.

Flo, 7 cours des Petites-Écuries, 10e. Until 1.30am.

Lipp, 151 bd St-Germain, 6e. Until 2am.

Le Muniche, 27 rue de Buci, 6e. Until 3am.

Le Petit Zinc, 25 rue de Buci, 6e. Until 3am.

Le Petit Prince, 12 rue Lanneau, 5e. Until 12.30am

Au Pied de Cochon, 6 rue Coquillière, 1er. 24hr.

Le Vaudeville, 29 rue Vivienne, 2e. Until 2am.

Music and nightlife

The strength of the Paris **music scene** is its diversity – a reputation gained mainly from its absorption of immigrant and exile populations. The city has no rivals in Europe for the variety of **world music** to be discovered: Algerian, West and Central African, Caribbean and Latin American sounds are represented in force. **Jazz** fans, too, are in for a treat, with new venues opening all the time, and all styles from New Orleans to current experimental, although in most clubs (*Le Dunois* is a rare, honourable exception) expense is a real drawback to enjoyment: admission charges are generally high and when they're not levied there's usually a whacking charge for your first drink, and subsequent drinks don't come cheap. One variety of home-grown popular music that survives is the tradition of **chansons**, epitomised by Edith Piaf and developed to its greatest heights by Georges Brassens and the Belgian Jacques Brel. This music is undergoing something of a revival. **Nightlife** recommendations – for **dance clubs and discos** – are to some extent incorporated with those for rock, world music and jazz, with which they merge. Separate sections, however, detail places that are mainly for dancing, or which cater for a primarily gay or lesbian clientele. Bear in mind that some clubs operate very snooty door policies. **Classical music**, as you might expect in this Neoclassical city, is alive and well and takes up twice the space of "jazz-pop-folk-rock" in the listings magazines. The Paris **Opéra** has a new palace with superb acoustics, if hideous exterior, at the Bastille. The need for advance reservations (except for the concerts held in churches) rather than the price is the major inhibiting factor here. If you're interested in the **contemporary** scene of Systems composition and the like, check out IRCAM at Beaubourg. At the end of the section are details of all the **stadium venues** for major events from heavy metal to opera.

Tickets and information

For exhaustive **listings of what's on** in the city, there are three weekly guides, published on a Wednesday: *Pariscope, L'Officiel des Spectacles* and *7 Jours à Paris. Pariscope* is probably the easiest to find your way around, but since all three are just listings, with a minimum of comment, there is not much difference between them. The best place to get **tickets** for concerts, whether rock, jazz, *chansons* or classical, is *FNAC Musique*, 4 place de la Bastille, 12ᵉ; Mº Bastille (Mon, Tues, Thurs & Sat 10am–8pm, Wed & Fri 10am–10pm) or the *Virgin Megastore*, 56–60 av des Champs-Élysées, 8ᵉ; Mº Franklin-Roosevelt (Mon–Thurs 10am–midnight, Fri & Sat 10am–1am, Sun 2pm–midnight).

Music venues

Most of the venues listed below are clubs. A few of them will have live music all week, but the majority host bands on just a couple of nights, usually Friday and Saturday, when admission prices are also hiked up.

Mainly rock

La Cigale, 120 bd de Rochechouart, 18ᵉ. Mº Pigalle (☎42.23.38.00). Rita Mitsouko, punk, indie etc, an eclectic programming policy in an old-fashioned converted theatre, long a fixture on the Pigalle scene. Music from 8.30pm.

Le Gibus, 18 rue du Faubourg-du-Temple, 11ᵉ. Mº République (☎47.00.78.88). For twenty years English rock bands on their way up have played their first Paris gig at Gibus, the Clash and Police among them. Fourteen nights of dross will turn up one decent band, but it's always hot, loud, energetic and crowded. It's also one of the cheaper clubs. 11pm–5am; Tues–Sat, Sat only in Aug.

La Locomotive, 90 bd de Clichy, 18ᵉ. Mº Blanche (☎42.57.37.37). Enormous hi-tech nightclub with two dance floors, one dedicated to British club scene sounds, the other to rock. Crowded and popular. Tues–Sun 11pm–5am. Concerts start at 1am. Tues–Fri 50F; Sat & Sun 90F.

Phil'One, Place de la Patinoire, 3ᵉ niveau, Parvis de la Défense (☎47.76.44.26); opposite CNIT building; Mº RER La Défense. An unprepossessing entrance and long corridor leads to one of the best clubs in Paris with a quirky musical policy encompassing Antillais, African, a bit of jazz and English and French rock, and a good mix of the well established and the new. Thurs–Sat, 10pm onwards.

Rex Club, 5 bd Poissonnière, 9ᵉ. Mº Montmartre (☎42.36.83.98). Tues, Wed & Fri–Sun 8.30pm–5am; sometimes closed Wed. Live music – rock, funk, soul, raï, rap (mainly on Tues and Sat from 8pm), charging 50–100F. Disco from 11pm, 60–90F.

Mainly Latin and Caribbean

L'Escale, 15 rue Monsieur-le-Prince, 6ᵉ (☎43.54.63.47). Mº Odéon. More Latin American musicians must have passed through here than any other club. The dance sounds, *salsa* mostly, are in the basement (disco on Wed), while on the ground floor every variety of South American music is given an outlet. 11pm–4am.

La Plantation, 45 rue de Montpensier, 1ᵉʳ (☎ 49.27.06.21). Mº Palais-Royal. In spite of the reputation for welcoming everyone, the doormen are fussy, particularly if you're white. Inside, excellent Cuban, Angolan, Congolese and Antillais music awaits you. Tues–Sun 11pm–dawn.

Les Trottoirs de Buenos Aires, 37 rue des Lombards, 1ᵉʳ (☎42.60.44.41). Mᵒ Châtelet. Argentinian tango is the only music performed on the stage of "the pavements of Buenos Aires". Drinks are very expensive and no one dances except professional artistes, but it's highly recommended. Tues–Sun 9.30pm onwards.

Bals musettes

Balajo, 9 rue de Lappe, 11ᵉ (☎47.00.07.79) Mᵒ Bastille. The old-style music hall of *gai* but straight *Paris* – extravagant 1930s décor, working-class Parisians in their weekend best and the music everything to move to from mazurka, tango, waltz, cha-cha, twist and the slurpy *chansons* of between the wars. Fri, Sat & Mon 10pm–4.30am.

Chapelle des Lombards, 19 rue de Lappe, 11ᵉ (☎43.57.24.24). Mᵒ Bastille. This erstwhile *bal musette* still plays the occasional waltz and tango but for the most part the music is salsa, reggae, steel drums, gwo-kâ, zouk, raï and the blues. The doormen are not too friendly but it's relatively cheap. Tues–Sat 10.30pm–dawn; bands Thurs–Sat only.

Le Tango, 13 rue Au-Maire, 3ᵉ (☎48.87.54.78). Mᵒ Arts-et-Métiers. The tango has been played here since the turn of the century and the décor looks as if it's retained layers from every decade since. No vetting, cheap admission and drinks, people dancing with abandon to please themselves, not the adjudicators of style. Wed–Sat 11pm–5am.

For afternoon dancing at the bals musettes, *see under "Afternoon Tangos" in the* Amusements *section.*

Mainly jazz

Les Alligators, 23 av du Maine, 15ᵉ (☎42.84.11.27). Mᵒ Montparnasse. A new, plush cocktail-style bar, with jazz on the stage. French and international musicians – Lee Konitz, for example. No admission charge, but 140F first drink. Mon–Sat 10pm–4am.

Baiser Salé, 58 rue des Lombards, 1ᵉʳ (☎42.33.37.71). Mᵒ Châtelet. A bar downstairs and a small, crowded upstairs room with live music every night from 11pm – usually jazz, rhythm & blues, Latino-rock, reggae or Brazilian. 8.30pm–4am.

Le Bilboquet, 13 rue St-Benoît, 6ᵉ (☎45.48.81.84). Mᵒ St-Germain. A very comfortable bar/ restaurant with live jazz every night – local and international stars, like baritone player Gary Smulyan. Music starts at 10.45pm. No admission; drinks 110F a shot. Mon–Sat 7pm–2.30am.

Le Dunois, 108 rue du Chevaleret, 13ᵉ (☎45.70.81.16). Mᵒ Chevaleret. Free and experimental jazz – and one of the few places in Paris to hear improvised music, as opposed to free jazz. Cheap and unsnobbish. Mon–Fri & Sun 8.30–11.30pm.

L'Eustache, 37 rue Berger, 1ᵉʳ (☎40.26.23.20). Mᵒ Châtelet-Les Halles.Cheap beer and very good jazz by local musicians in this young and friendly Les Halles café – cheapest good jazz in the capital. Mon–Sat 11am–4am; music from 10pm.

Lionel Hampton Bar, Hôtel Méridien, 81 bd Gouvion-St-Cyr, 17ᵉ (☎40.68.34.34). Mᵒ Porte-Maillot. First-rate jazz venue, with big-name musicians. Inaugurated by himself, but otherwise the great man is only an irregular visitor. Drinks from 120F. Mon–Sat 10pm–2am.

New Morning, 7–9 rue des Petites-Écuries, 10ᵉ (☎45.23.51.41). Mᵒ Château-d'Eau. Host to the big international names but not all it's cracked up to be. The sound is good but the décor, though spacious, is rather cold; no marks either for the ludicrous drink prices. 9pm–1.30am (concerts start around 10pm).

Le Petit Journal, 71 bd St-Michel, 5ᵉ (☎43.26.28.59). Mᵒ Luxembourg. Small, smoky bar, long frequented by Left Bank student types, with good, mainly French, traditional and mainstream sounds. Mon–Sat 10pm–2am.

Le Petit Journal Montparnasse, 13 rue du Commandant-Mouchotte, 14ᵉ (☎43.21.56.70). Mᵒ Montparnasse. Under the Hôtel Montparnasse, and sister establishment to the above, with bigger, visiting names, both French and international. Mon–Sat 9pm–2am.

Le Petit Opportun, 15 rue des Lavandières-Ste-Opportune, 1ᵉʳ (☎42.36.01.36). Mᵒ Châtelet-Les-Halles. It's worth arriving early to get a seat for the live music in the dungeon-like cellar where the acoustics play strange tricks and you can't always see the musicians. Fairly eclectic policy and a crowd of genuine connoisseurs. 9pm–3am; music from 11pm.

Le Sunset, 60 rue des Lombards, 1ᵉʳ (☎40.26.46.20). Mᵒ Châtelet-Les-Halles. Restaurant upstairs, jazz club in the basement, featuring the best musicians – the likes of Alain Jeanmarie and Turk Mauro – and frequented by musicians. Mon–Sat 9pm–5am.

Utopia, 1 rue Niepce, 14ᵉ; ☎43.22.79.66; Mᵒ Pernety. Good French blues singers interspersed with jazz and blues tapes playing to a young and studentish crowd. No admission charge and cheap drinks. Generally very pleasant atmosphere. Tues–Sat 8.30pm–dawn.

Mainly chansons

Le Caveau de la Bolée, 25 rue de l'Hirondelle, 6ᵉ (☎43.54.62.20). Mᵒ St-Michel. An ancient, ramshackle place where Parisian luminaries of the likes of Baudelaire used to go to hear their favourite singers. The music is still mainly *chansons* with occasional evenings of jazz. Affordable prices and a mainly student clientele. 9.30pm–6.30am.

Le Caveau des Oubliettes, 11 rue St-Julien-le-Pauvre, 5ᵉ (☎45.83.41.77). Mᵒ St-Michel. French popular music of bygone times – Piaf and earlier – sung with exquisite nostalgia in the ancient prisons of Châtelet. 9pm–2am.

Nightclubs and discos

Blue Moon, 160 bd St-Germain, 6ᵉ (☎46.34.01.04) Mᵒ St-Germain-des-Prés. The best reggae disco in town.

Le Cloître des Lombards, 62 rue des Lombards, 1ᵉʳ (☎42.33.54.09) Mᵒ Châtelet. 10.30pm–4am. More of a jazz club atmosphere though the music is definitely Caribbean.

Discophage, 11 passage du Clos-Bruneau (off 31–33 rue des Écoles), 5ᵉ (☎43.26.31.41). Mᵒ Maubert-Mutualité. A jam-packed and under-ventilated space, but all such discomforts are irrelevant for the best Brazilian sounds you can hear in Paris. Mon–Sat 9pm–3am, music begins at 10pm; closed Aug.

Le Malibu, 44 rue Tiquetonne, 2ᵉ (☎42.36.62.70) Mᵒ Étienne-Marcel. Around 150F. Black music from all over West Africa and the West Indies in a crowded basement beneath a restaurant. No strict admission policy: blacks outnumber whites and everyone is under thirty and well off. 8.30pm–5am.

L'Opéra Night, 30 rue Gramont, 2ᵉ (☎42.96.62.56) Mᵒ Richelieu-Drouot. A cinema during the day, transformed to a dance space every evening after the last film. Renowned for quality dancing to African and Caribbean funk, reggae and salsa. 11pm–5am.

Le Palace 999, 8 rue du Faubourg-Montmartre, 9ᵉ (☎.42.46.10.87). Mᵒ Montmartre. The best night out in Paris, packed nightly with revellers in their best party gear. Some nights it's thematic fancy dress, some nights the music is all African, other times the place is booked for TV dance shows. It's big, the bopping is good, and the clientele are an exuberant spectacle in themselves. Wed–Sun 11pm–dawn.

Whisky-a-Gogo, 57 rue de Seine 6ᵉ (☎.43.29.60.01). Mᵒ Odéon. This cellar bar currently plays Manchester-style dance music to flared French youth on the site of the original *Rock'n'Roll Circus* , where Jim Morrison made his last earthly appearance. Nightly 11.15pm–6am.

Lesbian and gay clubs and discos

Lesbian clubs find it hard to be exclusively female, and you may find that none of them are particularly agreeable. The pleasures of **gay men** are far better catered for, though AIDS has changed the scene and the wicked little bars with obscure backrooms around Les Halles have all but ceased to exist. Hi-tech, well-lit, sense-surround disco beat is the current style. For a complete rundown, consult *Paris Scene* (Gay Men's Press, £5.99) or the *Gai-Pied Guide*.

Women

Chez Moune, 54 rue Pigalle, 18ᵉ (☎45.26.64.61) Mᵒ Pigalle. In the red-light heart of Paris, this mixed but predominantly women's cabaret and disco may shock or delight feminists. The evening includes a strip-tease (by women) without the standard audience for such shows (any man causing the slightest fuss is kicked out). Sunday tea-dance afternoons from 4.30–8pm are strictly women-only. 10pm–dawn.

Entre Nous, 17 rue Laferrière, 9ᵉ (☎48.78.11.67). Mᵒ St-Georges. A small women-only club with an intimate atmosphere and catholic taste in music. Wed & Sat only 11pm–dawn.

Le Katmandou, 21 rue du Vieux-Colombier, 6ᵉ (☎45.48.12.96). Mᵒ St-Sulpice. The best-known and most upmarket of the lesbian nightclubs. Good music of the Afro-Latino variety, but not an easy place to meet people. 11pm–dawn.

Le New Monocle, 60 bd Edgar-Quinet, 14ᵉ (☎:43.20.81.12). Mᵒ Montparnasse. Revitalised women's cabaret. A scattering of men are allowed in every evening. 11pm–dawn; closed Sun.

Men

Bar Hôtel Central, 33 rue Vieille-du-Temple, 4ᵉ (☎42.78.11.42). Mᵒ St-Paul. An unfrenetic men-only bar catering mainly to over-30s. Midnight–2am.

Le BH, 7 rue du Roule, 1ᵉʳ; Mᵒ Châtelet-Les-Halles. Still one of the cheapest gay discos in the city; exclusively male. 10pm–6am.

The Broad Connection, 3 rue de la Ferronnerie, 1ᵉʳ (☎42.33.93.08). Mᵒ Châtelet-Les Halles. Young, chic and perennially popular. Next door, keeping the same hours, is the *Broad Side* cocktail bar – for quieter evenings. Tues–Sun 10.30pm–dawn.

Haute Tension, 87 rue St-Honoré, 1ᵉʳ (no phone). Mᵒ Châtelet. Discreet and rather subdued surroundings for a hot and sweaty bar-disco – a favourite with all gay men, irrespective of style and age. 11pm–dawn.

Le Piano Zinc, 49 rue des Blancs-Manteaux, 4ᵉ (☎42.74.32.42). Mᵒ Rambuteau. From 10pm when the piano-playing starts, this bar becomes a happy riot of songs, music hall acts and dance, which may be hard to appreciate if you don't follow French very well. It's one of the few venues patronised by both lesbians and gays. Tues–Sun 6pm–2am.

Classical and contemporary music

Paris is a stimulating environment for **classical music,** both established and contemporary. The former is well represented in performances within churches – often for free or very cheap – and in an enormous choice of commercially promoted concerts held every day of the week. Contemporary music, in the city that is home to Olivier Messiaen and Pierre Boulez, has an active and permanent base at the Beaubourg's *IRCAM* centre.

Concert venues

The **Cité de la Musique** project at La Villette has given Paris two new, major concert venues. The **Conservatoire,** the national music academy, has already opened its doors on av. Jean-Jaurès (information and bookings ☎40.40.46.46/40.40.46.47). Next door, a new **auditorium** due to be completed some time in 1992, and adaptable to all kind of novel configurations of instruments, will become home to *L'Ensemble Inter-Contemporain,* led by Pierre Boulez's orchestra.

These apart, the top **auditoriums** are: *Salle Pleyel,* 252 rue du Faubourg-St-Honoré, 8ᵉ, Mᵒ Ternes (☎45.63.88.73); *Épicerie-Beaubourg,* 12 rue du Renard, 4ᵉ, Mᵒ Hôtel-de-Ville (☎42.72.23.41); *Gaveau,* 45 rue de la Boétie, Mᵒ Miromesnil (xxxxxx); *Théâtre des Champs-Élysées,*15 av Montaigne, 8ᵉ, Mᵒ Alma-Marceau (☎47.23.47.77); and the *Théâtre Musical de Paris,* 1 place du Châtelet, 1ᵉʳ, Mᵒ Châtelet (☎42.33.44.44). **Tickets** are best bought at the box offices, though for big names you may find overnight queues, and a large number of seats are always booked by subscribers. The price range is very reasonable. Classical concerts also take place for **free** at *Radio France,* 166 av du Président-Kennedy, 16ᵉ, Mᵒ Passy (☎45.24.15.16).

Opera

The first performance of the Bastille opera house – the obscure, six-hour-long *Les Troyens* by Berlioz – cast something of a shadow on the project's proclaimed commitment to popularising its art. To judge the place for yourself, tickets (40–520F) can be booked Monday to Saturday 11am to 6pm on ☎40.01.16.16 or from the ticket offices (Mon–Sat 11am–6.30pm within two weeks of the performance). The cheapest seats are only available to personal callers; unfilled seats are sold at discount to students five minutes before the curtain goes up. For programme details phone ☎43.43.96.96.

Rather less grand opera is also performed at the **Épicerie-Beaubourg** in the Centre Beaubourg, and at the **Opéra-Comique**, Salle Favard, 5 rue Favard, 2e, M° Richelieu-Drouot (☎42.96.12.20). Both opera and recitals are also put on at the multi-purpose performance halls (see below).

Contemporary music: Pierre Boulez and IRCAM

Beneath the Beaubourg arts centre, the composer **Pierre Boulez** has been given space and funding to install a vast laboratory of acoustics and "digital signal processing" – a complex known as **IRCAM**. Here, amid banks of sophisticated synthesisers and computers, he and his team of scientists/technicians/musicians indulge in a "double dialectic" and study "psychoacoustics" towards "global, generalised solutions". To exactly what problems is unanswerable, but go and decide for yourself by playing around for free with tapes in the IRCAM lobby (entrance down the stairs by the Stravinsky pool on the south side of Beaubourg). If you're impressed, you might want to attend a performance by the resident *Ensemble Inter-Contemporain* (details from Beaubourg information desk).

Apart from Boulez, other names to look out for in this field are **Tod Machover**, also of IRCAM, **Iannis Xenakis and Olivier Messiaen**, at ninety the grand old man of Paris music. Concerts by any of these luminaries are quite regular events. Check *Pariscope*, etc, for details.

Festivals

Festivals are plentiful in all the diverse fields that come under the far too general term of "classical". The **Festival de Musique Ancienne** takes place at the end of May and beginning of June, and focuses on a particular civilisation or culture. The **Soirées de Saint-Aignan** at the Hôtel St-Aignan in May feature European music of the eighteenth and nineteenth centuries. There is also a **festival of sacred music** most years, a **Chopin festival**, a **Mozart festival**, and the *Festival de l'Orangerie de Sceaux* of chamber music all summer at the Château de Sceaux to the south of the city.

For details of these and more, pick up the current year's **festival schedule** from one of the tourist offices or the Hôtel de Ville.

The big performance halls

Events at any of the performance spaces listed below will be well advertised on billboards and posters throughout the city. Tickets can be obtained at the halls themselves, though it's easier to get them through agents like *FNAC* or *Virgin Megastore*.

Le Bataclan, 50 bd Voltaire, 11e. M° Oberkampf (☎47.00.30.12). One of the best places for visiting and native rock bands.

Forum des Halles, Niveau 3, Porte Rambuteau, 15 rue de l'Equerre-d'Argent, 1er. M° Châtelet (☎42.03.11.11). Varied functions – theatre, performance art, rock etc, often with foreign touring groups.

Maison des Cultures du Monde, 101 bd Raspail, 6e. M° Rennes (☎45.44.72.30). All the arts from all over the world and undominated for once by the Europeans.

Olympia, 28 bd des Capucines, 9ᵉ. Mᵒ Madeleine/Opéra (☎ 47.42.25.49). An old music hall hosting occasional well-known rock groups.

Palais des Congrès, place de la Porte-Maillot, 17ᵉ. Mᵒ Porte-Maillot (☎46.40.27.01). Opera, ballet, orchestral music, trade fairs and the superstars of US and British rock.

Palais des Glaces, 37 rue du Faubourg-du-Temple, 10ᵉ. Mᵒ République (☎46.07.49.93). Smallish theatre used for rock, ballet, jazz and French folk.

Palais Omnisports de Bercy, 8 bd de Bercy, 12ᵉ. Mᵒ Bercy (☎43.41.72.04). Opera, Bruce Springsteen, ice hockey, with seats to give vertigo to the most level headed, but an excellent space when used in the round.

Palais des Sports, Porte de Versailles, 15ᵉ. Mᵒ Porte-de-Versailles (☎48.28.40.10). Good place for seeing your favourite mega rock star in miniature half a mile away.

Zenith, Parc de la Villette, 211 av Jean-Jaurès, 20ᵉ. Mᵒ Porte-de-Pantin (☎42.08.60.00/ 42.40.60.00). Seating for six-and-a-half-thousand people in an inflatable stadium designed exclusively for rock and pop concerts. The concrete column with a descending red aeroplane is the landmark you should head for.

Film, theatre and dance

There are over 350 **films** showing in Paris in any one week, which puts moving visuals on an equal footing with the still visuals of the art museums and galleries. And they cover every place and period, with new works (excepting British movies) arriving here long before London and New York (and even big American films reach Parisian cinemas before London's). If your French is good enough for subtitles, go and see a Senegalese, Taiwanese, Brazilian or Finnish film that would never be seen in Britain.

Theatre can be less accessible to non-natives – especially the *café-théâtre* – but there is stimulation in the cult of the director (Peter Brook and other exiles, as well as the French), while, transcending language barriers, there are exciting developments in **dance**, much of it incorporating **mime**, which alas no longer seems to have a separate status.

Listings for all films and stage productions are detailed in *Pariscope* etc, with brief resumés or reviews. Venues with wheelchair access will say *"accessible aux handicapés"*. **Cinema tickets** rarely need buying in advance and are fairly cheap. Prices for **theatre tickets** vary between 70F and 150F on average and there are weekday student discounts. The easiest place to get **stage tickets** is at one of the *FNAC* shops (see above) or at two ticket kiosks: at the Châtelet-Les Halles RER station (Tues–Fri 12.30–7.30pm, Sat 2–7.30pm) and opposite 15 place de la Madeleine, 8ᵉ (Tues–Sat 12.30–8pm, Sun 12.30–4pm). They sell same-day tickets at half price, but queues can be very long. Most theatres are closed on Monday. **Booking** well in advance is essential for new productions and all shows by the superstar directors. These are sometimes a lot more expensive, quite reasonably so when they are the much-favoured epics, lasting seven hours or even carrying on over several days.

Cinema

Cinema-going in Paris is not exclusively an evening occupation: the *séances* (programmes) start between 1 and 3pm at many places and continue through to the early hours. The average price is 35F; most cinemas have lower rates on Monday, and reductions for students from Monday to Thursday. Some matinée *séances* also have discounts. All are **non-smoking**, and some have unwaged ushers who need to be tipped. Almost all of the huge selection of foreign films will be shown at some cinemas in the original – *v.o.* in the listings as opposed to *v.f.*, which means it's dubbed into French (*v.a.* means it's the English version of an international co-production).

An **International Festival of Women's Films** takes place at the end of March or beginning of April, organised by the *Maison des Arts* in Créteil, a southeastern suburb at the end of the Balard-Créteil métro line. Programme details are available from mid-March onwards, from the *Maison des Arts* on place Salvador-Allende, Créteil; M° Créteil-Préfecture (☎49.80.18.88), or from the *Maison des Femmes* (see below).

Cinemas

Cosmos, 76 rue de Rennes, 6e. M° St-Sulpice. Specialises in Soviet movies.

L'Escurial Panoramas, 11 bd de Port-Royal, 13e. M° Gobelins. A cinema that combines plush seats, a panoramic screen and more art than commerce in its screening policy (and films are never dubbed).

Le Grand Rex, 1 bd Poissonnière, 2e. M° Bonne-Nouvelle. Just as outrageous as the *Pagode* (see below), but in the kitsch line, with a Metropolis-style tower blazing its neon name, 2800 seats and a ceiling of stars and city skylines, plus flying whales and dolphins, all as a frame for the largest cinema screen in Europe.

Max Linder Panorama, 24 bd Poissonnière, 9e. M° Bonne-Nouvelle. Opposite *Le Grand Rex*, this always shows films in the original, and has almost as big a screen, state-of-the-art sound, and Art Déco décor.

L'Olympic Entrepôt, 7–9 rue Francis-de-Pressensé, 14e. M° Pernety. One of the best alternative Paris movie houses, which has been keeping ciné-addicts happy for years with its three screens dedicated to the obscure, the subversive and the brilliant. It also shows videos, satellite and cable TV, has a bookshop (Mon–Sat 2–8pm) and a restaurant (daily noon–midnight).

La Pagode, 57bis rue de Babylone, 7e. M° François-Xavier. The most beautiful of the city's cinemas, transplanted from Japan at the turn of the century to be a rich Parisienne's party place. The wall panels of the *Grande Salle* are embroidered in silk; golden dragons and elephants hold up the candelabra; and a battle between Japanese and Chinese warriors rages on the ceiling.

Le Studio 28, 10 rue de Tholozé, 18e. M° Blanche/Abbesses. In its early days, after one of the first showings of Bunuel's *L'Age d'Or*, this was done over by extreme right-wing Catholics who destroyed the screen and the paintings by Dali and Ernst in the foyer. The cinema still hosts avant-garde premières, followed occasionally by discussions with the director, as well as regular festivals.

Cinémathèques

For the seriously committed film-freak, the best movie venues in Paris are the **cinémathèques**: in the *Salle Garance* on the top floor of Beaubourg, 4e, M° Rambuteau (closed Tues); the *Cinémathèque Française* in the *Musée du Cinéma*, Palais de Chaillot, corner of avs Président-Wilson and Albert-de-Mun, 16e, M° Trocadéro; and in the Palais de Tokyo, 13 av du Président-Wilson, 16e, M° Trocadéro, with screenings every day. These give you a choice of over fifty different films a week, many of which would never be shown commercially, and tickets are only 20F. In 1994 a new *Palais des Arts de l'Image* is due to open in the Palais de Tokyo, with four cinemas amongst its treats.

The largest screen

There is one cinematic experience that has to be recommended, however trite and vain-glorious the film, **La Géode**, the mirrored globe bounced off the *Cité des Sciences* at La Villette. The 180-degree projection system is called Omnimax; there are less than a dozen of these things in existence, and their owners are not the sort to produce brilliant films. What you get is a Readers' Digest view of outer space, great cities of the world, monumental landscapes or whatever, on a screen wider than your range of vision into which you feel you might fall at any moment. Low-flying shots or shots from the front of moving trains, bobsleighs, cars etc are sensational.

There are several screenings a day, but you usually need to book in advance (Tues–Sun 10am–9pm; tickets 45F/35F or 70F/60F for combined ticket with *Cité des Sciences*; reservations ☎46.42.13.13; M° Porte-de-la- Villette/Corentin-Cariou). The film remains the same for months at a time (listed in *Pariscope* etc, under the 19ᵉ *arrondissement*), and not understanding French is a positive advantage.

Drama

Bourgeois farces, postwar classics, Shakespeare, Racine – all are staged with the same range of talent or lack of it that you'd find in London or New York. What you'll rarely find are home-grown, socially concerned and realist dramas. But foreign companies are always welcomed to the city, particularly for the **Festival d'Automne** from October to December.

The best contemporary work emanating from the city is from the superstar breed of directors such as **Peter Brook** at the *Bouffes du Nord* and **Ariane Mnouchkine** at the *Cartoucherie Théâtre du Soleil*. They treat playwrights as anachronisms and classic texts as packs of cards to be shuffled into theatrical moments where spectacular and dazzling sensation take precedence over speech. These are the shows to go to see: huge casts, extraordinary sets, overwhelming sound and light effects – an experience, even if you haven't understood a word. Many of the best productions are out in the suburbs but don't let that put you off.

Venues

Bouffes du Nord, 37bis bd de la Chapelle, 10ᵉ. Mᵒ Chapelle (☎46.07.34.50). Peter Brook has made this his permanent base in Paris, where he produces such events as the nine-hour show of the Indian epic *Mahabharata*.

Cartoucherie Théâtre du Soleil, rte du Champ-de-Manoeuvre, 12ᵉ. Mᵒ Château-de-Vincennes (☎43.74.24.08). The most memorable recent production of Russian-born Ariane Mnouchkine's workers' co-op company was the epic combination of Euripides and Aeschylus in *Les Atrides* (the House of Atreus).

Comédie Française, 2 rue Richelieu, 1ᵉʳ. Mᵒ Palais-Royal (☎40.15.00.15). The national theatre for the classics.

Odéon Théâtre de l'Europe, 1 place Paul-Claudel, 6ᵉ. Mᵒ Odéon (☎43.25.70.32). Roger Planchon's Lyon-based *Théâtre National Populaire* puts on its Paris performances on the main stage, while the smaller stage, the *Petit Odéon*, hosts foreign-language plays. In May 1968 this theatre was occupied by students and became an open parliament.

Renaud-Barrault at the **Rond-Point**, av Franklin-Roosevelt, 16ᵉ. Mᵒ Franklin-Roosevelt (☎42.56.60.70). The permanent home for the Renaud-Barrault troupe, where their performances of Beckett are unequalled.

Théâtre des Amandiers, 7 av Pablo-Picasso, Nanterre, 92. RER Nanterre-Université and theatre bus (☎47.21.18.81). The suburban base for Patrice Chéreau's exciting productions.

Théâtre de la Bastille, 79 rue de la Roquette, 11ᵉ. Mᵒ Bastille (☎43.57.42.14). One of the best places for new work and fringe productions.

Théâtre de la Colline, 15 rue Malte-Brun, 20ᵉ. Mᵒ Gambetta (☎43.66.43.60). The repertoire includes epic directors' works as well as less well-established innovators.

Théâtre National de Chaillot, Palais de Chaillot, pl du Trocadéro, 16ᵉ. Mᵒ Trocadéro (☎47.27.81.15). The great Antoine Vitez is no more, but the mega-spectacles go on.

Dance and mime

In the 1970s all the dancers left Paris for New York, and only **mime** remained as the great performing art of the French, thanks to the Lecoq school of Mime and Improvisation, and the famous practitioner, Marcel Marceau. Since Marceau's demise, no new mime artists of his stature have appeared. While pure mime is rarely seen (except on the streets, and Beaubourg's piazza in particular), a multi-dimensional performing art has been created by combining movement, mime, ballet, music from the medieval to contemporary jazz-rock, speech, noise and theatrical effects.

Many of the theatres listed above under drama include these new forms in their programmes. Plenty of space and critical attention is also given to tap, **tango, folk and jazz dancing**, and to visiting traditional dance troupes from all over the world. As for **ballet**, the principal stage is at the old opera house, the Opéra Garnier, with other major productions at the *Théâtre des Champs-Élysées* and the *Théâtre Musical de Paris*.

The **highlight of the year** is the *Festival International de Danse de Paris* in October and November, which involves contemporary, classical and different national traditions. Other **festivals** combining theatre, dance, mime, classical music and its descendants, include the *Festival du Marais* in June, the *Festival "Foire Saint-Germain"* in June and July and the *Festival d'Automne* from mid-September to mid-December.

Venues

Centre Mandapa, 6 rue Wurtz, 13e. Mo Glacière (☎45.89.01.60). The one theatre dedicated to traditional dances from around the world.

Le Déjazet, 41 bd du Temple, 3e. Mo République (☎48.87.97.34). Experimental dance productions, with the emphasis on mime.

Opéra de Paris-Garnier, place de l'Opéra, 9e. Mo Opéra (☎47.42.53.71). Now that the Bastille opera house has opened, this is given over exclusively to ballet.

Théâtre des Champs-Élysées, 15 av Montaigne, 8e. Mo Alma-Marceau (☎47.23.47.77). Forever aiming to outdo the *Opéra* with even grander and more expensive ballet productions.

Théâtre Contemporain de la Danse, 9 rue Geoffroy-l'Asnier, 4e. Mo Pont-Marie (☎42.74.44.22). Still innovative, but with more assured critical appeal than the performances at the *Café de la Danse*.

Théâtre Musical de Paris, place du Châtelet (☎40.28.28.40). A major ballet venue, where, in 1910, Diaghilev put on the first season of Russian ballet, assisted by Cocteau, Rodin, Proust and others.

Café-Théâtre

Literally a revue, monologue or mini-play performed in a place where you can drink, and sometimes eat, **café-théâtre** is probably less accessible than a Racine tragedy at the *Comédie-Française*. The humour or puerile dirty jokes, word-play and allusions to current fads, phobias and politicians can leave even a fluent French-speaker in the dark. If you want to give it a try, though, the main venues are concentrated around the Marais. Tickets average around 60F and it's best to book in advance – the spaces are small – though you have a good chance of getting in on the night during the week.

Blancs-Manteaux, 15 rue des Blancs-Manteaux, 4e. Mo Hôtel-de-Ville/Rambuteau (☎48.87.15.84). Somewhat cramped venue, beneath a restaurant.

Café de la Gare, 41 rue du Temple, 4e. Mo Hôtel-de-Ville/Rambuteau (☎42.78.52.51). This may not be operating its turn-of-the-wheel admission price system any more, but it has retained a reputation for novelty.

Listings

Airlines *Air France*, 119 av des Champs-Élysées, 8e (☎45.35.61.61); *Air Inter*, 12 rue Castiglione, 1er (☎42.60.36.46); *British Airways*, 91 av des Champs-Élysées, 8e (☎47.78.14.14). Full lists of the rest from any tourist office.

Babysitting There are two main agencies, both with English speakers: *Ababa* (☎45.49.46.46) and *Allo Maman Poule* (☎47.47.78.78). Apart from these, you could try the notices at the American Church, 65 quai d'Orsay, 6e, or, if you know someone with a phone, dial Babysitting on "Elletel" via *minitel*.

Banks and change To change money outside normal banking hours, the *Crédit Commercial de France*, 103 Champs-Élysées, 8e, is open on Sat until 8pm. At 66 av des Champs-Elysées, the 24-hour automatic exchange machine of the *Banque Régionale d'Escompte* accepts £10 and £20 notes, as well as dollars. The money exchange counter in the Gare du Nord is open until 10pm on weekdays, those at other stations until 8pm. Most of the major British banks have Paris branches – check the phone book in a post office for your nearest one.

Bike hire see "Getting Around the City".

Car hire and repairs see "Getting Around the City".

Chemists 24-hour service at *Dhery*, 84 av des Champs-Élysées, 8ᵉ, Mᵒ Charles-de-Gaulle Étoile (☎45.62.02.41).

Consulates/Embassies *Australia*, 4 rue Jean-Rey, 15ᵉ (☎40.59.33.00); *Britain*, 16 rue d'Anjou, 8ᵉ, Mᵒ Madeleine (☎42.96.87.19); *Canada*, 35 av Montaigne, 8ᵉ (☎47.23.01.01); *Ireland*, 12 av Foch, 16ᵉ, enter from 4 rue Rude (☎45.0089.43); *Netherlands*, 7–9 rue Eblé, 7ᵉ, Mᵒ St-François-Xavier (☎43.06.61.88); *New Zealand*, 7 rue Léonardo-de-Vinci, 16ᵉ (☎45.00. 24.11); *Sweden*, 17 rue Barbet-de-Jouy, 7ᵉ, Mᵒ Varenne (☎45.55.92.15); *USA*, 2 av Gabriel, 8ᵉ (☎42.96.12.02).

Dental treatment Emergency service: *Urgences Dentaires*, 9 bd St-Marcel, 13ᵉ, Mᵒ St-Marcel (☎47.07.44.44).

Emergencies *SOS-Médecins* (☎47.07.77.77) for 24-hour medical help; ☎18 or ☎45.67.50.50 for **24-hour ambulance service**.

Feminism Best place to make contact is the *Maison des Femmes*, 8 Cité Prost, off rue Chanzy, 11ᵉ, Mᵒ Faidherbe-Chaligny (☎43.48.24.91). It's run by *Paris-Féministes* who produce a fortnightly bulletin and organise a wide range of events and actions. It's also home to the lesbian group *MIEL* (*Mouvement d'Information et d'Expression des Lesbiennes;* ☎43.79.61.91, answering machine ☎43.79.66.07). A cafeteria run by *MIEL* operates most Friday evenings. Don't be put off by the back-alley entrance, and don't expect English speakers. See also details of the feminist library in the 13ᵉ (p.100).

Festivals There's not much in the carnival line, though kids armed with bags of flour and aiming to make a total fool of you appear on the streets during Mardi Gras (in Feb). There are marching bands and street performers and Gay Pride for the Summer Solstice (June 21), and July 14 (Bastille Day) is celebrated with official pomp in parades of tanks down the Champs-Élysées, firework displays and concerts. The French Communist Party hosts an annual Fête de l'Humanité in September at La Courneuve, just north of Paris, with representatives of just about every CP or ex-CP in the world and information tables, bands and eats that bring in Parisians of most political persuasions, and good times had by all.

Gay and lesbian life A few bars and clubs are listed in the "Nightlife" and "Eating & Drinking" sections. There are numerous gay organisations (far fewer lesbian ones): best place for information is the main gay and lesbian bookshop, *Les Mots à la Bouche*, 6 rue St-Croix-de-la-Bretonnerie, 4ᵉ; Mᵒ Hôtel-de-Ville. The Gay Switchboard equivalent is *SOS Gais* and *SOS Lesbia* (☎42.61.00.00; women Sat afternoons only).

Hitching out *Allostop*, 84 passage Brady, 10ᵉ (Mon–Fri 9am–7.30pm, Sat 9am–1pm and 2–6pm; ☎42.46.00.66).

Language schools French lessons from the *Alliance Française*, 101 bd Raspail, 6ᵉ, and numerous other establishments. A full list, *Cours de Français pour Étudiants Étrangers*, is obtainable from embassy cultural sections.

Launderettes Self-service places have multiplied in Paris over the last few years, and you'll probably find one near where you're staying.

Left Luggage There are lockers at all train stations and *consigne* for bigger items or longer periods.

Lost Bagage Orly: ☎46.75.40.38; Mᵒ Roissy/Charles de Gaulle: ☎48.62.12.12.

Libraries The British Council, 9 rue de Constantine, 7ᵉ, Mᵒ Invalides, and the US Institute, 10 rue du Général-Camou, 7ᵉ, Mᵒ Ecole-Militaire, have free access libraries, with daily newspapers. Interesting French collections include the *BPI* at Beaubourg (vast, including all the foreign press), *Forney* (books being a good excuse if you want to visit the medieval bishop's palace at 1 rue Figuier in the 4ᵉ), and the *Historique de la Ville de Paris*, a sixteenth-century mansion housing centuries of texts and picture books on the city at 24 rue Pavée, 4ᵉ.

Lost property Bureau des Objets Trouvés, 36 rue des Morillons, 15ᵉ, Mᵒ Convention (Mon–Fri 8.30am–5pm; ☎45.31.14.80).

Petrol 24-hr filling stations are *Garage St-Honoré*, 58 pl du Marché, St-Honoré, 1ᵉʳ; *Shell*, 109 rue de Rennes, 6ᵉ; 1 bd de la Chapelle, 10ᵉ; 4 av Foch, 16ᵉ; *Total*, 95 av des Champs-Élysées, 8ᵉ.

Police Dial ☎17 for emergencies. The main *Préfécture,* if you need to report a theft, is at 7 bd du Palais, 4ᵉ (☎42.60.33.22).

Post office Main office at 52 rue du Louvre, Paris 75001, M° Châtelet-Les-Halles: open 24hr for telephones and poste restante.

Train information See "Getting Around the City".

Travel firms *USIT Voyages*, 6 rue de Vaugirard, 15°, M° Odéon (☎42.96.15.88), is an excellent and dependable student–youth agency. *Nouvelles Frontières*, 66 bd St-Michel, 6° (☎46.34.55.30) has some of the cheapest charters going, and flights just about anywhere in the world. For national and international buses you can get information and tickets at the main terminus in Porte de la Villette – M° Porte-de-la-Villette (☎42.05.12.10).

VD clinic Free treatment at *Institut Prophylactique*, (36 rue d'Assas, 6°, M° St-Placide (☎45.44.38.94).

Work Not easy: look for ads in *Le Monde, Le Figaro* or *The International Herald Tribune*, or try the youth organisation *CIDJ*, 101 quai Branly, 15°, M° Bir-Hakeim, or the French job agency *ANPE* (*Agence Nationale Pour l'Emploi*) – check the phone book for the nearest office. The noticeboards at the British Council Library (see above) and the American church are worth a look.

Out from the city

The region around the capital – known as the **Île de France** – and the borders of the neighbouring provinces are studded with large-scale **châteaux**. Many were royal or noble retreats for hunting and other leisured pursuits; some, like Versailles, were for more serious state show. They are undoubtedly impressive but don't necessarily provide great fun days out. Indeed if you have even the slightest curiosity about church buildings, forget the châteaux and make instead for the cathedral of **Chartres**, which is all it is cracked up to be – and more. Closer in, on the edge of the city itself, **St-Denis** boasts a cathedral second only to Notre-Dame among Paris churches – a visit to which can be combined with a walk back along the banks of the **St-Denis canal**. Other waterside wanders include **Chatou** and the **Marne-side towns** with their memories of carrousing, carefree painters and musicians in the 1900s when these places were open countryside or small villages. Whether the various **suburban museums** deserve your attention will depend on your degree of interest in the subjects they represent – **china** at Sèvres, **French prehistory** at St-Germain-en-Laye, **Napoléon** at Malmaison, or **horses** at Chantilly. The biggest pull for kids is without question **Euro Disneyland** out beyond the bizarre satellite town of **Marne-la-Vallée**, but they might also like the **air and space museum** at Le Bourget, and the **Île de France** museum at Sceaux.

Some of the excursions detailed below would make sense as stop-offs on your way out from Paris – Anet en route for Normandy, Chartres on your way to Le Mans or Brittany, Fontainebleau as you head south, or Chantilly for heading north. Bear in mind that **Monet's** marvellous garden at **Giverny** (detailed Chapter Four, "Normandy") could also be a day trip from the capital.

For want of any other obvious logic, this section of the chapter is arranged in anticlockwise fashion, beginning with St-Denis and ending at Disneyland.

St-Denis

ST-DENIS has been one of the most heavily industrialised communities in France. Recession has taken its toll but it is still the bastion of the Red suburbs, stronghold of the Communist Party. Its centre retains traces of its small town origins, while all around the tower cranes swing hoppers of ready-mixed concrete over the rising shells of gimcrack workers' flats. The thrice-weekly **market** still takes place in the square by the Hôtel de Ville and the covered *halles* nearby. It is a multi-ethnic affair these days, and the quantity of offal on the butchers' stalls – ears, feet, tails and bladders – shows this is not wealthy territory. The town's chief claim to fame, though, is its magnificent cathedral, close by the St-Denis Basilique métro station – much the simplest way of getting to St-Denis.

Begun by Abbot Suger, friend and adviser to kings, in the first half of the twelfth century, **Basilique St-Denis** is generally regarded as the birthplace of the Gothic style in European architecture. Though its west front was the first ever to have a rose window, it is in the choir that you see the clear emergence of the new style: the slimness and lightness that comes with the use of the pointed arch, the ribbed vault and the long shafts of half-column rising from pillar to roof. It is a remarkably well-lit church, too, thanks to the clerestory being almost one hundred percent glass – another first for St-Denis – and the transept windows being so big that they occupy their entire end walls. Once the place where the kings of France were crowned, since 1000 AD the cathedral has been the burial place of all but three, and their very fine **tombs and effigies** are distributed about the transepts and ambulatory (Mon–Sat 10am–5pm, Sun noon–5pm). Among the most interesting are the enormous Renaissance memorial to François 1er on the right just beyond the entrance, and the tombs of Louis XII, Henri II and Catherine de Médicis on the left side of the church. To the right of the ambulatory steps you can see the stocky little general, Bertrand du Guesclin, who gave the English a run-around after the death of the Black Prince, and on the level above him, invariably graced by bouquets of flowers from the lunatic royalist fringe, the undistinguished statues of Louis XVI and Marie-Antoinette. Around the corner on the far side of the ambulatory is Clovis himself, king of the Franks way back in 500, a canny little German who wiped out Roman Gaul and turned it into France, with Paris for a capital.

Not many minutes' walk away on rue Gabriel-Péri, third right off rue de la Légiond'Honneur, the **Musée d'Art et d'Histoire de la Ville de St-Denis** (Mon & Wed–Sat 10am–5.30pm, Sun 2–6.30pm, closed hols) is housed in a former Carmelite convent. The exhibits are not of spectacular interest, save for the unique collection of documents relating to **the Commune**: posters, cartoons, broadsheets, paintings, plus an audiovisual presentation. There is also an exhibition of manuscripts and rare editions of the Communist poet, Paul Eluard, native son of St-Denis.

Canal St-Denis

To get to the canal at the St-Denis end, follow rue de la République from the Hôtel de Ville to its end by a church, then go down the left side of the church until you reach tl.e canal bridge. If you turn left, you can **walk** all the way back **to Paris** along the towpath – about an hour and a half to Porte de la Villette. There are stretches where it looks as if you're probably not supposed to be there. Just pay no attention and keep going.

Not far from the start of the walk, past some peeling *villas* with unkempt gardens, you come to a cheap friendly restaurant, *La Péniche*. Rue Raspail leads from there to a dusty square where the town council named a side street for IRA hunger-striker Bobby Sands. Continuing along the canal, you can't get lost. Sacré-Coeur is visible up ahead as you pass cottages with yards open on the water, patches of greenery, sand and gravel docks, waste ground where larks rise above rusting bedsteads and doorless fridges, lock-keepers' cottages with roses and vegetable gardens, decaying tenements and brightly painted shacks, derelict factories and huge sheds where trundling gantries load bundles of steel rods on to Belgian barges.

Le Bourget

The French were always adventurous, pioneering aviators and the name of **LE BOURGET** is intimately connected with their earliest exploits. Lindbergh landed here after his epic first flight across the Atlantic. From World War I to the development of Orly in the 1950s it was Paris's principal airport. Today it is used only for internal

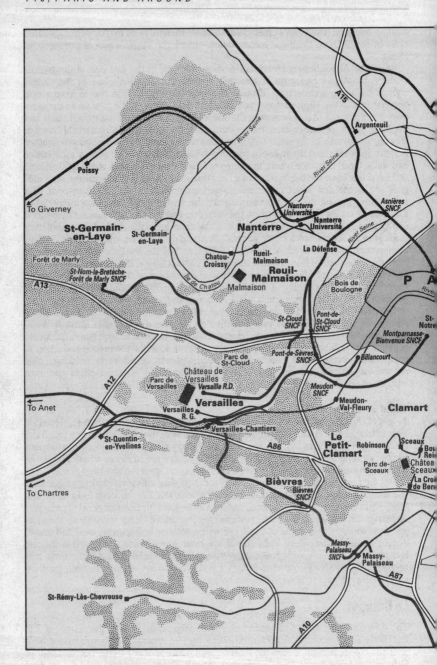

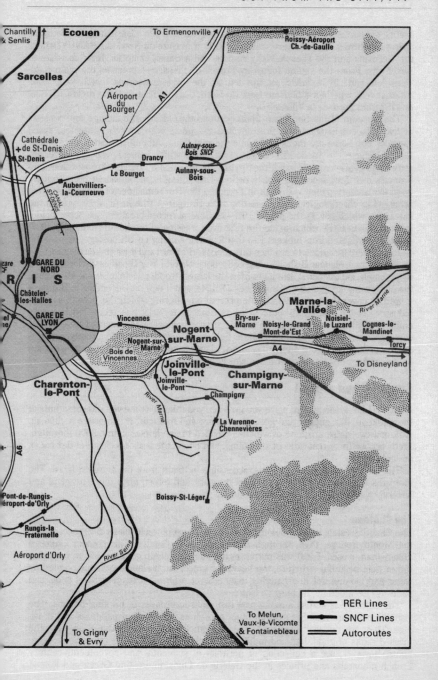

Chantilly & Senlis

Ecouen

To Ermenonville

Roissy-Aéroport Ch.-de-Gaulle

Sarcelles

Aéroport du Bourget

A1

Cathédrale de St-Denis

St-Denis

Aulnay-sous-Bois SNCF

Drancy

Le Bourget

Aulnay-sous-Bois

Aubervilliers-la-Courneuve

CANAL ST-DENIS

GARE DU NORD

Châtelet-les-Halles

GARE DE LYON

Vincennes

Marne-la-Vallée

River Marne

Bry-sur-Marne

Noisy-le-Grand Mont-de'Est

Noisiel-le Luzard

Cognes-le-Mandinet

Torcy

Nogent-sur-Marne

Nogent-sur-Marne

Bois de Vincennes

A4

To Disneyland

Joinville-le-Pont

Joinville-le-Pont

Champigny-sur-Marne

Charenton-le-Pont

River Marne

Champigny

A6

La Varenne-Chennevières

Pont-de-Rungis-Aéroport-de'Orly

Boissy-St-Léger

Rungis-la Fraternelle

Aéroport d'Orly

River Seine

To Grigny & Evry

To Melun, Vaux-le-Vicomte & Fontainebleau

■ RER Lines

◆ SNCF Lines

Autoroutes

flights, but some of the older buildings have been turned into a fascinating **museum of flying machines. To get there**, take the RER from Gare du Nord to DRANCY, where the Germans and the French Vichy regime had a transit camp for Jews en route to Auschwitz. From the station follow av Francis-de-Pressensé as far as the main road. Turn left and, by a *tabac* on the left at the first crossroads, catch bus #152. Alternatively, take bus #350 from Gare du Nord, Gare de l'Est or Porte de la Chapelle, or #152 from Porte de la Villette.

The museum (Tues–Sun 10am–5pm) occupies the old airport buildings, and consists of five adjacent hangars, the first devoted to **space**, with rockets, satellites, space capsules etc. Some are mock-ups, some the real thing. Among the latter are a Lunar Roving Vehicle, the Apollo XIII command module in which James Lovell and his fellow-astronauts nearly came to grief, the Soyuz craft in which a French astronaut flew, and France's own first successful space rocket. Everything is accompanied by extremely good explanatory panels – though in French only. The remainder of the exhibition is arranged in chronological order, starting with **Hangar A** (the furthest away from the entrance), which covers the period 1919–39. Several record-breakers are here, including the Bréguet XIX which made the first ever crossing of the South Atlantic in 1927, and the corrugated iron Junkers F13 that featured so long on US postage stamps; the Germans were forbidden to produce this after World War I and it was taken over instead by the US mail. Hangar B shows a big collection of World War II planes, including a V-1 flying bomb and the Nazis' last jet fighter, the largely wooden Heinkel 162A. Incredibly, the plans were completed on September 24, 1944, and it flew on December 6. **Hangars C and D** cover the years 1945 to the present day, during which the French aviation industry, having lost eighty percent of its capacity in 1945, has recovered to a pre-eminent position in the world. Its high-tech achievement is represented here by the super-sophisticated best-selling Mirage fighters, the first Concorde prototype and – symbol of national vigour and virility – the Ariane space-launcher (the latter two parked on the tarmac outside). Hangar E contains light and sporty aircraft.

Chantilly and around

CHANTILLY is the kind of place you go when you think it's time you did something at the weekend, like get out and get some culture and fresh air. It comprises a château, park and two museums, one of which is devoted to live horses. Some 3000 thorough-breds prance the forest rides of a morning, and two of the season's classiest **flat races** are held here.

The town is 40km north of Paris, accessible **by train** from the Gare du Nord. The footpaths **GR11** and **12** pass through the park and forest, for a more peaceful and leisurely way of exploring this bit of country.

The Château

The Chantilly estate used to belong to two of the most powerful clans in France: first to the Montmorencys, then, through marriage, to the Condés. The present **Château** (10am–6pm, closed Tues) was put up in the late nineteenth century. It's an imposing rather than beautiful structure, too heavy for grace, but it stands well, surrounded by water and looking out in a haughty manner over a formal arrangement of pools and pathways designed by the busy Le Nôtre.

The entrance is across a moat, past two realistic bronzes of hunting hounds. The visitable parts are mainly made up of an enormous collection of paintings and drawings. They are not well displayed, and you quickly get visual indigestion from the massed ranks of good, bad and indifferent, deployed as if of equal value. Some highlights, however, are a collection of portraits of sixteenth- and seventeenth-century French monarchs and princes in the Galerie de Logis; interesting Greek and Roman bits in the tower room called the Rotonde de la Minerve; a big series of sepia stained glass illustrating Apuleius's *Golden Ass* in the Galerie de Psyche, together with some very lively portrait drawings; and, in the so-called Santuario, some Raphaels, a Filippo Lippi and forty miniatures from a fifteenth-century *Book of Hours* attributed to the French artist Jean Fouquet.

The museum's single greatest treasure is in the library, the Cabinet des Livres, which you can enter only in the presence of the guide. It is *Les Très Riches Heures du Duc de Berry*, the most celebrated of all the Books of Hours. The illuminated pages illustrating the months of the year with representative scenes from contemporary (early 1400s) rural life – like harvesting and ploughing, sheepshearing and pruning, all drawn from life – are richly coloured and drawn with a delicate naturalism, as well as being sociologically interesting. Unfortunately – and understandably – only facsimiles are on display, but they give an excellent idea of the original. Sets of postcards, of middling fidelity, are on sale in the entrance. There are thousands of other fine books on display as well.

The Horse Museum

Five minutes' walk along the château drive, the colossal stable block has been transformed into a museum of the horse, the **Musée Vivant du Cheval** (Mon–Fri 10.30am–5.30pm, Sat & Sun 10.30am–6pm). The building was erected at the beginning of the eighteenth century by the incumbent Condé prince, who believed he would be reincarnated as a horse and wished to provide fitting accommodation for 240 of his future relatives. In the main hall horses of different breeds from around the world are stalled, with a ring for demonstrations (enquire at the ticket desk for details), followed by a series of life-size models illustrating the various activities horses are used for. In the rooms off here are collections of paintings, horseshoes, veterinary equipment, bridles and saddles, a mock-up of a blacksmith's, children's horse toys (including a chain-driven number, with handles in its ears, which belonged to Napoléon III), and a fanciful Sicilian cart painted with scenes of Crusader battles.

Ecouen

Midway between Chantilly and Paris, **ECOUEN** makes a good place to stop, if you have time, on the train from the Gare du Nord. Get out at Ecouen-Ezanville, the first stop outside the high-rise suburbs if you are approaching from Paris.

The Renaissance **château** here belonged, like Chantilly, first to the Montmorencys, then to the Condés, and has been converted into the **Musée National de la Renaissance** (9.45am–12.30pm & 2–5.15pm, closed Tues). In addition to some of the original interior decoration, including frescoes and magnificent carved fireplaces, the rooms display a choice and manageable selection of Renaissance furniture, tapestries, woodcarvings, jewellery and so forth. However, you need to know you have a definite interest in the period to make it worth the effort of getting there.

Senlis and Ermenonville

An attractive old town, 10km east of Chantilly, **SENLIS** (trains again from Gare du Nord) has a cathedral contemporary with Notre-Dame and all the trappings of medieval ramparts, Roman towers and royal palace remnants to entice hordes of day-trippers and weekenders from the capital. Another dozen kilometres away is the eighteenth-century château and park of **ERMENONVILLE**, where **Rousseau** died. He was buried on an island in the lake, but not long afterwards the Revolution moved his body to the Panthéon.

Malmaison

The château of **MALMAISON** was the home of the Empress Josephine, and, during the 1800–1804 Consulate, of Napoléon, too. According to his secretary, "it was the only place next to the battlefield where he was truly himself". After their divorce, Josephine stayed on here, occasionally receiving visits from the emperor, until her death in 1814. The **château** (10am–12.30pm & 1.30–5.30pm, closed Tues, guided tours only) is set in the beautiful grounds of the **Bois-Préau** and is a relatively small and surprisingly enjoyable place to visit. Tours include the private and official apartments, in part with original furnishings, as well as Josephine's clothes, china, glass and personal possessions. There are other Napoleonic bits in the **Bois-Préau museum** (10.30am–1pm & 2–6pm, closed Tues; same ticket as above).

To get there take the RER to LA DEFENSE, then bus #158A to MALMAISON-CHÂTEAU. Alternatively, if you'd like a walk, take the RER to RUEIL-MALMAISON and follow the GR11 footpath from the Pont de Chatou along the left bank of the Seine and into the château park.

Île de Chatou

A long narrow island in the Seine, the **Île de Chatou** was once a rustic spot where Parisians came on the newly opened rail line to row and dine and flirt at the riverside *guinguettes* (eating and dancing establishments). One of these, the **Maison Fournaise**, just below the Pont de Chatou road bridge, has finally been restored and is now once again a restaurant (☎30.71.41.91) with a small museum alongside dedicated to the artists of its heyday – Renoir, Monet, Manet, Van Gogh, Seurat, Sisley, Courbet – for whom it was a favourite haunt. Half of them were in love with the proprietor's daughter, Alphonsine; one of Renoir's best-known canvases, *Le Déjeuner des Canotiers*, shows his friends lunching on the balcony. Vlaminck and his fellow-Fauves, Derain and Matisse, were also habitués. It was in fact from here that Vlaminck set off for the 1905 *Salon des Indépendants* with the truckload of paintings that caused the critics to coin the term Fauvism.

The downstream end of the island has been made into a **park**, which tapers away into a tree-lined tail hardly wider than the path. The upstream end is spooky in the extreme. A track, black with oil and ooze and littered with assorted junk, bumps along past yellowed grass and bald poplar trees to a group of ruined houses stacked with beat-up cars. Beyond the rail bridge a louche-looking chalet, guarded by Alsatians, stands beside the track. A concrete block saying "No Entry" bars the way. If you're bold enough to ignore it, there's a view from the head of the island of the old market gardens on the right bank and the decaying industrial landscape of Nanterre on the left.

Access to the island is from the Rueil-Malmaison RER stop. Just walk straight ahead on to the Pont de Chatou. Bizarrely, there's a twice-yearly ham and antique fair on the island, which could be fun to check out (March and Sept).

St-Germain-en-Laye

ST-GERMAIN is not specially interesting as a town, but if you've been to the prehistoric caves of the Dordogne, or plan to go, you'll get a lot from the **Musée des Antiquités Nationales** (Wed–Sun 9am–5.15pm). It is in the unattractively renovated château (opposite the RER station), which was one of the main residences of the French court before Versailles was built.

The presentation and lighting make the visit a real pleasure. The extensive Stone Age section includes a mock-up of the Lascaux caves and a profile of Abbé Breuil, the priest who made prehistoric art respectable, as well as a beautiful collection of decorative objects, tools and so forth. All ages of prehistory are covered, right down into historical times with Celts, Romans and Franks: abundant evidence that the French have been a talented arty lot for a very long time. The end piece is a room of comparative archaeology, with objects from cultures across the globe.

From right outside the château, a **terrace** – Le Nôtre arranging the landscape again – stretches for more than 2km above the Seine with a view over the whole of Paris. All behind it is the **forest of St-Germain**, a sizeable expanse of woodland, although crisscrossed by too many roads to be convincing as wilderness.

Anet

The **château** at **ANET**, 20km or so north of DREUX, is a stop worth considering if you're driving towards western Normandy from Paris, or towards Rouen from Chartres, built for Diane de Poitiers, respected widow in the court of François 1er and powerful lover of the king's son Henri. Work started with Philippe de l'Orme as the architect in charge, and the designs are as delicate and polished as the Renaissance could produce. Within a year Henri inherited the throne and immediately gave Diane the château of Chenonceau, but the Anet project continued, luckily for Diane, since Henri's reign was brought to an untimely end and his wife demanded Chenonceau back. Diane retired to Anet where she died. Her grandson built a chapel for her tomb alongside the château which has remained intact. The château would have been completely destroyed by the first owner after the Revolution had it not been for a protest riot by the townspeople that sent him packing. As it is, only the front entrance, one wing and the château chapel remain, now restored to its former glorification of hunting and feminine eroticism, and with the swirling floor and domed ceiling of the chapel its climax. (March–Nov Mon & Wed–Fri 2.30–6.30pm, Sat 2–5pm, Sun & hols 10–11.30am & 2–6.30pm; Dec–Feb Sat 2–5pm, Sun & hols 10–11.30am & 2–5pm).

Versailles

The **Palace of Versailles** (Tues–Sun 9.45am–5.30pm; closed hols; 30F, Sun half price and free for under-18s) is one of the three most visited monuments in France. It's hard to know why so many tourists come out here in preference to all except the most obvious sights of Paris. Yet they do, and the château is always a crush of bodies. To **get there**, take the RER *ligne C5* to VERSAILLES-RIVE GAUCHE (40min), turn left out of the station and immediately right to approach the palace. You can get maps of the park from the tourist office on rue des Réservoirs to the right of the palace.

It is not a beautiful building by any means, its décor a grotesque homage to two of the greatest of all self-propagandists, Louis XIV and Napoléon, and more than anything else, is impressive for its size, which by any standards is incredible. You have a choice of itineraries and whether to be guided or not. Either way, the crowds won't give you much room to take your time. The most amazing room is perhaps the Hall of Mirrors, although the mirrors are smeared, scratched and not the originals – for these a Breton boy is currently serving fifteen years for breaking glass with explosives. You can also visit the state apartments of the king and queen, and the royal chapel, a grand structure that ranks among France's finest Baroque creations.

Outside, the **park** (open dawn–dusk) is something of a relief, although it's inevitably a very formal affair. The fountains are turned on every Sunday from 3.30pm to 5pm, May to September. The scenery gets better the further you go from the palace. There are even informal groups of trees near the lesser outcrops of royal mania, the **Grand** and **Petit Trianons** (Tues–Sun 9.45am–noon & 2–5.30pm, Petit Trianon afternoon only; closed hols; 10F each). Beyond is Le Hameau, where Marie-Antionette played at being a shepherdess. You may find bulldozers and chain saws wreaking havoc. Storm damage in 1990 prompted a massive restoration programme, which will involve, amongst other things, uprooting 20,000 chestnut trees because they weren't part of Le Nôtre's original creation.

The one competing attraction in Versailles town is a wonderfully snobbish **tearoom** in the *Hôtel Palais Trianon*, where the final negotiations for the Treaty of Versailles took place in 1919. It's near the park entrance at the end of bd de la Reine and much more worthwhile than shelling out for château admission, with trayfuls of *pâtisseries* to the limits of your desire for about 65F. The style of the *Trianon* is very much that of the town in general. The dominant population is aristocratic with the pre-revolutionary titles disdainful of those dating merely from Napoléon. On Bastille Day both lots show their colours with black ribbons and ties.

Southwest: a miscellany of museums

Meudon, **Sèvres** and **Sceaux**, once distinct villages, have expanded into each other over the last century, spreading across the steep hills above the Seine. The heights are dominated by luxury apartments these days, and for visitors the main attractions lie in museums: **Rodin** and **Jean Arp** at Meudon, **ceramics** at Sèvres and **Île de France history** at Sceaux.

Meudon-Val-Fleury

MEUDON-VAL-FLEURY, on the *C5/C7* RER lines, is the most easily accessible patch of Seine countryside. And to give a walk some purpose there is the **Villa des Brillants** at 19 av Auguste-Rodin, off rue de la Belgique, the house where **Rodin** spent his last years, with an annexe containing some of his maquettes, plaster casts and other bits and bobs.

From the station you make your way up the east flank of the valley through the twisty **rue des Vignes**. You can either go up rue de la Belgique until you reach av Rodin on the left towards the top, or turn down it to the rail line embankment, go through the tunnel and take the footpath on the right, which brings you out by the house. It stands in a big picnickable garden, where Rodin himself is buried, on the very edge of the hill looking down on the decimated Renault works in Boulogne-Billancourt. To the south, on the edge of Meudon's forest, is the **Musée et Jardin de Sculptures de la Fondation Jean Arp**, 21 rue des Châtaigniers (Fri–Sun 2–6pm; 15F/10F). This was Jean Arp's and Sophie Taeuber's home and studio, and both the house and garden have examples of their work.

Sèvres

The **Musée National de la Céramique** in **SÈVRES** is equally easy to reach. To get there take the métro to Pont-de-Sèvres/Boulogne-Pont-de-St-Cloud. The museum (10am–5.15pm; closed Tues) stands just to the right of the main road, close to the river-bank – an acquired taste, maybe, but if you do have it, there is much to be savoured, not just French pottery and china, but Islamic, Chinese, Italian, German, Dutch, English etc. There is also, inevitably, a comprehensive collection of Sèvres ware, as the stuff is made right here. Close by, overlooking the river, the **Parc de St-Cloud** is good for fresh air and visual order, with a geometrical sequence of pools and fountains delineating a route down to the river and across to the city.

The Musée de l'Île-de-France at Sceaux

The **château** of **SCEAUX** is a nineteenth-century replacement for the original – demolished post-Revolution – which matched the now-restored Le Nôtre grounds. As a park it's the usual classical geometry of terraces, water and woods, but if you fancy a walk you can get off the RER at La-Croix-de-Berny at the southern end. Otherwise it's a five- to ten-minute walk from Parc-de-Sceaux station (15min from Denfert-Rochereau): turn left on av de la Duchesse-du-Maine, right into av Rose-de-Launay and right again on av Le-Nôtre and you'll find the château gates on your left.

The château housing the **Musée de l'Île-de-France** (Mon & Fri–Sun 2–5pm, Wed & Thurs 10am–noon & 2–6pm; 10F) evokes the Paris countryside of the *ancien régime* with its aristocratic and royal domains; of the nineteenth century, with its riverside scenes and eating and dancing places, the *guinguettes*, that inspired so many artists; and of the new towns and transport of the current age. There are models, pictures and diverse objects: a backpack hot chocolate dispenser with a choice of two brews; 1940s métro seats; a painting of river laundering at Cergy-Pontoise alongside photos of the new town high-rise; early bicycles and a series of plates and figurines inspired by the arrival of the first giraffe in France in the 1830s. Though some of the rooms hold little excitement, most people, kids included, should find enough to make the visit worth it.

Temporary exhibitions and a summer festival of classical chamber music are held in the **Orangerie**, which, along with the **Pavillon de l'Aurore** (in the northeast corner of the park), survives from the original residence. The concerts take place at weekends, from July to October – details from the museum (☎46.61.06.71), or from the *Direction des Musées de France*, Palais du Louvre, Cours Visconti, 34 quai du Louvre, Paris 1er (☎42.60.39.26).

Chartres

About 35km beyond Versailles, an hour by train from Paris-Montparnasse, **CHARTRES** is a small and relatively undistinguished town. However, its **cathédrale Notre-Dame** (daily 7.30am–7.30pm) is one of the finest examples of Gothic architecture in Europe and, built between 1194 and 1260, perhaps the quickest ever to be constructed. Its facade is dominated by two towers, which rise up above portals heavily laden with sculpture that marks the transition from the Romanesque to Gothic styles – depictions of Christ, the Apostles, and the 24 Elders of the Book of Revelation. Inside, the chairs of the nave cover up the labyrinth on the floor – an original thirteenth-century arrangement and a great rarity, since the authorities at other cathedrals had them pulled up as distracting frivolities. The Chartres labyrinth traces a path over 200m long enclosed within a diameter of 13m, the same size as the rose window above the main doors. The centre used to have a bronze relief of Theseus and the Minotaur, and the pattern of the maze was copied from classical texts – the medieval Catholic idea of the path of life to eternity echoing Greek myth. During pilgrimages the chairs are removed so you may be lucky and see the full pattern.

But there are more than enough wonders to enthral: the geometry of the building, unique in being almost unaltered since its consecration in the thirteenth century; the details of the stonework, the Renaissance choir screen and the hosts of sculpted figures above each transept door; and the shining circular symmetries of the transept windows, virtually all of which are original, dating from the twelfth and thirteenth centuries. Among paying extras, the crypt and treasures can wait for another time but, crowds permitting, it's worth climbing the north tower (10–11.30am & 2–5.30pm). There are gardens at the back from where you can contemplate at ease the complexity of stress factors balanced by the flying buttresses. If, as you're wandering around, you hear a passionate and erudite Englishman giving guided tours, it is probably Malcolm Miller, almost an institution in himself and a world expert on Chartres Cathedral. He does two tours daily from April to November; the tourist office (see below) can provide details.

The town

Though the cathedral is why you come here, Chartres town is not without appeal. The **Musée des Beaux Arts** (10am–noon & 2–5pm; closed Tues) in the former episcopal palace just north of the cathedral has some beautiful tapestries, a room full of Vlaminck, and Zurbaran's *Sainte Lucie*, as well as good temporary exhibitions. Behind it, rue Chantault leads past old town houses to the river Eure and Pont des Massacres. You can follow this reedy river lined with ancient wash-houses upstream via rue des Massacres on the right bank. The cathedral appears from time to time through the trees and, closer at hand, on the left bank is the Romanesque church of **St-André**, now used for art exhibitions, jazz concerts and so on. Crossing back over at the end of rue de la Tannerie into rue du Bourg takes you back to the cathedral through the medieval town, decorated with details such as the carved salmon on a house on place de la Poissonerie.

Arriving at the **gare SNCF**, av J-de-Beauce leads straight up to place Châtelet. Past all the coaches on the other side of the *place*, rue Ste-Même crosses place Jean Moulin with the cathedral down to the left. Rue d'Harleville goes to the right to bd de la Résistance, a section of the main ring road around the old town. The memorial on the corner of the street and the boulevard is to **Jean Moulin**, Prefect of Chartres until he was sacked by the Vichy government in 1942. When the Germans occupied Chartres in 1940, he had refused under torture to sign a document to the effect that black soldiers in the French army were responsible for Nazi atrocities. He later became de Gaulle's number-one man on the ground, co-ordinating the Resistance. He died at the hands of Klaus Barbie in 1943.

The **SI** is on the cathedral *parvis*, at 7 Cloître Notre-Dame (Mon–Sat 9.30am–12.30pm & 2–6.30pm, Sun 10am–noon & 3–6pm), and can **supply free maps** and help with **rooms** if you want to stay. Rue du Cygne is a good place to look for **bars and restaurants**. If you want to splash out, have a meal at *Henri IV* at 31 rue Soleil-d'Or (☎37.36.01.55; closed Mon evening & Tues), which has one of the best selections of wines in France.

Vaux-le-Vicomte and Fontainebleau

VAUX-LE-VICOMTE, 46km southeast of Paris (daily except Jan 11am–5pm), is one of the great **classical châteaux**. Louis XIV's finance superintendent, Nicholas Fouquet, had it built at colossal expense, using the top designers of the day – Le Vau, the royal architect, Le Brun, the painter, and Le Nôtre, the landscape gardener. The result was magnificence and precision in perfect proportion and a bill that could only be paid by someone who occasionally confused the state's account with his own. The housewarming party, to which the king was invited, was more extravagant than any royal event – a comparison which other finance ministers ensured that Louis took to heart. Within three weeks Fouquet was jailed for life on trumped-up charges, and Louis carted Le Vau, Le Brun and Le Nôtre off to Versailles to work on a gaudy and gross piece of one-upmanship. The nearest station is at MELUN, 25 minutes by train from Gare de Lyon; however, there's no bus from the station, so call a radio cab on ☎64.52.51.50.

If you were feeling energetic, you could spend the morning at Vaux-le-Vicomte and continue by train from MELUN to **FONTAINEBLEAU** (daily except Tues 9.30am–12.30pm & 2–5pm; half-price Sun and hols) – an instructive and pleasant exercise in rapid châteaux touring. A hunting lodge from as early as the twelfth century, the château here began its transformation into a palace under François-1er in the sixteenth century. A vast, rambling place, unpretentious despite its size, it owes its distinction to a colony of Italian artists imported for the decoration – above all, Rosso Il Fiorentino, who completed the celebrated **Galerie François-1er**, a work that was seminal in the evolution of French aristocratic art and design. The gardens are equally luscious, but if you want to escape to the wilds, the surrounding **forest of Fontainebleau** is full of walking and cycling trails and its rocks are a favourite training ground for French climbers. Paths and tracks are all marked on Michelin map 196 (*Environs de Paris*). **Trains from Paris** take around 45 minutes from Gare de Lyon (25min from Melun), and there's a local bus to the gates from the train station.

In the loops of the Marne

The banks of the **Marne**, like the Seine at Chatou, were once dotted with *guinguettes* reached by poplar-lined paths through meadows and peasant villages. The surroundings have disappeared but the same combination of open-air eating, riverside views and live music can still be had in a *guinguette* established in the l900s: *Chez Gégène*, 162bis quai de Polangis, **JOINVILLE-LE-PONT** (March–Oct; midday *bals musettes* at weekends, noon–2pm; ☎48.83.29.43). Joinville-le-Pont is east of Paris, just across the Marne from the Bois de Vincennes (RER *ligne A2*, then buses #106 and #108 from rue J. Mermoz or walk to cross the river). Quai de Polangis runs upstream (northwards at this point). There are several places where you can hire canoes or pedalos, for much better **boating** than on the Vincennes lakes.

Champigny-sur-Marne

Downstream (or three stops on the RER, then buses #208/116 or bus #108A from Joinville) is **CHAMPIGNY-SUR-MARNE**, one of the few *banlieue* addresses which feels like a place in its own right. There are tiny terraced flats with wooden stairs and balconies beside the bridge; a gracefully sweet and ancient church, St-Saturnin, nestling on a cobbled square a block away from place Lénine and the central crossroads.

A short bus ride – #208 from the station or the centre (stop *Musée de la Résistance*) – takes you to the **Musée de la Résistance Nationale** at 88 av Marx Dormoy (Mon & Wed–Fri 10am–5.30pm, Sat, Sun & hols 2–6pm; 18F/9F). To its credit, this Resistance museum includes the immediate prewar period and the *Front Populaire*, acknowledges the major role of the Communists and covers the Socialist reforms after the liberation. But it can't quite escape the need to recuperate French glory nor can it relate the dignity it accords to this resistance with attitudes to contemporary resistance movements.

Boats are for hire from the *Centre Nautique* in Champigny (near the rail bridge three or four kilometres upstream from the road bridge), or you can wander down the quayside path on the left bank to the **Pont de Chennevières**. There are some good **riverside restaurants**, too, such as *L'Écu de France*, 31 rue de Champigny (☎45.76.00.03), before you reach the Chennevières bridge; *Le Pavillon Bleu*, a genuine *guinguette* at 66 promenade des Anglais (☎48.83.10.56), further on towards the Pont de Bonneuil on the right bank; and *La Bréteche*, 171 quai de Bonneuil (☎48.83.38.73), on the same side, past the Bonneuil bridge. The nearest RER station is La Varenne-Chennevières.

Nogent-sur-Marne

One other possible stop on these meanders of the Marne is **NOGENT-SUR-MARNE**, back by the Bois de Vincennes north of Joinville. The one remaining pavilion of the **old market at Les Halles** has been resurrected here in a bizarre setting of ocean-liner apartment blocks on one side and mismatched prewar houses on the other. Baltard's construction, all gleaming glass and paint above the diamond-patterned brickwork, is a pleasure to behold. In front of the entrance is a **"square of bygone Paris"**, replete with Wallace fountain, theatre ticket kiosk, cobbles and twirly lamp-post. But that is all there is to see, as the hall is given over to private functions for most of the year. From Nogent-sur-Marne RER you exit onto av de Joinville, cross over and turn left past the SI and then first left into av Victor Hugo, which brings you to the unmistakable building.

Charenton

Downstream from all these places, where the Marne meets the Seine just outside the city, is **CHARENTON**, where millions of bottles of wine are stored before reaching the Parisian throat. However, the museum to see here is dedicated to the other vital substance – bread, the **Musée Français du Pain**, situated above the flour milling firm *SAM* at 2bis rue Victor Hugo (Tues & Thurs 2–4.30pm). Gathered together in a small-ish attic room, this fussy but comprehensive collection has songs, pictures, bread tax decrees of the *ancien régime*, old *boulangerie* signs, baking trays, baskets and cupboards for bread, pieces sculpted out of dough and the thing itself – over 4000 years old in one instance. From Paris take the Créteil-Préfecture métro to Charenton-Écoles, exit place des Écoles: rue Victor Hugo goes down to the right of the *Monoprix* supermarket in front of you. From the Bois de Vincennes, av Cholet runs to place des Écoles from av de Grevelle on the edge of the wood, due south of Lac Daumesnil.

Mickey Mouse and Marne-la-Vallée

Since the 1960s a new feature to the Parisian outskirts has been the New Towns or *Villes Nouvelles*. Satellites to the city rather than places in their own right, they have spawned some extraordinary pieces of architecture. **Marne-la-Vallée,** where Terry Gilliam's totalitarian fantasy *Brasil* was filmed, has long topped the charts for most outrageous designs. It starts ten kilometres east of Paris and hops for twenty kilometres from one new outburst to the next, ending with Europe's first **Disneyland**.

You could just do a tour of Marne-la-Vallée, though the Disney Corporation may well have employed a persuasive Donald Duck for every eastbound RER train. If you can resist, stop at **NOISY-LE-GRAND**. You surface on the Arcades, a stony substitute for a town square and there you have the poetic panorama of a controlled community environment. The two acclaimed architectural pieces in this monolith are both low-cost housing units, gigantic, quite unlike anything you're likely to have seen before and unmitigatedly horrible. The **Arènes de Picasso** is in the group of buildings to the right of the RER line as you look at the lakes from the Arcades, about half a kilometre away. It's soon visible as you approach: two enormous circles like loudspeakers facing each other across a space that would do nicely for a Roman stadium. Prepare to feel as if the lions were waiting. At the other end of Mont d'Est, facing the capital, is the extraordinary semicircle, arch and half square of *Le Théâtre et Palacio d'Abraxas*, creation of Ricardo Boffil. Ghosts of ancient Greek designs haunt the facades but proportion there is none, whether classical or any other.

Further-flung delights of Marne-la-Vallée include the mosaic-coated **"Totem" water tower**, with clown and robot faces in the woods by LE LUZARD; another water tower, with plants growing through its grill cladding, at the head of bd Salvador Allende at NOISIEL MAIRIE; sympathetic small-scale housing in LE VAL MAUBOUE and, with easy access, an **RER station on a lake**, LOGNES-LE MANDINET.

Maps and information for Marne-la-Vallée as well as models and photos on view can be had from the CIVN, 3 place de l'Arche-Guédon, Torcy; bus #220 from Noisiel RER, direction Torcy, stop l'Arche-Guédon.

Disneyland

EURO-DISNEYLAND opens its mega-buck gates to the public in April 1992, an enormous project taking up a space one-fifth the size of Paris. At time of writing it's hard to give an appraisal of what to expect, but despite Disney Corporation promises that it would be "Europe-orientated", it seems likely that the place will in fact be a replica of Florida's Disneyworld minus some of the better rides. Certainly there won't be much that's genuinely "European" about it: each of the hotels has a region of the US as its theme; all the restaurants sell American food; the employees have learnt to say "have a nice day" in French; and claims that Sleeping Beauty's castle (*Le Château de la Belle au*

Bois Dormant) is modelled on a Loire château only confirm that all of Europe is fantasy-land to the American corporate mind. There's no doubt, however, that it will be successful, and the carrot for the French has been the amount of money they stand to make from it – estimated as a boost of some 0.25 percent to the country's GNP from the 11 million visitors expected annually.

For **getting there**, the French government have provided an RER extension, a new exit from the A4 motorway and, still to come, a TGV rail link. In 1995 Disney MGM Studios Europe and a waterpark will complete the ensemble on what used to be one of the rare stretches of open countryside near the city. **Entry charges** are likely to be around 200F for adults, 150F for kids.

travel details

Trains

From Gare du Nord through services to Britain via Calais and Boulogne (frequent) and Dunkerque (less so), and to Belgium, Holland and Amsterdam; also to Amiens (at least hourly; 1hr 45min), Arras (1hr 40min) and Lille (2hr 30min).

From Gare de l'Est frequent trains to Nancy (2–3hr), Reims (1hr 30min), Strasbourg (4hr), Besançon (3hr); Metz (2hr 30min).

From Gare St-Lazare to Dieppe (2 daily; 2hr 15min); frequent service to Le Havre (2–2hr 30min), Cherbourg (3–3hr 30min), Rouen (1hr 15min).

From Gare Montparnasse frequent service to Brest (5hr 30min–6hr), Nantes (3hr 30min); Rennes (2hr 30min).

From Gare d'Austerlitz numerous trains to Tours (2hr), Poitiers (3hr); Bordeaux (5hr); about 6 each to Bayonne (6–8hr) and Toulouse (7–8hr).

From Gare de Lyon almost hourly TGVs to Dijon (1hr 40min) and Lyon (2hr 30min; 7–8 regular trains to Dijon (2hr 30min) and Lyon (5–6hr); almost hourly service to Grenoble, changing at Lyon (3hr 45min by TGV); 10 or more to Marseille (5hr by TGV) and Nice (10hr 30min).

Buses

Regular connection to just about all points in France – and Britain, Belgium, Holland, Scandinavia, Spain, Morocco, Italy etc – from the terminal at **Porte-de-la-Villette** (M° Porte-de-la-Villette).

Hitching

Hitching out of Paris isn't easy, especially in high summer when you are likely to face long delays. It's much better to spend a few extra francs taking a train or bus 50km clear of the city. Alternatively, for a small fee, you can register with the hitching organisation *Allostop*; they will find you a ride and you just make a small contribution towards petrol (see above, "Listings" for details). If, however, you are determined, place yourself at one of the following points:

Heading south: M° to Porte d'Italie, then walk 300m south to the motorway slip roads – A6 for Lyon, Marseille, Nice or Perpignan, A10 for Tours, Bordeaux and Le Mans.

Heading east: M° to Porte de Charenton, then walk 500m south to the A4 slip road (for Reims, Metz, Strasbourg, Nancy) just north of the Pont National.

Heading north: M° to St-Denis-Porte de Paris and look for the blue highway signs – N1 for Boulogne, Calais and Amiens, N14 for Rouen, Dieppe and Le Havre.

Flights

Inter-Air and *Air-France* connect Paris with all major **French cities.** Contact them direct for details.

CHAPTER TWO

THE NORTH: CALAIS TO CHAMPAGNE

When conjuring up exotic holiday locations, **the north** of France is unlikely to get a mention. Even among the French, the most enthusiastic tourists of their own country, it has few adherents. Artois and Flanders include the most heavily industrialised parts of the country, while across the wheat fields of the more sparsely populated regions of Picardy and Champagne a few drops of rain are all that is required for total gloom to descend. It is likely, however, that you'll arrive and leave France via this region, and there are reasons to stop within easy reach of the channel ports – of which **Boulogne** is by far the most appealing.

The north of France has been on the obvious invaders' path into the country, from northern Europe as well as from Britain, and the events that have taken place in Flanders, Artois and Picardy have shaped French history. The bloodiest battles were those of the First World War, above all the **Battle of the Somme** which took place north of Amiens, and **Vimy Ridge** near Arras, where the trenches have been preserved in perpetuity. Throughout the north, but particularly around the villages of the Somme, there are powerful reminders, in monuments and cemeteries, of the devastating human wastage of those years.

Picardy boasts two of France's finest cathedrals at **Amiens** and **Laon**. Further south, the *maisons,* vineyards and produce of the **Champagne** region are the main draw, for which the best bases are **Épernay** and **Reims**, the latter with another fine cathedral. Other attractions include the bird sanctuary of **Marquenterre**; the wooded wilderness of the **Ardennes**; industrial archaeology in the coal fields around **Douai** where Zola's *Germinal* was set; the great medieval castle of **Coucy-le-Château**; and the battle sites of the Middle Ages – **Agincourt** and **Crécy** – whose names are so familiar in the history of Anglo-French rivalry.

Though the past is not forgotten, the present life of the region does not feed on it. In city centres from **Lille** to **Troyes**, you'll find your fill of food, culture and entertainment in the company of locals similarly intent on having a good time; and in addition to the more obvious pleasures of the Champagne region there's the possibility of finding relatively lucrative **employment** during the harvest season towards the end of September.

HOTEL ROOM PRICES

For a fuller explanation of these price codes, see the box on p.28 of *Basics.*

| ① Under 100F | ② 100–130F | ③ 130–180F | ④ 180–230F | ⑤ 230–300F |

THE CHANNEL PORTS AND THE ROAD TO PARIS

Apart from their attraction for day-trippers after a sniff of something foreign, a shopping-bag full of continental produce, or more commonly a few crates of cheap beer, the chief function of the **channel ports** in this section – **Dunkerque**, **Calais** and **Boulogne** – is to provide the cheapest and most efficient route between Britain and France. Details of the various crossings are listed in *Basics* (see p.9) and in the *Travel Details* at the end of this chapter. **Moving on** is just as easy. There are frequent **train** connections east to **Lille** and beyond, and south towards **Paris**, while the **autoroute** system will whisk you quickly off to your ultimate destination.

For a much more immediate immersion into *La France* – little towns, different-looking farms, a comfortable verge to sleep off the first *baguette* and *vin rouge* – the old *route nationale* **N1**, which shadows the coast all the way from Dunkerque to Abbeville before heading inland to Paris, is infinitely preferable. There are also interesting things to see en route: the cathedrals at **Amiens** and **Beauvais**, the hilltop town of **Montreuil** with its Vauban fortress, the remains of Hitler's Atlantic Wall along the bracing **Côte d'Opale**, and the **Marquenterre bird sanctuary** at the mouth of the River Somme.

Dunkerque

Frequently under a cloud of chemical smog and unstylishly resurrected from wartime devastation, **DUNKERQUE** is about as unappealing an introduction to France as could be imagined: hardly surprising given that it's the country's third largest port and a massive industrial centre in its own right, with oil refineries and steel works producing a quarter of the total French output. If you fancy a closer look at all this industrial muscle, there are **boat trips** from place du Minck, bassin du Commerce, at the northern end of rue Clemenceau (ask the **SI** for times).

The town

Save for the occasions when blockading French fishermen rule *aux quais*, there's little to detain you here. The only buildings of any significance to have survived the last war (or at least to have been rebuilt afterwards) are the tall medieval red-brick **belfry** that is the town's chief landmark (guided tours daily July & Aug 9.15am–5.30pm); the much restored fifteenth-century **Église St-Éloi**; and, a few blocks south of the church on place Jean-Bart, the turn-of-the-century **Hôtel de Ville**, a Flemish fancy to rival that of Calais.

If you're stuck with time on your hands, however, head for the unexpectedly brilliant **Musée d'Art Contemporain** (10am–6/7pm; closed Tues; 6F) with works by Karel Appel, Vasarely, César and many other stars of the post-war era, housed in a suitably serious, pared-down, white ceramic building in a landscaped canalside sculpture park off av des Bains (15min walk north of town centre towards Malo-les-Bains). Alternatively, there's the **Musée des Beaux-Arts** (10am–noon & 2–6pm; closed Tues; 6F), on place du Général-de-Gaulle by the **post office**, with good collections of Flemish, Dutch and French painting, natural history and, inevitably, a display on the evacuation of May 1940 (see box).

Practicalities

The ferry terminal is some 15km west of the town and **gare SNCF**, but it's linked by a **free shuttle service** – laid on by *Sally Lines*, the only ferry company which operates

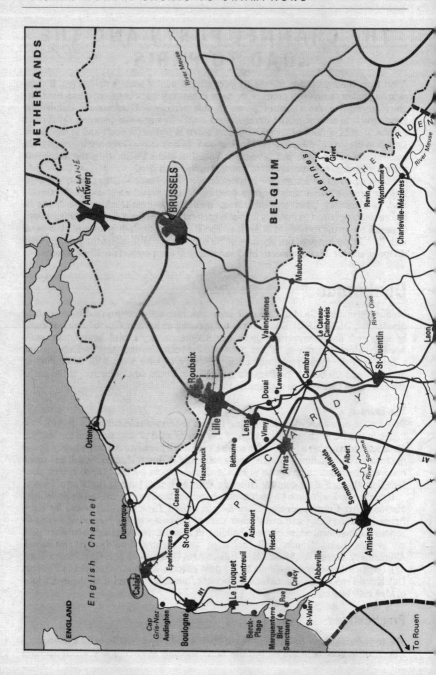

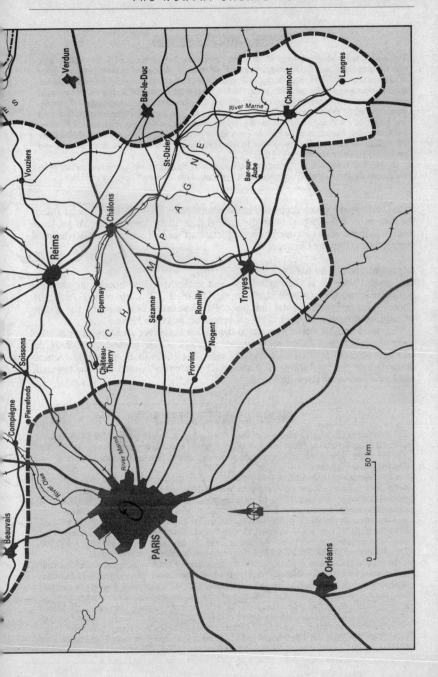

SHOPPING

The best area for shoppers to head for is the main drag, **bd Alexandre-III**, its continuation, **rue Clemenceau**, and the cross-street, **rue Poincaré**. In addition to clothes, perfume, fancy tobacconists and kitchenware shops, *Le Sanglier* stocks all manner of saliva-inducing edibles, including numerous take-out *plats*, while *Pimkie*, also on bd Alexandre-III, is a riotous press of style-conscious shoppers seeking fashion bargains. On place de la République just off the boulevard, the *Uniprix* department store stocks everything you can think of, including masses of food and booze. In rue Poincaré *Le Manoir* is good for groceries, *Boulangerie Hossaert* and *Poulain*, for tarts, cakes, biscuits and the like. As everywhere on this coast, crustaceans and shellfish are a tempting bargain buy, but if you want to take them home, you need to be quick about it and preferably arrive armed with a cool bag.

If you don't have time to wander from shop to shop, *Sally Lines* run a free bus service from the port to the three giant all-under-one-roof **hypermarkets**, *Auchan, Carrefour* and *Cora*.

---

from Dunkerque – which drops you in the central place Émile-Bollaert. The **SI** (Mon–Sat 9am–noon & 2–6.30pm) is on the ground floor of the town **belfry**. To get there from pl Bollaert, walk east one block to pl Jean-Bart (named after Louis XIV's licensed pirate), then left up rue Clemenceau.

Accommodation and eating

The grubby place de la Gare in town is best for **inexpensive hotels**, the cheapest being *Terminus Nord* (☎28.66.54.26; ②), and the best *XIX Siècle* (☎28.66.79.28; ④). There's also a **youth hostel** on place Paul-Asseman, 2km east of the centre (☎28.63.36.34; curfew 10.30pm; IYHF card required; bus #3 to *Piscine*).

You could do a lot worse than **eat** at the station buffet, the *Richelieu*. It's not especially cheap but they accept some brands of plastic. Other possibilities include the excellent pizzeria, *La Farigoule*, and the café, *Aux Halles*, both on rue de l'Amiral-Ronarc'h near the SI; *Auberge du Flamand*, 11 pl Charles-Valentin near the townhall, and *La Crêperie* on pl Roger-Salengro.

DUNKIRK 1940

The evacuation of 350,000 Allied troops from the beaches of Dunkirk from May 27 to June 4, 1940, has become one of those heroic wartime legends which conveniently conceals the fact that the Allies, through their own incompetence, almost lost their entire armed forces in the first few weeks of the war.

The German army had taken just ten days to reach the English Channel and could very easily have finished off the job. Unable to believe the ease with which he had overcome a numerically superior enemy, Hitler ordered his generals to halt their lightning advance. This allowed the Allied forces trapped in the Pas-de-Calais crucial breathing space in which to organise **Operation Dynamo**, the largest wartime evacuation ever undertaken. Initially it was hoped that around 10,000 men would be saved, though thanks to low-lying cloud and the assistance of over 1750 vessels – among them pleasure cruisers, fishing boats and river ferries – 140,000 French and over 200,000 British soldiers were successfully shipped back to England.

In France, the ratio of Brits to French evacuees caused bitter resentment since Churchill had promised that the two sides would go *bras dessus, bras dessous* ("arm in arm"). Meanwhile, the British media played up the "remarkable discipline" of the troops as they waited to embark, the "victory" of the RAF over the Luftwaffe and the "disintegration" of the French army all around. In fact, there was widespread indiscipline in the early stages as men fought for places on board; the battle for the skies was evenly matched; and the French fought long and hard to cover the whole operation, some 150,000 of them remaining behind to become prisoners of war. In addition, the Allies lost 7 destroyers and 177 fighter planes and were forced to abandon over 60,000 vehicles.

Malo-les-Bains and moving on

If you can't bear the thought of Dunkerque, you might want to consider staying in **MALO-LES-BAINS**, Dunkerque's nineteenth-century seaside suburb on the east side of town, from whose vast sandy strand the Allied troops were embarked in 1940 (see box). The *Hirondelle*, 46 av Faidherbe (☎28.63.17.65; closed Aug 15–Sept 7; ④) has **rooms** as well as a very reasonably priced restaurant, or if you fancy some **seafoood**, try *L'Iguane*, 15 digue des Alliés (daily 10am–10pm), or *Pavois*, 175 digue de Mer, both popular places on the seafront.

Moving on from Dunkerque by car, you'll be shepherded quickly (unless you take some pains to avoid it) onto the autoroute system, with links to Belgium and Germany as well as Paris. Heading west along the coast, on the other hand, brings you to Vauban-walled **GRAVELINES**, 16km from Dunkerque, site of one of France's many nuclear reactors.

Calais

CALAIS is under 40km from England – the Channel's narrowest crossing – and by far the busiest French passenger port. The port (and its accompanying petro-chemical works) easily dominates the town – in fact, there's not much else here. In the last war the British destroyed it to impede its use, fearing a German invasion. Ironically, the French still refer to it as "the most English town in France", an influence which began after the battle of Crécy in 1346, when Edward III seized it for use as a beach-head in the Hundred Years' War. It remained in English hands until 1558, when its loss caused Mary Tudor to make her famous schoolroom history quote: "When I am dead and opened, you shall find Calais lying in my heart." The association, however, has been maintained across the centuries by Brits both loved and unloved back home: Lady Emma Hamilton, Lord Nelson's mistress; Oscar Wilde on his uppers; Nottingham lace-makers who set up business in the early nineteenth century; and, most notably today, nine million British travellers per year, plus another million-odd day-trippers.

Arrival and accommodation

Don't bother walking into town from the ferry terminal (Calais-Maritime train station). There's a **free daytime bus service** to place d'Armes and the central Calais-Ville train station in Calais-Sud. The **gare routière** is at the southern end of bd Jacquard, by the municipal theatre. If you're intent on **hitching** to Paris, take a left out of the ferry terminal – the new autoroute bypass begins almost immediately, leading to both the A26 and the old N1. To phone the ferry companies, dial ☎21.96.67.10 for *Hoverspeed* or ☎21.34.55.00 for *Sealink SNCF*.

The town divides in two: **Calais-Nord**, the old town rebuilt after the war with the place d'Armes and rue Royale as its focus, is separated by canals from sprawling **Calais-Sud** which focuses on the Hôtel de Ville and the main shopping streets, bd Lafayette and bd Jacquard, named after the inventor of looms who mechanised Calais lacemaking.

Accommodation

Should you need to stay, there's plenty of cheap accommodation available, though it can be tricky finding a room late in the day in high season. If you're going to miss the boat home, phone before you arrive to book a room. Alternatively, you could use the **SI accommodation service**, at 12 bd Clemenceau (☎21.96.62.40; Mon–Sat 9am–7.30pm Sun 10am–1pm & 4.30–7.30pm), for which there is a small charge.

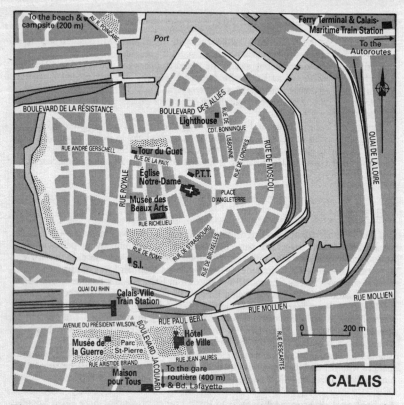

CALAIS

Hôtel du Cygne, 32 rue Jean-Jaurès (☎21.34.55.18). Behind the Hôtel de Ville and the cheapest place there is after the *Maison pour tous* youth hostel. ①

Hôtel Le Littoral, 71 rue Aristide-Briand (☎21.34.47.28). Large rooms and a popular choice, situated beside Parc St-Pierre. ②

Hôtel Richelieu, 17 rue Richelieu (☎21.34.61.60). More upmarket, but close to the park. ④

Hôtel Windsor, 2 rue du Cdt-Bonnique (☎21.34.59.40). Conveniently placed for the car ferry on the approach road to place d'Armes. ③/④

Hôtel Albert 1er, 51–53 rue de la Mer (☎21.34.36.08). Only hotel with seafront views. ④

Maison pour tous, 81 bd Jacquard (☎21.34.69.23; July & Aug; reception opens 5pm). 35F for hostel-type accommodation.

Camping municipal, 26 av Poincaré (☎21.46.62.00). An exposed site close to the beach.

The town

Although **Calais-Nord** is nominally the old town, its charms soon wear thin. The medieval **Tour du Guet** on the drab main square, place d'Armes, is the only building in the quarter to have survived wartime bombardment. From the Tour, rue de la Paix leads to the **Église Notre-Dame**, where Charles de Gaulle married local girl, Yvonne Vendroux, in 1921. Rather spuriously dubbed the only English Perpendicular church on the continent, it's not a particularly good example of the style, especially in its present state of dereliction. Frill fanciers can enjoy the unusual lacemaking exhibition in the **Musée des Beaux-Arts et de la Dentelle** (10am–noon, 2–5pm; closed Tues; 10F) on rue Richelieu.

Calais-Sud is scarcely more exciting. Just over the canal bridge, the town's landmark, its Flemish extravaganza of a **Hôtel de Ville**, which was finished in 1926 and, miraculously, survived the war, rears its belfry over 60m into the sky. Somewhat dwarfed by the building, Rodin's famous bronze **Burghers of Calais** records forever the self-sacrifice of these local dignitaries, who offered their lives to assuage the brutal lust of the victor at Crécy, Edward III – only to be spared at the last minute by the intervention of the Queen. For a record of Calais' wartime travails you can consult the **Musée de la Guerre** (daily March–Nov 10.30am–5.30pm; 10F) installed in a former German *Blockhaus* in the Parc St-Pierre across the street.

Eating

The area around place d'Armes is good for **restaurants**. Two that come highly recommended are *Le Touquet's*, 57 rue Royale (closed Mon) and the slightly more expensive *Channel*, 3 bd de la Résistance (closed Tues & Sun evening), overlooking the yacht basin. The *Café de Paris*, 72 rue Royale, and the self-service *Templier*, at the beach, offer cheaper fare. Remarkably, for the northern French provinces, there's also a popular (mostly male) gay bar called *Palm Beach* on rue Royale.

The Côte d'Escalles

The **coastal road** from Calais to Boulogne passes along some of the finest stretches of the Côte d'Opale (Opal Coast), where sea and sky merge in an opalescent, oyster-grey continuum and the air is tangy with salt. The long sandy beaches are exposed by huge tidal flows and backed by high chalk cliffs which the French have dubbed the **Côte d'Escalles**.

From Calais to Cap Gris-Nez

Right on the outskirts of Calais, BLÉRIOT-PLAGE commemorates Louis Blériot's epic first cross-channel flight in 1909. Six kilometres on, SANGATTE is set to be the French terminal for the **Channel tunnel** (see box). The nearby *Eurotunnel* information centre is disappointing, though at the weekends you can go on a slightly more interesting tour of the whole site. Thereafter, the road winds up on to the grassy windswept heights of **Cap Blanc-Nez**, topped by an obelisk commemorating the Dover Patrol who kept the channel free from U-boats during World War I. Better than the *Eurotunnel* centre for an overall history of chunnel exploits is the **Musée Transmanche** (April 15–Oct 15 daily 9am–noon & 2–6pm; rest of year weekends only; 15F), housed in the basement of a viewpoint café just off the D940 opposite the turnoff to the Cap Blanc-Nez obelisk. Hereafter, the road goes down to **WISSANT** and its enormous beach between the capes from which Julius Ceasar set sail in 55 BC to conquer Britain. The walk along the cliff tops past Wissant and up to **Cap Gris-Nez**, just 28km from the English coast, is an exhilarating one.

THE CHUNNEL

The notion of building a **tunnel** (or bridge) across the English Channel has long fired the imagination of the rulers and engineers of Britain and France. Napoléon was the first to toy seriously with the idea in 1802, but it wasn't until 1878 that the first real attempt was made, this time by the British, who got just 168m in five years before giving up. Edward Heath and Georges Pompidou had another go in 1973 in a fit of Euro-enthusiasm following the UK entry into the EEC, only for Harold Wilson to call it off after just 300m had been dug on each side. Finally it was left to the gigantic dual egos of Margaret Thatcher and François Mitterrand to go the whole way and commit both governments to completing the "chunnel" by 1993.

Eurotunnel were given the unenviable task of raising the billions needed to finance the project without government assistance – and of overcoming popular scepticism that this attempt, unlike the rest, would actually succeed. While anti-chunnel groups sprang up all over Kent and southeast England, protest in the sparsely populated and economically depressed northeast of France focussed on places bypassed by the tunnel rail-link. The town of Amiens, notably, set up shop in Victoria, London, selling ten-metre plots of French land in an attempt to foil the planned route.

More crucial to the survival of the project has been the spiralling cost of construction (effectively doubled since initial estimates). Arguments over money between *Eurotunnel* and the construction consortium *Transmanche Link*, who are actually building the fixed link, now look set to delay the opening of the tunnel, still optimistically scheduled to happen before the end of 1993. At the very least, only a limited service will operate to begin with – the British government, for one, don't intend to get their high-speed rail link sorted out until well into the next century. Moreover, there are serious doubts about the operational viability of the rapid cars-on-trains service (a 35-minute journey with departures every 20 minutes on a single line). And the pressure to finish the project on time has seen construction safety standards plummet, for which at least 12 workers have paid with their lives.

The Blockhaus at Audinghen

The entire Côte d'Opale is studded with massive concrete bunkers or *Blockhause*, that were part of the German World War II defences known as the **Atlantic Wall.** One of them, right beside the D940 at **AUDINGHEN**, equipped with a gun that could hit the English coast, has been converted into a rather rough and ready **museum** (daily Easter–Oct 9am–6pm; rest of year weekends only) of the paraphernalia of war. Burrowing two or three floors below ground level, it has curiosity value rather than any great attractions. The best exhibits are British propaganda material, and a poster, cautioning troops against the dangers of VD, in which a portly officer, buttons popping with excitement, is propositioned by a German fraülein ("Come mit me!").

Wimereux

Just 4km north of Boulogne is **WIMEREUX**, a traditional, turn-of-the-century seaside resort. Once favoured by the vacationing miners of the north of France, it still preserves a certain faded charm, with mock-Gothic and Tudor chalets holding out against the encroaching developers' bulldozers. Sale boards proliferate and it all looks set to become heavily gentrified. But the shore is pleasantly sandy and rocky, with plenty of wind-surfing and, to the north, walks along the cliffs.

The main drag through town, rue Carnot, has two good **hotels**: *Hôtel des Arts* at no.143 (☎21.32.43.13; ③), with a popular bar and restaurant, and *Hôtel les Promeneurs* at no.12 (☎21.32.41.13; ③). The SI is on place du Roi-Albert near the river, and the town itself is easily reached by bus or train (every couple of hours) from Boulogne-Ville to Wimille, the village just inland from Wimereux.

Boulogne-sur-Mer

BOULOGNE is quite different from Dunkerque and Calais – recommendation in itself. It has long been an important harbour and is claimed to be the largest fishing base in Europe. Rising above the port, an attractive medieval quarter, the Ville Haute, is flanked by grassy ramparts and dominated by a grand black-domed cathedral. Below, amid the newer shopping streets of the Ville Basse, are some of the best *charcuteries* and *pâtisseries* in the north, along with an impressive array of fish restaurants. Alone among the northeast channel ports this is a place that might actually tempt you to stay.

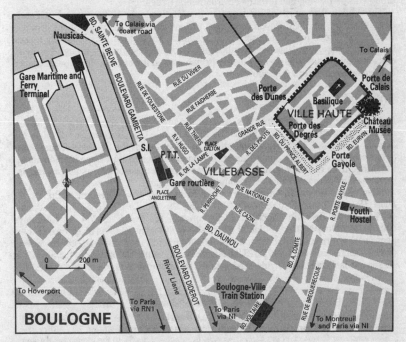

The town

The quiet cobbled streets of the **Ville Haute** make a pleasant respite from the noise and congestion of the Ville Basse. Within the walls, only the **Basilique Notre-Dame** is worth specially making time for. It's an odd building, raised in the nineteenth century by the town's vicar, without any architectural knowledge or advice. Against all the odds it seems to work. In the vast and labyrinthine crypt (Tues–Sun 2–5pm; 10F) you can see frescoed remains of the Romanesque building and relics of a Roman temple to Diana. In the main part of the church, the bizarre white statue of the Virgin and Child on a boat-chariot was drawn here (over the course of six years) on its own wheels from Lourdes during a pilgrimage in the 1940s.

Nearby, though less compelling, the **Château Musée** (May–Sept daily 10am–6/8pm; Nov–March 10am–1pm & 2–5pm; closed Tues; 20F), has items donated by a local-born Egyptologist, including a good collection of Greek pots. Alternatively – and free – you can stroll round along the **medieval walls**, decked out with rosebeds, gravel paths and benches for picnicking, with impressive views over the town and port.

Beyond the Ville Haute

Outside the Ville Haute the place to head for is the town's smart new aquarium at the *Centre National de la Mer* or **Nausicaá**, on bd Ste-Beuve (daily April–Sept 10am–8pm; Oct–March 10am–6pm; 45F). Ultra-violet lighting and New Age music create a suitably weird ambience, while hammerhead sharks circle overhead and giant conger eels conceal themselves in rusty pipes – definitely not for piscophobes. There's plenty of educational stuff, too (in French and English throughout), and a half-hour film show, though only a passing nod towards environmental issues.

Three kilometres north of Boulogne on the N1 stands the **Colonne de la Grande Armée**, where, in 1803, Napoléon is said to have changed his mind about invading Britain and turned his troops east towards Austria. The column was originally topped by a bronze figure of Napoléon symbolically clad in Roman garb – though his head, equally symbolically, was shot off by the British navy in the last war. It is now displayed in the chateau museum (see above).

Practicalities

Ferries dock within a few minutes' walk of the town centre. If you arrive by **hovercraft**, a little further out, you'll be met by a free shuttle bus (*Hoverspeed*, ☎21.30.27.26; *Sealink SNCF*, ☎21.30.25.11). If you intend to stay, stop at the **SI** (Mon–Thurs 9am–8pm Fri & Sat 9am–10pm Sun 10am–8am) – housed in a small Art-Deco pavilion across the bridge from the ferry terminal – which can supply a mass of information and advise on availability of rooms which, in summer, get taken early.

Most of the reasonable **hotels** are close to the port area. Cheapest of the lot are *Hôtel Hamiot*, 1 rue Faidherbe (☎21.31.44.20; ②) and *Le Castel*, 51 rue Nationale (☎21.31.52.88; ②). The small *La Plage* towards the beach at 124 bd Ste-Beuve (☎21.31.34.78; closed Dec 19–Jan 5; ④), is also worth a try, and has a reasonably inexpensive restaurant. Another good bet is the friendly and modern **youth hostel** (☎21.31.48.22; curfew 11pm; IYHF card necessary), southeast of the old town walls at 36 rue de la Porte-Gayole. It's a fair climb, so phone first to check for space. Ten minutes by bus along the bd Ste-Beuve, on the way to the sandy strand of Wimereux, is *Camping Moulin Wibert*, a three-star place (April–mid-Oct).

For **eating**, there are dozens of possibilities around place Dalton or up in the Ville Haute, but bear in mind the day-tripper trade and be selective. The *Hamiot*, right opposite the port is a basic standby, or, for beer drinkers, *La Houblonnière* on rue Monsigny (closed Sun & Aug) has a vast international selection of brews to wash down its *plats du jour*. The brasserie *Chez Jules*, on the *place*, is always a good bet, and serves food all day. For something more refined – and don't be put off by its name – try the *Welsh Pub* also on place Dalton (closed Mon), or *La Matelote*, 80 bd Ste-Beuve (closed Sun eve & late June), both of which specialise in seafood. **Vegetarians** should head for *La Vie Claire*, 15 rue Coquelin (lunchtimes only). For an early breakfast (5am onwards), chow down with the fishermen at *Bar Hamiot* on rue Faidherbe.

Inland: the Pas-de-Calais

Understandably, most tourists travel non-stop through the **Pas-de-Calais**, France's northernmost *département*, heading for warmer climes and more varied scenery. However, if you're on a short break to one of the channel ports, it's worth making the effort to venture inland – **Cassel** in particular is a minor gem for this part of France.

St-Omer

The first stop inland for many visitors to France is **ST-OMER**, a quiet, unassuming little town, though one which establishes an immediately distinct and foreign character. The landscape seems to expand and the town itself has flights of Flemish magnificence, especially in the **Hôtel de Ville** and some of the recently restored mansions on rue Gambetta. The Gothic **Basilique Notre-Dame** contains some noteworthy statuary, and there are some handsome exhibits in the eighteenth-century **Hôtel Sandelin** museum on rue Carnot (Wed–Sun 10am–noon & 2–6pm), in particular, a glorious piece of medieval goldsmithing known as the *Pied de Croix de St-Bertin*.

To get to the centre of town from the exuberant 1903 **gare SNCF**, cross over the canal and walk ten minutes down rue F-Ringot, past the PTT and into rue Carnot. **Accommodation** is satisfactory enough: *Le Comte de Luxembourg* in the street of the same name (☎21.38.10.09; ③), and the *St-Louis* at 25 rue d'Arras (☎21.38.35.21; ③/④), are both fine, if not especially cheap. The nearest **campsite** is near the Forêt de Clairmarais, 4.5km east of St-Omer (☎21.38.34.80; April–Oct; no bus). Place Maréchal-Foch is lined with cafés and **restaurants**; try the new Anglo-Indian place, *Sitar*, at no. 32, or for Flemish fare, the *Belle Époque*, just off the square at 3 pl P-Painlevé.

Aside from the pleasant **public gardens** to the west of town, there's also the possibility of exploring the nearby **marais**, a network of very Flemish-seeming waterways cut between plots of land on reclaimed marshes east of the town along the river Aa. You can **hire** boats from *Taverne Flamande*, 60 route de Clairmarais, or join one of the *bâteaux-promenade* which leave from the bridge on the D209, 2km west of the gare SNCF (daily July & Aug; Sun only May, June & Sept; 40F per person). The round trip takes roughly two hours, the longer one includes a ride down the unique vertical boat-lift at Arques. For more information go to the **SI** by the **gare routière** on pl P-Painlevé.

The Blockhaus at Eperlecques

Another interesting excursion is to the **Forêt d'Eperlecques** (3 or 4 trains daily from Calais to Watten station, on the eastern edge of the forest), 12km north of St-Omer. Here in 1943-44 the Germans, or rather 6000 half-starved slave labourers, built the largest ever *Blockhaus* from which to launch **V2 rockets** against London. Luckily the RAF and the French Resistance prevented its ever being ready for use. It's open daily from

June to September, 10am to noon and 2 to 7pm; in April, May and October 1 to November 11 daily 2.15 to 6pm; in March Sunday only, 2.15 to 6pm admission 20F by guided tour only).

Cassel

Twenty-three kilometres east of St-Omer is the hilltop town of **CASSEL**. Hills are rare in Flanders and Cassel was much fought over from Roman times onwards. Marshall Foch spent spent "some of the most distressing hours" of his life here during World War I, and it was up to the top of Cassel's hill that the "Grand Old Duke of York" marched his 10,000 men in 1793, though, as hinted in the nursery rhyme, he failed to take the town.

Cassel consists of little more than its very Flemish Grande-Place, lined with some magnificent mansions. The train station, 3km west of town, is linked only to Dunkerque, so you'll need your own transport to justify the trip. It's very worthwhile if you have it, to explore the narrow, cobbled streets which fan out from the square: southwards to a fine Gothic church; northwards to the public gardens from which you have an unrivalled view over Flanders (Belgium is just 10km away). Here among the trees is Cassel's only remaining wooden **windmill** – there used to be twenty-nine pounding their oil mills and driving the locals mad day and night – which revolves on its axis every Sunday. For refreshments, head for the café in the nearby nineteenth-century mansion, headquarters of the frequently banned Flemish radio staion, *Ulyenspiegel*.

There are one or two small **hotels** should you wish to stay over, including the fabulous eighteenth-century *Schoëbeque* on rue Foch (☎28.42.42.67; ④), where the marshal himself used to stay. Two gourmet **restaurants**, *Le Sauvage* and *Taverne Flamande*, are posed side by side on the Grande-Place, but you can get simpler fare opposite at the *Hôtel de Ville*.

From Boulogne to Amiens

Strictly speaking, there's no coast road south of Boulogne. The nearest thing to it, the D940, keeps a fair distance from the shores, as does the main Calais–Paris railway line. This makes the getting to the seaside resorts by public transport quite tricky, with the exception of the nobbiest of the lot, **Le Touquet**. One recommended diversion is the bird sanctuary at **Marquenterre**, one of only two in the country. A more direct road south is the N1, which cuts across some fairly dull countryside to **Amiens** – **Montreuil** being the single significant distraction en route.

Le Touquet

Among dunes planted with wind-flattened tamarisks and pines, **LE TOUQUET-PARIS-PLAGE** (to give it its full, pretentious title) is one of those peculiarly French northern resorts, once the height of fashion, now dully suburban. In the 1920s and 1930s, and for a spell after World War II, the town, with its broad sands and leafy luxury villas, ranked with places on the Côte d'Azur. At one time it is supposed to have had flights from Britain every ten minutes. The opening up of long-distance air travel put an end to this era, though not completely, nor forever. The new British rich, sensing a fresh field of elitism, are back in some force. Their private aircraft are now virtually the airport's only traffic.

It is an extraordinary set-up really and not one where many vistors will feel at home. With strict sociological intent, however, take a glimpse at the *Hôtel Manoir* on av du Golf, the most baronial of the town's bunch, which includes *Le Westminster* and *Le Bristol*. And if you're in town anyway, an expensive treat worth indulging in is Le Touquet's *Aqualud* **swimming complex** right on the front, which boasts no fewer than three giant waterslides (admission 60F). For those with kids (and still more money), there's the vast *Bagatelle* amusement park, 10km south of Le Touquet (daily May–mid-Sept 9.30am–7pm).

To get to Le Touquet, take the train from Boulogne to ÉTAPLES, a much more down-to-earth fishing village near the mouth of the River Canche, from where a local bus covers the last 4km. For somewhere reasonable to **spend the night**, try *L'Union*, 7 rue de Metz (☎21.05.08.88; ②), or *Hôtel Armide*, 56 rue Léon-Garet (☎21.05.37.21.76; ③ for half-board). There's also a **campsite**, on the waterfront of the Canche estuary, but this requires three nights minimum stay. The **SI** in the *Palais de l'Europe* on pl de l'Hermitage can furnish you with a free map of the town.

Montreuil-sur-Mer

Once a port, but now stranded 13km inland, **MONTREUIL-SUR-MER** is a far cry from Le Touquet. Strikingly situated on a sharp little hilltop above the river Canche, and enclosed by a ring of Vauban walls, it's an immediately appealing place. Lawrence Sterne spent a night here on his *Sentimental Journey*, and it was the scene of much of the action in Victor Hugo's *Les Misérables*, perhaps best evoked by the steep cobbled street of Cavée St-Firmin, first left after the Porte de Boulogne, a short climb from the **gare SNCF**.

Two minor Gothic masterpieces grace the main square: the **Église St-Saulvé**, and a tiny wood-panelled **chapelle** tucked into the side of the red-brick *Hôtel Dieu*. To the south there are numerous cobbled lanes to wander down, replete with half-timbered artisan houses. In the northwestern corner of the walls lies Vauban's **citadelle** (daily 9.30am–noon & 2–6pm; closed Tues; 8F) – ruined, overgrown and, after dark, pretty atmospheric, with subterranean gun emplacements and a fourteenth-century tower which records the coats of arms of the French noblemen killed at Agincourt.

The town's **youth hostel** (☎21.06.10.83) is by far the cheapest place to stay, housed in one of the citadel's outbuildings and giving access to the place long after the gates have been closed to the public. At the other end of the **accommodation** scale, there's the gastronomic **château-hôtel** opposite the citadel (☎21.81.53.04; ⑤ and above). For something in between, try *Le Darnétal* on place Darnétal (☎21.06.04.87; ④). In the second half of August, Montreuil puts on a surprisingly lively mini-arts festival of opera, theatre and dance, *Les Malins Plaisirs*.

Agincourt and Crécy

Two of the bloodiest Anglo-French battles of the Middle Ages took place near the attractive little town of **HESDIN** on the river Canche (a town familiar to Simenon fans from the TV series *Inspector Maigret*). Getting to either site is really only feasible with your own transport. The nearest train stations are Hesdin or Rue for Crécy (17km), and Blangy-sur-Ternoise for Agincourt (6km).

Crécy

Twenty kilometres southwest of Hesdin, at the **Battle of Crécy**, Edward III inflicted his first of many defeats on the French in 1346, thus beginning the Hundred Years' War. This was the first appearance of the new English weapon on the continent – the six-foot longbow – and the first use in European history of gunpowder. There's not a lot to see, just the **Moulin Édouard III** (now a watchtower), 1km northeast of the little town of CRÉCY-EN-PONTHIEU on the D111 to WADICOURT, site of the windmill from which Edward watched the hurly-burly of battle. And further south, on the D56 to Fontaine, the battered **Croix de Bohême** marks the place where King John of Bohemia died, having insisted on leading his men into the fight, despite being blind.

Agincourt

Ten thousand more died in the heaviest defeat ever of France's feudal knighthood at the **Battle of Agincourt**, which took place in 1415. Forced by muddy conditions to fight on foot in their heavy armour, the French were sitting ducks to the lighter, mobile English archers. The rout took place near present-day AZINCOURT, about 12km northeast of Hesdin on the D928; a **museum** in the village includes a short film about the battle, and notice-boards have been placed at strategic points on the battlefield indicating the sequence of fighting. Just east of the village, by the crossroads of the D104 and the road to Maisoncelle, a copse and a cross mark the position of the original grave pits whose reputation was once so grim it used to be called **"The Carrion"**.

The Marquenterre bird sanctuary

Ornithologists will need no persuasion, but if you know nothing of birds, the **Parc ornithologique du Marquenterre** will be a revelation. In terms of landscape, it is beautiful and strange: all dunes, tamarisks and pine forest, full of salty meres and ponds thick with water plants. It's "new" land, formed by the erosion of the Normandy coast and the silting of the Somme estuary, where thousands of cattle are grazed today to give their meat the much-prized flavour of the "salt meadows".

One of only two bird sanctuaries in the whole of France, Marquenterre is a tiny resrve in an area which gives new meaning to the word "sanctuary". From the opening of the water-fowl season – on July 14, Bastille Day, ironically – gunshots can be heard, day and night, all around. No species, however rare, is spared.

The sanctuary

Admission isn't cheap (currently around 40F), and unless you carry your own, you'll need to fork out to hire binoculars, too – there's no point in trying to manage without. Once inside, there's a choice of two itineraries, the longer being the more interesting. It takes you from resting area to resting area whence you can train your glasses on dozens of species – ducks, geese, oyster-catchers, terns, egrets, redshanks, greenshanks, spoonbills, herons, storks, godwits – some of them fat-cat residents, most taking a breather from their epic migratory flights to and from the ends of the earth. In April and May they head north, and they return from the end of August to October, so these are the best times to visit.

The sanctuary is open from April to November. The nearest town of any size is **RUE**, one of a number of attractive fishing villages in the area now stranded inland by the silting up of the Somme. Rue lies on the main Calais–Paris railway, but the final 7km to the sanctuary is only served by a bus in July and August.

The Somme estuary

After Marquenterre the bus meanders through yet more dry fishing hamlets, whose crouching cottages are reminders of their former poverty. Some, such as **LE CROTOY**, with enough sea still to attract the yachties, are enjoying the inevitable holiday- and second-home boom. Its south-facing beach attracted numerous writers and painters over the years: Jules Verne wrote *Twenty Thousand L:eagues Under The Sea* here; Colette, Toulouse-Lautrec and Seurat were also frequent visitors. **Rooms** are available at *Le Baie*, quai Léonard (☎22.27.81.22; ③).

In summer you can take a resuscitated steam train (Tues–Sun, July & Aug; rest of summer Sun only) around the bay to **ST-VALÉRY-SUR-SOMME**, from whose shores William the Conqueror set sail for England in 1066. With a fully intact *Ville Haute*, and a quayside of brightly painted fishermen's cottages, it easily outclasses Le Crotoy, its main rival across the estuary. There are **rooms** and fresh seafood available at both ends of the scale: cheap at *Hôtel du Port et des Bains* on quai Blavet (☎22.60.80.09; ①/ ②); expensive at the eighteenth-century *Château du Romerel*, quai du Romerel (☎22.26.93.23; ⑤ and above).

Between the two, near NOYELLES-SUR-MER, lies one of the most unusual war graves in France – the **Chinese Cemetery**. Nearly 1000 Chinese were drawn from north China to serve as dockers at St-Valéry, one of the major supply ports during the First World War, though most of them died in the 1919 yellow fever epidemic. Noyelles is also served by the steam train service, after which it's another 2km to the cemetery along the D111 to Nolette.

Abbeville

ABBEVILLE lies about half way from Calais to Paris, a convenient stop-off on the N1. Until a German air raid in May 1940, it was also a very beautiful town. Nowadays, all that remain of its former glories are a superbly ornate Flemish-style **gare SNCF**, what's reputed to be the oldest belfry in France, and the Gothic **Cathédrale St-Vulfran**, the latter on a par with those at Amiens and Beauvais, but under scaffolding since the war and still closed to the public. If you've time to kill, the best Abbeville has on offer is the country mansion of **Bagatelle** 2km south of town (not to be confused with the nearby amusement park of the same name).

Looking for somewhere to stay, *Le Conde*, 14–16 place de la Libération (☎22.24.06.33; ③) and *Le Jean Bart*, 5 rue Ste-Catherine (☎22.24.21.71; ③) have the cheapest **rooms** in town.

Amiens

Were it not for the cathedral, few travellers would stop at **AMIENS**. Badly scarred during both world wars, and with heavy traffic pounding along its ringroad built over the old city walls, it's not an immediately likeable place. Yet there is more to the town than first meets the eye – St-Leu, the canal-laced medieval *quartier*, north of the cathedral, has recently been renovated, and the town's university makes its presence felt.

Arrival and accommodation

Coming out of the main **gare SNCF** (Amiens-Nord) or **gare routière**, you find yourself in a rectangular square. At the opposite end is the slim, miserable-looking concrete **Tour Perret** – the tallest in Europe when it was built in 1952. In fact, the whole ensemble is the work of Auguste Perret, the architect of post-war Le Havre, whose only originality seems to have been the espousal of concrete and height.

From the Tour Perret, the cathedral is just five minutes' walk away. In summer, there are **SI** offices in front of both it and the station. The main SI is in the *Maison de la Culture*, 1 rue Jean-Catelas (Mon–Sat 10am–noon & 2–7pm), fifteen minutes' walk from the station, along rue de Noyon and its continuations. All three offices make **room** reservations, the cheapest options being *Hôtel La Renaissance*, 8bis rue André (☎22.91.70.23; ②); *Les Touristes*, 22bis place Notre-Dame (☎22.91.33.45; ②); and *Victor Hugo*, 2 rue de l'Oratoire (☎22.91.57.91; ③); all three are within spitting distance of the cathedral.

The **youth hostel** (☎22.44.54.21; IYHF card required; curfew 10.30pm; reception closes 8pm) is a twenty-minute walk from the station, along bd Alsace-Lorraine, then first left after the bridge, situated in the middle of Amiens' **campsite** by a lake with a great cathedral vista.

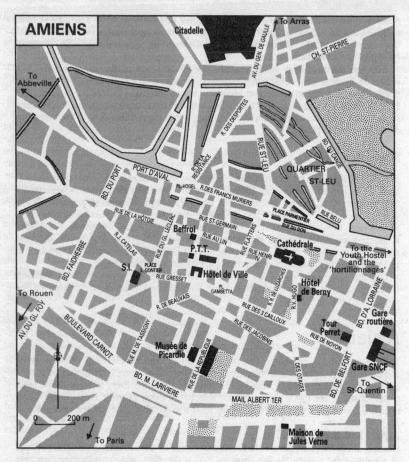

The Cathedral

The **Cathédrale Notre-Dame** provides the city's very obvious focus, whatever your interests. First of all, it dominates all else by its sheer size – it's the biggest Gothic building in France. But its appeal lies mainly in its unusual uniformity of style. Begun in 1220 under the architect Robert de Luzarches, it was pretty well complete by 1269, with just the tops of the towers unfinished; thus it escaped the influence of succeeding architectural fads that marred the "purity" of some of its slower sisters.

The **west front**, now in need of a good scrub, is best seen with early afternoon sun falling obliquely across it – not too easy given the climate – to give some good *chiaroscuro* effects and bring out the detail of the riot of sculpture (over 4000 pieces in all) adorning the three main porches. By way of contrast, the **interior** (daily 7.30am–noon & 2–5/7pm) is all straight up and no fuss: a light, calm and unaffected space. Ruskin thought the apse "not only the best, but the very first thing done perfectly in its manner by northern Christendom". If there is any pretence, it's in the later embellishments, like the sixteenth-century **choir stalls** (guided tours only), but they are works of such breathtaking virtuosity you might forgive anyone who could handle a chisel like that for wanting to show off. The same goes for the sculpted panels depicting the life of **St Firmin,** Amiens' first bishop, on the right side of the choir screen. The figures in the crowd scenes are shown in fifteenth-century costume, the men talking serious business among themselves, while their wives listen more credulously to the preacher's words.

Quartier St-Leu, the hortillonnages and the museums

Just north of the cathedral is the **quartier St-Leu**, a thoroughly Flemish network of canals and cottages which once belonged to Amiens' thriving textile industry. The town still produces much of the country's **velvet**, but the factories moved out to the suburbs long ago, leaving St-Leu to rot away in peace. That is, until the local property developers moved in. The whole area was certainly in bad need of renovation, and the rue de Don and rue Belu still retain some of the old character of the *quartier*, but many of the old houses have simply been torn down and turned into chi-chi riverside flats. Despite all that, it remains an interesting area to wander round.

Five minutes' walk up the towpath, on the edge of town, the canals still provide a useful function as waterways for the **hortillonnages** – a series of incredibly fertile market gardens, reclaimed from the marshes created by the very slow-flowing Somme. Farmers travel about them in black, high-prowed punts and a few still take their produce into the city by boat for the Saturday morning **market**, the *marché sur l'eau*, on the riverbank of place Parmentier. If you want a closer look round the *hortillon-nages*, there are inexpensive **boat trips** (mid-April–Sept) from the chemin de Halage, off bd de Beauvillé – ask the SI for details.

If you're interested in Picardy culture, you might take a look at Amiens' two regional museums. Close by the cathedral in the seventeenth-century **Hôtel de Berny** (Tues–Sun 10am–noon & 2–6pm; 15F) there are local history collections, including a portrait of Choderlos de Laclos, author of *Les Liaisons Dangereuses*, who was born in Amiens. Five minutes' walk south of central place Gambetta, a nineteenth-century mansion houses the **Musée de Picardie** (times as above), whose star exhibit is a collection of rare sixteenth-century paintings on wood donated to the cathedral by what was in effect a local literary society, some of the pictures still in their original frames carved by the same craftsmen who worked the choir stalls. A third museum-cum-documentation centre is the house, at 2 rue Dubois, of **Jules Verne**, who spent most of his life, and died, in Amiens (Tues–Sat 9.30am–noon & 2–6pm).

Food, festivals and transport details

Cheap brasseries and restaurants spread out below Tour Perret, while in the centre, around place Gambetta, there are numerous snackbars and food shops. More specifically recommended are the following places in St-Leu: *Le Vieil Amiens* on rue Belu (closed Wed), which gives another great view over the canal to the cathedral; *La Poissonade*, place du Don, a seafood snackery even closer to the cathedral; and *Memo*, a Turkish restaurant just off rue des Majots. For a more expensive and memorable meal, you couldn't do better than *Les Marissons*, on pont de la Dodane, a converted fifteenth-century boat-shed decked out in Picardy colours.

For one week in May Amiens bursts into life for its annual international **jazz festival**; on the third weekend in June, the local costumes come out for the **Fête d'Amiens**; and in November there's a cinema festival. In the summer, traditional Picardy **marionnettes** give performances (mostly evenings) at the *Maison du Théâtre*, 8 rue des Majots, in the quartier St-Leu.

Moving on from Amiens to Paris and beyond, you can choose between train, bus or *Allostop*, 45 rue des Otages (Mon–Fri 9.30am–12.30pm & 1.30–6.30pm; Sat mornings only). For St-Quentin or Beauvais you're best off by bus, while Albert is about 40 minutes by bus or train, both of which continue through the area of the Somme battlefields to Arras and the Canadian war memorial at Vimy Ridge.

Beauvais

As you head south from Amiens towards Paris the countryside becomes broad and flat – agricultural, though not rustic. **BEAUVAIS** seems to fit into this landscape. Rebuilt, like Amiens, after the last world war, it's a drab, neutral place, which – unlike Amiens – really is only redeemed by its radiating Gothic cathedral.

Beauvais is an hour by train from Paris, and the **gare SNCF** is a short walk from the centre of town – take av de la République, then right up rue de Malherbe. Just off the main square, on place Clemenceau, the **SI** can provide exhaustive further information. If you want to stay, two possible **hotels** are the *Bristol*, 58–60 rue de la Madeleine (☎44.84.33.85; ③), and *Le Brazza*, 22 rue de la Madeleine (☎44.45.03.86; ③). There's a **campsite** just out of town on the Paris road. For fine fare on the square, call in at the restaurant *Le Marignon* at 1 rue de Malherbe (☎44.48.15.15); the 98F menu offers cracking tuck.

If you happen to fly to Paris on a charter plane from London, you may well arrive at Beauvais airport ("BVA" on your ticket). Customs and immigration at the airport only take a moment, but as there's a bus link on to Paris, you wouldn't be likely to stay. What is now an innocuous-looking field five miles south of Beauvais was the site on October 5th, 1930 of the infamous R-101 **airship** crash.

Around town

The **Cathédrale St-Pierre** rises above the town, its roof, unadorned by tower or spire, seeming squat for all its height. It is a building that perhaps more than any other in northern France demonstrates the religious materialism of the Middle Ages – its sole intention and function to be taller and larger than its rivals. The **choir**, completed in 1272, was once 5m higher than that of Amiens, though only briefly – it collapsed in 1284. Its replacement, only completed three centuries later, was raised by the sale of indulgences – a right granted to the local bishops by Pope Leo X. This, too, however, fell within a few years and, the authorities having overreached themselves financially, the church remained unfinished, forlorn and mutilated. The appeal of the building, and its real beauty, is in its glass, its sculpted doorways and the remnants of the so-called **Basse-Oeuvre**, a ninth-century Carolingian church incorporated into the structure. It also contains a couple of remarkable clocks, including one 12m high which displays the night sky over Beauvais and features the Archangel Michael helping to weight souls at the Last Judgement.

Stopping at Beauvais to break the journey, you'll probably want to give the rest of the town no more than a passing look. The **Église St-Étienne**, a few blocks to the south of the cathedral on rue de Malherbe, houses yet more spectacular Renaissance stained-glass windows. There's also the **Galerie Nationale de Tapisserie** behind the cathedral (Tues–Sun 9.30–11.30am & 2–4.30/6pm; 15F), a museum of tapestry, for which Beauvais was once renowned, and the **Musée Départemental** (Tues–Sun 10am–noon & 2–6pm; 10F), devoted to painting, local history and archaeology, in the sharp, black-towered building opposite. The rousing statue in the central square is local heroine **Jeanne Hachette**, a fighter and inspiration in the defence of the town against Charles the Bold, Duke of Burgundy, in 1472.

THE INDUSTRIAL NORTH AND THE BATTLEFIELDS

Picardy, Artois and Flanders are littered with the monuments, battlefields and cemeteries of the two **world wars**, but nowhere as intensely as the region northeast of Amiens, between **Albert** and **Arras**. It was here, among the fields and villages of the **Somme**, that the main battle lines of the First World War were drawn. They can be visited most spectacularly at **Vimy Ridge**, just off the A26 north of Arras, where the trenches have been left *in situ*. Lesser sites, often more poignant, are dotted over the countryside around Albert and along the *circuit de souvenir*.

A more enduring and more domestic presence in the life of northern France has been that of the **coalfields** and all their related heavy industrial works. At their peak of production they formed a continuous stretch from Béthune in the west to Valenciennes in the east, though the industry is now in terminal decline. At **Lewarde** you can visit one of the pits associated with Zola's novel, *Germinal*, while at **Lille**, the "Coalville" of the north, or the pleasant town of **Douai**, you can see what the masters did with the brass from the muck.

Lille

LILLE, by far the largest city in the north, is the very symbol of French industry and working-class politics. Its mayor, Pierre Mauroy, was the first Socialist Prime Minister appointed by Mitterrand in 1981. In every direction the city spreads far into the countryside, a mass of suburbs and heavy industrial plants. Lille exhibits most of the problems and assets of contemporary France – some of the worst poverty and racial conflict in the country, a crime rate rivalled only by Paris and Marseille, and a certain regionalism; *Lillois* sprinkle their speech with a French-Flemish *patois* and, to some extent, assert a Flemish identity. But there is also classic French affluence. The city has a lovely central heart, Vieux Lille, some vibrant and obviously prosperous commercial areas, modern residential squares, a large university, a brand new métro system, and a very serious attitude to its culture and restaurants. Although you may not consider Lille a prime destination, if you're travelling through this region, it's worth at least a day and a night.

Arrival and accommodation

The central **Grande-Place** is just a few minutes' walk from the **gare routière** and adjacent **gare SNCF** (originally Paris' Gare du Nord, but brought here brick by brick in 1865). Despite being the fifth largest city in France, the centre of Lille is small enough to walk round, and, unless you choose to visit Villeneuve d'Ascq on the outskirts, you won't even need to use the city's efficient métro system.

There is an **SI** office in the station, but for more comprehensive information, it's best to go to the office in place Rihour (Mon 2–6pm Tues–Sat 10am–6pm; it also houses the *Allostop* hitching agency). Both SIs run a **free accommodation service**, but there should be few problems finding a cheap place to stay if you don't mind the slightly seedy station area.

Accommodation

Hôtel des Voyageurs, 10 place de la Gare (☎20.06.43.14). Slip of a building directly opposite the station offering basic, cheap rooms – worth it just for the wrought-iron lift. ①

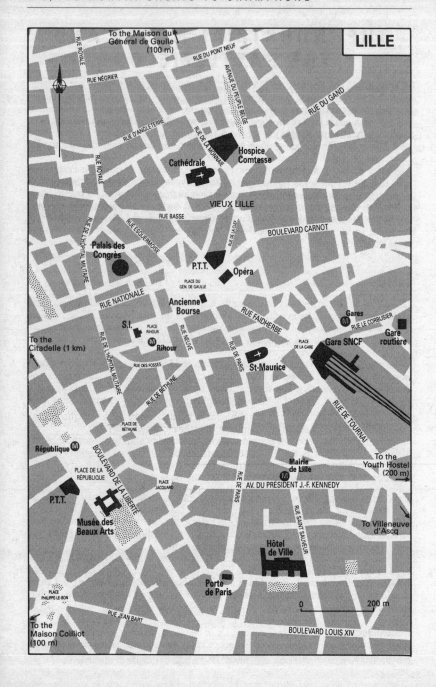

LILLE

RUE ROYALE

To the Maison du
Général de Gaulle
(100 m)

RUE DU PONT NEUF

RUE NÉGRIER

RUE DU GAND

AVENUE DU PEUPLE BELGE

RUE D'ANGLETERRE

RUE DE LA MONNAIE

Hospice
Comtesse

Cathédrale

RUE ROYALE

VIEUX LILLE

RUE BASSE

RUE ESQUERMOISE

BOULEVARD CARNOT

RUE DE LA CLEF

Palais des
Congrès

RUE DE L'HÔPITAL MILITAIRE

P.T.T.

Opéra

PLACE DU
GÉN DE GAULLE

RUE NATIONALE

Ancienne
Bourse

RUE FAIDHERBE

Gares
M
RUE LE CORBUSIER

S.I.

PLACE
RIHOUR

RUE NEUVE

PLACE
DE LA GARE

Gare SNCF

Gare
routière

To the
Citadelle (1 km)

M
Rihour

RUE DE L'HÔPITAL MILITAIRE

RUE DES FOSSÉS

RUE DE PARIS

St-Maurice

RUE DE BÉTHUNE

RUE DE TOURNAI

PLACE DE
BÉTHUNE

République
M

BOULEVARD DE LA LIBERTÉ

Mairie
de Lille
M

To the
Youth Hostel
(200 m)

PLACE DE LA
RÉPUBLIQUE

PLACE
JACQUARD

RUE DE PARIS

AV. DU PRÉSIDENT J.-F. KENNEDY

P.T.T.

RUE SAINT SAUVEUR

To Villeneuve
d'Ascq

Musée des
Beaux Arts

Hôtel
de Ville

PLACE
PHILIPPE-LE-BON

Porte
de Paris

0   200 m

RUE JEAN BART

To the
Maison Coilliot
(100 m)

BOULEVARD LOUIS XIV

Hôtel Continental, 11 place de la Gare (☎20.51.85.57). More upmarket version of the *Voyageurs*, complete with satellite TV. ③

Hôtel Constantin, 5 rue des Fosses (☎20.54.32.26). Right at the heart of things in the pedestrianised centre with clean rooms and a pleasant floral patio. ③

Auberge de Jeunesse, 1 av Julien-Destrée (☎20.52.76.02; no IYHF card needed; curfew 11pm). New Swiss chalet-type youth hostel, ten minutes' walk from the station. To get there walk southeast along rue de Tournai, cross the pedestrian underground walkway below the autoroute and you'll find it across the car park next to the *Foire Internationale*.

Camping Les Ramiers, Bondues (☎20.23.13.42; April–Oct). Lille's nearest site is actually in the village of Bondues, about 10km north of the city, and linked by bus.

Around the city

The point to make for is the **Grande-Place** (otherwise known as place du Général-de-Gaulle) which marks the southern boundary of the old quarter, **Vieux Lille**. To the south, is the central pedestrianised shopping area which extends along **rue de Béthune** as far as the adjacent squares of place Béthune and place de la République.

Vieux Lille

One side of the Grande-Place is dominated by the old exchange building, the lavishly ornate **Ancienne Bourse**, as perfect a representative of its age as could be imagined. To the merchants of seventeenth-century Lille, all things Flemish were the epitome of wealth and taste; they were not men to stint on detail, neither here nor on the imposing surrounding mansions. Recently cleaned up, the courtyard is now an organised flea market, with stalls selling books, junk and flowers. Lounging around the fountain at the centre of the *place* is a favourite *Lillois* pastime. At its centre is a column commemorating the city's resistance to the Austrian seige of 1792, topped by *La Déesse*, modelled on the wife of the mayor at the time.

North of the Bourse, you can see how the Flemish Renaissance architecture developed, becoming distinctly French, and combining brick with stone in grand flights of Baroque extravagance. The superlative example of this style is Lille's very own **Opéra**, which has a facade so strident it's almost ridiculous. It was built at the turn of this century by Louis Cordonnier, as was the equally inflated **belfry** of the neighbouring Nouvelle Bourse and Chamber of Commerce, now the city's main PTT.

Further north, the streets of the old town are pleasant to wander through, though the only specific sight is the **Hospice Comtesse** on rue de la Monnaie. Twelfth-century in origin, though much reconstructed in the eighteenth century, it served as a hospital until as recently as 1945. Its old ward, the *Salle des Malades*, can be visited (daily 10am–12.30pm & 2–6pm; closed Tues; entry 10F; free Wed & Sat am). Rue d'Angleterre, and the streets off it, was until quite recently an entirely **Arab quarter** of town. Gradually over the last decade, though, the boutiques and designer offices have taken over, and only a few families now remain.

In this unlikely part of town, at 9 rue Princesse, is the house where **Charles de Gaulle** was born in 1890. Predictably enough, it's now a **museum** (Wed–Sun 10am–noon & 2–5pm; 8F). Another must for military buffs is the neaby **Citadelle** which overlooks the old town to the northwest, constructed in familiar star-shaped fashion by Vauban. Still in military hands, it too can be visited, though only on Sundays, and by guided tour (details from SI; 30F).

Amid all the city's secular pomp, Lille's ecclesiastical architecture seems rather subdued. The city's cathedral, **Cathédrale Notre-Dame-de-la-Treille**, built in the last century, is undistinguished and still unfinished. Which means Lille's finest church is the cathedral-esque **Église St-Maurice**, close to the station off place de la Gare, a classic red-brick Flemish *Hallekerke*, with the characteristic five aisles of the style.

South of the Grande-Place

Just south of the Grande-Place is **Place Rihour**, a modern-looking leafy square with an old palace that now houses the **SI**, hidden behind an ugly war monument of gigantic proportions. Further south, the city's busiest shopping street, **rue de Béthune**, leads into place Béthune, another fine square, with some excellent cafés, and beyond to the **Musée des Beaux Arts** on place de la République (daily 9.30am–12.30pm & 2–6pm; closed Tues; 10F, free Wed & Sat afternoon). Like so many French art museums it studiously covers each art genre: paintings, ceramics, tapestries and so on. Here, though, the emphasis is very much on the Flemish painters, from "primitives" like Dieric Bouts, through the Northern Renaissance to Ruisdael, de Hooch and the seventeenth-century schools. It's an instructive display, helped by a small library of art books provided for browsing in the entrance hall. There's also an additional scattering of Impressionist paintings, including works by Monet and Corot.

A couple of blocks to the south of the museum, on rue de Fleurus, is **Maison Coilliot**, a ceramics shop, and one of the few houses built by Hector Guimard, who made his name designing the Art-Nouveau entrances to the Paris métro. Built at the height of the Art Nouveau movement, it's as striking today as it obviously was to the conservative burghers of Lille (there are no other such buildings in Lille), but it also displays the somewhat muddled eclecticism of the style, coming over as half brick-faced mansion, half timber-framed cottage. East of the museum, near the triumphal arch of **Porte de Paris**, the city's **Hôtel de Ville** is also worth a quick look, executed in a bizarre, Flemish Art-Deco style, with a tall belfry whose viewing platform is open to the public only on Sundays from April to September.

Villeneuve d'Ascq: Musée d'Art Moderne

One of the best escapes from the urban excess of Lille, amid the spaghetti junction of autoroutes east of the city centre, is the suburb of **VILLENEUVE-D'ASCQ**. Acres of parkland, an old windmill or two, and a whole series of mini-lakes form the backdrop for the **Musée d'Art Moderne** (June–Sept daily 10am–7/8pm; Oct–May daily 10am–6pm; closed Tues; 25F) which houses an unusually good collection in its uninviting red-brick buildings. To get there, take the métro to *Pont-de-Bois*, then bus #41.

The ground floor is generally given over to temporary exhibitions of varying quality by contemporary French artists. The permanent collection starts on the first floor with canvases by Picasso, Braque, Modigliani, Miró and a whole room devoted to Fernand Léger and Georges Rouault. There's also a small room – easy to miss but worth the search – on the top floor, devoted to graphics by many of the above. Meanwhile outside on the grass, Giacometti and Calder provide some playful picnic backdrops.

Eating, drinking and nightlife

Lille's main area for cafés, brasseries and **restaurants** is around pl Rihour and along rue de Béthune. *Le Grand Café* on pl Rihour is as good as any for sandwiches and light meals. **Mussels** are extremely popular in Lille and *the* place to eat them is *Aux Moules*, 34 rue de Béthune (daily 11.30am–11pm). Lille's best pizza place is *Piccolo Mondo* in rue des Molfonds, a side street off rue de Béthune. *Brasserie Jean* on place du Théâtre is a useful all-nighter. Rue Royale in the old town has good selection of (fairly pricey) ethnic eateries from Cambodian to Japanese. Also in the old town, a *crêperie*, *La Galetière*, 4 place Louise-de-Bettignies (closed Sun & Mon), is worth checking out.

The **cafés** around the Grande-Place and place Rihour are always buzzing with life, with *Café Leffe* top of the list. *Café au Bureau* on rue de Béthune is done out as all English pubs should be – plenty of brass and dark woodwork. Lille students with money hang around *Le Pubstore* at 44 rue de la Halle (evenings only); but a good bit cheaper is *La Petite Cour*, rue du Curé-St-Étienne, off rue St-Étienne.

Art and music **events** are always worth checking up on, either by picking up a copy of the free fortnightly listings magazine, *Sortir*, or the local paper, *La Voix du Nord*. The major festival of the year, the **Grande Braderie**, takes place over the Whitsun weekend (7th Sunday after Easter), when a big street parade and vast market fill miles of the city streets.

Douai and around

Situated in the heart of the mining country, 35km south of Lille, and badly damaged in both world wars, **DOUAI** is a surprisingly attractive and lively town, its streets of eighteenth-century houses cut through by both river and canal. Once a haven for English Catholics fleeing Protestant oppression in Tudor England, Douai later became the seat of Flemish local government under Louis XIV, an aristocractic past evoked in the novels of Balzac.

Centre of activity is the **place d'Armes**, overlooked by the massive Gothic belfry of the **Hôtel de Ville**, popularised by Victor Hugo and renowned for its *carillon* – the largest single collection of bells in Europe – which plays a great variety of tunes. Access is from rue de la Mairie (Mon–Fri 10am–noon & 2.30–5.30pm; Sat 2–6pm; admission by guided tour only 8F), and, in addition to peeling every half hour, there are hour-long concerts every Saturday at 10.45am, on public holidays at 11am, and on summer Monday evenings at 9pm.

One block north of the town hall, on **rue Bellegambe**, is an outrageous Art-Nouveau shop-front serving a very ordinary haberdashery store. Rising above the old town, at the end of the street, are the Baroque dome and tower of the **Église St-Pierre**, an immense, mainly eighteenth-century church with, among other treasures, a spectacular carved Baroque organ case. East of the place d'Armes, Douai's oldest church, the twelfth-century **Église Notre-Dame**, suffered badly in the last war, but has been refreshingly modernised inside. Beyond the church is the better of the town's two surviving medieval gateways, now a triumphal roundabout, the **Porte Valenciennes**.

With the exception of the 1970s extension to the old Flemish Parliament building, the riverfront west of the town hall is pleasant to wander along. Between the river and the canal to the west, on rue de Chartreux, the **Ancienne Chartreuse** is now a **museum** (daily 10am–noon & 2–5pm Sun 3–6pm; closed Tues; 8F) with a top quality collection of paintings by Flemish, Dutch and French masters including Van Dyck, Rubens, Rodin and Douai's own Jean Bellgambe.

Practicalities

The **gare SNCF** is a five-minute walk from place d'Armes – left down bd Faidherbe, then right down rue de Valenciennes. The SI is on the *place* facing the *Hôtel de Paris* (☎27.88.95.63; ④). For cheaper lodgings, try *L'Homme Sauvage*, 106 rue de Valenciennes (☎27.88.85.03; ②) or the *Grand Cerf*, 46 rue St-Jacques; ☎27.88.79.60; ③). Northeast of the place d'Armes is the PTT, whence buses leave (*Ligne* #1 orange) for Lewarde.

The mines at Lewarde

A visit to the pits at **LEWARDE**, 7km east of Douai, is a must for admirers of Zola's *Germinal*, perhaps the most electrifying "naturalistic" novel ever written, and fascinating even if you're not familiar with the writer. The bus from Douai heads east across the flat and featureless beet fields, down a road lined with poor brick dwellings that recall the company-owned housing of *Germinal*, intersected by streets named after

Pablo Neruda, Jean-Jacques Rousseau, Georges Brassens and other luminaries of the French and international Left. This is the traditional heart of France's coalmining country, always dispiriting and now depressed by closures and recession. Even the distinctive landmarks of slag heap and winding gear are fast disappearing with demolition and landscaping.

The Centre Historique Minier

The bus puts you down at the main square in Lewarde, leaving a fifteen-minute walk down the D132 towards Erchin. The **Centre Historique Minier** (daily 10am–5.30pm; office closes 4pm; 40F) is on the left in the old Fosse Delloye, sited, like so many pits, amid woods and fields. Visits are unavoidably guided, by retired miners, many of whom are not French, but Polish, Italian or North African – Polish labour was introduced in the 1920s, other nationalities successively after World War II. One Polish guide went down the pit at 14 and was brought up at 38 with silicosis, which had also killed his father at 52. *"Ce n'est pas un métier"*, he said – "it's not what you'd call a career".

The main part of the tour – in addition to film shows and visits to the surface installations of winding gear, machine shops, cages, sorting areas and the rest, (you can't yet go underground) – is a surface reconstruction of the pit-bottom roadways and faces, variously modelled and equipped to show the evolution of mining from the earliest times to today. These French pits were extremely deep and hot, with steeply inclined narrow seams that forced the miners to work on slopes of 55° and more, just as Étienne and the Maheu family do in Zola's story.

Accidents were a regular occurence in the old days: the northern French pits had a particularly bad record in the last years of the nineteenth century. The worst **mining disaster** occurred at Courrières in 1906, when 1100 men were killed. Incredibly, despite the fact that the owners made little effort to search for survivors, thirteen men suddenly emerged after twenty days of wandering in the gas-filled tunnels without food, water or light. The first person they met thought that they were ghosts and fainted in fright. More incredible still, a fourteenth man surfaced alone after another four days.

Cambrai and Le Cateau

CAMBRAI, like Douai 26km to the north, has kept enough of its character to repay a passing visit, despite the tank battle of November 1917 (see box) and the fact that the heavily defended Hindenburg Line ran right through the town centre for most of the First World War.

The huge, cobbled main square, **place Aristide-Briand**, dominated by the neo-Classical Hôtel de Ville, still smacks of the town's former wealth, based on the textile and agricultural industries. Cambrai's chief treasure is, for once, not its cathedral but the **Église St-Géry**, off rue St-Aubert west of the main square, which contains a celebrated *Mise au tombeau* by Rubens. The **Musée Municipal** (March–Dec daily 10am–noon & 2–5pm; closed Tues) on rue de l'Épée, south of the town square, is also worth a visit. The paintings of Velasquez feature prominently alongside various Flemish masters, works by Utrillo and, of course, Matisse, for more of whom, see Le Cateau, below.

Cambrai's **SI** is housed in the *Maison Espagnole* on av de la Victoire, south of place Aristide-Briand. *Le Mouton Blanc*, 22 rue d'Alsace-Lorraine (☎27.82.30.16; ③) is a convenient **hotel** close to the station with a cheap self-service restaurant round the corner and a posher one in the hotel itself. The nearest **campsite**, 10km away, is signposted off the D939 to Arras.

CAMBRAI 1917

At dawn on November 20, 1917, the first full-scale **tank battle** in history began at Cambrai, when over 400 British tanks poured over the Hindenburg Line. In just twenty-four hours, the Royal Tank Corps and British Third Army made an advance which was further than any made by either side since the trenches had first been dug in 1914. A fortnight later, however, casualties on both sides had reached 50,000, and the armies were back where they'd started.

Although in some respects the tanks were ahead of their time, they still relied on cavalry and plodding infantry as their back-up, and runners for their lines of communication. And before they even reached the "green fields beyond", most of them had broken down. First World War tanks were primitive machines, operated by a crew of eight who endured nigh intolerable conditions; with no ventilation system, the temperature inside could rise to 120°F. The steering alone required three men, each on separate gearboxes, communicating by hand signals through the din of the tank's internal noise. Maximum speed, 6kmph, dropped to almost literally a snail's pace – 1kmph – over rough terrain, and refuelling was necessary every 55km. Consequently, of the 179 tanks lost in the battle at Cambrai, very few had been destroyed by the enemy; the majority broke down and were abandoned by their crews.

Le Cateau

Twenty-two kilometres east of Cambrai along an old Roman road, the small town of **LE CATEAU-CAMBRÉSIS** is the birthplace of France's best-known twentieth-century painter, **Henri Matisse** (1869–1954). As a gift to his home town, Matisse bequeathed it a collection of his works. All of them are now displayed in the **Musée Matisse** (daily 10am–6pm; closed Tues; 20F) housed in the local château in the centre of town, and although there are no major works here, it still deserves a fleeting visit. Matisse's work occupies the first floor and includes several studies for the chapel in Vence and whole series of his characteristically simple pen-and-ink sketches. Also worth looking at is the work of local Cubist, **Auguste Herbin**, on the ground floor, particularly his psychedelic upright piano.

Arras, Albert and the Somme battlefields

Around Arras and Albert, some of the fiercest and most futile battles of the First World War took place. At one time the trenches cut through the main square in **Arras**, now restored to its former glory. At nearby **Vimy Ridge**, the Canadians fell in their thousands; at **Notre-Dame de Lorette**, the French suffered the same fate. **Albert**, unlike Arras, is not a place to linger, but makes a convenient base for exploring the many war cemeteries in the area. Note, however, that to get to most of the sights outside Arras and Albert, you need your own transport.

Arras

ARRAS has been rebuilt more times than any other town in France. Its history of conflict dates from the early fifteenth century – a temporary truce was signed here before Agincourt – and in addition to the destruction of this century, it has seen capture and bombardment by the Austrians, Spanish, British and Germans.

The town

Oddly enough the town bears few obvious battle scars. Reconstruction here, particularly after the last war, has been careful and stylish, and two grand arcaded squares in the centre – **Grande-Place** and the smaller **Place des Héros** – preserve their historic, harmonious character. On every side are restored Renaissance mansions, built in relatively restrained Flemish style, and, on pl des Héros, there's a grandly ornate **Hôtel de Ville**, its entrance hall housing a permanent photographic display documenting the wartime destruction of the town, and sheltering a pair of *géants* (festival giants) awaiting the city's next fête.

Also inside the town hall is the entrance to the belfry viewing platform and **les souterrains** (or *les boves*), cold, dark passageways and spacious vaults tunnelled beneath the centre of the city (Tues–Sat 2.30–6pm; Sun 10.30am–12.30pm & 3–6.30pm; guided tours 8F & 17F). Once down, you're escorted around an impressive area and given an interesting survey of local history. During World War I, the rooms, many of which have fine, tiled floors and lovely pillars and stairways, were used as a British barracks and hospital.

Arras' other main sight is the former Benedictine **Abbaye St-Vaast**, revived from its ruins after eighteenth- and twentieth-century wars. It now houses a city **museum** (daily 10am–noon & 2–5.30pm; closed Tues) with a mediocre collection of paintings including a couple of Jordaens and Breughels, fragments of sculpture, local ceramics and of course some of the tapestries or "screens" (*arras*; the final "s" is pronounced), which gave the town its name.

On the western edge of town, next to the Vauban barracks, is a **war cemetery** and **memorial** by Lutyens, a movingly elegiac, classical colonnade of ivy-covered brick and stone, commemorating 35,928 missing soldiers, the endless columns of their names inscribed on the walls. It's a long time ago now and the number of surviving relatives is dwindling fast; yet there are few sights as poignant as the fading posies left with a card beneath a name, an elderly hand reminding "Dad" she hasn't seen him since she was seven.

It is a mournful corner of town. Around the back of the old brick fortress, in an overgrown moat, is the **Mur des fusillés**, where some 200 Resistance fighters were shot by firing squad in the last war, most of them of Polish descent, most of them miners, and most of them Communists.

Accommodation, food and transport details

If you are staying the night there's a newly modernised **youth hostel** at 59 Grande-Place (☎21.21.07.83; IYHF card required; curfew 11pm), a **campsite** (April–Oct) 1km out of town on the Bapaume road, and two well-priced **hotels**: *Les Grandes Arcades* on the Grande-Place (☎21.23.30.89; ②/③), which is not as upmarket as it appears, and *Le Rallye*, 9 rue Gambetta (☎21.51.44.96; ③) near the station.

The *Arcades* also serves very good and not wildly expensive regional **food** (including the local speciality *andouillette* or tripe sausage – an acquired taste), as does *La Rapière*, 44 Grande-Place. Other places to try are *Le Win'Stub*, a little Alsatian bistro on rue Petit-Viéziers, or *La Cave*, 50 Grande-Place. The **SI**, 7 place du Maréchal-Foch, opposite the station (Mon–Sat 10am–noon & 2–5/6pm), are worth consulting on transport and tours of local battlefields; they also have a small branch bureau in the town hall.

For the Canadian memorial at Vimy you need your own transport or an organised tour, but to visit the smaller memorials at Neuville-St-Vaast, La Targette and Notre-Dame de Lorette, you can take buses from Arras, direction *Lens*, making sure you get out at the right stop.

Vimy Ridge and around

Eight kilometres north of Arras on the D49, **Vimy Ridge** or Hill 145, was the scene of some of the direst trench warfare of World War I: almost two full years of battle, culminating in its capture by the crack Canadian Corps in April 1917. It is a vast site, given in perpetuity to the Canadian people out of respect for their sacrifices, and has been preserved, in part, as it was during the conflict. There's an **information centre** (April–Sept daily 10am–6pm; free) supervised by bi-lingual Canadian students, who run guided tours and can fill you in on all the horrific details.

Nearby, long worms of neat, sanitised **trenches** meander over the now grassy ground, still heavily pitted and churned by shell bursts beneath the planted pines. There are examples of dug-outs, hideous places where men used to shelter during heavy bombardments and makeshift hospitals were set up. Beneath the ground lie some 11,000 bodies still unaccounted for and countless rounds of unexploded ammunition. Signs are still required to warn against straying from the directed paths.

On the brow of the ridge, 1.5km north of the information centre, overlooking the slagheap-dotted plain of Artois, a great white **monument** towers, like a giant funerary stele, rent down the middle by elemental force, with allegorical figures half-emerging from the stone towards the top, and inscribed with the names of 60,000 Canadians and Newfoundlanders who lost their lives during the war. An unenviable task to design a fitting memorial to such slaughter, but this one, aided by its setting, succeeds with great drama. At the time, Vimy was seen by many as the birth of the Canadian nation, yet you may feel a certain aversion to the victorious tone of the tourist handouts and the triumphalism of the memorial itself – it took eleven years to build, used up 6,000 tonnes of limestone and cost $1.5 million – a huge sum in the Depression years. It is also the only monument in the north to be constantly supervised – by Canadian guards intent on prescribing your movements around the plinth.

Back from the ridge, there's a subdued memorial to the **Moroccan Division** who took part at Vimy, and in the woods behind, on the headstones of another exquisitely maintained cemetery, you can read the names of half the counties of rural England.

La Targette

At the crossroads (D937/D49) of **LA TARGETTE**, 8km north from the centre of Arras, the **Musée de la Targette** (daily 9am–7pm) contains an interesting collection of World War I *objets de guerre*. It is the private collection of one David Bardiaux, assembled with passion and meticulous attention to detail, under the inspiration of tales told by his grandfather, a veteran of Verdun. Its interest lies in the absolute precision with which the thirty-odd mannequins of British, French, Canadian and German soldiers are dressed and equipped, down to their sweet and tobacco tins and such rarities as a 1915 British-issue cap with earflaps, very comfortable for the troops, but withdrawn because the top brass thought it made their men look like yokels. All the exhibits have been under fire; some belonged to known individuals and are complete with stitched up tears of old wounds. When you're finished, the *Café Flambeau* serves well-priced food.

Neuville-St-Vaast

More cemeteries lie a little to the south of La Targette (10km from Arras), nominally at **NEUVILLE-ST-VAAST**, though the village is actually 1km away to the east. There is a small British cemetery, a huge French one, and an equally large **German cemetery**, containing the remains of 44,833 Germans. If you haven't been to a German war cemetery before, the macabre, skeletal black crosses – each one represents four soldiers – come as quite a shock. So, too, do the handful of individual Jewish headstones which stand out from the rest. The Polish sculptor Henri Gaudier Brzeska died in action here in 1915 – a Polish memorial and Czech cemetery face each other across the main street of the village itself.

Notre-Dame de Lorette

On a bleak hill a few kilometres to the northwest of Vimy Ridge (and 5km north of Neuville-St-Vaast) is the church of **Notre-Dame de Lorette**, scene of a costly French offensive in May 1915. The original church was blasted to bits during the war and rebuilt in grim neo-Byzantine style in the 1920s, grey and dour on the outside, but rich and bejewelled inside. It now stands at the centre of a vast graveyard with over 20,000 crosses laid out in pairs, back to back, each one separated by a cluster of blood-red roses. 20,000 more are buried in the ossuary, and there's a small **museum** behind the church displaying photographs, uniforms and other military paraphernalia.

Albert and around

The church at **ALBERT** – now, with the rest of the town, completely rebuilt – was one of the minor landmarks of the First World War. Its tall tower was hit by German bombing early on in the campaign, leaving the statue of the Madonna on top leaning at a precarious angle. The British, entrenched over three years in the region, came to know it as the "Leaning Virgin". Army superstition had it that when she fell the war would end, a myth inspiring frequent hopeful potshots by disgruntled troops. Unless you have a really strong battlefield interest, however – in which case you could spend weeks here roaming the region – modern Albert does not invite much of a stay.

As you arrive (trains from Amiens or Arras) the town's new tower is the first thing that catches the eye, capped now by an equally improbably posed statue. The **SI** is close by on rue Gambetta (June–mid-Sept 2–5pm) together with a couple of good inexpensive **hotels**: *Basilique*, in the same street, and *La Paix* on rue Victor-Hugo.

THE BATTLE OF THE SOMME

On July 1, 1916, the British and French launched the **Battle of the Somme**, to relieve pressure on the French army defending Verdun. The front ran roughly northwest–southeast, 6km east of Albert across the valley of the Ancre and over the almost treeless high ground north of the Somme – huge hedgeless wheat fields now, their monotony relieved by an undulation as slow as the rhythm of a long sea swell. These windy open hills had no intrinsic value, nor was there any long-term strategic objective – the region around Albert was chosen simply because it was where the two allied armies met.

There were 57,000 British casualties on the first day alone, approximately 20,000 of them dead – making it the costliest defeat the British army has ever suffered. Sir Douglas Haig is the usual scapegoat for the Somme, yet he was only following the military thinking of the day, which is where the real problem lay. As A J P Taylor put it, "Defence was mechanised: attack was not". Machine guns were far more efficient, barbed wire more effective, and, most important of all, the railways could move defensive reserves far faster than the attacking army could march. The often ineffective heavy preliminary bombardment favoured by both sides only made matters worse, since the shells forewarned the enemy of an offensive and churned the trenches into a giant muddy quagmire.

Despite the bloody disaster of the first day, the battle wore on until bad weather in November made further attacks impossible. The cost of this futile struggle was 415,000 British, 195,000 French, and around 600,000 German casualties.

The *circuit de souvenir*

> *Was it for this the clay grew tall?*
> *O what made fatuous sunbeams toil*
> *To break earth's sleep at all?*

Wilfred Owen, *Futility.*

The **circuit de souvenir** conducts you from graveyard to mine crater, trench to memorial. There's not a lot to see; nothing, at least, that is going to satisfy any appetite for shocking atrocities or scenes of destruction. Neither do you get much sense of movement or even of battle tactics. But you will find that, even if you started out with the feeling that your interest in war was somehow puerile or mawkish, you have in fact embarked on a sort of pilgrimage, in which each successive step becomes more harrowing and oppressive.

The **cemeteries** are the most moving aspect of the region – beautiful cemeteries, the grass perfectly mown, an individual bed of flowers at the foot of every gravestone. And there are tens of thousands of them, all identical, with a man's name, if it is known (nearly half the British dead have never been found), and his rank and regiment. Just reading the names of the regiments evokes a world of experience quite different from today's: locally recruited regiments, young men from Welsh border farms, mill towns, and villages, who had never been abroad, wiped out in a morning, men from all corners of the Empire. In the lanes between Albert and Bapaume you'll see the cemeteries everywhere: at the angle of copses, halfway across a wheat field, in the middle of a bluebell wood, moving and terrible in their simple beauty. What follows is necessarily just a selected handful of some of the better known sites.

A good place to start is the station at **HAMEL** (7km by train north of Albert), where the 51st Highland Division walked abreast to their deaths with their pipes playing. Just across the river, towards the village of **THIEPVAL**, the 5000 Ulstermen who died in the Battle of the Somme are commemorated by the incongruously Celtic **Ulster Memorial**, a replica of the Helen's Tower at Clandeboyne near Belfast. South of Thiepval is probably the most famous of Edwin Lutyens' many memorials, the colossal **Memorial to the Missing**, erected in memory of the 73,357 British troops whose bodies were never recovered at the Somme. Half an hour's hike west of Hamel station, is the Newfoundlanders' memorial at **BEAUMONT-HAMEL**. Here, on the hilltop where most of them died, a series of **trenches** has been preserved, now grassed over and eroding, where German faced Canadian a few paces apart. It all seems so small scale now and almost more appropriate to the antics of the party of school children witnessed running around here shooting each other with their fingers than to anything as obscene as took place.

Twelve kilometres east at **LONGUEVAL**, on the other side of the Albert–Bapaume road, the **Musée 1914–1918** (daily 9.30am–6pm) consists mainly of a section of trench reconstructed in the back garden of a café and "equipped" with genuine battlefield relics. It's a bit amateurish, but quite interesting if you're passing through. The guide had first collected objects from the battlefield as a boy, to sell for pocket money. Farmers apparently still turn up about 75 tons of shells every year – not really surprising when you think the British alone fired one-and-a-half million in the last week of June 1916.

Another fine Lutyens memorial stands at **VILLERS-BRETONNEUX**, some 18km southwest of Albert near the Somme river itself. As at Vimy, the landscaping of the **Australian Memorial** is dramatic – for the full effect, climb up to the viewing platform of the stark white central tower. The monument was one of the last to be inaugurated in July 1938, when the prospects for peace were already looking bleak.

AISNE AND OISE

To the southeast, away from the coast and the main Paris through routes, Picardy, often rainwashed and dull, becomes considerably more inviting. Particularly in the *départements* of **Aisne** and **Oise**, where the region merges with neighbouring Champagne, there are some real attractions set amid lush, wooded hills. **Laon**, **Soissons** and **Noyon** all centre around handsome Gothic cathedrals, while at **Compiègne** Napoléon Bonaparte and Napoléon III enjoyed the luxury of its magnificent château.

Transport is good for once, too, with a network of bus connections from Amiens and good train and bus links with Paris.

St-Quentin

A pleasant and prosperous industrial centre, **ST-QUENTIN** is a convenient place to pause *en route* to somewhere else, but unless you have a passion for entomology (see below), the town makes no great demands on your time.

Thanks to St-Quentin's Communist mayor the central **place de l'Hôtel de Ville** is now completely closed to traffic. One side of it is dominated by a particularly good-looking arcaded late-Gothic **Hôtel de Ville**, whose bells ring protracted, syncopated changes every quarter hour. From the other side, rue St-André leads to the town's skyscrapingly massive, but outwardly rather uninspiring, Gothic **Basilique**. Inside, its main virtue is its sheer size. In fact, it's a miracle that it is still standing at all, since in 1918 the retreating Germans mined all 300 pillars and were only prevented from setting them off by lack of time – you can still see the marks left by the mines. Another curiosity is the maze in the paving of the nave designed for penitents to figure out on their knees.

Of much greater, if specialist, interest is the **Musée Antoine-Lécuyer**, on rue Lécuyer, at the end of rue Raspail (10am–noon & 2–5pm; Sun 2–6pm only; closed Tues), which contains a big collection of pastel portraits of the leading politicians, nobles, artists and socialites of eighteenth-century France, by locally born **Maurice-Quentin de Latour**. The other unique collection, and one of the largest in the world, is that of **butterflies** and other insects, more than half a million of them, housed in the **Musée d'Entomologie** on rue des Canonniers (Mon–Sat 2–6pm) – it could be the one thing to put St-Quentin on the map.

Practicalities

To get to the centre of town from the **gare SNCF**, follow rue Général-Leclerc over the Somme, and up rue d'Isle. The **SI** (Mon–Sat, 10.30am–6.30pm; Sun 10.30am–12.30pm & 2.30–6.30pm) is housed in the town hall and will recommend **accommodation**, which should not be a problem. You could try the bargain *Hôtel du Départ* on place du Monument-aux-Morts (☎23.62.31.69; ②), or the *Terminus*, 2 rue du Général-Leclerc (☎23.62.31.73; ③). The town's **campsite** and **youth hostel** (both ☎23.62.68.66; March–Nov) are on bd Jean-Bouin, 2km from the station by the river – bus #3 to rue H-Dunant.

Laon and around

Looking out over the plains of Champagne and Picardy from the spine of a high narrow ridge, girt still by its gated medieval walls, **LAON**, 36km southeast of St-Quentin, is one of the gems of the region. Dominating it all, and visible for miles around, are the five great towers of one of the earliest and finest Gothic cathedrals in the country. Of all the cathedral towns in Aisne, Laon is the one to head for.

Arrival and accommodation

Arriving by train or road, you find yourself in the disappointingly shabby and character-less lower town, or **Ville Basse**. To get to the upper town or **Ville Haute**, you can either walk – a stiff climb up the steps at the end of av Carnot – or take the world's first cable-hauled, pilotless, rubber-tired aerial métro, the **Poma 2000**, pride and joy of Laon. You board next to the train station and get out by the town hall on place Général-Leclerc; from there a left turn down rue Serurier brings you nose to nose with Laon's number-one attraction – its cathedral. The **SI** is right beside it (daily 9am–12.30pm & 2–6.30pm).

Cheap **accommodation** is mostly in the Ville Basse. Try *Le Welcome* (☎23.23.06.11; ③), *Le Nord-Est* (☎23.23.25.55; ③) or the unprepossessing but perfectly decent *Le Vauclair* (☎23.23.02.08; ③), which also boasts a good, no-frills restaurant. All are in the short av Carnot straight in front of the **gare SNCF**. For rooms in the **Ville Haute**, the cheapest solution is the *Maison des Jeunes* alongside the cathedral at 20 rue du Cloître (☎23.20.27.64; no curfew) – the official IYHF youth hostel is 5km out on the Soissons road and not worth the bother. As for Ville Haute **hotels**, *La Paix*, 52 rue St-Jean (☎23.23.21.95; ③; closed Aug) is a good bet, followed by *La Bannière de la France*, 11 rue Roosevelt (☎23.23.21.44; ④) and *Les Chevaliers* on rue Serurier (☎23.23.43.78; ④).

The **camping municipal** is on the south side of the Ville Basse, near the *stade municipal,* just off the N44.

Ville Haute

The magnificent **Cathédrale Notre-Dame,** built in the second half of the twelfth century, was a trend-setter in its day, elements of its design – the gabled porches, the imposing towers, and the gallery of arcades above the west front – being repeated at Chartres, Reims and Notre-Dame in Paris. Seen wrapped in thick mist, the towers seem quite other-worldly. The creatures craning from the uppermost ledges that appear to be reckless mountain goats borrowed from some medieval bestiary are reputed to have been carved in memory of the valiant horned steers who lugged the cathedral's masonry up from the plains below. **Inside**, the effects are no less dramatic – the high white nave is lit by the dense ruby, sapphire and emerald tones of the **stained glass,** which at close range reveals the appealing scratchy, smoky quality of medieval glass.

Crowding in the cathedral's lee are a web of quiet, grey, eighteenth-century streets. One, rue Pourier, leads past the **PTT** and on to the thirteenth-century **Porte d'Ardon** which looks out over the southern part of the Ville Basse. A left turn at the post office along rue Hermant leads to the little twelfth-century octagonal **Chapelle des Templiers** – the Knights Templar – set in a secluded garden by the local **museum** (daily 10am–noon & 2am–5pm; winter 2–6pm; closed Tues).

The rest of the Ville Haute, which rambles along the ridge to the west of the cathedral into the *Le Bourg* quarter around the early Gothic **Église St-Martin**, is good to wander in, with universally grand views from the **ramparts**.

Food and entertainment

Rue Châtelaine has a good range of *boulangeries* and *fromageries* for assembling a picnic. Simple **snacks** can be had at the *Café de Paris* overlooking the west front of the cathedral. *Crêperie Agora* is a cheap Breton place near the cathedral on rue des Cordeliers (open until 1am; closed Sat lunch & Mon) or you could try the *Pizzeria Florentina*, rue Châtelaine. Other restaurants in Laon tend to be expensive.

Like most northern French towns, Laon is short on **nightlife**, although there's usually something going on at the *Maison des Arts* on place Aubrey, and a concentration during the *Heures Médiévales* festival in the second and third weeks of September. If you feel like trying *pétanque,* the town also has an impressive **sports centre** in the Basse Ville, along with a tremendous heated **swimming pool** (daily 8am–1pm and 3–8pm; closed Sun afternoon & Mon morning).

Coucy-le-Château and the Forêt St-Gobain

About 30km west of Laon, on the far side of the forest of St-Gobain and set in hilly countryside (a worthwhile cycling trip in itself), lie the straggling ruins of one of the greatest castles of the Middle Ages, **Coucy-le-Château**. The power of its lords, the *Sires de Coucy,* rivalled and often even exceeded that of the king – "King I am not, neither Prince, Duke nor Count, I am the Sire of Coucy", was Enguerrand III's proud refrain. One of them, Enguerrand VII, who had fingers in all sorts of pies – he had powerful relatives among the English aristocracy – is the hero of Barbara Tuchman's brilliant account of the fourteenth century, *A Distant Mirror* (see "Books" in *Contexts*). He ended his days uncomfortably, in a Turkish jail.

The retreating Germans capped the destruction of World War I battles by blowing up the castle's keep as they left in 1917, but enough remains, crowning a wooded spur, to be extremely evocative (daily 10am–noon & 2–5pm; closed Tues). The entire modern village of COUCY-LE-CHÂTEAU-AUFFRIQUE is contained within the vast ring of walls, entered through the original gates, squeezed between powerful, round flanking towers. There is a footpath all around the outside, and the *Hôtel Bellevue* within (☎23.52.70.12; closed Feb; ①), should you be hungry or stuck here at night.

It's hard to get to Coucy-le-Château without a car, though several Laon–Soissons **trains** stop at ANIZY-PINON, which, if you're otherwise hitching, cuts the distance by about half – and there is an infrequent **bus** on to Soissons. If you continue into the nearby **Forêt St-Gobain**, include **ST-GOBAIN** itself, 13km north of Coucy, in your itinerary. The original eighteenth-century glassworks – the firm is now a vast conglomerate – hides behind a classical facade, pretending it's nothing so vulgar as a factory.

Soissons

Half an hour by train southwest of Laon (30km down the N2), **SOISSONS** can lay claim to a long and highly strategic history. Before the Romans arrived it was already a town, its kings controlling parts of Britain as well as northern France. And in 486 AD it was here that the Romans suffered one of their most decisive defeats at the hands of Clovis the Frank, making Soissons one of the first real centres of the Frankish kingdom. Napoléon, too, considered it a crucial military base, a judgement borne out this century in extensive war damage.

The town boasts the fine, if little sung, **Cathédrale Notre-Dame**, thirteenth century for the most part with majestic glass and vaulting, which stands at the west end of the main square, place F-Marquigny. More impressive still is the ruined **Abbaye de St-Jean-des-Vignes**, to the south of the cathedral down rue Panleu and rue Racine. The facade of this tremendous Gothic building rises sheer and grand, impervious to the now empty space behind it. The monastery, save for remnants of a cloister and refectory, was dismantled in 1804 (daily 10am–noon & 2–5pm; closed Tues; guided tours only).

Practicalities

Soissons is relatively compact. From the **gare SNCF** (with good services to Laon and Paris) the main square is a fifteen-minute walk away, along av du Général-de-Gaulle and then rue St-Martin. The **gare routière** is closer to the centre by the river on Le Mail: infrequent buses leave for Noyon and Compiègne as well as Laon. The **SI** is on the place de la République roundabout at the end of av du Général-de-Gaulle.

The town is a useful and attractive place to stay if you're exploring this part of the country. There are several moderately priced **hotels**: *Hôtel de la Gare* by the station (☎23.53.31.61; closed Mon & Aug; ②/③), *Hôtel du Nord* left out from the station on rue de Belleu (☎23.53.12.55; ③) and *Hôtel de la Marine*, 2 rue St-Quentin, in the centre (☎23.53.31.94; ②). Rooms are also sometimes available at the two youth *foyers*: women at 8 rue de Bauton; men at 20 rue Malieu. Alternatively there's a **campsite**, 1km from the station on av du Mail. One of the nicest places to **eat** in Soissons is *La Scala*, an exceptionally good Italian restaurant near the Hôtel de Ville. Alternatively, the *Lion Rouge*, off place de la République, is a good French fall-back (closed Sun).

Compiègne

Thirty-eight kilometres west of Soissons, **COMPIÈGNE**'s reputation as a tourist centre rests on the presence of a vast royal palace, built at the edge of the **Forêt de Compiègne** – in order that generations of French kings could play at "being peasants", in Louis XIV's words. It's worth a visit certainly, but the town is not the mecca built up by the hype: it tends to have a bland, Sunday-afternoon feel of somewhere that has lived too long in the stifling orbit of Establishment power. Perhaps that is due, above all, to its last royal tenant, Napoléon III.

Practicalities

Gares routière and **SNCF** (bike rental available) are adjacent. The centre of town is a few minutes' walk away: cross over the wide river Oise and walk up rue Solférino to place de l'Hôtel-de-Ville. As for **accommmodation**, there are cheapish rooms at the *Hôtel St-Antoine*, 17 rue de Paris (☎44.86.17.18; ②), *Hôtel de la Tour*, rue des 3-Barbeaux (☎44.23.37.18; ③), and the *Lion d'Or*, 4 rue du Général-Leclerc (☎44.23.32.17; ③). The **youth hostel** is 1km from the station at 6 rue Pasteur (☎44.40.26.00; bus #3 to rue des Fosses; IYHF card required; curfew 10pm), and there's a **campsite** along av Royale, into the forest beyond the palace.

Compiègne has no shortage of reasonably priced **restaurants** like *Cafétéria La Closeraie*, 37 rue Solférino, and *Á la Dernière Minute* on pl de la Gare. Slightly more expensive are *La Pizza Grill*, 10 rue des Boucheries (closed Mon & Aug), and an excellent Vietnamese place, *Le Phnom Penh*, 13 rue des Lombards. *Pâtisseries* are also rewarding, with liqueur-laced cream pastries. Lastly, on Saturdays, there's a big all-day **market** in the square by place de l'Hôtel-de-Ville.

The town and minor museums

The town itself is plain disappointing, though that shouldn't come as a surprise given that a platoon of German soldiers burnt it down in 1942, to provide their commander with evidence of a thoroughly subjugated community. A handful of half-timbered buildings remains, on the pedestrianised rue Napoléon and rue des Lombards, south of the main square, place de l'Hôtel de Ville. The most striking building, as so often in these parts, is the **Hôtel de Ville** itself – Louis XII-Gothic, with a riot of nineteenth-century statuary including, inevitably, Joan of Arc, captured in this town by the Burgundians before being handed over to the English. The **SI** has its offices here and, for a couple of francs, will provide you with a plan of the town, on which is conveniently marked an exhaustive visitors' route, including the forest paths (see below).

If you have an interest in Greek vases, the **Musée Vivenel** on rue d'Austerlitz (daily 9am–noon & 2–6pm; closed Tues) has one of the best collections around, especially a series illustrating the Panathenaic Games from Italy – a welcome dose of classical restraint and good taste compared with the palace. There is also a section on the forest's flora and fauna, which includes a wild boar the size of an armoured car. Another museum of specialist interest is the **Musée de Figurines** by the side of the town hall (Tues–Sun 9am–noon & 2–6pm; 10F), with reputedly the world's largest collection of wafer-thin military figurines in mock-up battles from Ancient Greece to World War II.

The Palais National and the Forêt de Compiègne

Compiègne's star attraction is two blocks east of the town hall down rue des Minimes. For all its pompous excess, there is a certain fascination about the **Palais National** (daily 9.30–11.15am & 1.30–4.30pm; closed Tues; guided tours only; all-inclusive admission 23F), particularly its **interior**: the lavishness of Marie-Antoinette's rooms, the sheer, vulgar sumptuousness of the First and Second Empire, and the evidence of the unseemly haste with which Napoléon I moved in, scarcely a dozen years after the

Revolution. The palace also houses the **Musée du Second Empire** and the **Musée de la Voiture**, the latter containing a wonderful array of antique bicycles, tricycles and fancy aristocractic carriages, as well as the world's first steam coach. The **Grand Théâtre** planned (but never finished) by Napoléon III has recently been completed at a cost of some thirty million francs. Originally designed with just two seats for Napoléon and his wife, it now seats 900 and is regularly used for concerts.

If you don't want to take the guided tour, a visit to the palace gardens or **petit parc** (daily 7.30am–6.30/8pm) is a pleasant alternative. Serene and formal, they include a long straight avenue extending far into the **Forêt de Compiègne** which touches the edge of town. Very ancient, and cut by a succession of hills, streams and valleys, this is grand rambling country for walkers or cyclists – the **GR12** goes through it. East of Compiègne, some 6km into the forest and not far from the banks of the Aisne, is a green and sandy clearing guarded by cypress trees, known as the **Clairière de l'Armistice**. Here, in what was then a railway siding for rail-mounted artillery, World War I was brought to an end on November 11, 1918. A plaque commemorates the deed: "Here the criminal pride of the German empire was brought low, vanquished by the free peoples whom it had sought to enslave". To avenge this humiliation, Hitler had the French sign their capitulation on June 22, 1940, on the same spot, in the very same railway car. The original car was immediately taken to Berlin and was destroyed by fire in the last days of the war. Its replacement, housed in a small **museum** (daily 8/9am–noon & 1.30pm/2–5.30/6.30pm; closed Tues; 3F), is similar, and the objects inside are the originals.

There are a couple of villages worth heading for right in the heart of the forest – VIEUX-MOULIN and ST-JEAN-AUX-BOIS – and 13km southeast of Compiègne at **PIERREFONDS**, connected by three buses daily from the train station in Compiègne, there's a classic medieval **château** (April–Sept daily 9.30am–6/7pm; closed Tues; Oct–March Wed–Sun 10am–noon & 2–4pm; 23F).

Noyon

Further up the Oise, and a possible day trip from Compiègne, is **NOYON**, another of Picardy's cathedral towns. Its present, quiet provinciality belies a long and relatively illustrious history; first as a Roman prefecture, then, in 531, as the seat of a bishopric. Here, in 768, Charlemagne was crowned king of Neustria – largest of the Frankish kingdoms; in 987, Hugues Capet was crowned king of France; and to cap it all, John Calvin was born here in 1509.

Rowing along the Oise on his *Inland Journey* of 1876, Robert Louis Stevenson stopped briefly at Noyon, which he described as "a stack of brown roofs at the best, where I believe people live very respectably in a quiet way". It is a bit like that, though the **Cathedral**, to which Stevenson warmed – "my favourite kind of mountain scenery" – is impressive, at least in passing. Spacious and a little stark, it successfully blends Romanesque and Gothic, and is flanked by the ruins of thirteenth-century cloisters and a strange, exquisitely shaped **Renaissance library** which contains a ninth-century illuminated bible (guided tours only; book in advance at the SI). Close by, signs direct you to the recently reconstructed **Musée Calvin** (Tues–Sun 9am–noon & 2–5pm), ostensibly on the site of the reformer's birthplace. The respectable citizens of Noyon were never among their local boy's adherents and tore down the original long before its tourist potential was appreciated.

If you intend to stay, the cheapest hotel is *Le Balto* on place de l'Hôtel-de-Ville (☎44.44.02.97; ②). The local **campsite** is 4km out of town along the N32 to Compiègne. **Buses**, mainly for Compiègne, leave from outside the **gare SNCF**. **Bicycles** are for hire there, too. Big days in Noyon are Saturday morning, when a colourful **market** spills out across pl de l'Hôtel-de-Ville, and the first Tuesday of the month, when a cattle market takes over virtually the entire town centre.

CHAMPAGNE AND THE ARDENNES

Bubbly is the reason most people visit **Champagne**. Away from the unusual landscape of the vineyards, the region's rolling plains are an uninspiring sight, and, while they grow more wheat and cabbages per hectare than any other region of France, it seems to bring the villages no great benefit. Some places look so run down you feel the shutters would fall off if you so much as popped a paper bag – and few are much more than hamlets, with grocery vans doing the rounds once a week and not a *boulangerie* in sight.

At least the official capital of Champagne, the cathedral city of **Reims**, is worth a visit in its own right, and has a reasonably full cultural calendar. For champagne-worshippers, however, **Épernay**, not Reims, is the place to head for out of preference, where you can sample vintages to your heart's content and go on free underground visits to the *caves* of the different *maisons*. Across the plains, neither **Châlons**, nor the smaller, further-flung towns like **Chaumont** or **Langres** dotted along the Marne towards its source, are much of an incentive to break your journey. Really the only major attraction in the rest of the region is the town of **Troyes**, some way off to the southwest, which is easily Champagne's most beautiful city.

CHAMPAGNE: THE FACTS

Nowhere else in France, let alone the rest of the world, are you allowed to make **champagne**. You can blend wines from chalk-soil vineyards, double-ferment them, turn and tilt the bottles little by little to clear the sediment, add some vintage liqueur, store the result for years at the requisite constant temperature and produce a bubbling golden liquid; but you cannot call it champagne. An outrageous monopoly to keep the region's sparkling wines in the luxury class, perhaps, but the locals will tell you the difference comes from the squid fossils in the chalk, the lie of the land and its critical climate, the evolution of the grapes, the regulated pruning methods, the legally enforced quantity of juice pressed. All of which is really rather irrelevant – like relating the effects of cocaine to the secretions of some Bolivian bug in the soil in which the coca bush grew. And the comparisons don't end there. In the promotional literature put out by the champagne industry – glossy, full-colour, multi-lingual, extravagant praise – not one mention is made of why people really buy the stuff and love it so much: champagne is a powerful, exhilarating drug.

The vineyards are owned either by *maisons* who produce the *grande marque* champagne, or by small cultivators, *vignerons*, who sell the grapes to the *maisons*. The **vignerons** also make their own champagne and will happily offer you a glass and sell you a bottle at half the price of a *grande marque* (ask at any SI in the Champagne region or at the CIVC in Épernay for a list of addresses). The difference between the two comes down to capital. The *maisons* can afford to blend grapes from anything up to sixty different vineyards and to tie up their investment while their champagne matures for several years longer than the legal minimum (one year for non-vintage, three years vintage). So the wine they produce is undoubtedly superior – and not a lot cheaper here than in a good discount off-licence in Britain.

If you could work the head offices of Cartier or Dior, the atmosphere would probably be similar to that in the champagne **maisons** whose palaces are divided between Épernay and Reims. While all the visits are free, some require appointments, but don't be put off – they all speak English and, with an individually arranged visit, you're more likely to get a *dégustation*. Their audiovisuals and (cold) cellar tours are on the whole very informative, and do more than merely plug brand names. The professional body regulating the industry is the *Comité Interprofessionel du Vin de Champagne* (*CIVC*), 5 rue Henri-Martin, Épernay. They can provide copious information and a full list of addresses and times for visits, as can any local SI.

If you want to work on the **harvest**, contact either the *maisons* direct; the *Agence Nationale pour l'Emploi*, 11 rue Jean-Moët, Épernay (☎26.51.01.33), or 57 rue Talleyrand, **Reims** (☎26.88.46.76); or try the youth hostel in **Verzy** where casual workers are often recruited, or work advertised – located at 14 rue du Bassin (☎26.97.90.10).

To the northeast, the scenery of the **Ardennes** region along the Meuse valley knocks spots off any landscape in Champagne. Most of the hills lie over the border in Belgium, but there's enough of interest on the French side to make it well worth exploring. Train and bus connections are good, and there are walking and boating possibilities, too.

Reims

Mostly laid flat by the bombs of World War I, **REIMS** doesn't make attractive first impressions, but there's a good reason for visiting – apart from its champagne world status – as it possesses one of the most impressive Gothic cathedrals in France, formerly the coronation church of dynasties of French monarchs. The expressway running along the Marne canal and the horrendous highway around its centre make it feel much bigger than it is. In fact the cathedral is less than ten minutes' walk from the **gare SNCF** and **gare routière**. And the **SI** is conveniently located next door (Mon–Sat 9am–7.30pm Sun 9.30am–6.30pm).

The city

The lure of the **Cathédrale** is threefold: firstly, the kaleidoscopic patterns in the stained glass, with Marc Chagall designs in the east chapel and champagne processes glorified in the south transept; secondly, a series of unusually lovely tapestries; and thirdly, and best, an inexplicable joke, running around the restored but still badly muti-lated statuary on the west front. The giggling angels who seem to be responsible for disseminating the prank are a rare delight. Not all the figures are the originals – some have been removed to spare them further erosion by the elements and are now at the former bishop's palace, the **Palais du Tau** (July & Aug 9.30am–6.30pm; rest of year 9.30am–noon & 2–6pm; 23F), next door. These oddities of sculpture are as expressive seen close up in the palace as in their intended monumental positions on the cathedral. Apart from the grinning angels, there are also some friendly-looking gargoyles and a superb Eve, shiftily clutching the monster of sin. As added narrative, embroidered tapestries of the *Song of Songs* line the walls.

The palace also preserves, in a state of unlikely veneration, the paraphernalia of the arch-reactionary Charles X's **coronation** in 1824, right down to the Dauphin's hat box. In being anointed here in purple pomp – after Revolution, Robespierre and Napoléon had tried to achieve a new France – Louis XVI's brother stated his intention to return the country to the *ancien régime*. His attempt turned out to be short lived, but the tradition he was calling upon dated back to 496 AD when Clovis, king of the Franks (and of the first identifiable French post-Roman entity), was baptised in Reims. Reims Cathedral was where Joan of Arc succeeded in getting the Dauphin crowned as Charles VII in 1429 – an act of immense significance when France was more or less wiped off the map by the English and their allies. In all, 26 kings of France were crowned in the Gothic glory of this edifice. Between July and September the upper parts of the cathedral are open to the public so you can look down and contemplate the vices and virtues of those who made the procession along its nave.

Most of the early French kings were buried in Reims' oldest building, the eleventh-century **Basilique St-Rémi**, ten minutes' walk away on rue Simon (Mon–Fri 2–6.30pm Sat & Sun 2–7pm; 8F), part of a former Benedictine abbey named after the 22-year-old bishop who baptised Clovis and 3000 of his warriors. An immensely spacious building, with aisles wide enough to drive a bus through, it preserves its Romanesque choir and ambulatory chapels, some of them with modern stained glass that works beautifully. The ticket to the basilica includes entrance to the other monastic buildings, where more stone sculpture and tapestries are displayed.

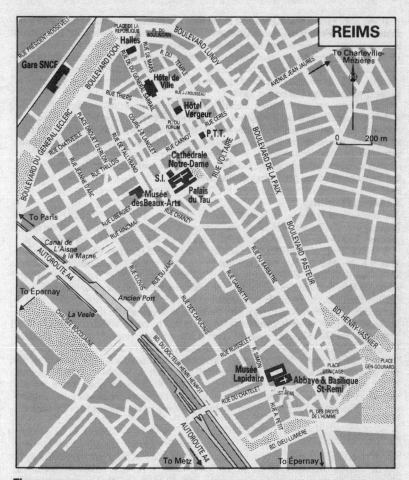

The museums

On rue Chanzy, the **Musée des Beaux-Arts** (daily 10am–noon & 2–6pm; closed Tues) is the city's principal museum, which, though ill-suited to its ancient building and very diverse, does effectively cover French art from the Renaissance to the present. Few of the works are among the particular artists' best, but the collection does contain one of David's replicas of his famous Marat death scene, a set of 27 Corots, two great Gauguin still-lifes, some beautifully observed sixteenth-century German portraits, and various interesting odds and ends, including an old *tabac* sign from nineteenth-century Reims. As long as you don't feel compelled to look at everything, an hour or so could be happily spent here. The same cannot be said for the museum in the **Hôtel Vergeur**, 36 place du Forum (Tues–Sun 10am–6pm; 15F), where you'll have to go through a long guided tour of the whole works, but it's nevertheless a stuffed treasure house of all kinds of beautiful objects, including two sets of Dürer engravings – an *Apocalypse* and *Passion of Christ*.

If you have even a passing interest in old cars you should head out to the **Centre de l'Automobile Française**, 84 av Georges-Clemenceau (March–Nov daily 10am–noon & 2–7pm; Dec–Feb Sat & Sun 10am–noon & 2–5pm; 30F), ten minutes' walk east of the cathedral. All 150 vehicles, dating from 1891 to the present day, are part of the private collection of Philippe Charbonneaux, designer of a number of the post-war classics on display. And, in addition to the full-scale cars, there's an impressive selection of models, antique toys and period posters.

On the opposite side of town, behind the station in rue Franklin-Roosevelt, is the rather more dull **Salle de Reddition** (10am–noon & 2–6pm; closed Tues; 8F), an old schoolroom which served as Eisenhower's HQ from February 1945. In the early hours of May 7, 1945, General Jodl agreed to the unconditional surrender of the German army, thus ending World War II in Europe. The room has been left exactly as it was (minus the ashtrays and carpet), but there's really not enough to warrant a special visit out here unless you're particularly motivated.

Champagne tasting

For the serious business of Reims, head to place des Droits-de-l'Homme and pl St-Niçaise, near the Basilique St-Rémi, which are both within striking distance of the Reims *maisons*. Unlike Épernay, the *maisons* here charge a small entrance fee for their tours.

If you're limiting yourself to one *maison* – not that there's any need for such abstinence – the **Maison Veuve Clicquot-Ponsardin**, 1 place des Droits-de-l'Homme (Mon–Sat 9–11.15am & 2–5pm; Nov–April by appointment only), is as good as they come. In the early days of capitalism, the widowed Mme Clicquot not only took over her husband's business, but later bequeathed it to her business manager rather than to her children – both radical breaks with tradition. In keeping with this past, the *maison* is one of the least pompous and its video the best. The *caves*, with their horror-movie fungi, are old Gallo-Roman quarries. The House of **Pommery**, 5 place du Général-Gouraud (March–Nov daily 9am–11am & 2–5pm), has also excavated Roman quarries for their cellars (they claim – in good champagne one-upmanship – to have been the first to do so). And at **Taittinger**, 9 place St-Niçaise (March–Nov Mon–Fri 9.30am–1pm & 2–5.30pm Sat & Sun 9am–noon & 2–6pm; Dec–Feb Mon–Fri only), there are still more ancient *caves*, with doodles and carvings added by more recent workers, and statues of St Vincent and St Jean, patron saints respectively of *vignerons* and cellar hands.

Practicalities

Accommodation is easy to come by: some hotels to try in the centre are *Thillois*, 17 rue de Thillois (☎26.40.65.65; ②/③); *Le Bon Accueil*, 31 rue de Thillois (☎26.88.55.74; ②/③); and *Alsace*, 6 rue du Général-Sarrail (☎26.47.44.08; ②/③). The youth hostel is at 1 chausée Bocquaine (☎26.40.52.60; curfew 11pm; no IYHF card required), fifteen minutes' walk from the station on the other side of the canal. The **camping municipal** is about 1.5km further out from the *maisons* on av Hoche (☎26.85.41.22; open April–Sept; bus Z, four stops after place des Droits-de-l'Homme).

Eating, drinking and nightlife

Place Drouet-d'Erlon, a wide boulevard lined with bars and restaurants, is where you'll find most of the city's nightlife (such as it is). Places on pl Drouet-d'Erlon itself are generally pretty good if a little overpriced; *Le Colbert* at no. 64 is a fair bet for decent food. For something cheaper, try some of the more unorthodox pizzas on offer at *Aux Côteaux*, on the same side of the street. If you've been visiting the *caves*, *Le St-Niçaise*, on place St-Niçaise, is cheap and convenient (closed Sun eve).

In the summer, over 100 classical **concerts** – many of them free – take place as part of *Les Flâneries Musicales d'Été*; pick up a leaflet at the SI. As a university city, Reims' cafés are livelier than most: try the *Café aux Loges* on pl Drouet-d'Erlon, where you can play pool or sit at the designer tables and drink till late; or the **jazz bar** *Croque-Notes*, 24 rue Ernest-Renan (Mon–Sat until 2.30am; closed Aug), which has live bands every night.

Épernay

Though a pleasant enough town, the only real reason for coming to **ÉPERNAY**, 26km south of Reims, is to visit the champagne *maisons*, whose tours, should you decide to take them all, could keep you fully occupied for a couple of days. Children over the age of four should be happy enough on the *caves* tours: toddlers may get chilly and scared.

The largest, and probably the most famous, is **Moët et Chandon**, 20 av de Champagne (April–Oct daily 9.30–11.30am/noon & 2–4/5pm; Nov–March Sat & Sun only; free *dégustation*), who own Mercier, Ruinart and a variety of other concerns, including, incidentally, Dior perfumes. By its own reckoning, a Moët champagne cork pops somewhere in the world every two seconds – or at least did before the slump of 1990. The cellars are adorned with mementoes of Napoléon, a good friend of the original M Moët, and the vintage is named after the monastic hero of champagne history, Dom Perignon.

Of the other *maison* visits, one of the most rewarding is **Mercier**, 73 av de Champagne (April–Oct Mon–Sat 9.30–11.30am & 2–5pm Sun 9am–5pm; Nov & March 9.30–11.30 & 2–4pm; Dec–Feb Sat & Sun only), whose glamour relic is a giant barrel that held 200,000 bottles-worth when M Mercier took it to the 1889 Paris Exhibition, with the help of 24 oxen – only to be upstaged by the Eiffel Tower. Visits round the cellars here are by electric train. They are fun, and again climax in *dégustation*.

Another *maison* worth visiting is **Castellane**, by the station at 57 rue de Verdun (May–Oct daily 10.30am–noon & 2–5.30pm), in a kind of neo-Classical signal box. If you go on a weekday, you'll see all the processes. The tour is less gimmicky and chic than Mercier's or Moët's, and the *dégustation* a lot more generous.

Practicalities

The cheapest **hotels** in Épernay are *St-Pierre*, 1 rue Jeanne-D'Arc (☎26.54.40.80; ②); *Hôtel de la Cloche*, 5 place Thiers (☎26.55.24.05; ②); *Le Progrès*, 6 rue des Berceaux (☎26.55.22.72; ②/③), in the centre; and *Hôtel de la Terrasse*, 7 quai de la Marne (☎26.55.26.05; ③), by the river. The **MJC** youth hostel, 8 rue de Reims (☎26.55.40.82), has dorm-style accommodation and a cheap cafeteria. The **campsite** is 1.5km to the north in the Parc des Sports, on the south bank of the Marne (route de Cumières). The **SI** is at 7 av de Champagne (Mon–Sat 9.30am–6.30pm Sun 11am–3pm; Nov–Feb Mon–Sat 10am–5.30pm). If you feel like roaming around the *vignerons*, **bikes** can be hired at the **gare SNCF** or c/o M Buffet, behind the church near the SI.

Troyes

TROYES, ancient capital of Champagne, is a gem. Its high narrow streets of restored, half-timbered houses protect an elegant Gothic cathedral, half-a-dozen superb lesser churches, a fistful of Renaissance mansions, and a couple of exceptionally good **museums**.

Around the town: churches and museums

Despite being raked by numerous fires in the Middle Ages, Troyes has retained many of its timber-framed buildings, particularly in the streets and alleyways of the old town off **rue Champeaux**. At the end of one such lane, rue Paillot-de-Montabert, is the

Église St-Jean, where **Henry V** married Catherine of France after being recognised as heir to the French throne in the 1420 Treaty of Troyes, his claim to the title being that he had successfully ravaged the already divided country – no doubt without a single one of the qualities attributed to him by Shakespeare. Two other Troyes churches worth seeking out are the **Église Ste-Madeleine** (daily, Easter–Sept), whose delicate stonework can be found down rue de la Madeleine, and the sumptuous **Église St-Pantaléon**, southwest of Église St-Jean, off place Audiffred (daily, July & Aug), which you can only peer into for most of the year.

As the tourist pamphlets are at pains to point out, the ring of boulevards round the town are shaped like a champagne cork. In fact they're just as much like a sock – a shape that's just as suitable since **hosiery and woollens** have been Troyes's most important industry since the end of the Middle Ages. In 1630 Louis XIII decreed that charitable houses had to be self-supporting, so the orphanage of the Hôpital de la Trinité set their charges to work making knitted stockings. Colbert introduced better machines, thanks to his spies in England, by the time the first generation of child labourers were experienced *bonnetiers*. Today the business still accounts for more than half the town's employment. Some of the machines and products can be seen in a **Musée de la Bonneterie** in the sixteenth-century Hôtel de Mauroy, 7 rue de la Trinité, one block east of Église St-Pantaléon (daily 9am–noon & 2–6pm; closed Tues; 15F). Beautifully restored and visually appealing, it sets an example for all crafts' museums with its respect for the traditions and lack of sentimentality.

Five minutes walk from the Église St-Jean up rue Urban IV is **la Cité**, the part of Troyes bounded to the south by the Seine canal and centred on the **Cathédrale St-Pierre-et-St-Paul** (daily 8/9am–noon & 2–5/6pm), its pale Gothic nave stroked with reflections from the wonderful stained-glass windows. Next door, housed in the old bishops' palace, is the **Musée d'Art Moderne** (daily 11am–6pm; closed Tues; 15F), an outstanding museum displaying part of an extraordinary private collection of art, particularly rich in Fauvist paintings by the likes of Vlaminck and Dérain – along with other works by Degas, Courbet, Gauguin, Matisse (a tapestry and three canvases), Bonnard, Braque, Modigliani, Rodin, Robert Delaunay and Ernst – all of them first class. On the other side of the cathedral, the **Musée St-Loup** (Tues–Fri 10am–noon & 2–6.15pm Sat 9am–5pm; 15F) is mostly **natural history**, but is worth a look for the ornate Baroque library situated on the first floor. In similar vein, the **Hôtel Dieu**, back down rue de la Cité, has a richly decorated sixteenth-century apothecary (prices and times as above).

Practicalities

The **gare SNCF** and **gare routière** are side by side off bd Carnot (part of the ring road). Not all buses use the main station, though, and if you're heading for the countryside, it's best to check first with the **SI** at 16 bd Carnot (June–mid-Sept, Mon–Sat 9am–8.30pm, Sun 10am–noon & 2.30–5.30pm; rest of year 9am–12.30pm & 2–6.30pm).

Places **to stay** around the station are plentiful; *Hôtel de la Gare*, 8 bd Carnot (☎25.78.22.84; ③); *Hôtel Splendid*, 44 bd Carnot (☎25.73.08.52; ③), and *Hôtel de Paris*, 54 rue Roger-Salengro (☎25.73.36.32; ③), are all reasonable. Cheaper and more central than any of the above is the rickety half-timbered *Marigny*, 3 rue Charbonnet (☎25.73.10.67; ②). More expensive but equally central is *Le Champenois*, 15 rue Pierre-Gauthier (☎25.76.16.05; ③/④). Outside of term-time there may be rooms in the city's *foyers* – the SI has details. The **youth hostel** is 6km out of town at 8 rue Jules-Ferry, Rosières (☎25.82.00.65; IYHF card required; bus #6B to the last stop, then bus #11, stop *Liberté*). Opposite the sign saying "Vielaines", a path leads down to the fourteenth-century priory – a youth hostel with a difference – where you can stay year round as well as camp in the grounds. The municipal **campsite** is 2km northeast of Troyes on the D960 at Pont-Ste-Marie (open April–Oct; bus #1).

For **eating** there's considerable variety, with plenty of brasseries around rue Champeaux. *Le Provençal* at 18 rue Général-Saussier with cheap and quick standard fare proves how unnecessary fast food is in France. On the same street further down there's quite a good African place. *Le Café du Musée*, on rue de la Cité near the cathedral, has a decent restaurant upstairs and a wide selection of beers downstairs. *Le Tricasse*, 2 rue Charbonnet, is perennially popular, with pool tables and the occasional live band.

The road to Dijon

The Seine, Marne and Aube and several other lesser rivers rise in the **Plateau de Langres** between Troyes and Dijon. Hunting for sources, though, is a thankless task – there are no bubbling springs promising bigger things to come, and you're more likely to be conscious of undifferentiated water everywhere, rather than emanations from specific fissures. Main routes from Troyes to the Burgundian capital of **Dijon** skirt this area; the eastern one, which the train follows, takes in CHAUMONT and LANGRES, two towns that could briefly slow your progress if you're in no hurry.

Between Troyes and Chaumont, there's one stop-off that might appeal if you have your own transport: the **Cristallerie de Champagne** below the church in BAYEL, 7.5km southeast of BAR-SUR-AUBE on the D396. The glassworks can be visited if you make an appointment (☎25.92.05.02; every day except Sun, 9.30am–5.30pm), or you can simply call at the shop (Mon–Sat 8.30am–12.30pm & 2.15–5.30pm, Sun 2.30–5.30pm). Most of the exquisite crystal on display is very expensive, but they also sell irregular and end-of-season items at greatly reduced prices.

Chaumont

Situated on a steep bank overlooking the Marne valley, **CHAUMONT**, 93km east of Troyes, is one of the few towns worth pausing at on the road to Dijon. The main building to go and look at is the **Basilique St-Jean-Baptiste**. Built with the same dour, grey stone of most Champagne churches, it has, nevertheless, a wonderful Renaissance addition to the Gothic transept of balconies and turreted stairway. The decoration includes a fifteenth-century polychrome *Mise en Tombeau* with muddy tears but expressive faces, and an *Arbre de Jessé* of the early sixteenth-century Troyes school in which all the characters are sitting, properly dressed in the style of the day, in the tree.

As for the rest of the town, there's not much to do except admire the strange, bulging towers of the houses in which the shapes of wide spiral staircases show through. Although not the most animated of places, Chaumont has recently set up an annual international poster festival held in the first week of July. Otherwise, try and go on Wednesday or Saturday, when a **market** is held on place des Halles.

If you're looking for a cheap **room**, try *Le St-Jean*, 2 place Aristide-Briand (☎25.03.00.79; ②), on the opposite side of town from the train station.

Langres

LANGRES, 35km south of Chaumont, and just as spectacularly situated above the Marne, suffered far less war damage and retains its encirclement of gateways, towers and ramparts. Walking this circuit, with views east to the hills of Alsace and southwest across the Plateau de Langres, is the best thing to do if you're just stopping for an hour or so. Wandering inside the walls isn't unrewarding either – Renaissance houses and narrow streets give the feel of a place time left behind, hidden by the mists of south Champagne. Langres was the home, for the first sixteen years of his life, of Diderot, the eighteenth-century Enlightenment philosopher, and people like to make the point that if he were to return to Langres today, he'd have no trouble finding his way around.

The **Musée de l'Hôtel du Breuil**, in one of the best of the town's sixteenth-century mansions (daily 10am–noon & 2–5/6pm; closed Tues), dedicates a room to Diderot with his encyclopaedias, various other first editions of his works, and one of Van Loos's portraits of the savant. In addition, the museum contains a collection of beautiful ivory pieces, and sets of dining knives for which this area was famous for several centuries. Local *faience* – glazed terracotta – is featured, too, though these nicely crafted pieces are upstaged by the sixteenth-century tiles from Rouen in one of the nave chapels of the **Cathédrale St-Mammès**. This grey stone edifice has not been improved by the eighteenth-century addition of a new facade, but, in addition to the Rouen tiles, there's an amusing sixteenth-century relief of the *Raising of Lazarus*, in which the apostles watch, totally blasé, while the locals look like kids at a good horror movie.

For **accommodation**, there's the *Auberge Jeanne d'Arc*, 26 rue Gambetta (☎25.87.03.18; ②), in the centre of town, or *Les Moulins*, 5 place des États-Unis (☎25.87.08.12; ③), near the SI and *Porte des Moulins*.

The Ardennes

In war after war, the people of **the Ardennes** have suffered protracted last-ditch battles down the valley of the Meuse – which, once lost, gave invading armies a clear path to Paris. The hilly terrain and deep forests (frightening even to Julius Caesar's legionnaires) gave some advantage to World War II's Resistance fighters when the Ardennes was annexed to Germany, but even peacetime living has never been easy. The main employment over the last century is coming to an end as the slateworks have all closed down, and the ironworks are following suit. The only offering from Paris has been a nuclear power station in the loop of the Meuse at Chooz, to which locals responded by etching "Nuke the Élysée!" high on a half-cut cliff of slate just downstream.

The land is rugged and unsuitable for crops, and tourism is the main growth industry. As yet the Ardennes is far from developed, which is its greatest attraction.

Charleville-Mézières

The usual starting point for exploring northwards is the twintown of **CHARLEVILLE-MÉZIÈRES** which spreads across the meandering Meuse before the valley closes in and the forests take over. Of the two, **Charleville** is the one to head for, though aside from its main square, its only virtue is as a base for the Ardennes countryside.

Charleville's main sight is the beautifully arcaded central **place Ducale**, the result of the seventeenth-century local duke's envy of the contemporary place des Vosges in Paris. The SI is in the Hôtel de Ville on the square and can provide information for the whole region. From the **gare SNCF**, place Ducale is a five-minute bus ride away (take any of the buses going to the right as you come out of the station and ask someone to tell you when you reach place Nevers, just below place Ducale): the **gare routière** is a couple of blocks north of place Nevers, between rues du Daga and Noël.

Rimbaud and puppetry

Charleville's most famous son is the poet **Arthur Rimbaud** (1854–91). He ran away from Charleville four times, the last time at the age of seventeen when he joined **Verlaine** in Paris, fought in the Commune and, after twice surviving attempts by the elder poet on his life, gave up poetry and fled the country (aged nineteen). For a while he journeyed between Europe and the Far East before establishing himself as a successful trader in Ethiopia and Yemen. He only returned to France at the age of 37 for surgery in a Marseille hospital, which killed him. His body was brought back to his home town – probably the last place he would have wanted to be buried. The **Musée Arthur Rimbaud**, in an old windmill on quai Arthur-Rimbaud, two blocks north of the main square (Tues–Sun 9am–noon & 2–6pm), contains a lot of pictures of this strange youth and those he hung out with, as well as facsimiles of his writings and related documents. A few steps down the quayside is the spot where he composed *Le Bateau Ivre*.

Charleville is also a major international **puppetry** centre (its school is justly famous), and every three years at the end of September or early October, it hosts one of the largest puppet festivals in the world, the **Festival Mondial des Théâtres de Marionnettes** (the next one is in 1994). For ten days groups from as far away as Mali and Burma put on something like fifty shows a day on the streets and in every available space in the town. Tickets are cheap and there are shows for adults as well as the usual stuff aimed at kids.

Accommodation

Three fairly central **hotels** to try are *Hôtel de Paris*, 24 av G-Corneau (☎24.33.34.38;④/⑤), *Europe*, 18 rue Porte-Lucas (☎26.51.80.28; ③), and *Pomme d'Or*, 12 rue E-Mercier (☎26.53.11.44; ③); for the **youth hostel**, 3 rue des Tambours (☎24.57.44.36), take bus #9, direction La Brouette from the station or place Nevers (stop *Auberge de Jeunesse*). The town **campsite** is south of place Ducale, over the river past the museum and off to the left.

Exploring the Ardennes

Georges Sand wrote of the stretch of the Meuse that winds through the Ardennes that "its high wooded cliffs, strangely solid and compact, are like some inexorable destiny that encloses, pushes and twists the river without permitting it a single whim or any escape". What all the tourist literature writes about, however, are the legends of medieval struggles between Good and Evil whose characters have given names to some of the curious rocks and crests. The grandest of these, where the schist formations have taken the most peculiar turns, is the **Roc de la Tour**, also known as the devil's castle, up a path off the D31, 3.5km out of MONTHERMÉ.

The journey through this frontier country should ideally be done on **foot or skis**, or by **boat**. The alternatives for the latter are good old *bateau-mouches* or live-in pleasure boats – not wildly expensive if you can split the cost four or six ways. If you're interested, contact *Loisirs Accueil en Ardennes*, 18 av G-Corneau, Charleville. At the same office you'll also find the Ardennes *Comité de Tourisme*, who can provide **walking maps** of the region. For **public transport** from Charleville, trains follow the Meuse into Belgium, and a few buses run up to Monthermé and LES HAUTES-RIVIÈRES, the latter on the river Semoy.

The **GR12** is a good walking route, circling the Lac des Vieux Forges (17km northwest of Charleville – and with canoe hire), then meeting the Meuse at BOGNY and crossing over to HAUTES RIVIÈRES in the even more sinuous Semoy Valley. There are plenty of other tracks, too, though beware of *chasse* signs – French hunters tend to hack through the undergrowth with their safety catches off and are notoriously trigger-happy. Wild boar are the main quarry being hunted, and nowhere near as dangerous as their pursuers: the bristly beasts would seem to be more intelligent, too, rooting about near the crosses of the Resistance memorial near REVIN while hunters stalk the forest at a respectful distance. The abundance of wild boar is partly explained when you rootle around on the forest floor yourself and discover, between the trees to either side of the river, an astonishing variety of mushrooms, and, in late summer, wild strawberries and bilberries. For connoisseurs of water, the faintly lemoned spring water of ST-VLADIMIR – just out of HAYBES on the HARGNIES road – makes for a pleasant goal.

travel details

Trains

London to Paris through-services run direct from the port stations at Calais or Boulogne, stopping en route only at Amiens.

From Calais-Ville 6 daily to Paris (3hr 30min), via Amiens (1hr 45min); 9 or 10 daily to Boulogne-Ville (30min) and Étaple-Le Touquet (1hr); frequently to Lille and stops en route (1hr–1hr 30min; some with change at Hazebrouck).

From Boulogne-Ville 8 daily to Paris (3 hr), via Amiens (1hr 15min); 9 or 10 to Calais-Ville (30min) and Étaple-Le Touquet (20min), Montreuil (30min) and Arras (2 hr).

From Dunkerque 7 or 8 daily to Paris (3hr 10min), via Arras (1 hr 20min); 3 or 4 daily, not Sun, to Calais-Ville (1hr).

From Amiens very frequently to Paris (1hr 45min–2hr); several daily to Compiègne (1hr 15min) and Laon (2hr).

From Beauvais 6 or 7 daily to Paris (1hr 10min).

From St-Quentin frequent service (7am–midnight) to Paris (1hr 45min), some via Compiègne (50min), a few stopping at all stations including Noyon and Tergnier (change for Laon); additional stopping trains run between Compiègne and Tergnier, and 4 daily from Tergnier to Laon (25min).

From Laon erratic service (mornings/evenings) to Paris (2hr 20min), via Soissons (1hr 40min); more frequent between Laon and Soissons.

From Lille very frequently to Paris (2–2hr 30min); TGV daily around 7am to Arras (40min), Longeau

(1hr 10min) and Lyon (4hr 40min); regularly to Brussels (2hr).

From Reims frequently to Paris (2hr); to Epernay (25min); to Charleville-Mézières (55min).

From Troyes frequently to Paris (1hr 30min).

Buses

From Dunkerque several daily to Calais.

From Calais 5 daily to Boulogne (1hr) and Le Touquet (2hr).

From Boulogne 5 daily to Calais (1hr) and Le Touquet (1hr).

From Amiens buses in all directions, including Beauvais (1hr 45min), St-Quentin (2hr 30min) and Albert (40min). South Picardy sporadic buses link most of the towns – Compiègne, Beauvais, Soissons, Chantilly, St-Quentin, Noyon – with each other and with Amiens and Paris.

From Reims 3 daily to Troyes (2hr 30min).

From Epernay 1 daily to Troyes, changing at Romilly (3hr 30min).

Ferries

For full cross-channel ferry details, see p.9 in Basics.

From Calais to Dover on *P&O* 15 daily (1hr 15min), on *Sealink* 20 daily (1hr 30min), on *Hoverspeed* 22 daily (35–45min);

From Dunkerque to Ramsgate on *Sally Lines* 5 daily (2hr 30min).

From Boulogne to Dover on *P&O* 6 daily (1hr 15min), on *Hoverspeed* 22 daily (35–45min).

CHAPTER THREE

ALSACE-LORRAINE AND FRANCHE-COMTE

F rance's eastern frontier provinces, **Alsace**, **Lorraine** and **Franche-Comté**, have had a complex and tumultuous history. For a thousand years they have been a battleground, disputed through the Middle Ages by independent dukes and bishops whose allegiance was endlessly contested by the kings of France and the princes of the Holy Roman Empire, and the scene, this century, of some of the worst fighting of both world wars.

The democratically minded burghers of **Alsace** created a plethora of well-heeled semi-autonomous towns for themselves centuries before their eighteenth-century incorporation into the French state. Sharing the Germans' taste for Hansel-and-Gretel decoration, they adorned their buildings with all manner of frills and fancies – oriel windows, carved timberwork and Toytown gables – and with Teutonic orderliness they still maintain them, festooned with flowers and in pristine condition. Not that you should ever call an Alsatian German. Alsatian is a Germanic dialect, but their neighbours across the Rhine have behaved in decidedly unneighbourly fashion twice in the last hundred years, annexing them along with much of Lorraine from 1870–1918 and again under Hitler. They remain fiercely and proudly Alsatian and French, in that order.

The combination of influences makes for a culture and atmosphere as distinctive as any in France. It is seen at its most vivid in the numerous little wine towns that punctuate the **Route du Vin** along the eastern margin of the wet and woody Vosges mountains, at **Colmar**, and in the great cathedral city – now European Community capital – of **Strasbourg**. But the province is not just a quaint setting for coach tours: it's also an industrial powerhouse, making cars, railway engines, textiles, machine tools, telephones – you name it – as well as half the beer in France.

By comparison **Lorraine**, although it has suffered much the same vicissitudes, is rather colourless. Apart from the elegant eighteenth-century provincial capital of **Nancy**, the cathedral city of **Metz** and the depressing and unforgettable World War I battlefield of **Verdun**, there's little to hold the attention or take up much of your time.

More impressive and dramatic are the wooded plateaux, pastures and valleys of **Franche-Comté** and the **Jura** further south, hilly-to-mountainous, rural and poor, but finding some compensation in the attentions of the leisure industry. *Ski de fond* – crosscountry skiing – is the speciality, and it's ideal terrain. It's good walking country, too, without the grinding ascents of the neighbouring Alps.

HOTEL ROOM PRICES

For a fuller explanation of these price codes, see the box on p.28 of *Basics*.

① Under 100F   ② 100–130F   ③ 130–180F   ④ 180–230F   ⑤ 230–300F

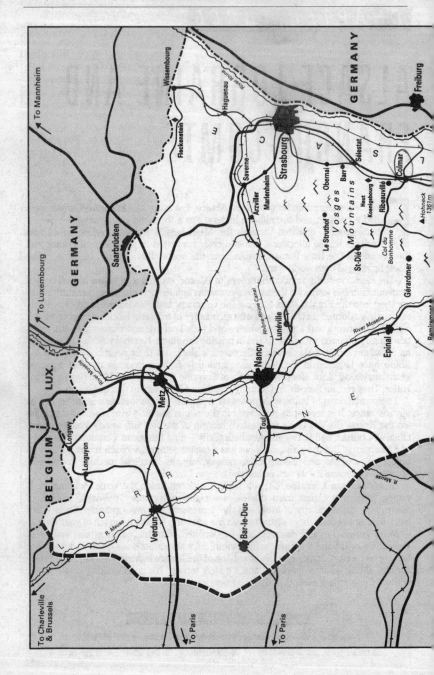

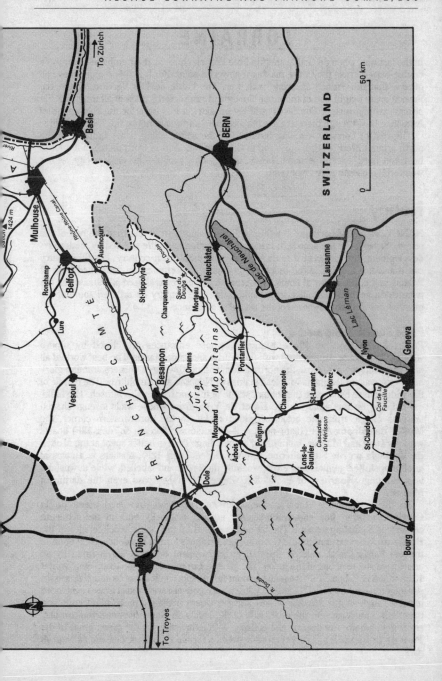

LORRAINE

In the last war, when de Gaulle and the Free French chose as their emblem **Lorraine's** double-barred cross they were making a powerful point. For it is this region, above all others, that the French associate with war. The battle field of **Verdun**, where the French army fought one of the most bloody and protracted battles of all time, is a site of national pilgrimage. The SNCF still lay on extra trains here for the celebration of Armistice Day, though there are few left alive who knew and mourn the 750,000 dead.

The rest of Lorraine – rolling farmland in the south, ailing heavy industry in the north around **Metz** – seems to stand in the shadows. And in truth there's not a lot to hold you here, except perhaps **Nancy**, the region's capital – an elegant city, with a wonderful museum of Art Nouveau.

Nancy

NANCY, capital of Lorraine, is lighter and more southern in feel than the rest of the region. Saved from the post-1870 Prussian occupation and little affected by modern re-development, the city centre remains classically eighteenth century. For this, Nancy can thank the the last of the independent dukes of Lorraine, the dethroned King of Poland, and father-in-law of Louis XV – **Stanislas Leszczynski** (see p.219). During the twenty-odd years of his office in the mid-eighteenth century he ordered some of the most successful urban renewal of the period in all France.

Place Stanislas and around

Pride of place goes to **Place Stanislas**, whose entrances are closed by superb wrought-iron gates, ornamented with florid urns and gilded twirls. The best work of all is in the railings which close the northeastern and northwestern corners, framing gloriously extravagant fountains with lead statues of Neptune and Amphitrite. The middle of the wide square belongs to the solitary statue of the portly Stanislas himself. The bulkiest building on the square is the **Hôtel de Ville**, from whose walls lozenge-shaped lanterns dangle from the beaks of gilded cocks. In the northwestern corner, the **Musée des Beaux-Arts** (10am–noon & 2–6pm; closed Mon am & Tues; 12F) boasts work by Dufy and Matisse, but nothing outstanding. Time is better spent at the **Musée de Zoologie** on rue Ste-Cathérine (2–6pm; closed Tues; 12F); upstairs is a colossal jumble of stuffed animals and birds, woefully displayed and labelled, while downstairs is a startling **aquarium** of exotic fish whose colours surpass even the daring of Matisse.

To the north, place Stanislas opens out into the long, tree-lined **place de la Carrière**, another fine eighteenth-century square, originally built in the sixteenth century as a jousting ground. The far end is closed by the classical colonnades of the **Palais du Gouvernement**, the Governor of Lorraine's former residence. Next door, in the old Palais Ducal, entered through an extravagant doorway surmounted by an equestrian statue of one of the dukes, the **Musée Lorrain** (summer 10am–6pm; winter 10am–noon & 2–5pm; 15F) contains a room full of superb etchings by the Nancy-born seventeenth-century artist, Jacques Callot, whose concern with social issues evidenced in series such as *The Miseries of War* and *Les Gueux* presaged much nineteenth- and twentieth-century art. On the other side of the Palais du Gouvernement, you can play crazy golf, admire the deer or just collapse with exhaustion on the green grass of the **Parc de la Pépinière**, a sort of cross between a formal French garden and an English park.

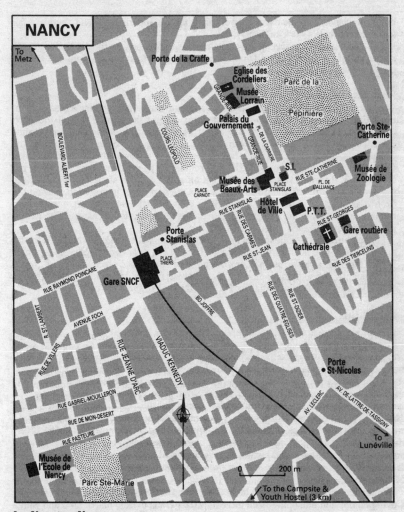

Art-Nouveau Nancy

A traditional handicraft and metal-working town, Nancy became, at the turn of the
century, a centre of Art Nouveau to rival Paris – the most famous and lasting exponent
of the "School of Nancy" being the manufacturer of glass and ceramics, Émile Gallé.
The town's moment of glory was short lived, and now all that remains are a handful of
buildings and – best of all – the **Musée de l'École de Nancy**, 38 rue Sergent-Blandan
(10am–noon & 2–5/6pm; closed Tues; 12F), housed in a 1909 villa built for the Corbin
family, founders of the big *Magasins Réunis* chain of department stores. Even if you are
not into Art Nouveau, this collection is exciting. Although not all of it belonged to the
Corbins, the museum is arranged as if it were a private house. The furniture is
outstanding – swirling curvilinear forms, whether the object is mantlepiece or sofa,

buffet or piano. The standards of workmanship are superlative – and there's a fair sprinkling of Gallé's work on display, too.

For a post-museum coffee in the same kind of atmosphere, try the Art-Nouveau café-restaurant of the former hotel *L'Excelsior*, opposite the train station, built in 1910 and preserved virtually intact to this day.

Accommodation and food

The **SI** on place Stanislas (Mon–Sat 9am–7pm, Sun 10am–1pm) provide a **free accommodation service**. The cheapest **rooms** are south of the **gare SNCF** at the *Hôtel Jean-Jaurès*, 14 bd Jean-Jaurès (☎83.27.74.14; ②), and the *Hôtel Moderne*, 73 rue Jeanne d'Arc (☎83.40.14.26; ①). The **youth hostel** is a long way from the centre in the Château de Rémicourt, Villers-lès-Nancy, southwest of town off the road to Dijon (☎83.27.73.67; curfew 10pm; no IYHF card required). To get there, take bus #6 on rue des Carmes, direction *Vandoeuvre*, and get off at the *Mangin* stop, then walk back to the main road, turn left and go straight across the first major intersection, leaving the *École d'Architecture* at the edge of a park on your left; take the next left, a small road running uphill beside the park, and a gate on the left leads to the château. The **campsite**, *Camping de Brabois* (open April–Oct), is nearby.

For **restaurants**, Grande-Rue and rue des Maréchaux offer the best choice. At the far end of Grande-Rue near Porte de la Craffe, the *Caveau de la Grand' Rue* serves simple French fare. For a classic *quiche Lorraine*, go to *Le Vaudemont*, place Vaudemont (open till midnight). For something different, *Le Bosphore*, further down on the opposite side, is an upmarket kebab joint with tasty Turkish starters like *borek* and *cacik*.

Lunéville

LUNÉVILLE, twenty-minutes' train ride east of Nancy, a half-hour drive along the banks of the Meuthe, was renowned for the **faience** – ceramic tile – works set up by Stanislas. There is a collection of it – too small to merit a detour unless you're a specialist – in the immense eighteenth-century **château** (9am–noon & 2–6pm; closed Tues), dubbed *Le Petit Versailles*. The rest of the château is occupied by cavalry uniforms and weaponry, Lunéville being a garrison town, but the gardens are good for picnicking.

What is worth a detour is M Chapleur's private motorcycle museum, the **Musée de la moto et du vélo** (Tues–Sun 9am–noon & 2–6pm; 16F), directly opposite the gates of the château,. Monsieur Chapleur started collecting in the 1930s when he was a mechanic at Citroën. He has over 200 models of different origins on display, all overhauled and in working order when they go into the museum. And they are beauties, works of art in copper, brass, chrome and steel. Some of the bicycles go back to 1865. The motorbikes date mostly from 1900 to 1940. Several of the older bikes are probably unique; one certainly is – a 1906 René Gillet 4.5hp belt-driven tandem. Many look like flying bombs and must have been incredibly dangerous to ride: bits of meccano with a couple of hefty cylinders welded on and capable of 100kph in 1900.

To get to the museum and château from the **gare SNCF**, take rue Carnot and keep going north until you hit the back of the old theatre which adjoins the château.

Metz

Very much a frontier city, **METZ** (pronounced "Mess") is solid, and confident of its hard-headed business values. As a barracks town from Roman times onwards, it has taken a battering over the centuries. Nevertheless, its soaring Gothic cathedral still stands, and, thanks to the university founded here in the 1970s, it's now a lively place whose nightlife is unrivalled in Lorraine.

The city

The **gare SNCF**, a vast granite building of 1900 in a mix of neo-historical styles, matched by the **post office** opposite, sets the tone of the **Ville Allemande** – the area around the station – built as a *Neustadt* by the occupying Germans between 1870 and 1918.

Five minutes' walk north of the station is the place de la République, a big parking square with shops and cafés to one side, army barracks to the south, and the formal gardens of the **Esplanade** overlooking the Moselle to the west. To the right, as you look down the esplanade, is the handsome, classical **Palais de Justice** in yellow stone; to the left, a gravel drive leads past the old arsenal to the **Église St-Pierre-aux-Nonnains**, not much to look at, but one of the oldest churches in France – parts of it fourth-century. Nearby, there's the thirteenth-century octagonal **Chapelle des Templiers**, an unusual building now converted into an arts centre. Further south, on the leafy square Giraud, the splendidly gabled and ivy-covered neo-Gothic **Palais du Gouverneur** is another legacy of the city's Prussian era.

North of place de la République, rue des Clercs leads through the principal shopping area to eighteenth-century **place d'Armes**, flanked by a pedimented and colonnaded **Hôtel de Ville**, but all rather dwarfed by the short-in-length but very tall **Cathédrale St-Étienne**. Its dark nave is the loftiest in France after Beauvais and Amiens, but its best feature is without doubt the stained glass, both medieval and modern, including windows by Chagall in the north transept and ambulatory.

A short walk up rue des Jardins brings you to the city's best museum, the **Musée d'Art et d'Histoire** (10am–noon & 2–6pm; closed Tues; 14F), a treasure house of Gallo-Roman sculpture, but equally strong on mock-ups of vernacular architecture from the medieval and Renaissance periods. The art section is less impressive, though again thoughtfully arranged, and including works by Corot and Delacroix.

To the west of the cathedral and worth a lesiurely stroll is the **Île de la Comédie**, a narrow island on the Moselle, laid out in classical eighteenth-century style and home to the city's main opera house.

Practicalities

The **SI** (Mon–Fri 9am–9pm Sun 10am–4pm) is conveniently located by the side of the Hôtel de Ville on place d'Armes. There are several reasonable **hotels** in front of the train station, though they fill up fast in season. The cheapest of the lot is the *Terminus*, on rue Lafayette (☎87.66.81.18; ③), followed by the *Métropole*, 5 place du Général-de-Gaulle (☎87.66.26.22; ③/④). Closer to the centre are *Lafayette*, 24 rue des Clercs (☎87.75.21.09; ③), and *France*, 25 place de Chambre (☎87.75.21.09; ③).

The official **youth hostel** is on the other side of town from the train station on allée de Metz-Plage (☎87.30.44.02; bus #3 or #11; IYHF card not required; no curfew but lock-out at 9am) – a clean and friendly place which also offers free bike rental. **Camping** *Metz-Plage* is also located here, on the banks of the Moselle (again, bus #3 or #11).

Eating, drinking, nightlife and events

Traditional French **restaurants** like *La Gargouille* on pl de Chambre are generally quite expensive (from 100F a head). *Les Arcades*, 5 rue Royale, will fill you fairly cheaply with mussels; *Crêperie du Pont* on the pont St-Marcel off Île de la Comédie will do the same with *crêpes*; a good standby is the self-service *Caféteria Flunch* on rue des Clercs.

Metz's hippest **bars** are all in the old centre between place St-Jacques and place de la République, *La Coupole*, rue du Palais, being the prime spot to be seen at. The *Café à la Lune* on place d'Armes has live rock at the weekend, as does *La 5th Avenue* on rue des Clercs. In late June and early July **classical music and dance** comes to town during the *Festival Étonnante Musique*. November's **music festival**, *Rencontres Internationales de Musique Contemporaine* is somewhat more adventurous. The *Fête de la Mirbelle* in late August/early September features a big **hot-air balloon exhibition** as well as floats, bands and fireworks. The SI produce a free listings monthly, *Calendrier des Manifestations* and the rather more critical free bi-monthly *Spectacles à Metz*.

Verdun and the battlefield

At Verdun even the pretence of rationality failed. The slaughter was so hideous that even a trench system could not survive . . . In the town, tourists inspect the memorials. One monument shows French soldiers forming a human wall of comradeship against the enemy. In another, France is personified as a medieval knight; resting on a sword, he dominates a steep flight of steps built into the old ramparts. There is another view of reality. Near the railway station, Rodin's statue shows a winged Victory as neither calm nor triumphant, but demented by rage and horror. Her legs are tangled in a dead soldier and she shrieks for survival.

Donald Horne: *The Great Museum*

You arrive in **VERDUN**, 68km west of Metz, and immediately the events of 1916 take over. For this place, which the German general Erich von Falkenhayn chose "to bleed the French army to death and strike a devastating blow at the morale of the French people", is, with Dresden, Stalingrad and Hiroshima, one of the names that have been chosen to denote the concept of war forever. It is a strange site to pass into tourism, but an instructive one. You never forget – or regret – seeing it.

The town

Given the hammering it took, and the fact that it is still a barracks town, Verdun itself is actually not as grim as you might expect. The **gares SNCF** and **routière** are at either end of av Garibaldi, on which stands the Rodin monument mentioned by Horne (above). A few minutes' walk down the central drag, rue St-Paul/rue Mazel, brings you to the much more militaristic **Monument de la Victoire**, "To the Victorious, living and dead", flanked by cannons and now part of an old fortress discovered under the ruins of 1916. Up the steps, there's a small, macabre safe-house for documents on the war dead run by local veterans. The main war museum is in Vauban's **citadelle souterraine** (daily 9am–noon/1pm & 2–5/6/7pm; closed Jan), further down the street on rue du Rû, in whose underground tunnels thousands of soldiers sheltered during World War I. If you need to make a quick escape from the town, climb the hill in the centre of Verdun and inspect its hybrid **Cathédrale Notre-Dame**.

Practicalities

The **SI** (May–Sept Mon–Sat 8.30am–7pm Sun 9.30am–noon & 1.30–4pm; Oct–April Mon–Sat 9am–noon & 2–5.30/6pm) is east of the centre, across the Pont Chausée and along av du Général-de-Gaulle. From May 1 to September 15 staff at the tourist office run daily minibus **tours of the battlefield**. They begin at around 2pm, last four hours (three hours on Sundays), and cost some 140F per person – not exactly cheap, but the guides are interesting and the expense is not one that you're likely to repeat. From Monday to Saturday, the tour covers the forts of Vaux and Douaumont, the Douaumont ossuary, the Trench of Bayonets and the Fleury museum; on Sundays, they skip Douaumont. Alternatively, you can **hire bicycles** throughout the year from *Cycles Flavenot*, 10 rue de la Marne, and make your own way to the battlefield.

For **accommodation**, start your search at the *Hôtel Verdunois*, 13 av Garibaldi near the station (☎29.86.17.45; ③), followed by *La Porte Chausée*, quai de Londres (☎29.86.00.78; ③), and the *Hôtel de France*, across the river on av du Général-de-Gaulle (☎29.86.09.85; ③).

The battlefield

The **Battle of Verdun** opened on the morning of February 21, 1916, with a German artillery barrage which lasted ten hours and expended two million shells. It concentrated on the forts of Vaux and Douaumont which the French had built after the 1870 Franco-Prussian War – Verdun lay outside the territory seized by the Germans. When the battle ended ten months later, the death toll was approaching a million, and nine villages had been pounded to nothing – not even their sites are detectable in aerial photos of the time and the land today still follows the curves of shell craters. It is said that the heavy artillery shells ploughed the ground to a depth of eight metres, and, though much of it is now reforested, there are parts that steadfastly refuse anchorage to any but the coarsest vegetation.

Douaumont

Ten kilometres northeast of Verdun, off the D913, and commanding the highest point of the ridge is the **Fort de Douaumont** (mid-March–Sept daily 9/9.30am–6/7pm; rest of the year Tues–Sun 10am–noon & 1.30/2–4/5/6pm; closed Jan; 13F). Completed in 1912, it was the strongest of 38 forts built to defend Verdun. But in one of those inexplicable aberrations of military top brass, the armament of these forts was greatly reduced in 1915. When the Germans attacked in 1916, twenty men were enough to overrun the garrison of 57 French territorials. The fort is built on three levels, two of them underground. Its claustrophobic, dungeon-like galleries are hung with stalactites. The Germans, who held it for eight months, had 3000 men housed in its cramped quarters with no toilets, continuously under siege, its ventilation ducts blocked for protection against gas, infested with fleas and lice and plagued by rats which attacked the sleeping and the dead indiscriminately. In one night, when their ammunition exploded, 1300 men died in the blast.

When the French retook the fort, it was with Moroccan troops in the vanguard. General Mangin, revered by officialdom as the heroic victor of the battle, was known to his troops as "the butcher" for his practice of shoving colonial troops into the front line as cannon fodder. Men who had no desire to kill were forced on pain of the firing squad to slaughter their fellow human beings. Official history accords little attention to their spontaneous mutinies and refusals. By 1918 the ground around Verdun was completely devoid of vegetation and covered in fragments of corpses. 120,000 French bodies were identified, just a third of the total killed.

Back on the main road, south of the fort, is the **cimetière nationale** containing the graves of 15,000 men, the Christians commemorated by rows of identical crosses, the Moroccans with gravestones facing the direction of Mecca. In the centre of the battlefield nearby is one of the most moving war memorials of all time, the vast **Ossuaire de Douaumont** (April–Sept daily 9am–5.30/6.30pm; March, Oct & Nov daily 9am–noon & 2–5/6pm; 14F). At its inauguration in 1932, the President of the Ossuary Committee observed: *"Douaumont, rempart contre l'envahisseur, est devenu le rempart contre l'oubli"* – "Originally a rampart against invasion, Douaumont has become a rampart against forgetfulness". Beneath each of the eighteen alcoves inside, and at either end of the building are vast sepulchral vaults filled with the bones of unidentified soldiers. The inlaid floor represents the different military orders and the names of the dead are inscribed all over the walls.

Not far from the ossuary along the D913 to Charny, a memorial marks the **Tranchée des Baïonnettes** (Trench of Bayonets), where two entire infantry platoons were buried alive during a German bombardment on June 11, 1916.

Fleury and Vaux

The events which demanded such a horrifying monument are all graphically documented in the **Musée-memorial de Fleury** (mid-March to mid-Sept daily 9am–6pm; rest of year daily 9am–noon & 2–5/6pm; 16F), 1km south of the cemetery along the D913. Contemporary newsreels and photos present the stark truth. In the well of the museum, a section of the shell-torn terrain which was once the village of Fleury has been reconstructed as the battle left it.

The tour's last call is at the **Fort de Vaux** (same times and price as the Fort de Douaumont but closed Wed low season), 4km east of Fleury, where after six days' hand-to-hand combat in the confined, gas-filled galleries, the French garrison, reduced to drinking their own urine, were left with no alternative but surrender. On the exterior wall of the fort a plaque commemorates the last messenger pigeon sent to the command post in Verdun vainly asking for reinforcements. Having safely delivered its message, the pigeon expired as a result of flying through the gas-filled air above the battlefield. It was posthumously awarded the *Légion d'Honneur.*

THE MAGINOT LINE

Constructed between **1930 and 1940** the defensive Maginot Line was the brain-child of the French Minister of War (1929–31), **André Maginot**. It was hugely expensive, spanned the entire French–German border and, when put to the test in 1940, proved totally useless – the Germans simply entered via Belgium. The **Fort de Fermont** (daily 1.30–4/5pm) was one of the largest forts, with nine fire points, served by six kilometres of underground tunnels and a garrison of 600. The entrance is hidden in woodland. Nothing shows above ground but the scarcely noticeable domes of the gun turrets. Below, the tunnels are equipped with power plants, electric trains, monorails, elevators and all the other technological paraphernalia necessary to support such a lunatic enterprise. The place has the feel of a nuclear bunker.

Getting there without your own transport can be difficult. There are trains to Longuyon from Metz and Verdun (change at Conflans), but you'll have to hitch or walk the last 5km to the fort.

ALSACE

There's no denying **Alsace**'s attractiveness, with its old stone and half-timbered towns set amid the thickly wooded hills of the Vosges, but it's a quaintness that has become a commodity. **Strasbourg**, the capital of Alsace, and along with Brussels, one of the main centres of the European Community, escapes the tweeness of some of the smaller towns of the foothills. **Saverne** and **Wissembourg**, to the north also avoid the worst of the tourist-brochure image, giving access to some spectacular ruined castles in the **northern Vosges**.

South of Strasbourg, along the **Route du Vin**, there are countless picturesque medieval villages and yet more ruined castles, which suffer to varying degrees from the attention of the tour coaches. A very different, sobering experience is the concentration camp of **Le Struthof**, hidden away in the Vosges forest. **Colmar** is almost excessively cute, yet still worth a visit for Grünewald's amazing Isenheim altarpiece. By contrast, **Mulhouse** is thoroughly industrial but boasts some unusually good museums devoted to cars, railways and printed fabrics.

Strasbourg

STRASBOURG is prosperous, beautiful and modern – big enough with a quarter of a million people to have a metropolitan air, but never overwhelming. It has one of the loveliest cathedrals in France, one of the oldest and most active universities and, an ancient commercial crossroads, is now home to the Council of Europe, the European Court of Human Rights and the European Parliament. You may not be planning time in eastern France, but if you're travelling through or near the region this is the one city worth a special detour.

Orientation and accommodation

It is not difficult to find your way around Strasbourg. The city centre is concentrated on a small island encircled by the River Ill. From the **gare SNCF** take rue du Maire-Kuss, cross the river onto rue du 22-Novembre and you'll soon notice **place Kléber** on your left, the commercial centre. From the other side of place Kléber, rue des Grandes-Arcades leads south to **place Gutenberg**, nominally the main square, where the **SI** is located at no.10 (June–Sept daily 8am–7pm; April, May & Oct 9am–6pm; rest of year Mon–Sat 9am–12.30pm & 1.45–6pm).

Accommodation

Room prices tend to be higher than you may be used to, but standards are correspondingly high.

Hôtel Weber, 22 bd de Nancy (☎88.32.36.47). Five minutes' walk from the station and all the better for not being right outside. ③/④

Hôtel Patricia, 1a rue de Puits (☎88.32.14.60). Great location, hidden away in the back streets of the old town not far from place Gutenberg. ③

Hôtel Jura, 5 rue du Marché (☎88.32.12.72). Just over the river from the station off rue du Vieux-Marché-aux-Vins. Midnight curfew won't suit everyone, nor the daily lock-out from 11am to 2pm, but it's cheap and central. ③

Hôtel Victoria, 7–9 rue du Maire-Kuss (☎88.32.13.06). Respectable, easy to locate, close to the station but no bargain. ⑤

CIARUS, 7 rue Finkmatt (☎88.32.12.12; curfew 1am). Shiny new hostel with a good central location just north of the old town. No lockout.

IYHF Auberge de Jeunesse René Cassin, 9 rue de l'Auberge de Jeunesse (☎88.30.26.46; curfew 1am). 3km west of the city centre; take bus #3, #13 or #23 from the next bridge upstream from Pont Kuss, stop *Auberge de Jeunesse*.

Camping *Montagne-Verte*, 2 rue Robert-Forrer (☎88.30.25.46; open March–Oct). Well-equipped site behind the IYHF youth hostel (see above for travel details).

The city centre

The small, central **Place Gutenberg** is named after the printer and pioneer of moveable type, whose statue occupies the middle of the square, and who lived in Strasbourg in the early fifteenth century. The west side of the square is taken up by the sixteenth-century **Hôtel de Commerce**, where the writer Arthur Young, fascinated, watched the night-time destruction of the magistrates' records during the Revolution.

The cathedral

As you stand in place Gutenberg, the one thing of which you're always aware is the **Cathédrale de Notre-Dame** (closed 11.40am–12.45pm), constructed out of the local pinky-brown sandstone, and soaring out of the close huddle of medieval houses around

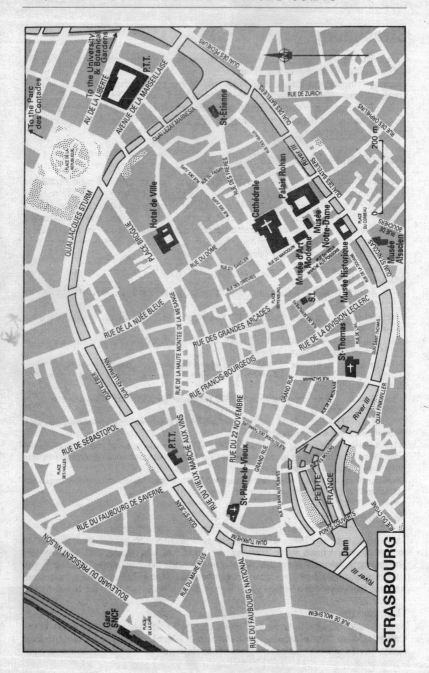

STRASBOURG

its base, with a single spire of such delicate, flaky lightness it seems the work of confectioners rather than masons. It's worth slogging up the 328 steps to the spire's **viewing platform** (daily July & Aug 8.30am–7pm; rest of year 9am–4.30/6.30pm; 7F) for the superb view of the old town, and, in the distance, the Vosges to the west and the Black Forest to the east.

The **interior**, too, is magnificent, the high nave a model of proportion, enhanced by a glorious sequence of **stained glass** windows. The finest are those in the south aisle next to the door, depicting the life of Christ and the Creation, but all are beautiful, including, in the apse, the modern glass designed in 1956 by Max Ingrand to commemorate the first European institutions in the city. On the left of the nave, the cathedral's **organ** perches precariously above one of the arches, like a giant gilded eagle, while further down on the same side is the late fifteenth-century **pulpit**, a masterpiece of intricacy in stone by the appropriately-named Hans Hammer.

In the south transept are the cathedral's two most popular sights. One is the slender triple-tiered central column known as the **Pilier des Anges**, decorated with some of the most graceful and expressive statuary of the thirteenth century. The other is the huge and enormously complicated **astrological clock** built by Schwilgué of Strasbourg in 1838: a favourite with the tour-group operators, whose customers roll up in droves to witness the clock's crowning performance of the day, striking the hour of noon, which it does, with unerring accuracy, at 12.30pm – that being 12 o'clock Strasbourg time. Death strikes the chimes; the Apostles parade in front of Christ, who occupies the highest storey of the clock; and as each one passes he receives Christ's blessing. As the fourth, eighth and twelfth pass, a cock crows. Entertaining enough, but the chief advantage of paying your 4F admission is that, since it is the only way of entering the cathedral at this time of day, there are fewer people about than at other times.

Strasbourg's museums

South of the cathedral, the majority of Strasbourg's **museums** are clustered together between the tree-lined place du Château and the river. **Opening hours** are the same for all the museums: 10am to noon and 2 to 6pm; closed Tuesday; admission charge is 15F for the Palais Rohan threesome, 10F for each of the other museums.

Right by the cathedral, place du Château is enclosed to the east and south by the Lycée Fustel and the **Palais Rohan**, both eighteenth-century buildings, the latter designed for the immensely powerful Rohan family, who, for several generations in a row, cornered the market in cardinals' hats. There are three museums in the Palais Rohan itself: the **Musée des Arts Décoratifs**, **Musée des Beaux-Arts** and **Musée Archéologique**. The rooms of the château are not especially interesting: vast, opulent and ostentatious. Of the three collections, only the Arts Décoratifs stands out – and that of slightly specialist interest – with its eighteenth-century faience tiles crafted in the city by Paul Hannong.

Next door, the **Musée de l'Oeuvre Notre-Dame** houses the original sculptures from the cathedral exterior, damaged in the Revolution and replaced today by copies – both sets are worth seeing. And there are other treasures here: glass from the city's original Romanesque cathedral; the eleventh-century Wissembourg Christ, said to be the oldest representation of a human figure in stained glass; the architect's original parchment drawings for the statuary, done in fascinating detail down to the different expressions on each figure's face.

Next door again, the **Musée d'Art Moderne** has an impressive permanent collection featuring such artists as Monet, Picasso, Klimt, Ernst, Klee and the Alsatian Dadaist Hans Arp and his wife, the Swiss Surrealist, Sophie Taeuber. Only a small selection are actually on display at any one time, due to the museum's acute lack of space. This problem should be alleviated in 1994 when the museum moves to new premises on the other side of La Petite France (see below).

On place du **Marché-aux-Cochons-de-Lait** (Suckling-pig market), the **Musée Historique**, housed in the old Grande Boucherie, is mainly concerned with the city, though it also has an odd-ball collection of mechanical toys upstairs. And last but not least, in a traditional house just across the Pont du Corbeau (Raven Bridge), off pl du Corbeau, there's the **Musée Alsacien**, containing painted furniture and other local artefacts.

The rest of the old town

On the far side of the Pont du Corbeau, the medieval **Cour du Courbeau**, still looks much as it must have done in the fourteenth century; downstream the **quai des Bateliers** was part of the old business quarter. Two bridges upstream is the Pont St-Thomas, leading to the **Église St-Thomas**, with a Romanesque facade and Gothic towers. Since 1549 it has been the city's principal Protestant church. Strasbourg was a bastion of the Reformation, and one of its leaders, Martin Bucer, preached in this church. The amazing piece of sculpture behind the altar is the tomb of the Maréchal de Saxe over which the eighteenth-century sculptor, Jean-Baptiste Pigalle, toiled for twenty-one years.

From here, it's a short walk upstream to the **Pont St-Martin**, which marks the beginning of the district known as **La Petite France**, where the city's millers, tanners and fishermen used to live. At the far end of a series of canals is the so-called **Ponts Couverts** (they are in fact no longer covered), built as part of the fourteenth-century city fortifications and still punctuated by watchtowers. Just beyond is a dam built by Vauban to protect the city from water-borne assault. The whole area is extremely attractive with winding streets – most notably rue du Bain-aux-Plantes – bordered by sixteenth- and seventeenth-century half-timbered houses, flower-bedecked and studded with carved woodwork, all perfectly restored and, predictably enough, a top-of-the-bill tourist hot spot.

The area east of the cathedral is good for a stroll, too, where rue des Frères leads to place St-Étienne. **Place du Marché-Gayot** off rue des Frères, behind the cathedral, is also very pretty with a couple of studenty cafés on one side. From the north side of the cathedral rue du Dôme leads to the eighteenth-century **place Broglie** with the Hôtel de Ville and *préfet*'s residence and some imposing eighteenth-century mansions around. It was at 4 place Broglie, in 1712, that Rouget de l'Isle first sang what later became known as the *Marseillaise* for the mayor of Strasbourg, who had challenged him to compose a rousing song for the troops of the army of the Rhine.

The German quarter and the Palais de l'Europe

Across the river here, **Place de la République** is surrounded by vast German neo-Gothic edifices erected during the post-1870 Imperial Prussian occupation – the main **post office** on av de la Liberté is one such. At the centre of the *place* is a war memorial showing a mother holding two dead sons in her arms, one German and one French, testifying to the split personality of this frontier city whose inhabitants fought on both sides during the war. At the other end of av de la Liberté, across the confluence of the Ill and Aar, is the city's university, where Göethe studied.

From here the wide and straight alleé de la Robertsau, flanked by confident turn-of-the-century bourgeois residences, leads to the **Palais de l'Europe**, an imposing and adventurous piece of architecture built in 1977. It is suitably vast, in aluminium, bronzed glass and Vosges sandstone, with the contemporary equivalent of a turret jutting from one corner. The interior, or at least the part you can visit (ask about guided tours at the SI), is surprisingly poky and cheaply finished, with the exception of the European Parliament's debating chamber, which looks as if it may finally get some legislative muscle after 1992. Opposite the Palais, the **Orangerie** is Strasbourg's best bit of greenery, and plays host to a variety of exhibitions and free concerts.

ALSATIAN

Travelling through the province, it's easy to mistake the language being spoken in the shops and streets for German. In fact it is **Alsatian** (*Elsässisch*), a High German dialect, known to philologists as Alemannic. To confuse matters further, there are two versions, High and Low Alemannic, as well as an obscure Frankish dialect spoken in the Wissembourg region and a Romance one called *Welche* located in the valleys around Orbey.

Most daily transactions are conducted in French, and *Elsässisch* has still not made it onto the school curriculum. Yet it remains a living language, with a rich medieval literary legacy, and is still spoken by young and old, throughout Alsace and even parts of Lorraine. A recent upsurge in nationalist feeling has meant that *Elsässisch* is beginning to start appearing again on menus and shop signs. In many ways, it's a miracle that it has survived at all, since both French and German rule have tended to discourage the Alsatian language.

The trouble started with the French Revolution when, in pursuit of national unity, the language was suppressed in favour of French, which was ousted, in turn, by German when the Prussians annexed the region in 1870. As a result, over 50,000 Alsatians went into exile in France. On its return to French rule, however, all things Germanic were disdained, and many Alsatians began to support the idea of autonomy. The Nazi occupation brought in manic Germanisation laws which made the speaking of French and even the wearing of berets imprisonable offences. Despite the good intentions of the Mitterrand administration, as recently as 1991, when Strasbourg's Socialist mayor, Catherine Trautman, proposed bi-lingual French and Alsatian street signs, the central government, uncomfortable at the idea of *strasse* being printed next to *rue*, intervened and overturned the decision.

Finally, a quick word on the subject of **four-legged Alsatians**: these are conspicuous by their absence in what English-speakers assume is their homeland. In fact they originated from Germany, and are known to the rest of the world as German Shepherds (*bergers allemands*).

Eating, drinking and entertainment

Strasbourg is full of overpriced Alsatian **restaurants**, particularly around the cathedral and La Petite France, which cater for the city's large political and business community. Listed here are a few of the exceptions.

L'Abécédaire, rue du Maroquin. One of the few places near the cathedral which doesn't insist on your ordering a full meal.

Panouche, opposite *L'Abécédaire*. Another good place for a quick snack, with tables outside.

Flam's, 27–29 rue des Frères (noon–2pm & 7–11.30pm; closed Sun evenings). *The* place to sample the local speciality, *tarte flambée*, a kind of onion tart with flecks of bacon.

Chez Faisan, 8 rue du Faisan. Strasbourg's best pizzeria, where you choose your own topping and salad ingredients. Extremely popular though, so avoid at weekends if possible.

FEC, place St-Étienne, near the church. The nicest of the city's cheap student restaurants.

Drinking

Unusually for a French city, Strasbourg abounds in **winebars** – *winstub* – and to a lesser extent **beer halls**, or *bierstub*. And if you happen to be in town in mid-August, there's a week-long **beer festival** at Schiltigheim, a suburb 3km north of the city centre (take the D468, direction la Wantzenau; or bus #4, #14 or #24) where *Heineken* have their main French brewery.

S'Burgerstuwel, 10 rue du Sanglier (closed Mon & mid-July–mid-Aug). Better known as *Chez Yvonne*, this is a classic Alsatian *winstub*.

Le Saint Sépulcre, 15 rue des Orfèvres. A family-run *winstub* not far from the cathedral.

L'Académie de la Bière, 17 rue Adolphe-Seyboth, near the Église St-Pierre (daily 9pm–3am). Strasbourg's most famous *bierstub*.

Le Trou, 5 rue des Couples, not far from place Corbeau, this is another of Strasbourg's more serious beer palaces.

Pub Nelson, 20 rue des Couples. An "Irish" pub with, among others brews, Guinness on tap.

Entertainment

Strasbourg usually has lots going on – in summer pick up the *Saison d'Été* listings leaf-let from the SI. If you're here during university term-time, you might want to check the noticeboards at the university as well. **Free concerts** are held regularly in the Parc des Contades and Parc de l'Orangerie, which also boasts a 24-lane bowling alley. The best of the annual **festivals** starts with international music in mid-June, followed by jazz in July, international contemporary music in mid-September and early October, and mime and clowning in November.

The student **club**, *Le Caveau*, 1 quai du Maire-Dietrich, off pl de l'Université, is far better than most of Strasbourg's rather staid nightspots, though for something differ-ent you could try the vast roller-disco, *Rollertime* (Tues–Sat from 8pm; bus #4, #14 or #24), 69 rte de Bischwiller – the D468 – in the suburb of Schiltigheim.

Listings

Bikes can be hired from the gare SNCF.

Boat trips Numerous boat companies ply the River Ill – ask at the SI for details.

Books *Librarie International Kléber*, 1 rue des Francs-Bourgeois, sells new books, French and English; *La Librocase*, 2 quai des Pêcheurs, sells second-hand books.

Buses leave from place des Halles.

Car hire *Avis*, Galérie Marchande, place de la Gare (☎88.32.30.44); *Hertz*, at the airport and 6 bd de Metz by the gare SNCF (☎88.32.57.62).

Cinemas *Le Club*, 32 rue du Vieux-Marché-aux-Vins, and *Le Star*, 27 rue du Jeu-des-Enfants (the parallel street), both show black-and-white classics and independent films all in *version originale*.

Consulates Canada, rue Ried, La Wantzenau 12km from the centre (☎88.96.25.00); Denmark, 1 rue du Bassin-d'Austerlitz south of the city centre (☎88.84.20.11); Finland, 2 av de la 2e-Division-Blindée, Shiltigheim (☎88.33.63.52); Norway, 2 rue Minoterie, Port-du-Rhin on the German border (☎88.61.14.14); Sweden, 11 rue du Canal (☎88.39.06.06); USA, 15 av d'Alsace (☎88.35.31.04).

Hiking information *Club Vosgien*, 4 rue de la Douane.

Hitching For Germany, take Pont du Corbeau, Pont d'Austerlitz and then route du Rhin. For *Allostop* call ☎88/37.13.13 or look in at the office at 5 rue Général-Zimmer, a couple of blocks south of the university.

Launderette at 18 rue Edel, near the botanical gardens (daily 7am–8pm).

Markets The city's biggest fruit and vegetable market takes place every Saturday morning around place de Bordeaux on the north side of Parc des Contades.

Rape Crisis *SOS Viol* ☎05.05.95.95.

Taxis *Station Centrale* ☎88.36.13.13 ; *Novotaxi* ☎88.75.19.19.

The northern Vosges

The **northern Vosges** lie to the northwest of Strasbourg, cut short by the German border where they continue as the Pfälzerwald. They don't reach the same heights as the southern Vosges, nor do they boast any vineyards as such: as a result, though, they are protected from the mass tourism of the southern range. Much of the region is designated a *Parc Naturel*, and there are numerous hiking possibilities, as well as a couple of attractive towns – **Saverne** and **Wissembourg** – built in the characteristic red sandstone of the Vosges.

Transport is patchy, as elsewhere in Alsace, though there are SNCF buses which wind their way through the villages and apple orchards along the German border. In addition, Saverne and Wissembourg are linked to Strasbourg by train. Even so, the easi-est way to explore the region is with your own transport – by car, bicycle or on foot.

Saverne and around

SAVERNE, seat of the exiled Catholic prince-bishops of Strasbourg during the Reformation, commands the only easy route across the Vosges into Alsace, at a point where the hills are pinched to a narrow waist. It is not as picturesque as some towns, but has the region's characteristic steep-pitched roofs, dormer windows and window-boxes full of geraniums. It's also a good launch pad from which to explore the northern Vosges, with a friendly **youth hostel** (☎88.91.14.84) in the château (see below), and inexpensive **rooms** nearby at the *National*, 2 Grand' Rue (☎88.71.19.50; ②/③).

A couple of things are worth seeing in town, not least the vast red sandstone **Château des Rohan**, built in a rather grim classical style by one of the Rohans who was prince-bishop at the time, and now housing the none-too-special local museum and the town's SI and youth hostel. The River Zorn and the Marne–Rhine canal both weave their way through the town, the latter framing the château's formal gardens with a graceful right-angle bend. Alongside the château, the **Église Notre-Dame-de-la-Nativité** contains another finely carved pulpit by Hans Hammer. Horticultural distraction can be found in Saverne's famed rose garden, **La Roseraie**, to the west of the centre by the river, which boasts over a thousand varieties, and the **botanical gardens** 3km out of town off the N4 Metz/Nancy road.

There are several relatively easy **walks** around Saverne (the SI can give details), the most popular being the one to the ruined **Château du Haut-Barr** (2hr return). Follow rue du Haut-Barr southeast along the canal past the leafy suburban villas until you reach the woods, where a signboard indicates the various walks possible. Take the path marked "Haut-Barr" through woods of chestnut, beech and larch. The castle stands dramatically on a narrow sandstone ridge with fearsome drops on both sides and views across the wooded hills and eastward over the plain towards Strasbourg. There's a **campsite** at the foot of the castle (☎88.91.35.65; April–Sept).

Wissembourg

WISSEMBOURG, 60km north of Strasbourg and hard against the German border, is one of the more interesting towns in the northern Vosges, unspoilt despite its popularity with German weekenders. A considerable section survives of its **medieval walls**, built, like the houses, in the local red sandstone. Branches of the River Lauter meander through the town – around the half-timbered quarter of **Le Bruch** to the west, the central, thirteenth-century **Église St-Paul-et-Pierre**, and the town's most striking

---

THE POLES OF WISSEMBOURG

Stanislas Leszczynski, born in the Polish–Ukrainian city of Lemberg (now Lvóv) in 1677, lasted just five years as the elected king of Poland before being forced into exile by the Russian Czar, Peter the Great. For the next twenty-odd years he lived on a French pension in Wissembourg, along with a motley entourage of Polish ex-pats. After fifteen years of relatively hum-drum existence in the town's Ancien Hôpital south of the main church, Stanislas' luck changed when he managed, against all odds, to get his daughter Marie betrothed to the fifteen-year old King of France, Louis XV. Marie was not quite so fortunate: married by proxy in Strasbourg Cathedral, and having never even set eyes on the groom, she subsequently had a total of ten children, only to be ultimately rejected by Louis, who preferred hunting and the company of his two, more powerful mistresses, Madame du Pompadour and Madame du Barry. Bolstered by his daughter's marriage, Stanislas had another brief spell on the Polish throne from 1733 to 1736, but eventually gave it up in favour of the comfortable dukedom of Bar and Lorraine. He lived out his final years in true aristocractic style in the capital Nancy, which was transformed by him into one of France's most beautiful towns.

secular building, the **Maison du Sel** (Salthouse) – creating a placid atmosphere of changelessness. The townspeople have one curious linguistic anomaly; they speak a very ancient dialect derived from Frankish, unlike their fellow Alsatians whose language is closer to modern German.

Should you want to stay, the best **hotels** to try are *Hôtel de la Gare* (☎88.94.13.67; ③), by the **gare SNCF**, or *Hôtel du Cygne* (☎88.94.00.16; ③/⑤), by the townhall on the central place de la République, which is quite luxurious and central, but has only one relatively inexpensive double.

Route des Châteaux

West of Wissembourg, along the **Route des Châteaux**, there are ruined castles on almost every hilltop, guarding the frontier with Germany. Buses will take you as far as LEMBACH (twice daily Mon–Sat), 15km from Wissembourg, but after that you'll need your own transport. Of the many castles, the ruins of the **Château du Fleckenstein** (daily 9.30am–5/6pm; 10F), 7km north of Lembach, are perhaps the most spectacular, rising above the forest on a narrow sandstone outcrop, just a stone's throw from the German border. Six kilometres further on at OBERSTEINBACH, there's an information centre, the **Maison des Châteaux-Forts**, with displays and maps on the other castles in the area.

The southern Vosges

The **southern Vosges** covers a much greater area than the northern range, stretching as far as Belfort in Franche-Comté. The major tourist atttractions are along the **Route du Vin**, following the Rhin at the foot of the mountains, where every turn in the road reveals yet another exquisitely preserved medieval village – many of them packed out with visitors – nestling below a precariously perched ruined fort. **Colmar**, the main centre for the *route*, also suffers from an overdose of visitors. If you want to escape from the crowds, you'll need to head for the hills proper, along the **Route des Crêtes** which traces the central ridge of the Vosges to the west.

The Route du Vin

Alsace is a region both blessed and cursed by tourism and no more so than along the **Route du Vin**, which stretches from MARLENHEIM, west of Strasbourg, to THANN, near Mulhouse. The problem with Alsace is that, left to its own devices, it stays on the right side of Disneyland, but, under the impact of tourism and the desire to make money, it comes close to caricaturing itself.

Set against the "blue line of the Vosges", the *route* winds north–south through the endless terraced vineyards which produce the region's famous fruity white wines. Opportunities for tasting the local produce are plentiful, with free *dégustations* along the roadside, in the *caveaux* of most villages, and at the region's countless wine festivals. You can take a closer look at the vines themselves courtesy of the region's SIs, or independently via the various *sentiers vinicoles* (vineyard paths). In the midst of this sea of vines are dozens of flowery and typically picturesque Alsatian villages, dominated from the heights above by an extraordinary number of ancient ruined castles, testimony to its turbulent past.

The *Route du Vin* is deceptively hilly work on a bike – but it's definitely easier to get around with your own **transport;** otherwise you're dependent either on the **railway,** which narrowly misses some of the best villages, or the region's more-or-less non-existent bus services.

Obernai and around

If you're heading south, the vineyards may begin at MARLENHEIM, but **OBERNAI**, on the D422, is the first place most people head for on the *route*. Miraculously unscathed during the last two wars, it has retained almost its entire **rampart system**, including no fewer than fifteen towers, as well as street after street of carefully maintained medieval houses. Not surprisingly, it also gets more than its fair share of visitors, though this shouldn't put you off visiting the town – it's just about big enough to absorb the crowds. If you're thinking of staying the night, the only remotely affordable **hotels** are the *Maison du Vin*, 1 rue de la Paille (☎88.95.46.82; ③), and *Hôtel zum Schnogaloch*, 18 place de l'Étoile (☎88.95.54.57; ④).

ROSHEIM, 7km north of Obernai and up in the hills a little to the west of the D422, is relatively off the beaten track for this busy region. Its two main sights are the Romanesque **Église St-Pierre-et-St-Paul**, whose roof is peppered with comical sculptured figures contemporary with the building, and the twelfth-century **Heidenhüs**, thought to be the oldest building in Alsace. The *Hôtel Alpina*, 39 rue du Lion (☎88.50.49.30; ③), is reasonable.

From Rosheim's gare SNCF, 1.5km northeast of the village, a steam train runs up the valley on Sundays and holidays, round the back of Rosheim, to **OTTROTT**, which produces one of the few red wines of Alsace. Ottrott brings you to within hiking distance, 6km, of **Mont Ste-Odile** (763m), whose summit is surrounded by a Celtic wall, originally built in the 7th century BC, which reaches a height of 3.5m in parts. Saint Odilia herself is buried in the small **chapel** on top of the hill, a pilgrimage site to this day. According to tradition, having been cast out by her father at birth on account of her blindness, she miraculously regained her sight during childhood and returned to found the convent on Mont Ste-Odile, where she is said to have cured thousands of blindness and leprosy.

Barr

For some unknown reason **BARR**, also west of the main road, is bypassed by many of the coach groups. Every bit as charming as Obernai, it's easy to while away a couple of hours wandering its twisting cobbled streets, at their busiest during the mid-July wine festival and on Sundays when the vintners come to ply their wines. The town has just one specific sight, **La Folie Marco** (daily, May–Sept 10am–12.30pm & 2.30–6pm; closed Tues), an unusually large eighteenth-century house on the outskirts of the town along the road to Obernai, with displays of French and Alsatian furniture. There are regular *dégustations* in the garden cellar, and a festival of dance and waltz at the end of May.

The cheapest **rooms** in Barr are at the *Hôtel du Parc*, 11 rue du Général-Vandenberg (☎88.08.92.91; ③). Alternatively, there's a **campsite** in ST-PIERRE, 3km south of Barr. The **gare SNCF** is 1km east of town in the neighbouring village of GERTWILLER.

Le Struthof concentration camp

Deep in the forests and hills of the Vosges, over 20km west of Barr, **Le Struthof-Natzwiller** (daily April–Aug 8–11.30am & 2–6.30pm; Sept–March 9–11am & 2–4.30pm; 10F) was the only Nazi concentration camp to be built on French soil (though at the time, of course, it was part of the Greater German Reich). Like the picture-postcard villages along the *route*, the site is almost perversely beautiful, its stepped terraces cut into the steep hillside, giving fantastic views across the Bruche valley. Set up shortly after Hitler's occupation of Alsace-Lorraine in 1940, it is thought that over 10,000 people died here. When the Allies liberated the camp on November 23, 1944, they found it empty – the remaining prisoners having already been transported to Dachau.

The barbed wire and watchtowers are as they were, though only two of the prisoners' barracks remain, one of which is now a **museum** on the deportations. Captions are in French only, but the pictures alone tell the story. An arson attack by neo-Nazis in 1976 only served to underline the need for such displays. At the foot of the camp is the crematorium with its ovens still intact; a couple of kilometres down the road to the west, towards Schirmeck, the Germans built a gas chamber – proof that Le Struthof was a fully integrated part of the Nazi killing machine. Alongside the gas chamber, in extraordinarily bad taste, is a tourist restaurant. To the east, the two main granite quarries worked by the internees still survive, clearly signposted from the main road.

Sélestat

Back on the *Route du Vin*, **SÉLESTAT**, midway between Strasbourg and Colmar, is a delightful old town, positively cosmopolitan compared with the wine route's villages, and a good base for exploring the central and most popular section of the *route*. The choice of reasonable accommodation is better than average, and the town itself contains a couple of interesting churches and a great museum for bibliophiles.

The oldest and finest of the two churches is the **Église Ste-Foy**. Built by the monks of Conques and much restored since, its clean, austerely Romanesque lines have not been entirely wiped out. Close by to the north, the much larger Gothic **Église St-Georges** sports spectacularly multi-coloured roof tiles and some very fine stained glass. For a brief period in the late fifteenth and early sixteenth centuries, Sélestat was the intellectual centre of Alsace, due mainly to its Latin School, which attracted a group of Humanists led by Beatus Rhenanus, whose personal library was one of the most impressive collections of its time. At the **Bibliothèque Humaniste** (July & Aug daily 9am–noon & 2–5pm; rest of the year weekdays only; 8F), housed in the town's former corn exchange just by St-Georges, Rhenanus' collection is now on display along with some unusual and very rare books and manuscripts from as far back as the seventh century.

Sélestat is comparatively well served transport-wise, with frequent **train** connections to Strasbourg and Colmar, as well as a branch line which heads north to Strasbourg via Molsheim; the **gare SNCF** is west of the town centre down av de la Liberté. To explore the castles around Sélestat (see next), you'll need your own transport – **bikes** can be hired from *Evao' Sport*, 21 rue des Chevaliers. There's a choice of three mid-range **hotels**: the *Lion d'Or*, 4 rue du 4e-Zouaves (☎88.92.06.13; ③); the *National*, 7 rte de Strasbourg (☎88.92.10.76; ③); and the *Riebel*, 35 rte de Colmar (☎88.92.14.27; ③). And there's also a **campsite** south of the centre behind Vauban's remaining ramparts. For further information, the **SI** is by the ring road on bd du Général-Leclerc.

Castles around Sélestat

Within easy range of Sélestat are a whole host of **ruined castles**. Seven kilometres north, and accessible by train, the village of **DAMBACH-LA-VILLE**, with its walls and three fortified gates all intact, is one of the highlights of the *route*, and has a cheap **campsite** (open June–Sept 15), 1km east, on the D210. A thirty-minute climb west of the village is the formidable castle of **Bernstein**. In the Middle Ages, Alsace was culturally more German than French and this is a typically German mountain keep, tall and narrow, with few openings and little use for everyday living. Around it are residential buildings, enclosed within an outer wall, the masonry cut into protruding knobs, which gives it a curious pimpled texture.

From SCHERWILLER, another attractive village just 3km northwest of Sélestat, you can reach the castle of **Ortenbourg** via a steep marked path. Like Bernstein, it has a lofty refuge-tower with courtyards outside, in a good state of preservation, protected by a rock-cut ditch. A few hundred metres to the southwest, **Ramstein** castle was originally built in 1293 to protect the besiegers of Ortenbourg.

The best cluster of castles, however, is southwest of Sélestat. Four kilometres away, **KINTZHEIM** boasts a small but luxurious ruined castle built around a cylindrical refuge-tower; today it's an aviary, the **Volière des Aigles** (daily April–Sept 2–5.30/6pm; Oct–March Wed, Sat & Sun only), for birds of prey, with magnificent displays of aerial prowess by eagles and vultures. If you have a yen to watch Barbary apes at play in the Vosgian jungle, you can do just that a couple of kilometres further west at the **Montagne des Singes** (daily mid-March–mid-Nov 10am–noon & 1.30–6pm; 22F).

Another 5km on, the ruins of **Oudenbourg** castle, its sizeable hall preserved among the trees, is dwarfed by the massive **Haut-Koenigsbourg** (9am–noon & 1–4/ 5/6pm; closed Jan 5 to Feb 5; 30F), one of the biggest, most popular, and – astride its 757-metre bluff – by far the highest, castles in Alsace. Ruined after an assault in 1633, it was heavily restored in the early years of this century for Kaiser Wilhelm II. It's easy to criticise some of the detail of the restoration, but it's an enjoyable experience and a remarkably convincing re-creation of a castle-palace of the age of Dürer. There are guided tours, but it's best on your own. The views all around are fantastic. There's a winding road down to Bergheim (see below) from here, if you'd rather not retrace your tracks to Sélestat.

Around Ribeauvillé

RIBEAUVILLÉ is the largest town between Sélestat and Colmar – not as pretty as some of its immediate neighbours, but right at the foot of the mountains and well placed for exploring the many castles and villages which surround it. However, unless you're **camping** at the *Camping des 3 Châteaux*, to the north of town, or the much plusher *Pierre-de-Courbertin* site, to the south (closed Feb–March 15), staying here is a costly business, with the *Hôtel du Cheval Blanc*, 122 Grande-Rue (☎89.73.61.38; ④), the cheapest option.

In the vicinity of Ribeauvillé is a threesome of fortresses built by the counts of Ribeaupierre: **St-Ulrich** castle, an hour's haul up a marked path; just north of it the smaller **Girsberg** castle, balanced on a pinnacle which somehow provides room for a bailey, two towers and other buildings; and further on the ruins of **Haut-Ribeaupierre**.

BERGHEIM, 3.5km northeast of Ribeauvillé, retains a good part of its old fortifications, with three towers still surviving; and despite being one of the most beautiful Alsatian villages, it rarely attracts the attentions of the tour groups.

Again within easy walking range of Ribeauvillé, this time to the south, the village of **HUNAWIHR** is another beguiling hamlet, with a fourteenth-century walled church standing out amid the green vines. Hunawihr is at the forefront of the Alsatian ecological movement aimed at reintroducing the stork – the *cigogne* – to the region, and there's a reserve to the east of the village.

Lastly, getting closer to the hub of Colmar, there are a couple of tourist targets you may want to avoid, or at least for which you might be advised to time your visits carefully. A couple of kilometres south of Hunawhir, the walled village of **RIQUEWIHR** is exceptionally well preserved, and consequently suffers more visitors per annum than any other village along the *route*. **KAYSERBERG**, still further to the southwest, also plays host to more than its fair share of tour buses. It boasts a fortified bridge and a handsome sixteenth-century wooden altarpiece in the main church. But the town's principal renown is as the birthplace of Nobel Peace Prize winner Albert Schweitzer, who spent most of his extremely active, and not always peaceful, life at the leprosy hospital he founded at Lambaréné in French Equatorial Africa, now Gabon. During World War I, he was interned by the French authorities as an "enemy alien", but nowadays he is suitably honoured with a **museum** dedicated to him at 124 rue de-Gaulle.

Colmar

COLMAR, a fifty-minute train ride south of Strasbourg, has sprawled unattractively on both sides of the train tracks, but the old centre remains typically and whimsically Alsatian, with crooked houses, half-timbered and painted, on crooked lanes – all extremely pretty and very touristy. Colmar's attractions don't stop at its buildings; it is also the proud possessor of one of the last and most extraordinary of all Gothic paintings – the altarpiece for St Anthony's monastery at Isenheim, painted by Mathias Grünewald.

Practicalities

The **SI** by the Musée d'Unterlinden sells *Club Vosgien* hiking maps and a booklet of **day walks** in the hills behind the town (daily mid-June–mid-Sept 9am–12.30pm & 1.30–7pm; rest of year Mon–Fri same hours, Sat 9am–noon & 2–6pm, Sun 9am–noon). They'll also give you details of the **buses** to the towns and villages of the *Route du Vin*, which leave from outside the gare SNCF, where it's also possible to hire **bikes**.

The **accommodation** possibilities are not as overpriced as you might expect, with a number of reasonable hotels on the av de la République – try *La Chaumière*, at no.74 (☎89.41.08.99; ③). There's a basic but clean **IYHF youth hostel** at 2 rue Pasteur (☎89.80.57.39; curfew midnight), across the railway tracks, twenty minutes' walk off av de la Liberté. Alternatively, there's the *Maison des Jeunes*, 17 rue Camille-Schlumberger (☎89.41.26.87; curfew 11pm), two blocks east of the station and just ten minutes' walk from town. The nearest **campsite** is ten minutes' walk along the N415 Neuf Brisach road (☎89.41.15.94; open Feb–Nov; bus #1, direction *Wihr*).

Restaurants in Colmar are generally overpriced, particularly Alsatian ones. One exception is *Bartholdi*, 2 rue des Boulangers near the Dominican church. *L'Amandine* on place de la Cathédrale serves cheap light snacks and salads. Otherwise, you could amass a sumptuous picnic from the town's numerous *pâtisseries* and *charcuteries* like *CCA* on the corner of place Unterlinden. There's a fuit and veg **market** every Thursday around the Koïfhus, and every Saturday on place St-Joseph.

The town

From the **gare SNCF**, the **Musée d'Unterlinden** (daily April–Oct 9am–6pm; Nov–March 9am–noon & 2–5pm; closed Tues; 5F) is a ten-minute walk down av de la République, in a former Dominican convent. Although displayed in an exploded format, the **Isenheim altarpiece** was designed to make a single piece. On the front was the luridly expressive Crucifixion, a tortured Christ with stretched rib-cage and outsize hands turned upwards, his fingers splayed in pain, flanked by his pale fainting mother, St John and Mary Magdalene. It would have been unfolded for holy days, to reveal an Annunciation, Resurrection, Virgin and Child, and finally a sculpted panel depicting saints Anthony, Augustine and Jerome. Completed in 1515, the painting is affected by Renaissance innovations in light and perspective but still rooted in the medieval spirit, with an intense mysticism and shifts of mood in its subject matter. Other works in the museum are, inevitably, secondary, but there's a surprisingly interesting collection of modern paintings in the basement, including works by Picasso, Léger and Vasarely.

A little to the southeast, the **Dominican church** has some fine glass and, above all, a radiantly beautiful altarpiece, known as *The Virgin in a Bower of Roses* (daily April–Oct 10am–6pm; 5F), painted in 1473 by Martin Schongauer, who is also represented in the Musée d'Unterlinden. Down rue des Serruriers you come to the **Collégiale St-Martin** on a café-lined square. Known locally as "the cathedral", it's also worth a quick peek for its stonework and stained glass. On the south side of the church is the sixteenth-century **Maison Pfister** with painted panels and, on the opposite side of the street, the birthplace of Frédéric Auguste Bartholdi, the nineteenth-century sculptor responsible for New York's Statue of Liberty. Now the **Musée Bartholdi** (daily April–Oct 10am–noon & 2–6pm; Nov–March Sat & Sun only; 10F), it contains Bartholdi's personal effects, plus the original designs for the statue, along with sundry Colmarabilia.

Rue des Marchands continues south to the *Ancienne Douane* or **Koïfhus**, its gaily painted roof tiles loudly proclaiming the city's medieval prosperity. This is the heart of Colmar's old town, a short step away from the archly picturesque quarter down the Grande-Rue, cut through by the River Lauch and known as **La Petite Venise**. The dolly-mixture colours of the old fishermen's cottages on quai de la Poissonnerie are more touristy even than Strasbourg's Petite France. Twice as tall, but similarly over-restored, are the black-and-white half-timbered tanners' houses on **quai des Tanneurs**, which leads off from the Koïfhus, with open verandahs on the top floor originally designed for drying hides.

ROUTE DES CRETES

If you're serious about hiking, it's best to leave the *Route du Vin* and take instead the **Route des Crêtes** (literally the Ridge Road), which forms the backbone of the Vosges. Although it's perfectly possible to drive or cycle down this *route*, the best way to appreciate the rounded peaks (known as *ballons*) is on foot – GR5 covers much of the same ground, and there are other footpaths in the *sentiers grand randonnées* network which criss-cross the hills (*Club Vosgien* in Colmar or Strasbourg will provide details).

Built for strategic purposes during World War I, it's a spectacular trail, which in winter becomes one long cross-country ski route. Starting in **Cernay**, 15km west of Mulhouse, it follows the main ridge of the Vosges, including the highest peak of the range, the **Grand Ballon** (1424m), north as far as **Ste-Marie-aux-Mines**, 20km west of Sélestat, once at the heart of a silver-mining district.

Mulhouse

Thirty-five kilometres south of Colmar, **MULHOUSE** is a large sprawling industrial city, popularly dubbed by the British the "French Manchester". It was Swiss until 1798 when, at the peak of its prosperity, based on printed cotton fabrics and allied trades, it voted to become part of France. Its only other minor claim to fame is as the hometown of Alfred Dreyfus, the unfortunate Jewish army officer who was wrongly convicted of espionage in 1894 (see *Contexts* for the full story). Not having much of an old town, it is no city for strollers, but it does have four or five unusually good **museums**, which together make Mulhouse worth at least a day's visit.

Practicalities

Place de la Réunion, nominally the centre of town, is five minutes' walk north of the **gare SNCF**. The **SI** is on the way at 9 av Foch (Mon–Fri 9am–8pm Sat 9am–7pm Sun 10am–1pm). **Hotels** in Mulhouse are not cheap by any standards. *Paon d'Or*, 13 av de Colmar (☎89.45.34.41; ③/④) is as economical as they come, but inconveniently located; the *Hôtel de Paris*, 5 passage de l'Hôtel-de-Ville (☎89.45.21.41; ④), and *Hôtel Bâle*, 19 passage Central (☎89.46.19.87; ④), are at least fairly central. If these are full, the **youth hostel** on rue de l'Illberg (☎89.42.63.28; bus #4 or #6, stop *Salle des Sports*) is about your best bet. If you're **camping**, there's a pleasant site on rue Pierre-de-Coubertin, near the suburb of Dornach, 4km from the city centre on the banks of the Ill (☎89.06.20.66, open April–Sept).

As at Colmar and Strasbourg, Mulhouse's Alsatian **restaurants** are none too cheap. The *Auberge du Vieux Mulhouse*, right on the main square (closed Sun), is one of the few exceptions. The *Crêperie Crampous Mad*, 14 rue des Tondeurs (closed Sun), is a good standby, or *Le Parthenon*, on rue des Franciscains (closed Sun & Mon lunchtimes). Alternatively, you can drown your sorrows at *Gambrinus*, which boasts over thirty beers on tap, and a bit of simple food to wash them down with.

In the first week of September, Mulhouse hosts the region's hottest **jazz festival**; to find out what's going on at other times of the year, get hold of a copy of *Mulhouse Poche*, the free listings quarterly.

The museums: in town and around

Closest to the **gare SNCF**, just along the canal to the right, is the excellent **Musée de l'Impression sur Étoffes** (daily summer 10am–12.30pm & 2–6pm; winter 10am–noon & 2–6pm; closed Tues; 24F or combined ticket with Musée du Papier-Peint 35F). It contains a vast collection of the most beautiful fabrics imaginable – eighteenth-century Indian and Persian imports which revolutionised the European ready-to-wear market in their time; silks from Turkestan; batiks from Java, Senegalese materials, some superb kimonos from Japan, and a unique display of scarves from France, Britain and the US. The **Musée du Papier-Peint**, a subsidiary of the printed fabrics museum, is housed in the former headquarters of the Teutonic Knights at 28 rue Zuber, 6km east in the village of Rixheim (times as above; train to Rixheim or bus #10, stop *Centre Europe*) and contains an equally stunning cornucopia of antique painted wallpaper.

Again out of the centre near the southwestern suburb of Dornach, is the railway museum, **Musée Français du Chemin de Fer** (daily 9am–6pm; bus #17, stop *Porte-Jeune Place*; 28F). Rolling stock on display includes Napoléon III's ADCs' drawing-room, decorated by Viollet-le-Duc in 1856, and a luxuriously appointed 1926 diner from the *Golden Arrow*. There are cranes, stations, signals and related artefacts, but the stars of the show are the big locomotive engines with their brightly painted boilers, gleaming wheels and pistons, and tangles of brass and copper piping. Cold steel they may be, but you could be forgiven for thinking they had life in them – real works of craft. In the same complex is the **Musée du Sapeurs-Pompiers** (times as above), its antique fire engines the personal collection of a retired local firefighter. In 1992, the above museums will be joined by a third, **Electropolis**, an exhibition devoted to the glories of the electricity industry.

A couple of kilometres north of the city centre, in the **Musée National de l'Automobile**, av de Colmar (daily 10am–6pm; bus #1, #4 or #17, stop *Porte-Jeune Schuman* or *Porte-Jeune Place*; 35F), are over six hundred cars, originally the private collection of local business sharks, the Schlumpf brothers. The vehicles range from the industry's earliest attempts, like the extraordinary wooden-wheeled Jacquot steam "car" of 1878, to 1968 Porsche racing vehicles and contemporary factory prototypes. The largest group is that of locally made **Bugatti** models: dozens of glorious racing cars, coupés and limousines, the pride of them the two Bugatti Royales, out of only seven that were constructed – one of them Ettore Bugatti's own, with bodywork designed by his son.

Ten kilometres northwest off the D430 just past Pulversheim, is Mulhouse's attempt at confronting environmental issues, the **Écomusée de Haut-Alsace** (daily 9am–7pm; regional bus, direction *Geubwiller*; 50F). "Eco" may be a somewhat misleading prefix for this open-air museum, but it's certainly plenty of fun for adults and kids, with over fifty traditional Alsatian buildings spanning the centuries, as well as on-site craft workers doing their various things. It's a vast complex already, and there are plans to enlarge it further, to incorporate the nearby potassium mine which recently ceased production.

FRANCHE-COMTÉ
AND THE JURA MOUNTAINS

The **Jura mountains** – gentle in the west, precipitous in the east, with wide, high forested plateaux in between – cover most of the old county of **Franche-Comté**, once part of the realms of the Grand Dukes of Burgundy, but properly French only since the late 1600s. With the exception of the city of **Besançon**, what there is to see is country-side – hundreds of square miles of woodland, lake and pasture: hard to get around without a car, but really best explored on foot. There are several **GR** footpaths in the area, including the marathon GR5. A winter mode of transport for the hardy could be **cross-country skiing** – very big in the Jura – down the marked, long-distance route, *Grande Traversée du Jura*. Of the many skiing possibilities, the valley of the Doubs, south of Belfort, and the heights overlooking Lac Léman, are perhaps the most rewarding.

Belfort and around

Nestled in the gap between the southern reaches of the Vosges and the northern outliers of the Jura mountains – the one natural chink in France's eastern geological armour, and therefore the obvious route for invaders – **BELFORT** is assured of a place in French hearts for its deeds of military daring. Its name is particularly linked with the 1870 Prussian War, when its long resistance to siege spared it the humiliating annexa-tion to Germany suffered by much of neighbouring Alsace-Lorraine. And its command-ing officer Colonel Denfert-Rochereau, earned himself the honour of numerous street names as well as that of a Parisian métro station. There are few real reasons, however, to give it much attention, though the train connections are good. Otherwise, it's a nondescript town, surrounded by zones of heavy industry.

Finding your way around Belfort is easy enough. The town is divided in two by the River Savoureuse: the **new town** to the west is the commercial hub; to the east lies the quieter **old town**, laid out below the château. If you're interested, you can visit the massive red **château** on the heights above, which was constructed by the ubiquitous fortress-builder Vauban (daily April–Oct 8/10am–noon & 2–5/7pm; Nov–March 8am–noon & 2–6pm; closed Tues; 10F). The gigantic red sandstone lion, sculpted by Bartholdi, which you pass on the way up to the castle, serves to commemorate the 1870 siege.

Practicalities

The **gare routière** and **gare SNCF** are at the end of Faubourg-de-France, the main pedestrianised shopping drag in the new town. The **SI** is on place de la Commune, just off Faubourg-de-France (July & Aug Mon–Sat 10am–7pm Sun 9am–noon; rest of year Mon–Sat 9.30am–12.15pm & 1.45–6/7pm).

There shouldn't be any problems with finding a **room**: try the *Vauban*, 4 rue du Magasin (☎84.21.59.37; ③), or the *Hôtel du Centre*, across the street (☎84.28.67.80; ②). There's no official **youth hostel**, but the *Foyer des Jeunes Travailleurs*, west of the rail line at 6 rue de Madrid (☎84.21.39.16), does the same job, though it gives priority to under-25s. Belfort's **campsite** is just before the *foyer*, in the Parc des Loisirs (open May–Oct).

Inexpensive **places to eat** include the pizzeria, *L'Ancêtre*, 4 Faubourg-des-Ancêtres, and *Le Cèdre*, a Lebanese restaurant (not bad for vegetarians) on the Grande-Rue not far from Vauban's stronghold.

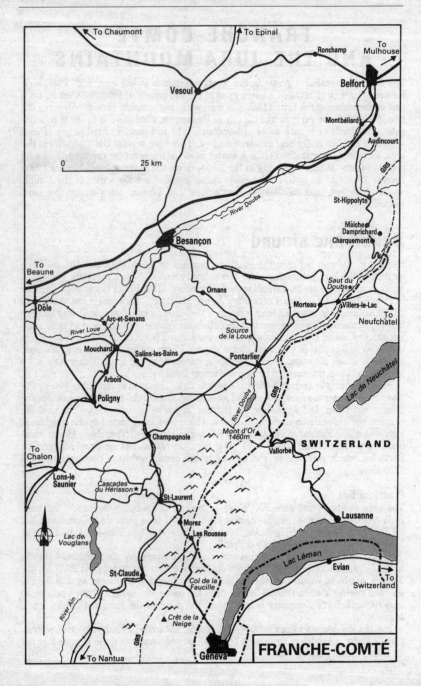

To Chaumont

To Epinal

Ronchamp

To Mulhouse

Belfort

Vesoul

Montbéliard

Audincourt

GR5

0   25 km

St-Hippolyte

River Doubs

Maîche
Damprichard

Besançon

Charquemont

Saut du
Doubs★

To
Beaune

Ornans

Morteau

Villers-le-Lac

Dôle

To
Neufchâtel

Arc-et-Senans

River Loue

Source
de la Loue

Mouchard

Salins-les-Bains

Pontarlier

Arbois

Lac de Neuchâtel

Poligny

River Doubs

GR5

To
Chalon

Champagnole

Mont d'Or
1460m

SWITZERLAND

Vallorbe

Lons-le-
Saunier

Cascades
du Hérisson★

St-Laurent

Lausanne

Morez

Les Rousses

N

Lac de
Vouglans

Lac Léman

Evian

St-Claude

Col de la
Faucille

To
Switzerland

River Ain

Crêt de la
Neige

GR5

To Nantua

Geneva

FRANCHE-COMTÉ

Ronchamp: Le Corbusier

Before you take to the hills, there is one-day trip from Belfort worth undertaking – the mining town of **RONCHAMP**, 20km west (train or bus), where the architect Le Corbusier built one of his most enduring and atypical masterpieces, the **Chapelle de Notre-Dame-du-Haut** (daily 9am–7pm; 5F). It stands, all in concrete, above the town on the top of a wooded hill, white and reflective, visible from miles away, with its aero-dynamic tower and wave-curved roof cutting into the sky beyond. **Inside**, the rough-textured walls are pierced with unequal embrasures, several closed by patterns of primary glass, whose reds, blues and yellows stain the dipping floor. Simplicity itself, with pared-down crucifix and steel altar rail, it's highly atmospheric.

If it's getting late and you're worried about a **place to stay**, there are **rooms** at *La Pomme d'Or*, 19 rue le Corbusier (☎84.20.62.12; ②), alongside the railway. Youth hostellers can take another twenty-minute train ride west to VESOUL, where the **hostel** is at 1 rue Paul-Petitclerc. Failing either of these, you'll have to beat a retreat to Belfort.

Up the Doubs and down the Loue

The Doubs runs a course like a hairpin, doubling back on itself repeatedly, flowing first northeast into Switzerland (off our map) and then southwest. In France, its most dramatic change of course happens at **AUDINCOURT**, a short way south of Belfort, where *Peugeot* bikes are made. The town's chief sight is the modern **Église Sacré-Coeur** which has windows and a tapestry by Fernand Léger.

From here, southwards and upstream, the D437 follows the valley of the Doubs, wind-ing and climbing steadily between steep, wooded banks, to the bridging point at **ST-HIPPOLYTE**. Without a car you'd have to hitch all this – manageable but slow. But it's beautiful country. Beyond St-Hippolyte the road climbs onto a wide **plateau** at around 800–900m altitude, with grassy cattle pastures encompassed by fir-clad ridges and dotted with broad-roofed farms and barns. Once up here, **cycling** is easy enough. Alternatively, it's a lovely, though long, **hike** (well over 50km) along the GR5 footpath from St-Hippolyte, across the plateau and up the Doubs valley to the plunging waterfall of the **Saut du Doubs** outside **VILLERS-LE-LAC**. By road, Villiers is 47km south of St-Hippolyte along the D437, turning east at MORTEAU. To reach the fall from Villers, it's a four-kilometre walk from the last houses above the north end of the **lake** along a track through the woods.

Staying in the Doubs valley and the plateau

For **accommodation** in the area there are **hotels** in the bigger villages, but their prices are at least fifty percent higher than places less dependent on seasonal tourism. When the icicles are hanging from the eaves up on the plateau, a cosy, well-heated shelter is *Hôtel de la Poste* opposite the church in Charquemont (☎81.44.00.20; ③), which has a good unpretentious restaurant. There are, however, numerous cheaper, if more primitive, alternatives. There are **campsites** in the valley at St-Hippolyte (open May–Sept), Goumois and Villers-le-Lac (open April–Oct), and plateau campsites up at Maîche and Le Russey; **gîtes** (or similar) on the plateau in Maîche (☎81.64.12.58), Trévillers (☎81.44.43.73), Fessevillers (☎81.44.43.07) and at the *Chalet du Ski Club* in Damprichard (☎81.44.23.10). In Villers-le-Lac there's *La Petite Ferme*, rte de Morteau, (☎81.68.08.33), and there's a gîte in Morteau, on rue des Moulinots (☎81.67.48.72).

Pontarlier

Thirty kilometres southwest of Morteau by train lies **PONTARLIER**, one of the bigger Jura towns and not very interesting except as a transit point and transport base.

There's a **youth hostel** on rue Marpaud near the station (☎81.39.06.57) and two **gîtes**: *Le Gounefay*, rte du Grand-Taureau (☎81.39.05.99); and the *Chalet-Refuge du Larmont* (☎81.46.44.03). Also close to the station are two or three cheap **hotels**; try the *Hôtel de France* at 8 rue de la Gare (②). The **gare routière** is nearby; the SI is in the Hôtel de Ville on the main street, rue de la République, as is the reasonable *Brasserie de la Poste*. For **campers**, there's *Les Gentianes* by the municipal stadium on av Paul-Robbe.

Moving on, there are trains and buses to BESANÇON, trains to FRASNE to pick up the *TGV* from Vallorbe and Lausanne to Dijon and Paris, and local buses to **Lac de St-Point**, where you can pick up GR5 again to make the ascent of **Mont d'Or** (1463m) overlooking Lake Geneva and the Alps, and to Mouthe, where the River Doubs emerges from an underground cavern.

Down the Loue

From Pontarlier, some 17km north (buses) lies OUHANS, a couple of kilometres above the source of the **River Loue**, which eventually flows into the Doubs below DÔLE. The river issues from an enormous rock mouth beneath a tiered cliff, in winter entirely fringed with icicles. From here you can continue by foot, along the GR595 footpath down the valley to Ornans.

ORNANS, roughly halfway between Pontarlier and Besançon on the D67, is the prettily archetypal Franche-Comté village. The Loue valley here is an abrupt trench with the river washing the foundations of Ornans' ancient balconied houses. The painter and *Communard* Gustave Courbet was born here: his house is now a **museum** (daily April–Nov 10am–noon & 2–6pm; winter closed Tues). There are **campsites** and **gîtes d'étapes** in Ornans, as well as in Vuillafans and Mouthier.

Besançon

BESANÇON, capital of Franche-Comté, is an ancient and attractive town enclosed in a loop of the River Doubs at the northern edge of the Jura mountains. The constriction of the wooded hills, which tightly enclose the town, and the sober grey stone of its facades, give it a slightly mournful air. It was the birthplace of **rayon**, in 1890, and, until the Far East emerged on the scene, a major centre of French **clock-making**.

The town

To reach the centre from the **gare SNCF**, follow av du Maréchal-Foch down to the river and cross over the Doubs by the second bridge. From here rue de la République leads to the central **Place du 8-septembre** in front of the sixteenth-century **Hôtel de Ville**.The principal street, **Grande-Rue**, cuts across the square along the line of the old Roman road, overlooked by a craggy hill above the river, capped by another of Vauban's prodigious citadels (see below). At its northwestern end – the livelier part with shops and cafés – there is an excellent **Musée des Beaux-Arts** (9.30am–noon & 2–6pm; closed Tues; 12F) with two magnificent Bonnards, other good representative nineteenth- and twentieth-century works, and a wonderful clock collection. Midway down the street, the **Palais Granvelle**, a fine sixteenth-century mansion, houses a not very illuminating local history museum. Continuing up the street, you pass place Victor-Hugo (he was born at no. 140) and arrive at the **Porte Noire**, a second-century Roman triumphal arch spanning the street and partially embedded in the adjoining houses. Beside it, in the shady little **Square Archéologique A-Castan**, are the remains of a *nymphaeum*, a small reservoir of water fed by an aqueduct. Beyond the Porte is the boring and pompous eighteenth-century **Cathédrale St-Jean**.

The **Citadelle** (late-March to Sept 9.15am–6.15pm; rest of the year 9.45am–4.45pm; closed Tues; 22F) is a steep, fifteen-minute climb from here, with a crow's nest view of the town and the noose-like bend in the river that contains it. It houses four highly worthwhile museums (times as above): the **Musée d'Histoire Naturelle**, which speaks for itself; the **Musée Populaire Comtois** with pottery, furniture and a good collection of nineteenth-century marionnettes; the **Section d'Agriculture Traditionnelle** with marvellous old farming implements; and – best of all – the **Musée de la Résistance et de la Déportation**, a superb aid to understanding post-war France's political consciousness. The first rooms document the rise of Nazism and French fascism through photographs and exhibits, including a bar of soap stamped *RIF* – Pure Jew Fat. Moving on to the Vichy government, there's a telegram of encouragement sent by Marshall Pétain to the French troops in the "Legion of Volunteers against Bolshevism", fighting alongside the Germans on the eastern front. Finally, as counterbalance, much is made of General Leclerc's vow at Koufra in the Libyan desert, whose capture in January 1941 was the first, entirely French, victory of the war: "We will not stop until the French flag flies once more over Metz and Strasbourg", a vow which he kept, when he entered the latter city at the head of a division in November 1944.

Practicalities

The **SI**, by the second bridge on rue de l'Armée-Française (mid-June–Aug Mon–Fri 9am–noon & 1.30–7pm, Sat 9am–noon & 1.45–5pm, Sun 9am–noon; rest of the year Mon–Fri 9am–noon & 1.30–6/6.30pm, Sat 9am–noon & 1.45–5pm), provide a free accommodation service. **Hotels** to check include the *Florel* opposite the station (☎81.80.41.08; ②/③); the *Levant*, 9 rue des Boucheries (☎81.81.07.88; ③); and, dead central, the *Regina* at 91 Grande-Rue (☎81.81.50.22; ③).

There is no official **youth hostel**, but the *Centre International de Séjour* in the new town at 19 rue Martin-du-Gard (☎81.50.07.54; bus #8, stop *L'Épitaphe*) fulfils the same function, though at slightly greater expense. Alternatively, there's the *Foyer des Jeunes Filles*, 18 rue de la Cassotte (☎81.80.90.01; women only), and *CROUS*, whose main office is at 38 av de l'Observatoire (☎81.50.26.88); but to get a room you must head for the university itself (open July–Sept; bus #7 direction *Campus*, stop *Université*). **Camping** is at Plage de Chalezuele, 5km out on the Belfort road (open March–Oct; bus #1 towards Palente).

For **eating**, the *Levant* hotel has a popular restaurant (closed Sat), or you could try the student restaurant, *Canot*, at the entrance to the old town by Pont Canot (closed evenings July & Aug). *Kabouli* is a Syrian/Lebanese place on rue Claude-Pouillet (closed Sun), and, unusually for France, there's a good sandwich bar, *La Boîte*, 21 rue du Lycée (closed Sat evening & Sun). The two biggest **cultural events** of the year in Besançon are *Jazz en Franche-Comté*, which takes place in June and July, and an international young conductors' competition in the first two weeks of September.

Transport: buses south for Pontarlier and Salins-les-Bains leave from the **gare routière** on rue Proudhon off rue de la République.

Dôle and the road to Geneva

Half way between Besançon and Dijon on the edge of the flat and fertile valley of the Saône, **DÔLE** is quiet and provincial. It's a place to stay overnight, or rest, and attractive enough in a subdued way. Grey stone houses with barred ground floor windows stand on narrow streets around its vast, stolid main church, **Église Notre-Dame**. The Rhône–Rhine canal washes the feet of the town, and along its bank below the church runs the narrow rue Pasteur, birthplace of **Louis Pasteur**, the politically reactionary French biologist and chemist, who discovered the rabies virus (and its cure), and whose name is commemorated in the process of "pasteurisation", another of his discoveries. He was the son of a tanner, and his house, like those of his father's workmates, backs on to a pretty waterside walkway leading to an island. The house is now a **museum** (April–Oct Mon & Wed–Sat 9am–noon & 2–7pm Sun 2–6pm; 10F).

Whatever happens in Dôle, happens between the **Grande-Rue** leading up from the bridge and **place Grévy**, with the SI at no. 6 (Tues–Sat 8.30am–noon & 2–5/6/7pm). There are some reasonable **hotels**: *Le Grand Cerf*, 6 rue Arney, near place Grévy (☎84.72.11.68; ③), and *Auberge du Père Guy* across the river on av Maréchal-Juin (☎87.72.40.32; ③). But the cheapest rooms, as usual, are at the **youth hostel**, in fact a mixed *foyer*, on place St-Jean XXIII (☎84.82.0036; no curfew; IYHF card required). To get there, take bus #1, direction *Mesnils-Poiset*, stop *Les Paters*; the hostel also does **bike hire**. There's a **campsite**, *Camping du Pasquier*, by the river (☎84.72.02.61; open March 15–Oct). Apart from pizzerias and *crêperies*, like the canal-side *La Demi-Lune*, 39 rue Pasteur (closed Wed), you should try *Restaurant Associative*, 8 rue Charles-Sauria, or the station's *Buffet de la Gare*, both of which have good local reputations. The **gare routière** is next to the train station.

The road to Geneva

As elsewhere in the Jura, it's scenery rather than special places that enlivens the **road to Geneva** – the old N5 from Dijon via Dôle. Most of the journey can be covered by train from Dôle or Besançon via Mouchard.

Salins-les-Bains and Arc-et-Senans

SALINS-LES-BAINS, 8km east of Mouchard, is worth the detour if you're an enthusiast of industrial archaeology. Confined in the bottom of a narrow valley, guarded by two lofty forts, Salins has been a salt-mining town for most of the last thousand years, and the **salt works**, with their ancient machinery, are the town's only real attraction (daily 9am–noon & 2–6pm). For any further information, the **SI** is next to the eighteenth-century Hôtel de Ville on the central place des Alliés. The main accommodation is the **campsite**, available from mid-June to mid-September, at av Général-de-Gaulle

More interesting from the architectural-historical point of view are the salt works at **ARC-ET-SENANS**, 7km north of Mouchard. They were to have been the centrepiece of a utopian model city dreamed up by the revolutionary architect Claude-Nicolas Ledoux (May–Sept, 9am–7pm; rest of year 9am–noon and 2–5pm).

Arbois

ARBOIS, a dozen kilometres to the southwest and on the railway to POLIGNY, the centre of Jura wine-making, is prettier and gentler than the salt towns. The SI, in the Hôtel de Ville by the river, will direct you to various *caves* for *dégustations*. The most distinctive local wines are the "yellow" *Château-Chalon*, with a much stronger aftertaste than most wines, and the powerful but scarce *vin de paille*, so called because it's made from grapes dried on beds of straw. The town was also the principal boyhood home of Louis Pasteur (after the family moved from Dôle), and the **Maison Pasteur**, on av Pasteur, is open to the public (April–Oct 9am–noon & 2–6.30pm; closed Tues; 10F). *Hôtel Mephisto*, 33 pl Faramand (☎84.66.06.49; ②), offers the cheapest **rooms**, there's **camping** at *Camping des Vignes*, on av Général-Leclerc (☎84.66.14.12; open April–Sept) 1km to the east of the town centre, and you can hire bikes from *Patrick Aviet*, 1 rue de Bourgogne.

From Champagnole to the Swiss frontier

At the small industrial town of **CHAMPAGNOLE**, 25km southeast of Arbois, the railway line rejoins the N5. It's no great place to stay, with the cheapest hotel, the *Franc-Comtois*, 11 rue Clemenceau (☎84.52.04.95; ④). Try instead the *Accueil Jeunes*, Base de la Roche-sur-Ain (☎84.52.07.76), or the **campsite** on rue Georges-Vallerey (open June–Sept 15). About 20km south by train through progressively wilder country, you reach **ST-LAURENT-EN-GRANDVAUX**, with the *Hôtel de la Poste* (☎84.60.15.39; ④) and a **campsite** (closed May & Oct).

A short distance west of the N5 and the railway is the hamlet of **ILAY**, from which a path leads down through the woods to a spectacular series of waterfalls, the **Cascades du Hérisson**, 3.5km away. A touristy spot in summer, you can have it to yourself in the spring, with the bonus of much more water and wild daffodils growing in the oak woods on the sides of the gorge. Be warned that the only **hotel** in Ilay, the *Auberge du Hérisson*, is much more expensive than it looks (☎84.25.58.18; open April–mid-Oct; ⑤).

Next stop on the way to the Swiss frontier is **MOREZ**, which makes watches and spectacles – another claustrophobic town squeezed along a slit-like valley floor. The **SI** is in the central place Jaurès, along with the **gare routière**, where buses leave for LA CURE on the Franco-Swiss frontier. From the Swiss side there are trains down to Nyon on Lac Léman and on to Geneva itself.

A couple of kilometres before the frontier, **LES ROUSSES** exists purely for skiing – downhill and, especially, cross-country – but just before it a lane to the right goes down to a very attractive **youth hostel** in an old red-shuttered farmhouse by a stream, 2km away at BIEF-DE-LA-CHAILLE (☎84.60.02.80; open Dec–mid-April & mid-June–mid-Sept). There's also a *gîte d'étape* at PRÉMANON on the D25 (☎84.60.54.82; mid-Dec–April & July–Aug). The footpath **GR9** passes through, beginning a magnificent hiking section all along the crest of the ridge to the Col de la Faucille and beyond (see below).

St-Claude

From Morez the railway leaves the N5 and heads instead for the industrial town of **ST-CLAUDE**, to the southwest, squeezed even more claustrophobically by even higher mountains than Morez. It makes pipes (the smokers' kind), and inevitably there's a collection of them on display in a building opposite the main church of St-Pierre. Should you find yourself here for the night, the *Hôtel La Poyat* at 7 rue de la Poyat off the main rue du Pré (☎84.45.49.81; ③) is a better bet than the *Hôtel de la Poste*, 1 rue Reybert (☎84.45.52.34; ③). **Camping** is at Le Martinet, 3km from town off the Col de la Faucille road. For **eating**, *Le Bayard* in the central place du Pré is wholesome and inexpensive.

The Col de la Faucille

What gives purpose to the rest of the onward route from either St-Claude or Les Rousses are the superb views from the crest of the great fir-clad ridge that overlooks Lac Léman (Lake Geneva) to the east. The N5 crosses the ridge at the **Col de la Faucille** (1323m). If it's clear, the **view** is unbelievably dramatic, from the Col or the GR footpath, with the whole range of the western Alps stretched out before you, dominated by Mont Blanc, with the steely, cusp-shaped Lac Léman laid at your feet. There's an even better view from the top of nearby Mont-Rond (1534m), accessible by chairlift. Of course, if it's not clear, after all that hitching or walking, you're going to be disappointed. But it's downhill all the way to Geneva, 30km or so to the south – with the thought of a couple or more revitalising bars of Swiss chocolate at hike's end.

travel details

Trains

From Verdun to Chalons-sur-Marne/Paris-Est up to 5 daily (1hr 20min/3hr); Metz via Conflans 1 daily (1hr–1hr 15min), changing at Conflans.

From Metz to Longuyon 2 daily (1hr 30min); Paris-Est 4 daily (3hr); Strasbourg every 2hr (1hr 30min); Mulhouse 7 daily (2hr 30min); Nancy hourly (1hr).

From Nancy Paris-Est hourly (3hr); Lunéville hourly (30min); Saverne 3 daily (1hr); Strasbourg 2 daily (1hr 20 min).

From Strasbourg to Paris-Est every 2hr (4hr 30min); Wissembourg up to 3 daily (1hr); Sélestat/Colmar/Mulhouse/Basel hourly (20min/50min/1hr 20min/1hr 30min–2hr); Molsheim/Rosheim/Obernai/Barr/Dambach/Sélestat 9 daily (20min/25min/40min/55min/1hr/1hr–1hr 20min); Besançon (8 daily (2hr 15min); Dôle 10 daily (3hr 30min).

From Mulhouse to Belfort up to 5 daily (30–45 min).

From Belfort to Paris-Est 2 daily (5hr); Ronchamp 12 daily (5 min); Besançon 5 daily (1hr–1hr 15min); Dôle 5 daily (1hr 30min).

From Besançon to Paris-Lyon direct up to 6 daily (2hr 30min); to Dijon 10 daily (1hr); Dôle 10 daily (30min); 4 or 5 to Bourg-en-Bresse (2hr 30min); several to Lons (1–1hr 30min), some via Mouchard (30min), Arbois (45min), Poligny (1hr 5min); St-Claude 4 daily (2hr 30min–3hr), via Champagnole (1hr 40min–1hr 30min), St-Laurent (1hr 40min–2hr), Morez (2hr 10min–2hr 30min); Morteau (1hr–1hr 45min).

From Dôle to Dijon 10 daily (30min); and Paris-Lyon 10 daily (4hr); Pontarlier 3 daily (1hr 20min).

From St-Claude to Bourg 4 or 5 daily (1hr 40min–2hr), connecting with TGV to Paris.

Buses

From Colmar to Mulhouse up to hourly (1hr), Sélestat hourly (1hr).

From Belfort to Ronchamp 1 daily (45min).

From Besançon to Ornans/Pontarlier 4 daily (30min/1hr); Salins-les-Bains 3 weekly (1hr).

From Arbois to Monchaud 7 daily (5min).

From Pontarlier to Frasne regularly (SNCF); infrequently to Vallorbe, Mouthe, Ouhans.

From Morez to St-Claude 3 weekly (1hr); to Lons 1 most days (1hr 45min); to Les Rousses Thursday & Friday.

From St-Claude Lyon daily (3hr 40min).

CHAPTER FOUR

NORMANDY

Though now firmly incorporated into the French mainstream, the seaboard province of **Normandy** has a history of prosperous independence as one of the crucial powers of medieval Europe. Colonised by Norsemen from Scandinavia, it began, in the eleventh and twelfth centuries, to colonise in turn; not only England, but as far afield as Sicily and parts of the Near East. Later, as part of France, it was instrumental in the settlement of Canada.

Normandy has always had large **ports**: Rouen, on the Seine, is the nearest navigable point to Paris; Dieppe, Le Havre and Cherbourg have important transatlantic trade. **Inland**, it is overwhelmingly agricultural – a fertile belt of tranquil pastureland, where the chief goal of most visitors will be the restaurants of towns such as Vire and Conches. Much of the **seaside** is a little overdeveloped. The last French emperor created towards, the end of the last century, a "Norman Riviera" around Trouville and Deauville, and an air of pretension hangs about their elegant promenades. But the ancient ports – **Honfleur** and **Barfleur** especially – are visual delights, and there are numerous seaside villages with few crowds or affectations. Along the Seine, too, are several idyllic resorts.

Normandy also boasts extraordinary **Romanesque** and **Gothic architectural** treasures, although only the much-restored capital, **Rouen**, has a complete medieval centre. The attractions are more often single buildings than entire towns. Most famous of all is the spectacular *merveille* on the island of **Mont St-Michel**, but there are also the monasteries at Jumièges and Caen; the cathedrals of Bayeux and Coutances; and Richard the Lionheart's castle above the Seine at Les Andelys. Bayeux has in addition its vivid and astonishing **Tapestry**, and among more recent creations are **Monet's garden at Giverny** and, at **Le Havre**, a fabulous collection of paintings by Dufy, Boudin and other Impressionists. Furthermore, Normandy's vernacular architecture makes it well worth exploring inland – the back roads through the countryside are lined with splendid centuries-old half-timbered manor houses. It is remarkable how much has survived or been restored since the Allied landings in 1944 and the subsequent **Battle of Normandy**, which has its own legacy in a series of war museums, memorials and cemeteries.

To the French, at least, the essence of Normandy is its **produce**. This is the land of Camembert and Calvados, cider and seafood, and a butter- and cream-based cuisine with a proud disdain for most things *nouvelle*. **Economically**, however, the richness of the dairy pastures has been Normandy's downfall in recent years. EEC milk quotas have liquidated many small farms, and stringent sanitary regulations have forced many small-scale traditional cheese factories to close. Parts of inland Normandy are now among the most depressed of the whole country, and in the forested areas to the south where life has never been easy, things have not improved.

Politically, Normans have a reputation for being mistrustful, closed and conservative, with a love of taking each other to court. The rural population identifies with the age-old *pays* and tends to use the phrase "gone east" with equal disapproval for a move of ten kilometres as for one to Alsace. However, there is no question of a separatist

HOTEL ROOM PRICES

For a fuller explanation of these price codes, see the box on p.28 of *Basics*.

① Under 100F   ② 100–130F   ③ 130–180F   ④ 180–230F   ⑤ 230–300F

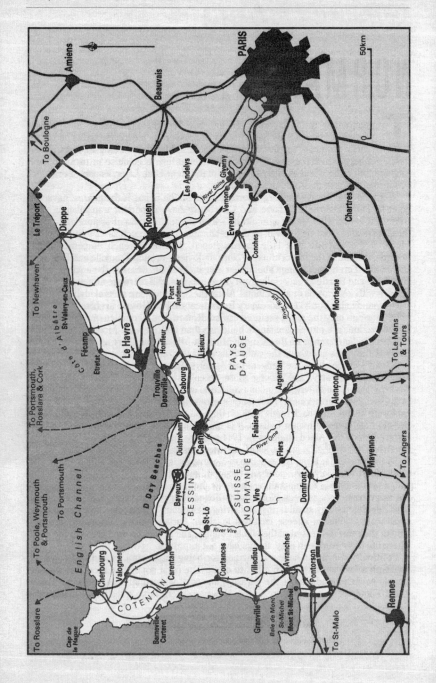

movement on the scale of that in neighbouring Brittany; most people would be unaware of the existence of the minuscule and bizarre **Normandy Nationalist Party**. These neo-Norse people use English as the next best language after Saxon, and talk about Sinn Féin and the Duchess of Normandy (the Queen of England) in equally glowing terms.

CÔTE D'ALBÂTRE

The Channel ports along Normandy's upper coast, **Dieppe** and **Le Havre**, unquestionably provide a better introduction to France than their counterparts further north in Picardy, though things get livelier and warmer to the west, and it's only a short train or bus ride to Rouen. An impressive display of white cliffs has earned this stretch of seashore the epithet of "Alabaster coast", and occasional surprises can be found beyond the windswept and tide-chased walks, such as a wonderful Lutyens fantasy at **Varengeville**, and the Hammer Horror Benedictine distillery at **Fécamp**.

Dieppe

Crowded between high cliff headlands, **DIEPPE** is an enjoyably small-scale port. It's industrious, with the commercial docks unloading half the bananas of the Antilles and forty percent of all shellfish destined to slither down French throats. The markets sell fish right off the boats, displayed with the usual Gallic flair, and the sole, scallops and turbot available in profusion at the restaurants may well tempt you to stay. Even if you do immediately head south by train, the railway line runs along the *quais* of the fishing port, so you can get a whiff of what you're missing.

The **town** used to be more of a resort; Parisians would take the sea air here in the days before fast cars took them further afield. In the nineteenth century, the French would promenade along the front while the English colony indulged in the peculiar pastime of swimming – hence the extravagant space allotted to the seafront and "salt water therapy centre" (now hemmed in by car parks). In the centre the streets are run down and in continual shadow – little advertisement for the eighteenth-century town planning to which they are supposed to be a monument. Livelier, particularly for its **Saturday market**, is the pedestrianised **Grande-Rue**.

For monuments, the obvious place to start is the medieval **castle** overlooking the seafront from the west, home of the **Musée de Dieppe** and two showpiece collections. The first is a group of carved **ivories** – virtuoso pieces of sawing, filing and chipping of the plundered riches of Africa, shipped back to the town by early Dieppe "explorers". The other permanent exhibition is made up of a hundred or so prints by the co-founder of cubism, **Georges Braque**, who went to school in Le Havre, spent summers in Dieppe and is buried just west of the town at Varangeville-sur-Mer (see below). Only a small number of prints are displayed at any one time, but in theory you can see the rest if you ask. (10am–noon and 2–6pm; closed Tues out of season.)

An exit from the western side of the castle takes you out onto a path up to the **cliffs**. On the other side, a flight of steps leads down to the **square du Canada**, originally a commemoration of the role played by Dieppe sailors in the colonisation of Canada. Now a small plaque is dedicated to the Canadian soldiers who died in the suicidal 1942 raid on Dieppe, justified later as a trial run for the 1944 Normandy landings.

Practicalities

Dieppe's **SI** is on the bd Général-de-Gaulle (May–Sept Mon–Sat 9am–noon & 2– 7pm; rest of year 9am–noon & 2–6pm; ☎35.84.11.77), alongside the very ordinary Hôtel de Ville. There are four daily Sealink **ferries** from Newhaven to Dieppe in summer and

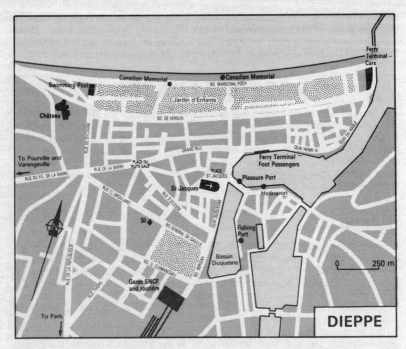

three each day in winter. The **gare maritime** is on quai Henri IV (reservations: foot passengers ☎35.84.22.60, cars ☎35.82.24.87). Connecting trains for the ferries draw up alongside on the quay, although the town's main **gare SNCF** (☎35.98.50.50) is 500m away on bd Clemenceau, 1km from the beach. The **gare routière** is right next to the gare SNCF.

Dieppe has plenty of **hotels**; on the whole, prices get progressively cheaper as you head further inland from the seafront. The **youth hostel** at 48 rue Louis-Fromager, 2km southwest of the gare SNCF in the quartier Janval (☎35.84.85.73), is open year round, except for two weeks in December and two weeks in February. It's on bus route #2, direction Val Druel; get off at the Château Michel stop.

The same bus continues to one of Dieppe's two **campsites**, the three-star *Camping Vitamin*, Chemin des Vertus (April–Oct; ☎35.82.11.11). The other, the two-star *Camping du Pre Saint-Nicholas* is west along the coast, 3km beyond the château on the route de Pourville (year-round; ☎35.84.11.39). The campsite which used to exist in Pollet at the mouth of the harbour disappeared during the re-development programme of 1991.

The biggest **hypermarket** in the Dieppe area is *Mammouth*, out of town at the Val Dunel commercial centre on the route de Rouen (RN 27).

HOTELS

Hôtel Les Arcades, 1–3 arcades de la Bourse (☎35.84.14.12). Restaurant with menu from 75F. Facing the port; particularly suitable for tired passengers arriving at midnight and not wanting to walk more than 200 yards to find a bed. ③

Hôtel Epsom, 11 bd de Verdun (☎35.84.10.18; ⑤). Facing the sea. Newly refurbished; bright and cheerful. English bar with tartan carpet and resident pianist. No restaurant. ⑤

Hôtel Select, 1 rue Toustain (☎35.84.14.66). Not far from the château at the western end of the rue de la Baine. Serves a "Great British Breakfast" for 59F all day long – to all-comers. No restaurant. ④

Hôtel Windsor, 18 bd de Verdun (☎35.84.15.23). Restaurant – *Le Haut Gallion* – with menu from 90F. Facing the beach. ③

RESTAURANTS

Ankara, 18 rue de la Rade (☎35.84.58.33). Turkish restaurant between quai Henri IV and bd de Verdun. Midday menu from 45F; evening menu from 69F; vegetarian menu from 75F. Closed Wed.

Les Rourelles, 43 rue du Commandant-Fayolle (☎35.84.15.88). Menu from 52F. Paella. Behind the casino.

Marmite Dieppoise, 8 rue St-Jean (☎35.84.24.26). Between St-Jacques church and arcades de la Bourse. Lunch menu from 80F. Small, rustic and busy, featuring the local speciality *marmite Dieppoise* (seafood pot). Closed Sun evening and Mon.

Les P'tits Bateaux, 23 quai Henri IV (☎35.06.14.74). Menu 80F and 100F. Sixteenth-century cellar with live music until late; last orders midnight. The more upmarket *Pergola* is on the ground floor.

Out from Dieppe: Varengeville

If the museum in Dieppe has awakened your interest in **Georges Braque**, you may be interested in visiting his **grave** in the clifftop church of **VARENGEVILLE**, 8km west of town (a 25-min ride on bus #311 or #312, afternoons only). The tombstone is monstrous and the view along the cliffs more appealing than the artist's stained-glass windows.

Back along the road from the church, the **Bois des Moutiers** was one of architect **Edwin Lutyens'** first commissions, and is un-French in almost every respect. The gardens are open from March 15 to November 15 (9am–noon & 2–7pm; closed Sat am; 25F), and the house in July and August (closed Sun am & Tues). Enthusiastic guides lead you through the highly innovative construction and composition of the house and grounds, replete with quirks and games. The colours of the Burne-Jones tapestry hanging in the stairwell were copied from Renaissance cloth in William Morris's studio; the rhododendrons were chosen from similar samples. Paths lead through vistas based on paintings by Poussin, Lorrain and other eighteenth-century artists; no modern roses are allowed to update the colours.

West along the coast

From Dieppe to Le Havre the coast is eroding at a ferocious rate, and it's conceivable that the small resorts here, tucked in among the cliffs at the ends of a succession of valleys, may not last more than another century or so. For the moment, however, they are quietly prospering, with casinos, sports centres and yacht marinas ensuring a modest but steady summer trade.

St-Valery-en-Caux

The first sizeable community west of Dieppe is **ST-VALERY-EN-CAUX**, a rebuilt town which is the clearest reminder of the fighting – and massive destruction – of the Allied retreat of 1940. A monument on the western cliffs pays tribute to the French cavalry division who faced Rommel's tanks on horseback, brandishing their sabres with hopeless heroism, while beside the ruins of a German artillery emplacement on the opposite cliffs another commemorates a Scottish division, rounded up while fighting their way back to Le Havre and the boats home. The *Terrasses*, 22 rue le Parrey (☎35.97.11.22; ④), is a nice seaside hotel-cum-restaurant.

Fécamp

FÉCAMP, roughly halfway between Dieppe and Le Havre, is a serious fishing port with an attractive seafront promenade. One compelling reason to pay a brief visit is to see the **Benedictine Distillery** on rue Alexandre-le-Grand, in the narrow strip of streets running parallel to the ports towards the town centre. A taste for nineteenth-century operatic horror sets is more important than a liking for the liqueur in question. Tours lasting 45 minutes (9.30–11.30am & 2–5.30pm) start with a small **museum**, set firmly in the Middle Ages with props of manuscripts, locks, testaments, lamps and religious paintings beneath a nightmarish mock-Gothic roof. The first whiff of Benedictine comes in the grim rust-and-grey-coloured *Salle des Abbés*, and at this point the script abruptly changes – from mysterious monks to PR for an exclusive product. The boxes of ingredients are a rare treat for the nose (take it easy with the myrrh), and there's further theatricality in the old distillery where boxes of herbs are thrown with gusto into copper vats and alembics. (Commercial production has long since moved to an out-of-town site). Finally you are offered a *dégustation* in their bar across the road – neat, in a cocktail, or on crêpes; make sure you hold on to your ticket to qualify.

If your aesthetic sensibilities need soothing after this, the soaring medieval nave and Renaissance carved screens of the **Église de la Trinité,** up in the town centre, may do the trick. Alternatively, you could feast your eyes on a Renaissance chancel on a grass floor with the open sky above and an intact Gothic lady chapel: the remains of the **Abbaye de Valmont,** 11km east from the coast (bus #261, #311 from Fécamp). This is open 10am to noon and 2 to 6pm, except Wednesday (and, from Oct–April, Sun).

The **hotels** in Fécamp tend to be set back away from the sea on odd side streets. It's a popular place; you need to reserve a room at the *Hôtel de l'Univers*, 5 pl St-Étienne (☎35.28.05.88; ③), or the *Angleterre*, 93 rue de la Plage (☎35.28.01.60; ③). The **youth hostel** (☎35.29.75.79; for reservations ☎35.29.36.35) is open from July to September 15; it's east of the port, along the route du Commandant-Roquigny, on the Côte de la Vierge. A superb **campsite**, the *Camping de Renneville* (☎35.28.20.97), is a short walk away on the western cliffs. The **SI** is just behind the seafront where it meets the yacht harbour; the **gares SNCF** and **routière** between the port and the town centre on av Gambetta

Étretat

The cliff formations of **ÉTRETAT** are splashed across most of the *département's* tourist brochures. Without the prior publicity, these could be quite thrilling as you first catch sight of the arches and needles from the beach or clifftop. You'll need transport though – Étretat is not on bus or train routes – and to explore them you have only three hours either side of low tide. The standard high vantage point on the eastern side has a life-size aeroplane in concrete relief and an arch inclining to the sky, a moving commemoration of two pilots last seen over Étretat attempting a Paris–New York flight in 1927.

Well sheltered from the elements, the town itself is a pleasant enough little resort and has a nice idiosyncrasy in the form of beached boats converted with thatched roofs into sheds or, these days, bars. If you want to stay, there's not much **accommodation** available. Try along av George V – either the *Windsor* (☎35.27.07.27; ③) at no. 9, or *de la Poste* (☎35.27.01.34; ③) at no. 6; or try the municipal **campsite** (☎35.27.07.67), 1km out on rue Guy-de-Maupassant. There is an **SI** on the central pl de la Mairie.

Le Havre

Most ferry passengers head straight out of the port of **LE HAVRE** as quickly as the traffic will allow, to escape a city most guidebooks dismiss as dismal, disastrous and gargantuan. While it is not the most picturesque or tranquil place in Normandy, it is not the soulless urban sprawl the warnings suggest, even if the port, the second largest in France after Marseille, does take up half the Seine estuary, extending way beyond the town. The city was originally built on the orders of François I in 1517. Its function was to replace the ancient ports of Harfleur and Honfleur, then silting up, and its name was soon changed from Franciscopolis to Le Havre – "the Harbour". It became the principal trading post of France's northern coast, prospering especially during the American

War of Independence and thereafter, importing cotton, sugar and tobacco. In the years before the outbreak of war in 1939, it was the European home of the great luxury liners such as the *Normandie, Île de France* and *France*.

Having suffered almost total destruction in World War II, it was rebuilt to the specifications of a single architect, **Auguste Perret**, between 1946 and 1964 – which makes it a rather rare entity, and one that has been the subject of much controversy. Perret is often quoted as having said "concrete is beautiful", and the "new" Le Havre certainly offers those who linger every opportunity to make up their minds for themselves.

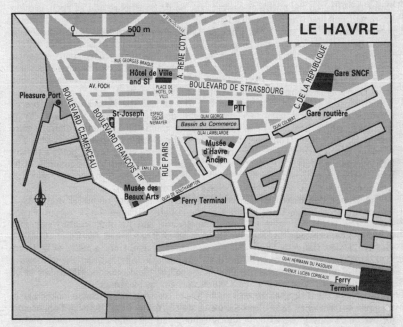

Arrival and accommodation

The **SI** is at Forum de l'Hôtel de Ville (April–Sept 8.45am–12.15pm & 1.30–7pm; ☎35.21.22.88). The **gare SNCF** (☎35.43.50.50) is 1.5km west, on Cours de la République, right alongside the **gare routière** (☎35.26.67.23) across bd de Strasbourg. **Bus #3** from the gare SNCF runs to the **P & O European Ferries Terminal** (☎35.21.36.50), while a separate shuttle goes to the Terminal d'Ireland (☎35.53.28.33).

Le Havre has two main concentrations of **hotels**: one group faces the gare SNCF, and there are more within walking distance of the ferry terminal. The nearest **camping** is at the 700-acre *Forêt de Montgeon* site (☎35.46.52.39), north of the town centre. Take bus #1 from the Hôtel de Ville or gare SNCF, direction *Jacques-Monod*, getting off at *Sainte-Cecile* or *Noisetriers*.

Hôtel Richelieu, 132 rue de Paris (☎35.42.38.71). Between the Hôtel de Ville and the ferry terminal. No restaurant. ③

Hôtel Séjour Fleuri, 71 rue Émile-Zola (☎35.41.33.81). On a side road off rue de Paris, close to the ferry terminal. Two hotels knocked into one make for some uneven corridors. No restaurant. ③

Hôtel Green, 209 bd de Strasbourg (☎35.22.63.10). Double glazing – and easy parking – near the gare SNCF. 10 percent discount weekends, Sept–March. No restaurant. ④

Hôtel-Restaurant Monaco, 16 rue de Paris (☎35.42.21.01). The closest hotel to the ferry terminal, with a highly recommended and good-value restaurant. Closed second fortnight in Feb and Mon July–Oct. ④

Hôtel Parisien, 1 cours de la République (☎35.25.23.83). A well-appointed place, with congenial management, facing the gare SNCF. ④

The town

Two projects in particular represent Perret's work at its most contentious. The central **Hôtel de Ville**, on the town's east–west axis, bd de Strasbourg and av Foch, is a low flat-roofed building which stretches for a full 120 yards, overshadowed by a 17-storey concrete tower. The severity of place de l'Hôtel-de-Ville has now been softened by flower beds, rustic fencing and pergola walks. His huge church of **St Joseph**, with its 99-metre bell tower, also has its critics; one regrets "the all-too-conspicuous octagonal concrete tower", another complains that "it simply does not look French – one could see it in Stalinist Moscow or 1930's New York". The Stalinist lines are perhaps attributable to the long-standing Communist control of the city council.

Between the Hôtel de Ville and the P & O terminal, the **Bassin du Commerce** provides a third focal point. The line of the dock is continued westwards by pl Gambetta, which has now been graced with a multi-million-pound cultural centre named for its equally controversial architect, the Brazilian **Oscar Niemayer**. The building, which resembles a gleaming white truncated cooling tower, holds a theatre and cinema, and has a steadfast socialist sentiment inscribed by the fountain at its base. A plaza for street performance and strolling slopes down to bars and shops as well as exhibition and concert space (what's on details from SI).

The **Musée des Beaux-Arts**, overlooking the port entrance on bd J.-F.-Kennedy, is one of the best designed art galleries in the country (10am–noon & 2–6pm; closed Tues). The lovely collection of French nineteenth- and twentieth-century paintings includes fifty canvases by Eugene Boudin, as well as works by Corot, Courbet, Pissarro, Sisley, Gauguin, Léger, Braque and Lurçat. Raoul Dufy, a native of Le Havre (1877–1953), has a whole room for his drawings and paintings, in which the windows at the base of the walls show waterlilies in a shallow moat outside. Waterlilies in oil appear along with Westminster and a snowscape sunrise by Monet.

If you have the time to spare, you might like to see what old Le Havre looked like in the pre-war days when **Jean-Paul Sartre** wrote *La Nausée* here. He taught philosophy for five years during the 1930s in a local school, and his almost transcendent disgust with the place cannot obscure the fascination he felt in exploring the seedy dockside quarter of St-François, in those spare moments when he wasn't visiting Simone de Beauvoir in Rouen. Little survives of the city Sartre knew, but pictures and bits gathered from the rubble are on display in one of the very few buildings that escaped, the **Musée de l'Ancien Havre** at 1 rue Jerome-Bellarmato, just south of the Bassin du Commerce (Wed–Sun 10am–noon & 2–6pm).

Eating

Few of the **restaurants** in Le Havre are worth making a fuss about, except perhaps for some in the suburb of **Ste-Adresse** (where the beachside bd Albert I commemorates the fact that this was the seat of the Belgian government in exile during World War I). There are, however, lots of bars, cafes and brasseries around the gare SNCF.

If you're **shopping** for food to take home, possibilities include *Halles Centrales* west of pl Gambetta, and two hypermarkets: *Mammouth* at Montivilliers (signed from the Tancarville road) or the larger *Auchan* at the *Mont Gaillard Centre Commercial* (follow cours de la République beyond the gare SNCF, through the tunnel, then look for signs). The *Flunch* (☎35.46.59.82) at *Auchan* is a good self-service cafeteria.

La Chope d'Or, 163 rue Victor-Hugo (☎35.43.62.15). Off rue de Paris, between the Hôtel de Ville and pl Gambetta. *Plat du jour* 32F, *menu économique* 48F. Mon–Fri only, 7.30am–8pm.

Le Channel, 4 rue de Paris (☎35.21.21.48). On the corner of quai Southampton and rue de Paris. Menus at 57F, 69F and 95F. Easy parking.

Lescalle, 39 place de l'Hôtel de Ville (☎35.43.07.93). Menu from 87F. Open every day, overlooking the huge town hall square.

Nice-Havrais, 6 pl Frederic-Sauvage, Ste-Adresse (☎35.46.14.59). Lovely sea views, excellent cooking, especially fish; moderately expensive. Closed Sun, and Mon pm.

THE SEINE VALLEY

The days of the **Seine's** tidal bore and treacherous sandbanks are over. Heavy ships serenely make their way up the looping river to the provincial capital of **Rouen**, the largest city of Normandy and the only one to merit a long stay. Further upstream, Monet's wonderful house and garden at **Giverny** and the medieval English frontier stronghold, the **Château Gaillard** at **Les Andelys**, also justify taking a slow route into Paris. The immense **Tancarville** suspension bridge spans the opening of the estuary just beyond Le Havre, while at Caudebec the yellow stays of the Pont de Brotonne produce magical optical effects on your way across; for unhurried river crossings there are *bacs* (ferries: cheaper for cars than the bridge tolls). Le Havre to Rouen buses (#191, #192) follow the north (right) bank, much the best in terms of scenery.

Upstream towards Rouen

Le Havre and Rouen being such vast industrial conglomerates, you might not expect the countryside between them to hold much appeal. In fact, it's a surprisingly beautiful area, designated the **Parc Naturel Régional de Brotonne** with imaginative projects run by local people to preserve the environment and traditional activities. Its highlight, to outsiders, is the majestic **Abbaye de Jumièges**, but if you have time there are less crowded attractions south of the river. **Details** on all aspects of the park can be obtained from the very helpful *Maison du Parc* (2 rond-point-Marbec, LE TRAIT). After the oil refineries of Le Havre, the *parc* comes as quite a shock. On the south bank Camargue horses and Scottish highland cattle graze in the Vernier marshes, and upstream the scenery on both sides of the Seine is soft and lush like a sleeping, giant green cat.

Caudebec-en-Caux

The first town of any size on the right bank of the Seine is **CAUDEBEC-EN-CAUX**. Most traces of its long past were destroyed by fire in the last war. The damage – and previous local history – is recorded in the thirteenth-century **Maison des Templiers**, one of the few buildings to be spared. The town has one cheap **hotel**, the *Cheval Blanc* (☎35.96.21.66; ③), and even there the food is pricey, and a **campsite**, *Barre Y Va* (☎35.96.11.12). You can **hire bicycles** from M. Jaubert on rue de la Vicomte. A **market** has been held every Saturday since 1390 in the main square.

St-Wandrille

Just beyond the Pont de Brotonne as you continue towards Rouen, the medieval **ABBAYE DE ST-WANDRILLE** was founded, so legend has it, by a seventh-century count who, with his wife, renounced all earthly pleasures on the day of their wedding. The abbey's buildings are an attractive if curious collection: part ruin, part restoration and, in the case of the main buildings, part transplant – a fifteenth-century barn brought in here just a few years ago from another Normandy village miles away. Monks will show you around every afternoon at 3 and 4pm, and at 11.30am on Sunday.

Jumièges

In the next loop of the Seine, 12km on from St-Wandrille, is the more famous **Abbaye de Jumièges**, a haunting ruin whose main outline dates from the eleventh century; William the Conqueror himself attended its consecration in 1067. The towers, nearly 60m high, still stand. So, too, does part of the nave, roofless now and even more impressive because of it. (Unescorted visits 9am–noon & 2–6pm summer; 10am–noon & 2–4pm winter). If you get off the Le Havre–Rouen bus at YAINVILLE or DUCLAIR you can pick up a connection (or hitch) down to Jumièges.

The south bank

Just across the river from Jumièges, near **HAUVILLE** (off the road to GUERANDE), you can look around a **windmill**, one of six owned by the abbey's Benedictine monks, who farmed and forested the entire area in the Middle Ages. Its outline – based on contemporary castle towers – looks just like a kid's drawing. Restored by the *parc*, it is open at weekends, from 2.30 to 7pm.

If you have time, move on from here to the neighbouring village of **LA HAYE-DE-ROUTOT**. The churchyard has a novelty – a pair of millennia-old yew trees shaped into a chapel and grotto – but the feature for which the village is best known (at least in Normandy) is its annual **Fête de Ste-Claire**, held on her feast day, July 16. The centre-piece of this is a towering, conical bonfire, topped by a cross, which must survive to ensure a good year. The smouldering logs are taken home as protection against light-ning. Should you miss the big day, a video recording of the events is shown in a recon-structed *boulangerie* (July & Aug daily except Tues 2.30–6.30pm; April–June, Sept & Oct, Sat & Sun only).

For **accommodation** in the *Parc* south of the river, there's a *gîte d'étape* at ROUTOT (c/o M Verhaeghe, ☎32.57.31.09) and a few rooms available at the *Maison des Métiers* (☎32.57.40.41) in BOURNEVILLE, which is also a beautifully presented **museum** of traditional farming and building techniques (April–Dec 2–7pm; closed Mon). The most practical places to stay are on the north bank, either at Caudebec or in **DUCLAIR** with a couple of cheap hotels: *L'Aigle d'Or*, 75 rue Jules-Ferry (☎35.37.50.38; ②), and *Le Tartarin*, 125 pl du Général-de-Gaulle (☎35.37.50.38; ②).

Rouen

You could spend a day wandering around **ROUEN** without realising that the Seine runs through the city. The war destroyed all the bridges, the area between the cathedral and the *quais,* and much of the left bank industrial quarter. The immediate riverside area has never been adequately restored, with the result that what you might expect to be the most beautiful part of this ancient city is in fact an abomination. Instead, enormous sums were devoted to a thorough restoration job on the streets a few hundred yards north of the river, which turned the centre into an idealised medieval city – it looks authentic and probably isn't in the slightest. Historians consulted on the project suggested that the houses would have been painted in bright, clashing colours – an idea not considered sufficiently evocative or picturesque by the city authorities. Still, the churches are extremely impressive and the whole place faintly seductive.

Outside the renovated quarters, things are rather different. The city spreads deep into the loop of the Seine to the south, and increasingly into the hills to the north, while the riverbank itself is lined with a fume-filled motorway. As the nearest point that large container ships can get to Paris, the port remains the country's fourth largest – albeit in decline. Rouen's docks and industries stretch endlessly away to the south. Many work-ers live outside the municipal boundaries, which might explain why the left is never elected to the town hall.

Arrival and accommodation

Rouen's **SI**, opposite the cathedral at 25 place de la Cathédrale, stands in an early sixteenth–century house known as the House of the Exchequer (May–Sept Mon–Sat 9am–7pm, Sun 9.30am–12.30pm & 2.30–6pm; Oct–April Mon–Sat 9am–12.30pm & 2–6.30pm; ☎35.71.41.77).

The main **gare SNCF** (☎35.98.50.50), at the top end of rue Jeanne-d'Arc, is referred to as Gare Rive Droite; Gare Rive Gauche on the south bank only handles goods traffic. It's not immediately conspicuous on most maps, because the train lines run underground. All town buses except #2A from here run the length of rue Jeanne-d'Arc to the Théâtre des Arts by the river. The **gare routière** is tucked away in rue des Charettes (☎35.71.81.71) behind the riverfront buildings, one block to the west of the bottom end of rue Jeanne-d'Arc. Out-of-town buses include #191 and #192 to Le Havre along the river via Jumièges and Caudebec, #193 to Dieppe via Totes and Bacqueville, #150 to Dieppe and Le Tréport, and #261 to St-Valéry.

You can hire **bicycles** from *Freeway* at 21 rue des Bonnetiers (☎35.70.04.04), just south of the cathedral.

Accommodation

There should be no difficulty in finding appropriate accommodation in Rouen, even at the busiest times. Few of the **hotels** have restaurants, but eating out is no hardship. The city's **youth hostel** is 2km from Gare Rive Droite, south of the river at 17 rue Diderot (☎35.72.06.45). From the Théâtre des Arts on the north bank, take bus #5, direction *Grand Quevilly*, as far as the *Diderot* stop. The **Camping Municipal** is 5km northwest on rue Jules-Ferry in Déville-lès-Rouen (☎35.74.07.59), reached by taking bus #2 from the Théâtre des Arts.

Hôtel-Restaurant le Cache Ribaud, 10 rue du Tambour (☎35.71.04.82). Between the Palais de Justice and the Gros Horloge. Restaurant with *plat du jour* 55F; evening menu from 88F. ③

Hôtel de la Cathédrale, 21 rue St-Romain (☎35.71.56.95). Quiet and central rooms alongside the cathedral. A quaint old courtyard and unexpected flowers in a street lined with fourteenth- century timber-framed houses. No restaurant. ⑤

Hôtel des Familles, 4 rue Pouchet (☎35.71.69.61). Very friendly and characterful place near the Gare Rive Droite. Incorporates the old *Hôtel de la Paix*; hence the two entrances. No restaurant. ③

Hôtel Lisieux, 4 rue de la Savonnerie (☎35.71.87.73). At the junction of rue de la Savonnerie and rue du Bec, between the cathedral and the river. The hotel "flier" has it that Pierre Cauchon, bishop of Beauvais, who prosecuted Joan of Arc at her trial in 1431, stayed and died here in 1442. If so, it has been considerably modernised since. No restaurant. ⑤

Hôtel Saint-Ouen 43 rue des Faulx (☎35.71.46.44). Near the Hôtel de Ville, on bus #2A from the Gare Rive Droite. No restaurant. ①

Hôtel Sphynx, 130 rue Beauvoisine (☎35.71.35.86). The cheapest rooms share showers. ①

The town

Rouen spends a bigger slice of its budget on **monuments** than any other provincial town, which annoys many a Rouennais. As a tourist, your one complaint may be the lack of time to visit them all. The obvious place to start is the **pl du Vieux-Marché** in which a small plaque and a huge cross, nearly 20m high, mark the site where Joan of Arc was burned to death on May 30, 1431. A new memorial church to the saint has been built in the square – a spikey, wacky-looking thing, said to represent an upturned boat, designed to accommodate some sixteenth-century stained glass rescued from the destroyed church of St Vincent. It is an architectural triumph, and part of an ensemble of buildings which manages to incorporate a covered food market – more for show than practical shopping. The square itself is surrounded by fine old brown and white half-timbered houses; many of those on the south side now serve as restaurants.

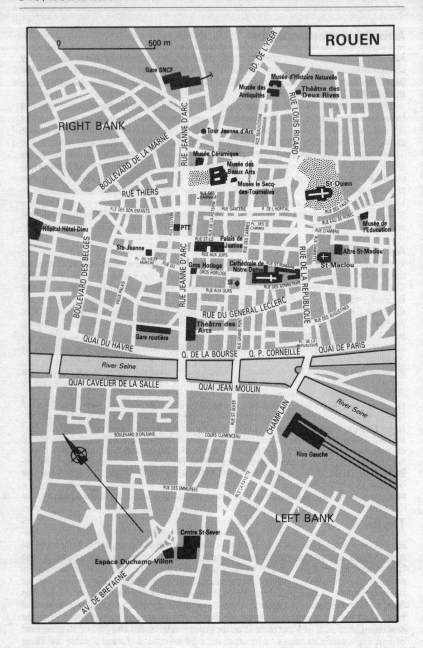

ROUEN

0   500 m

Gare SNCF

BD. DE L'YSER

Musée d'Histoire Naturelle

Musée des
Antiquités

Théâtre des
Deux Rives

RUE LOUIS RICARD

RUE BEAUVOISINE

RIGHT BANK

Tour Jeanne d'Arc

RUE JEANNE D'ARC

BOULEVARD DE LA MARNE

Musée Céramique

Musée des
Beaux Arts

St-Ouen

Musée le Secq-
des-Tournelles

RUE DES VAUX

RUE THIERS

RUE DES
BASNAGE

RUE DES BON ENFANTS

RUE GANTERIE

R. DE L'HOPITAL

RUE EAU DE ROBEC

RUE DES
ANTENNE

Musée de
l'Éducation

Hôpital Hôtel-Dieu

RUE D'AMIENS

RUE ST LO

RUE DE L'EPICERIE

PL. DES
CARMES

PTT

Aître St-Maclou

BOULEVARD DES BELGES

Ste-Jeanne

RUE DES CARMES

Palais de
Justice

St-Maclou

RUE JEANNE D'ARC

RUE AUX JUIFS

PL. DU VIEUX
MARCHE

RUE DU

Gros Horloge

GROS HORLOGE

Cathédrale de
Notre Dame

PL. ST ROMAINE

RUE ST ROMAINE

RUE DE LA RÉPUBLIQUE

PETIT PALAIS

SI

RUE DES BONNETIERS

RUE AUX OURS

RUE DU GENERAL LECLERC

RUE DES AUGUSTINS

Théâtre des
Arts

Gare routière

RUE GRAND PONT

PL. DE LA
RÉPUBLIQUE

QUAI DU HAVRE

Q. DE LA BOURSE

Q. P. CORNEILLE

QUAI DE PARIS

River Seine

QUAI CAVELIER DE LA SALLE

QUAI JEAN MOULIN

River Seine

RUE ST SEVER

CHAMPLAIN

BOULEVARD D'ORLEANS

COURS CLEMENCEAU

Rive Gauche

RUE DE LA FAYETTE

RUE DES EMMURÉES

LEFT BANK

Centre St-Sever

Espace Duchamp-Villon

AV. DE BRETAGNE

From pl du Vieux-Marché, rue du Gros-Horloge leads east towards the cathedral. Just across rue Jeanne-d'Arc you come to the **Gros Horloge** itself. A colourful one-handed clock, it used to be on the adjacent Gothic belfry until it was moved down by popular demand in 1529, so that people could see it better. You can climb the belfry (Easter–Sept 10am–noon & 2–6pm; closed Tues all day and Wed am) and see the surrounding towers and spires arraying themselves in startling density.

The **Cathédrale-de-Notre-Dame** somehow remains at heart the Gothic master-piece that was built in the twelfth and thirteenth centuries, although all kinds of vertical extensions have since been added. The west facade, intricately sculpted like the rest of the exterior, was Monet's subject for a series of studies of changing light, which now hang in the Musée d'Orsay in Paris. Inside, the carvings of the misericords in the choir provide a study of fifteenth-century life – in secular scenes of work and habits along with the usual mythical beasts. Unfortunately the ambulatory, whose recumbent English royals include Richard the Lionheart, is only accessible on guided tours.

St-Ouen, next to the Hôtel de Ville in a large open square to the north, is larger than the cathedral and has far less decoration, so that the Gothic proportions have that instant impact rivalled by nothing built since the Middle Ages. The world which produced it and, nearer the end of the era, the light and grace of St-Maclou, was one of mass death from the plague; the **Aître St-Maclou** (entrance between 184 and 186 rue Martainville) was a cemetery for the victims. It's now the tranquil garden courtyard of the Fine Arts school, but if you examine the one open lower storey of the surrounding buildings you'll discover the original deathly decorations and a mummified cat. In the square outside are several good antique bookshops, and a few art shops.

The museums

Of all Rouen's **museums**, the most interesting and unusual is the ironmongery museum, **Musée Le Secq des Tourelles**. Housed in the old and barely altered church of St-Laurent on rue Jacques-Villon, it is a brilliant collection of wrought-iron objects of all dates and descriptions. The museum is right behind the **Beaux-Arts**, and admission is by the same ticket, as is the Gros Horloge belfry. The Beaux-Arts itself is not very enthralling but it does include works by the Rouennais Géricault, Sisley and Monet in the Impressionist section, Dadaist pictures by Marcel Duchamp, and a collection of portraits by Jacques Émile Blanche (1861–1942) of his contemporaries – Cocteau, Stravinsky, Gide, Valéry, Mallarmé and others (both museums open 10am–noon & 2–6pm; closed all day Tues and Wed am).

Other museums include **Antiquités**, way up north on rue Beauvoisine, which is particularly good on tapestries, and **Ceramics**, a speciality of Rouen, very near the Beaux-Arts. On the corner of rue Eau-de-Robec and rue Ruissel there is, too, one of a new breed of intellectually self-conscious French museums – the **Musée de l'Éducation** (Tues–Sat 1–6pm), which covers the upbringing, education and general influences on children. If you're interested in conservative French ideology it's illuminating. If not, **rue Eau-de-Robec** is a good example of Rouen restoration: a pure, shallow stream makes aesthetic appearances between paved crossings to the front doors of neatly quaint houses, now inhabited by successful antique dealers. In an earlier age these were described by one of Flaubert's characters as a "degraded little Venice".

To understand more of Flaubert himself, and for an insight into the Rouen that he knew, the place to look is not the *Pavillon Flaubert* at Croisset-Canteleu, which like the other two literary museums – the two homes of Pierre Corneille – only prove the point-lessness of the genre. It is, rather, the **Musée Flaubert et de l'Histoire de la Médicine**, at the Hôtel-Dieu Hospital (10am–noon & 2–6pm; closed Mon; ring several times). This stands on the corner of rue de Lecat and rue du Contrat-Social, walkable from the centre (or bus #2a), and it's infinitely more relevant to Flaubert's writings than the manuscript copies and personal mementoes in the Pavillon museum.

Flaubert's father was chief surgeon and director of the medical school, living with his family in this house within the hospital. Even during the cholera epidemic when Gustave was eleven, he and his sister were not stopped from running around the wards or climbing along the garden wall to look into the autopsy lab. Some of the medical exhibits would certainly have been familiar objects to him – a phrenology model, a childbirth demonstrator like a giant ragdoll, and the sets of encyclopaedias.

Eating and drinking

Unlike the hotels, which sometimes have cheaper weekend rates, Rouen's upmarket restaurants tend to charge more over weekends, when families eat out. The greatest concentration of restaurants is in pl du Vieux-Marché, an area in which, perversely, there are few hotels. There's a daily **food market** in the square, while the area just north is full of Tunisian **take-aways, crêperies** and so forth.

Restaurants

Les Abysses, 136 rue Beauvoisine (above *Hôtel Sphynx*). *Plat du jour* 50F; *mese* 74F. An interesting experience; authentic Greek cuisine and fantastical decor.

Des Beaux-Arts, 34 rue Damiette (☎35.70.17.15). On pretty pedestrianised street north of St-Maclou church. Algerian cuisine: couscous or tajine from 50F. Closed Wed.

Le Chope d'Or, 55 rue Jeanne-d'Arc (☎35.71.00.68). Near Post Office. *Plat du jour* 35F; menu from 56.50F. Closes 10pm Mon–Thurs, midnight Fri & Sat; closed Sun. Young crowd.

Flunch, 60 rue des Carmes (☎35.71.81.81). Good self-service, just north of the cathedral.

Pascaline, 5 rue de la Poterne (☎35.89.67.44). North of Palais de Justice, near the flower market, and probably the most reasonable place to sample Rouennais *caneton* duckling. Menus 55F, 75F and 95F.

Le Queen Mary, 1 rue du Cercle (☎35.71.52.09). Off northwest corner of pl du Vieux-Marché. Brasserie upstairs: *plat du jour* 38F, *formule express* 50F, and a more expensive restaurant on the ground floor. Closed Mon. Named after the boat, hence gender; the staff are dressed to sail.

Walsheim, 260 rue Martainville (☎35.98.27.50). Alongside St-Maclou church. Menu from 59F. Austrian: lively atmosphere – and ask to see the two old cider presses.

Bars

Some of Rouen's most agreeable bars are in the maze of streets between rue Thiers and pl du Vieux-Marché. Incoming sailors used to head straight for this area of the city, and the small bars are still there even if the sailors aren't.

Big Ben Pub, 95 rue du Gros-Horloge (☎35.84.44.50). Right under the big clock – hence the name. A restaurant which incorporates an always-packed bar, strictly speaking entered from a side street – 30 rue des Vergetiers. Open noon–2am. Usually as crowded inside as street outside.

La Boite a Bières, 33 rue Cauchoise (☎35.07.76.47). On the corner with rue de Fontenelle, near pl du Vieux-Marché. "*Cool et pas cher*"; good choice of beers.

Au Gres d'Alsace, 13 pl Saint-Marc (☎35.71.55.88). More of a restaurant but, despite the title and the renowned *strudel d'Alsace*, there are "frequent evenings of Irish music played by expert Bretons".

Shopping

Most of the classier **shops** in Rouen are in the pedestrian streets near, and slightly north of, the cathedral. If you are looking for fancy foodstuffs, pâtisseries, chocolates and the like, there are shops on rue Jeanne-d'Arc around and just above rue du Gros-Horloge. For **hypermarkets** and cheap clothes, however – or just a laugh on a rainy day – go south of the river to the modern multi-storey St-Sever complex. Even if your pockets are empty, the long rides on the travelators are free. There's an open-air antiques and bric-a-brac **market** nearby in the pl des Emmurées.

Nightlife and entertainment

As you would expect in a conurbation of 400,000, there's always plenty going on in Rouen, from classical concerts in churches to alternative events in community and commercial centres. An annual handbook, *Le P'tit Normand*, available in all newsagents, is helpful with addresses and telephone numbers. For current events, pick up the free *Cette Semaine à Rouen* from the SI.

Rouen has four **theatres**, which mainly work to winter seasons, and a wide assortment of one-night performances (jazz, rock, dance, satire) is presented at *Espace Duchamp-Villon* (☎35.62.31.31) in pl de la Verrerie, Saint-Sever, south of the river. Further south, the *Exo 7* (militaristic pun) on pl des Chartreux is the centre of Rouen's **rock** scene, while nearer the centre, concerts and other spectacles are held in *Hangar 23* (☎35.70.04.07), a converted warehouse down by the river.

Upstream from Rouen

Upstream from Rouen towards Paris, high cliffs on the north bank of the Seine imitate the coast, looking down on waves of green and scattered river islands. By the time you reach Les Andelys, 25km out of Rouen, you're within 100km of the capital, meaning that accommodation and eating prices tend to be geared towards affluent weekend and day trippers. Large country estates abound in this agreeable countryside, and public transport, too, is minimal – it's assumed any visitor has, if not a residence, then at least a car. However, infrequent buses run from Rouen to Les Andelys, and an expensive but enjoyable boat trip from the POSES DAM (bus #130 from Rouen) goes to Les Andelys and on to Vernon – ask at Rouen SI for details. Trains from Rouen call at Vernon.

Les Andelys

The most dramatic sight anywhere along the Seine has to be Richard the Lionheart's **Château Gaillard**, perched high above LES ANDELYS. Constructed in a position of impregnable power, it looked down over any movement on the river at the frontier of the English king's domains. It was built in less than a year (1196–97) and might have survived intact had Henry IV not ordered its destruction in 1603. As it is, the dominant outline remains and, for once, there's free access at all times. The best route up is the path off rue Richard-Coeur-de-Lion in PETIT ANDELYS.

The cheapest hotel, *Au Soleil Levant* at 2 rue du Général-de-Gaulle (☎32.54.23.55; ②), is well back from the riverfront. The *Normandie* at 1 rue Grande (☎32.54.10.52; ③) has a more attractive Seine-side setting, and a good if not particularly cheap restaurant.

Giverny

Roughly 15km beyond the ancient fortifications of Les Andelys, you come to **Monet's gardens** (complete with waterlily pond) at **GIVERNY**. Monet lived here from 1883 till his death in 1926, and the gardens that he laid out were considered by many of his friends to be his masterpiece. Each month is reflected in a dominant colour, as are all the rooms in the house, which remain as he left them, covered floor to ceiling with his collection of Japanese prints. May and June, when the rhododendrons flower around the lily pond and the wisteria winds over the Japanese bridge in bloom, are the best times to visit. But any month, from spring to autumn, is overwhelmingly beautiful in this arrangement of living shades and shapes – the one drawback being the crowds of camera-happy visitors contending to capture their own impressions of the waterlilies (gardens and house open April–Oct only, Tues–Sun 10am–6pm; 30F for both, 20F for gardens only). Monet enthusiasts may be disappointed by the absence of any of his paintings; to see his renditions of the lilies, you need to go to the Orangerie and Musée d'Orsay in Paris.

You can hire bikes at the gare SNCF in nearby **VERNON**, or catch the bus to the gardens that leaves from the station at 1.15pm (and returns from the car park opposite the gardens at 3.15pm and 5.15pm; 12F return). In Vernon itself, there's a **youth hostel** at 28 av de l'Ile-de-France (☎32.21.20.51), while the busy *Hôtel de France* at 71 av de Rouen (☎32.51.43.83; ②) is a good-value place to eat and sleep, unfortunately closed at weekends and often booked far in advance.

BASSE NORMANDIE

As you head west along the coast of Lower Normandy, a succession of somewhat smug and exclusive resorts – of which only **Honfleur** is especially memorable – is followed first by the beaches where the Allied armies landed in 1944, and then by the wilder, and in some places deserted, shore around the Cotentin peninsula. There are two absolutely unmissable sights – the glorious island abbey of **Mont St-Michel**, and the **Bayeux Tapestry**.

The Norman Riviera

The only section of the Norman coast to have any serious delusions of grandeur is that stretch which lies immediately east of the mouth of the Seine. The scheduled completion of the new bridge across from Le Havre threatens to make such places as Trouville and Deauville altogether too hectic for comfort, but only Honfleur could really be said to have much that it would be a shame to lose.

Honfleur

HONFLEUR, the best-preserved of the old ports of Normandy and the first you come to on the eastern Calvados coast, is a near-perfect seaside town which lacks only a beach. It used to have one, but with the accumulation of silt from the Seine the sea has steadily withdrawn, leaving the eighteenth-century waterfront houses of bd Charles V stranded and a little surreal. The ancient port, however, still functions – the channel to the beautiful *Vieux Bassin* is kept open by regular dredging – and though only pleasure craft now use the moorings in the harbour basin, fishing boats tie up alongside the pier nearby. There is usually fish for sale either directly from the boats or from stands on the pier, still by right run by fishermen's wives. It's all highly picturesque, and very upmarket, but not altogether different to the town that had such appeal to artists in the second half of the nineteenth century.

Though the town has modern suburbs and developments, it's the old centre, around the **bassin**, to which you'll gravitate. At the *bassin*, slate-fronted houses, each of them one or two storeys higher than seems possible, harmonise despite their tottering and ill-matched forms, into a backdrop only rivalled by the **Lieutenance** – the King's Lieutenant's residence – at the harbour entrance. The church of **St-Stephen** nearby is now a **Musée de la Marine** (July–mid-Sept daily 10.30am–noon & 2.30–6pm; rest of year Sat & Sun only same hours; closed Jan–March). Just behind it, two seventeenth-century salt stores house temporary art exhibitions in summer.

Honfleur's artistic past – and its present concentration of galleries and painters – owes most to Eugène Boudin, forerunner of Impressionism. He was born and worked in the town, trained the fifteen-year-old Monet, and was joined for various periods by Pissarro, Renoir and Cézanne. At the same time, Baudelaire paid visits to the town, which was also home to the composer Erik Satie. There's a good selection of Boudin's works in the **Musée Eugène Boudin** – west of the port on pl Erik-Satie – and they're quite appealing here in context, particularly the crayon seascapes. But it's the Dufys, Marquets, Frieszes and above all the Monets that are so impressive (summer Wed–Mon 10am–noon & 2–6pm, winter Mon & Wed–Fri 2.30–5pm, Sat & Sun 10am–noon & 2.30–5pm; closed Jan to mid-Feb).

Admission also gives you access to one of Monet's subjects featured in the museum, the detached belfry of **Ste-Catherine**'s. The church and belfry are built almost entirely of wood – supposedly due to economic restraints after the Hundred Years War. It's a change from the great stone Norman churches and has the added peculiarity of being divided into twin naves, with one balcony running around both. From rue de l'Homme-de-Bois behind you can see yacht masts through the houses overlooking the *bassin* and, in the distance, the huge industrial panorama of Le Havre's docks.

Practicalities

Honfleur's **SI** is on the pl Arthur-Boudin (Mon–Sat 9am–noon & 2–6pm, Sun 10am–noon & 3–6pm; ☎31.89.23.30), in front of the **gare routière** at 33 cours des Fosses. The town is on the direct **bus** route #20 from Caen to Le Havre, with eight buses per day in each direction; the nearest train station is at Pont-l'Évêque, connected by the Lisieux bus, #50 (about a 20-min ride).

It's not quite as easy to live the Bohemian life in Honfleur these days; **accommodation** is far from cheap, with even the most reasonable place, the *Hôtel des Cascades* at 17 pl Thiers (☎31.89.05.83; ④), obliging its guests to eat in the restaurant. There is, however, a **campsite** at the west end of bd Charles V on pl Jean-de-Vienne. Of the many **restaurants** around the port, *Au Gars Normand* is recommended for its bargain-price mussels. Otherwise the best-value food, and liveliest **bar**, can be found on rue Haute, on the way up to the Boudin museum. The bar, *des Amis*, is at no. 35; the restaurants, *Les Frères de la Côte* and *Au P'tit Marayeur*, at nos. 3 and 4; a speciality (mainly Oct–Nov) is *crevettes grises*, tiny shrimp eaten with an unsalty Spanish-style bread, *pain brié*.

Trouville and Deauville

Heading **west along the corniche** from Honfleur, green fields and fruit trees lull the land's edge, and cliffs rise from sandy beaches all the way to Trouville (15km). The **resorts** aren't exactly cheap but they're relatively undeveloped, and if you want to stop along the coast this is the place to do it. The next stretch, from Trouville to Cabourg, is what you might call the **Riviera of Normandy** with Trouville as "Nice" and Deauville as "Cannes", within a stone's throw of each other.

TROUVILLE retains some semblance of a real town, with a constant population and industries other than tourism. But it is still a resort – and has been ever since the imperial jackass Napoléon III started bringing his court here every summer in the 1860s. One of his dukes, looking across the river, saw, instead of marshlands, money – lots of it, in the form of a racetrack. His vision materialised and villas appeared between the racetrack and the sea to become **DEAUVILLE**. Now you can lose money on the horses, cross five streets and lose more in the casino, then lose yourself across 200m of sports and "cure" facilities and private swimming huts before reaching the *planches*, 500m of boardwalk, beyond which rows of primary-coloured parasols obscure the view of the sea. French exclusiveness and self-esteem ooze from every suntanned pore and a visit to the **SI** on pl de la Mairie in Deauville – or by the casino in Trouville – is repaid with some spectacularly revolting brochures (in English).

Practicalities

Deauville and Trouville share their **gare SNCF** and **gare routière**, in between the two towns just south of the marina. As you might imagine, **hotels** are either luxurious or overpriced. The *Café-hôtel des Sports*, 27 rue Gambetta (☎31.88.22.67; closed Sun; ④), behind Deauville's fish market is the least expensive, while the *Charmettes*, 22 rue de la Chapelle (☎31.88.11.67; ⑤), is Trouville's closest equivalent. There are also three **campsites**, two in Trouville and one in Deauville. One possible reason to visit is the **American Film Festival** held in Deauville in the first week of September, when the public are admitted to a wide selection of previews.

Cabourg and Dives

The smaller **resorts west towards Cabourg** are equally crowded and equally short on inexpensive hotels, but they're less snobbish, and there are plenty of campsites. With an eye on the tides you can also walk beneath the **Vaches Noires** cliffs from VILLERS to HOULGATE (4.5km).

At **CABOURG**, the town centre fans out in perfect symmetry fronted by the straightest promenade in France. The resort, contemporary with Deauville, seems to be stuck in the nineteenth century, immobilised by Proust perhaps, who wrote for a while in the **Grand Hôtel** – one of an outrageous ensemble of buildings around the **Jardins du Casino**. There's an SI here with full details on places to stay such as the *Hôtel de Paris*, 39 av de la Mer (☎31.91.31.34; ③). Arriving by **bus** you'll be dropped off at the gardens on av Pasteur. Walking through them and turning right on av de la Mer will take you down to the Jardins du Casino.

By **train** you'll come in at Cabourg's much older neighbour, **DIVES**, which is across the river. It has nothing in common with the aristocratic resort except for its significance to Proust. The land's end church of Balbec in *Du Côté de Chez Swann* is Proust's dream version of **Notre-Dame** in Dives. There's a reasonable **hotel** here, *de la Gare* (☎31.91.24.52; ③), and a **campsite** in between Cabourg and Dives (and a couple of others off the Cabourg–Lisieux road). The town has a lively **Saturday market** around the ancient timbered *halles*; in early August it hosts a puppet festival.

Caen

CAEN, capital and largest city of Basse Normandie, is not a place where you're likely to spend much time. In the months of fighting in 1944, it was devastated. The central feature is a ring of ramparts that no longer have a castle to protect, and, though there are the scattered spires and buttresses of two abbeys and eight old churches, roads and roundabouts fill the wide spaces where pre-war houses stood. Approaches are along thunderous dual-carriageways through industrial suburbs – once an economic success story, currently hammered by unemployment. Even so, the city that nine hundred years ago was the favoured residence of William the Conqueror, remains in parts highly impressive.

Arrival and accommodation

Caen's **SI** is in the town centre, across the street from the church of St-Pierre in the beautiful sixteenth-century Hôtel d'Escoville at 14 pl St-Pierre (June–Sept, Mon–Sat 9am–7pm, Sun 10am–12.30pm & 3–6pm; rest of year Mon 10am–noon & 2–7pm, Tues–Sat 9am–noon & 2–7pm; ☎31.86.27.65). For details of forthcoming events in the city, pick up a copy of their free weekly *Caen Scope*. The **gare SNCF** (☎31.83.50.50) is 1km south of the town centre, with the **gare routière** so close at hand that you can walk directly to it from platform 1.

The *Brittany Ferries* service from Portsmouth, promoted as sailing to Caen, in fact docks at **Ouistreham**, 15km north; see below. Buses from the gare routière connect with each sailing.

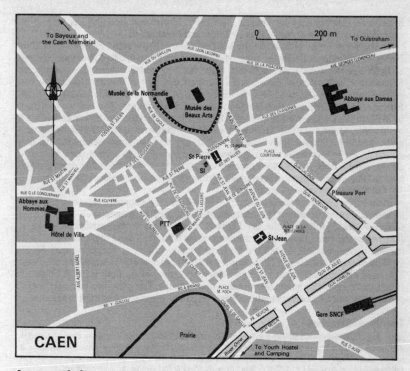

Accommodation

Although Caen has a great number of **hotels** – especially around the gare SNCF – surprisingly few are particularly central. With plenty of dedicated restaurants in town, few hotels other than those listed below bother to provide food. The summer-only **youth hostel** at 68 rue Eustache-Restout, Grace-de-Dieu (☎31.52.19.96) is 2km south of the gare SNCF. Take bus #17 from the town centre (Tour le Roi) or gare SNCF, direction Grace de Dieu, getting off at stop Lycée Fresnil. The municipal **campsite** Camping OMJ (☎31.72.60.92) is nearby, beside the River Orne, on route de Louvigny.

Hôtel-Restaurant Petite Auberge, 17 rue des Équipes-d'Urgence (☎31.86.43.30). On the way into town, just off av du 6-Juin opposite St-Jean church. Restaurant closed Sun pm and Mon. ②

Hôtel-Restaurant Rotonde, 4 place de la Gare (☎31.82.24.25). Facing gare SNCF. Restaurant closed Sat noon and Sun. ②

Hôtel-Restaurant Weekend, 14 quai Vendeuvre (☎31.86.39.95). In town, near the port de Plaisance. Restaurant closed Fri pm and Sun. ②

Hôtel Saint Pierre, 40 bd des Alliés (☎31.86.28.20). In town alongside the Tour le Roi bus stop and pl Courtonne. No restaurant. ③

The town

The **ramparts** of Caen's château are dramatically exposed, having been cleared of their attached medieval houses by aerial bombardment. Within are two museums (10am–noon & 1.30–6pm; closed Tues), devoted to Norman history and Fine Arts. The former is unmemorable but the **Beaux-Arts** is a treat. Amid comprehensive displays – from fifteenth-century Italian and Flemish primitives to contemporary French artists –

it includes masterpieces by Poussin, Géricault, Monet and Bonnard, as well as an exceptional collection of engravings by Dürer and Rembrandt.

To the north of the château lie the buildings of the **University**, founded in 1432 by Henry VI of England. Below the ramparts to the south is the fourteenth-century church of **St-Pierre**, its facade reconstructed since the war which spared the magnificent Renaissance stonework of the apse. To the west and east of the town stand the two great Romanesque constructions, the **Abbaye des Hommes**, with its church of **St-Étienne**, and the **Abbaye des Dames** with **La Trinité** church. The first was founded by William the Conqueror and designed to hold his tomb; the other was commissioned by his wife, Queen Matilda. Hers is more starkly impressive, with a gloomy pillared crypt, wonderful stained glass behind the altar, and odd sculptural details like the fish curled up in the holy-water stoup. It stands at the end of rue des Chanoines. William's abbey, reached via rue St-Pierre, incorporates the town hall (visitable during office hours). The great church, where much of Caen's population took shelter during the 1944 bombardment, towers beside it.

Most of the centre of Caen is taken up with busy new shopping developments and pedestrian precincts, where the cafés are distinguished by names such as *Fast Food Glamour Vault*. Outlets of the big Parisian stores – and of the aristocrats' grocers, *Hédiard*, in the cours des Halles – are here, along with good local rivals. If you're looking for books, records or tickets for local events, call in at the branch of *FNAC* (☎31.39.41.00) in the Centre Paul-Doumer, on the corner of rue Doumer and rue Bras. The main city **market** takes place on Friday, spreading along both sides of Fosse St-Julien, and there's also a Sunday market in pl Courtonne. The **pleasure port,** at the end of the canal which links Caen to the sea, is where most life goes on, at least in summer.

The Caen Memorial

June–Aug 9.30am–10pm, last entry 8.30pm; Sept–May 9.30am–7.30pm, last entry 6pm. Admission 40F, reductions for students, the young and the over-65s, World War II veterans free. The museum is just north of Caen, at the end of av Marshal-Montgomery in the Folie Couvrechef area. It's on bus routes #12 (Mon–Fri) and #14 (Sat & Sun) from the Tour le Roi stop in the centre of town.

The relatively new **Caen Memorial** – "a museum for peace" – stands on a plateau named after General Eisenhower, which ends on a clifftop beneath which the Germans had their HQ in June and July 1944. Funds and material for it came from the US, Britain, Canada, Germany, Poland, Czechoslovakia, the USSR and France. One section in this typically French high-tech, novel-architecture conception deals with the rise of fascism in Germany, another with resistance and collaboration in France. A third charts all the major battles of World War II and finally there's a film documentary on all the conflicts since 1945. Though a touch naive in its historical analysis, it is a great improvement on the older war-glorifying museums of Normandy.

Eating

The town centre offers two major areas for eating. In the attractive pedestrianised **quartier Vaugueux**, cosmopolitan restaurants include the Algerian *Couscous Kouba* and the Italian *Toscanne*, while the streets off rue de Geôle, particularly rue des Croisiers and rue Gemane, house more traditional French restaurants.

Garden Grill, 20 rue de Bernières (☎31.85.43.45). Lunch menu 49F, dinners from 63F. Last orders 11pm, midnight on Sat; closed Sun.

Tangosoa, 7 rue du Vaugueux (☎31.43.87.15). Midday menu 52F; evening menus from 82F. Dishes from Madagascar, Réunion and the Seychelles. Open every day.

Le Verseau, 41 rue Neuve-St-Jean (☎31.86.71.60). Vegetarian; menus at 70F and 90F. Closed Sun & Mon pm, and all day Wed.

Insolite, 16 rue du Vaugueux (☎31.43.83.87). Lovely half-timbered house, open until late, with menus from 95F. Closed Sun pm and Mon.

The D-Day beaches

It is hard now to picture the scene at dawn on **D-Day**, June 6, 1944, when Allied troops landed along the Norman coast between the mouth of the Orne and Les Dunes de Varneville on the Cotentin peninsula. For the most part, these are innocuous beaches backed by gentle dunes, and yet this foothold in Europe was won at the cost of 100,000 soldiers' lives. That the invasion happened here, and not nearer to Germany, was partly due to the failure of the Canadian raid on Dieppe in 1942. The ensuing **Battle of Normandy** killed thousands of civilians and reduced nearly 600 towns and villages to rubble but, within a week of its eventual conclusion, Paris was liberated.

The **beaches** are still often referred to by their wartime codenames: Sword, Juno, Gold, Omaha and Utah. Bits of shrapnel could still be found, and sold, along with packets of sand, in the junketings which surrounded the fortieth-anniversary celebrations. But more substantial traces of the fighting are rare. The most remarkable are the remains of the prefab **Mulberry harbour**, built in Britain while "doodlebugs" blitzed overhead. It now lies where it served its purpose on the seabed and beach at ARROMANCHES-LES-BAINS. At POINTE DU HOC on Omaha beach the cliff heights are still deeply pitted with German bunkers and shell holes. And the church at STE-MÈRE-ÉGLISE from which the US paratrooper dangled during heavy fighting and survived, his parachute entangled in the roof, still stands.

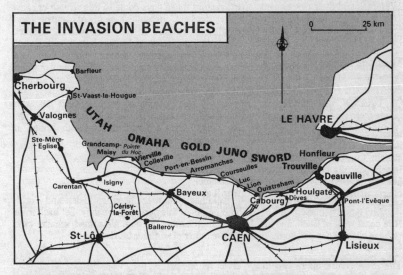

Just about every coastal town has its **war museum**, tending as a rule to shy away from the unbearable reality of war in favour of Boy's Own-style heroics. The wealth of incidental human detail can nonetheless be overpowering. There are also numerous cemeteries, each usually devoted to one specific country, and providing strong reflections of different national characteristics and experiences. The largest of the American cemeteries, at ST-LAURENT, is a disturbing place, with its clinical rows of impersonal crosses resembling nothing so much as a vast corporate balance sheet, and an air of martial exaltation – complete with maps and battle plans – that does little to inspire thoughts of peace; in comparison the German cemetery at ORGLANDES to the west is subdued, sombre and heavy with futility, free of slogans or monuments.

On a completely different tack, the beaches are good for **windsurfing**, too. In theory there are **buses** running all along this coast. **From Bayeux**, #74 goes to Arromanches and Corseulles, #70 to Port-en-Bessin and Vierville, #7 to Isigny. **From Caen**, #30 runs inland to Isigny via Bayeux, #1 to Ouistreham and on to Luc. None of these services, however, except for those linking Caen with the Ouistreham ferries, is reliable – you're better off cycling, or at least trying to hitch while you wait for the bus.

Ouistreham

The small community of **OUISTREHAM**, on the coast 15km north of Caen and connected to it by a fast dual carriageway, gives the impression that it can barely believe its luck at having become a major ferry port. Since *Brittany Ferries* started their service here in 1986, the easternmost of the D-Day resorts has developed an extensive array of reasonable hotels and restaurants. Any number of cafeterias and *brasseries* in the central pl Courbonne are eager to liberate passengers from their spare change, while *Le Chanel*, just around the corner at 79 av Michel-Cabieu (☎31.96.51.69; ③) is just about the best value for both eating and sleeping. Ouistreham's road system, at least in summer, is still not quite up to the task of coping with the volume of traffic, and motorists should allow plenty of time to catch their boats. All services are connected by bus with Caen.

Other bases along the coast

Veterans and their descendants apart, visitors these days come to this stretch of coast for its **seaside**: sand and seafood (best oysters at Courseulles), plenty of campsites and no Deauville chic. Each of the towns, which start more or less within walking distance west of Ouistreham, tends to have one or two quintessential resort hotels, with simple rooms upstairs above a large glass-fronted seaview dining room. **Luc** and **Arromanches** are perhaps the nicest, but the basic experience will be similar wherever you chose to stay. Possibilities include: at LUC-SUR-MER *Beau Rivage* (☎31.96.49.51; ③); at ARROMANCHES, the *Normandie*, pl du 6-Juin (☎31.22.34.32; ④); at GRANDCAMP-MAISY, *du Guesclin*, 4 quai Crampon (☎31.22.64.22; ③), and *Grandcopaise*, 84 rue A-Briand (☎31.22.63.44; ④); at ISIGNY-SUR-MER, *du Commerce*, 5 rue E-Demagny (☎31.22.01.44; ④). There's also a summer-only **youth hostel** at VIERVILLE-SUR-MER, in the Stade Municipal (☎31.22.00.33).

Bayeux

BAYEUX's perfectly preserved medieval ensemble, magnificent cathedral and world-famous tapestry make it one of the high points of this part of Normandy. Set back from the coast west of Caen, and just fifteen minutes away by train, it's a much smaller city, whose charms can pall somewhat with the influx of summer tourists.

The Bayeux Tapestry

Housed in the Centre   Guillaume-le-Conquérant, clearly signposted on rue de Nesmond. Daily mid-May to mid-Sept 9am–7pm; mid-March to mid-May & mid-Sept–mid-Oct 2–6.30pm; rest of year 9.30am–12.30pm & 2–6pm. 20F.

Visits to the world-famous **Bayeux Tapestry** are well planned and highly atmospheric, if somewhat exhausting. You start off with a projection of slides on swathes of canvas hung as sails, before moving on to an almost full-length reproduction of the original, complete with photographic extracts and detailed commentary. Upstairs in the plush theatre there's a film (French and English versions alternate) on the general context and craft of the piece – which you can skip if you feel you know the 1066 story well enough by now. Beyond this – and the souvenirs table – you finally approach the real thing, a seventy-metre strip of linen which recounts the story of the Norman Conquest

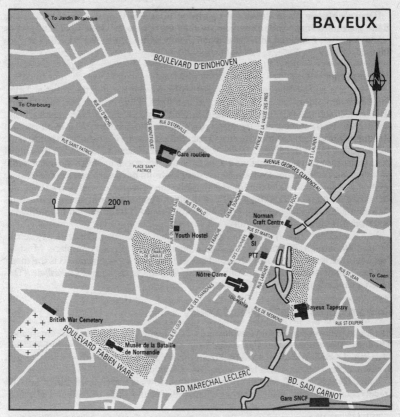

of England. Although embroidered nine centuries ago, the brilliance of its coloured wools has barely faded, and the tale is enlivened throughout with scenes of medieval life, popular fables and mythical beasts. The quality of the draughtsmanship, and the sheer vigour and detail, are stunning. The work is thought to have been done by nuns in England, working under commission from Bishop Odo, William's half-brother, for the inauguration of Bayeux Cathedral in 1077. Claims advanced by an English historian in the last few years that the tapestry was of more recent origin are not accepted by most authorities. He argued, amongst other things, that the "kebabs" grilled in one beach scene show it to be post-Crusades.

Around the town

The **Cathédrale Notre-Dame**, the first home of the tapestry, is a short and very obvious walk away from its latest resting-place. Despite such eighteenth-century vandalism as the monstrous fungoid baldachin that flanks the pulpit, the original Romanesque plan is still intact. The crypt, entirely unaltered, is a beauty, its columns graced with frescoes of angels playing trumpets and bagpipes, looking exhausted by their performance for eternity. Admission tickets for the tapestry are valid for the rather dull **Musée Baron-Gerard** in pl des Tribunaux (☎31.92.14.21) next to the west front of the cathedral in the shadow of the 200-year-old Liberty Tree.

Bayeux's **Musée de la Bataille de Normandie** is a particularly offensive example of the genre which appears to consider its chief purpose to be crude Cold War propaganda. It's a sorry contrast with the tranquil dignity of the British war cemetery across the road.

Practicalities

The **SI** is in a fourteenth-century half-timbered house overhanging the street at 1 rue des Cuisiniers (Mon–Sat 9am–12.30pm & 2–6.30pm, Sun, in summer only 10am–12.30pm & 3–6.30pm; ☎31.92.16.26). The **gare SNCF** (☎31.83.50.50) is 15 minutes' walk away to the west, just outside the "ring road", while the **gare routière** is on rue du Manche, alongside pl St-Patrice (used as a car park, except during Saturday's market).

Something called the *Family House* at 39 rue Général-Dais (☎31.92.15.20) describes itself variously as a youth hostel and a guest house; its prices are over the usual odds and it's a bit self-consciously jolly, but it does have its advocates and people return again and again. The pick of the **hotels** has to be the *Hôtel-Restaurant Notre-Dame*, 44 rue des Cuisiniers (☎31.92.87.24; ④), with its magnificent view of the cathedral. There's a summer-only campsite on bd d'Eindhoven (☎31.92.08.43), on the northern ring road (RN13) near the River Aure.

As for food, the *Family House* serves a filling and good-value dinner at 8pm each evening, for around 60F; non-guests should phone ahead to reserve a place. Most of the **restaurants** are in the pedestrianised rue St-Jean – *La Rapière* at no. 53 is the most popular. If they are all full, try the Chinese and Vietnamese cooking at *La Paillote d'Or*, 6 rue Génas-Duhomme (☎31.21.79.33).

On from Bayeux: Balleroy and Cerisy

Heading **southwest from Bayeux**, towards ST-LO, you pass close to two remarkable buildings: the **Abbaye de Cerisy-la-Forêt** (5km north, midway along) and the **Château de Balleroy** (3km southeast from the same junction). Neither is easy to get to without transport but with a bike or car they shouldn't be missed.

Romanesque CERISY, with its triple tiers of windows and arches, laps light into its cream Caen stone and makes you sigh in wonder at the skills of medieval Norman masons: it is open 9am to 6pm (free visit).

At BALLEROY, you switch to an era when architects ruled over craftsmen. The main street of the village leads straight to the château, masterpiece of the celebrated seventeenth-century architect, François Mansard, and standing like a faultlessly reasoned and dogmatic argument for the power of its owners and their class. Until his recent death, it belonged to the flamboyant American press magnate Malcolm Forbes, pal of Nixon, Ford and Nancy Reagan. His is the enlarged colour photograph sharing the stairwell with Dutch still lifes, and he left his mark on most other aspects of the house, too – only the *salon* remains in its original state of glory, with brilliant portraits of the then royal family by Mignard. Admission (expensive) includes a **hot-air balloon museum,** which was one of Mr Forbes' hobbies (9am–noon & 2–6pm, closed Wed).

Cherbourg and the Cotentin Peninsula

Until *Brittany Ferries* inaugurated its direct services to Brittany, the **Cotentin Peninsula**, in the far west of Normandy hard against the frontier with Brittany, provided many visitors with their first taste of western France. Now that Caen, too, has direct sailings, the port of **Cherbourg** sees only a fraction of the traffic it had twenty years ago, but the peninsula itself remains worth exploring.

Cherbourg

If the murky metropolis of **CHERBOURG** is your port of arrival, best to head straight out and on; the town itself is almost devoid of interest. Napoléon inaugurated the transformation of what had been a rather poor, but perfectly situated, natural harbour into a major transatlantic port, by means of massive artificial breakwaters. An equestrian statue commemorates his boast that in Cherbourg he would "recreate the wonders of Egypt". But there are as yet no pyramids nearer than the Louvre, and if you are waiting for a boat, the best way of filling time is to settle into a café or restaurant or do some last-minute **shopping**. Don't, however, leave your food shopping for the town. Unless you hit the Thursday market, held around rue des Halles, the standard fallback is *Le Continent* hypermarket, a real monster opposite the ferry quay.

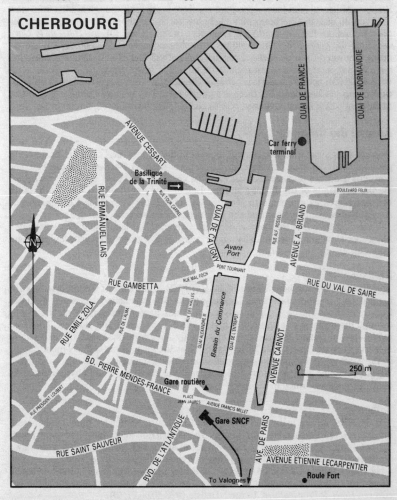

As for walking off lunch, the only area which really encourages a ramble is over by the Basilique de la Trinité and the town beach – an unexpected pleasure, even if you wouldn't dream of swimming from it. Over to the south, you could alternatively climb up to Roule Fort for a view of the whole port; the fort itself contains a museum of the war and liberation.

Practicalities

Cherbourg's **SI** is at 2 quai Alexandre III (June–Aug, Mon–Sat 9am–noon & 2–6pm; rest of year Mon 2–6pm, Tues–Fri 9am–noon & 2–6pm, Sat 9am–noon; ☎33.93.52.02). In summer there's also a tourist information kiosk near the *P & O* terminal, which is on quai de France (☎33.44.20.13). *Brittany Ferries* (☎33.22.38.98) sail from Poole to Cherbourg between May and September. The **gare SNCF** (☎33.57.50.50) is on av François-Miller/pl Jean-Jaurès; the **gare routière** is opposite, though hidden from view.

If you do stay in Cherbourg, it's likely just to be for one night. Among cheap but good **hotels** are the *Divette*, 15 rue Louis XVI (☎33.43.21.04; ②), the *Hôtel de la Gare*, very near the gares SNCF and routière at 10 pl Jean-Jaurès (☎33.43.06.81; ③), and the newly renovated *Croix de Malte*, 5 rue des Halles (☎33.43.19.16; ④). None of these has a restaurant; nice places to eat include the dramatic *Jaurès Brasserie*, 4 pl Jean-Jaurès (☎33.43.06.35), and the waterfront *Briqueville*, 16 quai de Caligny (☎33.20.11.66). You can't **camp** in Cherbourg, but there is a **youth hostel** on av Louis-Lumière, 1.5km east of the gare SNCF (April–Oct only; ☎33.44.26.31). Take bus #1 or #2, direction Diderot.

Around the Cotentin

Once you get away from Cherbourg, the rest of the largely rural Cotentin peninsula is geographically an area of transition. Little ports such as **Barfleur** on the indented northern headland presage the rocky Breton coast, while inland the meadows resemble the farmlands of the Bocage and the Bessin. The long western flank with its flat beaches serves as a prelude to Mont St-Michel; hill towns such as **Coutances** and **Avranches** contain architectural and historical relics associated with the abbey.

Travelling by bus is not easy in northern Cotentin. Nor is hitching: the local *patois* has a special pejorative word for "stranger" used for foreigners, Parisians and southern Cotentins alike.

Barfleur

The pleasant little harbour village of **BARFLEUR**, 25km east of Cherbourg, was the biggest port in Normandy seven centuries ago. The population has since dwindled from nine thousand to six hundred, and fortunes have diminished – most recently through the invasion of a strain of plankton which poisoned all the mussels. The more modest-priced **hotels** include the summer-only *du Phare* (☎33.54.02.07; ③) and *Le Moderne* (1 pl de Gaulle; ☎33.23.12.44; ③). Near the town, about a thirty-minute walk, is the **Gatteville lighthouse**, the tallest in France, guarding the rocks on which William, son and heir of Henry I of England (and recently "outed" by historians as being gay), was drowned in 1120.

Valognes

VALOGNES, on the main road south from Cherbourg, somewhat ludicrously passes itself off as "the Versailles of Normandy". The description might have had some meaning before the war, when the region was full of aristocratic mansions, but now only a scattering of fine old houses remain. There's a cider museum, a little public garden and a big empty square – activated only for the Friday **market**. But it's a quiet, convenient alternative to waiting around in Cherbourg: the best place to spend a night is the ivy-covered *Hôtel de l'Agriculture*, 16 rue L-Delisle (☎33.40.00.21; ③).

La Hague and the Nez de Jobourg

If you go west from Cherbourg to **LA HAGUE**, the northern tip of the peninsula, you'll find wild and isolated countryside where you can lean against the wind, watch waves smashing against rocks or sunbathe in a spring profusion of wild flowers. But the discharges of "low-level" radioactive wastes from the **Cap Hague nuclear reprocessing plant** may discourage you from swimming. In 1980, the Greenpeace vessel, *Rainbow Warrior*, chased a ship bringing spent Japanese fuel into Cherbourg harbour. The *Rainbow Warrior's* crew were arrested, but all charges were dropped when 3000 Cherbourg dockers threatened to strike in their support. In the spring of 1985 the French secret service finally took their revenge on the *Rainbow Warrior*, killing a member of the crew.

From the cape, bracken-covered hills and narrow valleys run west to the cliffs of the Nez de Jobourg, claimed in wild local optimism to be the highest in Europe. On the other side, facing north, PORT RACINE declares itself more plausibly the smallest port in France. **Accommodation** is distinctly lacking in these half-tumbled-down villages. There are **campsites** at OMONVILLE-LA-ROGUE, VAUVILLE and further afield at URVILLE-NACQUEVILLE, which also has the **hotel** *Beaurivage* (☎33.03.52.40; ③).

South of La Hague a great curve of sand – some of it military training ground – takes the land's edge to FLAMANVILLE and another nuclear installation. But the next two sweeps of beach down to CARTARET, with sand dunes like mini-mountain ranges, are probably the best beaches in Normandy if you've got transport and a desire for solitude. There are no resorts, no hotels and just two **campsites** – at LE ROZEL and SURTAINVILLE.

Coutances

The old hill town of **COUTANCES**, 65km south of Cherbourg, confined by its site to just one main street, has on its summit a landmark for all the surrounding countryside, the **Cathédrale de Notre-Dame**. Essentially Gothic, it is still very Norman in its unconventional blending of architectural traditions. The *sons et lumières*, on Sunday evenings and throughout the summer, are for once a true complement to the light stone building. Also illuminated on summer nights (and left open) are the formal fountained **public gardens**.

If you want to stay, the summer-only **SI**, in a new wing behind the Hôtel de Ville in pl Georges-Léclerc (☎33.45.17.79) will be happy to find you a room. The best place, for food as well as beds, is the **hotel** *Relais du Viaduc* (☎33.45.02.68; ②) at the junction of the D7 and D971 to the south of town.

Granville

From Coutances, the D971 runs down to the coast at **GRANVILLE**, the Norman equivalent to Brittany's St-Malo with a history of piracy and a severe citadel, the **haute ville**, guarding the approaches to the bay of Mont St-Michel. Though the most lively town and popular resort in the area, it can't quite match the appeal of its Breton rival. However, if you want to get to the Channel Islands, or to the offshore Îles Chausey whose granite was quarried for the Mont St-Michel, this is where you embark. Most of the shops and hotels, including *Terminus* (☎33.50.02.05; ④) and *de la Gare* (☎33.50.00.05; ④), are in the new town towards the **gare SNCF**. **Bikes** can be hired from *Le Coulant* (av de la Libération) and there's a covered **market** opposite the Mairie on Saturday mornings.

South of Granville the crowded towns and small resorts all compete for views and proximity to Mont St-Michel. ST-JEAN-LE-THOMAS is the first point from which you can walk at low tide across the bay to the abbey. This is not a walk to take on a drunken, or any other, impulse. The tide, as they like to tell you, comes up faster than galloping horses. A special phone line on ☎33.50.02.67 gives advice on timing.

Avranches

AVRANCHES is the nearest large town to Mont St-Michel, and it has always had close connections with the abbey. The Mont's original church was founded by a bishop of Avranches, spurred on by the Archangel Michael who supposedly became so impatient with the lack of progress that he prodded a hole in the bishop's skull (viewable in Avranches' St-Gervais basilica). Robert of Torigny, a subsequent abbot of St-Michel, played host in the town on several occasions to Henry II of England, the most memorable being when Henry was obliged, bare-footed and bare-headed, to do public penance for the murder of Thomas-à-Becket. The arena for this act of contrition was Avranches Cathedral, designed, most inexpertly, by de Torigny himself: it swiftly "crumbled and fell for want of proper support". All that marks the site is a fenced-off platform. A more vivid evocation of the area's medieval splendours comes from the illuminated manuscripts from the Mont, on display in the town **museum** (Easter–Sept 9am–noon & 2–6pm; closed Tues).

Though still some distance from the Mont, Avranches is not a bad place to base yourself. Reasonable **hotels** include *du Jardin des Plantes*, 10 pl Carnot (☎33.58.03.68; ③); *Le Central*, 2–4 rue du Jardin-des-Plantes (☎33.58.16.59; ③), and *Bellevue*, 2 pl du Général-Patton (☎33.58.01.10; ③). **Market** day is Thursday, and piped disco music on the streets goes on all summer. The **gare SNCF** is far below the town centre.

Mont St-Michel

The island of **MONT ST-MICHEL** was once known as the Mount in Peril from the Sea. The Archangel Michael was its vigorous protector, the most militant spirit of the Church Militant, with a marked tendency for leaping from rock to rock in titanic struggles against Paganism and Evil. Today his gilded statue gleams from the very pinnacle, brandishing a sword.

The Mont is barely an island anymore – the causeway that now leads to it is never submerged, and is silting up on both sides. Although it was once a large community – a fortress town – there were never more than forty monks until it was converted into a prison at the time of the Revolution. On its 1000th anniversary, in 1966, the Benedictines were invited to return; today, three nuns and three monks maintain a presence.

The abbey church, known since 1228 as the *Merveille*, is visible from all around the bay, and it becomes more awe-inspiring the closer you get. In Maupassant's words:

> *I reached the huge pile of rocks which bears the little city dominated by the great church. Climbing the steep narrow street, I entered the most wonderful Gothic dwelling ever made for God on this earth, a building as vast as a town, full of low rooms under oppressive ceilings and lofty galleries supported by frail pillars. I entered that gigantic granite jewel, which is as delicate as a piece of lacework, thronged with towers and slender belfries which thrust into the blue sky of day and the black sky of night their strange heads bristling with chimeras, devils, fantastic beasts and monstrous flowers, and which are linked together by carved arches of intricate design.*

The Mont's rock comes to a sharp point just below what is now the transept of **the church**. The Chausey granite was sculpted to match the exact contours of the hill and though space was always limited, the building has grown through the centuries in ever more ingenious uses of geometry. Not everything has lasted; the original church, choir, nave and tower have all collapsed and been superseded. To visit, you must join a **tour**. These run between 9.30am and 5.30pm in summer, when there are some tours in English, listed on a timetable at the entrance; in winter, French-only tours are held between 9.30 and 11.45am and 1.45 and 5pm. The visit lasts for about an hour, and the guides are experts, pointing out among much other useful information that the current unadorned state of the stone walls around you is a far cry from the way the medieval monastery would have looked, brightly painted and festooned with tapestries. There's a church service at 12.15pm every day, with a nursery provided below for children under eight years old.

The base of Mont St-Michel is a jumble of overpriced postcard and souvenir shops and restaurants, maintaining the great tradition of separating pilgrims from their money. The most famous **hotel**, *La Mère Poulard* (☎33.60.14.04; ③), uses the time-honoured legend of its fluffy omelettes, as enjoyed by Leon Trotsky and Margaret Thatcher, to justify extortionate charges. Higher up the one twisting street, however, prices fall to surprisingly realistic levels. The *Hôtel Croix Blanche* (☎33.60.14.04; ②) has some very inexpensive rooms and an exceptional restaurant.

The nearest **gare SNCF** is at **PONTORSON**, 6km south, where you can hire a bike from the station or take an expensive bus to the Mont. The best budget **hotel** is the *de France* at 2 rue de Rennes (☎33.60.29.17; ②), next to the railway crossing; it has a late and youthful bar, with pool and a good jukebox. Pontorson is otherwise eminently forgettable.

FROM THE SEINE TO THE BOCAGE: INLAND NORMANDY

It's hard to pin down specific highlights in **inland Normandy**. The pleasures lie in the feel of particular landscapes – the lush meadows and orchards, the classic half-timbered houses and farm buildings, and the rivers and forests of the Norman countryside. **Gastronomy** is of course another major motivation – the cheeses, creams, apple and pear brandies and ciders for which the region is famous. The **Pays d'Auge** country south of Lisieux and the **Vire Valley** to the west are the best for this. The **Suisse Normande** is canoeing and rock-climbing country, and there are endless good walks in the stretch along the southern border of the province designated as the **Parc Naturel Régional de Normandie-Maine**. Of the towns, **Conches** is the most charming. **Falaise** has William the Conqueror as a constant fall-back attraction, and **Lisieux** has religious myths and a spectacularly revolting basilica to back them up.

South of the Seine

Heading south from the Seine you can follow the RISLE river from the estuary just east of Honfleur, or the EURE and its tributaries from upstream of Rouen. Between the two stretches the long featureless **Neubourg plain**. The lowest major crossing point over the Risle is at **PONT-AUDEMER**, where medieval houses lean out at alarming angles over the criss-crossing roads, rivers and canals. From here, perfect cycling roads lined with timbered farmhouses follow the river south.

Bec-Hellouin

The size and tranquil ethos of the **ABBAYE DE BEC-HELLOUIN**, just before BRIONNE, give a monastic feel to the whole valley. Bells echo across the water and white-robed monks go soberly about their business. From the eleventh century onwards, the abbey was one of the most important centres of intellectual learning in the Christian world; the philosopher Anselm was abbot here before becoming archbishop of Canterbury in 1093. Due to the Revolution, most of the monastery buildings are recent – the monks only returned in 1948 – but there are some survivals and appealing clusters of stone ruins. Recent archbishops of Canterbury have maintained tradition by coming here on retreat. Tours are at 10am, 11am, 3pm, 3.45pm, 4.30pm, 5.15pm; Sunday and holidays at 9.30am, noon, 2.45pm, 3.30pm, 4.15pm and 6pm; closed Tues In the rather cute adjacent town of **BEC-HELLOUIN** is a **vintage car museum** and a distinctly un-ascetic **restaurant**, the wonderful *Auberge de l'Abbaye*.

Brionne and Beaumont-le-Roger

BRIONNE, which is on the Rouen–Lisieux rail line, is a small town with large regional **markets** on Thursday and Sunday. The fish hall is on the left bank, the rest by the church on the right bank. Above them both, with panoramic views, is a **donjon**. If you decide to **stay**, the *Auberge du Vieux Donjon* (☎32.44.80.62; ④) on the marketplace is good, though pricey.

The Charentonne river joins the Risle near SERQUIGNY. The town is also the meeting point of rail lines and main roads and the banks are clogged with fuming industrial conglomerations. But 7km upstream, at **BEAUMONT-LE-ROGER**, you are back in pastoral tranquillity. The ruins of a thirteenth-century priory church slowly crumble to the ground, the slow restoration of one or two arches unable to keep pace. In the village, little happens beyond the hammering of the church bell next door to the abbey by a nodding musketeer. Just across the Risle from here, on the D25 near LE VAL-ST-MARTIN, huge stables are spread across an absurdly sylvan setting, and horses are available for hire.

The next riverside village, **LA FERRIÈRE-SUR-RISLE**, has an especially beautiful church and old covered market hall. Paddocks and meadows lead down to the river and two small and inviting **hotels**, the *Croissant* (☎32.30.70.13; ③) and *Vieux-Marché* (☎32.30.70.69; ③).

Conches-en-Ouche

Fourteen kilometres east of La Ferrière across the wild and open woodland of the **Forêt de Conches**, **CONCHES-EN-OUCHE** is every Norman's favourite heartland town, standing above the Rouloir river on an abrupt and narrow spur. At the highest point, in the middle of a row of medieval houses, is the church of **Ste-Foy**, its windows a stunning sequence of Renaissance stained glass. Behind are the gardens of the **Hôtel de Ville**, where a robust, if anatomically odd, stone boar gazes proudly out over a spectacular view. Next to that, you can scramble up the slippery steps of the ruined twelfth-century **castle**. Conches is given a certain edge over other towns with equal lists of historic relics, by the pieces of modern sculpture that seem to lie around every other corner.

Across the main street from the castle is a long **park**, with parallel avenues of trees, a large ornamental lake and fountain, and the **hotel** *Grand Mare* (☎32.30.23.30; ③), which serves up very pricey gastronomic dinners; the *Cygne* (☎32.30.20.60; ②), at the north end of town, has some more affordable rooms but not such a good menu; or there's a **municipal campsite** (☎32.30.22.49). On Thursday the whole town is taken up by a **market**.

Evreux

If you're heading south to Conches from Rouen, you follow first the Eure river, and then its tributary the Iton, passing through **EVREUX**, capital of the Eure *département*. It's hardly an exciting place, but an afternoon's wander in the vicinity of the cathedral – a minor classic with its flamboyant exterior decoration and original fourteenth-century windows – and the ramparts alongside the Iton riverbank is pleasant. Most of the cheaper hotels in the town tend to shut during August. An evening is better spent in Conches or at **PACY-SUR-EURE**, where the *Hôtel de l'Étape* (☎32.36.12.77; ③) nestles at the water's edge.

Lisieux and the Pays d'Auge

The rolling hills and green twisting valleys of the **Pays d'Auge**, which stretches south of the cathedral town of **Lisieux**, are scattered with magnificent half-timbered manor houses. The pastures here are the lushest in the province, their produce the world-famous cheeses of Camembert, Livarot and Pont L'Évêque. And beside them are acres of orchards, yielding the best of Norman ciders, both apple and pear (*poiré*), as well as Calvados apple brandy.

Lisieux

LISIEUX, 35 minutes by train from Caen, is the main town of the Pays d'Auge, and a good place to get to know its cheeses and ciders, at the large **street market** on Wednesday and Saturday. Most people, however, come to Lisieux as a place of pilgrimage based around the cult of Ste-Thérèse, the most popular French spiritual figure of the last hundred years. Passivity, self-effacement and masochism were her trademarks, and she is honoured by the grotesquely gaudy and gigantic **Basilique de Ste-Thérèse**, completed in 1954 on a slope to the southwest of the town centre. Huge mosaics of her face decorate the nave, and every night at 9.30pm as part of a stunningly tasteless (and expensive) laser show, her face is simultaneously projected on every column in the church. The faithful can ride on a white, flag-bedecked fairground train around the holiest sites, which include the infinitely restrained and sober **Cathédrale St-Pierre.**

Practicalities

Lisieux's **SI**, at 11 rue d'Alençon (left out of the station, then right), is the best place to gather information on the rural areas further inland. The quantity of pilgrims means that Lisieux is full of reasonably priced places to stay. Try the **hotels** *de la Terrasse*, 25 av Ste-Thérèse (☎31.62.17.65; ③), *Condorcet*, 26 rue Condorcet (☎31.62.00.02; ③), or *de l'Avenue*, 4 av Ste-Thérèse (☎31.62.08.37; ③). There is also a large **campsite**, but campers would probably be better off somewhere more rural nearby, such as Livarot or Orbec.

Into the Pays d'Auge

Though the tourist authorities responsible for the pays d'Auge have laid out a **Route de Fromage** and a **Route du Cidre** – the manor houses of BEUVRON-EN-AUGE on the Cider route, and MONTPINÇON and LISORES on the Cheese route, are well worth finding – you won't be missing out if you don't follow these itineraries. For really good solid Norman cooking this is the perfect area to look out for *Fermes Auberges*, working farms which welcome paying visitors to share their meals. Local *Syndicats* can provide copious lists of these and of local producers from whom you can buy your cheese and booze.

Pont l'Évêque to Livarot

There was little left after the war of the old **PONT-L'ÉVÊQUE**, the northernmost of the Pays d'Auge towns. Since then it has become such a turmoil of major roads that it's no place to stay. **CORMEILLES** on the other hand is a tiny (Friday) market centre, with several half-timbered restaurants to its credit. **ORBEC** lies just a few miles along a pleasant valley from the source of its river, the Orbiquet. It consists of little more than the main road of classic Norman houses with patterned tiles and bricks between the beams, ending in the huge tower of Notre-Dame church.

The centre of the cheese country is the old town of **LIVAROT**, with the **hotel** and restaurant *du Vivier* (☎31.63.50.29; ③) in its centre. The main attraction is the **Conservatoire du Fromage**, a small-scale working cheese factory. For a few francs, you can see Camembert, Pont L'Évêque and Livarot cheeses at every stage of their production.

At **ST-PIERRE-SUR-DIVES**, the medieval market hall has been converted into a slightly academic annexe to the Livarot cheese museum. It's an impressive building, though, almost rivalling the Romanesque-Gothic church (whose windows depict the history of the town). A large **market** still takes place every Monday in the adjacent square.

Vimoutiers and Camembert

VIMOUTIERS, due south of Livarot, contains another **cheese museum**, this one specialising in labels – the cheeses underneath are mostly polystyrene. At the tiny village of **CAMEMBERT**, nearby, Marie Harel developed the original soft Camambert cheese early in the nineteenth century, promoting it with a skilful campaign which even involved sending free samples to Napoléon. The **hotels** *Soleil d'Or*, 16 pl Mackau (☎33.39.07.15; ②), and *Couronne*, 9 rue du 8-Mai (☎33.39.03.04; ③), are good, economic places to stay, and there is also a **campsite**. Just outside the village is the **Escale du Vitou**, a lake, beautifully sited, with everything you need for windsurfing, swimming and horseback riding.

Along the **valley of the Vie** south of Vimoutiers runs the D26 – a route that takes in many of the best features of Normandy, lined along the way with old ramshackle barns and farm buildings. Faded orange clay crumbles out from between the weathered wooden beams of these flower-covered beauties. At the intersection with the D13 is the **hotel-restaurant** *Relais St-Pierre*. For any sensible kid this should be a principal holiday target – mini 125cc motorcycles and three-wheelers are hired out to hurtle around a course of bales of hay. There's additional lodging available at a farm a little further north, and several further **hotels** at **GACÉ**.

Falaise

William the Conqueror, or William the Bastard as he is more commonly known over here, was born in **FALAISE**, 40km southwest of Lisieux. His mother, Arlette, a laundress, was spotted by his father, Duke Robert of Normandy, at the washing-place below the château. She was a shrewd woman, scorning secrecy in her eventual assignation by riding publicly through the main entrance to meet him. During her pregnancy, she is said to have dreamed of bearing a mighty tree that cast its shade over Normandy and England.

Both the keep of the **castle**, and the **Fontaine d'Arlette** on the riverside beneath it, still exist, though so heavily restored as to be scarcely worth the ten-minute tour. The town itself was devastated in the war. The struggle to close the "Falaise Gap" in August 1944 was the climax of the Battle of Normandy, as the Allied armies sought to encircle the Germans and cut off their retreat. By the time the Canadians entered the town on August 17, they could no longer tell where the roads had been and had to bulldoze a new 4-metre strip straight through the middle.

Practicalities

The SI can be found at 32 rue Georges-Clemenceau, the main Caen–Argentan road, which is also the (rather noisy) location of most of Falise's few **hotels**, such as the Poste at no. 38 (☎31.90.13.14; ②). The **campsite**, *Camping du Château* (☎31.90.16.55), next to Arlette's fountain and the municipal swimming pool, is in a much better location.

The Suisse Normande

The area known as the **"Suisse Normande"** lies roughly 25km south of Caen, along the gorge of the River Orne, between Thury-Harcourt and Putanges. The name is a little far-fetched – there are certainly no mountains – but it is quite distinctive with cliffs and crags and wooded hills at every turn. The energetic race along the Orne in canoes and kayaks, the less so are content with pedalos or a bizarre species of inflatable rubber tractor, while high above climbers dangle from thin ropes clawing at the sheer rockface. For mere walkers the Orne can be frustrating: footpaths along the river are few and far between and often entirely overgrown.

The Suisse Normande is usually approached from CAEN or FALAISE and contrasts dramatically with the prairie-like expanse of wheatfields en route. On wheels, the best access is via the D235 from Caen (signed to Falaise then right through Ifs). The *Bus Verts* #34 will take you to THURY-HARCOURT or CLÉCY on its way to Flers, and there are occasional special summer train excursions from Caen.

Thury-Harcourt

At **THURY-HARCOURT**, the **SI** on pl St-Sauveur can suggest walks, rides and *gîtes d'étape* throughout the Suisse Normande; *SIVOM* at 15 rue de Condé hires canoes. Unfortunately there's no very affordable hotel in the town, but there are a couple of **campsites** – *Vallée du Traspy* (☎31.79.61.80) and *Camping du Bord de l'Orne* (June–Sept only; ☎31.79.70.78). In summer, the public park allows access to the riverside.

Clécy

CLÉCY is a slightly better bet for finding a room, although its visitors outnumber its residents in peak season. The *logis* in town, *Au Site*, isn't as good value as the *Alpes Normands* (☎31.69.45.39; ③), a short way along the road which faces the church. For advice on accommodation and the wide variety of holiday activities available in Clécy, the SI is tucked in behind the church. The village centre is about a kilometre above the river at PONT DU VEY. On the way down, in the Parc des Loisirs, is a **Musée du Chemin de Fer Miniature** (June to mid-Sept 10am–noon & 2–7pm), featuring a model railway which may appeal to children. At the bridge is a restored watermill, run as a restaurant and hotel. The riverbank continues in a brief splurge of restaurants, takeaways and snackbars as far as the 100-pitch **campsite**.

Pont d'Ouilly

If you're planning on walking, or cycling, one good central spot to base yourself is **PONT D'OUILLY**, at the point where the main road from Vire to Falaise crosses the river. It's a small town, with a few basic shops, an old covered market hall and a promenade (with bar) slightly upstream alongside the weir; you can walk along the riverside down to Le Mesnil Villement. As well as the **campsite** overlooking the river, there's an attractive **hotel**, the *du Commerce* (☎31.69.80.16; ②), with cheap rooms and wonderful food, in a dining room appropriately filled with stuffed animals. About a kilometre north, the much more upmarket *Auberge St-Christophe* (☎31.69.81.23; ⑤) stands in a beautiful setting on the right bank of the Orne, covered with ivy and geraniums and opposite a roofless and now overgrown Art Deco factory. A *Grand Pardon du Ste-Roche* takes place along the river on the third Sunday in August.

A short distance south of Pont-d'Ouilly is the **Roche d'Oëtre**, a high rock with a tremendous view, not over the Orne but into the deep and totally wooded gorge of the Rouvre. The river widens soon afterwards into the **Lac du Rabodanges**, formed by the many-arched Rabodanges Dam. It's a popular spot where people practise every watersport, and with a **campsite**, *Les Retours*, perfectly situated between the dam and the bridge on D121.

The Bocage

The region centering on **St-Lô**, west of Caen and just south of the Cotentin, is known as the *bocage* from a word which refers to a type of cultivated countryside common in the west of France, in which fields are cut by tight hedgerows rooted into walls of earth well over a metre high. An effective form of smallhold farming, at least in pre-industrial days, it also proved to be a perfect system of anti-tank barricades. When the Allied troops tried to advance through the region in 1944 it was almost impenetrable – certainly bearing no resemblance to the East Anglian plains where they had trained. The war here was hand-to-hand, inch-by-inch slaughter; the destruction of villages often wholesale.

St-Lô

The city of **ST-LÔ** is still known as the "Capital of the Ruins". Memorial sites are everywhere and what is new speaks as tellingly of the destruction as the ruins that have been preserved. In the main square, the gate of the old prison commemorates Resistance members executed by the Nazis, people deported east to the concentration camps and soldiers killed in action; when the bombardment of St-Lô was at its fiercest, the Germans refused to take any measures to protect the prisoners and the gate was all that survived. Samuel Beckett was here during the battle and after, working for the Irish Red Cross as interpreter, driver and provision-seeker – for such things as rat poison for the maternity hospitals. He said he took away with him a "time-honoured conception of humanity in ruins".

All the trees in the city are the same height, all planted to replace the battle's mutilated stumps. But the most visible – and brilliant – reconstruction is the **Cathédrale de Notre-Dame**. Its main body, with a strange southward-veering nave, has been conventionally repaired and rebuilt. But the shattered west front and the base of the collapsed north tower have been joined by a startling sheer wall of icy green stone that makes no attempt to mask the destruction.

In contrast to such memories, a lighthouse-like 1950s folly spirals to nowhere on the main square; should you feel the urge to climb its stairway, ask at the Mairie opposite. More compelling, around behind the Mairie, is a **Musée des Beaux-Arts** (summer 10.30am–noon & 2.30–6pm; winter 10.30am–noon & 2.30–5pm; closed all day Tues & Sun am; free). This is full of treasures: a Boudin sunset; a Lurçat tapestry of his dog Nadir and the Pirates; works by Corot, van Loo, Moreau; a Léger watercolour; a fine series of unfaded sixteenth-century Flemish tapestries on the lives of two peasants, and sad bombardment relics of the town.

Practicalities

St-Lô makes an interesting pause but it's virtually abandoned at night. Most of the hotels, restaurants and bars are by the river and **gare SNCF**. The *Terminus*, 3 av Briovère (☎33.05.08.60; ②), one of a row of modern, slightly expensive riverside hotels, is a *Logis de France* with a good 60F menu. You can also get a good deal for rooms, assuming you get through the owners' eccentric selection process, at the *des Remparts*, 3 rue des Prés (☎33.57.08.06; ②). The **SI** is just off the central square at 2 rue Havin, and the **gare routière** is on the rue des 80e and 136e, a short way south.

The Vire Valley

Once St-Lô was taken in the Battle of Normandy, the armies speedily moved on for their next confrontation. The **Vire Valley**, trailing south from St-Lô, saw little action – and indeed its towns and villages have rarely been touched by any historic or cultural mainstream. The motivation in coming to this landscape of rolling hills and occasional gorges is essentially to consume the region's cider, calvados – much of it bootleg – fruit pastries and sausages made from pigs' intestines.

From St-Lô to Tessy

The best section of the valley is south of St-Lô through the Roches de Ham to TESSY-SUR-VIRE. The **Roches de Ham** are a pair of sheer rocky promontories high above the river. Though promoted as "viewing tables", the pleasure lies as much in the walk up, through lanes lined with blackberries, hazelnuts and rich orchards. Downstream from the Roches, and a good place to stop for the night, is **LA CHAPELLE-SUR-VIRE**. Its church, towering majestically above the river, has been an object of pilgrimage since the twelfth century. Next to the bridge on the lower road is the *Auberge de la Chapelle* (☎33.56.32.83; ②), a good but rather expensive restaurant that has a few cheap **rooms**.

An alternative base for the Roches, over to the east, is **TORIGNY-SUR-VIRE**, which was the base of the Grimaldi family before they attained princeliness in Monaco. A spacious country town, it boasts a few grand buildings and an attractive **campsite**, *Camping du Lac* (☎33.56.91.74). At **TESSY-SUR-VIRE** there's little to see other than the river itself, though the town has a luxurious **campsite**, along with a couple of **hotels** and Wednesday **market**.

Vire

VIRE itself is worth visiting specifically for the food. The town is best known for its dreaded *andouille* sausages, but you can gorge yourself instead on salmon trout fresh from the river, accompanied by local *poiré*. The biggest treats are to be found at the *Hôtel des Voyageurs* (☎31.68.01.16; ③), at the bottom of av de la Gare, by the station. For around 68F you can have a sublime and almost interminable meal in opulent surroundings. Good **restaurants** are to be found, too, at the more central *Hôtel de France*, 4 rue Aignaux (☎31.68.00.35; ④), and *Hôtel du Cheval Blanc*, 2 pl du 6-Juin-1944 (☎31.68.00.21; ④). The one problem is what to do when you're not eating; the only action in Vire is at the Friday **market**, again obsessively dedicated to food.

For some exercise (and you'll need it), head 6km south along D76 to **Lac de la Dathée**. Set in open country, the lake is circled by footpaths or can be crossed by hired sailboat or wind-surfer (contact the *Maison des Jeunes et de la Culture*, 1 rue des Halles, Vire; ☎31.68.08.04).

Villedieu-les-Poêles

VILLEDIEU-LES-POÊLES – literally "City of God the Frying Pans" – is a lively though touristy place, 28km west of Vire. Copper souvenirs and kitchen utensils gleam from its rows of shops, and the **SI** (on pl des Costils) has lists of dozens of local *ateliers* for more direct purchases and details of the copperwork museum. All of which seems a bit over-enthusiastic though there is more authentic interest at the **Fonderie Cornille-Havard** at 13 rue du Pont-Chignon, one of the twelve remaining bell foundries in Europe. Work here is only part time, but it's always open to visits during the week (summer 8am–noon & 2–6pm; winter 1.30–5.30pm only) and you may find the forge lit. If you're charmed into staying, there's a **campsite** by the river, and excellent basic food and accommodation at the *Hôtel de Paris* on route de Paris (☎33.61.00.66; ③).

Southern Normandy

In addition to the two more northerly routes across Normandy described above, motorists heading west from Paris towards Brittany may choose to get just a brief taste of the province by following the line of the N12 through Alençon and Domfront.

Alençon

ALENÇON, a fair-sized and busy town, is known for its traditional – and now pretty much defunct – lace-making industry. The **Musée des Beaux-Arts et de la Dentelle** (closed Mon) is housed in a former Jesuit school and has all the best trappings of a modern museum. The highly informative history of lacemaking, with examples of numerous different techniques can, however, be tedious for anyone not already fascinated by the subject. It also contains an unexpected collection of gruesome Cambodian artefacts, spears and lances, tiger skulls and elephants' feet, gathered by a "militant socialist" French governor at the turn of the century. The paintings in the adjoining *Beaux-Arts* section are nondescript, except for a few works by Courbet and Géricault. Wandering around the town might take you to Ste-Thérèse's birthplace on rue St-Blaise, just in front of the gare routière – if, that is, you haven't had a surfeit of the saint at Lisieux. The **Château des Ducs**, the old town castle close by the museum, looks impressive but doesn't encourage visitors. It is a prison, and people in Alençon have nightmarish memories of its use by the Gestapo during the war.

If you want to stay – and the town has good shops and cafés – the main concentration of **hotels** is around the SNCF station on the northeast side of town. The two *logis*, *L'Industrie*, 20 pl Général-de-Gaulle (☎33.29.06.51; ③), and the *Grand Hôtel de la Gare*, 50 av Wilson (☎33.29.03.93; ③), are very decent and have fixed-price menus for around 60F. There's a **youth hostel** out on the D204 towards Colombiers, at 1 rue de la Paix, DAMIGNI (☎33.29.00.48). If you're interested in **horseback riding** – along the Orne – the *Association Départmentale de Tourisme Equestre et d'Equitation de Loisir de l'Orne* has its headquarters in Alençon at 60 Grand-Rue. They can also tell you about the various stud farms open to the public – another speciality of this area.

The **Forêt d'Ecouves**, north of Alençon and inaccessible by public transport, is a dense mixture of spruce, pine, oak and beech, unfortunately a favoured spot of the military – and in autumn of deerhunters, too. You can usually ramble along the cool paths, happening on wild mushrooms and even the odd wild boar. The *gîte d'étape*, on the D26 near LES RAGOTIÈRES on the edge nearest Alençon, is an ideal spot from which to explore the forest (contact the local *gîte* office at 60 rue St-Blaise in Alençon; ☎33.32.09.00).

Carrouges

One alternative base at the western end of the Forêt d'Ecouves is the hill town of **CARROUGES**, which offers two appealing small hotels – the *Hôtel du Nord* (☎33.27.20.14; ③) or *St-Pierre* (☎33.27.20.02; ③).

Carrouges' **château** (10.30am–noon & 2–6.30pm), is a fine old-style castle set in spacious grounds at the foot of the hill. Its two highlights are a superb restored brick staircase, and a room in which hang portraits of fourteen successive generations of the Le Veneur family, an extraordinary illustration of the processes of heredity.

Bagnoles-de-l'Orne

West of Carrouges, the spa town of **BAGNOLES-DE-L'ORNE** is quite unlike anywhere else in this part of the world. The monied sick and convalescent come from all over France to its thermal baths. Business is so good they maintain a reservations office next to the Pompidou Centre in Paris. The layout is formal and spacious, centring on a lake with gardens where horse-drawn *calèches* take the clients to an enormous casino, and with so many visitors to keep entertained, and spending money, there are innumerable cultural events of a restrained and stressless nature. Whether you'd actually want to spend time in Bagnoles, though, depends on your disposable income as well as health. The innumerable **hotels** are expensive and sedate places, in which it's possible to be too late for dinner at 7pm and locked out altogether at 9pm, and the **campsite** is rather forlorn. You may do better at Bagnoles' less exclusive sister town of TESSÉ-LA-MADELEINE. **Restaurants** in both towns are reasonable; the *de la Terrasse* in Bagnoles is well tried and popular.

As the baths only open for the summer season in April, Bagnoles in winter is a gloomy and almost entirely closed place. However, away from its main roads, the surrounding **Forêt des Andaines** is pleasant, with scattered and unspoiled villages such as JUVIGNY and ST-MICHEL.

Domfront

The road west through the Forêt des Andaines from Bagnoles, the D335 and then D908, climbs above the lush woodlands and progressively narrows to a hog's back before entering **DOMFRONT**. Even less happens here than at Bagnoles, but it has the edge on countryside. A public park, near the **gare SNCF**, leads up to **castle ruins** on an isolated rock. Eleanor of Aquitaine was born in the castle in October 1162, and Thomas-à-Becket came to stay for Christmas in 1166, saying mass in the nearby church of Notre-Dame-sur-l'Eau. The views from the gardens surrounding the mangled keep are spectacular, including a very graphic panorama of the ascent you've made. Domfront is a useful stopover; the *Hôtel de la Poste* on the hill top (☎33.38.51.00; ②) is very reasonable, and there are others down by the station. Beware though that the **campsite** has only ten spaces.

The **SI** at Domfront on rue Fossés-Plissons can provide details of the neighbouring forests, the **Forêt de Lande-Pourrie** and **Forêt de Mortain**. The eleventh-century vestiges of **LONLAY L'ABBAYE**, 9km out on D22 towards TINCHEBRAY, is one destination. Another is the **Fosse d'Arthur** to the west, a waterfall plunging into deep grottoes, and one of the many claimants to King Arthur's death scene. At the town of **MORTAIN** there are **waterfalls** and a tiny chapel on a high rock from which the neighbouring province of Maine spreads before you.

St-Symphorien-des-Monts

If you're heading down into Brittany, a last Norman stop, 7km southeast of ST-HILAIRE-DU-HARCOUET, is **ST-SYMPHORIEN-DES-MONTS**, where the park of the now non-existent château is run as a **wildlife sanctuary**. Contented-looking beasts, like yaks and bisons, and threatened domestic animals, graze in semi-liberty in fields and woods around a lake inhabited by swans and flamingos. In order to attract French visitors, there are wolves, too. Admission (mid-March to mid-Nov only daily 9am–8pm) is expensive but worth it.

travel details

Trains

Through services to Paris connect with all ferries at Dieppe, Le Havre and Cherbourg: if you're doing this it's easiest to buy a combined rail-ferry-rail ticket from your point of departure.

From Dieppe 5 daily to Rouen (45min); 5 daily to Paris-St-Lazare (2hr 15min).

From Le Havre at least hourly to Rouen (45min) and Paris (2hr).

From Rouen 8 daily to Caen (2hr 15min); at least hourly to Fécamp (1hr) and to Paris-St-Lazare (1hr 15min).

From Caen at least hourly to Paris-St-Lazare (2hr 15min); 2 daily to Rennes (2hr) via St-Lô (1hr), Coutances (1hr 15min) and Pontorson, near Mont St-Michel (1hr 30min); 9 daily to Le Mans (2hr) and Tours (2hr 30min); hourly to Cherbourg (1hr to 1hr 30min).

Buses

From Dieppe 5 daily to Paris (2hr 15min); 1 daily to Fécamp (1hr 30min).

From Rouen hourly to Le Havre (2hr 45min); 2 daily to Dieppe (1hr 45min), Fécamp (2hr 30min) and Lisieux (2hr 30min).

From Caen 3 daily to Le Havre (3hr), via Cabourg, Deauville and Honfleur; 4 daily to Fécamp (1hr 30min).

From Lisieux 5 daily to Honfleur (45min).

Ferries

From Dieppe *Sealink* (☎35.82.24.87) 4 daily to Newhaven (4hr).

From Le Havre *P&O* (☎35.21.36.50) 2 daily to Portsmouth (5hr 30min); *Irish Ferries* (☎35.26.57.26) daily to Cork (21hr) and to Rosslare (21hr).

From Caen (Ouistreham) *Brittany Ferries* 1 or 2 daily to Portsmouth (6hr)

From Cherbourg *Sealink* (☎33.20.43.38) 1 daytime crossing to Portsmouth (4hr 45min), another to Weymouth (4hr 30min); *Truckline*

Ferries to Poole (4hr 30min); *P&O* (☎33.44.20.13), 3 daily to Portsmouth (4hr 45min); *Irish Continental* (☎33.44.28.96) to Rosslare (17hr) .

From Granville to Jersey, Guernsey and Chausey Islands. *Vedettes Armoricaines*, 12 rue Clemenceau, ☎33.50.77.45. *Vedettes Blanches*, 1 rue Le Campion, ☎33.50.16.36. *Jolie France*, gare maritime, ☎33.50.31.81.

From Carteret to Jersey. *Vedettes Armoricaines*, gare maritime, ☎33.04.60.60. *Vedettes Blanches*, gare maritime, ☎33.53.81.17.

Air

From Cherbourg *Aurigny-Air-Service* to Jersey, Guernsey and Aurigny; *Air Camelot* to Bournemouth, Bristol and Exeter. Both from Maupertus Airport, ☎33.22.91.32.

CHAPTER FIVE

BRITTANY

No one area – and certainly no one city – in **Brittany** encapsulates the province's character. That lies in its people and in its geographical unity. For generations Bretons risked their lives fishing and trading on the violent seas or struggling with the arid soil of the interior. And this toughness and resilience is tinged with Celtic culture: mystical, musical, sometimes morbid and defeatist, sometimes vital and inspired.

Though archaeologically Brittany is one of the richest sites in the world – the alignments at Carnac rival Stonehenge – its first appearance in history is as the quasi-mythical "Little Britain" of Arthurian legend. In the days when to travel by sea was safer and easier than by land, it was intimately connected with "Great Britain" across the water, and settlements such as St-Malo, St-Pol and Quimper were founded by Welsh and Irish missionary "saints" whose names are not to be found in any official breviary. Never as expansionist or prosperous as Normandy, Brittany nonetheless remained independent until the sixteenth century. Its last ruler, Duchess Anne, managed to protect Breton **autonomy** only through marriage to two consecutive French monarchs. After her death, in 1532, François I moved in, taking her daughter and lands, and sealing the union with an act supposedly enshrining certain privileges. These included a veto over taxes by the local *parlement* and the people's right to be tried, or conscripted to fight, only in their province. The successive violations of this treaty by Paris, and subsequent revolts, form the core of Breton history since the Middle Ages.

Maintained often as a near colony, Bretons have seen their language steadily eradicated, and the interior severely depopulated through lack of centralised aid. But people still tend to treat France as a separate country, even if few actively support Breton **nationalism** (which it's a criminal offence to advocate) much beyond putting **Breizh** (the Breton for Brittany) stickers on their cars. There have also been many successes in reviving the language. The recent economic resurgence, helped partly by summer tourism, has largely been due to local initiatives. Ignoring Paris pressures, **Brittany Ferries** has re-established an old trading link, carrying Breton produce as well as passengers across to Britain and Ireland. At the same time a Celtic artistic identity has consciously been revived. At local festivals, and above all the **Interceltic festival** at Lorient in August, traditional Breton music, poetry and dance are given great prominence and fellow Celts (Welsh-speakers will be understood) are treated as comrades.

For most visitors, it is **the Breton coast** that is the dominant feature. After the Côte d'Azur, this is now the most popular summer resort area in France – for both French and foreign tourists. The attractions are obvious: warm white sand beaches, towering cliffs, rock formations and offshore islands and islets, and everywhere the stone *dolmen* and *menhir* monuments of a prehistoric past. The most frequented areas are the **Côte d'Émeraude**, around **St-Malo**, and the **Morbihan coast** below **Auray** and **Vannes**. Accommodation and campsites here are plentiful, if pushed to their limits from mid-June to the end of August, and for all the crowds there are resorts as enticing as any in

---

HOTEL ROOM PRICES

For a fuller explanation of these price codes, see the box on p.28 of *Basics*.

① Under 100F   ② 100–130F   ③ 130–180F   ④ 180–230F   ⑤ 230–300F

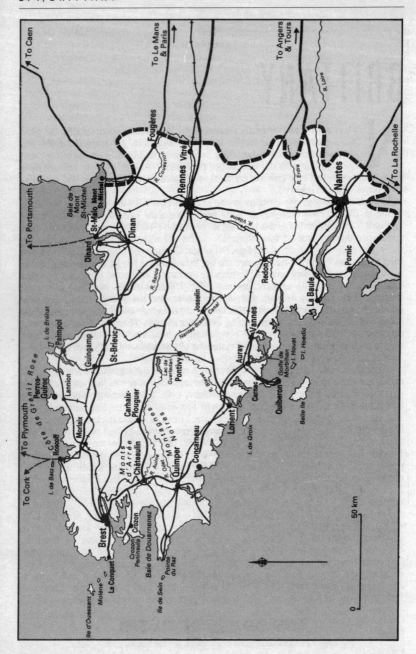

the country. Over in **southern Finistère** ("land's end") and along the **Côte de Granit Rose** in the north you may have to do more planning. This is true, too, if you come to Brittany out of season, when many of the coastal resorts close down completely.

Whenever you come, don't leave Brittany without visiting at least one of its scores of **islands** (such as the **Île de Bréhat**), or taking in cities like **Quimper** or **Morlaix**, testimony (like the parish *enclos* of Finistère) to the riches of the medieval duchy. Allow time, too, to leave the coast and explore **the interior**, particularly the western country around the **Monts d'Arées**. Here you pay for the solitude with very sketchy transport and few hotels, but Brittany is one of the few areas of France where *camping sauvage* (not in campsites) is tolerated. There are sporadic *gîtes*, boats for hire on the **Nantes–Brest canal**, and hitching is relatively easy.

Finally, a note on the **Pardons**, pilgrimage-festivals commemorating local saints, which guidebooks (and tourist offices) tend to promote as spectacles. These are not, unlike most French festivals, phoney affairs kept alive for tourists, but deeply serious and rather gloomy religious occasions. If you're looking for traditional Breton fun, and you can't make the Lorient festival (or the smaller *Quinzaine Celtique* at Nantes in June/July), look out for gatherings organised by **Celtic folklore groups** – *Circles* or *Bagadou*.

THE NORTH COAST AND RENNES

Medieval Brittany was obliged vigorously to defend its independence against potential incursors, and today its eastern approaches remain guarded by the heavily fortified citadels of **Fougères** and **Vitré**. Along the coast, too, from Mont St-Michel, which lies only just across the border in Normandy, are some of Brittany's finest old towns. One of the most spectacular introductions to the province is that which greets ferry passengers from Portsmouth; the **Rance River**, guarded by magnificently preserved **St-Malo** on its estuary, and **Dinan** 20km upstream. To the west stretches a varied coastline culminating in one of the most seductive of the islands, the **Île de Bréhat**, and the colourful chaos of the **Côte de Granit Rose**. Inland all roads curl eventually to **Rennes**, the Breton capital, which lies a short way north of the legendary forest of **Brocéliande** (Paimpont), the location of the Arthurian tales.

A BRETON GLOSSARY

Estimates of the number of Breton-speakers range from 400,000 to 800,000. You may well encounter it spoken as a first, day-to-day language by the very old, and by the young in parts of Finistère and the Morbihan. Learning Breton is not really a viable prospect for visitors without a grounding in Welsh, Gaelic or some other Celtic language. However, as you travel through the province, it's interesting to note the roots of Breton place names, many of which have a simple meaning in the language. Below are some of the most common:

Aber	estuary	*Hen*	old	*Mor*	sea
Bihan	little	*Hir*	long	*Nevez*	new
Bran	hill	*Inis*	island	*Parc*	field
Braz	big	*Ker*	town or house	*Penn*	end, head
Creach	height	*Koz*	old	*Plou*	parish
Cromlech	stone circle	*Lan*	church	*Pors*	port, farmyard
Dol	table	*Lann*	heath	*Roch*	stone
Dolmen	stone table	*Lech*	flat stone	*Ster*	river
Du	black	*Mario*	dead	*Stivel*	fountain, spring
Gavre	goat	*Men*	stone	*Trez*	sand, beach
Goat	forest	*Menez*	mountain	*Trou*	valley
Goaz	stream	*Menhir*	long stone	*Ty*	house
Guen	white	*Meur*	big	*Wrach*	witch

The frontier towns: Dol, Fougères and Vitré

If you're entering Brittany by road, from Normandy, Maine or Le Mans, you're likely to pass through Dol-de-Bretagne, Fougères, or close to Vitré – all, at one time or another, heavily fortified strategic sites.

Dol-de-Bretagne

DOL-DE-BRETAGNE, thirty kilometres west of Mont St-Michel, is the first Breton town. All approaches to it are guarded by the former island of **Mont Dol**, now eight rather marshy kilometres in from the sea. This abrupt granite outcrop, looking mountainous beyond its size on such a flat plain, was the legendary site of a battle between the Archangel Michael and the Devil. Various fancifully named indentations in the rock, such as "the Devil's Claw", testify to the savagery of their encounter, which as usual the Devil lost. The site has been occupied since prehistoric times – flint implements have been unearthed alongside the bones of mammoths, sabre-toothed tigers, and even rhinoceri. Later on, it appears to have been used for worship by the Druids, before becoming, like Mont St-Michel, an island monastery, all traces of which have long vanished. A plaque proclaims that visiting the small chapel on top earns a Papal Indulgence. The climb is pleasant, too, a steep footpath winding up among the chestnuts and beeches to a solitary bar.

Close to the **cathedral**, with its strange squat and square tiled towers, is a **Musée d'Histoire et d'Art Populaire** (summer only, daily 9.30am–6pm). Though a bit full of posed waxworks it has two rooms of astonishing wooden bits and pieces rescued in assorted states of decay from churches, often equally rotting, all over Brittany. These carvings and statues, some still brightly polychromed with their crust of eggy paint, range from the thirteenth to the nineteenth centuries.

There is not a great deal more to Dol, for visitors anyway. The commercial part of town is lively without being too modern; the *Katédral* bar, between the church and museum, is worth some of your time. And there's one very reasonable **hotel**, the *Bretagne*, 17 pl Chateaubriand (☎99.48.02.03; ②).

Cancale

Along the coast north of Dol, the pinnacle of Mont St-Michel is clearly visible from every vantage point, of which the most spectacular is the **Pointe du Grouin**, a perilous and windy height which also overlooks the bird sanctuary of the **Îles des Landes** to the east. Just south of the *pointe,* and less than 15km from St-Malo across the peninsula, **CANCALE** should not be missed by those who attribute magical properties to **oysters**. In the old church of **St-Méen** at the top of the hill, a small **Musée des Arts et Traditions Populaires** (July–Aug Mon 3.30–7.30pm, Tues–Sun 10.30am–12.30pm & 3.30–7.30pm; rest of year Mon–Sat 3.30–7.30pm) documents the town's obsession with meticulous precision. Cancale oysters were found in the camps of Julius Caesar, taken daily to Versailles for Louis XIV, and even accompanied Napoléon on the march to Moscow.

From the rue des Parcs next to the jetty of the port, you can, at low tide, see the *parcs* where the oysters are grown. The rocks of the cliff behind are streaked and shiny like mother-of-pearl; underfoot the beach is littered with countless generations of empty shells. The port area is lined with upmarket glass-fronted hotels and restaurants – of the **hotels** the *Continentale* (☎99.89.60.16; ④) and the *Emeraude* (☎99.89.61.76; ④) on quai Thomas are among the best value. The restaurants without exception specialise in every kind of seafood, but unfortunately oysters here are no less expensive than on a Paris boulevard.

Fougères

FOUGÈRES, which lies on the main Caen–Rennes road, has a topography impossible to grasp from a map; streets that look a few metres long turn out to be precipitous plunges down the escarpments of its split-levelled site, lanes collapse into flights of steps. The **castle** is built well below the level of the main part of town, on a low spit of land that separates, and is towered over by, two mighty rock faces. Its massive and seemingly impregnable bulk is protected by great curtain walls growing out of the rock, and encircled by a hacked-out moat full of weirs and waterfalls – none of which prevented its repeated capture by such medieval adventurers as du Guesclin. It is, however, eighteenth-century Fougères that is always featured in the summer-night theatrical performances at the château, based on the book that immortalised the town, Balzac's *The Chouans*. It tells, in rampant best-seller vein, the story of the counter-revolutionary *Chouan* rebellion in Brittany during the early 1790s, and makes great play of the strange layout of the town.

Within the castle, the focus is more prosaic. Footwear, to this day the main industry of the town, is presented in a **museum** included in the **château tours** (on the hour, March–Oct 9–11am & 2–6pm, closed Tues except in summer; weekends only in Nov; Sun only in Feb). The best approach to the castle is from **pl des Arbres** beside St-Léonard's church off the main street of the old fortified town. The formal terraces give way to the water meadows of the River Nançon which you can cross beside medieval houses still standing on the riverbank. Alternatively, take the longer route down rue Nationale, where you'll pass, at no. 51, the **musée de La Villéon**, an Impressionist who painted numerous lovely Breton landscapes (July–Aug daily 9am–7pm; April–June & Sept Sat & Sun 9am–7pm).

The **Forêt de Fougères**, a short way out on the D177 towards Vire (see p.269), is one of the most enjoyable in the province. The beech woods are spacious and light, with various megaliths and trails of old stones scattered in among the chestnut and spruce. It's quite a contrast to their normal bleak and windswept haunts to see dolmens sporting themselves in such verdant surroundings. If you have time, walk through the forest as far as **Le Chatellier**, a village set high in thick woods.

Practicalities

Fougères's **SI** at 1 pl Aristide-Briand (☎99.94.12.20) provides copious information on all aspects of the town and local countryside. The *Grand Hôtel des Voyageurs* at 10 pl Gambetta (☎99.99.08.20; ③) is a particularly nice place to stay, with a superb restaurant (closed Sat and the second half of Aug); the *Hôtel Balzac* at no. 15 in the pedestrian rue Nationale (☎99.99.42.46; ③) is also pleasant. There is a **youth hostel** at 11 rue Beaumanoir (☎99.99.22.06). A surprising alternative to French cooking is to be found in the excellent **Iranian restaurant** *Persépolis*, at 70 rue de la Pinterie, in front of the main gate of the castle, which serves an unusual but very appetising melange of Greek, Persian and Breton dishes.

St-Aubin-du-Cormier

Halfway between Fougères and Rennes, **St-Aubin-du-Cormier** has a sad tale to tell concerning English, French and Breton relations. A small monument in a field marks the battlesite where, in 1488, the forces of the Duke of Brittany were defeated by the French army. Many of the Breton soldiers had dressed in the English colours, a black cross on white silk, to scare the French into believing that the duke had extensive English reinforcements. The victorious French were told to spare all prisoners except the English; and so the hapless Bretons were massacred. St-Aubin's castle was then demolished – just one sheer wall survives, with a fireplace visible midway up. Should you wish to stop overnight there's a very cheap **hotel**, the *du Bretagne*, 68 rue de l'Ecu (☎99.39.10.22; ③), a wonderful rambling old building serving very good food.

Vitré

VITRE, just north of the Le Mans–Rennes motorway, rivals Dinan as the best-preserved medieval town in Brittany. Its walls are not quite complete, but what lies outside them has hardly changed. The **castle** has sharp-pointed towers with slate-grey roofs in best fairy-tale fashion though, unfortunately, the municipal offices and museum of shells, birds, bugs and local history inside are not exactly thrilling. Hours are 10am to 12.15pm and 1.30 to 6pm; closed Tuesday in winter.

Vitré is a market town rather than an industrial centre, with its principal **market** held on Mondays in the square in front of Notre-Dame church. The old city is full of twisting streets of half-timbered houses, a good proportion of which are bars. **Rue Beaudrairie** in particular has a fine selection. An unusual visual treat, if you happen to be using the **post office**, is its modern stained-glass window behind the counter.

Practicalities

Most of the **hotels** are around the station, where the ramparts have disappeared and the town imperceptibly blends into its newer sectors. This is a cheap as well as a pleasant place to stay; the *Petit-Billot*, pl du Général-Leclerc (☎99.75.02.10; ③), and *Chêne-Vert*, pl de la Gare (☎99.75.00.58; ③), are both good value, and the *Hôtel du Château*, 5 rue Rallon (☎99.74.58.59; closed Sun out of season; ②), on a quiet road just below the castle, is a delight. The nearby Escalier restaurant is also good value.

St-Malo and the Rance Estuary

ST-MALO, walled and built with the same grey granite stone as Mont St-Michel presents its best face to the sea; if you are not planning to arrive by Brittany Ferries from Portsmouth, you may well want to consider the ten-minute shuttle across the river Rance from Dinard as an alternative. The city was originally a fortified island at the mouth of the Rance, controlling not only the estuary but the open sea beyond. For centuries its pirate-mariners forced English ships passing up the Channel to pay tribute. They brought wealth from further afield, too. Jacques Cartier, who colonised Canada, lived in and sailed from St-Malo, and the Argentinian name for the Falklands, *Las Malvinas*, derives from the islands' first French colonists, *Les Malouins*.

These days, St-Malo is more visited than anywhere in Brittany – and not just for the use of its ferry terminal. The *intra muros* streets of the **old citadelle** are a unique experience: at times they can be sombre and grim (particularly beneath grey skies), but in high summer or at sunset they become light and almost unreal. Much of what you see today has been lovingly and precisely rebuilt stone by stone; eighty percent of the city was destroyed in August 1944.

Arrival and accommodation

Coming into St-Malo by bus or train, the old city is concealed by modern suburbs and dock-side industry almost until you're in it. Approaches by road are somewhat dismal; the signposts seem designed to confuse and all the roads seem to end on tramlined docksides. Lost and bewildered cars circle the port like seagulls.

The helpful **SI** (July–Sept Mon–Sat 8.30am–8pm, Sun 10am–noon & 2–6.30pm; rest of year Mon–Sat 9am–noon & 2–6.30pm; ☎99.56.64.48) is housed in a single-storey building beside Bassin Duguay-Trouin in the **Port des Yachts**. Officially, the **gare**

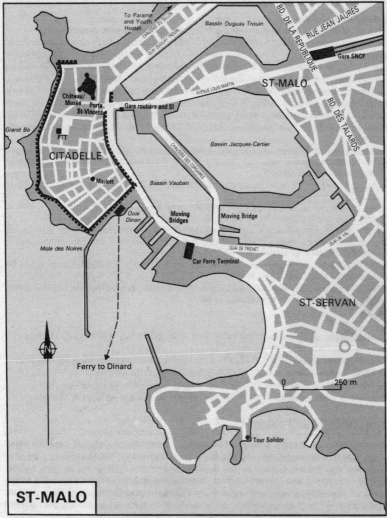

ST-MALO

routière (☎99.40.83.33) is right next to it, but most buses, whether local or long distance, coincide also with trains at the **gare SNCF** (☎99.65.50.50), 2km out from the citadelle on pl Hermine and not convenient for either the old town nor the ferry (take care if you're planning a tight connection).

As well as the *Brittany Ferries* sailings to Portsmouth, from the *Gare Maritime du Naye* (☎99.82.41.41), St-Malo is busy with other **boats**. You'll find details of the various services to the **Channel Islands** in the "Travel Details" at the end of this chapter, and there also regular ten-minute crossings to Dinard in summer, and pleasure cruises around the estuary.

Bicycles can be hired from *Cycles Diazo*, 47 quai Duguay-Trouin (☎99.40.31.63), or *Cycles Nicole*, 11 rue Robert-Schumann (☎99.56.11.06).

Hotels and hostels

Though St-Malo is said to have over 100 **hotels**, in high season it needs every one of them. Motorists intending to stay the night before catching a ferry should make reservations well in advance; if you don't have one, you do best to find a hotel somewhere else along the coast. You pay a premium for the privilege of staying within the walls of the citadelle; the many places in the station area tend to be cheaper.

There's also a **youth hostel** in the *Centre des Rencontres International*, 37 rue de Père-Umbricht (☎99.40.29.80). This is 2km northeast of the gare SNCF, on the main street of suburban Paramé, a short way back from the beach on bus routes #1, #2 or #5.

Hôtel Arrivée, 52 bd de la République (☎99.56.30.78). Very near the station. Open all year. No restaurant. ③

Hôtel-Restaurant Auberge au Gai Bec, 4 rue des Lauriers (☎99.40.82.16). The best bargain within the citadelle walls, some way from the Grande Porte near pl aux Herbes. Open all year. Menu from 85F (closed Mon). ②

Hôtel Le Croiseur, 2 pl de la Poissonerie (☎99.40.80.40). Inside the walls, near the Grande Porte. Open all year. No restaurant.③

Hôtel Europe, 44 bd de la République (☎99.56.13.42). Year-round cheap rooms in a genuinely friendly hotel near the station. No restaurant. ②

Hôtel-Restaurant Pomme d'Or, 4 pl du Poids-du-Roi (☎99.40.90.24). Just inside the citadelle near the ramparts – take a sharp left after entering through the Grande Porte. The patronne has an eccentric predeliction for animals. ④

Hôtel-Restaurant Porte St-Pierre, 2 pl du Guet (☎99.40.91.27). Comfortable place within the walls, near the small Porte St-Pierre. ⑤

Hôtel-Restaurant Terminus, 8 bd des Talards (☎99.56.14.38). Reasonable hotel near the station, with an inexpensive restaurant. Open all year. ③

Camping

St-Malo's four municipal campsites also tend to be full in July and August, and you may have to travel inland to find space.

La Cité d'Aleth, St-Servan (☎99.81.60.91). On the headland southwest of St-Malo. Open all year.

Les Ilôts, Rotheneuf (☎99.56.98.72). June–Sept only. Inland, to the northeast.

Le Nicet, Rotheneuf (☎99.40.26.32). April–Sept only. On the coast by Pointe de Nicet.

Les Nielles, Paramé (☎99.40.26.35). June–Sept only. On the beach at the plage du Minhic.

The citadelle and suburbs

The **citadelle** of St-Malo, very much the prime destination for visitors, was for many years joined to the mainland only by a long, single causeway, before the original line of the coast was hidden forever by the construction of the harbour basin. Although its streets of restored seventeenth- and eighteenth-century houses can be crowded to the point of absurdity in summer, away from the more popular thoroughfares random exploration is fun. You can surface to the sunlight on the ramparts to enjoy wonderful views all round, especially to the west as the sun sets over the sea.

Besides the prominent Grande Porte, the main gate of the citadelle is the **Porte St-Vincent**. The town **museum** in the castle to the right (daily 10am–noon & 2–6pm; closed Tues out of season) is something of a hymn of praise to the "prodigious prosperity" enjoyed by St-Malo during its days of piracy, colonialism and slave trading. Climbing the 169 steps of the castle keep, you pass a fascinating mixture of maps, diagrams and exhibits – chilling handbills from the Nazi occupation, accounts of the "infernal machine" used by the English to blow up the port in 1693, and savage four-pronged *chaussetrappes*, thrown by pirates onto the decks of ships being boarded to immobilise their crews.

It is possible to pass under the ramparts at a couple of points and on to the open shore, where a huge beach stretches away beyond the rather featureless resort-suburb of Paramé. When the tide is low, the most popular walk is out to the small island of **Grand-Bé** – sometimes you even need to queue to get on to the short causeway. Solemn warnings are posted of the dangers of attempting to return from the island when the tide has risen too far – if you're caught there, there you have to stay. The island "sight" is the tomb of the nineteenth-century writer-politician Chateaubriand (1768–1848), who was described by Marx as "the most classic incarnation of French vanité . . . the false profundity, Byzantine exaggeration, emotional coquetry . . . a never-before-seen mishmash of lies". Suitably enough he features heavily on all the tourist brochures, which – with no apparent irony – extol his "modesty" in choosing so "isolated" a burial spot.

St-Servan, within walking distance along the corniche to the south of the citadelle, was the city's original settlement, converted to Christianity by St-Malou (or Maclou) in the sixth century; later, in the twelfth century, they moved to the impregnable island we now call St-Malo. The town curves round several small inlets and beaches to face the tidal power dam across the river. Its **Tour Solidor**, three linked towers built in 1382, is open all year for 90-minute guided visits to a museum of clipper ships (summer daily 10am–noon & 2–6pm; Oct–March 2–6pm only, closed Tues).

Eating and shopping

Intra-muros St-Malo boasts even more **restaurants** than hotels, with a long crescent lining the inside of the ramparts to the left of the Grande Porte. Prices are probably higher than anywhere else in Brittany, however, inflated by the numbers of ferry-passengers having last-night blow-outs.

For last-minute **shopping**, the citadelle contains a few specialists, but buying in any quantity is best done in *Le Continent* **hypermarket** on the southwest outskirts of the town. There are markets in both St-Malo (intra muros) and St-Servan on Tuesdays and Fridays, and in Paramé on Wednesdays and Saturdays.

A new **festival** has been conceived for St-Malo. The **Étonnants Voyageurs** ("Amazing Travellers") takes place each May, and is dedicated to the film and literature of travel and adventure.

Restaurants

Astrolabe, 8 rue des Cordiers (☎99.40.36.82). Near Grande Porte. Menus from 98F. Serves until late. Open all year. Closed all day Mon, and Tues lunchtime.

Borsalino, 18 rue des Cordiers (☎99.40.24.22). Good Italian food, with menus from 45F. Open until late, all year round. Closed Sun.

Brick, 5 rue Jacques-Cartier (☎99.40.18.88). Near Porte St-Vincent; formerly the *Étoile de Mer*, and still maintaining the same tradition of good-value seafood. Menus from 70F. Serves until late, open all year but closed Wed.

Duchesse Anne, 5/7 pl Guy-la-Chambre (☎99.40.85.33). Almost opposite Porte St-Vincent. The best known of St-Malo's upmarket restaurants, which continues to work hard to keep up its reputation – and its prices. Menus from 220F. Closed Wed.

Dinard

The road **from St-Malo to Dinard** crosses the estuary along the top of the world's first **tidal power dam** which, unfortunately, failed to set a non-nuclear example to the rest of the province. You can see how it works in a half-hour visit (8.30am–9pm) from the entrance on the west bank, just downstream from the lock. If you're catching the bus between St-Malo (St-Vincent gate) and Dinard, get off at LE RICHARDAIS for the dam, and at *Gallic* for the centre of Dinard.

The tastes of the affluent nineteenth-century English can be blamed for the metamorphosis of **DINARD** from a simple fishing village into something along the lines of a

Côte d'Azur resort, with its casino, spacious shaded villas and social calendar of regattas and ballet. It's an expensive and not especially welcoming place to stay – the only hotel charging even slightly under 200F for a room is the *Hôtel-Restaurant Printania*, on the sea front near the Port de Plaisance at 5 avenue George-V (☎99.46.43.07; ④). There are, however, some unofficial **youth hostels**, of which the best is the Centre International du Port Blanc, rue du Sergent-Boulanger (April–Oct; ☎99.46.10.32). **Campsites** include the "municipal" *Port Blanc*, also near the Plage du Port-Blanc on rue de Sergent-Boulanger (☎99.46.10.74), and the four-star *Prieuré* (☎99.46.20.04), a little way back from the beach on av de la Vicomte, about 2km up the Rance from the Pointe du Moulinet.

If you just want to kill a little time in Dinard, a scenic coastal path, the *Promenade du Clair de Lune* goes up from the estuary beach, the *plage du Prieuré*, over the tiny port, and up to Pointe du Moulinet for views over to St-Malo. You can continue around the point to another beach, by the casino, and on around more rocky outcrops to a secluded stretch at neighbouring ST-ENOGAT. **Boat tickets**, either to St-Malo or, for a real pleasure trip, down the Rance to Dinan, are on sale in Dinard at 27 av George-V.

Dinan

The wonderful citadel of **DINAN** has preserved almost intact its three-kilometre encirclement of protective masonry, with street upon colourful street of late medieval houses. Like St-Malo, it's best seen when arriving by boat up the river Rance. Behind the houses on the left bank quay where the boats tie up, a steep and cobbled street with fields and bramble thickets on either side climbs up to the thirteenth-century ramparts, partly hidden by trees.

For all its slightly unreal perfection, Dinan is not excessively overrun with tourists. There are no very vital museums; the monument is the town itself, and time is most easily spent wandering from *crêperie* to café, admiring the overhanging houses along the way. Unfortunately, you can only walk along one small stretch of the ramparts, from the Jardin Anglais behind St-Sauveur church to a point just short of Tour Sillon overlooking the river. You can however get a good general overview from the **Tour de l'Horloge**, which dates from the end of the fifteenth century (July–Sept daily 10.45am– 1.15pm & 3–6pm).

The fourteenth-century keep which once protected the town's southern approach now houses a small local history museum. Together with the ancient **Tour Coëtgen**, this is known as the Château de Duchesse Anne (summer daily 10am–6.30pm; rest of year closed Tues). On the lower floor of the Tour Coëtgen a group of stone fifteenth-century notables looks for all the world like some kind of medieval time capsule, about to de-petrify at any moment.

St-Sauveur church, very much the town's focus, is a real mixture of ages with a Romanesque porch and an eighteenth-century steeple. Even its nine Gothic chapels feature five different patterns of vaulting in no symmetrical order; the most complex pair, in the centre, would make any spider proud. A cenotaph contains the heart of Bertrand du Guesclin, the fourteenth-century Breton warrior (and later Constable of France) who fought and won a single combat with the English knight Thomas of Canterbury, in what is now pl du Guesclin, to settle the outcome of the siege of Dinan in 1364. Relics of his life and battles are scattered all over Brittany and Normandy; in death, he spread himself between four separate burial places for four different parts of his body (the French kings restricted themselves to three burial sites). North of the church, rue du Jerzual leads down to the gate of the same name and on down (as rue du Petit-Fort) to the port and a majestic old bridge over the Rance, lined with artisans' shops and restaurants.

On the last weekend in September or the first weekend in October – check with the SI – the **Fête des Remparts** is celebrated with medieval-style jousting, banquets, fairs and processions, culminating in an immense fireworks display. There's a **market** every Thursday in the places du Champ and du Guesclin (the original medieval fairground).

Practicalities

Dinan's **SI** is in the beautiful sixteenth-century Hôtel Kératry at 6 rue de l'Horloge (☎96.39.75.40). The Art Deco **gare SNCF** (☎96.39.22.29) and the **gare routière** (☎96.39.21.05) are in pl du 11-novembre, ten minutes' walk outside the main entrance of the walled town. In summer, **boats** sail from the port downstream to Dinard and St-Malo; contact *Émeraude Lines* in Dinard (☎99.46.10.45) or St-Malo (☎99.40.48.40), or the *Agence Boutin* at 7 Grande-Rue in Dinan (☎96.39.12.32).

ACCOMMODATION

In addition to the **hotels** listed below, Dinan has an attractive year-round **youth hostel** in the Moulin de Méen, Vallée de la Fontaine-des-Eaux (☎96.39.10.83), 2km from the gare SNCF. Unfortunately it's not on any bus route; to walk there, follow the quay downstream from the port on the town side. The **Camping Municipal** is at 103 rue Chateaubriand (March–Nov; ☎96.39.11.96), just outside the western ramparts.

Hôtel le Consigne, 40 rue Carnot (☎96.39.00.12). Between the gare SNCF and pl de Général-Leclerc. No restaurant. ②

Hôtel du Théâtre, 2 rue Ste-Claire (☎96.39.06.91). Near the SI and Théâtre des Jacobins, under the same efficient management as the nearby *Restaurant Cantorbery* (see below). ③

Hôtel-Restaurant Duchesse Anne, 10 pl du Guesclin (☎96.39.09.43). Comfortable rooms, with a good-value restaurant where set menus start at 55F. ④

EATING

Cantorbery, 6 rue Ste-Claire (☎96.39.02.52). Excellent food served in an old stone house, with rafters, a spiral staircase, and a real wood fire. Menu from 60F.

Mère Pourcel, 3 pl des Merciers (☎96.39.03.80). Beautiful half-timbered fifteenth-century house in the central square. Closed Jan, Feb, and Sun pm and Mon out of season. Menu from 85F.

Les Terrasses, Port de Dinan (☎96.39.09.60). Lovely waterfront setting, with good menus from 90F. Closed Tues out of season.

Rennes

For a city which has been the capital and power centre of Brittany since the 1532 union with France, Rennes is – outwardly at least – uncharacteristic of the province, with its neo-Classical layout and pompous major buildings. What potential it had to be a picturesque tourist spot was destroyed in 1720, when a drunken carpenter managed to set light to virtually the whole city. Only the area known as **Les Lices**, at the junction of the canalised Ille and the river Vilaine, was undamaged. The remodelling of the rest of the city was handed over to Parisian architects, not in deference to the capital but in an attempt to rival it.

Today, Les Lices is dominated by two ugly market halls, but originally it was, as its name suggests, the place for tournaments – that is, jousting "lists". It was here, in 1337, that the hitherto unknown Bertrand du Guesclin, then aged seventeen, fought and defeated several older opponents. This set him on his career as a soldier, during which he was later to save Rennes when it was under siege by the English. However, after the Bretons were defeated at Auray in 1364, he fought for the French, and twice invaded Brittany. He may be a French hero but, for some Bretons, he is a knave and a traitor. In 1946, Breton separatists destroyed a memorial to him in the Thabor gardens.

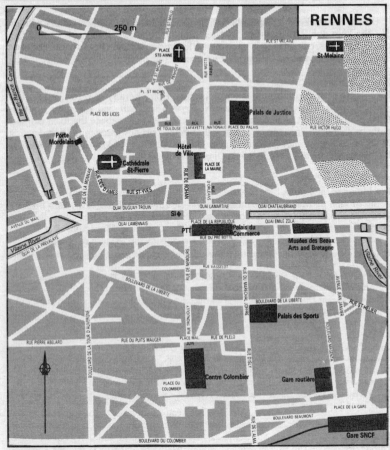

RENNES

Arrival and accommodation

Rennes' modern **gare SNCF** (☎99.65.50.50) is well south of the Vilaine, twenty minutes' walk from the central **SI** on the Pont de Nemours, where the river briefly disappears underground (mid-June to mid-Sept Mon–Sat 9am–7.30pm, Sun 10am–noon & 2–5pm; rest of year Mon 2–6.30pm, Tues–Sat 10am–12.30pm & 2–6.30pm; ☎99.79.01.98). The **gare routière** on bd Magenta (☎99.30.87.80) is a couple of blocks north of the gare SNCF, but most local buses start and finish on or near pl de la République, alongside the SI.

Accommodation

Besides its many hotels, Rennes has a year-round **youth hostel**, 3km out from the centre, next to the Canal d'Ille et Rance – the *Centre International de Séjour*, 10/12 Canal St-Martin (☎99.33.32.33). It's on bus routes #20 and #22 from the gare SNCF (or bus #2 at weekends), direction St-Gregoire, stop Coëtlogon. Open all year. The **Camping Municipal** is at rue de Professeur-Maurice-Audin (April–Sept; ☎99.36.91.22), on bus #3.

Hôtel d'Angleterre, 19 rue du Maréchal-Joffre (☎99.79.38.61). Not brilliant, but relatively cheap, a short way south of the river towards the station. No restaurant. ③

Hôtel de Brest, 15 pl de la Gare (☎99.30.35.83). A cheaper option near the station. No restaurant. ④

Hôtel le Pengouin, 7 pl des Lices (☎99.79.14.81). Newly rebuilt, very comfortable and friendly hotel in old Rennes. No restaurant. ④

Hôtel-Restaurant Rocher Cancale, 10 rue St-Michel (☎99.79.20.83). Between pl Ste-Anne and pl St-Michel, in all that remains of medieval Rennes. Beautifully restored frontage and ground floor, but with modern facilities upstairs. The restaurant, which is closed at weekends, has menus from 50F menu at midday and 80F in the evening. ④

Hôtel Tour d'Auvergne, 20 bd de la Tour-d'Auvergne (☎99.30.84.16). Ten minutes' walk from the SI, between the gare SNCF and the river. No restaurant. ②

The city

Rennes' surviving **medieval quarter**, bordered by the canal to the west and the river to the south, radiates from the **Porte Mordelaise**, the old ceremonial entrance to the city, which following building work in 1990 is now more prominently exposed. This is the liveliest part of town and it stays up late, particularly in the area around St-Aubin church and along rue St-Michel and rue de Penhöet.

The one central building to escape the 1720 fire was symbolically enough the **Palais de Justice** on rue Hoche downtown. It is possible to see round the building, where the Breton *parlement* – a mixture of high court and council with unelected members – fought battles with the French governor from the reign of Louis XIV up until the Revolution. Tours start from the far right-hand corner of the courtyard (daily except Tues 9.45, 10.30, 11.15am, 2.15 & 4.45pm). Each of the seventeenth-century chambers is more opulently gilded and adorned than the one before, culminating in the debating hall hung with Gobelin tapestries depicting scenes from the history of the duchy and the province. Every centimetre of the walls and ceilings is decorated – the Sun King style, but on a relatively small scale.

Two major museums are housed in former university buildings at 20 quai Émile-Zola, on the south bank of the Vilaine (both open daily except Tues, 10am–noon & 2–6pm). The **Musée de Bretagne** gives one of the best possible introductions to the history and culture of Brittany. The prehistoric section is good, and includes the bones of a woolly rhinoceros found at Dol, but the greatest strength of the museum is the audiovisual presentation of the transition from the last century to the present. The **Musée des Beaux Arts** owns some Leonardo drawings in addition to more local exhibits. Its specifically Breton room combines paintings of mythical themes – the Île d'Ys legend (see p.301) by Luminais – and of real life – a woman waiting for the fishermen to come back through stormy seas.

Eating

There are more restaurants than hotels in old Rennes. Along rue St-Malo in particular there are all sorts of ethnic places – Chinese, Turkish and so on – while the rue des Dames has mainly Greek and Spanish restaurants.

La Boutique Antillais, 5 pl du Bas-des-Lices (☎99.30.54.44). Midday menu from 55F, but *à la carte* in the evening. A small, friendly restaurant – booking advisable.

Le Chouin, 12 rue d'Isly (☎99.30.87.86). A fine fish restaurant, not far from the gare SNCF. Menu 99F midday, *à la carte* in the evening. Closed Sun and Mon.

L'Île aux Fruits, 21 rue de Penhöet (☎99.79.01.06). A little pricey, specialising in delicious South-Seas fish and fruit-based dishes.

Le Kalesche, rue St-Malo (99.79.47.30). Well-priced couscous and paella.

Le Louisiane, 7 pl St-Michel (☎99.79.25.94). Cajun-styled place in the old town. Menu from 66F weekday midday, but from 88F evenings and weekends. Closed Sat lunchtime.

Entertainment and culture

Rennes is seen at its best in the first ten days of July, when the **Festival des Tombées de la Nuit** takes over the whole city to celebrate Breton culture with music, theatre, film, mime and poetry in joyful recognition of the influences of both Paris and Hollywood. In the second week of December, an annual rock festival, **Les Transmusicales**, attracts big-name acts from all over France and the world at large, though still with a Breton emphasis; over the last decade it has helped to make Rennes an important centre for French rock. All year round, *Club Ubu* at 1 rue St-Helier (☎99.31.79.79) puts on large-scale gigs, and there's regular **jazz**, daily except Sundays, at *De Jazey*, 54 rue St-Malo (☎99.38.70.72). The varied season of the *Théâtre National de Bretagne*, 1 rue St-Helier (☎99.30.88.88), runs from mid-October to mid-June. The *Barantic* bar on rue St-Michel is currently a big favourite, putting on occasional live music for a mixed crowd of Breton nationalists and boisterous students.

The presence of so many students – 35,000 all told – gives Rennes a rather more visible level of political and cultural activity than most places in Brittany. The friendly co-operative bookshop *Breizh* at 17 rue Penhöet has cassettes of Breton and Celtic music along with books and posters. *L'Arvor* cinema at 29 rue d'Antrain (☎99.38.72.40) shows v.o. (original language) films, and there's a large selection of English books in the *FNAC* bookshop in the Colombier shopping centre south of the river.

Out from Rennes to Brocéliande – the Forêt de Paimpont

Thirty kilometres to the west of Rennes, the **Forêt de Paimpont**, known also by its ancient name of **BROCÉLIANDE**, is the forest of the wizard Merlin. Medieval Breton minstrels, like their Welsh counterparts from whom or with whom the stories originated, set the tales of King Arthur and the Holy Grail both in *Grande Bretagne* and here in *Petite Bretagne*. For all the magic of these shared legends, however, and a succession of likely sites, few people come out here. If you like the idea of roaming around for a day it isn't difficult. The bus from Rennes to Guer runs twice a day past the southern edge of the forest, stopping at FORGES-LES-PAIMPONT, and another, around the north corner, to **MAURON**.

Mauron is a good point to start. From the hamlet of **FOLLE-PENSÉE**, just south of the village, it's a circuitous but enjoyable twenty-minute walk to **La Fontaine de Barenton** – Merlin's spring. The path leads off from the end of the road at Folle-Pensée, turning to the right, running through pines and gorse to a junction of forest tracks: here take the track straight ahead for about 100m, where an unobvious path to the left goes into the woods and turns back north to the spring – walled, and filled by the most delicious water imaginable, as you might expect from the elixir of eternal youth. After drinking, stroke the great stone slab beside the spring to call up a storm, roaring lions and a horseman in black armour. Here Merlin first set eyes on Vivianne who bound him willingly in a prison of air.

Another forest walk, more scenic but without a goal, is the **Val sans Retour** (the Valley of no Return), off the GR37 from TRÉHORENTEUC to La Guette. The path to follow leads out from the D141 just south of Tréhorenteuc to a steep valley from which exits are barred by thickets of gorse and giant furze on the rocks above; at one point it skirts an overgrown table of rock, the *Rocher des Faux Amants*, from which the seducer Morgane le Fay enticed unwary boys.

Possible bases in the forest

If you feel like **staying** in these parts, **PAIMPONT** is the most enjoyable and easy place to base yourself. It's right in the centre of the woods and has two **campsites**, a **gîte d'étape** (c/o M and Mme Grosset; ☎99.07.81.40), a **youth hostel** (☎97.22.76.75; a couple of kilometres out on the Concoret road) and the **hotel** *Relais de Brocéliande* (☎99.07.81.07; ③). Next to the abbey on the edge of the lake is an **SI**. If you do head out to Concoret you'll find the **Étang du Comper**, overlooked by the château of the enchantress Vivianne. There's another *gîte d'étape* at FORGES-LES-PAIMPONT which is on the GR37, south of Paimpont (c/o Mme Farcy; ☎97.06.93.46). Or, for two cheap **hotels**, the *Orée de la Forêt* (☎99.06.81.15; ②) and the *Bruyères* (☎99.06.81.38; ②), you could stop at **PLÉLAN-LE-GRAND**, east of the forest on the main Rennes road.

The north coast from Dinard to Lannion

The coast which stretches from St-Malo to Finistère at the far western end of Brittany is divided to either side of the bay of St-Brieuc into two distinct regions. First come the exposed green headlands of the **Côte d'Émeraude**; beyond St-Brieuc itself the shore is more extravagantly indented, with a succession of secluded little bays, and an increasing proliferation of huge pink granite boulders seen at their best on the **Côte de Granit Rose** near Perros-Guirec.

Along the Côte d'Émeraude

To the west of the Rance, beyond Dinard, begins the green of the **Côte d'Émeraude**. Though composed mainly of developed family resorts, it also offers wonderful camping, at its best around the heather-backed beaches near **Cap Fréhel**. You can't camp within 5km of the headland itself, a high, warm expanse of heath and cliffs with views extending on good days as far as Jersey and the Île de Bréhat. The **Fort La Latte**, to the east, is used regularly as a film set, and you can take guided tours across its two drawbridges to the cannonball factory within its towers (June–Sept 10am–12.30pm & 2.30–6.30pm; rest of year Sun and holidays only, 2.30–5.30pm). The nearest places to stay are the ideal isolated **campsite** at PLÉHEREL, and a summer-only **youth hostel** at PLÉVENON (☎96.61.91.87).

Erquy and Le Val-André

Further round, Erquy and Le Val-André both have huge beaches. At **ERQUY**, a perfect crescent dominated in the centre by a sailing school, the tide disappears way beyond the harbour entrance, leaving gentle ripples of paddling sand. The *Hôtel Beauséjour* (☎96.72.30.39; ③) has a good view of the bay, and excellent fish dinners, while the more upmarket restaurant *l'Escurial* (☎96.72.31.56) by the seafront serves a five-course menu (for 180F) which consists entirely of scallops, the town's speciality. There are several campsites on the promontory (dotted with tiny coves) that leads to the Cap d'Erquy north of town.

At **LE VAL-ANDRÉ** the long pedestrian promenade at the seafront feels oddly Victorian, consisting solely of huge old houses undisturbed by shops or bars. What amusements there are lurk on rue A-Charner behind. The recently refurbished *Hotel de la Mer* at no. 63 (☎96.72.20.44) compares well with any hotel anywhere; as well as having good cheap rooms, it serves food that is utterly magnificent, transporting *moules marinières* onto a hitherto undreamed-of plane.

St-Brieuc

The major city on the **Côte d'Émeraude**, **ST-BRIEUC**. is far too busy being the industrial centre of the north to concern itself with entertaining tourists. It's an odd-looking city, with two very deep wooded valleys spanned by viaducts, at its core, and it's almost impossible to bypass, however you're travelling. The streets are hectic, with the town centre cut in two by a virtual motorway, unrelieved by any public parks, and not much distinguished either by a mega-shopping complex. Motorists and cyclists, unfortunately, have little choice but to plough straight through rather than attempting to negotiate the backroads and steep hills around.

The most central **hotel** is *A Tournebride,* 10 rue Mireille-Chrysostome (☎96.33.09.60; ④), though a preferable base is the **youth hostel**, two kilometres out, at rue Alphonse-Daudet, Ty Coat; this has bicycles and canoes for hire. There's a "biological" **restaurant** at 19 rue de Maréchal-Foch, *Le Grain de Sel*, which serves **vegetarian** meals made with the fresh organic produce it also sells both on the spot and at local markets.

Northward from St-Brieuc

Moving northwest towards Paimpol, the coast becomes wilder and harsher and the seaside towns tend to be crammed into narrow rocky inlets or set well back in river estuaries. **BINIC** is a narrow port surrounded by meadows, with a thin strip of beach and a decent hotel, the *Galion* (☎96.73.61.30; ③), while at the sedate family resort of **ST-QUAY-PORTRIEUX** just further on, the *Gerbot d'Avoine* (☎96.70.40.09; ④) beside the beach is the best place to stay, despite the hideous decor of its rooms.

After St-Quay, the coastal road shifts inland, through PLOUHA, the traditional boundary between French-speaking and Breton-speaking Brittany. It's a viable proposition to hitch to **KERMARIA-AN-ISQUIT** from here, signposted off the D21 from Plouha. The point of this complex detour is to see the extraordinary medieval frescoes of a **Dance Macabre** in the **chapel** of the village. They show Ankou, who is death or death's assistant, leading representatives of every social class in a dance of death. An encounter between three living nobles out hunting and three philosophical corpses is also depicted, and there's a statue of the infant Jesus refusing milk from Mary's proffered breast. To get into the chapel you'll need to get a key from Mme Hervé Droniou in the house just up the road on the left.

Paimpol

To the north, back on the coast, **PAIMPOL,** though still an attractive town, has lost something in its transition from working fishing port to pleasure harbour. It was once the centre of a cod and whaling fleet that sailed for the fisheries of Iceland in February of each year, sent off with a ceremony marked by a famous *pardon*. From then until August or September, the town would be empty of all young men. A haunting glimpse of the way Paimpol used to look can be seen in the recently re-released silent film shot here in 1924 of Pierre Loti's book *Pêcheur d'Islande*. The **hotels** in the ugly new block that lines one side of the tiny harbour are reasonable enough, while of the restaurants the *Cotriade* to the right is much better value than the *du Port* to the left. On the whole, though Paimpol may be a very pleasant place to arrive by yacht, threading through the rocks, you'll probably prefer if you're landbound to continue to the spectacular **Pointe de l'Arcouest** and Bréhat – or to little **LOGUIVY**, a beautiful village where Lenin once came on his summer holidays from Paris.

The Île de Bréhat

The **ÎLE DE BREHAT** – in reality two islands joined by a tiny bridge – gives the appearance of spanning great latitudes. On the north side are windswept meadows of hemlock and yarrow, sloping down to chaotic erosions of rock; on the south, you're in the midst of palm trees, mimosa and eucalyptus. All around is a multitude of little islets – some accessible at low tide, others *propriété privée*, most just pink-orange rocks. All in all, this has to be one of the most beautiful places in Brittany.

As you might expect, this island paradise has attracted Parisians and the like looking for holiday homes. Over half the houses now have temporary residents and young Bréhatins leave in ever-increasing numbers for lack of a place of their own, let alone a

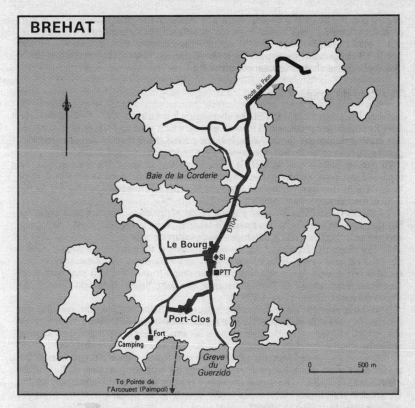

job. In winter the remaining 300 or so natives have the place to themselves, without even a *gendarme*; the summer sees two imported from the mainland, along with upwards of 3000 tourists. As a visitor, though, you should find the Bréhatins friendly enough – it's the holiday-home owners that they really resent.

The beach to swim from at low tide is the **Grève de Guerzido,** on the east side facing the mainland. Near **Le Bourg** – Bréhat village, which is the centre of all activity on the island, the sea tends to be a bit murky, and the east coast generally is less accessible because of private property. But in the north, even when Le Bourg is blocked up with visitors, you can walk and laze about in near solitude. Bréhat no longer has a castle (blown up twice by the English), but it does have a lighthouse, and a nine-teenth-century **fort,** in the woods near the campsite (see below).

Practicalities

Bréhat is connected regularly by **ferry** from POINTE DE L'ARCOUEST (hourly in high summer, slightly less otherwise, with the last boat back from Bréhat around 7pm). No cars are permitted on the island, and there's barely a road wide enough for its few light farm vehicles. You can rent bikes at the ferry port, but it's easy enough to walk from one end to the other in half an hour.

The island's three **hotels** are expensive and in any case permanently booked through the summer; all close in winter, though you may be able to find a room by inquiring in the **SI** (☎96.20.00.36), in the old Mairie in the main square in Le Bourg. Most days there's a small market here; restaurants are neither numerous nor cheap, so picnic food is the best bet. The SI can provide **campers** with information on the wonderful campsite in the woods high above the sea west of the port; when that's closed you can pitch your tent almost anywhere.

The Côte de Granit Rose

Between Bréhat and TRÉGASTEL the shoreline is known as the **Côte de Granit Rose** after its pink-tinged, glittery and smooth granite which wind and waves have sculpted into curious shapes and forms. Not only is the coastal chaos of rocks and promontories granite; so too are the houses, the breakwaters, the pavements, and so on.

In passing, take a look at **TRÉGUIER**, where the ancient cathedral contains the tomb of Saint Yves, a native of the town who died in 1303 and became the patron saint of lawyers for his incorruptibility. Attempts to bribe him continue to this day in the form of marble plaques and candles.

PERROS-GUIREC is the most popular resort of this coast, with the walk along the **Sentier des Douaniers** to Ploumanac'h leading past the region's most spectacular succession of bizarre granite outcrops – each complete with its own unlikely label as well. The **plage du Trestraou**, on the opposite side of the town to the port, is a good place to eat and drink – the *Homard Bleu* and *L'Excelsior* are particularly recommended. From here, boats sail on three-hour round trips to the bird sanctuary **Sept Îles** (June–Aug, usually at 2pm, sometimes also 9am; ticket office next door to the *Centre Nautique*, closed 11am–1.30pm).

The strangest sight along this coast, however, outdoing anything the erosions can manage, is just south of TRÉGASTEL-BOURG, on the route de Calvaire, where an old stone saint, halfway up a high calvary, raises his arm to bless or harangue the gleaming white discs and dome of the Lannion telecommunications research centre.

Between Lannion and Morlaix, on the bus route, there's a good place to witness the traditional Breton death figure of Ankou in all his majesty (see also p.295). In the church at PLOUMILIAU he stands 1m high, a wooden skeleton with spade and scythe. He used to travel with every coffin to the cemetery, the familiarity of his presence perhaps making death less sinister.

Practicalities

Public transport on the Côte de Granit Rose is pretty marginal. There are **buses** between Paimpol, Trégastel and LANNION but that's about it. Walkers have the GR34, which follows the coast a little inland.

There are **campsites** dotted all along the coast but little other accommodation. **Youth hostels** can be found at 6 rue du 73ᵉ-Territorial, Lannion (☎96.37.91.28), and at TRÉBEURDEN (*Le Toeno;* ☎96.23.52.22). There are a couple of **gîtes d'étape**, at LOUANNEC (c/o Mme Kremer, *Villa Stelle;* ☎96.23.15.62), east of Perros-Guirec, and south of Treguier near LA ROCHE DERRIEN (*Château de la Roche Jagu;* ☎96.95.62.35). In PLOUMANAC'H near Perros-Guirec, there are a couple of reasonable **hotels**, *Roch Hir* (☎96.23.23.24; ③) and *du Parc* (☎96.23.24.88; ③).

Guingamp

If you skip the Pink Granite Coast and head directly west towards Finistère you'll pass through **GUINGAMP**. It's the only town of any size in the centre of this northern peninsula and an old weaving centre – its name possibly the source of the fabric "gingham". It's an attractive place of cobbled streets, but there's not much to see beyond the main square, where a fountain bedecked in griffins and gargoyles is overlooked by a splendid pair of lopsided old timber-frame houses propping each other up, and the Black Virgin in the basilica. On the road out towards Morlaix is the "mountain" of the **Ménez Bré**, a spectacular height amid these plains. In the mid-nineteenth century, the local rector was often observed to climb to the mountain's peak on stormy nights, accompanied only by a donkey laden with books. For all his exemplary piety, his parishioners suspected him of sorcery and witchcraft; he was, it turned out, doing early research into natural electrical forces.

FINISTÈRE – LAND'S END

It's hard to resist the appeal of the **Finistère coast**, with its ocean-fronting cliffs and headlands. Summer crowds may detract from the best parts of the **Crozon** peninsula and the **Pointe de Raz** but there are miles and miles of coast where you can enjoy near solitude. If you've transport, explore the semi-wilderness of the **northern stretches** beyond Brest and the little fishing village of **Le Conquet**, or the misty offshore islands, **Ouessant and Molène**. From the top of **Ménez-Hom** you can admire the anarchic limits of western France, and in the two cities of **Morlaix** and **Quimper**, you'll witness distinctly Breton modern life as well as ancient splendours. Of these, the **parish closes** south of Morlaix reveal much of the mythology of the medieval past.

Roscoff

The opening of the deep-water port at **ROSCOFF** in 1973 was part of a general attempt to revitalise the Breton economy. The ferry services to Plymouth and to Cork are intended not just to bring tourists, but also to revive the traditional trading links between the Celtic nations of Brittany, Ireland and southwest England – links which were suppressed for centuries as an act of French state policy after the union of Brittany with France in 1532. In fact, Roscoff has long been a major port. It was here that Mary Queen of Scots landed in 1548 on her way to Paris to be engaged to François, the son and heir of Henri II of France. And it was here that Bonnie Prince Charlie, the Young Pretender, landed in 1746 after his defeat at Culloden.

Roscoff itself has, however, remained a small resort, where almost all activity is confined to **rue Gambetta** and the **old port** – the rest of the roads are residential back streets full of retirement homes and institutions. One factor in preserving its old character is that both the ferry port and the SNCF station are some way from the centre.

The town's main church, **Notre-Dame-de-Croas-Batz** at the far end of rue Gambetta (which becomes rue Amiral-Reveillère), was built in the sixteenth century. Bretons take a particular pride in ornate Renaissance belfries such as the one which embellishes this church, with its sculptured ships and protruding stone cannons. From the side, rows of bells can be seen hanging in galleries, one above the other like a tall, but narrow, wedding cake created by an early Walt Disney. Some way beyond is the grand **Thalassotherapy Institute** of Rock Roum, and a kilometre further on is Roscoff's best **beach**, at Laber, surrounded by expensive hotels and apartments.

The old **harbour** is livelier, mixing an economy based on fishing with relatively low-key pleasure trips to the **Île de Batz** (see below). The island looks almost walkable; a narrow pier stretches over three or four hundred metres towards it before abruptly plunging into deep rocky waters. The Pointe de Bloscon and the white fisherman's chapel, the Chapelle Ste-Barbe, make a good vantage point, particularly when the tide is in; the tide goes out a long way (and dictates the embarkation point for the boat trips). Below the headland are the *viviers,* where you can see trout, salmon, lobsters and crabs being reared for the pot.

In 1828, Henri Ollivier took **onions** to England from Roscoff, thereby founding a trade which flourished until the 1930s. In the bar of the *Hôtel du Centre* (see below), you can see old photographs of "Johnnies": men in black berets with strings of onions hanging over the handlebars of their bicycles. Older people of the town travelled as children with their fathers as far afield as Glasgow.

Practicalities

Brittany Ferries **boats** from Plymouth (6hr) or Cork (19hr), dock at the new Port de Bloscon (98.29.28.28), to the east of the town. The helpful **SI** is at 46 rue Gambetta in town (☎98.61.12.13), next to a *boulangerie*. Regular buses and trains run from town to Morlaix, with connections beyond. You can also hire **bikes** from *Desbordes*, 13 rue Brizeux (☎98.69.72.44).

For a small town, Roscoff is well equipped with **hotels**, which are well accustomed to late-night arrivals from the ferries (not that it's easy to get a meal much after 9pm). Be warned however that most of them close in winter. There's also a **youth hostel** on the Île de Batz (see below), and two summer **campsites** – the *Municipal de Perharidy*, 2km west, just off the route de Santec (☎98.69.70.86), and the *Manoir de Kerestat*, 2 km south towards St-Pol (☎98.69.71.92). Good **restaurants**, apart from those in the hotels below, include the welcoming seafront *Les Korrigans* on the Quai d'Auxerre (☎98.61.22.15), and *Chez Gaston*, rue J-Bara (☎98.69.75.65), inland near the station.

Hôtel des Arcades, 15 rue Amiral-Reveillère (☎98.69.70.45). Closed mid-Nov–March. Sixteenth-century building with fine views from some rooms and from the restaurant; menus 39–185F. ②

Les Chardons Bleus, 4 rue Amiral-Reveillère (☎98.69.72.03). Very friendly and helpful hotel with a good restaurant (closed Thurs out of season) but no sea views. Closed Dec and Jan. ④

Hôtel du Centre, 5 rue Gambetta (☎98.61.24.25). Very much a family hotel, facing the beach. Menus from 80F. Closed Jan. ③

Hôtel de la Gare, 2 rue Ropartz-Morvan (☎98.61.21.42). Cheap rooms near the station, open all year. Bar (and shop). Open all the year round. ②

The Île de Batz

The **ÎLE DE BATZ** (pronounced *Ba*), just off the coast of Roscoff, is a somewhat wind-swept spot, but well endowed with sandy beaches; for campers looking to have a stretch of coastline to themselves, it could be ideal.

The island's first recorded inhabitant was a "laidly worm", a dragon that infested the place in the sixth century. Such dragons normally symbolise pre-Christian religions, in this case perhaps a Druidic serpent cult. Allegorical or not, when Saint Pol arrived to found a monastery he wrapped a Byzantine stole around the unfortunate creature's neck and cast it into the sea. These days, there are no dragons; there aren't even any trees, just an awful lot of seaweed which is collected and sold for fertiliser.

Several sailings each day from Roscoff arrive at the quayside of the old island town. Walk uphill from here and you will come to the **youth hostel**, at the evocatively named Creach ar Bolloc'h (April–Sept; ☎98.61.77.69). Higher still, on the island's peak (all of 23m above sea-level) is a 44-metre lighthouse, which welcomes visitors. And beyond that, it's just the sands and seaweed.

St-Pol-de-Léon

The main road **south from Roscoff** passes by fields of the famous Breton artichokes before arriving after 6km at **ST-POL-DE-LÉON**. It's not an exciting place but – assuming you've got your own transport – it has two churches that at least merit a pause. The **Cathédrale**, in the main town square, was rebuilt towards the end of the thirteenth century along the lines of Coutances – a quiet classic of unified Norman architecture. The remains of Saint Pol are inside, alongside a large bell, rung over the heads of pilgrims during his *pardon* on March 12 in the unlikely hope of curing headaches and ear diseases. Just downhill is the original **Kreisker Chapel**, with access to the top of its sharp-pointed soaring granite belfry (now coated in yellow moss).

Morlaix

MORLAIX, one of the great old Breton ports, thrived off trade with England in between wars during the "Golden Period' of the late Middle Ages. Built up the slopes of a steep valley with sober stone houses, the town was originally protected by an eleventh-century castle and a circuit of walls. Little is left of either, but the old centre remains in part medieval – cobbled streets and half timbered houses. Its present grandeur comes from the pink granite viaduct carrying trains from Paris to Brest way above the town centre. Coming by road from the north, the opening view is of shiny yacht masts paralleling the pillars of the viaduct.

Arrival and accommodation

The **SI** is in a solitary one-storey building almost under the viaduct in pl des Otages (Mon–Sat 9am–12.30pm & 1.30–7.30pm, Sun 10am–12.30pm; rest of year Tues–Sat 9am–noon & 2–6.30pm; ☎98.62.14.94).

All **buses** conveniently depart from pl Cornic, right under the viaduct, but the **gare SNCF** (☎98.80.50.60) is on rue Armand-Rousseau, high above the town at the western end of the viaduct. To reach it on foot, you have to climb the steep steps of the Venelle de la Roche. **Bicycles** can be hired from Henri Le Gall, 1 rue de Callac (☎98.88.60.47).

Accommodation
Though Morlaix's municipal campsite is now closed, there's a **youth hostel** at 3 route de Paris (open all year; ☎98.88.60.47), 1km out from the town centre on the Kernégues bus route.

Hôtel les Arcades, 11 pl Cornic (☎98.88.20.03). Not far from the viaduct, opposite the new bus station. No restaurant. ②

Hôtel Au Roy d'Ys, 8 pl des Jacobins (☎98.88.61.19). Central hotel, across the square from the town museum. Closed Nov, no restaurant. ②

Hôtel-Restaurant les Halles, 23 rue du Mur (☎98.88.03.86). Friendly hotel facing the attractive pl des Halles, with a garage for motor bikes and bicycles. Good cheap restaurant; menus at 48F and 66F. ③

Hôtel-Restaurant le St-Melaine, 75–77 rue Ange-de-Guernisac (☎98.88.08.79). Self-styled family hotel, not easy to find, above pl Cornic and all but under the viaduct. Value for money, but dull. ①

The town

On her way from Roscoff to Paris, Mary Queen of Scots passed through Morlaix in 1548, and stayed at the **Jacobin convent** which fronts pl des Jacobins. She was at the time just five years old, an aspect which may have contributed to local interest in the spectacle. A contemporary account records that the crush to catch a glimpse of the infant was so great that the inner town's "gates were thrown off their hinges and the chains from all the bridges were broken down". The **town museum**, in the convent church, contains a reasonably entertaining assortment of Roman wine jars, bits that have fallen off medieval churches, cannons and kitchen utensils, and a few modern paintings (entrance on rue des Vigues; daily 9am–noon & 2–6pm; closed Tues in winter).

The church of **St-Mathieu**, off rue de Paris, contains a sombre and curious statue of the Madonna and Child; Mary's breast was apparently lopped off by a prudish former priest leaving the babe suckling at nothing. The whole statue opens down the middle to reveal a separate figure of God the Father, clutching a crucifix.

In the eighteenth century, Morlaix's wealth was sustained by boat building, textiles and tobacco, and it still has an active tobacco factory, by the port, on quai de Léon. It employs 500 people who produce annually 300 million cigars, 50 tons of chewing tobacco and 15 tons of snuff, and can be visited on Wednesday afternoons (ring ☎98.88.15.32).

In 1522, Morlaix pirates raided and looted Bristol. With hurt pride, and seeking revenge, Henry VIII sent a sizeable fleet to storm Morlaix. The citizens were absent at a neighbouring festival when the English arrived. When they returned, they found the English drunk in their wine cellars. The Bretons routed the English and, to forestall further attacks from the sea, they built the fortified **Château de Taureau** in Morlaix bay, off Pointe de Pen-al-Lann 12 km north of town. In the seventeenth century, it was used as a prison; now it's a sailing school. Meanwhile, the town adopted the motto which it keeps to this day – "If they bite you, bite them back".

Eating

The best hunting ground for **restaurants** in Morlaix is to be found between St-Melaine church and pl des Jacobins.

Dolce Vita, 3 rue Ange-de-Guernisac (☎98.63.37.67). Pizzeria, with an extensive menu, including pasta dishes. Menu starts at 120F, but you can choose *à la carte*.

El Marisco, 15 rue Ange-de-Guernisac (☎98.88.70.99). Specialises in seafood dishes from Galicia and paellas.

L'Agadir, 24 rue Ange-de-Guernisac (☎98.63.42.02). Despite the name, this is an Algerian restaurant, serving couscous and so on.

Le Marrakech Venelle du Four St-Melaine, (☎98.88.78.93). This is a Moroccan restaurant, just around the corner from L'Agadir: tagine, etc.

Nightlife and drinking

Morlaix has recently acquired its own small brewery, set up to produce real ale similar to that its owners had enjoyed on visiting Britain. You should be able to find the resultant brew, *Coreff*, in local bars, or you can visit the brewery itself at 1 pl de la Madeleine (groups of 10, Tues–Thurs by arrangement; ☎98.63.41.92).

Among clubs and bars to look out for are *Le Père Ubu*, at 37 rue de Callac (closed Sun & Mon), near the youth hostel, which has good taped mustic, boisterous Bretons playing darts, and puts on fortnightly café-théâtre, and the lively *Tempo Piano Bar*, facing the port on quai de Tréguier, (☎98.63.29.11), where there are regular jazz and blues concerts. The *Club Coätelan* (☎98.72.50.71) in Plougonven, 12km east of Morlaix, also books a wide assortment of jazz, rock and blues performers.

The Parish Closes

Morlaix makes an excellent base for visiting the **parish closes** (*enclos paroissiaux*), in the countryside towards Brest. **Breton Catholicism** has a very distinctive character, closer to the Celtic past than to Rome. There are hundreds of saints who've never been approved by the Vatican, but whose brightly painted wooden figures adorn every Breton church. Their stories merge imperceptibly with the tales of moving *menhirs*, ghosts and sorcery. Visions and miracles are still assumed; and death's workmate, Ankou, is a familiar figure, even if no one now would dread his manifestation.

Many of the churchyards in this part of Brittany have stone calvaries sculpted with detailed scenes of the Crucifixion above a crowd of saints, gospel stories and legends. In the richer parishes a high stone arch leads into the churchyard adjoining an equally majestic ossuary where the old bones would be taken when the tiny cemeteries filled up. Most date from the two centuries to either side of the union with France in 1532 – Brittany's wealthiest period – and nothing is more telling of the decline in the province's fortunes. Everywhere you'll find magnificence in the *enclos paroissiaux*, walled churchyards which incorporate a trinity of further elements – cemetery, calvary and ossuary – in addition to the churches themselves. The interiors of the churches are often decorated as richly as the architectural ensemble without, while their villages can now be not far removed from poverty.

The three most famous *enclos* are the neighbouring parishes of **GUIMILIAU**, **ST-THÉGONNEC** and **LAMPAUL-GUIMILIAU**, off the N12 between Morlaix and Landiviseau on a clearly signposted route served by the SNCF bus. At St-Thégonnec the entire east wall of the church is a carved and painted retable, with saints in niches and a hundred scenes depicted. The pulpit and the painted oak entombment in the crypt beneath the ossuary are the acknowledged masterpieces. At Lampoul-Guimiliau the painted wooden baptistery, the dragons on the beams and the suitably wicked faces of the robbers on the calvary are the key components. At Guimiliau poor **Katel Gollet** (Katherine the Damned) is depicted tormented in hell – for the crime of hedonism rather than manslaughter. In the legend she danced all her suitors to death until the reaper-figure **Ankou** stepped in to whirl her to eternal damnation. But at **LA ROCHE** (15km or so on towards Brest), where the ruined castle above the Elhorn estuary is said to have been her home, it is Ankou who appears on the ossuary with the inscription "I kill you all". If you've got transport, a 5km detour southeast of La Roche brings further variations at **LA MARTYRE** (where Ankou clutches his disembodied head) and its adjoining parish PLOUDIRY, the sculpting of its ossuary affirming the equality of social classes – in the eyes of Ankou.

If you have time and interest, **other calvaries** to take a look at include PLEYBEN, south of the Monts d'Arrée; LANRIVIAN, in the centre of Brittany; and GUEHENNO, southwest of Josselin. Another speciality to be seen in many Breton churches is the intricate carving and paintwork of **rood screens**: exceptional examples are the St-Fiacre chapel outside LE FAÖUET (between Lorient and the Montagne Noire) and the chapel at KERFONS (south of Lannion), though both wonderful works of art are kept locked up except in July and August and for the annual *pardon*.

The Abers and the western islands

The coast west from Roscoff is some of the most dramatic in Brittany, a jagged series of **abers** – deep, narrow estuaries – in the midst of which are clustered small, isolated resorts. It's a little on the bracing side, especially if you're making use of the numerous **campsites**, but that just has to be counted as part of the appeal. In summer, at least, the temperatures are mild enough, and things get progressively more sheltered as you move around towards LE CONQUET and BREST.

Around the Abers

If you're dependent on public transport, the only stop on the Roscoff–Brest bus before it turns inland is **PLOUESCAT**. Here you'll find **campsites** at each of its three adjacent beaches and the *Baie de Kernic* (☎98.69.63.41; ③), best bet of the **hotels**. An old wooden market hall can provide picnic provisions and at the edge of the bay, about 1km out from the centre, the *Auberge Le Kersabiec* serves good food. **BRIGNOGAN-PLAGE**, on the next *aber*, has a small natural harbour, once the lair of wreckers, with beaches and weather-beaten rocks to either side, as well as its own menhir. The two high-season **campsites** are the *Keravezan* (☎98.83.41.65) and the *du Phare* (☎98.83.45.06), and there are schools for both sailing and riding. Further west, at **PLOUGERNEAU**, the **hotel/restaurant** *Les Abériades* (☎98.04.71.01; ③) could make a good base.

The *aber* between Plougerneau and the yachting port of **ABER-WRAC'H** has a stepping-stone crossing just upstream from the bridge at LLANELLIS, built in Gallo-Roman times, and its long cut stones still cross the three channels of water (access off the D28 signposted Rascoll), and continue past farm buildings to the right to "Pont du Diable". For drivers and cyclists there's a beautiful corniche road west of TRÉMAZEN, whose ruined castle was the point of arrival in Brittany for Tristan and Iseult. Odd little chapels dot the route, and the views of sea and rocks are unhindered before turning inland just before Le Conquet.

Le Conquet

LE CONQUET, at the far western tip of Brittany 24km beyond Brest, is a wonderful place, scarcely developed, with a long beach of clean white sand, protected from the winds by the narrow spit of the Kermorvan peninsula. It is very much a working fishing village, the grey stone houses leading down to the stone jetties of a cramped harbour. It occasionally floods, by the way, causing great amusement to locals who watch the waves wash over cars left there by tourists taking the ferry out to Ouessant and Molène. A good walk 5km south brings you to the lighthouse at **Pointe St-Mathieu**, looking out to the islands from its site among the ruins of a Benedictine abbey.

The *Hôtel du Bretagne*, 16 rue Lt-Jourden (☎98.89.00.02; ③), has cheap **rooms** with a view across the grassy headland. Alternatives are the larger *Pointe Ste-Barbe* (☎98.89.00.26; ④), or either of two well-equipped campsites, *Le Théven* (☎98.89.06.90) and *Les Sablons Blancs* (☎98.89.01.64).

The Îles d'Ouessant and Molène

The island of **Ouessant** lies 30km northwest of Le Conquet, its lighthouse marking the entrance to the English Channel. It's at the end of a chain of smaller islands, mostly uninhabited, and half-submerged granite rocks, but **Molène**, midway, has a village and can also be visited. Boats leave Brest daily except Tuessay at 8.30am, calling en route at Le Conquet at 9.30am; from Le Conquet only there are additional sailings at 6.30pm on Friday and 1.30pm Saturday. Boats back from Ouessant leave at 5pm, with an additional sailing at 8.30am on Tuesday, Thursday and Saturday. Not all the sailings call at both islands, and it would be hard to visit more than one in a day.

Ouessant

You arrive on **OUESSANT** at the new **harbour** in the ominous-sounding Baie du Stiff. There is a scattering of houses here and dotted around the island, but the single town (with the only hotels and restaurants) is 4km away at LAMPAUL. Everybody from the boat heads there, either by the bus that meets each ferry or on bicycles hired from one of the many waiting entrepreneurs – a good idea, as the island is a bit too big to explore on foot. **LAMPAUL** has not a lot to it and quickly becomes very familiar. The best beaches are sprawled around its bay, and, in case you should forget the perils of the sea, the town cemetery's war memorial lists all the ships in which townsfolk were lost, alongside graves of unknown sailors washed ashore and a chapel of wax "*proëlla crosses*" symbolising the many islanders who never returned. You can also visit the Éco-Musée – a reconstruction of a traditional island house – at nearby NIOU. The **Creac'h lighthouse**, closed to the public, is a good point from which to set out along the barren and exposed rocks of the north coast. The star-shaped formations of crumbling walls are not extra-terrestrial relics, but built so that the sheep – peculiarly tame here – can shelter from the winds.

Staying overnight, you can camp almost anywhere on the island, making arrangements with the nearest farmhouse (which may well rent rooms, too). In Lampaul, the hotels *Océan* (☎98.48.80.03; ③), *Roch ar Mor* (☎98.48.80.19; ③) and *Fromveur* (☎98.48.81.30; ③) are all reasonably priced, for a fairly minimal standard. There is, too, a small official campsite, the *Pen ar Bed* (☎98.48.84.65). **Restaurants** are not outrageously priced, but if you want to picnic, it's best to buy provisions on the mainland as the Lampaul shops have limited and rather pricey supplies.

Molène

MOLÈNE is quite well populated for a sparse strip of sand. Its inhabitants make their money from seaweed collecting and drying – and to an extent from crabbing and from crayfish, which they gather on foot, canoe and even tractor at low tide. The tides here are more than usually dramatic, halving or doubling the island's territory at a stroke. It's not called "the bald isle" for nothing. Few people do more than look at Molène as an afternoon's excursion from Le Conquet, but it's quite possible to stay here and to enjoy it, too. There are rooms – very chilly in winter – at *Kastell en Doal* (☎98.84.19.11; ③), an old house by the old port.

Brest

BREST is set in a magnificent natural harbour, known as the Rade de Brest, and sheltered from the ocean storms by the Crozon peninsula to its south. It has always played an important role in war, and in trade whenever peace allowed. Today it is the base of the French Atlantic Fleet; the dry dock can accommodate ships of up to 500,000 tons; and, as a ship repair centre, it ranks sixth in the world.

During World War II, Brest was continually bombed to prevent the Germans from using it as a submarine base. When the Americans liberated it on 18 September, 1944, after a six-week siege, they found the town devastated beyond recognition. The architecture of the post-war town is raw and bleak. There have been attempts, as in Caen, to green the city, but despite the heaviest rainfall in France, the site has proved too windswept to respond fully to these efforts.

Arrival and accommodation

Brest's **SI** on avenue Clemenceau faces pl de la Liberté (summer daily 9am–7pm; winter Mon–Sat 9.30–12.30pm & 2–6pm; ☎98.44.24.96). The **gare SNCF** (☎98.80.50.50) and **gare routière** are together in pl du 19ème RIC at the bottom of avenue Clemenceau; Brest is very much at the end of the railway system, though now connected to Paris in just four hours thanks to the TGV.

As well as the sailings to Ouessant detailed above, in summer three **boats** per day cross from Brest's Port de Commence, Brest, to Le Fret on the Crozon Peninsula.

Accommodation

There's a **youth hostel** near Océanopolis on rue de Kerbriant, Port de Plaisance du Moulin-Blanc (☎98.41.90.41). It's 3km from the SNCF and bus stations, on bus routes #3, #8 or #72. The *Camping de Goulet* (☎98.45.86.84) is not easy to find, and not in any case warmly recommended. If you need to use it, it is on the outskirts of Brest, across the Pont de Recouvrance and then to the left of the Le Conquet road (D789) in Ste-Anne-du-Portzic – take bus #71. Several hotels are within walking distance of the stations.

Hôtel Bellevue, 53 bd Victor-Hugo (☎98.80.51.78). Not easy to find; look for St-Michel church. No restaurant. ④

Hôtel de la Gare, 4 bd Gambetta (☎98.44.47.01). Facing the stations; renovated in 1989. You pay a little more for an uninterrupted view of the Rade de Brest. No restaurant. ④

Hôtel le Regent, 22 rue d'Algesiras (☎98.44.29.77). A clean, newish hotel, but without its own restaurant. ③

Hôtel-Restaurant Vauban, 17 av Clemenceau (☎98.46.06.88). Restaurant closed Sun pm and all day Mon. ③

The town

As a tourist centre, Brest has little to offer. Few relics of the past remain. The fifteenth-century **castle** near the Pont de Recouvrance looks impressive on its headland, and offers a superb panorama of the city and the bay but, once inside, it is not especially interesting. Three of its towers house the **National Maritime Museum** (daily 9.15–11.30am & 2–6pm; closed Tues). The fourteenth-century **Tunguy Tower** on the opposite bank of the river Penfeld serves as the **Museum of Old Brest** (July & Aug daily 10am–noon & 2–7pm; June & Sept daily 2–7pm; Oct–May Thurs, Sat & Sun 2–5pm).

Oceanopolis, next to the Port de Plaisance du Moulin-Blanc, incorporates the largest aquarium in Europe (May–Sept daily 9.30am–6pm; Oct–April Tues–Sun 10am–5pm). Under its white dome, 2400 square yards of exhibits and 35,700 gallons of water contain all kinds of fish, seals, molluscs, seaweed and sea anemones.

Eating and drinking

Most of Brest's restaurants are to be found in the immediate area of the stations. There are a lot of lively **bars** in town. Students tend to congregate at the *Café de la Plage* in pl Guerin, at the top end of rue Jean-Jaurès, near the St-Martin church, while the *Bar Écossais*, also on rue Jean-Jaurès and positively festooned with Scottish memorabilia, attracts a lively Celtic crowd.

Le Rapide, rue Comtesse-de-Carbonnières, near pl de la Liberté. Menu from 45F. A new restaurant with a young following.

Le Ruffe, 1 rue Yves-Collet (☎98.46.07.70). Menu from 60F. Closed Sun.

La Taverne St-Martin, 92 rue Jean-Jaurès (☎98.80.48.17). Menu from 50F; open from 9am to 1am. Don't be put off by the pink fluorescent frontage – the restaurant at the back is warmer and more friendly.

Le Tire Bouchon, 20 rue le l'Observatoire (☎98.44.15.18). Menu from 100F, but a *plat du jour* midday at 35–40F. Closed Sat midday and all day Sun; rest of year open until 10.45pm. The *Café Record* next door stays open later.

The Crozon Peninsula

The **CROZON PENINSULA**, a craggy outcrop of land shaped like a long-robed giant, arms outstretched to defend bay and roadstead, is the central feature of Finistère's torn chaos of estuaries and promontories. Much the easiest way for cyclists, and travellers relying on public transport, to reach the peninsula from Brest is via the ferries to Le Fret (see above).

Motorists heading for Crozon have to follow a circuitous route skirting this complex coast through **PLOUGASTEL-DAOULAS**. At the church here, the calvary shows more torment for Katel Gollet, in this case being raped by devils. The sculpting of Katel herself is more sympathetic than at Guimillau, but it is not difficult to imagine how such graphically portrayed myths have been used in gender politics.

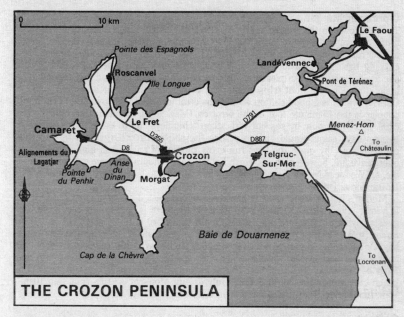

THE CROZON PENINSULA

The Musée de l'École Rurale

Inland from the peninsula, a short way east of the Menez-Hom hill on the intersection of the Argol–Dineault and Trégarven–Menez-Hom roads, is a **museum** that should fascinate anyone interested in how education can be used for subordination. The **Musée de l'École Rurale** is housed in the village's old secondary school, closed down due to lack of numbers in 1974 and re-opened a decade later as a re-creation of a 1920s Breton classroom. At the time all the kids would have spoken Breton at home and been forbidden to speak it here. The teacher gave a little wooden cow to the first child to utter a word in the mother tongue, and they could get rid of the *vache* only by telling on the next offender. The lesson, to parents and pupils alike, was obvious enough: that Breton was backward and a handicap. It was taught, with considerable success, throughout the province, and only recently have things begun to change. As well as Breton-language nursery and primary schools, there's one secondary school and a fund-raising campaign for a lycée. While a few years back SNCF had to be taken to account before it would accept a cheque made out in Breton, there is now a Breton bank. A battle for a Breton TV channel is also underway.

The museum is open from May to September from 2.30 to 7pm and is not accessible by bus.

Onto the peninsula

As you approach the Crozon peninsula, it's well worth making a slight detour to climb the hill of **MENEZ-HOM**, at the giant's feet, for a fabulous view of the land and water alternating out to the ocean. Getting down to the coastal headlands themselves can be a bit of a disappointment after this vision: those extremities that don't house military installations tend to be too crowded. But it is the cliffs that tourists head for here and some of the **beaches**, like **LA PALUE** on the southern arm, are almost deserted.

Crozon and Morgat

The first town on the peninsula proper, **CROZON**, is not much more than a one-way traffic system to distribute tourists among the various resorts – though it does keep a market running most of the week. **MORGAT**, just down the hill, is a more realistic and enticing base. It has a long crescent beach that ends in a pine slope, and a well-sheltered harbour full of pleasure boats raced down from England and Ireland. The main attractions are **boat trips** around the various headlands, such as the Cap de la Chèvre (which is a good clifftop walk if you'd rather make your own way). The most popular is the 45-minute tour of the **Grottes** (May–Sept), multicoloured caves in the cliffs, accessible only by sea but with steep "chimneys" up to the clifftops, where in bygone days saints would lurk to rescue the shipwrecked. Organised by two rival companies on the quay, the trips run every quarter of an hour in high season; they often leave full, however, so it's worth booking a few hours in advance. It's also possible, on Wednesdays and Sundays in July and August, to take a ferry service across to **Douarnenez** (☎98.27.09.54).

Morgat's **hotels** are all quite expensive. The cheapest, *des Grottes* (☎98.27.15.84; ③) is a long (albeit pleasant) walk from what centre there is, and in any case insists on guests paying for *demi-pension*. Better, if you can afford it, is to splash out on the *du Kador* (☎98.27.05.68; ④) where you can eat excellent seafood and enjoy the view of the bay. Or alternatively, **camp**. With a total of 865 pitches available, campers are spoilt for choice; best perhaps are the three-star sites at *Plage de Goulien* (☎98.27.17.10) and *Plage de Trez-Rouz* (☎98.27.93.96). The SI for the whole peninsula is at the start of the beach crescent on the bd du France (July & Aug Mon–Sat 9.30am–7pm, Sun 10am–1pm; June & Sept Tues–Sat 9.30am–noon & 2–6pm; ☎98.27.07.92).

Camaret

CAMARET is another sheltered port, at the very tip of the peninsula, with two beaches – a small one to the north and another in the rather marshy *Anse de Dinan*. The town itself is not large, though in season there are all the shops and supplies you could need. A little walk away from the centre, around the port towards its long protective jetty, the quai du Styvel contains a row of excellent **hotels**. The *Vauban* (☎98.27.91.36; ③) is especially hospitable, though the food in *du Styvel* (☎98.27.92.74; ③) is marginally better; both have rooms that look right out across the bay. There are also various **campsites** to fall back on, like the *Lambézen* (☎98.27.91.41) and the *Lannic* (☎98.27.91.31).

South towards Quimper

The Atlantic inlet to the south of the Crozon peninsula is officially the **Baie de Douarnenez**, although it has also earned itself the grim title of the **Baie du Trépassés** (Bay of the Dead), thanks to the shipwrecked bodies washed up here over the centuries.

Locronan

The fantasy village of **LOCRONAN**, a short way inland en route towards Quimper, is a sort of time capsule, perfectly preserved from its medieval days as a sail-making centre; subsequent economic decline has meant that its old buildings have never been destroyed or superseded. It's long been popular with film directors, such as Roman Polanski, who used it as the setting for *Tess*. For the filming, every visible porch had to be changed, and new windows were fitted to the Renaissance houses of the main square, to make the place more English. The town's main source of income is, in fact, high-budget tourists who buy carved wooden statues by local artisans, pottery from the Midi or leather jackets, provenance unknown. Every sort of craft artefact is sold in this village, some of it produced in open **ateliers**, others through the hands of third parties whose sleek cars are parked beside the shops. One of the artisans suggested converting the loft above his studio to a *gîte d'étape* for young people but the idea was rejected by the powers that be. As it is, there are two **hotels**, the *Fer à Cheval* (☎98.91.70.67; ⑤) and the *du Prieuré* (☎98.91.70.89; ⑤), both expensive and normally reserved well in advance.

Douarnenez

DOUARNENEZ is an unpretentious but also rather unexciting port, for which the holiday trade is only a sideline. The beaches around its bay look pretty enough, but they are dangerous for swimming. It is, however, a functional enough place to stay – and to eat. The part to make for is the **port de Rosmeur**, where the quayside is a line of cafés and restaurants. Sardines and crustaceans are still landed at Douarnenez in huge quantities – in 1923 the eight hundred fishing boats brought in 100 million sardines during the six-month season. You can buy fresh fish at the waterfront or go on a sea-fishing excursion yourself. Boats also cross the bay to Morgat (see above).

Although for most purposes the modern commercial harbour on the other side of town, **Port-Rhu**, is best avoided, in pl de l'Enfer there's a **Boat Museum** (May–Sept 10am–noon & 2–6pm, rest of the year by special arrangement only; ☎98.92.65.20). This doubles as a working boatyard, where visitors can watch or even join in the construction of seagoing vessels, using techniques from all over the world and from all different periods. The emphasis, unsurprisingly, is on fishing, and the craft on display include a *moliceiro* from Portugal and coracles from Wales and Ireland.

To stay in Douarnenez, try the **hotels** *de la Rade,* 31 quai du Grand-Port (☎98.92.01.81; ③) or *des Halles* in the old marketplace (☎98.92.02.75; ③). Close by on the bay, there's a **campsite**, *Croas Men* (☎98.74.00.18), at Tréboul/Les Sables Blancs. North of town, at the **Plage du Ris**, there's an excellent and fairly secluded hotel and restaurant, *Les Mouettes* (☎98.92.01.67; ③), facing the (treacherous) beach.

Quimper and the Land's End Pointes

QUIMPER, capital of the ancient diocese, kingdom and later duchy of Cornouailles, is the oldest Breton city. According to the only source – legends – the first bishop of Quimper, Saint Corentin, came with the first Bretons across the channel to the place they named Little Britain, some time between the fourth and seventh centuries. He lived by eating a regenerating and immortal fish all his life, and was made bishop by one King Gradlon, whose life he later saved when the seabed city of Ys was destroyed. According to one version, Gradlon built Ys in the Baie de Douarnenez, protected from the water by gates and locks to which only he and his daughter had keys. She seems to have been very nice, giving pet dragons to all the citizens to run their errands for them, but Saint Corentin saw decadence and suspected evil. He was proven right: the princess's keys unlocked the gates, the city flooded and Gradlon escaped only by obeying Corentin and throwing his daughter into the sea. Back on dry land and in need of a new capital, Gradlon founded Quimper.

Modern Quimper is very relaxed, active enough to have the bars – and the atmosphere – to make it worth going out café-crawling. Still "the charming little place" known to Flaubert, it takes at most half an hour to cross it on foot. The word "kemper" denotes the junction of the two rivers, the Steir and the Odet, around which are the cobbled streets (now mainly pedestrianised) of the medieval quarter, dominated by the cathedral towering nearby. As the Odet curves from east to southwest, it is crossed by numerous low flat bridges, bedecked with geraniums, and chrysanthemums in the autumn. You can stroll along the boulevards on both banks of the river, where several

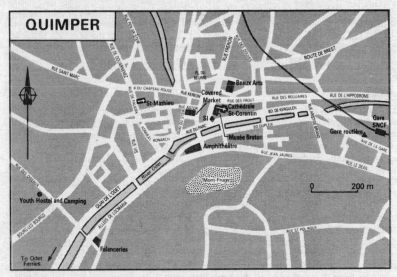

ultra-modern edifices blend in a surprisingly harmonious way with their ancient – and attractive – surroundings. Overlooking all is **Mont Frugy** (all of 87m the river) denuded following the devastation of the hurricane of 1987. There is no great pressure in Quimper to rush around monuments or museums, and the most enjoyable option may be to take a boat and drift down "the prettiest river in France" to the open sea at Bénodet.

Arrival and accommodation

Quimper's **SI** has moved several times in recent years. It can now be found in a small, single-storey building at 7 rue de la Déesse, pl de la Résistance (July & Aug, Mon–Sat 8.30am–8pm; mid-June to mid-Sept also Sun 9.30am–noon; rest of year Mon–Sat 9am–noon & 2–6pm).

The **gare SNCF** (☎98.90.50.50) and **gare routière** are next to each other on avenue de la Gare, 1km east of the centre. Local **buses** #1 and #6 connect with both, but all pass through pl de la Résistance near the SI; buses to Bénodet leave from here.

Between May and September you can **sail** from Quimper down the Odet to Bénodet, which takes about 1hr 15min, on *Vedettes de l'Odet* (Bénodet ☎98.57.00.58, Quimper ☎98.52.98.41). The boats leave from the end of quai de l'Odet; times vary with the tides so check with the SI (who also sell tickets). **Bicycles** can be hired from *Torch VTT*, 58 rue de la Providence (☎98.53.84.41).

Accommodation

Quimper has a summer-only **youth hostel** 2km downstream from town at 6 avenue des Oiseaux in Bois de Seminaire (☎98.55.41.67), on bus route #1, direction Penhass. You can **camp** either next to the hostel, or at the four-star *Orangerie de Lannion* site on the route de Bénodet (☎98.90.62.02).

There are remarkably few hotels in the centre of the town from which to choose, though more can be found near the station. Rooms can be especially difficult fo find in late July or early August, when reservations are advisable

Hôtel-Restaurant Celtic, 13 rue de Douarnenez (☎98.55.59.35). Economical rooms, a little way out from the centre. Restaurant closed Sat pm and Sun, except in July & Aug. ③

Hôtel Nantais, 23 av de la Gare (☎98.90.07.84). Hotel near the station, with a ground-floor café. ②

Hôtel-Restaurant Pascal, 19 av de la Gare (☎98.90.00.81). Also near the station; the restaurant is not very exciting. ④

Hôtel-Restaurant le Transvaal, 57 rue Jean-Jaurès (☎98.90.09.91). Comfortable and central old-fashioned *logis* just south of the Odet, with a good but rather dark restaurant. Garage available. ③

The town

The enormous **Cathédrale St-Corentin** is said to be the most complete Gothic cathedral in Brittany, though its neo-Gothic spires date from 1856. When the nave was being added to the old chancel in the fifteenth century, the extension would either have hit existing buildings or the swampy edge of the then unchanneled river. The masons eventually hit on a solution and placed the nave at a slight angle – a peculiarity which, once noticed, makes it hard to concentrate on the other Gothic splendours within.

The exterior, however, gives no hint of the deviation, with King Gradlon now mounted in perfect symmetry between the spires – though whether he would have advised a river bed nave is another question.

The heart of old Quimper lies to the west of pl St-Corentin, in front of the cathedral. This is where you'll find the liveliest shops and cafés, housed in the old half-timbered buildings, such as the Breton *Keltia-Musique* record shop in pl au Beurre, and the Celtic shop, *Ar Bed Keltiek*, nearby at 2 rue Grallon. The old market hall was burned down in 1976, but the light and spacious new **Halles St-Francis**, rue Astor, built to replace it is quite a delight, not just for the food, but for the view past the upturned boat rafters through the roof to the cathedral's twin spires.

In the **Musée des Beaux-Arts**, alongside the Hôtel de Ville at 4 pl St-Corentin (summer 9.30am–noon & 1.30–7pm; winter 10am–noon & 2–6pm; closed Tues), are amazing collections of drawings by Cocteau, Gustav Doré and Max Jacob (who was born in Quimper), paintings of the Pont-Aven school, and Breton scenes by the likes of Eugène Boudin. Only the old Dutch oils upstairs let the collection down.

Pottery has been made in and around Quimper since 1690 and, as you walk round the town, it is impossible to ignore its presence – you are invited to look and to buy on every corner. On weekdays, it's also possible to visit the two major *ateliers*, both to the southwest in the suburb of Locmaria just off the route de Bénodet: *H-B Henriot*, allées de Locmarion (☎98.90.09.36), and the more modern *Keraluc*, 71 rue du President-Sadat (☎98.53.04.50).

Eating and drinking

Although the pedestrian streets west of the cathedral are surprisingly short on places to eat, there are quite a few **restaurants** further east, towards the station. For *crêperies*, pl au Beurre is a good bet. Otherwise, rue Aristide-Briand, just north of the river, is a particularly promising area, which also contains a couple of lively **Celtic bars**; *Les Deux Cornouailles* at no. 2 and *Ceili* at no. 4.

Restaurants

L'Ambroisie, 49 rue Elie-Feron (☎98.95.00.02). Upmarket French restaurant, with menus from 105F; closed Mon pm, except in summer.

L'Astragale, 3 rue Aristide-Briand (☎98.90.53.85). Very popular Spanish place, serving excellent seafood paella.

La Couscousserie, 1 bd de Kerguélen (☎98.95.46.50). Wide range of Middle Eastern dishes.

Trattoria Mario, 35 rue des Réguaires (☎98.95.42.15). Italian meals; behind the post office.

Entertainment and culture

The **Festival de Cornouaille** started in 1923 and has gone from strength to strength since. This great jamboree of Breton music, costumes, theatre and dance is held in the week before the fourth Sunday in July, attracting guest performers from the other Celtic countries and a scattering of other, sometimes highly unusual, ethnic-cultural ensembles. The whole thing culminates in an incredible Sunday parade through the town. The official programme does not appear until July, but you can get provisional details from 2 pl de la Tour-d'Auvergne, BP 29103, Quimper (☎98.55.53.53).

Not so widely known are the **Seminaires Musicales** which follow in the first two weeks of August. The music is mainly classical and favours French composers such as Berlioz, Debussy, Bizet and Poulenc. Founded in 1978, it brings the rather stuffy nineteenth-century theatre on bd Dupleix alive every year.

Down the Odet – and out to the headlands

Once out of its city channel, the Odet takes on the anarchic shape of most Breton inlets, spreading out to lake proportions then turning narrow corners between gorges. The family resort of **BÉNODET** at the mouth of the river (reachable by boat from Quimper – see above) has a long sheltered beach on the ocean side, with amusements for children and beachside nurseries. Its **hotels** offer comparatively good value – you could try the *Beau Rivage* (☎98.57.00.22; ②) or *L'Hermitage* (☎98.57.05.37; ②), and there are several large **campsites** such as the enormous four-star *Du Letty*, southeast of the "village" by the plage du Letty (summer only; ☎98.57.04.69).

The Pays de Bigouden

The southwest corner of Brittany, the **Pays de Bigouden**, is the least touristed area of the province. Traditions have endured: it's the place you're most likely to see women wearing coiffes for non-promotional reasons. The local variety is fairly startling – 30-centimetre high tubes of lace that always stay on, defying the strong gusts of wind. World **windsurfing championships** are held at **POINTE DE LA TORCHE**, at the southern end of the Baie d'Audierne, and there are usually some aficionados twirling about with effortless ease. But warning signs about swimming should not be ignored. For safer seas framed by white sand beaches there's the coast from PENMARCH to LOCTUDY and beyond. It's about an hour on the bus from Quimper to this southern tip and it's one of the more frequent services.

Land's End

An hour and a half's bus ride east of Quimper takes you to the land's end of France, the **POINTE DU RAZ**. As you approach, the vision of the ocean is blocked by a gaggle of souvenir shops, and then military installations, but once past these you reach plummeting fissures, filling and draining with deafening force, and you can walk on precarious paths above them (shoes that grip are a good idea). A short way back towards Audierne, the fading graffiti on walls and hoardings is the only reminder that this is **PLOGOFF** where ecologists, autonomists and, principally, the local people fought riot police and paratroopers for six weeks in 1980 to stop the opening move in a nuclear power station project. Mitterrand pledged to abandon the plans if elected, and did so.

Audierne and the Île de Sein

The town of **AUDIERNE** remains an active fishing port, famous for its prawns and crayfish – the most affordable restaurant to try them is *Le Cornouaille*. From the town centre inland, it's roughly 2km to the long curving and surprisingly sheltered beach. The *Hôtel de Dunes* just back from the sea (☎98.70.01.19; ②) serves good fish menus from just 57F.

Boats leave from Audierne-Plage to the **ÎLE DE SEIN** (three daily in July and Aug; rest of year one daily at 9.30am except Wed; phone ☎98.70.02.38 for times; journey time 70min). A misty, windy, treeless, dry spot, the island is reputed to have been the last refuge of the Druids in Brittany. A few hundred people still live on it, gathering rain water and fishing scallops, lobster and crayfish. There is one summer-only hotel, the *Armen* (June–Sept; ☎98.70.90.77; ②).

Concarneau, Pont-Aven and Quimperlé

The first major town east of Bénodet is **CONCARNEAU**, a fishing port doing a reasonable job of passing itself off as a holiday resort. Its greatest asset is its **Ville Clos**, the old walled city situated across a slender causeway on an irregular rocky island in the bay. It has been inhabited for at least 1000 years and was originally a priory founded by King Gradlon of Quimper. It has also been fortified for centuries – its current ramparts are as Vauban remodelled them in the seventeenth century. From Easter to the end of September (9am–7pm) you can walk along the top of them, admiring the climbing roses and clematis on the restaurants, snack bars, and gift shops below.

The **Musée de la Pêche**, immediately inside the Ville Clos (daily summer 10am–7pm; rest of year 10am–12.30pm & 2.30–7pm; 25F), provides an insight into the traditional life Concarneau shared with so many other Breton ports. It details the history and practice of whaling, tuna fishing – with drag nets the size of central Paris – herring fishing and sardine processing; the building itself was a sardine cannery.

The one thing the Ville Clos lacks completely is **hotels**. Those that there are in Concarneau skulk in the back streets of the mainland, and tend to be full most of the time. The *Bonne Auberge*, Le Cabellou (☎98.97.04.30; ③), and the *Crêpe d'Or*, 3 rue du Lin (☎98.97.08.61; ③), are worth trying, but the best bet in Concarneau is probably the **youth hostel** (☎98.97.03.47), for once very near the city centre. It's just around the tip of the headland on pl de la Croix, with a good crêperie opposite. The town's main **market** is held in front of the Ville Clos on Friday, with a smaller one on Monday. For a cheap meal in the centre, *Ty Mad* near pl du Guesclin features on its menu a Breton rarity – affordable scallops.

Gauguin and Pont-Aven

PONT-AVEN, 14km east at the tip of the Aven estuary, is a small port packed with tourists and art galleries. It was where Gauguin came to paint in the 1880s, before shuffling off to Tahiti. In his wake developed a "Pont-Aven School" of painters, the best known of whom was Émile Bernard. The so-called **Musée Gauguin** (Easter–Sept 10am–12.30pm & 2–7pm) in the Mairie holds annual exhibitions of the many members of this school, but, for all the local hype, the town does not possess a single work by Gauguin himself. Even without the master, the town is pleasant in its own right and the countless galleries can easily while away an afternoon. There is a small and neat port, with a watermill and, so it is said, leaping salmon; occasional cruises run down to the sea at Port-Manech. Upstream, a walk can take you into the **Bois d'Amour**, wooded gardens which have long provided inspiration to visiting painters – and a fair number of poets and musicians, too. If you need to stay, be warned that the three **hotels** are expensive, and the nearest **campsite** is 4km away at ROZ PIN, on the road to Nevez.

Quimperlé

The final town of any size in Finistère, **QUIMPERLÉ** straddles a hill and two rivers, the Isole and the Elle, cut by a sequence of bridges. It's an atmospheric place, particularly in the medieval muddle of streets around **Ste-Croix** church. This was copied in plan from schema brought back by crusaders of the Church of the Holy Sepulchre in Jerusalem and is notable for its original Romanesque apse. There are some good bars nearby and, on Fridays, a market on the square higher up on the hill. The **hotels** *L'Europe* (☎98.96.00.02; ②) and *Auberge de Toulföen* (☎98.96.00.29; ③) both have reasonable rooms.

INLAND BRITTANY:
THE NANTES–BREST CANAL

The **Nantes–Brest canal** is a meandering chain of waterways from Finistère to the Loire, linking rivers with stretches of canal built at Napoléon's instigation to bypass the belligerent English fleets off the coast. Finally completed in 1836, it came into its own at the end of the century as a coal, slate and fertiliser route. The building of the dam at Lac Guerlédan in the 1920s chopped the canal in two, leaving a whole section unnavigable by barge. Road transport had already superseded water haulage; now tourism is breathing life back into the canal.

En route it passes through riverside towns, such as **Josselin** and **Malestroit**, that long pre-date its construction; commercial ports and junctions – **Pontivy**, most notably – that developed in the nineteenth century because of it; the old port of **Redon**, a patchwork of water, where the canal crosses the River Vilaine; and a sequence of scenic splendours, including the string of lakes around the **Barrage de Guerlédan** near Mur-de-Bretagne. As a focus for exploring **inland Brittany**, whether by barge, bike, foot or all three, the canal is ideal. Not every stretch is accessible but there are detours to be made away from it, such as the wild and desolate **Monts d'Arrée** to the north of the canal in Finistère.

The Finistère stretch

The **MONTS D'ARRÉE**. stretch from the base of the Crozon peninsula almost to Morlaix, of These hills, rising at their peaks to only 380m at the wild-looking ridge encircling the Lac de Brennilis, give the impression of being much higher than they are, due partly to the desolate infrequency of habitation and partly to the lack of anything higher in the whole province.

They form part of the **Parc Naturel Régional d'Armorique**, an area, in theory at least, of conservation and rural regeneration along traditional lines. The administrative centre is at **MENEZ-MEUR**, off the D342 near the Forêt de Cranou – just inland from the Brest–Quimper motorway. Menez is an official **animal reserve** with wild boar and deer roaming free (June–Sept daily 10.30am–7pm). At the reserve gate you can pick up a wealth of detail on the park and all its various activities (☎98.68.81.71).

To the north, at **SIZUN**, there's a research station, **aquarium** and fishing exhibition (mid-June to mid-Oct 10.30am–7pm; rest of year public holidays only). East of here, 3km along D764 to COMMANA, is the abandoned hamlet of **MOULINS-DE-KÉROUAT** (or MILIN KERROCH*)*, which has recently been restored as an Éco-Musée (July–Aug daily 11am–7pm; March–June & Sept–Oct Sat & Sun 2–6pm). Kérouat's last inhabitant died in 1967 and, like many a place in the Breton interior, it might have crumbled into indiscernible ruins, but one of the hamlet's watermills has been restored to working order, and its houses have been repaired and refurnished. The largest belonged in the last century to the mayor of Commana, who also controlled the mills – its furnishings are those of a wealthy family.

The **ridge** around Brennilis is visible as a stark silhouette from the under-used **campsite** at **NESTAVEL-BRAZ** on the eastern shore of the lake. From this deceptively tranquil vantage point, the army's antennae near **Roc Trévezel** to the north are obscured, as are those of the navy at Menez-Meur to the west. Right behind you, however, is the BRENNILIS nuclear power station. In a rare manifestation of separatist terrorism, Breton nationalists attacked it in 1975 with a rocket launcher; it survived. In 1987, the SAS conducted an outrageously offensive exercise in this area, when they were invited by the French government to subdue a simulated Breton uprising, and in the process managed to run over a local inhabitant. Perhaps appropriately, across the lake where the tree-lined fields around the villages end, is **Yeun Elez**, one of the legendary "holes to hell". You can walk around the lake – gorse and brambles permitting; be very careful not to stray from the paths into the surrounding peat bogs. The ridge itself is followed most of the way by a road, but in places it still feels like miles from any habitation.

Huelgoat

Up until October 1987, the **Forêt de Huelgoat** was one of the most beautiful places in Brittany, a too-good-to-be-true natural arrangement of rocks, waterfalls, grottoes and a gurgling stream. But the hurricane just about destroyed it, and it will take more than a lifetime to be restored. Though now a rather depressing place, **HUELGOAT** is still one of the best bases for this area, with accommodation at the *Hôtel l'Armorique*, 1 pl Aristide-Briand (☎98.99.71.24; ①), the *du Lac* (☎98.99.71.14; ②) on the lakeside, or the summer-only campsite (a short walk towards the lake along the Brest road). The **SI**, at 14 pl Aristide-Briand, or the Parc centre (see above) can provide details of the numerous campsites and **gîtes d'étapes** in the region. SIZUN, too, has a reasonable **hotel**, the *des Voyageurs*, 2 rue de l'Argoat (☎98.68.80.35; ②). **Bikes** can be hired at Huelgoat (from the garage at 1 rue du Lac) and several of the other villages.

Along the canal

As late as the 1920s, steamers would make their way across the Rade de Brest and down the Aulne River to CHÂTEAULIN, the first real town on the canal route. If you're walking the canal seriously, PONT-COBLANT and PLEYBEN are just 10km further away on the map, but be warned that the meanders make it a several-hour hike. Pick your side of the water, too; there are no bridges between Châteaulin and Pont-Coblant.

Châteaulin

CHÂTEAULIN is a quiet place, where the main reason to stay is the canal itself – or river as it is here. For its salmon and trout fishing, if you're interested, most bars (as well as fishing shops – some of which hire out tackle) sell permits. You should have little difficulty finding a room at the **hotel** *Le Christmas* (☎98.86.01.24; ④) on rue des Écoles, which climbs from the town centre towards Pleyben. Along **the riverbank**, there's a statue to Jean Moulin, the Resistance leader; the inscription reads *"mourir sans parler"* – to die without talking – which is exactly what he did. He was *sous-préfet* in Châteaulin from 1930 to 1933. Within a couple of minutes' walk upstream from the statue and the town centre, you're on towpaths full of rabbits and squirrels and overhung by trees full of birds.

Pont-Coblant

PONT-COBLANT is the first point on the canal at which you can **hire boats** – either canoes or houseboats (see the travel details at the end of this chapter). A small village, it also has a very basic (and cheap) forty-bed unofficial **youth hostel** (contact the *Moulin de Pont-Coblant*, 29190 Pleyben, ☎98.73.34.40 to reserve a bed) and a **campsite**.

Pleyben

PLEYBEN, 4km north of Pont-Coblant, is renowned for its **parish close** (see p.294). On its four sides the calvary traces the life of Jesus like a comic strip, with a naivety that is echoed by the hand-drawn and coloured exhibition in the repository of local customs, traditions, folktales and fountains. The church is still very visibly scarred by the 1987 hurricane, which ripped off much of its roof. There's an **SI** in the adjacent pl de Gaulle.

Châteauneuf-du-Faou and onwards

CHÂTEAUNEUF-DU-FAOU is similar to Châteaulin, sloping down to the tree-lined river. It's a little more developed, though, with a tourist complex, the *Penn ar Pont* (☎98.81.81.25), with swimming pool, *gîtes* and camping, as well as **cycle** and **boat hire**. The **canal proper** separates off from the Aulne a few kilometres to the east at PONT-TRIFFEN, staking its own path on past Carhaix, and out of Finistère. **CARHAIX**, an ancient road junction, has cafés and shops to replenish supplies, but not much to recommend it. Beyond it the canal – as far as PONTIVY – is navigable only by canoe.

The central stretch: Gouarec to Ploermel

Although the canal is limited to canoeists between CARHAIX and PONTIVY, it's worth some effort to follow on land, particularly for the scenery from GOUAREC to MUR-DE-BRETAGNE. At the centre is the trailing **Lac de Guerlédan**, created by the construction of a barrage near Mur, and backed, to the south, by the enticing **Forêt de Quénécan**. Approaching by road, the canal path is easiest joined at GOUAREC, covered by the five daily buses between Carhaix and Loudéac.

Gouarec

At **GOUAREC**, the River Blavet and the canal meet in a confusing swirl of water that shoots off, edged by footpaths, in the most unlikely directions. The old schist houses of the town are barely disturbed by traffic or development, nor are there great numbers of tourists. For a comfortable overnight stop, the *Hôtel du Blavet* (☎96.24.90.03; ③) is in an ideal waterside position; don't be put off by its extravagant menus – they have affordable meals as well. The municipal **campsite** (☎96.24.90.22) is next to the canal.

Quénécan Forest

For the 15km between GOUAREC and MUR-DE-BRETAGNE, the **N164** skirts the edge of **Quénécan Forest**, within which is the series of artificial lakes created when the Barrage of Guerlédan was completed in 1928. Though sadly once again damaged by the hurricane, it's a beautiful stretch of river, a little overrun by campers and caravans but peaceful enough nonetheless. The best places to stay are just off the road, past the villages of **ST-GELVEN** and **CAUREL**. At the former, you can walk down to Lac Guerlédan and the **campsite** at KERMANEC. From just before Caurel, the brief loop of the D111 leads to tiny, sandy beaches – a bit too tiny in season – with **campsites** *Les Pins* (☎96.28.52.22) and *Les Pommiers* (☎96.28.52.35). At the spot known as BEAU RIVAGE is a complex containing a campsite, hotel, restaurant, snackbar and mooring for a 140-seat glass-topped cruise boat.

Mur-de-Bretagne

MUR-DE-BRETAGNE is set back from the eastern end of the lake, a lively place with a wide and colourful pedestrianised zone around its church. It's the nearest town to the barrage – just 2km distant – and has a **campsite**, the *Rond-Point du Lac* (☎96.26.01.90), with facilities for windsurfing and horseback riding. There's also a **youth hostel** a short way along the N164 at **ST-GUEN** (☎96.28.54.34) – take the Loudéac bus and get off at *Bourg de St-Guen*.

Pontivy

You can again take **barges** – all the way to the Loire – from **PONTIVY**, the central junction of the Nantes–Brest canal, where the course of the canal breaks off once more from the Blavet. When the waterway opened, the small medieval centre of the town was expanded, redesigned and given broad avenues to fit its new role. It was even renamed Napoléonville for a while, in honour of the man responsible for its new prosperity.

These days, Pontivy is a bright market town, its twisting old streets contrasting with the stately riverside promenades. At its northern end, occupying a commanding hillside site, is the **Château de Rohan**, built by the lord of Josselin in the fifteenth century. Open to visitors, and used for low-key cultural events, the castle still belongs to the same family, who are slowly restoring it. At the moment, one impressive facade, complete with deep moat and two forbidding towers, looks out over the river – behind that, the structure peters out.

Pontivy has several **hotels**, among them the low-priced *Martin* (☎97.25.02.04; ①) and *Robic* (☎97.25.11.80; ②), as well as a very spartan **youth hostel** (☎97.25.58.27), 2km from the **gare SNCF** on the Île des Recollets. Its **SI** is on rue de Gaulle.

Bréhan and the Abbaie de Timadeuc

Following the canal beyond Pontivy to ROHAN is difficult unless you're on it. Between Rohan and Josselin is the Cistercian **Abbaie de Timadeuc**, which you can enter only to attend mass. But it's beautiful from the outside, with its front walls and main gate covered in flowers at the end of an avenue of old pines. The abbey also provides an excuse to stay at nearby **BRÉHAN**, a quiet little village whose **hotel**, the *Cremaillère* (☎97.51.52.09; ①), must be one of the best deals anywhere in the province, both for good rooms and excellent food at astonishingly low prices.

Josselin and Ploërmel

A short way south from Timadeuc, you come to the three Rapunzel towers embedded in a vast sheet of stone of the **château** in JOSSELIN. The Rohan family used to own a third of Brittany, the present duke contents himself with the position of local mayor. The pompous apartments of his residence are not very interesting, even if they do contain the table on which the Edict of Nantes was signed in 1598. But the Duchess's collection of **dolls**, housed in the *Musée des Poupées*, behind the castle, is something special. (Both open June–Sept daily 10am–noon & 2–6pm, March–May, & Oct to mid-Nov Wed, Sat, Sun & hols only 2–6pm.) The **town** is full of medieval splendours, from the gargoyles of the Basilica to the castle ramparts, and the half-timbered houses in between (of which one of the finest is the **SI** on pl de la Congrégation). **Notre-Dame-du-Roncier** is built on the spot where in the ninth century a peasant supposedly found a statue of the Virgin under a bramble bush. The statue was burned during the Revolution, but an important *pardon* is held each year on September 8.

If you want to **stay** at Josselin, there's a *gîte d'étape* right below the castle walls, where you can also hire **canoes**. Alternatively, the *Hôtel du Commerce* on rue Beaumanoir (☎97.22.22.08; ②) is reasonable.

For rail travellers, **PLOËRMEL**, though a bit north of the canal, may be a useful base. It doesn't have anything special to offer other than a few Renaissance houses – it's no match for its old rival Josselin 12km east. The **hotels** *Saint Marc* (☎97.74.00.01; ②) and *Cobh* (☎97.74.00.49; ②) are good value and there's an **SI** on pl Lamennais.

Guéhenno and the Domaine de Kerguéhennec

One of the largest and best Breton calvaries is at GUÉHENNO, south of Josselin on the D123. Sculpted in 1550, the figures include the cock that crowed after Peter's denials, Mary Magdalene with the shroud and a recumbent Christ in the crypt. Its appeal is enhanced by the naivety of its amateur restoration. After damage caused by Revolutionary soldiers in 1794 – who amused themselves by playing *boules* with the heads of the statues – all the sculptors approached for the work demanded exorbitant fees, so the parish priest and his assistant decided to undertake the task themselves.

Another unusual sculptural endeavour, this time contemporary, is taking place at the **Domaine de Kerguéhennec**, which is marked a short way off the D11 near ST-JEAN-BREVELAY. This innovative **sculpture park** has plans to build up a permanent international collection and if the first pieces to be installed are anything to go by, it should be an increasingly compelling stop. Its setting is the lawns, woods and lake of an early eighteenth-century château. Over to the east, off the D151, LIZIO has also set itself up as a centre for arts and crafts, with ceramic and weaving workshops its speciality. A **Festival Artisanal** is held on the second Sunday in August, along with street theatre (and pancakes). There are several **gîtes** in the town and a **campsite**.

Towards Nantes: Malestroit and Redon

Not a lot happens in **MALESTROIT**, but that, along with the unexpected details of its ancient buildings and the serenity of the canal, is what gives it its charm. As you come in to the main square, **pl du Bouffay** in front of the church, the houses are covered with unlikely carvings – an anxious bagpipe-playing hare looking over its shoulder at a dragon's head on one beam, while an oblivious sow in a blue-buckled belt threads her distaff on another. The **church** itself is decorated with drunkards and acrobats outside, demon torturers and erupting towers within; each night the display is completed by the sullen parade of metal-studded youth who weave in and out of the *Vieille Auberge* bar opposite. The only ancient walls without adornment are the ruins of the **Chapelle de la Madeleine**, where one of the many temporary truces of the Hundred Years War was signed.

Next to the grey canal, the matching grey slate tiles on the turreted rooftops bulge and dip, while on its central island overgrown houses stand next to the stern walls of an old mill. If you arrive by barge (this is a good stretch to travel), you'll moor very near the town centre, so you can lurch across to the only **hotel** and restaurant, the *Aigle d'Or*, 1 rue des Écoles (☎97.75.20.10; ③), where meals, if not rooms, are relatively cheap. The **gare routière**, served by buses from Vannes and Rennes, is on the main road, bd du Pont-Neuf; there's a **campsite** below the bridge that it crosses, and a **gîte d'étape** up at the canal lock (c/o M Halier, ☎97.75.11.66). The **SI** is also on bd du Pont-Neuf, and has details of **canoe and boat hire**; **bikes** can be hired from the *Aigle d'Or*.

The Musée de la Résistance Bretonne

West of Malestroit about 2km (and with no bus connection), just past the village of ST-MARCEL off the Vannes road, the **Musée de la Résistance Bretonne** rests on the site of a June 1944 battle (June–Sept 10am–7pm; rest of year 10am–noon & 2–6pm). Here the Breton *maquis*, joined by Free French Forces parachuted in from England, successfully diverted the local German troops from the main Normandy invasion movements. The museum's strongest feature is the presentation of the pressures that made the majority of French people collaborate: the reconstructed street corner from which all life has been drained by the occupiers; the big colourful propaganda posters offering work in Germany, announcing executions of *maquis*, equating resistance with aiding US and British big business; and, to counter them, the low-budget, flimsily printed Resistance pamphlets.

Redon

Thirty-four kilometres east of Malestroit, at the junction not only of the rivers Oust and Vilaine and the canal, but also the railways to Rennes, Vannes and Nantes, and six major roads, **REDON** is not an easy place to avoid. And you shouldn't try to, either. A wonderful grouping of water and locks, the town has history, charm and life. It's probably the best stop along the whole course of the canal. Up until World War I, Redon was the seaport for Rennes. Its industrial docks – or what remains of them – are therefore on the Vilaine, while the canal, even in the very centre of town, is almost totally rural, its towpaths shaded avenues. Ship-owners' houses from the seventeenth and eighteenth centuries can be seen along quai Jean-Bart by the *bassin* and quai Duguay-Truin next to the river. A rusted wrought-iron workbridge, equipped with a gantry, still crosses the river, but the main users of the port now are cruise ships heading down the Vilaine to La Roche-Bernard.

Redon was once also a religious centre, its first abbey founded in 832 by Saint Conwoion. The most prominent church today is **St-Sauveur**. Its unique four-storeyed Romanesque belfry is squat, almost obscured by later roofs and the high choir, and best seen from the adjacent cloisters; the Gothic tower is entirely separated from the main building by a fire. Inside the church, you'll find the tomb of the judge who tried the legendary Bluebeard – Joan of Arc's friend, Gilles de Rais.

The most reasonable place to **stay** in Redon is the *Hôtel Bretagne* on pl de la Gare (☎99.71.00.42; ②). Near the train station, five minutes' walk away from the centre, it also houses the *Doucet* restaurant, which serves a good 90F menu, in its attractive garden. The more central *Hôtel Asther*, in town at 14 rue des Douves (☎99.71.10.91; ③), has its own brasserie. Redon's **SI** is on pl du Parlement (☎99.71.06.04); in summer it has an additional annexe in the port. A large Monday **market** centres around the modern *halles*, where you can buy superb crêpes.

THE SOUTHERN COAST

Brittany's **southern coast** takes in the province's, and indeed Europe's, most famous prehistoric site, the **alignments of Carnac**, with the associated megaliths of the beautiful, island-studded **Golfe de Morbihan**. The beaches are not as spectacular as in Finistère, but there are more safe places to swim and the water is warmer. Of the cities, **Lorient** has Brittany's most compelling **festival** and **Vannes** has one of the liveliest medieval town centres. Further east, **La Baule** does a good impression of a Breton St-Tropez, and you can escape to the islands of **Belle Île**, **Hoëdic** and **Houat**. Inevitably it's popular, and in summer you can be hard pressed to find a room, but if you're prepared to make reservations, or you're camping, there shouldn't be much problem.

Lorient and around

LORIENT, Brittany's fourth-largest city, is an immense natural harbour – protected from the ocean by the Île de Groix and strategically located at the junction of the Rivers Scorff, Ter and Blavet. A functional, rather depressing port today, it was once a key base for French and English colonialism, and was founded in the mid-seventeenth century for trading operations by the *Compagnie des Indes*, an equivalent of the Dutch and English East India Companies. Apart from the name, little else remains to suggest the plundered wealth that once arrived here. During the last war, Lorient was a major target for the Allies; the Germans held out until May 1945, by which time the city was almost completely destroyed. The only substantial remains were the U-boat pens – subsequently greatly expanded by the French for their nuclear submarines.

Across the estuary in Port-Louis there's a museum of the *Compagnie des Indes*, a pretty dismal temple to imperialism. Time would be more enjoyably spent on a boat trip, either up the estuary towards Hennebont (see below) or out to the Île de Groix. This 8km-long steep-sided rock is a short way out to sea and has no permanent population, though there is a summer-operated **youth hostel** (phone Lorient's hostel, see below, for details). The coast around Lorient itself is unenticing, and plagued with thick drifts of seaweed.

The Inter-Celtic Festival

The overriding reason people come to Lorient is for the **Inter-Celtic Festival**, held for ten days from the first Friday to the second Sunday in August. The biggest Celtic event in Brittany, or anywhere else for that matter, sees representatives from all seven Celtic countries. In a genuine popular celebration of cultural solidarity, with up to 250,000 people in attendance at over 150 different shows, five languages mingle and Scotch and Guinness flow with the French and Spanish wines and ciders. There is a certain competitive element, with championships in various categories, but the feeling of mutual enthusiasm and conviviality is paramount. Most of the activities – which embrace music, dance and literature – take place around the central pl Jules-Ferry, and this is where most people end up sleeping, too, as accommodation is pushed to the limits.

For schedules of the festival, and details of temporary accommodation, contact the *Office du Tourisme du Pays du Lorient*, pl Jules-Ferry, 56100 LORIENT (☎97.21.07.84), bearing in mind that the festival schedule is not finalised before May. For certain specific events, you need to reserve tickets well in advance.

Lorient practicalities

Lorient's **SI**, on quai de Rohan (July & Aug Mon–Fri 9am–7pm, Sat 9am–noon & 2–7pm, Sun 2–6pm; rest of year Mon–Fri 9am–12.30pm & 1.30–6pm, Sat 9am–noon & 2–6pm; ☎97.21.07.84), can provide full details on local boat trips, and organises some excursions itself.

Apart from during the festival, there's a huge choice of **hotels**. Among the best are the *Hôtel-Restaurant Gabriel*, 45 av de la Perrière in the fishing port (☎97.37.60.76; ③), and the *Hôtel d'Arvor*, 104 rue Lazare-Carnot (☎97.21.07.55; ①), both of which have good-value restaurants. The *Poisson d'Or* on rue Maître-Esvelin (☎97.21.57.06) is a great **fish restaurant**, with menus from 90F. The **youth hostel** is at 41 rue Victor-Schoelcher, 3km out on bus line C from the gare SNCF, next to the River Ter (☎97.37.11.65). Place Aristide-Briand is much the best area of town in which to find a congenial **bar**, year-round.

Hennebont

A few kilometres upstream from Lorient, at the point where the Blavet estuary narrows to river proportions, and a short hop from the port by train, is the old walled town of **HENNEBONT**. The fortifications, and especially the main gate, the Porte Broerec'h, are imposing, and from the top of the ramparts there are wide views of the river below. What you see of the old city within, however, is entirely residential – an assortment of clothes lines, budgies and garden sheds. All its public buildings were destroyed in the war and now not even a bar (or rented room) is to be found in the former centre.

The one time Hennebont comes alive is at the **Thursday market**, held below the ramparts and through the squares by the church. It's one of the largest in the region, with a heady mix of good fresh food, crêpes and Vietnamese delicacies alongside livestock, flowers, carpets and clothes. On other days, the only places you'll find any activity are along pl **Maréchal-Foch** (in front of the basilica) and **quai du Pont-Neuf**, beside the river.

Practicalities

If you decide to **stay** in Hennebont – and few people do – the *Hôtel de France* at 17 av de la Libération (☎97.36.21.82; ②) is a good proposition near the town centre. The town's **campsite**, the *St-Caradec* (☎97.36.20.14; June–Sept only), has a prime site on the river bank opposite the fortifications. You can hire **bicycles** at 5 av de la République and 87 rue Maréchal-Joffre, and take **boat trips** either up the Blavet towards the Nantes–Brest canal or down the estuary to Lorient.

Lochrist

Just to the north, at **LOCHRIST,** the great chimneys of the Hennebont ironworks still stand, smokeless and silent, looking down on the Blavet. Strikes and demonstrations failed to prevent the closure of the foundry in 1966, and the only work since then has been to set up a museum, the **Musée Forges d'Hennebont**, which documents its 100-year history from the workers' point of view (Tues–Thurs 9am–noon & 2–6pm, Fri 9am–noon, Sat & Sun 2–6pm). Some of the men put out of work have contributed their memories and tools; for others the museum was a final bitter irony. It is excellent though, both in content and presentation, despite the sense of defeat after seeing the joyful pictures of successful strikes in the 1930s. If it's on your route it's worth a stop: the bus station is just opposite, on the other side of the river.

Auray

Some people find **AURAY**, with its over-restored ancient quarter, slightly dull – but it is a lot less crowded than Vannes, a lot cheaper than Quiberon town, and usefully placed for exploring Carnac, the Quiberon peninsula and the Gulf of Morbihan.

The natural centre of the town today is **pl de la République**, with its eighteenth-century Hôtel de Ville. In a neighbouring square, linked to the pl de la République by rue du Lait, is the seventeenth-century church of **St-Gildas**, with its fine Renaissance porch. A **covered market** adjoins the Hôtel de Ville, but on Mondays an open-air market fills the surrounding streets with colour – and stops all traffic for a considerable radius.

However, Auray's showpiece is undoubtedly the ancient quarter of **Saint-Goustan**, with its delightful fifteenth- and sixteenth-century houses, albeit restored. The bend in the River Loch, an early defended site, was a natural setting for a town – and, with its easy access to the gulf, it soon became one of the busiest ports of Brittany. Today, as you look at it from the Promenade du Loch on the opposite bank, with the small seventeenth-century stone bridge still spanning the river, it is not difficult to imagine it in its heyday. In 1776, Benjamin Franklin landed here on his way to seek the help of Louis XVI in the American War of Independence.

Practicalities

Auray's **SI** is on the ground floor of the Hôtel de Ville, pl de la République (☎97.24.09.75). A small annexe is maintained at the gare SNCF, twenty minutes' walk from the centre, in July and August.

There are a couple of **hotels** out near the station, including the *Hôtel Terminus*, pl de la Gare (☎97.24.00.09; ②), which has a snack-bar and *crêperie*, but Auray's most appealing accommodation is to be found at the more central *Hôtel le Celtic*, on the way into town at 30 rue Clemenceau (☎97.24.05.37; ②). The nearby *Olympic Bar*, 19 rue Clemenceau (☎97.24.06.69), is a friendly restaurant-cum-bar with menus at 58F and 90F.

Buses run from the gare SNCF through the centre of Auray and on to La Trinité, Carnac and the gare SNCF at Quiberon.

North of Auray

A short way north of Auray, on the B768 to Baud, beyond the station on the left, is the grandiose **Abbaye de Chartreuse** housing a black-and-white marble mausoleum with sculpted reliefs by David d'Angers of the 1790s Royalist rebellion – viewable, bones and all, 10am to noon and 2 to 5.30pm. Another counter-revolutionary failure is recalled by the **Champs des Martyres**, nearby to the right of the D120, where 350 *chouans* were executed. Two kilometres farther along the D120, towards BRECH, you come to the **Écomusée St-Degan** (July to mid-Sept only, 2–6pm). This consists of a group of reconstructed farm buildings, representing the local peasant life at the beginning of this century. It's all a bit too rustically charming, but at least it does attempt to escape the glass cases and wax models of most folk museums.

Ste-Anne-d'Auray

Perhaps the largest of the Breton **pardons** takes place at **STE-ANNE-D'AURAY** on July 26. Some 25,000 pilgrims gather for the occasion to hear mass in the church, mount the *scala sancta* on their knees, and buy trinkets from the street stalls. The origin of this *pardon*, typical of many, lies in the discovery in 1623 of a statue, of Saint Anne by a local peasant, one Nicolazic. He claimed to have been directed to the spot by visionary appearances of the saint (the Virgin's mother) and to have been instructed by her to build a church. Illiterate, speaking only Breton, and with no more than a subsistence livelihood, he managed to raise the necessary funds and construct his church (since destroyed, along with the statue during the Revolution). On his deathbed, twenty years later, the church authorities were still accusing him of making up his story and the debate continues today with the ongoing campaign to have Nicolazic canonised.

Ste-Anne's status as a pilgrimage centre led to its being chosen as the site for the vast **Monument aux Morts** erected to the memory of the 250,000 Breton dead of the Great War. Even the 200 metres of closely inscribed wall which surrounds the monument is insufficient to list all the victims by name. All in all, Ste-Anne is a sad and solemn place, not really somewhere to stop despite its abundant hotels.

Carnac

The **alignments** at **CARNAC** – rows of 2000 or so menhirs stretching for over 4km to the north of the village – constitute the most important prehistoric site in Europe, long predating Knossos, the Pyramids, Stonehenge or the great Egyptian temples of the same name at Karnak. Mercifully they now stand a few kilometres in from the sea, which means you can combine a reasonably tranquil visit to the stones with a stay in the modern seaside resort, pretty hectic by Brittany's mild standards.

The alignments

According to local legend, the standing stones at Carnac are Roman soldiers turned to stone by Pope St-Cornély. Another theory, with a certain amount of mathematical backing, says the giant menhir of Locmariaquer and the Carnac stones were an observatory for the motions of the moon – a sort of three-dimensional neolithic graph paper for plotting the movements of heavenly bodies. But history has seen them used as readyquarried stone, and dug up and removed by peasants to protect their precious crops from academic visitors when prehistoric archaeology became fashionable. It's impossible to say how many have disappeared, nor really to prove anything from what's left;

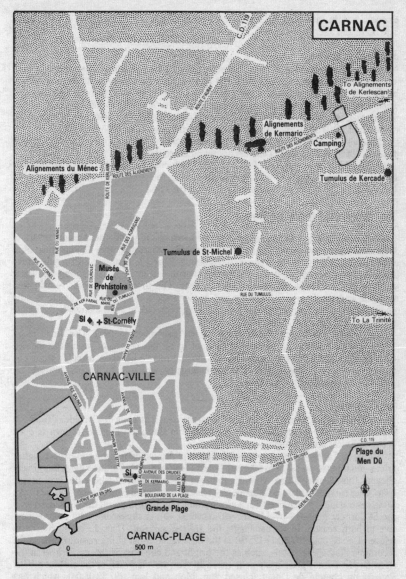

and in any case their actual arrangement may never have been particularly important, with their significance lying in some great annual ceremony as each one was erected.

Aside from strolling in wonder among them, you can get a good deal of information, and entertainment, too, from the **Musée de Préhistoire** on rue du Tumulus in Carnac-Ville (July to mid-Sept daily 10am–noon & 2–6.30pm; rest of year 10am–noon & 2–5pm, closed Tues). It combines serious scholarship with large blowups of the

French Asterix cartoons, and traces the history of the area from about 450,000 years ago up to and after the Romans.

Seeing the stones

Thanks to increasing numbers of visitors, special viewing platforms have recently been erected amidst the alignments, meaning that they are no longer quite as undisturbed as they were a few years ago. If you want to set off on your own, you can rent **bicycles** from several of the town's campsites (see below), or from *Le Randonneur*, 20 av des Druides, Carnac-Plage (☎97.52.02.55), or *Lorcy*, 6 rue de Courdiec, Carnac-Ville (☎97.52.09.73). The *Grande Metairie* site also arranges tours on **horseback**.

Probably the best way of all to see the alignments is from the **air**, which if you split the cost three or four ways, can cost not much more than a good meal. The year-round *Quiberon Air Club* (☎97.50.11.05) and the summer-only *Thalass Air* (☎97.30.40.00) both operate short flights over the Morbihan from the Aérodrome de Quiberon, near the tip of the Quiberon peninsula at Roc'h Priol (☎97.50.11.05).

The town and the beaches

Carnac itself, divided between the original **Carnac-Ville** and the seaside resort of **Carnac-Plage**, is extremely popular and crowded, swarming with holiday makers in July and August. For most of these, the alignments are, if anything, only a side show. But, as a holiday centre, it has its special charm, especially in late spring and early autumn when it is less crowded – and cheaper. The town and seafront remain well wooded, and the tree-lined avenues and gardens are a delight – the climate is mild enough for the Mediterranean mimosa and evergreen oak to grow alongside the native stone pine and cypress.

The town's five **beaches** extend for nearly two miles in total. The small plage Légenèse, nearest the yacht club, is reputed to be the beach on which the ill-fated *Chouan* Royalists landed in 1795. The two most attractive beaches, usually counted as one of the five, are **plages Men Dû** and **Beaumer**, which lie to the east towards LA TRINITÉ beyond Pointe Churchill.

Practicalities

The main **SI** for Carnac is slightly back from the beach at 74 av des Druides (Tues–Sat 9am–noon & 2–6pm; ☎97.52.13.52). An annexe in the pl de l'Église in town is open between Easter and September.

Hotels in Carnac are at a premium in July and August, when you can expect higher prices and intense pressure to take half board (*demi-pension*). Carnac-Ville is marginally cheaper than Carnac-Plage, although the distinction is blurred where the two merge. *Hôtel Chez Nous*, at 5 pl de la Chapelle in Carnac-Ville (closed Nov–March; ☎97.52.07.28; ③) is central and convenient, with a nice garden, but no restaurant; the *Hôtel d'Arvor*, 5 rue St-Cornély (closed Nov–March; ☎97.52.96.90; ④), is similar but a bit more expensive in high season. In Carnac-Plage, the *Hôtel-Restaurant Hoty*, 15 av de Kermario (closed Dec & Jan; ☎97.52.11.12; ③) is the best value. Most of the **restaurants** worth recommending are in hotels, such as the bright and cheerful *Bistrot du Pêcheur* in the *Hôtel La Marine* at 4 pl de la Chapelle (open all year; ☎97.52.07.33) or the old stone *Hôtel Ratelier* on chemin de Douet (closed Sun, Mon and Jan; ☎97.52.05.04), which has menus from 90F. *Chez Yannick*, 8 rue du Tumulus (closed Jan; ☎97.52.08.67) is a worthwhile *crêperie*. There's a **market** in Carnac on Wednesday and Sunday mornings.

As befits such a family-orientated place, there are as many as eighteen **campsites** in and around Carnac. Amongst the best are the *Men Dû* (☎97.52.04.23) near the sea, inland from the plage du Men Dû, and the more expensive *Grande Metairie* (☎97.52.24.01) near the Kercado tumulus.

The Presqu'île de Quiberon

The **Presqu'île de Quiberon**, south of Carnac, is well worth visiting on its own merits; **QUIBERON** is quite a lively port, and you can get boats out to the islands or walk the shores of this narrow peninsula. The ocean-facing shore, known as the **Côte Sauvage**, is a wild and highly unswimmable stretch, where the stormy seas look like flashing scenes of snowy mountain tops. The sheltered eastern side has safe and calm sandy beaches, and plenty of **campsites**.

Quiberon

The town of **QUIBERON** itself centres on a miniature golf course surrounded by bars, pizzerias and some surprisingly good clothes and antique shops. The cafés by the long bathing beach are the most enjoyable, along with the old-fashioned *Café du Marché* next to the PTT.

Port-Maria, the fishing harbour and **gare maritime** for the islands of Belle Île, Houat and Hoedic, is the most active part of town and has the best concentration of **hotels** and **fish restaurants**. Port-Maria was once famous for its sardines, canned locally, but those days are long gone.

Practicalities

Between June and September, the special *Tire Bouchon* (corkscrew) train links Quiberon's **gare SNCF**, which is a short way above the town proper, with Auray. There are also buses right to the gare maritime from Vannes (#23 and #24) and Auray (#24) via Carnac.

The **SI** at 7 rue de Verdun (July & Aug daily 9am–8pm; rest of year daily 9am–12.30pm & 2–6.30pm closed Sun in low season; ☎97.50.07.84), downhill and left from the gare SNCF, has an illuminated map outside which purports to show which hotels are full. Among the many good hotels-cum-restaurants along the seafront in Port-Maria facing the ferry terminal, the *Pension Au Bon Accueil* at 6 quai de Houat (closed Nov–March; ☎97.50.07.92; ②) is particularly recommended, for its friendly atmosphere, superb fish soup, and *assiette de fruits de mer*. *L'Océan Hôtel-Restaurant*, 7 quai de l'Océan (closed Nov–March; ☎97.50.07.58; ④), is also good – its higher prices are due to an insistence on half board. Nearer the station, the *Hôtel-Restaurant de Kermorvan*, 45 rue de Kermorvan (closed Nov–March; ☎97.50.11.33; ③), has an attractive garden.

The local **youth hostel** is *Les Filets Bleus*, inland at 45 rue du Roc'h-Priol (☎97.50.15.54), 1.5km southeast of the gare SNCF. **Campsites** on the sheltered east coast near Quiberon town include the *Do-Mi-Si-La-Mi*, St-Julien (☎97.50.22.52).

Belle-Île

BELLE-ÎLE, 45 minutes by ferry from Quiberon, has its own *Côte Sauvage* on its Atlantic coast, while the landward side is fertile, cultivated ground, interrupted by deep estuaries with tiny ports. To appreciate the island's contrasts, some form of transport is advisable – you can **hire bikes** at the port and main town of **LE PALAIS**, and if you're in a small car the ferry fare is relatively low.

The island once belonged to the monks of Redon; then to the ambitious Nicholas Fouquet, Louis XIV's minister; later to the English, who in 1761 swapped it for Minorca in an unrepeatable bargain deal. Docking at Le Palais, the abrupt star-shaped fortifications of the **Citadelle** are the first thing you see. Built along stylish and ordered lines by the great fortress builder, Vauban, it is startling in size – filled with doorways leading to mysterious cellars and underground passages, endless sequences of rooms, dungeons, and deserted cells. It only ceased being a prison in 1961, having numbered a succession of state enemies and revolutionaries among its inmates, including Ben Bella of Algeria. Less involuntarily, painters such as Monet and Matisse, the writers Flaubert and Proust, and the actress Sarah Bernhardt all spent time on the island. And presumably Alexandre Dumas, too, as Porthos' death, in *The Three Musketeers*, takes place here. A museum in the *citadelle* (9am–7pm) documents the island's history, in fiction as much as in fact.

For exploring the island, a coastal footpath runs on bare soil the length of the **Côte Sauvage**. At the Sauzon end you'll find the **Grotte de l'Apothicairerie**, so called because it was once full of cormorants' nests, arranged like the jars on a pharmacist's shelves. It's reached by descending a slippery flight of steps cut into the rock. Be careful: most years someone falls and drowns. Inland, on the D25 back towards Le Palais, you pass the two **menhirs**, Jean and Jeanne, said to be lovers petrified as punishment for wanting to meet before their marriage. Another larger menhir used to lie near these two; it was broken up to help construct the road that separates them.

Belle-Île's second town, **SAUZON**, is set at the mouth of a long estuary 6km to the west of Le Palais. If you're staying any length of time, and you've got transport, it's probably a better place to base yourself.

Practicalities

The **SI** for the whole island is next to the gare maritime as you arrive in Le Palais (daily July–Sept 8.30am–12.30pm & 2–7.30pm, rest of year 9.30am–noon & 2–6pm; ☎97.31.81.93). **Accommodation** in Le Palais includes the reasonably priced *Hôtel du Commerce*, pl Hôtel-de-Ville (☎97.31.81.71; ④), a **campsite** *Les Glacis* (☎97.31.41.76) and a **youth hostel** (reservations as for Quiberon, ☎97.50.15.54), a short way out of town along the clifftops from the *citadelle*, at Haute-Boulogne.

In Sauzon, there's a good, cheap **hotel** in a magnificent setting, the *du Phare* (☎97.31.60.36; ③) – which insists that guests eat its delicious fish dinners. There are also two **campsites**, *Pen Prad* (☎97.31.62.79) and *Prad Stivell*.

Houat and Hoëdic

The islands of **HOUAT** and **HOËDIC** (boats from PORT-MARIA, 90min; daily except Tues) are very much smaller versions of Belle-Île. Both feel as though they've been left behind by the passing centuries, although the younger fishermen of Houat have revived the island's fortunes by establishing a successful co-operative. HOUAT, in particular, has excellent **beaches** – as ever on its sheltered, eastern side – that fill up with campers in the summer. There is one **hotel** on each island: the *Cardinaux* on Hoëdic (☎97.30.68.31; ⑤) and the *Hôtel-Restaurant des Îles* on Houat (☎97.30.68.02; ④), both of which accept visitors on a *pension* basis only.

Vannes and the Golfe de Morbihan

It was from **VANNES** that the great Breton hero, Nominöe, set out to unify Brittany – giving the Franks a terrible beating and pushing the borders past Nantes and Rennes, where they remained up until the French Revolution nearly a millenium later. Here, too, the Breton *États* assembled to ratify the Act of Union in the building known as *La Cohue*. **Vieux Vannes**, the old centre of chaotic streets crammed around the cathedral and enclosed by ramparts and gardens and a tiny stream, has every reason to vaunt its historic charms.

The new town centre of Vannes is **pl de la République**; the focus was shifted outside the medieval city in the nineteenth-century craze for urbanisation. The grandest of the public buildings here, guarded by a pair of sleek and dignified bronze lions,

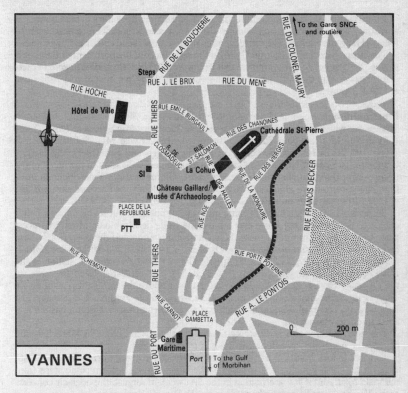

is the **Hôtel de Ville** at the top of rue Thiers. By day, however, the streets of the old city, with their overhanging, witch-hatted houses and busy commercial life, are the chief source of pleasure. **La Cohue**, which fills a block between rue des Halles and pl du Cathédrale, has recently reverted to its original use as a market place (*cohue* means "hubbub" or "throng"), having served at various times over the past 750 years as high court and assembly room, prison, revolutionary tribunal and theatre. Stalls downstairs now sell various arts and crafts, while upstairs is the local Beaux-Arts museum.

The **Cathédrale St-Pierre** is a rather forbidding place, with its stern main altar almost imprisoned by four solemn grey pillars. The light, purple through new stained glass, illuminates the dessicated finger of the Blessed Pierre Rogue, who was guillotined on the main square in 1796. For a small fee, you can in summer examine the assorted treasure in the chapter house, which includes a twelfth-century wedding chest, brightly decorated with enigmatic scenes of romantic chivalry.

The **Musée Archaeologie** on rue Noé is said to have one of the world's finest collections of prehistoric artefacts (June–Sept Mon–Sat 10am–noon & 2–6pm). But unlike the excellent display at Carnac, it's all pretty lifeless – some elegant stone axes, more recent Oceanic exhibits by way of context, but nothing very illuminating. Further collections of fossils, shells and stuffed birds, equally traditional in their display, are on show around the corner in the **Hôtel de Roscannec** at 19 rue des Halles (same hours).

The city's excellent **fish market** is active in the covered hall on pl de la Poissonerie each Wednesday, Friday and Saturday, with a general market spreading slightly higher up on the streets towards the cathedral on Wednesday and Saturday.

Place Henri IV, with its charming fifteenth- and sixteenth-century gabled houses, is attractive, as are the views from it down the narrow side streets. The ramparts can be followed for quite a length, the old moat often made into neat and colourful flower beds.

The **Aquarium**, in the parc du Golfe on the right bank of the port from pl Gambetta, claims the best collection of tropical fish in Europe, 400-odd electric eels, and a crocodile "discovered in the Paris sewers" (June–Aug daily 9am–7pm; rest of year 9am–noon & 1.30–6.30pm).

Practicalities

Vannes' SI, which has a well-restored seventeenth-century frontage, is at 1 rue Thiers (July & Aug Mon–Sat 9am–7pm, Sun 10am–noon; rest of year Mon–Sat 9am–noon & 2–6pm; ☎97.47.24.34), on the corner of rue du Drézen and rue Thiers and near pl Gambetta. The **gare SNCF** (☎97.42.50.50) is 25 minutes' walk away to the north of the town centre. Buses to Nantes, Auray, Carnac, Quiberon and other destinations leave from the gare routière alongside. **Boats** out to the islands, and around the gulf, are operated from the **gare maritime**, parc du Golfe, by *Navix* (☎97.63.79.99).

In peak season Vannes can become quite claustrophobic, but it still offers a better choice of **hotels** than anywhere else around the Golfe de Morbihan. Much the nicest place to stay, if you can get a room, is pl Gambetta overlooking the port. Hotels here include the *Hôtel-Restaurant la Voile d'Or* at no. 1 (☎97.42.71.81; ③) and the *Hôtel le Marina*, at no. 4 (☎97.47.22.81; ⑤). Among cheaper places nearer the station is the *Hôtel de France*, 57 av Victor-Hugo (☎97.47.27.57). The central *Hôtel la Bretagne*, 36 rue du Méné (☎97.47.20.21; ②), is on the first floor above the excellent restaurant *La Taverne de Maître*. It's also worth eating at *Le Brick*, 25 rue Ferdinand-le-Dressay, just left of the port from pl Gambetta, which has an upstairs restaurant with a basic menu and a good downstairs bar.

The nearest **campsite** is *Camping Couleau* at the far end of av du Maréchal-Juin, beyond the Aquarium, and alongside the gulf (☎97.63.13.88).

To listen to **folk bands** in a friendly atmosphere, call in at the *Cactus Bar*, open until 1am, on rue de la Boucherie, just north of the Hôtel de Ville – down some steps from the main road. And if you are visiting in the first week of August, the open-air concerts of the **Vannes Jazz Festival** take place in the Théâtre de Verdure.

Morbihan – and its islands

It comes as rather a surprise to discover that Vannes is on the sea. Its harbour is a channelled inlet of the ragged-edged **Golfe de Morbihan**, which lets in the tides through a narrow gap between the peninsulas of **Rhys** and **Locmariaquer**. By popular tradition the **islands** scattered around this enclosure used to number the days of the year, though for centuries the waters have been rising and there are now less than one for each week. Of these, thirty are owned by film stars and the like, while two – the Île Aux Moines and Île d'Arz – have regular populations and ferry services and end up being extremely crowded in summer. The rest are the best, and a **boat tour** around them, or at least a trip out to GAVRINIS near the mouth of the gulf, is a fairly compelling attraction. As the boats thread their way through the baffling muddle of channels you lose track of what is island and what is mainland; and everywhere there are megalithic ruins, stone circles disappearing beneath the water, and solitary menhirs on small hillocks.

Boat tours of the gulf

In season, there are dozens of different **gulf tours** available, leaving from VANNES, PORT NAVALO and LARMOR-BADEN. Full details are available from the Vannes SI; in addition to the trips from Vannes mentioned above, options include: **from Port-Navalo** (four buses daily from Vannes) more basic and economic *TVCP* cruises (mid-

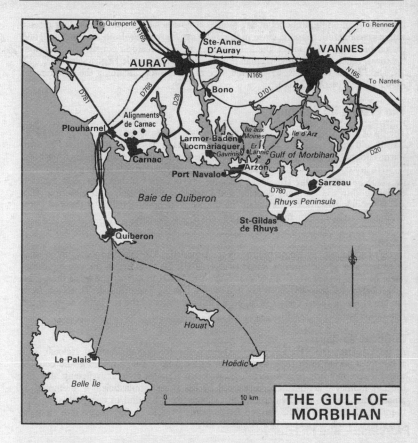

THE GULF OF MORBIHAN

March to mid-Sept); **from Locmariaquer** (buses from Auray or Carnac) *TVCP* trips around the gulf, up the Auray river and intermittently to Gavrinis; **from Larmor-Baden** (one bus daily from Vannes) there's a regular run to Gavrinis only, leaving on the hour and returning on the half hour (15min crossing).

Gavrinis and Locmariaquer

A dramatic group of menhirs, arranged in a figure of eight, is to be seen on the tiny barren island of **Er Lannic** – though only at low tide when the water gives these smaller islets the appearance of stranded hovercraft skirted with mud. The best island for megalithic monuments is, however, **GAVRINIS.** It contains, almost consists of, a tumulus that has been partially uncovered to reveal a chamber in which all the slabs of stone are carved with curving lines like fingerprints, axeheads and spirals – purely decorative according to archaeologists.

Thanks to the complex patterning, the stone of the roof on Gavrinis has been identified as part of the same piece as the dolmen known as the **Table des Marchands** at **LOCMARIAQUER.** Locmariaquer also has the **Grand Menhir Brisé,** supposedly the crucial central point of the megalithic observatory of Carnac. Before being floored by an earthquake in 1722, it was by far the largest known menhir – 22m high and weighing more than a full jumbo jet at 347 tonnes. It now lies on the ground in four pieces, with a possible fifth missing, close to the *Table des Marchands*. Both are fenced off and closed between 12.30 and 2.30pm. There are more prehistoric constructions around the town, which has a couple of small **hotels**, the *Lautram*, pl de l'Église (☎97.57.31.32; ③), and *l'Éscale* (☎97.57.32.51; ⑤), and several **campsites**, including the excellent *La Ferme Fleurie* (☎97.57.34.06).

The Presqu'île de Rhuys

The tip of the Presqu'île de Locmariaquer is only a few hundred metres away from Port Navalo and the **Presqu'île de Rhuys**. This peninsula has a micro-climate of its own, warm enough for pomegranates, figs, bougainvillaea and the only Breton vineyards. Oysters are cultivated on the muddy gulf shores, but the currents of the gulf make this no place for swimming. The ocean beaches are the ones to head for: east from St-Gildas-de-Rhuys is the most enticing and least crowded stretch with glittering gold- and silver-coloured rocks. For details on the whole peninsula, call in at the new information centre just off the main road as you come into Sarzeau.

Arzon

If you're spending any length of time on the peninsula, **ARZON** is probably the best of its towns; stay at the *Hôtel de Rhuys* (☎97.41.20.01; ⑤) or either of the two big campsites, *Le Tindio* (☎97.41.25.59) or *Port Sable* (☎97.41.21.98). Near the tip of the peninsula, clearly visible to the north of the main road, is the **Tumulus de Thumiac**, from the top of which Julius Caesar is supposed to have watched the sea battle in which the Romans defeated the Veneti.

St-Gildas-de-Rhuys

At **ST-GILDAS-DE-RHUYS**, Pierre Abélard, the theologian/lover of Héloïse, was abbot for a period from 1126, having been exiled from Paris. "I live in a wild country where every day brings new perils", he wrote to Héloïse, eventually fleeing after his brother monks – hedonists unimpressed by his stern scholasticism – attempted to poison him. By the beaches around the village are a handful of **campsites**, among them *Le Menhir* (☎97.45.22.88) and *Les Govelins* (☎97.45.21.67); there's also an average-priced **hotel**, the *Giquel* (☎97.45.23.12; ③).

The Château de Suscinio

Near SARZEAU, which also has accommodation if you're stuck, is the impressive fourteenth-century **Château de Suscinio**. This completely moated castle, set in marshland at the edge of a tiny village, contains a sagging but still vivid mosaic floor. You can take a precarious stroll around its high ramparts (April–Sept daily 9.30am–noon & 2–7pm; rest of year Tues, Sat, Sun & hols 9.30am–noon & 2–5pm; 15F).

South to the Loire

South of the **Vilaine** river, in leaving the Morbihan *département* you are technically also leaving Brittany itself. The roads veer firmly east and west – to Nantes or La Baule, avoiding the marshes of the **Grande-Brière**. For centuries these 20,000 acres of peat bog have been deemed to be the common property of all who lived in them. The scattered population, the *Brièrois*, made and make their living by fishing for eels in the streams, gathering reeds and – on the nine days permitted each year – cutting the peat. Tourism has arrived only recently, and is resented. The touted attraction is hiring a punt which will get you lost for a few hours with your pole tangled in the rushes.

But don't let this put you off the eccentric assortment of oddities of its museum collection: rhinoceros toenails, a coelecanth and an aepyornis egg, and slightly tatty stuffed specimens of virtually every bird and animal imaginable. There is an Egyptian mummy, too, as well as a shrunken Maori head and a complete tanned human skin – taken in 1793 from the body of a soldier whose dying wish was to be made into a drum.

The **Musée Jules-Vernes** on 3 rue de l'Hermitage (10am–noon & 2–5pm) on Île Feydeau commemorates the birthplace of the first serious writer of science fiction.

Eating

Nantes is a big enough city to cater to all tastes in food; wandering the pedestrian streets in the centre you're bound to come up with something.

La Cigale, 4 pl Graslin (☎40.69.76.41). Well-known late nineteenth-century brasserie. Menus 69F and 125F, served until midnight.

Delices de Tunis, 11 allée-du-Commandant-Charcot (☎40.74.30.91). Very cheap Middle Eastern food opposite the station.

Le Djerba, 1 rue Lekain (☎40.48.77.08) Tunisian restaurant behind the Théâtre Graslin. *A la carte* meal from 80F.

La Taverne Kronenburg, 23 allée-du-Commandant-Charcot (☎40.74.87.37). Brasserie and restaurant next to the château. Menus from 65F.

La Palmier, 10 rue des 3-Croissants (☎40.47.97.41). Moroccan food in the maze of pedestrianised streets; *à la carte* in the evening, lunch menu 42F.

Within reach of Nantes

Immediately **upstream from Nantes** you are into the Loire wine-growing country that produces the two classic dry white wines, *Gros-Plant* and *Muscadet*. Any **vineyard** should be happy to give you a *dégustation*. Almost without exception the grapes are picked by machine so there's no opportunity for casual harvest work.

To explore the **last section of the Nantes–Brest canal** (the rest of which is covered earlier in this chapter), you can take a river cruise from quai des Versailles at the end of cours des 50-Otages in the centre of Nantes. These cruises run up the Erdre to the point where it is joined by the canal coming from Redon. They thrive mainly because the Loire is not at present navigable by this sort of boat – although there are plans to change that. However, the Erdre is itself beautiful and wide, with a fine selection of châteaux along its banks, chief among them **La Gâcherie**. At least two boats run every day in high season, one with a top-class restaurant on board – contact *Lebert-Buisson*, 24 quai des Versailles (☎40.20.24.50).

The coast south of the Loire

In summer Nantes empties, as everyone heads west to the beaches, either to the more upmarket resorts beyond St-Nazaire, or **south of the Loire** to the almost unbroken line of holiday apartments, *pepsi* and *frites* stands of the **PAYS DE RETZ** coast. **PORNIC** is the one exception among these resorts, with a still-functional fishing port and one of Bluebeard Gilles de Reis' many castles. It is a small place: you can walk past the harbour and along the cliffs to a tiny beach where the rock walls glitter from the phosphorescent sea-water. The **hotels** in town are not cheap; the *Relais St-Gilles* (☎40.82.02.25; ②), just down the road from the post office, is the most reasonable.

Between the coast and Nantes, the countryside is a series of marshes and mostly inaccessible lakes. The largest, the **Grand-Lieu**, contains two drowned villages, Murin and Langon. Along the **estuary** itself, the towns are depressed and depressing, their traditional industries struck hard by unemployment.

Guérande

On the edge of the Grande-Brière marshes, just before you come to the sea, is the walled town of **GUÉRANDE**. The moat around the thick ramparts, long since filled in, forms a spacious promenade around the old city, whose best feature is a market by the church. It's quite a metropolis by Brière standards, though not one likely to delay you for too long. The *Hôtel les Floralies* on the chemin du Pradillon (☎40.24.96.50; ②) is something special; menus in its superb nearby restaurant, the *Dé d'Argent*, start at 75F.

There are more marshes between Guérande and the sea. This time, however, they are salt, a "white country" of bizarre-looking *oeillets* – pens measuring 70 to 80 square metres, in which sea water, since Roman times, has been collected and evaporated.

La Baule

There is something very surreal about emerging from the Brière to the coast at **LA BAULE**. This is Brittany's most upmarket pocket – an imposing, monied landscape where the dunes are no longer bonded together with scrub and pines, but with massive apartment buildings and luxury hotels. Around the crab-shaped bay, bronzed nymphettes and would-be Clint Eastwoods ride across the sands into the sunset against a backdrop of cruising lifeguards, horse-dung removers and fantastically priced cocktails.

Still, the beach is undeniably impressive; there is a wonderful ice cream shop, *A Manuel*, on the corner of the promenade; and, a little out of character, there's also an excellent bookshop, *Breizh* (at 9 av du Général-de-Gaulle), which specialises in Breton culture, language and politics.

Staying in town can be fun if you feel like a break from the more subdued Breton attractions – but it may well be expensive. Full details can be had from the **SI**, in a new post-modern office at 8 pl de la Victoire (☎40.24.34.44). La Baule has two **gare SNCFs**, the barely used La-Baule-les-Pins and the main La-Baule-Escoublac near the SI on pl Rhin-et-Danube (☎40.66.50.50), where the TGVs from Paris arrive. The **gare routière** is at 4 pl de la Victoire (☎40.60.25.58).

Few of the **hotels** are cheap, particularly in the high season, and in the low season more than half them are closed. The very cheapest are near the main gare SNCF, less than 1km from the beach; these include *Hôtel Violetta*, 44 av Clemenceau (☎40.60.32.16; ②), and *Hôtel-Restaurant la Coquille*, 10 av Clemenceau. (☎40.60.38.47; ②). The best of the **campsites**, 2km back from the beach, is *La Roserie*, 20 av Sohier (☎40.60.46.66).

Le Croisic

The small port of **LE CROISIC**, sheltered from the ocean around the corner of the headland, is probably a more realistic (and to many perceptions, more attractive) place to stay. These days it's basically a pleasure port, but fishing boats do still sail from its harbour and there's a modern **fish market**, near the long Tréhic jetty, where you can see the day's catch auctioned. The best **hotels** are *Les Nids*, 83 bd Général-Leclerc (☎40.23.00.63; ④), or *Perthuy du Roy*, 3 pl Croix-de-Ville (☎40.23.00.95; ④).

Close by, all around the rocky sea coast known as the **Grande Côte**, is a whole range of **campsites**. Just outside Le Croisic itself is the *Océan* (☎40.23.07.69), and at BATZ there's the *Casse Cailloux* (☎40.23.91.71). For equally good beaches and a chance of cheaper **hotel** accommodation, you could go east from La Baule to **PORNICHET** (though preferably keeping away from the plush marina) or to the tiny **ST-MARC**, where in 1953 Jacques Tati filmed "Monsieur Hulot's Holiday".

St-Nazaire

The best sandy coves in the region are to be found on the western outskirts of **ST-NAZAIRE**, linked by wooded paths and almost deserted. But it's a gloomy city. It was bombed to extinction in World War II, and its shipyards, in more or less continuous operation since constructing Julius Caesar's fleet, are now closing. The one reason you might want to stay is the relative ease of finding inexpensive **hotel** space. Options include the *Lapeyre*, 2 rue de la Paix (☎40.22.55.09; ②), and the new *Korail* opposite the station (☎40.01.89.89; ④). There's also a **hostel**, the *Foyer du Jeune Travailleur*, at 30 rue Soleil-Levant (☎40.22.51.04). Even if St-Nazaire is a familiarly depressing town in total industrial decline, it has one inspiring piece of engineering – the **Pont St-Nazaire**, a great elongated S-curved suspension bridge over the mouth of the Loire. Driving across it incurs a heavy toll, but bikes go over for free.

Nantes

NANTES, the former capital of Brittany, is no longer officially part of the province: it was transferred to the Pays de la Loire in 1962 when the modern administrative regions were established. Nonetheless, such bureaucracy is not taken too seriously in the city, and its history is closely bound up with Breton fortunes. A considerable medieval centre, it later achieved great wealth from colonial expeditions, the slave trade and shipbuilding – activities in turn surpassed by more recent industrial growth. Despite the tower blocks masking the Loire and motorways tearing past the city, it remains to its inhabitants an integral part of Brittany.

Arrival and accommodation

Nantes' **gare SNCF** (☎40.08.50.50), east of the château, has two exits; for most facilities (tramway, buses, hotels) use Accès Nord. There are two central **bus** stations. Local buses use the Gare des Bus on cours Franklin, alongside pl du Commerce, while the long-distance **gare routière** (☎40.47.62.70) is 400m away on allée Baco, near pl Ricordeau. Modern rubber-wheeled trams run along the old river front, past the gare SNCF and the two bus stations. Flat-fare tickets are valid for one hour, rather than just a single journey. Bicycles can be hired from *Seguir Bernard*, 38 rue des Alouettes (☎40.46.56.32).

The **SI** is in one of the most beautiful medieval buildings to survive in the city, in pl du Commerce, at the colonaded back door of the Palais de la Bourse (Mon–Fri 9am–7pm, Sat 10am–6pm; ☎40.47.04.51). It provides a free book-size guide, including an excellent town map.

Accommodation

As well as the hotels listed below, Nantes also has three **youth hostels**. The summer-only one in a former tobacco factory at 2 pl de la Manu (☎40.20.57.25) is easiest to reach, by taking tramway #1 towards Malachère and getting off at *Manufacture*. The other two don't require youth hostel cards and are at 1 rue Porte-Neuve (☎40.20.00.80), 2km from the gare SNCF on bus routes #36, #40 or #41, direction pl Viarne, and at 9 bd Vincent-Gache (☎40.47.91.64). The latter, which only has nine beds, is also 2km from the gare SNCF, and reached by taking the tramway west to the Commerce stop, and changing to bus #24 or #52.

Hôtel l'Atlantique, 9 rue Maréchal-de-Lattre-de-Tassigny (☎40.73.85.33). Just below *Hôtel de l'Océan*. No restaurant. ④

Hôtel Château, 5 pl de la Duchesse-Anne (☎40.74.17.16). Alongside the Château du Ducs 500m from the gare SNCF, with castle views from the best rooms. ③

Hôtel l'Océan, 11 rue Maréchal-de-Lattre-de-Tassigny (☎40.69.73.51). A pleasant hotel in between pl Graslin and the quai de la Fosse at the bottom of the hill, west of the gare SNCF, near the Mediathéque. ③

ORLÉANAIS AND BERRY

Orléanais is in many ways a country suburb of Paris, and visiting its principal châteaux (detailed below), though entertaining, won't fill up an enormous amount of time. The city of **Orléans**, however, has enough in itself, and nearby, to merit a stop between Paris and Touraine.

To the south, **Berry**, centred on **Bourges** and an obvious route if you're heading south, has medieval links and more modern literary connections, but the countryside has a tendency to be damp and dismal.

Orléans

Seemingly crushed by the oppressive weight of Paris to the north, **ORLÉANS** feels compelled to recoup its faded *gloire* from 1429, when Paris was infested by disease and the English, and the Loire valley was the capital of France. The city's deliverer on that date is honoured everywhere, though nothing contradicts the overriding feeling that **Joan of Arc** was, and is, a myth. In earlier times still, Orléans was capital of Clovis – one of the Frankish kingdoms – and in the days of Asterix it was one of the key Gallo-Roman cities. Today, not only do Orléanais go to Paris for their evenings out, they commute to work there as well.

From the busy **Centre d'Arc** – location of the **SI**, **Gare Routière** and **Gare SNCF**, and a shopping precinct – rue de la République leads south to the central **place du Martroi** and a nineteenth-century statue of the Maid.

The town

St Joan turns up all over town. The **Cathédrale Ste-Croix** (daily 9am–noon & 2–6pm) battered for the best part of 600 years, is splendid, and full of Joan, who celebrated her victory here. In the north transept, her pedestal is supported by two jagged and golden leopards, representing the English, on an altar carved with the battle scene. In the nave, the late-nineteenth-century stained glass windows tell the story, starting from the north transept, of her life, with caricatures of the loutish Anglo-Saxons and snooty French nobles. (Across place d'Étape from the cathedral, outside the red-brick Renaissance **Hôtel de Ville**, Joan appears again, in pensive mood, her skirt now shredded by twentieth-century bullets.)

Follow rue Jeanne d'Arc half a kilometre west and you come to the semi-timbered **Maison de Jeanne d'Arc**, 3 place Général-de-Gaulle (Tues–Sun, 10am–noon & 2–6pm; Nov–April 2–6pm only). Fun, most of all for children, this has good models and displays of the breaking of the Orléans siege. Despite the consistency in artists' renderings of Ste-Jeanne, it seems the page-boy hair cut and demure little face are part of the myth – there is no contemporary portrait of her (save for a trial clerk's doodle in the Paris archives) and certainly no death mask.

Visitors to the **Musée des Beaux-Arts**, 1 rue Fernand Rabier (10am–noon & 2–6 pm; closed Tues; 14F, students free), are encouraged to start by taking the lift to the second floor, for the collection of **sixteenth-century work**. If you'd rather escape back to more recent times, however, the best route is down to the **modern art collection** in

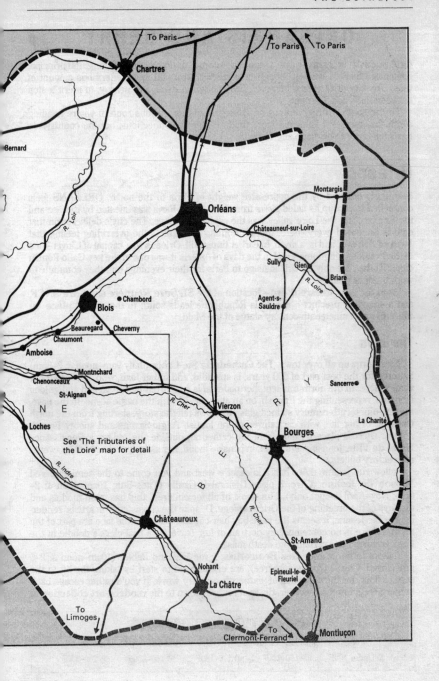

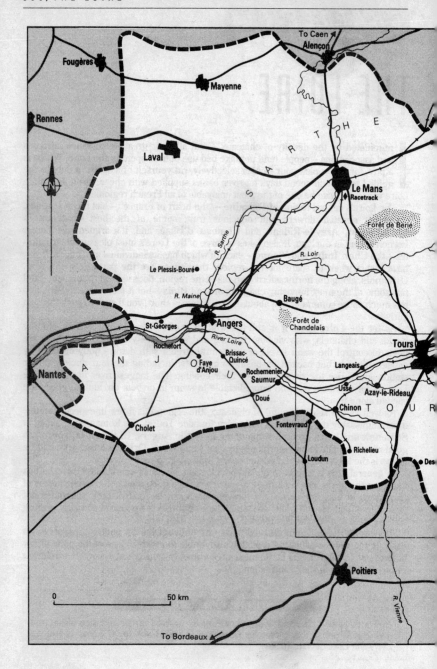

CHAPTER SIX

THE LOIRE

Intimidated by the density of châteaux – and all their great Renaissance intrigues and associations – people tend to make bad use of time spent in the Loire. Which is a pity, for if you pick your castles selectively, rid yourself of a sense of duty to the guided tours, and spend days on river banks supplied with cheese, fruit and white Loire wines, this can be one of the most enjoyable of all French regions.

The Loire's central region of **Touraine** – "the heart of France" – has the best wines, the most scented flowers and delicious fruit, some of the best **châteaux** in **Chenonceau, Azay-le-Rideau** and **Chateau d'Ussé**, and, it's argued, the purest French accent in the land. It also takes in three of the Loire's most pleasurable tributaries – the **Cher, Indre** and **Vienne** – each of which has its individual attractions. If you have just a week to spare for the region, then these are the parts to spend it in. **Orléanais**, along the northeastern margins of the region, does its best to compete – and has some of the most imposing châteaux around **Blois** – but it feels close to Paris and has much of the commuter belt about it, and, if time is short, you'll want to push through fairly fast.

As for the **Loire** itself, it is still the wild river of whirlpools, quicksands, shifting banks and channels, with vicious currents and a propensity to flood. But there are plans to control the water levels of the central stretch with dams – hotly opposed by conservationists but backed by business interests, including the four nuclear power statios which use the river water for their cooling. The longest river in France, the Loire is for the most part too unpredictable to swim in or boat on, and no goods are carried along it.

As well as the select handful of châteaux, the region has a few unexpected sights: most unmissably the gardens at **Villandry** (outside Tours), the Romanesque abbey at **St-Benoît-sur-Loire** and the stunning tapestries in **Angers**. Of the cities, **Tours** has good museums and is now starting to lose its stuffy name, **Orléans** has charm, and **Le Mans** is the least touristy and authentically lively, even outside race times.

In general, this is a right-wing, laid-back region where air-conditioned cars and bus tours are the norm. For exploring on your own, it's a good idea to hire some means of **transport**, at least for occasional forays. Buses can be sparse, their schedules not geared to outsiders, and trains are too limiting. But this is wonderful and easy **cycling** country, best of all on the floodbanks, or *levées*, of the Loire.

Arriving at the northern channel ports, the only **access** on public transport is via Paris. If you want to avoid the capital, it's advisable to make for the ports either in Brittany (change trains at Rennes) or Normandy (change at Caen). See relevant *Travel Details* for further information.

WHICH CHÂTEAUX?

Faced with limited time and a vast choice, many covered in the following pages, you could do a lot worse than plump for **Cheverny** (p.342), **Ussé** (p.347), **Azay-le-Rideau** (p.347) and **Chenonceau** (p.351).

travel details

Transport in Brittany can be a tricky and time-consuming business. Most of the main towns have train links with Rennes and/or Nantes and there's a rough loop of the coast. Aside from these, getting between towns is often a matter of fitting in with a web of independent private bus lines – their services, especially inland, often geared to schools and markets. The timetables supplied at stations are a help – there's one for each of fourteen sectors detailing both buses and trains – but this is one part of France where you may find it more rewarding to pick a couple of main bases and hire a bike.

Trains

From Rennes frequently to Paris-Montparnasse (3hr 15min) via Le Mans (2hr), to St-Malo (1hr), to Vannes/Lorient/Quimper (1hr/1hr 30min/2hr 15min) and to Morlaix/Brest (2hr/2hr 45min); 5 daily to Roscoff (2hr 45min; via Vannes – summer only) and Mont St-Michel (45min).

From Roscoff 5 daily to Morlaix (30min) and Rennes (2hr 45min).

From Brest 6 daily to Quimper (1hr 30min).

From Nantes very frequently to Paris-Montparnasse (3hr 30min); slightly less so to Angers (45min), La Baule/Croisic (1hr/1hr 15min) and Vannes/Quimper (1hr 45min/3hr 30min).

Buses

From Rennes more or less hourly to Dinan (1hr 45min); 8 daily to Dinard (1hr 45min); 3 daily to Nantes (2hr 30min) and Josselin (1hr 15min).

From Quimper 4 daily to Brest (1hr 30min); daily to Morlaix (1hr 45min).

From Lannion 9 daily to St-Brieuc (1hr); 6 daily to Trégastel (1hr); daily to Morlaix (1hr 15min).

From St-Brieuc 7 daily to Paimpol (1hr 30min); 4 daily to Dinan (1hr).

From Vannes daily to Malestroit (45min).

From Carnac 2 daily to Lorient (1hr 15min).

Ferries

From St-Malo Regular ferries to Dinard (10min) in season. *Émeraude Lines* (☎99.40.48.40) to Jersey (mid-March to mid-Nov) and to Guernsey and Sark (April–Sept). They also sail (May–Sept) along the Brittany coast to Cap Fréhel, Cezembre and Dinard; to Îles Chausney and Granville in Normandy; and to Dinan up the River Rance. *Condor Hydroglisseurs* (☎99.56.42.29) to Jersey and Guernsey (all year except mid-Jan to mid-March); and to Sark and Weymouth (mid-March to Sept). *Brittany Ferries* (St-Malo ☎99.56.68.40, Portsmouth ☎0705.827701) to Portsmouth (9hr overnight crossing).

From Roscoff *Brittany Ferries* (☎98.69.76.22, Plymouth ☎0752.21321) twice daily to Plymouth (6hr) and once daily to Cork (13–17hr). Also to the Île de Batz (several times daily in season, irregularly out; 15min).

From Dinan daily boat up the estuary to Dinard (2hr 30min) and to St-Malo (3hr); May–Sept only.

Dinard-St-Malo Regular boats (10min).

From Pointe de l'Arcouest Regular ferry to the Île de Bréhat (10min).

From Quimper Daily boat down the Odet to Bénodet (1hr 15min); May–Sept only.

From Nantes boats can be hired for the Nantes-Brest canal. Also at Malestroit, Josselin, Quimper and elsewhere.

From Lorient regular summer ferry to the Île de Groix (45min).

From Vannes/Port-Navalo/Lamor-Baden (and other ports) ferries to Île de Gavrinis and boat trips to other islands in the Gulf of Morbihan.

From Quiberon regular ferry to Belle-Île (1hr), less frequently to Houat and Hoëdic.

More details and ferry schedules for the Breton islands can be obtained from APIT (11 pl Joffre, Auray; ☎97.56.52.57) or principal tourist offices in the province, or Maison de la Bretagne, Centre Commercial, Maine-Montparnasse, 17 rue de l'Arrivée, 15ᵉ, Paris (☎45.38.73.15).

But don't let this put you off the eccentric assortment of oddities of its museum collection: rhinoceros toenails, a coelecanth and an aepyornis egg, and slightly tatty stuffed specimens of virtually every bird and animal imaginable. There is an Egyptian mummy, too, as well as a shrunken Maori head and a complete tanned human skin – taken in 1793 from the body of a soldier whose dying wish was to be made into a drum.

The **Musée Jules-Vernes** on 3 rue de l'Hermitage (10am–noon & 2–5pm) on Île Feydeau commemorates the birthplace of the first serious writer of science fiction.

Eating

Nantes is a big enough city to cater to all tastes in food; wandering the pedestrian streets in the centre you're bound to come up with something.

La Cigale, 4 pl Graslin (π40.69.76.41). Well-known late nineteenth-century brasserie. Menus 69F and 125F, served until midnight.

Delices de Tunis, 11 allée-du-Commandant-Charcot (π40.74.30.91). Very cheap Middle Eastern food opposite the station.

Le Djerba, 1 rue Lekain (π40.48.77.08) Tunisian restaurant behind the Théâtre Graslin. *A la carte* meal from 80F.

La Taverne Kronenburg, 23 allée-du-Commandant-Charcot (π40.74.87.37). Brasserie and restaurant next to the château. Menus from 65F.

La Palmier, 10 rue des 3-Croissants (π40.47.97.41). Moroccan food in the maze of pedestrianised streets; *à la carte* in the evening, lunch menu 42F.

Within reach of Nantes

Immediately **upstream from Nantes** you are into the Loire wine-growing country that produces the two classic dry white wines, *Gros-Plant* and *Muscadet*. Any **vineyard** should be happy to give you a *dégustation*. Almost without exception the grapes are picked by machine so there's no opportunity for casual harvest work.

To explore the **last section of the Nantes–Brest canal** (the rest of which is covered earlier in this chapter), you can take a river cruise from quai des Versailles at the end of cours des 50-Otages in the centre of Nantes. These cruises run up the Erdre to the point where it is joined by the canal coming from Redon. They thrive mainly because the Loire is not at present navigable by this sort of boat – although there are plans to change that. However, the Erdre is itself beautiful and wide, with a fine selection of châteaux along its banks, chief among them **La Gâcherie**. At least two boats run every day in high season, one with a top-class restaurant on board – contact *Lebert-Buisson*, 24 quai des Versailles (π40.20.24.50).

The coast south of the Loire

In summer Nantes empties, as everyone heads west to the beaches, either to the more upmarket resorts beyond St-Nazaire, or **south of the Loire** to the almost unbroken line of holiday apartments, *pepsi* and *frites* stands of the **PAYS DE RETZ** coast. **PORNIC** is the one exception among these resorts, with a still-functional fishing port and one of Bluebeard Gilles de Reis' many castles. It is a small place: you can walk past the harbour and along the cliffs to a tiny beach where the rock walls glitter from the phosphorescent sea-water. The **hotels** in town are not cheap; the *Relais St-Gilles* (π40.82.02.25; ②), just down the road from the post office, is the most reasonable.

Between the coast and Nantes, the countryside is a series of marshes and mostly inaccessible lakes. The largest, the **Grand-Lieu**, contains two drowned villages, Murin and Langon. Along the **estuary** itself, the towns are depressed and depressing, their traditional industries struck hard by unemployment.

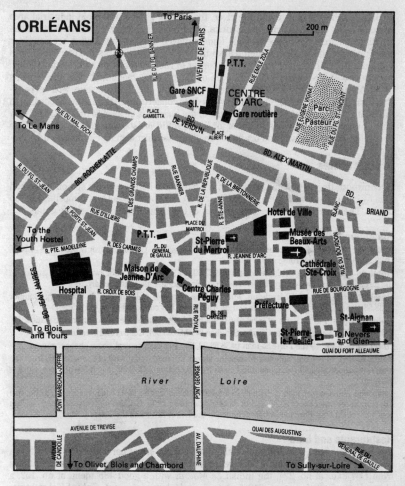

the basement, with canvasses by Picasso, Miró, Braque, Dufy, Renoir and Monet, as well as Auguste Rodin's studies of Gauguin, and photographs of Picasso by Man Ray.

If you read French, the **Centre Charles Péguy**, 11 rue Tabour (Mon–Sat, 2–6pm; free), down the road in a Renaissance mansion, is worth a visit. It takes its themes from the life and work of Charles Péguy (1873–1914), a Christian Socialist writer from Orléans. Though there are cartoons and drawings, the main exhibits are texts without translation, Zola's front page *J'accuse* letter to the President and the explanations by both sides in the Dreyfus affair; documentation of the 1907 general strike call for the 40-hour week (not in effect until 1936) and various books and pamphlets.

If you head back east, and down towards the river, you find the scattered vestiges of the old city. Rue de Bourgogne was the Gallo-Roman main street; in the basement of the modern **Préfecture**, 9 rue de Bourgogne, a spartan civic reception room provides odd surroundings for an excavated **first-century dwelling** – or bits of it – and the walls of a **ninth-century church**. It's not a site, as such: ask the receptionist if you can look.

Between the Préfecture and the river, the narrow streets of the old industrial area surround the **Dessaux vinegar works**, a turn-of-the-century establishment whose buildings encircle the house Isabelle Romée moved to a few years after her daughter was burned at the stake in Rouen. Down the road, a plaque marks the house of Joan's brother and companion-in-arms, on the corner of rue des Africains and rue de la Folie. At least two of the quarter's churches are on the precious monuments list: the remains of **St-Aignan** and its eleventh-century crypt, and the Romanesque **St-Pierre-le-Puellier**, the old university church, now used for concerts and exhibitions. According to the SI, it's only a matter of time until most of the quarter is cleared to make way for new offices; until then it provides an outlet for local **graffiti** artists, whose work covers acres of derelict warehouse wall and brightens an otherwise dilapidated neighbourhood.

Practicalities

Accommodation in Orléans is good, with a few cheap hotels near the station (not a bad area by comparison with the usual grim streets) and youth hostel and campsites not too far out. There's a selection of acceptable places to eat, but not a lot of nightlife going on.

Accommodation

Hôtel de Paris, 29 Faubourg Bannier, just across pl Gambetta from the Gare SNCF (☎38.53.39.58). Pleasant rooms. ①.

Hôtel de Trevise, 7 rue Croix de Malte (☎38.62.69.06). Five-minute walk away from the station in the direction of the town centre, left off rue de la République. Small and friendly. ②

Hôtel Touring, 142 bd Châteaudun, left after ten minute's walk up rue du Faubourg Bannier (☎38.53.10.51). The wrong side of the station from town, but comfortable for the price. ①

Hôtel de Blois, 1 av de Paris (☎38.62.61.61). Rather dingy, but a stone's throw from the station. ①

Hôtel Charles Sanglier, 8 rue Charles-Sanglier (☎38.53.38.50). Central and comfortable. ③

Hôtel Saint-Jean, 19 rue Porte-St-Jean (☎38.53.63.32). Two-star, central, some cheaper rooms. ②

Youth hostel, 14 rue du Faubourg-Madeleine across the road to the west of town, bus #B from the gare routière (☎38.62.45.75). Open mid-Feb to Nov, reception 7.15–9.30am & 5.30–10.30pm. Curfew 10.30pm.

Campsite Nearest one is at St-Jean-de-la-Ruelle, 2km out on the Blois road, rue de la Roche, bus #B, stop *Roche aux Fées* (☎38.88.39.39). Another campsite (☎38.63.53.94; high season only), is 7km south at rue du Pont-Bouchet in Olivet, between the Loiret River and the Loire.

Restaurants and bars

Rue de Bourgogne, the erstwhile Gallo-Roman main street parallel to the river, has a good choice of **restaurants** of different ethnic origins, including African and Antillais from *Le Dakar* at no. 224, the Indian *Le Madras* with a good 48F menu at no. 152, a cheap *Crêperie Breton* at no. 242, and even an Afghan restaurant, *Kaboul Kabab* at no. 151. For really cheap snacks try the studenty *Sunset* billiard bar at no. 174. There's also a trendy music bar, the *Bar Bourgogne*, at no. 248.

Listings

Bike hire From the Gare SNCF, the youth hostel and from *Société Alexis*, 14 rue des Carmes.

Car hire *Avis* 13 rue Sassonières, door H from the SNCF.

Launderette 178 rue de Bourgogne, 113 rue Faubourg Bannier.

Listing mags *Orléans Poche* is a free listings magazine with music and nightlife info, cinema listings and the rest.

Markets Food market at Halles de la Charpenterie, pl du Châtelet near the river; flea market on Saturdays at bd Alexandre-Martin.

Medical assistance SAMU (☎38.63.33.33), Centre Hospitalier, 1 rue Porte Madeleine (☎38.51.44.44).

Poste Restante Pl de Gaulle, 45031 Orléans Cedex 1.

Public transport Bus information available from SEMTAO office (☎38.84.41.11), pl Albert 1er in the Centre d'Arc, shopping mall, behind SI. For trains, phone SNCF (☎38.62.56.65).

SI Place Albert 1er (daily, 9am–7pm), provide a friendly and comprehensive service, with information on hotels, nightlife and sights.

Upstream from Orléans

Along the Loire **upstream from Orléans**, single lane roads run along the top of the flood banks, ideal for **cycling**. There are plenty of riverside **campsites** but the countryside is miserably dull, with the marsh-ridden Sologne to the south and the north bank much of a kind with the treeless wheat plain that stretches to Paris. There's no good wine in this direction, either, until SANCERRE and POUILLY on the Burgundy border – and heading for Burgundy is the best reason to pass this way. On the other hand, there are attractions en route, among them **St Benoît's abbey**, the châteaux of **Sully** and **Gien** and, if you're particularly interested in modern sculpture, **Argent-sur-Sauldre**. If you're out on, or in, the river (or camping on the bank), beware that the Loire's placid flow along these reaches is deceptive; it can swell within 24 hours and deluge the valley.

St-Benoît

An afternoon's bike ride – or a short drive – out of Orléans, crossing to the north bank at CHÂTEAU-NEUF-SUR-LOIRE, brings you to **ST-BENOÎT-SUR-LOIRE**. In the **Abbaye de Flery** at this village, a marble mosaic of Roman origin covers the chancel floor of one of the most awe-inspiring Romanesque churches in France, built in pale yellow and cream-coloured stone between 1020 and 1218. The oldest part, the porch, illustrates the *Vision of the Apocalypse* by the fantastically sculpted capitals and by the layout that follows the description of the New Jerusalem in *Revelations* – foursquare, with twelve foundations and three open gates on each side.

Sully-sur-Loire

SULLY-SUR-LOIRE is accessible by bus from Orléans (but it requires a wildly inconvenient change at **Montargis** over to the east), and if you don't have your own wheels you should try to hitch. The grand **château** (daily, summer 9–11.45am & 2–5.45pm, winter 10–11.45am & 2–4.45pm; closed Dec–Feb; 12F) is well worth the effort of getting there, despite savage wartime bombing which twice destroyed the nearby bridge over the Loire and caused incidental damage to the château itself. The interior doesn't really merit a look except for the fourteenth-century timberwork of the keep, but from the outside, rising massively out of its gigantic moat, it has all the picturebook requirements of pointed towers, machiolations and drawbridge. The imagination is further fired by the fact that Voltaire spent three years here in exile, after he was banished from Paris in 1716. The château is probably best seen at night when, in season, it's floodlit during the **Sully festival**. You can attend one of the concerts held in a medieval-style pavillion and in the Salle des Gardes. The festival features concerts of contemporary, jazz and classical music (mid-June–mid-July; details from local SIs).

If you want a place to stay in Sully, try the *Hôtel du Coq*, 21 Faubourg St-Germain; ☎38.36.21.30). Alternatively, there's a serene **campsite** (☎38.36.23.93) with an amazing location by the river, practically in the grounds of the château. The SI is on place Général-de-Gaulle.

Gien

Gien's château is basically a museum of hunting – weapons, victims stuffed or skeletal, horns and antlers, plus paintings, pottery and tapestries venerating the sport (daily, summer 9am–7pm; winter 10am–noon & 2–5pm; closed Nov–Dec & Feb–March; 23F). Even the squat, red-brick building itself is hardly worth the climb to reach it. The **town** of Gien, though, is pretty, having been restored to its late fifteenth-century quaintness after, like Sully, extensive wartime bombing, and the sixteenth-century stone **bridge** spanning the river – one of the oldest on the Loire – gives excellent views as you approach from the north.

The **SI** on rue Anne-de-Beaujeu are extremely helpful, and will make hotel reservations and plan routes for the whole region. The two-star *Camping Touristique de Gien* (☎38.67.12.50), situated 500m from the bridge across the river on rue des Iris, is quiet and well equipped, with a good view of the town. Possible hotels in town are the *Hôtel le Relais Normand*, 64 pl de la Victoire (☎38.67.28.56; ①), or the *Hôtel des Alpes*, 20 rue Victor-Hugo (☎38.67.28.56; ①/②).

Briare

The small village of **BRIARE** 10km from Gien (on the Orléans–Nevers road and the Paris–Nevers rail line) is fast gaining recognition for two sites, the Musée de l'Automobile and the *pont canal*, or canal bridge.

At the **Musée de l'Automobile**, 500m out of town on the Nevers road (daily, Aug 10am–7pm & noon–6pm; April–June & Nov–March 2–6pm), the junk-shop approach to curating lends a relaxed atmosphere, in marked contrast to the hi-tech regimentation of most French museums. Crammed into an assortment of warehouses, the exhibits range from electric bubble cars and penny-farthings to modern racing cars, steam engines and model car collections, all in a state of theme-less disorder. You can wander at your leisure and, having seen the tank in the garden, finish the visit in a suitably anomalous railway bar done out with antique furniture and racing trophies.

The **canal bridge**, signposted off the road to the museum in Briare is an aqueduct designed in collaboration with the engineer Eiffel to carry canal traffic across the Loire. There's a narrow towpath on which you can cross the 662-metre-long bridge – the longest of its kind in the world – on foot. The experience, enjoyably confusing to the senses, is more fun than taking one of the tourist boats, which are too low in the water for decent river views. If you're interested in the full, three-and-a-half-hour canal boat trip, contact *Croisière* (☎38.37.12.75), embarkation at the Pont de Briare. For accommodation there's a hotel right next to the bridge, the *Hostellerie du Pont Canal* (☎38.31.22.54; ③).

Argent-sur-Sauldre

The château just outside the village of **ARGENT-SUR-SAULDRE**, on the D940 between Gien and Bourges, houses an unmissable museum, a small, fascinating collection of modern ceramics, the **Musée Vassil Ivanoff** (Sat–Mon 10am–noon, 2–6pm; Tues–Fri 2–7pm). The Bulgarian Ivanoff discovered the clay of the Cher valley in 1945 and settled in Borne to produce a collection which has been described as a revolution in clay. The works on display – sensual forms expressing all the complexities of the human condition – demonstrate a range of techniques resulting in different surface textures and glazes, the most successful of which is a unique, ox-blood red.

The other museum in Argent-sur-Sauldre that you could visit while you're in the vicinity, is the **Musée des Métiers et Traditions de France** (May–Oct, Mon–Fri 2–7pm, Sat & Sun 10am–noon & 2–7pm) situated in the thirteenth-century château itself. This is a nostalgic exhibition of eighteenth- and nineteenth-century country crafts and trades including bizarre machines for making brooms and clogs, looms, a windmill gear, and a display about the production of weathercocks. The exhibits continue into the roofspace, giving a good opportunity to view the rafters of the château.

For accommodation and good food in Argent, the comfortable *Relais de la Poste* (☎48.73.60.25; ④) is directly opposite the château.

La Charité-sur-Loire

LA CHARITÉ-SUR-LOIRE, much further upstream, on the road between Bourges and NEVERS, could reasonably be described as sleepy, were it not for the local radio, piped through municipal loudspeakers in the main street, which vies with the noisy bells of the clock tower of the **church of Notre-Dame**. This, the town's best-known monument, was restored in 1695 but dates back to the twelfth century, when it was consecrated by Pope Pascal II. The most impressive remains of the church are the bell tower, presently being restored, and the ambulatory with its fluted pillars and stained glass, including nativity scenes with unusual palm trees.

There's a good rear view of the Notre-Dame church from the site of the eighth-century **monastery** – on the pl des Bénédictines, 43 Grand-Rue – from which La Charité derives its name. The original monastery, destroyed twice by invading Saracens soon after it was completed, waited 300 years before a monk from Cluny came to restore it. The home of 200 monks, and situated on the pilgrim route to St Jacques de Compostelle, it soon became an important centre of trade.

Behind the church, on a hill above the town, it's an easy walk up to the eleventh-century ramparts and the remaining three towers of the **ruined castle**. The ramparts and grassy slopes below are excellent for picnics and afford a fantastic view of the town and the river, spanned by an eighteenth-century, slightly off-centre bridge.

The *Musée Municipal*, 33 rue des Chapelains (daily, summer 10am–noon, 3–7pm; in winter weekends only 10am–noon & 3–7pm), displays findings from the excavations of the monastery as well as an exhibition of sculptures by Pina, a pupil of Rodin.

The **SI**, on pl Ste-Croix, have a useful hotel list. The cheapest **rooms** in town are over the *Café de Paris*, 60 rue de Paris (☎86.70.16.00; ①), and at the *Union*, 8 av Gambetta (☎86.70.08.58; ②). On the other side of the river the town's campsite (☎86.70.00.83) fronts onto a little beach with a bar and summer disco.

Bourges

A town small enough to be seen in a day but attractive and lively enough to keep you longer, **BOURGES**, the main town of the **Berry region**, would be good to visit even if it were not a handy stopover on the way to Burgundy. It also makes an alternative base to Orléans for neighbouring châteaux – Gien and Sully – and for the museums of Argent-sur-Sauldre, and is the obvious jumping-off point on the literary trail of Alain Fournier and George Sand. If you're travelling with small children, it's worth pointing out that Bourges Cathedral, while brilliant, is surrounded by cobbled streets and squares that create a terrible obstacle course for a buggy.

Bourges Cathedral

The exterior of the twelfth-century **Cathédrale St-Étienne** is characterised by the delicate, almost skeletal appearance of its flying buttresses. A much vaunted example of Gothic architecture, it is modelled on the Notre-Dame in Paris but incorporates improvements on the design of the better-known building; for example in the increased height of the inner aisles, which appear to ascend almost interminably. The tympanum of the church's main (west) **portal** could engross you for hours with its carved figures – faces alive with expression and bodies full of movement – representing the Last Judgement. The artist gave his imagination full rein in depicting the devils, with snake's tails and winged bottoms and faces appearing from below the waist, symbolic of the soul in the service of the lower appetites. A cauldron filling with merry souls, one of whom appears to be wearing a bishop's mitre, contrasts sorely with the depiction of the gloomy-looking saved, while God, sitting in judgement, appears exceptionally sanctimonious. The naked figures are surprisingly detailed, belying any impressions of medieval prudery.

Apart from the soaring effect of the aisles, the **interior**'s best feature is its **stained glass**. In the main body of the cathedral this is mostly twelfth to thirteenth century, and includes geometric designs in lovely muted colours. But the most glorious windows are those located behind the altar, with glass so bright that the effect is more like a nightclub than a church. A video on the monuments of Bourges and the River Cher is shown daily at 10.30am except Sunday; in July and August at 10am, 11am, 2.30pm, 3.30pm and 4.30pm, when the crypt is also open for visits.

Palais de Jacques-Coeur

The other old buildings and streets of Bourges are contained within a loop of roads northwest of the cathedral. On rue Jacques-Coeur stands the head office, stock exchange, dealing rooms, bank safes and home of Charles VII's finance minister, **Jacques Coeur** (1400–56). This medieval shipping magnate, moneylender and arms dealer dominates Bourges as Joan of Arc does Orléans, while the "King of Bourges" (Charles VII) doesn't get a look in. Jacques Coeur's career provides an early example

---

MUSICAL AND LITERARY BERRY

The drear southern reaches of the **Berry region**, while scenically unprepossessing, have found appeal for writers, and fans may want to see the sources of their inspiration for themselves. Of more popular interest is the annual music festival at St-Chartier.

RENCONTRES INTERNATIONALES DE SAINT-CHARTIER

The annual **festival of folk and traditional music** at St-Chartier began some years ago as an accordian and pipe festival, but it has spread its interests more widely over the years and is now one of the biggest in Europe. It all takes place around the old château, the village church and in parkland roundabout. The 1991 line-up included artists from Spain, Hungary, France, Algeria, the USA, Scotland, Italy, Greece, Norway, Burkina Faso, England, India, Egypt, Ireland, Czechoslovakia and Holland and offerings ranged from Kathryn Tickell on the Northumbrian small pipe to Blowzabella, the Musicians of the Nile and the Bonnie Doon String Band from the States. It's a highly recommended focus for a trip to this corner of France.

St-Chartier is 27km south of Châteauroux (10km north of La Châtre if you're coming that way). The festival runs for 4 or 5 days every July (11–14 July in 1991). Inclusive tickets cost around 300F, or you can just go for the day for about 150F. There's camping in the park. Details are available from the Comité George Sand, 141 rue Nationale, 36400 La Châtre (☎54.06.09.96).

NOHANT: GEORGE SAND

Nohant, on the Châteauroux road, just 3km from St-Chartier, is where **George Sand** (1808–76) spent half her life. After the publication of her novel *Valentine*, which was set locally and received considerable publicity, she wrote: "This unknown *Vallée Noire*, this quiet and unpretentious landscape . . . all this had charms for me alone and did not deserve to be revealed to idle curiosity". What the critics jumped on in this novel, and in the rest of her writings, were "anti-matrimonial doctrines", her view, reasonable enough, that ill-matched couples should be able to separate. Simone de Beauvoir described Sand as a

of the profitability of war. Until just a few years before his death, the English were still in control above the Loire, yet his business interests stretched from Paris to Damascus.

The **Palais de Jacques-Coeur** (daily, May–Oct 9–11.15am & 2.15–5.15pm; rest of the year 10–11.15am & 2–4.15pm) is one of the most remarkable examples of fifteenth-century domestic architecture. The visit, which is memorable and especially fun for children, starts with the fake windows on the entrance front from which two realistic sculpted half-figures look down. There are hardly any furnishings, but the decorations on the stonework (restored in the nineteenth century), including numerous hearts and scallop shells (*coeurs* and *coquilles-St-Jacques*), clearly show the mark of the man who had it built, and in the **Salle du Trésor** there are carved scenes from the romance of Tristan and Isolde. The tour includes the kitchen, with its original water-heating system, and dining hall, with minstrels' gallery. The Palais de Jacques-Coeur is also the only mansion where you are shown the original toilets.

Practicalities

The SI, 21 rue Victor-Hugo, near the cathedral (Mon–Sat 9am–6/7pm; Sun 9am–1pm & 2.30–6/7pm), provides a fairly comprehensive list of hotels and restaurants and a plan of the city. Rue Moyenne is the main street leading north from here, with the main restaurant and food shopping areas to the east. The **gare routière** is east of the city off bd Juranville, while the **gare SNCF** is 1km to the north of the centre, on av P-Sémard. The **youth hostel** and **campsite** are close to each other, ten minutes' walk from the gare routière. **Bikes** can be hired from *Loca Bourges*, rue Edouard-Vaillant.

"sentimental feminist", and, except for the brief period of the 1848 revolution, she was certainly no activist. But her male contemporaries called her a man-eater, and she is still too often referred to simply as Chopin's mistress. Though her literary output was enormous and the French recognise her as one of their great writers, her lasting reputation is based on her life – shocking at the time – as she willed and suffered it.

The **Château de Nohant** is open for quick guided tours (daily Oct–March 10–11.30am & 2–3.30pm; April & Oct 9–11.30am & 2–5.30pm; May–Sept 9–11.30am & 1.30–6pm). You're shown the dining room table where Flaubert, Turgenev, Dumas, Delacroix, Balzac and Liszt all dined on many occasions. In the drawing room with the family portraits sits a piano given by Sand to Chopin, her guest for ten years.

In **La Châtre** itself, where every other place name is connected with George Sand, the **Musée George Sand de la Vallée Noire**, 71 rue Venose (daily, 9am–noon & 2–5pm; closes 7pm in summer; 8F), dedicates a floor to the writer, with plenty of pictures: George Sand's caricatures of her friends, a photo of Chopin, her son Maurice's illustrations for his mother's work and the doodles on her manuscripts.

If you're looking for a room in Nohant, the SI is on the square George-Sand: try the *Hôtel La Boule d'Or*, 1 rue Maurice-Sand (☎54.48.33.58). There's also a riverside **campsite** at Montgivray, 2.5km along the La Châtre road, the *Château Solange Sand* (☎54.48.37.83).

"STE-AGATHE": ALAIN FOURNIER

More obscure are the scenes which inspired **Alain Fournier**, author of *Le Grand Meaulnes*, born near Bourges in 1886. Some scenes of the novel are set in the city, but the lost domaine of *la fête étrange* is somewhere near **Epineuil-le-Fleurial** (the Ste-Agathe of the novel), 25km south of St-Armand-Montrond (turn right off the Montluçon road to cross the Cher at Meaulne). "In the whole of the Sologne", he wrote "it would have been hard to find a more desolate spot". Albicoco's film of the book was shot around Epineuil and is more rewarding to see than searching for an actual château that fits all the details. Fournier spent his childhood in Epineuil, and the elementary school described in the book can be visited outside class hours.

Hotels

Hôtel de la Poste, 22 rue Moyenne (☎48.70.08.06). Comfortable and central. ③

Hôtel le Central, 6 rue du Docteur-Témoin, off rue Moyenne (☎48.24.10.25). A small hotel, worth booking, with showers down the corridor and a lively bar downstairs. ②

Hôtel de l'Agriculture, 15 rue du Prinal. (☎48.70.40.84). Further out to the west. ③

Hôtel l'Étape, 4 rue Raphael-Casanova (☎48.70.59.57). Also westwards, and handy for the gare SNCF and the gare routière. ②

Au Rendez-vous des Amis, 6 av Marx-Dormoy (☎48.70.81.80). A short walk from the gare SNCF, up av P-Sémard and right. Cheap but not convenient for the centre. ①

Youth hostel, rue Henri-Sellier (☎48.24.58.09). Red bus #1 to Maison de la Culture, stop *Auberge de Jeunesse*.

Camping Municipal (☎48.20.16.85). Across the stream on bd de l'Industrie, bus to #6 Justices from pl Cujas, stop *Joffre*. A three-star site.

Eating

If good **food** seems elusive in Bourges (the only possibility on rue Moyenne being *Tan Hong Phuc*, a Chinese–Vietnamese restaurant/takeaway at no. 34), it's becaue the main centre for **restaurants** is pl Gordaine, at the end of rue Coursarlon, which, if you're progressing north, is second right off rue Moyenne after the PTT. The square is attractively medieval, a lovely place to sit and eat in the daytime (despite the continuous piped music). Good options for food include *Le Compt de Paris*, the *Lion d'Or*, and *Le Brownie*, an American salad and hamburger joint. The *Arome du Vieux Bourges*, on the square, is a coffee shop offering all kinds of delicacies, but the best bet for picnic fare is to take rue E-Vaillant off pl Gordaine to the *Les Halles* shopping mall on nearby pl St-Bonnet (Tues–Sat 7.30am–1pm, 3–7.30pm, Sun 8am–1pm) with its *charcuteries*, cheese specialists and fresh produce. The **pâtisserie** on the corner of rue d'Auron and rue des Armuriers (100m southwest of the PTT; go down the cour des Jacobins), isn't Jacques Coeur's birthplace as claimed, but that doesn't detract from eating their good pastries in a partly medieval room.

Nightlife

For a small city Bourges doesn't do too badly for **late-night venues**, which include: *Le Guillotin*, 15 rue E-Vaillant, off pl Gordaine, a bar and restaurant with *café-théâtre* upstairs in winter; the *Scottish* pub next door (Guinness); the bar above the *Central* hotel, 6 rue du Dr-Témoin, with a video jukebox and *babyfoot*; a couple of cabaret bars – the *Star* – 24 rue Faidherbe, and *L'Estoril*, 89 av Carnot; and a number of night clubs including *Les Jardins de Cesar*, 10 pl H-Mirpied, and *Le Calypso*, 22 av Marx-Dormoy.

Blois and around: the great châteaux

A mild climate, attractive setting and proximity to Paris have made the Loire an ideal location for the **palaces and hunting lodges** of the French ruling classes. After the Hundred Years' War (1339–1453), fortifications began to give way to more elegant facades. The influence of the Italian Renaissance, however imperfectly understood by French craftsmen, is in evidence, particularly in the detail of Blois and Chambord. This is the châteaux heartland, with one imposing mansion seated after another across the gently undulating countryside.

Blois

The biggest drawback of a visit to the **château at Blois** is the modern town of **BLOIS**, and particularly the broad, fast-moving boulevard that rings the château as if it were a mere traffic island rather than a sensational piece of architecture. There are, however, plenty of places around pl Victor-Hugo, for example the steps of the SI, that offer excellent views of the exterior of the building, Italian loggias and all, and it's worth braving the traffic for the pleasure of a non-guided visit around rooms steeped in the history of power and intrigue.

Château de Blois

Daily, summer 9am–6pm, winter 9.30am–noon & 2–5pm/6pm; 27F.

All six kings of the sixteenth century spent time at the **château** and later, in the early nineteenth century, it was given to Louis XVIII's brother to keep him away from Paris. Hence the courtiers' mansions that fill the town and, given its earlier non-royal ownerships, the château's building montage of distinct, unmatching wings – medieval, Gothic, Renaissance and Classical – that you see today. Much of the château can be visited, from its oldest part, the thirteenth-century manorial assembly hall of the Salle des États to the flamboyant Gothic east wing of Louis XII and the Italianate north wing of François I, with its double loggias and gallery showing the French determination to embrace the Renaissance.

The Blois horror story is the murder of the Duc de Guise and his brother the Cardinal of Lorraine – they who had the Huguenots executed at Amboise – by Henri III. The king had summoned the States General to a meeting in the Grand Salle, only to find an overwhelming majority supporting de Guise, the stringing up of Protestants and aristocratic, rather than royal power. He panicked and had de Guise ambushed and hacked to death in a corridor of the palace. The cardinal was murdered in prison the next day and their deaths were avenged a year later when a monk assassinated the king himself.

The château at Blois was also home to Henri III's mother and manipulator, Catherine de Médicis, who died here a few days after the murders in 1589. The most famous of her suite of rooms is her study, where she kept poison hidden in secret caches behind some of the 237 carved wooden panels. In a later century, revolutionaries were tried in this hall for conspiring to assassinate Napoléon III, a year before the Paris Commune.

Orientation and accommodation

Blois is easy to get around: av Jean-Laigret is the main street leading from the **gare SNCF** south to pl Victor-Hugo and the château, and past it to the town centre. The Blois **SI**, 3 av Jean-Laigret (Mon–Sat, summer 9am–7pm, Sun 10am–1pm & 2–7pm; daily, winter 9am–12pm & 2–6pm), organise hotel rooms for a small fee and change money.

Hotels worth trying are the inexpensive *St-Nicolas*, 2 rue du Sermon (☎54.78.05.85; ①), the equally good-value *Étoile d'Or*, 7–9 rue du Bourg-Neuf (☎54.78.46.13; ②), the slightly more expensive *Hôtel du Bellay*, 12 rue des Minimes (☎54.78.23.62; ②), and the more comfortable *Savoie*, 6 rue Ducoux (☎54.74.32.21; ③), near the train station.

The Blois **campsite** is across the river 2km from the town centre on the Lac de Loire at Vineuil (☎54.74.22.78; bicycle and boat hire).

The **youth hostel**, 18 rue de l'Hôtel-Pasquier, Les Grouets (☎54.78.27.21; March–mid-Nov; closed daily 10am–6pm), is further out, 5km downstream, between the Forêt de Blois and the river. Take bus #4, direction Les Grouets, stop *Église des Grouets*.

Eating

Best bets for **food** are rue St–Lubin and rue Foulérie, including *La Tosca*, 36 rue Foulérie, with Swiss fondue and raclettes, and *Le Maidi*, 42 rue st-Lubin, with cheap *menus*. Another good bet, reasonably priced especially for weekday lunches, is *Hôtel de la Poste*, 11 av de Blois. Lastly, next to the **bus** office, 6 pl Victor-Hugo, there's a **bar that stays open late**. Blois, however, is not a town that delivers much nightlife.

Chaumont, Cheverny, Beauregard and Chambord

On the left bank of the river, within a 20km radius south and east of Blois, are a handful of impressive and easily visited **châteaux**. By car you could call at all of them in a couple of days. But they make ideal **cycling** targets – Chambord is a flat, beautiful ride – or, if you strike out along minor roads and woodland rides with a map, **walking** destinations. Of the two most imposing examples, Chaumont has frequent daily trains from Blois, but to get to Chambord on public transport you have to use the expensive châteaux tour buses that leave from from Blois, Tours or Amboise. **Accommodation**, if you wanted to stay near any of the châteaux, is limited to **campsites** at Chaumont (☎54.20.95.22) and Cheverny (☎54.79.90.01; March 30–Sep 30) and several pricey hotels at Cheverny (Cour-Cheverny), of which the *St-Hubert* (54.79.96.60; ⑤) is the cheapest.

Château de Chaumont

Daily, summer 9.15am–5.35pm; winter 9.15–11.35am & 1.45–3.30pm/5.35pm; 24F.

Catherine de Médicis forced Diane de Poitiers to hand over Chenonceau in return for the château de **CHAUMONT**, 16km downstream from Blois. That Diane got a bad deal is quite evident if Chaumont, as a building, is contrasted with the lovely Chenonceau, but this is still one of the more fascinating of the visitable châteaux.

Chaumont started life as a fortress – complete with towers, moat and drawbridge – defending the river and valley below. The wings you see today form three sides of a square, the fourth side having been demolished in 1739 to improve views over the river – which are spectacular. Chaumont's interior, unlike those of many Loire châteaux, is furnished in an early nineteenth-century style which, combined with its unkempt air, gives it a surprising, homely feel. Look out for the tiled floor with its depictions of hunting scenes, and a copy of a sixteenth-century portrait of the young Catherine de Médicis in the Salles des Fêtes, on the first floor.

More interesting than anything inside the château, however, are the remarkable, Belle-Époque **stables**, with their porcelain troughs and elegant lamps, all lit by electricity for the benefit of the horses at a time before it was used in the château itself – let alone in general use around the country. If you want to get a further feel of the château's equestrian character, the best way is to hire either a horse or a pony and trap, available in the château grounds from May to October (☎54.20.90.60; closed Tues in winter).

Château de Cheverny

Mon–Sat, July–Aug 10am–noon & 3–7pm, Sun 3–7pm; daily, winter 3–6pm; 23F.

Seventeenth-century purists have their treat 15km southeast of Blois at the château de **CHEVERNY**. Presenting an immaculate picture of symmetry and stasis, and still containing impressive displays of paintings, furniture and armour, it was built between 1604 and 1634 and never altered. It still belongs today to a descendant of the original owner: in winter he exercises his hounds and horses to the accompaniment of hunting horns and tourist buses. And it's in winter time when, not inundated by crowds, Cheverny appears at its best and you're most likely to enjoy it.

Château de Beauregard

Daily, summer 9.30am–6.30pm; winter 8.30–noon & 2–5pm /6.30pm; 16F.

If you want to take in another château near Blois – and one that's closer, too, at a cyclable 9km – the much less visited château de **BEAUREGARD** is planted amid the Forêt de Russy. The highlight of the castle, most of it dating from the same time as Cheverny, is a portrait gallery of 363 paintings of kings and their cohorts.

Château de Chambord
Daily, summer 9.30–5.45pm/6.45; winter 9.30–11.45am & 2–5.45/6.45pm; 30F.

CHAMBORD, François I's little "hunting lodge", is the largest of the Loire châteaux and one of the most extravagant commissions of its age. Its patron's principal object, to outdo the Holy Roman Emperor Charles V, would, he claimed, leave him renowned as "one of the greatest builders in the universe". It has its fans, though for many its mix of styles make it the single ugliest building in the Loire – nuclear power stations excepted, perhaps. Visits, at least, are unguided, and even if you loathe the château there's entertainment to be had from circling it on foot or by bike, with free access to the grounds, and roaming around inside, up and down the double spiral staircase, around the chimneys and through endless mostly unfurnished rooms and corridors. Judge for yourself.

As for its architectural history, the design employed was that of the Italian architect Domenico de Cortona. It was begun in 1519, in another bid to introduce prestigious Italian Renaissance art forms to France, but the building work was executed by French masons, and the overall result is essentially French medieval. This is particularly evident in the massive round towers with their conical tops, and the forest of chimneys and turrets, which bring to mind Flamboyant Gothic. The details, however, are pure Italian, for example the **Great Staircase** (attributed by some to da Vinci), panels of coloured marble, niches decorated with shell-like domes, and free-standing columns. Wandering through you can get a good feel for the contrasting architectural styles.

TOURAINE AND ANJOU

This is the lowest – and best – stretch of the Loire, languidly floating by long islands of reed and willows before it reaches its estuary. Travelling upstream from Brittany and Nantes, or downstream if you approach from Paris and **Tours**, is straightforward with bus and train routes following the river for most of the way. The Touraine and Anjou **wines** can become addictive, and the **food markets** in this key region, which, in the west, divides northern France from the south, are among the best in the country.

Touraine

Chief town of the Loire proper is **Tours**, an appealing place to spend a day or two. But the most popular sight in the Touraine is the **Château de Chenonceau**, best loved of all the Loire châteaux. Touraine is also excellent touring country, particularly by bicycle and the vineyards of this fertile, affluent belly of the Loire are famous, especially for the Chinon and Vouvray wines. The excellent chalky soil also lends itself to easy excavation; between Tours and Amboise there are a fair number of troglodyte dwellings. The **Gâtine** area of Touraine, stretching north from the Loire over the Loir to the Sarthe, is particularly attractive. Once a great forest, it is now heaveily cultivated, but there are still some woodland belts left, notably the large **Forêt de Bercé** and the smaller **Forêt de Chandelais**.

Tours

TOURS once had a reputation as a staid, bourgeouis city. If, as a traveller passing through, you decided to stay, it was likely to be for the museums – of wine, crafts, and an above-average *Beaux-Arts* – and for the pleasures (and *dégustations*) of the vineyards. An English travel writer wrote in 1913:

> *Tours has an immense air of good breeding . . . you have visions of portentously dull entertainments in lofty gilded saloons where everything is rather icily magnificent.*

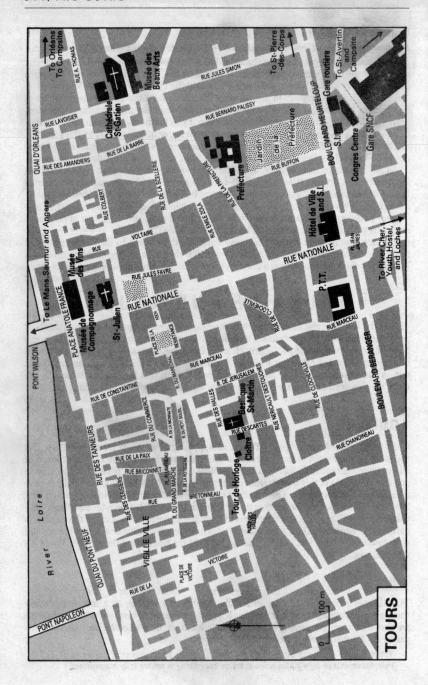

TOURS

But the city is now only an hour's journey from Paris on the *TGV* line, and this, together with the building of a new **conference centre** has meant an influx of business people, young commuters and students. Together they are effecting a gradual, enlivening change on what's fast becoming a Paris satellite. The metropolitan feel is heightened if you drive into Tours: it's virtually impossible to find anywhere to park.

The city: museums, the cathedral and Old Tours

At the head of **rue Nationale** – Tours' main street – statues of Descartes and Rabelais (looking, respectively, suitably doubtful and gleefully certain) overlook the Loire. A short walk back from the river and you come to the church of St-Julien and, hard by, two of the town's most compelling museums.

In the **Musée de Compagnonnage**, 8 rue Nationale (summer 9am–12pm & 2–7pm; winter 9am–12pm & 2–5pm; closed Tues; 10F), for once the people who built rather than ordered the châteaux and cathedrals are celebrated. As well as documents of the origins and militant activity of the "guilds", there are **masterpieces** (in the original sense of the term) of various crafts from cake-making and carpentry to locksmithery and brick-laying, with their relevant tools exhibited alongside.

The **Musée des Vins** next door (same opening hours; 10F) takes you through a comprehensive treatment of the history, mythology and production of **wine**, though there's nothing on recent technical innovations, and no tasting to look forward to. Still, it has some great quotations on the subject: Virgil on planting vines like an arrangement of cohorts in battle; Victor Hugo's "God only created water; man made wine"; and Colette, going over the top with "the barren chalk weeps in wine tears of gold". Behind the museum, a Gallo-Roman wine press from Cheillé sits in the former cloisters of St-Julien's church.

Over towards the **Cathédrale St-Gatien** – with its crumbling, Flamboyant Gothic front – you'll find the city's third museum, the **Beaux-Arts** (8am–12.45pm & 2–6pm; closed Tues; 20F), overshadowed by a huge and venerable Lebanon cedar. The museum has some beauties in its rambling collection: *Christ in the Garden of Olives* and the *Resurrection* by Mantegna; Franz Hals' portrait of Descartes; *Balzac* painted by Boulanger; prints of *The Five Senses* by the *Tourainais* Abraham Bosse; a sombre Monet; and a cheering tapestry by Caldor. The museum's top treasure, Rembrandt's *Flight into Egypt*, is unfortunately difficult to see through the security glass.

The **old part of Tours** crowds around **pl Plumereau**, over to the west of rue Nationale and past the **Hôtel Gouin** – a small archaeological museum (summer 10am–12.30pm & 2–6.30pm; winter closes at 5.30; closed Wed) with a Renaissance facade to stop you in your tracks. But it's the half-timbered houses and bulging stairway towers of the twelfth to fifteenth centuries (and 1970s restoration) that are the city's showpiece. Some of the earlier buildings look like cut-out models, but the Renaissance stone and brick constructions are sturdier – particularly the **Écoles des Langues Vivantes** on rue Briconnet with its wonderful sculpted dogs, drunks, frogs and monsters. West of rue Bretonneau modern artisans' workshops cluster between medieval dwellings. The pre-restoration inhabitants of Old Tours were Portuguese, some of whom remain, and Algerians – kicked out by the city council. Today it's a highly yuppified quarter.

Accommodation

Unless there's a conference in town, **accommodation** shouldn't be a problem. There's a **youth hostel** on av d'Arsonval in Parc de Grandmont, bus #6 or #2 from pl Jean-Jaurès to Chambray, stop *Auberge de Jeunesse* (☎47.25.14.45; reception 5pm–midnight; closed Dec and Jan; curfew 11pm), and a **hostel** for under-25s, *Le Foyer*, 16 rue Bernard-Palissy; (☎47.05.38.81; call first, they may be full). The closest **campsite** *Edouard Peron* (☎47.54.11.11; May 11–Sep 8) is on the north bank of the Loire about 1.5km from the town centre. Take bus #6, stop *Ste-Radegonde*.

The range of **hotels** is good and the following merely a selection of some of the cheaper options:

Mon Hôtel, 40 rue de la Préfecture (☎47.05.67.53). Towards the cathedral, clean and comfortable. ①

Hôtel Akilene, 22 rue du Grand Marché (☎47.61.46.04). Reasonably priced, comfortable and central. ②

Hôtel Grammont, 16 av de Grammont (☎47.05.55.06), on the southward continuation of Rue National. Not so central but very pleasant. ②

Hôtel l'Olympic, 74 rue B-Palissy (☎47.05.10.17). In the less salubrious area around the station – and not the cleanest of rooms. ②

Hôtel au Rhum, 4 pl des Aumônes (☎47.05.06.99). Also near the station, slightly better value. ①

Food and nightlife

The regional **food speciality** is greasy potted pork *rillettes*, or pieces of cold pork – *rillons*. But for sugar and chocolate freaks, Tours also has some excellent **pâtisseries**: *La Marotte* (3 rue du Change), *La Chocolatière* (6 rue de la Scellerie) and *Sabat* (76 rue Nationale).

Rue du Grand-Marché and rue de la Rôtisserie, on the periphery of old Tours, and rue du Commerce and rue Colbert (which run down to the cathedral), are the most promising **restaurant** streets; *Les Lionceaux*, 17 rue Jules-Favre, off rue Colbert, has the cheapest *menu fixe*. *Le Yaki Tour*, rue de la Rôtisserie, is a Japanese restaurant with 38F and 49F menus, and there's good Indian, Chinese and Vietnamese food in this area, too, particularly *Yang Tse* on rue du Commerce. The *El Patio* Spanish restaurant on 32 rue Briçonnet overlooks the subterranean gardens in the former foundations of a twelfth-century church and backs onto a small medieval square (see the *Atomic Café*, below, in the same courtyard). *Le Donjon*, 7 rue de la Monnaie, has interesting and cheap international fare from a good filling stroganoff to chilli, and if you're in a frivolous mood give *Le Medieval*, 50 rue du Grand Marché, a try, with its theme costumes, decor and *menus*. For an excellent oriental takeaway with chopsticks thrown in try the deli-style *Shanghai Express*, 24 Rue de la National.

Nightlife in the city is a lot more promising than in other towns in the Loire, with a fairly impressive selection of nightclubs, bars and cabaret-cafés. The youngest of the clubs are *Le Boléro*, 57 rue de la Scellerie (10.30pm–dawn; Tues & Thurs student nights 35F, weekends 60F), with various "theme" nights and *L'Excalibur*, 35 rue Briçonnet, nicely situated in a vaulted cellar (10.30pm–4am, 50F weekdays, 70F weekends, free for women). Cafés with shows include the popular *Petit Facheaux*, 23 rue des Cerisiers, best known for jazz, but also featuring comedians and darts, cards and chess at any time; and *Le Bateau Ivre*, 146 rue Edouard-Vaillant, with a varied programme including jazz, rock, theatre and comedy.

Place Plumereau is set out with the tables of expensive cafés and restaurants, and the bars in most of the surrounding streets are equally overpriced and exclusive, with silly names like *The Sherlock Holmes*. But just off the square, situated on a medieval courtyard is a refreshingly rough-looking bar, the *Atomic Café*, teeming with people and with a good atmosphere. A more serious establishment, only for those with a measure of dedication to alcohol, is the *Académie de la Bière*, 43 rue Lavoisier, at the other end of town, near the cathedral, where you can choose between 150 types of beer while playing darts.

Listings

Book shops English books from 2 rue du Commerce and 20 rue Marceau.

Bike hire From the Gare SNCF and from *Au Col de Cygne*, 46 rue Dr-Fournier; *Grammont Motocycles* 93 av de Grammont; *Loisirs Plus* (mountain bikes), 214 rue Jolivet. The ride west from Tours along the Cher is particularly idyllic.

Car hire *Acels Thrifty*, 157 av de Grammont; *Diffusion Location Service*, 30 rte de Bordeaux; *ELS Sobal*, 6 rue George-Sand.

Caravan & camper hire *Eurovan* RN10 Parçay Meslay; *Auto Loisirs Maginot*, 289 av Maginot.

Châteaux tours *Touraine Evasion* (☎47.66.52.32), or *Service Touristique de Touraine* (☎47.05.46.09), located in the Gare SNCF. The *Bureau des Châteaux de la Loire*, also at the Gare SNCF arranges minibus trips to Villandry, Ussé, Langeais and Azay-le-Rideau.

Cinema *Les Studios* on rue des Urselines shows eight good films a week (in the original) at reasonable cost.

Contraceptives Condom machines by pharmacies on bd Heurteloup, rue Nationale and rue Charles Gilles.

Gare SNCF Centrally positioned on pl Maréchal-Leclerc, off bd Heurteloup (☎47.20.20.50 for information). Many trains stop at St-Pierre-des-Corps, an industrial estate outside the city, from where buses #3 and #6 go into the centre.

Gare Routière Right next to the train station (☎47.05.30.49).

Kids There's a great, gleaming, and climbable SNCF **steam engine**, placed in a square by the intersection of boulevards des Deportés and Paul-Langevin in the suburb of St-Pierre-des-Corps (bus #3, stop *Deportés*).

Launderettes 21–23 pl Michelet; 56 rue du Grand-Marché.

Medical assistance SAMU ☎15; Hôpital Bretonneau, 2 bd Tonnelé (☎47.47.47.47).

SI In the Hôtel de Ville on pl Jean-Jaurès with an annexe near the Gare Routière on bd Heurteloup (summer 8.30am–7.30pm, Sun 10am–12.30 & 3–6pm, winter weekdays only 9am–12.30pm & 1.30–6pm). Well organised and helpful, they run an accommodation service.

Travel Agencies *Tourisme et Loisirs du Val de Loire*, 19 av de Grammont, *Turone Voyages* 13 rue Victor-Hugo.

Short trips west of Tours: châteaux, gardens, vineyards

Even if gardens aren't your thing, it's highly recommended you devote some time to getting out to the **garden** at **VILLANDRY** (daily, May–mid-Sept 9am–6pm; Nov–mid-March 9am–5pm; 34F). Thirteen kilometres west of Tours along the Cher – a superb **cycle trip** – this recreated Renaissance garden is no ordinary formal pattern of opposing primary colours, but more like a tapestry of that period, one that changes with the months and only fades in winter. Carrots, cabbages and aubergines are exalted to coloured threads woven beneath rose bowers; herbs and ornamental box hedges are part of the same artwork, divided by vine-shaded paths. From a terrace above, you can see the confluence of the Cher and the Loire and châteaux on the northern bank.

For drivers, or keen cyclists, the tiny, but paved, D16 road creeps alongside the river from Villandry to the **Château d'Ussé**, 33km from Tours (daily 9–12 & 2–6, closed Nov–mid-March; 44F). With its shimmering white towers and spires and idyllic wooded setting (best seen after dark when floodlit), this is the ultimate in fairytale châteaux, so much so that it's supposed to have inspired Charles Perrault's transcription of the Sleeping Beauty fairy story. Going inside for the visit, despite a display of models illustrating the Sleeping Beauty myth – which might be of interest to children – isn't half as compelling, and perhaps not worth the rather excessive entrance fee.

Crossing the river from Villandry at LANGEAIS and turning left onto the N152 brings you to ST-MICHEL-SUR-LOIRE and **Le Musée Cadillac** located in the **Château de Planchoury** (10am–6pm, Sept–May, closed Tues). This is the largest collection of Cadillacs outside the USA, comprising fifty different models of the American dream machine collected from all over the world – and all in remarkable condition.

Azay-le-Rideau and Cheillé

Even without its **château** (daily, summer 9.30am–5.30pm, closes 6.30pm July & Aug; winter 10am–noon, 2–4.30pm; 24F), **AZAY-LE-RIDEAU** would bask in its serene setting: the island in the Indre, the old mill by the bridge, the Carolingian statues embedded in the facade of St-Symphorien church, and a quiet village. The château **exterior**, however, on its little island in the Indre, is one of the loveliest, pure

Renaissance and required viewing. And while the guided tours of the **interior**, furnished in Renaissance style, don't add much to the experience, the **portrait gallery**, is worth seeing, since it has the whole sixteenth-century royal Loire crew – François I, Catherine de Médicis, the de Guises, and the rest – the highlight being a semi-nude painting of Gabrielle d'Estrée, Henri IV's lover.

Upstream from the château, there's a large **campsite** (☎47.45.42.72). Otherwise, **hotels** in Azay-le-Rideau don't come cheap, though *Le Balzac*, 4 rue A-Richer (☎47.45.42.08; ③), and *Le Grand Monarque*, 3 pl de la République (☎47.45.40.08; ④) are both comfortable possibilities. There are trains and buses to Chinon and Tours and you can hire **bikes** at the station or from *Le Provost*, 13 rue Carnot.

For something rather strange and totally off the tourist track, make your way to **CHEILLÉ**, a small village 6km west of Azay, on the south bank of the Indre, linked by some (not all) of the Chinon trains. In the church is a life-sized wooden crucifix that differs from almost every other representation of Christ – he has no beard. The effect is astounding: Christ no longer a hippy but someone whose face could belong to any period. It is the work of a very passionate artist, but who or when is not documented. If the church is locked, ask for the key at the house next door.

Upstream from Tours: Amboise

AMBOISE is a a prim little town trading on long-gone splendours, its one saving grace Leonardo da Vinci's residence of Clos-Lucé. It is the home power base of Michel Debré, de Gaulle's first prime minister, who strives to keep the Gaullist party pure, and also one of Mick Jagger's favourite residences – perhaps because few recognise him here.

The most notable thing in Amboise is **Max Ernst**'s prototype ET/toy bear and turtle **fountain**, with the Friday and Sunday **market** behind it on the riverside. What's left of the **château** is interesting enough, however (daily, summer 9am–noon, 2–6.30pm; July & Aug 9am–6.30pm; winter 10am–noon & 2–5pm; 27F). The *Tour des Minimes*, the original entrance and fifteenth-century forerunner of the multi-storey car park ramp, is architecturally the most exciting part. The Loire presents one of its best panoramas from the top. The hooks along the battlements were once smeared with the blood and guts of rebellious Huguenots. Caught plotting to get rid of the Catholic de Guise family, the power behind young François II, they were summarily tried in the *Salle des Conseils* and the whole town was hung about with their corpses. The last French king, Louis-Philippe, stayed in this château, hence the abrupt switch from solid Gothic furnishings to 1830s post-First Empire style.

One man, of far greater renown than any of the French kings, who died in Amboise in 1519, was **Leonardo da Vinci**, invited here by François I to bolster and encourage the French Renaissance. His home, **Clos-Lucé**, at the end of rue Victor-Hugo (summer 9am–7pm, winter 9am–6pm; 30F), does not contain any original works, but it does have forty models of Leonardo's inventions, recently constructed according to his detailed plans. It's wonderful to see the mechanical manifestations of da Vinci's technological achievements. But even the best model, the wooden tank, does not have the same effect as Leonardo's sketch, beetling along with manic velocity, kicking up a wake of dust.

While you're here, a museum of somewhat specialist interest is the **Musée de la Poste**, in the *Hôtel Joyeuse*, 6 rue Joyeuse (summer 9.30am–noon & 2–6.30pm; winter 10am–noon & 2–5pm; 12F), whose exhibits trace the history of the postal delivery service, from the pony express to air and sea mail.

Practicalities

From the practical viewpoint, apart from a good **campsite** on the island across from the castle, the Ile d'Or (☎47.57.23.37), Amboise's overpriced hotels and restaurants –

TOURAINE WINE AND CHEESE: SOME POINTERS

Vouvray, 10km east of Tours on the north bank, is the *appellation* for one of the most delicious white wines of the Loire. A good vintage lives to be 100, can be *sec, demi-sec* or *pétillant* (lightly sparkling) and is best from the grape of a single vineyard. The SI at the *Hôtel de Ville* in Vouvray can provide addresses of vignerons, but all the roads leading up the steep valleys are lined with *caves*. The view of the vines from the top of the hill is almost intoxicating in itself. Vouvray has a **campsite** between the Loire and the Cisse. Bus #61 runs from pl Jean-Jaurès in Tours to pl St-Vincent just south of the SI in Vouvray.

The other two famous Touraine *appellations* are **Chinon** and **Bourgueil**, which lies 5km north of the Loire on the D479. The Abbaye de Bourgueil has been making wine for nearly a thousand years and this is the best place to taste it. The *Clos de l'Abbaye* (☎47.97.76.30) in the abbey close, just east of the town centre, is open for visits every day except Sunday, from 2.30–7pm. Chinon produces mostly red wines, but also a few very dry whites. The SI (see p.000) can provide a list of producers and arrange visits.

The *appellation* **Touraine-Amboise** has fewer pretentions but still some excellent wines. Some 4.5km out from Amboise on the D81 to Chenonceaux, there's a farmhouse by a crossroads and a petrol station. Here M. Delecheneau sells his *sec* and *demi-sec* white wine and sublime *demi-sec* rosé across the kitchen table. He'll show you his barrels named after cows (Dauphine, Jolie, Violette etc) and the wine press his grandfather used.

To go with the wine, Touraine produces **chèvre** (goat's cheese); the best of those cylindrical and speckled miniature building blocks you see at cheese stands come from around the small town of **Ste-Maure-de-Touraine**, 30km south of Tours. The SI here on rue du Château can provide addresses for *dégustations* , and the medieval covered market will be well stocked. One producer is M. Raguin, by the Château d'Eau in **Noyant-de-Touraine**, 4km west on the Chinon road. Ste-Maure is on the bus route to Descartes (see p.000) from Tours.

and nothing open after 10pm – don't exactly encourage long stays. For information the **SI** is on the waterfront east of the bridge. The *Auberge de Jeunesse/Centre Charles Péguy* (☎47.57.06.36; reception 3–10pm; closed Mon and Sun in winter), on the west end of the Ile d'Or, has hostel-style rooms, and also hires out **canoes**.

Hotels worth trying are the central *Chaptal*, 13 rue Chaptal (☎47.57.14.46; ③), the *Plantanes*, rte de Nazelles (☎47.57.08.60; ②), in a pleasant rural setting behind the **gare SNCF** (though it's a fairly long walk from the centre on the north side of the river), and *La Brèche*, 26 rue Jules-Ferry, also near the station (☎47.57.00.79 ③).

For **bikes**, try either the gare SNCF or the campsite snackbar.

Along the Cher, Indre and Vienne

The rivers **Cher**, **Indre** and **Vienne** share none of the Loire's dangerous habits, but it can be somewhat difficult to get down to their banks unless you're prepared to hunt for the paths through the riverside farmland. At least most of the notices you see are more often about fishing restrictions than *defense d'entrer*. Trains and roads follow the Cher from **Tours** and the Indre from **Loches**. Obvious bases for the Vienne are **Chinon** and **Descartes**, but, along here, trains aren't very practical.

The best **places to stay** on the Cher are the village of Chenonceaux itself – if you can get a room – or MONTRICHARD, with its full complement of medieval houses and ruined castle, a couple of stops along the rail line. Other local possibilities are CHISSEAUX, located between Chenonceaux and Montrichard, or ST-AIGNAN, 30km southeast of Chenonceaux.

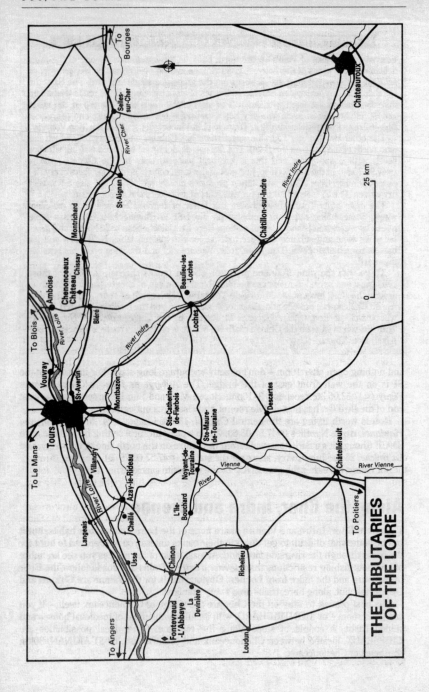

THE TRIBUTARIES
OF THE LOIRE

If you're travelling up the Indre, the overnight possibilities (and reasons for staying) are fewer. LOCHES has pricey hotel rooms and a campsite, but the next obvious target, CHÂTEAUROUX, is unappealing.

The Cher: Chenonceaux and east upstream

Unlike the anarchic Loire, the eminently reasonable River Cher keeps to its depth and flows so slowly and passively between the exquisite arches of the **Château de Chenonceau** that in the reflection it's as though two châteaux appear before you. This striking mansion is the very best of all the Loire châteaux for architecture, site, contents and organisation.

In the village of **Chenonceaux** (the village has the "x"), a convenient stone's throw from the château, the *Hostel du Roy* (☎47.23.90.17; ③) is excellent value for a comfortable hotel, and it's right next to the train station. For camping there's *Le Moulin Fort* (☎47.23.86.22; Easter–mid-Sept) in **FRANCEUIL** over the river. Just down the north bank road at **CHISSEAUX**, the best-value beds are to be found at the *Clair Cottage* (☎47.23.90.69; closed Jan; ②).

Château de Chenonceau

Daily 9am–7pm; closes 5pm first two weeks Nov, 5.30pm last two weeks Feb, 6pm Oct & first two weeks March, and 6.30pm last two weeks Sept; from mid-Nov–mid-Feb 9am–noon & 2–4.30pm; 30F

The building of the **Château de Chenonceau** was always controlled by women. Cathérine Briconnet, whose husband bought the site, hired the first architects in 1515 and had them begin building on the foundations of an old mill that stood on the granite bed of the Cher. The château's most characteristic feature, the set of arches spanning the river Cher, was begun later in the century by Diane de Poitiers (mistress of Henri II) and completed by the indomitable Catherine de Médicis (wife of Henri II) after she had evicted Diane. Mary Queen of Scots, child-bride of François II, also spent time here. After a long period of disuse, Mme Dupin brought eighteenth-century life to this gorgeous residence along with her guests Voltaire, Montesquieu and Rousseau, whom she hired as tutor to her son. Restoration back to the sixteenth-century designs was completed by another woman in the late nineteenth century. It is now a profitable business, owned and run by the Menier chocolate family firm.

During summer the place is teeming with people but visits are unguided – a luxurious relief. The best **approach** is not straight up the path to the front door, but through the gardens of Diane de Poitiers. After the pay-booths, cross the stream and follow signs to the maze. Follow the stream through the woods, turn right to the Cher and, upriver, there's a magnificent view of the château.

An endless number of arresting tapestries, paintings, ceilings, floors and furniture are on show. On the ground floor the **Chambre de François I** features a portrait of Diane de Poitiers by Primaticcio and a case containing copies of her signatures. Another exceptional picture is Zurbaran's half-dressed *Archimedes* with his clothes inside out and a face full of fear and justified suspicion that his theories will go unrecognised. The **Salle des Gardes** on the same floor, its painted rafters emblazoned with the device of Catherine de Médicis, is used to exhibit Flemish tapestries. The elegant **gallery** across the Cher, despite the potted plastic plants, is worth spending time in if only to evoke the parties – all naked nymphs and Italian fireworks – held there by Catherine.

In July and August you can take boats out onto the Cher, and there's a crèche if you've got small children. It's also worth bearing in mind that Chenonceau's *son et lumière* show, entitled *Les Dames de Chenonceau*, tracing the history of the château from fortified mill to elegant residence, takes place twice every evening from mid-June to mid-September (10pm & 10.45pm; 25F).

Upstream to Montrichard

Another delightful way to fill the time, if you don't mind a bit of a walk, is a visit to the **Fraise-Or**, 3km east of Chenonceaux, just beyond Chisseaux on the road to **MONTRICHARD**. It's an old-fashioned distillery (Easter–Sept 9–11.30am & 2–6pm), specialising in fruit liqueurs, and complete with shiny copper stills. The visit includes a *dégustation* of three of their eighteen liqueurs and eaux-de-vie – based on various fruits, herbs, spices, nuts and rose petals.

Two possibilities for rooms in **MONTRICHARD** are the **hotels** *du Courier,* 4 rte de Blois(☎54.32.04.42; ①), and *Gare,* 20 av de la Gare (☎54.32.04.36; ③); there's an **SI** at 1 rue du Pont and a **campsite**, the *Camping Municipal de L'Etourneau,* (☎54.32.10.16), on the river. Montrichard has a cheap pizzeria, *La Dolce Vita,* on rue St-Celerin. On the D17, the smaller of the two roads from Montrichard to St-Aignan (between Angé and Pouillé), a good-value restaurant, *Le Bosquet* (☎54.71.44.44), situated in an old wine cellar serves simple meat dishes cooked over a charcoal grill.

St-Aignan

Some 30km east of Chenonceaux, lies **ST-AIGNAN** where you can admire the **church** of the same name; the capitals are adorned with mermaids, a multi-bodied snake bites its own necks, a man's head is tunnelled by an eagle and doleful dragons and other wonders of the twelfth-century imagination fill the available space, while, in the crypt, if you can find the light switch, there are superb, brightly coloured medieval frescoes.

If you want to stay, try the **hotel** *du Moulin,* 7 rue Nouilliers (☎54.75.15.54; ②), or the riverside **campsite** (☎54.75.15.79; March 15–Oct 15), where **boats** can be hired for an afternoon at the island. For **food** the market and shops at St-Aignan are excellent. Fairly inexpensive dishes using local wines are served at the *Relais de la Poste,* 3 rue de l'Ormeau.

The Indre: Loches and around

The walled citadel of **LOCHES** is by far the most impressive of Loire valley fortresses, with its unbreached ramparts and the Renaissance houses below still partly enclosed by the outer wall of the medieval town. It is an hour's train journey away from Tours and hotel accommodation is expensive, but there is a good **campsite** across the Indre. From the station av de la Gare leads to place de la Marne and the **SI**.

The southern end of the **Citadelle** (daily, summer 9am–6pm; winter 9am–noon & 2–5pm; closed Wed; closed Dec–Jan; 22F) is taken up by dungeons and a keep, initiated by Foulques the Black, eleventh-century Count of Anjou, with cells and a torture chamber added in the fifteenth century. Climbing unescorted to the top of the keep is fun even if the surrounding countryside is unexciting. There is not much left of the fifteenth-century extension, thanks to the people of Loches who destroyed most of the torture equipment in the Revolution. The very professional guides make up for the lack of exhibits with their spiel, but the English text can't quite express the goriness.

At the other end are the **Royal Lodgings** of Charles VII and his three successors. The medieval half of the palace witnessed two women of some importance to Charles: Joan of Arc, victorious from Orléans, came here to give the defeatist Dauphin another pep talk about coronations. Some time after her death, the less significant but much sexier Agnès Sorel, Charles' lover, resided here. Even the pope took a fancy to her, which allowed Charles to be the first French king to have an officially recognised "mistress". Her tomb now lies in the fifteenth-century wing with her portrait by Fouquet and a painting of the Virgin in her likeness.

Just across the Indre from Loches is the village of BEAULIEU–LES–LOCHES – an extraordinary, unvisited place, thoroughly medieval in appearance and with its parish church built into the spectacular ruins of an **abbey** contemporary with the Loches keep. Its other church, **St–Pierre** holds the bones of Foulqes the Black.

Upstream into Berry

If you follow the Indre upstream into the region of Berry, the river itself tends to be the only source of interest – other than the Romanesque church in CHATILLON-SUR-INDRE on the Touraine–Berry border. CHÂTEAUROUX, the largest town on the banks of the Indre and a local route hub, is a grey and officious sort of place, but further south the river flows past NOHANT and LA CHÂTRE (see p.338).

The Vienne: Chinon and around

A fortress of one kind or another existed at **CHINON** from the Stone Age until the time of Louis XIV, the period of the most recent of its ruins. A favourite Plantagenet residence, the **château** (daily, July & Aug 9am–7pm; April–June & Sept 9am–6pm; Oct 9am–5pm; Nov–March 9am–noon & 2–5pm; 20F) was, much later, one of the few places in which Charles VII could stay while Henry V of England held Paris and the title to the French throne. Charles' situation changed with the arrival here in 1429 of Joan of Arc who recognised him, disguised in a crowd of courtiers, and persuaded him to give her an army.

In the château today all that remains of the scene of this encounter, the *Grande Salle*, is a wall and first-floor fireplace. Visits to this and to the restored Royal Lodgings – both guided – are not wildly exciting. More interesting is the *Tour Coudray*, over to the west, covered with intricate thirteenth-century graffiti carved by imprisoned and doomed Templar knights. Joan is said to have stayed here, too, and to have watered her horse at the pump and prayed in the church on rue Voltaire after her journey from eastern France.

Below, the **town** continues its celebration of the long dead, and in sterile fashion: medieval streets, a wine- and barrel-making museum with tacky, animated models and free tasting of the worst wine. Although the town has been ruined by commercialism, it's a short walk out into the open **countryside** with the added interest of some of the region's troglodyte dwellings on the way. The Coteaux Sainte-Ragonde (GR3) leads from pl Pitoche above the south bank of the Vienne. The route is lined with cave dwellings, some of which are still inhabited, and ends at the Chapel Ste-Radegonde, a rock-cut church which is part of a complex of cave dwellings in which St Radegonde lived with her followers. The sixth-century German princess renounced the world and her husband – probably not a great sacrifice since he eventually murdered her brother – in order to devote her life to God.

Practicalities

If you're looking for a **room** in Chinon, the two cheapest alternatives are the *Point du Jour*, 102 quai Jeanne-d'Arc (☎47.93.07.20; ①/②), and the *Jeanne d'Arc*, 11 rue Voltaire (☎47.93.02.85; ②), while the interesting eighteenth-century *Hôtel Diderot*, 4 rue Buffon (☎47.93.18.87; ③), is a more comfortable option. The most reasonable **restaurant** is *Les Annees 30*, 78 rue Voltaire.

There's a **youth hostel** (☎47.93.10.48 and 47.93.21.37; curfew 10.30pm) close to the **gare SNCF** on rue Descartes, (turn left out of the station onto av Gambetta, and first right into rue Descartes), and at the **campsite** (☎47.93.08.35; March 15–Oct 31) across the river on rue de la Digne de Faubourg you can hire **canoes** during summer and paddle the placid Vienne.

Transport: the SI, 12 rue Voltaire (Mon–Sat 9am–7pm; Sun 10am–12.30pm), has **bikes** for hire, as does the **gare SNCF**. The **gare routière** is on place Jeanne-d'Arc.

RABELAIS, RICHELIEU AND DESCARTES

The Vienne valley is associated with several historical figures. The man who, in Chinon, vies with Joan of Arc for snackbars, shops and streets named in his honour, is **Rabelais** (1494–1553), who wrote approvingly of wine, food and laughter in serious and rather difficult humanist texts, and whose most famous creations are the giant father and son Gargantua and Pantagruel. He was born at **La Devinière**, 6km southwest of Chinon in a steep-roofed farmhouse which is now a **museum** (summer 10am–7pm, winter 9am–noon & 2–5/6pm) completely furnished in the style of the time, right down to the stone kitchen sink.

The small town of **Richelieu**, 25km south of Chinon, didn't see the cardinal until he'd grown up, bought the place, built an enormous château and re-arranged the village into an enclosed town of model classical planning. The château has disappeared without trace; the town survives to please those with a penchant for right angles.

Another upper Vienne birthplace-cum-museum, is much further away, 45km southeast and upstream from Chinon at **Descartes**. Formerly La Haye, the town, on the banks of the Creuse a few kilometres from the Vienne, was renamed after its famous son, the great sceptic philosopher born here. There's a municipal **campsite** on the riverbank (☎47.59.85.90; March 23–Nov 1) – no great shakes but pleasant enough.

Saumur and around

Unlike many small Loire towns, **SAUMUR** is not completely dominated by its château. Nor is it dominated by the military – which it might well be as the home of the French Cavalry Academy, and its successor the Armoured Corps Academy, since 1763. Even the local sparkling wines are based elsewhere – in the suburb of St-Hilaire-St-Florent. Saumur is simply peaceful and pretty, with a number of interesting attractions to the north and south. The Hôtel de Ville strives busily to attract festivals and conferences, and, when they're successful, finding a room can be a problem. Even at the best of times, reservations are essential. But it's a good place to stay, with Angers, Chinon and plenty of vineyards within easy reach.

Saumur

You might begin a look around Saumur with the **Église St-Pierre's** interesting selection of dragons, which you can hunt at your leisure. There are at least seven monsters here, carved in stone and wood, and woven into the sixteenth-century tapestries that tell the legend of St-Florent, an early scourge of the beautiful beasts that symbolise sin.

The great hulk of a **château**, however, is the main crowd-puller (daily, July–Aug 9am–6.30pm & 8.30–10.30pm; rest of the year 9–11.30am & 2–6pm; 20F). The **dungeons** and **watch-tower** can be visited on your own; for the two larger museums, relaxed guides take over. The **Musée des Arts Décoratifs** in the former royal apartments has a huge collection of, among other items, European china, but it's the **Musée du Cheval**, situated in the attic of the château, that's the real treat. Progressing from a horse skeleton, through the evolution of bridles and stirrups over the centuries, you finally reach an amazing and diverse international saddlery collection. The **Musée de la Figurine-Jouet** located in an ancient powder magazine on the ramparts (summer 10am–noon & 2–6pm; winter 2–6pm), offers a display of 20,000 model soldiers.

By knocking at the guarded gate on av Maréchal-Foch, west of rue d'Orléans, you can also visit, escorted by a soldier, the **Musée de la Cavalerie** (Mon–Sat 2–5pm; Sun 9–11.30am; closed Fri and Aug). Among the uniforms, weapons and battle scenes (including some very recent engagements), there's a particularly moving room, dedicated to the cavalry cadets who held the Loire bridges between Gennes and Montsoreau against the Germans for three days in 1940, after the French government had surrendered. If this museum engages you, the **Musée des Blindés**, northeast of place du Chardonnet, is also reasonably worthwhile – an exhibition illustrating the history of **tank** warfare (daily 9–noon & 2–6pm) .

For a slightly less bellicose diversion, the **Riding School**, *L'École Nationale d'Equitation* at St-Hilaire-St-Florent just to the northeast of town (bus #B from the town centre) provides guided tours (Mon pm–Sat am, at 9.30am, 10.30am, 2.30pm & 4pm) and displays of dressage and anachronistic battle manoeuvres by the crackshot *Cadre Noir*. To leave the theme of war completely, a one-kilometre walk downriver along the D751 from the last bus stop in St-Hilaire, brings you to the **Musée de Champignon** (mid-March–mid-Nov, 10am–7pm) which organises tours through some of the region's 500km of underground *caves de champignons*, used to grow seventy percent of France's commonest cooking mushrooms, the *champignon de Paris*.

Practicalities

Orientation is straightforward. Arriving at the **gare SNCF** (bicycle hire) you'll find yourself on the north bank of the Loire: turn right onto av-David-d'Angers and either take bus #A to the centre or cross the bridge to the island on foot. From the island the old **Pont Cessart** takes you to the main part of the town on the south bank. The **gare routière** is in the centre – a couple of blocks from the Pont Cessart on pl St-Nicolas. Saumur's main street, **rue d'Orléans**, cuts back through the south bank sector: the **SI** is just across the river on the left, on pl de la Bilange. The old quarter, around St-Pierre and the castle, is reached along rue Dacier, also to the left of rue d'Orléans.

The best **hotel** by far is *Le Cristal,* 10 place de la République (☎41.51.09.54; ③), with river views from most rooms and very friendly proprietors. Other options include the *Volney*, 1 rue Volney (☎41.51.25.41; ③), and, all in the centre on the south bank: *La Croix de Guerre*, rue de la Petite-Bilange (☎41.51.05.88; ①), with a scruffy café downstairs; *Bretagne*, 55 rue St-Nicholas (☎41.51.26.38; ③); and *Central*, 23 rue Daillé (☎41.51.05.78; ③). On the eastern end of the Île d'Offard – connected by bridges to both banks of the town – there's also a good **youth hostel**, rue de Verden (☎41.67.45.00; reception 8–10am & 5–10pm; curfew 10pm), with boat and bike hire, and a **campsite** (☎41.67.45.00; closed Dec 21– Jan 4) next door. For once you can even **swim**, in the north stream.

Saumur's best **eating** area is around **place St-Pierre**: *Auberge St-Pierre*, 6 pl St-Pierre, sometimes has *langoustines* on a fairly cheap menu, and *les Cigognes* opposite at 1 pl St-Pierre, has an interesting 48F menu. There're a couple of **bars** on the square, too – *Le Swing* with its ancient *Wurlitzer* juke box and fruit cocktails and *Le Richelieu* with good music, Guinness and pool – and there are *crêperies* and other restaurants on the streets heading back to rue d'Orléans. The *Café de la Poste*, opposite the post office on pl du Petit-Thouars is a student meeting place which serves cheap snacks.

WINES AROUND SAUMUR

The **Maison du Vin** next door to the SI in Saumur, has information on local wines and addresses of wine growers. The speciality here is **sparkling** – *méthode champenoise* – wines, which can rival lesser champagnes. Names to look out for are Veuve Amiot and Château de Beaulieu. A good red is the *Saumur Champigny* from around the village of the same name. The *Caves Coopératives* at **St-Cyr-en-Bourg** (a short train hop south of Saumur and near the station) have miles of cellars, and you can taste different wines with no obligation to buy.

Baugé

In **BAUGÉ**, north of Saumur, the nuns at the **Chapelle des Incurables** claim to have a cross made from the True Cross. The wood is certainly Palestinian, though its history prior to its donation to an Angevin crusader is dubious. It is, anyhow, the double-armed cross that became the emblem of the dukes of Anjou and Lorraine and, in this century, of the Free French Forces. To see it, ring at 8 rue de la Girouardière (3–4.30pm, Sun 3–4pm & 6–7pm, closed Thurs; free). The **SI** in Baugé is worth visiting merely for the pleasure of walking freely into a fifteenth-century **castle**. And take a look, too, at the **Hospice St-Joseph** (east of the château up rue Anne-de-Melun) for its seventeenth-century pharmacy, to which the hospital receptionist will direct you (daily, summer 10am–noon & 3–5.30pm; winter closes 4.30pm; Sun 10.30am–noon; free), with its beautiful woodwork shelves, parquetry floor and sculpted ceiling, and the vials, *flacons* and contents as they were in 1874. If you have an interest in ecclesiastical architecture, three parishes around Baugé – PONTIGNÉ, FONTAINE-GUERIN and LE-VIEIL-BAUGÉ– have strange twisting towers (the last one leans as well). A stiff hike to the southeast (5km on the MOULIHERNE road) brings you to the pretty, forest remnant of **Chandelais**.

Staying in Baugé, there's a pleasant **campsite** (☎41.89.14.79; May 15–Sept 15) and a reasonably priced **hotel**, the *Boule d'Or*, 4 rue Cygne (☎41.89.82.12; ⑤).

Abbaye de Fontévraud

The **Abbaye** at **FONTÉVRAUD**, 13km southeast of Saumur (bus #16) is a key site in French and English history (guided or independent visits, summer 9am–7pm; winter 9.30am–12.30pm & 2–5.30pm; 23F). The community was established in 1099 as both a nunnery and a monastery with an abbess in charge – an unconventional move even if the post was filled solely by queens and princesses. The buildings still standing, dating from the twelfth century, are immense, built as they were to house and separate not only the nuns and monks but also the sick, the lepers and repentant prostitutes – there were originally five separate complexes, of which three still gracefully stand in Romanesque solidity. Used as a prison from the Revolution until 1963, its most famous inmate was the writer Jean Genet. But its chief significance is as the **burial ground of the Plantagenet kings**. Four tombstone effigies remain, of Henry II, Eleanor of Aquitaine, Richard the Lionheart and Isabelle of Angoulême (King John's queen).

Recently, the Chirac government brought **changes to the abbey** which have horrified local inhabitants. After massive public funds had been spent on restoration, a multinational corporation was given a say in the cultural activities of the abbey; until then, the site had been the exclusive responsibility of the public organisation *Centre Culturel de l'Ouest (CCO)*. The villagers fear desecration of the sanctity of the place and its tombs, which have already been covered by "viewing screens". For information about concerts at the abbey, phone the *CCO* (☎41.51.73.52) or ask at Saumur SI.

Troglodytes and the Zoo de Doué

The Saumur tourist board are busy promoting one of the region's most interesting phenomena, particularly for those who have had their fill of château-gazing. The "falun" or soft shellstone found in the Loire valley lends itself to troglodyte dwellings. One of the most interesting of the – no longer inhabited – rock-cut villages in the region is the underground village of **ROCHEMENIER**, between Louresse and Gennes 20km west of Saumur. The village (summer Tues–Sun 9.30–noon, 2–7pm; winter weekends only 2–6pm), is situated on a plain, from which a large crater was dug. The cave-dwellings, which housed a small nineteenth-century farming community, were carved out of the walls of the crater, and the excavated limestone was sold or used as fertiliser on the fields. The village includes an underground chapel, a modernised troglodyte dwelling, and a museum of domestic items, including wine and oil presses.

An unusual attraction is the **Zoo de Doué**, 17km southwest of Saumur on the N147 Bus #23 from pl St-Nicholas in Saumur runs to **DOUÉ LA FONTAINE**, then it's a couple of kilometres' walk outside the village. The natualistic zoo (summer 9am–7pm; winter 10–12.30 & 2–6pm) has been established in one of the region's complexes of quarried falun caverns. The natural setting has been used to full advantage for a cave of fruit bats, a vivarium (formerly a cave-dwelling but now home to pythons, anacondas and the like), and a lynx enclosure so spacious and overgrown it's refreshingly hard to spot the cat. Should you find yourself stuck for a **bed** in Doué, try *La Dagobert*, 14 pl Champ de Foire (☎41.59.14.44; ①).

Anjou

From Saumur down to **Angers** is the loveliest stretch of the Loire. The land to the south, under grapes and sunflowers, gradually rises away from the river, with long-inactive windmills still standing. Across the water cows graze in wooded pastures. For **transport** you can either take the train or one of three buses – #5 along the south bank, #11 crossing half way, or #10 staying north of the river. Angers stands on the banks of the Maine, which is the short stretch of river fed by the Mayenne, the Sarthe and the Loir. The Maine, in turn, feeds into the Loire itself.

Angers

"Black" **ANGERS**, Anjou's capital, gained its epithet from the gloomy-coloured slate and stone that has been quarried here since the ninth century. Despite the somewhat forbidding aspect it first presents, however, it's a well-kept town with a lively atmosphere. And it possesses two prize **tapestries**, more stirring and stunning than all the châteaux and their contents put together, the fourteenth-century *Apocalypse* and the twentieth-century *Chant du monde*. A single 35F ticket allows access to the tapestries, together with the town **museums and galleries** (summer daily 10am–1pm & 2–7pm; winter Tues–Sun 10am–noon & 2–6pm).

The château and tapestries

The **Château d'Angers** (daily summer 9am–7pm; winter 9am–12.30pm & 2–6pm; 23F) is a formidable early medieval fortress whose sense of impregnability is created by seventeen circular towers like elephants' legs gripping the rock below the kilometre-long curtain wall. Inside there are a few miscellaneous remains of the counts' royal lodgings and chapels, but the immediate and obvious focus is the **Tapestry of the Apocalypse**, whose 100-metre length (of an original 140m) is well displayed in a modern gallery. Woven between 1375 and 1378, it takes as its text **St John's Vision of the Apocalypse**, as described in the Book of Revelations. A bible would come in handy since, though the French biblical quotations are given, the English "translation" is just explanation. The vision is of the lead-up to the Day of Judgement signalled by seven angels blowing their trumpets. After this . . .

> *hail and fire mingled with blood . . . were cast upon the earth and the third part of trees was burned up and all green grass . . . and as it were a great mountain burning with fire was cast into the sea and the third part of the sea became blood . . . (Rev. 8:7-8).*

The battle of Armageddon rages, as Satan, "the great red dragon" (depicted with seven heads), and his minions of composite animals, mark their earthly followers. The

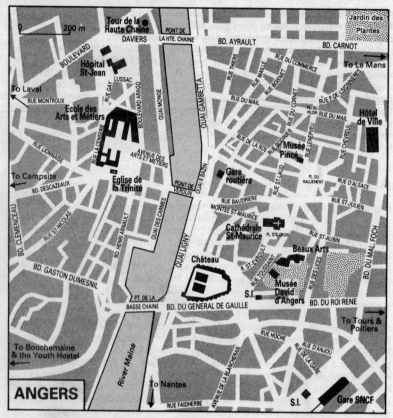

ANGERS

holy forces retaliate by breaking the seven vials of plagues. The vision ends with heavenly Jerusalem, and Satan buried for a thousand years. The slightly flattened medieval perspective has a hallucinatory quality, extraordinarily beautiful and terrifying, evoking the end of the world either in accordance with the first-century text or as a secular holocaust.

If you can take in anything else after that, there are more tapestries, of a gentler nature, in the sporadically open **Royal Lodgings** and **Governor's Lodge**.

THE APOCALYPSE TAPESTRY

The city's **modern tapestry** (daily summer 10am–1pm & 2–7pm; winter Tues–Sun 10am–noon & 2–6pm; 10F) is located across the river from the château, in the **Hôpital St-Jean**, bd Arago, about a fifteen-minute walk upstream from the château across Pont de la Haute Chaine. The tapestry sequence, **"Le Chant du Monde"**, was designed, in response to the *Apocalypse*, by Jean Lurçat, who began the project in 1957 but died nine years later before its completion (the artist's own commentary is available in English). The first four tapestries deal with *La Grande Menace*, the threat of nuclear war: first the bomb itself; then Hiroshima Man, flayed and burned with the broken symbols of belief dropping from him; then the collective massacre of the *Great Charnel House*; and the last dying rose falling with the post-holocaust ash through black space – the *End of*

Everything. From then on, the tapestries celebrate the joy of life and the interdependence of its myriad manifestations: fire, water, champagne, the conquest of space, poetry and symbolic language. Modern tapestry is an unfamiliar art, and the colours and Lurçat's style so unlike anything else, that initially you may be overwhelmed. You can, in any case, enjoy the **Hôpital St-Jean** itself which, from 1174 to 1854, was a hospital for the poor.

The town: churches, museums and sculpture

The far side of the Maine from the château, known as **La Doutre** (the other side, literally), has several mansions and houses dating from the medieval period and later. An official tour will get you into buildings you can't otherwise visit, such as the Romanesque galleries of the **Église de Ronceray**, with their beautiful murals. The abbey to which this church belonged, now the *École des Arts et Métiers*, juts into the twelfth-century **Église de la Trinité**, where an exquisite Renaissance wooden spiral staircase fails to mask this bizarre piece of medieval building joinery. Call at the SI for tour details.

If you cross the middle bridge, Pont de Verdun, back to the centre, just to the right after the quayside road, you'll see a long flight of steps leading up to the **Cathédrale St-Maurice** – the most inspiring approach, giving you the full benefit of the early medieval facade. Inside, the unusually wide, aisle-less nave with its dome-like Plantagenet vaulting is illuminated by twelfth-century stained glass. In the choir one window is dedicated to Thomas à Becket – it was made shortly after his death. Behind the cathedral, on place Ste-Croix, is the town's favourite carpentry detail – the unlikely genitals of one of the carved characters on the medieval **Maison d'Adam**. Old Angers does not extend much further: on place du Ralliement a giant turkey made of aeroplane wings is the central sculpture.

Apart from its cathedral, the other great Gothic edifice in Angers is the chancel of the **Église St-Serge**, on av M-Talet, just north of the centre near the Jardin des Plantes. Though nothing much to look at from the exterior, inside it has some of the most perfect vaulting rising from the slender columns.

The best sculptures elsewhere in the town are those of **David d'Angers** (1788–1856), exhibited in a brilliant gallery (10F) built by glassing over the ruins of a thirteenth-century church, the **Église Toussaint,** 37 bis, rue Toussaint. The building is full of the essential light required for viewing the statues, but the juxtaposition of figures of such different proportions does tend to work to comical effect. The main **Beaux-Arts** collection next door (5F) has delightfully purposeful babies as creative cupids in Boucher's *Génie des Arts*, as well as the beautiful *La Femme au Masque* by Lorenzo Lippi and representative works from the thirteenth to the twentieth centuries. Lastly, the **Musée Pince,** 32 rue Lenepveu (5F) exhibits antiquities and treasures from the Far East with an excellent Japanese collection.

Practicalities

The **gare SNCF** is south of the centre, about a ten-minute walk from the château. Bus #2 makes the journey to the SI and château, bus #22 to pl du Raillement, which is handy for cheap hotels. The **gare routière** is up by the Pont de Verdun, between pl de la République and the river. The main SI (summer Mon–Sat 9am–7pm, Sun 10.30am–6.30pm; winter Mon–Sat 9am–12.30pm & 2–6.30pm), which runs an accommodation service) is on pl Kennedy, facing the château, with, just up the road, the *Conseil Interprofessionel des Vins d'Anjou et du Saumur* vineyards. They can give you details of vineyards to visit (see suggestions below) and sell you Anjou wines.

For a room, the two most central and affordable **hotels** are the *Armor*, 13 rue Bodinier (☎41.88.06.06; ①) and the *Centre*, 12 rue St-Laud (☎41.87.45.07; ①) both located in quiet streets off rue de la Röe. The most comfortable of the reasonably priced places around the **gare SNCF** is *La Coupe d'Or*, 5 rue de la Gare (☎41.88.45.02;

①/②). There's a **youth hostel** (☎41.48.57.01; summer only), along with a **campsite** (☎41.73.05.03; closed Dec 21–Feb 9), at the *Centre d'Accueil du Lac du Maine*, rte du Pruniers, southwest of the town. Take bus #6 (#26 on Sun) either from the gare SNCF or bd Générale-de-Gaulle to stop *Bouchemaine*. You can **hire canoes** at the *Base Nautique* in the complex.

As for **eating** in town, the streets around place du Ralliement and place Romain have a variety of **restaurants** including: *Chez Taya*, rue Pocquet de Livonnières, an oriental café serving couscous; *Le Connétable*, 13 rue des Deux Haies, a good crêperie; *La Mamounia*, 17 rue des Jacobins off pl Frappel, a Moroccan restaurant with cheap *tajines*; *L'Acropole*, rue St-Georges (Greek); a café specialising in soufflés on pl Pilori; and the Californian *Street Line*, 13 rue des Poëliers, which serves excellent American chicken pie. For a good-value, high-quality French feed, best value is *Le Meridor*, 4 rue de l'Espine behind the Musée Pincée. There's also a **market** every day on pl Ste-Croix.

Transport: the *Allostop* phone number is ☎41.87.21.21 (5–7pm Mon–Fri), and you can **hire bikes** from *Cycl et Mob*, 67 bd Eugène-Chaumin (☎41.47.48.28), probably the best plan for easy-going explorations in the district.

Anjou vineyards and châteaux

By lazing around the Loire and its tributaries between visits to vineyards you could fill a good summer week **around Angers**, as long as you're mobile. Otherwise it is a two-bus-a-day problem, or no buses at all. Worthy exceptions are the **Savennières vineyards** which you can reach by train (see box). Just across the Loire bridge from here at **St-Aubin-de-Luigne** (south of Rochefort; take the #6 bus) you can hire **rowing boats** in the summer at the **SI**, next to the **campsite**.

There are also some reasonably easy hitching routes from Angers, if you want to see a couple more **châteaux** in these parts – Brissac-Quincé, 20km south of the town (also on the #9 bus), or Le Plessis Bourré (impossible to get to by public transport), 17km to the north. For a more accessible glimpse of a real monster of a mansion, try the **Château Serrant**, just outside ST-GEORGES-SUR-LOIRE on bus route #18 from Angers.

Château de Brissac

Daily summer 9.30–11.20am & 2.15–5.45pm; winter closes 4.15pm, closed Tues; closed Nov 16–Feb 6.

The **Château de Brissac** at BRISSAC-QUINCÉ has been owned since 1502 by the same line of dukes. It contains some beautiful **ceilings** and has a seventeenth-century addition outreaching the fifteenth-century **fortified towers** – which were supposed to have been pulled down in deference to the symmetry of the building. While it's a riot of aristocratic bad taste, it has an interesting portrait in the Gallery of Ancestors of Madame Cliquot, the first woman to run a champagne business, and her granddaughter, the present duke's grandmother – apparently one of the first women to get a driving licence.

Château du Plessis-Bourré

Daily July–Aug 10am–noon & 2–7pm; Sept–June closes 5pm and Wed & Fri am; closed Nov 15–Dec 15.

Five years' work at the end of the fifteenth century produced the fortress **Le Plessis-Bourré**, which still looks as if it expects an attack any day from across its vast moat. The Treasurer of France who commissioned the château had it redecorated luxuriously inside – best of all are the secular and allegorical scenes painted on the guard room ceiling. It is, however, impossible to get to on public transport.

SARTHE

Half way between Normandy and the Loire, the *département* of **Sarthe** shows France at its most gentle – boring if you're after spectacular landscapes – and less overrun by tourists than neighbouring regions. It contains more châteaux than both banks of the Loire put together, but most are privately owned and closed to the public. The River Sarthe has little to offer and the pastimes of wine-tasting, château-seeking and riverside walking are best done on the Loir (a tributary of the Loire) in southern Sarthe. **Le Mans**, capital of Sarthe, is not much visited, except for its annual 24-hour motor race and as a transit point en route to or from Brittany. But, unpackaged and untouristed, it can be an unexpected pleasure.

Le Mans

Le Mans is taken over by car fanatics in the middle of June for the famous 24-hour race. The rest of the year it's still lively enough, with good public services, free museums (courtesy of the Communist Town Hall) and one of the most beautiful old quarters of any city in France.

The modern centre is **place de la République**, lined by a mixture of Belle Époque and Americana office blocks. The SI is at no. 40, on the north side of the *place* nearest the *Vieille Ville*, and below it in the underground shopping centre is the city bus terminal. Buses #16, #5, #31, #3 and #41 run between here and the **gare SNCF** via av Général-Leclerc where the **gare routière** is located. The old town consists of the complicated web of streets beyond the Cathédral St-Julien on the hill above the Sarthe river.

The sights

The immense Gothic apse of the **Cathédrale St-Julien** rears up the hill above the River Sarthe, with its Romanesque nave, on place du Grente (also called du Château), the crowning point of the old town. According to Rodin, the now badly worn sculpted figures of the south porch were rivalled only in Chartres and Athens. Some of the stained glass windows here were in place when the first Plantagenet was buried in the church, but the brightest colours in the otherwise austere interior come from the tapestries.

The **old town** descends the hill from the cathedral to the river and is still encircled by its original third-to-fourth-century Gallo-Roman **walls**. Supposed to be the best preserved in Europe, they stretch for several hundred metres and encompass ten hectares of intricate Renaissance stonework, medieval half-timbering, sculpted pillars and beams and grand classical facades. Steep, walled steps lead up from the river and longer flights descend the southern side using the old Gallo-Roman entrances. In the 1850s a road was tunnelled under the quarter – a slum at the time – helping to preserve its self-contained unity.

The road tunnel comes out on the south side, by an impressive monument to Wilbur Wright, into **place des Jacobins**, the vantage point for St-Julien's flying buttresses and apse. From here, you can walk east through the park to the **Musée Tessé** (daily 9am–noon & 2–6pm), a mixed bunch of pictures and statues including Georges de la Tour's light at its most extraordinary in the *Extase de St-François* and copies of brilliant medieval populist murals in Sarthe churches. If you're intrigued you can see pictures, maps and plans of *Vieux Mans*, plus examples of its ancient arts and crafts, in the **Maison de la Reine Bérengère** (Tues–Sun 9am–noon & 2–6pm), one of the Renaissance houses on rue de la Reine-Bérengère.

Le Mans race track and the Musée de l'Automobile

Entrance to events at the **24-hour racetrack** (south of the town centre; take bus #3 to rte d'Angers followed by a short walk) is pricey – around 200F for a seat at the *24 Heures du Mans* car race in mid-June – but practice sessions are much cheaper, at around 40F, and all through the year motorcycles, go-karts and even trucks race on the Bugatti circuit, and some practising vehicle is bound to provide you with the appropriate soundtrack for the scene.

In 1908, **Wilbur Wright** took off in his prototype aeroplane, alongside what is now the fastest stretch of the racetrack, and stayed in the air for a record-breaking 1 hour 31.5 minutes. The invitation to use the grounds came from two brothers, busy manufacturing some of the first cars with internal combustion engines.

The refurbished **Musée de l'Automobile** (summer 10am–7pm weekends 10am–8pm; winter noon–6pm; closed Tues; 35F) is on the edge of the Bugatti and 24-hour circuits. It documents the early history of car racing, while the technical side examines research, automobile anatomy and automated assembly, with the emphasis on audience participation. The display includes a superb collection of cars, from 1885 to recent winners, almost all in working order, and the visit ends by examining the world of car racing through audiovisual displays including a simulated high-speed track.

Practicalities

If you're trying to hitch out, the **Allostop** number is ☎43.24.70.69. But unless your visit coincides with one of the big racing events in April, June or September, Le Mans is a good bet for a cheap **hotel**, especially in the area of the station: a good thing, too, since there's no youth hostel and no nearby campsites (ask at the SI for addresses of local *Foyers* and *Centres d'Hébergement*).

Hotels

Hôtel de la Terrasse, 15 bd de la Gare (☎43.24.91.00). Around the cheapest. ①

Hôtel Le Cristina 43 bd de la Gare (☎43.24.86.17). Another close contender. ①

Hôtel du Saumon, 44 pl de la République (☎43.24.03.19). Very central and comfortable and a good deal if you book into one of their cheaper rooms. ②

Hôtel Select, 13 rue du Père-Mersenne, off av du Général-Leclerc (☎43.24.17.74). Cheap and comfortable. ②

Hôtel Le Châtelet, 15 rue du Père-Mersenne (☎43.28.27.51). Located over a bar. ①

Hôtel Chantecler, 50 rue de la Pelouse (☎43.24.58.53). Upmarket option in the same quarter. ③

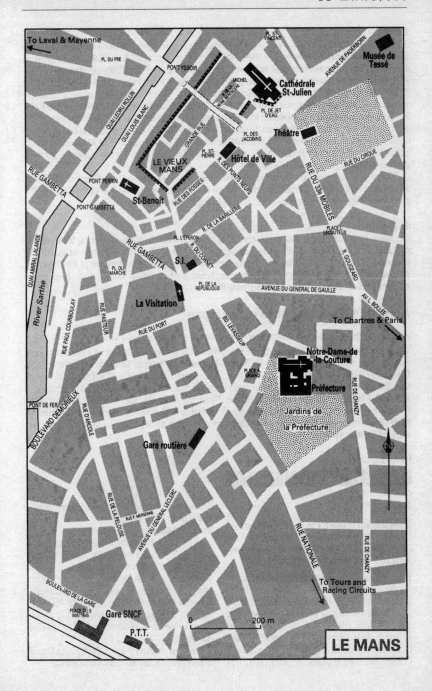

To Laval & Mayenne

PL. DU PRE

QUAI LEDRU ROLLIN

QUAI LOUIS BLANC

PONT YSSOIR

PL. ST. VINCENT

AVENUE DE PADERBORN

Musée de Tessé

MICHEL

NOTRE DAME

Cathédrale St-Julien

PL. DE JET D'EAU

GRANDE RUE

Théâtre

RUE DU CIRQUE

LE VIEUX MANS

PL. DES JACOBINS

PL. ST. PIERRE

Hôtel de Ville

R. DES PONTS NEUFS

RUE DU 33e MOBILES

RUE GAMBETTA

PONT PERRIN

RUE DES FOSSES

St-Benoît

PONT GAMBETTA

R. DE LA BARILLERIE

PLACE L. LECOUTEUX

RUE GAMBETTA

PL. L'ÉPERON

R. DU CORNET

S.I.

R. GOUGEARD

QUAI AMIRAL LALANDE

River Sarthe

PL. DU MARCHE

PL. DE LA RÉPUBLIQUE

AVENUE DU GENERAL DE GAULLE

AV. L. BOLLÉE

La Visitation

To Chartres & Paris

RUE PAUL COURBOULAY

RUE PASTEUR

RUE DU PORT

BD. LEVASSEUR

Notre-Dame-de-la-Couture

PONT DE FER

BOULEVARD DEMORIEUX

RUE D'ARCOLE

PLACE A. BRIAND

Préfecture

RUE DE CHANZY

Gare routière

Jardins de la Préfecture

RUE DE LA PELOUSE

RUE P. MERSENNE

AVENUE DU GENERAL LECLERC

RUE NATIONALE

RUE DE CHANZY

To Tours and Racing Circuits

BOULEVARD DE LA GARE

PLACE DU 8 MAI 1945

Gare SNCF

P.T.T.

0   200 m

LE MANS

Eating – and markets

The cafés and brasseries on place de la République stay open till late and there's a very good **restaurant**, *Le Grenier à Sel*, and a very cheap one, *La Brise*, on nearby pl l'Éperon. The best restaurants, however, are located in the labyrinthine **streets of the old town**, particularly on and around Grande-Rue. Good value for a blow-out is *Le Flambadou*, 14 rue St-Flaceau – which offers a very meaty menu, including a fantastic cassoulet Landaise – but you won't eat here for much under 150F. Moroccan food can be had in the darkly atmospheric *Sherazade*, 79 Grande Rue; *Le Pantagruel*, pl St-Pierre, is a good bet for fish and *fruits de mer*; and *Les Glycines*, pl du Hallai, is pretty with a pleasant atmosphere and reasonable *menus*. The *Truie qui File* **charcuterie**, 25 pl de la République, provides excellent picnic fodder, and if you want cakes to go with it, visit *Pasquier*, 33 rue Gambetta.

There's a large **general market**, the *Marché St-Julien*, on av Pierre-Piffault on Mondays, and a **bric-à-brac market** on pl du Jet d'Eau, below the cathedral on the new town side, on Wednesday, Friday and Sunday mornings.

Nightlife

Le Mans has a lively night-time scene. The best **cinema** in town, showing films in the original, is *Ciné Poche*, 97 Grande-Rue in the old town. There're a couple of good late night **bars** on bd Emile-Zola, and a **jazz** bar, *Le Stan*, open 4pm–4am on pl de l'Éperon. **Night clubs** are ubiquitous, but a couple worthy of mention are *Le City Bird* on pl d'Alger and *Le Yani's Club*, rue des Ponts Neufs.

Around Le Mans: the Abbaye de L'Epau

Abbaye de l'Epau: mid-April to mid-Sept 9.30am–noon & 2–6pm; closed Thurs.

If car racing holds no romance, there's another outing from Le Mans of a much quieter nature. The Cistercian **Abbaye de Notre-Dame de l'Epau**, 4km out of town off the Chartres/Paris road (bus #14 from place de la République in Le Mans, stop *Pologne*) was founded in 1229 by Queen Bérengère, consort of Richard the Lionheart. It stands, in a rural setting, on the outskirts of the **Bois de Changé** and is more or less unaltered since its fifteenth-century restoration after a fire. The visit includes the dormitory, with the remains of a fourteenth-century frescoe, the abbey church and the scriptorium, or writing room.

travel details

Trains

From Angers frequently to Paris (3hr 15min) via Le Mans (1hr); to Nantes (45min); and to Tours (1hr 30min) via Saumur (45min); to Savennières-Béhuard 8 daily (15min).

From Tours at least hourly to Paris (2hr 30min or 1hr for TGV) via Blois (30min) and Les Aubrais-Orléans (1hr 15min); to Angers at least 10 daily (1hr 30min) via Saumur (45min); to Le Mans at least 10 daily (1hr 15min); to Azay-le-Rideau/Chinon 8 daily (30min–1hr); to Loches 6 daily (1hr); to Chenonceaux-Chisseux/St-Aignan 5 daily (30min–1hr); to Bourges 5 daily (2hr); to

Montrichard 7 daily (35min); to Langeais several daily (20min).

From Orléans to Les Aubrais-Orléans every 5 minutes (4 min); to Sully 8 daily (1hr); to Gien 4 daily (2hr); to Briare 4 daily (2hr 10min); to Tours several daily (1hr 30min) .

From Les Aubrais-Orléans to Paris 2 every hour (1hr 15min); to Bourges 4 daily (1hr 15min).

From Le Mans frequently to Paris (1hr 45min), to Nantes (1hr 45min) and to Rennes (2hr); to Angers 22 daily (1hr 15min, or 30min for TGVs); to Saumur 3 daily (2hr).

From Gien to Briare 6 daily (20min); to La Charité 9 daily (1hr); to Nevers 12 daily (1hr 20min).

Buses

From Angers to Saumur 3 or 4 daily (1hr 30min; none Sun); to Doué 6 daily (55min).

From Saumur to Fontévraud 3 daily (30min); to Chinon daily (45min); to Doué 6 daily (30min).

From Tours to Amboise 7 daily (30min); to Loches 4 daily (45min); to Azay-le-Rideau/Chinon 3 daily (30min–1hr 15min); to Chenonceaux (1hr) and Ste-Maure 2 daily (45min); to Montrichard (1hr 15min) and Richelieu 2 daily (1hr 30min).

From Blois to Orléans 4 daily (1hr 30min); to Cheverny 1 or 2 daily (20min).

From Orléans to Gien 4 daily (1hr 40min); to Sully 6 daily (1hr 20min); to Blois 4 daily (1hr 30min).

CHAPTER SEVEN

BURGUNDY

Peaceful, rural **Burgundy** is one of France's most prosperous regions. For centuries its powerful dukes remained independent of the French crown, even siding with the English in the Hundred Years' War (when Philippe le Bon sold them the captured Joan of Arc). Their state was the best organised and richest in Europe, its revenues equalled only by Venice. The evidence of their former wealth and power lies everwhere: in the dukes' capital of **Dijon**; in the châteaux of **Ancy** and **Tanlay**; in the great abbeys of **Vézelay** and **Fontenay**; and in the ruins of the monastery of **Cluny**. By the fifteenth century the power of the Burgundian dukes embraced all of Franche-Comté, Alsace and Lorraine, Belgium, Holland, Picardy and Flanders, and it only fell to the French kings in 1477.

Because of its monastic foundations Burgundy became, with Poitou and Provence, one of the great **church-building** areas in the Middle Ages. Practically every village has its Romanesque church, especially in the country around Cluny and Paray-le-Monial. It is hard not to believe this had something to do with the reminders of its own illustrious Roman past so visible in the substantial Roman remains at **Autun**. And the record goes back further: **Bibracte** on the atmospheric hill of **Mont-Beuvray** was an important **Gallic capital** and **Alésia** was the scene of Julius Caesar's epic victory over the Gauls in 52 BC.

For voluptuaries, **wine** is, of course, the region's most obvious attraction, and devotees head straight for the great **vineyards**, whose produce has played the key role in the local economy since Louis XIV's doctor prescribed wine as a palliative – perhaps an analgesic – for the royal dyspepsia. If you lack the funds to indulge your taste for expensive drink, go in September or October when the *vignerons* are recruiting harvesters.

Burgundy's renowned cuisine supplies **good cooking** in abundance to go with the vintages. Best known of the region's specialities are its snails, *escargots à la bourguignonne*, stuffed with garlic, shallots, parsley and mushrooms; *boeuf bourguignon*, a beef stew cooked in red wine with baby onions and sliced mushrooms – not to be confused with *boeuf bourguignonne*, which is a *fondu*; and *coq au vin*, chicken braised in red wine. These are on many menus, but they need to be cooked in a good wine to taste their best, which makes them more expensive. Other delights to look out for are *jambon persillé*, ham in aspic with parsley; *gougère*, a kind of cheese pastry; *pochouse*, a freshwater-fish stew with white wine; and *chevrotons*, the little hard, dry goat cheeses.

Between bouts of indulgence, you can engage in moderate activity: for **walkers** there's a wide range of hikes, from the gentle to the relatively demanding, in the **Morvan Regional Park** and the **Côte d'Or**. There are also several long-distance canal paths – which also make great **bike** trips. As for the waterways themselves, aficionados rate most highly the **Canal de Bourgogne** and the **Canal du Nivernais**, both of which can be cruised by **hired barge**, though this is not an inexpensive option.

HOTEL ROOM PRICES

For a fuller explanation of these price codes, see the box on p.28 of *Basics*.

① Under 100F   ② 100–130F   ③ 130–180F   ④ 180–230F   ⑤ 230–300F

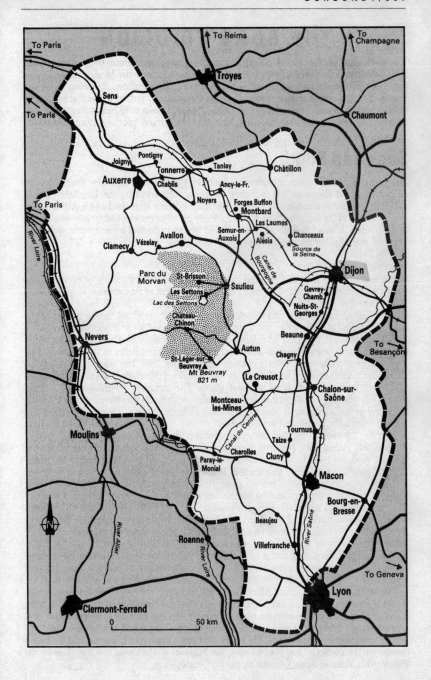

THE ROAD TO DIJON

The backbone of the broad corridor stretching southeast from the Seine outside Fontainebleau is the **N6 highway** – the old route from Paris to the Mediterranean, passing through the ancient towns of **Sens**, **Auxerre** and **Avallon**, following the river Yonne. But the corridor also reaches out to the north to pull in a fascinating bag of abbeys and châteaux, ironmasters and Celts. This may be a time-consuming route, but it's a lot more interesting than speeding along the bland curves of the Autoroute du Sud.

Sens and South

The name of **SENS** commemorates the Senones, the Gallic tribe whose shaggy troops all but captured Rome in 390 BC; they were only thwarted by the Capitoline geese cackling the garrison awake. Nowadays, the town is somewhat staid and unstimulating, the influence of its famous cathedral seemingly as all-pervasive today as it was in the Middle Ages. A short visit, though, is justified by the cathedral treasury (the richest in France), the adjacent museum and the cathedral itself.

The town

Contained within a ring of tree-lined boulevards where the city walls once stood, the town's ancient centre is still dominated by the **Cathedral of St-Étienne**. Begun around 1130 it was the first of the great French Gothic cathedrals. Though early, the Gothic elements of airiness, space and weightlessness are fully realised, in the height of the nave, the arcading of the aisles and the great rose window. The architect who completed it, William of Sens, was later to rebuild the choir of Canterbury Cathedral in England, the missing link being **Thomas-à-Becket**, who, though ten years in the grave by that time, had previously spent several years in exile around Sens. The story of his murder is told in the twelfth-century windows in the north aisle of the choir, just part of the cathedral's outstanding collection of **stained glass**. The **treasury** (10am–noon & 2–6pm; closed Tues & Sun mornings during 11am mass), which can be entered either from the cathedral or the museum, is also uncommonly rich, containing Islamic, Byzantine and French vestments, jewels and embroideries.

Just to the south is the thirteenth-century **Palais Synodal** with its roof of Burgundian glazed tiles, restored like so many other buildings in this region by the "purist" Viollet-le-Duc. Its vaulted halls, originally designed to accommodate the ecclesiastical courts, now house an excellent **museum** (10am–noon & 2–5pm in summer, and 6pm in winter; closed Tues all year; 10F), making all possible use of available space to display a prize collection of exhibits found in the region, including statuary from the cathedral and Gallo-Roman mosaics. Prize exhibits include the **Villethierry treasure**, which consists of 867 items of bronze jewellery in a jar, thought to be a jeweller's horde; a collection of bone combs; and the facade of Sens' second-century public baths. The vaults of the building, which partly constituted the remains of a Gallo-Roman building, including baths heated through the pavement, have now been incorporated into the museum, along with displays of Gallo-Roman metalwork, jewellery and textile crafts, many of which were discovered when the basement was excavated.

Facing the cathedral across **place de la République** are fine wood and iron *halles*, where a **market** is held all day Monday and Friday and Saturday mornings. The *place* stands right in the centre of town where the main streets, **rue de la République** and **Grande-Rue**, intersect. Lined with old houses now converted into shops, they are mainly reserved for pedestrians. There are two particularly finely carved and timbered houses on the corner of rue Jean-Cousin, the **Maison d'Abraham** and the **Maison du Pilier**, with **Maison Jean Cousin** on rue du Général-Alix.

Practicalities

At the far end of Grande-Rue, the road crosses two broad arms of the **river Yonne**, with houseboats moored at the bank, and leads straight ahead to the **gare SNCF**, about ten minutes' walk from the cathedral. The **SI** (summer 9am–noon & 2–6pm/7.30pm; winter 9.30am–noon & 2.30–5pm) is the temporary-looking structure on pl Jean-Jaurès.

Accommodation is rarely a problem. The *Hôtel du Chemin de Fer* (☎86.65.10.27; ②), which has cheap rooms, is opposite the station entrance. Try also *Hôtel du Centre*, 4 place de la République (☎86.65.15.92; closed mid-Sept–mid-Oct; ②), or the *Hôtel Esplanade*, 2 bd du Mail, the road leading from the SI away from the river, (☎86.65.20.95; closed Aug; ②). The **campsite**, *Entre-deux-Vannes* (☎86.65.64.71 June– Sept), is on rte de Lyon, just out of town, but there's no public transport in that direction.

For **cheap eating**, the self-service place, *Brasserie le Senonais*, at 99 rue de la République, and good *crêperie*, *Aux 4 Vents*, at 3 rue de Brennus, do the trick. There's also good, inexpensive Chinese food at the *Saigon* on Grande-Rue near the bridge, pasta at *La Bosa*, 162 rue des Déportés et de la Résistance near the museum, and a number of reasonable restaurants around pl de la République, including the *Roi St-Louis*, which has an excellent 60F menu.

Market days are all day Monday and Wednesday and Thursday mornings. **Ponies and horses** can be hired from *Haras de Villechétive*, Cersiers (☎89.96.28.28), and **bicycles** are available from *E Nibel*, 25 rue Victor-Guichard (☎86.65.11.27).

Joigny

Travelling south of Sens towards Auxerre, the next place of any size on the Yonne is the prosperous little town of **JOIGNY** (twinned with Godalming in Surrey for more than aesthetic reasons), with its elegant amphitheatre overlooking the river, and its share of medieval carving and Burgundian snobbery. It's not worth a prolonged visit, but isn't a bad rest stop. Buildings worthy of attention are the Château des Gondi, built by Cardinal Gondi in the sixteenth century and presently undergoing restoration; remains of the twelfth-century remparts on Chemin de la Guimbard; and a number of semi-timbered houses on rue Montant-au-Palais, the street leading up to the Église St-Jean, including the best-known **Maison du Pilori**, which combines Gothic and Renaissance styles, and displays some carvings strangely reminiscent of crocodile heads.

The SI is on quai Ragobert. Cheap **hotels** include the *Relais de L'Escargot*, 1 av Roger-Varrey (☎86.62.10.38; ①), and the *Lion d'Or*, 5 rue Roger-Varrey (☎86.62.17.00; ②). The *Marmite de Joigny* on rue Gabriel-Cortel (☎86.62.31.81; closed Wed) has a good 95F menu. There's a snazzy bar and pizzeria, the *Montmartre*, on pl de Jean-de-Joigny.

Auxerre

A pretty old town of narrow lanes and handsome squares, **AUXERRE** stands on a hill a further 50km up the Yonne. It looks its best seen from the riverside with its **churches** soaring dramatically above the surrounding rooftops. The most interesting of them is the disused abbey church of **St-Germain** (9am–noon & 2–6pm, closed Tues; 7.5F), at the opposite end of **rue Cauchois** from the cathedral. Partial demolition has left its belfry detached from the body of the building, but what gives it special interest is the **crypt**, one of the few surviving examples of **Carolingian** (ninth century and earlier) architecture, with its plain barrel vaults still resting on their thousand-year-old oak beams. Deep inside, the faded ochre frescoes of St Stephen (St Étienne) are among the most ancient in France (around 850).

The **cathedral** itself, despite the fact that its construction was drawn out over more than three centuries (1215–1560), remains unfinished. The southernmost of the two west front towers was never completed. Compensation for this lies in the richly detailed **sculpture** of the porches and the glorious colours of the original thirteenth-century **glass**, that, despite the savagery of the Wars of Religion and the Revolution, still fills the windows of the choir. There has been a church on the site since about 400 AD, though nothing visible survives earlier than the eleventh-century **crypt**. Among its **frescoes** is a unique depiction of a warrior Christ mounted on a white charger, accompanied by four mounted angels.

From in the front of the cathedral, **rue Fourier** leads to **place du Marché** and off left to the Hôtel de Ville and the old city gateway known as the **Tour de l'Horloge** with its fifteenth-century coloured clock face.

Rooms, eating and nightlife

If you arrive by train you'll find yourself across the river from the town: follow signs for the *centreville* and cross Pont Bert. The **SI** is down by the river – to the right as you cross the river towards town – at 2 quai de la République. There is a **Bureau d'Informations Jeunesse** (☎86.51.68.75) at 70 rue du Pont with information on travel and leisure activities. The cheapest accommodation is in the *foyers*: at 16 av de la Résistance (☎86.46.95.11; open May–Aug) and at 16 bd Vaulabelle (☎86.52.45.38) at the back of the courtyard of the *Peugot* and *Citroën* garage. Among **hotels**, you could try *Hôtel Saint Martin*, 9 rue Germain-Bénard (☎86.52.04.16; ②), which is probably the best value in town, or *Hôtel de la Porte de Paris* (5 rue St-Germain; ☎86.46.90.09; ②). The *Hôtel Seignelay*, 2 rue du Pont (☎86.52.03.48; ②/⑤), has a few cheap rooms if you're stuck. The two hotels opposite the station, *Hôtel des Deux Gares* (☎86.46.90.06; ①/②) and *Hôtel St-Sebastian*, are both rough-looking dives and only worth considering if you're desperate for somewhere cheap. There's a **camping municipal** at 8 rte de Vaux (☎86.52.11.15; mid-March–mid-Oct).

Finding somewhere to **eat** is easy, as there are numerous reasonably priced restaurants, including the *Marmite*, 34 rue du Pont (☎86.51.08.83; closed Mon and Sun in winter), and a self-service place, the *Novéco*, 9 place Charles-Surugue. **Nightlife** venues aren't exactly vying for custom, but there are three clubs, *Le Magis*, 36 rue Puits-de-Dames (☎86.52.34.14), with a dubious singles night on Tuesdays; *Le Passage*, 32 rue du Pont (☎86.51.73.45), with live cabaret, including rock and blues bands; and, if you're after a disco, *Le Paradisier* (☎86.51.73.45). Late-night bars include the *Bar American*, 34 pl Cordeliers (☎86.52.31.46; open till 2am), and the *Bar du Parc*, 6 av Foch (open till 1am).

East of Auxerre

On or close to the D965 and the Paris–Dijon railway, in the open, rolling country east of Auxerre, lie several minor attractions, ranging from **Greek treasures** to **Cistercian abbeys** and **Renaissance châteaux**. The aptly-named Sereine river is the location of the tranquil villages of CHABLIS, famed for its excellent vineyards, and the time-locked village of NOYERS-SUR-SEREINE, unlikely location of an excellent art gallery.

Pontigny

The ravages of time – in particular the 1789 Revolution – destroyed most of the great monastic buildings of the Cistercians, whose rigorous insistence on simplicity and manual labour under their most influential twelfth-century leader, St Bernard, was a revolutionary response to the worldliness and luxury of the Benedictine abbeys of Cluny (see p.394). Cîteaux and Clairvaux, the first Cistercian foundations, are unrecognisable today. The only places you can get an idea of how Cistercian ideas translated into bricks and mortar are **Pontigny** and **Fontenay**.

The beautifully preserved twelfth-century **abbey church of PONTIGNY** lies 18km northeast of Auxerre on the edge of Pontigny village, where its functional mass rises from the meadows. There is no tower, no stained glass and no statuary to distract from its austere, harmonious lines. The effects of cream-coloured stone flooded with light and permeated with the smell of fresh cut flowers are only slightly marred by the nineteenth-century choir screen which cuts the nave in two. Surprisingly, **three Englishmen** played a major role in the abbey's early history, all of them archbishops of Canterbury: Thomas-à-Becket took refuge in the abbey from Henry II in 1164, Stephen Langton similarly lay low here during an argument over his eligibility for the primacy, and Edmund Rich died here; his tomb in the church is a goal of pilgrimages to this day. The abbey was also the origin of a tourist attraction with which a nearby village is more often associated: the famous **Chablis wine**. It was the monks of Pontigny who originally developed and refined the variety, and the village and its unassuming neighbouring hamlets are better places to sample the wine than in the expensive wine bars of Chablis itself.

There are two hotels in Pontigny: the *Relais de Pontigny* on the N77 (☎86.47.42.83; ②); and the *Hôtel St-Vincent*, rue Paul-Desjardins (☎86.47.42.61; ①/②); and a good restaurant nearby at Ligny-le-Chatel, on the av de Chablis, the *Auberge de Bief* (☎86.47.43.42; closed Sun pm and Mon).

Chablis: the town

A little way to the south is the snobbish, pretty red-roofed town of **CHABLIS**, home of the region's light, **dry white wines**. The town lies in the valley of the **river Serein** – brim-full of fish waiting to be poached – between the wide and mainly treeless upland wheatfields typical of this corner of Burgundy.

While wandering around you could take a look at the side door of **St-Martin's church**, decorated with ancient horseshoes and other bits of rustic ironwork. Nearby, if you need to **spend the night**, *Hôtel de l'Étoile* in rue des Moulins (☎86.42.10.50; closed Nov–Feb; ②) is reasonable; and there's an attractive **campsite**, the *Camping du Serein*, beside the river just outside the village. If you're seeking sustenance, however, it's best to go on to **Tonnerre**, as establishments in Chablis are never good value.

CHABLIS: THE WINE

The neatly stacked **vineyards**, originally planted by the monks of Pontigny, cover the sunny, well-drained, stony slopes on both sides of the valley. The grape is the *chardonnay*, which is to white wine what the *pinot noir* is to red: raw material of all the greatest Burgundies. But the town milks its product for all it's worth. Overpriced wine bars and stuffy restaurants abound. You don't get the opportunity to taste the cheaper varieties and there's haughty disapproval if you hope to spend less then 100F a bottle. Better to head for for the co-operative, *La Chablisienne*, on bd Pasteur (Mon–Sat, 8am–noon & 2–6pm, Sun 9.30–noon & 2–6pm) or better still, drink in one of the other villages like Pontigny or Maligny. If you want to buy a **good wine**, go for the ones with an *appellation*; the *grands crus*, from the northern slopes of the valley are the best, with the *premiers crus* next in line. For information on the Chablis appelation ask at the *Maison de la Vigne et des Vins Chablis*, 26–28 rue Auxerrois (☎86.42.42.22).

Tonnerre and around

Sited on the Paris–Sens–Dijon railway, **TONNERRE** is a useful starting point for exploring this corner of the region. A pleasant if unremarkable town, its principal sight is a vast and well-conserved **medieval hospital** (guided tours June–Sept 10am–noon & 2–

5.30pm; closed Tues) right on the main road in the middle of town. In the chapel is one of the best super-expressive and realistic pieces of Burgundian *tableau* statuary, an **Entombment** of Christ, in the style pioneered by Claus Sluter. The **SI** is directly opposite and in the same street, rue de l'Hôpital, at no. 65, the *Hôtel du Centre* (☎86.55.10.56) offers the cheapest **accommodation**, and a reasonable little **restaurant**. There is also a **campsite** (May–Sept) between the **river Armançon** and the now more-or-less defunct **Canal de Bourgogne**.

A couple of blocks from the hospital, the Hôtel d'Uzès saw the birth of Tonnerre's quirkiest claim to fame, an eighteenth-century gentleman with the impossible handle of **Charles-Geneviève-Louise-Auguste-Andrée-Timothée Éon de Beaumont**. He tickled his contemporaries' prurience by going about his important diplomatic missions for King Louis XV dressed in women's clothes. His act was so convincing that while he was in London bookmakers took bets on his real sex. Oddly enough, he was also a fearsome swordsman, though history does not relate what he wore to fight in. When he died the results of the autopsy were eagerly awaited by the gossip columnists of the day.

Noyers-sur-Sereine

Twenty kilometres further south – there's no alternative to hitching if you don't have your own transport – you come to the beautiful little town of **NOYERS-SUR-SEREINE**, sealed from the modern world in a medieval time warp. Its half-timbered and arcaded houses, ornamented with rustic carvings – particularly those on pl de la Petite Étape aux Vins – are corralled inside a loop of the river and the town walls, and pleasant hours can be passed wandering the path between the river and the irregular walls with their robust towers. The Sereine here is as pretty as in Chablis but Noyers, being remarkably free of commercialism, has more authentic charm .

The main event, however, is the town's **Musée de l'Art Naïf** (June–Sept daily 2.30–6.30), comprising the remarkable collection of art historian, Jacques Yankel. The naïve painters (also known as "Sunday artists") had no formal training and were often workers lacking academic education (one, Augustine Lesage, worked as a miner for sixty years before he started painting). The perspectives are sometimes awkward, tending to lack depth, and meticulous detail is employed to compensate for this flatness. Some star exhibits include Gérard Lattier's morbid comic-strip-style work and the excellent collages of Louis Quilici.

There's a **hotel** – also the best place to **eat** – in the town centre, the *Hôtel de la Vieille Tour* (☎86.82.87.69; ③/④), with just five rooms beautifully furnished in old wood, and views across the gardens to the river.

Neighbouring châteaux: Tanlay and Ancy-le-Franc

Close to Tonnerre are two of the finest, though least-known and least-visited, **châteaux** in France, **Tanlay** and **Ancy-le-Franc**. The former has the edge for romantic appeal, the latter for architectural purity.

ANCY-LE-FRANC was built in the mid-sixteenth century for the brother-in-law of the notorious Diane de Poitiers, mistress of Henri II. More Italian than French, with its rather gloomy, austere classical countenance, it is the only accepted work of the Italian, **Sebastiano Serlio**, one of the most important architectural theorists, who had been brought to France in 1540 by François I to work on his palace at Fontainebleau. The **inner courtyard** is more elaborate, and some of the **apartments** are sumptuous (guided tours only, Easter–Oct 10am–noon & 2–6pm; 25F), decorated by the Italian artists, **Primaticcio** and **Niccolo dell'Abbate**, who also worked at Fontainebleau. The most impressive rooms are La Chambre des Arts with medallions by Primaticcio and La Galerie des Sacrifices with monumental battle scenes in monochrome by Abbate. Ancy has one small **hotel**, the one-star *Hôtel du Centre* (☎86.75.15.11; closed Jan ②), with restaurant, at 34 Grande-Rue.

TANLAY, by contrast, is much more French and full of *fantaisie*. It is only slightly later in date, about 1559, but those extra few years were enough for the purer Italian influences visible in Ancy to have become frenchified. It also feels much more feudal, the village crouching humbly at its gate and its approach road – a long straight tree-lined avenue – like a private drive, tying down the land on either side, proclaiming ownership.

Water-filled **moats** encircle the château and a wooded hill backs it. A grand lodge guards the entrance to a first grassy courtyard, from which you enter the château proper across a stone drawbridge. Domed and lanterned turrets terminate the wings of the *cour d'honneur*. Urns line the ridge of the roof, from whose slates project carved and pedimented dormers. The white stone and the round medieval towers, leftovers from the original fortress, add to the irregularity and charm.

The **interior** can be visited on guided tours only (April–Oct 9.30am, 10.30am & 11.30am; afternoons every 45min from 2.15 to 5.15pm; closed Tues; 25F). The most remarkable, if overpowering, room is the **Grande Galerie**, entirely covered by mono-chrome *trompe-l'oeil* frescoes.

Châtillon and the source of the Seine

If you're interested in pre-Roman France, as the French themselves are for nationalistic reasons, there is one compelling reason for going to **CHÂTILLON-SUR-SEINE**, and that is the so-called **Treasure of Vix**. Housed in the town's **museum**, Maison Philandrier, rue du Bourg, close to the centre (June–Sept Tues–Sun 9am–noon & 2–6pm; Oct–May Wed, Sat & Sun 10am–noon & 2–5pm; Tues, Thurs & Fri, pm only; 10F), it consists of the finds from the **sixth-century BC tomb** of a Celtic princess buried in a four-wheeled chariot. In addition to pieces of the chariot, these include stag-geringly beautiful jewellery, Greek vases and Etruscan bowls. But the best on show is a gloriously simple **gold tiara**, actually found on the princess's head, and the largest **bronze vase** (*krater*) of Greek origin known from antiquity. It stands an incredible 1.64m high on triple tripod legs and around its rim is a superbly modelled **high-relief frieze** depicting naked hoplites and horse-drawn chariots, with Gorgons' heads for handles. How these magnificent objects found their way to such a remote place is a mystery. The village of Vix is the **highest navigable point** on the Seine, and it is thought that the Celtic chieftains who controlled it received such gifts, possibly from traders in Cornish tin which was shipped south from Britain by this route on its way to the Adriatic, and perhaps to the bronze workers of Bibracte, the capital of the Aedui.

On the rocky bluff overlooking the steep-pitched roofs of the old quarter are the ruins of a castle and the early Romanesque **church of St-Vorles**. At its foot in a luxuri-antly verdant spot, a **spring** swells out of the rock to join the infant Seine.

The **SI** is off place Marmont, and there is a very welcoming **cheap hotel**, the *Jura* (☎80.91.26.96), on rue Docteur-Robert, and another, *Hôtel de la Montagne* (☎80.91.10.61), on place Joffre. Rooms at the *Hôtel de la Côte d'Or* (☎80.91.13.29), rue Charles-Ronot, are more expensive, but the restaurant is first class – not a cheapie, but it won't break the bank if you're careful.

Source of the Seine

To get to the **source of the Seine** you have to hitch 43km down N71 to the hamlet of **Courceau** or, on foot, take the **GR2** footpath. From there, by road, take D103 through the upland hamlet of St-Germain, all crumbling stone farms and barns; or, better still, because rides are unlikely, pick up the GR2 at the bridge in Courceau (2 hr).

The **Seine**, no more than a trickle, rises in a tight little vale of beech woods. The spring is now covered by an artificial grotto complete with a languid nymph, Sequana, spirit of the Seine. In Celtic times it was a place of worship, as is clear from the numer-ous votive offerings discovered there, including a neat bronze of Sequana standing in a bird-shaped boat, now in the Dijon museum. If you're here alone, it's a good place for rustic reverie, but if your arrival coincides with a coachload of Parisian Senior Citizens (the site belongs to the city of Paris) you'd be wise to retreat downstream. There's a **campsite** at Chanceaux 5km away on the N71.

Around Montbard: Forges du Buffon and Fontenay Abbey

Blessed with **iron ore** deposits, extensive forest for charcoal burning, and water for hydraulic power, Burgundy became the Ironbridge of France (see "Le Creusot", p.392) in the eighteenth century. The earliest **foundries** were small-scale rural affairs, dependent on one man's knowledge. Production was minimal and costly despite the invention of the blast furnace (*haut fourneau*) and the use of water power to drive hammers and bellows. The area around Montbard offers some insights.

MONTBARD town itself is nothing much, apart from being a handy base for cheap rooms and a good feed. Its predicament is typical of 1990s industrial Europe: a one-industry town – it makes steel tubes – it is seeing the bottom drop out of its livelihood. Comfortable **accommodation** is to be found opposite the train station at *Hôtel de la Gare*, 10 rue Maréchal-Foch (☎80.92.02.12; ③), and there's a cheap little **restaurant**, the *Auberge du Donjon*, on rue Févret. In the village of BUFFON (see below), on the main road, the *Marronier* hotel (☎80.92.33.65; ①) offers extremely cheap accommodation and *menus* starting at 50F.

The best **approach** to the Forge de Buffon is a pleasant hour's walk along the **canal path** from Montbard. If that doesn't appeal, there are buses from Montbard to St-Rémy, from where it's a mere two-kilometre hike to Buffon.

Fontenay Abbey is also quite accessible, 3km up a lane from D905, 6km altogether from Montbard (buses and trains). The best approach would be to walk it on the **GR213** footpath.

Forges de Buffon

June–Sept 2.30–6pm; closed Tues; July & Aug only open 10am–noon Wed, Thurs & Fri.

Just outside Montbard, 6km north on D905, beside the **river Armançon** and the **Canal de Bourgogne**, are the remains of one of the most influential eighteenth-century **foundries**, the **FORGES DE BUFFON**. Built in 1768 by **Georges-Louis Buffon**, distinguished scientist, landowner and lord of Montbard. Production was never more than 400 tons a year, but Buffon's main interest was experimental. The site, now owned by an Englishman and being restored as part of the growing French interest in industrial archaeology, comprises **model dwellings** for workers (woodmen, ox-drivers and miners along with foundry workers) as well as the **foundry workshops**. These are situated on the banks of the river, designed in a most unindustrial **classical style**, with special viewing galleries for royal visitors and a grand staircase. There's not a great deal to see (some reproductions of machinery made by kids from the local school), but you get a unique insight into a pre-capitalist approach to industry. The foundry's most notable product was the railings, still in place, of the Jardin des Plantes in Paris.

Fontenay Abbey

Guided tours only: 45-min duration, on the hour 9am–noon, on the half hour 2.30–6.30pm; 24F.

The privately owned abbey of **FONTENAY**, founded in 1118, is the only Burgundian monastery to survive intact, despite conversion to a paper mill in the early nineteenth century. It was restored earlier this century and is one of the most complete monastic complexes anywhere, comprising caretaker's lodge, guest house and chapel, dormitory, hospital, prison, writing and warming rooms, bakery, kennels, dovecote, abbot's house, as well as church, cloister, chapter house and even a forge. There's not much to be seen in the **forge**, but it is interesting that there should have been such a large one here, in the same countryside where France's industrial ironmasters set up shop 500 years later.

On top of all this, the abbey's **physical setting** is superb, at the head of a quiet stream-filled valley enclosed by woods of pine, fir, sycamore and beech. There is a bucolic calm about the place, but you still feel a *frisson* of unease at the Spartan simplicity of Cistercian life. Not a scrap of decoration softens the church; not one carved capital – the motherly statue of the Virgin arrived after St Bernard's death; no direct lighting in the nave, just an other-worldly glow from the square-ended apse, beautiful but daunting, the perfect structural embodiment of St Bernard's ascetic principles.

Alésia: Venarey and Alise-Ste-Reine

One train stop south of Montbard (or three hours on the footpath) brings you to **VENAREY-LES-LAUMES**, home to another ailing metal tube factory. Accommodation is at *Hôtel Restaurant de la Gare,* 6 av de la Gare (☎80.96.00.46; ③).

It was here, or rather behind and above the town, on the flat-topped hill of Mont Auxois, that **the Gauls**, united for once under the leadership of **Vercingétorix**, made their last stand against the military might of Rome at the **Battle of Alésia** in 52 BC. **Julius Caesar** himself commanded the Roman army, surrounding the hill with a huge double ditch and earthworks and starving the Gauls out, bloodily defeating all attempts at escape. Vercingétorix surrendered to save his people, was imprisoned in Rome for six years until Caesar's formal triumph and then strangled. The battle was a great turning point in the fortunes of the region, marking the end of Gallic independence and an end to life in Europe before Greece and Rome. Thereafter, Gaul remained under Roman rule for 400 years.

Towards the top of the hill the village of **ALISE-STE-REINE** has a small **museum** (daily Feb–Oct; 15F) displaying finds from the Gallic town of Alésia and Caesar's earthworks (the line of them still clearly visible in aerial photographs). On the first weekend of September the martyrdom of **Ste Reine** is celebrated in a **costume procession** through the village, a custom that goes back to the year 866. Ste Reine was a young Christian girl who was put to death in 262 for refusing to marry the proconsul of the Gauls, Olibrius. This martyrdom was the occasion for the conversion of Alesia.

Directly above the village, steps climb up to a great bronze **statue of Vercingétorix**. Erected by **Napoléon III**, whose influence popularised the rediscovery of France's pre-Roman roots, the statue represents Vercingétorix as a romantic Celt, half virginal Christ, half long-haired 1970s matinée idol. On the plinth is inscribed a quotation from Vercingétorix's address to the Gauls as imagined by Julius Caesar: "United and forming a single nation inspired by a single ideal, Gaul can defy the world". Napoléon signs his dedication, "Emperor of the French", inspired by a vain desire to gain legitimacy by linking his own name to that of a "legendary" Celt.

The site of **Alésia the town**, treeless and exposed, is back along the ridge 3km from the modern village. While you can see little more than the layout today, it is extensive, and the interest of the whole area lies in imagined atmosphere rather than in anything concrete.

Avallon and around

Approached from the north **AVALLON** hardly appears perched or medieval (both terms appropriate enough) as the main road into town, rolls through substantial industrial suburbs without any noticeable change in altitude. The southern aspect, however, is altogether more promising as Avallon is seen to stand high on a ridge above the wooded valley of the **River Cousin**, looking out over the hilly, sparsely populated country of the Morvan regional park. It is a small and ancient town of stone facades and comatose, cobbled streets, bisected wall-to-wall by the narrow **Grande-Rue-Aristide-Briand**. Under the straddling arch of the **Tour de l'Horloge**, whose spire dominates the town, this street brings you to the pilgrim church of **St-Lazare**, on whose battered **Romanesque facade** you can still decipher the graceful carvings of signs of the zodiac, labours of the months, and the old musicians of the Apocalypse. Almost opposite, in a fifteenth-century house, is the SI with the municipal **museum** (10am–noon & 2–7pm) behind it. Exhibits include a room of modern silverware designed by local boy Jean Despres, and a second-century mosaic from a Gallo-Roman villa. Following the road away from the town centre brings you to the lime-shaded **Promenade de la Petite Porte**, with precipitous views across the plunging valley of the Cousin. You can **walk** from here around the outside of the walls. From the **parc des Chaumes** on the east side of town there is a great **view** back to the old quarter, snug within its walls, with garden terraces descending on the slope beneath.

Practicalities

Commercial activity such as it is, including the main shopping centre, is concentrated in the new town north of the city walls, but there's a **Saturday market** in place Vauban. For cheap **accommodation** first try *Au Bon Acceuil*, 4 rue de l'Hôpital (☎86.34.09.33; ②); the comfortable *Hôtel du Parc*, opposite the train station at 3 place de la Gare (☎86.34.17.00; ①/②), both with good cheap restaurants; or the *Hôtel du Paris*, not far from the station at 45 rue de Paris (☎86.34.10.05; ②). The attractive **camping municipal** de Suous-Roche (☎86.34.10.39; open March–Oct), and camping *à la ferme* at *les Chatelaines* (☎86.34.16.37; April–mid-Oct), are located a couple of kilometres out of town in the Cousin valley. Reasonable **eating** is to be found on place Vauban at the *Hôtel du Centre* (☎85.34.03.53), or at *Cheval Blanc*, 55 rue de Lyon, and there's a snack bar on Place Vauban – the *Pub Vauban* – with hamburgers and the like. **Bike hire** is from the gare SNCF.

The road alongside the Cousin river, though something of a detour, is an attractive route to nearby VÉZELAY. Five kilometres out of town along the valley is the perfect little **Moulin de Ruats**, an expensive hotel (☎86.34.07.14; ⑤) with a good restaurant where you can dine al fresco in rural bliss beside the river.

Vézelay

If you can get a reliable bike, **cycling** would be a pleasant way of covering the distance to VÉZELAY (15–20km, depending on your route). Alternatively, there are **buses** from Avallon (*Cars de la Madeleine*; one a weekday) and **trains** to Sermizelles on the Auxerre–Avallon line with an SNCF bus link on to Vézelay.

La Madeleine

A hundred years ago the village of Vézelay was abandoned, although its **abbey church, La Madeleine** (open from sunrise to sunset; 6F), one of the seminal buildings of the Romanesque period, had already been saved from collapse by **Viollet-le-Duc** in 1840. Quintessentially picturesque and popular with the coach tours, it is undeniably an attractive place.

As you emerge puffing from the climb (the lane is literally festooned with ice-blue wisteria blossom in May) into the rather desolate square in front of the church, the first impression is disappointing: Viollet's reproduced west front does not look authentic. But veer to the right into the garden on the south side and you get an angle on the long buttressed nave and Romanesque tower that corrects the balance and sheds light on the nautical imagery of "nave" – *navis*, ship or hull.

Once **inside** you find yourself in a colossal **narthex**, added to the nave around 1150 to accommodate the swelling numbers of pilgrims attracted by the supposed presence of the bones of Mary Magdalen. The abbey was one of the main assembly points for the pilgrimage to St-Jacques de Compostelle. Your eye is first drawn to the superlative sculptures of the **central doorway**, on whose **tympanum** an ethereal Christ swathed in swirling drapery presides over a group of apostles and peoples, converted and unconverted, going about their business with cows, fish, crossbows and so forth. Among the figures supposed to represent the peoples of the world are giants, pygmies (one mounting his horse with a ladder), a man with breasts and huge ears, and dog-headed heathens. Somewhat better preserved, in the **outer arch**, are the charmingly small-scale medallions of the zodiac signs and labours of the months. In the **flanking portals** are depicted, on the right, nativity scenes and, on the left, Christ on the road to Emmaus after the resurrection.

From this great doorway you look down the long body of the church, vaulted by arches of alternating black and white stone, to a **choir** of pure early Gothic (completed in 1215), luminous with the delicacy of the inside of a shell by contrast with the heavier, more sombre Romanesque nave. Its arches and arcades are edged with fretted mouldings, and the supporting pillars are crowned with ninety-nine finely cut **capitals**, depicting scenes from the bible, classical mythology, allegories and morality stories. The finest of all is "**The Mystic Mill**" at the end of the fourth bay on the right, showing Moses pouring grain (Old Testament Law) through a mill (Christ), the flour (New Testament) being gathered by St Paul.

St Bernard preached the **Second Crusade** at Vézelay in 1146. Because the church was too small, he preached in the open below the hill. A commemorative cross marks the spot. Richard the Lionheart and Philippe Auguste, King of France, also made their rendezvous here before setting off on the **Third Crusade** in 1190. But the abbey's heyday came to an end in 1280 when it was discovered that the Magdalen's bones belonged to someone else. Its **decline** was hastened by Protestant vandalism in the sixteenth century and the whole establishment was disbanded during the Revolution.

Practicalities

The small **SI** (Easter–Oct 10am–1pm & 2–6pm; Sun 10.30am–6.30pm; closed Wed; closed Nov–March) is on the right in rue St-Pierre as you go up towards the abbey. Hotels and restaurants in the village are vastly overpriced although there are two **youth hostels**, both open July through August, one, on rue des Écoles, the *Centre de Rencontres Internationales*, run by the *Amis de Pax Christi* (☎86.33.26.73), the other an IYHF-affiliated *Auberge de Jeunesse* about 1km along the route de l'Étang (☎86.33.24.18; IYHF card required; with camping space and also open at Easter). Otherwise it's best to time your visit to avoid eating or sleeping here. Even picnic makings should be sought elsewhere, though on summer days the lawns shaded by horse chestnuts behind the church are an excellent picnic spot.

Transport: SNCF **buses** for Sermizelles and buses for Avallon leave from Garage de la Madeleine on the main square.

Clamecy

A better place to stay if you're restrained by a tight budget is the riverside town of **CLAMECY** to the west, which is altogether more accommodating if you're looking for no-frills bed and board. There's nothing special to see here, apart from the many ancient (fifteenth- to eighteenth-century) buildings in the centre, but the town does have an interesting **history**. William IV of Nevers died in Palestine, bequeathing one of his properties in Clamecy to a bishopric of Bethlehem, to serve as a sanctuary in the case of Palestine falling into the hands of the infidel. When the Latin Kingdom of Jerusalem fell, the first bishop arrived to claim his legacy, and from 1225 until the Revolution fifty bishops of Bethlehem suceeded each other in Clamecy, thus honouring the little town with the title of bishopric. More recently the town's claim to fame was the regulation of log trains from the upper Morvan to Montereau and Paris. The practice, dating from the sixteenth century to the completion of the Nivernais Canal in 1923, of floating vast quantities of logs down the river Yonne, is documented in the Romain Rolland **museum** (July–Sept 10am–noon & 3–7pm; closed Tues; 4F) on rue de la Mirandole.

The **SI** is on rue de la Promenade, leading from St Martin's church in the direction of Tannay. Cheap **eateries** include *La Vieille Rome* (closed Sun eve and Mon) on pl du 19-août opposite the church, and *Le Tour* snack bar on the same square beside the church. The *Hôtel de la Poste* on pl Émile-Zola (☎86.27.01.55; ⑤) has an excellent restaurant if you're prepared to spend upwards of 130F, and across the river, near the modern Chapel of Bethlehem on the road to Auxerre, *La Boule d'Or* (☎86.27.11.51; ①/②), is a good-value **hotel**, with an attractive restaurant located in a renovated thirteenth-century chapel.

Semur-en-Auxois

East of Avallon, the small, fortress town of **SEMUR-EN-AUXOIS** sits on a rocky bluff above the Armançon river. All roads here lead to **place Notre-Dame**, a handsome square dominated by the large thirteenth-century church of Notre-Dame, another Viollet-le-Duc restoration, characterised by its huge entrance porch and the narrowness of its nave. The twin-towered west front has had many of its statues removed and the niches left bare. The best view is from the east in **place de l'Ancienne-Comédie**, past the finely sculpted north transept door (the life of Doubting Thomas), with a couple of Burgundy snails, symbol of Burgundy's culinary traditions, carved on the flanking columns. Inside, the windows of the first chapel on the left commemorate American soldiers of the First World War – a reminder that the battlefields were not far away. Also on the left are further, fine **fifteenth-century windows** dedicated by the butchers' and drapers' guilds and illustrating their trades, and a masterly Sluteresque painted **Entombment**.

Down the street in front of the church and off to the left you come to the four sturdy towers of Semur's once powerful **castle**, dismantled in 1602 because of its utility to enemies of the French crown. There is a dramatic view of it from the **Pont Joly** on the river below. Less specifically, the whole town is full of interesting buildings: there is scarcely a street without something of note, and there's a pleasant shady **walk** around the fortifications. On rue J-J-Collenot, the **library** (Wed 2–6pm only), which is part of the **museum** (Wed & Fri 2.30–6.30pm June 15–Sept), has a fantastic collection of illuminated manuscripts and early printed books.

Practicalities

The **SI** is on the small place Gaveau, at the junction of rues de l'Ancienne-Comédie, de la Liberté and Buffon, where the medieval **Porte Sauvigny** and **Porte Guillier** combine to form a single long, covered gateway. There is a **youth hostel** at 1 rue du Champ-de-Foire, to the left off rue de la Liberté (☎80.97.10.22), and a **campsite** at Lac-du-Pont, 3km south of town. *Hôtel des Gourmets*, 4 rue de Varenne (☎80.97.09.41; ③), has the cheapest **rooms** and an excellent, reasonably priced restaurant, as has *Hôtel de la Côte d'Or*, 3 place Gaveau (☎80.97.03.13; closed mid-Nov to Dec; ④). Two pleasant cafés, *Le Trombone* and *Le Mont Arclet*, are on rue Buffon, just before the arches leading to the SI. They're not especially cheap but tables are arranged around a traffic-free square.

Saulieu and the Parc du Morvan

The **Parc du Morvan** is the region of countryside between the Nivernais – of which **Nevers** is the principal city – and Burgundy proper. According to Celtic etymology Morvan means Black Mountain, presumably a reference to the forested escarpments which characterise the region. The Morvan plateau covers an area seventy by fifty kilometres, with heavier than average rainfall – which explains the relative significance of its three small rivers: the Yonne, the Cure and the Cousin.

Saulieu

SAULIEU is a thriving market town and, on the eastern edge of the parc du Morvan, a possible base for a visit. But it's not somewhere you'd want to stay long. If you're after any kind of nightlife, Saulieu is one place that dies pretty convincingly after 9pm – when you might as well be tucked up with a mug of *Poulain* like the respectable locals. Nor is it easy to get to by public transport. **Bus** connections are unhelpful, with *Transco* doing evening runs from Dijon, Montbard and Semur, but not every day, while the **train** from Dijon takes 3hours 30minutes and involves two changes. By **car**, the drive from Dijon takes just 40 minutes.

Saulieu's principal sight is the twelfth-century **Basilique St-Andoche**, noted for its lovely **capitals**, probably carved by a disciple of **Gislebertus**, the master sculptor of Autun. The **museum** next door (Tues–Sun 2.30–6.30pm; 7F) is also surprisingly interesting, with good local **folklore displays** and a large collection of the works of the local nineteenth-century animal sculptor, **François Pompon**.

Arrival and practicalities

Coming from the station, walk up av de la Gare to the highway. Along to the right on rue d'Argentine is the **SI** (out of season, go to the *mairie* in place de la République). Opposite pl Alexandre-Dumaine is the monumental edifice of the *Hôtel Tour d'Auxois* (☎80.64.13.30; closed Dec; ②, half-board obligatory). Rue Grillot which runs from pl Alexandre-Dumaine to the left has a few cheap standbys, like *La Renaissance* at no. 7 (☎80.64.08.72; ①–③) and *La Vieille Auberge* at no. 17 (☎80.64.13.74; closed mid-Dec–mid-Jan; ②). The 3* **campsite** (☎80.64.16.19; April–Oct) is off the Paris road.

Saulieu's **gastronomic reputation** dates back to its days as a post house in the seventeenth century, but it tends to be expensive to put it to the test. An exception is the *Hôtel de la Poste*'s excellent **restaurant**, 1 rue Grillot (☎80.64.05.67; ④), with menus starting at 130F and specialities including pigeon in truffle liquor. Otherwise the other eating establishment of note is *La Côte d'Or*, 2 rue d'Argentine (☎80.64.07.66), where lunchtime menus start at 350F (680F Sat & Sun) and traditional Burgundian abundance gives way to *Nouvelle Cuisine*-style rations. The only night life venue (and it's not exactly swinging) is the *Café du Centre* on pl de la République.

Into the Parc du Morvan

If you are going into the **park**, it's worth consulting the SIs in Saulieu, Nevers or Vézelay. The **Maison du Parc**, the official information centre, is 13km from Saulieu at ST-BRISSON. There's no public transport there, but if you're walking or cycling it's a good place to head for as they have all available information on routes and facilities in the park, as well as a small **museum** devoted to the resistance movement in the region, and a **herbarium** of regional plants. The *maison*, about a kilometre outside St-Brisson on the D6, is located in beautiful grounds which include a deer park. The information centre is open from 8.45am–6pm on weekdays, but at the weekends the same service is provided by the exhibition centre, next to the museum.

Accommodation in the park includes a number of hotels and campsites. Likely locations include LES SETTONS and its nearby lake, on the right bank of which are the *Hôtel de la Plage* (☎86.84.53.78) and a number of campsites. St-Brisson itself has a municipal campsite (☎86.78.70.80; open June–mid-Nov), and there's a two-star campsite (☎86.76.81.18; June–Sept) at MOUX, 10km to the east of Settons. MONTSAUCH, northwest of Settons, is a good bet for provisions, including camping gas, and also has a *camping municipal* (☎86.84.51.05). **Bikes** are available from a number of outlets, including the train station in Saulieu (☎80.64.05.32), *Camping du Midi* on Lac des Settons (☎86.84.51.97) and *La Margelle* pizzeria in Montsauche (☎86.84.54.55).

A **map**, *Saulieu Vélo Tout-Terrain en Morvan*, marks cycling and walking routes. For **walkers** the most challenging trip is the **GR13** footpath, which crosses the park from Vézelay to MONT-BEUVRAY, taking in the major **lakes**, which are among the park's most developed attractions. There are also less strenuous possibilities: for example, the 4-kilometre walk to Lac Chamboux, leaving Saulieu by the D26 and taking a track to the left (blue and yellow markers) after about ten minutes. For a starting point deeper into the park, there is a bus to Moux.

Château-Chinon

The most substantial community in the park itself is the rather ugly village of CHÂTEAU-CHINON, set in beautiful country (bus connection to Autun). **President Mitterrand** was a local council member here until 1983, and the town has been the home base of his political life for half a century. Thanks largely to him it boasts a major hosiery factory and military printing works.

In the **Musée du Septennat** (June–Sept daily 10am–7pm; Oct–May weekends & public holidays 10am–6pm; 12F) you can see the extraordinary variety of gifts Mitterrand has received as head of state. The museum is light and airy, purpose-built to hold a collection of some of the finest handicrafts from their many countries of origin – carpets from the Middle East, ivory from Togo, Japanese puppets, beaded spears from Burundi and bizarre gifts like a table decorated with butterfly wings.

Mitterrand's preferred **hotel** is the *Vieux Morvan*, 8 place Gudin (☎86.85.05.01; closed mid-Nov to mid-Jan; ④). If you're not budgeting for such expense, you might be better off in the *Hostellerie l'Oustalet* on the route de Lormes (☎86.85.15.57; closed Sept 20–Oct; ③) or in the comfortable *Lion d'Or* (☎86.85.13.56; ②).

Nevers

Well to the west of the parc du Morvan, **NEVERS** is a large city on the confluence of the **Loire** and the **Nièvre**. In France it is known for its *nougatine* candies and fine **porcelain,** a hallmark since the seventeenth century, still produced in just three workshops and sold in a few elegant, expensive shops (*faïenceries*) around town. Parts of the **old town**, best viewed from the bridge over the Loire, date back to the twelfth century, and make for a relaxed stroll away from the busier town centre. This, combined with an open-air **concert programme** in summer and a few lively bars and restaurants, makes Nevers an excellent stopover if you're travelling in the region. Movie buffs might also know that Alain Resnais's *Hiroshima Mon Amour* was filmed here.

The town

The town centres around **place Carnot**, and the nearby **Ducal Palace**, the former home of the dukes of Nevers, with octagonal turrets and an elegant central tower decorated with sculptures illustrating the family history of the first duke, François de Clèves, in the mid-seventeenth century. The fifteenth-century building now houses an annexe of the law courts.

Nearby, opposite the **Hôtel de Ville**, is the **Cathédrale de St-Cyr**, a sort of wall display of French architectural styles from the tenth to the sixteenth century. It even manages to have two opposite apses, one Gothic, the other Romanesque.

More interesting and aesthetically satisfying is the late eleventh-century church of **St-Étienne** on the east side of the town centre. Behind its plain exterior, it is one of the **prototype pilgrim churches**, with galleries above the aisles, ambulatory and three radiating chapels around the apse.

From the **station**, av de-Gaulle leads to **place Carnot** via the city **park**, on the north side of which is the convent of St-Gildard, where **Bernadette of Lourdes** ended her days. If you have a religious inclination – or are merely ghoulish – the saint's embalmed body is on display in a glass-fronted shrine in the convent chapel.

On the other side of av de-Gaulle, five minutes' walk from the station by pl Mossé and the bridge over the Loire, you pass a section of the old town walls and the **Tour Goguin**, part of which goes back to the eleventh century. If you turn in here to the right you come to the **Porte de Croux**, a cream stone tower with a steep tiled roof like those of its surrounding buildings, and intact machicolations. Inside, the small local **archaeology museum** (daily 10am–noon & 2–6pm; closed Tues) displays mainly Greek and Roman statuary. Nearby in rue du 14-Juillet is a seventeenth-century **faïencerie** selling antique pieces such as huge Nivernais plates. To your right again you get back to the **oldest quarter** of town around the cathedral – rue Morlon and rue de la Cathédrale – with its dilapidated half-timbered houses, alleys and stairs extending down to the river.

To the north of the ducal palace on the way out of town towards Orléans, **Porte de Paris**, a triumphal arch, straddles rue des Ardilliers. It commemorates one of Europe's major conflicts, the battle of Fontenoy, fought out between Charlemagne's sons in 841 AD. The stakes were Charlemagne's empire, and the outcome the division of his lands east and west of the Rhine, which formed the basis of modern France and Germany.

Practicalities

The **SI**, which provides a map and information on events in the summer music festival, is at 31 rue du Rempart near pl Carnot.There are several **hotels** in the area of the **gare SNCF**, not all of which are affected by traffic noise: *Hôtel Thermidor*, 14 rue Claude Tillier (☎86.57.15.47; ①), reached by turning left out of the station and right after *Bar des Messages*, is good value and quiet; a little further away but also worth trying are *Hôtel Beauséjour* at 5 rue St-Gildard (☎86.61.20.84; ①) and the neighbouring *Hôtel Villa du Parc*, 16 rue de Lourdes (☎86.61.09.48; ③). These contiguous streets are reached by taking av Charles-de-Gaulle from the station, turning left along rue Jeanne-d'Arc and walking to the end of the Parc Roger-Salengro, which is to the right of the street. The **camping municipal** is on the other side of the Loire, just over the bridge. If you're just passing through and need a change of skin, there's a clean, well-run **bath house** on 18 rue Jean-des-Veaux, open till 7pm.

Av de-Gaulle, the street leading from the train station into town, has a few inexpensive **restaurants** and **cafés**, *Gambrinus*, for example, 37 av de-Gaulle (closed midday Sat & Sun). *Le Goemon*, 9 rue du 14-juillet (closed Sun & Mon evening), is a *crêperie* with good salads, and live jazz on Saturday nights. *Le Florentin pizzeria*, rue St-Genest (leading to Porte Croux), has cheap pizzas and pasta. More upmarket, the well-situated and classy *Auberge de la Porte du Croux*, 17 rue de la Porte-de-Croux (closed Fri evening & Sun), has good fish dishes at a price, and a big rear garden.

As for **nightlife**, *Le Moderne Bar* opposite the station has live music at the weekend, as do *Les Baladins* at 7 rue St-Didier and *Le Broadway* at 7 rue du Fer, and there are a couple of bars on rue de Nièvre: *L'Entracte* at no. 2 and *Le New Bar* at no. 8.

Transport: bike hire is from *Laroche*, 28 rue St-Genest, and buses go from the **gare routière** on rue du Chemin-de-Fer.

DIJON AND SOUTHWEST BURGUNDY

If the much touted image of "rural Burgundy" has conjured up slightly backward and ramshackle rustic charm in your mind, you'll have to do some adjusting when you encounter the slick prosperity of **Dijon** and the countryside to the south. It may look peacefully pastoral, but there is nothing medieval about the methods or the profits made in today's wine business. For any trace of the older traditions you have to head into the **southwestern corner** of the region.

Dijon

DIJON owes its origins to its strategic position in Celtic times on the tin merchants' route from Britain up the Seine and across the Alps to the Adriatic. It became **capital of the dukes of Burgundy** in around 1000 AD, but its golden age occurred in the fourteenth and fifteenth centuries under the auspices of Dukes Philippe le Hardi (the Bold), who as a boy had fought the English at Poitiers and been taken prisoner, Jean sans Peur (the Fearless), Philippe le Bon (the Good), who sold Joan of Arc to the English, and Charles le Téméraire (the Rash). They used their tremendous wealth and power – especially their control of Flanders, the dominant manufacturing region of the age – to make Dijon one of the greatest centres of art, learning and science in Europe. Though it lost its capital status on its incorporation into the kingdom of France in 1477, it has remained one of the country's pre-eminent provincial cities, especially since the railway and industrial boom of the mid-nineteenth century.

Today, Dijon is a smart, modern, young city, not in any way resting on its laurels. It's a good place for an extended stay, with lots to do. A city where **discos** have swimming pools, **swimming pools** have jacuzzis, and **restaurants** serve some of the best *haute cuisine* in the world just calls out to be explored.

Arrival and accommodation

Dijon isn't a huge city and pointing yourself in the right direction on arrival is not difficult. Rue da la Liberté, the main shopping street, is a ten-minute walk from the **Gare SNCF** and **gare routiére**, both clumped together to the west of the city centre. If you're driving, the *routes nationales* bring you right into the heart of Dijon and it's copable enough with a car: the station area is not a bad place to park (lock up).

Finding a **place to stay** is straightforward. For cheaper hotels, the station area is a good bet, if typically a little sleazy. For more expensive hotels, try the area around pl Bossuet (see listings, below). The *Foyer International d'Étudiants* on av Maréchal-Leclerc (☎80.71.51.01; bus #4, direction Grézille) is a cheap **student hostel**, while the **youth hostel** itself is in a modern complex with a cafeteria at 1 bd Champollion (☎80.71.32.12; IYHF card required; bus #5, direction Épirey, from place Darcy) 4km from the centre. The nearest **campsite** (☎80.43.54.72; bus #18, direction Plombières, stop *Pont des Chartreux*) is by the lake off bd Kir: follow the signs for Paris and it's about 1km out of town. There are any number of hotels, but better-value establishments include the following:

Hôtel Gare et Bossuet, 16 rue Mariotte, towards the cathedral (☎80.30.46.61; ②). On the gloomy side – and breakfast is obligatory.

Hôtel du Théâtre, 3 rue des Bons-Enfants (☎80.67.15.41 ①/②), right in the Palais des Ducs quarter. Good bet for a comfortable night – if there's room.

Lamartine, "Le Confort", 12 rue Jules-Mercier (☎80.30.37.47; ②). Cheap, comfortable, central.
Hôtel Monge, 20 rue Monge (☎80.30.55.41; ②). Overlooks a quiet courtyard, reasonably priced, friendly and comfortable.
Hostellerie Sauvage, 64 rue Monge (☎80.41.31.21; ②/③). Excellent value for pleasant rooms at the back of a vine-hung courtyard.

The city

You sense Dijon's former glory more in the lavish town houses of its rich burghers than in the former seat of the dukes, the **Palais des Ducs**. Though extensive in area, and still functioning as the town hall, the exterior of the palace is undistinguished. It has undergone so many alterations, especially in the sixteenth and seventeenth centuries when it became Burgundy's parliament, that the dukes themselves would scarcely recognise it. In fact, the only outward reminders of the older building are the fourteenth-century **Tour de Bar** above the east wing, which now houses the **Musée des Beaux-Arts** (see below), and the fifteenth-century **Tour Philippe-le-Bon** (daily summer 9.30–11.30am & 2.30–5.30pm; Nov–Easter Wed pm & Sun pm only; 7F, free on Sun), from whose terrace they say you can see Mont Blanc on a very clear day.

The south front of the palace looks on to a semi-circular classical square, **place de la Libération**, hemmed by houses of honey-coloured stone. Behind, it leads to a tiny, enclosed square, **place des Ducs**, and a maze of lanes to the west, especially **rue des Forges**, bordered by beautiful old mansions. No. 34, the **Hôtel Chambellan** (1490), housing the **SI** (one of two main offices) and **Club Alpin**, is a good example. From the courtyard you get a decent view of the building, with open galleries on the first and second floors, reached by a spiral staircase. There's a marvellous piece of stonemason's virtuosity at the top of the stairs: the vaulting of the roof springs from a basket held by the statue of a gardener. At the end of the street, with several other fine houses, you come to the attractive **place François-Rude** with its fountain graced by the bronze figure of a grape harvester. On sunny days this is a favourite hangout, with people crowding the café tables and sitting on the flagstones around the fountain. If you're interested in looking at more of the city's **mansions**, the tourist office issues a leaflet entitled *Maisons et Hôtels particuliers du XVe au XVIIIe siècle à Dijon*.

Near to rue des Forges, **rue de la Chouette**, with more splendid houses at nos. 8 and 10, passes the north side of the impressive thirteenth-century Gothic church of **Notre-Dame**. In the north wall is a small sculpted owl – *chouette* – which people touch for luck and which gives the street its name. The church's unusual **west front** consists of two galleries of arcades adorned with spectacular leaning **gargoyles**. The **interior** has some beautiful thirteenth-century windows, a twelfth-century black wooden Virgin (dear to the hearts of Dijon's citizens) and, in the north transept, a Gobelins tapestry commemorating the 1944 liberation from the Nazis.

Over to the west, the **cathedral** church of **St-Bénigne**, of similar date to Notre-Dame, with the characteristic glazed-tile roof, lies south of **rue de la Liberté** – the main street of stylish clothes and shoe shops. Its circular **crypt** is the original tenth-century Romanesque church.

But among the greatest of Dijon's artistic monuments are the remains of the **Chartreuse de Champmol**, some 2km west of the city centre on av Albert-1er. Founded by Philippe le Hardi in 1383 as a suitably sumptuous burial place for the ducal family, it was practically destroyed in the Revolution and today is a psychiatric hospital. To adorn it, Philippe recruited a talented team of artists, foremost among them the Dutchman **Claus Sluter**, pioneer of realism in sculpture and founder of the Burgundian school. Most of the surviving works of art are in the city's museums, but two of Sluter's finest, the so-called **Well of Moses** featuring six highly realistic portrayals of Old Testament prophets, and the **portal** of the chapel, remain *in situ*.

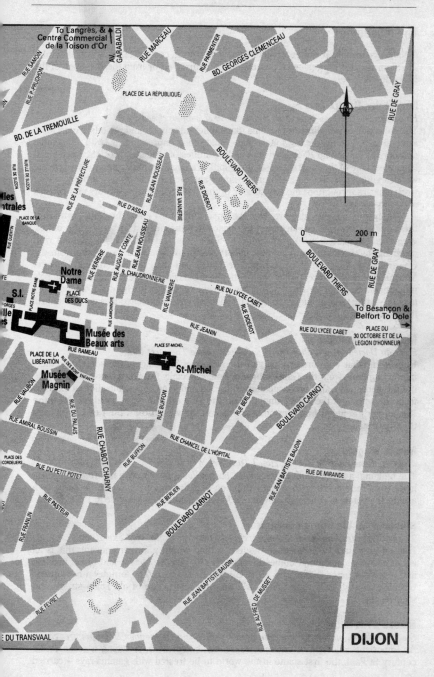

To Langrès, &
Centre Commercial
de la Toison d'Or

AV. GARABALDI

RUE MARCEAU

RUE PARMENTIER

BD. GEORGES CLEMENCEAU

RUE SAMSON

RUE P. PRUDHON

PLACE DE LA RÉPUBLIQUE

BD. DE LA TREMOUILLE

RUE DE GRAY

BOULEVARD THIERS

RUE DE LA PRÉFECTURE

RUE JEAN ROUSSEAU

RUE DIDEROT

RUE D'ASSAS

RUE VANNERIE

lles
ntrales

RUE DE BELLE SITUÉE

RUE DE BELLE SITUÉE

PLACE DE LA
BANQUE

RUE QUENTIN

BOULEVARD THIERS

RUE DE GRAY

RUE VERRERIE

RUE AUGUST COMTE

RUE JEAN ROUSSEAU

Notre
Dame

R. CHAUDRONNERIE

S.I.

PLACE NOTRE-DAME

PLACE
DES DUCS

RUE VANNERIE

RUE DU LYCEE CABET

FORGES

RUE LAMONNOYE

RUE DIDEROT

To Besançon &
Belfort To Dole

ille
s

Musée des
Beaux arts

RUE JEANIN

RUE DU LYCEE CABET

PLACE DU
30 OCTOBRE ET DE LA
LEGION D'HONNEUR

RUE RAMEAU

PLACE ST-MICHEL

PLACE DE LA
LIBÉRATION

RUE DES BONS ENFANTS

St-Michel

Musée
Magnin

RUE VAUBAN

RUE DU PALAIS

RUE BUFFON

RUE BERLER

BOULEVARD CARNOT

RUE AMIRAL ROUSSIN

RUE CHANCEL DE L'HÔPITAL

RUE DE MIRANDE

PLACE DES
CORDELIERS

RUE DU PETIT POTET

RUE BUFFON

RUE JEAN BAPTISTE BAUDIN

RUE CHABOT CHARNY

RUE BERLER

BOULEVARD CARNOT

RUE PASTEUR

RUE FRANLIN

RUE FEVRET

RUE JEAN BAPTISTE BAUDIN

RLE ALFRED DE MUSSET

DU TRANSVAAL

0   200 m

DIJON

The museums

A collective **museum ticket** for all of Dijon's museums, costing 12.6F, is available from the SI on rue des Forges, from the museums themselves, or from the reception of the Hôtel de Ville.

Musée des Beaux-Arts
Palais des Ducs: 10am–6pm; Sun 10am–12.30 & 2–6pm; closed Tues.
The collection of **paintings** represents many different schools and periods, from Titian, Rubens and Schongauer to Monet, Manet and other Impressionists, with substantial numbers of Italian and Flemish works and quantities of religious artefacts, ivories and tapestries. One of the most interesting exhibits is a small room devoted to the intricate woodcarving of the sixteenth-century designer and architect, **Hugues Sambin**, whose work appears throughout the old quarter of the city in the massive doors and facades of the aristocratic *hôtels*.

Visiting the museum also provides the opportunity to see the surviving portions of the original ducal palace, including the vast **kitchens** needed to service the dukes' gargantuan appetites and the magnificent **Salle des Gardes**, richly appointed with panelling, tapestries and a minstrels' gallery. Here are displayed the **tombs** from the Chartreuse de Champmol, of **Philippe le Hardi** and **Jean sans Peur** and his wife, **Marguerite de Bavière**. Sluter and his nephew Claus de Werve worked on Philippe's monument. Both follow the same pattern: painted effigies of the dead, attended by angels holding their helmets and heraldic shields and accompanied by a cortege of brilliantly sculpted mourners.

Musée Archéologique
5 rue du Docteur-Maret: 9am–noon & 2–6pm; closed Tues; free Sun.
Housed in what was formerly part of the Abbey of St Benigne, are some extremely interesting finds from the Gallo-Roman period, especially **funerary bas-reliefs** depicting the perennial Gallic preoccupation with food and wine and a collection of ex-votos from the source of the Seine, among them the little bronze of the **goddess Sequana** (Seine) upright in her bird-prowed boat. Also on show is **Sluter's bust of Christ** from the Chartreuse.

Musée Magnin
4 rue des Bons-Enfants: 2–6pm; closed Tues; free Wed & Sun.
The building, a seventeenth-century *hôtel particulier* complete with its original furnishings, is more interesting than the exhibition of **paintings** by good but lesser-known artists, the personal collection of Maurice Magnin, donated to the state in 1938.

Musée de la Vie Bourguignonne
17 rue Ste-Anne: 9am–noon & 2–6pm; closed Tues; free guided visit Sun 10am.
Housed in a stark, well-designed modern setting within a former convent, this is all about costumes, furniture, domestic industries like butter, cheese and bread making, and a reconstructed kitchen: in short **Burgundian life in the nineteenth century**. Opening shortly, on the first floor, will be a reconstruction of old Dijon streets and shop fronts.

Musée d'Art Sacré
Ste-Anne chapel, next to the Vie Bourgignonne Musesum: 9am–noon & 2–6pm; free Sun.
An important collection of **church treasures** is kept here, including a seventeenth-century St Paul, the first statue in the world to be treated with gamma-rays – carried

out in Grenoble as part of the Nucle-art project. Formerly crumbling to dust, it is now solid. There's a free guided visit that really perks up these special-interest exhibits.

Musée d'Histoire Naturelle

Jardin de l'Arquebuse; access from gare SNCF departures: 2–5pm; closed Tues.
In addition to just about every stuffed bird and mammal you can think of, including the wild boar, the best exhibits are an exquisite collection of butterflies and, for the morbid, a collection of animal mutants.

Musée Grevin

Av Albert-1er, 9.30am–noon, 2–7pm; 50F (not part of collective ticket).
Bizarre, rather overpriced experience – considering it's all just a tourist board PR job – in which you walk around a waxworks museum with a Walkman headset clamped to your ears and regard scenes from Burgundy's history. Perhaps of more interest is the free wine tasting in the foyer.

Eating, drinking and entertainment

Dijon has an inordinate number of **pâtisseries** in the town full of high-quality, tempting confectionery. For more substantial fare, there's no problem finding a good **restaurant**, though locating cheaper places is harder.

Eating: food and basic meals

Dijon's famous *pâtisseries* feature marzipan and fruit prominently. The more exotic places also promote the *pain d'épices*, a sweet bread made with honey and spices eaten with butter or jam (from *Moulot et Petitjean*, 13 pl Bossuet), and *cassissines* – blackcurrant candies – while on rue de la Préfecture, down from the *pâtisserie* at no. 84, you can watch **chocolate** being made in a traditional workshop.

In rue de la Liberté – the fashionable main street to which you're certain to gravitate – there's nowhere to **buy food** apart from the cake shops and food department in *Les Nouvelles Galeries*. The best food area in this part of town is the exceptionally good covered food market, the *halles centrales* (Tues & Fri am, & Sat). *Le Panier Campagnard*, 10 rue François-Rude, sells mountain sausages and very good but expensive *jambon persillé* – cheaper elsewhere, but nowhere near as delicious. The legendary **Burgundy snail** comes in all guises and sizes, fresh, pre-cooked with garlic butter in the shell, or canned, at the delicatessen *Simone Porcheret* at 14 rue Bannelier. This place resembles a museum of cheese making. Also tops for **cheese** is *Le Chalet Comtois*, 28 rue de la Musette, where the patient staff explain, in French, exactly what's what. This same area is peppered with bars and cafés offering sandwiches and cheap menus. The best place to buy local **bread** to make your own sandwiches is south of rue de la Liberté, at *Au Pain d'Autrefois*, 47 rue du Bourg, where the bread is baked in a wood-fired oven.

And you can hardly forget that Dijon is also the high temple of **mustard** and **wine**. For the former there is the shop of leading producer **Maille** in rue de la Liberté selling a range from the mild to the cauterising. On the same block, at no. 11, there is *Bourgogne Tour* for **wine tasting** and, at 3 rue Jeannin behind the Palais des Ducs, *La Cour aux Vins*, with books on wine in the shop and talks in English.

To consume all the food and wine *al fresco* there are several **green spaces** you can escape to. In or near the centre there's **place des Ducs** and **place Darcy**, or, if you prefer something more spacious and private, there are the very attractive and meticulously labelled botanical gardens, **Jardin de l'Arquebuse**, behind the station, as well as **Parc Colombière** a ten-minute bus ride away (bus #3 from rue de la Liberté) by the **river Ouche**.

There are three **university restaurants** in town where students can eat for 10.5F. They are at 3 rue du Dr-Maret in the town centre, and at 6 bd Mansart and 6 rue du Recteur-Bouchard, near the university to the southeast of the city. They all serve meals from 11.30am to 1.15pm and from 6.40 to 7.15pm.

Restaurants

Finally, if you want to shell out to sample some of Dijon's cuisine – local and otherwise – in more style, the listings that follow are just a small selection from a large number of excellent establishments in the town. For an **apéritif**, you should try *kir* – two parts dry white wine, traditionally *aligoté*, and one part *cassis* (blackcurrant liqueur) – and to round the evening off there are many liqueurs to choose from, but Burgundy is particularly famous for its *marcs*, of which the best are matured for years in oak casks.

TRADITIONAL FRENCH

Le Clos des Capucines, 3 rue Jeannin (☎80.65.83.03). Reasonably priced for such an upmarket establishment, serves excellent regional cooking in a pleasant environment.

La Dame d'Aquitaine, 23 pl Bossuet (☎80.30.36.23, closed Sun & Mon lunch). Excellent food found typically in the southwest, served in a former crypt.

Le Relais de la Gare, Gare SNCF (☎80.41.40.35 closed Sun pm, service till midnight), Upmarket station buffet, with fish specialities at reasonable prices.

Le Savoyard, 13bis rue d'Assas (☎80.72.27.67; dinner only, serving till 2am; closed Sun). Very popular for its fondues and *raclettes* (a Swiss cheese dish).

MID-RANGE AND SNACKS

Restaurant Buffon, 28 rue Buffon (☎80.65.39.91). A different 45F menu of traditional fare each day. Friday (in season) is mussels day.

Coum' Chez Eux, 67–68 rue JJ-Rousseau (☎80.71.57.72). Informal, cheaper lunchtime eatery with substantial dishes served in little pots.

Le Derly, 17 rue de la Poste near Arc de Triomphe (closes 10pm). Good for lunch or early supper, an inexpensive restaurant/*crêperie* with no menu but light, interesting dishes. You can just have a *galette* or put together your own meal.

Le Triskell, 31 rue Verrerie (☎80.30.65.84). Popular lunchtime *crêperie*.

Au Feu du Bois, 64 rue Monge (☎80.41.17.33). Busy lunchtime grill.

VEGETARIAN

Le Potimaron, 4 av de l'Ouche (☎80.43.38.07, closed Sun). Vegetarian and macrobiotic, with organic meat and fish dishes, too.

La Vie Saine, 27–29 rue Musette (☎80.30.15.10; lunches till 2.30 only; closed Sun).

INTERNATIONAL

Restaurant Thai, 44 rue Monge (☎80.30.49.88). Interesting decor, and traditional silk-clad waitresses. Good food, too, with amazing lunchtime menus at only 39F and 45F.

Le Marrakech, 20 rue Monge (☎80.30.93.81). Moroccan music and decor. Reasonable prices for large plates of couscous and *tajines* (thick soups).

Osaka, 13 rue Musette (☎80.50.17.51). Traditional restaurant; kimonos et al. It makes sense to eat Japanese in France as it tends to be good value – menus here from 39F.

Le Grand Mandarin de Côte d'Or, 53 rue Devosge (☎80.73.56.55). Good cheap menus in pleasant surrounds; nice service, huge portions.

American Way Café, Centre Commercial de la Toison d'Or (☎80.70.11.37). Tex-mex menus, as well as a good selection of whiskies and Stateside beer.

Le Cachemire, 8 rue Gagnereaux (☎80.74.10.13). Top-value Pakistani restaurant.

Bars and Nightclubs

Dijon is an important university city as well as one of France's main conference centres, so night spots and cultural centres at both ends of the range are worth exploring.

Palais de la Gare, at the corner of rue Piron and rue Berbissey. Charming, characterful spot, good for a daytime or early evening drink.

Café de la Cathedrale, 4 pl St-Bénigne, next to the *Café au Carillon*. Two bars popular with students, in front of the cathedral.

Le Café des Grands Ducs, 96 rue de la Liberté (open till 3am). Popular rendezvous for young people, with original decor and table juke boxes.

L'Acropole, 4 bd du Dr-Petitjean. Near the university on #9 bus route. Popular with students for cheap lunchtime snacks, games and occasional gigs.

Hunky Dory, av Maréchal-Foch. Dynamic bar with excellent decor, billiards and live music.

Pub Kilkenny, 1 rue Auguste-Perdrix. Irish bar: draught Guiness and week-night Irish bands.

Le Brighton, 33 rue Auguste-Comte. English pub with 200 different kinds of beer.

Rhumerie la Jamaïque, 14 pl de la République. Cocktails and ice-creams laced with alcohol in an exotic venue. Jazz bar in the basement.

Ragtime, 3 pl Émile-Zola. Jazz bar serving overpriced cocktails, reductions for students. Jazz sessions on Tues and Wed.

L'An-Fer, 8 rue Marceau. Popular nightclub with a jazz club, the *Kalimba*, upstairs. Free entry for women on Sun & Mon. Otherwise 50F.

Pimm's Club, Centre Dauphine. Popular, youthful venue which attracts a good crowd.

Le Prive, 20 av Garibaldi. Older clientele, dancing to rock and Lambada.

L'Escapade, Varois et Chaignot. Outdoor pool, and a huge dance floor.

Listings

Buses Distances are small enough to make walking easy, but if you plan to use buses a lot it's worth getting a pass and bus map, from STRD, in the middle of place Grangier. **Gare routière**: for out-of-town journeys, this is next to the gare SNCF at the end of av Maréchal-Foch, five minutes from pl Darcy.

Bike hire Try *Rousseau*, 3 place Notre-Dame by the Notre-Dame church and SI.

CIJ Helpful *Centre International de Jeunesse* office at 22 rue Audra on the north side of the Darcy gardens.

CROUS Student information service, 3 rue Maret near place Darcy.

Cinemas *L'Eldorado*, 21 rue Alfred-de-Musset (☎80.66.51.89), is a three-screens Arts cinema, showing all films in original language with a concentration of foreign films. *Le Devosges*, 6 rue Desvosges (☎80.30.74.79), shows some films in the original, and tries to deviate from the obvious classics.

Festivals The city has a good summer music season, with classical concerts through June in its *Été Musical* programme. *L'Estivade*, June 20–Aug 15, puts on endless music, dance and street theatre performances. *Fête de la Vigne* at the beginning of Sept is a traditional costume/folklore jamboree, and the *Foire Gastronomique* in the first week of Nov is a pretext for a disgusting pig-out to see you through the lean months of winter.

Gymnasium 9 rue Montgolfier, Chenôve, bus #7; Mon–Fri 9am–9.30pm, Sat 10am–5pm, Sun 9.30am–1pm. Sauna, hammam & solarium in addition to the gymnasium. 75F a session for non-members.

Hitching For Paris, follow av Albert-1er to Lac Kir; for Beaune and Lyon, cross the canal from place du 1er-mai and continue down av Jean-Jaurès.

Launderettes 41 rue Auguste-Comte, 57 rue de Mirande, 55 rue Berbisey.

Listings The SI produce an excellent directory of local facilities, called *Divio*.

Markets Tues, Fri & Sat mornings along the four streets surrounding the covered market – rue Bannelier, rue Quentin, rue C.-Ramey, rue Odebert. Markets also at Petit Citeaux, bus #21, Wed am and Fontaine d'Ouche, bus #12, Wed am.

Swimming Pools *Aqua Center les Cyclades*, Centre Commercial de la Toison d'Or, bus #16, Wed–Fri noon–10pm, Sat 10am–10pm, Sun 10am–6pm; toboggans, jacuzzi, & water slides.

Travel Agents *Agence Wasteels*, 20 av Maréchal-Foch near the station is a youth-orientated travel agent.

SIs 34 rue des Forges (Mon–Thurs 8am–noon & 2–6pm; Fri 8am–noon & 2–5pm); pl Darcy 9am–noon & 2–7pm, 9pm from mid-April–mid Oct). The regional **SI** office in place Darcy has a hotel reservation service and money exchange. The rue des Forges office sells a cheap **all-in-one ticket for the main museums** and sights in the Côte d'Or *département*. You can also buy the cheap general museum ticket from any of the city's museums.

Walking The *Club Alpin* in the rue des Forges SI produces a booklet, *Promenez-vous en Côte d'Or*, showing all the region's **marked paths**.

Autun and around

With its Gothic spire rising amid red-brown lichenous roofs against a backdrop of Morvan hills, **AUTUN**, even today, is scarcely bigger than the circumference of its medieval walls, and they in turn follow the line of the Roman fortifications which predated them. The emperor Augustus founded Autun in about 10 BC as part of his massive and, eventually, highly successful campaign to pacify and Romanise the broody Celts of defeated Vercingétorix. **Augustodunum**, as it was called, was designed to eclipse by its splendour the memory of BIBRACTE (see below), the neighbouring capital of the powerful tribe of the Aedui. And it became one of the leading cities of Roman Gaul.

Arrival, food and accommodation

Whether you arrive at the **gare SNCF or gare routière** – or drive in – you'll find yourself on av de la République. Opposite the station, *Hôtel de France* at 18 av de la République (☎85.52.14.00; ①) and *Hôtel Commerce et Touring* at no. 20 (☎85.52.17.90; closed Oct; ②) are both decent and cheap and the *Commerce et Touring* has a very acceptable, mid-priced **restaurant**. The cheapest **hotel** in town, possibly in the whole of Burgundy, is *Au Petit Paris*, 35 rue du Fbg-St-Andoche (☎85.52.11.92; ①), with just five small rooms. There's a scruffy café downstairs, but the location is peaceful, with a courtyard at the back, and it's a friendly, well-kept establishment. The municipal **campsite** is just across the river beyond Porte d'Arroux, (☎85.52.10.82; March–Oct).

The broad **av du Gén-de-Gaulle** (SI at no. 3; Easter–Sept, daily 9am–12.30pm & 1.30–7pm; Sun 10am–noon & 3–6pm; winter Mon–Fri 9am–noon & 2–7pm; Sat 9am–noon; closed Sun) leads from the station to the enormous central square, the **Champ de Mars**, where there are two **places to eat**, the *Auberge de la Bourgogne* at no. 39–40 (closed Sun pm & Mon) and the brasserie *Morvandiau* at no. 30. Other reasonable and well-priced eating houses in town are *Le Châteaubriant*, 14 rue Jeannin, off av Charles-de-Gaulle (closed Sun pm & Mon), and *Le Petit Rolin*, opposite the Cathédrale St-Lazare (closed Feb & Wed out of season), a reasonably priced restaurant and *crêperie*.

The town

The narrow streets of the **old town** (rue St-Saulge and rue Chauchien) climb from pl du Champ-de-Mars towards the cathedral, situated in the most southerly and best fortified corner of Autun. The unique importance of the twelfth- to fifteenth-century **Cathédrale St-Lazare** lies in its **sculptures**. These include depictions of over fifty nude figures, suggesting that the Middle Ages were not as constrained by prudery as historians once believed.

The sculptures are the work of **Gislebertus**, generally accepted as one of the greatest Romanesque sculptors. The typanum of the Last Judgement above the west door

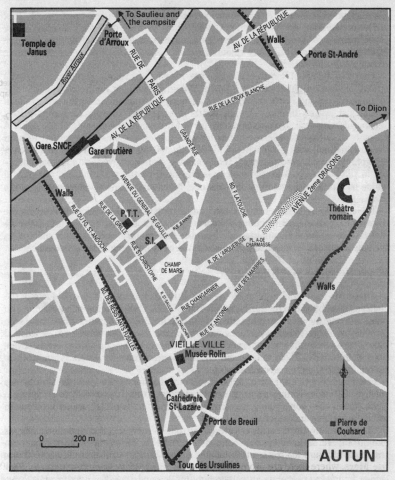

bears his signature – *Gislebertus hoc fecit*: "Gislebertus made this" – beneath the feet of Christ. To the left and right of Christ are depicted the elect entering heaven, the apostles, the Archangel Michael disputing souls with Satan who tries to cheat by leaning on the scales, and the flames of hell licking at the damned. Luckily, during the eighteenth century the local clergy decided it was an inferior work and plastered it over, which saved it from almost certain destruction during the Revolution. The **interior**, whose pilasters and arcading were modelled on the Roman architecture of the city's gates, was also decorated by Gislebertus, who himself carved most of the **capitals**. Conveniently for anyone wanting a close look, some of the finest are now exhibited in the old chapter library, up the stairs on the right of the choir, among them a beautiful *Flight into Egypt* and *Adoration of the Magi*.

Just outside the cathedral, on rue des Bancs, the **Musée Rolin**, in a Renaissance *hôtel* built by Nicolas Rolin, chancellor of Philippe le Bon, is definitely worth a look

(April–Sept 9.30am–noon & 1.30–6pm; Oct–March 10am–noon & 2–5pm; closed Tues; 10F). In addition to interesting Gallo-Roman pieces, the star attractions are **Gislebertus**'s representation of **Eve** as an unashamedly sensual woman and the **Maître de Moulins'** brilliantly coloured *Nativity*. Also in preparation are some cases of exhibits from **Bibracte**.

Traces of the era of Roman occupation are, in fact, surprisingly abundant. Two of the city's four **Roman gates** survive – **Porte St-André** spanning rue de la Croix-Blanche in the northeast and **Porte d'Arroux** in Faubourg d'Arroux in the northwest – while in a field just across the river Arroux stands the so-called **Temple of Janus**, a lofty section of brick wall that was probably part of the sanctuary of some Gallic deity. A measure of Autun's significance at that time are the few remains of the largest **Roman theatre** in Gaul, with a capacity of 15,000, situated off the Dijon road, av du 2ème-Dragon. It's not an evocative site – the remaining seats now overlook a football pitch – but in July and August its authenticity is enhanced by the performances of a play in which 600 locals, dressed in period costume, reconstruct the Gallo-Roman past of the town.

The most idiosyncratic of the Gallo-Roman remains in the region however is the **Stone of Couhard**, off faubourg St-Pancrace to the southeast of the town. It's a 33-metre stone pyramid thought to date from the first century, and since it's situated on the site of one of the city's necropolises, it could be either a tomb or a cenotaph.

Mont-Beuvray and Bibracte

The base for the climb up Mont-Beuvray and the visit to the 2000-year-old site of the Gallic capital of Bibracte is ST-LÉGER-SOUS-BEUVRAY, southwest of Autun. You reach it along the N81 for 16km, then right, up the D61 for another 10km, past scattered farms, coarse marshy pastures and brown streams, all set between close wooded hills. There's a morning and afternoon bus to St-Léger, or you can tackle the stiff seven-hour walk on **GR131** from the Croix de la Libération outside Autun. If you need to spend the night, there's a **youth hostel**.

From St-Léger, it's the best part of two hours further by the path, or 8km by the road, to **Bibracte** at the top of the *mont*, altitude 800m. If you want to recapture a Celtic mood, it's worth doing this last stretch on foot. The path winds up through woods of conifers and beech.

Close to the fortified earthwork which surrounds the site, great ceremonial stones like the **Pierre de la Wivre** are still standing. **BIBRACTE**, the lines of which you can still follow through the trees, was inhabited from 5000 BC. Capital of the Aedui, it was the sight of an assembly of all the Gallic nations in 52 BC to elect Vercingétorix their leader, in one last desperate attempt to fight off Roman imperialism. Although it is two millennia since Bibracte was abandoned, probably on Roman orders, vague memories of its significance were preserved in the folk tales of the Morvan and a fair was held on the summit every May until the beginning of World War I.

Le Creusot

LE CREUSOT means one thing to the French: the **Schneider iron and steel works**, maker of the first French railway engine in 1838, the first steamship in 1839, the 75mm field gun – mainstay of First World War artillery – the iron-work of the Pont Alexandre-III and the Gare d'Austerlitz in Paris. Now **Creusot-Loire** manufactures specialised steels and boilers for the nuclear industry, and, like many steel works in Britain, employs far fewer people.

The town

As you travel south through the wooded hills from Autun (25km away, with frequent buses because of the Montchanin TGV station), nothing prepares you for this former industrial powerhouse. You arrive to see, suddenly, over the brow of a hill, spilling down the bottom of a valley, abandoned factories and workers' housing.

A small street of rustic-looking workers' dwellings survives in the **Combes des Mineurs** across the valley from the Château de la Verrerie, while in place du 8-mai on the Montchanin road out of town a colossal 100-ton Schneider **drop-hammer** has been set up as a monument to past glories.

For a good **view** of the town from across the valley, climb to the rue des Pyrénées, above the Combe des Mineurs, from where you can see Le Creusot spread before you, including the modern Creusot-Loire steel works, the gleaming white Château de la Verrerie and the terraces of pastel-coloured houses, against a backdrop of hills which are the northeast border of the Massif Central.

The Château de la Verrerie and Écomusée

The town's main attraction is the **Écomusée de la communauté urbaine du Creusot-Montceau-les-Mines** situated in the **Château de la Verrerie** on place Schneider (Tues–Fri 10am–noon & 2–6pm; Sat & Sun 2–6pm; closed Mon; 12F). As well as being the home of the Schneider family until 1971, the château housed the **glassworks** of Marie-Antoinette from 1787, and many examples of the product are now on display, alongside a video explaining methods of production. The peculiar cone-shaped constructions in the courtyard of the château were formerly **glass ovens**, recently transformed into a theatre and a chapel.

The exhibits in the **écomusée**, also situated in the château, tell the story of heavy industry and agriculture in the area, with superb period photos, coin-slot push-button models of the works, steam cranes, reconstructed workshops, models of locomotives and a photo record of the great *Mistral* train's run from Paris to Marseilles.

The **Schneiders**, who in 1836 took over the former **Royal Foundry**, in which Louis XVI was a shareholder before losing his head, were typically paternalistic employers. They provided housing, schools and health care for their workers, but in return expected "gratitude and obedience". Thus the worker-mayor who proclaimed adherence to the Paris Commune in 1871 was sentenced to hard labour for life, while the army moved in to quell the unrest. The local mine owners organised a private police force to keep an eye on workers' reading matter and church attendance and handed out building plots for "good behaviour".

Other industrial sites in the area to which visits are organised by the *Association Communautaire de Développement du Tourisme Industriel* include the **Canal du Centre** and Maison du Canal at Écuisses, the **coal mines** at Blanzy and Montceau, and the town of Le Creusot itself. Inquire at the SI annexe at the entrance to the château.

Practicalities

The **SI** on rue Maréchal-Foch (the road out of town which leads past the station to the *Securité social* building) can provide information on tours of the town and of the TGV industry workshops. If you want to **stay** overnight, *Hôtel des Voyageurs* on place Schneider (☎85.55.22.36; ②) is cheap and has a good restaurant, and the *Hôtel Moderne* near the station at 41 rue Maréchal-Leclerc (☎85.80.80.80; closed Aug; ③) is old-fashioned and comfortable, and also has a good restaurant. Another cheap possibility near the SI is the *Beauclair*, 28 rue de l'Yser (☎85.5503.34; ①). There's a cheap café for midday snacks, *Au Lion de Belfort*, on place Schneider, and a few reasonable, no-frills **restaurants** in town, such as *La Taverne*, 4 rue Marcel-Sembat.

Cluny and nearby monasteries

The voice of the **abbot** of **CLUNY** once made monarchs tremble. His power in the Christian world was second only to that of the pope and his intellectual influence arguably even greater. The monastery was founded in 910 in response to the corruption of the existing church and a universal longing for some spiritual assurance at a time of great insecurity at the approach of the first millennium. All it took was a couple of vigorous early abbots to build the power of Cluny into a veritable empire. They established numerous subordinate houses, especially along the pilgrim routes of St-Jacques. Ironically, however, the growing wealth and secular involvement of the monastery led to the decline of its spiritual influence, which was superseded by the reforming zeal of St Bernard and his Cistercians based at Cîteaux. In time Cluny became a royal gift – a convenient device for dressing the king's temporal machinations up in a little spiritual respectability. Both Richelieu and Mazarin did stints as abbot.

Now, apart from the very attractive village, practically nothing remains. The Revolution suppressed the monastery and **Hugues de Semur's** vast and influential **eleventh-century church**, the largest building in Christendom until the building of St Peter's in Rome, was dismantled in 1810. All you can see of the former abbey now (daily 9am–6pm; regular optional tours 23F, half price off-season) is an octagonal belfry, the south transept and, in the impressive granary, the surviving capitals from its immense columns – disappointing, but evocative. From the top of the **Tour des Fromages** (entry inside the **SI**; mid-March–Oct am & pm, rest of the year pm only; 6F) you can reconstruct it in your imagination. The **Musée Ochier** (March–Sept 9.30am–noon & 2–6.30pm; Oct–Feb 10am–noon & 2–6pm; 6F) in the fifteenth-century palace of the last freely-elected abbot helps to flesh out the picture with reconstructions and fragments of sculpture, while the Romanesque belfry of the parish **church of St-Marcel** also recalls the belfries that once adorned the abbey.

Practicalities

If you're planning to stay, a municipal **hostel**, *Cluny Séjour*, on rue Porte-de-Paris (☎85.59.08.83; 10pm curfew), is the cheapest. The **campsite**, *Camping municipal St-Vital* (☎85.59.08.34; May 15–Sept) is on rue des Griottons across Pont de la Levée and on the right. *Hôtel de l'Abbaye* on av de la Gare (☎85.59.11.14; closed Dec–Feb; ③) has inexpensive rooms, as does the *Hôtel du Commerce*, 8 place du Commerce (☎85.59.03.09; ②). The *Marroniers* at 20 av de la Gare is a reasonable **restaurant**; otherwise the cheapest bet is one of the *crêperies* or picnic fare from *charcuteries*.

Taizé

Another powerful attraction for the converted might be the modern ecumenical community at **TAIZÉ**, 10km north of Cluny. Founded in 1940, its monks are drawn from both Protestant denominations and the Roman Catholic Church. It is unashamedly populist in outlook, attracting hordes of youngsters who come to take part in discussion groups and camp out under canvas. If you are seriously interested – and it is not likely to be to the taste of the merely curious – write to Communauté de Taizé, 71250 Cluny.

Paray-le-Monial

The old town of **PARAY-LE-MONIAL** on the banks of the river Bourbince 50km to the west across the **Charolais** countryside, has more to offer than Cluny, even though it is hardly recognised on the tourist circuit. Substantial medieval remains are to be seen, and the town is altogether a cheaper and more congenial place to visit than Cluny, and, except at times of **pilgrimage**, likely to be practically devoid of other tourists.

The town

The Bourbince River at Paray is slow moving, curtained by willow trees and graced by occasional families of swans. Alongside the river the very pretty town, idyllically quiet, shuttered, towered and red roofed, is largely pedestrianised, and visitors have to leave their cars outside the historic centre. Most spectacular of the buildings in the town centre is the fourteenth-century *Hôtel de Ville*, with its elaborate carved stone facade.

Architecture buffs can get a good idea of what Cluny must have looked like from the church of the **Sacré-Coeur** in the old town. The cult of the **Sacred Heart** (Sacré Coeur) originated with Marguerite-Marie Alacoque, a local nun. It was in Paray that she received revelations advocating the worship of the sacred heart, a cult later adopted by the entire Roman Catholic Church. The first **pilgrimage** in 1873, encouraged as a means of fighting the socialist ideas espoused by the Commune, raised the money to construct that great white cheese of the Sacré-Coeur on the hill of Montmartre in Paris. Paray is now second only to Lourdes as a pilgrim centre, its best-known visitor of recent times being **Pope John Paul II,** who visited in 1986.

Practicalities

Accommodation is better value than in Cluny. Try the *Hostellerie des Trois Pigeons*, 2 rue Daugard, just beyond the *Hôtel de Ville* (☎85.81.03.77; closed Dec; ①/②), or, near the station, *Hôtel Terminus*, 27 av de la Gare (☎85.88.84.45; closed Nov; ②), or *Hôtel du Nord*, 1 av de la Gare (☎85.81.05.12; ①); or else *Hôtel aux Vendanges de Bourgogne*, 5 rue Denis-Papin, south of the Canal du Centre off the N 79 (☎85.81.13.43; ②). There's also a *Foyer des Jeunes Travailleurs* on rue Michel-Anguier, a couple of kilometres from the town centre. The **campsite**, *camping municipal Le Pré-Barré* (☎85.81.05.05; all year) is by the river on bd Dauphin-Louis.

For **food**, the *Hôtel aux Vendanges* and the *Trois Pigeons* (above) both have reasonable restaurants, and there's a café – and a pub, *Le Palais de la Bière* – on av Charles-de- Gaulle which leads from the station across the Canal du Centre towards the river.

The **gare SNCF** hires out **bikes**, which is an excellent way of exploring the gentle **Brionnais country** to the south, peppered with small villages and Romanesque churches, precursors or offspring of Cluny.

THE WINE ROUTE

Burgundy farmers have been growing grapes since Roman times, and their rulers, the dukes, frequently put their **wines** to effective use as a tool of diplomacy. Today they have never had it so good, which is why they're reticent about the quirks of soil and climate and the tricks of pruning and spraying that make their wines so special. Vines are temperamental: frost on the wrong day, sun on the wrong day, too much water, or poor drainage and they won't come up with the goods. And they like a slope, which is why so many wines are called *Côte* something.

Detailed in this section are the main wine-producing areas of Burgundy: **Côte d'Or, Mâcon, Beaujolais**, and the smaller **Chalonnais** region. All lie close to the main Dijon-Lyon roads and are accessible and much visited. The fifth area, **Chablis**, is included with Auxerre (above, see p.371).

The Côte d'Or

The attractive countryside of the **Côte d'Or** is characterised by the steep scarp of the *côte*, wooded along the top and incised by steep little valleys called *combes*, where local rock climbers hone their skills (**footpaths GR7 and GR76** run the whole length of

THE SOIL AND THE GRAPE

Burgundy's best wines come from a narrow strip of hillside called the **Côte d'Or** that runs southwest from Dijon to Santenay. It is divided into two regions, **Côte de Nuits** and **Côte de Beaune**. With few exceptions the reds of the Côte de Nuits are considered the best: they are richer, age better and cost more. Côte de Beaune is known particularly for its whites, Meursault, Montrachet and Puligny.

The single most important factor determining the "character" of wines is the **soil**. In the **Côte d'Or**, the relative mixture of chalk, flint and clay varies over very short distances, making for an enormous variety of taste. Chalky soil makes a wine *virile* or *corsé*, in other words "heady" – *il y a de la mâche*, they say, "something to bite on" – while clay makes it *féminin*, more *agréable*.

These and other more extravagant judgements are made after the hallowed procedure of **tasting**, which, in order to do properly, by one account, you have to "introduce a draft of wine into your mouth, swill it across the tongue, roll it around the palate, churn it around emitting the gargling sound so beloved of tasters, which is produced by slowly inhaling air through the centre of your mouth, and finally eject it". The ejection is what has to be learned.

the wine country as far south as Lyon). Spring is a good time to visit this region, when you avoid the crowds and the landscape is a dramatic symphony of browns – trees, earth, vines, with millions of bone-coloured vine stakes wheeling past as you travel through, like crosses in a vast war cemetery.

The villages, strung along the N74 through Beaune and beyond, have names – **Gévry-Chambertin**, **Vougeot**, **Vosne-Romanée**, **Nuits-St-Georges**, **Pommard**, **Volnay**, **Meursault** – that all sound like Pavlov's bell to the ears of wine buffs and are familiar to the most casually interested; but they turn out to be sleepy, dull and exceedingly prosperous, full of houses inhabited by well-heeled *vignerons* in expensive suits and fat-cat cars. You make a very good living on a patch of four or five hectares (ten to twelve acres), the average-sized plot. Proof: none are ever up for sale.

There are numerous *caves* where you can **taste and buy**, but, as usual, the former is meant to be a prelude to the latter. And there's no such thing as a cheap wine, red or white, 100–120F being the minimum. The *Hautes Côtes* (Nuits and Beaune), from the top of the slope, are cheaper, but they lack the connoisseur cachet of the big names.

Château Clos-Vougeot

Though the whole French wine culture is fascinating, it is debatable whether making a special detour to see these vineyards is really worthwhile. The only "sight" you should perhaps go out of your way for is the **château de CLOS-VOUGEOT**, between Gévry-Chambertin and Nuits-St-Georges on the N74 (half-hour guided tours, May–Aug 9am–5pm; Oct–April 9–11.30am & 2–4pm; 12F), where you get to see the mammoth thirteenth-century wine presses installed by the Cistercian monks to whom these vineyards once belonged. The château today is the home of a sort of phony chivalrous order, the **Confrèrie des Chevaliers du Tastevin** (about which you get a video promo after the tour), whose principal reason for existence seems to be commerce and snobbery, though no doubt the food and wine are treated seriously at the trade's annual beanfeast, the so-called *Les Trois Glorieuses* on the third weekend in November.

Beaune

BEAUNE, the principal town of the Côte d'Or, has many charms but is totally devoted to tourism. If you want a **base** for getting around in the area, it's cheaper and pleasanter to use Dijon or Chalon, as both are easily accessible by train and *Transco* buses, which service all the villages down the N74. Beaune is situated at a major **autoroute junction** (A6 from Paris/Lyon–A31 from Metz) and its **hotels** are pricey and likely to be full.

The town

Beaune's town centre, a tightly clustered, rampart-enclosed *vieille ville*, is 500m from the **gare SNCF** (outside the old walls), down av du 8-septembre. If you arrive by bus, you're likely to by dropped at the main **gare routière** on the southwest side of town, just outside the walls at the end of rue Maufoux, a five-minute walk from the town's highlights.

The chief attraction is the fifteenth-century hospital, the **Hôtel-Dieu** (tours in French every 15min July & Aug 9am–6.45pm; Sept–June 9–11.45am & 2–6pm; 20F), on the corner of place de la Halle opposite the **SI** (see "Listings" for details). Once past the turnstile of the **Hôtel-Dieu** you find yourself in a cobbled courtyard surrounded by a wooden gallery overhung by a massive roof patterned with diamonds of gaudy tiles, green, burnt sienna, black and yellow – and similarly multi-coloured steep-pitched dormers and turrets. Inside is a vast paved hall with a painted timber roof, the **Grande Salle des Malades** which, until quite recently, continued to serve its original purpose of accommodating the sick. The last item on the tour is the **Polyptych of the Last Judgement**, a splendid fifteenth-century altarpiece by Rogier van der Weyden, commissioned by Nicolas Rolin, who also founded the hospital. It is here that a major wine auction takes place (see above for dates) during the *Trois Glorieuses*, the prices paid setting the pattern for the season.

The private residence of the dukes of Burgundy on rue d'Enfer now contains the **Musée du Vin** (daily summer 9am–noon & 1.30–7pm; winter 10am–noon & 2–5.30pm; 10F), with more giant wine presses and an interesting collection of tools of the trade. At the other end of rue d'Enfer the church of **Notre-Dame** is about the only thing free in town. Inside are five very special **tapestries** from the fifteenth century depicting the Life of the Virgin and commissioned, once again, by the Rolin family.

Accommodation and eating

If you're going to stay in Beaune, a couple of possibilities are *Auberge de la Gare,* near the train station at 11 av des Lyonnais (☎80.22.11.13; ②), which has a cheap restaurant, and *Hôtel Foch*, 24 bd Foch (☎80.24.75.59; ③), situated to the west of the town, outside the walls (from the SI take av de la République and turn right). There might also be room at the *Foyer des Jeunes Travailleurs* opposite the hospital on rue Guigone-de-Salins (☎80.22.21.83). The pretty *Les Cent Vignes* **campsite**, 10 rue Dubois (☎80.22.03.91), is about 1km out of town, off rue du Faubourg-St-Nicolas (the N74 to Dijon), before the bridge over the autoroute; but, again, booking is advisable as it fills up through the day.

Eating can be an expensive business. The best places to look for something **cheaper** are rue Monge, place Carnot and rue Madeleine. *Le Carnot,* 18 rue Carnot, is a good cafeteria; and decent, reasonably priced restaurants include the *Brelinette*, 6 rue Madeleine where *menus* start at 58F, *La Gouzotte* in the same street at no. 5, and *Le Bistrot Bourguignon*, 8 rue Monge.

Listings

Bikes Can be hired from the station, or from *Loc Car*, 6 av du 8-Septembre (☎80.24.17.17), who also hire out cars and trucks.

Buses Right outside the walls at the end of rue Maufoux (times on SI display board).

Launderette Off pl Madeleine, and at 24 rue du Fbg-St-Nicholas.

Market Place Carnot; and a *Casino* supermarket at 28 rue du Fbg-Madeleine.

SI Opposite the Hôtel-Dieu on rue de l'Hôtel-Dieu (Easter–June 9am–8pm; July–Sept 9am–10pm; winter 9am–7.15pm). They provide information and hype on wine-tasting in the region, as well as useful town info and, seasonally, free guided tours of Beaune.

Chalon-sur-Saône

CHALON, a sizeable port and industrial centre on a broad meander of the Saône, is not a place you'd want to stay very long, but its old riverside quarter does have an easy charm. Today it's a thriving business centre, and trade fairs frequently possess the town; however, more **festive occasions** are an important part of its appeal and good reasons to stop if you're around at the right time. Three major events are a **carnival in March**, which features a parade of giant masks, confetti battle and "laughter evening"; a national **festival of street artists in July**; and a **film festival in October**.

Around town

The **old town** is located just back from the river around Grande-Rue and rue du Châtelet. The **junction** of these two streets is the location of a fifteenth-century **timber-framed house**, and there're a number of semi-timbered overhanging facades in the quarter. Nearby, 200m to the west on **pl de l'Hôtel de Ville** is the **Musée Denon** (closed Tues; 12F), whose most vaunted exhibit is the 18,000-year-old **Volgu flint**, rated one of the finest stone tools yet discovered. Apart from the usual collection of locally excavated bits and pieces, also look out for the local furniture.

The one attraction you definitely won't want to miss is the **Musée Niepce** (9.30–11.30am & 2.30–5.30pm; closed Tues; 12F) on the river quays just downstream from Pont St-Laurent (rue du Pont leads to the bridge from the junction mentioned above). Niepce, who was born in Chalon, is credited with inventing **photography**, and the museum possesses a fascinating range of **cameras** from the first machine ever to the *Apollo* moon mission's equipment, plus a number of 007-type spy-camera devices, all attractively displayed under a set of glass domes. Upstairs is a **library** of works on the subject of photography, to be thumbed through at leisure, and space for temporary exhibitions monopolised by some of the greatest names in the history of the art.

The other interesting target in town is the **Maison des Vins**, on Promenade Ste-Marie (daily 8am–12.30pm & 1.30–8pm), where you can taste and buy Côte Chalonnaise wines, chosen blindly from the wines of 44 local villages by a choice committee of professional wine tasters. (If you want to explore the wines at source, SNCF buses go south to **MÂCON**, passing through some of the **Chalonnais** wine villages, best known for their whites: 14km west to **Mercurey** on the D978 and then down the D981 to **Givry**, **Buxy** and **Montagny**.)

Practicalities

The **SI**, on bd de la République five minutes' walk from the **gare SNCF**, gives out excellent listings and a useful map. The town is particularly convenient for youth hostellers, with an agreeably located riverbank **youth hostel** (☎85.46.62.77) on rue d'Amsterdam about a ten-minute walk north of the Pont St-Laurent, the last bridge upstream. From the bridge, follow quai de la Poterne, then quai Ste-Marie, upstream. If you're coming from the station direction, go straight ahead into bd de la République as far as place de l'Obélisque, then work your way diagonally right until you hit the river. Alternatively, take bus #11 from the SI.

The cheapest **hotel** in town is the *Gloriette* (☎85.48.23.35; ②), 27 rue Gloriette off bd de la République, behind the SI, but even two-star establishments like *Hôtel Central*, 19 pl de Beaune, beyond pl de l'Obélisque on bd de la République (☎85.48.35.00; ②) and *Nouvel Hôtel* (☎85.48.07.31; ②), 7 av Boucicaut – from the station turn left at the end of av Jean-Jaurès and left again – have some cheap rooms. *Camping de la Butte*, (☎85.48.26.86) 3km east of town in St-Marcel, is accessible on bus #9, or if you're walking, cross either Pont St-Laurent or Pont J-Richard and head east.

If you're staying at the youth hostel, the nearest and nicest places for cheap **eating** are on rue de Strasbourg on the **island** across Pont St-Laurent, where there are several establishments including pizzerias, *crêperies*, fish restaurants and a piano bar. **Live music** can be heard at *La Tête à l'Envers,* 9 rue Gloriette, where they also serve cold meals until 1am (3am at weekends).

Tournus

TOURNUS is a small walled town on the banks of the **Saône,** just off the autoroute and N6 between Chalon and Mâcon. As you enter from the **gare SNCF** through a narrow gateway flanked by medieval towers, it all seems almost too carefully preserved, especially around the old abbey church of **St-Philibert**, one of the earliest Romanesque buildings in Burgundy. Further into the town there are some lovely arcaded shopfronts and substantial hotels, and in **place de l'Hôtel-de-Ville** the remains of an arcaded pavement. From the **riverside quays**, you look out over the broad sweep of the river and its wide flat valley beneath the huge piling cloudscapes.

Prosperous today from its agriculture and light industry, Tournus owed its first flowering to the growth of the monastic community around 900 AD. **St-Philibert** bears witness to that wealth and importance. It has the massive qualities and clean, pared-down lines more associated with a fortress than a church. It is equally strong inside, not to say primitive, with its colossal round pillars and rough-looking stonework in the narthex. The **nave** is something of an architectural rarity in that the vaults of its ceiling run side to side instead of down the axis of the church; an ingenious idea, because it made it possible to have windows in the ends of the vaults opening directly into the nave – very unusual given the state of the art.

Beside the church, **Musée Perrin de Puycousin** (April–Oct 9am–noon & 2–6pm; closed Tues; 8F) is a moderately interesting museum of local life and costumes, while **Musée Greuze** nearby at 4 rue du Collège (April–Oct 9.30am–noon & 2–6.30pm; closed Sun am & Tues) displays the eighteenth-century paintings of Tournus's native son, Greuze.

Practicalities

If you're planning **to stay**, *Hôtel Le Terminus* (☎85.51.05.54; ④) near the station in av Gambetta is a good choice. The centrally located and popular bar, *La Petite Auberge*, in place Lacretelle, has simple rooms, as does the *Hôtel de l'Abbaye,* 12 rue Léon-Godin (☎85.51.11.63; ②), which also has a well-priced restaurant serving local specialities, which include *quenelles au brochet* – fish dumplings in a creamy sauce. **Camping** *Le Pas-Fleury* (☎85.51.16.58) is by the river just south of the town. Take av du 23-janvier out of town to the N6, direction "Lyon".

Apart from the *l'Abbaye*, other **eating houses** worthy of investigation are *Café de la Poste* on the corner of rue Jean-Jaurès, which has cheap snacks and meals, and *Le Voleur de Temps*, 32 rue Dr-Privey, with a vegetarian menu on offer.

Mâcon and Mâconnais

MÂCON is basically a large, modern conurbation, but it has a riverside district, with flamboyant facades, curly-tiled roofs and pavement cafés, looking out over the town's pleasure-boat harbour, that contributes to a southerly atmosphere reminiscent of a seaside town. Old houses include the extraordinary carved **Maison du Bois**, a half-timbered Renaissance mansion detailed with fantastic animals, on rue Dombey at the corner of pl aux Herbes.

The **SI** is at 187 rue Carnot. The **gare SNCF** and **gare routière** are located next to each other behind the busy T-junction of rue Gambetta, rue V-Hugo and rue Bigonnet. Cheap **hotels** include *La Savoie*, 87 rue Rambuteau (☎87.38.42.22; ①), which also has a good cheap restaurant, and *La Boiserie*, 56 rue V-Hugo, (☎85.38.00.90, ②). If you want to camp, there's a three-star **campsite** (☎86.38.16.22; mid-Mar–Oct) 3km north out of town on the N6.

For **food and nightlife** the *Café Noir* on pl des Cordelières is a trendy bar, open till 1am, with cheap lunchtime menus, and there's a good *pizzeria* on the same *place*. There are **piano bars** on rue Carnot, rue Franche-Chatillon and rue Mattieu and a **disco** across the river on quai Bouchecourt.

Transport: note that **TGV trains** leave from Mâcon-Loché station 6km out of town.

Mâconnais

The **Mâconnais wine-producing** country lies to the west. Its reds are good, but it is best known for the expensive **white wines** from the villages of **Pouilly, Fuissé, Vinzelles**, and **Prissé**. A curious phenomenon in the landscape is the 500-metre **Solutré** rock, which evidently puzzled prehistoric as well as modern visitors. An incredible quantity of horse, reindeer, bison and mammoth bones have been found here covering an area of 4 hectares (7 acres).

Bourg-en-Bresse and Brou

BOURG-EN-BRESSE, 32km east of Mâcon, means three things in France: chickens, Peugeot lorries and **Brou**. Poultry raising is the speciality of the flat surrounding farm-land and lorries are made in the town.

BROU is an uninteresting suburban village about 1km away to the southeast, which happens to have an early sixteenth-century **church** (daily; 20F) that generally sends guidebook writers into raptures. If you're heading east to Geneva or the Alps, take a look, but don't lose a lift or miss a train for it. Aldous Huxley found it "a horrible little architectural nightmare", its monuments "positively and piercingly vulgar". Certainly, it was a very rich woman's very expensive folly, crammed with virtuoso craftsmanship from the dying moments of the Gothic style, and it is interesting to see; but the place is soulless, without a trace of vision or inspiration. It was undertaken by Margaret of Austria after the death of her husband, Philibert, Duke of Savoy, and is in effect a mausoleum for the two of them and Philibert's mother. It's no longer a place of worship.

From Bourg **gare SNCF**, bus #2 goes to the town centre and #1 to Brou. The **SI** is in Centre Albert-Camus, 6 av Alsace-Lorraine with, in summer, an annex by Brou church. Wednesday is **market day** in place Carriat, and on the first and third Wednesdays of each month there's a livestock market as well. There are several reasonable **hotels** with inexpensive restaurants in av Baudin, about a two-minute walk from the station, while the **camping municipal** (74.22.27.79; April–mid-Oct) is on av des Sports, the N83 northeast of town on the road to Lons-le-Saunier.

Beaujolais

Imperceptibly, as you continue south, the Mâconnais becomes the **Beaujolais**, a larger area of terraced hills producing lighter, fruity red wines. The fashion now is to drink them very early, and this is taken to ridiculous extremes with **Beaujolais Nouveau**. The *vin de l'année* is transported to British wine bars at breakneck speeds by drunken young tearaways (and, increasingly, around the world by air) during the **Beaujolais run** in November: it should be polished off within six months.

The well-marked **route de Beaujolais** winds down through the wine villages to **VILLEFRANCHE**. Uninteresting in itself, Villefranche could be a useful starting point if you are coming from Lyon, and, if you're driving south, it's a usefully straightforward place to stop just before the big city. The **SI** at 290 rue de Thizy has all the information

BEAUJOLAIS: CRUS, NOUVEAU, VILLAGES & SUPÉRIEUR

The Beaujolais grape is the **Gamay**, which – in contrast to other parts of Burgundy – thrives here on this granite soil. Of the **four appellations** of Beaujolais, the best are the *crus,* including Morgon and Fleurie, which come from the northern part of the region between St-Amour (the northernmost *cru*) and Brouilly in the south. If you have transport you can follow the *cru*-trail south from Mâcon by turning right at Crêches-sur-Saône up the D31 to St-Amour and then south along the D68. **Beaujolais Villages**, which produces the best *nouveau*, comes from the middle of the Beaujolais region, south of the *cru* belt, while plain **Beaujolais** and **Beaujolais supérieur** are produced in the vineyards southwest of Villefranche not far from Lyon.

about *caves*, visits and wine tours, though they're not overly helpful. There are numerous cheap **hotels**, almost all near the **gare SNCF**. A good one to try is the friendly and clean *Hôtel la Colonne*, 6 place Carnot (☎74.65.06.42; ②), with a popular cheap **restaurant**, open every night – including Sunday when everything else is dead. Most of the cafés on **rue Nationale** are good for snacks or cheap menus, too.

travel details

Trains

From Sens to Paris, frequent (50min–1hr 30min); to Dijon, 11 daily (2hr 10min), via Joigny (27min) Laroche-Migennes junction (30min), Tonnerre (55min) and Montbard (1 hr 27min); 3–5 daily to Auxerre (45min) and Avallon (2hr), a few continuing to Autun (4hr).

From Auxerre to Paris, 7 or 8 daily (1hr 45min), some changing at Laroche-Migennes; 4/5 daily to Avallon (1hr 5min) and Autun (about 3hr).

From Avallon direct to Paris, 2 or 3 weekly (2hr); to Auxerre, 4 to 5 daily (1hr 5min); to Autun, 4 to 5 daily (about 2hr); to Dijon, 4 daily (2 hr); to Semur-en-Auxois, 3 daily (40min).

From Tonnerre to Paris, 6 daily (1hr 45min); to Dijon, 6 daily (1hr 15min).

From Dijon to Paris, 9 direct TGVs daily (1hr 40min); 6 stopping trains to Paris (3hr) via Les Laumes (30min), Montbard (45min), Tonnerre (1hr 15min), Laroche-Migennes (1hr 40min), Sens (2hr 10min); several, late night and early morning only non-stop to Lyon (1hr 40min); about 14 others daily to Lyon (1hr 45min) stopping variously at Nuits-St-Georges (20min), Beaune (25min), Chalon (40min), Tournus (1hr), Mâcon (1hr–1hr 20min), Villefranche (1hr 40min) – journey times vary.

From Beaune to Paris, 2 TGVs daily (2hr); to Dijon, about 7 daily (20min); about 7 daily to Lyon

(2hr), some stopping everywhere, others only at Chalon and Mâcon.

From Mâcon to Paris, 5 direct TGVs daily (1hr 40min); 4 TGVs daily to Bourg-en-Bresse (20min) and Geneva (1hr 50min); around 14 daily to Dijon (1hr 10min) and Lyon (40min).

From Bourg-en-Bresse to Paris 4 TGVs daily (2hr) via Mâcon (20min); to Geneva 4 TGVs daily (1hr 30min); to Dijon 2 daily direct trains (1hr 45min–2hr 30min); to Mâcon 8 daily (30min); to Lyon 14 daily(about 1hr).

From Autun 4 to 5 daily to Avallon (2hr), Auxerre (3hr), Sens (4hr).

From Nevers to Paris, about 5 daily non-stop (2hr) and several stopping trains daily (3hr); to Clermont-Ferrand 5 daily (1hr 50min).

Buses

From Sens to Auxerre, 4 daily (2hr 5min), via Joigny (1 hr 10min); to Troyes, 4 to 5 daily (1hr 45min).

From Auxerre to Sens, 4 daily (2hr 5min); other sporadic village buses, including to Chablis and Tonnerre.

From Avallon to Vézelay, 1 daily (30min); to Dijon, 1 daily (2hr 30min–3hr) via Semur.

From Semur to Les Laumes (on Paris–Dijon line), Saulieu and Montbard (with SNCF buses); to Auxerre 1 daily .

From Dijon daily services through villages to Avallon; Beaune; Nuits and other wine villages; Autun.

From Mâcon 7 SNCF buses daily to Chalon (2hr 15min) via Cluny (45min); 2 to 5 daily to Paray-le-Monial, Charolles, Cluny, and everywhere on route N79.

From Bourg-en-Bresse to Lyon, 1 SNCF bus daily (1hr 40min).

From Nevers to La Charité, Cosne and Moulins on N7, several daily.

From Cluny 7 SNCF buses daily to Chalon (1hr 20min) and Mâcon (45min); to Charolles and Paray, 2 to 5 daily.

From Autun several SNCF buses daily to Montchanin TGV station (1hr) via Le Creusot (30min); to Château-Chinon, 1 daily (1hr); to St-Léger-sous-Beuvray, 2 to 3 daily (1hr 15min); to Chalon (1hr 20min); to Beaune and Dijon, 1 daily.

From Paray-le-Monial to Digoin, Charolles, Cluny, Mâcon, 2 to 5 daily.

From Montbard to Châtillon-sur-Seine and Chaumont (with SNCF buses); to Châtillon and Langres (with Cars CDA).

CHAPTER EIGHT

POITOU-CHARENTES, THE ATLANTIC COAST AND LIMOUSIN

Newsstands selling *Sud-Ouest* remind you where you are: this is not the Mediterranean, certainly, but in summer at least, in the quality of the light, the warm air, the fields of sunflowers and the shuttered siesta-silence of the farmhouses, you get the first exciting promises of the south.

The **coast**, on the other hand, remains unmistakably Atlantic – dunes, pine forest, reclaimed marshland and misty mud flats. While it has great charm in places, particularly out of season on the islands of **Noirmoutier, Ré** and **Oléron**, it's a family, camper-caravanner seaside, lacking the glamour and excitement of the Côte d'Azur. The principal port in the north, **La Rochelle**, is one of the prettiest and most distinctive towns in France. The sandy beaches are beautiful everywhere, though can occasionally be disappointing where the waster is murky and shallow for a long way out: this applies more to the northern stretches. On the dune-backed **Côte d'Argent**, south of **Bordeaux**, however, the sea can be lively, not to say dangerous, and often surfable.

Inland, the **valley of the Charente river**, slow and green, epitomises blue-overalled, Gauloise-smoking, peasant France. The towpath is accessible for long stretches, on foot or mountain bike, and there are boat trips from Saintes and Cognac. The **Marais Poitevin** marshes, too, with their groves of poplars and island fields reticulated by countless canals and ditches, are both unusual landscape and good walking or cycling country.

But perhaps the most memorable aspect of the countryside – and indeed of towns like Poitiers, too – is the presence of exquisite **Romanesque churches**. This region formed a significant stretch of the medieval pilgrim routes across France and from Britain and northern Europe to the shrine of **Saint Jacques** (St James, or Santiago as the Spanish know him) at Compostela in northwest Spain, and was well endowed by its followers. The finest of the churches, among the best in all of France, are to be found in the countryside around **Saintes** and **Poitiers**: informal, highly individual and so integrated with their landscape they often seem as rooted as the trees.

Lastly, of course, remember that this is a region of **seafood** – fresh and cheap in every market for miles inland – and, around Bordeaux, some of the world's top **vineyards**.

HOTEL ROOM PRICES

For a fuller explanation of these price codes, see the box on p.28 of *Basics*.

① Under 100F ② 100–130F ③ 130–180F ④ 180–230F ⑤ 230–300F

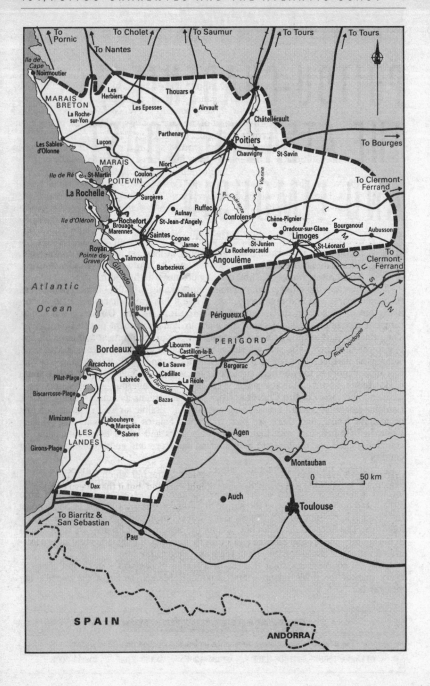

POITIERS AND INLAND POITOU

Most of the old **province of Poitou** is a huge expanse of rolling wheat land, sunflower and maize plantations where the combines crawl and giant sprinklers shoot great arcs of white water over the fields in summertime. Villages are strung out along the valley bottoms. Heartland of the domains of Eleanor, Duchess of Aquitaine, whose marriage to King Henry II in 1152 brought the whole of southwest France under English control for 300 years, it is also the northern limit of the *langue d'oc*-speaking part of the country, whose **Occitan** dialect survives among old people even today.

Hitching is the easiest way of **moving around** within the area, though the main destinations are all directly accessible by train from Paris. Poitiers is just three hours away, with frequent connections on to La Rochelle, Bordeaux and the Atlantic coast.

West of Poitiers the open landscape of the **Poitou plain** gradually gives way to *bocages* – small fields enclosed by hedges and trees. The local farmers' co-operatives say that grubbing up woodland and creating vast windswept acreages in the name of efficiency and productivity is going out of fashion. And not just for aesthetic reasons: wind erosion has left scarcely fifteen centimetres of top soil.

Poitiers and around

Heading south from Tours on the *Autoroute de l'Aquitaine*, you'd hardly be tempted by the cluster of towers and office blocks rising from the plain, which is all you see of **POITIERS**. But approach more closely and things look very different. No seething metropolis, Poitiers is a country town with a charm that comes from a long and sometimes influential history – as the seat of the dukes of Aquitaine, for instance – discernible in the winding lines of the streets and the breadth of civic, domestic and ecclesiastical architectural fashions represented in its buildings. A hilltop town overlooking two rivers,with plenty of pedestrian precincts, restaurants and pavement cafés – and some wonderful central gardens – it makes for comfortable sightseeing.

For the dedicated, there are two **Romanesque churches** not far from Poitiers, at ST-SAVIN and CHAUVIGNY, both of which have some great sculpture and frescoes (see p.409).

Arrival and hotels

Arriving by train, you'll find yourself at the foot of the hill which forms the kernel of the town. It's a pretty run-down, desolate neighbourhood, but if that doesn't bother you there are several **places to stay** right opposite the gare SNCF. For more entertaining surroundings it's only a short uphill walk – bd Solférino, then right up the steps – to the **town centre** on place du Maréchal-Leclerc. There's also a **youth hostel** at 17 rue de la Jeunesse (☎49.58.03.05; bus #9 from the gare SNCF to *Bellejouanne*: 3km) and a **camping municipal** (☎49.41.44.88) on rue du Porteau, north of the town (bus #7). If you have any difficulty with accommodation, ask the **SI**, whose principal office is at 8 rue des Grandes-Écoles (Mon–Sat 9am–7pm; closed lunchtime Sept–June), with a summer annexe by the station.

Station hotels

Hôtel de Paris, 123 bd du Grand-Cerf, (☎49.58.39.37; closed Mon). Run-down, fairly unfriendly and suffers from traffic noise front and back, but cheap. ②

Le Grand Cerf, 137 bd du Grand-Cerf (☎49.58.20.85; closed 6–27 Aug & Mon). Much of a muchness with the *Paris* and the other hotels in the street. ②

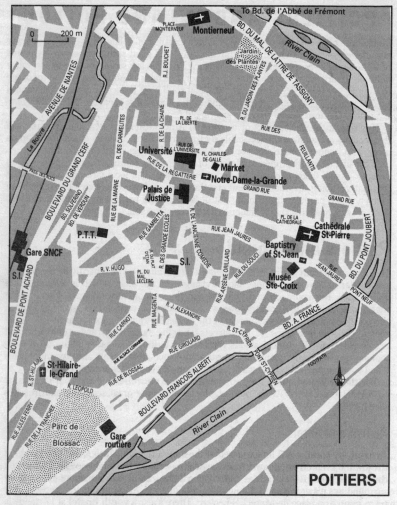

POITIERS

La Renaissance, 179 av de Nantes (☎49.58.22.27; closed Sun afternoons). Comfortable hotel within walking distance of the railway station. ①

La Petite Villette, 14 bd de l'Abbé-de-Frémont (☎49.41.41.33; closed Sun). Easily accessible from the station, just continue along bd du Grand-Cerf till you reach the roundabout and turn right. ①

Town centre hotels

Hôtel du Plat d'Étain, 7 rue du Plat-d'Étain (☎49.41.04.80). Situated in a quiet street, this is well run and attractive and infinitely preferable to the above selection. ③

Hôtel Jules Ferry, 27 rue Jules-Ferry (☎49.37.80.31). Clean, recently decorated, fairly central. ③

Le Carnot, 40 rue Carnot (☎49.41.23.69). Small, with a noisy restaurant downstairs. ①

Le Victor Hugo, 5 rue Victor-Hugo (☎49.41.12.16). Central and very cheap. ①

The town

Tree-lined **Place du Maréchal-Leclerc** and **Place Charles-de-Gaulle** a few streets north are the two poles of communal life, the first with popular **cafés**, the second with a big and bustling **market**. Between is a warren of prosperous streets, with rue Gambetta cutting north past the **Palais de Justice**, whose nineteenth-century facade hides the twelfth-century great hall of the dukes of Aquitaine, into rue de la Chaine, full of half-timbered medieval houses, and down to the river by the heavily restored church of St-Jean-de-Montierneuf. **Inside**, the Palais de Justice is a magnificent room nearly 50m long, where Jean, Duc de Berry held his sumptuous court in the late fourteenth century seated on the intricately carved dais at the far end. In one corner, stairs give access to the old **castle keep**. Joan of Arc was once put through her ideological paces here by a committee of bishops worried about endangering their own immortal souls and worldly positions by endorsing a charlatan or a heretic. They also had her virginity checked by a posse of respectable matrons. The stairs lead out on to the roof with a fantastic view over the town.

Right behind you, you look down upon one of the greatest and most idiosyncratic churches in France, **Notre-Dame-la-Grande**, begun in the reign of Eleanor. Access is via rue de la Régatterie or rue du Marché. The weirdest and most spectacular thing about it is the **west front**. You can't call it beautiful, at least not in a conventional sense. It is squat and loaded with detail to a degree that the modern eye finds fussy. And yet it is this **detail** which is enthralling, ranging from the domestic to the disturbingly anarchic. In the blind arch to the right of the door, a woman sits in the keystone with her hair blowing out from her head. In the frieze above, Mary places her hand familiarly on Elizabeth's pregnant belly. You see the newborn Jesus admired by a couple of daft-looking sheep and gurgling in his bath-tub. Higher still are images of the apostles, and at the apex, where the eye is carried deliberately and inevitably, Christ in Majesty in an almond-shaped inset. Such elaborate sculpted facades – and domes like pinecones on turret and belfry – are the hallmarks of the Poitou brand of Romanesque. The **interior**, crudely overlaid with nineteenth-century frescoes, is not nearly as interesting.

There is another unusual Poitiers church towards the southern tip of the old town, where the hump of the hill narrows to a point now occupied by the **Parc de Blossac**, a great spot to sit among the clipped limes and gravelled walks, to watch the *boules* and munch a baguette. This is the eleventh-century **St-Hilaire-le-Grand** on rue du Doyenné – unbelievably, pruned of part of its nave in the last century. Take the trouble to admire the **chevet** from the outside; the apse has a particularly beautiful group of chapels surrounding it. Inside, there is the usual **ambulatory** to accommodate the many pilgrims who flocked in, one of whom perhaps caused the fire around 1100 that destroyed the original wooden roof and necessitated the improvised arrangement that makes St-Hilaire architecturally unique. Eight heavy domes introduced for the re-roofing had to be supported somehow, hence the forest of auxiliary columns making three aisles either side of the nave.

And this is neither the oddest nor the oldest building in town. Literally in the middle of rue Jean-Jaurès, as you go down towards the river Clain, you come upon a chunky, square edifice with the air of a second-rate Roman temple. It is the mid-fourth-century **Baptistère St-Jean** (April–Sept 10.30am–12.30pm & 3–6pm; Oct–March 2–4pm), reputedly the oldest Christian building in France and until the seventeenth century the only place in town you could have a proper **baptism**. The "font" was the octagonal pool sunk into the floor. The guide argues that the water pipes uncovered in the bottom show that the water could not have been more than 30 to 40cm deep, which casts doubt upon the popular belief that early Christian baptism was by total immersion. There are also some very ancient and faded **frescoes** on the walls, including the Emperor Constantine on horseback, and a collection of Merovingian sarcophagi.

Nearby is Poitiers' **cathedral of St-Pierre**, an enormous building on whose broad, pale facade pigeons roost and plants take root. Some of the **glass** dates from the twelfth century, notably the crucifixion in the centre window of the apse, in which the features of Henry II and Eleanor are supposedly discernible. The **choir stalls**, too, are full of characteristic medieval detail: a coquettish Mary and child, a peasant killing a boar, the architect at work with his dividers, a baker with a basket of loaves.

Opposite, in the side street across rue J-Jaurès, is Poitiers' museum, **Musée Ste-Croix** (10am–noon & 2–6pm; closed Tues; free). Downstairs is an interesting collection of farming implements, among them an *alambic ambulant* or itinerant still, of a kind in use until surprisingly recently. There is also a good Gallo-Roman section with some handsome glass, pottery and sculpture, notably a white marble Minerva of the first century.

If you still have an appetite for buildings, there's a seventh-century subterranean chapel, the **Hypogée martyrium**, on rue de la Pierre-Levée across the **Pont Neuf**, and the Pierre Levée dolmen itself, where Rabelais came with fellow-students to talk, carouse and scratch his name. Descartes, Poitiers University's other most illustrious student, was rather more serious.

Alternatively, you could take a more relaxed **walk along the riverside path** – on the right across Pont Neuf – upstream to Pont St-Cyprien. On the far bank, you can see a characteristic feature of every French provincial town: neat, well-manured *potagers* – vegetable gardens – coming down to the water's edge with a little mud quay at the end and a moored punt, where *monsieur* spends many a weekend hour patiently waiting for a fat carp. Sometimes you find such scenes right in the heart of a town: an atavistic refusal to become totally urban.

Eating and nightlife

As for **eating**, there are good opportunities for fine food whatever your culinary persuasions. If you know where to head, the town offers everything from cheap fast food to high-priced restaurants with so many recommendations you can't see in the windows for stickers. There's a good range of ethnic options if you're bored with French *haute cuisine*. If you're not too long in the tooth, you could also try wangling a university restaurant ticket; ask **CIJ** at 64 rue Gambetta or phone ☎49.01.83.69.

RESTAURANTS

Jack Rolland, 16 rue Carnot (☎49.88.14.41; closed 13 July–16 Aug, Sun eve & Mon). Specialises in exquisite fish dishes, but menus start at 140F. If you can't countenance such expense there are a number of other options in this street.

Le Poitevin, 76 rue Carrnot. Regional food at reasonable prices.

Patatorium, 185 Fbg du Pont-Neuf, just over the Pont Neuf bridge (open Tues–Sat, 2–7pm). French and Moroccan food in café connected to an exhibition centre and record store.

Notre Dame, pl Charles-de-Gaulle. Cheap snacks, pizzas, cups of tea or *menus*, situated opposite Notre-Dame church with tables out on the square.

Makossa, 20 rue des Vieilles-Boucheries (☎49.01.74.72). Plain and simple African restaurant, with lots of cheap options and vegetarian dishes.

Pizza Rosa and **Snooker Bar**, on espace Régratterie, off rue de la Régratterie. Very cheap pizza slices to eat at the bar, and English beers in the *Snooker Bar* on the same courtyard.

Le Cappucino, 5 rue de l'Université (closed Sun eve & Mon). One of a number of Italian restaurants in this area.

Chez Pierrot, place Montierneuf. Inexpensive restaurant with several studenty bars nearby.

Le Regal, rue de la Régatterie, a plain *brasserie*.

La Trattoria, rue de la Régatterie. Flash pizzeria.

El Sombrero, 51 rue Arsène-Orillard (☎49.88.64.14). Mexican restaurant.

NIGHTCLUBS
Two clubs worth a visit are **Privilege**, 195 av du 8-mai 1945, and **La Nuit Blanche**, 15 bd du Grand-Cerf.

Listings

Bike hire *Cyclamen*, 49 rue Arsène-Orillard.

CIJ Youth centre, 64 rue Gambetta (☎49.88.64.37).

Gare routière, off the D4 on the way, north, out of town towards Châtellerault (bus #11 from the train station), 500m north of place Montierneuf. Most buses, however – except to Loudun and local villages – leave from pl Thézard below Parc de Blossac. Contact *Rapides du Poitou*, 20 rue de la Plaine (☎49.46.27.45) for buses to St-Savin and Chauvigny.

Launderette, rue René-Descartes, off pl de la Liberté.

Poste restante, 16 rue Arthur-Ranc.

Walkers can get a guide to the regional opportunities from the SI. The GR364 sets out from here, reaching the Vendée coast via Parthenay.

St-Savin and Chauvigny

You need to get an early start if you want to do both Chauvigny (23km east of Poitiers) and St-Savin (42km) in one day using public transport. Alternatively, both places have two or three reasonable **hotels** and Chauvigny also has a **campsite**. In Chauvigny, try *Le Lion d'Or*, 8 rue du Marché (☎49.46.30.28; closed Dec 15–Jan 15; ③), or, in St-Savin try *Hôtel du Midi* (☎49.48.00.40, closed Jan; Sun evening & Mon; ②) on route Nationale.

Chauvigny

CHAUVIGNY's pride is the set of sculpted capitals of the **church of St-Pierre**. A busy market town on the banks of the Vienne, Chauvigny's half-dozen porcelain factories and lumber mills provide work for the area. If you can manage it, the Saturday **market** gives an extra dimension to a visit. Held between the church of Notre-Dame and the river, it offers a mouthwatering selection of food – oysters, prawns, crayfish, cheeses galore, pâtés in pristine aspic, including the spectacular *amandes*, decorated with yellow segments of scallop flesh. The cafés are fun, too, bursting with noisy wine-flushed farmers mixing business with pleasure.

To get to the church you take rue du Château opposite Notre-Dame, winding up the spur on which the old town stands. Past the ruins of a castle that belonged to the bishops of Poitiers and the better-preserved Château d'Harcourt, you come first to the attractive and unusual east end of **St-Pierre**. Once inside, however, it turns out to be damp, and in poor repair.

The **choir capitals** are a visual treat. Each one is different, evoking a terrifying, nightmarish world. Graphically illustrated monsters – bearded, moustachioed, winged, scaley, human-headed with manes of flame – grab hapless mortals, naked, upside down and puny, and rip their bowels and crunch their heads. The only escape offered is in the naively serene events of the nativity. On the second capital on the south side of the choir, for instance, the angel Gabriel announces Christ's birth to the shepherds, their flock represented by four sheep that look like Pooh's companion Eeyore, while just around the corner the archangel Michael weighs souls in hand-held scales and a devil tries to grab one for his dinner. The oddest scene is on the north side: a Siamese-twin dancer grips the hindlegs of two horse-like monsters which are gnawing his upper arms. You get a strong feeling that here was an artist who came from the same peasant background as his audience, prey to the same fears of things that went bump in the night or lurked in the wet woods.

St-Savin

In **ST-SAVIN** – which is scarcely more than a hamlet in comparison with bustling Chauvigny – the bus puts you down beside the abbey near the modern bridge over the poplar-lined River Gartempe. Walk downstream a little way to the **medieval bridge** for a perfect view of the **abbey church** – built in the eleventh century, possibly on the site of a church founded by Charlemagne – rising strong and severe above the gazebos, vegetable gardens and lichened tile roofs of the domestic dwellings at its feet. The soaring crocketed spire, which first catches the eye today, is a Gothic addition.

Inside (July–Sept 9am–12.30pm & 2.30–7pm, Sun 9–11am & 2.30–7pm; closes 5pm Oct–June) steps descend to the narthex and thence to the floor of the nave, which stretches away from you to the raised choir: high, narrow, barrel-vaulted and flanked by bare round columns, their capitals deeply carved with interlacing foliage. The whole of the vault is covered with **paintings**. The colours are few – red and yellow ochres, green mixed with white and black. Yet the paintings are full of light and grace, depicting scenes from the stories of Genesis and Exodus. Some are instantly recognisable: Noah's three-decked ark, Pharoah's horses rearing at the engulfing waves of the Red Sea, graceful workers constructing the Tower of Babel.

Parthenay and around

On the edge of the plain, served by regular SNCF buses from Poitiers, stands the small town of **PARTHENAY**, once an important staging point on the pilgrim routes to Compostela and now the site of a major weekly cattle market every Wednesday. It's not a place to make a special detour for, but worth a stopover if you're heading north for Brittany or west to the sea.

Arrival and accommodation

Finding your way around is easy. From the **gare SNCF**, **av de Gaulle** leads directly west to the central square, with the **SI** on the righthand corner. The main part of town – essentially the medieval core, and fairly restricted in area at that – lies ahead to the west, towards the river Thouet. Rue Jean-Jaurès and rue de la Saunerie cut in through the largely pedestrian shopping precinct to the Gothic **Porte de l'Horloge**, the fortified gateway to the old citadel on a steep-sided neck of land above a loop of the Thouet.

If you're after shelter, a reasonable **hotel** in bd Meilleraye by the main square is *Grand Hôtel* at no. 85 (☎49.64.00.16; closed Sat evening & Sun out of season; ②). Another possibility is *Hôtel du Nord* at 86 av de Gaulle, opposite the station (☎49.94.29.11; closed Sat; ①/②). **Campers** have to head out to LE TALLUD, about 3km west on D949.

The town

Parthenay has nothing very remarkable to see. The **mairie** faces the attractively simple Romanesque **church of Ste-Croix** across a small garden with a view over the ramparts and the **gully of St-Jacques** with its medieval houses and vegetable plots climbing the opposite slope. Further along is a house where Cardinal Richelieu used to visit his grandfather, and then a handsome but badly damaged Romanesque door, all that remains of the castle chapel of **Notre-Dame-de-la-Couldre**. Of the castle itself practically nothing is left. From the tip of the spur where it once stood you look down on the twin-towered gateway and bridge of the **Pont St-Jacques**, dating back to the thirteenth century, through which the nightly flocks of pilgrims poured into the town for shelter and security. To reach it, turn left under the Tour de l'Horloge and down the **Vaux St-Jacques**, as this medieval lane is called. It is highly evocative of that period, with its crooked half-timbered dwellings crowding up to the bridge. They are only now beginning to be restored. Some look as if they have received little attention since the last pilgrim shuffled up the street.

Romanesque churches near Parthenay

There are three more beautiful Romanesque churches you might like to see within easy reach of Parthenay. One – with a sculpted facade depicting a mounted knight hawking – is only a twenty-minute walk on the Niort road, at PARTHENAY-LE-VIEUX. The others are at AIRVAULT, 20km northeast of Parthenay and easily accessible on the Parthenay–Thouars SNCF bus route, and ST-JOUIN-DE-MARNES, 9km northeast of Airvault (you'll have to hitch or walk that). Or, you could go on north to THOUARS, 21km from Airvault or 16km from St-Jouin (cheap hotels and *Camping municipal*), and combine St-Jouin with a visit to the sixteenth-century Château d'Oiron.

Niort

NIORT, too, is a stop-over rather than a destination, most immediately and conveniently if your goal is the Marais Poitevin, the so-called *Green Venice*. In itself Niort is a pleasant morning's stroll and, if you're in a car, probably the best place to stay. If you're on foot, it's the last place before the marshes to get a really wide choice of provisions.

The **most interesting part** of the town is the mainly pedestrian area around **rue Victor-Hugo** and **rue St-Jean**, full of stone-fronted or half-timbered medieval houses. Coming from the **gare SNCF**, take rue de la Gare as far as av de Verdun with the **SI** and main **Post Office** on the corner. Turn right into **place de la Brèche**. Rue Ricard leaves the square on the left; rue Victor-Hugo is its continuation, following the line of the medieval market in a gully separating the two small hills on which Niort is built. Up to the right, opposite the end of rue St-Jean, is the old **town hall**, a triangular building of the early sixteenth century with lantern, belfry and ornamental machicolations, perhaps capable of repelling drunken revellers but no match for catapult or sledgehammer.

At the end of the street is the river, the **Sèvre Niortaise**, not to be confused with the Sèvre Nantaise which flows northwards to join the Loire at Nantes. There are gardens and trees along the bank and, over the bridge, the ruins of a glove factory, the last vestige of Niort's once thriving **leather industry.** At the time of the Revolution it kept more than thirty cavalry regiments in breeches. Today Niort's biggest industry is **insurance**: the most bourgeois town in France, so it is said, because of the prosperity brought by the large number of major insurance firms making their headquarters here.

Just downstream, opposite a riverside car park, is the **market hall** (with a café doing a good cheap lunch) and, beyond, vast and unmistakeable on a slight rise, the **keep of a castle** begun by Henry II of England. Now a **museum** (summer 9am–noon & 2–6pm; closes 5pm in winter; closed Tues), it displays mainly **local furniture and costumes**, an extraordinary variety of which were still commonly worn in the villages until the beginning of the twentieth century.

Practicalities

The SI, with plenty of information to hand about the Marais, is on pl de la Poste. If you have decided to stay, there is the usual crop of **hotels** close to the station: *L'Univers*, 22 rue Mazagran, place de la Gare (☎49.24.41.70; ②); *Terminus*, 82 rue de la Gare (☎49.24.00.38; closed Sat; ④); and *Bordeaux*, 117 rue de la Gare (☎49.24.00.74; ②). The *Saint-Jean*, 21 av St-Jean (☎49.79.20.76; ①/②), is another good bet for cheap, comfortable rooms. The **station** has a convenient, if not particularly economical, **restaurant.** The three-star **camping de Noron** (☎49.79.05.06) is on bd S-Allende next door to the stadium, bus #6 from pl de la Brèche.

Transport practicalities: bicycles are for hire at the gare SNCF, and, although the maximum period of rental is three days, if you find a trustworthy machine, you could make a bike tour of the Marais – the pleasantest way to see it – within that time: it's completely flat and small enough to pretty well cover. Before setting out, pick up the collection of walking itineraries available from the SI. If you're using the buses, the **gare routière** is just off place de la Brèche on rue Viala.

The Marais

The **Marais Poitevin** is a strange, lazy landscape of fens and meadows, shielded by poplar trees and criss-crossed by an elaborate system of canals, dykes and slow-flowing rivers. Recently declared a National Park, the French know it as *La Venise Verte* – the Green Venice – and a tourist industry of sorts has been developing around the villages. This, sadly, seems destined to be the region's future. But the marshes are not yet dead, or completely phoney, and the flat-bottomed punts remain the principal means of transport for many farmers – indeed there's no dry land access to many of the fields. Be sure to avoid weekends, when the evidence of the coming transformation is all too clear.

Coulon and around the marshes

Access is easiest at the village of **COULON**, on the river Sèvre, at the eastern edge of the marsh – just 11km from NIORT, by bike or occasional bus. As you would expect in a marshland village, Coulon's houses are small, low and obviously poor. **Punts**, with or without a guide, can be hired here by the half day – touristy perhaps, but fun on a sunny day with a picnic. There are two **hotels** in the village, both likely to be full in season: the *Central*, 4 rue d'Autremont (☎49.35.90.20; closed 13 Jan–7 Feb, 22 Sept–17 Oct, Sun & Mon; ③), and the pricey *Au Marais* (☎49.25.90.43; closed Dec 22–Jan 22; ⑤). A better bet if you're **camping** is the attractively sited *Camping Venise Verte* in a meadow about 2km downstream – or a 25-minute walk – or the *camping municipal* la Niquière (☎49.35.81.19; open mid-June–mid Sept) situated north of Coulon on the road to Benet.

For **getting around** the Marais, **bicycles** are ideal. However, if you **walk**, it's best to stick to the lanes since cross-country routes tend to end in fields surrounded by water and you have to back-track continually. Once you're away from the riverside road from Coulon to ARÇAIS (10km west), there's practically no traffic, just meadows and cows. At the **seaward end of the marsh** – the area south of LUÇON – the landscape changes, becoming all straight lines and open fields of wheat and sunflowers. The villages cap low mounds that were once islands.

WESTERN POITOU: LA ROCHELLE AND THE ISLANDS

This stretch of coast, especially the **islands**, is great for young families, with miles of safe sandy beaches and shallow water. Beware, however, that in August, unless you're camping or have booked something in advance, accommodation is a near-insuperable problem. Out of season you can't rely on sunny weather, but that shouldn't deter you if you like the slightly melancholy romance of quiet misty seascapes and working fishing ports. **Nantes** in the north (covered separately in *Chapter five*, "Brittany") and **La Rochelle** and **Royan** in the south – all well served by train – are the best bases. Away from these centres you'll have to take pot luck with the rather quirky bus routes.

Les Sables d'Olonne and Les Épesses

The area around **LES SABLES-D'OLONNE** and northwards has been heavily developed with Costa-style apartment blocks. If you're passing through, though, there's a surprisingly good **modern art** section in the Musée de l'Abbaye Ste-Croix on rue Verdun (10.30–noon & 2.30–6.30pm), and an automobile museum 8km southeast of town on the road to Talmont (April–Sept 9.30am–noon & 2–7pm). Beyond these, and despite the town's clean **beach**, there seems little reason to stay. If you do, there's a **youth hostel** (July–Aug only) and municipal campsite (☎51.95.10.42; March–Oct) on rue des Roses 400m from the beach and several **campsites** in the PIRONNIÈRE district, 3km south of town on the D949. Hotels get booked up well in advance for July and August, but a couple worth trying are *Le Merle Blanc* near the beach at 59 av Aristide Briand (☎51.32.00.35; ①/②) and *Hôtel les Olonnes*, 25 rue Patrie (☎51.32.04.12; ②).

Two possible attractions which might make you want to linger longer in this part of the country are the *spectacle* that takes place at the château at **Les Épesses** every evening in the summer months and the **Île de Noirmoutier**, one of the more desirable locations on this coast.

Les Épesses: the spectacle at the Château du Puy

Some 80km inland from Les Sables (on the N160 if you're driving), at the ruined **Château du Puy du Fou** in LES ÉPESSES, a remarkable **lakeside extravaganza** is put on most nights from June to August. This is a weird affair: the enactment of the life of a local peasant from the Middle Ages to World War II, complete with fireworks, lasers, dances on the lake and *Comédie Française* voice-overs. The story, summarised in a brief English text, is interesting but incidental – the spectacle is the thing. For details ask at the the **SI** in Les Sables (rue Leclerc) or, nearer to the event, at LES HERBIERS.

To get to Les Épesses by public transport, you'll need to get to CHOLET (reasonably connected by train) and take a bus south from there; Puy du Fou itself is 2.5km from Les Épesses, on the D27 to CHAMBRETAUD. There is one reasonably priced **hotel** in Les Épesses, *Le Lion d'Or*, 2 rue de la Libération, and a wider choice (*Relais, Le Centre* or *Chez Camille*) 10km west at Les Herbiers.

The Île de Noirmoutier

The **ÎLE DE NOIRMOUTIER**, spared the high-rise development of its adjoining coast, was an early monastic settlement. It is now very much a tourist resort, and a relatively plush one: villas here are in great demand. But though this is the island's main economy, it doesn't dominate everything. Salt marshes here are still worked, spring potatoes sown and fishes fished. The island can be reached in three hours by bus from Les Sables: it's connected to the shore by a tollbridge.

The island town, **Noirmoutier-en-l'Île**, boasts a twelfth-century castle (with a couple of museums), a church with a Romanesque crypt, an excellent market (Tues & Fri) and most of the nightlife – piano bars which extend normal café hours. There are **campsites** dotted around the island – maps from the **SI** on the main road from the bridge at MARMATRE. **Bike hire** is from *Vel-hop*, 55 av Joseph-Pineau, or *Fabre*, rue du Centre, Marmatre. Among **hotels** to try in the town are *Le Bois de la Chaize*, 23 av de la Victoire, *La Marée*, 2bis Grande-Rue, or at BARBATRE in the south of the island: *La Fosse*, 57 rue de la Pointe, or *Le Marina*, 1 route du Gois.

As for exploring **around the island**, the western coast, with its great curves of sand, resembles the mainland, while the northern side dips in and out of little bays with rocky promontories between. Inland, were it not for the salt-water dykes, the horizon would suggest that you were miles from the sea. It is a strange place with only one hostile element apart from the storms in spring – a vicious mosquito population. The more southerly resorts, though built up, have not been the main targets for the developers. In the village centres there are still the one-storey houses that you see throughout La Vendée and southern Brittany – whitewashed and ochre-tiled with decorative brickwork around the windows and S- or Z-shaped coloured bars on the shutters.

La Rochelle

LA ROCHELLE is the most attractive and unspoiled seaside town in France. Thanks to the foresight of Michel Crépeau, the left-wing 1970s mayor and subsequently Mitterrand's Minister for the Environment, its historic seventeenth- to eighteenth-century centre and waterfront were plucked from the clutches of the developers and its streets freed of traffic for the delectation of pedestrians. A real shock-horror outrage at the time, the policy has become standard practice for preserving old town centres across the country – more successful than Crépeau's picturesque yellow bicycle plan, designed to relieve the traffic problem, and now somewhat watered down (see below).

La Rochelle has a long history, as you would expect of such a sheltered Atlantic port, and the inevitable English connection. Eleanor of Aquitaine gave it a charter in 1199, which released it from its feudal obligations, and it rapidly became a port of major importance, trading in salt and wine, and skilfully exploiting the Anglo-French quarrels. The Wars of Religion, however, were particularly destructive for La Rochelle. It turned Protestant and, because of its strategic importance, drew the remorseless enmity of Cardinal Richelieu, who laid siege to it in 1627. To the dismay of the townspeople, who reasoned that no one could effectively blockade seasoned mariners like themselves, he succeeded in sealing the harbour approaches with a dyke. The English dispatched the duke of Buckingham to their aid, but he was caught napping on the Île de Ré and badly defeated. By the end of 1628 Richelieu had starved the city into submission. Out of the pre-siege population of 28,000 only 5000 survived. The walls were demolished and the city's privileges revoked.

After this disastrous interlude, La Rochelle later became the principal port for trade with the French colonies in the Caribbean Antilles and Canada. Indeed, many of the settlers, especially in Canada, came from this part of France.

Arrival and accommodation

Finding your way around La Rochelle is absolutely straightforward. Everything you want to see is in the area behind the waterfront: in effect, between the **harbour** and the **place de Verdun**, about a ten-minute walk away. There is no need to bother about public transport, except for getting to the campsite or youth hostel. If you arrived at the **gare SNCF**, take **av de Gaulle** opposite to reach the town centre. On the left as you hit the waterfront, quai du Carénage, is a **free municipal bike park**, heir to Michel Crépeau's original no-identity-check, no-restrictions, pick-up-and-leave scheme.

Accommodation
Accomodation in La Rochelle can be a bit of a problem in the summer season, so book ahead wherever you're staying. Expect to pay seaside-type prices in the **hotels**, especially in season. There's a handful of cheapies in the town centre, but be sure to book in advance from May well into autumn. There's also a **youth hostel** in Port des Minimes to the west – left as you come out – of the gare SNCF (☎46.44.43.11; bus #10 from place de Verdun) and two **campsites**: *Camping Le Soleil*, by the hostel (☎46.44.42.53; open May–Sept; bus #10) and *Camping Municipal de Port-Neuf* on the northwest side of town (bus #6 from Grosse Horloge, direction Port-Neuf).

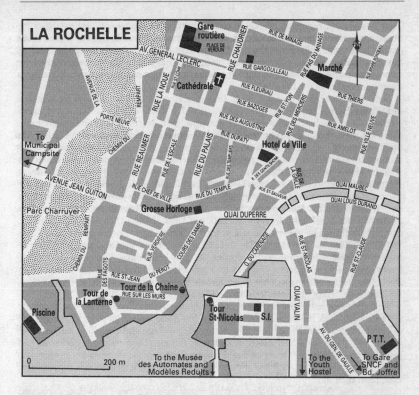

LA ROCHELLE

0   200 m

To the Musée
des Automates and
Modèles Reduits↓

To the
Youth
Hostel

To Gare
SNCF and
Bd. Joffre

Hôtel Bordeaux, 43 rue St-Nicholas (☎46.41.31.22). Comfortable, friendly hotel nicely situated between the train station and the port. ③

Hôtel Henri-IV, 31 rue des Gentilshommes (☎46.41.25.79). Excellent, very popular hotel right in the town centre. If you haven't booked don't bother trying to get in. ②

Hôtel Printania, 9 rue Brave-Rondeau (☎46.41.22.86). Pleasant, unpretentious and central. ②

Fasthotel, Village Informatique, les Minimes (☎46.45.46.00). Small quiet hotel of modern bungalows, near the port des Minimes and the beach. ③

Hôtel François-I, 15 rue Bazoges (☎46.41.28.46). Historic building with a walled courtyard. ⑤

Hôtel Atlantic, at 23 rue Verdière behind the waterfront off cours des Dames (☎46.41.16.68). Eighteenth-century ivy-clad affair with some studio apartments. ④

The town

Dominating the inner harbour, the heavy Gothic gateway of the **Porte de la Grosse Horloge** straddles the entrance to the old town. The quays in front are too full of traffic to encourage loitering. For that, it's best to head out along the tree-lined **cours des Dames** towards the fourteenth-century **Tour de la Chaine,** so called because of the heavy chain that was slung from here across to the opposite tower, **Tour St-Nicolas,** to close the harbour at night. Today the only night-time intruders are likely to be yachties from across the Channel. Their craft far outnumber the working boats – mainly garishly painted trawlers. Beyond the tower, steps climb up to **rue Sur-les-Murs,** which follows the top of the old sea wall to a third tower, the **Tour de la Lanterne** or

Tour des Quatre Sergents, named after four sergeants imprisoned and executed for defying the Restoration monarchy in 1822 (9.30am–12.30pm & 2–7pm; closed Tues except June–Aug; 18F). From the great views here there's a way up onto what's left of the **city walls**, planted with unkempt greenery. Beyond is the **beach**, backed by casino, hot dog stands and amusement booths, and a belt of park, which continues up the western edge of the town centre.

But for the real charm of the place, turn in under the Grosse Horloge on to **place des Petits-Bancs**, where you are confronted with a statue of Eugène Fromentin, nineteenth-century Rochelais painter, writer and traveller in North Africa and the Sahara. In front, the main shopping street, **rue du Palais**, stretches away to place de Verdun. On both sides are superb eighteenth-century houses, some grey stone, some half-timbered, with their woodwork protected from the weather in distinctive Rochelais style by slates overlapped like fish-scales, while the shop fronts are set back beneath the ground floor arcades. Among the finest are the **Hôtel de la Bourse** – in fact the Chamber of Commerce – and the **Palais de Justice** with its colonnaded facade, both on the left hand side. A few metres further on, in **rue des Augustins**, there is another grandiose affair built for a wealthy Rochelais in 1555, the so-called **Maison Henri II**, complete with loggia, gallery and slated turrets, where the regional tourist board has its offices. **Place de Verdun** itself is dull and characterless, with an uninspiring, hump-backed classical **cathedral** on the corner. Its only redeeming feature is the marvellously opulent Belle Époque *Café de la Paix*, all mirrors, gilt and plush, where La Rochelle's ladies of means come to sip lemon tea and nibble daintily at sticky cakes. And there is a tempting *charcuterie* and seafood shop next door.

To the west or left of rue du Palais, especially in **rue de l'Escale**, paved with granite setts brought back from Canada as ballast in the Rochelais cargo vessels, you get the discreet residences of the eighteenth-century ship-owners and chandlers, veiling their wealth with high walls and classical restraint. A rather less modest gentleman had installed himself on the corner of **rue Fromentin**: a seventeenth-century doctor who adorned his house-front with the statues of other famous medical men – Hippocrates, Galen and their ilk.

East of rue du Palais, and also starting out from place des Petits-Bancs, **rue du Temple** takes you up alongside the **Hôtel de Ville**, protected by a decorative but seriously fortified wall. It was begun around 1600 in the reign of Henri IV, whose initials, intertwined with those of Marie de Médicis, are carved on the ground floor gallery. It's a beautiful specimen of Frenchified Italian taste, adorned with niches and statues and coffered ceilings, all done in a stone the colour of ripe barley. And if you feel like quiet contemplation of these seemingly more gracious times, there's no better place for it than the terrace of the *Café de la Poste*, right next to the Post Office, in the small, traffic-free square outside. For more relaxed vernacular architecture nearly as ancient, carry on up **rue des Merciers**, the other main shopping area, to the cramped and noisy **market square**.

Museums

A number of excellent, well-sign-posted **museums** in the city provide entertainment for just about everybody. The following listings cover only a selection. If you intend to do some serious sightseeing, a 35F ticket covers the *Nouveau Monde*, the *Orbigny-Bernon* and the *Beaux-Arts*, as well as two more not listed here – the *Histoire Naturelle* and the *Musée Océanographique*).

Musée du Nouveau Monde, rue Fleuriau (Mon–Sat 10.30am–12.30pm & 1.30–6pm, Sun 3–6pm; closed Tues; 12F). Out of the ordinary, this occupies the former residence of the Fleuriau family, rich shipowners and traders, who, like many of their fellow-Rochelais, made fortunes out of the slave trade and Caribbean sugar, spices and coffee. There is a fine collection of prints, paintings and photos of the old West Indian plantations; seventeenth- and eighteenth-century maps of America;

photogravures of Native Americans from around 1900, with incredible names like Piopio Maksmaks Wallawalla and Lawyer Nez Percé; and an interesting display of aquatint illustrations for Marmontel's novel *Les Incas* – an amazing mixture of sentimentality and coy salaciousness.

Musée d'Orbigny-Bernon, 2 rue St-Côme (10–noon & 2–6pm; closed Sun am & Tues; 12F). Consists mainly of a collection of local ceramics.

Musée des Beaux-Arts, rue Gargoulleau (2–5/6pm, winter till 5pm; closed Tues; 12F). Exhibition centred around a few Rochelais artists, illustrating the history of art from the Primitives to the present day.

Musée des Automates, rue de la Desirée, La Ville en Bois (June–Aug 9.30am–6pm; rest of the year, 10am–noon & 2–6.30pm; 30F, under-10s 15F). Highly recommended for children and adults alike. A collection of 300 automated puppets draws you into an irresistible fantasy world. Some of the puppets are interesting from an historical angle; others, like one which writes the name "Pierrot", are interesting from a mechanical viewpoint.

Musée des Modèles Réduits, rue de la Desirée, La Ville en Bois (same hours & prices as the *Automates*, joint ticket for both museums 50F, under-10s 25F). The prices may be a bit prohibitive for families – especially considering the whole tour takes barely half an hour – but this does combine well with a visit to the neighbouring Musée des Automates. Scale models of every variety and era, starting in typical French fashion with cars and including models of a submerged shipwreck and La Rochelle train station.

Aquarium, port des Minimes, near the youth hostel (June 9am–7pm, July & Aug 9am–11pm, Sept– May 10–noon & 2–7pm). One of the largest aquariums in France with species from around the world. Emphasis on hi-tech display.

Musée Maritime Bassin des Chalutiers (10am–6.30pm; 33F). An entire frigate, *France I*, kitted out to give you some idea of the realities of ocean life.

Eating, nightlife and practicalities

For **eating**, try the rue du Port/rue St-Sauveur area just off the waterfront, or else rue St-Nicolas or rue St-Jean (which has everything from crêperies and pizzerias to expensive fish restaurants).

Pub Lutèce, rue St-Sauveur. Reasonably priced *brasserie*.

Café-Resto à la Villette, behind the market. Good *plats du jour*.

L'Ouvreboîte, rue Verdière, opposite the *Atlantic* hotel. Good selection of fish options and *menus* starting at 52F.

La Datcha, rue St-Jean. Serves a mixture of Turkish, Greek and French food in bright, pleasant surroundings.

Le Coquelicot, 2 rue du Collège (closed Sun). Offers a slightly more expensive evening with live folk-singing.

Nightlife

For **nightlife**, rue des Templiers is promising, with a couple of good late-night music bars: the *Piano Pub* and the *Mayflower*. Nightclubs include *L'Oxford*, plage de la Concurrence, and *Le Triolet*, 8 rue des Carmes.

Listings

Ambulances *Ambulance Atlantique* 71 bd Joffre (☎46.27.25.19)

Bike hire at the gare SNCF, from M Salaün-Benard, 3 place de la Solette on the left bank of the canal, from *Dock Moto*, bd Émile-Delmas near the bridge to the Île de Ré, and from *Vel'Oxygène*, 29 bd de la République (☎46.56.07.58) – not forgetting the municipal bike pound on quai du Carénage.

Boat trips around La Rochelle and to neighbouring islands, organised by *Océcars*, 14 cours des Dames (☎46.41.78.95).

Car Hire *Ada/Budget*, 1 av Général-de-Gaulle, *Citer Sorda*, 99 bd Cognehors, *Locarwest*, 14 quai Georgette, *Tonic Car*, 16 quai Georges-Simenon.

CDIJ Youth Centre 14 rue des Gentilshommes has an information service, including *Allostop*, for young people.

Emergencies Centre Hospitalier ☎46.27.33.33; Police ☎17; lost children ☎92.83.63.19.

Festivals July, *"Francofolies"*, music festival takes place in selected venues and in the streets. June–July, international film festival.

Gare routière, pl de Verdun. For certain destinations you'll need to use to use other terminals. *Citram*, pl de Verdun, run to Angoulême, Saintes, Cognac, St-Jean-d'Angeley and Rochefort; *Océcars*, pl de Verdun, & 44 cours des Dames, is more local, serving the coastal towns and villages.

Horse riding Ferme St-Mathurin, La Jarne (direction Surgères) (☎46.44.32.34).

SI, quai de Gabut, excellent free maps and hotel information, open June–Sept Mon–Sat 9am–8pm, Oct–May Mon–Sat 9am–12.30pm & 2.30–6pm.

Walking The regional tourist board produce a pamphlet called *Promenades à Pied en Charente-Maritime*, covering the Île de Ré, Île d'Oléron, Brouage, Rochefort and Saintonge.

The Île de Ré

A half-hour drive from La Rochelle, the **ÎLE DE RÉ** is a low, narrow island some 30km long, fringed by sandy beaches to the southwest and salt marshes and oyster beds to the northeast. The central districts are a motley mix of small-scale vine, asparagus and wheat cultivation. All the buildings on Ré, restricted to two storeys, are required to incorporate the typical local features of whitewashed walls, curly orange tiles and green-painted shutters which give the island villages a southerly holiday atmosphere.

Out of season the island has a slow, misty charm, and life in its little ports revolves exclusively around the cultivation of oysters and mussels. In season, though, it's extraordinarily crowded, with upwards of 400,000 visitors passing through. The crowds mainly head for the southern beaches; those to the northeast are covered in rocks and seaweed, and the sea is too shallow for bathing.

ST-MARTIN, the island's capital, is an atmospheric fishing port with whitewashed houses clustered around the stone quays of a well-protected harbour. Trawlers and flat-bottomed oyster boats, piled high with cage-like devices used for "growing" oysters, slip out every morning on the muddy tide. The quayside *Café Boucquingam* recalls the military adventures of the duke of Buckingham. To the east of the harbour, you can walk along the almost perfectly preserved **fortifications** – redesigned by Vauban, after Buckingham's attentions – to the citadel, long used as a prison. It was from here that the *bagnards* – prisoners sentenced to hard labour on Devil's Island in Guyana or New Caledonia in the Pacific – set out. Most did not return. One who eventually did was the notorious *Papillon*.

Getting there

The island is connected to the mainland at **La Pallice**, a suburb of La Rochelle, by a 3km-long toll bridge constructed in 1988 (82F per car). *Rébuses* run by *Aunis & Saintonge* leave from pl Verdun, passing *Grosse Horloge* and the train station every hour (62F return), but the timetable can be awkward if you want to tour the island. It's probably best to take all day and do this by bike. **LA PALLICE** was a big commercial port with important shipyards. Although it still serves as a naval base, times have changed. As you ride by in the bus, you notice some colossal weather-stained concrete sheds, submarine pens built by the Germans to service their Atlantic U-boat fleet during World War II. Too difficult to demolish, they are still in use.

As an alternative to the toll bridge connection, *Interiles*, 14 cours des Dames, also run a bus and boat service to SABLONCEAUX on Ré (70F return), and combine trips to the Îles de Ré and Oléron.

Once on Ré, **bikes and motorbikes** are for hire all over the island, the former in the Sablanceaux bus depot and from *Cyclo-Surf Location* at 14 rue Henri-Lainé, LA FLOTTE; Clos Vauban, av V-Bouthillier, ST MARTIN; and 2 rte Joachim, LA COUARDE.

Accommodation and restaurants

Hotels and **campsites** are plentiful in all the island villages, though obviously packed to the gills through July and August. The following, located in various villages across the island, are the most reasonably priced. *Le Sénéchal*, 6 rue Gambetta, ARS-EN-RÉ (☎46.29.40.42; ②); *Hôtel de l'Océan*, 4 rue St-Martin, LE-BOIS-PLAGE (☎46.09.23.07; ③); and *L'Hippocampe*, 16 rue du Château-des-Mauléons (☎46.09.60.68; ①), and *Le Français*, 1 quai de Sénac, both in **la Flotte** (46.09.60.06; closed mid-Nov–mid-March).

There are even more **campsites** on the island than there are hotels, and it shouldn't be difficult finding a place except perhaps in desirable locations near the southern beaches at the height of the rush. A few names, if you want to advance-book, are the 3* *Camping du Soleil* in ARS (☎46.29.40.62); 2* *Les Pins*, route de la Blanche; *Le Bois Plage* (☎46.09.35.45) and 3* *L'Océan*, La Passe in LA COUARDE (☎46.29.87.70; Easter–Sept).

Good-value **food** is available on the quayside in St Martin at *Les Remparts*, 4 quai Daniel-Rivaille, which has a piano-bar upstairs; from *La Salicorne*, 16 rue de l'Olivette, in la Couarde, which has a high standard of cuisine starting at 85F for lunchtime menus, and from *Le Bistrot de Bernard*, 23 rue de l'Église in Le Bois Plage.

Fouras and the Île d'Aix

The tiny **Île d'Aix**, where Napoléon spent his last days in Europe, is a good trip. **Fouras**, on the other hand – the embarkation point for it, some 30km south of La Rochelle – is a dull town, redeemed by a clutch of popular beaches and the **presqu'île**, the peninsula which extends 3km out to sea from the town centre, terminating at the ferry dock, **Pointe de la Fumée**. The finger of land is hemmed by sea-dashed **fortresses** – originally intended to protect the Charente, and particularly La Rochelle, against Norman attack – which were later employed against Dutch invasions in the seventeenth century and English in the eighteenth. The peninsula is bordered by **oyster beds**, and off its westernmost tip at low tide can be seen the *bouchots à moules*, lines of mussel-encrusted stumps. At high tide this is a popular place from which to fish for *crevettes* – shrimp.

Fouras practicalities

Fouras' **SI** is situated in the fifteenth- to seventeenth-century Fort Vauban, which also houses a small local **maritime museum**. The esplanade of the fort (mid-June to mid-Sept Tues & Fri am only) offers a magnificent panorama of neighbouring forts and islands. As for places to stay, Fouras has a posse of overpriced **hotels**, the exception being an excellent establishment behind the gare routière, the *Hôtel Continental* at 9 av Lucien-Lamoureux (☎46.84.58.38; ②). There are also three **campsites** around the town: the *Fumée* (☎46.84.26.77) near the ferry port; the *L'Esperance* off av Philippe-Jannet (☎46.84.24.18); and the 2* *Cadoret* near to plage Nord, on av du Cadoret (☎46.84.02.84). The best-value **food** in town is probably from *Jetée* at Pointe de la Fumée (closed in Jan), serving excellent seafood at affordable prices.

The island

Less frequented than the bigger islands, **l'Île d'Aix** is small enough – just 2km long – to be walked around in about three hours, giving a greater sense of its island status than is felt on Ré. **Access** is by frequent ferry (half hourly in season) from Pointe de la Fumée (☎46.41.76.24), or with *Interîles* from La Rochelle (May–Sept 2–4 times daily). The only **hotel** on the island is the *Napoléon*, rue Gourgard (☎46.84.66.02; ③), and there's also a 2* campsite, the *Fort de la Rade* (☎46.84.50.64).

The crescent-shaped island is well defended with a pair of forts and ramparts around its southern tip. The island, and particularly Fort Liédot, served as a prison for members of the Paris Commune and later held Russian prisoners in the Crimean and First World wars. There's a **museum** (Thurs–Tues 10am–noon & 2–6pm) situated in the house constructed to Napoléon's orders and inhabited by him in 1815. Extensive displays fill ten rooms with the emperor's works of art, clothing, portraits and arms. The white dromedary from which he conducted his Egyptian campaign is lodged nearby in the **Musée Africain**, which houses an entire collection of African wildlife.

Rochefort to the Île d'Oléron

With the exception of Rochefort, which has regular **train** connections with La Rochelle, you may find the simplest solution to travelling along this whole section of coast is **hitching**. Many of the towns, however, are also served by the Aunis and Saintonge **buses**. Unless you have your own transport, however, ROCHEFORT is a useless base for nearby Royan or the Île d'Oléron. Bus times are inconvenient and buses to Oléron generally involve a wait at BOUCREFRANC.

Rochefort

ROCHEFORT dates from the seventeenth century. It was created by Colbert, Louis XIII's navy minister, as a naval base to protect the coast from English raids. Built on a grid plan with regular ranks of identical houses, the town may be a joy to the military mind or to a new town planner, but if you're looking for hidden back alleyways or irregular architecture you'll be disappointed.

The sights
If you have a taste for the bizarre, then there's one good reason for visiting Rochefort – the house of the novelist Julien Viaud, alias **Pierre Loti**. Forty years a naval officer, he wrote numerous best-selling romances with exotic oriental settings and characters, and revealed his immense vanity by refusing to marry any woman taller than himself.

The house at 141 rue Pierre-Loti (July–Sept closed Sun am; tours at 10 & 11am and on the hour from 2–5pm, Wed & Thurs at 8.30pm; Oct–June closed Sun & Tues; no tours at 5pm or 8.30pm; 30F) is part of a row of modestly proportioned grey stone houses, outwardly a model of petty-bourgeois conformity and respectability. The experience has been dimmed somewhat by the introduction of the obligatory **guided tours**, and if you don't want to be herded in a large group through claustrophobically small rooms while someone reads you an interminable commentary in French you might decide to give it a miss, but that would be a pity: once inside, surprise heaps on surprise. Typical rooms are a medieval banqueting hall complete with Gothic fireplace and Gobelin tapestries, a monastery refectory with windows pinched from a ruined abbey, a Damascus mosque; a Turkish room, with kilim wall-hangings and a ceiling made from an Alhambra mould. To suit the mood of the place, Loti used to throw extravagant parties: a medieval banquet with swan's meat and hedgehog and a *fête chinoise* with the guests in costumes he had brought back from China where he took part in the suppression of the Boxer rebellion.

A possible rainy hour's worth of museum is the **Centre International de la Mer**, (every day 10am–6/7pm; July & Aug 10am–10pm) situated in the **Corderie Royale**, or the royal ropeworks, off rue Toufaire. At 372m the Corderie is the longest building in France, and a rare example of seventeenth-century industrial architecture, substantially restored after damage in World War II. From 1660 until the Revolution, the Corderie Royale furnished the entire French navy with **rope**, and the building now houses an exhibition on ropes and rope-making, including machinery from the nineteenth century.

Lastly, the **Musée de la Marine**, pl de la Gallossinnière (10am–noon & 2–6pm; closed Tues), houses an excellent collection of model ships, figureheads, navigational instruments and other naval paraphernalia.

Practicalities

Should you want to **stay**, hotels need to be booked in advance to ensure reasonably priced accommodation. The **SI**, which should be able to help if you haven't done so, is off rue du Dr-Pelletier, near the **gare routière** .

There's a small youth hostel at 20 rue de la République (☎46.99.74.62), but the cheapest hotel rooms are at *Les Messageries*, pl de la Gare (☎46.99.00.90; ②). Otherwise, the *Hôtel de France*, at 55 rue du Dr-Pelletier (☎46.99.34.00; ②) – left out of the gare routière – also has some cheap rooms, as does the extremely comfortable *Caravelle*, 34 rue Jaurès, off av de-Gaulle (☎46.99.02.53; ③), which leads to the naval museum from directly opposite the gare routière, and the *Colbert*, 23 rue A.-de-Puyravault (☎46.99.08.28; ③, singles from ①), left out of the gare routière and third right, opposite the post office .

The **camping municipal** (☎46.99.14.33) is a long haul if you've arrived at the **gare SNCF**. Take av du Président-Wilson and keep going straight, until you reach the bottom of rue Toufaire, where you turn right, then left – about half an hour all the way.

For inexpensive **meals**, either the *Self-Service* by the Arsenal on rue Toufaire, or *l'Étalon*, also on rue Toufaire, is adequate and convenient, and there's a good Chinese, *L'Asie*, on the same street at no. 45. The *Pub Keaton* on pl Colbert serves good beer.

Brouage, Marennes and the oysterbeds

Eighteen kilometres southwest of Rochefort, **BROUAGE** is another seventeenth-century military base, this time created by Richelieu after the siege of La Rochelle. It's surrounded by salt marshes, now reclaimed and transformed into meadows grazed by white Charolais cattle and intersected by dozens of reed-filled drainage ditches where herons watch and yellow flag blooms. It's a strangely beautiful landscape with huge skies specked with wheeling buzzards and kestrels.

To reach it, leave Rochefort by the D733 to ROYAN, which crosses the Charente river near the disused **Pont Transbordeur**, a great iron gantry with a raft-like platform suspended on hawsers, on which a dozen cars were loaded and floated across the river – a technological wonder in its time. There, either turn right for SOUBISE and MOEZE or go on to ST-AGNANT. Flat as a pancake, this is good cycling and walking country.

The way into Brouage is through the **Porte Royale** in the north wall of the totally intact fortifications. Locked within its 400m square, it seems abandoned and somnolent. Even the sea has retreated, and all that's left of the harbour are the partly freshwater pools or *claires* where oysters are fattened in the last stage of their rearing.

Within the walls, the streets are laid out on a grid pattern, lined with low two-storey houses. On the second cross street to the right is a memorial to **Samuel de Champlain,** the local boy who founded the French colony of Québec in 1608. In the same century Brouage also witnessed the last painful pangs of a **royal romance**. Here, Cardinal Mazarin, successor to Richelieu, locked up his daughter, **Marie Mancini**, to keep her from her youthful sweetheart, the Sun King, **Louis XIV**. Geopolitics of the time made the Infanta of Spain a more suitable consort for the king of France than his daughter – in his own judgement. Louis gave in, while Marie pined and sighed on the walls of Brouage. Returning from his marriage in St-Jean-de-Luz, Louis dodged his escort and stole away to see her. Finding her gone, he slept in her room and paced the walls in her footsteps.

Half a dozen kilometres south, on a narrow, drier spit of land, past the graceful eighteenth-century **Château de la Gataudière** (built by the man who introduced rubber to France), you come to the village of **MARENNES**. This is the centre of **oyster production** for an area which supplies over 60 percent of France's requirements. If you want to visit the oysterbeds, and see how the business works, you can do so here; just ask any of the local SIs. For **accommodation** in the village, there's a **youth hostel** (☎46.85.22.78; open July and Aug only) and the very agreeable and inexpensive *Hôtel du Commerce*, with a restaurant, on rue de la République (☎46.85.00.09, ②).

OYSTERS

Marennes' speciality is fattening the **oysters** known as *creuses* – the other, tastier, type being the *plates*. It's a lucrative but precarious business, extremely vulnerable to storm damage, changes of temperature or salinity, the ravages of starfish and umpteen other improbable natural disasters.

Oysters begin life as minuscule larvae, which are "born" about three times a year. When a "birth" happens, the oystermen are alerted by a special radio service, and they all rush out to place their "collectors" – usually arrangements of roofing tiles – for the larvae to cling to. There the immature oysters remain for eight or nine months, after which they are scraped off and moved to *parcs* in the tidal waters of the sea, sometimes covered, sometimes uncovered. Their last move is to the *claires* – shallow rectangular pools where they are kept permanently covered by water less salty than normal sea water. Here they fatten up, and acquire the greenish colour the market expects. With "improved" modern oysters, the whole cycle takes about two years, as opposed to four or five with the old varieties.

The Île d'Oléron

The **ÎLE D'OLÉRON** is France's largest island after Corsica. It's up the road from Marennes, joined to the mainland by a toll bridge. Buses from Rochefort are awkward, changing at SAINTES or BOUCREFRANC. It's easier to go direct from Saintes, from where there are several *Citram* buses daily, stopping on the island at LE CHÂTEAU, DOLUS, ST-PIERRE, LA BRÉE and ST-DENIS.

Flat and more wooded than the Île de Ré, with extensive pine woods at BOYARDVILLE and ST-TROJAN, Oléron has miles of beautiful **sandy beaches**, though the water tends to be shallow on the east coast facing the mainland. The best beaches are to the northeast, at LA BRÉE-LES-BAINS. Most of the little towns, inevitably, have been ruined by the development of hundreds of holiday homes – and it can be a real battle in the summer season to find a place to stay.

The **island interior** is pretty and distinctive. Waterways wind right into the land, their gleaming muddy banks overhung by round fishing nets suspended from ranks of piers. There are so many oyster *claires* that, from above, the island must look like an Afghan mirrored cushion. The stretch from Boyardville to ST-PIERRE, with its pines, tamarisks and woods of evergreen oak, is the most attractive and St-Pierre is the best of the towns. Boyardville has no interest except for the ranks of *bouchots* – stakes for growing mussels – along the shore. It's tempting to help yourself, but these are private property and you'll be in trouble if someone sees you.

The island's most interesting attraction is the **bird park** of *Le Marais aux Oiseaux*, situated off the D126 between St-Pierre and Dolus (June–Aug 10am–8pm; April–Nov 10am–noon & 2pm–dusk). It was originally established as a hospital for injured birds found in the wild, but has been developed as a breeding centre and was opened to the public to further the interest in rare species. From 300 to 400 species of birds are given the freedom of twenty hectares of beautiful countryside, while sixty species are caged for observation alongside public walkways.

Practicalities

The main town in the south of the island, **LE CHÂTEAU**, named after the citadel still standing, thrives on its traditional oyster farming and boat building. The **SI** is on pl de la République, the location of a **market** every morning, and of a couple of cheap **restaurants**. **Bike hire** is from *Lacellerie Michel*, rue Maréchal-Foch. The chief town in the north is **ST-PIERRE**, whose SI is on pl Gambetta. Cycles are available from *Lespagnol*, rue de la République, and there are a couple of **supermarkets** on av Général-Leclerc.

Cheap **accommodation** on the Île d'Olérion is at *Les Tamaris* in the port of St-Denis (☎46.47.86.04; closed Oct–mid-March; ②) and at *Hôtel de la Petite Plage à Domino*, rue de l'Ocean, Saint-Georges (☎46.76.52.28; ③). There are **campsites** all over the island. At La Brée, where the best beaches are located, the 2* site is *Pertuis d'Antioche* (☎46.47.92.00), situated 150m from the beach off the D273. Also on the east coast, *Signol* at Boyardville (☎46.47.01.22; 3*) is pleasantly sited near pine forests.

Royan and the Gironde

Before World War II, **ROYAN**, at the mouth of the Gironde, was a fashionable resort for the bourgeoisie. It is still popular though no longer exclusive, and the modern town has lost its elegance to the dreary rationalism of 1950s town planning: broad boulevards, car parks, shopping centres, planned greenery. Ironically, the occasion for this planners' romp was provided by Allied bombing, an attempt to dislodge a large contingent of German troops who had withdrawn into the area after the D-Day landings. But the **beaches**, the most elegant and fashionable of which has long been **Pontaillac** to the northwest, are beautiful: fine pale sand, meticulously harrowed and raked near town, and wild, pine-backed and pounded by the Atlantic to the north.

There is one sight worth seeing in Royan – the 1950s **Église Notre-Dame** designed by Gillet and Hébrard, in a tatty square behind the main waterfront. Though the concrete has weathered badly, the overall effect is dramatic and surprising. Tall V-sectioned columns give the outside the appearance of massive fluting with a stepped roof-line rising dramatically to culminate in a 65m belltower like the prow of a giant vessel. The **interior** is even more striking. Using uncompromisingly modern materials and designs, the architects have succeeded in out-Gothicking Gothic. The **stained glass** panels, in each of which a different tone predominates, borrow their colours from the local seascapes – oyster, sea, mist and murk – before a sudden explosion of colour in the Christ-figure above the altar.

The most attractive area in Royan is around **Boulevard Garnier** (leading southeast from Rond-Pointe-de-la Poste along the beach), which once housed Parisian high society in their purpose-built Belle Époque-style holiday villas. Some of these have survived, including *Le Rêve*, 58 bd Garnier, where **Emile Zola** lived and wrote, and *Kosiki*, 100 av du Parc (running parallel to bd Garnier), a nineteenth-century folly of Japanese inspiration, and *Tanagra*, 34 av du Parc, whose facade is covered in sculptures and balconies.

Practicalities

The **SI** and **PTT** are close to the Rond-Point-de-la-Poste at the east end of the seafront; **gare routière** and **gare SNCF** are in the nearby cours de l'Europe. **Bike hire** is from the SNCF, the bike shops in bd de Lattre-de-Tassigny near the station, or 37 cours de l'Europe; and car hire is from *Budget-Milleville*, bd Albert-1er and *Automobiles 17*, rue Lavoisier.

Accommodation in Royan is expensive and, in season, in short supply. Your best bet would be to camp up the coast to the north or visit for the day from Saintes or Rochefort. Cheaper **hotels** if you're booking ahead are: *Les Mouettes*, 60 bd de Lattre-de-Tassigny (☎46.05.03.68; mid-June to mid-Sept; ②), right off pl de la Gare, in front of the station; *Nouvel Hôtel de la Plage*, 18 av de Cognac (☎46.39.00.18; ②), off Pontaillac beach to the west of town – frequent *Aunis & Saintonge* buses from the train station via pl Charles-de-Gaulle; and the *Hôtel du Centre*, 88 bd Aristide-Briand (☎46.05.29.00; ③), off pl Charles-de-Gaulle. Alternatively, 3km southeast of Royan, in SAINT-GEORGES-DE-DIDONNE, there's an excellent little hotel, the *Colinette*, 16 av de la Grande-Plage (☎46.05,15,75; ②), situated in pleasant surroundings 100m from the sea.

There are a number of **campsites** in the region and around Royan itself, including the *Clairefontaine* (☎46.39.08.11; June–Sept), a fairly pricey 4* site at av Louise, allée des Peupliers, PONTAILLAC, and the municipal *La Triloterie* (☎46.05.26.91) off av d'Aquitaine – the road to Bordeaux.

As for **food**, good-value *menus* are to be found at the *Relais de la Mairie*, 1 rue du Chay, and from *Le Chalet*, 6 bd de la Grandière, which serves imaginative seafood dishes reasonably cheaply. Several **crêperies**, **pizzerias** and **snack bars** are situated on Front de Mer, the street leading from the SI to the beach and Port-de-Plaisance. Otherwise there's a large covered **market**, the *Marché Central*, situated at the end of bd A-Briand, open every day (except Mon out of season), but particularly crowded and lively on Wednesday and Sunday mornings.

Nightlife is fairly restricted considering the size of Royan: there's a disco, *Tropicana*, and a jazz bar at Plage de Pontaillac, and a piano bar, *Le Mylord*, and jazz bar, *le Yachtman*, at Voûtes-de-Port .

Out of Royan: cruises, the zoo and Talmont

Various **cruises** are organised from Royan in season, including one to the **Cordouan lighthouse** commanding the mouth of the Gironde, first erected by the Black Prince. There's a twenty-minute **ferry** crossing to the Pointe de Grave, whence a **bicycle trail** and the GR8 head down the coast through the pines and dunes to the bay of Arcachon.

It's worth knowing about the **zoo park** in **PALMYRE**, 10km northwest of Royan up the D25 coast road, especially if you're travelling with children. Exotic species – including wild cats, gorrillas and monkeys – are housed in enclosures covering ten hectares. To reach it there are buses all day from Royan gare routière and pl de-Gaulle.

An ideal bicycle/picnic excursion – just over an hour's ride from Royan – is to **TALMONT**, 16km up the Gironde on the GR360. Apart from a few ups and downs through the woods outside Royan, it is all level. Talmont's twelfth-century **church** stands at the edge of a cliff above the Gironde, with the low-crouching village clustered about. With gabled transepts, a squat tower, an apse simply but elegantly decorated with blind arcading – all in weathered tawny stone, and pocked like a sponge – it stands magnificently, in sun or cloud, against the forlorn browny-grey seascapes typical of the Gironde. Entrance is through the north transept, where the rings of carving in the arched doorway depict acrobats standing on each other's shoulders and, in the outer braid, two tug-of-war teams hauling roped lions up the arch. The inside is as unpretentiously beautiful as the exterior.

AQUITAINE

In Roman times, **Bordeaux** was capital of the province of *Aquitania Secunda*. With the marriage of Eleanor of Aquitaine and King Henry II of England in 1152, it quickly became the principal English foothold for their three-hundred-year Aquitanian adventure, and it was to their presence, and particularly their taste for its red wines, that the region owed its first great economic boom. The second boom, which financed the spacious **eighteenth-century centre** of Bordeaux, and which is still visible today, came with the expansion of colonial trade in the eighteenth century.

The surrounding countryside is not the most enticing. The **vineyards** are mainly flat and monotonous: you go for the wines, not the scenery. More interesting is the vast pine-covered expanse of **les landes** and the huge wild Atlantic beaches of the **Côte d'Argent**. But it is not a landscape that charms. Its appeal, like desert, is more in its size and uniqueness – and you definitely need your own transport to explore it.

Bordeaux

The city of **BORDEAUX** is something of a disappointment for a casual visitor. It's big, with a population of over half a million, and obviously rich, yet the only part you could call attractive is the relatively small eighteenth-century centre, paid for by the expansion of colonial trade. The rest is scruffy and, even with its long history, contains far fewer sights than many a lesser place. But if you're just passing through – it's the main regional transport centre – there are a couple of sights worth checking out, and plenty of cheap places to sleep and eat.

Arrival and accommodation

Arriving by train, you'll find yourself at the **gare St-Jean**, the heart of a somewhat insalubrious area, half an hour's walk south of the city centre (and off our map to the bottom right); buses #7 or #8 will save you the hike. Tickets are available on the buses, but it's cheaper to buy a *carnet* of ten from a *tabac*. You must punch your ticket on the bus; then it is valid for half an hour, even if you change bus and direction. The **gare routière** is just a short walk north of the centre on rue Fondaudège near place Tourny. The **SI**, 12 cours du 30-juillet (June–Aug Mon–Sat 9am–8pm, Sun 9am–3pm; Oct–May Mon–Sat 9am–6.30pm), has loads of useful information on the city and the surrounding vineyards.

Accommodation

The area right by the station, particularly rue Charles-Domercq and cours de la Marne, is full of one- and two-star hotels, reasonably priced but no great treat to stay at. The hotels listed below are either in the city centre itself or in the quieter neighbourhood around the gare routière.

Hôtel Huguerie, 67 rue Huguerie (☎56.81.23.69; ①). Just about the cheapest hotel in Bordeaux, right next door to the gare routière.

Hôtel de la Boétie, 4 rue de la Boétie (☎56.81.76.68; ②). Surprisingly cheap for such a central location, on a quiet street near the Musée des Beaux-Arts.

Hôtel du Centre, 8 rue du Temple (☎56.48.13.29; ③). Still very central, and with breakfast thrown in for free.

Dauphin, 82 rue du Palais-Gallien (☎56.52.24.62; ③). Situated near the gare routière and the *palais*, so not too far from the action.

Hôtel Etche-Ona, 11 rue Mautrec (☎56.44.36.49; ⑤). Very central location, and at the cheaper end of the luxury bracket.

YOUTH HOSTELS AND CAMPSITES

Auberge de Jeunesse, 22 cours Barbey (☎56.91.59.51; curfew 11pm; IYHF card not necessary). Situated off cours de la Marne (400m off the edge of our map); from gare St-Jean it's 15 minutes' walk or take bus #7 or #8.

Maison des Étudiantes, 50 rue Ligier (☎56.96.48.30; no curfew). Women-only from October to June, it will also accept men in July and August.

Camping les Gravières, Pont-de-la-Maye, Villeneuve-d'Ornon (☎56.87.00.36). A 3* site, 8km south of gare St-Jean, in a forest by the River Garonne. Take bus B from pl de la Victoire.

BORDEAUX

The city

Bus #7 or #8 from the train station will take you as far as place Gambetta (see below), but it's more fun to get off at place de la Victoire, near the **Porte d'Aquitaine**, and explore the run-down area to the northeast of the *porte*. A short way up rue Ste-Catherine, you come to cours Victor-Hugo in the middle of which is a heavy Gothic tower, the **Grosse Cloche**, originally part of the medieval town hall. A largely North African market sets up in the streets around here on Sundays. The tall landmark to the east is the **Église St-Michel**, or rather the colossal 114-metre tower which stands in front of it – there's no reason to give either a closer inspection. Instead, backtrack and walk north up **rue Ste-Catherine**, clean, modern, partially pedestrianised and the city's main shopping street.

This is the beginning of the elegant, eighteenth-century city, especially the **quartier St-Pierre**, to the right towards the river. Much of this area has been done up in the last ten years, though some streets remain incongruously seedy. Particularly pleasing are **place du Parlement** and **place St-Pierre**, both lined with typical *Bordelais* mansions, all tastefully renovated and peppered with wrought-iron balconies. Much more imposing is **place de la Bourse** with the old customs house and stock exchange looking out over the quayside. Further south down the riverbank is the fifteenth-century **Porte Cailhau**, so named for the stones (*caillou – cailhau* in dialect) unloaded on the neighbouring quay to be used as ballast for boats. Apart from a few sleazy bars, the once-impressive quayside is little more than a noisy six-lane freeway now. A little further to the south, only the **Pont de Pierre** – "Stone Bridge", though in fact it's brick – built at Napoléon's command during the Spanish campaigns, with seventeen arches in honour of his victories, testifies to a nobler past.

The real hub of the eighteenth-century city was the impeccably classical **Grand Théâtre** on place de la Comédie at the northern end of rue Ste-Catherine. Built in 1780 by the architect Victor Louis, it is faced with an immense colonnaded portico topped by Muses and Graces. Smart streets radiate from here. The sandy, tree-lined **allées de Tourny** leads to a statue of Claude Boucher, Marquis of Tourny – the eighteenth-century administrator who was prime mover of the city's "Golden Age".

North of the Grand Théâtre, cours du 30-juillet leads into the bare gravelly expanse of the **Esplanade des Quinconces**, said to be Europe's largest municipal square. At the quayside end are two tall columns, erected in 1829, and topped by allegorical statues of Commerce and Navigation; at the opposite end of the *esplanade* is the **Monument aux Girondins**, a glorious *fin-de-siècle* ensemble of statues and fountains built in honour of the influential local deputies to the 1789 Revolutionary Assembly, later purged by Robespierre as moderates and counter-revolutionaries. During the last war, in a fit of anti-French spite, the occupying Germans made plans to melt the monument down, only to be foiled by the local Resistance, who got there first and, under cover of darkness, dismantled it piece by piece and hid it in a barn in the Médoc for the duration of the war.

To the northwest, and a welcome relief, is the **Jardin Public** (summer 7am–9pm; winter 7am–6pm), containing the city's botanical gardens and, further west still, the dilapidated third-century amphitheatre, **Palais Gallien** – all that remains of *Burdigala*, Aquitaine's Roman capital.

Place Gambetta, the cathedral and the Centre Mériadeck

Cours de l'Intendance, a street lined with chic shops, links place de la Comédie with café-lined **place Gambetta**, a pivotal square for the city's museums, shops and the cathedral. Once a majestic space, conceived as an architectural whole in the time of Louis XV, pl Gambetta's house fronts, arcaded at street level, are decorated with rows of carved masks, and, in the middle, a so-called English garden soaks up some of the traffic fumes. The guillotine lopped 300 heads here at the time of the Revolution. In one corner stands the eighteenth-century arch of the **Porte Dijeaux**.

South of place Gambetta is the **Cathédrale St-André**, whose most eye-catching feature is the great upward sweep of the twin steeples over the north transept, an effect that is heightened by the adjacent but separate *campanile*, the fifteenth-century **Tour Pey-Berland**. The interior of the cathedral is not particularly interesting, apart from the choir, which is one of the few complete examples of the florid late-Gothic style, known as *Rayonnant*, and there's some fine carving in the north transept door and the Porte Royale to the right. The surrounding square, **place Pey-Berland**, is attractive with enticing pavement cafés like the old-fashioned *Musée* on the south side, and another on the west by the classical Hôtel de Ville. To the west is Bordeaux's acknowledgement of twentieth-century architectural fashions, the **Centre Mériadeck**. Herald of a brighter future to some *Bordelais*, and a carbuncle to others, it delivers its streets to the automobile and elevates its humans to mid-air plazas and walkways. Despite some interesting shapes and textures, it's not user-friendly, and your most likely welcome will be an embrace around the legs by yesterday's windblown newspaper.

The museums

The city's main museums are clustered around the cathedral. A handsome eighteenth-century house in rue Bouffard, the Hôtel de Lalande, houses the **Musée des Arts Décoratifs** (2–6pm; closed Tues; 15F, free Wed). The collections include some beautiful, mainly French, porcelain and *faïence*, period furniture, glass, miniatures, Barye animal sculptures and prints of the city in its maritime heyday. Just around the corner on cours d'Albret, the **Musée des Beaux-Arts** (10am–noon & 2–6pm; closed Tues; 15F, free Wed) has a small and worthy collection of Perugino, Veronese, Delacroix, Rubens, Matisse, Marquet (a native of the city) as well as Kokoshka's superb painting of the city's cathedral. Smaller still is the Resistance museum and archive, the **Centre Jean-Moulin** (Mon–Fri 2–6pm), one of the most comprehensive of its type in the country.

Best of the city's museums, though, is the **Musée d'Aquitaine** (10am–6pm; closed Tues; 15F, free Wed) at 20 cours Pasteur. Imaginatively laid out, with a stimulating variety of objects and types of display, the museum emphasises regional ethnography and covers the three main facets of the region's development: maritime, commercial and agricultural. Drawings and writings on the period enable you to see why eighteenth-century Bordeaux was so extolled by contemporary writers, who compared it to Paris. Take a look at the section on the wine trade before venturing off on a vineyard tour.

Another museum worth checking out, to the north of the city centre, is the city's new **Musée d'Art Contemporain** (Tues–Sun 11am–7pm; 20F, free daily noon–2pm) on rue Ferrère. There are no permanent collections, so it's hit-and-miss as to whether you'll like the stuff, but the building alone – a converted nineteenth-century warehouse for exotic goods – is worth the trek. There's also a superb collection of glossy art books in the first-floor library and an elegant designer café-restaurant on the roof.

Eating, drinking and entertainment

There are numerous cheap **eating places** around the station, and ethnic restaurants in the area around Église St-Michel. In the centre of town, slightly pricier establishments are scattered through the quartier St-Pierre. Wholesome meals and terrace drinks are available from the very popular *Café des Arts* on the corner of rue Ste-Catherine and cours Victor-Hugo. There's French-Antillaise cooking at *Le Balafon*, 15 rue des Bahutiers, and – somewhat cheaper – big, fresh salads at *Aux 3 Arcades* on pl du Parlement. Seafood features prominently on many a *Bordelais* menu: fairly cheaply at *La Flambée*, 26 rue du Mirail, or, for a lot more money, at Bordeaux's top fish restaurant, *Chez Philippe*, 1 pl du Parlement (closed Sun, Mon & Aug).

For **picnic** fodder, there is a marvellous, round covered **market** near the church of Notre-Dame behind cours de l'Intendance. And on rue de Montesquieu, off place des Grands-Hommes, Jean d'Alos runs the city's best *fromagerie*, with over 150 farm-produced cheeses.

If you're just after a **drink**, *Chez Auguste*, on pl de la Victoire, is a regular student hang-out. For **live music**, the places to go are *L'Alligator*, 3 place du Général-Sarrail (closed Sun), and *Le Borie*, 43 rue Borie, both of which host jazz ensembles towards the end of the week. The *Cricketers*, 72 quai de Paludate (southward continuation of quai Richelieu), has a more regular live spot, of more variable quality. To find out the latest on events happening in and around Bordeaux, get hold of a copy of the regional newspaper *Sud-Ouest*, or the free bi-monthly listings booklet *Clubs & Concerts*.

Listings

Airlines *British Airways*, galerie Frantel, Centre Mériadeck (☎56.81.24.59); *Air France*, 29 rue Esprit-des-Lois (☎56.44.64.35).

Airport Bordeaux-Mérignac, 10km west of the city (☎56.34.84.84): connected on weekdays by half-hourly shuttle to and from the SI (40min).

Bike hire From gare St-Jean (open 24hr).

Books *Mollat*, 83–91 rue Porte Dijeaux. The city's largest bookstore with French and English titles, and a separate record store next door. *Bradley's*, 32 place Gambetta, has a fair selection of English and French-language textbooks, as well as a bulletin board for job adverts.

Consulates UK, 15 cours de Verdun (☎56.52.28.35; Mon–Fri 9am–noon & 2.30–5pm); Canada, Immeuble Croix-du-Mail, 8 rue Claude-Bonnier (☎56.96.15.61; Mon–Fri 9am–12.30pm & 1.30–4.45pm); USA, 22 cours du Maréchal-Foch (☎56.52.65.92; Mon–Fri 9am–noon & 2–5pm).

Hitching For a prearranged ride, *Allostop* is at 59 rue des Ayres (☎56.81.24.59). Operating under your own steam, take the following buses to get clear of the city: for Bergerac, bus #5, from just across the Pont de Pierre to the corner of av Clemenceau; for Paris, #92, from Porte Cailhau to Ambares; for Toulouse, #B, from place de la Victoire to the terminus; for Bayonne-Biarritz, #G, from place de la Victoire to the terminus.

Laundrettes On cours de Marne and rue de la Boétie.

Money exchange On Sundays you can change money at the SI or *Thomas Cook* at the train station.

Postcards Vast selection of period post- and playing-cards, new and second hand at *Au Bonheur du Cartophile*, 4bis rue de Cursol.

Second-hand clothes *Steak Fripes*, 12 rue Fernand-Philippart. Agreeable small shop off place du Parlement.

Swimming pools *Olympique*, Grand Parc; *Judaique*, 166 rue Judaique.

Women visitors Counselling and information at *CIDF*, 5 rue Duffour-Dubergier (☎56.44.30.30; Mon–Fri 9am–12.30pm & 1.30–4pm).

The Médoc

The landscape of the **Médoc** is rather monotonous. Its gravel plains, which occupy the west bank of the brown, island-spotted Gironde estuary, rarely swell into anything resembling a hill, but, paradoxically, this poor soil is ideal for viticulture. Vines root more deeply if they don't find the sustenance they need in the topsoil: firmly rooted, they are less subject to drought and flooding; while the stable conditions required by the plant are further ensured by the insulating properties of the gravel.

The problem of accommodation is common to the entire wine region, so it's a good idea to visit on a day trip from Bordeaux. There are regular *CITRAM* buses to PAUILLAC, but it's worth considering **car rental** (*Citer*, opposite the train station in Bordeaux is a cheap option).

BORDEAUX WINES – THE FACTS

With Burgundy and Champagne, the **wines** of Bordeaux form the "Holy Trinity" of French viticulture. Despite producing as many whites as reds, it is the latter – known as *claret* to the English – which have graced the tables of the discerning for centuries. The countryside that produces them stretches north, east and south of the city, enjoying near perfect climactic conditions and a soil which ranges from limestone hills to sand and pebbles. It is the largest quality wine district in the world, turning out around 500 million bottles a year – over half the country's quality wine output.

The **classification** of Bordeaux wines is an extremely complex affair. Apart from the usual *appellation d'origine contrôlée* (AOC) labelling – guaranteeing the origin, but not the quality of the wine – the wines of the Médoc châteaux are graded into five *crus*, or growths. These were established as long ago as 1855, based on the prices the wines had fetched over the previous hundred years. Yet with the exception of Château Mouton-Rothschild, which moved up a class in 1973, there have been no official changes, so that the divisions between the *crus* should not be taken too seriously. Since then, to confuse matters further, additional catagories have been devised, for instance *Crus Bourgeois*, which has three categories of its own.

If you are interested in **buying wines**, it is possible to find bargains at some of the châteaux, but bear in mind that anything pre-1987 is likely to be cheaper in Britain. The advantages of buying at source include the opportunity of tasting the wines before purchasing, and the possibility of receiving expert advice about the different vintages. In Bordeaux, the best place to go is *La Vinotèque* next to the SI (Mon–Sat 9.15am–7.15pm). In recent years tales of machine oil and chemical additives have shaken many people's confidence in wine-drinking; as a result, there's a growing fashion for organic methods and "green" wines, already available on many good labels.

If you're interested in **visiting the châteaux**, the Bordeaux SI has a leaflet detailing all the places that allow visits and wine-tasting. For general **information** on the region's wines, the place to go is the *Maison du Vin* in Bordeaux on the opposite side of the street from the SI. In addition, each wine-producing village has its own SI and *Maison du Vin* who can provide the same service. Since getting to any of these places except St-Émilion without your own transport is hard work, the simplest thing is to take one of the SI's own **guided tours**, which leave at 1.30pm (June–mid-Oct; daily except Wed & Sat). They currently cost around 110F per person, but are generally interesting and informative and an English translation for the commentary is available.

Château Margaux, Fort Médoc and Blaye

Easily the prettiest of the Bordeaux châteaux, **Château Margaux** is an eighteenth-century villa situated in extensive, sculpture-dotted gardens. Its wine, world famous in the 1940s and 1950s, went through a rough patch in the two succeeding decades, but improved in the 1980s after the estate was bought by a Greek family. Château Margaux (☎56.88.70.28) is not included in Bordeaux's SI tours and advance booking is essential.

The seventeenth-century **Fort Médoc**, off the main road between Margaux and St-Julien by the banks of the estuary, is a good place to tuck into a few purchases between châteaux. It was designed by Vauban, the greatest military architect of his century, to defend the Gironde estuary against the British. The remains of the fort are scant but scramble-able, and in summer its toytown aspect has a leafy charm, marred only by a splendid view of the nuclear power station across the river just north of Blaye.

From LAMARQUE, seven or eight ferries a day cross the Gironde to **BLAYE**, another place fortified by Vauban. The green slopes behind the river, the *Côtes de Bourg* and *Côtes de Blaye*, were home to wine production long before the Médoc was planted. The wine is a rather heavier, plummier red, and cheaper than anything found on the opposite side of the river. To stay inside in the medieval town itself at *Hôtel La Citadelle*, place d'Armes (☎57.42.17.10; above ⑤), will cost you an arm and a leg; for half the price you could try *Hôtel Toison d'Or*, 15 cours du Port (☎57.42.00.41; ③), near the SI who can give you details on wine tasting in the region.

Pauillac and around

PAUILLAC is the largest town in the Médoc region and central to the most important vineyards of Bordeaux – no fewer than three of the top five *Grands Crus* come from around here. The town's rapid growth in recent years, however, is due not to its vineyards, but to the giant oil refinery which now dominates the town and accounts for the bleak, industrial appearance of the place. It's not a great place to stay, but should you wish or need to, try the *Hôtel Yachting*, Port de Plaisance (☎56.59.06.43; ④).

The most famous of the Médoc châteaux are situated in the Pauillac commune: **Châteaux Lafite-Rothschild**, **Châteaux Latour** and **Châteaux Mouton-Rothschild.** Their vineyards occupy larger single tracts of land than elsewhere in the Médoc, and consequently the qualities of the wines differ to a greater extent than other châteaux on neighbouring land: a good vintage *Lafite* is perfumed and refined, whereas a *Mouton-Rothschild* is strong and dark, and should be kept for at least ten years. A shared distinction of all three is their phenomenally high prices. Château Mouton-Rothschild and its wine museum (☎56.59.22.22; Mon–Fri only; closed Aug) are not included in tours from Bordeaux and must be booked in advance. As well as the viticultural stuff, you also get to see the Rothschilds' amazing collection of post-war art, which includes work by Picasso, Dali and Warhol.

Saint-Émilion

ST-ÉMILION is well worth a visit in its own right. Its old grey houses straggle down the south-hanging slope of a low hill, the green froth of the summer's vines pressing right to its walls and street ends. Many of the growers still keep up the old tradition of planting roses at the ends of the rows, which in pre-pesticide days served as an early warning system against infection, the idea being that the commonest bug, *oidium*, went for the roses first, giving three days' notice of its intentions.

The Église Monolithe

The town's belfry belongs to the rock-hewn **Église Monolithe** beneath it. Entry to the church is off a small square with a large locust tree in the middle, below the cliff on which the belfry stands. The church can only be visited on a guided tour which lasts 45 minutes (9.45am–12.30pm & 1.45–6.30pm; tickets 25F from the SI). The **guided tour** starts in a dark hole in someone's back yard, supposedly the cave where Saint Émilion lived a hermit's life in the eighth century. A rough-hewn ledge served as his bed and a carved seat as his chair, where, so you're told, barren women still come to sit in the hope of getting pregnant. Above is a half-ruined Benedictine chapel that the Revolution converted into a barn. Fragments of frescoes include one of Saint Valérie, patron saint of wine-growers. On the other side of the yard, a passage tunnels beneath the belfry, where three chambers have been dug out of the soft limestone, used as ossuary and cemetery from the eighth to the eleventh century. In the innermost chamber, discovered by a neighbour enlarging his cellar some fifty years ago, a large tombstone bears the inscription: "Aulius is buried between saints Valérie, Émilion and Avic".

The ninth- and twelfth-century **church** itself is an incredible place. Simple and huge, the entire structure, barrel-vaulting, great square piers and all, has been hacked out of the rock. The windows of Chartres Cathedral were stored here for safekeeping during the 1939–45 war. The whole interior was painted once, but only faint traces survived the Revolution, when a gunpowder factory was installed in the church. These days, every June, the wine council – *La Jurade* – assembles here to evaluate the previous season's wine and decide whether each *viticulteur*'s produce deserves the *appellation contrôlée* accolade.

Behind the SI the town comes to an abrupt end with a grand view of the moat and old walls. To the right, is the collegiate church of the Cordeliers with a handsome but badly mutilated doorway and a fourteenth-century cloister, which you have to consult the SI about visiting.

Practicalities – and wine

The **SI**, on place des Créneaux (daily 9.30am–12.30pm & 1.45–6pm), by the aforementioned belfry, is a good source of information and organises tours of the various châteaux in the region, but it's unlikely to be of much help in solving St-Émilion's chronic shortage of budget **accommodation**. The only remotely reasonable accommodation is at the *Auberge de la Commanderie* on rue des Cordeliers (☎57.24.70.19; ④).

There are two distinct wine districts of St-Émilion: the **plateau** and the **Côtes de St-Émilion**. The product of the former are called *Graves* wines because of the gravelly soil in which they are grown. *Côtes* wines grow in alkaline soil which gives them added strength: St-Émilion *Côtes* contain an average of one percent more alcohol than Médoc wines. The most famous wine of the region originates at **Château Ausone**, south of St-Émilion. The cellars (which can be visited) have been dug out of limestone directly beneath the vineyards. If you are interested in seeing the vineyards, ask at the **Maison du Vin** at the top of the hill by the prominent belfry.

Entre-Deux-Mers

The landscape of **Entre-Deux-Mers** ("between two seas" – so called because it is sandwiched between the tidal waters of the Dordogne and Garonne) is much more attractive than the other wine regions, with its gentle hills and scattered medieval villages. Its wines, which include the *Premières Côtes de Bordeaux*, are regarded as good but inferior to the Médocs or super-dry Graves to the south. It's also a region which can be explored, at least in part, by public transport, should you feel like avoiding the SI tour.

La Sauve

The one place you should really try to get to is the ruined abbey at **LA SAUVE**, an important stop for pilgrims *en route* to Santiago de Compostela. The bus from Bordeaux drops you off in the middle of a tranquil valley of small vineyards and corn fields, but you can see the ruin as you approach. Once it was all forest here, the abbey's full name, **La Sauve-Majeure**, being a corruption of the Latin *silva major* (big wood). It was founded in 1079, and the treasure of what remains is the twelfth-century Romanesque apse and apsidal chapels and the outstanding **sculpted capitals** in the chancel. The finest are the ones illustrating stories from the Old and New Testaments (Daniel in the lions' den, Delilah shearing Samson's hair and so on), while others show fabulous beasts and decorative motifs. There is a **mini-museum** at the entrance (9am–noon and 2–6pm), with some excellent photos and keystones from the fallen roofs. But what makes the visit so worthwhile is not just the capitals themselves, but the remote, undisturbed nature of the site. If you have the time, stroll over to the abbey's parish church, visible on the hill – take rue de l'Église.

THE TRUTH ABOUT CADILLAC

According to the tourist office at the medieval town of Cadillac, the founder of Detroit (home of General Motors), **Antoine Laumet**, originally came from Cadillac. Sadly, this is just too good to be true. In fact Antoine Laumet was born in 1658 in St-Nicolas-de-la-Grave, halfway between Agen and Toulouse, and never set foot in Cadillac itself. On emigrating to Canada, he took the name of Lamothe-Cadillac, a family who had nothing whatsoever to do with Cadillac the town. In 1701, he founded Detroit, and in 1958, in honour of on the 300th anniversary of his birth, General Motors named their new limousines "Cadillacs".

Around Langon

If you're heading south from Entre-Deux-Mers, LANGON is the first town of any size you come to. But **ST-MACAIRE**, across the Garonne from Langon, and **LA RÉOLE** on the north bank 18km further east, are both better for a rest or food stop. St-Macaire still has its original gates and battlements, and the Maison du Pays serves as an *écomusée* and information centre on the region and its products.

Thirteen kilometres south of Langon, the town of **BAZAS** has a laid-back, southern air. Its most attractive feature is the wide, arcaded cathedral square, place de la Cathédrale, overlooked by the lichenous grey **Cathédrale St-Jean** that manages, against all odds, a harmonious blend of Romanesque, Gothic and Classical in its west front.

Circling back east and north towards Sauternes, you could pass through **UZESTE**, a quiet little place, where Pope Clement V – who caused a schism by moving the papacy to Avignon in the fourteenth century – erected the old church on the *place*; and then through neighbouring **VILLANDRAUT**, where Clement was born and built a colossal castle whose curtain walls and corner towers still stand beside the road.

The Côte d'Argent

The **Côte d'Argent** is the long stretch of coast from the mouth of the Gironde estuary to Biarritz, which, at over 200km, is the longest, straightest and sandiest in Europe. The endless beaches are backed by high sand dunes, while behind lies the largest forest in western Europe. Despite these attractions, the lack of conventional tourist sights means that the coast still gets comparatively few visitors, and away from the main resorts, it is still possible to find deserted stretches of coastline.

Arcachon and around

On summer weekends, the *Bordelais* escape *en masse* to **ARCACHON**, the oldest resort on the Côte d'Argent, forty minutes' train ride across flat sandy forest from Bordeaux. There's nothing much to see in the town, but the beaches of white sand are magnificent, albeit crowded. To get to them from the **gare SNCF**, go straight down the av de-Gaulle past the **aquarium** run by Bordeaux University (March–Sept 9.30am–8pm). The town, a sprawl of villas great and small, is expensive, though there are a couple of reasonable **hotels** – *Le Provence*, 106 bd de la Plage (☎56.83.10.78; ③), and *Saint-Christaud*, 8 allée de la Chapelle (☎56.83.38.53; ③/④) – and lots of **campsites**. If you're stuck, there's an **SI** to the left of the station on place Roosevelt. A cheap place to try some of the local **seafood** is *La Marée*, 86 rue de Lattre-de-Tassigny.

The Côte d'Argent's chief curiosity is the **Dune du Pilat**, at 114 metres, the highest sand dune in Europe – a veritable mountain of wind-carved sand, about 8km south of

Arcachon. Buses leave from the gare SNCF (where you can also hire bikes) every half hour in July and August – about five a day at other times. From the end of the line the road continues straight on uphill for about fifteen minutes. There is the inevitable group of stands selling ice cream, *galettes* and junk and, from the top, a superb view over the bay of Arcachon and the forest of the *landes* stretching away to the south. There is also a great slide down to the sea – with a long haul back up.

At **LE TEICH**, about 14km east of Arcachon in the southeast corner of the Bassin d'Arcachon, one of the most important expanses of wetlands remaining in France has been converted into a bird sanctuary, the **Parc ornithologique du Teich** (March–Sept daily 10am–7pm; Oct–Feb Sat & Sun 10am–6pm; 23F), one of only two in the country. The only accommodation in Le Teich is the campsite beside the sanctuary, but you can easily come here on a day trip by train from Arcachon.

Les Landes

Travelling south from Bordeaux by road or rail, you pass for half a day through an unremitting, flat, sandy pine forest known as **les landes**. Until the nineteenth century it was a vast, infertile swamp, badly drained because of the impermeable layer of grit deposited by the glaciers of the quaternary age and steadily encroached upon by the shifting sand dunes of the coast. Today it supports over two million acres of trees (nearly 10,000 square kilometres) and since 1970 has been designated a *parc naturel régional* .

At LABOUHEYRE, on the N10 and railway line from Bordeaux to Bayonne, you can take a restored steam train to SABRES (at least daily June–Sept; check at other times) via the **Écomusée de Marquèze** (Palm Sunday–Oct daily 10.15am–5.40pm; rest of year Sat & Sun only; 30F), set up by the park authorities to illustrate the traditional *landais* way of life, when shepherds used to clomp around the scrub on long stilts.

THE CHARENTE

It is hard to believe that the peaceful fertile valley of the **river Charente**, which has given its name to the two modern *départements* that cover much of this chapter, was once a busy industrial waterway, bringing armaments from **Angoulême** to the naval shipyards at **Rochefort**. Low ochre-coloured farms crown the valley slopes, with green swathes of vineyard sweeping up to the walls. The turrets of minor châteaux – properties of wealthy cognac-producers – poke from the woods. The towns and villages may look old-fashioned, but the prosperous shops and classy new villas on the outskirts are proof that where the grape grows, money and modernity are not far behind.

The valley itself is easy to travel as the main road and railway to Limoges run this way. North and south, Poitiers, Périgueux (for the Dordogne) and Bordeaux are also easily reached by train. Otherwise, for cross-country journeys, you are heavily reliant on your own transport or patient hitching.

Saintes

SAINTES was formerly much more important than its present size suggests. Today a busy market for the surrounding region, it was capital of the old province of Saintonge and a major administrative and cultural centre in Roman times. It still retains some impressive remains from that period, as well as two beautiful Romanesque pilgrim churches and an attractive centre of narrow lanes and medieval houses. It also has the doubtful distinction of being the birthplace of Dr Guillotin, who advocated execution by decapitation.

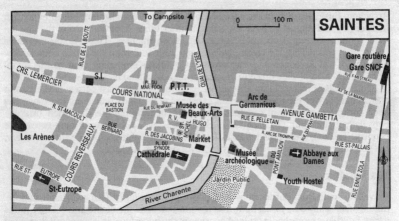

Practicalities

The modern town is bisected by av Gambetta, which becomes the cours National on the west/south side of the Charente. Arriving by train you'll find yourself on av de la Marne at the east end of av Gambetta, with several cheap **hotels** in the vicinity. Avoid the dirty and noisy *Hôtel de la Gare* on rue F-Mestreau. The *Hôtel de France* (☎46.93.01.16; ③) and the *Parisien* (☎46.74.28.92; ②) on this street may be slightly more expensive, but they're worth the difference. One cheapy that you should look into is the *Té-Gé-Vé* (☎46.93.07.06; ①), which is actually a good snack bar at 45 av de la Marne with a few rooms above it. Another good choice off av Gambetta is the *Hôtel St-Pallais*, 1 pl St-Pallais (☎46.92.51.03; ①), in the courtyard of an abbey but with a bar downstairs: coming from the gare SNCF take rue du Perat to the left.

Another accommodation option is the **youth hostel**, 6 rue Pont-Amilion (☎46.92.14.82), just beyond St-Palais Abbey. Over the river, a right turn (north) on the far bank leads to the **camping municipal** (☎46.93.08.00) on riverside rue de Courbiac.

For **eating**, there's a good **restaurant**, the *Petit Bidou*, by the river on place Blair, and **crêperies** at 20 rue Victor-Hugo and 11 rue St-Palais. *Le Jardin du Rempart*, 36 rue du Rempart, off Cours National serves top-value *menus* including salads, seafood and grills. Out of town, the *Restaurant de la Charente* (☎46.11.00.73; closed Sun), 10km upstream at CHANIERS, is the Sunday haunt of prosperous locals and makes a more expensive but fulfilling gastronomic experience.

If your plan is to move on to COGNAC, you might consider getting there by river, on one of the SI's summer boat trips.

The sights

The abbey church, the **Abbaye-aux-Dames**, is as quirky as Notre-Dame in Poitiers. It stands back from the street – rue St-Pallais – in a sanded courtyard behind the smaller Romanesque church of St-Pallais. An elaborately sculpted doorway masks a plain, broad interior space roofed with two big domes, evocative of a barefoot, vigorous faith. Its rarest feature is a tower, flanked with pinnacles and by turns square, octagonal and lantern-shaped, capped with the Poitou pinecone. It was built in the eleventh century.

From here rue Arc-de-Triomphe brings you out on the **riverbank** beside an imposing **Roman arch** that originally stood on the bridge until it was demolished in the nineteenth century to make way for the modern one. It is not in fact a triumphal arch, though it looks like one. It was dedicated to the emperor Tiberius, his son Drusus and nephew Germanicus in 19 AD. And in a shed of a building next door, there is an

archaeological museum (10am–noon & 2–6pm; winter Sun 10am–noon only; closed Tues; free), with a great many more Roman bits and pieces strewn about, mostly rescued from the fifth-century city walls into which they had been incorporated.

A footbridge crosses from this point to the covered **market** on the west bank of the river and **place du Marché** at the foot of the rather uninspiring **cathedral of St-Pierre**, which began life as a Romanesque church but was significantly altered in the aftermath of damage inflicted during the Wars of Religion, when Saintes, like La Rochelle, was a Huguenot stronghold. Its enormous, heavily buttressed tower, capped by a hat-like dome instead of the intended spire, is the town's chief landmark.

In front, the lime trees of **place du Synode** stretch away to the municipal buildings, with the old quarter up to the right and the Hôtel Martineau library in the rue des Jacobins with an exquisite central courtyard full of trees and shrubs. Back towards the bridge, a seventeenth-century mansion on rue Victor-Hugo houses the **Musée des Beaux-Arts** (10–noon & 2–6pm; closed Tues), containing a collection of local pottery and some unexciting paintings.

If you continue along rue des Jacobins, past the library and up the hill to the Capitol, with an impressive view back over the cathedral tower, you eventually come to the broad **cours Reverseaux**. To the left the road dips downhill through an avenue of trees with a steep little valley on the right. Two signs advise you to see the concierge if you want to visit **Les Arènes**, the Roman arena, whose ruins you can see at the head of this valley. The conventional approach is from rue St-Eutrope, past the church and right on rue Lacurie. Much more interesting, but involving an illicit scramble over the fence, is straight down the path into the valley bottom.

The arena – in fact, an **amphitheatre** – is dug into the end of the valley. Dating from the early first century, it is one of the oldest surviving. Most of the seats are grassed over, but it is still evocative. You can easily imagine the echoes of the alien Latin mingling with some local Gaulish patois all those centuries ago, when Saintes had twice its present population.

On the way back from the amphitheatre, it's no extra trouble to take in the eleventh-century church – really two churches – of **St-Eutrope**. The upper church, which lost its nave in 1803, has some brilliant **capital-carving** in the old choir – best seen from the gallery. But it's the **crypt** – entered from the street – which is more atmospheric and primitive. Massive pillars carved with stylised vegetation support the vaulting in semi-darkness. There is a huge old font and the third-century tomb of Saintes' first bishop, Eutropius himself.

Aulnay and other churches

If you have a car there are several marvellous Romanesque churches within easy reach of Saintes, notably FENIOUX to the north towards ST-JEAN-D'ANGELY and RIOUX to the south. There is also the fine château of ROCHE-COURBON off the Rochefort road.

But car or no car, one place worth any amount of trouble to get to if you are into Romanesque is the twelfth-century pilgrim church of **St-Pierre** at AULNAY. Without your own transport, the simplest route there is by train from Saintes to St-Jean-d'Angely, a journey of 25 minutes. St-Jean has some pretty old houses but is not worth a stop in its own right. Thereafter you have to hitch. After 3km on the D939 Poitiers–Angoulême road, take the left fork for Aulnay on D950: St-Pierre is off to the right before you reach the town.

Aulnay church's **finest sculpture** is on the west front, south transept and apse. On the former, two blind arches flank the central portal. The tympanum of the right depicts Christ in Majesty; the left, St Peter, crucified upside down with two extraordinarily lithe and graceful soldiers balancing on the arms of his cross to get a better swing at the nails in his feet. On the **south side**, the doorway is decorated with four bands of even more intricate carving. The **apse**, too, is a beauty, framed by five slender columns and lit by three perfectly arched windows, the centre one enclosed by figures wrapped in the finest twining foliage. **Inside**, there is more extraordinary carving: capitals depicting Delilah cutting Samson's hair, devils pulling a man's beard, human-eared elephants, bearing the Latin inscription *"Hi sunt elephantes"*, "These are elephants" – presumably for the edification of ignorant locals. **Outside**, in the cemetery, is a *croix hosannière*, so-called because on Palm Sunday the priest and congregation would re-enact Christ's entry into Jerusalem, with the priest reading the story while the congregation filed past laying branches by the cross and crying "Hosanna".

If you have a car, you might also visit NUAILLÉ-SUR-BOUTONNE, 9km west of Aulnay. And even nearer, just down the D129 east of Aulnay, you can walk to SALLES-LES-AULNAY (20 minutes), or ST-MANDÉ (1 hour). They all have humbler churches of the same period, each in its way, as charming as that of Aulnay.

Cognac

Anyone who does not already know what **COGNAC** is about will quickly nose its quintessential air as they stroll about the medieval lanes of the riverside quarter. For here is the greatest concentration of *chais* or warehouses, where the precious liquid is matured, its fumes blackening the walls with tiny fungi. Cognac is cognac, from the tractor-driver and pruning-knife-wielder to the manufacturer of corks, bottles and cartons. Untouched by recession (80 percent of production is exported), it is likely to thrive as long as the world has sorrows to drown – a sunny, prosperous, respectable, self-satisfied little place.

Practicalities

The simplest way of **getting there** is by train – 20 minutes from Saintes, 45 minutes from Angoulême. From the **gare SNCF**, go down rue Mousnier, right on rue Bayard, past the **PTT**, up rue du 14-juillet, with a good supermarket and the reasonably priced *Sens Unique* restaurant, to the central **place François-I**, dominated by an equestrian statue of the king rising from a bed of begonias. There are a couple of **cafés** and a **brasserie** on the square. Close by is the **SI**, where you can ask about visiting the various *chais*, the St-Gobain glass works (second biggest bottle-maker in Europe) and river trips – upstream through the locks to JARNAC is a particularly beautiful excursion.

Upstream from the bridge, the oak woods of the **Parc François-I**, where there's **swimming** in the river or a pool, stretch along the riverbank to the **Pont Chatenay** and the town **campsite** (45.32.13.32). As for **rooms**, the cheapest are *Tourist Hôtel*, 166 av Victor-Hugo (the Angoulême road) (☎45.82.09.61; ②), and *Le Cheval Blanc*, 6–8 place Bayard (☎45.82.09.55; ②). For something a bit more expensive and more comfortable, try *La Résidence*, 25 av Victor-Hugo (☎45.32.16.09 ②/③), or *L'Étape*, a little further out on the N141 at 2 av d'Angoulême (☎45.32.16.15; ③).

The town

From the north side of the square, **rue d'Angoulême** leads past shops specialising in those archetypal French frivolities – pastries and ladies' knickers – to the **market** square overlooked by the tower of St-Léger (entrance on rue Aristide-Briand). Straight on down, you come to **Grande-Rue** winding through the old quarter to the *chais*. On the right is all that remains of the château where King François I was born in 1494.

To the left are the *chais* and offices of the **Hennessy cognac** company. Like the other main **warehouses** they are open, free, from 9–11am and 2–5pm except weekends; only *Polignac* and *Otard* are open at weekends, and then only in July and August. The consensus is that *Hennessy* – a seventh-generation family firm – are the best to visit. The first Hennessy, an officer in the Irish brigade serving with the French army, hailed from Ballymacnoy in County Cork. He gave up soldiering in 1765 to set up a little business here.

The **Hennessy visit** begins with a film explaining what's what in the world of cognac. Only an *eau de vie* distilled from grapes grown in a strictly defined area can be called cognac, and this stretches only from the coast at La Rochelle and Royan to Angoulême. It is all carefully graded according to soil properties: chalk essentially. The inner circle, from which the finest cognac comes – Grand Champagne and Petite Champagne (not to be confused with bubbly) – lies mainly south of the Charente River.

Hennessy alone keep 180,000 barrels in stock. All are regularly checked and various *coupages* or blendings made from barrel to barrel. Only the best is kept. And what is the best? That – and, in effect, the whole enterprise – depends on the tastebuds of the *maître du chais*. For six generations the job has been in the same family. The present heir apparent has already been sixteen years under his father's tutelage and is not yet fully qualified.

Around Cognac

There are several attractive **walking possibilities** around Cognac. The best is the **towpath** or *chemin de hâlage* which follows the left (south) bank of the Charente upstream to **Pont de la Trâche**, then on along a track to BOURG-CHARENTE, with an excellent **restaurant** called *La Ribaudière* at the bridge and a Romanesque church – about three hours all in all. A by-road leads back to ST-BRICE on the other bank, past sleepy farms and acres of shoulder-high vines. From there another lane winds up the hill and over to the **ruined abbey** of CHÂTRE, abandoned amid brambles and fields about 3km away. Alternatively, at the hamlet of RICHEMONT, 5km northwest of Cognac, you can swim in the pools of the tiny **river Antenne** below an ancient church on a steep bluff lost in the woods.

Further afield, 18km northwest of Cognac between the villages of MIGRON and AUTHON, there's the fascinating **Écomusée du Cognac** (☎46.94.91.16; free) which illustrates the history of the distillation process, and the various tools involved, finishing off with *dégustation* of Cognacs, liqueurs and cocktails. Follow the D731 to St-Jean-d'Angely out of Cognac for 13km as far as BURIE, then turn right on the D131 4km to Migron.

Angoulême and the road to Limoges

The cathedral city of **ANGOULÊME** turned Christian in the third century under the influence of Ausonius, a Gallo-Roman landed gent, poet and saint. It was heavily fought over in the Anglo-French squabbles and again in the Wars of Religion – when it was another Protestant stronghold. After the revocation of the Edict of Nantes, a good proportion of its citizens – among them many of its skilled papermakers – emigrated to Holland, never to return. Marguerite de Valois, sister of François I, author, and one of the "characters" of French royal history, was born here.

The **old town** occupies a steep-sided plateau overlooking a bend in the Charente. Its scruffy labyrinthine streets, only just beginning to undergo gentrification, fit every visitor's stereotype of what a French working-class neighbourhood should look like. The papermills which employed the workers and made the city's prosperity are now almost completely defunct.

On the southern edge of the plateau stands the **cathedral**, whose west front, like Notre-Dame at Poitiers, is a fascinating display board for some very expressive and lively **medieval sculpture**, most of it twelfth century and culminating, as ever, in a

Risen Christ with angels and clouds about his head, framed in the habitual mandorla. The **frieze** beneath the tympanum to the right of the west door is interesting. It commemorates the recapture of Spanish Zaragoza from the the Moors and shows, on the left, a bishop transfixing a Moorish giant with his lance and, on the right, Roland killing the Moorish king who, having invited Charlemagne to his aid, refused to let him into his city, thus forcing him to make the retreat that led to the massacre of his rearguard by the Basques above St-Jean-Pied-de-Port. Unfortunately much of the rest of the building has suffered from the attentions of the reviled, nineteenth-century busy-body restorer, **Abadie**, and his desire to rediscover the pure Romanesque by destroying everything that followed it.

From the front of the cathedral, you can **walk** all around the **ramparts** encircling the plateau, with long views over the surrounding country, now largely filled with urban sprawl. There are **public gardens** below the parapet at the far end and a gravelly esplanade by the *lycée* where locals gather to play *boules*.

To the east of Angoulême, there are two interesting places on the way to Limoges – **La Rochefoucauld** and **Confolens**.

Practicalities

Angoulême is easily accessible **by train**: 45 minutes from Cognac, 50 minutes from Limoges and an hour from Poitiers. There is a branch office of the **SI** outside the **gare SNCF**, from which **av Gambetta**, with the **gare routière** and several cheap **hotels**, leads uphill to the town centre through **place Pérot**. Among the cheapest rooms are those of the *Les Messageries*, pl de la Gare (☎45.92.07.62; ②); *Hôtel Le Crab*, 27 rue Kléber (☎45.95.51.80; ②), left out of the station then first right off av Maréchal-de-Lattre-de-Tassigny; and *Hôtel Gaste*, 381 rte de Bordeaux (☎45.91.89.98; ①), a long haul from the station on the opposite side of town. A little pricier are *Hôtel des Pyrénées,* 80 rue St-Roch (☎ 45.95.20.45; ②), *Hôtel d'Orléans*, 133 av Gambetta (☎45.92.07.53; ③), and the excellent *Hôtel de Bordeaux*, 236 rte de Bordeaux (☎45.91.60.66; ⑤).

Alternatively, there's a **youth hostel** (☎45.92.45.80; with canteen) on an island in the Charente. Take bus #7 from pl du Champ-du-Mars, or turn right at the first lights on av Gambetta, cross the railway bridge and go right again down to the river. Cross by the footbridge and the hostel is on your left. The **camping municipal** (☎45.92.83.22) is nearby, beyond the Pont de Bourgines.

Likely **restaurant** areas are rue de Genève, with a number of options including traditional French and international, rue Massilon or *Le Mektoub*, 28 rue des 3 Notre Dames, for oriental cuisine and pl des Halles for anything from cheap snacks and salads at *Le Chat Noir* to gastronomy at *Jardin des Arceaux*. One of the best restaurants in the region, with *menus* starting at 85F, is the *Margaux*, 25 rue de Genève (☎45.92.58.98). **Discos** are *Le Rayon Bleu* at 2 rue de Paris and *Le Must*, 71 bd Besson-Bey, near Pont St-Antoine.

For additional information consult the **SI** at 2 pl St-Pierre behind the Cathédrale St-Pierre to the west of town, or the **CIJ** behind the Hôtel de Ville. Either can provide, among other things, route details for **walks** in the area – *circuits pédestres*. **Bike hire** is from rue d'Arceaux. Angoulême **festivals** include a brief **jazz** blow at the beginning of June and, in February, the *Bande Dessinée*, a convention of comic-strip writers and artists. Comics (*"BD"*) from politics to pornography, are high art in France.

East of Angoulême: La Rouchefoucauld...

LA ROUCHEFOUCAULD, 15km from Angoulême, is on bus and train routes. By road you pass through RUELLE, now an Exocet-missile-manufacturing centre, formerly a naval armaments foundry, specialising in casting gun barrels, which were shipped down the Charente to the yards at Rochefort.

La Rochefoucauld itself is the site of a huge Renaissance **château** on the banks of the river Tardoire, which still belongs to the family that gave its name to the town. It is only open in August, when there is a brigade-sized cast for the *son et lumière*. Unfortunately, you cannot quite see the courtyard, the château's best architectural feature, from outside. Two **hotels**, if you need them, are the *Hôtel de France*, 13 Grand-Rue (☎45.63.02.29), and *Vieille Auberge*, Faubourg La Souche (☎45.62.02.72). The **camping municipal** is on rue des Flots.

...and Confolens

East of Angoulême the country becomes hillier and more wooded, with buttercup pastures grazed by liver-coloured Limousin cattle. **CONFOLENS** is about 40km north-east of Rochefoucauld (buses do the 55-kilometre trip from Angoulême) and off the main N141 to Limoges. Travelling by train, it's better to go to ST-JUNIEN on the Limoges line and hitch back. You enter the valley of the **river Vienne** and Confolens is on the left bank, a small, quiet town of ancient houses stacked on a hill above the river. The chief claim to fame of Confolens today is an **International Folklore Festival**, held every year in the second and third weeks of August.

If you're planning an overnight, try the *Hôtel de Vienne*, 4 rue de la Ferrandie (☎45.84.09.24) – or there's a **camping municipal**.

LIMOGES AND THE LIMOUSIN

The **Limousin** – the country around Limoges – is hilly, wooded, wet and not overly fertile: ideal pasture for the famous Limousin breed of cattle and, higher up to the east, for sheep. Herdsman's country; whence, presumably, the widespread use of the shepherd's cape called a *limousine* gave its name to the big, wrap-around, covered twentieth-century car.

The only town of any consequence in the region is **Limoges** itself, whose turn-of-the-century reputation for revolutionary workers' politics struck terror in bourgeois hearts. Transport in the region, so long as you're on an axis between Limoges and another significant town, presents no problem. Off such axes, however, you have to find your own solutions. An obvious and agreeable one is a bicycle, but be warned that in the beautiful eastern half of the province the climbs are long and steep towards the **Plateau de Millevaches**. A satisfying rural route would be to follow the course of the **river Vienne** – easier, of course, if you start from the source above **Eymoutiers** and roll downstream.

Limoges

LIMOGES is not a city that strikes you as calling for a long stay. It is worth a look, however, for a magnificent railway station and the craft industries which made its name a household word: **enamel** in the Middle Ages and, since the eighteenth century, some of the finest **china** ever produced. If these appeal, then the city's unique museum collections – and its Gothic cathedral – will reward a visit. But it has to be said that the industry today seems a spent tradition, hard hit by recession and changing tastes among the rich and barely clinging on now the local kaolin (china clay) mines are exhausted. The workshops survive mainly on the tourist trade.

Nothing daunted by recession, Limoges' annual **porcelain exhibition** still takes place every July and August. In September and October there's the **Festival des Francophonies** with numerous concerts, lectures and drama productions. For gour-

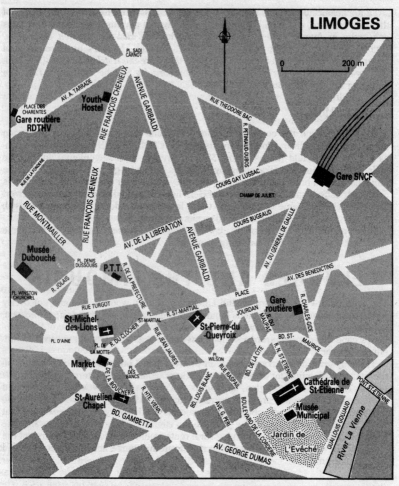

mets the big attraction is the **Fête des Petits Ventres** staged on the third Friday in October, when the entire populace turns out to gorge on everything from pig's trotters to sheep's testicles in the old butchers' quarter, rue de la Boucherie.

Arrival and practicalities

From the magnificent **Gare des Bénédictins** train station, the quickest route to the city centre is up **av du Général-de-Gaulle** to place Jourdan, where a left turn takes you towards the cathedral, while a diagonal right leads into the old town. The **SI** is just across place Jourdan at 1 bd de Fleurus (Mon–Sat 9am–noon & 2–6.30pm).

For a place to stay, there's a clean, hospitable **youth hostel** in the *Foyer des Jeunes Travailleuses* (☎55.77.63.97), on the tiny rue Encombe-Vineuse to the right off rue Chenieux south of **place Carnot**, with private rooms available, and a canteen. Alternatively, two reasonable **hotels** close to the railway station are *Hôtel du Faisan*, 25 av du Général-de-Gaulle (☎55.77.15.45; ②), and *Le Concorde*, 2–4 rue Pétiniaud-Dubous (☎55.77.09.00; ②). If you're **camping**, the nearest site is *La Vallée de l'Aurence* (☎55.38.49.43; open all year), 5km north of town on the N20 Paris road.

Two very good-value **eating places** are *Le Sancerre*, 18 rue Montmailler off place Denis-Dussoubs (closed Sat and Sun pm), with menus from 50F, and the self-service *Flunch* in rue Dalesme near the church of St-Pierre (daily 11am–10pm). For **drinking** and generally **hanging** out, *Le Duc Étienne* (till 1am) in rue de la Boucherie is popular. For beer drinkers, *Le Paris* (till 3am) on place Denis-Dussoubs brews its own and the *Lord John* on av de-Gaulle near the station is a good imitation of a British pub in all but closing time (3am), complete with darts.

Transport: the **gare routière** for private buses is at 9 rue Charles-Gide near the **gare SNCF**; local buses leave from pl des Charentes on av Adrien-Tarrade off pl Carnot.

The city: museums, the cathedral and the old quarter

The best of the museums – with its showpiece collections of **enamelware** dating back as far as the twelfth century – is the **Musée Municipal de l'Évêché** (July–Sept; daily 10–11.45pm & 2–6pm; Oct–June closed Tues) in the old Bishop's Palace overlooking a classic eighteenth-century formal garden. There's an interesting progression to be observed here, from the simple, sober, Byzantine-influence *champlevé* done on copper plate, to the later, especially seventeenth- and eighteenth-century work, which used a far greater range of colours and indulged in elaborate virtuoso portraiture. By the nineteenth century, however, the spirit and vigour had dissipated, and although there are contemporary artisans in the city using the medium, their work, too, judging from this display, is not much more successful.

Outside, if the weather is good, the **garden** is an inviting prospect (all year 7.45am–5.30/9pm; free), descending gracefully towards the river Vienne.

For collections of the **porcelain**, and extensive representative china displays from around the world, continue to the **Musée Adrien-Dubouché** (10am–noon & 1.30–5pm; closed Tues), off pl Winston-Churchill and close to **pl Dussoubs**. Various celebrity services are included: Napoléon Bonaparte, Royalty, Charles and Di . . . The exhibits are well laid out, with explanatory panels describing the processes for making the different wares – more interesting than you might expect. And if your interest is sufficiently aroused, the **SI** in bd de Fleurus can arrange visits to a number of active workshops.

The cathedral

Opposite the municipal museum is the city's **cathedral** of St-Étienne. Begun in 1273, it was planned on the model of the cathedral of Amiens, though only the choir, completed in the early thirteenth century, is pure Gothic. The rest of the building was added, piecemeal, over the centuries, the western part of the nave not until 1876. The most striking external feature is the sixteenth-century **facade of the north transept**, built in full Flamboyant style with elongated arches, clusters of pinnacles and delicate tracery in window and gallery. The doors are carved with scenes from the lives of St-Étienne (St Stephen) and St-Martial.

At the west end of the nave, the **tower**, which was erected on a Romanesque base that had to be massively reinforced to bear the weight, has octagonal upper storeys, in common with most churches in the region. It once stood as a separate campanile and probably looked the better for it. **Inside**, the effects are much more pleasing. The rose stone looks warmer than on the weathered exterior. The sense of soaring height is accentuated by all the upward-reaching lines of the pillars, the net of vaulting ribs, the curling, flame-like lines repeated in the arcading of the side chapels and the rose window, and, above all, as you look down the nave, by the narrower and more pointed arches of the choir.

The old quarter

Over to the west of the cathedral is the **old quarter** of the town, partly renovated. Make your way through to **rue de la Boucherie**, for 1000 years the domain of the Butchers' Guild (with several good but expensive restaurants). The dark, cluttered chapel of **St-Aurélien** with a fourteenth-century butter cross outside belongs to them. At the top of the street is the **market** in **place de la Motte** and to the right, partly hidden by adjoining houses, the church of **St-Michel-des-Lions** (fourteenth–fifteenth century), named after the two badly weathered Celtic lions guarding the south door and topped by one of the best towers and spires in the region. The **inside** is dark and atmospheric, with two beautiful densely-coloured fifteenth-century windows either side of the choir, one of which – in the south aisle – depicts the Tree of Jesse.

From place de la Motte, rue du Clocher leads to rue Jean-Jaurès, with the **PTT** a couple of blocks up to the left. Straight across, **rue St-Martial** leads past the car park on place de la République – where the fourth-century crypt of the long-vanished **abbey of St-Martial** (July–Sept only 9.30am–noon & 2.30–5pm) was discovered during building operations in 1960 – to the church of **St-Pierre-du-Queyroix**, whose belfry was the model for the cathedral and the church of St-Michel. The interior, partly twelfth-century (the exterior was remodelled in the sixteenth century), gains a sombre strength from the massive round pillars which still support the roof. Like St-Étienne it has a slightly pink granite glow. There is a fine window at the end of the south aisle depicting the Dormition of the Virgin, signed by Jean Pénicault, one of the great enamel artists, in 1510.

Around Limoges: Oradour and the Limousin

The following **villages** are all within an easy day's reach of Limoges. **Solignac** can be reached on foot. And you'll need the walk from **Oradour** to the train station to recover from the macabre shock of the ruined village.

Oradour-sur-Glane

Twenty-five kilometres northwest of Limoges and a few kilometres north of the N141 road to Angoulême, the village of **ORADOUR-SUR-GLANE** stands just as the soldiers of the SS *das Reich* Division left it on June 10, 1944, after killing all the inhabitants in reprisal for attacks by French *maquisards*. It seems irreverent to approach it as a "sight"; perhaps it should be treated more as a shrine.

There are **buses** from pl des Charentes in Limoges, but the best, if most strenuous, approach is by **train** to ST-VICTURNIEN on the Angoulême line – about 25 minutes; you can get there and back in a day. Then walk the 7km to Oradour in a couple of hours.

St-Victurnien is a tiny village on the Vienne, with a **hotel** and **campsite** (open only in season). Turn right out of the station, through the village and up a wooded hill past meadow and hedge to the main N141 road – 2km. Cross straight over and continue 5km through quiet, woody country with orchids and Lady's Smock in the verges, buttercups and asphodels in the pasture. You might get a lift, but there is very little traffic. Turn left at the next main road, and **Oradour** is in front of you, a modern village built beside the old, with a 1950s concrete church trying, but failing, to be impressive – and it would be difficult to devise an architectural space commensurate with the task of commemorating, forgiving and transcending that dreadful act.

A gate into **the old village** admonishes: "*Souviens-toi*", "Remember". The village street leads past roofless houses gutted by fire. Telephone poles, tram cables and gutters are fixed in tormented attitudes where the fire's heat left them. Pre-war cars rust in the garages. A yucca, grown into an enormous clump, still blooms in the notary's garden. Last year's grapes hang wizened on a vine whose trellis has long rotted away.

Behind the square is a **memorial garden**, a plain rectangle of lawn hedged with beech. A dolmen-like slab on a shallow plinth covers a crypt containing relics of the dead, and the awful list of names. Beyond, by the stream, stands the church where the women and children – five hundred of them – were burnt to death.

The Lionheart route: around St-Junien, Châlus and Nexon

The Limoges tourist office has worked out a route linking several châteaux and places of interest on the south bank of the Vienne, detailed in a leaflet called the **Route Richard-Coeur-de-Lion**. Visiting all of them really requires a car, but some at least are accessible by a combination of public transport and patient hitching.

The St-Junien area
A 35-minute train journey along the river on the Angoulême line takes you to ST-JUNIEN, whence a further 10km on the N141 Angoulême road leads to the eleventh-century **Château de Rochebrune** at **ST-ÉTAGNAC**. The more interesting **Château de ROCHECHOUART** (July–Sept 9am–noon & 2–6pm) in the pretty walled town of the same name (**SI** at 6 rue Victor-Hugo) is some 11km southwest of St-Junien, an hour by bus from the gare SNCF in Limoges. With its oldest parts dating from the thirteenth and fifteenth centuries and with a fine interior courtyard and frescoed hunting gallery added in Renaissance times, the château now serves as town hall, magistrates' court and **museum of contemporary art** (July–Aug 10am–noon & 2–6pm closed Tues; June & Sept 2–6pm closed Tues; March to mid-June & Oct to mid-Dec 2–6pm, closed Mon & Tues). Take a look also at the wind-carved spiral spire on the **church of St-Sauveur**.

A further 20km to the southwest, and worth the trip for Romanesque buffs, though it is really only practicable by car, the **church of St-Eutrope** in **LES SALLES-LAVAUGUYON** boasts some very early frescoes, from around 1100, only uncovered by restorers in 1986. Les Salles-Lavauguyon lies well to the west of the D675 Rochechouart–Nontron road, 11km from VAYRES LA CHAISE or 7.5km from ST-MATHIEU. If you're really keen on walking, the ROCHECHOUART SI's **walking route**, which joins Rochechouart with Les Salles-Lavauguyon, is a handy publication.

Around Châlus
CHÂLUS is best reached direct from Limoges, 35km along the N21 or one hour by bus. Its principal point of interest is the ruined **château** (daily July to mid-Sept 10am–noon & 2–6pm; April–June Sun & holidays only) where Richard the Lionheart was mortally wounded by an archer shooting from the still extant keep in 1199. Richard, son of Eleanor of Aquitaine and himself as much French as English, was campaigning to suppress a local rebellion against English rule. The archer was flayed to death for his marksmanship. For real enthusiasts there are two further castles, **Brie** and **Montbrun**, a short distance west of Châlus (both visitable on request, and either of them reachable on foot in a couple of hours).

Nexon
Eighteen kilometres east, past two more early medieval fortresses at CARS and RILHAC-LASTOURS, the village of **NEXON**, also directly accessible by bus and train from Limoges, is of more general interest, with a fine, heavily restored late medieval château (only open to the public in summer), set in magnificent parklands with a stud farm renowned for its Anglo-Arab breeds (daily 9am–noon & 2–7pm). You can **camp** in Nexon at *Étang de la Lande* and, for a **meal**, try the *Dexet* in av de la Gare.

Chalusset and Solignac

South of Limoges, trains down to BRIVE stop infrequently at the station of SOLIGNAC-LE-VIGEN, the closest point of access to the ruined castle of Chalusset and the abbey of Solignac, in the wooded valley of the Briance. This is perhaps the most attractive day excursion you could make from Limoges – and, if you're feeling energetic, you could even forget the trains and walk the whole way (13km to Solignac; 19km if you hike to Chalusset, too, and back). If you decide to do this, cross the Vienne in Limoges by the Pont St-Martial and take the back road to Solignac. If hitching, leave by Pont-Neuf on the Brive/Toulouse road. Turn right after a few hundred metres and continue uphill out of town. After 6km take the St-Yrieix turning on the right. It is 6km from there down into the green valley of the Briance at LE VIGEN.

The twelfth-century **Château de CHALUSSET**, which the English held during the Hundred Years' War, is 4km on from here, up a lane to the left. At the highest point of the climb, about 40 minutes from Le Vigen, an iron belvedere in the wood on the right of the road gives a dramatic view across the valley to where the ruined keep rises above the trees. To get there, turn downhill to the right for 1km until you cross the Briance. Opposite the end of the bridge a path climbs up to the castle. It's about an hour from Le Vigen and an hour back.

SOLIGNAC is a 15-minute walk to the other side of Le Vigen. You can see the **abbey** ahead of you with the tiled roofs of its octagonal apse and neat little brood of radiating chapels. The twelfth-century facade is plain with just a little sculpture; the granite of which it is built does not permit the intricate carving of limestone. Inside it is beautiful. A flight of steps leads down into the nave with a dramatic view the length of the church. There are no aisles, just a single space roofed with two big domes, and no ambulatory either – an absolutely plain Latin cross in design. It is a simple, sturdy church, with the same feel of plain robust Christianity as the crypt of St-Eutrope in Saintes.

St-Léonard-de-Noblat

ST-LÉONARD-DE-NOBLAT is 25 minutes by train from Limoges or 45 minutes by bus: to **hitch** out of Limoges in this direction, take bus #1 from place Carnot, across Pont-Neuf to the last stop on the St-Léonard–Bourganeuf–Aubusson road. St-Léonard is a small market town of narrow streets and medieval houses with jutting eaves and corbelled turrets. There's a very lovely eleventh- to twelfth-century **church**, whose six-storey tower looks out over the rising hills and woods where the river Vienne threads its course down from the heights of the Massif Central. The interior is strong and simple: barrel vaults on big, square piles, a high dome on an octagonal drum, domed transepts – the whole in grey granite.

Aubusson

AUBUSSON (buses and trains from Limoges) is 90km east of Limoges. A neat grey stone town in the bottom of a ravine formed by the river Creuse, it is of no great interest in itself. What makes it unique is its enormous reputation as a centre for weaving tapestries, second only to the Gobelins in Paris. If you're interested, the place to aim for is the **Musée Départemental de la Tapisserie** in av des Lissiers (daily 9am–12.30pm & 2–6.30pm; closed Tues am in summer, Tues all day in winter). For information about further exhibits, ask the **SI** in rue Vieille. If you want to **stay**, there are two inexpensive **hotels** in the main Grande-Rue: *Hôtel du Lissier*, nos. 84–86 (☎55.66.14.18; ②; with restaurant), and *Hôtel du Chapitre*, at nos. 53–55 (☎55.66.18.54; ②). **Camping** is by the river on the Felletin road.

travel details

Trains

From Poitiers frequent to Châtellerault (20min); frequent to Paris-Austerlitz (2hr 50min); frequent to Niort (1hr); frequent to Surgères (1hr 25min); frequent to La Rochelle (1hr 45min); several daily to Limoges (2hr 30min); several daily to Angoulême (1hr) continuing to Bordeaux (2hr 10min), Dax (3hr 30min), Bayonne (4hr), Biarritz (4hr 30min), St-Jean-de-Luz (4hr 40min), Hendaye (4hr 55min) and Irun (5hr 5min) – all stops on the same line.

From Les Sables-d'Olonne several daily to Nantes (1hr 30min) and Paris-Montparnasse (4hr 45min).

From La Rochelle several daily to Nantes (1hr 50min); several daily to Bordeaux (4hr) via Rochefort and Saintes.

From Royan frequent to Angoulême (2hr) via Saintes (40min) and Cognac (1hr).

From Bordeaux frequent to Paris-Austerlitz (4–5 hr), stopping at Angoulême (1hr) and Poitiers (2hr); frequent to Bayonne-Biarritz (1hr 40min); frequent to St-Jean-de-Luz (2hr 15min); frequent to Toulouse (2hr 20min); 5 or 6 daily to Marseille (6–7hr); 4 daily to Nice (9–10 hr); 5 daily to Périgueux (1hr 20 min); 5 daily to Brive (2hr 30min); 6 daily to Bergerac (1hr 30min); frequent to Arcachon (45min); up to 4 daily to Sarlat (2hr 20min).

From Angoulême 4 daily to Limoges (1hr 30min–2hr).

From Limoges frequent to Paris-Austerlitz (3hr 30min–4hr); 4 daily to Poitiers (2hr–2hr 30min); 5 daily to St-Léonard-de-Noblat (25min), Eymoutiers (50min), Meymac (1hr 50min) and Ussel (2hr); frequent to Brive (1hr 10min) some stopping en route at Solignac-le-Vigen.

Buses

From Poitiers several SNCF to Parthenay (1hr–1hr 30min); 3 daily to Châteauroux (3hr 30min) via Chauvigny (35min), St-Savin (1hr) and Le Blanc (1hr 25min); daily to Ruffec (2hr 30min); daily to Limoges (3hr).

From Parthenay several SNCF to Thouars (1hr) via Airvault (25min); several to Niort (50min).

From Les Sables d'Olonne 4 SNCF to Luçon (2hr); 4 SNCF to Nantes (5hr 30min) – both via the coast road.

From Bordeaux: frequent to Blaye (1hr 45min); daily but infrequent to Pauillac (1hr); 5 daily to St-Émilion (1hr 15min).

From Saintes 2 daily to St-Denis-d'Oléron (2hr).

From Limoges 2 daily to Aubusson (2hr), 3 to St-Léonard (35min); up to 3 daily to Oradour and St-Junien (more in school term time); 1 daily to Châlus (1hr)

CHAPTER NINE

THE DORDOGNE AND LOT

T his is the south without the aridity of the Mediterranean. Steamy, moist and green, it can feel like a kind of lower-latitude England – which is no doubt why it attracts so many urban Brits in search of the good life and, increasingly, a second home. In the **Dordogne** heartlands, the country is certainly beautiful, but the regional authorities are all too well aware of their assets, hyping up the landscape, food and medieval towns as hard as they can. The result is that the famous spots, especially around **Sarlat**, are oppressively crowded in season. Don't let this deter you from seeing the region, though, particularly the **prehistoric cave paintings**, either in the **Vézère valley**, or at the quieter **Pech-Merle** caves in the Lot valley.

Heavily contested by the French and English during the Hundred Years' War, the Dordogne and Lot valleys are scattered with **ruined castles**, like **Bonaguil**, **Castelnaud** and **Beynac**, and **bastides** – the small military settlements constructed by both sides to secure their respective patches – like **Monpazier** and **Domme**. The **towns** – **Bergerac**, **Périgueux**, **Brive** and **Cahors** – are not really interesting enough to hold your attention beyond a brief stay, though they are useful bases for exploring the region. If you're interested in ecclesiastical architecture, there is rich fare, especially the **Romanesque sculpture** at **Beaulieu**, **Souillac** and, above all, **Moissac**.

There is rich culinary fare, too, for the Dordogne has the **richest regional cuisine** in the country, thanks to the preference for goose fat over any other cooking medium and the widespread use of *confits* – preparations of cooked meats preserved in their own juices. But it is renowned, too, for its *foie gras* (goose-liver pâté), truffles (the mushroom variety), *cèpes* or wild mushrooms, *cabécou* (goat's cheese), *coq au vin*, stuffed poultry, walnut oil (not to mention walnut salad and preserves) and the custom of *faire chabrol*, that is, pouring red wine into the remnants of your soup and slurping the delicious sludge directly from the bowl; formerly considered a low-class peasant habit this is gaining ground among gourmets.

Transport throughout the region is very poor. There's a sporadic train service which serves parts of the Lot valley, the Dordogne as far as Castelnau, and another line further north which passes through Périgueux and Brive, but you'll need your own wheels to get to most of the caves and castles, not to mention the Bordeaux vineyards. Otherwise, **walking** and **cycling** are the best ways to explore the region fully. Several **GRs** (marked footpaths), including the cross-country GR36, bisect the central and eastern parts of the region, and **bicycle hire** throughout the region is pretty good. The landscape of the east and north is small scale and intimate, just right for slow travelling, and the hills are not too strenuous either, until you get up into the wilder foothills of the Massif Central to the northeast beyond Brive. An increasingly popular way of seeing the region is by **canoe**: numerous companies hire out *kayaks*, and most of them will pick you up by minibus, once you've paddled downstream (see box on p.457 for further details).

HOTEL ROOM PRICES

For a fuller explanation of these price codes, see the box on p.28 of *Basics*.

① Under 100F ② 100–130F ③ 130–180F ④ 180–230F ⑤ 230–300F

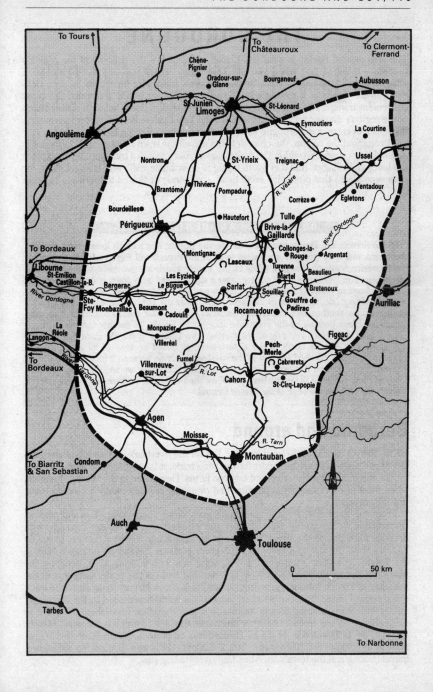

THE DORDOGNE

The area around **Sarlat** is what the British and Dutch – the majority of the region's tourists – think of first when you say **Dordogne**: where you find the picture-book villages and cliff-top castles (and the coach tours), and where the cuisine is at its richest and the prices at their highest. If you're relying on public transport, the most convenient transport base is **Périgueux**, no great shakes itself, but within easy reach of the region's famous prehistoric caves around **Les Eyzies**. For the eastern periphery, the upper Corrèze and Dordogne valleys, you are better off using **Brive** as a base.

Throughout the region, the chief delights are off the main routes – the Dordogne is nothing if not rustic. So within the limitations of your means of transport, try to explore the lanes and villages. And it is worth trying to co-ordinate visits with **market days**, for then even places that otherwise seem dead – or merely dedicated to tourists – come to life.

DORDOGNE – AN IDENTITY CRISIS

To the French, the **Dordogne** is a river. To the British, it is a much looser term, which covers a vast area (roughly equivalent to what the French call **Périgord**), which starts somewhere south of Limoges, takes in the Vézère and Dordogne valleys and much in between. The Dordogne is, of course, also a *département*, with fixed boundaries which pay no heed to either definition. The central part of the *département*, around Périgueux and the River Isle, is known as *Périgord Blanc*, after the light, white colour of its rock outcrops; the southeastern half around Sarlat as *Périgord Noir*, said to be darker in aspect than the *Blanc* because of the preponderance of oak woods. To confuse matters further the tourist authorities recently added another two colours to the Périgord patchwork: *Périgord Vert*, the far north of the *département*, so called because of its fertile green pastureland; and *Périgord Pourpre* in the southwest, purple because it includes the wine-growing area around Bergerac. For the purposes of this guide, we use the departmental boundaries, except in the east where we follow the Dordogne, Corrèze and Vézère rivers upstream as far as the edge of the Massif Central.

Bergerac and around

BERGERAC, capital of *Périgord Pourpre*, lies on the riverbank in the wide plain of the Dordogne. Once a flourishing port for the wine trade, it is still the main market centre for the surrounding maize, vine and tobacco farms. Devastated in the Wars of Religion, when most of its Protestant population fled overseas, it is essentially a modern town, but still attractive.

From the **gare SNCF** it's a ten-minute walk down cours Alsace-Lorraine and its continuation to the **vieille ville**, a calm and pleasant area to wander through, with drinking fountains on the street corners and numerous late medieval houses. In rue de l'Ancien-Pont, the splendid seventeenth-century **Maison Peyrarède** houses a **Musée du Tabac** (Tues–Sat 10am–noon & 2–5/6pm; Sun 2.30–6.30pm; 12F), detailing the history of the weed, with collections of pipes and tools of the trade. Bergerac is the mainstay of French **tobacco growing**, somewhat in the doldrums today since the traditional *brune* – made of air-cured brown tobacco – is being superseded by the seemingly milder but more harmful *blonde*, oven cured and therefore less labour-intensive to make. Bergerac has a couple of other museums, the best of which is the small **Musée du Vin, de la Batellerie et de la Tonnellerie** on pl de la Myrpe (Tues–Fri 10am–noon & 2–5.30pm, Sat 10am–noon, Sun 2–6.30pm; 12F), with displays on viticulture, barrel making and the town's once-bustling river-trading past.

CYRANO DE BERGERAC

Bergerac's most famous association is with **Cyrano de Bergerac**, the big-nosed lead character in Edmond Rostand's play, recently turned into the most expensive French film ever made, starring Gérard Dépardieu. Rostand's Cyrano, though fictional, was inspired by the seventeenth-century philosopher of the same name, who, sadly, had nothing to do with the town. Seemingly unperturbed by this historical fact, Bergerac has nevertheless erected a statue in honour of Cyrano on the pl de la Myrpe in the centre of town.

For **accommodation** in Bergerac, there are several small hotels in the back streets. A popular choice is the *Hôtel Pozzi*, 11 rue Pozzi (☎53.57.24.90; ③); more expensive is *Le Cyrano*, 2 bd Montaigne (☎53.57.02.76; ④); and there's a **campsite**, *La Pelouse* (☎53.57.06.67; open all year), a short way west of the centre by the river. The **SI** is at 97 rue Neuve-d'Argenson (summer daily 9am–7pm; winter Tues–Sat 9am–noon & 1.30–5.30pm). There is a vast **market** in the covered *halles* off the Grande-Rue in the old town on Wednesday and Saturday.

Château de Monbazillac

Half a dozen kilometres south of the town and best reached by **bicycle** (hire from 11 place Gambetta or 114 bd de l'Entrepôt) is the small **Château de Monbazillac** (June–Sept 10am–12.30pm & 2–7pm; Oct–May 10am–noon & 2–5/6pm; 20F), situated on gently rising slopes among its long-famous vineyards. The wine – out of fashion for many years – is white, velvety and sweet, best consumed with desserts or chilled as an apéritif. Red Bergeracs, on the other hand, often produced by small growers on the slopes north of the river and for many years known only to local connoisseurs, are beginning to enjoy much greater popularity, particularly among the British, at prices far more reasonable than the better known clarets of Bordeaux. The tour of the château includes a glass of *Monbazillac* at the end.

Château de St-Michel-de-Montaigne

Some 35km west of Bergerac, on the edge of the Dordogne *département*, committed fans of the French essayist, Michel Eyquem de Montaigne (1533–92), can visit his tower-study. This is all that remains of the ancient **Château de St-Michel-de-Montaigne**, burned down in 1885 and rebuilt in neo-Gothic style. Getting there entails a train journey to Lamothe-Montravel, followed by a 3.5-kilometre walk. A further complication is the need to telephone ahead for an appointment (☎53.58.69.74), which can only be arranged from Wednesday to Saturday, 9am to noon and 2 to 7pm.

Abbaye de Cadouin

More rewarding – the effort here is a 6-kilometre hike or bike ride up from LE BUISSON – is the twelfth-century Cistercian **Abbaye de Cadouin**, around 40km east of Bergerac. Until 1935 it drew flocks of pilgrims to wonder at a piece of cloth thought to be part of Christ's shroud. Since that date, when the shroud was shown not to be authentic, the main attraction has been the finely sculpted capitals of the flamboyant Gothic **cloister** (July–Aug daily 9am–noon & 2–6/7pm; rest of year 10am–noon & 2–5pm; closed Tues; 12F). Beside it is a Romanesque **church** (daily 8.30am–7pm) with a stark, bold front and wooden belfry roofed with chestnut shingles (chestnut trees abound around here, the timber used in furniture making and the nuts ground for flour in the once-frequent famines). Inside, it is apparent that the nave is slightly out of alignment. This is thought to be deliberate, perhaps a vestige of pagan attachments; for the three windows are aligned so that at the winter and summer solstices the sun shines through all three in a single shaft.

BASTIDES

In the thirteenth and fourteenth centuries, the kings and overlords of France and England – not to mention the Church – were busy trying to establish a foothold in southwest France. To do this, they began to construct fortified settlements known as **bastides** (a corruption of the word *bastille*), from which they could defend their interests. As an incentive to local inhabitants, anyone who was prepared to build, inhabit and defend them, was granted various perks and concessions, including a degree of self-government remarkable in feudal times. During this period, over 300 *bastides* were founded stretching from the Pyrenees to the Massif Central, all designed along rational, standardised lines – grid-plan streets, centred around a central arcaded market place with covered *halles*, all enclosed within a thick swath of walls. Most have lost their original aspect, but a handful retain their street layout, while fewer still have kept their walls – Domme being the exception.

Three bastides and a château

Three *bastides* – **Monpazier**, **Villeréal** and **Beaumont** – form a convenient triangle southeast of Bergerac, midway between the Dordogne and the Lot. Along with the nearby château at **Biron**, they make a pleasant and peaceful day's rambling if you have your own wheels. Public transport is almost non-existent: there is a bus from Périgueux to Monpazier (Mon–Sat; 2hr 30min), but the easiest way to get around is to hire a bicycle from Bergerac, Le Buisson or Siorac, all within 20–30km of the *bastides*.

Monpazier

MONPAZIER is the most impressive of the *bastides*, suffering none of the suffocating commercialism of DOMME (see p.455). Built in 1284 by King Edward I of England, who was also Duke of Aquitaine, it hasn't spread far beyond its original limits. Picturesque and placid though it is today, the village has a hard and bitter history. Twice, in 1594 and again in 1637, it was the centre of peasant rebellions, provoked by the misery that followed the Wars of Religion* and brutally suppressed: the 1637 peasants' leader was broken on the wheel in the square.

It is now severely depopulated. As the street ends the fields begin and you look out over the surrounding country. There is an ancient *lavoir*, where women used to wash their clothes, a much-altered church, and a gem of a central square – sunny, still and slightly menacing, like a Sicilian piazza at siesta time. Deep, shady arcades pass under all the houses, which are separated from each other by a small gap to reduce fire risk. At the corners the buttresses are cut away to allow the passage of laden pack animals.

It is possible to **stay overnight** in Monpazier, either at the *Hôtel de France*, 21 rue St-Jacques (☎53.2.60.06; ③), or at the choice of **campsites**: the *municipal*, 2km northwest, or *camping à la ferme*, 5km along a country lane at Le Bouyssou, signposted as you enter Monpazier – a great spot. If there are not too many people, the old couple who run the farm let you camp under the pines by the house and provide meals. They still speak Occitan together, the old language of the south and west of France. It's their first language; they only learnt French when they went to school.

---

* Sully, the Protestant general, describes a rare moment of light relief in the terrible wars, when the men of the Catholic *bastide*, Villefranche-de-Périgord, planned to capture Monpazier on the same night as the men of Monpazier planned to capture Villefranche. By chance, both sides took different routes, met no resistance, looted to their hearts' content and returned home congratulating themselves on their luck and skill, only to find in the morning that things were rather different. The peace terms were that everyone should return everything to its proper place.

Biron

A short distance to the south (8km from Monpazier), dominating the countryside for miles around, is the vast **Château de Biron** (July–Aug daily 9am–noon & 2–7pm; rest of year 9/9.30am–noon & 2–6pm; closed Tues; 30F). You can only see the place on a guided tour – and that means everything, including the grassy courtyard within its walls, where there is a Renaissance chapel and guardhouse with tremendous views over the roofs of the feudal village below.

A single street runs through the **village**, past a covered market on timber supports iron-hard with age, and out under an arched gateway. Well-manured vegetable plots interspersed with iris, lily and Iceland poppies lie under the tumbledown walls. At the bottom of the hill, another group of houses stand on a small *place* with a broken well in front of a half-ruined church, its Romanesque origins covered by motley alterations, and with a massive home-made ladder leading to the belfry.

Villeréal

Built a decade or so earlier than Monpazier, the *bastide* of **VILLERÉAL**, 15km to the southwest, was founded by Alphonse de Poitiers in an attempt to check English expansion in the Dordogne. It failed to do so and was taken by the English during the Hundred Years' War. Its most outstanding feature is the oak-beamed *halles* in the central *place*, which dates from the fourteenth century. You can stay at the *Hôtel de l'Europe*, 1 rue Mirabeau (☎53.36.00.35; ③), or at one of the many nearby **campsites**; the *camping municipal* (☎53.36.05.63; mid-June to mid-Sept), is off the D207 to Bergerac.

Beaumont

BEAUMONT, 17km north of Villeréal on the D676, is another thirteenth-century English *bastide*, founded by Edward I. Like many *bastides*, its church, **Église St-Front**, was built for military as well as religious reasons – a kind of final outpost of defence in times of attack, hence the bulky tower at each of the four corners, and the well inside the church. There's a **campsite**, *Les Remparts* (☎53.22.40.86; April–Oct), to the southwest of town off the D676.

The grands châteaux

East of ST-CYPRIEN, the Dordogne is at its most appealing, forming great loops (*cingles*) between rich fields, wooded hills and craggy outcrops. The 10km between LES MILANDES and DOMME are particularly spectacular, with cliff-top châteaux facing each other across the valley, for the most part dating from the Hundred Years' War when the river marked the frontier between French-held territory to the north and English-held territory to the south. Public transport is confined to the train station at LA ROQUE-GAGEAC, but all the places are within easy walking or cycling distance from there. A good way to see the châteaux without enduring the compulsory guided tours is to paddle downstream by canoe (see box on p.457 for details).

Châteaux: Les Milandes, Fayrac and Castelnaud

The first château you come to east of St-Cyprien is **Les Milandes** (Palm Sunday–mid-Oct daily 9.30–11.30am & 2–6.30pm; 20F), perched high on the south bank. Built in 1489, it was the property of the De Caumont family until the Revolution, but its most famous owner is the *Folies-Bergères* star, **Josephine Baker** (see box), who owned it from 1936–69. The stories surrounding the place are more intriguing than the château itself, which contains de Caumont treasures as well as Ms Baker's effects.

Further along on the same side of the river, the **Château de Fayrac**, all slated pepperpot towers, and closed to the public, was an English forward position in the Hundred Years' War, built to watch over Beynac, on the opposite bank, where the French were holed up.

A little to the south of Fayrac are the ruins of the **Château de Castelnaud** (April–Oct 10am–6/7pm; 20F), the true rival to Beynac in terms of impregnability – although it was successfully captured by the bellicose Simon de Monfort as early as 1214. The English held it for much of the Hundred Years' War, and it wasn't until the Revolution that it was finally abandoned. Fairly heavily restored in the last two decades, none of the architecture can match the views up and down the valley.

JOSEPHINE BAKER AND THE RAINBOW TRIBE

Born on June 3, 1906, in the black ghetto of East St Louis, Mississippi, **Josephine Baker** was one of the most remarkable women of this century. Her mother washed clothes for a living and her father was a drummer who soon deserted his family, yet by the late 1920s Josephine was the most celebrated cabaret star in France, primarily due to her role in the legendary *Folies Bergère* s show in Paris. On her first night, de Gaulle, Hemingway, Piaf and Stravinsky were among the audience; her notoriety was further enhanced by her long line of illustrious husbands and lovers, which included the crown Prince of Sweden and the crime novelist Georges Simenon; she mixed with the likes of le Corbusier and Adolf Loos, and kept a pet cheetah, called Mildred, with whom she used to walk round Paris. During the war, she was active in the Resistance, for which she won the *Croix de Guerre*. Later on, she became involved in the civil rights movement in North America, where she insisted on playing to non-segregated audiences, a stance which got her arrested in Canada and tailed by the FBI in the US.

By far her most bizarre project, though, was the château of **Les Milandes**, which she bought in 1936, after her marriage to the French orchestra leader, Jo Bouillon. Having equipped the place with two hotels, three restaurants, a mini-golf course, tennis court and an autobiographical wax museum, she opened the château to the general public as a model multi-cultural community, popularly dubbed the *"village du monde"*. In the course of the 1950s, she adopted babies (mostly orphans) of different ethnic and religious backgrounds from around the world. By end of the decade, she had brought twelve children to Les Milandes, including a black Catholic Colombian and a Buddhist Korean, along with her mother, brother and sister from East St Louis. Over 300,000 people a year visited the château in the 1950s, but the conservative local population were never very happy about Les Milandes and the "Rainbow Tribe". In the 1960s, financial problems, divorce and two heart attacks spelled the end for the project, and despite a sit-in protest by Baker herself (by then in her sixties), the château was sold off in 1969. Josephine died of a stroke while on stage, in 1975, and was given a grand state funeral at La Madeleine in Paris, mourned by thousands of her adopted countryfolk.

Beynac

Clearly visible on an impregnable cliff edge on the north bank of the river, the eye-catching village and castle of **BEYNAC-ET-CAZENAC** was built in the days when the river was the only route open to traders and invaders. By road it is 3km to the **château** (daily 10am–noon & 2–5.30/6.30pm; 22F), but a steep lane leads up through the village (15min by foot). It is protected on the landward side by a double wall; elsewhere, the sheer drop of almost 200m does the job. The flat terrace at the base of the keep, which was added by the English, conceals the remains of the houses where the beleaguered villagers lived; one of the houses has been partly excavated. Richard the Lionheart held the place for a time, until a gangrenous wound received while besieging the castle of Châlus, north of Périgueux, ended his term of bloodletting.

Originally, to facilitate defence, the rooms inside the keep only communicated via a narrow spiral staircase – in stone, not wood, as in the reconstruction, because of the danger of fire. The division of domestic space into dining rooms and so forth only came about when the advent of artillery made these old *châteaux-forts* militarily obsolete. From the roof, there is a stupendous – and vertiginous – view up river to the **Château de Marqueyssac**, whose beautiful seventeenth-century gardens are open to the public in the summer.

La Roque-Gageac

The village of LA ROQUE-GAGEAC is almost too perfect, ite ochre-coloured houses sheltering under dramatically overhanging cliffs. Regular winner of France's prettiest village contest, it inevitably pulls in the coaches, and since the main road separates the village from the river, the noise and fumes of the traffic can become oppressive. The best way to escape is to slip away through the lanes and alleyways which wind up through the terraced houses. The other option is taking the rowing-boat ferry service to the small island where you can picnic and enjoy a much better view of La Roque than the crowds milling around beneath the village, at its best in the burnt-orange glow of the evening sun.

Most people just come here for the afternoon, so there's usually space if you want to stay the night, most cheaply at *La Belle Étoile* (☎53.29.51.44; closed mid-Oct to Palm Sunday; ③/⑤). In the low season this can be a good deal, but in high season, prices rocket and availability plummets. There are also four **campsites** in the vicinity, and a reasonably priced restaurant, *L'Ancre d'Or,* overlooking the Dordogne.

Domme

High on the scarp on the opposite bank of the river, **DOMME** is one of the best preserved of the *bastides*. The best way to get there is by bicycle, so do your renting in Sarlat and come up by the back road – about 45 minutes. Somewhat petrified by too careful grooming, Domme's attractions include three of the original thirteenth-century gateways and a section of the old walls. From the northern edge of the village, known as the *barre*, marked by a drop so precipitous fortifications were deemed unnecessary, you look out over a wide sweep of river country. Underneath the village are hundreds of metres of caves – entrance opposite the **SI** on the main square – in which the towns-people took refuge in times of danger.

If you decide to **eat** here, you might as well succumb to the tourist blandishments and sample the sickly local walnut liqueur or the *eau de vie de prune* as a *digestif*. But it makes more sense to eat down by the river at CÉNAC among the saggy, tea-cosy roofs and escape the worst of the crowds. While you're there, don't miss the round tile roof of the chapel or the beautifully proportioned twelfth-century church on rue St-Cybranet.

Sarlat

SARLAT-LA-CANÉDA, capital of *Périgord Noir*, is held in a hollow between hills 10km or so back from the Dordogne valley. As so often, one hardly notices the modern town, but the mainly sixteenth- to seventeenth-century vieille ville is alluring – busy in a friendly, rustic sort of way, mellow with time and warm with the honey colour of the local limestone.

The vieille ville

The **vieille ville** is an excellent example of medieval organic urban growth, violated only by the straight swathe of "La Traverse", the **rue de la République** – now thank-fully pedestrianised – which cuts through its middle. The west side alone remains un-chic and grubby; the east side is where most people wander. As you approach from the station, turn right down rue Lakanal which leads to the large and unexciting **Cathédrale St-Sacerdos**, mostly dating from its seventeenth-century renovation. Opposite stands arguably the town's finest house, **Maison de La Boétie**, one-time home of Montaigne's friend, Étienne de La Boétie, with its gabled tiers of windows and characteristic steep roof stacked with heavy limestone tiles (*lauzes*).

Beneath the house, a plaque pays tribute to de Gaulle's Minister of Culture, André Malraux, "...member of the Resistance, government minister and author of the law on the renovation of historic towns...". In one sense the renovation that has taken place in Sarlat since the passing of the **Loi Malraux** in 1962 is a marvellous illustration of the success of that policy, yet it also exemplifies the negative side. In season, the town goes overboard, with caparisoned dames, jousting in the streets and other heritage junketing.

For a better sense of the medieval town, wander through the cool, shady lanes and courtyards around the back of the cathedral – **cour des Fontaines** and **cours des Chanoines**. To one side of the cours des Chanoines is the curious twelfth-century coned tower, the **Lanterne des Morts**, whose exact function has escaped historians, though the most popular theory is that it was built to commemorate St-Bernard who performed various miracles when he visited the town in 1147.

There are more wonderful old houses in the streets to the north, especially **rue des Consuls**, and up the slopes to the east. Eventually, though, Sarlat's labyrinthine lanes will take you back to the central **place de la Liberté**, where the big Saturday **market** spreads its stands of geese, flowers, *foie gras*, truffles and mushrooms in season, as well as various people trying to make a living from the hordes who hit Sarlat in the summer. Another recent development is the increasing number of museums which are cropping up in Sarlat as the town turns more and more to tourism. The only one worth anything more than a passing nod is the **Musée des Miniatures**, 17 rue de la République (July & Aug daily 10am–12.30pm & 2–7pm; rest of the year Tues–Sun only; 20F). Staying just on the right side of kitsch, it's a firm favourite with the many kids who are dragged around Sarlat with their parents.

Practicalities

The **gare SNCF** is 1.5km south of the old town (there's a free bus shuttle between the two). If you have no transport of your own, you can hire **bicycles** from: *Sarlat Sport* on rue Jean-Leclaire; the youth hostel; the train station; or *Garage Matigot*, 52 rue Gambetta. The **SI** lodges in the sixteenth-century Hôtel de Maleville on place de la Liberté (mid-June to mid-Sept Mon–Sat 9am–7pm; Sun 10am–noon & 4–6pm; rest of year Mon–Sat 9am–noon & 2–6pm). For a small fee, they'll find you a room, though it's almost impossible to find cheap **accommodation** in season.

Hotels worth trying include the *Marcel*, 8 av de Selves (☎53.59.21.98; closed mid-Nov–Feb; ③/④); the very central *Hôtel de la Mairie*, place de la Liberté (☎53.59.05.71; ③/⑤); and, again central, *Les Récollets*, 4 rue J-J-Rousseau (☎53.59.00.49; ③/⑤). As throughout this part of the Dordogne, prices vary enormously between the high and low seasons. Fortunately, the **youth hostel** on av de Selves (☎53.59.47.59; open May–Sept; no curfew), a ten-minute walk from the vieille ville along the Périgueux road, is cheap year-round; the nearest **campsite**, *Les Périères*, is expensive and often full in high season, but there's a simpler and more prettily sited campground, *Les Acacias*, about 2km beyond the railway viaduct in LA CANEDA (☎53.59.29.30; open Easter–Sept).

Restaurants are generally overpriced compared with the rest of the Dordogne, but mercifully nowhere near Côte d'Azur prices. To stay the right side of 100F, you'll be confined to *brasseries* like the *Brasserie de la Mairie* on the main square – tables in the shade for lunch, and not that expensive despite its prime location. *Le Planon*, around the side of Église Ste-Marie is smaller, cooler but similarly priced. If you're prepared to pay a bit more, try *Rossignol*, up rue Fénelon (open until 8pm only).

CANOEING IN THE DORDOGNE

Canoeing is becoming increasingly popular in the Dordogne, with hire outlets at just about every twist in the Vézère and Dordogne rivers. In the summer both rivers are shallow and slow-flowing and ideal for beginners. Although it's possible to hire one-person kayaks or two-person canoes by the hour, it's best to take at least a half day or longer, and simply cruise downstream – you'll be picked up by the company's minibus at your final destination and get taken back to where you began. Prices for one full day vary from 90–110F for a kayak, 130–180F for a canoe; most places function daily in July and August, on demand in May, June and September, and are closed the rest of the year. All companies are obliged to equip you with lifejackets (*gilets* or *ceintures*) and teach you basic safety procedures – most importantly how to capsize and get out without drowning – and you must be able to **swim**. Below are just some of the choices on offer.

RIVER DORDOGNE

Copeyre, based in Martel (☎65.37.33.51). Twelve outlets from Argentat to Beynac; choose your own route, or longer accompanied trips up to seven days (900F).

Canoë Cénac, Le Port de Domme (☎53.28.22.01). Carsac–Beynac (full day); Carsac–Cénac or Cénac–Beynac (half day); longer accompanied trips possible.

Safaraid, in summer based in Argentat (☎55.28.80.70). Seven outlets from Argentat to Beynac; choose your own route for the day, or longer trips up to 15 days.

Kayak-Club, Castelnaud-en-Périgord (☎53.29.52.06). Groléjac–Castelnaud (full day); Vitrac–Castelnaud (half day); Castelnaud–Les Milandes (half day).

Maison du Plein-Air, 16 rue Fénelon (☎53.31.24.18). St-Julien–Vitrac (full day; canoe 130F/kayak 100F); Vitrac–Les Milandes (full day; canoe 120F/kayak 90F); half day trips possible.

RIVER VÉZÈRE

L'Animation Vézère, Pont Routier, rte de Périgueux, Les Eyzies (☎53.06.92.92). Also based at Montignac; you can choose your distance, stopping anywhere between Montignac to Les Eyzies.

Randonnée Vézère, Condat-sur-Vézère (☎53.51.38.35). Choice of distance from Condat to Les Eyzies.

The Vézère Valley: prehistoric caves

Half an hour or so by train from Périgueux lies the **Vézère Valley**, a luxuriant cliff-cut region riddled with **prehistoric caves** and subterranean streams. It was here that the first skeletons of **Cro-Magnon people** – the first *Homo sapiens*, tall and muscular with a large skull – were unearthed in 1868 by labourers digging out the Périgueux–Agen railway line, and here, too, that an incredible wealth of archaeological and artistic evidence of the life of late-Stone-Age people has since been found. The many cave paintings are remarkable not only for their great age but also for their exquisite colouring and the skill with which they are drawn.

LES EYZIES is the main base for the caves, but the most spectacular of all is at LASCAUX, further to the north near MONTIGNAC. **Transport** is not bad for the region; four trains run daily to Les Eyzies from Périgueux; two from Bordeaux, with a change at LE BUISSON. For getting around the area once you've arrived, the SI in Les Eyzies hire **bikes** by the day, half day or week.

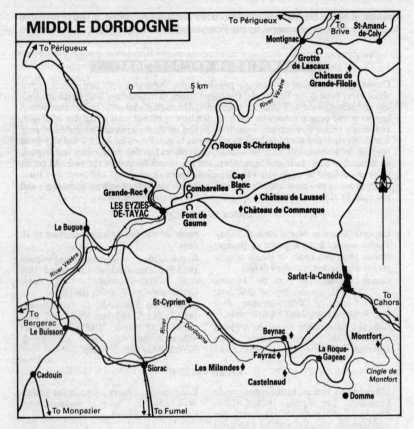

MIDDLE DORDOGNE

To Périgueux
To Brive   St-Amand-de-Coly
Montignac

To Périgueux

Grotte de Lascaux

Château de Grande-Filolie

0   5 km

River Vézère

Roque St-Christophe

Cap Blanc
Combarelles
Grande-Roc♦
Château de Laussel♦
LES EYZIES-DE-TAYAC
Font de Gaume
Château de Commarque♦

N

Le Bugue

River Vézère

Sarlat-la-Canéda

To Cahors

To Bergerac
Le Buisson

St-Cyprien

River Dordogne

Beynac

Montfort

Fayrac♦
La Roque-Gageac
Cadouin
Siorac
Les Milandes♦
Cingle de Montfort
Castelnaud

Domme

To Monpazier   To Fumel

Les Eyzies

The main base for visiting the Vézère valley is **LES EYZIES-DE-TAYAC**, an unattractive one-street village completely dedicated to tourism. However, there are a couple of things worth checking out before (or after) heading out to one or more of the caves.

Firstly, there's the **Musée National de Préhistoire** (9.30am–noon & 2–5/6pm; closed Tues; 10F). It exhibits numerous prehistoric artefacts including copies of one of the most beautiful pieces of Stone-Age art, two clay bisons from the Tuc d'Audoubert cave in the Pyrenees, and the small bas-relief of an exaggerated female figure holding what looks like a slice of watermelon, found near Laussel (see below), known as the *Vénus à la Corne* (Venus with the horn of plenty): the orginal is in the Musée d'Aquitaine in Bordeaux.

In April 1990, local farmer, M Pataud, opened his own extensive private collection of prehistoric finds, next door in the **Musée de l'Abri Pataud** (July–Aug Tues–Sun 9.30am–7.30pm; rest of the year 10am–noon & 2–5.30pm; closed Jan; 20F). Much of the stuff was discovered during archaeological digs in the 1950s and 1960s on Pataud's own farmland, which, it transpired, lay over an *abri* (shelter) used by reindeer hunters for over 20,000 years.

Practicalities

The **SI** is on Les Eyzies' one street (July & Aug daily 9am–7pm; rest of the year Mon–Sat 9am–noon & 2–6pm). In addition to bicycle hire, they also give out information on private rooms in the area (roughly 150F per person). **Hotels** are pricey and likely to ask for *demi-pension*; the cheapest is the *Hôtel du Périgord*, near the Grotte de Font-de-Gaume on the D47 (☎53.06.97.26; ③), followed by the *Hôtel de France* on rue du Moulin (☎53.06.97.23; closed Nov–Palm Sunday; ④/⑤). Alternatively, stay in LE BUGUE, 10km downstream, where the *Hôtel de Paris*, 14 rue Paris (☎53.07.28.16; ②/③), has much cheaper rooms.

There's a riverside **campsite**, *La Rivière* (☎53.06.97.14; mid-March to mid-Oct), on the rte de Périgueux, or hostel-priced beds at a very attractive self-catering **gîte d'étape**, *La Ferme Eymaries* (☎53.06.94.73; April–Oct), thirty minutes by foot from the village. To find it, cross the bridge on the Périgueux road, turn sharp left and continue to the rail track, where there's a signpost to the right.

Eating out in Les Eyzies can be expensive, unless you go for the no-nonsense *brasserie*-style food at *La Grignotière*, near the SI.

The caves

There are more **prehistoric caves** around Les Eyzies than you could possibly hope to visit in one day. Besides, the compulsory guided tours are tiring, so it's best to select just a couple of the ones listed below.

Grotte de Font-de-Gaume

1.5km along the D47 to Sarlat; April–Sept daily 9am–noon & 2–6pm; Oct–March 10am–noon & 2–4pm, closed Tues; 22F; Sun half price. Maximum of 20 on each tour (tickets sell out fast: get to the ticket office as soon as possible).

Since its discovery in 1901, dozens of polychrome paintings have been found in the tunnel-like **Grotte de Font-de-Gaume**. The cave mouth is no more than a fissure from which a resurgent stream once flowed. Concealed by rocks and trees, it now stands above a small lush valley, but when Stone-Age people first settled here during the last Ice Age – about 25,000 BC – the Dordogne was tundra, the domain of roaming bison, reindeer and mammoth.

Inside, the cave is a narrow twisting passage of irregular height. There's no lighting, and you quickly lose your bearings in the dark. The first **painting** you see is a frieze of bison, at about eye level: reddish-brown in colour, massive, full of movement, and very far from the primitive representations you might expect. Further on, in a side passage, two horses stand one behind the other, forelegs outstretched as if to attempt, as the guide suggests with some relish, *un début d'accouplement* (the beginnings of copulation). But the most miraculous of all is a frieze of five bisons discovered in 1966 during cleaning operations. The colour, remarkably sharp and vivid, is preserved by a protective layer of calcite. Shading under the belly and down the thighs is used to give three-dimensionality with a sophistication that seems utterly modern. Another panel consists of superimposed drawings, a fairly common phenomenon in cave painting, sometimes the result of work by successive generations, but here an obviously deliberate technique. A reindeer in the foreground shares legs with a large bison behind to indicate perspective.

Stocks of artists' materials have also been found: kilos of prepared pigments; palettes – stones stained with ground-up earth pigments; and wooden painting sticks. Painting was clearly a specialised, perhaps professional, business, reproduced in dozens and dozens of caves located in the central Pyrenees and areas of northern Spain.

THEORIES ABOUT THE CAVES

Font-de-Gaume is only 130m long, but many caves are far longer, with terrifyingly difficult access through twisting slippery passages, passable only on your belly. The artists had just the most primitive lamps to light their way and paint by.

No one ever lived in these caves, and there are various theories as to why these inaccessible spots were chosen. Most agree that the caves were sanctuaries: if not actually places of worship, they at least had religious significance. One theory is that making images of animals that were **commonly hunted**, like reindeer and bison, or feared, like bears and mammoths, was a kind of sympathetic magic intended to help men either catch or evade these animals. Another is that they were part of a **fertility cult**: sexual images of women with pendulous breasts and protuberant rumps are common, and it seems, too, that certain animals were associated with the feminine principle. Others argue, from parallels with aboriginal Australians who used similar images to teach the young vital survival information as well as the history and mythological origins of their people, that these cave paintings served **educational purposes**. But much remains unexplained – for instance, the abstract signs that appear in many caves and the arrows which clearly cannot be arrows, because Stone-Age arrowheads looked different from these representations.

Grotte des Combarelles

2km along the D47 to Sarlat; hours and admission prices as Font-de-Gaum (unlike Font-de-Gaume, afternoon tickets are not for sale in the morning – arrive early for both sessions to be sure of a place).

Discovered in 1910, the innermost part of the **Grotte des Combarelles** is covered with engravings from the Magdalenian period about 12,000 years ago, many superimposed, as they were drawn over a period of 2000 years. They include horses, reindeer, mammoths and crude human figures. Among the finest are the heads of a horse and a lioness.

Abri du Cap Blanc

7km east of Les Eyzies: take the D47 to Sarlat, then left after the Grotte des Combarelles up the D48; July–Aug 9.30am–7pm; rest of the year 10am–noon & 2–5pm; closed mid-Nov–mid-March; 17F (no discounts because the site is privately owned).

Not a cave but a rock shelter, the **Abri du Cap Blanc** contains a **sculpted frieze** of horses and bison dating from the Middle Magdalenian period, 14,000 years ago. The design is deliberate, with the sculptures polished and set off against a pock-marked background. But what makes this place extraordinary is not just the large scale, but the **high relief** of some of the sculptures. This was only possible in places where light reached in, which in turn brought the danger of destruction by exposure to the air. Of the ten surviving prehistoric sculptures in France this is the best. Cro-Magnon people actually lived in this shelter, and a female skeleton has been found some 2000 years younger than the frieze.

Château de Commarque

If you're looking for a non-cave detour, continue a little further up the primitive-looking and heavily wooded Beune Valley from Cap Blanc, to the elegant sixteenth-century Château de Laussel (closed to the public). On the opposite side of the valley stand the romantically overgrown ruins of the **Château de Commarque**. Built in the thirteenth century, it was occupied by the English during the Hundred Years' War, and substantial sections of the fortifications still stand. You can reach it on foot via the GR6 footpath, which leaves the D47, past the Font-de-Gaume and just after *Pizzeria Girouteaux*.

Grotte du Grand Roc

2km north of Les Eyzies, off the D47 to Périgueux; July–mid-Sept 9am–7pm; rest of the year 9am–noon & 2–6pm; closed Nov–March; 25F.

As well as prehistoric cave paintings, you can also see some truly spectacular stalactites and stalagmites in the area around Les Eyzies. Some of the best examples are in the **Grotte du Grand Roc**, whose entrance is high up in the cliffs which line much of the Vézère Valley. There's a great view from the mouth of the cave and, inside, along some fifty metres of tunnel, a fantastic array of rock formations.

La Roque St-Christophe

9km northeast of Les Eyzies, along the D706 to Montignac; times and prices as for Grotte du Grand Roc.

The enormous prehistoric dwelling site, **La Roque St-Christophe**, is made up of about one hundred caves on five levels, hollowed out of the limestone cliffs, 700–800m long and 80m above the ground, where the river Vézère once flowed. The earliest traces of occupation go back over 50,000 years. The view is pretty good, and the guided tour instructive, but most of the finds are actually on display at the Musée National de Préhistoire in Les Eyzies.

Around Montignac: the Lascaux caves

Some 26km up the Vézère Valley, **MONTIGNAC** is the main base for visiting the **Lascaux** caves. It's a more attractive place than Les Eyzies, with several wooden-balconied houses leaning appealingly over the river, and a lively annual arts festival in mid-July.

Unfortunately, the shortage of moderately priced accommodation is even more acute. Apart from *Le Bon Acceuil*, rue du 4-septembre (☎53.51.82.99; ③), only the *Hôtel de la Grotte*, further along the same street (☎53.51.82.99; ③/⑤), has cheapish rooms; otherwise it's the *Hôtel du Périgord* on place Tourny (☎53.51.80.38; ⑤), or the 3* **campsite**, *Municipal le Bleufond*, a little to the south of town (☎53.51.83.95; April to mid-Oct). The **SI** can be found on place Bertran-de-Born, with a bicycle hire shop opposite.

In the same building as the SI is the **Musée Eugène-Le-Roy** – displaying local crafts and trades – which includes a reconstruction of the household of Jacquou le Croquant, the peasant protagonist of the novel of the same name by Eugène le Roy, the Dordogne's native novelist, who lived and died here in Montignac. His *L'Année Rustique en Périgord* is also a good read for getting the feel of the region in the nineteenth century.

Grotte de Lascaux

The **Grotte de Lascaux** was discovered in 1940 by four boys who were, according to popular myth, looking for their dog and fell into a deep cavern decorated with marvellously preserved animal paintings. Executed by Cro-Magnon people 17,000 years ago, the paintings are among the finest examples of prehistoric art in existence. There are five or six identifiable styles, and subjects include the bison, mammoth and horse, plus the biggest known prehistoric drawing, of a five-and-a-half-metre bull with astonishingly expressive head and face. In 1948, the cave was opened to the public, and over the course of the next fifteen years, more than a million tourists came to Lascaux. Sadly, because of deterioration from the body heat and breath of visitors, the cave had to be closed in 1963. If you want to see the original you can put your name on the waiting list, but there's a two-year backlog. Since 1983, though, it has been possible to see an exact replica – known simply as Lascaux II.

Lascaux II

2km south of Montignac on the D104e; July–Aug daily 9.30am–7pm; rest of the year Tues–Sun 10am–noon & 2–5pm; tickets must be bought from Montignac SI in July–Aug; 45F.

Opened in 1983, **Lascaux II** is the result of eleven years' painstaking work by twenty artists and sculptors, under the supervision of Monique Peytral, using the same methods and materials as the original cave painters. While the visit can't offer the excitement of a real cave, the reconstruction – which cost over 500 million francs – rarely disappoints the thousands who trek here every year. The guided tour lasts 40 minutes (commentary in French, with English translations available), and the tickets include entrance into the **prehistoric theme park**, 5km down the Vézère at LE THOT, with Disney-esque mock-ups of prehistoric scenes and live examples of some of the animals which feature in the paintings: European bison, long-horned cattle and Przewalski's horses (a rare and beautiful animal from Mongolia that is believed to resemble the prehistoric wild horse: notice the erect mane).

St-Amand-de-Coly and the Château de la Grande Filolie

An arduous but rewarding nine-kilometre cycle ride east of Montignac is the village of **ST-AMAND-DE-COLY**, which boasts a superb fortified Romanesque church. Despite its bristling military architecture, the **church** – built in the twelfth century – manages to combine great delicacy and spirituality. With its purity of line and simple decoration, it is at its most evocative in the low sun of late afternoon or early evening. Its defences left nothing to chance. The walls are four metres thick, a ditch runs all the way around, and a passage once skirted the eaves, with numerous positions for archers to rain down arrows, and blind stairways to mislead attackers.

There is a guard on hand to give **guided tours**, including an informative and evocative 30-minute film. Although not officially sanctioned, he will usually agree to show you the roof and galleries if you make a special request. If you don't mind heights, you'll be rewarded with a magnificent view down into the church and you can climb secret stairs for a bird's-eye view of the roof.

Between Montignac and St-Amand-de-Coly, 100m off the D704, is the **Château de la Grande Filolie**, an amalgam of medieval and seventeenth-century buildings, including a farm and chapel – an attractive diversion, if you have the time. The château itself is closed to the public, but the gardens are accessible.

Périgueux

PÉRIGUEUX is a suitably busy and prosperous market town for a province made rich by tourism and specialised farming. The local Gaulish tribe, the *Petrocorii*, gave the town its name, but it was the Romans who transformed it into an important settlement. A few Roman remains, and the medieval vieille ville, survive to this day, and are pleasant enough, but hardly compelling. However, if you're dependent on public transport, Périgueux can be a useful base for exploring the northern half of *Périgord*, with particularly good transport links to the prehistoric caves around Les Eyzies (see p.458–59).

The town

Place Bugeaud and the long **Boulevard Montaigne** mark the western edge of the vieille ville, known as the **quartier St-Front** (after the cathedral), with the River Isle as its natural eastern border. Between the station and the vieille ville lies the heart of what used to be Roman Périgueux, known as **La Cité**.

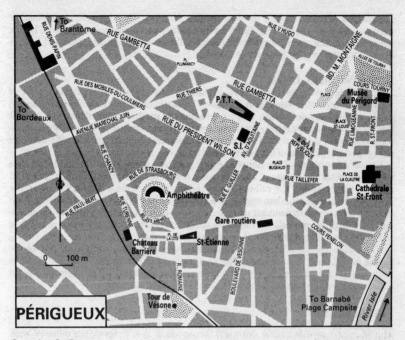

PÉRIGUEUX

Quartier St-Front

East of pl Bugeaud, down rue Taillefer, is the town's principal building, the domed and coned **Cathédrale St-Front**, its square, pineapple-capped belfry still surging far above the roofs of the surrounding medieval houses. Unfortunately, it's no beauty, having suffered, like Angoulême Cathedral, from the zealous purist attentions of the nineteenth-century restorer, Abadie, best known for the Sacré-Coeur in Paris. The result is too white, too new, too regular, and the roof is spiked all over with ill-proportioned nipple-like projections serving no obvious purpose. "A supreme example of how not to restore," Freda White tartly observed in her classic travelogue, *Three Rivers of France*. It's a pity, for it was one of the most distinctive Romanesque churches undertaken in France, modelled on St Mark's in Venice and the Holy Apostles in Constantinople. Nevertheless, the Byzantine influence is still evident in the interior in the Greek-cross plan – most unusual in France – and in the massive clean curves of the domes and their supporting arches. The big Baroque **altarpiece**, carved in walnut wood, in the gloomy east bay, is worth a look, too, depicting the Assumption of the Virgin, with a humorous little detail in the illustrative scenes from her life, of a puppy tugging the infant Jesus' sheets from his bed with its teeth.

At the west end of the cathedral in **place de la Clautre** beneath the blank facade of the original eleventh-century building there is a bi-weekly **market**, on Wednesday and Saturday. From the terrace below you look across to the wooded hills beyond the River Isle, while north and south of the *place* crowd the renovated buildings of the medieval **vieille ville**. The longest and finest street is the narrow **rue Limogeanne**, lined with Renaissance mansions, now turned into shops and *pâtisseries*. The surrounding streets are also scattered with fine Renaissance houses; a particularly handsome one is the Hôtel de Gamançon, 3 rue de la Constitution, now the seat of the *Conservation des*

Monuments Historiques, with the more sedate Hôtel de Crenoux next door. Another curious one is 17 rue de l'Éguillerie on the corner of the attractive **place St-Louis**, where a turretted watch tower leans out over the street. There are other old houses down along the river by the Pont des Barris.

Roman Périgueux: La Cité

For an insight into the days when Périgueux was the provincial Roman town of *Vesunna*, head for the **Musée du Périgord** (10am–noon and 2–5pm; closed Tues; 5F), on the shady cours de Tourny, which runs along the northern edge of the vieille ville. It has some very beautiful Gallo-Roman mosaics, an extensive but badly displayed prehistoric collection, again of local origin, and some exquisite Limoges enamels near the exit, especially portraits of the twelve Caesars.

For actual remains of the Roman heyday you have to go to the Jardin des Arènes which conceals the ruins of an enormous **amphitheatre**, dismantled in the third century, while over by the railway at the end of rue Romaine a high brick tower, the **Tour de Vésone**, is the last vestige of a temple to the city's guardian goddess. More bits and pieces, chiefly jumbled masonry, are visible in the so-called **Maison Romane** and the **Porte Normande** off rue Turenne, defensive works hastily cobbled together to keep the invading Visigoths at bay in the fourth century.

The rather mutilated church in this neighbourhood is the former cathedral of the **Église St-Étienne**, condemned to life as a traffic island on place de la Cité. Partially destroyed by the Huguenots when the town was occupied in 1577, it's nevertheless an equal match for the present cathedral in terms of height and majesty.

Practicalities

The **SI** is at 1 av d'Aquitaine (Mon–Fri 9am–noon & 2–4.30/6pm), ten minutes' walk from the **gare SNCF**. Other useful sources of information include the **CIJ**, next to the SI in av d'Aquitaine and, if you're interested in **walking**, the **GR office** at 15 av Lattre-de-Tassigny: ask for their booklet, *Randonnées Pédestres en Périgord*.

If you're after a **hotel**, you'll find a number of cheap ones right by the station: *Hôtel du Midi et Terminus* (☎53.53.41.06; ②); *Hôtel des Voyageurs* (☎53.53.17.44; ①); and *Hôtel des Charentes* (☎53.53.37.10; closed mid-Dec–mid-June; ③), which has an inexpensive restaurant. There's really little to choose between them. Alternatively, there is **hostel accommodation** at the *foyer, Résidence Lakanal* (☎53.53.52.05; reception 5–7/8pm), off 32 bd Lakanal (follow the rail track south of the station to the far edge of town), and **camping** – at *Barnabé-Plage* on the east bank of the River Isle and *l'Isle*, 2km out on the BRIVE road (☎53.53.41.45; open all year).

There's no shortage of good **restaurants** in Périgueux, though they tend to be expensive. Exceptions, and good standbys, include *Lou Chabrol*, 22 rue Éguillerie, and *Pizzeria Les Coupoles*, 7 rue de la Clarté, both near the cathedral and both closed on Sunday and Monday. Also worth a try and nearby is the restaurant, *Au Vieux Pavé*, 4 rue de la Sagesse, and *Au Petit Chef*, by the *halles* on pl du Coderc. As for nightlife, you can occasionally hear jazz at *Benson's* on pl St-Louis.

Around Périgueux

This is one of the hardest regions in France to explore without transport of your own. Buses are infrequent, trains almost non-existent and hitching uncertain, to say the least. If you're interested in the sights, it can be worth considering coach trips from Périgueux. The **Office Départemental de Tourisme**, on rue Wilson, organises trips from mid-June to mid-September.

Brantôme

BRANTÔME, 27km north of Périgueux on the Angoulême road, and beloved of British tourists, sits in a bend of the River Dronne, whose still, water-lilied surface mirrors the limes and weeping willows of the riverside gardens. On the north bank of the river are the church and convent buildings of the **ancienne abbaye** that for centuries has been Brantôme's focus. Its stone facades, now masking the secular offices of the **Hôtel de Ville**, have that pallor and blank stare so characteristic of the self-denying institutional life, be it monastery, home or school. Not that there was much of the flagellant about this monastery's most notorious abbot, **Pierre de Bourdeilles**, the sixteenth-century author of scurrilous tales of life at the royal court.

Take a look at the **église abbatiale**, for the palm-frond vaulting of the chapter house and the font made from a carved and grounded pillar capital. There is a fine stone staircase, too, in this end of the Hôtel de Ville. But Brantôme's best architectural feature is the Limousin-style Romanesque **belfry** standing behind the church against the wooded and cave-riddled scarp that forms the backdrop to the village.

There are no other specific sights in Brantôme, but a walk through the nearby gardens and the balustraded riverbanks is a must. The café/*brasserie*, *Au Fil de l'Eau*, on quai Bertin, with tables down by the river, is as cheap as Brantôme's restaurants come, as long as you don't go for the *omelette aux truffes*. For **accommodation**, try the *Hôtel de la Poste*, 33 rue Gambetta (☎53.05.78.55; ②), the *Auberge du Soir* (☎53.05.82.93; ③), or the **campsite** to the north of the village on the D78 (☎53.05.75.24; open June–Sept). Getting to Brantôme without your own transport can be problematic: there are buses, but only for school and the Wednesday market. Should you need the **SI**, it is in a lime-shaded Renaissance pavilion on the river bank.

Bourdeilles

BOURDEILLES, 16km down the Dronne from Brantôme by a beautiful back road, is relatively hard to reach. Perhaps the most appealing way is by canoe – you can hire kayaks or canoes from Porte des Réformés in Brantôme. It's a sleepy backwater, an ancient rural village clustering around its **château** on a rocky spur above the river (daily 9–11.30am & 2–6pm; Sept 15–June 15; closed Tues; closed Dec 15–Jan & first week in Oct). The château consists of two buildings, one a thirteenth-century fortress, the other an elegant Renaissance residence begun by the lady of the house as a piece of unsuccessful favour-currying with Catherine de Médicis; unsuccessful, because Catherine never came to stay and the château stayed unfinished. Climb the octagonal keep to look down on the clustered roofs, the weir and the boat-shaped mill parting the current, and beyond to the cavernous shade of the Dronne's course, the cornfields and the manors hidden among the trees.

The house is now home to an exceptional collection of **furniture** bequeathed to the state by its former owners. Among the more notable pieces are some splendid Spanish dowry chests; a sixteenth-century Rhenish entombment with life-sized statues, embodying the very image of the serious, self-satisfied medieval burgher; and a fifteenth-century primitive Catalan triptych of an exorcism, with a bull-headed devil shooting skywards out of a kneeling princess.

Château de Hautefort

From the same period, but much grander in scale and style is the **Château de Hautefort**, 35km northeast of Périgueux (Palm Sun–Oct 9.15–11.30am & 2.15–6.30pm; rest of the year Sun only 2–5pm; 20F). Standing proud at the end of a wooded spur above its feudal village, it has an elegance that is out of step with the usual rough stone fortresses of *Périgord*. You approach across a wide esplanade flanked by formal gardens, cross the moat by a drawbridge through the oldest part of the building and emerge into a stylish Renaissance courtyard backed by an arcaded gallery and enclosed by slated towers. Once the property of the troubadour Bertrans de Born, it passed into the hands of the Hautefort family in the seventeenth century and was extensively remodelled. It was the childhood home of Marie de Hautefort, the young beauty who so captivated Louis XIII.

It is impossible to get to Hautefort and back in one day using public transport: although there is a morning **bus** from Périgueux via CUBJAC (Wed & Sat), on other days there's only an evening service. You stand a reasonable chance **hitching** from Périgueux, or you could get a Brive train as far as La Bachellerie, and hitch the final 15km. **By car** the most attractive route is along the river Auvézère via Cubjac and TOURTOIRAC, where Antoine-Orélie I, "King of Araucania", died in 1878. This bizarre character was a Périgueux lawyer who, deciding he was destined for higher things, borrowed money and set sail for Patagonia, where he proclaimed himself king of the Araucanian Indians.

Brive and the Corrèze

Brive-la-Gaillarde is a major rail junction and the nearest thing to an industrial centre for miles around. As such, it makes an agreeable base for exploring the Corrèze *département*, which encompasses beautiful villages like **Turenne and Collonges-la-Rouge**, as well as the upper reaches of the Vézère and Dordogne rivers.

Brive-la-Gaillarde

Though it has no commanding sights, **BRIVE-LA-GAILLARDE** does have a few distractions, aside from its usefulness as a base for exploring the region. Right in the middle of town is the much-restored **Église St-Martin**, originally Romanesque, though now only the transept, apse and a few comically carved capitals survive from that era. Saint Martin himself, a Spanish aristocrat, arrived in pagan Brive in 407, on the feast of Saturnus, smashed various idols, and was promptly stoned to death by the outraged onlookers.

Numerous streets fan out from the surrounding square, place du Général-de-Gaulle, with a number of turreted and towered houses, some dating back to the thirteenth century. The most impressive is the sixteenth-century **Hôtel de Labenche** on bd Jules-Ferry, which now houses the town's archaeological finds (10am–6/6.30pm; closed Tues; 22F).

Practicalities

From the **gare SNCF**, it's a 10-minute walk up av Jean-Jaurès to the nucleus of the old town, encircled by a tight ring of modern boulevards. Just south of the old town is the attractive square Auboiroux, with the **PTT** and **gare routière** nearby. The **SI** is north of the ringroad on place 14-juillet (July & Aug 9am–12.30pm & 2.30–7pm; Sun 10am–1pm; rest of the year Mon–Sat 9am–1pm & 2.30–6pm), alongside a slick, Scandinavian-style timber-frame **market** (Tues, Thurs & Sat).

There are numerous cheap **hotels** on av Jean-Jaurès: *Hôtel de la Gare* (☎55.74.14.49; ②), *Majestic et Voyageurs* (☎55.24.10.20; ②) and *Hôtel de France* (☎55.74.08.13; ②), to name but three. In addition, there's a clean new **hostel** on the other side of town from the train station at 56 av Maréchal-Bugeaud (☎55.24.34.00; curfew 11pm; 25min by foot from the gare SNCF), with a **campsite**, *Les Îles*, just across the river.

Turenne

TURENNE, just 16km south of Brive (one train a day), is the first of two very pictu-resque villages close to the town. Capital of the viscounty of Turenne, whose most illus-trious seigneur was Henri de la Tour d'Auvergne, the "Grand Turenne", whom Napoléon rated the finest tactician of modern times, the village today would not surprise him. The same mellow stone houses still crowd in the lee of the sharp bluff whose summit sprouts the towers of their castle. One forms part of someone's house. The other, known as **La Tour de César**, can be visited (mid-March–Oct 9am–noon & 2–7pm; rest of the year Sun only 10am–noon & 2–5pm). One of the highest points for miles around, it's worth climbing for the views away over the ridges and valleys to the mountains of Cantal.

Collonges-la-Rouge

COLLONGES-LA-ROUGE, 7km east of Turenne, is the epitome of rustic charm with its red-sandstone houses, pepperpot towers and pink-candled chestnut trees. Though small scale, there is a grandeur about the place, as if the Turenne administrators, who lived here, were aping, within their means, the grandiloquence of their superiors. On the *place* a twelfth-century church testifies to the imbecility of shedding blood over religious differences: here, side by side, Protestant and Catholic conducted their services simultaneously. Outside, the covered market hall still retains its old-fashioned baker's oven.

An additional reason for visiting Collonges is the unpretentious **hôtel-restaurant**, the *Relais de St-Jacques* (☎55.25.41.02; ③/④), which has comfortable beds and memor-able food. If you're not tempted, you have to head downhill a few minutes to MEYSSAC, a town built in the same red sandstone, though less grandly, for the cheaper accommodation at the *Relais du Quercy* (☎55.25.40.31; ③), or the **campsite**, *Moulin de Valane* (☎55.25.41.59; open April–Oct).

Getting to Collonges without your own wheels is difficult, though worth the effort. The prettiest route on foot from Turenne is along the back lanes through meadow and walnut orchards via SAILLAC (3hr), whose Romanesque church sports an elaborately carved tympanum upheld by a column of spiralling animal motifs.

Uzerche and Arnac-Pompadour

A half-hour train ride north of Brive along the course of the bubbling river Vézère, the town of **UZERCHE** is impressively located above a loop in the river's course. It's worth a passing visit as the town has several fine old buildings. From the **gare SNCF**, the old town is a five-minute walk south along the main road which tears through the town. The **SI** – behind the main church – provides information on landmarks, but the place is so small you can easily find your own way around. For a grand view of Uzerche, well worth the extra march, turn left onto rue du Champ-de-Foire as you come down from the station; pass the church and keep on to rue Ste-Eulalie, turning right at the end to cross the river on rue du Pont. If you need a place to stay, the *Hôtel Teyssier* by the river (☎55.73.10.05; ④) is about all there is.

Roughly 20km west of Uzerche (40min by train, on a different line, from Brive) is **ARNAC-POMPADOUR**, a town dominated by its grey, turreted **château** (only the terraces can be visited), presented by Louis XV to his mistress, Madame de Pompadour, in 1745, though she never actually visited it. Set in the green countryside of southern Limousin – reminiscent of parts of Ireland – the château is home to one of France's best known **stud farms** (*haras*), first created by Louis XV in 1761. For horse-lovers it's a must, and it is interesting even for the non-specialist. Its speciality is the Anglo-Arab breed, descendants of horses brought back from the Crusades. The stallions are kept at the Puy-Marmont stables west of the château (July 15–Feb 21; free guided tours every 40 min; closed Sat), the mares 4km away at La Jumenterie de la Rivière (afternoons only). From May to October there are frequent race meetings and open days. In spring the fields are full of mares and foals, the best being kept for breeding, the rest sold worldwide as two-year-olds. The **gare** SNCF is southeast of the town, close to the racecourse and opposite the château. And there's even a reasonable place to stay, and eat, by the station, the *Hôtel-Restaurant de l'Hippodrome* (☎55.73.35.03; ③).

Northeast to Ussel

As you climb northeastwards towards the Massif Central, the country becomes progressively wilder and hillier, full of streams and woods of beech, birch, chestnut and conifer, good only for grazing sheep. Signs of human habitation are few and far between and mostly consist of isolated hamlets and grey stone farms peopled by weatherbeaten peasants inured to the hardships of upland life.

Château du Ventadour

Near the rather gloomy little town of EGLETONS, on the main Brive to Clermont-Ferrand route, a minor road runs past modest farms to the romantic ruins of the **Château du Ventadour**, perchèd on a precipitous ridge above the woods, where the troubadour Bernard de Ventadour was born, son of a castle servant. A path climbs up to the ruined walls and towers, with plummeting views into the valley below.

Ussel and the Plateau de Millevaches

Some 30km further, the town of USSEL is a pleasant old place, with a folk art and crafts **museum** split between the Hôtel du Juge-Choriol on rue Michelet and the Chapelle des Pénitents-Blancs on rue Pasteur (July–Aug 10am–noon & 3–7pm; same hours for both). Among the old houses is the Renaissance residence (behind the **market**) built by the Ventadours to replace their draughty and uncomfortable castle. For **accommodation**, there's a choice between the *Hôtel des Messageries* by the train station, the **youth hostel** on rue Pasteur, in the town centre (☎55.96.13.17), and a **campsite**, *Municipal de Ponty*, 2.5km off the rte de Tulle (☎55.72.30.05; open March–Nov).

West of the Brive–Clermont road lies the starkly beautiful moorland of the **Plateau de Millevaches** (plateau of a thousand cows), with high ground up to 1000m – all bog, bracken and conifer plantations under wide skies. The easiest access is by train on the Limoges–Ussel line, which serves several small stations on the western edge of the plateau between EYMOUTIERS and MEYMAC. The principal walking centre is La Courtine on the east side (*SNCF* bus from Ussel). For more on these parts, see p.441.

The upper Dordogne

The upper reaches of the Dordogne lie confusingly in the Lot and Corrèze *départements*. This is still what the British call the Dordogne, but to the French it is best known by its ancient name of *Quercy*. In many ways the scenery here is more akin to parts of the Massif Central – all treeless plateaux (*causses*) and limestone bluffs – rather than the more lush, gentle valley of the middle Dordogne around Sarlat. As a result, despite being no less attractive, it receives considerably fewer visitors.

Souillac

The first place of any size east of Sarlat is **SOUILLAC**, which lies at the confluence of the Borrèze and Dordogne rivers. Virginia Woolf stayed here in 1937, and was pleased to meet "no tourists...England seems like a chocolate box bursting with trippers afterward". There are still few tourists, since Souillac's only real point of interest is the twelfth-century domed **Église Ste-Marie** close to the river and the Sarlat road. On the back of the west door are some of the most wonderful **Romanesque sculptures**, including a seething mass of beasts devouring each other. The greatest piece of craftsmanship, though, is a bas-relief of Isaiah, fluid and supple, thought to be by one of the artists who worked at MOISSAC (see p.479).

Behind the church, a new museum has opened to try and draw a few more visitors to Souillac, the **Musée de l'Automate** (July & Aug 10am–7pm; rest of year 10am–noon & 3–6pm; Nov–March closed Mon & Tues; 25F). Under-12s are the ones most likely to enjoy the mostly nineteenth-century mechanical dolls, who dance, sing and perform magical tricks.

The **SI** is between the old belfry and the main road through town, bd L-J-Malvy. The *Hôtel-Restaurant du Beffroi*, 6 place Martin (☎65.37.80.33; ②), offers the cheapest **accommodation**, and is also a good place to eat. Alternatively, there's the large riverside **campsite**, *Les Ondines* (☎65.37.86.44; open July–Sept). You can hire **bicycles** from the gare SNCF, 1.5km northwest of the centre, or from *Évasion Sport*, 36 bd L-J-Malvy. Lastly, and unlikely-sounding, Souillac puts on a fairly good **jazz festival** in the third week of July.

Martel

About 15km east of Souillac, and set back even further from the river, **MARTEL** is a minor medieval gem, built in a pale, almost white, stone, offset by the warm reddish-brown roofs, yet it suffers none of the crowds endured by the likes of Sarlat. Another Turenne-administered town, its heyday came during the thirteenth and fourteenth centuries, when the viscounts established a court of appeal here.

The main square, **place des Consuls**, is mostly taken up by the large eighteenth-century covered *halles*, but on every side there are reminders of the town's illustrious past, most notably in the superb Gothic **Hôtel de la Raymondie**. Begun in 1280, it served as the Turenne law courts, though it doubled as the town's refuge, too, hence

---

THE TALE OF HENRY SHORT-COAT

At the end of the twelfth century, Martel was the stage for one of the tragic events in the internecine conflicts of the Plantagenet family. When Henry Plantagenet (King Henry II of England), imprisoned his estranged wife Eleanor of Aquitaine, the sons took up arms against their father. The eldest son, **Henry Short-Coat** (Henri Court Mantel to the French) even went so far as to plunder the viscounty of Turenne and Quercy. Furious, Henry II immediately stopped his allowance, and handed over his lands to the third son, Richard the Lionheart. As the normally very restrained *Michelin* guide puts it: "the royal household was a royal hell". Financially insecure, and with a considerable army of soldiers to feed and clothe, Henry Short-Coat began looting the treasures of every abbey and shrine in the region. Finally he decided to sack the shrine at Rocamadour, making off with various artefacts including Roland's famous sword, *Durandal*. This last act was to be his downfall, for shortly afterwards he fled to Martel and fell ill with a fever. Guilt-ridden, and afraid for his life, he confessed his crimes and asked his father for forgiveness. Henry II was busy besieging Limoges, but sent a messanger to pardon him. On his arrival in Martel, Henry Short-Coat died, and Richard the Lionheart became heir to the English throne.

the distinctive corner turrets. Facing the *hôtel* is the **Tour des Pénitents**, one of the many medieval towers which gave the town its epithet, *"la ville des sept tours"*. Henry Short Coat (see box on p.469) died in the striking building in the southeast corner of the square, the **Maison Fabri**, while, one block south, rue Droite leads east to the town's main church, the **Église St-Maur**, built in a fiercely defensive, mostly Gothic style, with a finely carved Romanesque typanum depicting the Last Judgement above the west door.

If you'd rather stay here than in Souillac, head for the *Lion d'Or* on av de Turenne (☎65.37.30.16; ③ for *demi-pension*) or *Le Turenne* on av J-Lavayssière (☎65.37.30.30; ③ for *demi-pension*). The nearest **campsite**, *Les Falaises* (☎65.37.33.59; open May–Sept), is 5km south of Martel on the Dordogne itself.

Carennac

CARENNAC is without doubt one of the most beautiful villages in this part of the Dordogne. Elevated just above the south bank of the river, 13km or so east of Martel, it's best known for its typical *Quercy* architecture, its Romanesque priory, where the French writer, Fénelon, spent the best years of his life and, invitingly, for its greengages.

It's a tiny little village with just the **Église St-Pierre** in the way of specific sights. Its best feature, as so often in these parts, is the Romanesque tympanum above the west door, in the Moissac style. Christ sits in majesty with the Book of Judgement in his left hand, with the apostles and adoring angels below him. Inside the church, you can gain access to the old **cloisters** (daily 10am–noon & 2–7pm; 7F), which contain an exceptionally expressive life-size entombment of Christ, quite simply one of the best in the Dordogne.

The *Hôtel-Restaurant des Touristes* (☎65.38.47.07; ③) is the cheapest place to sleep and eat, but for a more stylish meal, try the restaurant in the *Hôtel Fénelon* (☎65.38.67.67; ⑤), which overlooks the river.

Castelnau-Bretenoux

The sturdy towers and machicolated red-brown walls of the eleventh-century **Château de Castelnau-Bretenoux** (July & Aug daily 9.30am–6.30pm; rest of year 9am–noon & 2–5/6pm; closed Tues; 25F) dominate a sharp knoll above the Dordogne, making a harmonious whole with the village piled at its feet. Most of it has now been restored and refurnished. Below, on the banks of the River Cère, you come to the graceful little *bastide* of **BRETENOUX**, with two sides of its cobbled and arcaded square still intact. For **accommodation**, there's the *Hôtel de la Cère* (☎65.39.71.44; ③), and a grassy and shady **campsite** beside the river.

St-Céré and St-Laurent-les-Tours

A short detour up the valley of the Bave, a minor tributary of the Dordogne, is the medieval town of **ST-CÉRÉ**, dominated by the brooding ruins of the **St-Laurent-les-Tours**. The latter has been partially rebuilt and now encompasses within its walls a **musée/atelier** (Lent–Sept daily 9.30am–noon & 2.30–6.30pm; 15F) originally set up by the late, maverick, experimental artist, Jean Lurçat (1892–1966). The town itself has just one distraction, the **Musée Automobile du Haut-Quercy**, out on the rte de Monteil (Easter–May 10am–noon & 2–6pm; closed Tues; June–Sept daily 10am–noon & 2–7pm; 15F). St-Céré has two reasonable **places to stay**: *Le Quercy*, av A.-de-Monzie (☎65.38.04.83; ③), and *Le Limonaire*, pl A-de-Monzie (☎65.38.20.26; ③).

Beaulieu-sur-Dordogne

Beautifully situated on the banks of the Dordogne, 8km upriver from Castelnau-Bretenoux, **BEAULIEU-SUR-DORDOGNE** boasts another of the great masterpieces of Romanesque sculpture on the porch of the **Église St-Pierre** in the centre of town. This doorway is unusually deep-set, with a tympanum presided over by an Oriental-looking Christ with one arm extended to welcome the chosen. All around him is a complicated pattern of angels and apostles, executed in characteristic "dancing" style, similar to that at Carennac. The dead raise the lids of their coffins hopefully, while underneath a frieze of monsters crunches heads. Take the opportunity to wander through to the peaceful medieval Quartier de la Chapelle, to the north of the town centre, which boasts some handsome **fourteenth-century houses** with sculpted facades.

The *Hôtel Fournié* (☎55.91.01.34; ③/④) has the cheapest rooms on offer, but much more appealing is the magnificent half-timbered and turreted **youth hostel**, in the Quartier de la Chapelle (☎55.91.13.82). There are river-bathing and canoeing possibilities, and a riverside **campsite** close by.

Argentat

An *SNCF* bus can take you still further upstream to **ARGENTAT**, the last major town on the Dordogne, and the last part of the river accessible by anything other than foot. Beyond Argentat, the Dordogne changes character entirely due to the series of hydro-electric dams (*barrages*), which turn the river into a succession of grand reservoirs.

Argentat's whitewashed houses and rather sombre grey slate rooftops make a distinct change from the warm yellow stone of the rest of the Dordogne. It's easy enough to while away an hour or so sitting at one of the riverbank cafés, or exploring the cobbled *petites ruelles* which slope down to the river. But there's nothing else to make you stay. Should you need to, however, there's a good choice of reasonable **hotels** – kicking off with the basic *Espérance* (☎55.28.11.92; ②), or the rather more amenable *Hôtel des Xaintries* (☎55.28.01.41; ③) – and a whole host of **campsites** in the vicinity.

The Causse de Gramat

South of the Dordogne valley, the land climbs to the **Causse de Gramat,** one of the high limestone plateaux characteristic of the old province of *Quercy*, which begins around here. There is a distinct change of vegetation once you leave the valley behind. The soil is poor, the grass yellow, the ground littered with stones and patches of rock breaking through. Scrub oak and juniper abound; caves and underground rivers riddle the substrata. On the plateau are two of the area's best-known tourist traps, the pilgrim shrine of **Rocamadour** and the **Gouffre de Padirac**. Neither is easy to get to without your own transport and unless you have a specific interest both could be skipped, especially since there are equally interesting sights – such as Castelnau – within much easier reach.

Gouffre de Padirac

July–Aug daily 8/8.30am–6.30/7pm; rest of the year 9am–noon & 2–6pm; closed mid-Oct–March; guided tours 1hr 30min; 33F.

The **Gouffre de Padirac** is an enormous limestone sink-hole, about 100m deep. There are some impressive formations of stalactites and waterfalls created by the accumulation of lime, but the natural beauty of the place is spoiled by the lift apparatus and all the tourist paraphernalia. Visits are partly on foot, partly by boat. In wet weather you'll need a waterproof jacket. The nearest **gare SNCF** is Rocamadour-Padirac, over 10km west of the cave itself; the only alternative to walking or hitching is the summer-only bus which costs over 50F for the round trip.

Rocamadour

Tucked under a cliff in the deep and abrupt canyon of the Alzou stream, the spectacular setting of **ROCAMADOUR** is hard to beat. The village itself must have been beautiful once, too. However, for centuries now it has been inundated by religious pilgrims (and latterly more secular-minded coach tours), whose constant stream has turned the place into something of a nightmare, with every house displaying mountains of unbelievable junk. The reason for its popularity since medieval times is the supposed miraculous ability of the shrine's Black Madonna. Nowadays, pilgrims are outnumbered by tourists who come here to wonder at the sheer audacity of its location, built almost vertically into its rocky backdrop.

Practicalities

Getting to Rocamadour without your own transport is awkward, unless you're prepared to pay through the nose for the **summer-only buses** from the SIs in Brive, Sarlat and Souillac, or walk the 5km from the Rocamadour-Padirac **gare SNCF** on the Brive–Capdenac line. If you arrive **by car**, you'll have to park in L'Hospitalet, 1.5km from Rocamadour (and with the best view of the town there is), or else in the car park, several hundred metres below the town. If you're carrying luggage, you can leave it at the **SI** in the Hôtel de Ville on the main street, rather than lug it up the chapel steps.

Rocamadour is not a place to hang around in, although its **hotels** are actually not that expensive, it's just that they're completely booked out in the summer. If you ring ahead, you might get in at the *Lion d'Or*, Porte Figuier (☎65.33.62.04; ②/④), or the *Terminus*, pl de la Carretta (☎65.33.62.14; ②/④), both in Rocamadour itself, and both closed from November to Easter. There are also several **campsites** in L'Hospitalet, the nearest one being *Le Relais du Campeur* (☎65.33.63.28).

ROCAMADOUR – A BRIEF HISTORY

The history of **Rocamadour** begins with the arrival of Zacchaeus, husband of Saint Veronica, who fled to France to escape religious persecution, and lived out his last years here as a hermit. When in 1166, a perfectly preserved body was found in a grave high up on the rock, it was declared to be Zacchaeus, who thereafter became known as Saint Amadour. Rocamadour soon became a major pilgrimage site, on a par with Lourdes. Saint Bernard, numerous kings of England and France and thousands of others crawled up the chapel steps on their knees to pay their respects and seek cures for their illnesses. Henry Short-Coat was the first to plunder the shrine, but he was easily outclassed by the Huguenots who tried in vain to burn the saint's corpse, but finally resigned themselves simply to hacking it to bits. What you see today, therefore, is not the real thing, but a nineteenth-century reconstruction, carried out in the hope of reviving the flagging pilgrimage.

The Parvis

Rocamadour is easy enough to find your way around – there's just one street, rue de la Couronnerie, strung out between two medieval gateways, while above sits the **Parvis**, the main complex half way up the cliff, with no fewer than seven churches. The indolent take the lift dug into the rockface (12F up and back), while the devout drag themselves on their knees up the 223 steps of the *Via Sancta* to the smoke-blackened and votive-packed **Chapelle Notre-Dame** where the miracle-working twelfth-century Black Madonna resides. The tiny macabre, walnut-wood statue is appropriately lit in the mysterious half light of her protective black cage, but the rest of the chapel is unremarkable. High up in the rock, above the entrance to the chapel is a sword, supposedly Roland's legendary blade *Durandal*.

There's no relief for the non-religious in the **Musée Francis Poulenc** (daily July & Aug 9am–6pm; rest of the year 9am–noon & 2–6pm; 10F), which contains sacred art treasures, reliquaries and various historical documents. It's dedicated to the French composer, Francis Poulenc (1899–1963), because he was one of the modern pilgrims who received miraculous inspiration from the shrine, though in his case the results were musical rather than medical.

Other sights

You can climb still further to the ancient **ramparts** above the chapel, or take the winding shady path, *La Calvarie*, past the stations of the cross: either way the views across the valley are stunning.

Coincidentally, it seems, there are three different wildlife centres in Rocamadour: the **Rocher des Aigles**, a breeding centre for birds of prey (demonstrations of falconry at 11am and hourly from 3–6pm; 28F); the **Forêt des Singes**, off the D673, where 150 Barbary apes roam the relative freedom of a reserve in the baking hot plateau behind L'Hospitalet (daily June 15–Aug 9am–7pm; rest of the year 10am–noon & 2–6pm; closed Dec–March; 25F); and the **Jardin des Papillons**, just off the rte de Gramat, which breeds an international cast of wild butterflies (July–Aug 9am–6.30pm; rest of the year 10am–noon & 2–5.30pm; closed mid-Oct to March; 22F).

THE VALLEY OF THE LOT

Travelling south from the Dordogne takes you into the drier, poorer and more sparsely populated province of *Haut Quercy*, through which the **River Lot** flows roughly parallel with the Dordogne. There aren't many facilities for tourists and, except in the Lot valley itself, not much help from public transport. So it's an ideal area to hike, bike and camp, and, away from the main centres of **Cahors** and **Figeac**, you'll have most of it to yourself.

Villeneuve and around

VILLENEUVE-SUR-LOT, capital of the Lot-et-Garonne *département*, does not have a great deal to commend it: there are no very interesting sights, though the handful of attractive timbered houses in the old town go some way to compensate. And if you're reliant on public transport, it's worth remembering there's no train station, and bus links are poor – just AGEN and FUMEL/CAHORS.

The town's most striking landmark is the red-brick tower of the **Église Ste-Catherine**, completed as late as 1937 in typically garish neo-Byzantine style, but rather unusually built on a north–south axis. In the streets around the main square, **place La Fayette**, a couple of towers alone survive from the fortifications of this originally *bastide* town, and a bridge resembling the Pont Valentré in Cahors, but devoid of towers. There is, however, and rather unexpectedly, a good museum, the **Musée Gaston Rapin** (2–7pm; closed Tues) on bd Voltaire, on the south bank of the river beyond the Porte de Pujols, with sections on traditional crafts and local history, as well as typically very good, temporary exhibitions.

If you **stay overnight**, the centrally placed *Hôtel de l'Espoir*, 5 place de la Marine (☎53.70.71.63; ③), is clean and welcoming, or you could try the *Remparts* (②) on bd de la Marine, two blocks west of the main street. For reasonable **eating** there's *Le Parmentier*, along with two popular Italian places, *L'Intermezzo* and *Nando*, all on rue Parmentier.

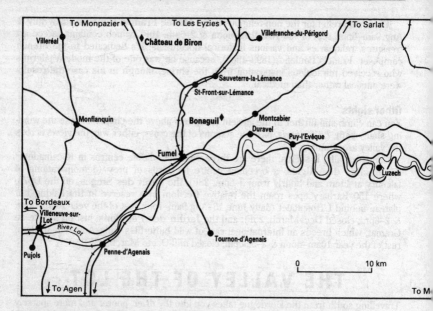

Pujols and Penne: and plums and prunes

For a pleasant **short walk** – about half an hour from the Porte de Pujols – you can climb south to the tiny walled village of **PUJOLS** with faded Romanesque frescoes in the Église Ste-Foy and great views over the surrounding country. Another side trip could be to the old fortress town of **PENNE**, 8km upstream on a steep hill also on the south bank – take the **bus** to ST-SYLVESTRE on the north bank and walk. There are great views from the top, and excellent home cooking to be enjoyed at the **hotel-restaurant** *Chez Madame Bonnet* on place Gambetta (☎53.41.22.17). Otherwise, there's a **campsite** by the river and a **gîte d'étape** near the **gare SNCF** on the Agen–Paris line.

This region is the **plum centre** of France, the plum said to have been brought back from Damascus during the Crusades. Most highly regarded are the *prunes d'ente*, from the Old French *enter*, to graft, while star prunes (in the dried sense) come from Agen – *pruneaux d'Agen*. You can buy or ogle them at the *Boutique des Pruneaux* next to the Porte de Paris in Villeneuve; they come straight or armour-plated with chocolate, Armagnac-soaked or *fourrés*, that is, stoned and stuffed with more prune flesh.

Beyond Fumel

From Villeneuve as far as FUMEL, the valley is ugly and industrial. But upstream, the vine-cloaked banks are dotted with small and ancient villages. An **SNCF bus** threads through them, and because there are six daily it's possible to get off, look around and pick up the next bus – not that any of the villages is worth more than a brief stay.

The first place worth heading for east of Fumel – the **Château de Bonaguil** (daily summer 10am–noon & 3–6pm; rest of the year Sun only 3pm; 30F) – is more difficult to get to. The site is superb: perched at the end of a wooden spur commanding two valleys, about 8km northeast of Fumel. Built during the fifteenth–sixteenth centuries, with a double ring of walls, five huge towers and a narrow boat-shaped keep, it was the last of the really medieval castles to be constructed, albeit designed to resist artillery.

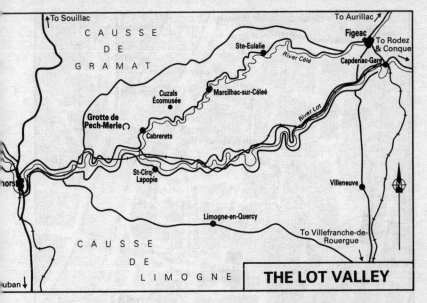

THE LOT VALLEY

The only way to get there by public transport is to take the train to ST-FRONT-SUR-LEMANCE, about 7km northwest of Bonaguil and hardly any closer than Fumel itself.

Back on the Lot, the first place worth pausing at is **PUY-L'ÉVÊQUE**, 15km east of Fumel and probably the prettiest village in the entire valley, built in honey-coloured rock and overlooked by both church and castle. For the best view, stand on the suspension bridge which crosses the Lot.

Several bends in the river later – 15km by road – you come to **LUZECH**, with Gaulish and Roman remains and the Chapelle de Notre-Dame-de-l'Île dedicated to the medieval boatmen who transported Cahors wines to Bordeaux. It stands in a huge river loop, overlooked by a thirteenth-century keep, with some picturesque alleys and dwellings in the quarter opposite place du Canal.

Cahors

CAHORS, on the river Lot, was the capital of the old province of *Quercy*. In its time, it has been a Gallic settlement; a Roman town; a briefly-held Moorish possession; governed by the English; a bastion of Catholicism in the Wars of Religion, sacked in consequence by Henri IV; 400 years a university town; and birthplace of Gambetta, after whom so many French streets and squares are named. Despite all this, modern Cahors is a sunny southern backwater. Its two most interesting sights are its **cathedral** and the remarkable fourteenth-century **Pont Valentré**.

Practicalities
The **gare SNCF** and **gare routière** are at the end of av Jean-Jaurès off rue du Président-Wilson which leads to the Pont Valentré. For further information on the area, make for the **SI** on the corner of bd Gambetta and allées Fénelon close to the cathedral. **Bicycle hire** is possible either from *Ets Combes*, 117 bd Gambetta, or the gare SNCF.

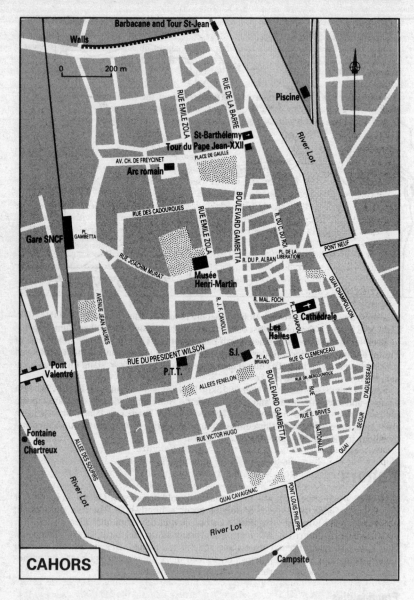

CAHORS

For **accommodation**, try the *Hôtel L'Escargot*, 5 bd Gambetta (☎65.35.07.66; ②), or *Hôtel de la Paix*, place St-Maurice by the cathedral (☎65.35.03.40; ②). Otherwise, there's a *foyer* at 20 rue Frédéric-Suisse (☎65.34.64.71; no curfew); turn right out of the station, second left – a 10-minute walk. As a last resort, there's the ragged **camping**

municipal just across the Pont Louis-Philippe. For **restaurants** try the convivial *La Brasérade* on rue du Dr-Bergougnoux. More commonplace is the *Le Palais brasserie* at 12 bd Gambetta, a great people-watching spot. Cahors boasts two vegetarian restaurants, *Marie-Colline*, 173 rue Clemenceau, and the only slightly more expensive *L'Orangerie*, 41 rue St-James. For picnic fodder, there are the *halles*, close to the cathedral.

While you're in the Cahors area, don't miss out on the **local wine**: heady, almost black in colour, but dry to the taste, and not at all plummy like the Gironde wines from Blaye and Bourg, which use the same Malbec grape.

The town

The town is sited on a peninsula formed by a tight loop in the river, and is bisected by the north–south main drag of **rue de la Barre** and **bd Gambetta**. The surviving vieille ville lies to the east of this thoroughfare.

Consecrated in 1119, Cahor's **Cathédrale** is the oldest and simplest in plan of the *Périgord*-style churches. Like St-Étienne at Périgueux, it has a nave without aisles or transepts, roofed with two big domes. In the first are fourteenth-century frescoes of the stoning of St Stephen. The Gothic choir and apse are extensively but crudely painted. To their right a door opens into a delicate **cloister**, in the Flamboyant style, which, though damaged, still retains some intricate carving. On the northwest corner pillar a graceful girl with broad brow and ringlets to her waist serves as a model for the Virgin. In the northeast corner an arch opens on to a courtyard by the fine Renaissance **archdeacon's house.**

The **exterior** of the church is not exciting. A heavy square tower dominates the plain west front. The best feature is the elaborately decorated **portal** in the street on the north side, where a Christ in Majesty dominates the **tympanum**, surrounded by angels and apostles, while cherubim fly out of the clouds to relieve him of his halo. Side panels show scenes from the life of St Stephen. On the outer ring of voussoirs a line of naked figures are being stabbed in the behind and hacked with axes.

Around the cathedral, towards the river bank, there's a warren of narrow lanes and scruffy alleys. Many of the houses, turreted and built of flat, thin, southern brick, date from the fourteenth–sixteenth centuries. On the south side, the lime-bordered place Jean-Jacques-Chapou commemorates a local trade-unionist and Resistance leader, killed in a German ambush on July 17, 1944.

Lastly, and most dramtically, there's the **Pont Valentré** – the single reason most people come to Cahors. Its three powerful towers, originally closed by portcullises and gates, made it effectively an independent fortress, guarding the river crossing on the west side of town. One of the finest surviving bridges of its time, it is, rightly, one of the most photographed monuments in France. Just upstream a resurgent river, known as the **Fontaine des Chartreux**, flows from the valley-side. The Roman town was named *Divona Carducorum* after it, and it still supplies Cahors with drinking water.

Upriver to Figeac

East of Cahors, *SNCF* buses follow the beautiful, deep-cut, twisting valley of the Lot to FIGEAC, via CONDUCHÉ. From here, it's a further 5km up the tributary valley of the Célé to CABRERETS, then 1.5km to the marvellous **prehistoric cave** of **Pech-Merle**. You'll need to hitch or walk if you've no transport – no hardship along this minor road through thick-wooded limestone hills. If you want to camp rough, there are numerous discreet sites between Cabrerets and Pech-Merle.

Grotte de Pech-Merle

Easter–Sept daily 9.30am–noon & 2–6pm; rest of year phone ☎65.31.23.33; 35F.

Discovered in 1922, the **Grotte de Pech-Merle** is bigger and less accessible than those at Les Eyzies, and doesn't suffer from the same problems of overcrowding and consequent dangers of deterioration. The admission charge includes a film and excellent **museum**, where the prehistory is illustrated by colourful and intelligible charts, a selection of objects (rather than the usual 10,000 flints) and beautiful slides displayed in wall panels. It is interesting, too, to see the skulls of Neanderthals and Cro-Magnon people side by side – the jaw muscles of the former much cruder, to chomp and tear food without benefit of knives or other stone utensils.

The **cave** itself is far more beautiful than those at Padirac or Les Eyzies, with galleries full of the most spectacular stalactites and stalagmites – structures tiered like wedding cakes, hanging like curtains, or shaped like whale baffles, discs or cave pearls. Yet the visit is less awe-inspiring than, say, Font-de-Gaume. The cave is wired for electric light and the guide, who talks like a recorded message, makes sure you're processed through in the scheduled time.

The first drawings you come to are in the so-called **Chapelle des Mammouths**. They are done on a white calcite panel that looks as if it's been specially prepared for the purpose. There are horses; bison charging head down, with tiny rumps and arched tails; tusked and whiskery mammoths. Then you pass into a vast, magical chamber where the glorious **horse panel** is visible on a lower level. Here is another remarkable example of the way in which the artist used the contour and relief of the rock to do the work: an utterly convincing mammoth is suggested by just two strokes of black. The cave ceiling is covered with finger marks, preserved in the soft clay. You pass the skeleton of a cave hyena that has been lying there for 20,000 years – wild animals used these caves for shelter and sometimes, unable to find their way out, starved to death in them. And finally, the most moving and spine-tingling experience at Pech-Merle – the **footprints** of a Stone-Age adult and child preserved in a muddy pool.

Cuzals: Écomusée du Quercy

June–Sept daily except Sat 9.30/10am–6.30/7pm; May Sun & holidays only 10am–7pm; Oct Sun only 1–5.30pm; 44F.

Five kilometres up the Céré from Peche-Merle is the **Écomusée du Quercy**, one of the better open-air museums, set up in the 1980s in an attempt to preserve the distinctive rural architecture of France. Reconstructions that range from a half-timbered eighteenth-century farmhouse to a garage from the 1920s, are scattered around the site, which is centred around a twentieth-century château burnt down by the Nazis in the last war. The information is dished out with an appealing blend of humour and didactics, and the whole place is less blantantly commercial than many such *écomusées*.

St-Cirq-Lapopie

If you have your own transport you could easily make a side trip to the cliff-edge village of **ST-CIRQ-LAPOPIE** perched high above the south bank of the Lot. Though it is an irresistible draw for the tour buses with its cobbled lanes, half-timbered houses, gardens and fantastic site, it's still worth the trouble, especially if you visit early or late in the day. Public transport in the form of an **SNCF bus** will get you from Cahors to Gare-St-Cirq in the valley bottom; thereafter, there's no alternative but to leg it up the steep hill. For **accommodation** there is the *Hôtel du Causse* (☎65.31.24.16; ④), and a **campsite** at LA TRUFFIÈRE, 3km to the southeast and over the rim of the valley, while upstream, approximately 10km and 20km respectively, there are **hostels/gîtes** at CALVIGNAC (*La Ferme de Pars*; ☎65.40.64.54) and CAJARC (*gîte d'étape*; ☎65.40.65.20).

Figeac

FIGEAC, on the edge of the sombre country of the Auvergne, is a quietly busy little town, long a Protestant stronghold, with well-preserved and still inhabited medieval quarters. To reach the centre of town from the **gare SNCF** head down to the river and over the bridge. The **vieille ville** lies straight ahead of you, with street signs directing you to the most interesting streets – place Carnot, rue Gambetta, rue Colomb, rue Boutaric – labelled bilingually in French and Occitan.

Figeac's prosperity first grew out of its importance as a station on the pilgrim road from Conques to Compostela. In the thirteenth century it enjoyed the privilege of minting money: the original mint building, the **Hôtel de la Monnaie**, now houses the **SI**, on place de la Raison, on the first floor of which is the uninspiring **museum** of old Figeac. A very different class of museum is the **Musée Champollion** (May–Sept Tues–Sun 10am–noon & 2.30–6.30pm; 25F), opened by President Mitterrand in 1986. It is dedicated to the life and work of native-born Champollion, the man who (almost) cracked Egyptian hieroglyphics by deciphering the triple text of the Rosetta Stone. Very well designed, with films and exhibits, it's an incredibly instructive and interesting place. Just below the museum, the cobbled alley of rue Delzhem leads to the **Église Notre-Dame-du-Puy**, where you get a good view of the town.

If you're staying, there's a choice of reasonable **hotels**: *Le Pourquoi Pas*, 2 av J-Loubet (☎65.34.03.28; ③); *Hôtel la Courte Paille*, 12 place Carnot (☎65.34.21.83; ③); and the *Croix Blanche*, 2 rue Croix-Blanche (☎65.34.13.66; ③), which also has a generous and fairly-priced menu in its restaurant. In addition, there's a **campsite** – *Camping des Carmes* – beyond the sports fields.

Moissac

MOISSAC stands on the junction of the rivers Tarn and Garonne. It's most easily accessible **by train** from AGEN or MONTAUBAN or by bus from Villeneuve (or, alternatively, part of SI-run tours from Cahors in high season). Its claim to fame is the **cloister** of the abbey of St-Pierre, generally regarded as the finest achievement of Romanesque stone-carvers in the country. To find it from the **gare SNCF**, turn left and keep going straight until you see the sign for *cloître*. (The **SI** is right next to the cloister, so they can't be much help in finding it.)

Built between 1059 and 1131 the cloister has seventy-six delicate pointed arches supported on alternating single and double pillars, all of whose capitals are carved with animal or decorative motifs or anecdotal biblical scenes. Equally magnificent is the tympanum of the **south doorway** of the church. Dating from the early 1100s this illustrates a passage from the book of Revelations (iv.2-4): 24 old men, with marvellously expressive faces, strain their necks upwards to admire **Christ in Majesty** – just as vistors have to. To the side are other beautifully carved and decorated scenes, including the flight into Egypt and a Jeremiah and St Paul. The church itself is not very interesting, although inside there is a moving twelfth-century wooden sculpture of a suffering Christ on the cross. Behind the church is a **museum** of local arts and traditions, shabby but with an atmospheric mock-up of a nineteenth-century Bas Quercy farm room.

travel details

Trains

From Bergerac 4 daily to Le Buisson (30min); 3 daily to Sarlat (1hr 30min); daily to Périgueux (1hr 50 min); 6 or 7 daily to Bordeaux (1hr 15min–3hr).

From Le Buisson 4 daily to Sarlat (30min); 5 daily to Bergerac (40min); 3 daily to Bordeaux (2hr).

From Périgueux 5 daily to Le Buisson (50min); 5 daily to Bordeaux (1hr 30min–2hr); 5 daily to Brive (1hr–1hr 15min); 5 daily to Les Eyzies (30min); 3 daily to St-Front-sur-Lémance (1hr 30min); 4 daily to Agen (2hr 30min); 10 daily to Limoges (1–1hr 30min); for Paris-Austerlitz, change at Limoges.

From Brive 2 daily to Pompadour (40min); 2 daily to St-Yrieix (1hr 30min); 2 daily to Uzerche (30min); 1 daily to Turenne (15min, plus one morning train on Sundays); 4 daily to Souillac (30min); 3 daily to Rocamadour-Padirac (40min); 10 daily to Cahors (1hr 15min–1hr 30min); 5 daily to Figeac (1hr 30min); 7 daily to Toulouse (2hr 30min); 5 daily to Meymac (11/2hr); 3 daily to Ussel (1hr 45min); 3 daily to Clermont-Ferrand (3hr 40min); 6 daily to Aurillac (1hr 45min–2hr); 5 daily to Bordeaux (2hr 30min).

From Cahors to Brive; Toulouse; Souillac; 4 daily to Montauban (1hr – with bus connection to Moissac in 20min).

From Agen 3 daily to Moissac (25min, with bus connection from Villeneuve-sur-Lot to Agen).

Buses

From Sarlat 5 daily to Souillac (SNCF – 30min, connecting with trains to Brive and Cahors); 2 or 3 daily to Le Buisson (SNCF – 50min) via Beynac; frequent to Montignac.

From Brive 2 daily to Souillac (50min); 1 daily to Montignac (30min).

From Cahors infrequently to Figeac and Capdenac via Conduché and St-Cirq (2hr); 6 daily to Montsempron (1hr 20min) via Luzech (20min), Puy-l'Eveque (40min), Duravel (1hr).

CHAPTER TEN

THE PYRENEES

B asque-speaking and wet in the west, craggy, snowy, patois-speaking in the middle, dry and Catalan in the east, the **Pyrenees** are physically beautiful, culturally varied and – so far – a great deal less developed than the Alps. The whole range is marvellous walkers' country, especially the central region around the **Parc National des Pyrénées**, with its 3000-metre peaks, streams, forests, flowers and wildlife. If you're a committed hiker, it's possible to go all the way across, from Atlantic to Mediterranean, along the **GR10** or the more difficult **Haute Randonnée Pyrénéenne** (HRP); and there are numerous local walking centres as well – **Cauterets, Luz-St-Sauveur, Barèges, Ax-les-Thermes** – with hikes to suit all temperaments and abilities. The hiking season is mid-June through to September; earlier in the year few refuges are open and you will run into snow even on parts of the GR10. Whatever you intend, bear in mind that these are big mountains and should be treated with respect: to cover any of the main walks you'll need hiking boots and, despite the southerly latitude, warm and wind-proof clothing.

As for more conventional tourist attractions, the **Basque coast** is lovely but very popular, suffering from seaside sprawl and a massive surfeit of campsites. **St-Jean-de-Luz** is by far the prettiest of the resorts, **Biarritz** the most over-rated; **Bayonne** is the most attractive town, with an excellent Basque museum, although sadly this is in abeyance right now due to local political wrangles. The foothill towns are on the whole dull, though **Pau** is worth a day or two, while **Lourdes** is such a monster of kitsch that it has to be seen. The east – Catalan-speaking **Roussillon** – has beaches every bit as popular as those in the Basque country, but on the whole less inviting. Its interior, however, is another matter: craggy landscapes split by spectacular canyons, a crop of fine Romanesque abbeys, of which **St-Martin-de-Canigou** and **Serrabonne** are the most dramatic, and a climate bathed in Mediterranean heat and light.

EUSKAL-HERRI: THE PAYS BASQUE

The three **Basque provinces** – Labourd, Basse-Navarre and Soule – share with their Spanish neighbours a common language, *Euskara*, and a strong sense of separate identity. The language is universally spoken, and Basques refer to their country as a land in itself, **Euskal-herri**, or, across the border in Spain, Euskadi. Unlike the Spanish, however, few French Basques favour an independent state or secession from France. There is no equivalent of ETA here, and there are signs that the old sympathy, which allowed refuge to Spanish Basques wanted on terrorist charges, is waning. It was hatred of the Franco regime that provided the political momentum.

HOTEL ROOM PRICES

For a fuller explanation of these price codes, see the box on p.28 of *Basics*.

① Under 100F ② 100–130F ③ 130–180F ④ 180–230F ⑤ 230–300F

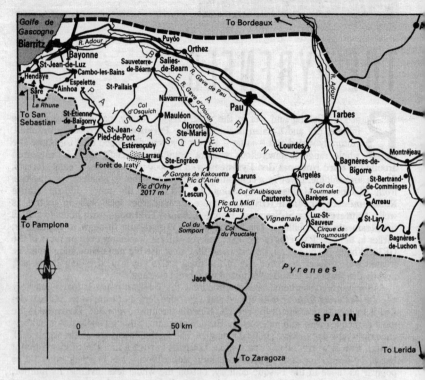

Administratively, the three French Basque provinces were organised together with Béarn in the single *département* of Basses-Pyrénées, now Pyrénées-Atlantiques, at the time of the 1789 Revolution, when the Basques' thousand-year-old *fors* (rights) were abolished. It was a move designed to curtail their nationalism, but ironically has probably been responsible for preserving their unity.

Apart from the language and the *beret basque*, the most obvious manifestation of Basque national identity are the ubiquitous *frontons* or *jaï alaï*, the huge concrete courts in which the national game of *pelota* is played. This game is a bit like fives. Pairs of players wallop a hard leather-covered ball, either with their bare hands or a long basket-work extension of the hand called a *chistera*, against a high wall blocking one end of the court. It's quite extraordinarily dangerous – as you'd expect at speeds of up to 200kph – and knock-outs and worse are not uncommon. Trials of strength, rather like Scottish Highland games, are also popular – tugs-of-war, lifting heavy weights, turning massive carts, sawing through giant tree trunks and the like.

The *cuisine*, too, is quite distinctive and appropriately hearty. In addition to air-cured Bayonne ham, common dishes are *pipérade*, a cross between scrambled egg and omelette filled with green peppers, red pimentoes and tomato; *ttoro*, the Basque version of *bouillabaisse*; *piballes* – young eels; cod *vizcaina* or à la Biscayenne; *poulet basquaise* – chicken casseroled with pimentoes, tomatoes, mushrooms and wine; and the cream-filled *gâteau basque*. The only Basque wine – very drinkable – is *Irouléguy*. And if you have a taste for the harder stuff, you'll enjoy the potent *Izarra* green and yellow liqueurs.

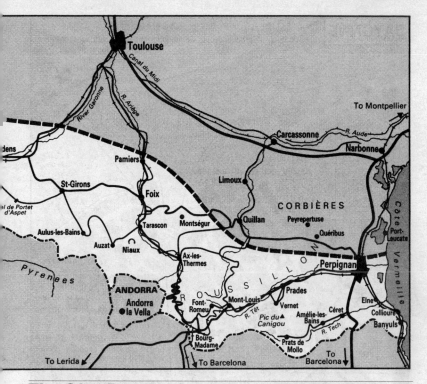

The Côte Basque

Hardly more than 30km long and well served by bus and train, the Basque coast is easily accessible, and, perhaps surprisingly, reasonably priced hotel accommodation is not that difficult to find – although space can be limited in summer. The most popular budget place is **Anglet**, which has a youth hostel and is within easy reach of the magnificent beaches and Biarritz hot spots. **Biarritz** itself is a rather exhausting place to stay in full season; families will certainly prefer **St-Jean-de-Luz** – in any case much the most attractive town.

Bayonne

BAYONNE stands back some 6km from the Atlantic, a position that has protected it from any real exploitation by tourism. It bestrides the confluence of the River Adour, which rises far to the east in the region of the the Pic du Midi de Bigorre, with the much smaller Nive, which rises in the Basque Pyrenees above St-Jean-Pied-de-Port. Although purists dispute whether it is truly a Basque rather than a Gascon city, it is the effective economic and political capital of the Pays Basque.

To the layman, at least, there seems no doubt about its Basque flavour, with its tall half-timbered houses with their woodwork painted in the peculiarly Basque tones of green and red. Here, too, Basques in flight from Franco's Spain came without hesitation to seek refuge among their own. For many years the Petit Bayonne quarter was a

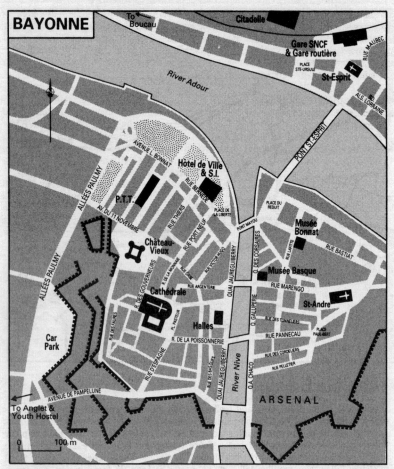

BAYONNE

To Boucau
Citadelle
Gare SNCF & Gare routière
RUE MAUBEC
River Adour
PLACE STE-URSULE
St-Esprit
ALS. LORRAINE
AVENUE L. BONNAT
ALLÉES PAULMY
AV. DU 11 NOVEMBRE
Hôtel de Ville & S.I.
RUE BERNÈDE
P.T.T.
RUE THIERS
RUE PORT NEUF
PLACE DE LA LIBERTÉ
PLACE DE LA LIBERTÉ
PLACE DU RÉDUIT
PONT ST-ESPRIT
Château-Vieux
ALLÉES PAULMY
R. DE LA MONNAIE
RUE LORME
RUE VICTOR HUGO
PONT MAYOU
Q. DES CORSAIRES
QUAI JAUREGUIBERRY
Musée Bonnat
RUE LAFITTE
RUE BASTIAT
RUE DES GOUVERNEURS
Cathédrale
RUE ARGENTERIE
PL. PASTEUR
Musée Basque
RUE MARENGO
RUE DES FAURES
RUE D'ESPAGNE
Halles
R. DE LA POISSONNERIE
Q. GALUPERIE
RUE DES TONNELIERS
St-André
PLACE PAUL-BERT
Car Park
RUE DES BASQUES
QUAI JAUREGUIBERRY
River Nive
Q.A. CHAO
RUE PANNECAU
RUE DES CORDELIERS
RUE PELLETIER
AVENUE DE PAMPELUNE
To Anglet & Youth Hostel
ARSENAL
0   100 m

hotbed of Basque nationalist ferment, until the French government clamped down on such dangerous tendencies.

The city's origins go back to Roman times, since when its Latin name of Lapurdum, corrupted to Labourd, has been extended to cover the whole of this westernmost of the three Basque provinces. For 300 years until 1451 it enjoyed prosperity and security under English domination. Around 1500, Sephardic Jews fleeing the Spanish Inquisition arrived bringing their chocolate manufacturing trade with them. The city reached the peak of its commercial success in the eighteenth century, when it was also a centre of the armaments industry (it gave its name to the invention of the bayonet). Later, its prestige suffered a blow in the 1789 Revolution when the anti-regionalist centralising zealots of the Paris government subsumed the three Basque provinces under a single *département* with its capital at Pau. More recently, there has been a renewal of economic activity based on the processing of by-products from the natural gas field at Lacq near Pau, but this, too, has been affected by the current hard times, leaving Bayonne with a higher than average level of unemployment.

These problems don't immediately impinge on the visitor, however, and first impressions are likely to be favourable – it's a small-scale, easily manageable city. Whether your intention is to head inland or down the coast, it may – as the nodal point of all major road and rail routes from the north and east – be your first encounter with the Pays Basque. Cheaper and quieter than neighbouring Biarritz, it could be worth considering as a base even for a seaside sojourn.

Arrival and accommodation

The **train and bus stations** are next door to each other just off place de la République in the slightly shabby district of St-Esprit on the north bank of the River Adour. The heart of the city lies straight across the wide Pont St-Esprit from here. If you're driving, there's a conveniently placed **car park** on the left side of allées Paulmy, heading south, under the old city walls. The SI has its offices on place de la Hôtel de Ville on place de la Liberté (daily except Sun 9.30–noon & 2.30–6pm), close by the river.

The best and most agreeable budget **hotel** is the old-fashioned *Hôtel des Arceaux*, 26 rue Port-Neuf (☎59.59.15.53; ③) below the cathedral; the cheapest – basic but spotless – is the *Hôtel des Basques*, on place Paul-Bert (☎59.59.08.02; ①). A clean and reasonable alternative is the *Hôtel Monbar*, 24 rue Pannecau (☎59.59.26.80; ③). Other possibilities are the *Hôtel de Bordeaux*, 4 rue Maubec (☎59.55.04.07; ⑤), and *Hôtel Vauban*, 13 place Ste-Ursule (☎59.55.11.31; ③), both close to the station.

Another possibility is the **youth hostel** in Anglet, at 19 route des Vignes, Quartier Chiberta (☎59.63.86.49). Friendly and well run (no night-time curfew; canteen in summer), it's a great international meeting-place for surfers and summer travellers. There is room for tents under the pine trees, where you can fall asleep to the sound of the breakers on the shore. From Biarritz take the bus to the beaches, get off by the Fontaine-Laborde campsite, turn up the road by the camp, then left into promenade des Sables and left again into route des Vignes. From Bayonne, take the *ligne bleue* bus, direction Biarritz-La Négresse, from the Hôtel de Ville to Cinq Cantons: there take a left down promenade de la Barre, then fifth left into promenade des Sables, and right into route des Vignes – about 25 minutes on foot.

Campers can choose between *La Chêneraie* (mid-March to mid-Oct), off the N117 Pau road close to the Bayonne-nord exit from the autoroute, and the pleasanter *Camping Barre de l'Adour* at 130 av de l'Adour (mid-June to mid-Sept), by the mouth of the Adour. Or try one of the Anglet sites (see below).

The city

Although there are no great sights, it's a pleasure to wander the deep narrow streets of **Grand Bayonne**, the quarter around the cathedral, and **Petit Bayonne** across the Nive. The smartest streets are those radiating from the cathedral: **rue d'Espagne**, the old commercial centre, and **rue de la Monnaie**, leading into **rue du Port-Neuf**, with its aromatic *pâtisseries* and *confiseries*. Behind the cathedral, along **rue des Faures** and the streets above the old walls, there is a distinctly Spanish feel, with washing strung at the windows and strains of music drifting from the dark interiors.

The **cathedral** itself, on the magnolia-shaded **place Pasteur**, with its twin towers and steeple rising with airy grace above the houses, is best seen from a distance. Up close, the yellowish stone reveals bad weathering, with most of the decorative detail lost. Inside, its most impressive features are the height of the nave and some sixteenth-century glass, set off by the prevailing gloom. Like other southern Gothic cathedrals of the period (about 1260), it was based on more famous northern models, in this case Soissons and Reims. On the south side is a quiet, secretive cloister with a lawn, cypress trees and beds of begonias.

Below the cathedral, past the monstrous market building (home to especially good markets on Tues, Wed and Sat), the riverside **quays** of the Nive are the city's most picturesque focus, with sixteenth-century arcaded houses on the far, Petit Bayonne side, one of which used to contain the excellent Basque ethnographic museum, the **Musée Basque**. Unfortunately, the museum is closed at the time of writing, ostensibly because the floors are unsound – though more likely due to the petty political squabbles which are delaying a decision on its future. The word is that it will reopen in the fifteenth-century *château neuf* a few blocks east. The exhibits illustrate Basque life through the centuries, and include reconstructed farm buildings, house interiors, implements and tools, *makhilas* – a kind of offensive walking stick, often elaborately carved from medlar wood – a section on Basque seagoing activities (Columbus' skipper was a Basque and another Basque, Sebastian de Caro, made the first circumnavigation of the globe in 1519–22), and rooms on *pelota* - its history and stars – and famous Basques, among whom are Simon Bolivar and de Lesseps, of Suez canal fame.

The city's second museum, the **Musée Bonnat**, close by at 5 rue Jacques-Lafitte (June 15–Sept 10 daily 10am–noon & 3–7pm, closed Tues; rest of year Mon, Wed, Thurs 3–7pm, Fri 3–9pm, Sat & Sun 10am–noon & 3–7pm), is an unexpected treasury of art, and a welcome change from most run-of-the-mill provincial galleries, with an array of works that includes thirteenth- and fourteenth-century Italian primitives, especially a *Virgin and child* by Matteo di Giovanni and Isenbrandt, Brussels tapestries, paintings by Goya, Constable, Rubens, Géricault, Delacroix, and some fine society portraits by Léon Bonnat, whose personal collection formed the basis of the museum.

Apart from savouring the wide river skies there is little to draw you to the northern bank of the Adour. There is a synagogue in rue Maubec, a reminder that it was here that Bayonne's Jewish community settled first on arrival from Spain. The **church of St-Esprit** opposite the station is all that remains of a hostel that once ministered to the sore feet and other ailments of the St-Jacques pilgrims – worth a look for an interesting wood sculpture of the *Flight into Egypt*. Just behind the station, Vauban fans might take a look at the massive **Citadelle** he built in 1680 to defend the town against Spanish attack, though it did not see much action until the Napoleonic wars, when its garrison resisted a siege by Wellington for four months in 1813.

If you have a car, it's worth making an evening trip through the Communist-run industrial suburb of **BOUCAU** out to the breakwater that protects the mouth of the Adour. Sit at the bar and watch the leaden-backed Atlantic rollers come in; if you are tempted to bathe from the beautiful white beach that stretches from here to Bordeaux, just remember that there are lethal currents close inshore and you must be extremely careful.

Eating, drinking and entertainment

Apart from the much-frequented *Café du Théâtre* on place de la Liberté there are no obvious major gathering points in the city. The best place to look for **eating and drinking places** is in the back streets of the Petit Bayonne quarter on the right bank of the Nive, especially round rue Pannecau, rue des Cordeliers and rue des Tonneliers. The *Xan Xan Gorri*, a friendly and popular wine bar at 9 rue des Cordeliers (open until 2am) serves *tapas*-style food in the evenings; the nearby *Bar des Amis* at 13 rue des Tonneliers (open until 9.30pm) is a cheap and cheery local restaurant. More sophisticated, with greater choice, is the *Restaurant de la Tour* at 5 rue des Faures (closed Sun) behind the cathedral, which has menus for 60–120F. Good for a midday meal or a dawn snifter (it opens at 5am) is the *Bar du Marché* in rue des Basques directly opposite the market – *plats du jour* for less than 40F.

As far as **festivals** go, Bayonne's biggest thrash of the year is the *Fêtes Traditionelles*, which opens on the first Wednesday in August, and consists of five days and nights of continuous boozing and entertainment, finishing up with a *corrida* on the following Sunday. This is followed by three or four days of bullfighting, starting on August 15. The last two years have seen a jazz festival in mid-July, which is set to become a regular feature, and every October there is a Franco-Spanish theatre festival.

Biarritz

A few minutes by rail or road from Bayonne, **BIARRITZ** was the Monte Carlo of the Atlantic coast. Today, however, it has something of a faded air, and while still to some extent drawing in the wealthy punters as successfully as ever, the overriding impression is the town's slightly sad combination of the chic and the shabby.

Practicalities

The **SI** in square d'Ixelles (summer daily 9am-7.30pm; rest of year Mon–Fri 9am–12.30pm & 2.15–6.15pm, Sat 9am–12.30pm & 3–6pm, closed Sun) has information about excursions into the surrounding country and local **festivals** (of which the most interesting is the end-of-September **film festival**). Contrary to what you might think, there are two or three very reasonably priced hotels right in the middle of town, though it is wise to book in advance in July and August. Try the family-run, friendly and clean *Hôtel de la Marine*, on the corner of rue des Goélands (☎59.24.34.09; ②), or *Hôtel Palym* (no. 7; ☎59.24.16.56; ②), both in rue du Port-Vieux. Slightly more expensive but superbly placed overlooking the Plage du Port Vieux, *Le Welcome* (☎59.24.10.42; ⑤) has a very charming English-speaking *patronne* and a restaurant, pizzeria and bar. Of the three Biarritz **campsites** (all in the southern part of town), *Le Biarritz* at 28 rue d'Harcet (April 28–Sept 30; ☎59.23.00.12) and *Le Splendid*, nearby in route d'Harcet (April–Sept; ☎59.23.01.29), are about 500m from Plage de la Milady; the cheapest, *Camping Municipal*, is near the station in av Président-Kennedy (June–Sept; ☎59.24.52.50). It would be wise to phone ahead for any of them in July and August.

Town and beaches

The only part of town worth a stroll is the area of streets between the Casino Municipal and the Plage du Port Vieux. One centre of Biarritz life is the oblong **place Clemenceau**, where you can nibble a cake or sip a lemon tea at Dodin's *pâtisserie* or Miremont's *salon de thé* – prissy and frightfully superior places. To the west, **place Ste-Eugénie** with its faded old-time hotels, and **place Attalaye**, down by the port, are also worth a look as you go by, as is the workaday **rue du Port-Vieux**, nearby.

The **shore**, however, is beautiful. White breakers crash on sandy strands on which the beautiful people bronze their limbs cheek-by-jowl with suburban families and ageing Californian and Australian surf bums against a backdrop of casinos and ocean-liner hotels, Gothic castles and unfinished apartment blocks which the developers are obliged to paint prematurely to hide the raw cement. The **beaches** – served by a special bus or *navette* in summer – extend from Plage de la Milady in the south through Plage Marbella, Côte des Basques, Plage du Port Vieux, Grande Plage, Plage Miramar to the Pointe St-Martin to the north, though most of the action takes place between the Plage du Port Vieux and the huge **Hôtel du Palais** overlooking the Plage Miramar, formerly the *Villa Eugénie*. This was built by Napoléon III in the mid-nineteenth century for his wife, whom he had met and courted in Biarritz, and it was this imperial patronage that transformed the town into a playground for monarchs, aristos and *glitterati* up until World War II. Just beside the **Plage du Port Vieux**, the most sheltered and intimate of the beaches, a rocky promontory sticks out into the sea ending in an iron catwalk anchoring the **Rocher de la Vierge**, an offshore rock adorned with a white statue of the Virgin that has become Biarritz's hallmark. Around it are scattered other rocky islets where the swell heaves and combs. It seems irresistible to lovers, for the seaward view is always obscured by pairs of backs and interlocking arms apparently in thrall to the ocean. On the bluff above the Virgin stands a **Musée de la Mer** (July–Aug 9am–7pm; rest of year 9am–noon & 2–7pm), hardly a must, but with interesting exhibits to do with the fishing industry, the region's birds, and an aquarium of North Atlantic fish. Beyond here is the postcard-pretty harbour of the **Port des Pêcheurs,** backed by tamarisks and pink and blue hydrangeas. The fishermen have gone, but you could afford a snack at one of the waterfront *tapas* bars or indulge in some good if overpriced seafood at the doughty *Chez Albert* (menus for 160–200F). Beyond here lies the **Grande Plage**, taking you in one immaculate sweep of sand past the tatty Casino Municipal all the way to the lighthouse on the Pointe St-Martin.

Anglet

Immediately north of Biarritrz, **ANGLET** sprawls amorphously up the coast from the Pointe St-Martin to the mouth of the Adour. There is nothing to see except for two superb beaches – the **Chambre d'Amour**, so named for two lovers trapped in their trysting place by the tide, and the **Sables d'Or**, much favoured by the surfers (boards for hire). Here, too, the swimming is very dangerous and you should heed the warning signs.

There are buses from the Hôtel de Ville in Biarritz, and the *navette des plages* runs during the summer. Alternatively you can walk it in about thirty minutes, along av de l'Impératrice, av MacCroskey, then second left down to the seaside bd des Plages. Anglet is also a good place to stay if you're hostelling (see above) – though if you're not, the only **accommodation** is in one of two **campsites**: *Fontaine Laborde* (June–Sept), near the hostel, and *Chambre d'Amour* (April–Sept) in route de Bouney. For **eating** there is no alternative to picnicking or making do with overpriced snacks and pizzas from the seaside establishments.

St-Jean-de-Luz

With its fine sandy bay and magnificent harbourfront houses, **ST-JEAN-DE-LUZ** is far and away the most attractive resort on the Basque coast. Despite this, it has not been submerged by tourism and remains one of the busiest fishing ports in France, and the principal one for landing anchovy and tuna.

As the only natural harbour on the coast between Arcachon and Spain, it has been a major port for centuries, with whaling and cod fishing the traditional preoccupations of its fleets. Its sailors voyaged as far afield as Newfoundland, which indeed they claimed to have discovered 100 years before Columbus. In the seventeenth century, they were driven from their traditional ports-of-call in Arctic waters by Dutch and English whalers – a problem which an enterprising Basque overcame by devising a method of boiling down the blubber on board ship, thus enabling the ships to stay at sea much longer and in effect inventing the factory whaler. Then, in the eighteenth century, under the provisions of the Treaty of Utrecht, they lost their cod-fishing grounds in Newfoundland and were only saved from ruin, like their counterparts in Bayonne, by turning privateer and seizing other nations' shipping.

Practicalities

The train station is on the southern edge of the centre, opposite which, on and around av Verdun, there are several reasonable **hotels**, of which you might try the *Hôtel Toki-Ona*, 10 rue Marion-Garay (☎59.26.11.54; ②; closed Nov–March), the *Hôtel de Verdun*, 13 av de Verdun (☎59.26.02.55; ③), or *Hôtel de Paris*, 1 bd du Comandant-Passicot, on the corner of av Labrouche(☎59.26.00.62; ④). The last is in the process of renovation, which will push the prices up a notch. There are numerous **campsites**, all grouped in the so-called *zone des campings* to the left of the N10 between St-Jean and Guéthary.

The **SI** is in place Maréchal-Foch behind the Hôtel de Ville (daily 9am–noon & 2–7pm; July–Aug Sun 10am–noon). On Friday and Tuesday there is a **market** in the adjacent bd Victor-Hugo. **Bikes** can be hired at the station or *ADO* on av Labrouche. **Pelota** matches take place every Saturday at the *fronton* at the far end of rue Gambetta.

The focus of life for visitors is **place Louis XIV** with its bandstand (free concerts), cafés and plane trees. Leading off it to the huge curving beach, **rue de la République** with its numerous touristy restaurants is the easiest, if not the cheapest place to eat. *Le Kaiku,* in a handsome old house at no. 17, has an excellent reputation for its fish and seafood, but is likely to cost upward of 200F. A cheaper, more family-oriented place to try is *La Sardinerie* (open 11.30am–2.30pm & 6–10pm) in the car park behind the Hôtel de Ville, where dishes of tuna, sardines or omelettes cost in the region of 40–50F.

The town

The wealth and vigour of St-Jean's seafaring past is evident in the town, most notably in the surviving seventeenth- and eighteenth-century houses of the merchants and ship-owners. One of the finest, adjacent to the **Hôtel de Ville** on **place Louis XIV**, is the turreted **Maison Louis XIV** (June–Sept daily 10.30am–noon & 3–6pm), built for the ship-owning Lohobiague family in 1635 but taking its name from the fact the young King Louis stayed here in 1660 during the preparations for his marriage to Maria Teresa, Infanta of Castile, while she lodged in the equally impressive pink Italianate villa with loggias overlooking the harbour on **quai de l'Infante.** (The corner house on rue Mazarin nearby was the Duke of Wellington's HQ during the 1813–14 winter campaign against Marshal Soult.) In the school-book history of St-Jean-de-Luz this wedding was a major event. The couple were married in the **church of St-Jean-Baptiste** on **rue Gambetta**, the main shopping street today, and the door through which they left the church has been walled up ever since. The extravagance of the event defies belief. Cardinal Mazarin alone presented the queen with 12,000 pounds of pearls and diamonds, a gold dinner service and a pair of sumptuous carriages drawn by teams of six horses – all paid for by money made in the service of France. Plain and fortress-like on the outside, the church inside is the biggest of all Basque churches, with a barn-like nave roofed in wood and lined on three sides with tiers of dark oak galleries. These are a distinctive feature of Basque churches, and were reserved for the men, while the women sat at ground level in the nave. Equally Basque is the elaborate gilded retable of tiered angels, saints and prophets behind the altar. The walled-up door through which Louis and his bride passed is on the right of the main entrance. Hanging from the ceiling is an *ex-voto* model of the Empress Eugénie's paddle-steamer, *Eagle*, which narrowly escaped wrecking on the rocks outside St-Jean in 1867.

On the other side of the harbour, **CIBOURE** looks like a continuation of St-Jean but is in fact a separate *commune*. Its streets are even prettier, especially opposite the end of the bridge from St-Jean, the waterfront **quai Maurice-Ravel** (the composer was born at no. 12) and the parallel **rue Pocolette** behind. Wide-fronted, half-timbered, gaily painted and sometimes balconied, they epitomise the Labourdian Basque style. The octagonal tower protruding above the houses belongs to the sixteenth century church of **St-Vincent**, where you'll find more characteristic Basque galleries and Baroque altarpiece; the entrance is in rue Pocolette through a paved courtyard with gravestones embedded in it. From the bridge the **fish dock** sticks out into the harbour, stacked with nets and blackened lobster traps, with grubby blue-painted tuna boats redolent of diesel oil tied up alongside. Upstream, smaller boats lie heeled over on the tidal mud flats of the little River Nivelle against a backdrop of green fields and the emerald flanks of the 900-metre peak of La Rhune (3/4 buses daily Mon–Fri from gare SNCF to Col de St-Ignace and Sare for ascent of La Rhune; see below).

Hendaye and the Spanish frontier

HENDAYE, 16km south of St-Jean-de-Luz, is the last town in France before the Spanish frontier. Neither the town itself, **Hendaye-Ville**, nor the seaside quarter, **Hendaye-Plage**, is of any intrinsic interest, although the latter has a fine beach.

The town, which is served by the Paris–Bordeaux–Irun main rail line, lies on the estuary of the River Bidassoa which here forms the border with Spain. Just upstream, a tiny wooded island known as the Île des Faisans – or Île de la Conférence – was once used as a meeting place for the monarchs of the two countries. François I, taken prisoner at the battle of Pavia in 1525, was ransomed here. In 1659 it was the scene of the signature of the Treaty of the Pyrenees and in the following year of the marriage contract between Louis XIV and Maria Teresa. On the latter occasion, it was here that the painter Velasquez, who was responsible for the decor, caught the cold which resulted in his death. Another interesting encounter was the meeting between Hitler and Franco at Hendaye station on October 23, 1940, when Hitler refused to commit himself to supporting Franco's colonial claims on Morocco. **Pierre Loti** fans might like to see the house in rue des Pêcheurs, on the waterfront below bd de Gaulle, where the author died in 1923.

If you are **planning to stay**, hotel prices are cheapest in Hendaye-Ville. Try *Chez Antoinette*, in pl Pellot-Belcenia (☎59.20.08.47; ⑤). The **campsites** are mainly grouped around Hendaye-Plage. *Le Moulin,* off the D658 (between the N10 and coastal D912), is one of the cheaper ones. For further information, consult the **SI** at 12 rue des Aubépines in Hendaye-Plage.

Around Hendaye: up the coast and inland

The best thing about Hendaye is in fact getting there, for the stretch of **coast** from St-Jean south has remained miraculously unspoilt, especially in the region of the Château d'Abbadie and the **Pointe Ste-Anne** promontory, accessible from the **Chemin Piéton Littoral** footpath, which runs parallel to the coastal D912 Corniche Basque road. It is equally accessible from the beach at Hendaye-Plage.

Moving **inland**, both trans-Pyrenean walking routes – the **GR10 and HRP** (Haute Randonnée Pyrénéenne) – begin their course in Hendaye-Plage, at the casino on the front. The first stage is dull and gives no sense of the glories that lie ahead: along bd Général-Leclerc, through the town on rue des Citronniers, under the rail line, then 50m east on the N10 before following the waymarks to the right towards the A63 autoroute. A cattle track passes underneath and continues to the tiny hilltop village of **BIRIATOU**, where the walking starts to get interesting. (If you are not concerned about the romance of starting at the very beginning, splash out on a taxi and start at Biriatou.) A short steep section leads to a Basque church with a collection of weather-worn Celtic-type tombstones, next door to the pretty *Auberge Hirribarren,* a temporary haven for many escaping Allied soldiers during World War II. From here the main footpaths and a number of local variations rise rapidly above the coast to semi-isolation where only the buzzing power lines (soon left behind) and the occasional walker or jogger disturb the peace.

Inland: Labourd and Basse Navarre

If you don't have your own transport, the simplest forays into the soft, seductive landscapes of the **Basque hinterland** are along the St-Jean-de-Luz/Sare bus route and the Bayonne-St-Jean-Pied-de-Port railway. Either gives a representative sample of places.

La Rhune, Ascain, Sare

The 900-metre cone of **LA RHUNE** on the Spanish border is the last skyward thrust of the Pyrenees before they decline into the Atlantic. It is *the* landmark of Labourd, in spite of its unsightly TV mast, and since it is also equipped with a rack-and-pinion railway it is predictably popular with the seekers of views – and very fine they are, way up the Basque coast and east to the rising Pyrenees. Three or four **buses** a day ply the 30-

minute route from the gare SNCF in St-Jean-de-Luz, stopping at ASCAIN, COL DE ST-IGNACE (for La Rhune) and SARE.

ASCAIN, where Pierre Loti wrote *Ramuntcho,* is like so many Labourd villages – pretty as a picture and in danger of caricaturing itself, with its galleried church, *fronton* and half-timbered houses. To shake off this sweetness you could walk up La Rhune from here in about two and a half hours, or take the little train from Col de St-Ignace (July–Sept daily every 35min from 9am; May 1–June 30 & Oct 1–Nov 15 weekends only 10am & 3pm; Easter and the spring holiday daily 10am & 3pm; 35F, children 17F). The ascent takes 30 minutes, but you need to allow up to two hours for the round trip.

It is worth going on to **SARE** even if you've missed the bus. You can either walk on the GR10 from the station just below the summit of La Rhune in about an hour and a quarter or follow the road from St-Ignace in about the same time. If you plan to continue further east, you can make an overnight stop at the *Hôtel Lastiry* on pl du Fronton (☎59.54.20.07; ③) or the *Hôtel Baratchartea* (☎59.54.20.48; ③), or at one of two **campsites**, *La Petite Rhune* and *Goyenetche*, both just south of the village.

Instead of going back to St-Jean-de-Luz, an easy three to four-hour stint on the GR10 would take you on to **AINHOA** to link up with the valley of the Nive (see below). Another gem of a village, once patronised by the Duke of Windsor and touristy in season, it consists of scarcely more than a single street lined with substantial houses, whose stone lintels are carved with the dates of their construction and details of their families' history – mostly seventeenth century. The heavy-towered church is worth a look with its rich altarpiece of prophets and apostles in niches framed by Corinthian columns and capped with pediments. There is a **gîte d'étape** at the Maison Elissaldia (☎59.29.25.29).

The **Spanish frontier** is 3km away at **DANCHERIA**, where there is a **campsite**, the *Xokoan*. There is a back road through the woods, ending at a stream crossed by a plank bridge, with a *venta* on the Spanish side, much frequented in the days before Spanish membership of the European Community when so many products could be bought more cheaply across the border. While a certain amount of smuggling was tolerated, there was always the risk of encountering the *douane volante* – mobile customs vans – lurking on back roads.

Smuggling has long been an appropriately virile occupation all along this frontier, and it's said that some sizeable fortunes have been made. Wartime was particularly profitable, with an almost money-no-object trade in refugees from the Vichy and Nazi-occupied territories. And a pretty ruthless business it was: French fugitives were charged a "reasonable" rate, while Jews had to pay £1000 a head whether they were alone or in a group. If it was not trading in people, it was blackmarket coffee or any other commodity in short supply one side of the border or the other.

The Valley of the Nive

The **River Nive** is the only public transport artery into the Basque interior, with four or five trains a day making the riverside journey from Bayonne to St-Jean-Pied-de-Port in about an hour. The landscape, scattered with villages untouched by speculative development, remains as peaceful and harmonious as you approach the mountains as it was in the lowlands. The dominant note is green: a luminous green, as distinctive as an Irish or an English green, but quite different and specific.

Cambo-les-Bains

The first major stop is **CAMBO-LES-BAINS**, an old spa town whose favoured micro-climate (camelias flower a month earlier here, the locals maintain, than elsewhere in the region) made it an ideal centre for the treatment of tuberculosis in the last century. It is an attractive town, green and open, but suffers from the usual genteel stuffiness of spas. The "new" town, with its ornate houses and hotels, radiates out from the baths over the heights above the River Nive, while the old quarter, typically Basque with its whitewashed houses and galleried church, lies beside the river. For an **overnight stay** try the *Auberge de Tante Ursule* in Bas Cambo (☎59.29.70.23; ③) by the *fronton;* the nearest year-round **campsite** is *Ur-Hégia* in route des Sept-Chênes.

The main thing to see is the **Villa Arnaga**, just out of town on the Bayonne road (May–Sept daily 10am–noon & 2.30–6.30pm, March 20 to April 30 & Oct 2.30–6pm), built for Edmond Rostand, author of *Cyrano de Bergerac*, who came here to cure his pleurisy in 1903. It's a larger-than-life Basque house overlooking an almost surreal formal garden with discs and rectangles of water and segments of grass punctuated by blobs, cubes and cones of box, lined by limes and blue cedars, with a distant view of green hills. It's very kitsch inside, with a minstrels' gallery, fake pilasters and allegorical frescoes, chandeliers and numerous portraits and other memorabilia. Nothing as yet about the Depardieu movie.

Around Cambo

It's 5km southwest from Cambo by bus or on foot to **ESPELETTE,** a village of wide-eaved houses, with a church notable for its heavy square tower, carved doors, painted ceiling and disc-shaped gravestones. The village's principal source of renown is its large red **pimentoes**, much used in Basque cuisine, and its *pottok* **sales**. *Pottoks* are a small stocky Basque breed of pony, once favoured for work in British coal mines, but now reared mainly for meat and riding – herds of them are a common sight on the upland pastures. The annual sales take place on the last Wednesday in January; the pimento jamboree takes place on the last Sunday in October. There is a very good hotel-restaurant in the village, too, the *Euzkadi*, on the Cambo road (☎59.93.91.88; ④;), with menus specialising in Basque country cooking from 60F. The *Hôtel Chilar*, on the same road, has slightly cheaper rooms (☎59.93.90.01; ③).

About the same distance from Cambo-les-Bains, next stop up the rail line (though there's only one train a day), **ITXASSOU** is another lovely village, quieter than most of the others in the area, surrounded by green wooded hills. Nearby, the River Nive cuts through a narrow looping defile by the so-called **Pas de Roland** – hardly more than a roadside boulder with a hole in it, supposedly struck by the hooves of the great knight's horse. Even without a car it would be a great place for a gentle recharge of the batteries, especially if you were to stay at the *Hôtel Arza Mendi* on the place du Fronton (☎59.29.75.29; ③–④), which has attractive, old-fashioned rooms and a restaurant with prices which begin at 52F; the proprietor speaks excellent English. Nearly as enticing, but shut from November to March, is the *Etchepare,* on the same square (☎59.29.75.14; ③), also with a restaurant from 55F.

St-Étienne-de-Baïgorry

The next major stop is the station of OSSÈS-ST-MARTIN-D'ARROSSA, from where it's about 8km south to **ST-ÉTIENNE-DE-BAIGORRY.** SNCF buses meet the trains. Like other Basque villages St-Étienne is divided into quite distinct quarters, more like separate hamlets than a unified village. A prosperous, sleek place, its business is still very much agriculture rather than tourism, with the Pays Basque's only vineyards centred here, producing a good strong red wine, named *Irouléguy* after a neighbouring village; a local shop offers *dégustation* (June 15–Aug 31 daily 9am–noon & 2–7.30pm; July–Aug Sun 10am–12.30pm).

There are no great sights here: a seventeenth-century church with a sumptuous Baroque retable, a picturesque bridge, posing against a backdrop of romantic castle and distant hills, and the **hills** themselves. St-Étienne lies in the mouth of the **Vallée des Aldudes**, with the GR10 running along the **Cresta de Iparla** ridge to the west, the classic ridge walk of the Basque country. The GR10 goes directly up from the village, or you could hitch a ride on the D949 to the Col d'Ispéguy. There are plenty of other gentler walks, too.

The *Hôtel Hargain* has **rooms** from 160F (☎59.37.41.46; ③–④) and a restaurant with menus from 65F. There is a municipal **campsite**, *Camping Irouléguy*, on the banks of the river (mid-June to mid-Sept), and another, *Camping à la Ferme Mendy*, in the Lespars quarter, with a **gîte d'étape** (☎59.37.42.39).

St-Jean-Pied-de-Port

The old capital of Basse Navarre, **ST-JEAN-PIED-DE-PORT** lies in a circle of hills at the foot of the Roncevaux pass into Spain. It owes its name to its position "at the foot of the *port*" – a Pyrenean word for pass. Only part of France since the Treaty of the Pyrenees in 1659, it was an important pilgrim centre in the Middle Ages. The routes from Paris, Vézelay and Le Puy converged here, and it was the pilgrims' last stop before struggling over the pass to the Spanish monastery of Roncesvalles (Roncevaux in French), where Roland, Charlemagne's general celebrated in medieval romance, sounded his horn in vain.

THE CHANSON DE ROLAND

Roland, with his sword Durandal, is the hero of the medieval *Chanson de Roland*. But he was also a historical character, warden of the Breton marches who in 778 accompanied the Emperor Charlemagne on a campaign against the Moors in Spain, in the course of which the Navarrese capital of Pamplona was sacked. In revenge the Basques ambushed and decimated Charlemagne's rearguard, commanded by Roland, as it withdrew through the gorges above Roncevaux. The *chanson* has it that infidel Saracens were the dastardly foe, but this was propaganda designed to make poor Roland's end more heroic.

The town lies on the River Nive, enclosed by walls of pinky-red sandstone. Above it rises a wooded hill crowned by the inevitable Vauban fortress, while to the east a further defensive system guards the road to Spain. The more recent overspill, pleasant but unremarkable, spreads down across the main road on to lower ground.

The **old town** consists of a single cobbled street, **rue de la Citadelle**, which runs downhill from the **Porte St-Jacques**, so named because it was the gate by which the pilgrims entered, to the **Porte d'Espagne**, commanding the bridge over the Nive. Many of the houses, painted except for their cornerstones, bear inscriptions on their lintels from the sixteenth, seventeenth and eighteenth centuries. A plain red church, **Notre-Dame-du-Bout-du-Pont** (fourteenth century), stands beside the Porte d'Espagne, and, opposite, a short street leads through the **Porte de Navarre** to the modern road. From the Porte d'Espagne, with its view of balconied houses overlooking the stream, rue d'Espagne leads uphill to the so-called Route Napoléon.

Off to the left is the town *fronton*, where a barehanded *pelota* match – the most macho kind – is held every Monday at 4.30pm throughout the year. On the other side of the river, the **SI** is in pl de-Gaulle opposite the *mairie* (Mon–Fri 9am–noon & 2–6pm, Sat 10am–noon). The **gare SNCF** is at the end of av Renaud, on the northern edge of the centre. Just beyond the *fronton* is the **camping municipal**, on the banks of the Nive, or there's another campsite, the *Narbaïtz*, 2.5km from here along the Bayonnne road. Among **hotels**, the *Remparts* in 16 pl Floquet (☎59.37.13.79; ③), just before you cross the Nive coming into town on the Bayonne road, is the cheapest; more expensive are the *Ramuntcho* just inside the city walls at 1 rue de France (☎59.37.03.91; ⑤), with a good and reasonably priced restaurant, and *Hôtel Central* on pl de-Gaulle (☎59.37.00.22; ⑤–6x). There is a **gîte d'étape** (M. Etchegoin) on route d' Uhart (the Bayonne road).

South from St-Jean: hikes and walks

Numerous tracks lead **south from St-Jean** up into the mountains towards the Spanish border. It is sheep country, and if you are interested in getting an idea of what the old pastoral life was like, this is a good place to do it. If you are a walker, the last leg of the **GR65** pilgrim route starts from St-Jean and follows the line of the old Roman road across to Spanish Asturia.

Follow rue d'Espagne out through the city walls. The waymarks begin on the first telephone pole on the left. A little further on you turn up a lane to the right; GR10 and GR65 run together here. Follow the lane, between grassy banks, past fields and isolated farms. The farmhouses have immensely broad roofs, one side short, the other long enough to cover space for stalls and tools; it's all very quiet and rural, with long views out across the valleys. The climb becomes steeper above a little group of houses known as **HOUNTO**. It is no good asking the way, even if you can find someone to ask, for, although everyone speaks French, the Basque names are impossible for a foreigner to pronounce. Above Hounto you come out on top of a grassy spur. The GR65 turns left up what looks like an old drove road to rejoin the tarmac higher up by two small sheds at the edge of beech woods. It is about two hours to these sheds. You get your first glimpse of the higher Pyrenean peaks to the east. Above the trees you come out on grassy uplands dotted with sheepfolds or *cayolars*.

The route continues along the track to a fork (3hr 30min) with a small white statue of the Virgin. Here, the GR65 turns right towards Spain (another 90min) and the GR10 turns left. For a while it follows the road before veering away to the right to Béhérobie (see opposite), while the road continues its twisting descent to the tiny hamlet of ESTERENÇUBY, then down along the Nive and back to St-Jean-Pied-de-Port.

TRANSHUMANCE

Like other shepherds in southern or Mediterranean climes, the Basques are forced to take their flocks to the high **mountain pastures** in summer in search of better grazing. They live out on the mountainside in stone huts with a couple of dogs, milking the ewes twice a day and making cheese, the *fromage de brebis*, whose soft and hard versions are a speciality throughout the pastoral Pyrenees. Most *cayolars* today are accessible by car, at least at the gentler Basque end of the Pyrenees, so the shepherds' life is not as isolated as it used to be – though there are still areas in the higher mountains which are only accessible with mules or ponies. A measure of the pre-eminence of sheep in the Basque economy is the Basque word for rich, *aberats* – whose literal meaning is "he who owns large flocks".

Much of the grazing is owned in common by various communes, who have over the centuries made elaborate agreements to ensure a fair shareout of the best pasture and avoid disputes. One of the oldest of these *faceries*, as they are called, concluded by the inhabitants of Roncal and Baretous in 1375, is still in force, renewed each year on payment of three white heifers.

East from St-Jean

About 30km east of St-Jean, **MAULÉON,** the ancient capital of the viscounty of Soule, lies in the bottom of the flat, hot valley of the River Saison. It used to claim fame as the world capital of espadrille manufacturing, but has since lost its pre-eminence to the Far East, and, apart from the sombre but elegant Renaissance *Hôtel d'Andurain* in the middle of town, there is little to hold the attention.

The GR65 passes to the north, but if you are vaguely following the pilgrim route by car, then the road from St-Jean through Col-d'Osquich and then on towards Navarrenx is the most attractive to take. There is a riverside **campsite**, *Le Saison* (June–Sept), just outside Mauléon on the Tardets road, and another, *Le Landran* (Easter–Oct) at ORDIARP back towards the Col d'Osquich. And there's a couple of reasonable and agreeable **hotels** just after Ordiarp at MUSCULDY: *Hôtel du Col d'Osquich* (☎59.37.81.23; ④; open July 1 to Nov 11) and *Hôtel le Chistera* (☎59.28.06.74; ②).

Into the mountains: la Haute Soule

Le bout du monde – the end of the earth – is what they used to call Ste-Engrâce locked in its cul-de-sac valley beneath the Spanish frontier at the easternmost extremity of the Basque country. And although a new road has been built, the place still feels utterly remote, especially if you've approached it over the hills from St-Jean-Pied-de-Port either on foot by the GR10 or along the tortuous lane that accompanies it.

There are no shops, no hotels, no villages except Larrau. It's a land of open skies where griffon vultures turn on the thermals without so much as a flick of their huge wings, of countless flocks of sheep and thousands of acres of whispering beech woods. Although the overall distance is not very great, the slowness of the road and the grandeur of the scenery seem to magnify it. There is no public transport. Carrying a tent would give you the greatest flexibility. No one objects if you pitch it discreetly, and to be on the safe side you can always ask the nearest shepherd.

Estérençuby, Béhérobie and the Col d'Errozaté

From St-Jean-Pied-de-Port the D301 follows the deepening valley of the Nive for 8km past small red- and green-shuttered farms to **ESTERENÇUBY**, and on a further four or five kilometres to **BÉHÉROBIE**. The river, now no more than a mountain stream, runs sparkling down between steep green slopes, whose only crops are hay and bracken. In late June and early July entire families are out on the mountainside scything the meadows or turning the sweet-smelling hay with wooden rakes. In the farmyards, stacks of bracken impaled on wooden stakes are dried for winter bedding.

At Béhérobie the road climbs up to the right to the border and the Col d'Arnostéguy. In the valley bottom beside the infant Nive the only building is the *Hôtel de la Nive* (☎59.37.10.57; ③) – closed in January and invariably booked out in October for the *palombes* shooting season – but, with a restaurant whose prices start from 50F and a terrace overhanging the river, a marvellous place for a quiet stay. There is an equally attractive hotel a little way back towards Estérençuby, the *Artzain-Etchea* (☎59.37.11.55; ⑤).

Just before the bridge at Béhérobie a lane keeps up to the left, then drops down to cross a tributary stream of the Nive by an ancient barn and cottage with beautiful shady pools to bathe in. You are on the **GR10**. To the right a secondary path heads into the beech woods, bringing you to the bank of the Nive in about half an hour – a fantastic picnic spot – while the GR10 itself bears left over the bridge by the cottage, before climbing back to the right, contouring high along the sides of the valley until after about an hour you emerge above the tree line in a huge ravine of shining knee-deep grass. If you feel like continuing, it's another hour to the **Col d'Errozaté** (1076m) or two hours to the **summit of Errozaté** (1345m).

The Iraty Forest

A kilometre or so on the Estérençuby side of Béhérobie a lane turns up left towards **IRATY**. It is very steep and full of tight hairpins but, as you climb higher up the steep spurs and round the heads of labyrinthine gullies, ever more spectacular views open beneath you. You can see way back over the valley of the Nive, St-Jean and the hills beyond. Stands of beech fill the gullies, shadowing the lighter grass whose green is so intense it seems almost theatrical – an effect produced, apparently, by the juxtaposition of outcrops of rock whose purplish hue brings out the cadmium yellow in the grass.

Along the cols and ridges stand ranks of shooting butts, from which the well-heeled urban bourgeoisie open murderous fire every October on the millions of migrating *palombes*, as they call woodpigeons in the southwest, heading north over the western Pyrenees from Spain. Of the four and a half million birds that attempt the crossing, some one and a half million end up in the pot. Conservationists oppose the massacre, but for the moment they are too few to have significant influence. Many other species – not destined to be eaten – can be seen, too, among them honey buzzards, black kites, red kites, cranes and storks. Herds of healthy-looking horses and ponies and big sleek caramel cows with bells at their throats on wooden collars marked with their owners' names wander across the road. Flocks of white sheep graze on the hillsides. There are superb places to camp, with views west to the orange and crimson striations of the sunset and the revolving beacon of the Biarritz lighthouse visible in the dark.

Over the col below **Occabé** (1456m) the road loops down past scattered *cayolars* to the **plateau d'Iraty** where there is a small lake and a snack bar and flat ground to camp on. A road leads south to OCHAGAVIA in Spain, via the **Chalet Pedro** (1km) where the GR10 swings right and up on to the flat-topped Occabé (90min), with its Iron-Age stone circle and views across the forest and south to the Sierra de Abodi. Continuing east from the plateau, the road enters the densest part of the forest, climbing past a **campsite** half-hidden in the magnificent beeches, to an unsightly collection of chalets at the Col de Bargaguiac (*gîte d'étape*: ☎59.28.51.29) and the **Col d'Orgambideska**, which is one of the prime viewing – and killing – fields for the autumn bird migrations. As you come over the top, the ground drops sharply away into the valley of LARRAU six hundred metres lower. To the right the brilliant grassy swards of the **Pic d'Orhy** (2017m) culminate in swirling strata of rock below the summit, barring the way to Spain. And ahead, for the first breath-stopping time, you see the serrated horizon of peaks that dominate the **cirque of LESCUN**, a harbinger of the central Pyrenees.

Larrau, the gorges and Ste-Engrâce

The first thing you notice coming into **LARRAU** from the west is how different the architecture is. In contrast to the gaily painted facades and tiled roofs of Labourd and Basse Navarre, the houses here are grey and stuccoed, with slate roofs, the mood secretive and inward looking. And although it's the biggest place since St-Jean-Pied-de-Port, it is nonetheless very small and quiet – almost dead out of season.

There are two friendly and simple **hotels** with restaurants, the *Hôtel Etchémaïté* (☎59.28.61.45; ③; closed late Jan) and *Hôtel Despouey* (☎59.28.60.82; ③; closed Dec). There is an excellent baker, a **campsite** and a **gîte d'étape** 3km away at LOGIBAR (☎59.28.61.14) close to the mouth of the **Gorges d'Holzarte** – one of several in the region, cutting deep into northern slopes of the ridge that forms the frontier with Spain. A short track leads from Logibar across the turbulent and freezing stream to a car park, from where a steep path, part of the GR10, climbs through the beech woods to the junction of the Holzarte gorge with the Olhadybia in about one hour. Slung across the mouth of the latter is a spectacular Himalayan-style **suspension bridge**, which bounces and swings dizzily as you walk out over the 180-metre drop. The GR10 continues to Ste-Engrâce in seven hours or down to the beginning of the Gorges de Kakouetta in about six. But it is definitely worth coming this far. In June and July the open spaces are full of flowers: columbines,, cranesbills, orchids and vetches, and if you're lucky you might see the beautiful, long-stemmed *bimbette des Pyrénées*.

The Gorges de Kakouetta and Gorges d' Ehujarré

East of Larrau, the **Gorges de Kakouetta** (open daily 8am–nightfall; Easter to Nov 1 15F) is reachable by turning right off the D26 down the D113. Just over halfway down, the minuscule hamlet of LA CASERNE is the site of the only food shop for miles around – opposite the *mairie* – and a **campsite**, *Ibarra* (June 1–Sept 30). Kakouetta is on the tourist trail, but do not be put off: the gorge is truly dramatic and outside peak season is not crowded at all. It pays to be well shod for the path is precarious and very slippery in places; you are glad of the handrail. The walls of the gorge are very high – up to 300m – and scarcely more than 5m apart. They are jungle-thick with a luxuriant vegetation that thrives on the hothouse atmosphere produced by the myriad seepages and waterfalls that fill the air with a fine spray, that refracts and filters what sunlight gets in. There is a range of ferns that you wouldn't expect to see outside a houseplant nursery. The path continues for about an hour with a small cave at the end and just before it a full-blown waterfall spewing out of a hole in the rock.

There's a third gorge a short way southeast from Caserne, the **Gorges d'Ehujarré** at SENTA, the eastern-most of the three hamlets that comprise Ste-Engrâce. It's a straightforward walk – the route has been used for centuries for moving sheep up to the pastures of Pic Lakhoura – but requires about seven hours.

Ste-Engrâce

As for **STE-ENGRÂCE** itself, although the road now continues east over the head of the valley, reducing its isolation, it remains a beautifully remote and peaceful place, enclosed by hay meadows and green mountainsides and largely untroubled by the rhythms of the twentieth century. Life is not so simple for the locals; there is no work and the young won't stay. But for the outsider not caught in the rural poverty trap it has great charm. Its hallmark is the eleventh-century Romanesque church at Senta, which features in all the coffee-table books on the Pyrenees. It stands just as it should, with its heavily buttressed walls, belfry and penthouse roof, a sharply defined and angular assertion of humanity against the often mist-shrouded bulwarks of the mountains behind. Very simple inside, it has some good carved capitals, and the graveyard is full of traditional disc-shaped headstones.

There's a **gîte d'étape** (☎59.28.61.63) opposite the church, with an adjacent field to pitch a tent, and a **café-bar** which will serve meals. There's also the *Hôtel de la Pierre-St-Martin* (☎59.28.63.12; ③) at Calla.

On from Ste-Engrâce

The new road up to **ARETTE-LA-PIERRE-ST-MARTIN** – which is a typically ugly modern ski resort – gives fabulous views of the Ste-Engrâce valley, through magnificent forests of pine and beech, though if the cloud is down (which it often is) you'll be lucky to see much at all. Just south of the resort is the **Col de la Pierre-St-Martin**, where every July 13 the mayors of Barétous and Roncal exchange heifers in renewal of an ancient grazing treaty (see above). Also nearby is the **Goufre de la Pierre-St-Martin**, at 728m one of the deepest potholes in the world. To the east begins the descent into the valley of the Aspe, which belongs to the ancient county of Béarn.

THE CENTRAL PYRENEES

The area immediately east of the Pays Basques – the **Central Pyrenees** – is home to the highest peaks, and is the most spectacular part of the region. The southernmost part is protected, contained within the **Parc National des Pyrénées Occidentales**. Getting to the area is simple enough, at least as far as the foothill towns, by train on the

Bayonne–Toulouse line. But travelling around once there can be very slow. The few buses – and most other traffic – keep to the north–south valleys, which is frustrating when you want to switch from one valley system to the next without having to come all the way out of the mountains each time.

The **GR10** provides a good link if you are ready to walk all the way, and it's possible to hitch, at least up the valleys and across the main passes at **Col d'Aubisque** and **Col du Tourmalet**, though you will find you invariably get left on the top by drivers, who come up for the view and go back the same way.

Highlights, apart from the lakes, torrents, forests and 3000-metre peaks around Cauterets, are the *cirques* of **Lescun**, **Gavarnie** and **Troumouse**, each with its distinctive character. And for less hearty interests, there is many a flower-starred mountain meadow accessible by car, in which to quaff and gorge on a well-chosen picnic. The only real urban centres are **Pau**, which you may use as your entry-point to the area, dull **Tarbes**, and the strikingly tacky pilgrimage target of **Lourdes**. Great monuments of the bricks and mortar kind – with the exception of the fortified church at **Luz-St-Sauveur** – are equally scarce.

The Parc National des Pyrénées Occidentales

The **Parc National** was created in 1968 to protect at least part of the high Pyrenees from the development brought about by modern tourism – ski resorts, roads, mountaintop restaurants, car parks and other amenities. Through the banning of hunting it has (apart from the traditional mountain peasants' pursuit of poaching or *braconnage)* also provided sanctuary for many rare and endangered species of birds and mammals. Among them are chamois, marmots, genets, griffon vultures, golden eagles, eagle owls and capercaillies, to say nothing of the rich and varied flora. The most celebrated animal – and the most depleted by hunting – is the **Pyrenean brown bear**, the prewar numbers of which were perhaps as high as two hundred but which are now reduced to barely a dozen individuals. Although largely herbivorous, bears will take the occasional sheep or cow, and the mountain shepherd communities are their remorseless enemies. To appease them, the Park pays prompt and generous compensation for any losses, but this is not always enough to overcome the atavistic fear of the bear.

The park's main defect is its size. It is not big enough and access is too easy. It was meant to be much bigger, and more than anything it was supposed to protect the bears, which it does not do, because most of their regular habitat falls outside. In many ways its boundaries were a very bad compromise, forced on the park's creators by the conflict of countless local interests. Hunting organisations were prominent in creating obstacles, but so also were the 87 communes, who had to be consulted and who remain fiercely attached to the ancient charters which regulate the use of their mountain pastures.

The park's current president is a controversial local politician from the Vallée d'Aspe, who, in addition to supporting the incorporation of his valley, part of which falls within the park, into the Zaragoza–Bordeaux autoroute, actually promoted the construction of a ski resort at Somport within the park boundaries. Luckily the latter scheme was stopped after environmentalists took the matter to court. But the park has, in consequence, been the object of an aggressive media campaign, slating it for not doing enough to protect the bears – an accusation which angers the hard-pressed rangers, who complain that distant planners have no conception what it is really like trying to reconcile legitimate local economic needs with the protection of wild species and unsullied landscapes, to say nothing of coping with the litter, wear and tear on footpaths, illicit camping and other problems caused by modern tourism.

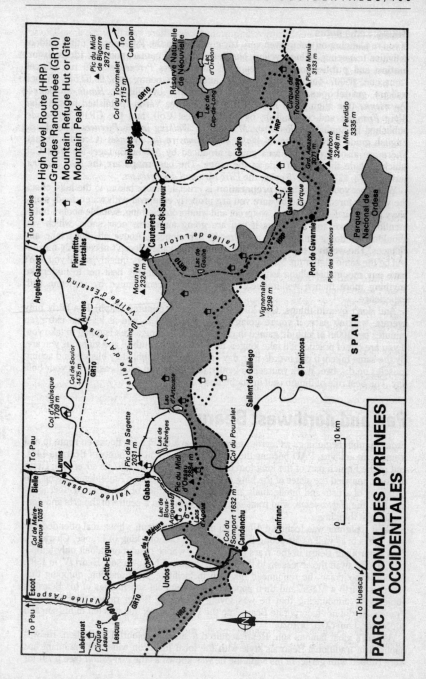

PARC NATIONAL DES PYRENEES
OCCIDENTALES

Hiking: some notes

If you're planning on doing even very basic walking in the Pyrenees, or other outdoor activities (canoeing, riding, cycling, *parapente*), a good contact point for **ideas, information** and **publications** (in French) is *Randonnées Pyrénéennes*, 29 rue Marcel-Lamarque, 65007 Tarbes (☎62.93.66.03; information centre, ☎62.93.57.57). French walkers' **guidebooks** include *Pyrénées Occidentales* by Ollivier. *Haute Randonnée Pyrénéenne* (the High Level Route/HRP) by Georges Véron (published by the *Club Alpin Français* and, in English, by Gastons-West Col), and the GR10 *Topo-guide*, published in English by *Robertson McCarta* as *Walking in the Pyrenees*. The classic English guide is Kev Reynolds' *Walks and Climbs in the Pyrenees* (Cicerone Press). There are also three small area guides produced by Arthur Battagel for West Col, which include the Spanish side of the range. The best **maps** are the *IGN* 1:25,000 series; #273, #274 and #275 cover the *Parc National des Pyrénées*.

Wherever you plan to hike, **preparation** is crucial. Before taking to the hills, check the weather forecasts, and be sure you are properly equipped with water, food, maps, bivvy bag, whistle, knife, warm, wetproof and windproof clothing, suitable boots – not to mention ice axe and crampons if you are going anywhere near snow, which you shouldn't be doing unless you are already experienced. Above all, don't take any chances. The weather being sunny and warm in the valley doesn't necessarily mean it will be the same higher up. Mountain weather can change very quickly, and if you don't have any mountain-walking experience yourself, it's probably best not to undertake anything more than a well-frequented path unless accompanied by someone with experience.

And don't overdo things. One kilometre in twelve minutes (5kph) is a fairly nifty average walking pace; if you're going uphill, you need to add at least an extra ten minutes per 100m of altitude gained in calculating how long a trek is going to take you. If you are out of practice it'll take longer, no matter how youthful and vigorous you are. By the same token, if you overdo it on day one, you'll be hobbled by blisters and aching muscles on day two. Work yourself in gently; otherwise you could easily ruin your holiday. The best rule of thumb is: if in doubt, don't do it.

Pau and northwest Béarn

From humble beginnings as a crossing on the Gave de Pau for flocks en route to and from the mountains, **PAU** became the capital of the ancient viscounty of Béarn in 1464, and of the French part of the kingdom of Navarre in 1512. In 1567 its sovereign, Henri d'Albret, married the sister of the king of France, Marguerite d'Angoulême, friend and protector of artists and intellectuals and herself the author of a celebrated Boccaccio-like tale, the *Heptameron*, who transformed the town into a centre of the arts and non-conformist thinking.

Their daughter was Jeanne d'Albret, an ardent Protestant, whose zeal offended her own subjects as well as attracting the wrath of the Catholic king of France, Charles X, thus embroiling Béarn in the Wars of Religion – whose resolution, albeit only temporary, had to await the accession to the French throne of her own son, Henri IV, in 1589. An adroit politician, he renounced his faith to facilitate this transition, quipping that "Paris is worth a Mass" and then appeasing the regional sensibilities of his Béarnais subjects by announcing that he was giving France to Béarn rather than Béarn to France. He did not incorporate Béarn into the French state; that was left to his son and successor, Louis XIII, in 1620.

As Pau's most famous son, Henri acquired a suitably colourful reputation. He was baptised in traditional Béarnais style with the local Jurançon wine and his infant lips were rubbed with garlic. In his adult life he was known as the *vert-galant* (see p.79) for his prowess as a lover. He also gave France one of its most famous recipes, *poule au pot* – chicken stuffed and boiled with vegetables; he is reputed to have said that he did not want anyone in his realm to be so poor as not to be able to afford a *poule* in the *pot* once a week.

The least expected thing about Pau is its English connection, which dates from the arrival of Wellington and his troops after the defeat of Marshal Soult at Orthez in 1814. Seduced by its climate and persuaded of its curative powers by the Scottish doctor Alexander Taylor, the English flocked to Pau throughout the nineteenth century, leaving behind their peculiar cultural obsessions – fox hunting, horse racing, polo, croquet, cricket, golf (the first eighteen-hole course in continental Europe in 1860), tearooms and parks. When the railway opened in 1866, the French came, too: writers and artists like Victor Hugo, Stendhal and Lamartine, as well as the socialites. The first rugby club in France opened here, in 1902, after which the sport spread throughout the southwest. In the 1950s, natural gas was discovered at nearby Lacq, bringing new jobs and subsidiary industries, as well as massive production of acid pollution, now reduced by filtration but still substantial. In addition there is a well-respected university.

Arrival and accommodation

Pau lies on the still incomplete **A64** *Pyrénéenne* **autoroute** and on the **main east–west rail route**, with connections to Bayonne and Biarritz in the west and with Lourdes, Tarbes and Toulouse in the east, as well as to Bordeaux and Paris. Buses run south down the Vallée d'Ossau and to Oloron-Ste-Marie, with connections to the Vallée d'Aspe. Its international **airport** (information ☎59.33.21.29; *Air Inter* ☎59.27.66.29; *Air Littoral* ☎59.33.26.64) has flights to London and Paris. The **gare SNCF** is on the southern edge of the city centre, across av Jean-Biray: *SNCF* buses leave from here; private buses from the **gare routière** in rue Michel-Houneau. A **free funicular** carries you up from the train station to the boulevard des Pyrénées opposite place Royale at far end of which is the **SI** (July–Aug daily 9am–12.30pm & 2–7pm; rest of year Mon–Sat 9am–noon & 2–6pm; closed Sun).

For a very friendly, cheap and quiet **hotel** try the *Hôtel d'Albret*, 11 rue Jeanne-d'Albret, close to the castle (☎59.27.81.58; ①). Good alternatives, almost equally central, include the *Hôtel du Musée,* 17 rue Mathieu-Lalanne, opposite the Musée des Beaux-Arts (☎59.27.73.80; ③), and the *Pomme d'Or*, 11 rue Maréchal-Foch (☎59.27.78.48; 2–③). There are two **youth hostels**, at 30 rue Michel-Houneau (☎59.30.45.77) and at 3 av de Saragosse (☎59.02.88.46) in the Cité Universitaire, and three **campsites** – a municipal site on bd du Cami-Salie off av Sallenave towards the autoroute on the northern edge of town (Whitsun–Sept 16), *Camping de Gelos* behind the gare SNCF at the Base Plein Air, Bizanos (May 15–Oct 15), and *Le Terrier* in av du Vert-Galant in Lescar to the west off the N117 and D105 (open all year).

The town

Pau has no great sights or museums, which leaves you free to enjoy its relaxed and friendly elegance without guilt. The parts to wander are the streets behind the **boulevard des Pyrénées**, especially the western end, which stretches along the rim of the scarp above the Gave de Pau from the castle to the casino in the English-style Parc Beaumont. On a clear day the view from the boulevard is out of this world, encompassing a sixty-mile sweep of the highest Pyrenean peaks, with the distinctive Pic du Midi d'Ossau slap in front of you.

In the narrow streets **around the castle**, rue du Château, rue Henri IV, rue Fournets, rue Maréchal-Joffre, in rue des Cordeliers and down in the gully of the Chemin du Hédas are numerous cafés, restaurants, bars and boutiques, with the main market taking place at the *halles* in place de la République on Wednesday and Saturday mornings. The **Château** itself (daily 9.30–11.45am & 2–5.45pm, mid-Oct–mid-April until 4.45pm; guided tours only for royal apartments) is very much a landmark building. Not much remains of its original appearance beyond the brick keep built by Gaston Fébus in 1370. The handsome Renaissance windows and other details on the inner courtyard were added by Henri d'Albret. Louis-Philippe renovated it in the nineteenth century after it had stood empty for two hundred years, and Napoléon III and Eugénie titivated it further to make it suitable for weekend house parties. The visitable **apartments** are essentially theirs, with some fine tapestries and bits of Henri-IV memorabilia, like the turtle shell that allegedly served him for a cradle, while the ethnographic **Musée Béarnais** on the top floor has a good collection of costumes, Pyrenean animals, birds, butterflies and objects illustrative of the pastoral life.

A short distance northeast of the château, the mildly interesting **Musée Bernadotte,** 5 rue Tran, (10am–noon & 2–6pm; closed Mon) is the birthplace of the man who, having served as one of Napoléon's commanders, went on to become Charles XIV of Sweden. As well as fine pieces of traditional Béarnais furniture, the house contains some valuable works of art collected over his lifetime. Pau's other museum, the **Musée des Beaux-Arts** in rue Mathieu-Lalanne (daily 10am–noon & 2–6pm closed Tues) has a splendidly eclectic collection of works, including Spanish, Italian, Dutch and French schools and works by El Greco, Rubens and Degas.

Eating, drinking...and information for walkers

Of the several **restaurants** in the area of the château *La Brochetterie* at 16 rue Henri-IV serves good grills and fish in a pleasant, family atmosphere for around 100F *à la carte* or from 68F for a *menu fixe. La Taverne du Roy* at 7 rue de la Fontaine on the north side of the Hédas gully (closed Sat noon & Sun) offers more interesting if slightly more expensive menus. *El Mammounia* in rue d'Étigny, just off pl Grammont, is a good Moroccan, at around 100F *à la carte*, while the *Lotus d'Or* at 1 pl Grammont, with menus from 89F, is *the* Chinese. **Brasseries** include *Le Berry* on pl Clemenceau and the *Forum* in av de l'Université, popular with the students. The small *O'Gascon* on the corner of rue Bordenave-d'Abère and rue du Château, is a fun bar, as are *Le Sully*, with music, at 13 rue Henri-IV, and the student hangouts, *Bar de la Poste* in cours Bosquet and *Le Béarnais* at the eastern end of rue Guichenné.

Several organisations have **information on walking and climbing**: the local *CAF*, 5 rue Fournets (☎59.27.71.81), *Amis du Parc National,* 32 rue Samonzet (☎59.27.15.30), *Pyrénéa-Sports,* 12 rue des Bains (☎59.27.23.11), and *Randonneurs Pyrénéens,* 9 rue Latapie (☎59.30.22.48). The *Librairie des Pyrénées* in rue St-Louis stocks a wide range of books on the mountains. For the latest weather over the western Pyrenees, call ☎59.92.13.49.

Around Pau: northwest Béarn

Thirty kilometres northwest of Pau and renowned for the exploits of its basketball team, **ORTHEZ** was the original capital of Béarn, its wealth due in large part to its beautiful and still surviving **fortified bridge**, which controlled the most important commercial route across the Gave de Pau for English and Flemish textiles, Aragonese wool, olive oil and wine. It was also a major centre on the **pilgrim routes** to Compostella; the modern route, the **GR65**, which you might be interested in following for the last few days to the Spanish frontier, crosses the river just 8km east of Orthez at ARAGNON. It can also serve as a gateway to the hinterland of the Pays Basque: *SNCF* buses run from PUYÔO, 12km west, to SALIES-DE-BÉARN, SAUVETERRE and MAULÉON.

The **SI** occupies the sixteenth-century **Maison Jeanne d'Albret**, and there are other fine old houses in the centre of town, especially in **rue Moncade**. The **church of St-Pierre**, close to the SI, still has some interesting Gothic sculptures, though it was badly damaged when the town was sacked by Jeanne d'Albret's Protestant general

Montgomery in 1569. Should you need to **stay overnight**, there is a **campsite**, *La Source* (June to mid-Sept) on the east side of the town, and a couple of **hotels** – *Hôtel Terminus,* 14 rue St-Gilles (☎59.69.02.07; ②), and *Hôtel des Voyageurs* on the D933 (☎59.67.5.29; ③).

Fifteen kilometres from Orthez (*TPR* bus from Pau), **SALIES-DE-BÉARN** is a typical Béarnais village of winding lanes and flower-decked houses with brightly painted woodwork. The River Saleys, hardly more than a stream, runs through the middle separating the old village from the nineteenth-century development that sprang up to exploit the saline waters for which it has long been famous. It is a charming, if unremarkable place, good for an overnight stop, with a municipal **campsite** (mid-March–mid-Oct) and a tiny **youth hostel** (☎59.38.29.66), both on the rugby pitch.

Heading south again, the D933 winds over hilly farming country to **SAUVETERRE-DE-BÉARN,** another pretty country town beautifully sited on a scarp high above the Gave d'Oloron. From the terrace by the thirteenth-century church you look down over the river and the remains of another fortified bridge. At the end of the terrace a ruined castle dominates the steep slope, its empty joist sockets making perfect pigeon holes. There is a **campsite** by the bridge and the *Hostellerie du Château* in rue Léon-Bérard (☎59.38.52.10; closed Jan; ③).

Just across the river the D936 bears left along the flat valley bottom to **NAVARRENX**, 18km away, on Pau–Mauléon bus route, an old-fashioned market town built as a *bastide* in 1316 and still surrounded by its ancient walls. You enter by the fortified **Porte-St-Antoine**. The pleasure of the place is its sleepy rural atmosphere. The *Hôtel du Commerce* (☎59.66.5.16; ③) by the Porte St-Antoine makes an agreeable place to stay; there's a municipal **campsite** (mid-June to mid-Sept) in Chemin des Lauriers.

The **GR65** passes through the town. You pick up the markers on the telephone poles in SUSMIOU at the western end of the bridge. Turn left over the bridge on the MAULÉON road, then right on a back road shortly after. The path meanders westward following by-roads, farm tracks and footpaths to the vicinity of ST-PALAIS, where it turns southwest to follow the main St-Palais to ST-JEAN-PIED-DE-PORT road. To hitch to Mauléon, keep going to the intersection with the Sauveterre–Oloron road and go straight on. It is wooded, hilly country all the way. You are now in Basque territory.

Lourdes

LOURDES, about 30km southeast of Pau, has just one function. Over six million Catholic pilgrims arrive here each year, and the town is totally given over to looking after and exploiting them. Lourdes was hardly more than a village before 1858, when Bernadette Soubirous, the fourteen-year-old daughter of an ex-miller, had the first of eighteen visions of the Virgin Mary in the so-called Grotte de Massabielle by the Gave de Pau. Since then Lourdes has grown a great deal, and it is now one of the biggest attractions in this part of France, many of its visitors hoping for a miraculous cure for scientifically intractable ailments.

Practicalities

Lourdes' **gare SNCF** is on the northeast edge of the town centre, at the end of av de la Gare; the **gare routière** is in the central place Capdevielle, and the **SI** in place du Champ-Commun (Easter–mid-Oct daily 9am–noon & 2–7pm, Sun 10am–noon; rest of year closed at 6pm and all day Sun).

Although it is not an ideal place to stay, Lourdes has more **hotels** than any city in France outside Paris. There is masses of **cheap accommodation** in the small central streets around the castle, while **hostel-style** accommodation can be had at the *Centre Pax Christi,* route de la Forêt, and *Camp des Jeunes, Ferme Milhas,* av de Monseigneur-

Rodhain, both on the western edge of town. The nearest **campsites** (both open May–mid-Oct) are the *Poste*, 16 rue de Langelle, just south of the gare SNCF, and the *Fronton*, 60 rue de Bagnères, the next parallel street to the south.

The town and pilgrimages

The first large-scale **pilgrimage** took place in 1873, organised by a reactionary Catholic movement called the *Assomptionnistes*, whose avowed purpose was to stem the advancing tide of republicanism and rationalism. They took over the management of Lourdes, shoving aside the local priest who had wanted to organise the pilgrimages himself; adroit propagandists and agitators, they sought to promote their cause by publishing a cheap mass-circulation paper called *La Croix*, aimed at the poor and uneducated, and by organising these massive pilgrimages.

These days, especially bearing this in mind, it's hard to be charitable about the place. Practically every shop is given over to the sale of indescribable religious kitsch: Bernadette in every shape and size, adorning barometers, thermometers, plastic tree trunks, key rings, perfume bottles, bellows, candles, sweets, and illuminated plastic grottoes. Clustered around the miraculous grotto are the churches of the **Cité Réligeuse** – the first to be built, **Basilique du Rosaire et de l'Immaculée Conception** (1871), and the massive subterranean **Basilique St-Pie-X**, which claims to be able to house 20,000 people at a time. But the less said about their architecture, the better: Woody Allen, who joked that he'd come here when he'd completed psychoanalysis, would be impressed. The **Grotte de Massabielle** itself, the focus of the pilgrimages, is no more than a moisture-blackened overhang by the riverside with a statue of the Virgin in waxwork white and baby blue. Suspended in front are a row of rusting crutches, offered as ex-votos by the putative cured.

Lourdes' only secular attraction is its **castle**, poised on a rocky bluff guarding the approaches to the valleys and passes of the central Pyrenees. Briefly an English stronghold in the late fourteenth century, it later became a state prison. Inside, it houses the surprisingly excellent **Musée Pyrénéen** (daily 9am–noon & 2–7pm; mid-Oct–March closed Tues). Its collections include Pyrenean fauna, and all sorts of fascinating pastoral and farming gear. In the rock garden outside are some beautiful models of various Pyrenean styles of house, as well as of the churches of St-Bertrand-de-Comminges and Luz-St-Sauveur. There is also an interesting section on the history of Pyrenean mountaineering .

Tarbes

Twenty minutes away by train to the north, **TARBES** is useful as a base for visiting Lourdes, or launching into the mountains to the south, although apart from that there is little to draw your attention. If you have an interest in military history, the **Musée Massey** (daily 10am–noon & 2–6pm), in the very attractive jardin Massey near the train station, houses an extensive collection of cavalry uniforms – principally nineteenth- and twentieth-century hussars, but including samples of other European and US cavalry regiments. They are splendidly extravagant, the epitome of that old-fashioned quality of "dash", which was supposed to make ladies' hearts flutter at glittering balls. The Napoleonic stud farm, **Les Haras**, 70 av du Régiment-de-Bigorre, set in acres of beautiful grounds, is also worth seeing. The farm is best known for the *cheval Tarbais*, bred from English and Moorish stock as a cavalry horse. You can watch them drilling, July–Feb Mon–Fri 2.30–5.30pm. A final sight is the house where **Maréchal Foch**, supreme Allied commander in World War I, was born at 2 rue de la Victoire (daily 8am–noon & 2–5.15pm; closed Tues & Wed). Fans will find various family and personal mementoes.

Practicalities

The **gare SNCF is** on av Joffre, north of the centre, and the **gare routière** on the other side of town in pl au Bois, off rue Larrey. The **SI** is on pl de Verdun, where rue Massey meets rue Lassalle (Mon–Sat 8.30am–noon & 2.30–6pm). Tarbes has a **youth hostel** at 88 av Alsace-Lorraine (☎62.36.63.63) and some reasonable **hotels** in the vicinity of the station: try *Hôtel Isard*, 70 av Joffre (☎62.93.06.69; ③), or *Hôtel Normandie*, 33 rue Massey (☎62.93.08.47; ③).

The valleys of the Aspe and Ossau

The parallel north–south valleys of the **Aspe** and **Ossau** are the French Pyrenees at their most *sauvage*, and the region in which the Pyrenean brown bear most tenaciously resists extinction. About a dozen survive on the slopes of the valleys, in the Cirque de Lescun and in the adjoining parts of Spain.

Tourism is less developed here, especially in the Vallée d'Aspe, because of the unreliable snow conditions for skiing, but what tourism has failed to do, a major roadbuilding scheme threatens to achieve two-fold. To see the best of the region you should get out your map and walk, camping – with permission, of course – in the isolated farms along the way.

Along the Aspe

The valley of the Aspe begins at the grey town of **OLORON-STE-MARIE**, where the *gaves* of Aspe and Ossau meet. It is served by train from Pau as well as by *Citram* buses, with five daily *SNCF* buses continuing on down the valley to URDOS and three to CANFRANC in Spain. The town's claim to fame is as the centre of the manufacture of the famous woollen pancake-shaped *beret Basque*, once the standard titfer for all French men but now seldom seen on any but greybeards. However, the only real points of interest for the visitor are its two churches: **Sainte-Croix**, one of the oldest Romanesque buildings in Béarn, which has unusual interior vaulting copied from the Great Mosque at Cordoba, and the **cathedral of Sainte-Marie**, which boasts an unusually beautiful Romanesque portal in Pyrenean marble, supported by two chained slaves. In the upper arch the elders of the Apocalypse play violins and rebecs, while in the second arch scenes from medieval life are represented – a cooper, the slaying of a wild boar, fishing for salmon. The gallant knight on horseback over the outer column on the right is Gaston IV, Count of Béarn, who commissioned the portal on his return from the first Crusade at the beginning of the twelfth century, hence the reference to Saracens in chains among the sculptures. The magnificent studded doors were a present from Henri IV. Inside, well away from the main area of worship is a stoup reserved for the use of the Cagots, a stark reminder of the centuries-long persecution and segregation of this mysterious group of people, thought by some to have been lepers and by others to have been perhaps of Visigoth origin.

Should you find yourself stuck here, there is a municipal **campsite** (June–Oct) on the D919 Arrette road, and a couple of reasonable **hotels** – the *Hôtel de la Paix*, 24 av Sadi-Carnot near the train station (☎59.39.35.78; ③–④), and *Le Nautilus* in pl Clemenceau (☎59.39.04.72; ②). The **SI** is in place de la Résistance (summer Mon–Sat 9am–12.30pm & 2–7.30pm, Sun 9am–12.30pm; rest of year Tues–Sat 9am–noon & 2–6pm).

The Goutte d'Eau and Chemin de la Mâture

The narrow enclosed world of the valley proper begins south of Oloron at the village of **ESCOT**, where a beautiful side route, the D294, climbs through beech woods to the **Col de Marie Blanque** and down to BIELLE in the Vallée d'Ossau. It's a steep green world where the eye is perpetually carried upwards. South of Escot, the road follows the river through narrow defiles, past the attractive riverside villages of **SARRANCE** where there is **gîte** accommodation at *Accueil au Monastère* (☎59.34.72.07); there's also a youth hostel close by up the mountain at Lourdios (☎59.34.46.39); buses run as far as ASASP. Beyond Sarrance, **BEDOUS** has more accommodation – and food – at the cheap and very friendly *Le Choucas Blanc*, 4 rue Gambetta (☎59.34.53.71), and a **gîte d'étape** *(*☎59.34.73.23) in nearby **OSSE-EN-ASPE.** There's another **gîte** a little further south at l'Estanguet, near the turning for Lescun (☎59.34.72.30). Beyond here **CETTE EYGUN** has, in its old train station between the road and the river, an extremly friendly **restaurant-bar-gîte**, *La Goutte d'Eau* (☎59.34.78.83) – co-operatively run, and also a centre for information about the surrounding mountains and a bulwark of resistance to the planned Pau–Oloron–Col du Somport road improvement scheme (see below). There is additional accommodation in an old train carriage parked on the tracks, which, although much overgrown, still run along the valley, and camping space on the banks of the river.

Beyond Eygun the road continues up the valley to **ETSAUT**, where there's a food shop, a *gîte d'étape* *(*☎59.34.88.98), and the *Hôtel des Pyrénées* (☎59.34.88.62; ③), **BORCE**, an attractive medieval village on the west flank of the valley, is home to another *gîte d'étape* *(*☎59.34.70.87) and the squat menacing **Fort du Portalet**, in which Léon Blum was imprisoned by Pétain's Vichy government, and then Pétain himself after the liberation of France. Just before the fort, at the Pont de Cebers a track up to the left (the GR10) leads to the **Chemin de la Mâture**, an eighteenth-century mule path hacked out of the precipitous rock slabs that form the sides of a dizzy ravine to facilitate the transport of tree trunks felled for use as ships' masts. The path is broad enough, but if you don't like heights keep away from the edge. The GR10 runs this way, reaching the **Lacs d'Ayous refuge** opposite the Pic du Midi d'Ossau (see p.508) in about five hours. Further on, at URDOS, you pass through French customs; you can stay at *Hôtel des Voyageurs* (☎59.34.88.05; ③–④). From here, three buses a day continue over the **Col de Somport** and the Spanish frontier post (mid-June to mid-Sept open 24hr; rest of year daily 8am–10pm) and on to CANFRANC in Spain, the terminus for trains from Jaca.

Lescun

Six steep kilometres above the N134 at L'Estanguet, the ancient grey stone houses of **LESCUN** huddle tightly together on the north slopes of a huge and magnificent green cirque. The bowl of the cirque and the lower slopes, dimpled with vales and hollows, have been gently and harmoniously shaped by generations of farming, while to the west it is overlooked by the great grey molars of Le Billare and Le Petit Billare, beyond whose shoulders bristle further leaning teeth of rock and the snow-slashed bulk of the **Pic d'Anie** (2504m). Below the village in the hollow of the cirque, the *Camping Le Lauzart* must be one of the best placed anywhere, with an uninterrupted view of the peaks and no sound to disturb beyond the chiming of cow bells. If you're on foot be sure to take provisions with you – it is some way from the village and the only food shop. Lescun also has a **hotel**, the *Pic d'Anie* (☎59.34.71.54; ④), and a **gîte d'étape** 1500m west of the village (☎59.34.71.61).

The obvious **walk** in the area is along the GR10 in the direction of La-Pierre-St-Martin. From Lescun it keeps close to the road as far as the refuge of **Labérouat** (☎59.34.50.43) – around a two-hour walk. Thereafter it crosses meadows before entering beech forest beneath the organ-pipe crags, **Les Orgues de Camplong**, with fantastic views of the pine-stippled ridges of the Billares. It emerges above the tree line in a long flower-strewn hanging valley by the primitive **Cabane d'Ardinet** and reaches the shepherds' hut at **Cap de la Baitch** at around 1700m in a further ninety minutes. From there you can either continue on the GR towards La-Pierre-St-Martin via the Pas d'Azuns or swing south for the Col des Anies and the Pic d'Anie – a good two to three hours.

SOS VALLÉE D'ASPE

Under pressure from the Spanish, eager to modernise their communications with Europe, and from local French commercial and political interests, work has already begun on a project to transform the old N134 from Oloron-Ste-Marie to the Col de Somport into a *voie express* – **expressway** – linking a Pau–Oloron section of autoroute with a tunnel under the Col de Somport. This will facilitate the passage of a projected 1000 heavy trucks a day. However, it will also mean concreting the banks of the Gave d'Aspe, blasting away sections of pasture and mountainside, destroying the small-scale tourist economy of the riverside villages and degrading one of the few remaining places in Europe where a traditional mountain agricultural economy still persists, at least part of which is actually within the boundaries of the Parc National des Pyrénées. The road will also disturb the habitat of the last Pyrenean bears, not to mention other rare species like eagle owls, capercaillies and lammergeiers. The suspicion is that the expressway is in fact merely the thin end of the wedge, and that the ultimate aim is to upgrade the whole route to autoroute status – a suspicion supported by an element of chicanery already practised in pushing forward the project thus far: the fact that it is split into different stages – the valley express route, and the Somport tunnel – cleverly circumvents the EC requirements on the environmental impact of such projects .

The opposition claims that on the most sensitive section of the route the old Oloron–Canfranc rail route could be reactivated and improved to carry a greater volume of traffic at far less cost – financially and environmentally. Despite this, work has already started on the tunnel access road, and, in the hope that the Minister for the Environment will eventually intervene, the *CSAVA* and its allies have begun an indefinite occupation of the site. If you're interested in helping, or just finding out more, call in at the *Goutte d'Eau* (see above) or write – best of all with a contribution – to *Coordination pour la Sauvegarde Active de la Vallée d'Aspe (Secrétaire Générale, Florence Corbier), 64490 Eygun, France.*

Along the Ossau

The Ossau valley is served by both *Citram* and *SNCF* **buses** as far as Laruns. At weekends in July and August one *SNCF* bus goes on to Gabas and Artouste-Fabrèges, while *Citram* continues to Gourette every day from July to mid-September and again in the skiing season.

Between Pau and Laruns the only place worth stopping at is **ARUDY**, principally to see the **Maison d'Ossau** (July–Aug daily 10am–noon & 2.30–6.30pm; rest of year Sat & Sun pm only), which offers a comprehensive account of the prehistoric Pyrenees and an exhibition of the flora and fauna of the Parc National.

LARUNS, enclosed in the valley bottom by steep wooded heights, is of little interest in itself, although there are some fine old farms towards the river in the quarter known as Le Pon. If you find yourself here for the night, try *Hôtel de France* in rue de la Gare (☎59.05.33.71; ④), *Hôtel Le Lorry* on route des Cols (☎59.05.31.22; ③), or the refuge, *L'Embaradère*, 13 av de la Gare (☎59.05.41.88). The nearest **campsites** are *Le Gourzy* and *Le Lauguère* in Le Pon. The **SI** is in the main place de la Mairie. If you are heading for the Pic du Midi d'Ossau, it is best to stock up with **provisions** in Laruns. There is nothing in Gabas, though *Camping Bious-Oumettes* (see below) has a shop which opens around June 15.

Gabas

The road to **GABAS**, 13km away, winds steeply into the upper reaches of the Gave d'Ossau valley south of Laruns. On days when there is no bus, you should get a lift without much difficulty from other walkers or employees of the National Park, especially early in the morning. Primarily a base for climbers and walkers, there is nothing to it beyond a minuscule chapel, the **Maison du Parc** (for walking information), a

CAF **refuge** (☎59.05.33.14), and a couple of **hotels** – *Le Biscau* (☎59.05.31.37; ③) and *Le Vignau* (☎59.05.34.06; ②–③), both with restaurants.

Pic du Midi d'Ossau

The **Pic du Midi**, with its rocky twin-peaked summit (2884m), is a classic Pyrenean landmark, visible for miles around. From Gabas it is a steep 4.5-kilometre climb up a wooded ravine to the artificial **Lac de Bious-Artigues**, so named because it flooded the *artigue* – a Pyrenean word for mountain pasture – that formerly existed beside the infant *gave*. Just below the dam are the stony terraces of *Camping Bious-Oumettes* (July–Aug) Beside the lake, right under the Pic, is the *Refuge Pyrénéa Sports* (☎59.05.32.12; June 6–Oct 31). The area within immediate reach of the road gets very crowded in summer and the refuges are likely to be full at weekends; it's worth phoning ahead.

A **round trip** of the peak, excluding the summit, takes about seven hours. It can be broken by a stay at the *CAF Refuge de Pombie* (☎59.05.31.78; mid-June to Sept) below the vast southern walls. From the lake, follow the GR10 up the left bank of the *gave* and past the turning to the Lacs d'Ayous (see below). Cross the Pont de Bious and continue upstream across an expanse of flat meadow until you come to a signpost indicating **Lac de Peyreget** to the left. There follows a steepish zigzagging climb to the timber line and a long traverse right to the junction with the HRP path (1hr from *Pyrénéa Sports*). Keep left, with the ground falling away on your right. At the Lac de Peyreget, you can either follow the HRP steeply left towards the **Col de Peyreget**, or alternatively keep right – due south – to the **Col d'Iou**. From the latter, traverse leftwards following the contour to the **Col de Soum**, where you turn north towards the **Refuge de Pombie** (about 4hr). The path continues northwards back to *Pyrénéa Sports* (about 3hr) via the Col de Suzon, where the standard ascent of the Pic begins, the Col de Moundelhs and the Col Long de Magnabaigt.

There is a path **off the mountain** from the Col du Soum, and another from the Pombie refuge. The latter leads due east down the valley of the *Pombie* stream, through meadows full of daffodils, orchids, violets and fritillaries in June, where you might catch a glimpse of izards. At the **Cabane de Puchéou**, a shepherd's hut, cross to the left bank of the stream and carry on down to the next bridge. The HRP continues on the left bank past the Cabane d'Arrégatiou and comes out at the southern end of the Lac de Fabrèges. The right-hand path crosses the bridge and descends through woods to the Gave de Brousset at Soques (about 2hr from *Pombie*), where you join the Col du Pourtalet road (which leads to the Spanish frontier) and can hitch back to Gabas.

Lac d'Artouste

A short distance out of Gabas the Pourtalet road passes the **Lac de Fabrèges** whence a *téléférique* swings up to the Pic de la Sagette (2032m) to connect with a **miniature rail line** that runs for 10km through the mountains to the **Lac d'Artouste**. Built in the 1920s to service a hydroelectric project, it was later converted for tourist purposes. Weather permitting, the train normally starts operating in early June and keeps going until mid- or late September. It is a beautiful trip, lasting about four hours, including time to walk down to the lake. The first train leaves at 10am, but you need to allow half an hour on the *téléférique*. Don't forget to take warm clothes, as you'll be at an altitude of 2000m.

The Lacs d'Ayous

In the opposite direction from Gabas, this is another classic walk, in some ways more impressive than doing the Pic itself, especially if you spend the night by the lakes to get the quintessential dawn view of the peak silhouetted against the rising sun and reflected in the slaty waters of Lac Gentau.

It's a steady ninety-minute climb from *Pyrénéa-Sports*. Instead of crossing the Pont de Bious, turn up the GR10 to the right through woods of pine and beech, with ever-widening views of the valley scattered with herds of horses and cows and flocks of sheep. The meadows are full of orchids and the stream banks thick with azalea-like alpenrose. You pass three small lakes. The third and largest is **Lac Gentau**, whose reddish shallows are full of minnows that presumably turn into the trout so sought after by numerous fishermen. On its banks there's an expanse of flat, soft meadow for camping, while above it stands the *Refuge d'Ayous* (1960m; ☎59.05.37.00; June 6 to Sept 15). Over the Col d'Ayous behind it the GR10 continues west to the Chemin de la Mâture and the Vallée d'Aspe (see above).

The Col d'Aubisque and the road to Cauterets

The only way of reaching Cauterets by road without going back towards Pau is via the **Col d'Aubisque**, a grassy rounded ridge 17km and nearly 1000m above Laruns. There's a café on the top, served in July and August by a single afternoon bus from Laruns. It is also hitchable; if you're hitching on, remember that the next possible stopping place is 18km away, so it's best to stay close to the café.

The Col is an important grazing ground, with tremendous views over the valleys below and the rocky precipices of the Pic de Ger (2613m) to the south. It is also a favourite place for slaughtering the migrating *palombes* in autumn, as witness the numerous shooting butts along the ridge. The *Tour de France* passes this way, making the col an irresistible challenge to any French cyclist worth his salt. You see swarms of them toiling up, making it a matter of pride to find the breath for a cheery *bonjour*.

Cauterets and the Cirques of Gavarnie and Troumouse

Further east, **Cauterets** and **Gavarnie** are established resorts, but the country they give access to is so spectacular you should not miss it. Both are served by *SNCF* buses from Lourdes via the valley of the Gave de Pau. As ever, if you pick your season right or even the time of day, you can still enjoy the most popular sites in relative solitude. At Gavarnie, for instance, few people stay the night, so it is quiet in the early morning and evening, and **Troumouse**, which is just as impressive in its way though much harder to get to without a car, has very few visitors. As for more conventional sights, there are interesting churches at **Luz-St-Sauveur** and **St-Savin**.

Argèles, Aucun and St-Savin

Between Lourdes and Cauterets, **ARGELES-GAZOST** is a dull town, but, a little way southwest, **AUCUN** is worth a short detour for its small but fascinating private folk museum, the **Musée du Lavedan**, while, heading south from Argelès, it's worth taking a look at the twelfth-century abbey church of **ST-SAVIN**, to the right of the main road, with its fortifications and fine Romanesque doorway. Inside it boasts a magnificient Spanish wooden Christ, a Cagot stoup and amusing organ cabinet carved with grotesque faces designed to pull grimaces as the music played.

Cauterets

Thirty kilometres south of Lourdes, **CAUTERETS** is a pleasant, if unexciting, little town which owes its fame and its rather elegant neo-Classical architecture to its waters, much in demand now for the treatment of ear, nose and throat complaints and rheumatism. In modern times it has also become one of the main Pyrenean ski and mountaineering centres.

Its origins as a spa began with Count Raymond de Bigorre's grant of the land to the monks of St-Savin in 945. In the seventeenth century Marguerite d'Angoulême came to take the waters, in fact wrote her *Heptameron* here (see above). The eighteenth and especially the nineteenth century, with its Romantic adoration of mountains, were its heyday. Hugo visited, as did Chateaubriand, Baudelaire, Debussy, Edward VII and many other celebrities.

The modern town is so small there is no difficulty in finding your way around. Most of it is still squeezed between the steep wooded heights that close the mouth of the Gave de Cauterets valley. Next door to the **gare routière** on the north edge of the centre, the **Maison du Parc** (daily 9am–noon & 2–6pm) has a small museum of the flora and fauna, and film shows on Wednesday and Saturday in season. In the small centre of the town, bisected by the foaming river, two minutes' walk from here, you'll find the **SI** in place Clemenceau, (July–Aug Mon–Sat 9am–7pm, Sun 9am–noon & 4–7pm; rest of year Mon–Sat 9am–12.30pm & 2–6pm, Sun 9am–noon). Not far away, the **Maison de la Montagne** at 5 av Leclerc (☎62.92.58.16) has information on the state of the mountain paths and climbs, book and map shops, and **places to eat**.

If you're staying, the cheapest **accommodation** is in one of two **gîtes** – *Le Cluquet*, on av du Dr-Domer past the *télésiège du Lys* and the tennis courts (no phone; summer only; space for camping), and *Le Pas de l'Ours*, 1 rue Galliéni (☎62.92.58.07). Affordable **hotels** include *Le Béarn*, 4 av Leclerc (☎62.92.53.54; ①), *Le Centre-Poste*, 11 rue de Belfort (☎62.92.52.69; ③), and *Le Bigorre*, 15 rue de Belfort (☎62.92.52.81; ②–④). There are several **campsites** along the Lourdes road. One of the quietest is *Les Bergeronnettes* (June–Sept), across the river on the right before you reach the roadside *Les Glères*. For **food**, the *Brasserie Le Paris* in pl Clemenceau is a friendly and very reasonable establishment. Other places to try include the cafés *Le Béarn* and *Le Commerce* in av Leclerc, the pizzeria *Giovanni* in rue de la Raillère, or, for something a bit more special in the same street, *La Casa Manolo* (with menus from 70F).

Around Cauterets: some hikes

The classic excursion from Cauterets is up the Val de Jéret to the **Pont d'Espagne**, where the Gave de Gaube and Gave du Marcadau hurtle together in a boiling spume of spray before rushing down to Cauterets over a series of spectacular waterfalls. For a beautiful and tourist–free route, take the **Parc National path** from La Raillère, 3km from Cauterets (regular buses). It runs all the way beside the stream through woods of beech and pine to come out by the café-bar at Pont d'Espagne (about 2hr up, 90min down).

From Pont d'Espagne you can fork right up the **Vallée du Marcadau** to the *Refuge Wallon* (about 5hr round trip), or left up into the alpine valley of the Gave de Gaube, with the lovely little **Lac de Gaube** backed by the snowy wall and glaciers of **Vignemale** (3298m). There is even a *télésiège* to save you the first part of the ascent. Beyond the lake the path continues to the *CAF Refuge des Oulettes* below the north face of Vignemale (about 3hr from Pont d'Espagne), whence you can return to La Raillère via the *Refuge de Baysellance* and the beautiful and quieter **Vallée de Lutour** (7hr round trip).

A less-frequented walk from Cauterets is to the **Lac d'Ilhéou** along the GR10 (about 3hr). To avoid the initial steep climb you can take the *télécabine du Lys* to the **gare intermédiaire de Cambasque**, crossing the stream there and continuing up the right bank to the end of the tarmac at the **Cabane de Courbet**, where you follow a track, first on the left bank, then on the right. After a short distance – keep a good look-out – the GR10 leaves the track and climbs up the slope to the left, steadily gaining height to cross a chute of boulders beside the long white thread of the **Cascade d'Ilhéou** waterfall. Over the rim of the chute you come to a small lake, with the **Refuge d'Ilhéou** in sight ahead, on the shore of the lake – very pretty in June with snow still on the surrounding peaks and ice floes drifting on its still surface.

Luz-St-Sauveur and the road to Bagnères de Bigorre

The only approach to Gavarnie and Troumouse, best known of the Pyrenean cirques, is through **LUZ-ST-SAUVEUR** on the GR10 and the daily bus route from Lourdes. It, too, was a nineteenth-century spa, patronised by Napoléon III and Eugénie, and it owes its elegant neo-classical facades in the centre to this period.

Its principal sight is the church of **St-André**. Built in the late twelfth century and fortified in the fourteenth by the Knights of St John, it's a classic of its kind, with a crenellated outer wall and two stout towers. The entrance, beneath one of the towers, sports a handsome porch surmounted by a Christ in Majesty carved in fine-grained local stone. The lanes round about are crammed with **market stalls** every Monday.

The **SI**, with a *Bureau des Guides* (daily 9am–noon & 2.30–6pm) is in the central place du 8-mai by the crossroads for Gavarnie, along with *Camping Le Toy* (Jan–April & June–Sept). There's another **campsite** and **gîte d'étape** (☎62.92.82.15) at *Les Cascades* uphill from the church. Two **hotels** to try are the *Remparts* (☎62.92.81.70; ③), beside the church, and the *Londres* (☎62.92.80.09; ④; closed Nov & Dec) on the riverbank in the town centre. Another very agreeable and only slightly more expensive place to stay is the *Hôtel La Brêche de Roland* (☎62.92.48.54; ④; closed Oct–mid-Dec; restaurant from 75F), 12km south in GÈDRE, where the road divides for the Cirque de Troumouse. There are a couple of campsites nearby as well.

The road to Bagnères de Bigorre

From Luz-St-Sauveur begins the 18-kilometre pull up to the Col du Tourmalet, one of the major torments of the *Tour de France*. The only village in between is **BARÈGES**, 7km away, linked with Lourdes by buses via Luz. It has been popular as a spa – its waters renowned for the treatment of gunshot wounds – since 1677, when it was visited by Mme de Maintenon with her infant charge, the seven-year-old Duc de Maine, son of Louis XIV. Today it is a skiing and mountaineering centre. The **GR10** passes through and numerous other trails lead off into the **Néouvielle massif**, full of lakes and highly recommended as a walking area.

Above Barèges, the road continues up a huge denuded valley, with clusters of stone *bergeries* dug into the slope. At its head the **Pic du Midi de Bigorre** (2872m) comes into view, crossed by the **Col du Tourmalet**, which at 2115m is the highest road pass in the Pyrenees. It's a desolate windy spot with a track – you have to pay – leading off left to the Pic and its observatory, still going strong and continuously staffed since its opening in 1882. There's a small museum inside (open in summer daily 1–6pm).

Over the col the road descends steeply past the monstrously ugly ski resort of **LA MONGIE** into lovely woods of spruce, pine and beech, which continue down to the gentle green **Vallée de Campan**, whose meadows are dotted with farms all turned south in ranks to face the sun. The architecture is quite distinct from the valleys to the west. The roofs are still slate, but house and barn are built in line as one building, with the balconied living quarters always to the right as you face the sun. In the village of **CAMPAN** there is an interesting sixteenth-century covered market, old houses and another curious-looking fortified church. School buses cover the 6km from here to **BAGNÈRES-DE-BIGORRE**, another Pyrenean spa town trying to refurbish its somewhat faded image, and it is not a place to make a special stop. *SNCF* **buses** leave for TARBES from the **gare SNCF** on av de Belgique just north of the town centre. Two buses daily continue south to Ste-Marie-de-Campan and, in summer, on to the Lac de Payolle, whence it is possible to hitch on over the pine-covered Col d'Aspin to Arreau in the Vallée d'Aure. The **SI** (Tues–Sat 9am–noon & 2.30–6pm) is in pl Lafayette close to the leafy allées des Coustous, the main drag, lined with cafés. If you need to stay, there are reasonable **rooms** at the *Hôtel de Nice* (☎62.95.04.65; ③) and *Hôtel de l'Horloge* (☎62.95.00.20; ③) in rue de l'Horloge near the market. There are several **campsites** around the town, too.

The Cirque de Gavarnie

South of Luz-St-Sauveur, **GAVARNIE**, a further 8km up the ravine from Gèdre, is connected with Luz by two daily bus connections, or, if you're really into hiking you could walk it on the GR10. The village is a tacky and unpleasant mess of souvenir shops, car parks and snack bars. Poor and depopulated, it has found the attractions of mass tourism, much of it the excursion trade from Lourdes, too seductive to resist. It stinks, too, from the droppings of the dozens of mules, donkeys and horses used to ferry visitors up to the Cirque. However, the **Cirque** itself is magnificent – "Nature's Colisseum," Victor Hugo called it – a natural amphitheatre scoured out by a glacier, of which barely the roots of the tongue remain. Nearly 1700m high, it consists of three sheer bands of rock discoloured by the striations of seepage and waterfalls, and separated by sloping ledges covered with snow. To the east it is dominated by the jagged peaks of Astazou and Marboré, both over 3000m. In the middle, a corniced ridge sweeps round to Le Taillon, hidden behind the Pic des Sarradets, which stands slightly forward of the rim of the Cirque, obscuring the **Brèche de Roland**, a curious vertical slash, 100m deep and about 60m wide, said to have been hewn from the ridge by Roland's sword, Durandal.

Practicalities

If you are carrying a **tent**, there's nothing to beat *Camping La Bergerie* (with bar and breakfast) on the true right bank of the *gave* on the Cirque side of the village. The facilities leave something to be desired, but the site is away from the crowds and the view is right into the Cirque. The other campsite, *Le Pain de Sucre* (July–Sept), is on the Luz side of the village. As for **hotels**, the historic and unspoilt *Les Voyageurs* at the entrance of the village is much the nicest (☎62.92.48.01; ③–⑤); its "Golden Book" contains the signatures of Count Henry Russell, the eccentric pioneer of Pyrenean mountaineering, George Sand, Flaubert and Hugo among others; its beds witnessed the conception, so the whisper goes, of Napoléon III in an illicit encounter between Hortense de Beauharnais and a local *berger*. Otherwise the best bets are the *CAF* **refuge**, *Les Granges de Holle* on the Port de Gavarnie road (☎62.92.48.77), which also does meals, or the **gîte d'étape** near the *Voyageurs* (☎62.92.40.57). For a **place to eat**, *La Ruade*, also by the *Voyageurs*, is the best. For **weather, snow conditions** and the like, ask the *CRS* mountain rescue unit opposite *La Bergerie*. For **park information** there's the *Maison du Parc* (daily 10am–noon & 2.30–5.30pm) as you come into the village.

The Cirque and around

It's an easy fifty minutes' walk from the village to the Cirque. Luckily, the scale of it is sufficient to dwarf the tourists, but it is still best to go up before 10am or after 5pm, when the grandeur and silence are almost alarming, and the dung less overpowering. The track ends at the *Hôtellerie du Cirque*, once a famous meeting place for mountaineers and now a snack bar. To get to the foot of the Cirque walls you have to clamber over slopes of frozen snow. Take care not to stand too close, especially in the afternoon, because of falling stones. To the left, the **Grande Cascade**, at 423m the highest waterfall in Europe, wavers and plumes down the rock faces – a fine sight in the morning when it appears to pour right out of the eye of the sun. Scaling the cliffs is obviously a matter for climbers, but the relatively intrepid can get a powerful impression of the majesty of the place – and a superb vantage point for photography – by climbing the first stage of the **HRP path** to the *CAF* **Refuge des Sarradets** which begins in the right-hand corner of the Cirque at the edge of the first band of rock. The first hundred metres or so could be a little nerve-wracking if you are not used to heights, but in dry weather are perfectly safe.

If you do not want to retrace your steps, an enjoyable and not too demanding walk back to Gavarnie is to take the path from the *Hôtellerie* up the east flank of the Gavarnie valley to the **Refuge des Espuguettes** (about 3hr). It is a beautiful path cut into rocky pine-shaded slopes. At the top you emerge into open meadows, with the *Cabane de Pailla* in a hollow and the *Refuge des Espuguettes* (July–Sept) on a grassy bluff about a 45-minute climb above you. The climb is worth it for the views of the Cirque and the Brèche de Roland. The committed may want to go from here on to **Piméné**, the bare peak above you. It's a couple of easy, if tedious, hours' climbing, but the view is fantastic: the Cirque d'Estaubé, Monte Perdido and away into Spain. To return to Gavarnie, turn right at the signpost below the refuge (allow 90min).

La Brèche de Roland

This is *the* walk to do in Gavarnie. It is high, and involves crossing a glacier, which means being properly equipped, preferably with ice axe and crampons. It is, however, extremely popular in summer, so there is a good chance of being able to team up with someone more experienced.

There are three approaches to the *Brèche*, all converging on the *Refuge des Sarradets* (July–Oct; ☎62.92.48.24); contact *CRS* Gavarnie for reservations at the refuge, which are always necessary in high season. The easiest route is up the road to the Port de Gavarnie/Col de Boucharo, where a clear path climbs under the north face of Le Taillon to join (1hr) the footpath coming directly from Gavarnie. This path starts beside the church, climbs steadily up the valley of Pouey Aspé, then zigzags steeply up to join the Port de Gavarnie path (4hr). From the junction of these two paths it's less than an hour to the refuge.The third route (about 6hr in all from Gavarnie) is via the **Échelle des Sarradets** section of the HRP path mentioned above. The *Brèche* is about 40 minutes above the refuge.

The Cirque de Troumouse

A vast, wild, desolate place, much bigger than Gavarnie and, in bad weather, rather frightening (in spite of the car park smack in the middle), the **Cirque de Troumouse** lies up an equally desolate valley, whose only habitations are the handful of farmsteads that make up the hamlet of **HÉAS** – until the making of the road one of the loneliest outposts in France. There is **camping à la ferme** on the road to Héas and **chambres d'hôte** in the hamlet. As you reach the head of the valley there is a toll gate, after which the road climbs in tight hairpins up treeless slopes to the *Auberge Le Maillet* (☎62.92.48.97; June–Sept) by the side of a small tarn. After this it climbs again, even more steeply, beneath bare shining crags, to another car park with a white statue of the Virgin Mary crowning a grassy knoll enclosed by the wide sweeping walls of the Cirque. There is enough pasture here to feed thousands of sheep. The close moorland turf is channelled with streams and cut into dingles and hummocks, where gentians and saxifrage and sedums and houseleeks grow among the rock crevices. Beneath the walls of the Cirque is a scatter of clear blue glacial lakelets, the **Lacs des Aires**. A *Parc National* path does the circuit from Héas.

The Comminges

Stretching from Bagnères-de-Luchon (Luchon for short) almost as far as Toulouse, the **Comminges** is an ancient feudal county that encompasses the upper valley of the River Garonne, whose source, long disputed and finally proven only in 1931 by Norbert Casteret, father of French speleology, is a glacier of the Pico d'Aneto on the Spanish side of the frontier. The area also has one of the Pyrenees' few monumental buildings of any note, in the magnificent cathedral at St-Bertrand-de-Comminges, the product of three distinct periods of architecture.

St-Gaudens and Montréjeau

Access to the mountains is along the Garonne and its tributary, the Pique. Buses and trains run from the town of **ST-GAUDENS**, an unexciting place but home to a **youth hostel**, at 3 rue de la Résidence (☎61.95.65.37), and a reasonable hotel – the *Esplanade*, 7 pl Mas-St-Pierre, by the church in the town centre (☎61.89.115.90; ③–④) – and **MONTRÉJEAU** on the main Bayonne–Toulouse line, following the valley south to Luchon.

Valcabrère and St-Bertrand-de-Comminges

A short way south of Montréjeau, reachable by taking an *SNCF* bus (direction Luchon) to the hamlet of LABROQUÈRE, by the Garonne, and walking across the river, the village of **VALCABRÈRE**, with its rough stone barns and open lofts for hay drying, boasts an exquisite Romanesque church in **St-Just-St-Pasteur** (May–Oct daily 9am–noon & 2–7pm; rest of year Sat & Sun 2–5pm), whose square tower rises above a cemetery full of cypress trees. The porch is elegantly sculpted and the apse, decorated with a kind of inverted arcading, is quite remarkable. Both interior and exterior are full of recycled masonry from the old Roman settlement of **Lugdunum Convenarum**, whose remains are visible at the crossroads just beyond the village. Founded by Pompey in 72 BC this was a town of some 60,000 inhabitants at its apogee, making it one of the most important in Roman Aquitaine. Josephus, the Jewish historian, says it was the place of exile of Herod Antipas and his wife Herodias, who had John the Baptist decapitated. It was destroyed by Vandals in the fifth century and again by the Burgundians in the sixth century, after which it remained deserted until Bishop Bertrand began to build his cathedral around 1120.

Further on, the grey fortress-like **cathedral** (July–Aug daily 9am–7pm; April–June & Sept 9am–noon & 2–7pm; Oct–March 9am–noon & 2–6pm; Sun 9–10.30am & 2–6/7pm) commands the plain from the knoll ahead, the austere white-veined facade and heavily buttressed nave totally subduing the clutch of fifteenth- and sixteenth-century houses that gather at its feet. To the right of the west door a mainly Romanesque cloister looks out across a green valley to hills where a local *maquis* unit had its lair during the war. In the aisleless interior, the small area at the west end reserved for the laity has a superbly carved sixteenth-century oak organ loft, pulpit and spiral stair, although the church's great attraction are its choir stalls, built by Toulousain craftsmen and installed in 1535 in the great Gothic choir – an addition ordered by the future pope Clement V. The elaborately carved stalls – 66 in all – are a feast of virtuosity, mingling piety, irony and malicious satire, each one the work of a different craftsman. It is in the misericords and partitions separating them that the ingenuity and humour of their creators is best seen. Each of the gangways dividing the misericords has a representation of a cardinal sin on top of the end partition. In the middle gangway on the south side, for example, Envy is represented by two monks, faces contorted with hate, fighting over the abbot's baton of office, pushing against each other foot to foot in a furious tug-of-war. The armrest on the left of the roodscreen entrance depicts the abbot birching a monk, while the bishop's throne has a particularly lovely back panel in marquetry, depicting St Bertrand himself and St John. In the ambulatory a fifteenth-century shrine depicts scenes from St Bertrand's life, with the church and village visible in the background of the top right panel.

In July and August the cathedral and St-Just in Valcabrère play host to a **music festival**. Across the small square in fornt of the cathedral, the *Hôtel du Comminges* (☎61.88.31.43; ④–⑤), makes a nice place to stay and has a restaurant. The nearest **campsite** is *Es Pibous* (May 15–Sept) on the St-Just road, with the nearby *La Vieille Auberge* serving good basic food. Cars are no longer allowed in the village itself, but a minibus operates a shuttle service from the nearby car park.

The Grotte de Gargas
About 6km from St-Bertrand in the direction of Mazères-de-Neste, the **Grotte de Gargas** (guided tours afternoons only 2.30–4.30pm, with some mornings in high season; ☎62.39.72.07) is renowned for its 231 prehistoric painted hand prints. Outlined in black, red, yellow or white, they mostly seem mutilated or deformed – perhaps the result of disease or ritual sacrifice, although no one really knows. There are representations of animals as well.

Bagnères-de-Luchon

There's none of the usual spa town fustiness about **BAGNÈRES-DE-LUCHON**. It is small, but the main street, the **allée d'Étigny**, has a distinctly metropolitan elegance and bustle, lined with cafés and numerous places to eat. There is not, however, anything to see, apart from the moth-eaten **museum** by the SI (daily 9am–noon & 2–6pm), which has an extraordinarily eclectic collection, and the **baths** at the end of allée d'Étigny in the **Parc des Quinconces** (guided tours Tues & Thurs 2pm).

Luchon is best as a comfortable **base for exploring** the surrounding mountains. The **gare SNCF**, which is also the bus stop, is in av de Toulouse across the River One in the northern part of the town. The **SI** is at 18 allée d'Étigny (April–Oct daily 9am–7pm; Nov–March daily 9am–noon & 2–6pm; closed Sun pm) and includes a *Bureau des Guides* for walking information. For an all-in **accommodation** package including food and mountain sports, the *Accueil des Jeunes*, 12 allées des Bains (☎61.79.00.14; ③), is the cheapest deal going for under-25s, but it is mainly for groups, and there is no guarantee that passing individuals will find room. An excellent-value **hotel** is the *Deux Nations* at 5 rue Victor-Hugo (☎61.79.01.71; ③), which has an equally good restaurant with menus from 50F. Alternatively, try the *Bon Accueil*, 1 pl Maréchal-Joffre (☎61.79.02.20; ④), also with a good restaurant. There are numerous **campsites** in and around the town. Less cramped than the in-town ones: *Camping La Lanette* is only 1500m away across the River Pique in Montauban-de-Luchon (down rue Lamartine from allée d'Étigny). However, the best deal of all, for sleeping and eating, is the romantically sited *Le Jardin des Cascades* (☎61.79.83.09; ②), in a wild steep garden uphill from the church in Montauban. In summer you eat on a shaded terrace overlooking Luchon and the mountains to the west, where the hang-gliders and *parapentes* float hazily in the sunset. The food and service are excellent, the price with wine around 180F per person.

Around Luchon: some hikes
There are two classic hikes south of Luchon, to the **Lac d'Oô** and **Port de Vénasque** on the Spanish frontier. For the first, you can either follow the **GR10** to Superbagnères (3hr), then on west to the *Refuge d'Espingo* (☎61.79.20.01; June–Sept) and the lake (another 5hr), or take the road to **Granges d'Astau**, where there is a **gîte d'étape** (☎61.79.35.63) and refuge (☎61.79.14.92; July–Oct). From there it's an hour's

walk to the lake or two hours to the Espingo refuge. It's possible to continue into Spain via the Port d'Oô or the Lac du Portillon.

For the second hike, walk – or hitch – down the D125 to its end about 30 minutes' walk from the **Hospice de France**, an ancient inn founded by the Knights of St John. From here a signposted path climbs the narrow valley to the frontier ridge past four small lakes where there is a small unmanned *CAF* refuge. After that it's a steep climb up scree (subject to avalanches in spring) to the narrow passage of the **Port de Venasque** (3hr), with superb views of the Maladetta massif and the Pico d'Aneto, the highest summit of the Pyrenees (3404m).

THE EASTERN PYRENEES

The dominant climatic influence of the **Eastern Pyrenees** is the Mediterranean. The climate is hotter and drier here, the landscape more arid, and Mediterranean plants like the cistus, broom and thyme make their appearance. The lower slopes of the hills are planted with vines. The way of life is more laid back and outdoor. The proximity of Spain is evident, too, and much of the region is Catalan, incorporated into France a mere three hundred years ago. As with the rest of the Pyrenees the countryside is spectacular and densely networked with well-organised hiking trails. The historical sights, with the exception of the prehistoric caves at Niaux and the Cathar castle of Montségur, are most richly concentrated in the east, in what is essentially French Catalonia.

Along the Ariège

The first clear herald of the approaching Mediterranean, whether you're coming from the western Pyrenees or heading south from the major transport nodule of Toulouse, is the **valley of the Ariège**, thorny scrub and white eroded limestone cliffs beginning to make their appearance from Tarascon onwards. Transport is no problem as long as you stick to the valley, but for side trips – into the Couserans and the hike to Montségur – you really need a car.

Foix

Administrative centre of the *département* of Ariège, **FOIX** lies 82km south of Toulouse on the main Paris–Barcelona railway and the N20 road to Ax-les-Thermes and the Spanish border. It is an agreeable country town of narrow alleys and half-timbered houses, with an attractive old quarter squeezed between the rivers Ariège and Arget, full of houses of the sixteenth and seventeenth centuries.

Dominating it all is the town's hallmark, the three distinctive hilltop towers of the **castle of the counts of Foix**, which contains the somewhat tedious **Musée d'Ariège** (July–Aug daily 9.45am–6.30pm; June & Sept daily 9.45am–noon & 2–6.30pm; Oct–May daily 10.30am–noon & 2–6pm). Determined opponents of the territorial ambitions of the Capetian kings of France and stout defenders of Catharism, the counts drew upon themselves the wrath of Simon de Montfort, who four times laid unsuccessful siege to the castle, though he did capture the town in 1211. Their resistance was finally broken in 1229 when Roger-Bernard, the count of the time, was obliged to accept the feudal overlordship of the French king. Foix's age of glory came in 1290 when its counts married into the house of Béarn. Although they transferred their court to Orthez in the fourteenth century, this was the beginning of a powerful Pyrenean mini-state whose influence lasted three centuries and came to include the kingdom of Navarre, leading finally to the throne of France with the accession of Henri III of Navarre as Henri IV of France in 1589.

Practicalities

The **bus and train stations** are together in av de la Gare, off the N20 on the right bank of the Ariège. The **SI** is at 45 cours Gabriel-Fauré (Mon–Sat 8am–noon & 2–6pm, Sun 9am–noon). For **a place to stay**, try the *Hôtel Audoye-Lons* on pl G-Duthil, by the Pont-Vieux (☎61.65.52.44; ③–⑤), with a restaurant with menus from 59F, or *Hôtel Eychenne* at 11 rue Noel-Peyrevidal (☎61.65.00.04; ③). There's a municipal **campsite**, *Lac de Labarre*, on the N20 (May–Oct). Except on Sundays there's a daily **bus** service east via Lavelanet to Quillan and four buses a day west to Saint-Girons.

Mas d'Azil

West of Foix, the **Mas d'Azil** is one of the most impresssive, albeit overcommercial-ised, prehistoric caves in the region, although it's not easy to reach without your own transport. It lies 12km north of the Foix–St-Girons bus route: get off at Vic after La-Bastide-de-Sérou and take the D15. It's a pretty road, but without a lift it'll take a good two hours on foot. Failing that, four *SEMVAT* buses a day run from Toulouse.

As you approach along the River Arize its waters are suddenly engulfed by an enor-mous cavern, which the road traverses, too. Inhabited in prehistoric times for more than 20,000 years and used as a refuge by Cathars and Protestants in more recent years, the caves are open to guided tours only (June–Sept daily 10am–noon & 2–6pm; April–May 2–6pm; rest of year by appointment; ☎61.69.97.22) and include displays of tools, animal bones and other objects found during excavation.

In the village of **LE MAS-D'AZIL** 1km beyond the cave, the **Musée de la Préhistoire** (June–Sept daily 10am–noon & 2–6pm; rest of year daily 2–6pm) contains, among other engravings and tools from the cave, a beautiful carved antler known as *le faon aux oiseaux*, perhaps used as a spear-thrower. If you wish to stay, there's a munici-pal **campsite** (July–mid-Sept), 1500m distant on the Pamiers road, or the *Hôtel Gardel* on the main square (☎61.69.90.05; ③).

Tarascon and the Vicdessos valley

TARASCON-SUR-ARIEGE lies 16km south of Foix, where the N20 crosses the Ariège. Once a centre for the local iron-mining industry — there is still an aluminium plant in operation — it is a hot and unexciting little town, enclosed by high wooded ridges. However, it is useful as a base for the Vicdessos valley and the prehistoric cave of Niaux.

The **cafés** on the east bank of the river, dominated by the clock tower, are pleasant sunny places to sit. Apart from that it is worth taking a stroll up the narrow **rue de Barri** to the wide square by the church, with just one arcaded side and a single wooden house still in existence, to the **Porte d'Espagne**, the only surviving piece of the town walls. Above the gate is a minuscule **museum** (daily except Mon 9.30am–noon & 2.30–7pm) of prehistoric artefacts and Cathar memorabilia, dating back to the time when hunted *bonshommes*, the Cathar "priests", took refuge in the caves hereabouts after the fall of Montségur (see below).

Quietest and most attractive of the **hotels** is the *Francal* on the riverside quai Sylvestre (☎61.05.60.24; ②–③). Otherwise try the *Bellevue*, also on the river at the head of the bridge on pl Jean-Jaurès (☎61.05.60.45; ③), or the *Hostellerie de la Poste* on the N20 (☎61.05.60.41; ③–④). All have restaurants, the best of which is that of the *Hostellerie*. **Camping**, the *Pré Lombard* site is on the left bank of the river, ten minutes' walk upstream from the bridge, while the **gare SNCF** is a few minutes' walk to the right. The **SI** is in pl du 19-mars-1962.

Niaux and the prehistoric caves

Just south of Tarascon, by the aluminium plant, the D8 cuts up right into the green valley of the Vicdessos past the riverside remains of a Catalan ironworks. The hamlet of NIAUX lies in the valley bottom 5km further on, and is home to a campsite (June to mid-Sept). At its entrance the **Musée Paysan** (April–Sept daily 9am–8pm; Oct–March daily 10am–6pm) has an unrivalled collection of tools, furnishings, old photos and odds and ends illustrating the vanished traditions of peasant Ariège. Opposite the church a lane turns up left to the entrance to the **Grotte de Niaux**, under an enormous rock overhang high on the south flank of the valley (July–Sept guided visits every 45min 8.30–11.30am & 1.30–5.15pm; Oct–June 3 visits daily at 11am, 3pm & 4.30pm). Only twenty people are allowed in at a time, and reservations (☎61.05.88.37; 9.30–11am & 2.30–4.30pm) are essential in summer, preferably 48 hours in advance.

There are about 4km of galleries in all, mostly closed to the public, with **paintings** of the Magdalenian period (circa 11,000 BC) widely scattered throughout. The paintings you can see are in a vast chamber, a slippery 800-metre walk from the entrance of the cave along a subterranean riverbed. The subjects are horses, ibex, stags and bison. No colour is used, just a dark outline and shading to give body to the drawings, which have been executed with a "crayon" made of bison fat and manganese oxide. They are an extraordinary mix of bold impressionistic strokes and delicate attention to detail: the nostrils, pupils and the tendons on the inner thighs of the bison are all drawn in.

Two other caves – less impressive – in the vicinity are **La Grotte de la Vache** (July–Aug daily 10am–5.30pm; April–June, Easter & Sept 2.30–4pm; closed Tues) in Alliat right across the valley from Niaux and **Bedeilhac** (July–Aug daily 10am–5.30pm; April–June, Easter & Sept 2.30–4pm; closed Tues) in the side of the jagged Roc de Sédour ridge overlooking Tarascon on the D618 Massat road. The former is the more interesting, a relatively rare example of an inhabited cave where you can observe hearths, bones, tools, etc, *in situ*.

Vicdessos and Auzat

From Niaux the road continues deep in the valley bottom, overlooked by the romantically pinnacled ruins of the **château of Miglos** to VICDESSOS and AUZAT, the latter with an unsightly aluminium works. The villages themselves are not of much interest except as bases for exploring the magnificently wooded country round about. The GR10 passes nearby on its way from Mérens above Ax-les-Thermes to Aulus-les-Bains, and from the **gîte d'étape** at MOUNICOU (☎61.64.87.66), beyond Auzat, you can undertake the gruelling ascent of the **Pic de Montcalm**.

For **accommodation**, Auzat and Vicdessos have one hotel each, the *Hôtel Denjean* in Auzat (☎61.64.88.36; ①), and the *Hôtel Hivert* in Vicdessos (☎61.64.88.17; ①–②). Both have year-round **campsites**. GOULIER, across the valley, has a **gîte** (☎61.64.85.19), and in CAPOULET back towards Niaux a Dutch couple offer very comfortable **chambres d'hôtes** (☎61.05.89.88; 190F for two). The SI in Auzat are extremely helpful (July–Aug daily 8am–noon & 2–7pm; rest of year Mon–Sat 8am–noon & 2–6pm, Sun 2–6pm).

Into the Couserans

From Vicdessos a really stunning route – the D18, not much chance of a lift – climbs the **valley of the Suc**, tunnelling through trees, past abandoned barns and occasional cottages in lush meadows, past waterfalls and streams, to the pass at the **Port de Lers** (1517m). On the far side, herds of grey cows graze the alpine meadows down to the Étang de Lers, where there is a snack bar in process of construction. Then the road climbs again to another col overlooking the head of the valley of the little **River Garbet**. Below, the steep slopes are luxuriant with beech, while straight ahead you look into a high-walled crenellated *cirque* formed by the **Pic Rouge de Bassiès** and the **Pic des Trois Comtes** above the **Étang de Garbet**, where the heights are underlined by wedges of snow lying beneath the sheerest faces.

Aulus-les-bains

Down in the valley the road heads west to **AULUS-LES-BAINS**, a remote village lying among moist and fragrant meadows ringed by dramatic peaks. This is the beginning of the **Pays de Couserans**, one of the poorest, least developed and most depopulated regions of the Pyrenees. Its villages, Aulus in particular, were once renowned for their bear-trainers, who, driven by poverty, toured the lowland towns with their performing beasts.

Aulus, like other spas, enjoyed its moment of glory and fell again into rustic somnolence. There are signs, however – some rather ominous, like the tower crane erecting apartments four times the height of the traditional houses – that a new and ruder awakening may be coming. This is country for walking and enjoying the landscapes: there's nothing else, and, remote though it is, it is not inaccessible – there are two daily weekday **buses** and one on Saturdays to St-Girons.

For all information, consult the **SI** in the allée des Thermes. The classic walk is along the GR10 to the **Cascade d'Ars** (about 5hr round trip). Among **places to stay**, try the *Hôtel La Terrasse* (☎61.96.00.98; ③; closed Oct–May), or the *Grand Hôtel* (☎61.96.01.34; ②–③). There's also a **gîte d'étape** in the village and **camping** at *Le Couledous* 500m to the north.

For routes on to St-Girons, both the Garbet and Ustou valleys are beautiful. For a brief stopover, there is a great little inn by the river a little way beyond Ustou at **PONT DE LA TAULE** – *Auberge des Deux Rivières* (☎61.66.83.57; ②–③), with a restaurant.

St-Girons

With several *SNCF* buses a day from BOUSSENS, on the main Tarbes–Toulouse rail line, and connections on to Aulus, Ustou, Massat and St-Lary near the Col de Portet d'Aspet, **ST-GIRONS** may be your first taste of this out-of-the-way region. Apart from its long association with making cigarette papers, the most striking thing about St-Girons is its pavements, made of a local dark grey marble veined with white with finely chiselled gulleys to take the rainwater from the down-pipes. And although there are no other memorable sights, it's a far from unpleasant town.

The simplest centre for orientation is the **Pont-Vieux**. Straight ahead on the right bank of the River Salat it points you into the old commercial centre of the town, with some marvellously old-fashioned shops, their fronts and fittings unchanged for generations. To the left, on the riverbank, is the **SI**, to the right the typically provincial **place des Poilus**, its cachet largely due to the faded elegance of the *Grand Hôtel de France* and the equally old-fashioned *Hôtel de l'Union*, opposite, which rubs shoulders with the *Grand Café de l'Union*, a splendidly balconied period café facing the *mairie* across another square. Beside it, along the riverbank, a wide gravelled *allée* of plane trees, the **Champ de Mars**, provides the site for a big general market on the second and fourth Mondays of every month, and to a regular produce market every Saturday morning.

On the left bank of the river the main point of interest is **place des Capots**, the terminus for **buses**, where there are also a couple of cheap **places to eat**. Another workaday **eating place** is the restaurant of the old *Hôtel Madrid* (menus from 55F) opposite the end of the Pont-Vieux. Nearby at 37 Grande-rue Villefranche is a magnificent **wine shop**, *Ferré Frères*, with barrels lining the walls. If you're **staying over**, the *Grand Hôtel de France* is actually in course of renovation (☎61.66.00.23), which will put its prices broadly into the ④ bracket; it also has a good restaurant with menus from 85F. The *Hôtel de l'Union* is a little cheaper (☎61.66.09.12; ②–③), or there's the *Centre* *de Séjour du Parc de Paletès* (☎61.66.06.79) – take av des Évadés from the church behind the *mairie* and keep going for about 2km – with space for camping, some rooms, and a nice terrace restaurant overlooking the valley.

Saint-Lizier
SAINT-LIZIER, five minutes by bus from the old gare SNCF on the St-Gaudens road, totally outclasses St-Girons in the tourism stakes. It sits on a hilltop; it's full of history; it's walled, arcaded, cobbled, cathedralled, half-timbered and pretty and totally overrated.

Architecturally the most interesting building is the **cathédrale de St-Lizier** cloister, with some lovely Romanesque basketwork carving on the supporting columns, and the cathedral itself has some fine medieval frescoes, especially a Christ Pantocrator in the apse. On clear winter days its octagonal Toulouse-style tower poses photogenically against the snowy mountains to the south. There is a second cathedral, N**otre-Dame-de-Sède**, which boasts fine seventeenth-century choir stalls and can be visited along with the **bishop's palace** (7.30am–noon & 2–7pm). But that, really, is about it. If you want to know more, the **SI** (mid-June to mid-Sept daily 10am–noon & 2–6pm) is next door to the cathédrale St-Lizier.

Ax-les-Thermes and around

Twenty kilometres south of Tarascon, still on the river, the spa town of **AX-LES-THERMES** is completely walled in by mountains. It is small and pleasant enough, but once you've wandered the streets of the quarter to the right of the N20 (rue de l'École and rue de la Boucarie are the only old bits), which forms the main street, there is nothing to see, and Ax's principal value is as a base for exploring the surrounding mountains and as a staging-post on the way to Andorra or on down the N20 to FONT-ROMEU and, ultimately, PERPIGNAN and the Mediterranean.

The **SI** in place du Breilh (Mon–Sat 8am–noon & 2–6pm, Sun 9am–noon) has hiking information and lists of walks. Opposite, the church of **St-Vincent** with its Romanesque tower is the only surviving structure of architectural interest. Just across the road you can dandle your feet for free in the **Bassin des Ladres**, a pool of hot sulphurous water which is all that remains of the hospital founded in 1260 by St-Louis for soldiers wounded in the Crusades.

There are two particularly nice **places to stay** in Ax: the *Hôtel La Terrasse* at 7 rue Marcaillou (☎61.64.20.33; ③), with a restaurant from 60F, run by a young jazz-loving couple; and *Le Couloubret,* more like a private house than a hotel (☎61.64.21.88; ②; closed Nov–April), behind the sad-looking casino by the church of St-Vincent. A third possibility is *Hôtel Les Pyrénées* (☎61.64.21.01; ②–③), with a restaurant from 50F, on the main av Delcassé opposite the casino. There is a **campsite**, *Le Malazéou*, on the riverbank just before the **gare SNCF** as you come into town from Tarascon. The most atmospheric **places to drink and eat** are the old *Grand Café* next to *Hôtel Les Pyrénées* and *Brasserie Le Club*, which also does jazz and food, on the market square, place Roussel. Alternative places are the pizzeria opposite the *Hôtel de France* on the main road, and the *Terminus Bar* near the station.

Around Ax: some hikes
MÉRENS-LES-VALS, 8km south along the N20, lies on the GR10, which heads east to the Carlit massif and Font-Romeu/Mont-Louis (see p.536). It has a **gîte d'étape** (☎61.64.32.50), and you could use it to link up with the GR7, making a tour of the **Réserve Nationale du Burrus** via the lakeside *Refuge d'En Beys* (☎61.64.24.24; July–Sept) and **Forges d'Orlu**.

Montaillou and Montségur: the Cathar strongholds

Barely 20km northeast of Ax, the almost deserted hamlet of **MONTAILLOU** was the subject of a fascinating study by the French historian, Le Roy Ladurie. Based on Inquisition records, his book covers the years around 1300 when the Inquisition was trying to extirpate the Cathar heresy from its last strongholds. What the poor victims revealed to their interrogators amounts to an extraordinarily detailed and intimate portrait of contemporary life. Much of the book reads like good gossip: who is sleeping with whom, where the sheep are being pastured this year, which paths are best for crossing into Spain. You really need your own transport to get to Montaillou from Ax, although it is possible to hitch the D613 over the steep **Col de Chioula** (1400m). The village lies above the road to the right just after Prades.

The remaining inhabitants still bear the names of their Cathar ancestors; the graveyard is full of them. There is little left to see, but it is a pretty and highly atmospheric place, especially for anyone who has read the book. All that remains of the castle is the stump of the tower, which was once 45m high to facilitate visual communication with MONTSÉGUR, the Calvary of Cathardom, about 11km northwest as the crow flies.

Montségur

The easiest approach to **MONTSÉGUR** is probably from LAVELANET about 12km to the north or VILLENEUVE-D'OLMES (6km closer), both with weekday bus connections from QUILLAN. Lavelanet also has connections with Carcassonne via Mirepoix, with Foix, and with Toulouse via Mirepoix and Pamiers. Far and away the most dramatic route, however, is on foot from COMUS, where there is a **gîte d'étape** attached to the *Centre École Pleine Nature* (☎68.20.33.69), 45 minutes' walk below Montaillou.

Walking time is about four hours. Head west along the GR7B, following a lane beside the stream (masses of flowers in May) for about 3km until the lane doubles back hard to the left, leaving the stream to continue into the deep sunless ravine of the **Gorges de la Frau**. The path descends steeply on the old mule road until you hit the dead end of the D5 from Bélesta. Continue along the tarmac to the first farm on the left, where the route turns up the lane between the buildings, becomes a track, then a narrow footpath beside a stream in a deep gully thickly wooded with beech, ash, wild cherry and fir. It crosses to the left flank of the gully (the true right bank of stream) and the angle of ascent increases sharply, bringing you finally to an ancient quarry mule road that turns sharply and horizontally right back across the head of the valley to a signposted locality called Liam, where from a patch of rough meadow you get your first glimpse of the ruined walls of Montsègur castle ringing the summit of a rocky pyramid. Turn left at the signpost, down a good path with open pastures in a shallow valley on your right with a tarmacked lane. When you hit the tarmacked lane, turn left for a short distance and then right on a clear path down through trees to a riverside campsite. Cross the river to a road and make your way across allotment-like vegetable plots to the village of **MONTSÉGUR**. The houses are strung out in terraced lines, not the usual fetal huddle, at the foot of the castle rock. Silent and depopulated now, the place comes to life only with the influx of tourists, most of them day trippers.

Before going up to the castle (same ticket covers both visits), it's worth a glance at the one-room **museum** (May 1–Sept 30 daily 10am–1pm & 2–7pm; rest of year ask at the *mairie*), with its collection of bits and pieces from the castle. A footpath from the top of the village shortens the way up to the saddle of the hill, where the last steep half-hour climb to the castle (June 21–Sept 30 same times) begins in the *prats dels cramats*, the field where the Cathar martyrs were burned. All that remains of the castle are its stout and now truncated curtain walls and keep. The space within is terribly cramped and one can easily imagine the sufferings of the besieged. A somewhat precarious stair leads to the top of the walls, whence you look out over miles of forested hills and snowy peaks, giving a sense of solitude and airy isolation that is in itself highly evocative.

There are a couple of **hotels**, the nicest of them the old-fashioned *Hôtel Couquet* (☎61.01.10.28; ③–④), run by Madame Couquet and fronted by pollarded lime trees. There is a café and restaurant on the first floor (menus at 55F and 90F). The alternative is the more expensive *Hôtel Costes* (☎61.01.10.24; ④–⑤), also with a restaurant (65F and 90F). There is a **gîte d'étape** in the village (☎61.01.20.97).

THE FALL OF MONTSEGUR

In the early years of the thirteenth century the castle was reconstructed by a local feudal lord as a strong point for the Cathars under attack by the Crusade. In 1232 it became the capital of the banned Cathar Church, with a population of some five hundred people, bishops and clergy as well as ordinary believers on the run from the persecution of the Inquisition, under the protection of a garrison commanded by Pierre-Roger de Mirepoix.

Provoked by a raid on Avignonet in May 1242, which successfully assassinated the Inquisitors, the forces of the Catholic Church and the king of France laid siege to the castle in the spring of 1243. By March 1244, Pierre-Roger, despairing of relief, agreed terms with them. At the end of a fortnight's truce, the 225 Cathars who still refused to recant were burnt on a communal pyre on March 16.

Four men who had made good their escape recovered the Cathar "treasure" which had been hidden in a cave for safekeeping since the preceding Christmas and vanished. Two of them later reappeared in Lombardy where it seems probable these funds were used to support the refugee Cathar community established there. But numerous legends have grown up, especially in German writings, identifying this "treasure" with the Holy Grail and the Cathars themselves with the Knights of the Round Table.

Lavelanet and Mirepoix

LAVELANET has nothing to offer beyond its bus connections and a very clean and modern municipal **campsite** (March 20–Nov 1), from which you can just see Montségur nudging over the brow of the intervening ridges. There is a *crêperie* and a couple of restaurants off the main square.

If you are heading north in the Carcassonne direction, take a look at **MIREPOIX**. It's a late thirteenth-century *bastide* built around one of the loveliest surviving arcaded market squares in the country, with a relatively harmonious modern *halle* on one side and a not very exciting cathedral behind it. *Hôtel Le Commerce*, on the boulevard encircling the old town near the church (☎61.68.10.29; ②), is a safe place to stay, with a very agreeable restaurant in a lime-shaded courtyard (menus 65–130F). There's a municipal **campsite** on the Limoux road.

Along the Aude

South of Carcassonne, road and rail track climb steadily up the twisting valley of the Aude between scrubby hills and vineyards and ever deeper and more forested ravines to Quillan. From there, the road squeezes through the **Gorges de l'Aude** in a sunless bottom before emerging once again towards the river's headwaters above Les Angles on the east side of the Carlit massif in the high Pyrenees. It is a magnificent drive, and quite hitchable as it is one of the main routes to Andorra; public transport runs out at Axat, some 10km beyond Quillan.

Limoux and Quillan

First stop on the road, 24km from Carcassonne, **LIMOUX** is served several times daily by both the *SNCF* and the private *Cars Teissier* buses. It stands astride the Aude, which for much of the year is a powerful grey flood of snow melt. Life revolves around the pretty place de la République in the heart of the old town, with its Friday market, and the nineteenth-century promenade du Tivoli, in effect a bypass. Famed in the past for its woollens and the tanning of hides brought down from the mountains, the town's claim to fame today is the production of its excellent sparkling wine, *Blanquette de Limoux,* much cheaper than champagne and not at all inferior.

There is nothing special to see in Limoux, but if you've got your own transport the Romanesque abbeys of **St-Hilaire** and **St-Polycarpe** in the lovely green hills to the east are worth the effort. For a **place to stay** there's the *Hôtel Flassian*, 2 av du Languedoc (☎68.331.78.18; ①), *Hôtel des Arcades*, 96 rue St-Martin (☎68.31.02.57; ③), and, best and most expensive, the *Hôtel Moderne et Pigeon*, place Général-Leclerc (☎68.31.0.25; ⑤). Just upstream from the main part of town on the right bank of the river is an agreeable poplar-shaded municipal **campsite** (June–Sept). For an unusual and characterful **eating place**, try the *Maison de la Blanquette* on promenade du Tivoli, which promotes the local wines and serves excellent food (closed Wed pm; menus from 60F). If you are interested in sampling or buying any wine, the best place to go is the co-operative, *Aimery-Sieur d'Arques* in av du Mauzac (June–Aug daily 8am–7pm).

QUILLAN, 27km further upstream, is a pleasant little town, useful as a staging post on the way south into the mountains or east to the Cathar castles – it has daily bus connections with Perpignan, via St-Paul-de-Fenouillet. The only monument of interest is the ruined **castle**. It was burned by the Huguenots in 1575 and partly dismantled in the eighteenth century, but the remnants are still worth a scramble.

For an **overnight stay** try the *Hôtel Terminus*, 45 bd de-Gaulle (☎68.20.05.72; ③), or the slightly more expensive *Cartier* on the same street at no. 31 (☎68.20.05.14; ④). The **campsite** *La Sapinette* is at 21 rue René-Delpech. Other alternatives for accommodation are the riverside **campsite** at Pont d'Aliès (with a canteen), another 11km along the D117, or a couple of cheap **hotels** in AXAT: the *Hôtel de la Poste* (☎68.20.50.35; ③), which has a dining room overlooking the river, and the *L'Ensoleillé* (☎68.220.51.43; ③).

The Gorges du Rebenty and Gorges de l'Aude

From Pont d'Aliès, just before AXAT, there is a beautiful route up the **valley of the Rebenty** on the tiny D107 through woods of beech, fir and oak, with a magnificent early summer display of orchids and other Pyrenean flowers. It's a marvellous cycling route, too, except for the agony of the climb out of the valley. The road continues to Ax-les-Thermes over the Col du Pradel, or you can escape on to the Plateau de Sault at Espezel.

As to the **gorges de l'Aude,** the narrowest and deepest stretch is that between Axat and Usson. If you want to admire the scenery, don't drive: the road is much too danger-ous to take your eyes off it. Towards the end there is a magnificent cave to investigate, the **Grotte de l'Aguzou**. It's expensive, but as near the real thing as you can get without being a pukka caver; you spend the entire day underground, accoutred like a profes-sional (visits by arrangement: ☎68.20.45.38). *Camping sauvage* is allowed by the river, or there is a **gîte d'étape** at FONTANES-DE-SAULT, 3km away (☎68.20.37.07).

Continuing upstream the road divides just after USSON-LES-BAINS. On a shaggy bluff between the arms of the fork, dwarfed in turn by the heights either side, stand the forlorn ruins of the **Château d'Usson**, allegedly the hiding place for the "Cathar treas-ure" during the 1244 siege of Montségur. Passing its foot, a road winds up through the attractive grey tiers of houses at MIJANES – where there's a **hotel**, the *Relais de Pailhéres* (☎68.20.45.76; ②) – to the pass at the **Col de Pailhères**, which is at its loveli-est in June when a cornice of snow still lines the crests above the small round lake.

From Mijanès another road branches up the valley to **QUÉRIGUT**, passing through the village of Le Pla where there is a primitive **campsite**. (There is a thrice-weekly bus from Quillan to Quérigut, run by *Petit Charles* of Carcanières, on Monday, Wednesday and Friday afternoons.) Quérigut, where there is another **campsite** and a **hotel**, *Hôtel du Donezan* (☎68.20.42.40), stands at the head of a slope of neglected terraces, guarded by the ruin of its castle, last refuge of the Cathars who held out for eleven years after the fall of Montségur. Above, the forest begins: miles of beech and pine, interspersed with lush meadows, stretching to the windy plateau above Font-Romeu. This is the Donezan region, beautiful but the poorest, most neglected and depopulated corner of Ariège.

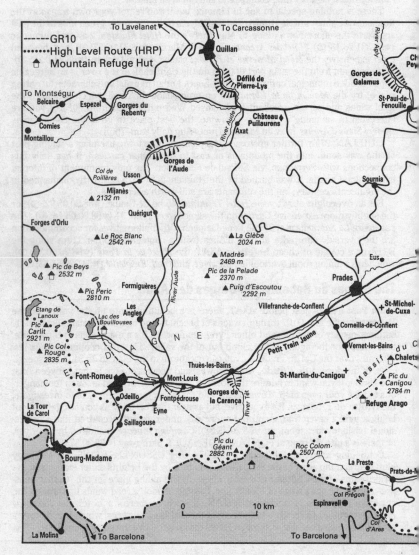

French Catalonia

The area the makes up the eastern fringe of the Pyrenees and the flatter stretch of land down to the Mediterranean coast is known as **Roussillon**, or **French Catalonia**. Catalan power first came into its own in the tenth century under the independent counts of Barcelona, who then became kings of Aragon as well in 1137. They attempted to create a joint power base with Occitan France under the counts of Toulouse, but that came to an unhappy end with the death of Pedro I at the battle of Muret in 1213, when he came to the aid of Raymond VI of Toulouse against Simon de Montfort in the anti-

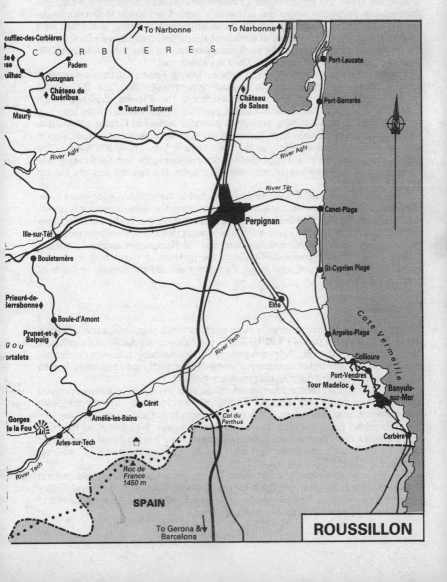

ROUSSILLON

Cathar crusade. The height of Catalan power was reached in the thirteenth and four-teenth centuries, when the Franco-Catalan frontier was fixed along the base of the Corbières hills north of Perpignan. But Jaime I made the mistake of dividing his king-dom between his two sons at his death . What is now the French part became the king-dom of Majorca with its capital at Perpignan, but, coveted by the rival brother, the king of Aragon, it sought alliance with the kings of France, who saw this as a splendid oppor-tunity to straighten out their southern border, thus ensuring continuous squabbling that was only finally ended by the Treaty of the Pyrenees, negotiated by Louis XIII in 1659.

After the Treaty the French began a ruthless process of Frenchification, which was successful in Perpignan where the bourgeoisie tended to identify their commercial interest with central power, but left the mountain hinterland largely untouched until modern times, when the collapse of traditional agriculture, compulsory education and the devastation of the vineyards by phylloxera combined to drive the peasantry off the land – a process which still continues, albeit at a slower rate.

Although there is no real separatist impetus among French Catalans today, their sense of identity is still strong: the language is very much alive, and the national colours of yellow and red are much in evidence. The **Pic du Canigou**, which completely dominates the French Catalan province of Roussillon, much larger in presence than its actual 2784m, remains a powerful symbol of Catalan nationalism, attracting hordes of Catalans from Barcelona to celebrate the summer solstice. And in the little town of **Prades**, which, as the place of exile from Franquista Spain of the cellist Pablo Casals, became a symbol of Catalan resistance, the first Catalan-language primary school in France has recently opened its doors. It is also the seat of a Catalan summer university.

Most of the region's attractions are easily reached from the region's one major town, **Perpignan. The coast** and immediate hinterland above the Spanish frontier is beauti-ful, though predictably crowded, and the finest spots are in the **Tech** and **Têt valleys** which cut back west into the Pyrenees, where you can view the Romanesque monaster-ies of **Serrabonne**, **St-Michel-de-Cuxa** and **St-Martin-du-Canigou**, Vauban's fortress town of **Villefranche-de-Conflent**, the museum at **Céret** with its unique series of Picasso ceramics, and **Mont Canigou** itself and the foothill orchards of peaches and cherries.

Perpignan

This far south climate and geography alone would ensure a palpable Spanish influence. But in addition a large part of **PERPIGNAN's** population is of Spanish origin, refugees from the Civil War and their descendants. The southern influence is further augmented by a substantial admixture of north African, both Arabs and white French settlers repatriated after Algerian independence in 1962.

While there are no memorable monuments to visit, Perpignan is a lively, pleasant city which lives its life very much on the public street. Its heyday was the thirteenth and fourteenth centuries, when the kings of Majorca held their court here, and it is from this period that most of its historical interest derives. Well placed on the main Mediterranean coast international lines of communication, it is much the best base for exploring the eastern end of the Pyrenees, and the Cathar castles of the Corbières, described in Chapter 11, "Languedoc".

The midsummer **Feux de Saint Jean** are the occasion for music and general Catalan merrymaking. But Perpignan's most distinctive festival is the Good Friday procession of penitents, **La Procession de la Sanch**, which goes from the church of St-Jacques to the cathedral between 3pm and 5pm.

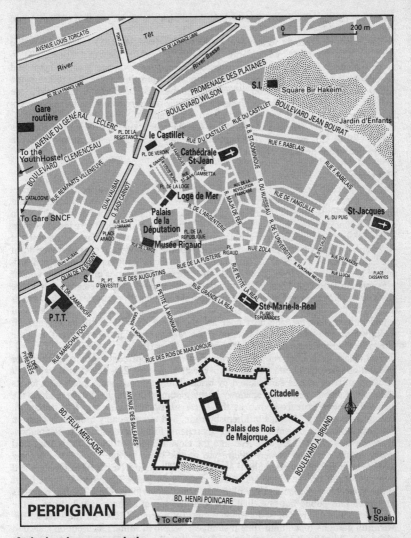

Arrival and accommodation

To reach the centre of town from the **gare SNCF**, which is also the terminus for long-distance coaches, walk up av Général-de-Gaulle to place de la Catalogne; turn right across the River Basse, then left along the flower- and palm-lined riverbank, past the **regional SI** on quai de Tassigny to place Arago, named for the city's most famous native son, a scientist and member of the revolutionary government of 1848. Continue along the riverside for a few minutes to the brick fortress of Le Castillet. The old town is on your right and the **municipal SI** is in the Palais des Congrès a few minutes' walk further on at the end of bd Wilson (summer daily 9am–8pm; winter Mon–Sat 8.30am–

noon & 2–6.30pm). The **gare routière** for local buses is at the junction of Pont Arago and av Général-Leclerc.

There is a delightfully welcoming **youth hostel** (☎68.34.63.32) behind the public gardens of La Pépinière by Pont Arago (entrance around the back of the police HQ on av de Grande-Bretagne), and two **campsites**, *La Garrigole* on rue Maurice-Lévy, and *Le Catalan* on route de Bompas, both signposted from the centre. There are some cheap **hotels** near the station, of which the best is *Le Berry*, 6 av de la Gare (☎68.34.59.02; ①). Another, very cheap possibility is the *Expéditeurs* on the rather desolate av Leclerc, at no. 19, with a good cheap restaurant (☎68.35.15.80; ①). The *Bristol* is more agreeably situated close to Le Castillet at 5 rue des Grandes-Fabriques (☎68.34.32.68; ③), as is the very comfortable and more expensive *Athéna* at 1 rue Quéya near place de la République (☎68.34.37.63; ③–⑤).

The town

The best place to begin your exploration of the town is at **Le Castillet** , built as a gateway in the fourteenth century, and now home to the *Casa Pairal*, an interesting **museum** of Roussillon's Catalan folk culture (summer daily except Tues 9.30–11.30am & 2.30–6.30pm; winter daily 9–11.30am & 2–5.30pm). From the roof there is a great view of the dominant pile of Canigou, and, if you know where to look, you can see the castle of Quéribus (see p.565), standing clear of its ridge to the northwest. A short distance down rue Louis-Blanc you come to the **place de la Loge**, focus of the renovated and pedestrianised heart of the old town. Dominating the cafés and brasseries of the narrow square is Perpignan's most interesting building, the Gothic **Loge de Mer**. Designed to hold the city's stock exchange and maritime court, and decorated with gargoyles and lacy balustrades, its ground floor has been somewhat incongruously taken over by a fast-food establishment. Side by side next door are the **Hôtel de Ville**, with its magnificent wrought-iron gates and Maillol's statue of *La Méditerranée* in the courtyard, and the fifteenth-century **Palais de la Députation**, once the parliament of Rousillon.

From place de la Loge rue St-Jean runs down to the fourteenth-century **Cathédrale St-Jean** on place Gambetta (site of a gypsy festival on June 21), its external walls built of bands of river stones sandwiched by brick. The interior is most interesting for its elaborate Catalan altarpieces, shadowy in the gloom of the dimly lit nave, and for the tortured wooden crucifix known as the *Dévôt Christ* in a side chapel to the south. Dating from around 1400, it's of Rhenish origin, and was probably brought back from the Low Countries by some travelling merchant. From here rue de la Révolution-Française and rue de l'Anguille lead into the close dilapidated lanes of the **Arab and gypsy quarter** where women congregate on the more private inner lanes but are seldom seen on the more public thoroughfares. There are North African shops and cafés, especially on rue Llucia and a daily **market on place Cassanyes**. At the heart of the quarter the wide and grimy **place du Puig** is overlooked by a Vauban barracks converted into public housing. Just past it, at the top of a shady uphill street, is the elegant Catalan church of **St-Jacques**, dating from around 1200, on the edge of the **Miranda** gardens (open until 7pm in summer, 5.30pm in winter), laid out on a section of the old city walls. It is from this church that the *Procession de la Sanch* (see below) sets out on Good Friday.

About twenty minutes away, through place des Esplanades, crowning the hill which dominates the southern part of the old town, is the palace of the kings of Majorca, the **Palais des Rois de Majorque** (summer daily except Tues 9.30am–noon & 2.30–6pm; winter daily except Tues 9am–noon & 2–5pm). Vauban's walls surround it now, but the two-storey palace and its great arcaded courtyard date originally from the late thirteenth century. Thanks to the Spanish–Moorish influence, there's a sophistication and finesse about the architecture and detailing – for instance, in the beautiful marble porch to the lower of the two chapels – which you don't often find in the heavier styles of the north.

Finally, at 16 rue de l'Ange near place Arago, there is Perpignan's museum of art, the **Musée Rigaud** (summer daily except Tues 9.30am–noon & 2.30–7pm; winter daily 9am–noon & 2.30–6pm), dedicated to the work of the portraitist Hyacinthe Rigaud, who became official painter to the court of Versailles in the early eighteenth century. The collection also includes works by Dufy, Maillol, Picasso, Tapiès, Appel and others.

Eating and drinking

For **eating**, there is nothing to beat the popular *Perroquet*, right outside the station on the corner of av de-Gaulle with a good selection of very reasonably priced Catalan dishes (closed Thurs pm & Fri). The *Expéditeurs* hotel restaurant is almost as good (closed Sat pm & Sun), or, for something smarter, there is the brasserie *Le Vauban* on quai Vauban near Le Castillet (closed Sun). Even the fast-food establishment in the Loge de Mer won't disappoint. For a **drink**, the *Café de la Grande Poste* on place de Verdun under the plane trees in front of Le Castillet is a great place to watch the world go by. It is here, too, that in summertime, on Tuesday and Thursday evenings, you will see the Catalan dance, the *sardana*, being performed by kids, grandparents, anyone whom the spirit moves. The *Bodega Castillet* in the nearby alley, rue Fabrique-Couverte, is a favourite bar with the locals, and there are several cafés on pl Arago.

Aound Perpignan: the coast

For a **swim**, the simplest thing is to take a 25-minute bus ride from Promenade des Platanes (2–3 an hour) to **CANET-PLAGE**. There is nothing to recommend the place, except that the beach is wide and sandy and the sea is wet. The same goes for the other resorts around here: PORT-LEUCATE, PORT BACARÈS (complete with weathered Greek ferry beached to make a casino and nightclub) and ST-CYPRIEN.

Perhaps more interesting, 15km north, served by several trains a day, is the **Château de Salses** (summer daily except Tues 9–11am & 3–6pm; winter daily 9am–noon & 3–5pm), built for the king of Aragon in the early fifteenth century, and one of the first forts to be designed with a ground-hugging profile to protect it from artillery fire. Its superior design apparently put Vauban's nose so out of joint that he wanted it demolished, a task that proved impossible.

Another place, with not so much to see but very moving because of its associations, is the vine-girt village of **TAUTAVEL**, 25km northwest, off the St-Paul-de-Fenouillet road. For here in 1971 were discovered the remains of the oldest known European human being– dated to around 450,000 BC. A reconstruction of the skull is on display in the village's **Musée de la Préhistoire** (daily 10am–noon & 2–6pm, until 8pm in July and Aug) along with various finds from the cave where he was unearthed, the Caune d'Arago, which can itself be visited by arrangement with the museum between June and August. The local wines are worth sampling, too, along with those of Estagel and Rivesaltes.

Thirteen kilometres to the south, on the way to the resorts of the Côte Vermeille and served by the same buses and trains, lies the small town of **ELNE**, which once had the honour of seeing Hannibal camp at its walls en route for Rome, and used to be the capital of Roussillon. It was only overtaken by Perpignan when the latter became the seat of the kings of Majorca. Today, it's worth a stop for its fortified, partially Romanesque **cathedral** and extremely beautiful **cloister** (April–May daily 9.30am–12.15pm & 2–5.45pm; June–Sept daily 9.30am–6.45pm; Oct–March daily 10–11.45am & 2–4.45pm). Though only one side of the cloister is strictly Romanesque, immaculately carved with motifs such as foliage, lions, goats and Biblical figures, the three later ones – fourteenth-century Gothic – have been made to harmonise perfectly. It's the best introduction to Roussillon Romanesque you could want, especially if you're planning to visit places like Serrabonne and St-Michel-de-Cuxa further west. Below the cathedral there are still a few streets of the old town left, twisting back down to the drab and unremarkable modern development.

The Côte Vermeille

Known as the **Côte Vermeille**, the last few miles of shore before Spain, where the Pyrenees sweep down to the sea, once held a handful of attractive seaside villages. Tourism has put paid to that, though all are well served by buses and trains from Perpignan.

ARGELÈS, the first of the resorts with the last of the wide sandy beaches on this stretch of coast, is lively and friendly, but packed out with foreign tourists. The **Musée Catalan** in rue de l'Égalité (Mon–Fri 9am–noon & 3.30–6pm, Sat 9am–noon) has some interesting exhibits of local arts and traditions.

COLLIOURE, set on its bay and once by far the prettiest of these places, inspiring Matisse and Derain in 1905 to embark on their explosive Fauvist colour experiments, is now overly quaint. Palm trees line the curving beach, and the seaward view is dominated by the landmark buildings of the **Château des Templiers** and the seventeenth-century church of **St-Vincent** with its distinctive round belfry, formerly the harbour lighthouse, while behind the town slopes of vines and olives rise to ridges crowned with ruined forts and watch towers. The château (Easter–Oct daily 2.30–7.30pm), founded by the Templars in the twelfth century, has undergone numerous alterations, especially at the hands of the kings of Majorca and Aragon in the fourteenth century and again after the Treaty of the Pyrenees gave Collioure to France. Today it is largely given over to summertime exhibitions. The church (daily 7.30am–noon & 2–6pm) contains some exuberant Baroque altarpieces. Behind it two small **beaches** are divided by a causeway leading to the chapel of St-Vincent built on what used to be a rocky islet, while to the left a concrete path follows the rocky shore to the bay of **Le Racou** back towards Argelès.

Behind the château lies the **old harbour**, where half a dozen brightly painted lateen-rigged fishing boats are often beached, all that remains of Collioure's traditional fleet. The attractive surrounding streets of pink- and beige-washed houses are the centre of tourist activity. The SI is here on place du 18-juin (summer Mon–Sat 9.30am–noon & 3.30–7pm, Sun 10am–noon; rest of year Mon, Tues, Thurs–Sat 9.30am–noon & 2–6pm; closed Sun & Wed). Two pleasant places to stay are the **hotels** *Triton* (☎68.82.06.52; ③–⑤) and *Boramar* (☎68.82.07.06; ③–⑤; closed Nov–April), on the main beach close to the through road. Cheaper, though a little grim, is the *Majorque*, 16 av de-Gaulle (☎68.82.29.22; ③). The best **campsite** is the seaside *La Girelle* (April–Sept), but there are numerous others in the area should it be full.

PORT-VENDRES, 3km down the coast, is a functional sort of place. Although the harbour has never been as busy as it was in the nineteenth century with colonial trade and ferries from North Africa, it still lands more fish than any other on this stretch of coast. If you're interested, the boats come in between about 4.30 and 6pm every day, except Sunday. You can watch them unload and auction the catch on the dock at the far end of the harbour. Otherwise, there is little to see here.

South towards **BANYULS**, 7km further on, where the **GR10** finally comes down to the sea, the road winds through attractive scenery with the Albères hills rising steeply on the right. The town, built round a broad sweep of pebble beach, is pleasant but lacks the charm of Collioure and the energy of more popular resorts. There are, however, two things to do before moving on. One is to visit the seafront **aquarium** of the Laboratoire Arago, run by the Sorbonne's marine biology department (daily 9am–noon & 2–6.30pm, until 10pm in summer), whose tanks contain a comprehensive collection of the region's fish and submarine life. The other is to sample the dark, full-bodied *Banyuls* **wine**, an *appellation* which, apart from Banyuls itself, applies only to the vineyards of Collioure, Port-Vendres and Cerbère. The best place to do this is the *Cellier* *des Templiers* on route du Mas-Reig, just under the rail line at the foot of the steep brown stone terraces of Banyuls' own vineyards (daily 9am–7pm; closed Oct–April). For further information consult the **SI** opposite the Hôtel de Ville on the seafront (July–Aug daily 9am–12.30pm & 2.30–7pm; April–June & Sept Tues–Sat 2–6pm). If you're **camping** there's a municipal **site** on the route du Mas-Reig (April 1–Oct 15). For a **hotel**, try *Le Manoir* at 20 rue du Maréchal-Joffre (☎68.88.32.98; ③).

If you've got a car, there's a magnificent winding drive up through the vineyards to the **Tour Madeloc**, a watch tower built by Jaime I of Majorca at the end of thirteenth century, on the crest of a ridge at about 650m, whence on a clear day you can see down into Spain, along the coast, across to Montpellier and over the Corbières, with the castles of Quéribus and Peyrepertuse easily visible. Otherwise, continuing down the coast brings you to **CERBÈRE**, 10km away, the last stop before the Spanish frontier, where there is nothing but a handful of hotels, a scrubby little beach and a large and grubby international train station. It's not worth getting off the train for.

Vallespir and the Valley of the Tech

The first stop on the D115, the main road which follows the **Tech valley** inland all the way up to the Spanish border at PRATS-DE-MOLLO, is **CÉRET**, capital of the Vallespir region, and served like the rest of the valley by regular buses from Perpignan's gare routière. It is a delightful place, friendly and bustling, with a wonderfully shady old town overhung by huge plane trees. The streets are typically narrow and winding, opening on to small squares like the **place des Neuf-Jets**, so called because of its trickling fountain. There's a large and varied Saturday **market** spilling out of place Pablo-Picasso into the main street, av d'Espagne, where two remnants of the medieval walls, the **Porte de France** and **Porte d'Espagne** are visible. In summer, Céret is also a big centre for *corridas*; the arena is on the other side of town from the market, out towards the AMÉLIE-LES-BAINS road. Other high points include the Easter Sunday procession of the Resurrected Christ, at a time of year when Céret's famous cherry harvest is also getting under way. And there is an international *sardana* jamboree on the second to last Sunday in August.

Céret's main sight, however, is the remarkable **Musée d'Art Moderne** just off bd Maréchal-Joffre near the SI (10am–noon & 2–6pm; closed Tues; ☎68.87.27.76), hopefully re-opened now after major building works. In the early years of this century, Céret's charms, coupled with the presence here of the Catalan artist and sculptor, Manolo, drew a number of avant-garde artists to the town, including Matisse and Picasso, and the museum contains work by Matisse, Picasso, Chagall, Dali, Dufy and Manolo, among others. Both Picasso and Chagall actually dedicated some pictures specifically to it, scrawling "pour le musée de Céret" across the bottom of each work. Among the Picassos is a marvellous series of ceramic bowls illustrating bullfighting scenes, and a sketch of a *sardana*, which he gave to the local branch of the *PCF*, who in turn donated it to the museum.

You can get more information on the *corridas* and other aspects of the town from the **SI** on av Clemenceau. If you're **stopping over**, the *Hôtel Vidal* in the place du 4-septembre (☎68.87.00.85; ②–③), with a restaurant from 68F, is a very attractive and reasonably priced place to stay. The municipal **campsite** is just out of town on the Maureillas road. **Eating**, there is a good cheap restaurant-cum-*crêperie*, *Le Pied dans le Plat* on place des Neuf-Jets.

To the Spanish frontier

West from Céret, past the leaping single span of its fourteenth-century **Pont du Diable**, the view opens north towards the towering imminence of the Canigou massif. **AMÉLIE-LES-BAINS**, the next place you come to, is hardly worth a stop, a rather stodgy health spa for the elderly and rheumatic. If an **overnight stay** is necessary, *Hôtel La Chaumière* at 2 av du Vallespir (☎68.39.05.35; ②), right on the river in the middle of town, is an attractive place, and there are various **campsites**, including the *Hollywood* back towards Céret at La Forge (April 15–Nov 15).

ARLES-SUR-TECH, 4km up the valley, is a more interesting proposition. It has a beautiful Romanesque church, whose Carolingian origins in the ninth century are thought to account for its back-to-front alignment of altar at the west end and the entrance at the east. The massive interior is impressive, but the church's most renowned feature is the cloister (closed lunchtime), whose pointed white marble arches and twin columns prefigure the Gothic, showing its relative lateness compared to other examples of Romanesque in the region, like Serrabonne (see below). Twin towers flank the church, while against the wall outside the east front – whose plainness is beautifully relieved, as the sun turns, by the shadow of blind arcading – stands a very ancient sarcophagus, known as the Sainte Tombe, which has the mysterious and scientifically inexplicable habit of slowly filling with very pure water.

The **GR10** passes through Arles, climbing north towards the Cortalets refuge on Canigou and south towards the Roc de France. Other points of interest include the probably prehistoric festival of the *Fête de l'Ours*, traditionally held at the end of February, when the bears woke from their winter hibernation, and designed to exorcise human fear of the bear. There is also a torchlight *Procession de la Sanch* at Easter.

The **SI** is in rue Barjau and you can **stay** at the attractive *Hôtel des Glycines* on rue du Jeu-de-Paume (☎68.39.10.09; ④), with a good restaurant and wisteria-shaded terrace. The **campsite** is on the west side of town.

A couple of kilometres from Arles in the direction of PRATS-DE-MOLLO, on the right, is the entrance to the **Gorges de la Fou**, some 2km in length, very narrow and up to 250m deep. It's spectacular but unfortunately something of a tourist trap, with a car park, admission charge, snacks, and a metal catwalk all along the bottom of the gorge.

After the gorge the road climbs on towards the border, between valley sides thick with walnut, oak and sweet chestnut, to **PRATS-DE-MOLLO**. Prats is the last French town before the border with Spain, and has a very Spanish atmosphere. Most of the population seems to sit around or play *pétanque* in El Firal, the main square. It's surprisingly unspoilt for a border town, but the only notable attraction is the **Ville Haute**, with its steep cobbled streets and weather-worn grey church with marvellous iron work on the door under a porch. The encircling walls were rebuilt in the seventeenth century after the suppression of a local revolt against the taxation newly imposed by Louis XIV after the Treaty of the Pyrenees brought these lands under his sway. The **Fort Lagarde** (April–Nov pm only), on the heights above the town, also dates from this period, built to keep the local population in check as much as keeping the Spanish out. **Camping**, there's a municipal site 1km along the road towards La Preste. For a **bed**, try *Hôtel des Touristes* in av du Haut-Vallespir (☎68.39.72.12; ③).

From here it is only 13km to the border on the **Col d'Ares.** The next place of any size on the other side is **CAMPRODÓN**, a village about 18km away. Alternatively, if you're feeling energetic, you can bus or hitch the 8km north to the spa town of LA PRESTE, and then walk over the **Col Prégon**. It's about an hour's steep climb to the top, followed by another hour's more gentle descent down to the small village of **ESPINAVELL**. (Leave the road at the first turning on the right before you get into La Preste, and then take the path from La Forge.)

From Tech to Têt

The only practical route between the **valleys of the Tech and the Têt**, especially if you're hitching – and it would be hard work – is the D618 across the eastern spurs of Canigou from Amélie-les-Bains to BOULETERNÈRE. It's 43 slow kilometres of mountain road, twisting and climbing through magnificent woods of holm oak, cork oak, regular oak, chestnut, ash and cherry, with explosions of yellow broom and tangles of wild honeysuckle, past isolated half-derelict farms or *mas*, some still tenanted by survivors of the post-1968 migration from the towns. About halfway along, the three-house hamlet of BELPUIG stands on the road. One of its buildings is the **Chapelle de la Trinité**, a tiny dark Romanesque church in grey and yellow stone with elaborate doors and a particularly fine crucifix from the twelfth century. Past the cemetery and up the hill beside a pine plantation a path climbs to the ruined **Château de Belpuig**, some fifteen minutes' walk from the road with long-range views over the surrounding country

From here the road descends into the valley bottom through the pretty hamlet of **BOULE D'AMONT** before climbing again to the remarkable **Prieuré de Serrabonne** (daily except Tues 9.30am–noon & 2–6pm) some 4km up an asphalt lane above the road. Even without its carvings, Serrabonne (consecrated in 1151) would still be impressive purely by virtue of its location: high on the scrub-covered mountainside, with massive views over the rocky Boulès valley and into the valley of the Têt. Yet it is also one of the finest – perhaps *the* finest – example of Roussillon Romanesque. The interior of the church is breathtakingly simple, making the beautiful carvings on the capitals of the pillars in the tribune even more striking: vividly carved lions, centaurs, griffins and human figures with oriental faces and haircuts – motifs brought back from the Crusades – all in the local pink marble. The altar is made of the same stone, as are the pillars and equally elaborate capitals of the cloister, which is set to one side of the church on a high terrace. Despite the rigours of monastic life here – all abandoned now – the settlement was well developed, and the remains of terraced cultivation and irrigation systems are still visible.

When you reach the Têt at Bouleternère, a 4km detour would take you to **Ille-sur-Têt**, where there is a very interesting museum of sacred art, the **Centre d'Art Sacré** (summer daily except Tues 10am–noon & 4–7pm; Oct–April 10am–noon & 3–6pm), whose exhibits include both temporary and permanent shows.

Canigou and the valley of the Têt

The upper part of the Têt valley, known as the **pays de Conflent**, is utterly dominated by **Canigou**. The bottoms are lush with peach and apple orchards – with the possibility of work as a picker from June onwards – but the mountain presides over all, vast and uncompromising.

The valley capital is **PRADES**, easily accessible by train and bus on the Perpignan–Villefranche–La Tour-de-Carol route, and, whether or not you stay, the obvious starting point for all excursions in the Canigou region. It is an attractive place, although there are no great sights beyond the church of **St-Pierre** in the town centre, but it enjoys a standing way out of proportion to its size or economic power. This is largely thanks to the Catalan cellist, Pablo Casals, who set up home here as an exile and fierce opponent of the Franco regime in Spain. In 1950 he instituted the internationally renowned **music festival** now held every year in the abbey of St-Michel-de-Cuxa (see overpage) from the end of July to the middle of August. Prades is also a centre of ardent Catalan feeling. It hosts a summertime Catalan university (mid- to end Aug) and boasts the first Catalan-language primary school in France.

The pillar of the **SI** at 4 rue Victor-Hugo is a bilingual English woman called Christine Hicks, who is a mine of information about the area; the SI can also sort out advance bookings for the music festival. However, the town isn't very good for **hotels**. The *Hostalrich* on the route Nationale (☎68.96.05.38; ④) is probably the best bet. If you had a car you could try across the river in Molitg-les-Bains or, better still, up in Vernet-les-Bains (see p.535). The municipal **campsite** (May–Oct) is by the river on the road to Molitg.

For an undemanding walk that will give you a sense of country life, at least as it used to be in these parts, head over to EUS on the far side of the valley from Prades. The upper, medieval, part of the village grouped round its fortress church has been largely taken over by Parisians and foreigners to the displeasure of the farming inhabitants of the lower, more modern, part – a phenomenon that is common in these picturesque but depopulated villages. To the left of the church an old mule road climbs up through the *garrigue* to the derelict village of COMES, with a single shepherd and his family in residence, in about one hour.

Climbing the Pic

You can get at least part of the way up the **Pic du Canigou** by car or on foot. **Cars** – and you would be well advised not to try it in a much-loved saloon – can get as far as the *Chalet des Cortalets* refuge either by the track from Villerach or the even steeper and rougher mining road that begins by the *Al Pouncy* campsite near Fillols, and passes the *Refuge de Balatg* and the now vandalised *Cabane des Cortalets*, where herds of cows and horses graze untended. (They are the best barometer of mountain weather, the locals say, descending to lower altitudes when bad weather is imminent.) Both routes take about an hour. You can also **hire** a **jeep** and driver from *LeBohec* in Prades (☎68.05.20.48) or from the *Garage Louis Villaceque* in Vernet-les-Bains (☎68.05.51.14). For **walkers** the standard ascent is from Vernet on a path that begins about 1km along the road to Fillols, joining up with the GR10 at the *Refuge de Bonaigua* (about 3hr) which you leave (about 90min) below the **Pic Joffre** to follow the HRP up the ridge to the summit (about 1hr).

From the *Chalet des Cortalets* (☎68.96.36.19; May–Oct), which has a restaurant, or the smaller *CAF* refuge next door, it's an easy 90-minute walk to the top. Strike west from the refuge through the last trees, past the little lake with a magnificent view into the *cirque* below the summit, round the back of the Pic Joffre, and up the long stony ridge to the cross and Catalan flag that crown the summit.

Although the **ascent** by this route is straightforward in good weather you should be properly shod and clothed and have good large-scale maps. If you are not experienced and encounter frozen snow, turn back: a German couple slid to their deaths on the slopes between Pic Joffre and the summit in 1991. **Midsummer** is a great time to do the climb. Catalans for miles around, including half the population of Barcelona, gather on the top on the night of June 21, which often coincides with the full moon, to light the bonfire from which a flame is carried to kindle all the *feux de St-Jean* of the Catalan villages, although the scene around the refuge can be pretty horrendous, with tents, ghetto-blasters and litter galore – not much respect for a wild place.

Vernet and the abbeys

Close to Prades and Vernet are two of the loveliest abbeys in the country, **St-Michel-de-Cuxa**, 3km from Prades, and **St-Martin-du-Canigou** just above Vernet. **St-Michel-de-Cuxa** (Mon–Sat 9.30–11.50am & 2–5pm, Sun 2–5pm, until 6pm in summer), mutilated after the Revolution but still beautiful, with its crenellated tower silhouetted against the wooded slopes of Canigou, dates from around 1000 AD. The bare stone crypt and church – the altar slab was rediscovered doing duty as a balcony on a house in the village of Vinça – are impressive enough, but the glory of the place is **the cloister**. Although some of the capitals were shipped off to the Cloisters Museum in New York in the early years of this century, those that remain are a feast for the eyes. Carved in the twelfth century in rose-pink marble from Villefranche, they are decorated with exact and highly stylised human, animal and vegetable motifs. The monastery, inhabited by a small community of Benedictines from Monserrat in Spain, hosts both the annual Casals music festival and the *Journées Romanes* (mid-July), a study session on the Romanesque architecture of Rousillon.

St-Martin-du-Canigou, on the other hand, lies a half-hour walk above the hamlet of CASTEIL – with restaurants under the apple orchards, and a **campsite**, *Camping St-Martin*, with swimming pool – 2km from Vernet-les-Bains. Resurrected from its ruins at the turn of the century, the monastery occupies a narrow promontory of rock at over 1000m altitude. Utterly quiet and serene, it is surrounded by the deep shade of chestnut and oak woods. Above it rise the precipitous slopes and eroded pinnacles of Canigou. Below, the ground drops sheer into the ravine of the Cady stream that rushes down from the Col de Jou. The buildings are visitable, in silent groups (summer daily at 10am and 11.45am, 2pm, 3pm, 4pm & 5pm; winter daily 10am, 11.45am, 2.30 & 4.30pm; closed Tues). What you see is a beautiful little garden and cloister overlooking the ravine, a low dark atmospheric chapel beneath the church and the church itself. Founded in the tenth century, St-Martin was the inspiration for the Romanesque architecture of the region. The graves of the founder, Count Guifred of Cerdagne, and his wife lie in the rock by the church door. It is possible, on request, to do a week's retreat as part of the community.

From the reception building a **path** leads up to a rocky viewpoint from which you can look down on the monastery and away across the valley to the surrounding mountains. As you go up, you pass a signpost to Moura on a path which leads first to the Col de Segalès on the GR10, then, on the HRP, to the *Refuge Arago* and finally to the summit of Canigou – the last stretch involving a rather steep hands and feet scramble which might alarm the inexperienced. For a different route back to Casteil, a path drops down into the Cady ravine just at the start of the monastery buildings.

Vernet-les-bains

A quiet and not unpleasant little spa, Vernet can make a useful base for picking up provisions and information. It has an **SI** in place de la Mairie (June–Sept daily 9.30am–12.30pm & 3–7pm, Sun 9.30am–12.30pm; rest of year Mon–Fri 10am–noon & 2–5pm, Sat 10am–noon) and plenty of **eating and drinking** possibilities in the main square. It's also a good place to **stay the night**, either at *Hôtel Moderne*, 7 av des Thermes (☎68.05.52.17; ③), or *Hôtel des Thermes*, 22 av des Thermes (☎68.05.50.06; ②; closed Dec–Feb). There's a **campsite**, *Camping Le Cady*, just up the road towards Casteil. In Casteil, there is a **gîte d'étape** in av St-Saturnin (☎68.05.51.30). Returning to the valley bottom at Villefranche-de-Conflent, you might want to stop off and look at the magnificent Romanesque church in **CORNEILLA** (key from the caretaker next door).

Villefranche-de-Conflent and the Petit Train Jaune

A medieval garrison town suffering from arrested development, **VILLEFRANCHE** is a tourist classic and lives off it. But it is interesting: founded around 1100 by the counts of Cerdagne to bar the road to Moorish invaders, remodelled by Vauban in the seventeenth century after rebelling against annexation by France, its streets and fortifications have remained untouched by subsequent development. The church of **St-Jacques** is worth a look and you can walk the **walls** for a fee (9am–noon & 2–6pm). If you do so, you will see why Vauban constructed the **Libéria fortress** on the heights overlooking the town to protect it from "aerial" bombardment. The way up to the Libéria (daily except Mon 9am–6pm) is a stairway of a thousand steps beginning just across the old bridge and rail line at the end of rue St-Pierre. If you don't fancy the climb, ask at the **SI** by the church for the minibus. For hiking and other miscellaneous information ask at the *Association culturelle de Villefranche* at 38 rue St-Jean. For accommodation it's better to try Vernet or Prades.

Villefranche is the terminus for trains from Perpignan. From here up to **La Tour-de-Carol** on the Spanish frontier *SNCF* transport is by bus, or, far nicer, the narrow-gauge **Petit Train Jaune**, which climbs to the valley head at a pace that allows you a walker's or cyclist's proximity to the scenery, especially in summer when some of the carriages are open air.

On up the Têt

Just beyond THUÈS-ENTRE-VALLS, southwest of Villefranche on the left of the main N116, the wild wooded canyon of the **Gorges de la Carança** cuts south into the mountains towards Spain. A path follows the gorge to a junction with the the GR10 at the refuge of the *Ras de la Carança* (3–4hr), while a further path continues on to meet the HRP on the frontier in another four hours.

At **FONTPÉDROUSE**, 5km beyond Thuès, a road branches south across the river and up a grassy spur above the River Aigues towards the village of PRAT-BALAGUER. From the top of the rise directly opposite Fontpédrouse, a path leads down to the Aigues where water from **hot springs** forms three separate pools at different temperatures, where you can skinny-dip for free.

Another 10km up the main road brings you onto the wide **plateau of the Cerdagne**, whose once powerful counts controlled lands from Barcelona to Roussillon and endowed the monasteries of St-Michel-de-Cuxa, St-Martin-du-Canigou and Ripoll, now well inside Spain. It's an area that has never been sure whether it is Spanish or French. After the French annexation of Roussillon, it was partitioned, with Spain retaining – as it does today – the enclave of LLIVIA.

The first place you come to is the little garrison town of **MONT-LOUIS**, built by Vauban in 1679 and still used as a base for paratroops and marines. There isn't much to see, but it is a far pleasanter place to stay than the monstrous ski resort of **FONT-ROMEU** just down the road, and it has an **SI** office (mid-June to mid-Sept daily 10am–noon & 2–6pm) and a delightful **hotel**, the *Lou Raballou* (☎68.04.23.20; ③–④) towards the back of the town near the barracks, with an excellent **restaurant** (menus from 120F). There is a **campsite** at PLA DE BARRES 3km away on the road to the Lac des Bouillousses (June–Sept), a **gîte d'étape** at La Cassagne farm (☎68.04.21.40) half an hour back down the main road, and a **youth hostel** 12km west along the N116 at SAILLAGOUSSE (☎68.04.71.69).

Of things to do round about, there is a good four-hour walk from the pretty mountain village of **EYNE** up a valley renowned for its flowers and medicinal plants to the Col d'Eyne, and numerous walks in the **Carlit massif** around the **Lac des Bouillousses** – where there's a *CAF* refuge (☎68.04.20.76), though the lake itself and parts accessible by car get very crowded in season. The region's curiosity is the **Four solaire** or solar power station (daily 10am–12.30pm & 1.30–5.30pm) at ODEILLO just below Font-Romeu, although the most impressive part of this, a screen composed of thousands of mirrors, can in fact be seen from the road.

travel details

Trains

From Bayonne frequent to Bordeaux via Dax (1hr 50min); frequent to Hendaye (35min), most stopping at Biarritz (10min), St-Jean-de-Luz (30min), with at least 5 continuing to Irun (1hr); 4 to St-Jean-Pied-de-Port (1hr 10min), via Cambo (20min); 4 daily to Toulouse (4hr) via Orthez (50min), Pau (1hr 15min), Lourdes (1hr 40min), Tarbes (2hr), Lannemazan (2hr 40min), Montréjeau (2hr 50min), St-Gaudens (3hr), Boussens (3hr).

From Pau 4 daily to Oloron-Ste-Marie (30min), connecting with *SNCF* bus to Canfranc (1hr 40min) via Bedous (25min), Lescun-Cette-Eygun (38min), Somport (1hr 20min); 4 daily to Buzy (20min), connecting with *SNCF* bus to Laruns (35min); frequent to Tarbes (40min) via Lourdes (30min).

From Tarbes frequent to Lourdes (20min).

From Luchon 3 daily to Montréjeau (35min).

From Montréjeau several daily to Toulouse (1hr 15min) via Saint-Gaudens (10min), Boussens (25min); several daily to Pau (1hr 35min) via Tarbes (35min) and Lourdes (50min); 3 daily to Luchon (35min).

From Foix 5 daily, one with bus from Ax, to Latour-de-Carol, 1hr 40min–2hr 10min), via Tarascon (20min) and Ax-les-Thermes (45min), with two continuing to Barcelona (5hr 15min–6hr 15min); 6–8 daily to Toulouse (50–70min).

From Quillan 3 daily to Carcassonne (1hr). via Limoux (30min).

From Perpignan frequent to Port-Bou (50min) and Cerbère (55min), via Elne (10min), Argelès (18min), Collioure (23min), Port-Vendres (27min), Banyuls (33min); frequent to Narbonne (40min) with many stopping at Rivesaltes (7min), Salses (15min), Leucate (25min), Port-la-Nouvelle (33min); with connections on to Montpellier and Toulouse; 6 daily to Barcelona (2hr 15min–5hr); 7 daily to Villefranche-de-Conflent (52min) via Prades (40min), with 5 *Petit Train Jaune* connections on to Latour-de-Carol (2hr 30min) via Mont-Louis (68min) and Font-Romeu (1hr 25min).

Buses

From Bayonne frequent to St-Jean-de-Luz (40min) via Biarritz (15min); 4 daily to San Sebastian; 7 daily to Cambo-les-Bains (30min).

From Biarritz 4 daily to Pau (2hr 30min) via Bayonne (15min), Salies-de-Béarn (1hr 20min) and Orthez (1hr 45min); frequent to St-Jean-de-Luz (35min).

From St-Jean-de-Luz frequent to Hendaye (35min); 3 daily to Sare-la-Rhune (30min); 3 daily to Espelette (35 min), Cambo-les-Bains (45 min) and Hasparren (1hr 5min).

From Pau 4 daily to Lourdes (1hr 30min); 6 daily to Tarbes (1hr); 1 daily to Mauléon (1hr 50min) via Navarrenx (1hr 35min); 1 daily to Orthez (1hr 10min); 4 daily to La Gourette (1hr 45min) via Laruns (1hr 5min) and Eaux-Bonnes (1hr 15min) with 1 continuing to Col d'Aubisque (2hr) July 1–Sept 15; 1 daily to Artouste and Gabas (summer weekends only; 1hr 45min).

From Lourdes frequent to Tarbes (30min); 4 daily to Pau (1hr 15min); several daily to Argelès-Gazost (20min), with 10 going on to Pierrefitte-Nestalas (30min); 5 daily to Cauterets (50min); 2–3 daily to Barèges (1hr) via Luz-St-Sauveur (45min); 3 daily to Gavarnie (June–mid-Sept, changing at Luz); 3 daily to Bagnères-de-Bigorre (45min–1hr).

From Tarbes 3 daily to Lannemazan (1hr); 1 daily to St-Lary (2hr 10min); several daily to Bagnères-de-Bigorre (40min); frequent to Lourdes (30min); 1 daily to Tarbes-Ossun-Lourdes airport (30min–1hr).

From Lannemazan 4–5 daily to St-Lary (1hr) via Arreau (30min).

From Saint-Girons several daily to Boussens (45min) with rail connections to Toulouse; 2–4 daily to Toulouse; 4 daily to Foix (1hr); 1–2 daily to Aulus-les-Bains (1hr 15min); 1 daily to Massat; 2 daily to Ustou; 1 daily to Sentein (1hr); term-time 1–2 daily, otherwise 2 on Mon, Wed & Fri to St-Lary.

From Foix 1 daily except Sun to Carcassonne (2hr 35min), via Lavelanet (35min), and changing at Mirepoix (1hr 30min); 4–6 daily to Toulouse (1hr 50min), via Pamiers (25min); 3 daily to Ax-les-Thermes (55min), via Tarascon (20min); 1 daily to Quillan (3hr).

From Tarascon Mon, Fri & Sat 1 daily to Auzat (1hr 20min).

From Quillan 2 daily to Comus (1hr 5min); 2 daily to Perpignan (1hr 30min), via Axat and St-Paul-de-Fenouillet; 4 daily to Carcassonne (1hr 15min).

From Perpignan 12 daily to Argelès (30min), with 5 going on to Collioure (45min), Port-Vendres (55min), Banyuls (1hr 10min); frequent to Céret (55min), with 10 going on to Amélie-les-Bains (1hr 10min) and Arles-sur-Tech (1hr 20min), and 5 to Prats-de-Mollo (1hr 50min) and La Preste (2hr 5min); 7 daily to Villefranche-de-Conflent (1hr 15min) via Prades (1hr), with 3 continuing to Mont-Louis (1hr 30min) and Latour-de-Carol (2hr), 1 passing through Font-Romeu (2hr 25min).

CHAPTER ELEVEN

LANGUEDOC

Languedoc is more an idea than a geographical entity. The modern region covers only a fraction of the lands where once **Occitan** or the *langue d'oc* – the language of *oc*, the southern Gallo-Latin word for *oui* – was spoken. These stretched south from Bordeaux and Lyon into Spain and northwest Italy.

The heartland today is the **Bas Languedoc**, the coastal plain and dry stony vine-growing hills between Carcassonne and Nîmes. It is here that the Occitan movement has its power base. Its demands, separatist only on the lunatic fringe, are for greater independence and recognition of its linguistic and cultural distinctiveness. Its appeal derives from widespread resentment against subservience to the bureaucrats of remote and alien Paris. In recent times this has been focused on Parisian determination to drag the province into the twentieth century, with massive tourist development on the coast and the drastic transformation of the cheap wine industry. But it is also mixed up in the

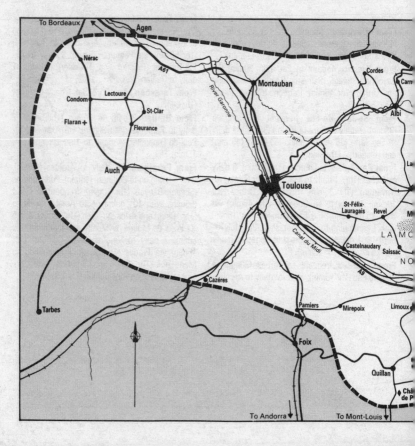

collective folk-memory with the brutal repression of the Protestant Camisards around 1700, the thirteenth-century massacres of the Cathars, and the subsequent obliteration of the brilliant *langue d'oc* troubadour civilisation. It is a hostility that has made an essentially rural and conservative population vote – paradoxically – massively for the Left.

It's a quirky, eccentric part of the world, and, although things are changing under the impact of a modernised economy, the Occitanian identity remains strong. Thousands of students take the language at school and follow courses at the universities of Montpellier and Toulouse. The Cathars have become a boom industry, and a number of writers use Occitan as their normal medium of expression, though none with the distinction of the poet Frédéric Mistral, who won a Nobel Prize in 1904 for his work in resuscitating Provençal (the same language as Occitan with different dialects).

Toulouse, the cultural capital, though included in this chapter, lies outside the official region but is a deserved high spot among numerous and various other attractions. There are great stretches of dramatic landscape and river gorges, from the **Cévennes** foothills in the east to the **Montagne Noire** and the **Corbières** hills in the west. There's superb ecclesiastical architecture in **Albi** and **St-Guilhem-le-Désert**, medieval towns in **Cordes** and **Carcassonne**, with the unforgettably romantic **Cathar castles** to the south. **Nîmes** has extensive Roman remains, and there are great swathes of beach, too, where, away from the major resorts, you can still find a mile or two to yourself.

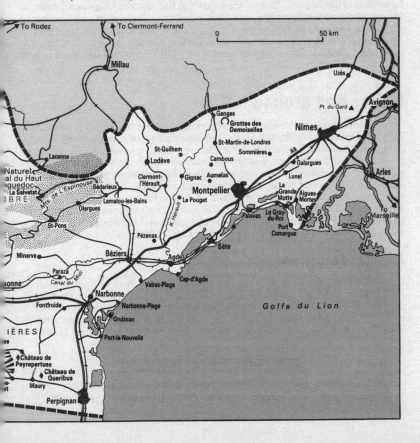

EASTERN LANGUEDOC

Heading south from Paris, via Lyon and the Rhône valley, you can go one of two ways: east to Provence and the Côte d'Azur, which is what most people do, or west to Nîmes, Montpellier and the comparatively untouched northern Languedoc coast. **Nîmes** itself, while not officially part of the modern Languedoc region, makes for a good introduction to the region, a hectic modern town impressive both for its Roman past and for some scattered attractions – the **Pont du Gard** for one – nearby. **Montpellier**, also, is worth a day or two, not so much for any historical attractions as for a heady vibrancy, and ease of access to the ancient villages, churches and fine scenery of the upper **Héraul valley**. This is the part of Languedoc most affected by the spread of **Protestantism** in the sixteenth century, an experience that has marked the region's character more than any other. The Protestants, with their attachment to rationality and self-improvement, espoused the cause of French over Occitan, supported the Revolution and the Republic, fought Napoléon III's coup against the 1848 revolution and adhered to the anti-clerical and socialist movement under the Third Republic. They dominated the local textile industry in the nineteenth century and, interestingly, were extremely active in the Resistance to the Nazis.

They also suffered a great deal for their cause, as did the whole region. After the Revocation of the Edict of Nantes – the treaty that had restored religious toleration at the end of the sixteenth century – in 1685, persecution drove their most committed supporters, especially in the Cévennes to the north, to form clandestine *assemblées du Désert* and finally, in 1702, to take up arms in the first guerrilla war of modern times, *la guerre des Camisards*. These conflicts are still very much present in the minds of both Huguenot and Catholic families.

Nîmes and around

On the border between Provence and Languedoc, the name of NÎMES is inescapably linked to two things – denim and Rome. The latter's influence is highly visible in some of the most extensive Roman remains in Europe, while the former, equally visible on the backsides of the populace, was first manufactured in the city's textile mills (denim = *de Nîmes*), and exported to the southern USA in the nineteenth century to clothe the slaves. It's worth a visit, in part for the ruins and, nowadays, for the city's new-found energy and direction, inspired by its mayor of the last ten years, Jean Bousquet. The former boss of the fashion house *Cacharel* has enlisted the services of a galaxy of architects and designers, including Norman Foster, Jean Nouvel and Philippe Starck, in his bid to wrest southern supremacy from neighbouring Montpellier.

Arrival and accommodation

If you're **driving** down the A9 autoroute the chances are you'll end up in av Jean-Jaurès, where there is a reasonable chance of finding parking space. Any street heading east will take you to the town centre. Travelling by bus or train, the **gare SNCF** is on bd Sergent-Triaire, southeast of the city centre at the end of av Feuchères, which leads down from Esplanade de-Gaulle, with the **gare routière** just behind in rue Ste-

---

HOTEL ROOM PRICES

For a fuller explanation of these price codes, see the box on p.28 of *Basics*.

① Under 100F ② 100–130F ③ 130–180F ④ 180–230F ⑤ 230–300F

Félicité. There's an **SI annexe** in the station which handles hotel bookings (daily 9.30am–12.30pm & 2–6.30pm), and a **main SI office** at 6 rue Auguste, by the Maison Carrée (summer daily 8am–7pm; winter daily 8am–noon & 2–7pm).

There are several recommended **hotels** within easy walking distance of the station. *Hôtel La Couronne* is just to the right at 4 square de la Couronne (☎66.67.51.73; ③), but be warned that the street-side rooms are very noisy. The *Concorde* is on the other side of the boulevard at 3 rue des Chapeliers beside the Palais de Justice (☎66.67.91.03; ③). Closer in to the centre, *Le France* is at 4 bd des Arènes behind the arena (☎66.67.23.05; ③), *La Mairie* is at 11 rue des Greffes near the Hôtel de Ville (☎66.67.65.91; ③), and *Les Voyageurs* at 4 rue Roussy off bd Amiral-Courbet (☎6.67.46.52; ③–④). Slightly more expensive but still central, there's *La Bourse* at 2 rue Tedenat (☎66.67.33.64; ③–④), near the church of St-Paul off bd Victor-Hugo.

There's a **youth hostel** with tent space on chemin de la Cigale (☎66.23.25.04); take bus #8 from the gare SNCF to stop *Stade*. The last bus goes at 8pm. Alternatively, *Espace Puech du Teil* on impasse Messager (☎66.64.13.37; ⑤) and *Résidence de la Reinette* on rue de Garons (☎66.23.25.04) have some individual rooms, but phone first. The municipal **campsite** is on route de Générac beyond the new Stade Costières and the autoroute.

The city

Most of what you'll want to see is mostly contained with the boulevards, Libération, Amiral-Courbet, Gambetta, Victor-Hugo. Beyond the gardens of the Esplanade de-Gaulle, **Les Arénes** is a first-century AD Roman **arena** (mid-June to mid-Sept daily 8am–8pm; rest of year daily 9am–noon & 2–6pm; free, as are all monuments and museums except the Beaux-Arts) and still the city's most spectacular building. One of the best preserved Roman arenas anywhere, its arcaded two-storey facade conceals massive interior vaulting, riddled with corridors and supporting raked tiers of seats with a capacity of more than 20,000 spectators. The blood and guts of gladiatorial combat was the staple fare. When Rome's sway was broken by the barbarian invasions, the arena became a fortress and eventually a slum, home to an incredible 2000 people when it was cleared in the early 1800s. Today it has recovered something of its former role, with the passionate summer crowds still turning out for some real-life bloodletting – Nîmes is the number-one European bull-fighting scene outside Spain.

Behind the arena, through the beautiful little **place du Marché**, rue Fresque leads towards the city's other famous landmark, the **Maison Carrée**, a neat, jewel-like temple, celebrated for its integrity and almost Greek harmony of proportion. Built in 5 AD, it is dedicated to the adopted sons of the Emperor Augustus: all part of the business of blowing up the imperial personality cult. No surprise then that Napoléon, with his love of flummery and ennobling his cronies to boost his own legitimacy, should have taken it as the model for the church of the Madeleine in Paris. The temple stands in its own small square opposite rue Auguste, where the Roman forum used to be. Around it are scattered pieces of Roman masonry. The interior (mid-June to mid-Sept daily 9am–7pm; rest of year daily 9am–noon & 2–6pm) is for the moment home to three enormous canvases by the American painter, Julian Schnabel. On the north side of place de la Maison Carrée, there's another example of French architectural boldness under construction, a building by **Norman Foster** destined to be the city archive, contemporary art museum and *médiathèque*.

Though already a prosperous city on the *via Domitia*, the main Roman road from Italy to Spain constructed in 118 BC, Nîmes did especially well by Augustus. He gave it its walls, remnants of which surface here and there around the town, and its gates, as the inscription on the surviving **Porte d'Auguste** at the end of rue Nationale – the Roman main street – records. He also, indirectly, gave it the chained crocodile of its

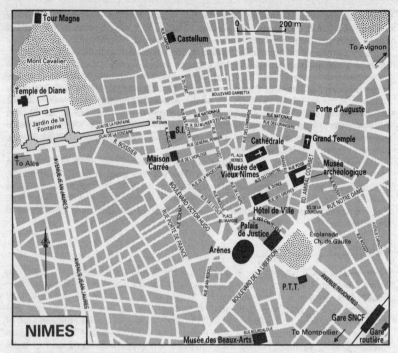

NIMES

coat of arms. The device was copied from an Augustan coin struck to commemorate his defeat of Antony and Cleopatra. And he settled his veterans on the surrounding land.

Cutting back east into the old quarter, **rue de l'Horloge** leads to the delightful **place aux Herbes**, with two or three cafés and bars and a fine twelfth-century house on the corner of rue de la Madeleine. The **Musée du Vieux Nîmes** (mid-June to mid-Sept daily 9am–7pm; rest of year daily 9am–noon & 1.30–6pm, closed Sun), in the bishop's palace here, has displays of Renaissance furnishings and décor and documents to do with local history. Opposite, the **cathedral of Notre-Dame-et-St-Castor** sports a handsome sculpted frieze on the west front illustrating the story of Adam and Eve and a pediment inspired by the Maison Carrée. It is practically the only existing medieval building. The rest were destroyed in the turmoil that followed the *Michelade*, the St Michael's Day massacre of Catholic clergy and notables by Protestants in 1567. Despite brutal repression in the wake of the *Camisard* insurrection of 1702, Nîmes was, and remains, a doggedly Protestant stronghold. Apart from that, it is of little interest, having been seriously mutilated in the Wars of Religion and significantly altered in the last century. Alphonse Daudet was born in its shadow, as was Jean Nicot – a doctor, no less – who introduced tobacco into France from Portugal in 1560, and gave his name to the world's most popular drug.

Banned from public office, the Protestants, like the Jews elsewhere, put their energy into making money. The results of their efforts can be seen in the seventeenth- and eighteenth-century *hôtels* they built themselves in the streets around the cathedral – rues de l'Aspic, Chapitre, Doré, Grand-Rue, among others. Their church is the serious-looking **Grand Temple** on bd Amiral-Courbet. On the same street, the **Musée**

Archéologique, housed in a seventeenth-century Jesuit chapel at no. 13, is full of Roman bits and bobs (mid-June to mid-Sept daily 9am–7pm; rest of year daily 9am–noon & 1.30–6pm, closed Sun). There's another museum, the **Musée des Beaux-Arts**, south of the Arènes in rue de la Cité-Foulc (mid-June–mid-Sept daily 9am–7pm; rest of year daily 9am–noon & 1.30–6pm, closed Sun) prides itself on a huge Gallo-Roman mosaic showing the *Marriage of Admetus*, but is mainly pretty ordinary.

The interior of the **Hôtel de Ville**, between rue Dorée and rue des Greffes, has been redesigned by the architect Jean-Michel Wilmotte, combining hi-tech with classical stone. Most of the other major examples of revolutionary building are out on the southern edge of town: Jean Nouvel's Mississippi steam boat housing project, **Nemausus**, off the Arles road behind the gare SNCF, named after the deity of the local spring which gave Nîmes its name, and the magnificent sports stadium, the **Stades des Costières**, by Vittorio Gregotti, close to the autoroute along the continuation of av J-Jaurès. There's also a **bus depot** by Philippe Starck on av Carnot, just east of the centre.

Perhaps the most refreshing thing you can do while in Nîmes is head out to the **Jardin de la Fontaine**, northwest of the centre at the top end of av Jean-Jaurès, France's first public garden, created in 1750. At its foot flows the gloriously green and shady **Canal de la Fontaine** built to supplement the rather unsteady supply of water from the *fontaine*, the Nemausus spring, whose presence in a dry, limestone landscape gave Nîmes its existence. Behind the formal entrance, where fountains, nymphs and formal trees enclose the so-called **Temple of Diana**, steps climb the steep wooded slope, adorned with grots and nooks and artful streams to the **Tour Magne** (mid-June–mid-Sept daily 9am–7pm; rest of year daily 9am–noon & 2–5pm), a 32-metre tower from Augustus' city walls, with a terrific view out over the surrounding country – as far , it is claimed, as the Pic du Canigou on the edge of the Pyrenees.

Eating and drinking

For **eating**, bd de la Libération and bd Amiral-Courbet harbour a stock of reasonably-priced **brasseries** and **pizzerias**, and the **café scene** is lively along here, too, as it is in bd Victor-Hugo, where the *Napoléon* and *Café de la Bourse* are city classics. *La Truye qui Filhe*, 9 rue Fresque (closed Sun), is an agreeable self-service in the old town. *Les Persiennes*, 5 pl de l'Oratoire (closed Mon), is good for traditional family cooking, and the popular and congenial *Nicolas*, 1 rue Poise, off bd Amiral-Courbet, is good, too, though there won't be much change out of 100F after you've had wine and coffee. *Les Vendanges* wine bar at 1 rue de la Violette makes a nice alternative, though the various *plats* work out quite expensive. For **music** there's the jazz bar *Le Mondial* on bd Gambetta and the *Musique en Stock* at 28 rue Jean-Reboul, which has jazz, salsa, etc. For up-to-the-minute information, you can't do better than ask at Laurent Maréchal's music shop, *Broc 'n Roll*, 3 rue des Flottes, near the Maison Carré.

There's always a lot going on in Nîmes: a Sunday morning **fleamarket** at the Stade Costières; on Monday, clothes and odds and bobs on bd Gambetta, antiques and flowers on av Jean-Jaurès on Friday, a **produce market** on av J-Jaurès, and a morning market at **Les Halles** on rue Général-Perrier, near the Maison Carrée.

Between May and September, dozens of other events take place, most notably **bullfights**, which are Nîmes' particular passion and raise the city's temperature to fever pitch. The principal *fierias* to watch out for are the **La Fieria du Carnaval** in February, when the inflatable "roof" of the *Arènes* is pulled over for protection from the weather; the ten-day madness of the Whitsun **Fieria de Pentecôte**, including bull-running in the streets, and the **Fieria des Vendanges** in the third week of September. You can pick up information on these and other happenings at the **SI** on rue Auguste.

Around Nîmes: the Pont du Gard and Uzès

Several buses a day head east from Nîmes' gare routière along the Avignon road to **UZÈS**, at the source of the Eure – the start of the 50-kilometre aqueduct built by the Romans in 19 AD to bring fresh water into Nîmes. With just 17m difference in altitude between start and finish, it was quite an achievement, running as it does up hill and down dale, through a tunnel, along the top of a wall, cut into trenches, and over rivers. The greatest surviving stretch is the bridge that carries it over the River Gard, the **Pont du Gard**, 21km from Nimes, at which Uzès buses stop. Today it is something of a tourist trap, but is nonetheless a supreme piece of engineering, a brilliant combination of function and aesthetics. It made the impressionable Rousseau wish he'd been born Roman.

Three tiers of arches span the river, with the covered water conduit on the top, rendered with a special plaster waterproofed with a paint apparently based on fig juice. Whatever the recipe, it's in need of a powerful descaler to remove the lime deposits of centuries. You can walk across, if the height does not bother you. The whole structure narrows as it rises and is slightly bowed on the upstream side for extra resistance to flooding. A visit was a must for French journeymen masons on their traditional tour of the country, and many of them have left their names and home towns carved on the stone work. You can also see markings left on individual stones in the arches by the original builders, for example *FR S III – frons sinistra*, front side left no. 3.

UZÈS is 17km further on, an attractive old town perched on a hill above the River Alzon, though a bit of a backwater until renovation put it on the tourist circuit. Half a dozen medieval towers – the most fetching the windowed Pisa-like **Tour Fenestrelle**, tacked on to the much later cathedral – rise above its tiled roofs and narrow lanes of Renaissance and neo-Classical houses, the residences of the seventeenth- and eighteenth-century local bourgeoisie, grown rich like their Protestant co-religionists in Nîmes on textiles. From **Le Portalet**, with its view out over the valley, walk past the classical church of **St-Étienne** into the medieval **place aux Herbes**, where there's a Sunday morning market, and up the arcaded **rue de la République**. The Gide family used to live off the square, the young André spending summer vacations with his granny there. To the right of rue de la République the castle of **Le Duché** (daily 9.30am–noon & 2.30–6.30pm), still inhabited by the same family a thousand years on, is dominated by its original keep, the **Tour Bermonde**. Opposite, the courtyard of the eighteenth-century **Hôtel de Ville** holds summer concerts.

For details of these and other summer events, including more bull-running *corridas*, consult the **SI** in av de la Libération next to the **bus station**. Should you need a **bed**, the *Hôtel La Taverne*, 7 rue Xavier-Sigalon (☎66.22.47.08; ③–④), and the *Hostellerie Provençale*, 1 rue Grande-Bourgade (☎66.22.11.06; ③), are the best cheap bets. Alternatively, there is a municipal **campsite** (mid-June to mid-Sept) off av Pascal, the Bagnols-sur-Cèze road.

More Roman ruins... and Sommières

About 25km west of Nîmes, off the Sommières road out of LUNEL and close to the A9 autoroute, the Roman **via Domitia** crosses the vineyards from the village of Gallargues to the bank of the River Vidourle, where one isolated arch of the original **Roman bridge** remains. On the west bank a fine stretch of the old **cobbled way** is visible climbing the slopes of the former Roman settlement of **Ambrussum**, a fortified staging-post on the road. From the top of the hill you look down on the modern international traffic still passing the same way, on the autoroute and parallel rail line. About 10km to the north, 28km from Nîmes, still on the Vidourle, the little medieval town of **SOMMIÈRES**, with a much modified Roman bridge, is where Lawrence Durrell spent the last years of his life. There is nothing special to see: just wander the hilly old streets.

There are three daily buses from Nîmes (one only at weekends – very early), which pass through the village of **NAGES**, where there are the ruins of another Roman town. There is a municipal **campsite** in rue Eugène-Rouch, and a pleasant cheap **hotel**, *Le Commerce*, 15 quai Gaussorgues (☎66.80.97.22; ③), with a restaurant.

Montpellier

A thousand years of trade and intellect have made **MONTPELLIER** a teeming, energetic city. Benjamin of Tudela, the tireless twelfth-century Jewish traveller, reported its streets crowded with traders, Christian and Saracen, Arabs from the Mahgreb, merchants from Lombardy, from the kingdom of Rome, from every corner of Egypt, Greece, Gaul, Spain, Genoa and Pisa. A few hiccups – like being sold to France in 1349, almost total destruction for its Protestantism in 1622, and depression in the wine trade in the early years of this century – have done little to dent this progress, and today it vies with Toulouse and Nîmes for the title of most dynamic city in the south. The reputation of its university especially, founded in the thirteenth century and most famous for its medical school, is a long-standing one, its 50,000 students still setting the intellectual and cultural tone of the city – the average age of which is said to be just twenty-five.

Arrival and accommodation

The **gare SNCF** and **gare routière** are next door to each other at the opposite end of rue Maguelone from the central place de la Comédie. If you're **driving**, don't attempt to enter the city centre: the one-way system is extremely complicated and parking nonexistent. The easiest place to park at the time of writing was south of place de la Comédie, around the new Antigone development. The **airport**, Montpellier-Fréjorgues, is 8km to the southeast beside the Étang de Mauguio. The **SI** is off place de Comédie, in allée du Tourisme down some steps towards the *Sofitel* hotel (daily 9am–7pm), and there's an annexe in the gare SNCF.

Most **hotel** accommodation is conveniently concentrated in the streets between the train station and place de la Comédie. The cheapest and simplest – entirely acceptable despite the price – is *Hôtel des Touristes*, 10 rue Baudin (☎67.58.42.37; ①); the *Central*, nearby on the corner of rue Broussairolles and rue Bruyas (☎67.58.39.28; ②), is also passable if you are looking for something cheap. The other recommended hotels in the area are comfortable and clean, if somewhat lacking in character: best of the bunch are *Le Mistral*, 25 rue Boussairolles (☎67.58.45.25; ④), the *Imperator*, 20 rue Boussairolles (☎67.58.40.97; ④–⑤), and the *Hôtel de la Comédie*, 1 bis rue Baudin (☎67.58.43.64; ⑤), although far the nicest and most central of the hotels is the *Hôtel du Palais*, 3 rue du Palais (☎67.60.47.38; ⑤), off to the right of the top end of av Foch. Two other good hotels, a little further out, are *La Plantade*, 10 rue Plantade (☎67.92.61.45; ②), off rue du Faubourg-du-Courreau, and the *Hôtel du Polygone*, 16 av du Pont-Juvénal (☎67.65.81.41; ④), near L'Antigone. There is a **youth hostel** at 2 impasse de la Petite-Corraterie in the old town (☎67.79.61.66). **Campers** should head towards the coast, to the semi-engulfed suburbs of Lattes and Pérols, in the direction of Palavas, where you'll find *Eden Camping* (June–Sept) and *L'Oasis Palavasienne* on the D986, and *Camping l'Estelle* on the edge of Pérols.

The city

Montpellier's hub, **Place de la Comédie** – *L'Oeuf* to the initiated – is a colossal oblong square, paved with cream-coloured marble, with a fountain in the middle and cafés either side. One end is closed by the **Opéra**, an ornate nineteenth-century thea-

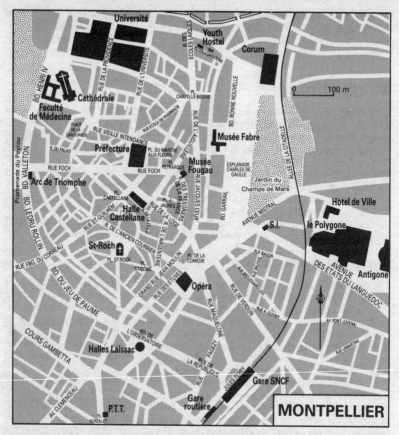

tre; the other opens on to the **Esplanade**, a beautiful tree-lined promenade which ends in the **Corum** concert hall, a sort of robotic bunker-palace in pink granite, with splendid views from the roof. The city's most trumpeted museum, the **Musée Fabre** (daily 9am–5.30pm; closed Mon; free Wed), is close by on bd Sarrail, and contains a large and historically important collection of seventeenth- to nineteenth-century French, Spanish, Italian, Dutch, Flemish and English painting.

From the top side of the *Oeuf*, rue de la Loge and rue Foch, opened in the 1880s in Montpellier's own Haussmannising spree, slice through the heart of the old city. Either side of them, a tangled maze of narrow lanes slopes away to the encircling modern boulevards. Few buildings survive from before the 1622 siege, but the city's busy bourgeoisie quickly made up for the loss, proclaiming their financial power in lots of austere seventeenth- and eighteenth-century mansions. Known as *Lou Clapas* ("the rubble"), the quarter is a curious mix of chic restoration and squalid disorder, a pleasure to wander through – the chic tending to the south side, the lively to the north up rue de l'Aiguillerie.

First left off rue de la Loge, is **Grand-Rue Jean-Moulin**, where Moulin, hero of the Resistance, lived at no. 21. To the left, at no. 32, the present-day Chamber of

Commerce is located in one of the finest eighteenth-century *hôtels*, the **Hôtel St-Côme** (open daily except weekends; free), originally built as a demonstration operating theatre for medical students. On the opposite corner, rue de l'Argenterie forks up to **place Jean-Jaurès**, on which, through the Gothic doorway of no. 10, is the so-called palace of the kings of Aragon, who ruled Montpellier for a stretch in the thirteenth century. With its morning **market** and cafés, the square is a nodal point in the city's commercial life. Close by is the **Halles Castellane**, Montpellier's answer to Paris' famous iron-framed *Halles*.

A short walk from place Jean-Jaurès, the *Hôtel de Varenne* on place Pétrarque houses two local history museums of somewhat specialised interest, the **Musée du Vieux Montpellier** (Mon–Fri 1.30–5pm), concentrating on the city's history, and the more interesting, private **Musée Fougau** (Wed & Thurs 3–6.30pm), dealing with the folk history of Languedoc and things Occitan. Off to the right, the lively little rue des Trésoriers-de-France has one of the best seventeenth-century houses, the *Hôtel Lunaret*, at no. 5 – also the **Musée de la Société Archéologique** (guided tours only Mon, Wed & Fri at 2.30pm).

On the hill at the end of rue Foch, from which the royal artillery bombarded the Protestants in 1622, the formal gardens of the **Promenade du Peyrou** look out across the city and away to the Pic St-Loup, which dominates the hinterland behind Montpellier, with the distant smudge of the Cévennes beyond. At the farther end a swagged and pillared water-tower marks the end of an eighteenth-century aqueduct modelled on the Pont du Gard. Beneath the grand sweep of its double tier of arches there is a huge Saturday **flea market**, which on Sundays moves to Nîmes. At the city end of the promenade, a vainglorious **triumphal arch** shows Louis XIV-Hercules stomping on the Austrian eagle and the English lion, tactlessly reminding the locals of his victory over their Protestant "heresy".

Lower down the hill on bd Henri IV, the **Jardin des Plantes** (May–Oct daily 9am–noon & 2–6pm; Nov–April 8.30am–noon & 2–5pm; closed Sun), lovely but slightly rundown with its alleys of exotic trees, is France's oldest botanical garden, where, in the poet Paul Valéry's words, "the pensive, the careworn and talkers-to-themselves come towards evening". Across the road is the long-suffering **cathedral** with its massive porch, sporting a patchwork of styles from the fourteenth to the nineteenth century. Inside is a memorial to the bishop of Montpellier who sided with the half-million destitute vinegrowers who came to demonstrate against their plight in 1907 and were fired on by government troops for their pains. Above it, on rue de l'École-de-Médecine in the university's prestigious medical school, the **Musée Atger** (Mon–Fri 1.30–4.30pm) has a distinguished academic collection of French and Italian drawings, and the macabre **Musée d'Anatomie** (2.15–5pm; closed weekends) displays all sorts of revolting things in bottles. Close by is the pretty little **place de la Canourgue**, and, beyond, down rue d'Aigrefeuille, the old university quarter, with some good **bookshops** on rue de l'Université. .

L'Antigone

South of place de la Comédie stretches the controversial and still not complete quarter of **L'Antigone**, a chain of post-modern squares and open spaces designed to provide a mix of fair-rent housing and offices, aligned along a monumental axis from the place du Nombre-d'Or, through place du Millénaire, to the glassed-in arch of the Hôtel de la Région. It's more interesting in scale and design than most attempts at urban renewal. The enclosed spaces in particular work well, with their theatrical references to classical architecture, like oversized cornices and columns supporting only sky. The more open spaces are, however, disturbing: there is something totalitarian and inhuman about their scale and blandness.

Eating and drinking

For something quick and uncomplicated to **eat** you need look no further than place de la Comédie. For something more interesting, there are various alternatives. One of the cheapest and best is *Le Petit Landais*, 14 rue du Palais, with menus from 45F. Others include the *Pizzeria La Provençale*, 7 rue de l'École-de-Pharmacie (closed Mon & Tues), *Chez Marceau* and the slightly more expensive *Le Vieil Écu* in the beautiful little pl de la Chapelle-Neuve, and a nameless local restaurant at 7 rue Lamartine (menus at 45F), off av du Pont-Juvénal. More upmarket and well regarded is *Le Ménestrel* (menu at 120F; closed Sun & Mon) in the tiny and easily missed impasse Perrier opposite the *Préfecture* on av Foch. Other good, more expensive restaurants include *Le Louvre*, 2 rue de la Vieille (120F; closed Sun & Mon), by the *Halles Castellane*; the Indian *Le Kachemire* in the same street (110F), which has vegetarian alternatives, and *Le Janus* at 11 rue Aristide-Olivier(110F upwards; closed Sun & Mon pm), near the station.

As for **drinking**, there is always plenty of activity in p de la Comédie, pl du Marché-aux-Fleurs, pl Castellane and pl St-Côme – and, gradually coming to life, the brand new place du Millénaire in L'Antigone. *Melody sur Place* by the cathedral and the *Brasserie des Facultés* on bd Henri IV, near the medical school, are well-populated student haunts. **By night** the *Irish Tavern*, 13 rue de Lunaret, is the most crowded, smoky young hangout in town. *Arts et Buffet* on pl St-Roch is a delightful gallery-cum-bar; *Le Movida*, 2bis rue Legendre-Hérail (closed Sun) hosts exhibitions and live music of the rock and blues variety. *La Pleine Lune*, 23 rue du Faubourg-de-Figuerolles (5pm–1am) is the pl for beer, as is the *Vert Anglais* on pl Castellane. The *Summertime Café* at 98 av du Pont-Juvénal (closed Sun) is fashionable for its cocktails and live jazz, while the old perennial for rock, jazz and everything is the *Rockstore* at 20 rue de Verdun. This has discos 10pm–4am, rock concerts Mondays & Fridays (free admission 10–11pm), and jazz on Sunday, with free admission all night.

Listings

Bikes Free bikes are available from *Vélos pour Tous* in the Esplanade de-Gaulle, but you have to leave a deposit of 800F. Summer daily 9am–9pm, winter daily 10am–5pm.

Buses Urban and district, including Palavas and the seaside, leave from 23bis rue Maguelone.

CROUS Service for foreign students, 11 rue Baudin (Mon–Fri 9–11.30am & 1–4.30pm).

Doctors *SAMU* (☎67.33.78.95); *SOS Médecins*, 148 rue Marius-Carrieu (☎67.45.62.45).

Festivals Montpellier is renowned for its cultural life, and hosts a number of annual festivals. *Le Printemps des Comédiens* (mid-June to mid-July) is a theatre festival; *Montpellier Danse*, from end June to mid-July, is a festival of dance. There's also the music festival, *Le Festival de Radio-France et de Montpellier*, held in the second half of July, and the *Festival du Cinéma méditerranéen*, in the second half of September. The SI will provide information about programmes and booking.

Markets The best central food markets are *Halles Castellane* on rue de la Loge and the open-air one on pl Jean-Jaurès.

Post Office The main office is on pl Rondelet.

Shopping The most convenient place is the *Polygone* mall, with a *FNAC* and *Galeries Lafayette*.

Swimming The nearest beaches for a dip are at Palavas, the best slightly to the west of the town.

What's on Free listings mags: *Montpellier Votre Ville* (monthly) and *Edito* (weekly).

The Coast: Aigues-Mortes to Agde

On the face of it the **Languedoc coast** isn't particularly enticing, the beaches bleak and treeless strands, often irritatingly windswept and cut off from their hinterland by marshy *étangs*. But the area does have long hours of sunshine, 200km of sand still only sporadically populated, and relatively unpolluted water. This could change, as for the last couple of decades the French government has poured money into this area at an amazing rate, building seven new resorts in twice as many years. But for the moment, as long as you steer well clear of the new towns – ugly, soulless places for the most part, anyway – deserted beaches are still there for the walking.

First built of the new resorts, on the fringes of the Camargue, **LA GRANDE-MOTTE** is an extravagant futuristic vision of concrete and glass pyramids and cones ranged around a broad sandy beach. In summer its seaside and streets are crowded with semi-naked bodies; in winter, it's a depressing, wind-battered place with few permanent residents.

A little way east are **PORT-CAMARGUE**, with a sparkling new marina, and **GRAU-DU-ROI**, the second of which manages to retain something of its character as a working fishing port. Tourist traffic still has to give way every afternoon at 4.30pm when the swing bridge opens to let in the trawlers to unload the day's catch on to the quayside, whence it is whisked off to auction – *la criée*, conducted today largely by electronic means rather the harsh-voiced shouting of former times. For a reasonable **place to stay**, try the *Hôtel du Quai d'Azur* on rue du Vidourle near the harbour entrance (☎66.53.41.94; ③).

Eight kilometres inland lies the appealingly named town of **AIGUES-MORTES**, built as a fortress port by Louis IX in the thirteenth century for his departure on the Seventh Crusade. Its massive walls and towers remain virtually intact. Outside the walls, amid drab modern development, flat salt pans lend a certain other-worldly appeal, but inside all is geared to the tourist. If you visit, climb up the **Tour de Constance** on the northwest corner (July to mid-Sept daily 9am–7pm; Oct–March daily 9.30am–noon & 2–4.30pm; April–May daily 9am–noon & 2–5.30pm; June daily 9am–6pm), where Camisard women were imprisoned (Marie Durand was incarcerated for 38 years) and walk the wall, gazing out over the weird mist-shrouded flats of the Camargue.

Palavas and Maguelone

A dozen kilometres by road, **PALAVAS** is the bathing station for the citizens of Montpellier – a concrete sprawl with little to recommend it apart from the presence of the sea, though there is plenty of summertime activity in the discos and the rip-off quayside bars and restaurants. The best place to swim and sunbathe is a little way to the west off the long flat strand that borders the marsh, in the direction of the **cathedral of Maguelone**, where flamingos feed and herons, egrets and other seabirds squabble and dive. The cathedral itself (daily 9am–6pm), dating mainly from the twelfth century, appears in the distance, pale and grey and fortress-like on an island of vines and pines in the middle of the marsh. Cavernous and cool, the strong and simple interior is the venue for a music festival in the second half of June. In the Dark Ages the island served as a base for Arab corsairs until Charles Martel drove them out in 737. Construction of the church began in the mid-tenth century.

Sète

Some 28km southeast of Montpellier, twenty minutes away by train, **SÈTE** has been an important port for three hundred years. The upper part of the town straddles the slopes of the Mont St-Clair, which overlooks the vast Bassin de Thau, breeding ground of mussels and oysters, while the lower part is intersected by waterways lined with tall terraces and seafood restaurants. It has a lively workaday bustle in addition to its tourist activity, at its height during the summer *joutes nautiques*.

The pedestrian streets, crowded and vibrant, are scattered with café tables. Climb up from the harbour to the **Cimetière marin**, the sailors' cemetery, where the poet Paul Valéry is buried. A native of the town, he called Sète his "singular island", and the **Musée Valéry** in rue Denoyer (summer daily 10am–noon & 2–6pm; winter closed Tues), opposite the cemetery, has a room devoted to him, as well as a small but strong collection of modern French paintings. Georges Brassens has a room to himself, too.

Singer-songwriter, an associate of Sartre, and the radical voice of a whole generation in France, **Brassens** was also born and raised in Sète and is buried in the Cimetière le Py on the other side of the hill in spite his song, "Plea to be buried on the beach at Sète".

> *My family tomb*
> *alas, is not that new.*
> *To be blunt, it's chock-a-block.*
> *If I wait for someone to move out,*
> *It'll be too late; and I can't*
> *Say to these good folk, 'Budge up a bit,*
> *make way for the young.*

If you're feeling energetic, you should keep going up the hill through the pines to the top, for the view, if it isn't engulfed in sea mist.

Below the sailors' cemetery, couched neatly above the water, is Vauban's **Fort St-Pierre**, which hosts a Brassens festival in mid-June. On the subject of **festivals**, the *joutes nautiques* are always spectacular: water jousting contests, and highly virile events, unchanged for three hundred years, in which young men in rival boats try to knock each other into the canal with long lances to the accompaniment of music and lots of drinking. They take place throughout the summer, though August 25 is the high point.

Practicalities

The **gare routière** is awkwardly placed on quai de la République, and the **gare SNCF** further out still on quai Midi-Nord – though it is on the main bus route which circles Mont St-Clair (last bus about 7pm). The **SI** has a central office at 60 Grand'Rue Mario-Roustan, a summer desk at the **gare SNCF** and a main office on quai d'Alger, opposite the **ferry port** for boats to Morocco and the Balearic islands.

For **accommodation,** there is a new annexe to what used to be a grotty old **youth hostel** (☎67.53.46.68) high up in the town on rue Général-Revest. Otherwise the chances of a cheap room are not very good. *Hôtel Le Family* at 28 quai Lattre-de-Tassigny (☎67.74.05.03; ③), or *Hôtel P'tit Mousse* on rue de Provence (☎67.53.10.66; ②) are worth a try. **Campers** should ask the SI for details of the numerous campsites in the area. When leaving, keep in mind that **hitching out** is horribly difficult: you're better off taking a train or bus to the nearest town and trying from there.

Agde

Midway between Béziers and Sète at the western end of the Bassin de Thau, **AGDE** is historically the most interesting of the coastal towns. Originally Greek, and maintained by the Romans, it thrived for centuries on trade with the Levant. Outrun as a seaport by Sète, it later degenerated into a sleazy fishing harbour.

Today, it is a major tourist centre with a good deal of charm, notably in the narrow back lanes between rue de l'Amour and the riverside where the fishing boats tie up. But it has few sights apart from its heavily battlemented **cathedral**. The town's most distinctive and surprising feature is its colour – black – from the volcanic stone of the Mont St-Loup quarries which built it. The waterfront is attractive, and by the bridge the Canal du Midi slips quietly and modestly into the Hérault on the very last leg of its journey from Toulouse to the Bassin de Thau and Séte.

Hotel rooms are expensive, but if the budget is healthy, the *Donjon* on pl Jean-Jaurès (☎67.94.12.32; ④) and *Les Arcades* at 16 rue Louis-Bages (☎67.94.11.66; ③–④) are comfortable and close to the river. If you're **camping**, it's best to seek guidance from the **SI** in place Molière near the bridge. **Places to eat** are numerous. The most convenient area to look is in La Promenade. Two specific restaurants to try are the *Orient Express* at 8 rue Jean-Roger and the *Clara Belle* at 11 rue André-Chassefière.

To get down to the sea at Cap d'Agde, there is a half-hourly bus service, which you can pick up at the **gare SNCF** at the end of av Victor-Hugo, at the bridge and in La Promenade. To explore the **Canal du Midi**, there are boat trips from 7 quai du Chapitre (*Bateaux du Soleil*). Alternatively you could walk or cycle the tow path (bike hire is available from the gare SNCF).

Cap d'Agde

CAP D'AGDE, 7km from Agde, lies to the south of Mont St-Loup. The largest and by far the most successful of the new resorts, it sprawls laterally from the volcanic mound of St-Loup in an excess of pseudo-traditional modern buildings, that offer every type of facility and entertainment – all expensive. It is perhaps best known for its colossal **quartier naturiste**, one of the largest in France, with the best of the beaches, space for 20,000 visitors, and its own restaurants, banks, post offices and shops. Access is possible, though expensive, if you're not actually staying there. But if you want to get inside for free, you can simply walk along the beach from neighbouring MARSEILLAN-PLAGE, and remove tell-tale fabrics en route.

If you have time to fill, the unattractively named **Musée de la Clape** (April–Sept daily 9am–noon & 2–7pm; winter daily 9am–noon & 3–6pm, closed Mon) displays antiquities discovered locally, many of them from beneath the sea. It's worth a visit for the beautiful little Hellenistic bronze known as the **Ephèbe d'Agde**, until recently one of the treasures of the Louvre in Paris.

Inland from Montpellier

For getting out into the country of the Bas Languedoc, there are two good routes from Montpellier, both served by regular buses: the D986 to GANGES and the N109 to LODÈVE.

The Ganges route

The Ganges road weaves north across the plateau of the *garrigue*, a landscape of scrubby trees, thorns and hot-smelling herbs cut by torrent beds. The distance is dominated by the high limestone ridge of the **Pic St-Loup** until you reach the first worthwhile stopping place, **ST-MARTIN-DE-LONDRES,** 25km on, whose name derives from the Occitan word, *loundres* – otters. It's a lovely little place of arcaded houses and cobbled passageways, set around the roadside place de la Fontaine, where the **SI** is housed in a round tower. Its pride is an exceptionally handsome early Romanesque church, reached through a vaulted passage just uphill from the square. The honey-coloured stone is simply decorated with Lombard arcading, the plain rounded porch with a worn relief of St-Martin on horseback, while the interior has an unusual clover-shaped ground plan. There's a **campsite** just out on the Pic St-Loup road, and the *Hôtel des Touristes* on the main road through the village (☎67.55.70.95; ③).

About 6km south, off the Gignac road near VIOLS-LE-FORT (on the bus route) and the Château de Cambous, there is a marvellous **prehistoric village** dating from 2000 BC and only discovered in 1967 (July–Aug daily 2–7pm; rest of year Sun & hols 2–6pm). The ground is incredibly rocky and densely covered with oak scrub. The site consists of a group of cabins, each about twenty metres long, their outlines clearly delineated, with the holes for the roof supports and the door slabs still in place. A reconstruction shows them to have been much like the sheep stalls in the old *bergeries* that dot the *causse*.

Further north, almost as far as Ganges, through dramatic river gorges, you reach the **Grotte des Demoiselles** (April–Sept daily 8.30am–noon & 2–7pm; rest of year daily 9.30am–noon & 2–5pm), most spectacular of the region's many caves: a set of vast cathedral-like caverns hung with stalactites descending with millenial slowness to meet the limpid waters of eerily still pools. Deep inside the mountain, it is reached by funicular (regular departures).

GANGES itself, 46km from Montpellier and also connected by regular buses, which continue to LE VIGAN on the southern edge of the Cévennes, is an attractive and busy market town (Friday's the day) of small squares, tree-lined walks and vaulted alleys designed for defence in the Wars of Religion – it, too, was a Protestant town, peopled by refugees from the plains, who made it famous for its silk stockings. It was here, too, that the last-ditch revolt of the Camisards earned its name. The rebels sacked and pillaged a shirt factory and went off wearing the shirts – *chemises/camises*.

For a **place to stay**, try *Hôtel de la Poste*, plan de l'Ormeau (☎67.73.85.88; ③), or *Hôtel Aux Caves de l'Hérault*, on av Jeu-de-Ballon (③), both in the town centre near the market. The **SI is** on plan de l'Ormeau.

The Gignac route

The second inland route runs west to the small town of **GIGNAC**, 30km from Montpellier, amid vineyards where a fine eighteenth-century bridge spans the Hérault. With its *Hôtel du Commerce* at 1 bd Pasteur (☎67.57.50.97; ③), and *Camping Le Pont*, it makes a viable stopover, especially if you're on your way to or from the glorious abbey and village of **ST-GUILHEM-LE-DÉSERT**, 16km north.

Hitching, it's best to go through ANIANE (with the imposing classical church of St-Sauveur) and across the eleventh-century **Pont du Diable**, supposedly the earliest medieval bridge in the country, where children used to dive into the pool beneath until it was banned. The narrowest part of the Hérault gorge begins here. St-Guilhem is in a side ravine 6km on. With a ruined **castle** spiking the ridge above, the ancient tiled houses of the village ramble down the banks of the rushing Verdus, everywhere channelled into carefully tended gardens. The grand focus is the tenth- to eleventh-century **abbey** on place de la Liberté, founded at the beginning of the ninth century by St-Guilhem, comrade-in-arms of Charlemagne and scourge of the Saracens. It is a beautiful and atmospheric place, though architecturally impoverished by the dismantling and sale of its cloister – now in New York – in the nineteenth century. It stands on place de la Liberté, surrounded by honey-coloured houses and arcades with traces of Romanesque and Renaissance domestic styles in some of the windows .The interior of the church is plain and somewhat severe compared to the warm colours of the exterior, best seen from rue Cor-de-Nostra-Dama/ Font-du-Portal, where you get the classic view of the perfect apse.

There are a couple of easy and worthwhile **walks** you can make from here – up the valley of the Verdus into the red-stained walls of the **Cirque du Bout-du-Monde** (from place de la Liberté, take rue du Bout-du-Monde out of the village and continue for about half an hour), or up the zigzagging path of the **GR74** through the sweet-scented shrubs and flowers towards the castle ridge (also about half an hour). From the crest of the ridge the view down on to the village is magnificent. The path divides here: one branch leads back right to the ruins of the castle, while the other continues along the GR74 to the **Ermitage Notre-Dame-de-Belle-Grâce** (90min), and on, if you so wish, to join the GR7 at St-Maurice-Navacelles on the Causse de Larzac.

In season the village is on every tour operator's route, making early mornings and late afternoons the best times for visiting. An **overnight stay** is possible at the *Hôtel Fonzes* on the main road (☎67.57.72.01; ③; closed Dec–Feb), or at *Camping Moulin de Siau* (mid-June to mid-Sept). Three kilometres back down the road, cave enthusiasts will enjoy the **Grotte de Clamouse** (April–Nov 15 open daily; rest of year Sun and hols).

Clermont-l'Hérault and around

Eight kilometres west of Gignac **CLERMONT-L'HÉRAULT** – accessible by bus from Montpellier – is the principal market town of the area and a major producer of grapes for the table. The most interesting quarter to explore is between the huge Gothic **cathedral**, fortified in 1351 for protection against English raiders, and the ruined château on the hill above. From the plane-shaded **place de la République** outside the cathedral, follow the back streets, passage des Jacobins, rue de la Fontaine-de-la-Ville, rue Barbès, then right past the church of Notre-Dame-de-Gorjan, uphill to the steps that lead to the **château**. Tumbledown and overgrown it affords a fantastic view of the surrounding country – a good place to picnic.

For a **place to stay**, try *Hôtel La Ramasse* on pl des Martyrs (☎67.96.02.68; ③) or the *Grand Hôtel* at 2 rue Coutellerie (☎67.96.00.04; ④). If you're **camping**, there's a local site, *Le Salagou*. For a reasonable **meal**, there's the *Restaurant des Remparts* at 3 rue Louis-Blanc.The **SI** is at 9 rue René-Gosse close to the cathedral.

Nearby, though not really worth the trouble without a car, is the cramped medieval village of **MOURÈZE**, set in the weirdly eroded landscape of the **Cirque de Mourèze**. Nearer – only 3km – on the main road to Bédarieux, and far more interesting, is **VILLENEUVETTE**, a model factory and workers' settlement created in the seventeenth century for the production of woollen cloth and subsidised by the royal government under Colbert's policy of trying to break the industrial supremacy of the Dutch and English. Although the last production ceased in 1954, the handsome buildings are still intact and partly inhabited. There is also a very nice, if somewhat pricey, **hotel** adjoining – *La Source* (67.96.05.07; ⑤), with a good restaurant and garden.

Three other interesting and little-visited places east of Clermont are only feasible if you have a car. The first is a very fine **dolmen** like a miniature version of Agamemnon's tomb at Mycenae on the end of a low ridge overlooking the D32 – best reached from the village of **LE POUGET**, where it is signposted. Continuing along the D139, you come within sight of the pale grey ruins of the keep and chapel of the **Château d'Aumelas** romantically silhouetted on the edge of the plateau of the *causse*. To reach it by road – considerably further – you need to bear right on to the D114 and then take a dirt track opposite a farm. It's a beautiful and silent place, and the chapel is in near perfect condition. By curious historical chance, the property is connected with the English crown.

Two kilometres further along the D114, down an unsigned and bumpy track leading right on to the *causse*, there is a marvellous and remote silvery chapel, **St-Martin-de-Cardonnet**, built in the twelfth century – all that remains of an ancient priory.

On to Lodève

Heading north from Clermont to **LODÈVE,** 19km away, the road passes country scarred by uranium mining – the area around the village of **ST-MARTIN-DU-BOSC** has some of the highest soil concentration of radioactivity in the world. **LODÈVE**, entirely enclosed by vine-terraced hills at the confluence of the Lergues and Soulondres rivers, is almost in the shadow of the Causse de Larzac. The **cathedral** is worth a look, as is the unusual World War I **Monument aux morts** in the adjacent park by the local artist, **Paul Dardé** – more of whose work is on display in the unmemorable **town museum** in the Hôtel Fleury.

There are really no sights, but Lodève is a pleasant old-fashioned place to pause on your way up to Le Caylar or La Couvertoirade on the Causse. The hub of life is **Grand-Rue** and **rue de la République**, where the cafés and restaurants are. A good **place to stay** is the *Hôtel du Nord* at 18 bd de la Liberté (☎67.44.10.08; ④), with a good restaurant from 60F. There is a big Saturday market for food shopping. The **SI** is at 7 place de la République, next door to the **gare routière**, where you can catch buses to Montpellier, Béziers, Millau, Rodez and St-Affrique.

FROM BÉZIERS TO THE HILLS

The southern portion of Languedoc cuts a slender triangle west, its watery coastal flats rising to low undulating hills as you move inland. Though the coast is not generally noteworthy, **Narbonne** and **Béziers** are enjoyable diversions on the way to the more refreshing and spectacular upland delights of the **Monts de l'Espinouse** and the **Parc Naturel Régional du Haut Languedoc**. Transport can be difficult, but a patient hitchhiker with an eye for scenery can get about without much hassle.

Béziers and around

Though no longer the rich city of its nineteenth-century heyday, **BÉZIERS**, birthplace of Resistance hero Jean Moulin, is still the capital of the Languedoc wine country and a focus for the Occitan movement. The fortunes of the movement and the vine have long been closely linked; Occitan activists have helped to organise the militant local vine-growers, and there were ugly events during the mid-Seventies, when blood was shed in violent confrontations with the authorities over the importation of cheap foreign wines and the low prices paid for the essentially poor-grade local product. Things are calmer now, as the conservatism of Languedoc farmers has given way to more modern attitudes in the face of public demand for something better than the traditional table wine. As a result, some of the steam has also gone out of the movement; interest today is more in the culture than in anti-Paris separatist feelings.

Practicalities

If you arrive at the **gare SNCF** on bd Verdun, the best way into town is through the Plateau des Poètes opposite the station entrance and up the allées Paul-Riquet. Halfway along on the left is place Jean-Jaurès, where you'll find the **gare routière**. The **SI** is at the end of the next street on the left, at 27 rue du 4-septembre (summer daily 9am–7pm; rest of year daily 9am–noon & 2–6.30pm).

For a **place to stay**, try the *Angleterre* at 22 pl Jean-Jaurès (☎67.28.48.42; ③), *La Dorade* at 10 rue Nougaret (☎67.49.35.39; ②–③), or – rather better – the *Hôtel des Poètes*, 80 allées P–Riquet (☎67.76.38.66; ④). There's a municipal **campsite**, though open in July and August only.

Béziers has one of the star **rugby** clubs in France. Its HQ, for *aficionados*, is at 6 places des Trois–Six. **Bullfighting** is also big in Béziers with the main *feria* on August 15. The principal cultural activity is a **music festival** in the second half of July. For more information on the Occitan movement, call in at the **Centre International de Documentation Occitane** at 7 rue Rouget-de-l'Isle (9am–noon & 2–6pm Mon–Fri).

The city

The finest view of the old town is from the west, as you come in from Carcassonne or the *Béziers-ouest* exit from the A9. Crossing the willow-lined River Orb by the Pont-Neuf, you look upstream at the sturdy arches of the **Pont-Vieux**, with the cathedral of **St-**

Nazaire crowning the steep-banked hill above – more like a castle than a church, with its crenellated towers silhouetted against the blue line of mountains behind. The best approach is up the medieval lanes at the end of Pont-Vieux, rue Canterelle and passage Canterellettes. The surviving building is mainly Gothic, the original having been burnt in 1209 during the sack of Béziers, when Simon de Montfort's crusaders massacred some five thousand people at the Église de la Madeleine for refusing to hand over about twenty Cathars. It's an atrocity Béziers has never forgotten or forgiven.

From the top of the cathedral **tower,** there's a superb view out across the vine-dominated surrounding landscape. Next door, you can wander through the ancient cloister (daily 9.30am–noon & 2–6pm) and out into the shady **bishop's garden** overlooking the river. In the adjacent **place de la Révolution**, where a brasserie deploys its tables under the trees, a monument commemorates the people who died resisting Napoléon III's coup d'état in 1851, and their leader, Mayor Casimir Péret, who was shipped off to Cayenne where he drowned in a Papillon-style escape attempt. Also on the square, the Hôtel Fabrégat houses a **Musée des Beaux-Arts** (Tues–Sat 9am–noon & 2–6pm, Sun 2–6pm), which, apart from an interesting collection of Greek Cycladic vases, won't keep you long.

The city's other museum, the **Musée du Biterrois** in the old St-Jacques barracks on av de la Marne near the train station (Tues–Sat 9am–noon & 2–6pm, Sun 2–6pm) displays a variety of entertaining exhibits, ranging from Greek amphorae and nineteenth-century door-knockers to distilling manuals, clogs and wine-presses. Away from the medieval streets round the cathedral, the centre of life in Béziers is the **allées Paul-Riquet**, a broad, leafy esplanade lined with cafés, *crêpes* stalls, restaurants, banks and shops, named after the seventeenth-century tax-collector who lost health and fortune in his obsession with building the **Canal du Midi** to join the Atlantic and the Mediterranean. Laid out in the last century, the allées run from an elaborate nineteenth-century theatre on place de la Victoire to the gorgeous little park of the **Plateau des Poètes**, with its ponds and palms and lime trees designed in the so-called English manner by the man who created the Bois de Boulogne in Paris.

Around Béziers: Pézenas

PÉZENAS lies 18km east on the old N9. Market centre of the coastal plain, it looks across to rice fields and shallow lagoons, hazy with heat and dotted with pink flamingos. Despite its size, local tourist pamphlets have dubbed it the Versailles of Languedoc – a reference to its long-standing political importance as the seat of the provincial *États-généraux* for Bas Languedoc. It has, however, retained the air of a gentrified resort, with its seventeenth-century centre, the **vieille ville**, carefully protected from development.

The town also plays up its association with **Molière**, who visited several times with his troupe in the mid-seventeenth century, when he enjoyed the protection of the local Conti lords. He put on his own plays at the **Hôtel Alphonse** on rue Conti, which now has an ice-cream parlour in its coach-house. When in town, he lodged at the **Maison du Barbier-Gély** in the unspoiled **place Gambetta**, today occupied by the **SI**. Although he figures prominently in the **Musée Vulliod St-Germain** (July–Aug daily 10am–noon & 3–6pm; rest of year daily except Tues, Wed & Thurs 10am–noon & 3–5pm, closed Tues), housed in an eighteenth-century palace just off the square, it does not fully convince with its recreated interiors and seventeenth- and eighteenth-century paintings.

The SI sells a guide to all the town's eminent houses, but you can just as easily follow the explanatory plaques posted all over the centre. Included in the route is the former **Jewish ghetto** on rue des Litanies and rue Juiverie. **Place de la République** is the location of an enormous Saturday **market**, and it's also the place to take a bus to Montpellier, Béziers or Agde. For **somewhere to eat**, try looking on place du 14-juillet, a five-minute walk away.

Narbonne and around

On the Toulouse–Nice main rail line, 25km west of Béziers, **NARBONNE** was the capital of Rome's first colony in Gaul, *Gallia Narbonensis*, and a thriving port and communications centre in classical times and again in the Middle Ages. Plague, war with the English and the silting-up of its harbour, finished it off in the fourteenth century. Today, despite the ominous presence of the Malvesi nuclear power plant just 5km out of town, it's a pleasant provincial city of tree-lined walks and esplanades converging on graceful squares.

In the summer of 1991 it acquired notoriety as a new flashpoint in France's continuing problems with its ethnic minorities, but with a difference. This time a long-suffering and long-forgotten minority forced itself on public attention. Among its mixed population of relative newcomers – fugitive Spanish Republicans, returning French settlers from Algeria and Algerian migrant workers – Narbonne has for thirty-odd years been home to a group of **Harkis**, Algerians who had enlisted in the French forces and fought with them against their own people in the Algerian war of independence in the late Fifties. After the war they were settled in France for their own protection, and since then have received little or no help. This summer's unrest was the protest of their children, angry at finding themselves still last in the pecking order in spite of their parents' sacrifice.

Practicalities

The **gare routière** is on the canal-side quai Victor-Hugo and the **gare SNCF** on the north side of town at the end of av Pierre-Sémard. If you want to head straight to the **SI**, it's in place Salengro next to the cathedral.

The best budget **accommodation** is the modern and friendly *MJC Centre International de Séjour* in pl Salengro (☎68.32.01.00) or, from May to September only, the *Foyer des Jeunes Travailleurs Le Capitole*, at 45 av de Provence (☎68.32.07.15). For a couple of reasonable **hotels**, try the *Hôtel du Lion-d'Or*, 39 av Pierre-Sémard (☎68.32.06.92; ⑤), which has a good restaurant, or the cheaper *Hôtel de la Gare*, 7 av Sémard (☎68.32.10.54; ②), and *Hôtel Novelty*, 33 av des Pyrénées (☎68.42.24.28; ②). The nearest **campsite** is the *Languedoc* on chemin de Cresseil, off av de la Mer on the south side of town not far from the *Narbonne–est* exit off the A9.

The city

The only surviving legacy of Rome in Narbonne is the **horreum** at the north end of rue Rouget-de-l'Isle (June–Oct daily 10–11.50am & 2–6pm; Nov–May closes at 5pm), an unusual and interesting site, consisting of two 'streets' lined with small cubby-hole shops. Well preserved though now entirely underground, it was used to store grain and other produce. At the opposite end of the same street, close to the attractive tree-lined banks of the **Canal de la Robine**, which bisects the town, is Narbonne's other principal attraction, the enormous Gothic cathedral of **St-Just-et-St-Sauveur**. With the Palais des Archévêques and its 40-metre keep, it forms a massive pile of masonry that completely dominates the restored lanes of the old town, and – like the cathedral of Béziers – can be seen for miles around. In spite of its size, it is actually only the choir of a much more ambitious church, whose construction was halted to avoid weakening the city walls. The immensely tall interior has some beautiful fourteenth-century stained glass in the chapels on the northeast side of the apse and imposing Aubusson tapestries. The high north tower is open for a panoramic view of the surrounding vineyards.

The adjacent **place de l'Hôtel-de-Ville** is dominated by the great towers of St-Martial, the Madeleine and Bishop Aycelin's keep. From there the passage de l'Ancre leads through to the **archbishop's palace**, housing a tedious **museum of art** (daily 10am–11.50am & 2–6pm in summer; winter closed Mon, and open until 5pm) but a good **archaeology museum** (same hours) with interesting Roman remains, including a milestone from the *via Domitia* bearing the name of Domitius Ahenobarbus – vital to the dating of the construction of the road.

If you're going across into the southern part of the town, beyond the bisecting **Canal de la Robine** and the built-over Pont des Marchands, the small palaeo-Christian crypt of the church of **St-Paul**, off rue de l'Hôtel-Dieu (daily 10am–noon & 2–6pm) is worth a quick look, and perhaps the eerily empty deconsecrated church of **Notre-Dame-de-la-Mourgié** (10am–noon & 2–6pm in summer; till 5pm in winter), though the jumbled Roman stones of the **Musée Lapidaire** it houses aren't very exciting.

Around Narbonne: Fontfroide

For a side trip from Narbonne – only 15km, but nigh impossible without transport of your own – the lovely abbey of **FONTFROIDE** enjoys a beautiful location, tucked into a fold in the dry cypress-clad hillsides. The extant buildings go back to the twelfth century, with some elegant seventeenth-century additions in the entrance and court-yards, and were in use from their foundation in the eleventh century until 1900, first by Benedictines, then Cistercians. It was one of their monks, Pierre de Castelnau, whose murder as papal legate set off the Albigensian Crusade against the Cathars in 1208.

Visits are only possible with a guide (mid-June to mid-Sept daily 9.30am–noon & 2–5.30pm every 30min; mid-March to mid-June & mid-Sept to mid-Nov daily 9.45am–noon & 2–5pm every 45 min; mid-Nov to mid-March Sat & Sun 10am–noon & 2–5pm). Star features are the cloister with its marble pillars and giant wisteria, the church itself, some fine iron work, and the rose garden. The stained glass in the windows of the lay broth-ers' dormitory are fragments from churches in eastern France damaged in World War I. Incidentally, if you do have transport, the **D611** is a beautiful route south into the Corbières (see p.565).

The coast: Valras to Gruissan

The coast close to Beziers and Narbonne enjoys the same attributes – and problems – as the rest of the Languedoc shoreline: fantastic sand but not a stitch of shade, and endless tacky development buffetted by a wind that would flay the shell off a tortoise.

For a quick escape from Béziers, you can take a twenty-minute bus ride across the flat vine-covered coastal plain to **VALRAS** at the mouth of the River Orb, whose old-fashioned family resort status is still just discernible. Further south, ST-PIERRE and NARBONNE-PLAGE (reachable by bus from Narbonnne) are horrible, and the only redeeming feature of this stretch of coast is the mini-landscape of the **Montagne de la Clape**, a former island, pine-covered and craggy, and not more than 200m above sea level in spite of its name. At its further end the fishing village of **GRUISSAN**, 13km from Narbonne (there are buses), built in concentric rings around the hub of the Tour Barberousse, is the only real place of character left, and it, too, is under assault by the developers. Out along the beach is a section of houses originally built on stilts to keep them clear of the sea, but since the danger of flooding has receded many have now added ground floors.

The one really worthwhile thing to do is go up to the **Chapelle Notre-Dame-des-Auzils** about 4km up a winding lane on to the Montagne – a quiet and beautiful spot in the pine woods, highly atmospheric. From the road a path climbs up to the ridge where the chapel stands. All along it are ranged moving **memorials** to the people of Gruissan lost at sea in merchantmen, trawlers and warships, from Haiti to the Greek island of Skiros. The inside of the chapel is full of ex-votos offered by grateful seamen and their families, many of them now painted on to the walls, the originals having been stolen in the Sixties.

The Parc Naturel Régional du Haut Languedoc

Embracing Mont Caroux in the east and the Montagne Noire in the west, the **Parc Naturel Régional du Haut Languedoc** is the southernmost extension of the Massif Central. The west, above Castres and Mazamet, is Atlantic in feel and climate, with deciduous forests and lush valleys, while the east is dry, craggy and calcareous. Except in high summer you can have it almost to yourself. Buses serve the **Orb valley** and cross the centre of the park to **La Salvetat** and **Lacaune**, but you really need transport of your own to make the most of it.

Bédarieux to St-Pons: the valley of the Orb and Jaur

Some 34km north of Béziers, the pleasant if unremarkable town of **BÉDARIEUX** lies right on the edge of the park. Served by buses from both Béziers and Montpellier, and by train from Béziers, it makes a good base for entering the park, especially as the service continues on along the Orb and Jaur valleys to St-Pons beneath the southern slopes of the Monts de l'Espinouse.

The best part of town is across the river around **place des Herbes**, where the tall and crumbly old houses are redolent of a rural France long since vanished in more prosperous areas. On the square itself are a couple of extremely old-fashioned shops, one selling excellent fresh sheep's milk cheese, *fromage de brebis* – worth keeping an eye open for anywhere in the park, where sheep are the only creatures that thrive. Also on the square, the *Hôtel Le Central* makes a cheap and atmospheric place to stay (☎67.95.06.76; ③), with a good and inexpensive restaurant. There's a municipal **campsite** on bd Jean-Moulin (mid-June–mid-Sept), and an **SI** at 77 rue Alexandre.

The Orb valley and Mons

Continuing **west**, the road is an easy hitch (if you don't want to wait for the bus) through spectacular scenery, with the peaks of the **Monts de l'Espinouse** rising up to 1000m on your right. The spa town of LAMALOU-LES-BAINS, 8km on, is quite missable, but at the village of COLOMBIÈRES a path leaves the road to take you up into the **Gorges de Madale** where it joins the GR7, which crosses the southern part of the park to Labastide–Rouairoux beyond St-Pons.

A further seven or eight kilometres brings you to **MONS**, where there is a **gîte** (☎67.97.72.80; M. Cabrol), **camping** at *Le Clap* on the D14, and the small *Auberge des Gorges d'Héric* (☎67.97.72.98; ②; closed Sept) – with good-value restaurant by the suspension bridge at Tarassac, 2km away. From the village a road climbs 5km up the dramatic **Gorges d'Héric** to the hamlet of HÉRIC.

Olargues

Shortly after, you reach the medieval village of **OLARGUES** scrambling up the south bank of the Jaur above its thirteenth-century single-span bridge. The steep twisting streets, presumably almost unchanged since the bridge was built, lead up to a thousand-year-old belfry crowning the top of the hill. With the river and gardens below, the ancient and earth-brown farms on the infant slopes of Mont Caroux beyond, and swifts screaming round the tower, you get a powerful sense of age and history.

There's a tiny **SI** on rue de la Place. The *Hôtel Laissac* down near the old station, served only by *SNCF* buses now, has reasonable rooms and a restaurant (☎67.97.70.89; ③) and there's *Camping Le Baous* by the river.

St-Pons-de-Thomières

ST-PONS-DE-THOMIÈRES, 18km further west, is a little larger and noisier: it's on the Béziers–Castres and Béziers–La Salvetat bus routes, as well as the SNCF's

Bédarieux–Mazamet bus route. It is the "capital" of the park, with the **Maison du parc** at 13 rue du Cloître by the cathedral – a strange mix of Romanesque and classical. It also boasts a small, reasonably interesting **Museum of Prehistory** (May–Sept daily 10am–noon & 3–6pm; rest of the year Wed, Sat & Sun 2–5pm). If you need to stay, there are several cheap **hotels** – try *Hôtel Le Somail*, 2 av de Castres (☎67.97.00.12; ③) or ask at the **SI** near the cathedral, and there's also a **gîte d'étape** at *La Ferme Tailhos* (☎67.97.27.62). There's no nearby campsite, however.

North, the D907 leads to LA SALVETAT in the heart of the park.

The uplands of the park

There's no transport, but the prettiest **route into the park** to Mont Caroux and L'Espinouse is the D180 from LE POUJOL-SUR-ORB 2km west of Lamalou-les-Bains. The road winds up through cherry orchards to the village of **COMBES**, where there is a **Bureau des Guides** and a **gîte d'étape** on the GR7 (☎67.95.66.55), and thence through the **Forêt des Écrivains-Combattants**, named after the French writers who died in World War I. Just above the hamlet of ROSIS, the road levels out in a small mountain valley (whose slopes are brilliant yellow with broom in June).

Douch and Héric

A left fork leads to the hamlet of **DOUCH**, beneath the 1091-metre summit of **Le Caroux** – a perfect place where time has really stood still. Half a dozen rough stone houses, inhabited by a handful of elderly residents, cluster tightly together for protection against the elements. There's a **gîte d'étape** and a small **auberge**. In the meadows below nestles a jewel of a church with an ancient cemetery full of graves like iron cots.

The University of Toulouse maintains a research unit here to survey the largest **moufflon** population in France. If you go out early in the morning or just before dark in the evening, there is a good chance of seeing them, and wild boar, too, as they come out to feed. The road provides some good vantage points a little further north round the **Col de l'Ourtigas** and the Pas de la Lauze.

The best short **walk** to do is down the GR7 to the hamlet of **HÉRIC** in the gorge of the same name. The path starts on the left at the end of the road in Douch and follows the telephone line. Once over the col and into the head of the gorge it becomes a beautiful paved mule track looping down through beech and chestnut woods. In the past people lived off the chestnuts, selling them, eating them and making flour from them. It takes about forty minutes to reach the two or three brown stone houses of Héric, inhabited for several generations by the Clavel family (and 90min to climb back up). They run a **gîte** and can provide **food**, too (☎67.97.77.29).

Into the Agout valley

Continuing north from Douch, the road climbs another 12km above deep ravines and long easterly views to the summit of **L'Espinouse**, where the landscape changes from Mediterranean cragginess to marshy moor-like meadow and big conifer plantations, and the road begins to descend west into the valley of the **Agout river**. It runs through tiny **SALVERGUES**, where there's a striking fortress-church, **Cambon**, where the natural woods begin, and postcard-pretty **FRAISSE-SUR-AGOUT** – home to *Camping Le Pioch* and a refuge at the *Maison du Parc* (☎67.97.61.14) – to **LA SALVETAT-SUR-AGOUT**. Situated between the artificial lakes of La Raviège and Laouzas, this is another attractive mountain town built on a hill above the river and half asleep except at holiday time, when it becomes a busy outdoor activities centre. With several **campsites** and the *Hôtel-Restaurant Cros* (☎67.97.60.21; ③; closed Nov–March), it's a convenient stopover for the centre of the park. There's a municipal **campsite** by the sports ground off the D907, and an **SI** in rue de la Poterne at the top of the hill.

Lacaune

Twenty kilometres further north, **LACAUNE** makes another agreeable stopover if you're heading for Castres. Surrounded by rounded wooded heights around the 1000m mark, it, too, is very much a mountain town, one of the centres of Protestant Camisard resistance at the end of the seventeenth century, when its inaccessibility made the region ideal for clandestine worship. There are bus connections most days – not at very convenient times, usually afternoon or very early morning – to Castres, Albi and Bédarieux.

The air is fresh. The town, though somewhat grey in appearance because of the slates and greyish stucco common throughout the region, is cheerful enough. For a **place to stay**, the *Fusiès*, an erstwhile coaching inn opposite the church on rue de la République (☎63.37.02.03; ⑤; closed first half of Jan), offers an old-fashioned classiness and has a restaurant (closed Nov–Jan), while the *Hôtel Calas*, a little way up the hill (☎63.37.03.28; ③; also closed first half of Jan), is simpler and also has a reasonable restaurant (closed Oct–Feb).

From here to Castres the most agreeable route is along the wooded **Gijou valley**, following the now defunct train track, past minuscule Gijounet and **LACAZE**, where a nearly derelict **château** stands picturesquely in a bend of the river and the small *Auberge du Gijou* has a restaurant and three bargain-priced rooms.

CARCASSONNE AND THE CATHAR CASTLES

Sited on the main Toulouse–Montpellier train link, **Carcassonne** couldn't be easier to reach; and for anyone travelling through this region it is a must – one of the most dramatic, if also most visited, towns in the whole of Languedoc.

Carcassonne is also a good historical introduction to the wild and ruinous **Cathar strongholds** to the north and south. These castles and fortified villages were the ultimate refuges of the Cathars, a sect strong in this part of France, who were literally hounded to death, first in the **Albigensian Crusade**, promulgated by the Vatican and launched in 1208 under the leadership of the abbot of Cîteaux, then by the notoriously cruel **Simon de Montfort**, and finally by the king of France. The name derives from the Greek word for clean or pure, *katharos*. The Cathars believed in the simple and humble Christianity of the Sermon on the Mount. They abhorred the materialism and worldly power of the established Church. Their clergy or *parfaits* renounced the physical world as inherently evil, the creation of the Devil. Though they saw themselves as good Christians, in the eyes of Rome they were abominable heretics – not least because among their adherents (probably never acounting for more than ten percent of the population) were many members of the nobility and the influential classes.

Cathars who were caught were burned in communal conflagrations, a hundred or two hundred at a time. Their lands were laid waste or seized by northern barons, de Montfort himself grabbing the properties of the count of Toulouse. The effect of this brutality was to unite Catholic and Cathar in southern solidarity against the barbarian north. Though military defeat became irreversible with the capitulation of Toulouse in 1229 and the fall of the castle of Montségur in 1244, it took the informers and torturers of the Holy Inquisition another seventy years to root them out completely.

If you're interested, the *Centre National d'Études Cathares* (☎68.77.10.21) in the Château Villegly, at CONQUES-SUR-ORBIEL, 8km northeast of Carcassonne is the place to contact for more information.

Carcassonne

CARCASSONNE owes its division into two separate "towns", the Cité and the Ville Basse, to the wars against the Cathars. Following Simon de Montfort's capture of the town in 1209, its people tried in 1240 to restore their traditional ruling family, the Trencavels. In reprisal King Louis IX expelled them, only permitting their return on condition they built on the low ground by the River Aude.

Arrival and practicalities

Encircling the old town walls of the **Ville Basse** are the modern boulevards – the main traffic thoroughfares. It is easy to find your way about within them for the old town is built on the traditional *bastide* grid pattern. For the medieval **Cité**, unmistakeable on its rocky bluff to the southeast, cross the river by the Pont-Vieux.

Arriving by train, you'll find yourself in the **Ville Basse** on the north bank of the Canal du Midi at the northern limits of the town. You can hire **bicycles** from the gare SNCF (or from *Fun Sports*, 14 rue Jean-Monnet). To reach the **town centre** from the train station, you cross the canal bridge by an oval lock, pass the Jardin Chénier and follow rue Clemenceau, which will take you through the central **place Carnot** and out to the exterior boulevard on the southern side of town (a fifteen-minute walk). If you arrive by bus, the **gare routière** is just off bd de Varsovie on the northwest side of town, south of the canal (for the bus up to the Cité, take no. 4 from square Magenta).

The **SI** (daily July–Aug 9am–7pm; rest of year 9am–noon & 2–6.30pm/7pm in Sept and Easter–June; Sun during school holidays. 10am–noon) is at 15 bd Camille-Pelletan at the end of square Gambetta, where the main road from Montpellier enters the town across the Pont-Neuf over the River Aude. If you're aiming to walk in the Montagne Noire, you should consult the *Comité Départemental des Randonnées*, 13 rue de la République.

Accommodation

With the exception of the terminally overbooked **youth hostel** on rue Trencavel (☎68.25.23.16), the price of staying in the Cité may make it unrealistic to seek a room there. There are, however, some very reasonably priced **hotels** in the Ville Basse. Pride of place goes to the *Hôtel Bonnafoux*, old-fashioned but spotlessly clean, at 40 rue de la Liberté (☎68.25.01.45; ②–③). *Hôtel de la Poste*, 21 rue de Verdun (☎ 67.25.12.18; ③), and *Le Cathare*, 59 rue Jean-Bringer (☎68.25.65.92; ②), are acceptable if fairly basic alternatives. More upmarket, the *Bristol*, 7 av Foch (☎68.25.07.24; ④), is situated on the canal bank opposite the gare SNCF. There are also two *foyers* worth checking out: *Foyer de la CAF*, 2 rue Zola (☎68.47.42.90), and *Foyer Mixte du Viguier*, rue Jules-Verne, Le Viguier (down av Henri-Gout; ☎68.25.13.93). The **campsite**, *Les Campéoles*, is just west of the Cité off route de St-Hilaire and the D104.

Eating and entertainments

For a **place to eat,** try the *Brasserie La Rotonde* on the corner of rue Clemenceau by the Jardin Chénier; alternatively the Indo-Chinese *Le Long An*, 84 rue 4-septembre, and *Le Vietnam*, 3 rue de Verdun, or the *Crêperie Kreiz–Avel*, 15 rue de Verdun (closed Sun noon), or the *Bon Pasteur*, 29 rue Armagnac (closed Sun & Mon). The *Hôtel Cathare* (see above) also has a reasonable restaurant. For picnic provisions, the **market** (Tues, Thurs and Sat) is on rue de Verdun.

There is **dance, theatre and music** in the annual *Festival de Carcassonne* through-out July and, in the first fortnight of August, *Les Médiévales*, a medieval junket of lasers and special effects on themes like the Cathars and the Holy Grail.

The Cité

The attractions of the Ville Basse notwithstanding, what everybody comes for is the **Cité**, a double-walled and turretted fortress crowning the hill above the Aude. From a distance it's the epitome of the fairy-tale medieval town. Viollet-le-Duc rescued it from ruin in 1844, and his "too-perfect" restoration has been furiously debated ever since. It is, as you would expect, a real tourist trap. Yet, in spite of the chintzy cafés, arty-crafty shops and the crowds, you'd have to be a very stiff-necked purist not to be moved at all.

Walking from the Ville Basse, across the Pont-Vieux, up rue Barbacane, past the church of St-Gimer, you enter the Cité through the sturdy bastion of the **Porte d'Aude**, all now peacefully integrated with the ancient lichened houses standing in their garden plots below. For a map, room, or details, the **SI** run a summer annexe in the **Porte Narbonnaise**, the other main gateway, on the east side.

There is no charge for admission to the streets or the grassy *lices* – lists – between the walls. However, to see the inner fortress of the **Château Comtal** and to walk the walls you have to join a guided tour (April–Oct 9/9.30am–12.30pm & 2–5/6.30/7.30pm; closed midday except July & Aug; 25F). The tours – in French only – assume some knowledge of French history, pointing out the various phases in the construction of the fortifications, from Roman to Visigothic to Romanesque and to the post-Cathar adaptations of the French kings.

In addition to wandering the narrow streets, don't miss the beautiful church of **St-Nazaire** towards the southern corner of the Cité at the end of rue St-Louis. It's a serene combination of Romanesque nave with carved capitals and Gothic transepts and choir adorned with some of the loveliest stained glass. In the south transept is a tombstone believed to belong to Simon de Montfort.

The Canal du Midi and Minerve

For 240km from the River Garonne at Toulouse via CASTELNAUDARY, Carcassonne and BÉZIERS to the Étang de Thau between Agde and Sète, the **Canal du Midi** traces a peaceful green alley, lined with plane trees and yellow irises, across the whole of western Languedoc. Both landscape and canal – navigable by houseboat, but no longer by modern barge – have remained much as they were when the canal was constructed between 1666 and 1681.

The canal was the brainchild of **Pierre-Paul Riquet**, a minor tax-collector from Béziers, who succeeded in firing the imagination of Louis XIV against the soberer counsels of his minister, Colbert, with the idea of joining the Mediterranean and the Atlantic via the Garonne. Riquet ruined himself financially in the process, but the canal was a great success for a couple of centuries as a means of moving freight and passengers. It's also a great architectural monument, marrying function and aesthetics in perfect classical style, as in the 1676 **Pont de Répudre** close to PARAZA about 45km east of Carcassonne, where the canal crosses a marshy stream among the sun-beaten vineyards.

DOING THE CANAL DU MIDI

The way to use the canal today is to **hike** it, **bike** it or rent a **boat**, with numerous villages to stop at along the way. Agencies to contact include: *Blue Line Midi*, Le Grand Bassin, Castelnaudary (☎68.23.17.51); *Connoisseurs Cruisers*, 7 quai d'Alsace, Narbonne (☎68.65.14.55); *Bateliers du Midi*, 5 quai Elie-Amouroux, Capestang (☎67.93.38.66); and *Les Croisières du Soleil*, Homps (☎68.91.38.11).

Minerve

The village of **MINERVE** lies a dozen kilometres north of the canal in the middle of the Minervois wine country, on a shelf-like terrain of rocky outcrops and magnificent views. Its location is extraordinary, isolated on an island of rock between the gorges of the Briant and Cesse rivers, the latter of which has cut its course through two enormous tunnels in the rock known as the *Ponts naturels*.

The village turned Cathar at the beginning of the thirteenth century, which made it a target for Simon de Montfort's crusade. On July 22, 1210, after a seven-week siege, he took the castle and promptly burned 180 *parfaits*. There is a memorial to them by the church and, inside, one of the most ancient altars in Gaul, dated 456 – but you won't be allowed in for love nor money. Nothing remains of the castle but the ruins of a tower.

If you want to stay, **camping** is free: ask at the *Mairie* by the church. There's a *gîte d'étape* (☎68.91.22.92) in the village as well as the *Hôtel Chantovent* (☎68.91.14.18; ④; closed Jan & Feb; closed Sun pm and Mon out of season). The **SI** (10am–noon & 3–5pm) has information about other accommodation possibilities in the area.

As for **getting to Minerve**, it's a manageable hitch from Carcassonne on the D610, then D5, turning north at CABEZAC. Alternatively, there are buses from LÉZIGNAN-CORBIÈRES on the Carcassonne–Narbonne railway to HOMPS on the canal and OLONZAC – where you could stay at the *Hôtel du Parc*, av d'Homps (☎68.91.24.77; ③). Lastly, the **bus route** between Narbonne and St-Pons (several daily) passes within 5km of Minerve.

The Montagne Noire

There are two good routes from Carcassonne into the **Montagne Noire**, which forms the western extremity of the *Parc du Haut Languedoc*, Carcassonne–Revel and Carcassonne–Mazamet by the valley of the Orbiel. Neither is served by public transport, but both offer superlative scenery.

The Revel route: Saissac, Revel and around

The **Revel route** follows the N113 out of Carcassonne, then the D629 through Montolieu (17km) and Saissac. **MONTOLIEU**, semi-fortified and built on the edge of a ravine, has set itself the target of becoming the Hay-on-Wye of France, **capital of books**, secondhand, antiquarian, and everything to do with them. Book-lovers should drop in at the *Librairie Booth* by the bridge over the ravine.

SAISSAC, another 8km, is much more an upland village. Conifers and beech woods, interspersed with patches of rough pasture, surround it. Gardens are terraced down the steep slopes. Remains of towers and fortifications poke out among the ancient houses and on a spur below the village stand the romantic ruins of its castle and the Église St-Michel. The *Hôtel de la Montagne Noire* (☎68.24.46.36; ③) stands on the road, and there are, in addition, two **campsites**.

If you're camping, though, the best place for miles around and an experience in itself is the *Camping du Bout du Monde* (☎68.94.20.92 – all year round), signposted to the left about 8km up the road after the hamlet of LA RÉGINE. It's at a beautiful tumble-down farm called Rodes, near VERDUN-EN-LAURAGAIS. You camp among the broom at the edge of the woods (though it's also a *gîte d'étape*), but, best of all, the owner is a genius of a cook, and she uses only their own farm-grown produce. It is not a regular restaurant: you have to order a meal, but you certainly won't regret it if you do – non-campers are welcome.

Some 14km west of Saissac on the D103 (or just a few kilometres southwest of the *Bout du Monde* campsite), the ancient village of **ST-PAPOUL** with its walls and cathedral make a gentle side trip. The fourteenth-century **cloister** is always open, but the church, in poor condition and undergoing restoration, may not be. The *Château de Ferrals* (3km east), though not visitable, is worth a sneaking glance from the road.

Back on the "main" D629, continuing on from La Régine, the road winds down through the forest, past the Bassin de St-Férréol constructed by Riquet to supply water to the Canal du Midi, to **REVEL** (15km). Revel is a *bastide* dating from 1342, with an attractive arcaded central *place* with a superb wooden-pillared *halle* in the middle. Now a prosperous market town (market day Sat), it makes an agreeably provincial stop-over. The *Hôtel du Midi*, 34 bd Gambetta (☎61.83.50.50; ④) has a restaurant, much appreciated by local gourmets, with menus from 90F. A simpler place to stay and eat is the *Adelscott*, 19 bd de la République (☎61.83.51.39; ②).

Lastours and the valley of the Orbiel

This is the region known as the Cabardès. Cut by the deep ravines of the Orbiel and its tributary streams, it's covered with Mediterranean scrub lower down and forests of chestnut and pine higher up. Extremely poor and depopulated, with rough stone villages and hamlets crouching in the valleys, its people lived off beans and chestnut flour and the meat from their pigs, and worked from very ancient times in the region's copper, iron, lead, silver and gold mines. Nothing now remains of that tradition save for the gold mine at **Salsigne** (of which more below).

The most memorable site in the Orbiel valley is the **CHÂTEAUX DE LASTOURS**, the most northerly of the Cathar castles, 16km north of Carcassonne. As the name suggests, there is more than one castle – four, in fact, their ruined keeps jutting super-bly from a sharp ridge of scrub and cypress that plunges to rivers on both sides. The two oldest castles, Cabaret (mid-eleventh century) and Surdespine (1153), fell into de Montfort's hands in 1211, when their lords gave shelter to the Cathars. The other two, Tour Régine and Quertinheux, were added after 1240, when the site became royal property, and a garrison was maintained here as late as the Revolution. Today, despite their ruined state, they look as impregnable and beautiful as ever. A path winds up from the roadside, bright in early summer with iris, cistus, broom and numerous other flowers.

For **cave** enthusiasts, there are the weirdly shaped rock and crystal formations of the **Grottes de Limousis** about 6km east of Lastours – hitchable, if you're lucky.

The **SALSIGNE gold mine**, over the hill to the west, atop a bleak windswept plateau, is a huge and unsightly opencast pit. A forlorn row of miners' cottages stands nearby, with *PCF* slogans and a *Mine Occupée* sign, the only evidence of political passions anywhere in the district. Apparently the only material now going through the treatment plant comes from Greece – thousands of tons of rubble shipped through Port-La Nouvelle and Marseille to be sifted for a few ounces of the stuff that glisters.

About 7km upriver from Lastours, the road and river divide. The left fork leads to the village of MAS-CABARDÈS, hunkered down defensively in the river bottom. The right goes to ROQUEFÈRE whose ancient *château* hosts summertime theatre. In a riverside apple orchard near the Orbiel–Rieutort confluence is a very welcoming and beautifully sited **campsite** and **gîte d'étape**, *Les Eaux Vives* (☎68.26.31.05).

From Roquefère a steep, serpentine road winds up through magnificent scenery to the tiny hamlet of CUPSERVIES, balanced on the edge of a sudden and deep ravine where the Rieutort stream drops some 90m into the bottom. A couple of kilometres further, by the crossroads at Caninac, there's a very early – tenth century – **chapel of St-Sernin** in the middle of the woods. To get here without transport, there's a marked footpath from Roquefère, which then returns via LABASTIDE-ESPARBAIRENQUE (four-and-a-half hours round trip). For other walking ideas, ask at *Les Eaux Vives*.

From CANINAC the road crosses the partly wooded, partly arable Plateau de Sambres, before dropping down to the dull town of MAZAMET.

The Cathar castles

The best of the so-called Cathar castles – they sought refuge in them, but did not build them – are in the arid, herb-scented **hills of the Corbières** to the south of Carcassonne. **Walking** is undoubtedly the most direct way to experience them, and there are numerous paths, of which the **GR36**, crossing from Carcassonne to St-Paul-de-Fenouillet, and the *Sentier Cathare*, crossing east to west from Port la-Nouvelle to Foix, are the most exciting. The *Sentier Cathare* is divided into twelve stages with *gîtes d'étape*, described in the *Sentier Cathare* pamphlet produced by *Comité Départemental de Randonnée*, 13 rue de la République, BP 143, 11003 Carcassonne.

Without transport or walking boots, the best way to tackle them is from the south, for the most spectacular ones are close to the **Perpignan–Quillan road**, which has a bus service. With transport it becomes possible to explore the wilder back roads and utterly ruinous castles like Durfort and Termes and cross the cols where orchids and cowslips shudder in the spring winds and the views southward all end in the snowy Pyrenean bulk of Canigou.

Puilaurens

From QUILLAN the road runs south through the incredibly narrow **defilé de Pierre-Lys** to the Pont d'Aliès before swinging east to the village of LAPRADELLE (17km) and the first of the castles, the **château de Puilaurens** (July–Sept 10am–6pm).

You can either drive up, or there's a shorter and fairly gentle path from the hamlet of Puilaurens. It's a steep climb up to the castle, perched on top of a high, wooded hill at 700m. There are fine crenellated walls built around the very top of the rock outcrops and a keep. Although the existence of a castle here dates from the tenth century, it seems more likely that it was fortified to something like its present extent in the early thirteenth century, when it passed from the king of France to the count of Roussillon, and then to the king of Aragon. It sheltered many Cathars up to 1256, when Chabert de Barbera, effective controller of power in the region, was captured and forced to hand over his strongholds here and at QUÉRIBUS further east, to secure his release. The castle remained strategically important, being close to the Spanish border, until 1659, when France annexed Roussillon and the border was pushed away to the south. The **view** from the battlements, which you can climb up to at one point, is quite breathtaking.

Quéribus, Cucugnan and Duilhac

The **Château de Quéribus**, 30km further east towards Perpignan, stands on the ridge above the vine-ringed village of MAURY – with a good chance of a lift up the six-kilometre side road. Again, it is spectacularly situated, balanced on a pillar of rock above a sheer cliff, whose crevices nourish a beautiful variety of wild flowers (Easter–Oct 10am–6pm/8pm, though nobody ever seems to shut the gate). Until 1659 this was the border with Spain.

Because of the extreme, cramped topography of the rock, the space within the walls is stepped in terraces, dominated by the polygonal keep and accessible by a single stairway. Inside, at the heart of the keep, is the remarkable **chapel** of St-Louis-de-Quéribus, surprisingly high and wide when you consider the keep's tortured position, and supported by a single pillar. The stairs to the roof are broken, but from the window halfway up there are fantastic views to Canigou and Perpignan, with other castles and watchtowers of the Spanish Marches dotting the peaks and ridges. To the northwest you're within easy eye contact of Peyrepertuse.

The history of Quéribus is similar to that of Puilaurens, though the fortifications visible today are thirteenth-century. It was the last stronghold of Cathar resistance, holding out until 1255, eleven years beyond the fall of Montségur. Never reduced by siege, its role as a sanctuary for the Cathars ended with the capture of the luckless Chabert.

If you're provided with water and food, you could camp discreetly on the slopes to the north of the castle behind the ticket office. There is no accommodation in CUCUGNAN, the village to the north below, though its two **restaurants**, *Auberge de Cucugnan* (closed first half of Sept) and *Auberge du Vigneron*, draw in the gourmets from miles around. The nearest **rooms** are in DUILHAC about 4km away below Peyrepertuse at the *Auberge du Vieux Moulin* (✆68.45.47.12; ①) or in the *gîte d'étape* (✆68.45.01.74). There is also an *alimentation* in the village, with bread, open even on Sunday morning.

Peyrepertuse

The access road for the **Château de Peyrepertuse** (Easter–Oct 9am–7/8pm) starts in Duilhac (see above). Alternatively, you can walk up from ROUFFIAC on the north side by the GR36, marked "Fontaine de la Jacquette" just outside the village; in summer it's a tough, hot climb that takes the best part of an hour. But either way the effort is rewarded, for Peyrepertuse is one of the most awe-inspiring castles anywhere, clinging to the crest of a long, wickedly jagged spine of rock on the top of a mountain ridge, surrounded by sheer drops of hundreds of metres.

You enter on the north side through thickets of box wood. The heaviest fortifications enclose the lower eastern end of the ridge, with a keep and barbican controlling the main gate. The castle is much larger than the others despite its precarious hold on the earth, with extensive buildings inside the outer wall, culminating in a keep and tower shutting off the highest point of the ridge, where such a pit of air opens at your feet that no artificial defence is necessary.

Surprisingly, the castle was taken by the French without much difficulty in 1240, and most of the existing fortifications were built after that. Whatever you do, don't go up in a thunderstorm; there can be some fierce ones in summer, and the ridge brings down the lightning as sure as a high-tension cable.

If you need to stay the night and are camping, you might prefer ROUFFIAC to Duilhac. It has a **campsite and hotel**, *Auberge de Peyrepertuse* (✆68.45.40.40; ② – with restaurant), but no shop. There is, however, a bus on Wednesday and Saturday to ST-PAUL-DE-FENOUILLET on the main Perpignan D117 road, returning at noon; also one on Monday to and from Perpignan.

Moving on

Moving on from Peyrepertuse, by car or by the GR36, you can return to St-Paul-de-Fenouillet through the **Gorges de Galamus**, as narrow and bristling as any nineteenth-century mountain engraving, and in many places you can get down to the river for a swim. There is even a *gîte d'étape* in the eagle's nest **Hermitage St-Antoine** (✆68.59.20.49) built into the side of the ravine.

Alternatively, the drive eastwards offers more castles, including **Padern** and the especially fine **Aguilar**, near TUCHAN, which overlooks the hills and vales of the *Côtes de Roussillon-Villages* wine area, with magnificent views from the twisty climbing roads. From here you have the possibility of heading either north towards NARBONNE or south through TAUTAVEL to Perpignan.

TOULOUSE AND THE WEST

In addition to its own sunny, cosmopolitan charms, **Toulouse** is a very accessible kick-off point for any destination in the south and west of France. Of immediately adjacent places **Albi** is the number one priority, with its highly original cathedral and unique collection of Toulouse-Lautrec paintings. Once you've made it that far, it's worth the extra hop to the time-warped medieval town of **Cordes**.

Toulouse

TOULOUSE, with its beautiful historic centre, is one of the most vibrant and metropolitan provincial cities in France. This is a transformation that has come about since the war, under the guidance of the French state, which has poured in money to make Toulouse the think-tank of high-tech industry and a sort of premier trans-national Euroville. Always an **aviation centre** – St-Exupéry and Mermoz flew out from here on their pioneering air mail flights over Africa in the 1920s – Toulouse is now home to *Aérospatiale*, the driving force behind Concorde, Airbus and the Ariane space rocket. The national Space Centre, the European shuttle programme, the leading aeronautical schools, the frontier-pushing electronics industry . . . it's all happening in Toulouse, whose 60,000 students make it second only to Paris as a university centre. But it's not to the burgeoning suburbs of factories, labs, shopping and housing complexes that all these people go for their entertainment, but to the old *ville rose* – pink only in its brickwork, no longer in its politics.

This is not the first flush of pre-eminence for Toulouse. From the tenth to the thirteenth century the counts of Toulouse controlled most of southern France. They maintained the most resplendent court in the land, renowned especially for its **troubadours**, the poets of Courtly Love, whose work influenced Petrarch, Dante and Chaucer and thus the whole course of European poetry. Until, that is, the arrival of the papal thugs in the Albigensian Crusade; in 1271 Toulouse became crown property.

Arrival and accommodation

The part of the city you'll want to see is a rough hexagon clamped around a bend in the wide, brown **River Garonne**. **Arriving by train or bus**, you'll find yourself at the **gare Matabiau** (☎61.62.50.50 for information) about a twenty-minute walk from the heart of things. There's an **SI** annexe here, shower facilities, a **city bus terminal**, with the **gare routière** to the right at 70 bd Pierre-Sémard and the *SEMVAT* regional bus depot a short distance away on the corner of rue Bertrand-de-Born and rue Stalingrad, in a *quartier* whose former red light seediness has all but disappeared.

The simplest route from the station to the **city centre** is to cross the Canal du Midi; turn left and then second right down the broad **allées Jean-Jaurès**; cross bd de Strasbourg into pl Wilson; then take rue Lafayette, across rue d'Alsace-Lorraine to the central **place du Capitole**. Just before you get to it, in the small leafy garden of the square Charles-de-Gaulle, the sixteenth-century *donjon* that used to house the city archives now hosts the main **SI** (May–Sept daily 9am–7pm; rest of year 9am–6pm, closed Sun and holidays).

Accommodation

Contrary, perhaps, to expectations, the centre of Toulouse still contains some very reasonable and agreeable **hotels**.

Hôtel Grand Balcon, 8 rue Romiguières (☎61.21.48.08; closed Aug 4–Aug 25), on the corner of pl du Capitole. A real classic this, frequented by St-Éxupéry and co in their pioneering days, it has retained its decor and period charm. ③.

Hôtel des Arts, 1bis rue Cantegril (☎61.23.36.21), off rue des Arts. Simpler but equally enjoyable alternative to the *Gd Balcon*. ②.

Hôtel Anatole-France, 46 pl Anatole-France (☎61.23.19.96) by the university. Quiet, and less obviously charming. ②.

Hôtel du Palais, 4 allées Paul-Feuga (☎61.52.96.23; closed mid-July–mid-Aug) near Pont-St-Michel. ②.

The **youth hostel** (☎61.80.49.93) – pokey but friendly – is at 125 av Jean-Rieux. Take bus #14 from the station to place Dupuy (not far, just across a canal bridge), then #22

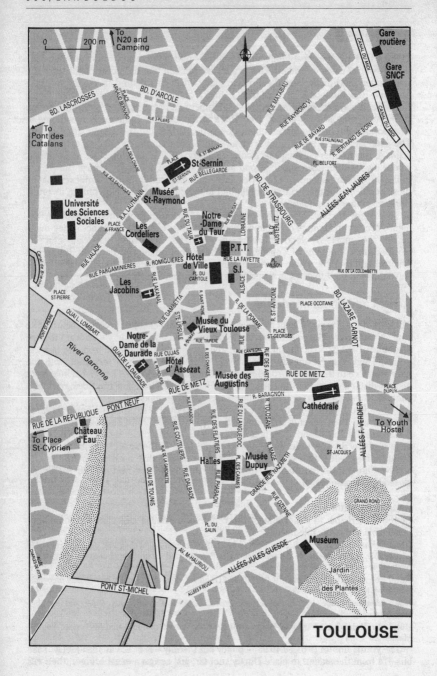

TOULOUSE

going back towards the canal and up the avenue. There are several cheap eating places in the *quartier*.

Campers are less well served. The **camping municipal** – scruffy but usable, and not worth the trouble unless you have some form of transport – is on the north side of the city. Take av des Minimes from the Canal du Midi and fork left at the Barrière de Paris into av des États-Unis (the main N20 Bordeaux road). The campsite is signposted, but keep a sharp look-out to your left. It's across the rail tracks in chemin du Pont-de-Rupé, near the Sesquières leisure centre.

The city

In addition to the pleasures of soaking up the atmosphere of the streets, old Toulouse offers some real architectural goodies in the two **churches of St-Sernin and Les Jacobins** and the ornate **Renaissance mansions** – *hôtels particuliers* – of the merchants who grew rich on the woad-dye trade, which formed the basis of the city's economy from the mid-fifteenth to mid-sixteenth century, when the importing of indigo from the Indian colonies wiped it out.

Toulouse's centre of gravity is the **pl du Capitole**. Southeast lies the small and attractive **pl St-Georges**, a major focus for the fashion-conscious young, with its bars, cafés and street performers. To the south, across the central dividing boulevard of rue de Metz, the central streets around the *halles* in pl des Carmes – rue du Languedoc, prolongation of rue d'Alsace-Lorraine and rue des Filatiers – are busy with shoppers, while towards the river and the allées Jules-Guesde they are quietly residential, with some beautiful houses overlooking secret gardens. Across the *allées*, the **Jardin des Plantes** with the adjacent gardens of the Grand Rond, provide the city centre's only green space.

Place du Capitole and district: the hôtels and the riverside

The heart of the city, seat of its government since the twelfth century, is the huge **capitole** or **town hall**, where once sat the *capitouls*, the relatively democratic and independent city council – an institution found in other Languedoc towns under the name of *consulat*, that may have inspired the son of Simon de Montfort who created the first English parliament. Today the *capitole*'s medieval origins are disguised by an elaborate pink and white Classical facade (1750) of columns and pilasters. Appropriately, the square it dominates – **pl du Capitole** – is a great meeting-place and talking-shop with numerous **cafés**, and a mammoth Wednesday **market** of clothes, trinkets and food.

From this *place* radiate the labyrinthine and now largely pedestrianised streets of the old city, elegantly constructed almost exclusively of the flat Toulousain brick, whose rosy colour gives the city its nickname of *ville rose*. It's a most attractive material, lending a small-scale, detailed finish to otherwise plain facades and setting off admirably any wood or stonework. Along these streets many of the **Renaissance** *hôtels* survive, not usually open to the public, so you have to do a lot of nonchalant sauntering into courtyards to get a look at them. Best known is the **Hôtel Assézat**, towards the river end of rue de Metz, a vast brick extravaganza adorned with Doric, Ionic and Corinthian columns. Several others can be found just to the south: on rue de la Dalbade, where no. 25, the **Hôtel Clary**, is unusual for being built in stone; on rue Pharaon; pl des Carmes; rue du Languedoc; and then northwards on rue St-Rome, rue des Changes, rue de la Bourse, and rue du May.

Cutting the old town in half, the late nineteenth-century **rue de Metz** at its western end leads to the river and the **Pont-Neuf** (begun in 1544 despite its name), to link up with the St-Cyprien quarter on the left bank where the *château d'eau*, erected in 1822 to supply clean water to the city's drinking fountains, now houses the photography gallery (see overpage). Here the **riverside** is at its best, with a grassy waterside walk backed by the plane-tree-lined *quais* in front of the art school and eighteenth-century church of La Daurade. Downstream you come to Pont St-Pierre, then the wildest and quietest stretch of *quai*, between the mouth of the lovely tree-lined Canal de Brienne and the Chaussée du Bazacle, formerly a ford across the Garonne.

Ecclesiastical Toulouse: St-Sernin, Les Jacobins and St-Étienne

From the north side of place du Capitole, **rue du Taur**, full of new and second-hand bookshops, takes you past the belfry wall of **Notre-Dame-du-Taur**, whose diamond-pointed arches and decorative motifs represent the acme of Toulousain bricklaying skills, to place **St-Sernin**. Here you're confronted with the largest Romanesque church in France, the **basilica of St-Sernin**. Begun in 1080 tó accommodate the passing hordes of St-Jacques pilgrims, it is one of the loveliest examples of its genre. Its most striking external features are the octagonal brick **belfry** with rounded and pointed arches, diamond lozenges, colonnettes and mouldings picked out in stone, and the **apse** with nine radiating chapels. Entering from the south, you pass under the **Porte Miégeville**, whose twelfth-century carvings launched the influential Toulouse school of sculpture. **Inside**, the great high nave rests on brick piers, flanked by double aisles of diminishing height, surmounted by a gallery running right around the building. To get into the **ambulatory** (Mon–Sat 10–11.30am & 2.30–7pm; 10F) you have to pay a small fee, but it's well worth it for the exceptional eleventh-century marble reliefs on the end wall of the choir.

Right outside St-Sernin is the town's archaeological museum, **Musée St-Raymond** and, on Sunday mornings, an impressively shambolic **flea market**.

A short distance west of place du Capitole, on rue Lakanal, the church of **Les Jacobins** is another ecclesiastical building you can't miss. Started in 1230 by Dominicans who had set up here in the wake of their founding father, St Dominic, who himself had come to preach against the Cathars, the church is a huge fortress-like rectangle of unadorned brick, buttressed, like Albi, by plain brick piles – quite unlike the architecture you normally associate with Gothic. The **interior** is a single space divided by a central row of ultra-slim pillars from whose minimal capitals spring an elegant splay of vaulting ribs – twenty-two from the last in line, like palm fronds. Beneath the altar lie the bones of the philosopher St Thomas Aquinas. On the north side you step out into the calming hush of a **cloister** with a formal array of box trees and cypress in the middle, and a superb view of the belfry.

By contrast, the city's **Cathédrale St-Étienne**, at the eastern end of rue de Metz, is an eminently missable hotch-potch of a building, constructed in so many phases that its ends literally do not know its beginnings.

Culture and museums

The best guide to what's going on in and around the city – and usually there is a lot, from opera to cinema – is the weekly **listings magazine**, *Le Flash*, which comes out on a Wednesday. The monthly *Toulouse Culture* has more exclusively highbrow interests.

The July–August *Musique d'Été* festival features Toulouse's own *Orchestre National du Capitole,* whose home base is the *Halle aux Grains* in pl Dupuy (☎61.22..29.22), as well as visiting ensembles. September is the regular slot for the *Festival International Piano* which takes place mainly in the beautiful cloister of the Église des Jacobins.

Major venues are: the splendid *Théâtre du Capitole* in pl du Capitole (☎61.23.21.35) for music, dance and opera; *Le Sorano*, 35 allées Jules-Guesde (☎61.25.66.87) for theatre; and *Odyssud*, 4 av du Parc, Blagnac (☎61.30.45.31). There's a *cinémathèque* at 3 rue Roquelaine (☎61.48.90.75) with programmes that change daily.

Toulouse has a good number of **museums** and various **galleries**, too – the following is just a selection.

Musée des Augustins

21 rue de Metz (☎61.22.21.82); June–Sept 10am–5/6pm; Wed 10am–9pm; closed Tues; 8F.

Incorporating the two surviving cloisters of an Augustinian priory, the **musée des Augustins'** collections of **Romanesque and medieval sculpture** – much of it saved from the now-vanished churches of Toulouse's golden age – are outstanding. As so often, what is interesting, regardless of the ostensible theme, is the highly naturalistic representation of contemporary manners and fashions. Merchants with forked beards touch one another's arms in a gesture of familiarity and collusion that says, "We understand each other. We're men of business. We belong to the same class". *Notre-Dame-de-Grâce* represents the Virgin as a pretty, bored young mother looking away from her child, who strains to escape her hold. A headless Saint Barbara is characteristically posed with weight on one leg, hips and tummy thrust slightly forwards, slender-waisted, bodice framed by long tresses – more a fashionable young woman than a saint.

Musée St-Raymond

Place St-Sernin (☎61.22.21.85); daily 10am–5/6pm; 8F.

The city's archaeological museum, housed in what remains of the poor students' block of the medieval university, contains principally a large collection of Roman objects, lamps, keys, bronze figurines, the labours of Hercules in relief and similar items.

Musée Paul-Dupuy

13 rue de la Pléau (☎61.22.21.83); daily June–Sept 10am–5/6pm; closed Tues.

A surprisingly good collection of arts and crafts from the Middle Ages to today, including watches and clocks, pottery, enamels from Limoges and furniture.

Musée Georges-Labit

43 rue des Martyrs-de-la-Libération (☎61.22.21.84); 13 rue de la Pl'eau; daily June–Sept 10am–5/6pm; closed Tues.

One of the best provincial collections of oriental art.

Musée du Vieux-Toulouse

7 rue du May; Mon–Sat June–Sept 3–6pm; May & Oct Thurs 2.30–5.30pm only; closed Nov–April; 8F.

Housed in the Hôtel du May, this illustrates somewhat unexcitingly the city's history.

Galerie municipale du Château d'Eau

Place Laganne (☎61.42.61.72); April–Oct 1–7pm; Nov–March weekdays noon–6pm, Sat & Sun 1–7pm; closed Tues.

This is an 1822 circular water tower transformed into an influential photography exhibition space and information centre. Frequent changes of exhibition. Call to see what's on.

Centre municipal de l'affiche, de la carte postale et de l'art graphique

58 allées Charles-de-Fitte (☎61.59.24.64); Mon–Fri 9am–noon & 2–6pm.

Exhibitions and information, library etc on all aspects of graphic art.

Eating, drinking and nightlife

There are several good areas to look for a place to eat. One of the most popular is the North African quarter around **place Arnaud-Bernard** just north of the church of St-Sernin: or try the *place* itself, where there is an organic fruit and veg market; or in the adjoining streets – rue Arnaud-Bernard, rue de la Chaine and rue des Trois-Piliers.

Snacks and restaurants

Rue du Taur has several **Vietnamese** places and **sandwich bars**. There's an **all-night crêperie** *St-André* at 39 rue St-Rome and another *crêperie, Le Bolbu*, at no. 8 in the adjoining rue du May (closed Sun). Or fill up on the cheap and plentiful fare of *La Place du May* (closed Sun lunch) at 4 rue du May. Another purveyor of cheap food in copious amounts is the *Auberge Louis XIII*, 1bis rue Tripière (parallel to rue du May; closed Sat & Sun), while a good home-cooked meal can be had for 50F at *Mami's* in the *Hôtel des Pyrénées*, rue de la Colombette. For similarly convenient, uncomplicated eating there are numerous **brasserie**-style establishments on bd de Strasbourg near the junction with allées Jean-Jaurès: *La Grillothèque*, 16 bd de Strasbourg is good. The much fancier and very popular *Brasserie des Beaux-Arts* with its Belle-Époque decor is right on the corner of the Pont-Neuf (open till 1am; from around 100F). Another good traditional and rather conventional restaurant is *La Bascule*, 14 av Maurice-Hauriou near the Pont St-Michel (closed Sun & Mon pm). For tasty Franco-Spanish **tapas** there's the *Tantina de Burgos*, 27 rue de la Garonnette near the Pont-Neuf (closed Sun & Mon).

Cafés and bars

Regular daytime **café-lounging** can be pursued around the popular student/arty hang-out of pl Arnaud-Bernard. *Café St-Sernin*, nearby in rue St-Bernard by the eponymous church, is an easy-going, sunny place to sit. **Place du Capitole**, with its huge Wednesday market, is another very popular meeting-place. The most distinguished establishment is the *Bibent* at no. 5 on the south side, with its exuberant plasterwork, marble tables and cascading chandeliers. Place St-Georges is still very popular, though its clientele is no longer convincingly bohemian. Place Wilson has its enthusiasts. A *branché*, designerish number is the *Café Classico* at 37 rue des Filatiers. Nearby, *Le Diagonal*, at 37 pl des Carmes, is *the* modish, hip nighttime bar (open till 2am; closed Sun).

Nightlife

If you want to tackle the **discos**, *L'Apocalypse* in Montaudran (☎61.54.67.60) is particularly popular in summer; *Le Bikini*, route de Lacroix-Falgarde (☎61.55.00.29), is casual and renowned for its rock, as is *La-Voie-12*, 7 chemin Lanusse in Croix-Daurade on the N88 Albi road; *Mélodie en sous-sol*, 23bis bd Riquet (☎61.62.35.91), is a subterranean cavern determined to lead the way in sound and wear; *Le Broadway*, 11 rue des Puits-Clos (☎61.21.10.11), is gay and *Le New Shanghai*, 12 rue de la Pomme (☎61.23.37.80) mixed.

But away from the flashing lights, many **night-time bars** have **music**, and good music at that.

Le Mandala, 23 rue des Amidonniers (☎61.21.10.05) on the corner of av Séjourné near the Pont des Catalans. At the time of writing, this is where serious jazz fans and musicians head.

Le Blue's Note, 14 rue Peyrolières (☎61.22.16.12; 6pm–2am; closed Sun). Popular hang-out with more comfortable fans and established groups.

Erich Coffie (Irish coffee!), 9 rue Joseph-Vié, just west of the river in the *quartier* St-Cyprien. (☎61.42.04.27; 9–2am; closed first half of Aug). One of the city's liveliest and most enjoyable music bars (food available) with a fairly eclectic music policy.

Le Ragtime, 14 pl Arnaud-Bernard (☎61.22.73.01). Good bar offering jazz, salsa and blues until 2am, or 5am on Saturday nights.

Le Piano Bar, 8 pl Arnaud-Bernard (☎61.21.78.36). Offers more the opportunity to talk to the accompaniment of the playing.

Le Bijou, 123 av de Muret (turn left at the end of Pont St-Michel; ☎61.42.95.07; closed Sun), with concerts and dancing. Popular and musically interesting joint.

Listings

Airlines *Air France*, 2 bd de Strasbourg (☎61.62.70.76); *Dan-Air* at the airport (☎61.30.04.04); *British Airways* (☎61.30.45.50); *Air-Inter*, 76 allées Jean-Jaurès (☎61.30.68.68).

Airport 7km west at Blagnac; ☎61.42.44.00 for info.

Airport bus from *gare routière* Mon–Fri 5.20am–10.20pm, Sat & Sun 6am–8.20pm.

Ambulance ☎61.31.56.56.

Bookstores *Gibert*, corner of rue du Taur/pl du Capitole – good general bookshop; *Librairie Occitania*, 46 rue du Taur – for regional books; *IGN*, 43 rue Peyrolières – for maps and guides.

Canal boats 2 port St-Étienne (☎61.36.24.24).

Chemist/all night 17 rue Rémusat (☎61.21.81.20).

CRIJ 17 rue de Metz (☎61.21.20.20).

CROUS 7 rue des Salenques: for student services.

Launderette By far the best is *Laundromatique*, 20 rue Arnaud-Bernard.

Police rue du Rempart-St-Étienne (☎61.29.70.00 or 17).

Post office 9 rue Lafayette.

Taxis 24hr: square Wilson ☎61.21.55.46; gare Matabiau ☎61.62.37.34; pl Esquirol ☎61.21.56.42.

Weather forecast ☎36.65.02.31; for the Pyrenees – ☎36.65.04.04.

Albi

ALBI, 77km northeast of Toulouse (an hour's train ride), is a small industrial town with two unique sights: a museum containing the most comprehensive collection of **Toulouse-Lautrec's** work (Albi was his birthplace) and the most remarkable Gothic cathedral you'll ever see. Its other claim to fame comes from its association with Catharism; though not itself an important centre, it gave its name – Albigensian – to both the heresy and the crusade to suppress it.

If you've any choice in the matter, you might decide to visit Albi at **festival time**. The town hosts three good festivals over the course of the year: jazz in April, theatre at the end of June/beginning of July, and music, at the end of July/beginning of August. During July and August there are also free organ recitals given in the cathedral (Wed 5pm).

Practicalities

From the **gare SNCF** on place Stalingrad it's a ten-minute walk into town along av de-Gaulle. The **gare routière** is on the right in place Jean-Jaurès just as you reach the limits of the old town.

Of Albi's **hotels**, the *Terminus* (☎63.54.00.99; ②), right opposite the station on the corner of place Stalingrad, or, in the heart of the old town near the cathedral, *Hôtel St-Clair*, 8 rue St-Clair (☎63.54.25.66; ④), are reasonable enough. Two cheaper possibilities are *La Fouillade* (☎63.54.21.86; ②) and *le Parking* (☎63.54.09.07; ②), both on place Pelloutier across from place Jaurès. Otherwise, there's a **youth hostel** at 13 rue de la République (☎ 63.54.53.65) and **camping municipal** in the *Parc de Caussels* about 2km east on the D999 Millau road.

The simplest and cheapest place for a **meal** is *Le Petit Bouchon*, 77 rue de la Croix-Verte off place du Vigan. An alternative is the vegetarian *Le Tournesol* in rue de l'Orten-Salvy on the west side of the *place*. *Auberge Saint-Loup*, 26 rue Castelviel at the west end of the cathedral, is a reasonable, traditional restaurant, and *La Tartine*, the café on the cathedral square, does salads and desserts. More expensive restaurants include *Le Jardin des Quatre Saisons* (closed Mon) at 19 bd de Strasbourg just across the river – good value for its prices.

The city

The **cathedral of Ste-Cécile** (8.30–11.45am & 2–5.45pm, except during services; 18F), begun about 1280, is visible the moment you arrive at the train station, dwarfing the town like some vast bulk carrier run aground, the belfry its massive superstructure. If the comparison sounds unflattering, perhaps it is not amiss, for this is not a conventionally beautiful building; it's all about size and boldness of conception. The sheer plainness of the exterior is impressive on this scale, and it is not without interest: arcading, buttressing, the contrast of stone against brick – every differentiation of detail becomes significant. Entrance is through the **south portal**, by contrast the most extravagant piece of Flamboyant sixteenth-century frippery. The **interior**, a hall-like nave of colossal proportions, is covered in richly colourful paintings of Italian workmanship (also sixteenth century). A good screen, delicate as lace, shuts off the choir: Adam makes a show of covering himself, Eve strikes a flaunting model's pose beside the central doorway, and the rest of the screen is adorned with countless statuary.

Next to the cathedral, a powerful red-brick castle, the thirteenth-century Palais de la Berbie (**SI** in one corner: daily 9am–7pm, Sun 10am–noon & 2–5pm), houses the **Musée Toulouse-Lautrec** (10am–noon and 2–5pm; closed Tues; 20F), containing paintings, drawings, lithographs and posters from the earliest work to the very last – an absolute must for anyone interested in *Belle Époque* seediness and, given the predominant Impressionism of the time, the rather offbeat painting style of its subject. The artist's house at 14 rue Toulouse-Lautrec is visitable in theory, but the hours seem very uncertain, dependent on the whim of the owners.

Opposite the east end of the cathedral, rue Mariès leads into the shopping streets of the **old town**, mostly impeccably renovated and restored. The little square and covered passages by the **church of St-Salvy** on the right are worth a look as you go by.

Eventually you come to the broad **Lices Pompidou**, the main thoroughfare of modern Albi, leading down to the river and the road to CORDES. Less touristy, it is the best place to look for somewhere to eat and drink. On place Vigan, for example, there's the *Grand Café de la Poste* and *Grand Café Poutre*, with useful supermarkets nearby.

Around Albi

Somewhat unexpectedly the country between Albi and CARMAUX, 16km to the north, has long been a coal-mining and industrial area, associated in particular with the political activity of **Jean Jaurès**, father figure of French socialism. Elected deputy for Albi in 1893, after defending the striking miners of Carmaux in his newspaper, *La Dépêche*, he then championed the glassworkers in 1896 in a strike which led to the setting up of a pioneering workers' co-operative, *La Verrerie Ouvrière*, which still functions today, albeit automated and monitored by computer (open to visits by groups only).The SIs in Carmaux (place Gambetta) and Albi publish a list of interesting industrial sites in the area, including the pit at **CAGNAC-LES-MINES**, which you can visit as a museum, including a trip down the shaft (visits at 2.30pm, 3.30pm and 4.30pm Mon–Sat; Sun 3pm & 4pm; ☎63.36.94.36).

Of more conventional tourist interest, the town of **CORDES**, is 24km northwest of Albi, a brief train ride (as far as Vindrac 3km away, with **bike hire** from the station) or bus ride on Tuesday and Saturday at 11.45am (return at 5pm) or an easy hitch. It was founded in 1222 by Raymond VII, Count of Toulouse, and remains pretty much untouched, perched on its conical hill. It was a Cathar stronghold and the ground beneath the town is riddled with tunnels for storage and refuge in time of trouble. It is worth seeing because it is such a perfect example of a medieval walled town, complete with thirteenth- and fourteenth-century houses climbing its steep cobbled lanes. It is also, however, a major tourist attraction: medieval banners flutter in the streets and artisans practise their crafts – unfortunately, the kiss of death. It's not a good place to stay, with no very affordable or recommendable hotels, though there is a **campsite** 1km down the GAILLAC road.

Castres

In spite of its industrial activities, **CASTRES**, 71km east of Toulouse, has kept a lot of its charm, in the streets on the right bank of the Agout and, in particular, the riverside quarter where the old tanners' and weavers' houses overhang the water. The centre is a bustling, business-like sort of place, with a **market** from Wednesday to Saturday on place Jean-Jaurès.

Arrival and practicalities

Arriving from Toulouse by train you'll find the **gare SNCF** on av Albert I. The **gare routière** is on pl Soult, with buses to Mazamet and Lacaune. Whether you come by train or bus or drive into Castres, however, you will inevitably find yourself by the **municipal theatre**, with the **SI** (Mon–Sat 9.15am–12.30pm & 2–6.30pm/7pm; Sun 10.30am–12.30pm in summer only), and the classical Mansart-designed **Hôtel de Ville** opposite, with a beautiful formal garden in front, of yew and clipped box and avenues of limes, designed by Le Nôtre.

For a place to stay, there are several reasonable **hotels**. Among the cheaper are *Le Périgord*, 22 rue Émile-Zola (☎63.59.04.74; ①), *Hôtel de France*, 8 rue des Trois-Rois (☎63.59.04.89; ③), and *Hôtel Rivière*, quai des Jacobins (☎63.59.04.53; ③). Best of the lot, and only a little more expensive, is the grandiose and old-fashioned *Grand-Hôtel* right on the riverbank at 11 rue de la Libération (☎63.59.00.30; ③). If you're **camping** there's a site on av Roquecourbe.

In addition to the hotel restaurants, you can **eat** at the *brasseries*, *Grand Café de l'Europe* and *Le Glacier* on pl Jean-Jaurès, where there's a **market** every Tuesday, Thursday, Friday and Saturday. Alternatives are *La Feuillantine* opposite the Jaurès museum, *La Périchole*, 6 rue d'Empare, and, going more upmarket, *Aux Crus d'Alsace*, 21 rue Thomas, or *L'Eau à la Bouche*, 6 rue Malpas.

The town

The *Hôtel de Ville* is home to the **Musée Goya** (Tues–Sun 9am–noon & 2–5pm/6pm; open Mon only in July & Aug). That is something of a misnomer, for it's really a collection of sixteenth- and seventeenth-century mainly Spanish painting, with just three Goyas, including a good self-portrait, the huge canvas of the **Philippines junta**, and a fair number of predictably macabre drawings.

Castres' other specialist museum is the **Musée Jean-Jaurès**, dedicated to its native son. Located in place Pélisson (same hours as the Musée Goya), getting to it takes you through the streets of the old town, past the splendid seventeenth-century **Hôtel Nayrac**. The museum, beautifully laid out according to the latest notions of museum design, was opened in 1988 by President Mitterrand – appropriately enough, because Mitterand's Socialist Party is the direct descendant of Jaurès' SFIO, founded in 1905, which split at the Congress of Tours in 1920, with the "Bolshevik" element leaving to form the French Communist Party. The museum, although slightly hagiographic as you might expect, nonetheless pays well-deserved tribute to one of France's boldest and best political writers, thinkers and activists of modern times. Jaurès supported Dreyfus, founded the newspaper *L'Humanité*, campaigned against the death penalty and colonialism, and was murdered for his courageous pacifist stance at the outbreak of the First World War – oddly enough, by a man called Villain! There could be no better epitaph than his own last article in *L'Humanité*, in which he wrote "The most important thing is that we should continue to act and to keep our minds perpetually fresh and alive…That is the real safeguard, the guarantee of our future".

Around Castres: le Sidobre

Just east of Castres rises the westernmost extremity of the *Parc du Haut Languedoc*, cut by deep river valleys and covered with marvellous woods. It's an area renowned for its **granite**: huge boulders litter the woods, often carved by the millennia into zoomorphic or other shapes – *les Trois Fromages* and *l'Oie*, for example – that give them commercial value in the eyes of the tourist industry. This is the **Sidobre** – certainly best explored on foot: the **GR36** footpath passes this way.

LACROUZETTE, 15km from Castres, is the main town, and capital of the granite industry. The demand for tombstones being impervious to recession, the town continues to prosper, judging by the number of Jaguars and Mercs in what is otherwise a thoroughly dreary place. However, if you're on your way up the Agout and Gijou valleys to Lacaze and Lacaune and feel homesick for the English tongue, the English-run *Hôtel Relais du Sidobre* (☎63.5060.06; ③) makes a convenient and pleasant stopover.

The Gers

The *département* of **Gers** west of Toulouse lies at the heart of the historic region of Gascony. In the long struggle for supremacy between the English and the French in the Middle Ages it had the misfortune to form the frontier zone between the English base at Bordeaux and the French at Toulouse – hence the large number of fortified villages or *castelnaux* dominating the hilltops. It is attractive, if unspectacular, rolling agricultural land dotted with ancient semi-fortified farms. Settlement is sparse and, with the exception of Auch, the capital, major monuments largely lacking, which keeps it well off the beaten tourist trails.

The region's traditional sources of renown are its stout-hearted mercenary warriors – of whom Alexandre Dumas' **d'Artagnan** and Edmond Rostand's **Cyrano de Bergerac** are the supreme literary exemplars – and its rich cuisine and Armagnac. The food and brandy still flourish: the Gers is the biggest producer of *foie gras* in the country. Other traditional dishes are *magret* of duck, Henri IV's *poule au pot* (the chicken that he promised to provide for every peasant's Sunday dinner), *confit* of chicken and goose and *daube de porc* – cassoulet, too, flavoured with the sausage of neighbouring Toulouse. Then there's *croustade*, a tart of apple and Armagnac, the speciality of Gascon *pâtissiers*. And to wash it all down there are the red wines of Madiran, Buzet and Saint-Mont and the whites of the Côtes de Gascogne.

If you're car-borne and prefer to keep away from the towns, there could be no more congenial or economical base for exploring the region than the English-run *Hôtel Rison* in St-Clar (see below).

Auch

The sleepy, provincial capital of Gers, **AUCH** is most easily accessible by rail from Toulouse, 78km to the east. The old town, which is the only part worth exploring, stands on a bluff overlooking the tree-lined River Gers with the cathedral prominent at its edge.

It is this building – the **Cathédrale Ste-Marie** (9am–noon & 2–5.30pm) – which makes a trip to Auch worthwhile. Although not finished until the latter part of the seventeenth century, it is basically late Gothic, almost expiring Gothic in fact, with a Classical facade. But what is of particular interest are the **choir stalls and the stained glass**. Although both were begun in the early 1500s, the windows are of clearly Renaissance inspiration, while the choir remains Gothic. The stalls are thought to have been carved by the same craftsmen who executed the stalls at St-Bertrand-de-Comminges, and show all the same extraordinary virtuosity and detail. The eighteen windows, nearly unique in being a complete set, parallel the scenes and personages depicted in the stalls. They are the work of a Gascon painter, Arnauld de Moles, and are equally rich in detail.

Immediately south of the cathedral, the tree-filled place Salinis by the fourteenth-century ecclesiastical court and prison, the forty-metre-tall **Tour d'Armagnac**, leads to a **monumental stairway** descending to the river with a statue of d'Artagnan on one of the terraces. From the west front of the cathedral rue d'Espagne, with a number of old houses, connects with rue de la Convention and what is left of the narrow medieval stairways known as the **Pousterles**, which gave access to the lower town. Opposite the cathedral front, on the corner of place de la République and **rue Dessolles**, the **SI** (9am–noon & 2–5.30/6pm; Sun & Mon pm only, and closed these days out of season) inhabits a splendid half-timbered house dating from the fifteenth century, with other fine houses further along the street and the only reasonably priced eating places in town. Beyond the SI place de la Libération leads to the allées d'Étigny, with the **gare routière** off to the right.

Just below rue Dessolles on place Louis-Blanc, the former **Couvent des Jacobins** houses one of the best collections of pre-Colombian and later **South American art** in France, left to the town by an adventurous son, M. Pujos, who had lived in Chile in the last years of the nineteenth century. Now known as the **Musée des Jacobins** (May–Oct daily except Mon 10am–noon & 2–6pm; Nov–April daily except Sun & Mon 10am–noon & 2–4pm; 6F), it also boasts a comprehensive collection of traditional Gascon tools, pottery, furniture and so forth, as well as paintings and Roman remains.

Practicalities

For a very central **place to stay**, try the modest *Hôtel des Trois Mousquetaires* at 5 rue d'Espagne near the cathedral (☎62.05.13.25; ②). Slightly superior alternatives are the *Hôtel de Paris*, 38 av de la Marne (☎62.63.26.22; ③), and *Le Relais de Gascogne*, 5 av de la Marne (☎62.05.26.81; ④). To reach av de la Marne from the gare SNCF, turn right on av de la Gare, follow it to the end and turn left.

There's also a **youth hostel**, *Foyer des Jeunes Travailleurs* (☎62.05.34.80), in a housing development at Le Garros, about 25 minutes' walk from the station: take rue Voltaire opposite the station, turn left at the end and keep straight on into rue Eugène-Sue, then follow rue Augusta until you reach the Nervol gas station, where you turn left, then right into rue du Bourget. The **camping municipal** is also off to the right of rue Augusta and there's a GR653 *gîte d'étape* 4km east at the Château St-Cricq (☎62.63.10.17)

Bus connections can take you on to Fleurance, Lectoure and Condom.

Fleurance, Lectoure, Condom

These are quiet **country towns** with no great sights, but, with the surrounding countryside, they make for a lazy taste of French provincial life. Away from the main roads, however, – the N21 for Fleurance and Lectoure, the D930 for Condom – you'll be stymied without your own transport.

Fleurance

FLEURANCE, 24km north of Auch, has a typical *bastide* central square, pl de la République, bordered by arcaded shops and houses, with the difference that its medieval *halle*, now the town hall, was most successfully converted into mellow classical stone in the nineteenth century. There's a market on Tuesdays. The church is worth a look, too, for its octagonal Toulouse-style belfry and, more particularly, the three stained-glass windows executed by Arnaud de Moles, the artist of Auch cathedral. *Hôtel Capelli* at 72 rue Gambetta (☎62.06.11.88; ③) makes a good place to stay. The **SI** is at 100 rue Pasteur.

ST-CLAR: A COUNTRY BASE

For a really welcoming place to stay, especially if you have a hankering to speak English, you can't do better than the *Hôtel Rison* (☎62.66.40.21; ①–②) in the village of **ST-CLAR**, 15km east of Lectoure and about the same distance from Fleurance. It's simple and cheap and kept authentically provincial by its English owners, who also specialise in traditional provincial cooking in their restaurant. In addition to pointing you in the direction of St-Clar's own magnificent market square and wooden-pillared *halle* (market on Thursdays; from July to October garlic's the thing – one of the biggest garlic markets in the country) they can also feed you with information about the whole region.

Lectoure

LECTOURE, 11km further north, is the smallest and prettiest of these three towns, built astride a high ridge looking out over the surrounding farmland. Capital of the colony of *Novempopulania* in Roman times and of the counts of Armagnac until their demise at the hands of Louis XI in 1473, it is now renowned for its melons. In the middle of the main street its **Cathédrale de St-Gervais-et-de-St-Protais** raises its enormous tower above the town, while down the rue Fontelié among the scarcely altered medieval houses you come to the **Fontaine de Diane** which, except for the handsome Mairie (**SI**) with its **Musée lapidaire** (daily 9am–noon & 2–5pm/6pm) containing some interesting Roman bits and pieces, pretty much exhausts the sights. Quite surprisingly, however, there is a **youth hostel** and **GR65** *gîte d'étape* – in rue St-Gervais by the cathedral (☎62.68.76.98; open April–Oct). Alternatively, there's the old-fashioned *Hôtel de France* in the main street (☎62.68.70.65; ③), and **camping municipal** on the edge of town.

Condom and environs

Some 43km north of Auch and 21km west of Lectoure, **CONDOM**'s road signs have been interfered with predictably by passing Brits: there's sadly no connection between the place and the device. Unremarkable in every other sphere, Condom is nonetheless good for a quick visit or an overnight stop, with its cathedral and attractive old streets in the centre. Armagnac drinkers will be interested in the **Musée de l'Armagnac**, 2 rue Jules-Ferry (Mon–Sat 10am–noon & 2–6pm) and the **Chais Ryst-Duperon** where the liquor is aged (June–Sept 9am–noon & 2–5pm, Sat 10am–noon & 2.30–7pm, Sun 2.30–6.30pm). For places to taste and buy Armagnac, ask the SI in place Bossuet. If you want to stay, try the *Hôtel Continental* at 22 rue Maréchal-Foch (☎62.28.00.58; ④). There's another GR65 **gîte** at the *Centre Salvandy* (☎62.28.23.80) and **camping municipal** near the river on the road to Eauze. For a straightforward **place to eat** try the pizzeria *L'Origan* at 4 rue Cadéot in the town centre (closed Sun & Mon).

Just 5km west of Condom, the tiny walled village of **LARRESSINGLE** is certainly very pretty, but is totally given over to the heritage industry, with twee tearooms or equivalent inside – and it only takes one coachload of visitors to swamp it.

More interesting is the very fine abbey of **FLARAN** 8km along the road to Auch (daily July–Aug 9.30am–7pm; June 9.30am–noon & 2–7pm; rest of the year 9.30am–noon & 2–6pm). Built by the Cistercians in 1151 in pale white stone it has the same scrubbed, ascetic appeal as Fontenay in Burgundy, with scarcely a hint of ornament – an effect totally destroyed by the decadent, incongruous plasterwork introduced into the monks' dormitory in the seventeenth century. Used as an Armagnac store until 1970, after undergoing many other vicissitudes in its long history, the monastery has only recovered its true identity in the last twenty years. With luck the spacious garden and herb patch will also receive some attention soon.

travel details

Trains

From Nîmes 5–6 TGVs daily to Paris (4hr 30min); frequent to Avignon (30min), Montpellier (30min), Sète (1hr); Béziers (1hr 30min), Narbonne (1hr 50min) and Perpignan (2hr 30min) or Carcassonne (2hr 30min); 4 daily to Paris via Alès (40min), Génolhac (1hr 25min), Villefort (1hr 40min), La Bastide-St-Laurent (2hr 10min), Clermont-Ferrand (5hr), and Vichy (6hr), including, from June to September, *Le Cévenol*, a *train touristique*, more frequent between Nîmes and Alès only; 3–4 daily to Arles (20min) and Marseille (1hr).

From Montpellier 5–6 TGVs daily to Paris (5hr); frequent to Lyon via Nîmes (30min) and Avignon (1hr); and to Sète (30min), Béziers (1hr), Narbonne (1hr 20min), Perpignan (2hr) or Carcassonne (2hr), and Toulouse (3hr 15min); 3–4 daily to Arles (1hr) and Marseille (1hr 40min); 1 daily to Mende (3hr 10min) via Nîmes and Alès.

From Sète frequent to Montpellier (30min), Nîmes (1hr), Avignon (1hr 30min); and to Béziers (30min), Narbonne (50min), and Perpignan (1hr 30min) or Carcassonne (1hr 30min); 3–4 daily to Marseille (2hr 10min) via Arles (1hr 30min).

From Béziers frequent to Paris (8hr 40min) via Montpellier, Lyon, and Dijon; 4 daily to Bédarieux (40min), Millau (2hr), and into the Massif Central; 3–4 daily to Marseille (2hr 30min) via Sète (30min), Montpellier (1hr), Nîmes (1hr 30min), Arles (2hr); more frequent continuing to Avignon (2hr) from Nîmes; frequent to Narbonne (20min) and Perpignan (1hr) or Carcassonne (1hr); several to Agde (12min) and Sète (25min).

From Narbonne frequent to Carcassonne (40min); 8 daily continue to Toulouse or Bordeaux; several daily to Perpignan (30–40min), Cerbère (1hr–1hr 30min), Port-Bou (1hr 20min–1hr 40min), and on into Spain; frequent to Béziers (20min), Sète (50min), Montpellier (1hr 20min), Nîmes (1hr 50min), Avignon (2hr 20min); 3–4 via Nîmes and Arles (2hr) to Marseille (2hr 40min).

From Carcassonne 8 daily to Toulouse (45min) or Bordeaux (3hr 20min); frequent to Narbonne (40min); several daily to Béziers (1hr), Sète (1hr 30min), Montpellier 2hr), Nîmes (2hr 30min), Avignon (3hr); 3–4 daily via Nîmes and Arles (3hr 20min) to Marseille (4hr); several daily to Quillan (1hr).

From Toulouse 8–10 daily to Bordeaux (2hr 45min) and Paris (8hr); 4 daily to Bayonne (4hr) via Tarbes (2hr), Lourdes (2hr 20min), Pau (2hr 30min); several to Auch (1hr), to Albi (1hr) and Castres (1hr 20min); 5–6 daily to Mazamet (1hr 40min) via Castres; 4 daily to Brive (4hr 10min); several to Barcelona (7hr 15min) via Pamiers (50min), Foix (1hr 5min), Tarascon (1hr 20min), Ax-les-Thermes (1hr 45min) and La-Tour-de-Carol (1hr 55min); 4– 5 daily to Luchon (2hr – some involve bus from Montréjeau); 6 daily to Lyon (6hr); 10 daily to Marseille (4hr 30min).

Buses

From Nîmes 6 daily to Aigues-Mortes (50min) and Grau-du-Roi (1hr); 5 to La Grande-Motte (1hr 15min); several daily to Pont-du-Gard (40min) and Uzès (55min); several to Avignon (1hr 30min); hourly to Montpellier (1hr 30min); 1–3 to Sommières (50min); 3–4 to Ganges (1hr 20min) and Le Vigan (1hr 40min).

From Montpellier good network radiating out, with about 6 daily on N9 to Gignac (45min), Lodève (1hr 5min), Le Caylar, La Cavalerie (1hr 50min), Millau (2hr 15min) and Rodez (3hr 55min); 4–5 to Clermont-l'Hérault (1hr) and Bédarieux (1hr 35min), with connections on to St-Pons; several to Viols-le-Fort (40min), St-Martin-de-Londres (50min), Ganges (1hr 15min), Le Vigan (1hr 40min); frequent to Palavas (20min), Aigues-Mortes (1hr 30min), La Grande-Motte (45min), Grau-du-Roi (1hr), Nîmes (1hr 45min) and Sète (1hr); 2–5 daily to Pézenas and Béziers; occasional to Sommières and Alès.

From Sète several daily to Montpellier (1hr).

From Béziers frequent to Montpellier (1hr 35min); 5 daily to Narbonne (40min); several to Pézenas (40min); 1–2 daily to La Salvetat (2hr 10min) via St-Chinian (50min) and St-Pons-de-Thomières (1hr 20min); 2 daily to Castres (3hr 30min) via St-Pons and Mazamet (3hr); frequent to Valras.

From Bédarieux 4–5 daily to St-Pons-de-Thomières (1hr) via Pont-de-Tarassac (30min) and Olargues (40min); 1 daily (except Tues & Sun) to Lacaune.

From Narbonne 4–5 daily to Béziers (40min); 3 to Perpignan (1hr 40min); 1 to Carcassonne (1hr

20min); 4–5 to Gruissan (35min); several to Narbonne-Plage.

From Carcassonne 2 daily to Quillan; 3 to Toulouse (2hr 30min) via Castelnaudary (1hr); daily coach tours with *Cars Teissier* to Lastours and Mas-Cabardès.

From Toulouse several daily to Ax-les-Thermes (3hr 10min) via Pamiers (1hr 25min), Foix (2hr) and Tarascon (2hr 25min); several to Albi (1hr 30min); 2–3 to Castres (1hr 30min); 1 daily to Auch (3hr 35min).

From Castres 6 daily to Mazamet (30min); 2 to Carcassonne; 2–3 to Toulouse (1hr 30min); 1 daily to Lacaune.

From Auch 4 to 6 daily to Agen (1hr 30min) via Fleurance (20min) and Lectoure (40min); 2 daily (except Sun) to Montauban (2hr); 3–4 to Tarbes (2hr 10min); 1 daily to Condom (40min) and Bordeaux (3hr 40min).

CHAPTER TWELVE

THE MASSIF CENTRAL

One of the loveliest spots on earth . . . a country without roads, without guides, without any facilities for locomotion, where every discovery must be conquered at the price of danger or fatigue . . . a soil cut up with deep ravines, crossed in every way by lofty walls of lava, and furrowed by numerous torrents.

So one of George Sand's characters described the Haute-Loire, the central *département* of the **Massif Central**, and it's a description which could still be applied to most of the region. Thickly forested, and sliced by numerous rivers and lakes, these mountains are geologically the oldest part of France, and culturally one of the most firmly rooted in the past. Industry and tourism have made few inroads here, and the people remain rural and taciturn (they have a reputation, largely unfounded, for unfriendliness), with an enduring sense of regional identity.

The Massif Central takes up a huge portion of the centre of France, but only a handful of towns have gained a foothold in its rugged terrain. **Le Puy**, spiked with jagged pinnacles of lava and with a majestic cathedral, is the most compelling, but there is appeal, too, in the elegant spa city of **Vichy** and in the capital **Clermont-Ferrand** – both of which make convenient bases for explorations. The heart of the region is the **Auvergne**, a wild, inaccessible landscape dotted with extinct volcanic peaks known as *puys*, much of it now incorporated into the *Parc Naturel Régional des Volcans d'Auvergne*, France's largest regional park. Among the poorest regions in France, it is startlingly insular and staunchly religious, sheltering Romanesque churches in almost every village, and rigid, black sculptures of the Madonna and Child. To the southeast are the gentler wooded hills of the **Cévennes**, where Robert Louis Stevenson and his donkey made one of the more famous literary hikes in the late nineteenth century – now also part of a national park, the *Parc National des Cévennes*. The two together make for some of the finest walking in the land.

NORTH AND EAST AUVERGNE

The northern and eastern portions of Auvergne make up much the most densely populated part of the Massif Central, taking in Clermont-Ferrand, Vichy and Le Puy, and the industrial (and soccer) centre of **St-Étienne**. **Clermont** and **Vichy** both have good train links with Paris and make obvious jumping-off points – not just for parts in this section but for much of the vast National Park of the Auvergne. To the west, **Le Puy**, a slow haul through the central mountains, gives access to the Cévennes and Ardèche.

HOTEL ROOM PRICES

For a fuller explanation of these price codes, see the box on p.28 of *Basics*.

① Under 100F ② 100–130F ③ 130–180F ④ 180–230F ⑤ 230–300F

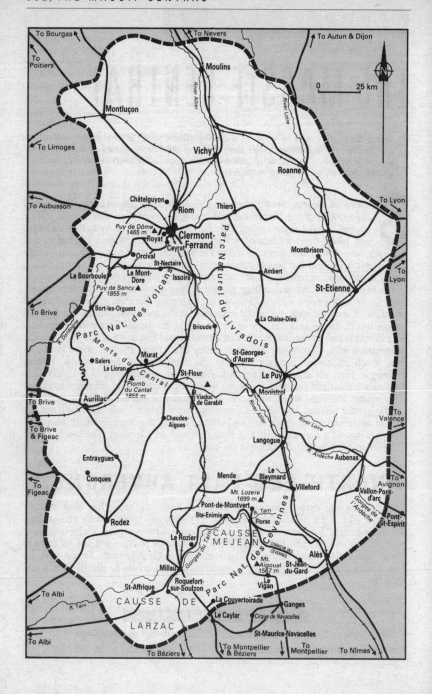

Clermont-Ferrand and around

Geographic and economic centre of the Massif Central, big industrial **CLERMONT-FERRAND** is an incongruous capital for rustic Auvergne, a lively, youthful place with a major university and a manufacturing base that – with St-Étienne and Paris – has been steadily depopulating the villages of the province. However, as a base for this side of the Massif it's ideal, with a wide choice of rooms and some good restaurants and bars. It is interesting in its own right, too, with a well-preserved historic centre and the nearby spectacles of the **Puy de Dôme** and the **Parc des Volcans**.

You're likely to spend most of your time in CLERMONT, since what is left of Vieux MONTFERRAND stands out on a limb to the north. Montferrand once greatly outshone its neighbour and rival but has gradually become no more than a suburb of the larger Clermont, which is a pity – for what remains of the original town, with its streets of ancient houses, is elegant and has recently been immaculately restored. (For a break from the more frenetic atmosphere of Clermont, you can get out here easily enough on bus #7 from place de Jaude.)

Both towns, despite long and vaguely illustrious pasts, were peacefully obscure by the time of their union in 1631. It took the arrival of one Mme Daubrée, niece of Charles Macintosh (of raincoat fame), to change things. She brought all the skills of her uncle to France with her and made rubber into bouncing balls for her children, an idea taken up by her entrepreneurial husband when he opened a small factory in 1832 dedicated to making and marketing rubber goods. His partner's grandsons, Édouard and André Michelin, adapted the factory to the demands of the emerging pneumatic tyre industry and so the Michelin empire was forged, and with it the city's (continuing) industrial base.

Arrival and accommodation

The **gare SNCF** is on av de l'URSS, east of the city centre, and is connected by regular bus with place de Jaude. The **gare routière** is next to the main **SI** office, which is at 69 bd Gergovia (Mon–Sat 8am–7pm, Sun 9am–noon & 2–6pm; Oct–May Mon–Fri 9am–6.30pm, Sat 9am–noon & 2–6pm), with annexes at the gare SNCF (Mon–Sat only), on place de Jaude (June–Sept only) and rue de la Rodade in Montferrand (June–Sept). At any of these you should be able to pick up a copy of *Le Mois à Clermont*, which details everything that's happening in the city. Other sources of information include the *Centre d'Information Jeunesse* at 8 place Regensburg, which concentrates on long-term accommodation and jobs, and the student-orientated *CROUS* office, 26 rue Étienne-Dollet, south of the main SI. The focal point of the **city transport system** is place de Jaude: you can get just about anywhere in town from here, and there's an information and ticket booth to find out how. You can either buy a single ticket which lasts an hour, or, much cheaper, invest in a book of ten tickets or a daily *carte de jour*.

Cheap beds are easy to find. There's a **youth hostel** at 55 av de l'URSS (☎73.92.26.39; March–Oct), two minutes' walk from the train station, and a *Foyer International des Jeunes* at 12 place Regensburg (☎73.93.07.82), in the midst of a noisy housing development, with beds for a little more. The *Foyer St-Jean* at 17 rue Gaultier-de-Biauzat (☎73.37.14.31) charges slightly more but is much the nicest option of the three and has a bargain canteen. There is a cluster of **cheap hotels** in av de l'URSS right outside the station, of which the most reliable is *Le Bellevue*, 1 av de l'URSS (☎73.92.43.12; ②). There's also the *Moderne*, opposite at 57 av Charras (☎73.91.50.63; ②), the *Hôtel de la Gare*, 76 av Charras (☎73.92.07.82; ②), or, for something nearer the centre, *Hôtel Foch*, 22 rue Maréchal-Foch (☎73.93.48.40; ③), close to place de Jaude. For **campers**, ROYAT has 1* and 4* sites, and there's a 3* site a little further out in CEYRAT.

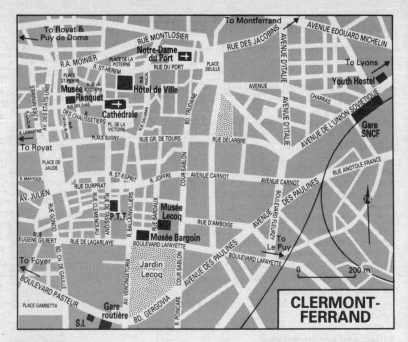

The city

Clermont's "ville-noire" aspect – so-called after the local black volcanic rock used in the construction of many of its buildings – becomes immediately apparent on entering the remnants of pre-rubber Clermont. Dark and solid, it clusters untidily around the summit of a worn-away volcanic peak.

The main streets of this quarter are **rue des Gras** and, running roughly parallel, **rue de la Boucherie**, a fragrant bazaar of tiny shops selling all kinds of food and spices. The **Musée Ranquet** on Petite-Rue-St-Pierre (May–Sept 10am–noon & 2–6pm; rest of year 10am–noon & 2–5pm; closed Sun am & Mon) is one of the city's best museums, with displays on local history back to Roman times.

These streets gather up to the dark and soaring **Cathédrale Notre-Dame**, its black-grey volcanic stone evocatively and accurately described by Freda White as "like the darkest shade of a pigeon's wing". This stone, black lava brought from nearby Volvic, was first used in the thirteenth century (the cathedral dates from 1248 – until then tools were not strong enough to cut it), and its uncommon strength permitted a radical change in construction and design, making it possible to build vaults and pillars of unheard-of slenderness and height. Inside, the building is Gothic at its most movingly inspired, delicately aspiring heavenwards out of the gloom, despite its heavy nineteenth-century fixtures (the originals were destroyed in the Revolution). Off the nave, there is access to the **Tour de la Bayette** (small admission charge), which has extensive views across the city. From this vantage point, too, you can understand why locals use the cathedral as a short cut – something the authorities have been trying to put a stop to for years, though these days at least there aren't any flocks of animals in tow.

A short step northeast of the cathedral stands Clermont's other great church, the **Basilique Notre-Dame-du-Port** – a century older and in almost total contrast both in style – Romanesque – and substance, built from softer stone in pre-lava-working days, and consequently corroding badly from exposure to Clermont's polluted air. For all that, it's a beautiful building, pure Auvergnat Romanesque with a Madonna and Child over the south door in the strangely stylised local form, both figures stiff and upright, the child more like a dwarf than an infant. Inside, it exudes the broody mysteriousness so often generated by the Romanesque style. Put a franc in the slot and you can light up the intricately carved ensemble of leaves, knights and biblical figures on the church's pillars and capitals. Outside, in **place Delille**, Pope Urban II preached the First Crusade in 1095 to a vast crowd who received his speech with the Occitan cry of "Dios lo Volt" (God wills it) – a phrase adopted by the crusaders in justification of all subsequent massacres.

On the edge of old Clermont, the huge and soulless **place de Jaude** is by day the noisome hub of the city centre and its main shopping area, and by night a desolate no-man's-land of drunks and glue-sniffers. In the centre stands a rousing statue of the Gallic chieftain Vercingétorix, who in 53 BC led his people to their only – and indecisive – victory over Julius Caesar, on the high windswept plateau of Gergovie south of town. North from place de Jaude, **place St-Pierre** is Clermont's principal marketplace, with a morning food **market** (Tues–Sat) that's at its liveliest on Saturday morning. South of the old centre on the busy bd La Fayette, there are a couple of museums that may be interesting if you've got an hour or so to kill: **Musée Lecoq**, opposite a large park of the same name, where you can't walk or even lie on the grass, has a fair natural history collection, while the almost adjoining **Musée Bargoin**, which forms the other half of the Musée Ranquet (see above), has exhibits of archaeology, religious sculpture and visual arts. Both museums keep the same hours as the Musée Ranquet.

Practicalities

For **eating**, there's a *Flunch* cafeteria at 8 av des États-Unis for a straightforward cheap and cheerful meal. *Le Stromboli* at 18 rue du Cheval-Blanc serves good pizza and pasta; *La Couscousserie*, 20 rue Cadène, off place de Jaude, is a good North African place, and the *Pied de Cochon*, at 4 rue Lamartine, again near place de Jaude, offers an amazingly cheap three-course menu. For something a little fancier, try *Le Charade*, 51 rue Bonnabaud, with menus from 110F. As for **places to drink**, try *Le Clown* at 65bis rue Anatole-France, or the *Horn Pub* at no. 31 (closed Mon), both just behind the train station, and both often with live music.

Moving on, *Le Cévenol*, a stopping train through the mountains to Nîmes, is one of the most enchanting French rail journeys you can take – so much so that during the summer the *SNCF* runs a *train touristique* with entertainment on board. If you're planning on exploring the surrounding countryside on foot, *Chamina* (the Occitan word for walking), 5 rue Pierre-le-Vénérable, has information on the paths, *gîtes d'étapes*, and anything else to do with the hills of the Massif Central. There's also a **Parc des Volcans** information office at 28 rue St-Esprit.

West of Clermont: Royat and Puy de Dôme

Clermont's main western suburb, **ROYAT**, to the west, began as a spa resort in the nineteenth century. Higher and breezier than Clermont, it too provides an attractive hour or so's respite. There are few particular sights – the ruins of Roman baths in the park, a fortified Romanesque church – but the centre has a pleasant villagey feel, leading out to riverside walks along the valleys of the Tiretaine and the Charade. If you've got the energy to make the climb, there are also fine views over the city and the surrounding country from the nearby *puys* of Montaudou and Chateix.

A longer walk – a couple of hours from Royat – or a bus ride from Clermont, is the **Puy de Dôme**, one of the tallest of the *puys*, with sweeping views back towards the town and over to the Parc des Volcans, stretching away amid shreds of cloud. Close to the summit, ruins survive of a Roman temple to Mercury, in its time considered one of the marvels of the Empire, fashioned from over fifty different kinds of marble and with an enormous bronze statue of Mercury where a TV antenna now stands. Walking out to the *puy* from Clermont, or Royat, allow a good half day – and take food. The restaurant on the top enjoys a monopoly and makes full use of it.

North of Clermont: Riom

Just 15km north of Clermont, **RIOM** is sedate and provincial. One-time capital of the entire Auvergne, its Renaissance architecture now secures the town's status as a highlight of the northern Massif. In 1942, just before the first trains of Jewish deportees were shipped to Nazi Germany, Léon Blum, Jewish Prime Minister and architect of the Socialist Popular Front government, was put on trial in Riom by Pétain, France's collaborationist ruler, in an attempt to blame the country's ills on the Left. Defending himself, Blum turned the trial into an indictment of collaboration and Nazism. Under pressure from Hitler, Pétain called it off, but none the less deported Blum to Germany, an experience which he survived, to give evidence against Pétain himself after the war.

You may not want to stay for more than a morning's wandering, but it provides a worthwhile stopover for lunch if you're on the way up to Vichy. It's an aloof, old-world kind of place, still Auvergne's judicial capital, with a nineteenth-century **Palais de Justice** that stands on the site of a grand palace built when the dukes of Berry controlled this region in the fourteenth century. Only the **Ste-Chapelle** survives of the palace, with some fine stained glass and tapestries (guided visits only; July & Aug Mon–Fri 3–5.30pm; Sept Wed & Fri 3–5.30pm; May & June Wed 3–5.30pm; 15F).

There is an interesting museum on the region's folk traditions nearby at 10 bis rue Delille, the **Musée Régional d'Auvergne** (daily except Tues 10am–noon & 2.30–5.30pm; 15F), with the **Musée Mandet**'s displays of Roman finds and unexciting paintings not far away at 4 rue de l'Hôtel-de-Ville (same hours). At 44 rue du Commerce, the **Église Notre-Dame-du-Marthuret** holds Riom's most valued treasures, two statues of the Virgin and Child – one a Black Madonna, the other, the so-called *Vierge à l'Oiseau*, a touchingly realistic piece of carving that portrays the young Christ with a bird fluttering in his hands. A copy stands in the entrance hall of the church (its original site), where you can see it with the advantage of daylight.

Practicalities

Riom's **SI** is at 16 rue du Commerce in the town centre (Mon–Sat 9am–noon & 2–6pm). If you decide to stay, the *Grand Hôtel Desaix*, 1 pl Martyrs-de-la-Résistance (☎73.38.20.36; ②), *Hôtel du Square*, 26 bd Desaix (☎73.38.46.52; 2–③), *Hôtel de Lyon*, 107 Faubourg-de-la-Bade (☎73.38.07.66; ②; closed May–mid-Sept), are all good value, and the first two have their own **restaurants** with inexpensive menus.

Around Riom

SNCF buses run to **MOZAC**, on the edge of town, with a twelfth-century **abbey church**, its Romanesque sculpture beautiful as ever, and on to the bourgeois spa-resort of **CHÂTEL-GUYON** (10–20 min). With thirty different **hot springs**, great views over the surrounding countryside and *puys*, and a couple of well-equipped **campsites**, this is as good a place as any if you want to rest up for a night. And for an easy stroll, you can wander out along the leafy **valleys of the Sardon and Prades** to the château of **Tournoël**.

South of Clermont: the plateau de Gergovie and Issoire

In the opposite direction from Clermont, heading south to LE PUY by the backroads, buses run from place de Jaude to **ROMAGNAT**, just beyond the **southern outskirts** of the city. From here it's a short walk to the **plateau of Gergovie**, where the Gauls won their only victory over the Romans in 53 BC (see above: "The City"). Beyond, you can stroll on through the villages of JUSSAT and CHANONAT to take in the medieval château of OPME.

By way of the main N9 and N102 – a quick but not terribly spectacular alternative – **ISSOIRE** is the only place of any note you pass, a small, rather drab industrial town, gathered into a tight centre within a wide circle of boulevards. A stronghold of Protestantism, it was decimated during the seventeenth-century Wars of Religion; a pillar erected in the *place* bears the simple legend, *Ici fut Issoire* ("Here was Issoire"). Just about the only thing to survive was the church – **St-Austremont** – Romanesque in style, with marvellously carved capitals and a beautiful crypt. Otherwise there's not a great deal to see: Issoire is a popular spot for a stopover, but its hotels are not as cheap as they might be.

Vichy

VICHY is famous for two things: its World War II puppet government under Marshal Pétain and its curative sulphurous springs, which attract thousands of ageing and ailing visitors – *curistes*, they're called – every year. There's no trace of the former, but the fact that Vichy is one of France's foremost spa resorts colours everything you see here. The population is largely elderly, genteel and rich, and swells several-fold in summer; they come here to drink the water, wallow in it, inhale its steam or be sprayed with it, and the town is almost entirely devoted to catering to them.

All of which should make it a place to avoid. Yet it's hard to dislike. There's a real *fin-de-siècle* charm about Vichy, and a curious fascination in its continuing function. The town revolves around the **Parc des Sources**, a stately tree-shaded park that takes up most of its centre. At its north end stands the **Palais**, an enormous iron-framed greenhouse in which people sit around and chat or read newspapers, while from a large tiled stand in the middle the various waters emerge from their spouts. The *curistes* line up to get their prescribed cupful, and for a small fee you can join them. The *Célestin* is the only one of the springs that is bottled and widely drunk: if you're into a taste experience, try the remaining five. They are progressively more foul and sulphurous, with the *Source de l'Hôpital*, which has its own circular building at the far end of the park, an almost unbelievably nasty creation. Each of the springs is prescribed for a different ailment and the tradition is, conveniently for the local hotel and tourist business, that apart from the *Célestin* they must all be drunk on the spot to be efficacious – a dubious but effective way of drawing in the crowds.

Although all the springs technically belong to the nation, and treatment is partially funded by the state, they are in fact run privately for profit by the *Compagnie Fermière*, first created in the nineteenth century to prepare for a visit by the Emperor Napoléon III. The *Compagnie* not only has a monopoly on selling the waters but also runs the casino and numerous hotels, including Vichy's grandest, the *Pavillon Sévigné*. Even the chairs conveniently dotted around the Parc des Sources belong to the *Compagnie*. And Vichy never fails to make money: there are over 200 hotels in town – one reason that it was chosen for the wartime government. Marshal Pétain's own offices were at the *Pavillon*, while the Gestapo had their headquarters at the *Hôtel du Portugal*. There is absolutely nothing to commemorate either.

After the waters, Vichy's curiosities are limited. There is pleasant wooded riverside in Parc de l'Allier, created again for Napoléon III. And, not far from here, the old town boasts the strange **Église de St-Blaise**, actually two churches in one, with a 1930s Baroque structure built onto the original Romanesque – an effect that sounds hideous but is rather imaginative. Inside, another Auvergne Black Virgin, *Notre-Dame-des-Malades*, stands surrounded by plaques offered by the grateful healed who stacked their odds with both her and the sulphur.

Practicalities

Vichy's **gare SNCF** is on the eastern edge of the city centre at the end of rue de Paris. The **gare routière** is on the corner of rue Doumier and rue Jardet, by the central place Charles-de-Gaulle. The building that used to house the wartime Vichy government at 19 rue du Parc is home to the **SI** (daily May–Sept 9am–7pm; Oct–April 9am–noon & 2–6pm, Sat am only), though they are, not surprisingly, very careful to make no reference at all to what once went on upstairs.

Inexpensive and adequate **hotels** can be found around the gare SNCF and along rue des Célestins. Two to try are the *Hôtel Les Antilles,* 16 rue Desbrest (☎70.98.27.01; ②), and *Hôtel Lion d'Or* (☎70.98.33.34; ③). There's also a **youth hostel** – invariably empty – across the river at 19 rue du Stade (☎70.32.25.14).

For **food** and **nightlife**, Vichy, despite the *curistes*, can be surprisingly active. The area to head for, full of cafés and *brasseries*, is around the junction of rue Clemenceau, rue de Pans, rue Lucas and rue Jean-Jaurès, a corner known locally as *les quatre chemins*. Most of the places here serve cheap meals and snacks (*vichyssoise*, inevitably, is available) and they're the obvious places to drink. If you want to move on from here, *Greenfields* is – despite the name – generally the most animated of the discos.

South to Le Puy

The slowest and most beautiful route south from Vichy is along the *Sentier de la Loire*, **GR3**, starting at CHÂTEL-MONTAGNE, heading down the ridges of the Forez mountains east of Thiers and through the Loire gorges to Le Puy. It's a serious commitment, requiring a ten-to-fourteen-day walk.

Somewhat gentler, the parallel **D906** road winds through the forested valleys a short distance west. **THIERS**, the first town, on the banks of the fast, twisting Durolle river, is a pleasant surprise, its steep streets hiding some lovely fifteenth-century timbered houses and a couple of interesting Romanesque churches, as well as stupendous views over the surrounding mountains. Thiers is noted, in France at least, for its cutlery, and scores of shops sell fine quality knives and other implements. If you want to stay, **accommodation** is limited, but there's a **campsite** at nearby LE BREUIL and a reasonable **hotel** 6km west at PONT-DE-DORE on the N89, *Hôtel de l'Avenue* (☎73.80.10.14; ③; closed 2 weeks in Aug & mid-Dec to mid-Jan).

To the southwest, and only realistically accessible for drivers, are a scattering of medieval **castles** – **Aultéribe, Ravel** (April–Nov daily 10am–noon & 2–7pm), **Mauzun and Martinanches** (mid-June to mid-Sept daily 2–7pm) – while to the southeast you can drive and hike up to the 1634-metre peak of **Pierre-sur-Haute**, the highest point of the eastern Auvergne.

Climbing higher, the road winds on to **AMBERT**, the centre of a once thriving paper-milling district, with a mill still functioning at nearby **RICHARD-DE-BAS** – well worth a visit (July & Aug daily 9am–8pm; rest of year daily 9am–noon & 2–6pm). Thirty kilometres on you reach **LA CHAISE-DIEU**, a hill village dominated by the sturdy square towers of an impressive medieval **abbey church**, one of the finest monastic buildings in the country and home to an eerily unfinished fresco of the *Dance of Death*, which shows the shadowy figure of Death plucking delicately at the coarse plump bodies of the living, who staunchly refuse to notice. "It is yourself", says the fifteenth-century text below, as indeed it might have been in the age of the Black Death and Hundred Years' War. Nearby, on place de l'Écho, the **Salle de l'Écho** is another product of the risk of contagion, if not from plague then from leprosy. In this room, once used to hear confession from the sick and dying, two people can turn their backs on each other and stand in opposite corners and have a perfectly audible conversation just by whispering.

The **SI** is to the right of the church in the central **place de la Mairie**. A couple of hotels – the *Hôtel Terminus*, av de la Gare (☎71.00.00.73; ③; closed Dec–Feb), and *Hôtel Au Tremblant* on the D906 (☎71.00.01.85; ②–④; closed mid-Nov to mid-April) – and a campsite offer a feasible chance of a bed for the night if you can't get down to LE PUY.

St-Étienne

Over to the east, on another possible approach to Le Puy from Lyon, **ST-ÉTIENNE** or *La ville où l'on fabrique de tout* (the town that makes everything), is not an especially appealing town, almost unrelievedly industrial, a major armaments centre, and enclosed for miles around by grim mineworkings, factory chimneys and warehouses. The centre is bland and characterless, the mood one of decline, since the closure of the coalfields. One thing that redeems it for a visitor (and probably for most residents, too) is the soccer team, *les Verts*, whose stickers you see on car windows all over the country. Its **Musée d'Art Moderne** at La Terrasse (daily except Tues 10am–7pm) justifies a detour for anyone interested in twentieth-century art – a quite unexpected treasure house of contemporary work, both pre- and post-World War II, with a good modern American section, in which Andy Warhol and Frank Stella figure prominently, work by Meunier, Rodin, Matisse, Léger and Ernst, and rooms filled entirely with French art, imaginatively laid out to exciting effect. The **Musée d'Art et d'Industrie** at 2 pl Louis-Comte (daily except Tues 9am–noon & 2–6pm) is also good on St-Étienne's industrial background, including the development of the revolutionary Jacquard loom.

Bus #10 runs from the **train station** into the centre of town and the **SI** on place Roannelle (daily except Sun 9am–12.30pm & 1.30–6pm). If you are forced to stay, there are several reasonable **hotels** around the station – the *Voyageurs*, 2 rue du Gris-de-Lin (☎77.32.20.95; ②), and the *National*, 3 rue Cugnot (☎77.33.11.97; ③).

Le-Puy

A strange town in a strange setting, **LE-PUY** (full name: Le Puy-en-Velay) sprawls across a broad basin in the mountains, a muddle of red roofs barbed with tall poles of volcanic rock. Capital of the Haute Loire, it isn't easy to get to – from Clermont or Nîmes you have to change trains at St-Georges-d'Aurac – but it's well worth the effort. In medieval times it was the assembly point for St-Jacques pilgrims coming from the east of France and Germany, and amid the cobbled streets of the old town are some of the most richly endowed churches in the land. The surrounding countryside is an added attraction. Try if you can to be around for the **Roi de l'Oiseau** in the second week in September – Le Puy's annual junket, when medieval archers, minstrels and jokers patrol the streets for a week before crowning the town's best archer.

Arrival and accommodation

Arriving by bus or train leaves you on place du Maréchal-Leclerc, a ten-minute walk from the central **place du Breuil,** and the SI (daily except Sun 8am–6.30pm), focus of the new town and within easy striking distance of some reasonably priced **hotels**. Of these, pride of place goes to the *Grand Hôtel Lafayette*, 17–19 bd St-Louis (☎71.09.32.85; ②), in a quiet, leafy courtyard off the main traffic artery. Though sadly dilapidated – and due for metamorphosis into an old people's home – it is one of the sights of the town, with once grand rooms that still contain period furniture and marble fireplaces, and a Gothic dining room with coffered ceiling and frescoed walls. Other possibilities include *Hôtel La Verveine* in place Cadelade (☎71.02.00.77; ②), with musical plumbing and a good restaurant, *Le Progrès*, 51 bd Maréchal-Fayolle (☎71.09.34.35; ②), in the same square, and *Les Cordeliers* – also hidden in its own courtyard – at 17 rue des Cordelières (☎71.09.01.12; ③), off rue Portail d'Avignon – the latter with a good restaurant with 69F menus. There's a **youth hostel**, the *Centre Pierre Cardinal*, at 9 rue Jules-Vallès (☎71.05.52.40) at the top of rue Général-Lafayette on the hill, and a municipal **campsite**, the 3* *Bouthézard*, off av d'Aiguilhe, in the northwest corner of town.

The old town

The main focus of the **old town**, reached up the steep sequence of streets and steps that terrace the town's *puy* foundation, the **cathedral** (daily July & Aug 8.30am–7pm; Sept–June 8.30am–noon & 2–6.30pm) is almost Byzantine in style, striped with alternate layers of light and dark stone and capped with a line of small cupolas. Oddly enough, you enter from below, the nave level reached by clambering up yet more steps. On the way, take a look at the *Fever Stone – La Pierre aux fièvres* – reputed to have the power of curing fevers by sending those who lie down upon it into a health-restoring slumber. Patchy gold frescoes pull you inside the church – dark and gloomy because of the volcanic rock of which it's built – and towards the city's own *Black Virgin*, copy of a revered original burnt during the Revolution, and still taken out, dusted, and paraded through the town every August 15. Other lesser treasures are displayed at the back of the church in the sacristy, beyond which is the entrance to the twelfth-century cloister, disarmingly beautiful and patterned with the same stripes as the cathedral facade. The surrounding ecclesiastical buildings – together with some splendid nineteenth-century stone mansions – form a small, independent *Ville Sainte*.

The cathedral is simply one of several strange and unique sights in this town, most of them stacked on wearisome heights. Behind the cathedral, visible from any street you might find yourself on, is the giant crimson statue of **Notre-Dame-de-France**, a fabulous monster fashioned from the metal of guns captured in the Crimean War, while beyond, at the end of bd Montferrand, the church of **St-Michel-d'Aiguilhe** (daily mid-June to mid-Sept 9am–7pm; mid-Sept to mid-Nov 9.30am–noon & 2–5.30pm; mid-Nov to mid-March 2–5pm; mid-March to mid-June 10am–noon & 2–6pm) sits precariously on the summit of another, even steeper and more pointed *puy*, the Rocher d'Aiguilhe, the eleventh-century construction seemingly growing out of the rock itself. It's a tough ascent, but one you should definitely make – a quirky little building decorated with mosaics, arabesques and trefoil arches, its bizarre shape forced to follow that of the available flat ground.

Back down below, lacemakers – a traditional, though now commercialised industry – do a fine trade, doilies and lace shawls hanging enticingly outside souvenir shops. But it's surface only; deeper into Le Puy's maze of narrow streets the old lanes are uncluttered and wonderful. In the **new part of town**, beyond the squat **Tour Pannessac**, **place de Breuil** joins **place Michelet** and forms a social hub, backed by the spacious Henri Vinay public gardens, where the **Musée Crozatier** (daily 10am–noon & 2–6pm; closes 4pm Oct–April; closed Tues, Sun am & Feb; 10F) is best known for its collections relating to the region's traditional lace-making activities. Busy bd Maréchal-Fayolle converges with place Cadelade, where there's another of Le Puy's crazier aspects: the extraordinary bulbous tower of the **Pages Verveine distillery**. The *verveine* (verbena) plant is normally used to make *tisane* (herb tea), but in this region provides a powerful digestive liqueur instead.

Eating and drinking

The cheapest places to **eat** in Le Puy are the *Self du Breuil*, in the same building as the SI, and the *Cafétéria Casino* in the *Casino* supermarket in av de la Dentelle. Other good bets are the *Cordeliers* hotel restaurant (see above) and the North African *Marrakesh*, 24 rue Portail-d'Avignon. Be sure to try the local specialities: fat sausages, called *Jésus*, and green lentils, invariably cooked in pork fat or served with pork like most Haute Loire dishes. *Salade auvergnat* also features on most menus, a substantial dish of green lentils cooked in lard, with chunks of ham, egg, potatoes and mayonnaise. **Market day** is Saturday, when there's something going on in practically every one of the town's squares.

Around Le Puy: hiking and excursions

Outside Le Puy, committed walkers can tackle the **GR40** *Tour du Velay*, basically a high ridge walk encircling the town and taking in an enormous variety of scenery, ranging from the "lookouts" of the Devès overhanging the Allier gorges to the high pastures of the Mézenc, the volcanic plugs of the Meygal, and the woods and meadows of the Loire valley. Other worthwhile excursions include the ruins of the thirteenth-century château at **Polignac**, the restored château of **Lavoûte-Polignac** (home of the dukes of Polignac for forty generations) beyond the Peyredeyre gorges on the Loire and, to the west, the spectacular **gorges of the Allier** between MONISTROL and ST-ARCONS.

THE PARC DES VOLCANS AND SOUTHERN MASSIF

Much of western Auvergne falls within the 3,500 square kilometres of the **Parc Naturel Régional des Volcans d'Auvergne** – the Auvergne Volcano Park – a wild country of peaks, gorges and lakes serrated by a phenomenal concentration of *puys*, most of them fragments of gigantic volcanoes that have been weathered away. The park is divided by three ranges: the Monts Dômes, the Monts Dores and the Cantal mountains. Few people live here; those that do are mainly involved in sheep and cattle farming, and now, for better or worse, in tourism. Solitude is the order of the day. If you meet anyone on the great grassy expanses of pasture covering the lava plateaux, it's likely to be the occasional shepherd or forester. Within all this are scattered traditional villages, a handful of stylish spa towns – most notably **Le Mont-Dore** and **La Bourboule** – and a growing number of winter sports resorts. **GR footpaths** cross some of the most interesting and difficult terrain (information from the office in Clermont-Ferrand – see above). Further south the cold, hard *causses* – plateaux – of the **southern Massif**, the quiet, wild hills of **the Cévennes**, and, to the east, the mountainous **Ardèche**, are all arguably parts of the southern province of Languedoc, but have an identity shaped by the mountains, quite different from that of the Mediterranean provinces.

The Monts Dômes and Monts Dores

The **Monts Dômes** range, west of Clermont-Ferrand, is the youngest in the region at 4000 years old, and includes 112 small volcanoes. The **Monts Dores**, slightly to the south, had only three centres of volcanic activity but it was much more intense, leaving hundreds of jagged projections.

Orcival

Twenty kilometres southwest of Clermont, lush pastures and green hills punctuated by the abrupt eruptions of the *puys* enclose the village of **ORCIVAL** (buses from Clermont), the home town of ex-President Valéry Giscard d'Estaing. A pretty if over-touristed little place, founded by the monks of La Chaise-Dieu in the twelfth century, it makes a suitable base for hiking in the region. It's dominated by the stunning Romanesque church of **Notre-Dame**. Built of the same grey volcanic stone as the cathedral in Clermont, the exterior, topped with a spired octagonal tower and fanned with tiny chapels, is a treat, though unfortunately the interior is marred by Gregorian muzak designed to encourage piety in the visitors, and an electronic alarm system sectioning off the choir. The purpose of the alarm is to protect another *Black Virgin*, this time enamelled and gilded, the object of pilgrimage since before the sixth century and still carried through the streets on Ascension Day. In the Middle Ages she was known as "Our Lady of Iron and Chains", and was revered by former convicts who had survived imprisonment – ironic that today she is the one who is confined in high security.

There's modest **accommodation** at the *Hôtel du Mont-Dore* (☎73.65.82.06; ②; closed mid-Nov–Dec), a couple of **campsites** and a **gîte d'étape**, *La Fontchartoux*, 1km away on GR30/GR441, with meals available in the adjoining restaurant run by the *gîte* proprietor.

Along GR441 and other walks

The footpath **GR441** continues right around the Monts Dômes on the hike known as the *Tour de la Chaine des Puys*. It's a seven-day outing, passing among more than forty extinct volcanoes, and is only really feasible between May and October.

For something less drastic, an hour's walk away along a section of GR41 is the **Château de Cordès**, a grand manor house rather than a castle, dating from the thirteenth century with extensive alterations in the seventeenth century. Its elegant suites and gardens designed by Le Nôtre provide a worthy focus for those who seek a purpose to their strolls.

Other walking possibilities out of Orcival include trips to **Lac Servière** and **Lac de Guéry**. The first takes two and a half hours, the second some five hours. For Lac Servière, follow GR4-GR30 through the woods above the valley of the Sioule. The lake is a beauty; it's 1200m up, with gently sloping shores surrounded by pasture and conifers. You can either head southeast to the *gîte d'étape* at PESSADE or continue on to the larger Lac de Guéry, lent a slightly eerie air by the black basaltic boulders strewn across the surrounding meadows. The town of MONT-DORE is only 9km further on from here.

Saint-Nectaire and around

ST-NECTAIRE lies on the other – eastern – side of the Monts Dores from Orcival. It comprises the tiny spa of St-Nectaire-le-Bas, with its main street lined with grand but fading Belle Époque hotels – there's a *gîte d'étape* just beyond – and the old village of St-Nectaire-le-Haut, overlooked by its magnificent Romanesque **church.** It also gives its name to a great cheese, widely produced in the Puy-de-Dôme and Cantal *départements*.

For a good aerial view of the local landscape, take the D150 out of the old village towards the 919-metre **Puy de Mazeyres** and turn up a path to the right for the short final climb to the summit – an hour's walk. An equally easy walk is along the D966, following the valley of the Couze de Chambon to SAILLANT, where the stream cascades down a high lava rock face in the middle of the village. For a good view, cross the bridge and continue a short distance along D26E. Stouter hearts can tackle a couple of longer hikes to local lakes. Particularly beautiful is the **Lac Chambon** (3hr), ringed with woodland and set with numerous islets. The waymarked GR30 will take you there, passing over lightly forested heath before reaching the vast medieval **castle of Murol** (June–Sept 10am–noon & 2–7pm) perched on a basalt cone with commanding views over the lake to the mountains beyond. If you don't want to go back the way you came, there are **hotels** and **campsites** near the lake and a *gîte d'étape* on down GR30 at COURBANGES. Somewhat further north – five hours – is the volcanic **Lac Aydat**, with **campsites** and a *gîte d'étape* in the nearby hamlet of PHIALEIX.

Le Mont-Dore and La Bourboule

Built along the banks of the young and shallow Dordogne, here hardly more than a trickle, **LE MONT-DORE** is an old established spa resort in the best tradition – good food and drink, walks in pleasant countryside, and a hopefully bearable cure at the baths for some not-too-serious ailment. Altogether a wholesome and civilised sort of place. The **Établissement Thermale** stands right in the town centre, and early every morning *curistes*, easily identifiable by tight-drawn scarves and overcoats, stream into the building, self-proclaimed "world centre for the treatment of asthma". Walkers frequent the town, too, using it as a base for hikes out to the **Puy de Sancy** (see below), 15km away – at 1885m, Auvergne's rooftop.

The town is brimming with **hotels**, and there's usually no problem finding a room; try *La Rûche*, 25 av des Belges (☎73.65.05.93; ③; closed Oct to mid-May Mon–Fri), or *Hôtel Terminus*, av Guyot-Dessaigne (☎73.65.00.23; ②; closed Oct–Dec & mid-April to mid-May). **Campsites**, too, are in good supply; the municipal *Les Crouzets* opposite the train station is the most convenient; and there's a big and comfortable **youth hostel** 3km out on Route du Sancy (☎73.65.03.53); take a bus from the station or the post office on pl de-Gaulle. For more general information, ask at the **SI** on av de la Libération for a copy of *La Semaine au Mont-Dore*, and also for their pamphlet on walks and drives in the area.

LA BOURBOULE is 7km down the road, an easy hitch. Known as the sister to Le Mont-Dore, it is another traditional spa – the "capital of allergies" – but with a more open feel and, due to its lower altitude, temperatures a degree or two warmer. The big casino, the domed Grands Thermes baths and several other turn-of-the-century buildings which used to house privately run baths, are ornate, gilded and wonderfully vulgar, with a faded, permanently off-season look to them – much like the whole town. All in all, it's a cool, tranquil place to unwind: as the SI's leaflet says, "You will be able to put your vital node to rest in La Bourboule".

The **SI**, in the Hôtel de Ville on place de la République, also sells a booklet of local walks. Behind the Hôtel de Ville, the large wooded **Parc Fenestre** has a *téléférique* taking you right up to **Plateau de Charlannes** at 1300m, where it's possible to stroll in the woods or ski in winter. **Hotels**, as at Le Mont-Dore, are plentiful, three good bargains being *Hôtel de la Poste*, on bd Clemenceau (☎73.81.09.66; ③; closed Oct–April), *Le Pavillon*, av d'Angleterre (☎73.65.50.18; 3–④; closed Oct–April), and the *Lutétia*, on rue des Frères-Roziers (☎73.81.05.75; ③). There is also a good selection of **campsites**, for example at MURAT-LE-QUAIRE 4km away, and along the Mont-Dore road; there's also a municipal site on av Lattre-de-Tassigny, while 2km east in the hamlet of LE PREGNOUX there's a **gîte d'étape**.

Some walks

Fit and serious walkers may want to conquer the **Puy de Sancy**, a six-hour hike south from La Bourboule on GR30-41, passing on the way (after about two hours) the two fine waterfalls of the **Cascade de la Vernière** and **Plat à Barbe** – themselves a satisfying destination for a walk. From the summit of Puy de Sancy you can take the *téléférique* down to Le Mont-Dore. For a less strenuous outing you could take it up and walk down. An easier walk out of La Bourboule is to the 1500-metre summit of the **Banne d'Ordanche**. Pick up the GR path to the east of the town where it crosses the D130 road and the railway line, then take the signposted GR41 where it diverges from GR30.

During winter months, both Le Mont-Dore and La Bourboule double as ski resorts – centres of a **ski-de-fond** (cross-country) network of circular pistes, some over 20km long. Skiable paths also connect La Bourboule to other ski villages in the locality – SANCY, BESSE, CHASTREIX and PICHERANDE. Downhill skiing is possible, too, on the Puy de Sancy.

Aurillac and the Cantal Mountains

Just south of the Monts Dores the landscape is dotted with **volcanic lakes**, among them Pavin, Chauvet and Montcineyre, with more to the west in the densely wooded country below the Plateau d'Artense. Apart from driving south on the ÉGLISENEUVE-D'ENTRAIGUES and CONDAT road (both good bases for exploring), the best way to see them is again **on foot**. The **GR30**, *Tour des Lacs d'Auvergne*, takes in the Puy de Sancy, Orcival and St-Nectaire as well as the lakes – about ten days in all – though it's not passable in winter. Alternatively, a section of the Atlantic-to-Mediterranean **GR4** passes through, crossing the Puy de Dôme and the Monts Dores, over the pastures of the Plateau du Limon and up the ridges of the **Plomb du Cantal** to the high town of ST-FLOUR (10–14 days).

The Cantal mountains, geologists say, contained a 3000-metre-high volcano, which no longer exists but has left a number of high crests. A relatively strenuous GR circuit encompasses the Cantal volcano – which with Etna is the largest, albeit extinct, volcano in Europe. Seventy kilometres in diameter, it is shaped like a wheel without a rim, the hub formed by its three spectacular conical peaks – Plomb du Cantal (1855m), Puy Mary (1787m) and Puy de Peyre-Arse (1686m) – and the spokes by deep valleys. The landscape is green and lush and devoted to sheep and dairy farming.

A convenient base for exploring the massif is **LE LIORAN**, where you can stay in the *Auberge du Tunnel* (☎71.49.50.02; ③; closed Nov), or at a **gîte** in nearby SUPER-LIORAN (June–Sept) in the centre of the mountains. **THIÉZAC** is also handy, with the possibility of staying either at the *Hôtel du Commerce* (☎71.47.01.67 – ②) or at the town campsite, on the southern outskirts, or at the pretty but touristy town of **SALERS** to the west. Here there's the *Hôtel des Remparts* (☎71.40.70.33; ④; closed mid-Nov to Dec) and *Camping le Mouriol*, though this is open summer only.

Aurillac

Southwest lies the provincial capital of **AURILLAC**, a pleasant enough town, although with little tangible to see apart from a couple of small **museums** concealed in the pedestrianised *vieille ville*, and a good one devoted to volcanoes in the Château St-Étienne (July & Aug daily except Sun & Mon 10am–6.30pm; rest of year daily 8.30am–noon & 2–5.30pm, Sat 8.30am–noon closed Sun & Mon). Wednesdays or Saturdays are the best times to be here, when peasants and farmers flock into town to sell their produce and livestock. Aurillac and the Cantal generally are noted for a traditionally rustic cuisine, with dishes like *tripoux* – stuffed sheep's feet wrapped in pieces of sheep's stomach – seen on menus from here to St-Flour and down to Chaudes-Aigues on the southern edge of the Cantal. More enticing perhaps is Cantal cheese – similar to cheddar, and one of the least expensive and most popular in France.

From the **gare SNCF** it's a fifteen-minute walk into the centre and the vigorous **place du Square**. Here you'll find the **SI** (Mon–Sat 9am–12.30pm & 2–7.30pm, Sun 10am–noon & 2–7pm; Sept–June Mon–Sat 9am–noon & 2–6.30pm), which books hotel rooms and dispenses maps, including the invaluable *IGN Monts du Cantal*. If you're staying, two reasonable **hotels** to try are *Hôtel des Voyageurs*, 4 pl Pierre-Sémard (℡71.48.01.44; ③), and *Hôtel le Square*, 15 pl du Square (℡71.48.24.72; ③). There's also a *Foyer des Jeunes Travailleurs*, with a good canteen, at 25 av de Tivoli (℡71.63.56.94; bus #1 from the station, direction Arpajon), and a riverside municipal **campsite** 1km away just off the D17. **Buses** leave daily from the main square for villages on the road to St-Flour and Conques.

East from Aurillac: Murat, St-Flour and around

"A clambering little town", Freda White called **MURAT**, 50km northeast of Aurillac, close-huddled and grey but attractive. Beyond here, you leave the Cantal mountains behind; the *puys* thin out and the country becomes high and flat all the way to **ST-FLOUR**, 25km away, whose inviting old centre is worth the long haul uphill from the **gare SNCF** (catch a bus up to allées Pompidou, on the old city's western fringe). The focal point of the old city is the **place d'Armes**, busy with a market on Saturday mornings and dominated by a severe fourteenth-century **cathedral**, built of dull grey rock, a square, rather plain building, from the outside at least. At first glance the interior seems equally austere, but it's big and beautifully vaulted, with bare stone blocks, slight traces of frescoes and some elaborate woodcarving – most prominently, a fifteenth-century figure of a black Christ on the cross. Behind the cathedral, expansive vistas take in the lower town and its two rivers. Back on place d'Armes, in the Hôtel de Ville, you'll find a museum of local life and traditions, the **Musée de la Haute-Auvergne** (daily 9am–noon & 2–6pm; closed Sat & Sun Oct–May), and, on the opposite side of the square, a rag-bag of collections in the **Musée Douet** (daily May to mid-Oct 9am–noon & 2.15–6pm) housed in the old Maison Consulaire.

For information, the **SI** can be found on place d'Armes (July & Aug daily 9am–noon & 2–7.30pm; rest of year closed Sun). If you're intending to stay, there are numerous **hotels**: try *Hôtel du Nord*, 18 rue des Lacs (℡71.60.07.33; ③) in the upper town, or *Hôtel l'Ander*, 6 av du Cdt-Delorme (℡71.60.21.63; ③; closed Jan to mid-May), in the lower. There is a **campsite** – *Les Orgues* (Easter–Oct) – in the upper town on av du Dr-Mallet.

Pushing on **south from St-Flour**, you reach a district in which the *Maquis* were very active: 15,000 Resistance fighters operated in this immediate locality, often having full-scale shootouts with the German army. A **monument** near the junction of the D4 and N9 marks the site of a battle that left a thousand *maquisards* dead. If you have your own transport, the D4 also makes a slow but spectacular route to Le Puy, crossing the wooded heights of **Mont Mouchet**, where there's another Resistance memorial and the best of all views back west to the Cantral mountains. Further south, the N9 winds below the **Garabit Viaduct**, an extraordinarily delicate tracery of steel, built by Eiffel of tower fame in 1884, to carry the railway over the River Truyère. This is wild, sparsely populated country whose grandeur and solitude not even the vast hydroelectric installations can mar. If you have an urge for the romantic, the ruins of the **Château d'Alleuze** about 20km south of St-Flour are well worth the stop. Otherwise there are no towns of any size in the area except **CHAUDES-AIGUES**, to the southwest on the D921, whose domestic hot water supply has been provided by natural springs since Roman times.

Larzac and the Causses

High **plateaux**, bleak, windswept and sparsely populated with primitive villages, the **Causses** of the southern Massif – **Causse de Larzac**, **Causse Noir**, **Causse Méjean** and **Causse de Sauveterre** – present some rugged, independent countryside. All four are riddled with strange caves, rock formations, grottoes and underground tunnels in between deep and narrow gorges: the Vallée de la Dourbie between Larzac and the Causse Noir, the Gorges de la Jonte between the Causse Noir and Méjean; and, most spectacular of all, the Gorges du Tarn between Méjean and Sauveterre.

The Causse de Larzac

In the 1970s, the **Causse du Larzac** was continually in the headlines over sustained political resistance to the high-profile presence of the French military. Originally there was a small military camp outside the village of LA CAVALERIE on the N9, long tolerated for the cash its soldiers brought in. But in the early 1970s, the army decided to expand the place and use it as a permanent strategic base, expropriating a hundred or so farms. The result was explosive. A federation was formed – *Paysans du Larzac* – which attracted the support of numerous ecological, left-wing and regionalist groups in a protracted campaign of resistance under the slogan "Gardarem lo Larzac". Successful acts of sabotage were committed, and three huge peace festivals were held here, in 1973, 1974 and again in 1977. The army's plans were scotched by Mitterrand when he came to power in 1981, but you still find Larzac graffiti from here to Lyon, shorthand for opposition to the army, the state and the Parisian central government, and in favour of self-determination and independence for the south.

The best way to immerse yourself in the empty, sometimes eerie atmosphere of Larzac is to walk: **GRs 7**, **71** and **74** cross the plateau, though you shouldn't attempt it without a *topo-guide*. Further information is available from the *Fédération interdépartementale des sentiers de pays*, BP600, Millau (☎65.61.06.57). The plateau's best-known village, **ROQUEFORT-SUR-SOULZON** – off the Millau-St-Affrique road (reachable by bus from Millau, Albi and Toulouse) – is home to Roquefort cheese, one of the most revered cheeses in France, sharp and creamy, blue-streaked and made from local ewe's milk. Its delicate maturity can only be reached in the caves here, and efforts to reproduce the conditions artificially elsewhere have failed.

A little way east the N9 cuts south from Millau to Lodève, and on eventually to Montpellier. If you have no time for anything else, the area between La Couvertoirade, Le Caylar and Ganges in the foothills of the Cévennes will give you a real sense of life on the *causse*.

LA COUVERTOIRADE lies 5km off the main road, a perfect Templar village, still completely enclosed by its towers and walls and almost untouched by renovation. Its forty remaining inhabitants live by tourism, and you have to pay just to enter the place (July & Aug daily 9.30am–6pm; rest of year daily 10am–noon & 2–5pm). Just outside the walls on the south side is a *lavogne*, a paved water-hole of a kind seen all over the *causse* for watering the flocks whose milk is used for the making of Roquefort. If you want to stay, there's the GR71 gîte d'étape in the far corner from the entrance.

Half a dozen kilometres south, the village of **LE CAYLAR** clusters in similar fashion at the foot of a rocky outcrop, the top of which has been fashioned into a fortress – worth clambering up for the aerial view of the surrounding *causse*: mean little patches of cultivated ground stolen from among the merciless upthrusts of rock.

If you've got your own transport and a good map, the backroad from here, via St-Michel to ST-MAURICE-NAVACELLES, is strongly recommended. Wild box grows along the lanes, often meticulously clipped into hedges. Here and there among the scrubby oak and thorn or driving home along the road at milking time you pass flocks of sheep. Occasional farmhouses materialise, like *Les Besses* – one of the few still in use – huge, self-contained and fortress-like, with the living quarters upstairs and the sheep stalls down below. **SAINT-MAURICE** itself, on the GR7 and GR74, is small and sleepy, with a shop and the *Hôtel des Tilleuls* opposite a moving World War I memorial by Paul Dardé. There is no official campsite, but if you ask you are directed to a grassy place by the cemetery, where a traditional *glacière* – a stone-lined pit for storing snow for use as ice before the days of refrigerators – has been restored. Its chief advantage is as a base for visiting the **Cirque de Navacelles**, 10km north on the D130 past the beautiful ruined seventeenth-century sheep farm of *La Prunarède*. The *cirque* is a widening in the 150-metre deep trench of the Vis gorges, formed by a now dry loop in the river that has left a neat pyramid of rock sticking up in the middle like a wheel hub. An ancient and scarcely inhabited hamlet survives in the bottom – a bizarre phenomenon in an extraordinary location, and you get literally a bird's eye view of it from the edge of the cliff above. Both road and GR7 go through. Continuing on to LE VIGAN or GANGES via MONTDARDIER you pass a prehistoric stone circle on the left of the road, a silent and evocative place, especially in a close wet *causse* mist. There are other stones and dolmens in the vicinity.

Millau

At the foot of the Causse Noir and Larzac, near the junction of the rivers Tarn and Dourbie, **MILLAU** is beautifully situated no matter how you approach it – a vivacious town, renowned for its glove-making, with broad streets arcaded by the branches of pollarded plane trees. There's not much to see, apart from the unusual octagonal belfry and fountain in the central square, but it has a pleasant southern feel and makes a wise overnight stop. For local history and things pertaining to glove-making there are interesting collections in the **Musée Archéologique et la Maison de la Peau et du Gant** in pl Foch (May–Oct daily 10am–noon & 2–6pm; closed Sun in winter).

The **gare SNCF** and **gare routière** are at the end of av Merle, on which you'll also find the SI – at no. 1 (Mon–Fri 9am–noon & 2–6pm, Sat 9am–noon) – and the town's most reasonable hotel, the *Grand Hôtel de Paris*, 10 av Alfred-Merle (☎65.60.00.52; ③–④), which also has a restaurant. There's a **youth hostel** at 26 rue Lucien-Costes (☎65.60.15.95), and two **campsites** just across the Pont de Cureplat. A couple of good **places to eat** in the most attractive part of the old town are *La Camargue*, 36 rue de la Capelle, with *plats* around 50F, and the *Auberge Occitane*, 15 rue Droite, for traditional regional cuisine.

The Gorges du Tarn

Northeast of Millau, a narrow difficult road jammed with crawling traffic follows the **Gorges du Tarn** all the way along its course – a dramatic ride. The most spectacular stretch starts at **LE ROZIER** and continues up as far as the beautiful little town of **STE-ÉNIMIE**, full of cafés and places to rent bikes, or canoes for trips on the river. Le Rozier is a good walking centre and base for exploring some of the weird geological features of the *causses*: the caves at DARGILAN in the gorge of the River Jonte and ARMAND on the Causse Méjean, as well as the extraordinary rock formations around MONTPELLIER-LE-VIEUX (16km from Millau), above the gorge of the Dourbie. Bear in mind, though, that, like Ste-Énimie, it can get very busy in July and August. If you want to **stay**, there are two decent places – the *Hôtel Arnal* (☎65.62.62.91; ③) and *Hôtel Doussière* (☎65.62.60.25; ②; closed Dec–March), both in the main street – and a **camping municipal**.

Mende and the Causse de Sauveterre

Continuing on from Ste-Énimie, the Tarn road runs to FLORAC and the Cévennes, while a minor route scurries up on to the **Causse de Sauveterre**, through the desolate village of SAUVETERRE to **MENDE**, capital of the Lozère, lounging comfortably in the valley of the Lot. The old and twisting streets of Mende enclose an immense, overbearing **cathedral**, destroyed by Huguenots during the religious wars but conscientiously restored by a bishop of the town in 1600. Inside it is dark and powerful, the air heavy with the lingering odour of incense; when your eyes adjust, take a look at the Aubusson tapestries, impressively carved choir stalls and stained glass. Just outside, in the dense network of medieval streets and Renaissance houses, is the municipal **Musée Ignon-Fabre** (daily 10am–noon & 2–5pm; closed Sun), worth half an hour for its local and prehistoric collections.

The **SI** is at 16 rue Soubeyran and the departmental office for the Lozère at 14 bd Henri-Bourillon. The **gare SNCF** is on the northern edge of town in av Clemenceau. **Buses** leave from place du Foirail for various Cévennes villages, as well as FLORAC, LE PUY and RODEZ. **Foodwise**, Mende is blessed with an unusual number of good *pâtisseries* and *charcuteries*, but there isn't too much cheap **accommodation**. *Hôtel du Gévaudan* on rue d'Aigues-Passe (☎66.65.14.74; ①) is the most reasonable place. Otherwise, there are two **campsites**, on opposite sides of town on the N88.

Florac and the Parc National des Cévennes

The **Parc National des Cévennes** spreads out southeast of Mende, the second largest national park in France, a wild and lonely range of high limestone hills cut by deep wooded valleys that make for prime walking country. The most famous person to have toured the region on foot is Robert Louis Stevenson, who walked from Le Monastier to St-Jean-du-Gard in 1878 accompanied by a donkey, and wrote a book detailing his experiences, *Travels with a Donkey in the Cévennes*. If you should feel moved to do the same trip, there is no better companion than the biographer Richard Holmes' *Footsteps* (see *Contexts*), the first part of which recounts how he retraced Stevenson's journey in 1964.

At the centre of the park, **FLORAC** is an attractive old town, home to the main information bureau on the park (daily June–Oct), housed in its massive hilltop château, with details about footpaths, *gîtes*, local history and wildlife. For further information, the **SI** is in av Jean-Monestier (summer daily 9am–6pm; rest of year 9am–noon). Florac is well stocked with **gîtes** and **hotels**, and could serve as a comfortable base for walking the GR68 *Tour du Mont Lozère* (see below), which crosses the Tarn 1km north at Pont-du-Tarn (*gîte d'étape*; ☎66.45.05.51). There are two **gîtes** in town, in rue du Four (☎66.45.14.93) and rue du Pêcher (☎66.45.05.51/46.90.39.92). More commodious **accommodation** can be found at the *Grand Hôtel du Parc*, 47 av Jean-Monestier (☎66.45.03.05; ③–④; closed Dec–Feb), which has a restaurant, and the cheaper *Hôtel Central de la Poste* in av Tours (☎66.45.00.01; ③; closed mid-Jan to Feb) – also with a restaurant. There's a municipal **campsite** at Pont-du-Tarn (April to mid-Sept). Buses connect with Alès, Pont-de-Montvert, Genolhac and Millau.

Hugeuenot villages

If you have any interest in guerrilla warfare or are at all moved by stories of obdurate resistance to oppression, then the Huguenot stronghold of **SAINT-JEAN-DU-GARD** is the place to go, 53km to the southeast of Florac down the winding ridge-top road known as the *Corniche des Cévennes*. When you've taken a stroll around the town, look in at the **Musée des Vallées Cévenoles** at 95 Grand-Rue (May–Sept daily except Sun am & Mon 10.30am–12.30pm & 2–7pm), which boasts some very interesting displays illustrating the life and times of the people of the Cévennes, the silk industry and the cultivation of the staple sweet chestnut. The **SI** is in place Rabaut-St-Étienne. You can **camp** by the river at Le Mas de La Cam, 3km away on the D907 on the Florac side of town. The *Hôtel Central*, 11 rue Pellet-de-la-Lozère (☎66.85.30.20; ③), with a restaurant, and the *Corniche des Cévennes* (☎66.85.30.38; ③), on the Florac road, are both convenient places to stay.

For the real shrine to the history of Huguenot resistance, you have to go a further eleven or so kilometres east to the hamlet of **MAS SOUBEYRAN** just beyond the village of Mialet on the River Gardon. Here, in the house of the Camisard leader, Roland, is the **Musée du Désert** (daily July–Sept 9.30am–6.30pm; rest of year 9.30am–noon & 2.30–6pm; closed Dec–Feb), recounting the history of the Reformation, persecution, the Camisard guerrilla campaign, and the "wandering in the wilderness" – this is what they mean by *désert* – that followed the suppression of the Camisards in 1704 up to the Act of Toleration passed by Louis XVI in 1787, which allowed them to practise their religion once more.

Hiking in the park

The principal **hiking areas** of the Cévennes Park are the **Mont Aigoual** (1565m) massif to the south, circled by the **GR66** *Tour du Mont Aigoual* path – which takes about a week, starting at the village of L'ESPÉROU – and the 1699-metre **Mont Lozère**, just north of Florac, circled by the **GR68**. The usual starting point for this is VILLEFORT; it also takes about a week. To walk anywhere in the area, the maps to get are IGN354 *Parc des Cévennes* and IGN265 *Mont Lozère*.

The second route takes in the village of **LE PONT-DE-MONTVERT**, where a seventeenth-century bridge crosses the Tarn by a stone **tower** that once served as a toll-house. In this building in 1702 the Abbé du Chayla, a priest appointed by the crown to reconvert the rebellious Protestants enraged by the revocation of the Edict of Nantes, set up a torture chamber to persuade the recalcitrant. Incensed by his brutality, a group of them under the leadership of Esprit Séguier attacked and killed him on July 23. Reprisals were extreme; nearly 12,000 were executed, so precipitating the Camisards' – most of them shepherds and peasant farmers – guerrilla war against the state. There is also an *écomusée* on the life and character of the region, the **Maison du Mont Lozère**, on the edge of the village (June–Sept daily 10.30am–12.30pm & 2.30–6.30pm; rest of year same hours but in school hols only). If you are tempted to stay in Le Pont-de-Montvert, there's the small *Hôtel des Cévennes* (☎66.45.80.01; ②; April–Oct) – with restaurant.

From the town a lane climbs north to the tiny hamlet of FINIELS 5km away, and from there up out of the trees and over the **Col de Finiels**. The GR7 branches left from the hamlet to gain the 1699m summit. On the far side it drops down across alpine turf jewelled with rising springs, through pine woods and into the village of LE BLEYMARD – basically the route Robert Louis Stevenson followed with his donkey in 1878.

The Ardèche

Heading east, the rolling hills of the Cévennes give way to the craggier heights of the **Ardèche**, a region cloaked with chestnut forests that produce delicious and much sought after *marrons glacés* and *purées*. It's savagely beautiful here, but far too popular with the outdoor brigade for its own good. Between Alès and Aubenas, where the gorges of the river Ardèche cut through from VALLON-PONT-D'ARC to the Rhône, canoeists are as numerous as lemmings – with an equivalent penchant for going over edges. For drivers there is a magnificent road high above the north flanks of the gorge from Vallon-Pont-d'Arc, reaching the Rhône at PONT-ST-ESPRIT.

During the summer holidays **VALLON-PONT-D'ARC** (reachable by bus from Montélimar and Avignon) is a major canoeing centre, with umpteen places to hire them (around 150F/day, with return lift by road). Firms offering canoe hire generally don't operate in July and August as there are just too many canoes in the water to make it fun. The traditional starting point for descents of the gorge by canoe is the natural rock bridge over the river at Pont-d'Arc 5km downstream from Vallon. For information, the **SI** is in pl de la Gare (daily except Sat pm and Sun). There is a **gîte d'étape** in pl de la Mairie (☎75.88.07.87) and a very reasonable **hotel**, *Hôtel de Château*, also in pl de la Mairie (☎75.88.021.20; ②–③), as well as numerous **campsites**.

travel details

Trains

From Clermont-Ferrand to Paris 4 daily (4 hr) via Riom (12min), Vichy (38min) and St-Germaine-des- Fosses (46min); to St-Étienne 3–6 daily (2hr 40min); 2–3 daily to Nîmes (4hr 50min) and Marseille (6hr), stopping at all stations including St-Georges-d'Aurac, where you change for Le Puy (2hr); 4 daily to Royat (6min), Laqueille (1hr 9min), La Bourboule (1hr 20min), Le Mont Dore (1hr 30min); 4 others daily just to Laqueille, for connections into the Dordogne; 4–5 daily to Toulouse (6hr) via Issoire (27min), Arvant (48min), Neussargues (1hr 33min), Le Lioran (1hr 57min), Vic-sur-Cère (2hr 14min), Aurillac (2hr 30min); change at Neussargues for St-Flour, Le Monastier (for Mende), Millau and into Languedoc.

From Riom to Paris 4 daily (3hr 30min) via Vichy (26min); very frequent to Clermont-Ferrand (12 min).

From Vichy to Nîmes 1–2 daily (7hr); to Paris 4 daily (3hr 30min); frequent to Clermont-Ferrand (38min).

From Le Puy 3–4 daily to St-Étienne (1hr 15min) and Lyon (3hr 30min); sporadic to St-Georges-d'Aurac where you change for Clermont-Ferrand (2hr) and Nîmes (4hr).

From St-Étienne 2 early morning trains daily to St-Germain-des-Fosses (3hr); 3 TGVs daily to Lyon (45min) and Paris (2hr 50min); 3–6 daily to Clermont-Ferrand (2hr 40min).

From Aurillac 4–5 daily to Vic-sur-Cère (15min), Le Lioran (30min), Neussargues (1hr), Arvant (1hr 45min), Issoire (2hr), Clermont-Ferrand (2hr 30min); 3 daily to Bort-les-Orgues (2hr); 4–5 daily to Toulouse (4hr 30min).

From St-Flour 2–3 daily to Neussargues, Le Monastier (change for Mende), Millau and Béziers.

From Mende 3 daily to La Bastide-Puylaurens, with connections to Paris and Marseille; to Marvejols, for junction with Paris-Béziers line.

Buses

From Clermont-Ferrand daily departures to St-Étienne, Volvic, Riom, Châtelguyon, Le Puy (3hr 30min), Vichy (1hr 30min).

From Riom daily to Vichy frequent (45min); Clermont-Ferrand (30min).

From Le Puy daily to La Chaise-Dieu (1hr 10min); Thiers; Clermont-Ferrand (4hr); St-Étienne (2hr 30min); Lyon (4hr); daily to local villages, including Le Monastier-sur-Gazeille.

From Aurillac to Le Lioran 3 daily (1hr 10min); St-Flour (2hr); 2 to Vic-sur-Cère (30min).

From Millau 3 daily to Rodez; 4 daily to Montpellier; 3 daily to Toulouse.

From Mende to Florac, Villefort, Langogne.

CHAPTER THIRTEEN

THE ALPS

Rousseau wrote in his *Confessions,* "I need torrents, rocks, pine trees, dark forests, mountains, rugged paths to go up and down, precipices at my elbow to give me a good fright". He might have added wild flowers – best seen in the first half of July – but these are certainly the great summer joys of **the Alps**. The best, though not the only, way to appreciate them is on foot. The obvious, winter alternative is to ski: although this chapter is not designed as a skier's guide, a round-up of the resorts is included on p.623.

There are four national or **regional parks** in the area covered by this chapter – Vanoise, Écrins, Queyras and Vercors – all with round-the-park trails, requiring one to two weeks' walking. The **Tour of Mont Blanc** path is of similar length. Then there are two transalpine routes: the **Grande Traversée des Alpes**, which crosses all the major massifs from St-Gingolph on Lake Geneva to Nice, and **Le Balcon des Alpes**, a gentler, village-to-village itinerary through the western foothills.

All these **routes** are clearly marked, equipped with refuge huts and *gîtes d'étape*, and described in *Topo-guides*. The *CIMES* office in Grenoble (see below) will provide detailed information on all GR paths. In addition, local SIs often produce detailed maps of walks in their own areas (Chamonix and Sixt, for example). You should not, however, undertake any **high-level**, **long-distance hikes** unless you are an experienced hillwalker. If you aren't, but nonetheless like the sound of some of these trails, read a specialised hiking book before making any plans, or simply limit your sights to more **local targets**. You can find plenty of day walks from bases in or close to any of the parks; and there are some satisfying road routes, too. A tent will give you greatest flexibility, since hotels are often seasonal and their prices inflated. The **Vercors**, **Chartreuse**, **Aravis** (east of Annecy), **Faucigny** and **Chablais** (Morzine, Sixt) areas are the gentlest and quietest introductions.

The Alps are crowded in mid-summer with mountain holidays and walking much in vogue. Unfortunately, you are more or less obliged to go in **season** if you want to walk; unreliable weather aside, anywhere above 2000m will be snowbound until the beginning of July. The Chamonix-Mont Blanc area is the worst for overcrowding and best avoided, unless you're going to get out on the mountain where other people cannot go. The **Parc du Queyras** is perhaps the least touristy and sunniest of the high parks. Together with parts of **Haute Tarentaise** it still has a few "genuine" Alpine villages – a species that has become more or less extinct since the Alps have been turned into one great resort.

THE FOOTHILL TOWNS AND VERCORS MASSIF

Strung in a line along the western edge of the French Alps, **Grenoble**, **Chambéry** and **Annecy** are the gateways to the highest parts. Of the three, Grenoble with its large university is the liveliest, but all are interesting enough for a short stay. (There is a fourth town, Aix-les-Bains, but it's a dull and elderly spa.) You can't really avoid them anyway, as nearly all Alpine traffic – road and rail – is routed through them.

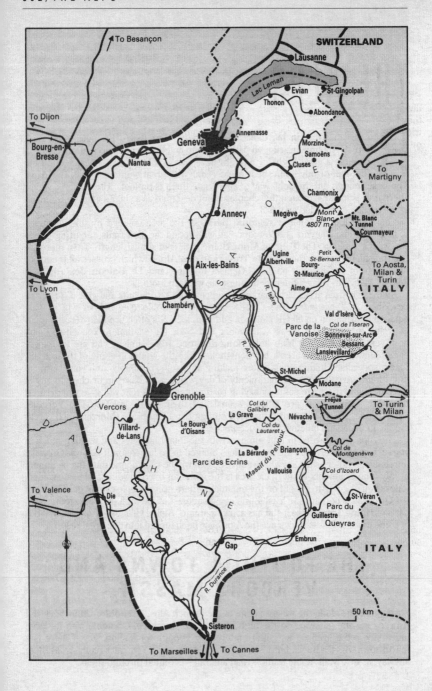

Grenoble

The economic and intellectual capital of the French Alps, **GRENOBLE** is a lively, thriving, modern city, beautifully situated on the Drac and Isère rivers, surrounded by mountains and home to a university of more than 30,000 students. The city's prosperity was originally founded on glove-making, but in the nineteenth century its economy diversified to include mining, cement, papermills, hydro-electric power (white coal, as they called it) and metallurgy. Today, it is a centre of chemical and electronics industries and nuclear research. The Atomic Energy Commission has big new laboratories on the banks of the Drac.

Grenoble has also been at the forefront of social, environmental and cultural innovation, particularly during the twenty-year mayoralty of Hubert Dubedout, who was killed in a climbing accident in 1986. His Villeneuve housing project (between av Jean-Jaurès and cours de la Libération), though tatty and of ill repute today, started out as an idealistic attempt to provide integrated living space for a complete mix of social classes, including Arab and other immigrant workers, together with open schooling and other community-based programmes. The current mayor, previously Chirac's environment minister, has revived one of Dubedout's ideas in the construction of the city's pride and joy, its pollution-free tram network.

Arrival and orientation

The visit-worthy sections of the city are easily accessible on foot, just ten minutes from the **gare SNCF** (**gare routière** next door) down av Félix-Viallet, mainly on the left bank of the Isère, where, not far from place Grenette at 14 rue de la République, you will find the **SI** (Mon–Fri 9am–6.30pm, Sat 9am–12.30pm & 1.30–6.30pm; winter closes 6pm). At the office you can buy copies of the *Guide DAHU*, a restaurant and nightlife guide compiled by local students and available in English translation, and you'll also find the local SNCF and **public transport** information offices: the splendid new trams and the buses each operate on a fixed fare of 6F – 42F for a book of ten tickets.

For **accommodation**, there's a **youth hostel** (☎76.09.33.52; open all day, year-round) at 18 av du Grésivaudan, Échirolles, a ten-minute bus ride south (#8 from cours Jean-Jaurès) to the *La Quinzaine* stop, by a large *Casino* supermarket which has excellent takeout dishes and salads, and a cafeteria serving good, reasonably priced meals. The hostel is 150m down av Grésivaudan, well placed if you are hitching south: just keep on down cours Jean-Jaurès. Other hostel-type possibilities are: *Le Foyer de l'Étudiante* – for both sexes, despite the name – at 4 rue Ste-Ursule (☎76.42.00.84), during the summer vacation only, and *Le Foyer La Houille Blanche*, 57 av du Grand-Châtelet (☎76.54.56.01; July–Sept).

For **hotels**, the railway station is the most convenient area. The *Colbert*, 1 rue Colbert (☎76.46.46.65; ③), is only a few minutes' walk south along the street that parallels the railway line. The *Lakanal* is nearby at 26 rue des Bergers (☎76.46.03.42; ②–③) off cours Jean-Jaurès. The *Bellevue* (☎76.46.39.64; ④) has a better location, as its name suggests, on the corner of quai Stéphane-Jay and rue Belgrade near the *téléférique*. The most central cheap rooms are in the *Hôtel du Moucherotte*, 1 rue Auguste-Gaché near pl Ste-Claire (☎76.54.61.40; ②), and *Hôtel de la Poste* (☎76.46.67.25; ②) at 25 rue de la Poste off place Vaucanson – the entrance is grubby and wicked-looking, but the hotel itself is spotless and friendly.

HOTEL ROOM PRICES

For a fuller explanation of these price codes, see the box on p.28 of *Basics*.

| ① Under 100F | ② 100–130F | ③ 130–180F | ④ 180–230F | ⑤ 230–300F |

Campers should make for the left bank of the Drac, where there are campgrounds in Sassenage – (*Camping de Sassenage*) and Seyssins (*Les Trois Pucelles*).

Focus of life for **eating and drinking** are the *places* Grenette, St-André and Notre-Dame. St-André, with its daily **market**, is frequented day and night by the young and cool. The streets to the east, round place des Herbes, rue Renauldon and rue Chenoise, form the **Arab quarter**, much the best area for cheap and copious food, whether full-blown meals or snacks. Two to try are: *Le Djerba*, 9 rue Chenoise, and *Le Tunis*. On place Notre-Dame, try the student café *Le Progrès* and *Le Tonneau de Diogène*, where you can also eat very reasonably. For fancier traditional cuisine try *La Panse*, 2 rue de la Paix (closed Sun and mid-July–mid-Aug)

Other practicalities

Walkers and climbers should check out the *CIMES* office at 7 rue Voltaire (☎76.54.76.00; Mon–Fri 9am–6pm, Sat 10am–noon & 2–6pm), and maybe the *Club Alpin Français* as well at 32 av Félix-Viallet (☎76.87.03.73).

If you fancy a **mountain-bike** tour and haven't brought your machine with you, head for *Mountainbike Grenoble*, on the right bank *quais* opposite Pont St-Laurent, where you can hire a bike and buy a *forfait évasion* bus ticket to get you and the bike clear of the town.

The main **PTT/Poste Restante** is on bd Lyautey, miles away near the park, but there's a small branch post office attached to the tourist office. There are **launderettes** at 65 place St-Bruno (on the way to Pont du Drac) and 18 rue Chenoise. The *CRIJ* youth information service is opposite *Cimes* at 8 rue Voltaire.

The City

The best way to start your stay is to take the **téléférique** (9/10/11am–6pm/7.30pm/midnight) from the riverside quai Stéphane-Jay to **Fort de la Bastille** on the steep slopes above the north bank of the Isère. It may be a touristy thing to do, but if you eschew all *téléfériques* in the Alps – and there are hundreds of them – you'll miss out on a lot of spectacular views. The ride is hair-raising, for you are whisked steeply and swiftly into the air in a sort of transparent egg, which allows you to see very clearly how far you would fall in the event of an accident.

Though the fort is of little interest, the **view** is fantastic. At your feet the Isère, milky-grey and swollen with snow-melt, tears at the piles of the old bridges which join the St-Laurent quarter, colonised by Italian immigrants in the nineteenth century, to the nucleus of the medieval town, whose red roofs cluster tightly around the church of St-André. To the east, snowfields gleam in the gullies of the Belledonne massif (2978m). Southeast is Taillefer and south-southeast the dip where the *Route Napoléon* passes over the mountains to Sisteron and the Mediterranean – this is the road Napoléon took after his escape from Elba in March 1815 on his way to rally his forces for the campaign that led to his final defeat at Waterloo. To the west are the steep white cliffs of the Vercors massif; the highest peak, dominating the city, is Moucherotte (1901m). The jagged peaks at your back are the outworks of the Chartreuse massif. Northeast on a clear day you can see the white peaks of Mont Blanc up the deep glacial valley of the Isère, known as La Grésivaudan. It was in this valley that the first French hydro-electric project went into action in 1869. Heading back, you can walk down through the public gardens.

Upstream from the *téléférique* station is the sixteenth-century **Palais de Justice** (open to the public) with **place St-André** and the church of St-André behind. Built in the thirteenth century and heavily restored, the church is of little architectural interest, but the narrow streets leading back towards *places* Grenette, Vaucanson and Verdun take you through the liveliest and most colourful quarter of the city, the focus of life for shoppers and strollers alike.

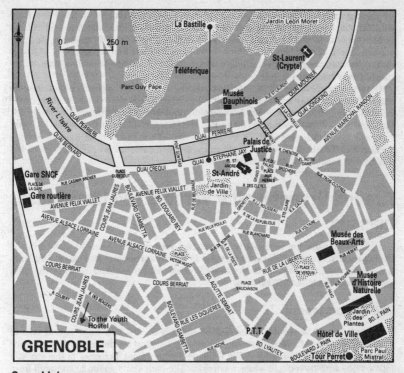

GRENOBLE

Grenoble's museums

Close to place Grenette at 14 rue J-J-Rousseau is a small **museum** dedicated to the French Resistance (Wed–Sat 3–6pm), who were particularly active in the Vercors massif. **Stendhal** was born in the house, though the city's museum of Stendhaliana at 20 Grand-Rue is itself in a corner of the public gardens just behind the St-André church.

Across the river, up a cobbled path opposite the footbridge by the Palais de Justice, the **Musée Dauphinois** (daily except Tues 9am–noon & 2–6pm; free on Wed) occupies the former convent of Ste-Marie-d'en-Haut. Imaginatively laid out, it is largely devoted to the history, arts and crafts of the province of Dauphiné (unlike neighbouring Savoie, which was only relinquished by the Italians in 1860, Dauphiné has been French since the fourteenth century). There are exhibits on the life of the mountain people, "*les gens de là-haut*", the people from up there, who like most poor mountaineers were obliged to travel the world as peddlers and knife-grinders. Many, too, were involved in smuggling, and there is a fascinating collection of body-hugging flasks used for contraband liquor. The most unusual section is the so-called *Roman des Grenoblois*, the story of the people of Grenoble told in an excellent audio-visual presentation through the lives of various members of a representative selection of families, ranging from immigrant workers to wealthy industrialists. France's first trade union was established in Grenoble in 1803 by the glove makers.

Should you go to the **Musée de Peinture et de Sculpture** (daily except Tues 10am–noon & 2–6pm; free on Wed) on the handsome nineteenth-century place de Verdun, which has an impressive collection of contemporary and representative works by the big names in twentieth-century art, you should continue on to the **Parc Paul Mistral**. On the corner at the end of rue Haxo, standing amid the fine trees of the public garden, is the **Natural History Museum** (Mon–Sat 9.30am–noon & 1.30–5.30pm, Sun 2–6pm; closed Tues; free on Wed) which has a huge collection of fossils and rocks, animals and birds, including specimens of all the Alpine birds of prey, unfortunately very badly displayed.

Opposite, at the edge of the park, stands the steel, glass and concrete **Hôtel de Ville**: all straight lines and square corners, but refreshingly contemporary – one of the earliest of France's now numerous and bold architectural experiments with its public buildings. In the park behind is an earlier and more frivolous structure, an 87-metre concrete tower designed in 1925 by Perret, one of the pioneers of modern French architecture. The concrete looks shabby now and you could hardly call it attractive, but it is bold and unapologetically modern.

Around Grenoble: the Vercors and Chartreuse massifs

Both these **massifs**, but particularly Vercors, are very close to Grenoble. They are relatively gentle, too, so if you're starting your Alpine ventures here, you can use them to break your feet in. The Grenoble *CIMES* office publishes route descriptions with extracts from the IGN 1:25,000 map.

The Vercors massif

Simplest and most accessible of the *CIMES* walks is no. 4: a **four-hour round trip to St-Nizier**, just over the rim of the Vercors mountains. Start by taking bus #5 from place Victor-Hugo and get off in SEYSSINET village by the school. For most of the way you follow **GR9** with its red and white waymarks. The path starts about 200m uphill from the school on the right. It is not difficult, but the path crosses the D106 a few times, and the continuation is not always obvious, so it is worth getting the leaflet. It is about two-and-a-half hours to **ST-NIZIER** (return the same way) by a beautiful path through thick woods with long views back over Grenoble to the mountains beyond. The lovely purplish Martagon lily blooms in the woods in early July. St-Nizier has **hotels** and a small **campsite**. It is a further three-and-a-half hours (there and back) to the top of **Moucherotte** on GR91.

The best way to explore the Vercors further would be to **base yourself** in the mountains – in VILLARD-DE-LANS, for example (**camping** and **hotels**: *Hôtel du Centre* – ☎76.95.14.12: ③) – and backpack around. Two other good, though more strenuous, walks are described in leaflets 6 and 11. **6** heads from Villard-de-Lans down to CLAIX, not far from Grenoble – a descent of 1700m in about seven hours. **11** follows a long (9hr) and a shorter (6hr 30min) **circuit of Mont Aiguille**, starting from the railway station in CLELLES (1hr by train south of Grenoble). Both are highly recommended, and by all accounts rightly so, by the *CIMES* office.

By road through the Vercors

If you just want **to travel through** – it is very pretty and undeveloped – you will have to drive or hitch, which is perfectly possible. To get started, take the #11/14 trolley just off place Victor-Hugo to *Sassenage Air Liquide* and get off at *La Rollandière*, one stop before the terminus. Start hitching on the road to LANS-EN-VERCORS more or less opposite the stop. The road winds up through a steep wooded gorge before coming out

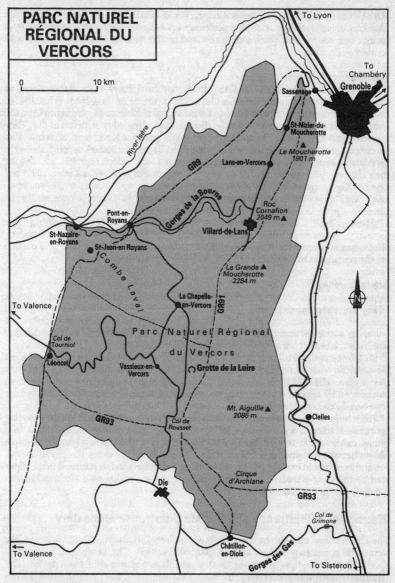

PARC NATUREL RÉGIONAL DU VERCORS

0   10 km

To Lyon

To Chambéry

Grenoble

Sassenage

St-Nizier-du-Moucherotte

River Isère

GR9

Le Moucherotte
1901 m

Lans-en-Vercors

Gorges de la Bourne

Roc
Cornafion
2049 m ▲

Pont-en-Royans

Villard-de-Lans

St-Nazaire-
en-Royans

St-Jean-en-Royans

Combe Laval

La Grande ▲
Moucherotte
2284 m

To Valence

La Chapelle-
en-Vercors

GR91

Parc Naturel Régional

du Vercors

Col de
Tourniol

Léoncel

Vassieux-en-
Vercors

Grotte de la Luire

Mt. Aiguille ▲
2086 m

Clelles

GR93

Col de
Rousset

Cirque
d'Archiane

Die

GR93

Col de
Grimone

To Valence

Châtillon-
en-Diois

Gorges des Gas

To Sisteron

into a wide valley full of hay meadows towards LANS and VILLARD. Turn right at Villard on the Pont-en-Royans road into the **Gorges de la Bourne**. The gorge becomes rapidly deeper and narrower with the road cut right in under the rocks, the river running far below, and tree-hung cliffs almost shutting out the sky above. Take a left fork here and you climb up to a lovely green valley before descending to ST-

MARTIN and LA CHAPELLE (*gîtes d'étape, Nouvel Hôtel, Hôtel des Sports*); thence the road climbs again to the wide dry **plateau of Vassieux**, bordered to the east by a rocky ridge rising from thick pine forest and to the west by low hills covered with scrubby vegetation.

Vassieux

It was here around the village of **VASSIEUX** that the fighters of the Vercors *maquis* suffered a bloody and bitter defeat at the hands of the SS in July 1944. From 1942–3 they had been gradually turning the Vercors into a Resistance stronghold, to the annoyance of the Germans who finally, in June 1944, decided to wipe them out. They encircled and attacked the *maquisards* with vastly superior forces and parachuted an SS division on to Vassieux. The French appealed in vain for Allied support and were very bitter about the lack of response. The Germans took vicious reprisals, and despite their attempts to disperse into the woods, 700 *maquisards* and civilians were killed and several villages razed. The Germans' most ferocious act was to murder the wounded, along with their nurses and doctors, in the **Grotte de la Liure**, a cave off the La Chapelle–Col de Rousset road, now a sort of national shrine.

Vassieux itself, a dull little village now rebuilt (*gîte d'étape*: Mme Chapays), has a memorial cemetery and small **museum** (April–Oct 9am–6pm; free) with documents, photos and other memorabilia to do with the *maquis* and the battle. In the field outside are the remains of two gliders used by the German paratroops.

Die to Grimone

From Vassieux, the **Col de Rousset** road winds through woods of pine and fir before taking the steep twisting descent to **DIE**, with terrific views of the white crags and pinnacles of the southeast end of the massif. Although an attractive little place, Die (*camping municipal* and **hotels**) is worth no more than a brief stop. Its most alluring feature is the bubbly white wine it produces, *Clairette de Die*.

Six kilometres south along the river Drôme at the **Pont de Quart** the road forks left for Châtillon – not a bad place to wait on a hot day, for you can swim in the river below the bridge. **CHÂTILLON** village is lovely, lying in a narrowing valley bottom surrounded by apple and peach orchards, vineyards, walnut trees and fields of lavender (two **hotels** and *camping municipal*).

From here on, the road enters the sunless trench of the **Gorges des Gas**, winding up between sheer rock walls to **GRIMONE**, a mountain hamlet on the flanks of a grassy valley with fir trees darkening the higher slopes. The Col de Grimone is visible above the village. If you have to walk it, a path cuts across the valley directly to the col. From the col it's about 7km down to the main Grenoble road, a tarmac trudge alleviated by the view eastwards to the mountains. If you are fed up with hitching you can get the train back to Grenoble.

Massif de la Chartreuse and Grande Chartreuse monastery

The **Chartreuse massif** stretches north from Grenoble towards Chambéry, and like Vercors it is not easy to visit without your own vehicle. The landscape, however, is spectacular: precipitous limestone peaks, mountain pastures and thick forest. The **Grande Chartreuse monastery**, the main local landmark, lies up the narrow Gorges des Guiers Mort, southeast of ST-LAURENT-DU-PORT. It is not open to visitors, though there is a museum nearby at LA CORRERIE illustrating the life of the Carthusian Order to which the monastery belongs (April–Sept Mon–Sat 9am–noon & 2–5.30pm; bus to VOIRON, where the *Caves de la Grande Chartreuse* offer a free visit and tasting of the sticky yellow or green liqueur).

Chambéry

CHAMBÉRY, 55km north of Grenoble, lies just south of Lac du Bourget in a valley separating the Massif de la Chartreuse from the Bauges mountains: historically, an important strategic position commanding the entrance to the big Alpine valleys leading to the passes into Italy. The earliest settlement was on the rock of Lemenc, behind the railway station – the church of St-Pierre-de-Lemenc off bd de Lemenc has a sixth-century baptistery in its crypt.

The present town grew up around the castle built by Count Thomas of Savoie in 1232, when Chambéry became capital of the ancient province, and flourished particularly in the fourteenth century under the three Amadeuses – the last of whom served ten years as anti-pope. Although superseded as capital by Turin in 1563, it remained an important commercial and cultural centre and the emotional focus of all French Savoyards: "the winter residence of almost all the nobility of Savoy", Arthur Young reported in 1789, before its mid-nineteenth-century incorporation into France.

Exploring the town

As usual, the most interesting district is the **old city centre**. To reach it, turn left out of the **gare SNCF** (**gare routière** just outside in place de la Gare) down rue Sommeiller to the crossroads at the end, and take another left into the tree-lined bd de la Colonne, where all the **city buses** stop – the **SI** is on the left at no. 24 (☎79.33.42.47; Mon–Sat 9am–noon & 2–6pm). Halfway down the street is the splendidly extravagant **Fontaine des Éléphants**, with the heads and shoulders of four large bronze elephants projecting from a stone pediment supporting a tall column, on top of which stands a statue of Comte de Boigne, a native son who made a fortune in the French East India Company in the eighteenth century and spent some of it on his home town. Past this, on the right, and you're at the **Musée Savoisien**, square de Lannoy-de-Bissy (daily 10am–noon & 2–6pm; closed Tues), a Savoyard parallel to the Musée Dauphinois at Grenoble and, like it, recording the lost rural life of the mountain communities. On the first floor are some very lovely paintings by Savoyard primitives and painted wood statues from various churches in the region; up above are tools, carts, hay-sledges, old photos, and some very fine furniture from a house in Bessans, including a fascinating kitchen range made of wood and lined with *lauzes* – slabs of schist.

Next to the museum, in the enclosed little place Métropole, the **cathedral** has a handsome, though much restored, Flamboyant facade. The inside is painted in elaborate nineteenth-century *trompe-l'oeil*, imitating the twisting shapes and whorls of the Flamboyant style. During the Revolution it became the seat of the National Assembly of the Allobroges in a Revolutionary attempt to revive pre-Roman tribal identity.

A passage leads from the *place* to **rue de la Croix-d'Or**, with numerous restaurants and, to the right, the long, rectangular **place St-Léger** with a fountain and cafés, hub of the city's social life, where street musicians and players perform on summer evenings. **Rousseau** and Mme de Warens lived here in 1735. They also had a country cottage, *Les Charmettes*, just 2km south of the town on the rustic chemin des Charmettes. It's now a small museum (daily April–Sept 10am–noon & 2–6pm; Oct–March 10am–noon & 2–4.30pm; closed Tues).

Towards the further end of the *place*, the town's smartest street, **rue de Boigne**, leads back to the Elephant Fountain. Past this intersection, on the left, a narrow medieval lane, rue Basse-du-Château, brings you out beneath the elegant apse of the **Ste-Chapelle**, the castle chapel, whose lancet windows and star vaulting are the building's best feature. It was built to house the Holy Shroud, that much-venerated and today highly controversial piece of linen brought back from the Crusades and reputed to be Christ's winding sheet. The dukes took it with them to Turin where it still lies in the cathedral. The entrance to the *château* (guided tours only; 5 daily in July & Aug; 2 daily June & Sept; March–May & Oct–Nov Sat 2.15pm, Sun 3.30pm) is on the left. A massive and imposing structure, it was the home of the dukes of Savoie until they transferred to Turin.

Practicalities

If you're staying, inexpensive accommodation is not hard to find. Try the *Hôtel du Château*, 37 rue Jean-Pierre Veyrat (☎79.69.48.78; ②); the *Home Savoyard*, 15 place St-Léger (☎79.3347.80; ②–③); *Les Voyageurs*, 3 rue Doppet (☎79.33.57.00; ③), or the more expensive *Revard*, 41 av de la Boisse (☎79.62.04.64; 4–e). But for rural peace and a lovely view there's no better than *Hôtel Aux Pervenches* (☎79.33.34.26; ②) next to Rousseau's house in Les Charmettes. For hostel-type beds, try the **Maison des Jeunes et de la Culture** at 311 Faubourg-Montmélian (☎75.75.13.23). You'll find good **food** at restaurants and cheap pizzerias around the rue la Croix d'Or.

The nearest **campsite** is *Camping Nivolet* (☎79.33.19.48) at BASSENS: bus *ligne C*, direction Albertville, from the SI.

Chambéry's **PTT** is on av Général-Leclerc, opposite the station.

Annecy

Sited at the edge of a turquoise lake, and bounded to the east by the eroded peaks of La Tournette (2351m) and to the west by the long wooded ridge of Le Semnoz (1699m), **ANNECY** is very much a transit point for hikers. Easily accessible from Geneva, Lyon and other centres, it offers good access to the Mont Blanc area and the northern pre-Alps. Historically, it enjoyed a brief flurry of importance in the early sixteenth century, when Geneva opted for the Reformation and the fugitive Catholic bishop decamped here with a train of ecclesiastics and a prosperous, cultivated elite.

The most interesting core of the city lies at the foot of the castle mound. It is a warren of lanes, passages and arcaded houses below and between which flow branches of the **Canal du Thiou**, which drains the lake into the river Fier. The houses, canal-side railings and numerous restaurants and cafés are stacked with displays of geraniums and petunias. It is picture-book pretty and, inevitably, full of tourists.

The annual **Festival de la Vieille Ville** brings plenty of visitors, too. It takes place in the first two weeks of July, with music (pop, rock, classical and mostly free). The first Saturday in August sees a major fireworks jamboree on the lake with the **Fête du Lac**.

Arrival and Centre Bonlieu

If you're coming from the **gare SNCF**, go straight ahead to **rue Royale** and turn left. Rue Royale becomes the arcaded **rue Paquier**, with the seventeenth-century **Hôtel de Sales** at no. 12, once a residence of the kings of Sardinia. Opposite the end of the street is the **Centre Bonlieu**, a modern shopping precinct which also houses the **SI** (summer daily 9am–6.30pm; Oct–May Mon–Sat 9am–noon & 1.45–6.30pm, Sun 9am–noon & 3–6pm; good maps and help with accommodation).

St-Maurice and Rousseau

Beyond Bonlieu, the tree-lined av d'Albigny leads west past the lakeside lawns of the **Champ de Mars**, joined by a bridge to the shady public gardens at the back of the Hôtel de Ville. Opposite is the fifteenth-century church of **St-Maurice**, originally built for a Dominican convent. (Numerous Savoyard churches are dedicated to St-Maurice. He was the commander of a Theban legion sent to put down a rebellion in the late third

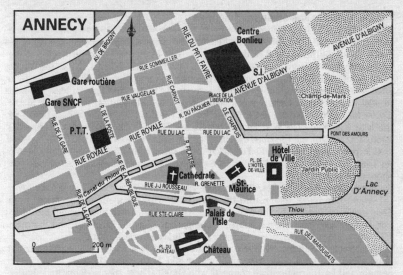

century. Converted to Christianity, he and his soldiers refused to sacrifice to the pagan gods of Rome and were put to death for their scruples.) Inside, the apse, with attractive Flamboyant windows, is badly distorted, the walls leaning outwards to an alarming degree; on the left of the choir is a fine fresco dated 1438, all in tones of grey.

Opposite the church door, rue Grenette leads into **rue Jean-Jacques Rousseau**. Just past the uninteresting Gothic cathedral where Rousseau sang as a chorister is an eighteenth-century bishop's palace, now the police commissariat, built on the site of the house where Mme de Warens, Rousseau's lover, lived. Converted from Protestantism, she was paid by the Catholic authorities to save other lost souls. The 16-year-old Rousseau, on the run from his miserable engraver's apprenticeship in Geneva, came to lodge with her on Palm Sunday 1728. She was 28. Their first meeting took place on the steps of the church, Rousseau recording: "in a moment I was hers, and certain that a faith preached by such missionaries would not fail to lead to paradise . . .". His admirers have placed his bust in the courtyard of the commissariat.

The Old Town, castle and museum

Continuing across the canal bridge, with a view of the grand old **Palais de l'Île** (prison, mint and courtroom in its time), you come to rue de l'Île and **rue Ste-Claire**, the main street of the old town, with arcaded shops and houses. No. 18 is the Hôtel Favre, where in 1606 Antoine Favre, an eminent lawyer, and François de Sales founded the literary-intellectual *Académie Florimontane* "because the Muses thrive in the mountains of Savoie". At the end of the street is its original medieval gateway.

From rue de l'Île the narrow Rampe du Château leads up to the **Castle**, former home of the counts of Genevois and the dukes of Nemours, a junior branch of the house of Savoy. There has been a castle on this site from the eleventh century. The Nemours, finding the old fortress too rough and unpolished for their taste, added living quarters in the sixteenth century, which now house the miscellaneous collections of the **Musée du Château** (daily 10am–noon & 2–6pm; closed Tues): archeological finds from Roman Boutae; Bronze- and Iron-Age metallurgy with comparative photos of similar still-surviving skills like scythe- and axe-making; Savoyard popular art, furniture and wood carving; and, on the top floor, an excellent display illustrating the geology of the Alps.

Accommodation and other practicalities

The **youth hostel** (*Grande Jeanne*, route du Semnoz; ☎50.45.33.19) is a good 45-minute walk from the old town (or take the bus, marked *Semnoz*, from opposite the Hôtel de Ville): .cross the main canal bridge along rue des Marquisats, and turn right at the lights into av de Trésum, then left on bd de la Corniche, which loops up into the woods of Le Semnoz, becoming the Route de Semnoz; the hostel stands in a clearing by a small zoo (there's a shortcut through the woods but for the first time, at least, it's best to stick to the road). **Other good hostel-type accommodation** is available at the *Centre International de Séjour des Marquisats*, 52 rue des Marquisats (☎50.45.08.80) by the lake (canteen). The best bet for **hotels** are *Rives du Lac*, 6 rue des Marquisats (☎50.51.32.85; ②), and the *Hôtel des Alpes*, 12 rue de la Poste (☎50.45.04.56; ⑤).

Camping municipal is off bd de la Corniche – turn right up a lane opposite Chemin du Tillier; it's on the left past *Hôtel du Belvédère*. There are other sites all around the shore of the lake.

As to **other practicalities**, there's **bike hire** from the *gare SNCF* and *Loca Sport* (37 av de Loverchy), and **round-the-lake boat trips**, at a reasonable price, from *Compagnie des Bateaux* by the mouth of the Thiou canal. You'll find a useful **launderette** in the *Nouvelles Galleries* shopping complex at 25 av du Parmelan, and the main **PTT** on rue de la Poste opposite the *gare SNCF* (**gare routière** next door).

Of interest to **walkers**, a 1:50,000 **map of the Annecy area** showing **walking trails** is on sale from the SI. The best and longest hike is the **tour du Lac**, taking in Le Semnoz and La Tournette (path connects with GR96). There are also loops and shorter sections suitable for day walks. *CAF* is at 38 av du Parmelan (☎50.45.52.76; afternoons only).

THE NATIONAL PARKS

The trouble with designating an area a **national park** is that it draws attention, and hordes of people, to it. Luckily, the scale of the mountains is big enough to absorb considerable numbers of visitors, and these parks remain exceptionally beautiful. But you won't have the paths to yourself after about 10am in July and August – which are the only **times of year** when hiking is really practicable. As for **accommodation**, you can **camp** freely on the fringes of the parks, but once inside you are supposed to pitch a tent only in an emergency and move on after one night. **Gîtes** and **refuges** are probably the best solution, and not having to carry equipment saves weight, too. Hotels are out – overpriced and overbooked.

For **guides**, there are the GR *Topo-guides* and *CIMES La Grande Traversée des Alpes* in French, the Mountaineers/Cordee *100 Hikes in the Alps* and Cicerone Press's *GR5* by Colin Turner in English.

Access to the **Vanoise** park is easiest from Chambéry (with frequent trains to Modane). For **Queyras** and **Écrins** it's best to set out from Grenoble: either by bus via Bourg-d'Oisans to Briançon (starting off point for the Écrins), or by train via Gap to Mont-Dauphin (for Queyras) and on beyond to Briançon. If you hitch – not hard if you look like a healthy hiker – you could follow any of these routes.

Parc Régional du Queyras

The **railway** from Grenoble to Gap seems an obvious approach to Queyras. At first it follows the **route Napoléon**, the road taken by the Emperor on his escape from Elba in 1815, running through the town of VIZILLE, where there's a vast *château*. This was the meeting place in 1788 of the Estates of Grenoble, whose demand for liberty for all

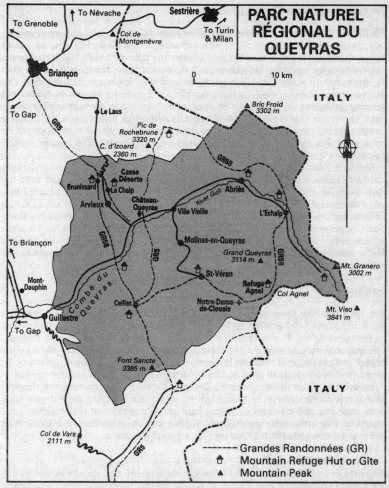

PARC NATUREL RÉGIONAL DU QUEYRAS

To Grenoble

To Névache

Sestrière

Col de Montgenèvre

To Turin & Milan

Briançon

0   10 km

ITALY

To Gap

GR5

Le Laus

Bric Froid
3302 m

Pic de Rochebrune
3320 m

C. d'Izoard
2360 m

GR58

Casse Déserte

La Chalp

Brunissard

Château-Queyras

Arvieux

River Guil

Ville Vieille

Abriès

L'Echalp

GR58

GR5

Molines-en-Queyras

To Briançon

Grand Queyras
3114 m

GR58

Mont-Dauphin

Combe du Queyras

St-Véran

Refuge Agnel

Col Agnel

Mt. Granero
3002 m

Ceillac

Notre-Dame-de-Clousis

Mt. Viso
3841 m

Guillestre

To Gap

Font Sancte
3385 m

ITALY

Col de Vars
2111 m

GR5

------- Grandes Randonnées (GR)
🏠 Mountain Refuge Hut or Gîte
▲ Mountain Peak

Frenchmen and suspension of parliament is often thought of as the catalyst for the French Revolution. Beyond Vizille the rail line and road diverge, the road climbing steeply to the village of LAFFREY, where Napoléon, finding his way barred by troops from Grenoble, melodramatically threw open his coat, challenging: "Soldiers, I am your Emperor! If anyone among you wishes to kill me, here I am!" The commanding officer ordered the soldiers to fire, but, instead, there were cries of "*Vive l'Empéreur!*" So, with his own party augmented by these soldiers, Napoléon entered Grenoble in triumph. He wrote in his memoirs: "As far as Grenoble, I was merely an adventurer. At Grenoble, I became a prince".

From GAP (105km; numerous **hotels** and three **campsites**) the railway and D64 strike east for 40km to Embrun. The landscape becomes increasingly Mediterranean in appearance, with low scrub covering the mountainsides, poor shallow soil and white friable rock.

Embrun and Mont-Dauphin

EMBRUN stands on a rock overlooking the huge man-made lake of **Serre-Ponçon**, now developed as a summer resort with campsites and wind-surfing schools (**youth hostel** at Savines-le-Lac, where the road crosses the lake; ☎92.44.20.16). It has been a fortress town for centuries. Hadrian made it the capital of the Maritime Alps, and from the third century to the Revolution it was the seat of an important archbishopric. The **SI**, in a former chapel of the Cordeliers, doubles as a bureau for **mountain guides** and **accompagnateurs**, organising a daily programme of walks in the surrounding mountains. The town's chief sight is its twelfth-century **cathedral**, with a porch in alternating courses of black and white marble in the Italian Lombard style, its roof supported on columns of pink marble resting on lions' backs – an arrangement that inspired numerous imitators throughout the region.

Eighteen kilometres up the road you come to **MONT-DAUPHIN**, where **buses** leave for Ceillac, Ville-Vieille and St-Véran in the Queyras national park. They meet the Paris–Briançon trains: the 7.40am bus going all the way to St-Véran (arriving 9.10am, every day except Sun throughout the year), others only as far as VILLE-VIEILLE (the 4.55pm operates only in the summer season). It is, however, easy to get a lift in these parts; there are always climbers and hikers with transport. Mont-Dauphin itself is just a station, with – opposite – an abandoned but formidably bastioned village, one of many Alpine fortifications designed by Vauban in the seventeenth century commanding the entrance to the valley of the Guil.

Into the park: Guillestre...

The road into the Queyras park follows the river Guil from Mont-Dauphin, through to the village of **GUILLESTRE**, its houses in typical Queyras style with open granaries on the upper floors, its church with a lion-porch emulating the cathedral at Embrun. You may want to stop here a night: there are several **hotels**, **campsites** and a **youth hostel** (☎92.45.04.32; in route de la Gare) – with another youth hostel, open July 7–Sept 9 (☎92.46.50.39), high up at the Col de Vars 20km along the Barcelonnette road.

Beyond the village, in the Combe du Queyras, the river gorge narrows to a claustrophobic crack with walls up to 400m high. Far below the road, the clear stream boils down over red and green rocks. It was only in this century that road-building techniques became sufficiently sophisticated to cope with these narrows. Previously they had to be circumvented by a detour over the adjacent heights.

... and around Ville-Vieille

At the upper end of the Combe, the valley broadens briefly, and ahead you see the fort of **Château-Queyras** barring the way so completely that there is scarcely room for the road to squeeze around its base – Vauban at work again, though the original fortress was medieval. Just beyond is **VILLE-VIEILLE**, where the road for St-Véran branches right over the Guil and up the ravine of the Aigue Blanche torrent. A smaller place than Guillestre, it has only a few old houses still intact and a church with the square tower and octagonal steeple flanked by four short triangular pinnacles characteristic of this corner of the Alps. A Latin inscription in the porch says the church was destroyed in 1574 by the "impiety of the Calvinists" and restored by the "piety" of the Catholics. There is a painted sundial on the tower, which is also characteristic of the region.

Straight on, the road follows the Guil through the villages of AIGUILLES, ABRIÈS, LA MONTA (all with *gîtes d'étape*), to the **Belvédère du Viso**, close to the Italian border and **Monte Viso**, at 3841m the highest peak in the area. Above the Belvédère is the **Col de la Traversette**, where in 1480 the Marquis of Saluces drove a 70-metre tunnel through the mountain. It has been reopened at various times through history, but is finally closed now.

East of L'ÉCHALP a variant of the **GR58**, which does the circuit of the park, climbs up to the **Col de la Croix**, used in former times by Italian peasants bringing their produce to market in Abriès. South of the village the path climbs to the pastures of **Alpe de Médille**, where you can see across to Monte Viso, then on past the **lakes** of Egourgéou, Bariche and Foréant to **Col Vieux** and west to the **Refuge Agnel**, from where you can continue on to St-Véran.

St-Véran

At 2040m **ST-VÉRAN** claims to be the highest permanently inhabited village in Europe. It lies on the east side of the valley of the Aigue Blanche torrent, backed by acres of steep lush mountain pasture. Opposite, rock walls and slopes of scree rise to snowy ridges. In the valley bottom and on any treeless patch of ground, no matter how steep, you can see the remains of abandoned terraces. They were in use up until World War II, though, as with most high Alpine villages, traditional farming activity has now practically died out. Only one Provençal shepherd still brings his flocks to the village pastures in summertime. Today the principal economic activity is entertaining tourists.

The houses are part stone, part timber. The upper storeys, usually timber, consist of long granaries with two or three tiers of rickety wooden balconies tacked on to the front for drying hay or firewood and ripening crops. The roofs are pine planks or huge slabs of schist – *lauzes* – arranged in diamond patterns. There are several refurbished old drinking fountains, made entirely of wood. The stone church stands prettily on the higher of the two "streets", its white tower silhouetted against the bare crags across the valley, as a mountain church should. It, too, has a porch whose columns rest on crudely carved lions, one holding a man in its paws. The interior is surprisingly rich, with Baroque altars and retables.

Just south of the village, past a triple cross adorned with the instruments of Christ's passion and an inscription urging the passer-by to choose between the saintly and conventional or rebellious life ("*l'homme révolté qui n'est jamais content*"), **GR58**, waymarked and easy to follow, turns right down to the river, beside which there are some good places to camp. The path continues up the left bank through woods of pine and larch as far as the chapel of Notre-Dame-de-Clausis. There, above the timberline, it crosses to the right bank of the stream and winds up damp grassy slopes to the **Col de Chamoussière**, about three-and-a-half hours from St-Véran. The ridge to the right of the col marks the frontier with Italy. In the valley below you see the **Refuge Agnel**, about an hour away, with the Pain de Sucre (3208m) behind it. From there you can continue on to L'Échalp. In early July there are glorious flowers in the meadows leading up to the col: violets, *Potentilla*, Black Vanilla Orchids, *Jovibarba*, pinks, *Silene acaulis*, *Hypericum*, anemones, *Trollius europaeus*, Mountain Buttercup, gentians, *Soldanella* and *Campanulas*.

For a **base in these parts**, you're really best off camping. There are, however, two reasonable **hotels** in St-Véran, the *Hôtel Étoile des Neiges* (☎92.45.82.19; ②) and *Le Perce-Neige* (☎92.45.82.23; ①), a *gîte d'étape* and the *Refuge Gabelous* (☎92.45.81.39). If you are feeding yourself, there are only two small shops and they have a tendency to run out of bread, fruit and vegetables.

Walking back down to Ville-Vieille takes about two-and-a-half hours. It's all road work save for an initial short cut to MOLINES, but downhill and pretty. Molines and its neighbours, La Rua and Fontgillarde, seem to have preserved their traditional rural character better than St-Véran. The houses are better kept, the hay meadows still mown – there is nothing prettier than these little patches of Alpine meadow, always steep and irregular in shape, full of wild flowers and neatly scythed by hand.

Queyras to Briançon

The direct route from Queyras to Briançon, crossing the 2360m **Col d'Izoard**, is a beautiful trip and saves backtracking to Mont-Dauphin. There are no buses, but it's reasonably promising hitching at holiday time.

The road turns up right just west of Château-Queyras along a wooded ravine to the village of **ARVIEUX**, lying in a high valley surrounded by fields and meadows. A church with the characteristic tower and steeple stands guard at the entrance to the village. The **GR5** passes through. *Hôtel Casse Déserte* has dormitory accommodation. Further up the valley at LA CHALP and BRUNISSARD are *gîtes d'étape*.

Going up to **the col**, above the timberline, you cross the **Casse Déserte**, a wild, desolate region with huge screes running down off the peaks and weirdly eroded orangey rocks. From the top the view extends over miles and miles of mountain landscape. On the other side, the road loops down through thick forest to LE LAUS, a cluster of old stone houses with long, sloping, wooden roofs set in meadows beside the stream, before swinging west into the deep valley of the Durance at BRIANÇON, dominated by the vast **Massif des Écrins**.

Briançon and the Parc National des Écrins

Imposing and fortified, built on a rocky height overlooking the valleys of the Durance and Guisane, **BRIANÇON** guards the road to the desolate and windswept **Col de Montgenèvre**, one of the oldest and most important passes into Italy, marked by a column commemorating Napoléon's construction of the road. Originally a Gallic settlement, the town was fortified by the Romans to guard their *Mons Matrona* road from Milan to Vienne. In the Middle Ages it was the capital of the "*république des escartons*", a federation of mountain communities grouped together for mutual defence and the preservation of their liberties and privileges.

The **old town**, mainly eighteenth century, is enclosed within another set of Vauban's walls. If you come in a car the best thing is to stop at the **Champ de Mars** at the top of the hill and look around from there; otherwise you'll have to struggle up from the unprepossessing modern town that has grown up on the more accessible ground at the foot of the hill. You enter the walls by the **Porte Pignerol**. In front of you the narrow main street, bordered by ancient houses, tips steeply downhill. It is known as the *grande gargouille* because of the stream running down the middle. To your right is the sturdy, plain **church of Notre-Dame**, designed by Vauban, again with an eye to defence. Beyond it there is a fantastic **view** from the walls, especially on a clear starry night, when the snows on the surrounding barrier of mountains give off an icy, silvery glow. Vauban's **citadel** above the Porte Pignerol, the highest point of the fortifications, can be visited, but only as part of an organised tour (ask the SI). In marked contrast to the relatively untouristy Queyras, Briançon and all the other towns and villages on this side of the Écrins park are crawling with people in summer.

Briançon practicalities

The **SI** is by the Porte Pignerol, on the right (Mon–Sat 9am–noon & 1.30–6.30pm, Sun 9am–noon & 2–6pm; there's a **mountain guides**' desk here). For **places to stay**, try *Hôtel aux Trois Chamois* in the Champs de Mars (☎92.21.02.29; ③), still reasonably priced with the obligatory *demi-pension* (full board July & Aug) – and the food is good. Alternatives in the old town include *Le Rustique* on rue Pont-d'Asfeld to the left of Grande-Rue (☎92.21.00.10; ③) and *L'Escale*, 59 Grande-Rue (☎92.21.00.69; ③). More expensive, but perhaps a better bet than the latter two is the *Edelweiss* at 32 av de la République (☎92.21.02.94; ④), the main road down to the new town. There's a **youth hostel** at Serre-Chevalier (☎92.24.74.54), 8km north on the main Grenoble road.

The nearest campsite is **Camping la Schappe** (mid-June–mid-Sept) in the lower town at the end of rue Centrale, which starts opposite the SI. Turn left after the bridge on the Durance. There is also a *gîte d'étape* at LE FONTENIL, 2km along the Montgenèvre road.

As for **eating** options, if you are not eating in a hotel, try one of the *crêperies* at the top of Grande-Gargouille or the *Café du Centre* on place du Temple by the church or the nearby *Entrecôte* in Porte Gargouille.

Névache

For a really beautiful day excursion from Briançon, head for the valley of the **River Clarée**. Without your own transport, you'll have to hitch or walk, but that should be no hardship because the scenery is truly magnificent.

Leave Briançon by the Montgenèvre road and take the left fork after 2km. A lane follows the wooded riverbank in the bottom of a narrow ravine parallel to the Italian frontier. On foot you could follow **GR5**, which passes through the main villages. If you want to spend a night up here, the half-ruined hamlet of PLAMPINET has both hotel and hostel-type **accommodation** in a vast renovated farm, *La Cleida* (☎92.21.32.48), as well as at the *Auberge de la Clarée* by the bridge. And there is more at **NÉVACHE**, where the valley widens. There's already been a good deal of holiday development here, though the old village nucleus of wide-roofed houses still huddles protectively around the church – this is worth a look for its carving, Baroque altarpiece, and a few items in the treasury, including some venerable, spiked eleventh-century doors. In addition to hotels and pensions, there are three **gîtes**: *Le Creux des Souches*, *Le Pontée* and *Paschalet*.

The finest country is beyond Névache towards the head of the valley, where in May the meadows are running with snow melt and carpeted with crocuses, and fat marmots whistle from the rocks. Six kilometres after the village, there are two refuges by the first bridge – *Fontcouverte* and *La Fruitière*, – another at the end of the road, as well as a *CAF* refuge on the slopes of Mt Thabor, none of which are open for much more than the summer season.

Into the park: towards Mont-Pelvoux

The usual **approach to the Parc des Écrins**, with some serious climbing goals at its end, is from the train station at ARGENTIÈRES-LA-BESSÉE, a scruffy, depressed little place with a recently closed aluminium works, south towards Mont-Dauphin. From here a small road cuts into the valley towards VALLOUISE, with the ice-capped monster of **Mont-Pelvoux** (3946m) rearing in front of you all the way.

The Vaudois and Les Vigneaux

On the right by the first village you come to, LA BATIE, are the remains of the so-called **Mur des Vaudois**. Despite the name, the origins of the wall are uncertain. It was probably built either to keep out companies of marauding soldiers-turned-bandits, or to control the spread of plague in the fourteenth century. These Vaudois (Waldensians in English) are not to be confused with the inhabitants of the Swiss canton of Vaud. They were members of a religious sect, sort of precursors of Protestantism, founded in the late twelfth century by Pierre Valdo, a merchant from Lyon, who preached against worldly wealth and the corruption of the clergy. Practising as he preached, he gave his wealth to the poor. Excommunicated in 1186, the Vaudois came more and more to deny the authority of the Church, and they sought refuge from persecution in the remote mountain valleys of Pelvoux, especially in the area around Vallouise and Argentières. Their numbers were also probably augmented by refugees from the Inquisition's persecutions of the Cathars in Languedoc.

There was a crop of executions for sorcery in the early fifteenth century, and many of the victims were probably Vaudois, burnt to death in wooden cabins built for this purpose. In 1488, Charles VIII launched a full-scale crusade against them. There is a spot west of Ailefroide known as Baume Chapelue where they were smoked out by the military and butchered. They were finally exterminated in the eighteenth century after the revocation of the Edict of Nantes, when 8000 troops went on the rampage, creating total desolation and "leaving neither people nor animals".

On the right beyond La Batie, the village of LES VIGNEAUX (with a *gîte d'étape*) shrugs off such a past: a lovely place, surrounded by apple orchards and backed by the fierce crags of Montbrison. The church has a fine old door and lock under a vaulted porch. Beside it on the exterior wall of the church are two bands of paintings depicting the Seven Deadly Sins. In the upper band the sins are naive representations of men and women riding various beasts (lion, hound, monkey) and chained by the neck. A man carrying a leg of mutton and drinking wine from a flask represents gluttony; a woman with rouged cheeks, green stockings and displaying an enticing expanse of thigh, represents lust. In the lower band they are all getting their come-uppance, writhing in the agonies of Hell fire.

Vallouise

VALLOUISE lies under a steep wooded spur at the junction of two valleys, the Gyrond (or Gyr, as it is called upstream of Vallouise) and the Gérendoine. The great glaciered peaks visible up the latter valley are Les Bans; up in front still is Mont-Pelvoux. The nucleus of the old village – narrow lanes between sombre stone chalets – is again its church, fifteenth century with characteristic tower and steeple and a sixteenth-century porch on pink marble pillars. A fresco of the adoration of the Magi adorns the tympanum above the door, itself magnificent with carved Gothic panels along the top and an ancient lock-and-bolt with a chimera's head at one end. Remains of an enormously long-legged figure, partially painted over, cover the end wall of the apse. Inside, as at Les Vigneaux, are more frescoes, including at the back of the church six naive statues on painted wood.

There is a **campsite, gîte d'étape** and several **hotels** (Dec–April & July–Sept/Oct). The *Edelweiss* is cheapest, but all rooms in the village are likely to be full in July and August.

GR54, which does the circuit of the Écrins park, passes through Vallouise; and the stage on from here to LE MONETIER via **Lac de l'Eychauda** is one of the best. Another good walk is to the hamlet of PUY AILLAUD high on the west flank of the Gyr valley. The path starts just to the right of the church and zigzags up the steep slope behind it with almost aerial views of the valley beneath. The Vallouise *Maison du Parc des Écrins* provides **hiking information**. There is a **minibus** service as far as AILEFROIDE in summer, starting from the bar next to the *Edelweiss* hotel; to walk takes two hours or so.

Ailefroide

AILEFROIDE, under the last slopes of Pelvoux (three **campsites**), is also a major centre for climbers and walkers. There is a **Bureau des Guides**. A path follows the road on up the valley as far as the so-called **Pré de Madame Carle** by the old *Refuge Cézanne* (1hr 30min). In fact, it is not a *"pré"* or meadow at all, but a jumble of rocks brought down by the torrent from which you can see the **Barre des Écrins** towering above the Glacier Noir. At 4102m, this is the highest peak in the massif – and one of the major Alpine climbs. From the bridge another path runs north up to the **Refuge du glacier Blanc** on the edge of the glacier at 2550m (about 2hr 30min). Anywhere beyond this on the **Pelvoux massif** is snow and ice – strictly experienced climbers' territory.

From the North: La Grave, Lautaret and Le Casset

Coming into the mountains from Grenoble along the **N91**, you have various alternative approaches to the **Parc des Écrins** – and the possibility of a substantial two-day circuit between LA GRAVE and LE CASSET. The road itself, though, is grand enough, twisting through the precipitous valley of the Romanche and up and over the 2058-metre **Col du Lautaret**, which is kept open all year round and served regularly by the Grenoble–Briançon bus.

La Bérarde and Bourg d'Oisans

For **LA BÉRARDE**, right in the midst of the park's mightiest peaks, you leave the road just after Bourg-d'Oisans (49km from Grenoble; buses). A tiny hamlet and mountaineering centre 38km up a very narrow lane, La Bérarde has a *CAF* refuge, mountain rescue base and the small *Hôtel Tairraz* (☎76.79.53.46; ③). There are plenty of accessible valley walks without the need to risk your neck, including the approach to the back side of the magnificent La Meije with its dazzling square glacier, *le Glacier Carré*.

Although **BOURG-D'OISANS** is of no great interest in itself, it's a good place to catch your breath and pick up information from the **SI** (quai Girard, close to the main road in the middle of town) and the **park information centre** on av Gambetta. There are also numerous **places to stay**, although they will be crowded in summer: **camping municipal** on rue Humbert near the town centre and a concentration of sites across the river on the ALPE D'HUEZ road. Among the cheaper **hotels** to try are *Beau Rivage* (☎76.80.03.19; ③–④) and *Le Rocher* (☎76.80.01.53; ③), all next to each other on the main street. If you like the idea of cycling in sharp mountain air, **bikes** can be hired from *Cycles d'Oisans* on rue Viennois – not such a crazy undertaking as you might think, for if you keep to the valley bottoms, the gradients aren't too fearsome.

La Grave and Valloire

LA GRAVE, 26km on at the foot of the Col du Lautaret, faces the majestic glaciers of the north side of La Meije (3983m). It's a good base for walking. **GR54** climbs up to Le Chazelet on the slopes northwest of the village and continues to the **Plateau de Paris** and the **Lac Noir**, which numerous walkers recommend for its breathtaking views of La Meije. And it's only 11km to the top of the col, with the still higher Col du Galibier just beyond. There is no public transport up Galibier – which is closed by snow from mid-October to mid-June – but in season you should be able to hitch up, and back to La Grave or on to Le Casset in a day.

The **Col du Lautaret** has been in use for centuries. The Roman road from Milan to Vienne crossed it, and its name comes from the small temple (*altaretum*) the Romans built to placate the deity of the mountains. They called it *"collis de altareto"*. Around the col is a huge expanse of meadow long known to botanists for its glorious variety of Alpine flowers, seen at their best in mid-July. There is a **Jardin Alpin**, maintained by the University of Grenoble (July 1–Sept 15 daily 8am–noon & 2–6pm), which includes plants from mountain ranges throughout the world. This is a great spot for picnicking or lounging waiting for a ride, for you look straight into the glaciers hanging off La Meije and the sight is intoxicating. On a clear sunny day the dazzling luminosity of the ice and the burning intensity of the sky above is such that you can hardly bear to look.

The **Col du Galibier** is less frequented – a tremendous haul up to 2556m, utterly bare and wild, with the huge red-veined peak of the Grand Galibier rearing up on the right and a fearsome spiny ridge blocking the horizon beyond. To the north you can see Mont Blanc. The pass used to mark the frontier between France and Savoie. A monument on the south side of the col commemorates Henri Desgranges, founder of the Tour de France: crossing the col is one of the most gruelling stages in the race, with a long, brutal ascent and terrifying descent at breakneck speed. The road loops down in hairpin after hairpin, through **VALLOIRE**, a sizeable ski resort, whose church is one of the most richly decorated in Savoy, over the Col du Télégraphe at 1570m and down into the deep wooded valley of the Arc, known as la Maurienne, with the Massif de la Vanoise rising abruptly behind. Valloire has a **gîte d'étape** (☎79.59.01.54) and a pleasant, reasonably priced **hotel**, *Les Gentianes* (☎79.59.03.66; ③–④).

Le Casset

LE CASSET, back on the D28 just before MONETIER-LES-BAINS, is a hamlet of dilapidated old houses clustered around a church with a bulbous dome. The site is superb: streams and meadows everywhere, reaching to the foot of the larch-covered mountainsides, the Glacier du Casset imminent, white and dazzling above the green of the larches. There is a **campsite** and **gîte d'étape** (☎92.24.45.74) near the church, with another (☎92.24.76.42) at neighbouring Les Boussardes. But provided you choose a spot where the hay has already been mown it seems you can camp anywhere. There is a café and grocery store in the village, which in season is overcrowded.

The **GR54** goes through the village. A good day's walk is to follow it as far as the **Col d'Arsine**, about three hours, from which point you can either turn back or go on down to **La Grave** on the north side of the park, making an overnight stop at the *Refuge de l'Alpe* below the col.

The path crosses the Guisane near the *gîte* and follows a track through the woods, first on the left, and later on the right bank of the Petit Tabuc stream. From the end of the track you cross some grassy clearings before entering the trees again and climbing up to a milky-looking lakelet, the **Lac de la Douche**, at the foot of the Glacier du Casset. From here a clear path zigzags up a very steep slope coming out in a long valley, and eventually leading to the Col d'Arsine. Masses of ground-hugging red rhododendrons grow along the banks of the stream. About halfway up are some tumbledown huts, the **Chalets d'Arsine**, by a series of blue-grey tarns. Up on the left are a whole series of **glaciers**. The biggest is the Glacier d'Arsine, hanging from the walls of the long jagged ridge suspended between the Montagne des Agneaux and the Pic de Neige Cordier to the west. Early in the morning there are colonies of marmots playing above the banks of the stream.

Other cheap accommodation nearby includes a *gîte d'étape* (☎92.24.41.13) in Monetier and the **youth hostel** at Serre-Chevalier (☎92.24.74.54).

Parc National de la Vanoise

The Parc National de la Vanoise occupies the eastern end of the **Vanoise massif**, the area contained between the upper valleys of the Isère and Arc rivers. It is extremely popular, with over 500km of marked paths, including the **GR5**, **GR55** and **GTA** (*Grande Traversée des Alpes*), with numerous refuges along the trails. For information on the spot, the SIs in **Modane**, **Val d'Isère** and **Bourg-St-Maurice** are helpful. The *Maison du Parc* in Chambéry (135 rue St-Julien) also gives advice and sells maps.

Modane and the Haute-Maurienne

MODANE is a dreary little place, destroyed by Allied bombing in 1943 and now little more than a railway junction. Nonetheless, it's a good kicking-off point for walkers on the south side of the park – easily accessible by train and with a well-sited grassy **camping municipal** just up the road to the Fréjus tunnel (which leads to Bardonecchia in Italy). The *Hôtel de l'Europe*, just beyond the Fréjus turning on the street parallel to the main road, is a friendly place if you want a **room** – and serves good home-cooked meals designed for the road weary.

PARC NATIONAL DE LA VANOISE

The **GR5** sets out from the northern edge of the transpontine section of Modane and leads up to the **Refuge de l'Orgère**, where a path joins up with the **GR55** leading north to PRALOGNAN, over the **Col de la Vanoise** and right across the park to Val Claret on the Lac de Tignes – a tremendous walk. The GR5 itself keeps east of La Dent Parrachée, describing a great loop through the **Refuge d'Entre-Deux-Eaux** before continuing up the north flank of the Arc valley and over the Col de l'Iseran to Val d'Isère.

The Arc Valley: churches and Baroque art

The **Arc valley**, dark and enclosed below Modane, widens and lightens above it, with meadows and patches of cultivation in the valley bottom and the lighter foliage of larches gracing the mountainsides. It is hardly a joyous landscape, especially under a stormy sky. Bare crags hang above the steep meadows on the north flanks, glaciers threaten to the south and east. The villages, though attractive to the modern eye, are poor and humble places, the houses squat and built of rough grey stone, the homes of people who have had to struggle to wring a living from harsh weather and unyielding soil. It is surprising at first to find such a wealth of exuberant **Baroque art** in the outwardly simple **churches**. But probably it is precisely because of the harshness and poverty of their lives that these mountain people sought to express their piety with such colourful vitality. Schools of local artists flourished, particularly in the seventeenth and eighteenth centuries, inspired and influenced by itinerant Italian artists who came and went across the adjacent frontier.

Haute Maurienne Information in **LANSLEBOURG** organise tours of the churches in AVRIEUX, BRAMANS (where Horace Walpole's dog Toby was eaten by a wolf), TERMIGNON, LANSLEVILLARD and BESSANS. Lanslebourg is also the start of the climb to the **Mont Cenis pass** over to Susa in Italy, another ancient trans-Alpine route. Last stop before the perils of the trek, it was once a prosperous and thriving town. Relief at finishing the climb from the French side was tempered by an alarming descent *en ramasse*, a sort of crude sledge, which shot downhill at breakneck speed much to the alarm of travellers. "So fast you lose all sense and understanding", a terrified merchant from Douai recounted in 1518.

BESSANS, further up the valley, retains its village character better than most. Its squat dwellings are built of rough stone with tiny window openings, and roofed with heavy slabs to withstand the long hard winters. Most have south-facing balconies to make the most of the sun and galleries under deep eaves for drying *grebons*, the bricks of cow dung and straw used locally for fuel. The **church** has a collection of seventeenth-century painted wooden statues and a retable, signed by Clappier. The Clappiers were a local family who produced several generations of artists. On the other side of the small cemetery, where old women in black tend the graves, the **chapel of St-Antoine** has exterior murals of the Virtues and Deadly Sins and fine sixteenth-century frescoes; ask the priest to unlock the chapel – his house is on the right of the road leading east from the village square. Two kilometres up the road you pass the chapel of Notre-Dame-des-Grâces on the right, with another ex-voto by Jean Clappier. On the opposite side of the river, the hamlet of LE VILLARON has a *gîte d'étape*.

BONNEVAL-SUR-ARC (1835m), 10km upstream, lies at the foot of the **Col de l'Iseran** in a rather bleaker setting close to the timberline. At the head of the Arc valley to the east you can see the huge glaciers of the *Sources de l'Arc*. Better preserved and more obviously picturesque than Bessans, Bonneval stops a lot of tourists on their way to and from the col. It is in danger of becoming twee.

Nonetheless, like all these Haute-Maurienne villages, Bonneval has a highly individual identity – quite different to Bessans. Its houses cluster tightly around the church, with only the narrowest of lanes between them. You feel the need for mutual protection and warmth even more strongly here, and sense how very isolated these places were until only a few years ago, cut off for months by heavy snow, forced in upon their own resources. Life was dangerous, too, even for experienced locals. Several graves in the churchyard record deaths by avalanche.

Alternative bases to Modane and Bessans in Haute-Maurienne include the **campsites** at Termignon, Lanslebourg and Lanslevillard; *gîtes d'étape* at Termignon, Sardières, Bramans and Le Villaron; or the **youth hostel** at Lanslebourg (☎79.05.90.96). **Hotels** are also numerous, but expensive and hard to find space in during summer.

The Col de l'Iseran and Haute Tarentaise

As with all the other high Alpine passes the **Col de l'Iseran** has been used for centuries by local people. Despite the dangers of weather and the arduous climb, it was by far the quickest route between the remote **upper valleys** of the Arc and Isère. The volume of traffic was too small to disturb the nature of the tiny communities that eked out an existence on the approaches. But twentieth-century roads and the development

SKIING THE ALPS: A RESORT ROUND-UP

Skiing in the French Alps is a highly organised business – which received a big boost from the 1992 Winter Olympics centred on Albertville – based around resorts that are either purpose-built or have been ruthlessly modernised. If skiing is what you're here for this is great: you can ski away from your front door in the morning and ski straight back at night, and rarely have to queue much along the way. The downside is that these places offer little else. Many are astonishingly ugly 1960s (and even 1970s and 1980s) functionalist brutes isolated in the middle of open snow fields – even worse if you see them in summer – which offer nothing in the way of après-ski and often little entertainment at all. There's certainly none of the alpine atmosphere here that you might associate with Austria, for example.

What you get instead, at the best of the resorts, is vast linked territories with some of the best high-altitude skiing in Europe. At **Val d'Isère** or **Chamonix** you can at least get some of the atmosphere of older-established resorts as well, though both are too large to be at all picturesque. Val d'Isère is very British-oriented in the ski season, and one of the liveliest resorts in France, with a magnificent ski terrain linked to **Tignes** (among the ugliest of the resorts), and endless challenges and off-piste possibilities, plus impressive new facilities built for the Olympics – the downhill and other blue riband events were held here. Chamonix is bigger still, and with even more going on, but as a place to ski is definitely less attractive – the local pass covers a wide area, but it's positively un-French in the lack of links between ski areas and relatively awkward transport. The other obvious choice is **Les Trois Vallées** – Courchevel, Méribel and Val Thorens/Les Menuires – which claims to be "le plus grand domaine skiable du monde". This may be true, but it often seems less exciting than the Val d'Isère area: of the resorts, Courchevel (actually four separate villages at different heights) is the most glamorous; Méribel, in the central valley, the best placed but very British-yuppie in season; Val Thorens and Les Menuires the ugly ducklings in terms of both architecture and cachet. Of the smaller, pure resorts, the pick are probably **Les Arcs** – cleverly designed, with varied terrain and no walking at all – **Flaine** – especially for beginners – **La Plagne** – one of the less ugly modern places with a vast area, though no great challenges – and **Valmorel**, among the newest and prettiest developments.

At any of these places you can simply turn up, buy a pass (90–200F a day, 450–800F a week) and hire equipment for a day. If you want to stay longer you'll almost certainly get a better deal by arranging a package before you leave – and accommodation can often be very hard to arrange on the spot.

of winter sports have changed all that. Val D'Isère, for instance, once a tiny mountain village, has become a hideous agglomeration of cafés, supermarkets and apartments for skiers – with some of the finest skiing in Europe.

From October to June **the pass** is usually blocked by snow. But in summer, being the highest pass in the Alps at 2770m, it is one of the "sights" that motorised tourists feel they must see; consequently it's relatively easy to hitch. A word of warning, though: if you do try, don't do it in light summer clothing, especially on a cool cloudy day. My lift put me down at the chalet on the col. It had been drizzling in Bonneval. On the col the temperature was 2°C, and it was blowing a blizzard – on July 18th.

The climb begins above Bonneval, offering splendid views of the glaciers at the head of the Arc, and then follows the rocky gully of the Lenta stream (marmots galore) through a narrow defile and out into a desolate cirque, where the Lenta rises and masses of anemones bloom in the stony ground. Behind the chalet on the col a path climbs west to the **Pointe des Lessières** (2hr 30min round trip), where on a clear day you have views of the Italian side of Mont Blanc and the whole of the frontier chain of peaks.

Val d'Isère

VAL D'ISÈRE (buses from BOURG-ST-MAURICE) at the foot of the col on the north side, is a convenient centre for walking (details from the SI), but no place to stay unless you're feeling extremely rich. There's a **campsite** on the edge of the resort at LE LAISINANT and a **youth hostel** (☎79.06.35.07) about 12km away at **TIGNES**, an unattractive, purpose-built resort on the artificial Lac de Chevril. But thereafter the valley is lovely, deep and wooded, with villages perched on grassy shoulders high on either flank.

The Isère Valley

If you're interested in exploring the valley, make for **Les Brevières**. Seven kilometres beyond, a lane turns left into the valley bottom to LA SAVINAZ and LA GURRAZ, whose creamy church tower is a landmark for miles around. High above, though looking dangerously close, the green ice cliffs that terminate the Glacier de la Gurraz hang off the edge of Mont Pourri (3799m). From the turn, the lane veers steeply down through trees and hay meadows full of flowers, past ruined houses, to the river. The climb up the opposite bank is hard going, past impossibly steep fields. You take a right fork for La Gurraz across a rickety plank bridge in the jaws of a defile. It's about an hour's walk, once you're on the lane.

And **LA GURRAZ** shouldn't disappoint you. Tiny and untouched by tourism, its dozen old houses have wide eaves and weathered balconies spread with sweet drying hay, and firewood stacked outside. Only the old people remain, but they keep the traditional agricultural economy ticking over. The houses are all sited in the lee of a knoll for protection against the avalanches which come thundering off the glacier above the village, thousands of tons of snow and rock, almost sheer down into a cwm behind. If you are unlucky enough to be out of doors when one occurs, the blast knocks you off your feet, and can even suffocate you. There are no provisions available, so bring your own. Other hamlets on the opposite flank of the valley look just as interesting. The prettiest is LE MONAL, in the mouth of a small hanging valley, also accessible by car from La Thuile further along the Bourg-St-Maurice road.

From La Gurraz a signposted path climbs to **Refuge de la Martin** in an hour and a half. It zigzags up the slope behind La Savinaz, on to a spur by a ruined chalet, where a right-hand path goes up the rocks overhead to the edge of the glacier. The refuge path continues left along the side of a deep gully, whose flanks are thick with the white St Bruno's lily. It crosses a ferocious torrent by a plank bridge and follows a mule track up to the *alpage* by the refuge, where cows and sheep graze. The **Mont Pourri glaciers** are directly above. Opposite is the big **Glacier de la Sassière** and up to your right Val d'Isère with the Col de l'Iseran behind.

Bourg-St-Maurice

Continuing down the valley, **BOURG-ST-MAURICE** is the mid-point of the Tarentaise. Again, of little interest itself, it can be a useful place to stop. The big purpose-built ski resorts of LES ARCS and LA PLAGNE are nearby and the classic pass into the Italian Val d'Aosta, the **Col du Petit St-Bernard**, right behind. With its Swiss twin, the Grand St-Bernard, it was the only route around the Mont Blanc massif until the tunnel was opened in 1965. It's a rather spooky crossing, reaching a height of 2188m, with a couple of barrack-like buildings and a row of statues of St Bernard. It's at its most dramatic when you're coming over from the Italian side in the early evening, right into the eye of the setting sun. (There is one daily bus crossing in July and August.)

There are no very appealing **places to stay** in the town. It's best to look on Grande-Rue, the old main street, where you could try the *Hôtel du Centre* (☎79.07.05.13; ③) or the slightly more expensive *Vallée de l'Arc* (☎79.07.04.12; ④). There are other places on the dreary main road, av Leclerc, where you'll also find the **gares SNCF** and **the gare routière**, with the **SI** almost opposite. The **campsite**, *Camping le Versoyen* (79.07.03.45; open all year) is in rte des Arcs on the right just past the sports ground on the Val d'Isère road.

Towards Chambéry

Heading west towards Chambéry, there are a couple of places worth a brief stop. The first is **AIME**, whose Grande-Rue recalls what an Alpine village would once have looked like. Its principal sight, however, is the rough stone **church of St-Martin**, whose origins go back to a first-century Roman temple, swept away by the Isère in spate in the third century – an indication of how dangerous these mountain rivers could be in the days before flood control. What survives today is basically early Romanesque.

The other place that rewards a brief detour is **CONFLANS**, a small medieval town on a spur overlooking grim modern ALBERTVILLE (centre of the 1992 winter Olympics), and rather too cutely revived for its own good. From the public garden by the Tour Sarrazine, you can contemplate the contrast in town planning styles: spreading below are gaunt, rectangular blocks of appartments separated by rushing highways, against a steep backdrop of verdant slopes, vineyard terraces and hay meadows.

MONT BLANC AND LAKE GENEVA

Mont Blanc is the biggest tourist draw in the Alps, but so spectacular it's worth seeing despite the crowds. If you're going to walk in the area, you soon get away from the most of the visitors. ANNECY is the easiest place to approach the mountain from, and of the two road routes, the one via the old ski resort of MEGÈVE is the more interesting – though, from Ugine onwards, difficult to hitch. The alternative route goes through CLUSES.

Mont Blanc

The two main **approach roads** to the "Blonk" – as English climbers insist on calling the mountain – come together at LE FAYET, where the **tramway du Mont-Blanc** begins its 75-minute haul to the **Nid d'Aigle**, a vantage point on the northwest slope. CHAMONIX-MONT BLANC, the base camp for all Mont Blanc activities, is just 30km further on.

Chamonix-Mont Blanc

If Mont Blanc with its eery green glaciers was anything less than outstanding there would be no point in going to **CHAMONIX**. Its village identity has been submerged in a sprawl of development. It is extremely expensive, and always crawling with tourists, accoutred with the latest fashionable ski or mountaineering gear. And the town itself has no sights. The **Musée Alpin** off av Michel-Croz in the town centre (June–Sept daily 2–7pm; Christmas–Easter 3–7pm) will interest mountain freaks, but is not as exciting as you would expect; among various bits of equipment, documents and letters is Jacques Balmat's account of his first ascent of the "Blonk", written in almost phonetically spelled French.

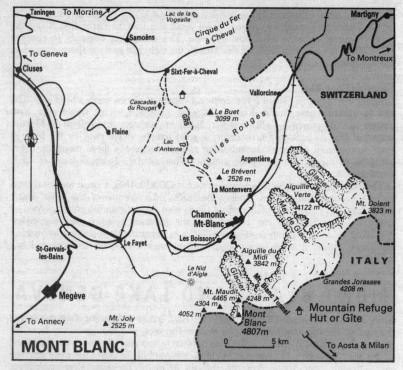

MONT BLANC

Accommodation and food

The biggest headache in Chamonix can be **finding a bed**. There is no such thing as a cheap hotel, and the only real alternative is to go for the hostel accommodation, of which there is at least a fair supply.

The official **youth hostel** itself is perhaps the best option; largely modernised, comfortable and friendly, it's at Les Pèlerins, just west of Chamonix proper (bus to les Houches and get off at *Pèlerins École*: the hostel, signposted, is at 103 Montée Jacques-Balmat; ☎50.53.14.52; meals, if you book). Arriving by car or on foot from the west, it's very easy to miss the turning: look out for the Pèlerins-d'En-Bas sign on your left not long after the Bossons glacier – the hostel road is opposite, on your right. Similar accommodation can be found at *Chalet Ski-Station*, 6 route des Moussoux, under the Brévent *téléférique* (☎50.53.20.25); *Le Chamoniard Volant*, 45 route de la Frasse (☎50.53.14.09) on the right towards the Bois du Bouchet; *La Montagne*, 789 promenade des Crémeries (☎50.53.11.60) in the Bois du Bouchet. Also at Argentière, 8km down the road: *Le Belvédère* (☎50.54.02.59) and *La Boerne*, 292 Tré-le-Champ (☎50.54.05.14), in an old farm just on the Swiss side of the village.

Campsites are numerous, though in high season there may only be room for a small mountain tent. Two convenient ones are *Les Molliases* (June–Sept 15), on the left of the main road going west from Chamonix towards the Mont Blanc tunnel entrance, and *Les Rosières* (year round) off the route des Praz. Mecca for the impoverished hard-nut climbers, and replacement for Snell's Field of yore, is the zero-amenities *Pierre d'Orthaz*.

If you have to go for **a hotel**, you'd certainly get a better deal away from Chamonix. But if you're determined to stay here, try *Hôtel du Faucigny* (☎50.53.01.17; ④) near the church and drop in at the **SI** (summer daily 8.30am–7.30pm; winter 8.30am–12.30pm & 2–7pm).

Getting a square **meal** at an affordable price is another of Chamonix's little drawbacks. Take advantage of hostel canteens where you can. *La Poêle*, 79 av de l'Aiguille-du-Midi, specialises in omelettes, but like its competitors tends to become very crowded. *Le Fer à Cheval*, place du Mont-Blanc, is a treat and its prices for *fondue* etc very reasonable in spite of its desperate popularity. There is standard *brasserie* fare at the *Brasserie des Sports* in rue Joseph-Vallot, and edible fast-foodish and pizza fare at *Le Bar à Papa* at the wrong end of rue Paccard, in av Ravanel.

And, once at least, you should take a look at *Le Choucas* right in the centre of town, at the right end of rue Paccard, the hangout of the climbers and their groupies.

Around Chamonix: the easy way up

There are various touristy things to do around Chamonix that in other circumstances you might baulk at. Here, though, if you don't do them there is not much else, unless you're an experienced walker or climber. The first is to take the **rack railway** from the Gare du Montenvers to the vast glacier known as the **Mer de Glace**, a favourite with Victorian travellers. The second, and best of all, is the very expensive *téléférique* to the **Aiguille du Midi** (3842m): if mountains excite you, you won't regret the outlay, and penny-pinching by buying a ticket only as far as the Plan du Midi is a waste of money – you won't see anything. You must, however, go before 9am; first, because the summits usually cloud over towards midday and, second, because any later there will be huge crowds and you may have to wait for hours. And take warm clothes: even on a summer day it will be well below zero on the top. You need a steady head, too, for the drop beneath your little bubble of steel and glass is truly appalling.

The Aiguille is a terrifying granite pinnacle on which the *téléférique* dock and a restaurant are precariously balanced. The view is incredible. At your feet is the snowy plateau of the **Col du Midi**, with the glaciers of the Vallée Blanche and Géant crawling off left at their millennial pace. To the right a steep snowfield leads to the "easy" ridge route to the summit with its cap of ice (4807m).

Away to the front, rank upon rank of snow-and-ice-capped monsters recede into the distance. Most impressive of all, closing the horizon to your left, from the east to south, is a mind-blowing cirque of needle-sharp peaks and precipitous couloirs: the Aiguille Verte, Triollet, the Jorasses, with the Matterhorn and Monte Rosa visible in the far distance across a glorious landscape of rock, snow and cloud-filled valleys – the lethal testing-ground of all truly crazed climbers. And there are plenty of them still at it, swapping tales in the valley campsites of difficult pitches, rockfalls and other people's accidents, so casually you'd think the whole thing was a picnic.

MONT BLANC: THE FIRST CLIMBS

The mountain was first climbed in **1786** by Dr Paccard and Jacques Balmat, both natives of Chamonix, inspired by the offer of a reward by de Saussure, a Genevese naturalist. The first woman to climb the mountain was Marie Paradis, who ran a tea shop in Chamonix. Alpine exploration and climbing developed quickly in the nineteenth century. Early technique was primitive and extremely dangerous. Even when guides began to use rope at all, they did not bother to rope themselves to their parties. When Edward Whymper, one of the most renowned early alpinists, made the first successful ascent of the Matterhorn in 1865, his party lost four members because the old, worn piece of rope they casually attached themselves to simply snapped.

Chamonix Valley: some possible hikes

Opposite Mont Blanc, the north side of Chamonix valley is enclosed by the lower but nonetheless impressive **Aiguilles Rouges**, with another *téléférique* to Le Brévent, the 2525-metre peak directly above the town. Classic walks this side of the valley include the **Lac Blanc**, starting from Les Praz and the Flégère *téléférique*, and the **Grand** and **Petit Balcon Sud** trails, giving spectacular views of Mont Blanc. A highly recommended **two-day hike** is the **GR5** stage north from Le Brévent to the village of SIXT via **Lac d'Anterne**, with a night at the **Refuge d'Anterne**. The classic **long-distance route** is the two-week **Tour du Mont Blanc** (TMB), described in a *Topo-Guide* and Andrew Harvey's *Tour of Mont Blanc* (Cicerone Press).

For up-to-the minute **walking and climbing information**, consult the **SI** or the **Maison de la Montagne** (☎50.53.03.40), both near the church in the centre of Chamonix. The Maison de la Montagne houses the *Bureau des Guides*, *Office de Haute Montagne* and a meteorological service. The SI publishes a large-scale **map of summer walks** in the area, while the guides run rock- and ice-climbing schools and will, if you wish, accompany you on any mad-cap expedition they reckon is within your capabilities.

Northern pre-Alps: the Cirque du Fer-à-Cheval

The **Northern pre-Alps**, climbing back from the shore of Lake Geneva, are cooler, softer and greener country. They are less well known than the mightier ranges further south but they're also a lot less crowded. For walkers, there's considerable potential – the only real problem is access off the main routes. To get into the **Giffre valley**, with its **Fer-à-Cheval** hikers' circuit, you need to hitch or bus over to TANINGES and thence to SAMOËNS and SIXT.

Samoëns

The gentle and attractive village of **SAMOËNS**, 21km from Cluses, lies at the foot of the Aiguille de Criou, with the tall peak of Le Buet in the distance. Its principal architectural claim to fame is its church – very late Gothic on a Romanesque base with a doorway of crouching lions like those in the Queyras. Built in the sixteenth century, it was already well behind its times, given that the Renaissance was in full swing elsewhere – although this architectural conservatism is very much a pattern in remote Alpine valleys.

The village is chiefly known for its stonemasons and for Marie-Louise Cognacq-Jay, who left to seek her fortune in Paris at the age of fifteen in 1853, and found it – as the founder of the famous department store, *La Samaritaine*. Hers was an exceptional success, but part of the pattern of local life: up to World War I the men of the village would set out every spring with their tools on their backs to seek work in the cities of France and Switzerland. Their guild, *les frahans*, evolved its own peculiar dialect, *le mourne*, so they could communicate secretly among themselves.

Sixt and the Cirque

East of Samoëns the valley narrows into the Gorge des Tines before opening out again at SIXT (7km), another pretty village on the confluence of two branches of the Giffre, the Giffre-Haut which comes down from Salvagny, and the Giffre-Bas which rises in the **Cirque du Fer-à-Cheval.**

The Cirque begins about 6km from Sixt – there is a footpath along the left bank of the Giffre-Bas. It is a vast semicircle of rock walls up to 700m in height and 4–5km long, blue with haze on a summer's day and striated with long, tumbling chains of white water from the waterfalls. The left-hand end of the Cirque is dominated by a huge spike of rock known as the Goat's Horn, *La Corne du Chamois*. At its foot the valley of the Giffre bends sharply north to its source in the glaciers above the Fond de la Combe. The bowl of the Cirque is thickly wooded except for a circular meadow in the middle where the road ends.

There is an **SI** and a **park office** here, though nowhere to buy provisions. The park office produces a folder of walks in the region – useful and well illustrated. They recommend, in particular, the walk to the **Refuge du Lac de la Vogeale** (3hr 30min); the **Chalets de Sales** via the spectacular Cascade du Rouget waterfalls on GR5 and GR96; and the GR5 stage to the **Lac d'Anterne** and on to Le Brévent and Chamonix.

Sixt, Samoëns and Taninges are all equipped with **campsites**, and there are two **gîtes d'étape** in Samoëns – *Les Couadzous* (☎50.34.41.62), in the centre, and *Les Moulins*, 1km away on the road up to Les Allamands – and one in Sixt.

Évian and Lake Geneva

The most agreeable way to reach ÉVIAN, or any of the **lakeside towns**, is by boat from GENEVA (3hr to Évian). Some 72km long, 13km wide and an amazing 310m deep, the lake – **Lac Léman** to the French – is fed and drained by the Rhône. It is a real inland sea, subject to violent storms, as Byron and Shelley discovered to their discomfort in 1816. On a calm day, though, sailing slowly across its silk-smooth surface is a serene experience.

The boat calls first at a series of flower-decked villages on the Swiss shore with the long level ridge of the Jura mountains in the background. The first stop on the French side is the walled village of YVOIRE, its houses packed on a low rise behind the shore, guarded by a massive fourteenth-century castle and wholly devoted to tourism. Mont Blanc and a host of other peaks appear shining in the distance. Next stop is THONON-LES-BAINS, flanked, just outside the town, by the fifteenth-century **Château de Ripaille,** built by Duke Amadeus VIII and used by him as a retreat before and after his stint as anti-pope. *"Faire la ripaille"* has come to mean "have a really riotous time" in French, which is apparently rather unfair to the duke, who led a much quieter life than popular imagination wanted to believe. Thonon was also the place from which St François de Sales set out on his donkey to reclaim the erring Protestants of Chablais for Rome.

Why visit ÉVIAN? Well, unless you are a well-heeled invalid or gambler, there probably isn't much point, except as the end of a pleasant, leisurely trip on the lake. The famous water is now bottled at Amphion, but the **Source Cachat** still bubbles away behind the Évian company's beautiful nineteenth-century offices, all wood, coloured glass, cupolas and patterned tiles – the best building in town. Anyone can go along and help themselves to spring water.

The waterfront is elegantly laid out with squares of billiard-table grass, brilliant flowerbeds and rare trees. It is pretty, restful and not very exciting, like most spa towns. For a little distraction, there are daily ferries across the lake to Lausanne in Switzerland. For further information about things to do, ask the **SI** in place d'Allinges (Mon–Fri 8.30am–noon & 2–6.30pm; June–Sept also Sat & Sun 10am–noon & 3–6pm).

If you stay, there are several **hotels** that would make a large hole in your budget, and one or two that would wipe it out completely. Two affordable options are the *Régina*, 25 rue Nationale near the port, at the east end of the street (☎50.75.21.09; ④ – with restaurant from 72F), and the *Hostellerie du Lac* on the lakeside av Grande-Rive (☎50.75.02.92; ②; closed Oct to mid-March). The nearest **campsite** is the *Grande Rive* off av Grande-Rive (April–Sept).

travel details

Trains

From Grenoble several daily to Paris-Lyon (7hr 15min – 3hr 12min by TGV.); very frequent to Lyon (1hr 30min–1hr 45min); several daily to Chambéry (1hr); several to Annecy (2hr); 2 daily to Gap (2hr 30min) and Briançon (4hr), changing at Veynes-Dévoluy.

From Annecy 10 daily to St-Gervais (1hr 15min–2hr); several daily to Grenoble (2hr); several to Chambéry (45min); several to Lyon (2hr); frequently, including 8 TGV to Paris (4hr 30min).

From St-Gervais 7 daily to Chamonix (35min).

From Chambéry frequent to Modane (40min–1hr 20min); 5 daily to Bourg-St-Maurice (2hr); very frequent to Lyon (1hr 30min–2hr 30min); several daily to Grenoble (1hr); several to Aix-les-Bains (10min); frequent to Annecy (45min); several to Geneva (1hr 30min); frequent to Paris (5hr 30min).

From Briançon 3 daily to Marseille (4hr 30min).

From Annemasse very frequent to Évian (35min); 4 or 5 daily to Annecy, changing at La-Roche-sur-Foron (1hr 30min) and 1 through train daily; 1 through train to Paris (8hr).

From Geneva 4 daily to Paris (3hr 45min).

Buses

From Chambéry several daily to Annecy (1hr); several to Aix-les-Bains (20min); several to Grenoble (1hr).

From Chamonix 3 to Annecy via La-Roche-sur-Foron (3hr); 1 to Annecy via Megève (3hr); 1 to Geneva (2hr 30min); 1 to Grenoble (3hr 30min).

From Bourg-St-Maurice 1 or 2 daily to Val d'Isère (50min–1hr 20min); 1 daily to Aosta (July–Aug only: 2hr 30min).

From Grenoble 1 daily to Briançon (3hr) via Bourg-d'Oisans (1hr), La Grave (1hr 40min), Col du Lautaret (2hr) and Monetier-les-Bains (2hr 25min); 5 daily to Bourg-d'Oisans (1hr 20min); 1 daily to Gap (2hr 45min); several daily to Chambéry (1hr); 2 daily to Alpe-d'Huez (45min); several to Briançon (2hr); at least 1 daily to Villard-de-Lans (45min).

CHAPTER FOURTEEN

THE RHONE VALLEY AND PROVENCE

O f all the areas of France, Provence is the most irresistible. Geographically it ranges from the high mountains of the **southern Alps** to the plains of the **Camargue**; and has the greatest European canyon, the **Gorges du Verdon**. Fortresses like **Sisteron** and **Tarascon** guard its old borders and countless citadels perch defensively at strategic heights. The sensual inducements of Provence include warmth, even in winter, food and wine, and the perfumes of Mediterranean vegetation. Along with its coast (see the following chapter), it has attracted the rich and famous, the artistic and reclusive, and countless arrivals who have found themselves unable to conceive of life lived elsewhere.

In appearance, despite the throngs of foreigners and French from other regions, **inland Provence** remains remarkably unscathed. The history of its earliest known natives, of the Greeks, the Romans that squeezed them out, raiding Saracens, schismatic popes, and shifting allegiances to different counts and princes, is still in evidence. Provence's complete integration into France dates only from the nineteenth century, and though the Provençal language is rarely heard, the common accent is distinctive even to a foreign ear, and in the east the intonation is Italian.

Unless you're intending to stay for months the main problem with Provence is choosing where to go. In the west, along the Rhône valley are the Roman cities, **Orange**, **Vaison-la-Romaine**, **Carpentras**, **Arles** and the papal city of **Avignon** with its brilliant summer festival. **Aix-en-Provence** is the mini-Paris of the region, and home to Cézanne, for whom the **Mont Ste-Victoire** was an enduring subject. Vasarely's works are on show in Aix and **Gordes**; Van Gogh's links are with **St-Rémy** and Arles. The **Gorges du Verdon**, the **Parc National du Mercantour** along the Italian border, **Mont Ventoux** northeast of Carpentras, and the flamingo-filled lagoons of the **Camargue** are only a selection of the landscapes that really should not be missed.

Before you reach Provence there are the **vineyards of the Rhône valley** and, before them, the French centre of gastronomy and the second largest city of the country, **Lyon**. With its choice of restaurants, clubs, culture and all the accoutrements of an affluent and vital Western city, it stands in opulent contrast against the medieval hilltop villages of Provence.

HOTEL ROOM PRICES

For a fuller explanation of these price codes, see the box on p.28 of *Basics*.

① Under 100F   ② 100–130F   ③ 130–180F   ④ 180–230F   ⑤ 230–300F

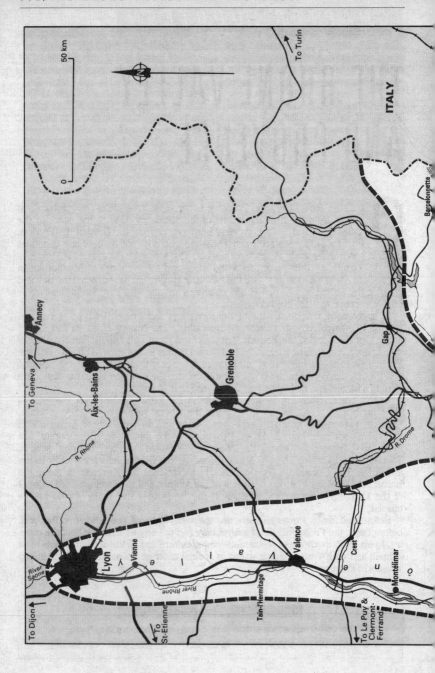

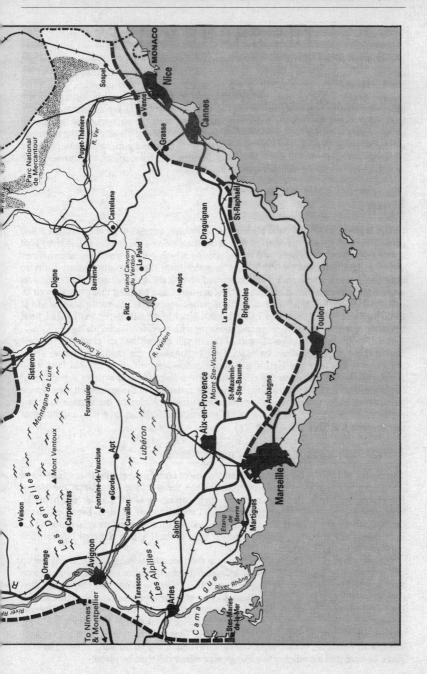

THE RHÔNE VALLEY

The **Rhône valley**, the north–south route of ancient armies, medieval traders and modern rail and road, is nowadays as industrialised as the least attractive parts of the North. Though the river is still a means of transport, it also provides, on a fairly massive scale, irrigation and hydro-electric power. Its waters cool the reactors of the Marcoule nuclear power station and act as a dustbin for the heavy industries along its banks. Following **the Rhône** holds few attractions, with the exceptions of the stretch of **vineyards** and fruit orchards between the Roman cities of **Vienne** and the distinctly southern city of **Valence**. But the big magnet is, of course, **Lyon**, with everything that big cities get bright lights for – good food, hundreds of bars, music and movies – and people without provincial chips on their shoulders.

Lyon

LYON is physically the second biggest city in France, a result of its uncontrolled urban sprawl. Viewed at high speed from the *Autoroute du Soleil* the impression it gives is of a major confluence of rivers and roads, around which only petro-chemical industries thrive. In fact, **silk** was the city's main industry from the sixteenth century right up until the present dominance of metalworks, chemicals and transport. But what has stamped its character most on Lyon is the commerce and banking that grew up with its industrial expansion. It is a city of political consequence, too: the race riots that swept through France in the summer of 1991 left a bitter aftermath here; and Michel Noir, the city's mayor, is an independent right-winger with presidential ambitions.

Staid, stolid and somewhat austere, Lyon is still not without its charms. Foremost among these is **gastronomy**, for which Lyon is, for many, the capital of France. There are more restaurants per Gothic and Renaissance square foot of the old town than anywhere else on earth and the city could form a football team with its superstars of the international chef circuit. While the **textile museum** is the second famous reason for stopping here, Lyon's nightlife, cinema and theatre (including the famous Lyonnais puppets), its antique markets and music and cultural festivals (see box) might tempt you to stay a few days.

Arrival, city transport and accommodation

The centre of Lyon is the *Presqu'île*, the tongue of land between the rivers Saône and Rhône just north of their confluence. Across the Saône is the old town at the foot of **Fourvière** on which the Romans built their capital of Gaul. To the north of the Presqu'île is the old silk-weavers' district, **La Croix Rousse**. Modern Lyon lies east of the Rhône with the *TGV* station and the assertive cultural and commercial centre of **La Part-Dieu**. The suburb of **Villeurbanne**, home to the Théâtre National Populaire, is northeast of the TGV station.

Ordinary **trains**, and **buses**, too, arrive at the *Gare de Perrache*, on what was the tip of the Presqu'île before 1770, when Monsieur Perrache shifted the confluence some 2km south. The *Autoroute du Soleil* crosses the Presqu'île alongside the station then runs down the east bank of this extension past such unprepossessing structures as St-Paul's prison and the wholesale market before recrossing the Saône just before the current merging of the rivers. Perrache is the exit to take from this manic highway. The **international airport, Satolas,** is off the Grenoble autoroute, with a 45-minute bus link to Perrache, or 30 minutes to La Part-Dieu. If you're thinking of flying in from Paris, beware that it's quicker to go by *grande vitesse* rail than by plane.

```
                    ██████ LYON FESTIVALS ██████
            ANNUAL                          BIENNIAL
September Festival de la Marionnette    June (1992) Festival International de la
October Festival des Arts Contemporains  Musique Mécanique
November Festival Lumière (Cinéma       June (1993) Biennale du Théâtre
Jeune Public)                            September (1992) Biennale de la Danse
                                         September (1993) Festival Berlioz

    The SI (see listings) is the best source of information for these and many more.
```

There's an **SI** in the *Centre Perrache* in front of the station where you can pick up a **métro, bus, tram** and **funicular** map (also available at Perrache métro station) or just hop two stops on the métro to **place Bellecour** where the central **SI** is on the southeast corner. You can buy tickets in *carnets* of six or a *billet de tourisme* valid for 48 or 72 hours. The ordinary tickets are flat rate within an hour's duration and limited to three changes using any combination of means of transport.

Accommodation

As a result of Lyon's commercial pre-eminence **hotel rooms** can be a problem to find, particularly in the week. If you don't book ahead, you could end up paying well over the odds for inferior accommodation. There will almost definitely be nothing in the area around Perrache station and pl Bellecour, but you may be luckier around Terreaux, especially if you take the precaution of **phoning ahead**. Again, if you phone ahead, *Bed et Breakfast à Lyon*, 4 rue Joliot-Curie (☎78.36.37.19; ②/③) offers a variety of accommodation in typical Lyonnaise homes, with the option of staying with English speakers.

PERRACHE AND BELLECOUR, 2ᵉ

Hôtel Vaubecour, 28 rue Vaubecour (☎78.37.44.91). One block back from the Saône quays. Comfortable, well furnished and friendly. ②/③.

Hôtel Célestins, 4 rue des Archers (☎78.37.63.32). Popular, but not especially cheap for a rundown establishment. ③/④.

Hôtel St-Vincent, 9 rue Pareille (☎78.28.67.97). Good position, just above the footbridge to *Vieux Lyon*. ④.

Hôtel d'Ainay, 14 rue des Remparts d'Ainay (☎78.42.43.42). One of a number of cheap and shabby establishments – which fill fast – off rue Victor-Hugo. ②/③.

Hôtel Alexandra, 49 rue Victor-Hugo (☎78.37.75.97). Large, well-run old hotel. ③/④.

Hôtel du Théâtre, 10 rue de Savoie (☎78.42.33.32). Expensive – singles prohibitively so – but comfortable and well run. ⑤.

TERREAUX, 1ᵉ

Hôtel Croix-Paquet, 11 pl Croix-Paquet (☎78.28.51.49). Take rue Romarin off pl de Terreaux. Good value for fairly comfortable rooms. ①/②.

Hôtel le Terme, 7 rue Ste-Catherine (☎78.28.30.45). Cheap and shabby, but well situated. ③.

Hôtel St-Vincent, 9 rue Pareille (☎78.28.67.97). More comfortable than *Le Terme*, but still nothing special for the price. ④.

VIEUX LYON, 5ᵉ

Celtic, 5 pl St-Paul (☎78.28.01.12). Large, fairly comfortable and cheap. ③/④.

There's a **youth hostel** 4km southeast of the centre in Vénissieux, 51 rue Roger-Salengrol; buses #53, #80 from Perrache or #36 from Part-Dieu, stop États-Unis-Viviani or Viviani Joliot-Curie (☎78.76.39.23; reception 8.30am–noon & 5–11pm). Not far away

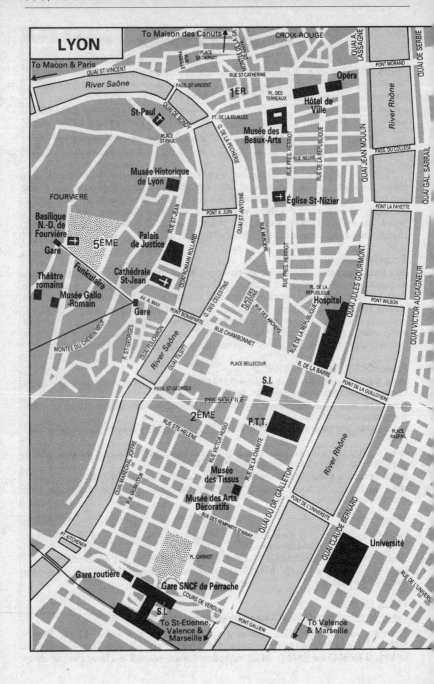

LYON

To Macon & Paris

To Maison des Canuts

CROIX-ROUGE

QUAI ST-VINCENT

River Saône

PASS. ST-VINCENT

RUE ST-CATHERINE

QUAI A. LASSAGNE

QUAI DE SERBIE

PONT MORAND

RUE PARGILLE

PLACE SATHONAY

MONTÉE DE LA GR...

1ER

PL. DES TERREAUX

Opéra

Hôtel de Ville

St-Paul

QUAI DE BONDY

PLACE ST-PAUL

PT. DE LA FEUILLÉE

Q. DE LA PÊCHERIE

Musée des Beaux-Arts

RUE PRES. HERRIOT

RUE NEUVE

RUE DE LA REPUBLIQUE

QUAI JEAN MOULIN

River Rhône

PASS. DU COLLEGE

QUAI GAL. SARRAIL

FOURVIÈRE

Musée Historique de Lyon

RUE ST-JEAN

Basilique N.-D. de Fourvière

Gare

5ÈME

Palais de Justice

QUAI ST-ANTOINE

PONT A. JUIN

RUE MERCIÈRE

Église St-Nizier

PONT LA FAYETTE

RUE PRES. HERRIOT

Funiculaire

Théâtre romains

Musée Gallo-Romain

Cathédrale St-Jean

QUAI ROMAIN ROLAND

AV. A. MAX

Gare

PONT BONAPARTE

Q. DES CELESTINS

PL. DE LA REPUBLIQUE

Hospital

QUAI JULES GOURMONT

QUAI VICTOR AUGAGNEUR

PONT WILSON

MONTÉE DU CHEMIN NEUF

R. ST-GEORGES

QUAI FULCHIRON

QUAI TILSITT

River Saône

PLACE DES CELESTINS

RUE DES ARCHERS

RUE CHAMBONNET

RUE DE LA REPUBLIQUE

R. DE LA BARRE

PONT DE LA GUILLOTIERE

PASS. ST-GEORGES

PLACE BELLECOUR

S.I.

PRESQU'ILE

2ÈME

RUE STE-HELENE

RUE VICTOR HUGO

P.T.T.

PLACE RASPAIL

QUAI MARECHAL JOFFRE

RUE HUBECOUR

Musée des Tissus

RUE DE LA CHARITE

Musée des Arts Décoratifs

RUE DES REMPARTS D'AINAY

QUAI DU DR. GAILLETON

River Rhône

PONT DE L'UNIVERSITE

QUAI CLAUDE BERNARD

Université

RUE DE L'UNIVERS...

PT. KITCHENER

PL. CARNOT

Gare routière

Gare SNCF de Perrache

COURS DE VERDUN

S.I.

To St-Etienne, Valence & Marseille

PONT GALLIENI

To Valence & Marseille

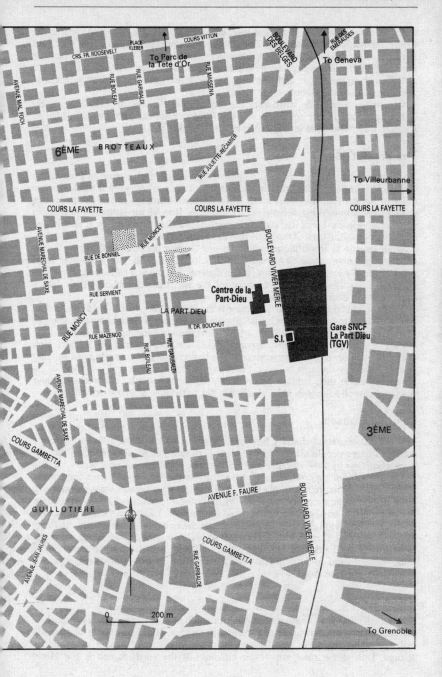

and a lot more expensive, though at least out of earshot of the main ring road, is the *Centre International de Séjour de Lyon*, 48 rue Commandant-Pégoud; bus #53 from Perrache or #36 from Part-Dieu, stop États-Unis-Beauvisage (☎78.01.23.45). If you have time, stop by the *Centre Régional d'Information Jeunesse*, 9 quai des Célestins, close to pl Bellecour on the Saône, and they may be able to fix you up in student lodgings or residences closer to the centre.

Campsites a bus ride away from the city are *Les Barolles* (☎78.56.05.56), at St-Genis- Laval on the #10 bus route, and the *Porte de Lyon* campsite (☎78.35.64.55) at Dardilly, a 10-minute ride by bus #19 from the Hôtel de Ville.

The Presqu'île

If you're walking, two streets link the pleasant greenery of **pl Carnot** in front of the **Centre Perrache** with the gravelly acres of pl Bellecour, where even Louis XIV in the guise of Roman Emperor looks small. **Rue Auguste-Comte** is full of antique shops selling heavily framed eighteenth-century artworks. **Rue Victor-Hugo** is a pedestrian precinct, a welcome break that continues north of pl Bellecour on rue de la République all the way up to the back of the Hôtel de Ville below La Croix Rousse.

While **rue de la République** is full of people jostling back and forth between café-*brasseries* and shops, quai St-Antoine on the bank of the Saône has a morning **food market** (daily except Mon), in which the cheeses are the star attraction. Two local varieties, from the *département* of Isère, of the sort that squash beautifully into a *baguette*, are *St-Félicien* and *St-Marcellin*.

To the right at the top of quai St-Antoine is the *quartier Mercière*, the old commercial centre of the town with sixteenth- and seventeenth-century financial houses lining rue Mercière, and the **Église St-Nizier**, whose bells used to announce the closing of the city's gates. In the silk-weavers' uprising of 1831, workers fleeing the soldiers took refuge in St-Nizier only to be massacred. The bourgeoisie had certainly been running scared, with only the area between the rivers, pl des Terreaux and just north of St-Nizier still under their control. Unfortunately for the *canuts* (the silk workers), their bosses could call on outside aid – which they did, to the tune of 30,000 extra troops.

La Croix-Rousse

The old **silk-weavers' district** (see box) is still a working-class area, but barely a couple of dozen people work on the modern high-speed computerised looms that are kept in business by the restoration and maintenance of palaces and châteaux.

The streets running down from bd de la Croix-Rousse, and many across the river in Vieux Lyon, are intercut with alleyways and tunnelled passages known as *traboules*. Their exits and entrances are sometimes visible; others have doors like any street door that often lead to an upstairs apartment and the *traboule*. You can get a map of them at the SI, but, for a good example: try going up past the right of St-Polycarpe on rue Réné-Leynaud above pl Terreaux; then take the *traboule* opposite 36 rue Burdeau; to the right around pl Chardonnet; through 55 rue des Tables-Cludiennes; opposite 29 rue Imber-Colomés and up the stairs into 14bis; across and up three more courtyards; and you should come out at pl Colbert.

Vieux Lyon

The streets pressed close together beneath the hill of Fourvière on the right bank of the Saône form an operatic set of Renaissance facades, bright night-time illumination and a swelling chorus of well-dressed Lyonnais in search of supper or a midday splurge. One of the most impressive buildings at the northern end is the **Hôtel**

THE SILK STRIKE OF 1831

The modern machines are no different in principle from the **Jacquard loom** of 1804 which made it possible for one person to produce 25 centimetres in a day instead of it taking four people four days. But this was not the undoing of the *canuts*: both masters and apprentices, and especially women and child workers, were badly paid whatever their output. And over the three decades following the introduction of the Jacquard the price paid for a length of silk was reduced by over fifty percent. Attempts to regulate the price were ignored by the dealers, even though hundreds of skilled workers were languishing in debtors' jails. On November 21, 1831 the *canuts* called an all-out **strike**. As they processed down the Montée de la Grande Côte with their black flags and the slogan "Live working or die fighting", they were shot at and three people died. After a rapid retreat uphill they built barricades, assisted by half the National Guard who refused to fire canons at their "comrades of Croix-Rousse". For three days, until the reinforcements were brought in, the battle raged on all four banks. Some 600 people were killed or wounded, and in the end the silk industrialists were free to pay whatever pitiful fee they chose. But the uprising was one of the first instances of organised labour taking to the streets during the most revolutionary fifty years of French history. In 1834, Lyonnais workers again built barricades, this time with overtly political demands and were repressed with even greater ferocity.

Paterin at 4–6 rue Juiverie, best viewed from the bottom of Montée des Carmes-Déchaussés just up from place St-Paul.

The central and pedestrian street, rue St-Jean, ends at the **Cathédrale St-Jean**, a twelfth- to fifteenth-century construction. The damage of religious wars and revolutions to the most recent part, the west facade, is slowly being repaired, but the thirteenth-century stained glass above the altar and in the rose windows of the transepts are in perfect condition. In the northern transept is a fourteenth-century clock rivalling modern digital watches for superlative functions: you can compute religious feast days till the year 2019. On the strike of noon, 1pm, 2pm and 3pm (most days), figures of the Annunciation go through an automated set-piece.

Just beyond the cathedral, opposite av Adolphe-Max and Pont Bonaparte is the **funicular station** from which you ascend either to the **Roman remains** (direction St-Just; stop *Minimes*) or to **Notre-Dame-de-Fourvière** (*Fourvière* terminus). The former consists of two theatres (entrance at 6 rue de l'Antiquaille; 9am–sunset) and an **underground museum** of Lyonnais life from prehistoric times to 7 AD. A mosaic illustrates the circus and various Roman games; bronze inscriptions detail ecomomic, legal and bureaucratic matters; there's a Gaulois lunar calendar and models aid the imagination in reconstructing the theatres outside. From there it's a very short walk to the late nineteenth-century creation of **Basilique de Notre-Dame**, an unenchanting miasma of multi-coloured marble and mosaic. As a visual antidote, make your way to the belvedere behind and you may well find Lyon and its curving rivers the epitome of graceful beauty by comparison.

Modern Lyon

On the skyline you'll see a gleaming cylinder with a pointed top and other Manhattanish protuberances around it. This is **La Part-Dieu**, a business-culture-commerce conglomerate including one of the biggest public libraries outside Paris, a mammoth concert hall and a shopping centre said to be the largest in Europe (métro *Part-Dieu*). On the corner of rue Garibaldi and cours Lafayette in front of these less than homely structures are the main **market halls** of Lyon.

For a break from city buildings head north to the **Parc de la Tête d'Or** (tram #4 from Part-Dieu, métro *Foch* or *Perrache*). There are ponds and rose gardens, and, just when you thought things were beginning to relax, the international headquarters of Interpol beside the river. The park and the university to the east are divided by bd de Stalingrad where there's another **antique market** around nos. 113–15 on Thursday and weekends.

The museums

Lyon and its environs have museums on practically every aspect of the history of the area, from the city's Roman origins and the occupations and endeavours of its inhabitants right up to today's motor industry. In Lyon itself, unmissable museums include the fascinating **Musée Historique des Tissus**, a unique collection of the world's fabrics; an entertaining collection of puppetry at the **Musée de la Marionette**; and the **Fondation Nationale de Photographie**, located in the birthplace of cinematic art, the family home of the Lumiére brothers.

Musée Historique des Tissus
Rue de la Charité, the Presqu'île; Tues–Sun 10am–noon & 2–5.30pm; 20F; ticket also covers Musée des Arts Décoratifs next door.

The museum doesn't quite live up to its claim to cover the history of decorative cloth through the ages. What it does have is brilliant collections from certain periods, most notably third-century Greek-influenced and sixth-century Coptic **tapestries**, woven **silk** and painted **linen** from Egypt. The fragment of woven wool *aux poissons* (second–third century AD) has an artistry unmatched in European work until at least the eighteenth century. Some of the Coptic designs have the style of modern cartoons, others are more like Roman mosaics. There are silks from Bagdad contemporary with the *1001 Nights* and carpets from Iran, Turkey, India and China. The most boring stuff is produced in Lyon itself – the sort of seventeenth- to eighteenth-century hangings, chair covers and the rest that go with all the pastoral cherubs in the paintings of that era. Sadly, there's almost nothing from the period of the Revolution, but there are some lovely twentieth-century pieces – Sonia Delaunay's *Tissus simultanés*, Michel Dubost's *L'Oiseau bleu* and Raoul Dufy's *Les Coquillages*.

Musée de la Marionette
Place du Petit-Collège; 10.45am–6pm; closed Tues; free; located in the same building as the Musée Historique de Lyon.

Located on the first floor of this fifteenth-century mansion, this is a lot more entertaining than its more self-important neighbour, the **Musée Historique de Lyon**. As well as the eighteenth-century Lyonnais creations, *Guignol* and *Madelon* (the French equivalents of Punch and Judy), there are glove puppets, shadow puppets and every type of rod-and-string toy actors from Europe and the Far East. If you want to see them in action, check out the times of performances at the **Nouveau Théâtre de Guignol** in the conservatory on rue Louis-Carrand by quai de Bondy (☎78.37.31.79; 10am–noon & 2–6pm; ☎78.28.92.57).

Musée des Beaux-Arts and Musée St-Pierre d'Art Contemporain
20 pl des Terreaux; 10.30am–6pm; closed Mon and Tues; free.

Thankfully this museum is free, so you don't need to worry if you can't handle more than ten rooms at a time. The second floor is dedicated to **paintings**, starting with medieval works to the right of the stairs and progressing chronologically counter-clockwise around the wings, the last of which is given over to temporary exhibitions. If you've started off with the Lyonnais paintings downstairs, you'll find a stairway leading up to the room of twentieth-century drawings and sketches and the most contemporary of the main collection – so you can work backwards if you want. There are some wonderful works among the modern stuff – to mention just a few: Gino Severini's *La Famille du Peintre* of 1939; spring and summer light in Bonnard's canvases beside wintry port scenes by Marquet; Van Dongens and de la Fresnayes throwing amused looks at their women friends; one of Monet's Thames series; *La Petite Niçoise* by Berthe Morisot. Of the early nineteenth-century collection *La Maraichère* attributed to David is outstanding, and you can work your way through Rubens, Zurbaran, El Greco, Tintoretto, and a hundred others back to the Middle Ages. Downstairs are numerous objects lifted at the turn of the century from Egypt, Iran and elsewhere, some ancient, some fourteenth/fifteenth-century.

The **Museum of Contemporary Art** devotes three huge spaces to one or more artists to do with them as they wish for six weeks or so.

Fondation Nationale de la Photographie and the Institut Lumière

25 rue du Premier-Film; Tues–Sun 2–6pm; free except for special exhibitions; bus #9, direction Bron Libération, stop Frères Lumières.

The building was the home of Antoine Lumière, father of Auguste and Louis who made the first ever films, and the exhibits range from magic lanterns to the cameras used by the brothers, and various art photographs (the temporary exhibitions are more exciting – enquire at the SI). The *Institut* also hosts various **film festivals**.

La Maison des Canuts

10–12 rue d'Ivry, one block north of pl de la Croix-Rousse; Mon–Fri 8.30am–noon & 2–6.30pm, Sat 9am–noon & 2–6pm; closed first two weeks and Mon in Aug; métro Croix-Rousse.

Traditional looms can be seen in action in this establishment founded by the Lyonnaise home weavers' co-operative (*Cooptiss*), as well as some of the rare and beautiful cloths they produced, including silk, damask and brocade.

The Musée Gallo-Romain

17 rue Cléber; 9.30am–noon & 2–6pm; closed Mon & Tues; free.

Traces the history of the region, particularly of *Lugdunum* (Lyon), the capital of the Gauls, from neolithic times to the seventh century. Mosaics, inscriptions and imperial busts abound.

Musée de L'Automobile Henri Malartre

Château of Rochetaillée-sur-Saône; daily 9am–6pm; ☎78.22.18.80; bus #33.

Situated 10km north of Lyon, the **Musée de L'Automobile Henri Malartre** houses a collection of cars dating from the last hundred years, as well as cycles, motorbikes and public transport vehicles, all in good working order and many of them unique. Exhibits range from early steam-driven cars to Enzo Ferrari's personal racing model, and include Adolf Hitler's armoured Mercedes (1942) and John-Paul II's popemobile, in which he visited Lyon in 1986.

Food and nightlife

Lyon's carnivorous **specialities** revolve around different preparations of heads, feet, testicles and innards: even the *salade Lyonnais* is a combination of eggs, bacon and fried bread on a bed of lettuce and tomatoes. If you're vegetarian it's not an ideal city. There is one dish that comes in many different flavours and sauces, including non-meaty ones – *quenelles*, dumpling things like solidified béchamel sauce.

Lyon being a great gastronomic centre, however, you'll find specialities from every region of France and overseas. One very major plus: local wines are affordable, and the most affordable type of Lyonnaise eating establishment, the **Bouchon** ("cork"), derived its name from the vast quantities of Lyonnaise wine consumed there. Tradition has it that wine bottles were lined up as the evening progressed, and at the end of the night the bill was determined by measuring from the first cork to the last. **Vieux Lyon** is the area with the greatest concentration of eateries, though you'll find cheaper and less busy ones between pl des Jacobins and pl Sathonay at the top of the Presqu'île. The possibilities are endless, but on weekends you'll see a lot of hotel-style *complet* signs: **booking ahead** is always a good idea.

Le Vieux Fourneau, 1 rue Tramassac, 5ᵉ (☎78.37.67.28). Good menu at a decent price, and lively.

L'Amphitryon, 33 rue St-Jean, 5ᵉ (☎78.38.24.30). Open daily till midnight, usually packed.

La Grille, 106 rue Sébastien-Gryphe, 7ᵉ (☎78.72.46.58). You won't have a hope unless you book. Home cooking *à la Lyonnaise*: sausages, broths, sweetbreads and mackerel.

La Meunière, rue Neuve (☎78 28 62 91). Booking is essential, but worthwhile for a 75F menu of course after course of Lyonnaise specialities. There are several *bouchons* located in the streets between Cordeliers and Terreaux, particularly in rue Mercière, but *Meunière* is the best.

Café des Fédérations, 8 rue du Major-Martin, 1ᵉʳ (☎78.28.26.00; closed Sat, Sun and Aug). Typical bouchon serving the earthiest of Lyonnaise specialities, (marinated tripe, black pudding and fish *quenelles*) in an atmosphere to match: there's even sawdust on the floor.

Chez Léa, la Voûte, 11 pl Antoine-Gourju (☎78.42.01.33). Excellent traditional Lyonnaise cooking, especially good salads. 80F menu.

Bidon 5, 44 rue Mercière (☎78.42.21.69, 5am–8pm, closed Sun afternoon & Mon). Popular for breakfast among local chefs, including Paul Bucuse.

Nightlife

If you haven't overindulged yourself at the meal table, Lyon is almost as good a place for **clubbing** as eating, though the entry and drinks prices are predictably stiff.

DANCE CLUBS AND DISCOS

Intellect, 3 rue St-Georges, 5ᵉ (Wed–Sat 10pm–3am). Plays a selection of reggae, house and funk.

Madness, 18 quai R-Rolland (10.30pm–3/4am; closed Aug). Play anything with a dance beat.

Factory, corner of rue Lavoisier and rue des Georges, 5ᵉ (10.30pm till dawn Fri, Sat and eve of holidays). More upmarket and avant-garde.

ARTS AND LIVE MUSIC CLUBS

Atmosphères, 9 montée des Carmelites, 1ᵉʳ (11am–1am, Sat from 5pm, Sun from 8pm). Tapas bar with painting and photo exhibitions, videos in the afternoon, music, theatre and mime.

Espace Gerson, 1 pl Gerson, 5ᵉ. Has *café théâtre* some nights, otherwise jazz or performance art.

New Peoples' Café, 12 quai St-Vincent (☎78.28.80.88; closed Sun). Live music, mainly jazz but also rock, country, Brazilian.

Hot Club, 26 rue Lanterne 1ᵉʳ (Tues–Sat 9–12pm). All styles of jazz, jam sessions Sat 4–8pm.

ANGLOPHILE BARS

Albion Public House, 12 rue Ste-Catherine. English pub with draught beer where you can play darts and listen to jazz on Sat nights.

Ecossais, 7 rue C-Dulin, 2ᵉ (5pm–4am). Scots-style piano bar serving 100 different whiskeys.

The Cornishman, 51 quartier de la Gare, St-Germaine-au-Mont-d'Or (☎78.98.18.51). "English" pub open till 1am.

GAY CLUBS

Le Mylord, 112 quai P-Scize, 5ᵉ (every night 10.30–4). Transvestite cabaret and disco, interesting decor including statues and a sculpted stone bar.

Paradiso Club, 24 rue Pizay, 1ᵉʳ. Funky music and transvestite cabaret.

Broad'way, 9 rue Terraille, 1er. Cocktail bar with videos.

Damière, 8 rue St-Georges (late nights Wed, Fri & Sat). Exclusively lesbian club with a very friendly atmosphere. Shows, songs and cabaret acts.

Listings

Airport information ☎78.71.92.21.

Bike rental *Motobécane François* ,139 av Maréchal-de-Saxe.

Boat trips *Bateaux-Mouches "Lui"*, *Société Naviginter*, 13bis quai Rambaud (☎78 42 96 81) from quai des Célestins; up the Saône or down to the confluence to the Île Barbe; daily April–Nov. The *Société Naviginter* also run a boat, *Le Calabrun*, down the Rhône to Vienne.

Books English bookshop, *Eton*, 1 rue du Plat, near pl des Terreaux.

Changing money *Thomas Cook*, Gare de la Part-Dieu (Mon–Fri 6am–8pm, weekends & holidays 6am–6pm); in summer, SI, pl Bellecour (Mon–Fri 9am–7pm, Sat 9am–6pm, Sun 10am–6pm).

Cinemas Offbeat, undubbed films at *Sully 129*, 129 rue Sully (métro Masséna), between Part-Dieu and the park.

Consulates USA: 7 quai Général-Sarrail, 6ᵉ (☎78.24.68.49); UK: 24 rue Childebert (☎78.37.59.67).

Hitching *Allostop*, 8 rue de la Bombarde, and *Lyon-Stop*, 29 rue Pasteur.

Hospital *Hôtel-Dieu*, 1 pl de l'Hôtel-Dieu, 2ᵉ (☎78.42.70.80), *Hôpital Edouard-Herriot*, pl d'Arsonval, 3ᵉ (☎78.53.81.11).

Launderette, 10 rue Mourget in the old city (cross the pont Bonaparte).

Post office PTT pl Antonin-Poncet, 1ᵉʳ.

Rape crisis *Stop Viol*, 9 Montée des Carmelites, 1ᵉʳ (☎ 78.39.77.77; 8pm–6am).

SIs at pl Bellecour (☎78.42.25.75) and *Centre Perrache* in front of the gare SNCF (☎78.22.42.07).

Theatre Roger Planchon's *TNP*, 8 pl Lazare-Goujon, Villeurbanne, métro Gratte-Ciel; (☎78.03.30.30), is the most famous; programme details and bookings available from the SI.

What's on *Lyon-Poche* out every Wed, available from any newsagent.

Women's info *Les Dames* bookshop on pl Célestines.

Around Lyon

Within easy reach of the city, the **Lyonnaise mountains** to the south and west may not reach spectacular heights but they offer quiet and solitude among steep, forested hills and unassuming villages surrounded by **cherry orchards**, the region's main source of income. Tourism is low key, but food and accommodation in the hostels of the mountain villages are rarely a problem for visitors to the area's **parks and museums**. Transport poses more difficulties, although by rural French standards services from Lyon to the larger villages are reasonably frequent. Be prepared to encounter snow as late as May, and lower temperatures throughout the year.

The mountains can be visited every Sunday from June until the middle of September by **steam train**, leaving from L'Arbresle just west of Lyon. You can either organise your own itinerary or take part in organised trips to major sites of the region. For reservations, phone ☎74.70.90.64.

West of Lyon: Le Parc Courzieu and museums to the west

A small and unassuming wildlife park in the heart of the Lyonnaise mountains to the west of the city, the **Parc Courzieu**, 24km from Lyon, is remarkable for its ecological and educational initiatives rather than for a dazzling collection of exotic species. By car, take direction Tassin-la-Demi-Lune from Lyon, followed by the D407 and left onto the D489 through CRAPONNE; then, after 3km, turn right onto the D50, and drive 11km, following signs to the park. By bus take #72 from Lyon to POLLIONNAY (the last stop) and hitch the remaining eight kilometres.

All the species in the park are native to Europe, including an enclosure of **wolves**, and a number of cat species, including the **Scottish wild cat**. All the exhibits are meticulously explained (in French); the **lynx** can be viewed from the safe confines of a child-size glass pyramid; and even the **trees** surrounding the enclosures are part of a grand-scale adventure trail prepared for local school children. The park specialises in **birds of prey** and is currently running a programme whose intent is to reintroduce endangered species, such as the golden eagle and black vulture, into the French mountains. **Flight displays** (April–Nov 2.30 & 4.30pm) give an opportunity to see the them in action, and to get a close look at the trained birds

Worth a visit if you're not returning straight to Lyon, the **Musée de la Mine de St-Pierre-la-Palud**, 10km from the Parc de Courzieu, is guaranteed to instill admiration for the endurance of the miners who put up with working conditions like those simulated in the reconstructed mine shaft which forms the main exhibit. Going down into the copper sulphate mine shaft while an ex-miner explains its workings in meticulous detail (two hours, in French) is not recommended if you're claustrophobic. Back on the surface, you move on to an exhibition on the former mining village and pit.

Easier to recommended is the extraordinary display of hats and hat-making tools in the **Musée du Chapeau** at CHAZELLES on the D2, 20km due north of St-Étienne (Wed–Mon 2–6pm; demonstrations of traditional hat-making methods first and third Sun of every month). The **Atelier de Souffleur de Verre**, the glass-blowing workshop at ST-GALMIER, 10km further along the same road to the southwest (after it becomes the D12), is good as well. Phone the local SI (☎77.54.06.08) for details.

Most of the villages in the Lyonnaise mountains have some form of *auberge* serving food and providing a bed for the night. A typical, attractive example is the tiny village of **YZERON**, 12km south of the wildlife park, on whose main square are an SI, a *crêperie* and the excellent *Auberge de Tonton* (☎78.81.01.42, ②), which serves duck and salmon as part of a 110F menu and has reasonably priced accommodation. There are a couple of hotels and restaurants in the village of ST-MARTIN-EN-HAUT, eight winding kilometres south of Yzeron, and a 2* municipal campsite just outside the village on the D122, direction Ste-Catherine (☎78.48.62.16). Information on local farms with camping facilities is available from Mme Bissardon (☎78.48.63.93). A five-minute drive from the wildlife park, the village of COURZIEU has no accommodation but an excellent little restaurant, open only at weekends. Ask at the park for details.

If you're heading north, **L'ARBRESLE**, an austere-looking market town reminiscent of a coal town in the north of England, 22km northwest of Lyon and accessible from the city by train, has accommodation at *Le Lion d'Or* (☎74.01.00.16; ②), with a restaurant serving excellent-value set menus.

Medieval cities: Pérouges and Crémieu

To the east of Lyon, **Pérouges** and **Crémieu** are two small medieval cities within easy reach, both accessible by train. Neither, however, is a must, and, if you've only time to visit one then Pérouges, originally the home of a colony of immigrants from Perugia, is a more *sympa* place, with a convincing historical ambiance, in which to lose yourself in tortuous cobbled alleyways.

The ambiance has not gone unnoticed by the **French film industry** – historical dramas such as *The Three Musketeers* and *Monsieur Vincent* were filmed within the walls of **PÉROUGES** – nor by some of the residents of the city, who have fought long and hard for preservation orders on its most interesting buildings. And the city's traditional commercial life is also thriving, in the hands of a hundred or so workers who still weave locally grown hemp. No particular monument stands out, but the central square of the city, the place du Halle, and its main street, the rue du Prince, are some of the best preserved French medieval remains. The lime tree on pl du Halle is a symbol of liberty, planted in 1792.

CRÉMIEU is less compelling, despite its local **sausages** (*sabodet*), monumental architecture and early origins (traced to 835 AD). The city was once an important commercial centre, signified by the fourteenth-century market buildings on rue du Lt-Col-Bel, and a border post of the kingdom of Dauphiné, signified by a number of fortified doorways which are all that remain of the medieval fortifications of the city.

Vienne

On leaving Lyon, it's tempting to head straight for the Med, and the first stretch of motorway between Lyon and **Vienne** is unlikely to distract you from that goal. There is absolutely nothing but oil refineries, steel, chemical and paper works, cement, fertiliser and textile factories, all spewing plumes of grey and orange pollution into the air and water.

VIENNE is still a bit too close to all this for comfort and too close to the lures of Provence. Taking a reluctant exit off the Autoroute du Soleil is well worth the trouble, however, as it contains extensive remnants of its ancient history as a major seat of Roman power in Gaul. Every street corner seems to sprout some monument: a Roman temple, a medieval church or cloister. The old quarter is criss-crossed with pedestrian precincts which make for enjoyable menu-browsing around rue des Clercs and place du Temple. And there's a feeling that despite the distant rumble of the autoroute calling you to sunnier climes, the town has maintained a character and sense of purpose.

Practicalities

The centre of life in Vienne, the **cours Brillier**, runs at right angles to the river, with the SI at no. 3, near quai Jean-Jaurès (Mon–Sat 8.30am–noon & 2–6pm; open Sun in July & Aug), and the **gare SNCF** at the other end. Halfway along the *cours*, rue Bosun leads up to the gothic **Cathédrale St-Maurice** – with various treasures including some superb stained glass. The Roman remains are close to the cathedral except for the **Cité Gallo-Romaine** on the right bank of the river, in the suburb of ST-ROMAIN-EN-GAL.

If you plan to stay over, there's a **youth hostel** on the other side of the park from the SI at 11 quai Riondet (☎74.53.21.97). Some **hotels** to try are *Hôtel de la Poste*, 47 cours Romestang (☎76.85.02.04; ④), between the station and the central pl de Miremont; *Hôtel de la Gare*, 37 cours Brillier (☎76.85.38.10), and *Hôtel Union*, 5 pl St-Louis, ☎76.85.63.15), off quai Jean-Jaurès at the northern end of town. *Le St-Maurice* (754.85.08.48; ④) is well situated in the square in front of the cathedral.

The old town has a number of promising eating houses, including a good selection of cheapies in the rue de la Table Ronde (near the Église St-André-le-Bas): the *Chez Soi* with a 55F menu (☎74.85.19.77), the *Estancot* (☎74.85.12.09) and the very basic *Café de la Table Ronde*. Near the SI, there's a very pleasant Thai Restaurant.

The town

A ticket covering the antique theatre and Vienne's three major museums can be bought at any museum ticket office. Hours are Tues–Sun 9am–12pm & 2–6pm; mid-Oct–March closed Sun am, Mon & Tues.

Roman monuments are scattered liberally around the streets of Vienne, and it requires little effort to take in the magnificently restored **Temple d'Auguste** on place du Palais or the scanty remains of the **Théâtre de Cybèle**, off pl de Miremont. The **antique theatre** is more of a haul, located off rue du Cirque at the base of Mont Pipet. It's worth making the trip for the view of the town and river from the very top seats. The theatre is the venue of an international **jazz festival** for the first two weeks of July, when it plays host to some of the biggest names on the jazz circuit: 1991 saw one of Miles Davies' last concerts as well as Chick Corea and John McLaughlin.

The **Musée Lapidaire** (hours above) is situated in one of Vienne's oldest monuments, the **Église St-Pierre**, possibly the first cathedral ever built in France. Since its origins in the fifth century, the building has suffered much destruction and rebuilding, but despite a short period when it was used as a factory in the nineteenth century, it is still one of Vienne's most graceful and attractive buildings. The museum itself is predictably dominated by finds from Vienne's Roman past, including mosaics. The most spectacular of these is the **mosaïque d'Orphée**, depicting birds and animals whose subtle colouring is beautifully preserved.

The buildings of the twelfth-century **Cloître de St-André-le-Bas** on rue des Clercs lend themselves well to a shady, quiet **pottery museum** (hours above) containing a collection which includes eleventh-century turned wooden vessels. The cloister itself is a tiny grassed courtyard surrounded by a collonade, and sets of pillars whose capitals are diversely decorated with mythological and biblical figures.

The other major museum in Vienne is the **Musée des Beaux-Arts et Archéologie** (hours above) on pl de Miremont, with an unfortunate preponderance of eighteenth-century French pottery and some pretty pieces of third-century Roman silverware.

Off the D41, leading from the modern road bridge in the direction of GRENOBLE, there's a fifteenth-century **humpback bridge** crossing the Gere (a tributary of the Rhône), on the far side of which – and the main reason for crossing it – is the **Église St-Martin**, containing twentieth-century frescoes by Maurice Denis celebrating the Eucharist, and an ancient wooden sculpture of Christ.

The most prominent – and vaunted – of Vienne's monuments is the **Cathédrale St-Maurice** which dominates the *place* of the same name. Its facade is a combination of Romanesque and Gothic so unwieldy that it appears as if its upper half had been dumped on top of a completely alien building. The interior, with its 90-metre long vaulted nave, is impressive though, best experience during the festival of sacred music which takes place throughout June, July and August.

St-Roman-en-Gal

Across the Rhône from Vienne, several hectares of Roman ruins constitute the site of **ST-ROMAN-EN-GAL**, which is also the name of the town which faces Vienne on the right bank of the Rhône. The excavations, situated to the right of the N86 as you head away from Vienne (direction Lyon) are low lying, but immaculately restored and well preserved, particularly the frescoes. They attest to a significant community dating from the first century BC to the third AD, and give a vivid picture of the daily life and domestic architecture of Roman France. Particularly evocative is the **House of the Sea Gods**, with a beautiful mosaic floor featuring bearded Neptune and other marine images.

Onward from Vienne: Hauterives and Tain

Between Vienne and Valence are some of the oldest, most celebrated **vineyards** in France: the renowned *Côte Rotie*, *Hermitage* and *Crozes-Hermitage appellations*. If you've got any spare luggage space it's well worth stopping to pick a bottle up from the local co-op; even their *vin ordinaire* is superlative, and unbelievably cheap considering its quality. Just south of AMPUIS, on the right bank, is the tiny area producing one of the most exquisite French white wines – *Condrieu*, and close by one of the most exclusive – *Château-Grillat* – an *appellation* covering just this single château.

Between ST-VALLIER and TAIN even the Rhône becomes quite scenic, and after Tain you can see the Alps. You may even conclude that it's worth slowing down. In spring you're more likely to be conscious of orchards everywhere rather than vines. Cherries, pears, apples, peaches and apricots, as well as bilberries and strawberries, are cultivated in abundance.

If you can choose your route, then head southeast towards BEAUREPAIRE on the D538, then follow it south. At **HAUTERIVES**, 11km south of Beaurepaire, is one of the main reasons for taking this route – to view the manic creation of a postman by the name of Ferdinand Cheval (1836–1912). His tombstone is bizarre enough but nothing compared to his **Palais Idéal** which took him thirty years to carve. Various surrealists have paid homage to it; psychoanalysts have given it their all, but it defies all classification (daily 8am–7pm in summer; 8am–8pm in winter; closed Jan). Tuesday is market day and there's a **campsite**, and one **hotel**, *Le Relais* (☎75.68.81.12).

Tain-l'Hermitage

TAIN L'HERMITAGE, accessible from both the N7 and the A7, is unpretentious and uneventful. The only reson to stay here is to drink. If your travel plans are flexible, you can sample a good selection of *Hermitage* and *Crozes-Hermitage* at the *Cave Coopérative des Vins Fins*, 22 route de Larnage (☎75.08.20.87).

If you need to stay, there are several reasonably priced **hotels** on place Taurobole, off av Jean-Jaurès in the centre of town: *L'Éscale*, 9 pl Taurobole (☎75.08.31.67; ②; closed Nov) and *Le Taurobole*, 2 pl Taurobole (☎75.08.25.88; ③/④; closed Sun eve & Mon). More upmarket, *Les 2 Côteaux*, 1 rue Joseph-Péala, running off Jean-Jaurés south of pl Taroboule (☎75.08.33.01; ③/④; closed Feb) is nicely located beside the Rhône.

If you're looking for a **cheap meal** in Tain, the *crêperie La Récré*, 8 pl du Taroboule (☎75.08.19.00) is an alternative to the stuffier establishments on av Jean-Jaurès.

From mid-September to December the different wine-producing villages celebrate their cellars with drunken *Fêtes des Vins*. The SI in Tain, 70 av Jean-Jaurès (Mon–Sat 9am–noon & 2–6pm) can give you lists of addresses if you want to buy a few bottles, or take N86 for some 30km north of Tain along the right bank, following the *dégustation* signs and then crossing back over between SERRIÈRES and CHANAS.

Romans-sur-Isère

South of Hauterives and 15km east of the Rhône at Tain, is **ROMANS-SUR-ISÈRE**. It's not the most exciting of towns, and its **museum of shoemaking**, the industry that has kept it going for the last five centuries – isn't one you would automatically alter your itinerary for. But the *Musée de la Chaussure et d'Ethnographie Régionale*, in the former Convent of the Visitation on rue Ste-Marthe (Wed–Sat 9–11.45am & 2–5.45pm; Sun 2.30–6pm; Mon 9–11.45) turns out to be interesting and well worth the stop. The toes curl in horror at the extent to which women have been immobilised by their footwear from ancient times to the present – and on every continent – while at the same time you can't help but admire the craziness of some of the shoes.

If you need information there's an **SI** on place Jules-Nadi. The municipal campsite in Romans, *Les Chasses* (☎75.72.35.27), is located a kilometre off the N92 northeast of the city, near to the aerodrome. In Romans itself there are a number of fairly expensive **hotels**, the exception being the *Hôtel des Voyageurs*, 9 rue Félix-Fauré, (☎75.02.22.07; ②; closed Sun), which is basic but cheap, as is its restaurant. The *Acropole* nightclub (☎75.05.16.95) is surprisingly good, and certainly better than any nightlife that Valence can offer.

From Romans, if you keep going south on D538, you meet the River Drôme at CREST beneath the massive ruin of a medieval castle. Snow-capped peaks lie east across an open rocky plain of pumpkin and sunflower fields, grazing goats, and vines for the speciality of DIE – the next town upstream on the Drôme – the sweet white wine *Clairette de Die*. This makes for an exciting route into eastern Provence, but if you're taking the more direct route south, following the autoroute, then Valence is your next port of call.

Valence and south

At an indefinable point along the Rhône, there's an invisible sensual border. By the time your reach **VALENCE** you know you've crossed it. The quality of light is different and the temperature higher, bringing with it the scent of eucalyptus and pine. The colours and contours have suddenly become worlds apart from the cold lands of Lyon and the north. The city is the obvious place to celebrate your arrival in the *Midi* (as the French call the South), with plenty of good bars and restaurants in the old town.

Practicalities

If you come in on the autoroute, running along the Rhône's left bank, you exit onto av Gambetta, with **Vieux Valence**, its ramparts replaced by boulevards, to your left. The N7 follows the eastern edge of the old town, and runs straight through place du Général-Leclerc where you'll find the **SI** (9am–12.30pm & 2–7pm, 1.30–7.30pm in summer).

Other practical information: the **gare SNCF** is alongside the N7, 500m south of pl du Gén-Leclerc; the **gare routière** and **PTT** are on pl Aristide-Briand, which runs south off av Gambetta; and if you're getting hot and dusty, there's a **launderette** on rue Madier-Montjau (8am–8pm).

For mid-range **hotel** rooms, try the *Logis de France* establishments, *California,* 174 av Maurice-Faure (☎75.44.36.05; ④), *de France,* 16 bd Général-de-Gaulle (☎75.43.00.87; ⑤), or *St-Jacques,* 9 fbg St-Jacques; (☎75.42.44.60; ③/④). Cheaper options include the *Hôtel d'Angleterre,* 11 av Félix-Faure (☎75.43.00.35; ②/③), *Splendid,* 20 av P-Sémard (☎75.44.09.18; ①/②), and *Oasis,* 91 av Sadi-Carnot; (☎75.43.48.51; ②/③).

The **youth hostel** *L'Epervière,* chemin de l'Epervière (☎75.42.32.00), is by the Rhône 2km south of the city. It's quite expensive but has good sports facilities – swimming pool, sailing – and **bike hire**. The 3* **camping municipal** is in the youth hostel grounds and open all year (also ☎75.42.32.00).

Around town: Vieux Valence

The focus of Vieux Valence, the **Cathédrale St-Apollinaire**, was founded in 1095 and largely reconstructed in the seventeenth century – after a local baron went on the rampage, avenging the execution of three Protestants during the Wars of Religion. More work was carried out later, including the horribly mismatched nineteenth-century tower, but the interior still preserves a Romanesque grace, and the old baron would be pleased by the event commemorated by the bust of Pope Pius VI above the choir stalls. The pope was taken prisoner by French revolutionaries and exiled to Valence where he died in 1799.

The **Église St-Jean**, to the north, has preserved its Romanesque tower and porch capitals, and between the church and cathedral are some of the oldest and narrowest streets of Vieux Valence. They are known as **côtes**: côte St-Estève just northwest of the cathedral; côte St-Martin off rue du Petit-Paradis; and côte Sylvante off rue du Petit-Paradis' continuation rue A.-Paré. Diverse characters who would have walked these steep and crooked streets include Rabelais, a student at the university founded here in 1452 and suppressed during the Revolution, and the teenage Napoléon Bonaparte, who began his military training as a cadet at the artillery school.

Though Valence lacks the cohesion of the medieval towns and villages further south, it does have several vestiges of the sixteenth-century city, most notably the Renaissance **Maison des Têtes** at 57 Grande-Rue, with its eroded but still bizarre statuary, and the **Maison Dupré-Latour** on rue Pérollerie, with a superbly sculptured porch and spiral staircase. Valence's **museum** on pl des Ormeaux (Mon–Tues & Thurs–Fri 2–6pm; Wed, Sat & Sun 9am–noon & 2–6pm) has little to distinguish it apart from an eighteenth-century collection of chalk drawings by Hubert Robert, a reminder of the days when the Rhône valley was an essential part of the Grand Tour of Classical Europe.

Eating and entertainments

To go with the local **wines** there are good **food markets** till noon on pl des Clercs (Thurs & Sat) and pl St-Jean (Tues): fruit is Valence's speciality. As for restaurants, *L'Épicerie-Restaurant,* 18 pl Belat (☎75.42.74.46; closed Sat lunchtine & Sun) is one of the most congenial **places to eat**, with art exhibitions on the fifteenth-century walls, jazz some nights, and imaginative food at reasonable prices. *La Taverne,* 4 pl des Clercs (closed Sat lunch), serving fish and pizzas, makes a good second choice. For Turkish, Greek and Armenian food try *Le Bosphore* at 14 rue Balthazar-Bargo (☎75.55.24.33), and, for a cheap, attractive little *crêperie* go to the *Crêperie du Musée,* at 10 pl des Ormeaux. If you want to eat very well, and are prepared to pay over 350F for the pleasure, *Restaurant Pic,* 285 av Victor-Hugo (☎75.44.15.32; closed Sun evening, Wed & Aug), is the city's top-notch eating house. Roast lobster with truffles, asparagus with hollandaise and caviar, and frozen nougat are some of the delights.

A good place if you need to fill in time, is the **Parc Jouvet** overlooking the river (and the motorway) south of av Gambetta. At evening-time around sunset, or even better at dawn, this is definitely the best place to be in the city – with a bottle of *Cornas* or sparkling *St-Peray* from the vineyards across the water.

The focus of Valence's somewhat down-at-heel **café scene** is the pl de la Gare, near the train station. *Le Continental* and *Le Régina* are ideal places from which to look on if you're past partaking in the more youthful pleasures indulged in at *Magic Studio* and *Le Look,* which cater to a younger, *baby-foot*-playing clientele. Valence's main disco, the *Bacana,* is near the SI at bd Maurice-Clerc.

Montélimar and its region

South of Valence, to the east of the river, a wide plain stretches towards the Alpine foot-hills, planted with strict rows of fruit trees (there are no further vineyards on the banks of the Rhône until you reach BOLLÈNE in Provence). To the west, the Massif Central pushes its final crest of rocks right to the river's edge.

Initial impressions of **MONTÉLIMAR** suggest a developing country or some provincial backwater in the USA. Every street proclaims the glory of the **nougat** that has been made here for centuries, and is the town's sole *raison d'être*. But it's quite lively and its **vielle ville** has some charm – so not at all bad for a stopover. Around the pastel facades and old arcades of **place du Marché**, in the vielle ville, you'll find: *Le Métro* bar, done up as an old Paris métro station with a young clientele playing chess and backgammon; a cheap and excellent Italian **restaurant** *Pizza Nino*; and the **market** on Wednesday and Saturday. Above the old town to the east is the fourteenth-century **Château des Adhémar** on rue du Château (guided visits 10am–noon & 2–7pm; closed Tues & Wed am), which contains a collection of seventeenth-century tapestries.

Practicalities

The main street of the old town, rue Pierre-Julien, runs from the one medieval gateway on the nineteenth-century ring of boulevards at pl St-Martin, down past the Cathédral Ste-Croix with its well-populated *place* and the market place, and on down to pl Marx-Dormoy. The **gare SNCF** is a short way west of the old town, with the **SI** nearby on the allée Champs-de-Mars.

There are plenty of **hotels** around the boulevards, but within the vieille ville you could try the *Logis de France Hôtel Pierre,* 7 place des Clercs (☎75.01.33.16, ③; closed Feb) – peaceful, apart from the nearby bell of Ste-Croix tolling the hours. The *Auberge la Cassoulet,* 80 av St-Lazare (☎75.01.07.34; ①) is basic but extremely reasonable, as is *La Friogoule* at no. 95 (☎75.01.26.18; ①). There's a **campsite** not too far away, the *International Deux Saisons* (☎75.01.88.99; mid-Feb to Nov), 500m east on the D540, then right towards Alexis.

Enticing smells emanate from *La Papillote* **restaurant** on pl du Temple (☎75.01.79.28; closed Sun & Mon). For slightly greater outlay, you can feast on beautifully presented food at *Le Grillon*, 40 rue Cuiraterie (☎75.01.79.02; closed Wed & Sun lunchtime). *Crêperies* and other snack food places are almost as ubiquitous as *confiseries* (sweet shops). The **SI** can fix up visits to a nougat factory; if you just want to buy, try *Chabert et Guillot*, 1 rue André-Ducatez (closed July), opposite the gare SNCF.

WESTERN PROVENCE

The richest area of Provence, the Côte d'Azur apart, is **the west**. Most of the large-scale production of fruits, vegetables and wine is based here in the low-lying plains beside the Rhône and the Durance rivers. The only heights are the rocky outbreaks of the **Dentelles** and the **Alpilles**, and the narrow east–west ridges of **Mont Ventoux**, the **Lubéron** and the **Mont Ste-Victoire**. Communications have always been relatively easy – the number of major Roman cities stands testimony to this. The two dominant cities of inland Provence, **Avignon** and **Aix**, both have rich histories and contemporary fame in their **festivals of art**. Around the Rhône delta, the **Camargue** is a unique self-contained region, as different from the rest of Provence as it is from anywhere else in France.

Orange

ORANGE, which gave its name to the Irish Protestant Orange Order, is best known for its spectacular Roman theatre – nowadays host to two important summer music festivals. But while the rest of the town is attractive enough, with its medieval street plan, fountained squares and houses with ancient porticos and courtyards, there's not a lot to detain you once you've visited the theatre and adjacent museum.

The **gare SNCF** is about 1500m east of the centre, at the end of av Frédéric-Mistral. The nearest bus stop is at the bottom of rue Jean-Reboul, the first left as you walk away from the station. Bus #2, direction Nogent, takes you to the *Théâtre Antique* and the next stop, *Gasparin*, to the **SI** on cours Aristide-Briand. The **gare routière** is close by the railway station on av Frédéric-Mistral.

In July and August, Orange is packed with opera fanatics for the *Chorégies* or **choral festival** performed in the Roman theatre. Regrettably it has turned away from productions of the spoken classics which actors such as Sarah Bernhardt performed here at the turn of the century, but if you're interested, and prepared to make a reservation well in advance, details can be had from the *Maison du Théâtre*, pl des Frères-Mounet, 84100 Orange (☎90.34.15.52).

The theatre

April–Sept 9am–6.30pm; Oct–March 9am–noon & 1.30–5pm; ticket, 15F, also good for the museum.

Days off in Orange circa 5 BC were most entertainingly spent from dawn to dusk at the **theatre**, watching farce, clownish improvisations, song and dance, and occasionally, for the sake of a visiting dignitary, a bit of heavy Greek tragedy (in Latin). The acoustics allowed a full audience of 10,000 to hear every word. The hill of St-Eutrope into which the seats were built, and a vast awning from the top of the stage wall protected the spectators from the weather. If they got bored with the play, according to rival archaeologists' theories, they either slipped out by the west door to the baths and gym with three 180-metre running tracks, or had a chat and a drink at the Forum. There is no

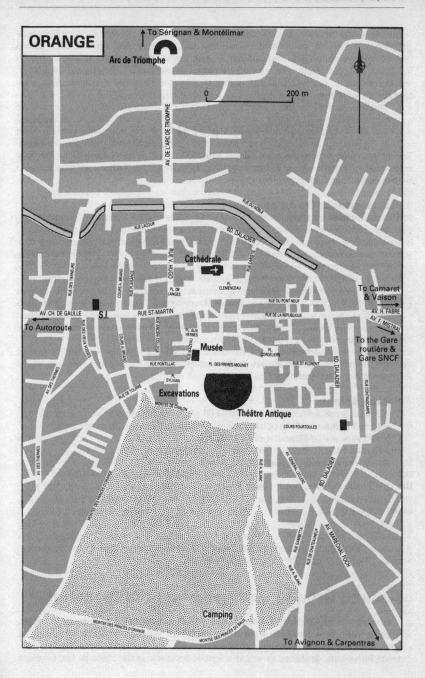

ORANGE

To Sérignan & Montélimar

Arc de Triomphe

0   200 m

AV. DE L'ARC DE TRIOMPHE

RUE DU NOBLE

RUE LACOUR

BD. DALADIER

RUE DES TANNEURS

RUE V. HUGO

Cathédrale

RUE CARISTIE

PL. DE LANGES

PL. CLEMENCEAU

COURS A. BRIAND

RUE R. PLASANCE

RUE DU PONT NEUF

To Camaret
& Vaison

AV. CH. DE GAULLE

S.I.

RUE ST-MARTIN

RUE DE LA REPUBLIQUE

AV. H. FABRE

AV. F. MISTRAL

To Autoroute

RUE DE L'ANCIEL COLLEGE

PL. AUX HERBES

To the Gare
routière &
Gare SNCF

COURS A. BRIAND

Musée

PL. CORDELIERS

RUE PONTILLAC

PL. DES FRERES-MOUNET

RUE ST-FLORENT

BD. DALADIER

AV. DES VIEUX FOSSES

RUE MAZEAU

PL. SYLVIAN

RUE CONTRESCARPE

AV. DES THERMES

RUE DE TOURRE

Excavations

MONTEE DE CHALON

Théâtre Antique

COURS POURTOULES

AV. DES THERMES

MONTEE DE PRINCE S. TOURRE

RUE A. BLANC

AV. GENERAL LECLERC

BD. DALADIER

AV. MARECHAL FOCH

RUE GAMBETTA

RUE DE CHATEAUNEUF

RUE A. BLANC

MONTEE DES PRINCES D'ORANGE

Camping

MONTEE DES PRINCES DU BAUS

To Avignon & Carpentras

question, however, about the Roman theatre. It is the best preserved example in existence, and the only one with the stage wall still standing. And stand it does, across 103m to a height of 36m, and completely plain like some monstrous prison wall when you see it from outside. The interior, although missing much of its original decoration, has its central, larger-than-lifesize statue of Augustus, and the columned niches for other lesser statues.

The best view of the theatre in its entirety is from St-Eutrope hill. If you go past the Forum or gymnasium remains, across pl Sylvian and take montée de Chalon to the left off rue de Tourre, you can follow a path up the hill until you are looking directly down onto the stage. The ruins around your feet are those of the short-lived seventeenth-century castle of the princes of Orange. Louis XIV had it destroyed and the principality annexed to France – a small price to pay for the ruler of the Netherlands who was also to become king of England.

The museum and the Arc de Triomphe

The **municipal museum**, across the road from the theatre entrance (summer 9am–6.30pm; winter 9am–noon & 2–5pm), has documents concerning the Orange dynasty, including a suitably austere portrait of the very first Orangeman, Guillaume "the taciturn". It was William III, grandson of William the Taciturn, who secured the everlasting devotion of Protestant Ulstermen by defeating the Catholic James II at the Battle of the Boyne in 1690, a victory still commemmorated by the Orangemen of northern Ireland.

In the best traditions of provincial town museums, upstairs on the second floor is an unlikely collection of works by one **Frank Brangwyn**, a Welsh painter with no connections with Orange, who learned his craft with William Morris and whose commissioned designs for the House of Lords were rejected as being better suited to a nightclub. The pictures here are stark portrayals of British workers early this century.

If you've arrived by road from the north you will have passed the town's second major monument, the **Arc de Triomphe**, whose intricate friezing and relief celebrates imperial victories against the Gauls.

Rooms and food

The *Fréau*, 3 rue Ancien-Collège (☎90.34.06.26; ②; closed Aug) is central, simple and cheap, and immaculately kept by two elderly women. Advance bookings are advisable. Others to try are *St-Florent*, 4 rue de Mazeau (☎90.34.18.53; ②/③), and *Arcotel,* 8 pl aux Herbes (☎90.34.09.23; ②/③), both as central, but less inviting.

Orange's **campsite**, *Le Jonquier*, rue Alexis-Carrel (☎90.34.19.832), to the northwest, is equipped with tennis courts. It's open from mid-March to the end of October.

For food, cheap *frites* with *plats du jour* to eat there or take away can be had at *La Fringale* on rue de Tourre (closed Wed). *Le Yaca,* 24 pl Silvain, (closed Tues evening & Wed), gives a generous choice of efficiently served dishes in an old vaulted chamber. If it's full, try the neighbouring *Galois*, or *Le Bec Fin* at 14 rue Segond-Weber. The *Café des Thermes* on rue des Vieux-Fossés is a billiards **bar** with youngish clientele. For a standard drinking place the square opposite the Mairie has *Les Négociants* and the less chic *Commerce*, which has a much better jukebox.

Around Orange: Sérignan and Châteauneuf

The village of **SÉRIGNAN-DU-COMTAT** is just a short drive northeast of Orange. This was the final home of **Jean-Henri Fabre**, a remarkable self-taught scientist famous for his insect studies, who composed poetry, wrote songs and painted his specimens with artistic brilliance as well as scientific accuracy. In the 1860s he had to resign from his teaching post at Avignon because parents and priests thought his lectures on the fertilisation of flowering plants to be licentious, if not downright pornographic. It was his friend John Stuart Mill who bailed him out with a loan, allowing Fabre to settle in Orange. Darwin was also a friend though Fabre was no evolutionist. In his house, which he named the **Harmas** (summer 9–11.30am & 2–4pm; winter 2–6pm; closed Tues), you can see his jungly garden, the study with his complete classification of the herbs of France and Corsica and, on the ground floor, a selection from his extraordinary watercolour series of the fungi of the Vaucluse. At the crossroads in the centre of the town (the Harmas is on N976 towards Orange) there's a flattering statue of Fabre in front of the red-shuttered buildings of the church and Mairie.

Châteauneuf-du-Pape

If you're heading down to Avignon, the slower route through **CHÂTEAUNEUF-DU-PAPE** (also taken by four buses daily) exerts a strong pull. The village takes its name from the summer palace of the Avignon popes. But neither the rather miserable ruins of the fourteenth-century château nor the medieval streets around place du Portail – the hub of the village – give Châteauneuf its special appeal. The wines produced by the local vineyards – warmed at night by the large pebbles that cover the ground, soaking up the sun's heat during the day – are its real attraction. The rich ruby red is one of France's most renowned, but the white, too, is exquisite.

Wine tasting

The *appellation Châteauneuf-du-Pape* does not, alas, come cheap, and there's no single place where you can taste a good selection from the scores of *domaines*. The SI on place du Portail, or the *Fédération des Syndicats de Producteurs* on route d'Avignon, can provide a complete list or you can visit an *Association de Vignerons* such as *Prestige et Tradition* on rue de la République, who bottle the wine of ten producers. For a casual introduction, the *Cave Père-Anselme* on av B-X-Pierre-de-Luxembourg has a **Musée des Outils de Vigneron** (9am–noon & 2–6pm) plus free tasting of its own and other Rhône wines to attract visitors.

And if you can coincide your visit with the first weekend of August you'll find free *dégustation* stalls throughout the village as well as parades, dances, equestrian contests, folkloric floats and so forth, all to celebrate the reddening of the grapes in the **Fête de la Véraison**. As well as wine, a good deal of grape liqueur – *marc* – gets consumed.

Accommodation

Getting too drunk to leave Châteauneuf is not advisable unless you're prepared to pay dearly for your excesses. The options are confined to two expensive hotels: *Le Logis d'Arnavel* on route de Roquemaure (☎90.83.73.22; ⑤) and *La Garbure*, 3 rue Joseph Ducos (☎90.83.75.08; ⑤; closed Wed), which has only four rooms.

East: Vaison-la-Romaine

For all its built-in attractions – a medieval town with a ruined cliff-top castle, a cloistered former cathedral, and the remarkable remnants of a Roman settlement – **VAISON** is surprisingly uncommercialised. Straddling the River Ouvèze, 27km northeast of Orange, the town divides into the *haute ville*, whose pale stone houses cluster under the castle, and the eighteenth-century town and its Roman predecessor, linked to the *haute ville* by an ancient stone bridge.

The town and monuments

Of all the distinctive epochs, it is the vestiges of **Roman civilisation** which intrigue the most. Two separate residential districts have been excavated on either side of the SI on pl du Chanoine-Sautel, at the other end of Grande-Rue from the bridge: **Puymin** to the east and **La Villasse** to the west (daily 9am–5/6/7pm). The **Puymin** *fouilles* (excavations) contain the theatre, several mansions and houses thought to be for rent, a colonnade known as the *portique de Pompée* and the museum for all the items discovered. The *fouilles* of **La Villasse** reveal a street with sidewalks and gutters with the layout of arcaded shops running parallel, more patrician houses (some with mosaics still intact), a basilica and the baths. The houses require a certain amount of imagination, but the street plan of La Villasse, the colonnade with its statues in every niche, and the theatre, which still seats 7000 people during the July festival, make it easy to visualise a comfortable, well-serviced town of the Roman ruling class.

Most of the detail and decoration of the buildings is displayed in the **museum** (daily 9am–5/6/7pm) in the Puymin district. Tiny fragments of painted plaster have been jigsawed together with convincing reconstructions of how whole painted walls would have looked. There are mirrors of silvered bronze, lead water pipes, taps shaped as griffins' feet, dolphin door knobs, weights and measures, plus impressive busts and statues.

Tickets can be bought at the Puymin entrance just by the SI or in the **cloisters** of the former **Cathédrale Notre-Dame** west down chemin Couradou which runs along the south side of La Villasse (included on the same ticket). The apse of the cathedral is a confusing overlay of sixth-, tenth- and thirteenth-century construction, some of it using pieces quarried from the Roman ruins. The cloisters are fairly typical of early medieval workmanship – pretty enough but not wildly exciting. The only surprising feature is the large inscription visible on the north wall of the cathedral, a convoluted precept for the monks.

Practicalities

Buses to and from CARPENTRAS, Orange and Avignon stop at the **gare routière** on av des Choralies near the junction with av Victor-Hugo. There's not a great choice of **hotels** and few bargains, though one of the nicer ones, the *Hôtel du Théâtre Romain*, place de l'Abbé-Sautel (☎90.36.05.87; closed mid-Nov to mid-Feb) has some low-priced rooms (②/③) for which you need to book in advance. The *Burrhus* hotel on pl Montfort (☎90.36.00.11; ④/⑤) is more upmarket and characterless but has the possible advantage of being in the thick of all the bars, with wide *terrasses* that stay open late. *Les Voconces* (☎90.36.00.94; ②/③) is also on pl Montfort and a cheaper option. On the route de St-Marcellin, 1km east of town down av Geoffroy from the bridge, you'll find the *Centre Culturel à Coeur Joie* with simple rooms (☎90.36.00.78; ③), and next door, the terrific top-notch **campsite**, *Le Moulin de César* (mid-March–Oct), which in summer should also be phoned first (☎90.36.06.91).

For really **stylish lodgings**, however, the *haute ville* is by far the best locality. Rue du Pont climbs upwards towards pl des Poids and the fourteenth-century gateway to the town. More steep zigzags take you past the Gothic gate and overhanging portcullis of the belfry and into the heart of this sedately quiet, uncommercialised and rich *quartier*. A sixteenth-century residence on rue de l'Évêché is Vaison's best hotel and restaurant, *Le Beffroi* (☎90.36.04.71; ⑤ and above). One other restaurant, and a *crêperie* and pizzeria on pl des Poids make up the sum of the *haute ville*'s public life.

Back on Grande-Rue, the *Muscade*, at no. 19, serves wonderful French and Indonesian dishes. More standard fare is to be had at the *brasseries* on pl Montfort – along with *Whitbread* pale ale at the *Café du Commerce* – and there are more *menus* to consider on cours Taulignan and pl de la Poste. Place Montfort is the obvious drinking place to gravitate towards, but if you want to be in a more "local" ambiance try *Vasio*

Bar on cours Taulignan. Vaison's weekly **market** takes place on Tuesday along the Grande-Rue, and there's an exceptional *fromagerie* on rue Raspail.

The Dentelles

The **Dentelles**, a row of jagged limestone pinnacles, run across an arid, windswept, and near-deserted upland area, the **Massif Montmirail-St-Amand** just south of Vaison-la-Romaine. Their name refers to lace – the limestone protrusions were thought to resemble the contorted pins on a lace-making board – though the word's alternative connection with "teeth" is equally appropriate.

On the western and southern slopes lie the **wine-producing villages** of **Gigondas**, **Beaumes-de-Venise**, **Sablet**, **Séguret**, **Vacqueyras** and, across the Ouzère river, **Rasteau.** Each one carries the distinction of having its own individual *appellation contrôlé* within the *Côtes du Rhône* or *Côtes du Rhône Villages* areas: in other words, their wines are exceptional. In addition, some of the villages are alluringly picturesque, with **Séguret** super-conscious of its Provençal beauty.

Besides *dégustation* and bottle buying, you can go for long walks in the Dentelles, stumbling upon mysterious ruins or photogenic panoramas of Mont Ventoux and the Rhône valley. The pinnacles are favourite scaling faces for apprentice rock-climbers – though their wind-eroded patterns can be appreciated just as well without risking your neck on an ascent. The place to go for **walking** and **climbing** information and maps is the *Club Alpin, Café de la Poste*, **Gigondas**.

Practicalities

Although it's possible to get to BEAUMES, VACQUEYRAS, GIGONDAS, SÉGURET and SABLET by **public transport** (there are two buses daily from Vaison and CARPENTRAS), hitching may be easier. There are **campsites** in Sablet, Beaumes and Vacqueyras and a **youth hostel** on route de Sablet in Séguret (☎90.36.93.31). In Beaumes the *Auberge St-Roch* (☎90.62.94.29; ③; closed mid-Aug to mid-Sept) and *Le Relais des Dentelles* (☎90.62.95.27; ③), past the old village and over the river, are quiet, old-fashioned **hotels** and middle of the range: note that both are closed on Monday. Out of season, you may be able to get one of the six rooms at *L'Oustalet*, pl du Portail, in GIGONDAS (☎90.65.85.30).

Places to stop for a **drink** or **food** are few and far between once you leave the main villages – basically one café in SUZETTE and a restaurant in LAFARE. In Sablet the *Café des Sports* on the last spiral of the dome-shaped village feeds you for 80F with no fooling around with menus. For a real treat, and not too expensive, *Lou Brasero* on the route de Lafare to MALAUCÈNE, 1.5km from Beaumes, serves beautiful home-made pizzas preceded by local specialities such as hot goat's cheese with salad.

Wines

The tourist offices in Gigondas on pl du Portail and the *Cave des Vignerons* or Mairie in Beaumes can provide lists for the villages of particular *domaines* or *caves* grouping several *vignerons*. If the art and science of wine and the whole business of wine-tasting is a mystery to you, then take a visit to the **Musée du Vigneron** between RASTEAU and ROAIX on the D975 (April–Oct 9.30am–12.30pm & 1.30–6pm; Nov–March daily 1.30–5.30pm, weekends 9.30am–12.30pm & 1.30–6pm; closed Tues all year). A *dégustation* is offered and there's no obligation to buy.

The most reputed **wine** in the Dentelles is made at **GIGONDAS** – it's almost always red, and quite strong with an after-taste of spice and nuts. You can taste the produce from forty different *domaines* and buy *en vrac* (in bulk) – a real bargain for this wine – at the *Caveau des Vignerons* (closed Wed) on pl de la Mairie in the village.

The most distinctive wine, and elixir for those who like it sweet, is the pale amber-coloured *Beaumes-de-Venise* **muscat** which you can buy from the *Cave des Vignerons* (8.30am–noon & 2–6pm; closed Sun) on the D7 just outside Beaumes.

MONT VENTOUX

Some 20km east of Vaison rises **Mont Ventoux**, whose outline repeatedly appears upon the horizon from the Rhône or Durance valleys. White with snow, black with storm-cloud shadow or reflecting myriad shades of blue, the barren pebbles of the uppermost 300m are like a colour weather-vane for all of western Provence. Winds can accelerate to 250km per hour around the meteorological, TV and military masts and dishes on the summit, but if you can stand still for a moment the view in all directions is unbelievable. A road, the D974, climbs all the way to the top, though no buses take it. If you want to make the **ascent on foot**, the best path is from LES COLOMBETS or LES FÉBRIERS, hamlets off the D974 east of BÉDOIN – whose **SI** in the Mairie on Portail-Olivier (☎90.65.63.95) can give details. Bédoin has five **campsites**, including the municipal *Pinède* (☎90.65.61.03; April–Sept), and over a dozen **gîtes ruraux** for anyone considering spending a week or more in the area.

Mont Ventoux is a sporadic highlight of the **Tour de France**, hence its appeal in summer for passionately committed cyclists in shiny skin-tight gear. Around the treeline is a memorial to the great British cyclist **Tommy Simpson**, who died here from heart failure, on one of the hottest days ever recorded in the race; his last words – "Put me back on the bloody bike"

Carpentras

With a population approaching 30,000, **CARPENTRAS** is a substantial city for this part of the world. It is also a very old city, its known history starting in 5 BC as the capital of a Celtic tribe. The Greeks who founded Marseille came to Carpentras to buy honey, wheat, goats and skins, and the Romans had a base here. For a brief period in the fourteenth century it became the papal headquarters and gave protection to Jews expelled from France. In May 1990, *Front National* supporters desecrated the town's Jewish cemetery – an event which sparked off a series of copycat anti-semitic attacks on Jewish graves throughout Europe.

The town

For all its ancient remains, Carpentras seems incapable of working up an atmosphere to imbue the present with its past. Friday is **market day** and one of the best reasons for being in Carpentras. **Festival** time (July 15–Aug 8) also makes it more worthwhile: information on all events can be had from the *Bureau du Festival* on pl d'Inguimbert.

Otherwise, the local history museum – the **Musée Comtadin** on bd Albin-Durand – is dark and dour. The **synagogue** (Mon–Fri 10am–noon), near the *hôtel de ville*, although the oldest in France, was rebuilt in the seventeenth century, and is only worth seeing if you've never been into one. The erotic fantasies of a seventeenth-century cardinal frescoed by Nicolas Mignard on what is now the **Palais de Justice**, in the centre of town, were effaced by a later incumbent. The *palais* is attached to the **Cathédrale St-Siffrein** and behind, almost hidden in the corner, stands a Roman *arc de triomphe* inscribed with happy imperial scenes of prisoners in chains. Fifteen hundred years after its erection, Jews, coerced, bribed or otherwise persuaded, entered the cathedral in chains to be unshackled as converted Christians. The door they passed through – the *Porte Juif* – is on the southern side and bears strange symbolism of rats encircling and devouring a globe. Apart from the *Porte Juif*, though, the cathedral is exceedingly dull, as is the space around it.

Practicalities

Buses (the trains are freight only) arrive either on av Victor-Hugo, or a short distance away on pl Aristide-Briand. From the latter, rue de la République runs north to the cathedral, past which rue d'Inguimbert leads off right towards the synagogue and Mairie. There's an **SI** at 170 av Jean-Jaurès (☎90.63.00.78) which hands out free maps. If you want, or need, to **stay**, *La Lavande* on bd A-Rogier (☎90.63.13.49; ②) has eight basic doubles but is often full. If so, the hotel-restaurant *Mont-Ventoux*, pl de la Mairie (☎90.63.04.89; ①/②), is another pauper option, with *Le Cours*, bd Albin-Durand (☎90.63.10.07; ②/③), running it a close second.

As far as **eating** goes, *La Saladine*, at 88 rue Porte-de-Mazan, serves main-course salads, snacks and *glaces* at reasonable prices. For more substantial fare at no more cost, try *Le Marijo* at 73 rue Raspail (closed Sun). Café-crawling is best done on pl Aristide-Briand or around the cathedral.

Avignon

Outside festival time **AVIGNON**, great city of the popes and for centuries one of the major artistic centres of France, can leave you feeling rather cold. There's a positively daunting list of monuments and museums that can't be missed (without bringing on a bad attack of tourist conscience) and no particularly cosy area of knotted medieval streets for café-lounging where you can feel good enough about just lazing. Parts of some streets are pleasant to wander down; a great many buildings have impressive decoration; there are the churches and chapels and convents. But it's easy to feel like an outsider, unless you're here during the **Festival d'Art Dramatique et de Danse** from **mid-July to mid-August**.

The papal city: some atmosphere

Central Avignon is enclosed by medieval walls, built by one of the nine popes that based themselves here throughout most of the fourteenth century, away from the anarchic feuding or, in the case of the last two, away from the rival popes, in Rome. Avignon was a lively place while the papacy had its headquarters here. Every vice and crime flourished in the overcrowded, plague-ridden ratbag of papal entourage and hangers-on, natives and visiting dignitaries with their retinues. According to Petrarch it was "a sewer where all the filth of the universe has gathered". In 1403 the anti-Pope Benoit, who had built the walls in a fit of justified paranoia during the shifting alliances of the Great Schism, was ousted and the city had to content itself with mere cardinals.

Arrival, orientation and accomodation

Avignon's walls still form a complete loop. They appear far too low to be a serious defence, but half the full height is buried since it was impossible to excavate the moat during the nineteenth-century restoration work. All the gates and towers, however, were successfully repaired, and there's little problem when you arrive of knowing which direction to take for the city centre.

Both the **gare SNCF** and the **gare routière** are set beside porte de la République on bd St-Roch. Cours Jean-Jaurès runs inside the gate with, at no. 41, the **SI** (Mon–Fri 9am–6pm, Sat 9am–1pm & 2–6pm; July Mon–Sat 9am–8pm, Sun 10am–1pm & 2–6pm), before changing its name to **rue de la République**. This is the main axis of the old town, leading straight up to the café-lined **place de l'Horloge**, the central square whose clock tower is part of the imposing Hôtel de Ville. If you're **driving**, it's best to park outside the walls as – once stuck on the narrow one-way system – driving in the city can become tiresone.

AVIGNON

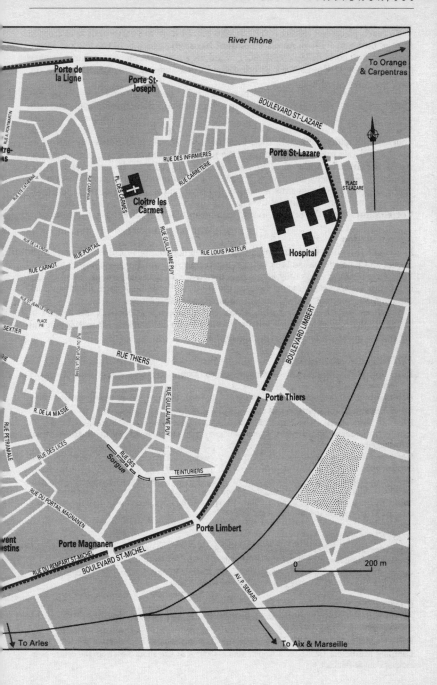

To reach place de l'Horloge you can take bus #4 from the gare routière or from in front of the main **PTT** on **av du Président-Kennedy**, which is to the left just as you come through porte de la République. Beyond the square, within easy walking distance are the **Palais de Papes**, the **cathedral**, the **Petit Palais** and St-Bénézet's bridge, the famous **Pont d'Avignon**.

Between *St-Pierre* and *St-Didier* churches are the pedestrian precincts of **rue des Marchands** and **rue du Vieux-Sextier**, with their complement of chapels and late-medieval mansions, in particular the *Hôtel des Rascas* on the corner of rue des Marchands and rue Fourbisseurs, and the *Hôtel de Belli* on the corner of rue Fourbisseurs and rue Vieux-Sextier. One block south, rue de la Bonneterie runs east past the hideous **market hall** on place Pie (open every morning except Monday) into **rue des Teinturiers**, the most atmospheric street in Avignon. Its name refers to the eighteenth- and nineteenth-century business of calico printing. The cloth was washed in the Sorgue which still runs alongside the street turning the wheels of long-gone mills. Following rue des Lices at the top of rue des Teinturiers brings you to **place des Corps-Saints** (near the SI), the second main focus of city life after place de l'Horloge.

Accomodation

Even outside festival time, **finding a room** in Avignon can be a problem: cheap hotels fill fast and it's never a bad idea to book in advance. It's worth remembering, too, that Villeneuve-lès-Avignon is only just across the river and may have rooms when its big neighbour is *complet*. Between the two, the Île de la Barthelasse is an idyllic spot for camping, and you may find the odd farmhouse advertising rooms.

Vaucluse Tourisme Hébergements (Mon–Fri 9am–6pm, Sat 10am–5pm), located in the gare SNCF, provide comprehensive information on accommodation in Avignon and the region, including lists of hostels and foyers.

HOTELS

Hôtel Splendid, 17 rue Agricole-Perdiquier (☎90.86.14.46). Near pl des Corps-Saints. Cheap, but not very cheerful. ②.

Hôtel Innova, 100 rue Joseph-Vernet (☎90.82.54.10). Small, friendly, and well worth booking. ③.

Hôtel Mignon, 12 rue Joseph-Vernet (☎90.82.17.30). Good value and stylish. ③/④

Hôtel de l'Angleterre, 29 bd Raspail (☎90.86.34.31) A *Logis de France* hotel in traditional style with some very reasonably priced rooms, located well away from nighttime noise in the southeast corner of the old city. ③/④.

Hôtel de Mons, 5 rue de Mons (☎90.82.57.16). Very central. Thirteenth-century chapel converted imaginatively. ④/⑤.

La Ferme Jamet, Île de la Barthelasse (☎90.86.16.74). A sixteenth-century farm on the island in the Rhône (signed right off Pont Daladier as you cross over from Avignon) with a choice of farm-house bedroom with period furniture, your own outhouse building, an ultra-modern flat or a gypsy caravan. Tennis courts and swimming pool. ⑤.

HOSTELS AND FOYERS

Foyer des Jeunes, 75 rue Joseph-Vernet (☎90.86.10.52). Centrally located women-only hostel; double and single rooms available, the latter a bit overpriced.

Centre d'Hébergement, 32 bd Limbert (☎90.85.27.78); bus #2 direction Pont des Deux-Eaux, from the PTT to Thiers stop. The city's extremely small youth hostel.

CAMPSITES

All campsites are located on the Île de la Barthelasse; take bus #10 from the PTT, stop La Barthelasse.

Foyer Bagatelle (☎90.86.30.39). 3* campsite with dormitory rooms; the closest to the city centre.

Camping Municipal (☎90.82.63.50; open March–Oct). A 3* site about 3km from the centre over-looking Pont St-Bénézet.

Unlike most provincial festivals of international renown, Avignon's is dominated by **theatre and film** rather than classical music, though there is plenty of that. The *Théâtre National Populaire,* one of the leading French companies, founded and directed for its first twelve years by Jean Vilar, comes to the *Palais des Papes* for the festival every year (**mid-July–mid-Aug**). The streets are taken over by the fringe – *"le off"* as opposed to the mainstream *"in"* – and by 250,000 non-native spectators; getting around or doing anything normal becomes virtually impossible.

The headquarters of the festival is the *Maison Jean-Vilar* (Tues–Fri 9am–noon & 2–6pm, Sat 10am–5pm) in the *Hôtel de Crochans,* 8 rue de Mons (☎90.86.59.64/90.82.67.08). As well as providing programmes and information they show free videos and have a collection of festival memorabilia dating back to its inception in 1947.

If you want to take part as an **impromptu performer,** all you need do is force a space in the pl de l'Horloge, the pl du Change, or wherever else the inspiration hits you, and begin.

Les Deux Rhônes, chemin de Bellegarde, Île de la Barthelasse (☎90.83.45.98; open June–Sept) 4km from the city, but cheaper than the municipal site.

The City

Avignon's major monuments occupy a compact quarter, spread about the **Rocher des Doms park** inside the northern loop of the walls. The **Palais des Papes,** home of the medieval popes, is obviously the major sight, but there are cardinals' and secular **palaces** dotted about the centre and, as you'd expect, a fair smattering of **churches** – most, frustratingly, kept locked outside of services. The best of the city's **museums** is the **Musée Calvet,** and, for a break from the monumental, the area east of the centre, around **rue des Teinturiers,** is the most enjoyable, atmospheric quarter.

Palais des Papes

July–Sept 9am–6pm, with English tours on offer; April–June 9–11.15am & 2–5.15pm; Oct–Mar 9–11.15am & 2–6.15pm; 30F guided, 22F unguided.

The **Palais des Papes** is a monster of a building, doing to the vertical what Versailles does to the horizontal. If you want to get a dramatic neck-cricking view of the whole towering pile, follow rue Peyrolerie around the south end of the Palais. So little remains of the original decoration and furnishings that you can be deceived into thinking that all the popes and their retinues were as pious and austere as the last official occupant, Benoît XII. The denuded interior certainly gives sparse indication of the corruption and decadence of fat, feuding cardinals and their mistresses, the thronging purveyors of jewels, velvet and furs, the musicians, chefs and painters competing for patronage, the riotous banquets and corridor schemings.

The first part of the tour takes you through the **Vieux Palais,** starting with the **Consistoire** where sovereigns and ambassadors were received and the cardinals' council held. The flooring and the frescoes covering all the walls were destroyed by fire in 1413. The only decoration now is fragments of frescoes moved from the cathedral and a nineteenth-century line-up of the popes, in which all nine look remarkably similar thanks to the artist using the same model for each portrait.

Some medieval artistry is in evidence, however, in the **Chapelle St-Jean,** off the Consistoire, and in the **Chapelle St-Martial** on the floor above. Both were decorated by a Sienese artist, Matteo Giovanetti, and commissioned by Clement VI who demanded the maximum amount of blue – the most expensive pigment, derived from lapis lazuli. The frescoes have suffered at the hands of soldiers, who tried to chip off all the heads in one piece to sell when the palace was a barracks in the nineteenth century. But this allows you to see something of the technique – the outline drawn on the stone, which was then covered up bit by bit with the plaster on which the paint was applied.

The **kitchen** on this floor also gives an idea of the medieval times, and a hint of the scale of papal gluttony – the square walls transform into an octagonal chimney piece for a vast central cooking fire.

In the **Palais Neuf**, Clement VI's **bedroom** and **study** are further evidence of this pope's secular concerns, with wonderful food-orientated murals and painted ceilings. Beautifully restored, they illustrate in detail fishing, falconry, hunting and other courtly pursuits. But austerity resumes in the cathedral-like proportions of the **Grande Chapelle** or *Chapelle Clementine* and in the **Grande Audience**, its twin in terms of volume on the floor below.

The cathedral and Petit Palais

The **Cathédrale Notre-Dame-des-Doms** just north of the Palais des Papes might once have been a luminous Romanesque structure, but the interior has had a bad attack of Baroque. In addition, nineteenth-century maniacs mounted an enormous gilded Virgin on the belfry, which would look silly enough anywhere, but when dwarfed by the 50-metre towers of the popes' palace, is absurd.

There's greater reward behind, in the **Rocher des Doms park**. As well as ducks and swans and views over the river to Villeneuve and beyond, it has a sundial in which your own shadow tells the time.

The **Petit Palais** (summer 9.30–11.50am & 2–6.15pm; winter 9.15–11.50am & 2–6pm; closed Tues; 16F), just below the Dom rock, also has treats, though the scale of the collections in this episcopal palace is dauntingly extreme – almost a thousand paintings and sculptures, most of them thirteenth- to fifteenth-century Italian. It's easy to get stuck, with more than a dozen rooms still to go, on the mastery of colour and facial expressions of a Simone Martini or Fabriano. Or to pass out from a surfeit of Madonnas and Childs before you've got to Louis Bréa or Botticelli.

Sur le Pont d'Avignon...

Easter–Oct 10am–1pm & 2–6pm; Nov–Easter 10am–noon & 1–5pm; 10F.

One theory has it that the song about the **Pont d'Avignon** says "Sous le pont (*under* the bridge)", rather than "Sur le pont (*on* the bridge)", and refers to the thief and trickster clientele of a tavern on the Île de la Barthelasse (which the bridge once crossed) dancing with glee at the arrival of more potential victims. Repairing the bridge from the ravages of the Rhône was finally abandoned in 1660, three and a half centuries after it was built, and only four of the original 22 arches remain. It can be walked, danced or sat upon, but if you take small children, beware the precipitous, barely protected drops on either side. To reach it from pl du Palais, follow the signs through the housing development to the left of the Petit Palais.

Churches and palaces

Around place de l'Horloge, on rues de Mons, Molière and Corneille, famous faces appear in windows painted on the buildings. Many of these figures from the past were visitors to Avignon, and of those that recorded their impressions of the city, it was the sound of over a hundred bells ringing that stirred them most. Of a Sunday morning, traffic lulls permitting, you can still hear a myriad different peels from **churches, convents and chapels** in close proximity – not quite as numerous after the centuries, but nearly. Many ecclesiastical buildings went during the Revolution and the years up until 1815, when a minority were still fighting against union with France. It was a bloody time: in 1791 a supporter of the new order was murdered in a church and in response sixty counter-revolutionaries were buried alive in the ice-house tower of the Papal Palace.

To either side of pl de l'Horloge and northwards are the most desirable Avignon addresses – both now and 300 years ago. High, heavy facades dripping with cupids, eagles, dragons, fruit and foliage range along rue Joseph-Vernet, rue Petite-Fusterie and rue St-Étienne. The **Église St-Agricole**, just behind the Hôtel de Ville, has recently been restored and is one of Avignon's best Gothic edifices. Opposite the Papal Palace a flamboyant griffin decorates the **Hôtel des Monnaies** – the old Mint, now the Music Conservatory. The **quartier de la Banasterie** behind the Palais des Papes is almost solid seventeenth- and eighteenth-century. The heavy wooden doors with highly sculptured lintels bear the nameplates of lawyers, psychiatrists and dietary consultants.

The most spectacular doorway in this area, which like the others is firmly closed, is the Renaissance creation of the **Église St-Pierre** on pl St-Pierre. In the scene of the Annunciation on the right-hand door, Mary looks as if she's saying "Who the hell are you?" to Gabriel, who points to the dove as his credentials. More Renaissance art is on show in the **Église St-Didier** (open except Sun pm), chiefly the altarpiece in which the realism of Mary's pain has prompted the somewhat uncomfortable name *Notre-Dame-du-Spasme*. There are also some fourteenth-century frescoes in the left-hand chapel.

Museums

Avignon's best museum, the **Musée Calvet**, 65 rue Joseph-Vernet (10am–noon & 2–6pm; closed Tues), has a bit of everything – from an Egyptian mummy of a five-year-old boy to a Vaserely tapestry, taking in along the way Renaissance armchairs, Géricault adventure-tableaux, Utrillos, Laurençons and Dufys, Dutch still lifes, Gallo-Roman pots, sixteenth-century clocks, and masses of wrought iron. The eighteenth-century palace housing this eclectic collection is in itself a delight to walk around, and its layout, unlike the Petit Palais, makes it easy to return to treasures glimpsed while passing earlier.

The remaining crop of museums is considerably less compelling. Next door to the *Musée Calvet* is the **Musée Requien** (Tues–Sat 9am–noon & 2–6pm). Its subject is natural history and its sole advantage is in being free and having clean loos. Also free, and with little more to recommend it, is the **Lapidary Museum** of Roman and Gallo-Roman stone, housed in the Baroque chapel at 27 rue de la République (10am–noon & 2–6pm; closed Tues). Finally, at the **Musée Vouland** on rue Victor-Hugo (Tues–Sat 9am–noon & 2–6pm; winter Wed–Sat 2–5pm only; free) you feast your eyes on the fittings, fixtures and furnishings that French aristocrats indulged in both before and after the Revolution. There's some brilliant Moustiers faïence, exquisite marquetry and Louis XV ink-pots with silver rats holding the lids – but little that you can't see better *in situ* elsewhere.

Food and entertainment

Good value midday **meals** are two a penny in Avignon and eating well in the evening needn't break the bank. The large terraced *café-brasseries* on pl de l'Horloge, rue de la République, pl du Change and pl des Corps-Saints all serve quick basic meals. Rue des Teinturiers is good for menu-browsing if you're budgeting, and the streets between pl de Crillon and pl du Palais are full of temptation if you're not.

There's a fair amount of **nightlife and cultural events**, too; the best place for information on concerts and theatre is the *Conseil Culturel* at 8bis rue des Mons.

Meals under 100F

La Tache d'Encre, 22 rue des Teinturiers (☎90.85.46.03). Live music Fri and Sat nights, occasionally weekdays, too; booking advisable. The food isn't brilliant but the musicians – jazz, rock, chansons, African or salsa – usually are. Congenial atmosphere and not expensive.

Le Venaissin, 16 pl de l'Horloge (☎90.86.20.99). In the height of summer you'd be lucky to get a table here – the only cheap eaterie on pl de l'Horloge that serves much more than *steak-frites*.

Le Corail, 64 bd St-Roch (☎90.27.03.26; closed Sun). Reasonably priced Provençal cuisine, including aïoli.

Le Pain Bis, 6 rue Armand-de-Pontmartin (☎90.86.46.77; closed weekends). Ninety percent of the dishes are vegetarian and all ingredients organically grown.

Le Megafaune, 36bis, rue Remparts-St-Lazare (☎90.85.64.75). Salads, chilli and grills, to the accompaniement of live music and theatre.

Meals over 150F

Le Petit Bédon, 70 rue Joseph-Vernet (☎90.82.33.98; closed Sun and last two weeks in June; last orders 10.30pm). According to fellow chefs, the "Pot-belly" does the best meal for under 250F to be had anywhere in the city.

Le Salon de la Fourchette and **Fourchette II**, 7 rue Racine (☎90.82.56.01; closed Sun and last two weeks in June; last orders 9.30pm). Two restaurants serving the same menus, inspired by the cuisine of Hiély-Lucellus, and differentiated only by fad and fashion.

Hiély-Lucullus, 5 rue de la République (☎90.86.17.07; closed Mon, Tues and the last two weeks of June; last orders 9.15pm). This is Avignon's top gastronomic palace, serving beautiful Provençal cuisine. The Rhône wines are the very best, and will add a good whack to an already groaning bill.

Markets

Place Pie Daily covered market for all produce.

Porte Magnanen Open market every weekend outside the ramparts.

Place des Carmes Organic market every Thurs morning.

Cafés and bars

La Grand Siècle, and **Les Célestins**, pl des Corps-Saints. A young, hippy-to-hip clientele and radical reputations.

Pub Z, corner of rue Bonneterie and rue Artaud. Café catering for the designer chic.

Grand Café du Commerce, 21 rue St-Jean-de-Vieux. Pleasant café for all tastes.

Le Bistrot d'Avignon, 1 rue Jean-Vilar. Cafe-winebar, for upmarket bibbing of Rhône specialities.

L'Esclave Bar, 12 rue du Limas. Gay bar, open 10pm–5am.

Bar du Change, pl du Change. Cheap snack bar.

Other student snack bars are located on and off rue des Lices, including the popular *Studio*, 13 rue du Portail-Magnanen.

Music

AJMI Jazz Club, c/o *Théâtre du Chêne Noir*, 8bis rue Ste-Catherine (☎90.33.84.23/90.86.03.61). Hosts major acts and some adventurous new groups. Jazz night is Thurs.

La Tache d'Encre (see restaurant above) and **Le Caf 'Conce**, 25 rue Carnot (☎90.85.79.71). Two more venues with jazz among their music mix.

Avignon Opéra. Programme details on ☎90.82.23.44.

Classical concerts are performed in the churches of the city, usually for free.

Theatre and cinema

Le Chêne Noir (see *AJMI Jazz Club* above). A company worth seeing – they may have mime, a musical or Molière on offer.

Utopia, 15 rue Galante. Cinema showing avant-garde, obscure or old time favourites, always in the original language.

Listings

Bike hire, *Dopieralski Cycles Peugeot*, 84 rue G-Puy; *Masson Richard Cycles Peugeot*, pl Pie; *Transhumance* (☎90.95.57.81).

Boat trips *Le Mireio*, allées de l'Oulle (☎90.85.62.25; all year round, 2-week advance booking recommended), upstream towards Châteauneuf-du-Pape and downstream to Arles.

Buses Single tickets or, more economically, a pack of ten can be bought from the driver or from the TCRA kiosks at porte de la République and pl Pie. A detailed bus map is available free from TCRA.

Car hire *Ardam Location*, garage St-Valéry, bd Limbert is the cheapest option. Located on bd St-Ruf are *Europcar* at nos. 27–29, *Eurorent* at no. 3, and *ACA* at no. 15.

Car repairs The SI has lists of the main manufacturers' concessionaires.

Change Outside banking hours at the SI, or the *Bureau d'Information Touristique* at the *gare SNCF*.

Emergencies Doctor, *SOS Médecins*, 31 rte de Morières (☎90.82.65.00); Hospital, *Centre Hospitalier de la Durance*, 305 rue Raoul-Follereau (☎90.89.91.31); Ambulance, ☎90.88.11.11; night chemist, call police on ☎90.85.17.17 for addresses.

French courses *Alta*, 4 impasse Romagnoli (☎90.85.86.24).

Launderettes 8 rue Pontmartin; 19 rue des Lices; 9 rue Chapeau-Rouge.

Poste restante PTT, av du Président-Kennedy, Avignon 84000.

Swimming pool *Piscine de la Barthelasse* on the Île de la Barthelasse; summer only.

Taxis pl Pie; ☎90.82.20.20.

Trains Information, ☎90.82.50.50; reservations, ☎90.82.56.29.

Travel agencies *Havas Voyages*, 35 rue de la République (☎90.82.51.28); *ATHO*, 64 pl des Corps-Saints (☎90.82.06.09).

Women *Vaucluse Information Femmes*, 9 rue Carnot (☎90.88.41.00) 9am–noon & 2–6pm; closed Fri.

Villeneuve-Lès-Avignon

VILLENEUVE-LÈS-AVIGNON rises up a rocky escarpment above the west bank of the river, looking down upon its older neighbour from behind far more convincing fortifications. Historically, Villeneuve operated largely as a suburb to Avignon, with palatial residences constructed by the cardinals and a great monastery founded by Pope Innocent VI.

To this day Villeneuve is technically a part of Languedoc not Provence, and would score better in the hierarchy of towns to visit were it further from Avignon – whose monuments it can almost match for colossal scale and impressiveness. In summer at least it benefits, providing venues for the Avignon Festival, as well as accommodation overspill; and it's certainly worth a day, whatever time of year you visit.

Getting there and accommodation

From Avignon's gare SNCF, one of the #10 buses runs direct to Villeneuve and Les Angles every half hour to place Charles-David in Villeneuve, taking less than ten minutes, or five if you catch it from Porte d'Oulle. After 8pm you'll have to take a taxi or walk – it's only 3km.

On **pl Charles-David** you'll find the **SI** (8.45am–12.30pm & 2–6pm) and, on Thursday mornings, a Provençal **market** of food, clothes and bric-à-brac. Rue Gabriel-Péri leads west off the *place* past the Mairie to place St-Marc. From here, the main street, **rue de la République**, runs due north.

For **reasonably priced accommodation**, try *Hôtel Beauséjour*, 61 av Gabriel-Péri (☎90.25.20.56; ①–④), *Auberge du Canard*, 65 bd Mistral (☎90.25.45.18; ③), or the *Central*, 15 rue de la République (☎90.25.44.12; ①/②), a restaurant with some cheap rooms. The *YMCA* hostel at 7bis chemin de la Justice (☎90.25.46.20) is an attractive alternative – though no cheaper than the above. It is beautifully situated overlooking the river by Pont du Royaume, has balconied rooms for two to six people, and an open-air swimming pool; if you're staying more than one night you have to pay full or half board (bus #10 from Avignon, get off at _Pont d'Avignon_, or _Général-Leclerc_ if via Les Angles). The **camping** _Municipal de la Laune_ is at chemin St-Honoré (☎90.25.76.06) off the D980, near the sports stadium and swimming pools. Another likely option, worthwhile for a prolonged stay or self-catering opportunities, is _Les Logis St-Eloi_, 14 pl de l'Oratoire (☎90.25.40.36; ③–⑤): a complex of studio flats with kitchenettes situated in sixteenth and seventeenth-century buildings.

If **money** is less of an object, _Le Prieuré_, pl du Chapitre (☎90.25.18.20; ⑤), is indisputably the first choice, both for the rooms and for its restaurant. For a quarter the price, you could stay in equally ancient surroundings at _l'Atelier_, 5 rue de la Foire (☎90.25.01.84; ④/⑤), a sixteenth-century house with huge open fireplaces and a walled garden. Alternatively there's a Louis XIV mansion, _Les Cèdres_, 39 bd Pasteur (☎90.25.43.92; ⑤), with pool and restaurant.

The town

For a good overview of Villeneuve – and Avignon – make your way to the **Tour Philippe-le-Bel** at the bottom of montée de la Tour (bus stop _Philippe-le-Bel_). This tower was built to guard the French end of Pont St-Bénézet, and a climb to the top (10am–noon/12.30pm & 2/3–5/6.30pm; closed Tues and Feb) will be rewarded with stunning views.

Even more indicative of French distrust of its neighbours is the enormous **Fort St-André** (daily 10am–noon & 2–6pm; closed Nov–mid-March), whose bulbous double-towered gateway and vast white walls loom over the town. Inside, refreshingly, there's not a hint of a postcard stall or souvenir shop – just tumbledown houses and the former abbey, with its gardens of olive trees, ruined chapels, lily ponds and dovecots. Its cliff-face terrace is the classic spot for artists to aim their brushes, or photographers their cameras, over Avignon. You can reach the approach to the fortress, montée du Fort, from pl Jean-Jaurès on rue de la République, or by the "rapid slope" of rue Pente-Rapide, a cobbled street of tiny houses leading off rue des Recollets on the north side of pl Charles-David.

La Chartreuse du Val de Bénédiction

Almost at the top of rue de la République, on the right, allée des Muriers leads from pl des Chartreux to the entrance of **La Chartreuse du Val de Bénédiction** (April–June & Aug–Sept 9am–noon & 2–6.30pm; July 9am–6.30pm; Oct–March 10am–noon & 2–5pm). This Charterhouse, one of the largest in France, was founded by the sixth of the Avignon popes, Innocent VI, whose sharp profile is outlined on his tomb in the church. The buildings, which were sold off after the Revolution and gradually restored this century, are totally unembellished. With the exception of the Giovanetti frescoes in the chapel beside the refectory, all the paintings and treasures of the monastery have been dispersed, leaving you with a strong impression of the austerity of the Carthusian order – when strictly practised. The only communication allowed was one hour of conversation a week plus the rather less congenial public confessions. Monks left the enclosure for one three-hour walk each week; within, their time was spent as much on manual labour as on prayer, and their diet was strictly vegetarian.

You're free to wander around unguided, through the three cloisters, the church, chapels, cells and communal spaces with little to see but plenty of atmosphere to absorb. Contemporary inspiration and creativity are given rein here by _CIRCA_, a cultural organisation that invites practitioners of the plastic and audiovisual arts to take up residence over the summer. They host concerts and performances, both as part of the Avignon Festival and at other times of the year: details are available from the ticket office (☎90.25.05.46).

Notre-Dame and the Musée Municipal

Another festival venue is the fourteenth-century **Église Collègiale Notre-Dame** and its cloister on pl St-Marc. Notre-Dame's most important treasure is a rare fourteenth-century smiling Madonna and Child made from a single tusk of ivory, now housed, along with many of the paintings from the Chartreuse, in the **Musée Municipal**. The museum, part of which was a cardinal's residence in the fourteenth century, is on rue de l'Hôpital below place St-Marc (April–Sept 10am–12.30pm & 3–7.30pm; Nov–March 10am–noon & 2–5pm). The spacious layout includes a single room, with comfortable settees and ample documentation, given over to the most stunning painting in the collection – *Le Couronnement de la Vierge*, painted in 1453 by Enguerrand Quarton as the altarpiece for the church in the Chartreuse. With fiercely contrasting red, orange, gold, white and blue, the statuesque and symmetrical central figures of the coronation form a powerful and unambiguous subject. To either side of them, in true medieval style, the social hierarchy is defined. Along the bottom of the painting the scale of detail leaps several frames, with flames engulfing sinners; devils and their assistant beasts carrying away victims; walled towns with pin-size figures; and in the distance Mont Ste-Victoire and the cliffs of Estaque.

No other painting in the collection matches Quarton's work and many are too obviously public relations pieces for their patrons – placing the pope, lord or bishop in question beside the Madonna or Christ.

Restaurants

Villeneuve's centre has perfectly reasonable places to eat for **under 120F**. Try *La Calèche*, 35 rue de la République, (☎90.25.02.54); *La Mamma Lucia*, pl V-Basch; (☎90.25.00.71) or the *crêperie La Fontaine Morgane,* 28 rue de la République. For a blowout meal, at **around 350F**, *La Magnaneraie*, off rue de la Magnanerie between av Paul-Ravoux and rue du Camp-de-Bataille (☎90.25.11.11), is the posh and perfect answer. Or you could eat very acceptable fresh Provençal fare – on a terrace over the Rhône at the foot of Philipe-le-Bel's tower – at *l'Anglore* restaurant in the *Hostellerie du Vieux Moulin,* rue du Vieux-Moulin (☎90.25.00.26).

St-Rémy-de-Provence and the Alpilles

The watery and intensely cultivated scenery of the Petite Crau plain changes abruptly with the eruption of the **Chaîne des Alpilles**, whose peaks look like the surf of a wave about to engulf the plain. At the base of the Alpilles nestles **St-Rémy-de-Provence**, a dreamy place, ideally situated for exploration of the hills (or La Petite Crau), while along the ridge is the medieval stronghold of **Les Baux** and the remains of an ancient city known as **Glanum**.

St-Rémy-de-Provence

The **vieille ville** of **ST-RÉMY** is contained within a circle of boulevards no more than half a kilometre in diameter. Outside this ring, the modern town is sparingly laid out – so, for once, you don't have to plug your way through dense developments before you reach the city's heart. It is a beautiful place, as unspoilt as the villages around it.

Orientation and accommodation

Arriving by **bus** from Avignon, Cavaillon, Tarascon, Aix or Arles (daily connections), you'll be dropped at pl de la République, the main square abutting the old town on the east. The **SI** (9am–noon & 2–6pm) is just south of the centre, reached by following bd

Marceau until it becomes av Durand-Maillane on pl Jean-Jaurès. They have excellent free guides on **cycling and walking routes** in and around the Alpilles and can provide addresses for **hiring horses**. If you want to **hire a bicycle, tandem** or **car**, go to *Florelia* 35 av de la Libération (the road to Cavaillon).

The town has a fairly wide choice of **accommodation**, though real bargains are hard to come by. In the old town, pleasant **hotels** with some cheaper rooms are *Le Provence* 36 bd Victor-Hugo, on the eastern edge of the old town (☎90.92.06.27; ③/④; closed Oct to mid-March); and *L'Oustalou* on rue du 8-mai-1945 (☎90.92.17.66; ②/③). The *Ville Verte*, av Fauconnet (☎90.92.06.14, ②/③), is central and has some cheap rooms. *Villa Glanum,* 46 av Vincent-Van-Gogh (☎90.92.03.59; ④/⑤; half-board compulsory; closed mid-Jan to mid-Feb), next door to the archaeological site, is pleasant and not too over-priced and has a swimming pool; at greater expense, *Canto Cigalo,* chemin de Canto Cigalo (☎90.92.14.28; ⑤; closed Nov–Feb) is top-notch; *Auberge La Reine Jeanne*, 12 bd Mirabeau, is restful and charming (☎90.92.15.33; ⑤) with a wonderful, good-value restaurant.

There are three **campsites** near St-Rémy: the 4* *Municipal du Mas de Nicolas* 2km along the route de Mollèges (☎90.92.27.05/90.92.28.55; open all year); 2* *Monplaisir* 1km along the route de Maillane (☎90.92.22.70/90.92.12.91; closed mid-Nov to Feb); and 3* *Pegomas* 1km along the route de Cavaillon (☎90.92.01.21; closed Nov–Feb).

The town

To reach the old town from pl de la Résistance, take av de la Résistance, which runs alongside Église St-Martin, and start wandering up alleyways, into immaculate, leafy squares. For an introduction to the region, a good first visit is to the **Musée des Alpilles**, on pl Favier, housed in the *Hôtel Mistral de Mondragon* (10am–noon & 2–5/ 6/7pm; closed Jan–March). The museum features interesting displays on folklore, festivities and traditional crafts, plus some intriguing local landscapes, some creepy portraits by Marshall Pétain's first wife, and souvenirs of local boy Nostradamus.

You can buy a combined ticket for the Musée des Alpilles and the neighbouring **Musée Archéologique** in the *Hôtel de Sade* (guided visits several times daily; closed Jan–March). This collection comes from the archaeological digs at the Greco-Roman town of Glanum (see below), for which the combined ticket is also valid. The hour's tour may be a bit much for the non-committed, but there are some stunning pieces, in particular the temple decorations.

In addition to the two fifteenth- to sixteenth-century *hôtels* that house the museums, you'll find more ancient stately residences as you wander through the **vieille ville**, particularly along rue Parage. On rue Hoche is the birthplace of Nostradamus – though only the facade is contemporary with the futuristic savant, and it's not open to visits. The town's main church, the **Collégiale St-Martin** opposite pl de la République, is in a very dilapidated state throughout, save for its surreally lime-green organ (recitals on Saturday mornings). Outside the old town enclosure, a short way south of the SI on rue Jean-de-Nostredame, is the beautiful Romanesque **chapel of Notre-Dame-de-Pitie**, used for exhibitions of religious art.

If you keep heading south, following av Vincent-Van-Gogh, you'll come to **Les Antiques** – a triumphal arch celebrating the Roman conquest of Marseille and a mausoleum thought to commemorate two grandsons of Augustus. Save for a certain amount of weather erosion, the mausoleum is perfectly intact; the arch less so, but both display intricate patterning and the unaesthetic proportional sense of the Romans.

The Antiques would have been a familiar sight to one whose aesthetic sense was always on the side of the angels. In 1889 **Vincent Van Gogh**, then living in Arles, requested that he be put away for several months. The hospital chosen by his friends was in the old monastery **St-Paul-de-Mausole**, a hundred yards or so east of the Antiques, and still a psychiatric clinic today. Although the regime was more prison than hospital, Van Gogh was allowed to wander out around the Alpilles and painted prolifically during his twelve-month stay. The *Champs d'oliviers*, *Le Faucher*, *Le Champ clôturé* and *La Promenade du soir* are among the 150 canvases of this period. The driveway with a statue of the artist, the church and cloisters can be visited from 9am to noon and 2 to 6pm (no charge). Take av Edgar-Leroy or allée St-Paul from av Vincent-Van-Gogh, go past the main entrance of the clinic and into the gateway on the left at the end of the wall. A permanent **Van Gogh Centre**, (March–Nov 10am–noon & 3–7pm) with documentation concerning the artist's stay in Provence and temporary exhibitions of contemporary artists, is now open in the *Hôtel d'Estrine* on rue Estrine in the old town.

Food and entertainment

The best **time to visit** St-Rémy is for the *Fête de Transhumance*, on Whit Monday, when a 2000-strong flock of sheep, accompanied by goats and donkeys, does a tour of the town before being packed off to the Alps for the summer. Or come for the *Carreto Ramado*, on August 15, a harvest thanksgiving procession in which the religious or secular symbolism of the floats reveals the political colour of the various village councils. A pagan rather than workers' Mayday is celebrated with donkey-drawn floral floats on which people play fifes and tambourines. On July 14, August 15 and the fourth Sunday in September, intrepid local youths attempt to set loose six bulls that are herded round the town by their mounted chaperons.

At all times of the year, you'll find plenty of **brasseries** and **restaurants** in and around old St-Rémy. *Lou Planet*, 7 pl Favier near the Musée d'Alpilles is a scenic spot to dine on crêpes. *Le Jardin de Frédéric*, 8 bd Gambetta (closed Tues), has a 100F menu, and usually some interesting dishes on offer. There are a few good options on rue Carnot (leading from bd Victor-Hugo east through the old town to bd Marceau) including the *Haricot Vert Palace* at no. 48, *La Gousée d'Ail* at no. 25 and *Le Gaulois* at no. 57 which, though not brilliant, is at least generous.

If you're after picnic fare, do your shopping at the Wednesday **market** on the pedestrian streets of the old town or at the Saturday market in pl de la Mairie. If it's raining or you don't feel like doing anything active, check out the films at the *Ciné Palace* **cinema** on av Fauconnet that has some screenings in the original language.

Transport: it's difficult to get to Glanum or Les Baux except by foot or taxi, and you may end up hitching to Tarascon or Arles if you miss a connection. Some **taxi** numbers are ☎90.92.09.71, ☎90.92.10.82 and ☎90.92.09.95.

Glanum

One of the most impressive ancient settlements in France, **GLANUM** (9am–noon & 2–5/6pm) was dug out from alluvial deposits at the very foot of the Alpilles, just south of Les Antiques. The site was originally a neolithic homestead; then, between the second and first centuries BC, the Gallo-Greeks, probably from Massalia (Marseille), built a city here, on which the Gallo-Romans, from the end of the first century BC to the third century AD constructed yet another town.

Though Glanum is one of the most important archaeological sites in France, it can be very difficult to get to grips with. Not only were the later buildings moulded on to the earlier, but the fashion at the time of Christ was for a Hellenistic style. You can distinguish the Greek levels from the Roman most easily by the stones: the earlier civilisation used massive hewn rocks while the Romans preferred smaller and more accurately shaped stones. The leaflet at the admission desk is helpful as, too, are the attendants if your French is good enough.

As the site narrows in the ravine at the southern end you find a Grecian edifice around a **spring** – the feature that made this location so desirable. Steps lead down to a pool, with a slab above for the libations of those too disabled to descend. An inscription records that Agrippa was responsible for restoring it in 27 BC and dedicating it to Valetudo, the Roman goddess of health. But **altars** to Hercules are still in evidence, while up the hill to the west are traces left by prehistoric people whose life depended on this spring. The Gallo-Romans directed the water through canals to heat houses and, of course, to the **baths** that lie near the entrance to the site. There are superb sculptures on the Roman **Temples Geminées** (twin temples) as well as fragments of mosaics, fountains of both periods, and first-storey walls and columns.

Les Baux

At the top of the Alpilles ridge, southwest of St-Rémy, lies the distinctly unreal, fortified village of **LES BAUX**. Unreal partly because the ruins of the eleventh-century citadel are hard to distinguish from the edge of the plateau whose rock is both foundation and part of the structure. And unreal, too, because the "Ville Morte" and a vast area of the plateau around it is accessible only via a turnstile, and payment, at the Lapidary museum in the living village below. The "profiting village" might be a better term for this oh-so-perfect collection of sixteenth- and seventeenth-century churches, chapels and mansions.

Once upon a time Les Baux lived off the power and widespread possessions in Provence of its medieval lords, who owed allegiance to no one. When the dynasty died out at the end of the fourteenth century, however, the town, which had once numbered 6000 inhabitants, passed to the counts of Provence and then to the kings of France, who eventually, in 1632, razed the feudal citadel to the ground and fined the population into penury. From that date until the nineteenth century both citadel and village were inhabited almost exclusively by bats and crows. The discovery in the neighbouring hills of the mineral **bauxite** (from Les Baux), brought back some life to the village. But it was the discovery in more recent times that large amounts of money can be made from ancient wealth, that has transformed the place. Today the population stays steady at around 400, while the number of visitors exceeds 1.5 million each year.

The village

It has to be conceded that the lower village has a great many, very beautiful, buildings, and the view beside the statue of Mistral beyond the **Ville Morte** at the southern edge of the plateau is superb. There are four **museums**, including the *Musée d'Art Contemporaine* in the *Hôtel des Porcelets* and a *Musée des Santons*, as well as three temporary exhibition spaces. If you're a good tourist you'll spend at least a whole day here, but don't expect anything to come cheap (and don't even think of staying – accommodation is absurdly overpriced).

The Ville Morte and the plateau are accessible every day in July and August from 8.30am until 8pm: through the rest of the year hours are from 9.30am to 5.30pm. The SI is on the impasse du Château on your left after you've entered the village.

The Val d'Enfer

Within walking distance of Les Baux, along the D27 leading northwards, is the valley of quarried and eroded rocks named the **Val d'Enfer** – the Valley of Hell. Dante, it is thought, came here while staying at Arles, and took from it his inspiration for the nine circles of the Inferno. Jean Cocteau used the old bauxite quarries and the contorted rocks for his film *Le Testament d'Orphée* (which also has scenes in Les Baux itself).

More recently, the very same quarries have been turned into an audio-visual experience under the title the **Cathédrale des Images** (March 20–Nov 11 10am–6/7pm; closed Tues) signposted to the right downhill from Les Baux's compulsory car park. The projection is continuous so you don't have to wait to go in. You're englobed by images projected all over the floor, the ceilings and the walls of these vast rectangular caverns, and by music that resonates strangely in the captured space. The content of the show, which changes yearly, does not really matter. It just is an extraordinary sensation, wandering on and through these changing shapes and colours. As an erstwhile worksite put to good use, it couldn't be bettered.

Tarascon and Beaucaire

To the south of the ridge of La Montagnette, the **castles of Beaucaire and Tarascon** face each other across the Rhône, Beaucaire on the west bank, Tarascon on the Provençal side. Neither of the towns set below them is wildly alluring but the castles are classics. In addition Tarascon has one of the most famous Provençal carnivals, based on an amphibious monster known as the *Tarasque*.

Both towns have **railway stations** and good **bus links** with Avignon, Arles, St-Rémy and Nîmes. Tarascon has more **accommodation** to offer, and a youth hostel, but in either town it should be easy enough to find a room. It doesn't really matter which of the two you choose, as the centre of Beaucaire is just a kilometre's walk away from Tarascon, across the bridge.

Tarascon and its Château

TARASCON castle – the **Château du Roi Réné** – is a vast impregnable mass of stone, beautifully restored to its determinedly defensive fifteenth-century pose (Easter–Sept 9am–7pm; Oct–Easter 9am–noon & 2–5pm; guided visits several times daily). Its towers facing the enemy across the river are square, those at the back round, and nowhere on the exterior is there any hint of softness.

Inside, however, is another matter. The château was a residence of King Réné of Provence – and of his father who initiated the building – and it was designed with all the luxury that the period permitted. The mullioned windows and vaulted ceilings of the royal apartments and the spiral staircase that overlook the *cour d'honneur* are all of graceful Gothic line, and the reconstruction currently taking place plans for at least one room to be fully furnished *à la Roi Réné*.

As it is, there are tapestries of a later date (François I) in the **Salon du Roi**, where traces remain of painted medieval monsters on the wooden ceiling. In several rooms graffiti dating from the fifteenth to the twentieth centuries testifies to the castle's long use as a prison. There's an inscription by an eighteenth-century English prisoner in the Salon du Roi, and, in the **Salles des Gallères**, carvings of boats, some of which date from the Crusades, done by prisoners awaiting judgement. In the **Salle des Gardes** the base of one vault column shows a man reading a book – sculpted at a time when such an activity was truly novel.

The visit ends with the climb up to the **roof**, from which revolutionaries and counter-revolutionaries were thrown in the 1790s. It's likely to be a bad experience for anyone with vertigo, and, depending on the winds, a bit unpleasant for everyone due to the fumes from Tarascon's paper mill just downstream from the town.

The town

It's apparent from a wander round Tarascon that the castle creams off most of the budget for old building restoration but it's quite a pleasant change not to be surrounded by immaculate historic heritage. The streets of Renaissance *hôtels*, interspersed with older houses with Gothic decoration, the classical Town Hall and medieval arcades along rue des Halles are all very subdued, with just the shutters adding a soft diversity of colour. Only during the Tuesday morning **market** does the town come to life.

The **Collégiale Royale Ste-Marthe**, which stands across from the castle, has the saint lying in stone on her tomb in the crypt and appearing in the paintings by Provençal artists that decorate the Gothic interior. In the centre of the town, on pl Frédéric-Mistral off rue Rollin-Lebrun, the sixteenth-century **Cloître des Cordeliers** (10am–noon & 3–7pm; winter 10am–noon & 2–5.30pm; closed Jan–Feb) has had its three aisles in light cream stone beautifully restored. It's used for exhibitions of contemporary paintings, often by young artists. Other exhibitions are organised in the **Chapelle de la Perseverance** (summer only 10am–noon & 3–7pm) on rue Proudhon, part of an erstwhile "refuge" for putting away women and girls suspected of living "bad lives".

Practicalities

The Tarascon **gare SNCF** is south of the centre on bd Gustave-Desplaces. **Buses** from other towns use the *Café des Fleurs* stop, in front of the station. Beyond the car park, across the boulevard, **cours Aristide-Briand** leads to the road bridge across the Rhône and, to your right, the city centre. The **SI** is at 59 rue des Halles. You can **hire bikes** at *Cycles Christophe*, 70bis bd Itam, or at the *Auberge de Jeunesse*, 31 bd Gambetta.

Two bargain **hotels**, both on pl Colonel-Bérrurier in front of Tarascon's station, are the *Rhône* (☎90.91.03.35; ②/③) and the *Terminus* (☎90.91.18.95; ③). The *St-Jean*, 24 bd Victor-Hugo (☎90.91.13.87④/⑤), is considerably more luxurious with a good **restaurant** serving Provençal food, and the neighbouring *Provence* at no. 7 (☎90.91.06.43; ⑤) is more upmarket again, with balconies where you can take your breakfast. The restaurant of the *Echevins*, 26 bd Itam (☎90.91.01.70; closed Sat) is better value than the hotel. Other **places to eat** in Tarascon include the cheapies *Le Roi Réné*, 13 rue A-Perrot, and *Le Français*, 7 cours Aristide-Briand.

The Tarascon **youth hostel** is at 31 bd Gambetta (☎90.91.04.08; open March–Sept), about 500m northeast of the gare SNCF, with sixty beds and **bikes** for hire. You can also hire bikes at the *St-Gabriel* **campsite** (☎90.91.19.83) at the Mas Ginoux, quartier St-Gabriel. Closer to the town centre, on the road to Vallabrègues, beyond the castle, is the *Tartarin* campsite (☎90.91.01.46).

THE TARASQUE

The **Tarasque** is said to have been tamed by Ste Marthe after a long history of clambering out of the Rhône, gobbling people and destroying the ditches and dams of the Camargue with its long croc-like tail. On **the last Sunday of June** it storms the streets of Tarascon in the form of a 6-metre-long Chinese dragon, with glaring eyes and shark-size teeth, the tail swishing back and forth to the screaming delight of all the kids. The monster represents paganism, predictably enough, but it also serves as a reminder of natural catastrophe, in particular floods, kept at bay in this region by the never totally dependable drainage ditches and walls.

Beaucaire

A statue of a bull standing at the head of the Rhône-Sète canal greets you as you arrive in **BEAUCAIRE** from Tarascon. And to the north, between the castle and the river, is a bullring plus a theatre on the site of the old fairground. The fair, founded in 1217, was one of the largest in medieval Europe, attracting traders from all around the Mediterranean as well as merchants from the north along the Rhône. The fairs reached their heyday in the eighteenth century but died in the nineteenth century with the onset of rail freight.

The town today is even more dilapidated than Tarascon, though it retains the classical mansions and arcade – in rue/pl de la République – that speak of former fortunes. For details and a map, the **SI** is at 6 rue de l'Hôtel-de-Ville. If you've arrived by **train** you'll find yourself just south of the bridge. If you want to go straight to the **castle**, you can follow the ramparts north of the bridge and then cut into the town as you come alongside the southern end of the battlements: from pl du Château steps lead up to the entrance.

The **Château de Beaucaire** (10am–dusk; full information available from the attendant) is an immense ruin, destroyed on Richelieu's orders for the support given by the town to one of the cardinal's rivals, the duc de Montmorency. One irregularly sided tower still stands intact with the battlements and machicolations typical of thirteenth-century military strategy. When you climb to the top you appreciate the great advantage it had over Tarascon, whose castle lies far below.

Accommodation is limited in Beaucaire. *Les Doctrinaires,* quai du Gén-de-Gaulle (☎66.59.41.32; ⑨), is an expensive hotel where, in summer, you have to take half-board, but its restaurant is reasonable, given the seventeenth-century decor. For a cheap **snack** at any time of the day, head for *Chez Brigritte* at 45 rue Nationale. Beaucaire's **campsite**, *Le Rhodanien* (☎66.59.25.50), is on the river by the site of the ancient *champs de foire*, and is open all year round.

Arles

ARLES is a major town on the tourist circuit, its fame sealed by the extraordinarily well-preserved Roman arena (*Les Arènes*) at the city's heart, and backed by an impressive variety of other stones and monuments – both Roman and medieval. It was the key city of the region in Roman times, then, with Aix, main base of the counts of Provence before unification with France. For centuries it was Marseille's only rival, profiting from the inland trade route up the Rhône whenever the enemies of France were blocking Marseille's port. It was a centre for counter-revolutionary activity in 1792 and is to this day an arch-reactionary town – a French establishment town par excellence, whose one claim to contemporary fame is the trendily folkloric rock group, the *Gypsy Kings* (their caravan base is under the ring road motorway).

Arles has a crowded calendar of **festivals**, of which the most worthwhile are the **Rencontres Internationales de la Photographie** and the dance-orientated **Festival d'Arles** in July. For locals, the key event is the crowning of the **Reine d'Arles**, once every three years, and the annual opening of the bullfighting season with the **Fête des Gardiens** on May 1.

Orientation and accommodation

Arriving by train eases you gently into the city, with the **gare SNCF** conveniently located a few blocks to the north of the *Arènes*. Most buses also arrive here at the adjacent **gare routière**, though for Aix, Marseille and the Crau, the stop is in the centre at 22 bd G-Clemenceau. From the stations, av Talabot leads to pl Lamartine and one of the old gateways of the city, **Porte de la Cavalerie**. From there rue de la Cavalerie takes you up to the *Arènes* and the centre. **Rue Jean-Jaurès**, with its continuation **rue Hôtel-de-Ville**, is the main axis of old Arles. At the southern end it meets bd Georges-Clemenceau and **bd des Lices**, the promenading and market thoroughfare, with the **SI** directly opposite (daily 9am–6/7.30/8pm). You can hire **bikes** at the train station or from *Ets Montuori* on rue du 4-Septembre which runs off rue de la Cavelerie.

Accommodation

Arles is well used to visitors and there's little shortage of hotel rooms at either end of the scale. The best place to look for cheap rooms is in the area around Porte de la Cavalerie near the station. If you get stuck, the **SI** will find you accommodation for a small fee.

HOTELS

Hôtel Lamartine, rue Marius-Jouveau (☎90.96.13.83). A gloomy but adequate hotel. ②/③.

Hôtel le Rhône, pl Voltaire (☎90.96.43.70). Slightly more character than its neighbours. ③.

Hôtel Gaugin, 5 pl Voltaire (☎90.96.14.35). Comfortable, cheap and well-run. Advisable to book. ②.

Hôtel Constantin, 59 bd de Craponne, off bd Clemenceau (☎90.96.04.05). Pleasant, well kept and comfortable, with prices kept down by the proximity of the Nîmes highway (some traffic noise) and its location some distance from the centre. ②.

Hôtel Diderot, pl de la Bastille (☎90.96.10.30). A lot nicer than any of the above. ③/④.

Hôtel Calendal, 22 pl Pomme (☎90.96.11.89). Generous rooms overlooking a garden. ④/⑤.

Hôtel Musée, 11 rue du Gd-Prieuré (☎90.96.04.49). Quiet location opposite Musée Réattu. ④/⑤.

Hôtel le Forum, 10 pl du Forum (☎90.93.48.95; closed mid-Nov to mid-Feb). Spacious rooms in an old house at the ancient heart of the city, with a swimming pool in the garden. ④/⑤.

YOUTH HOSTEL

Auberge de Jeunesse, 20 av Maréchal-Foch (☎90.96.18.25). The hostel is open all year; reception 7.30–10am and 5–11.30pm; 11.30pm curfew; bus from pl Lamartine to Foch.

CAMPSITES

Camping City, 67 rte de Crau (☎90.93.08.86; March–Sept). Close to town on the Crau bus route.

La Bienheureuse, 7km out on the N453 at Raphèles-les-Arles (☎90.98.35.64; open all year; regular buses from Arles). Best of Arles' half dozen campsites, the restaurant here is furnished with pieces similar to those displayed in the *Musée Arlaten*, and full of pictures of popular Arlesian traditions.

The city

During the city **festival** in July, or the **bullfight** season, which starts in May (see box below), the town has entertainment enough to justify a prolonged visit. Other times, given Arles' prestigious history, visits centre inevitably on monuments and museums. The SI and the Musée Reattu sell a 50F **global ticket** which covers admission to most of Arles' sites and museums. Otherwise, the town's saving grace is its Saturday market, when the streets are packed and the generally staid and conservative Arlesian atmosphere is whipped up a little by blaring Arab music and gypsy dancers.

Les Arènes and Roman Arles

Roman Arles provided grain for most of the Western empire and was one of the major ports for trade and shipbuilding. Under Constantine, it became the capital of Gaul, Britain and Spain. While being on the key road and river routes, however, it found itself, once the empire crumbled, isolated between the Rhône, the Alpilles and the marshlands of the Camargue – an isolation that allowed it to preserve considerable vestiges of an arrogant past. Today, all of the city's Roman remains have been classified by UNESCO as world heritage sites. Most are covered on the general ticket, though parts that you can see for free include the remnants of the **aqueduct** within the medieval ramparts east of the *Arènes*, and of the Roman **bridge** on the other side of the river opposite rue Marius-Jouveau.

The amphitheatre, known as the **Arènes** (summer 9am–7pm; winter 9am–12/12.30 & 2–4.30/6.30pm; 15F) is the most impressive of the Roman monuments. To give an idea of its size, it used to shelter over two hundred dwellings and three churches –

BULLFIGHTING

Bullfighting in Arles and the Camargue is not usually the Spanish-style *mise-à-mort*. Though the bulls probably don't enjoy their appearances very much, it is the bullfighters, or *razeteurs*, who get hurt, not the beast. Bulls are fêted and adored, and before retirement are given a final tour around the arena while people weep and throw flowers.

It's a passion with the populace, who treat the champion *razeteurs* like football stars. The **shows** involve various feats of daring, but the most common form is where the bull has a cockade at the base of its horns and ribbons tied between them. Using blunt razorcombs the *razeteurs* have to cut the ribbons and get the cockades. There's no betting but people add to the prize money as the game progresses. The drama and grace of the spectacle is the stylish way the men leap over the barrier away from the bull. You are much closer to the scene than with other dangerous sports and there are occasional casualties. For some shows involving horsemen arrows are shot at the bull though these don't go in deep enough to make the animal bleed.

All this may leave you feeling cold, or sick, but it's your best way of taking part in local life, and of experiencing the Roman arena in Arles, whatever your feelings are about the parallels with Roman barbarity. The SI, local papers and publicity around the arena will give you the details – be sure to check shows are not *mise-à-mort*.

built into the two tiers of arches that form its oval surround. This medieval *quartier* was cleared in 1830 and the *Arènes* once more used for entertainment. Today, though not the largest Roman amphitheatre in existence, and missing its third storey and most of the internal stairways and galleries, it is a very impressive structure and a stunning venue for performances. It can still seat 20,000 spectators.

The **Théâtre Antique** (summer 9am–7pm; winter 9am–12/12.30 & 2–4.30/6.30pm; 11F) just south of the *Arènes*, comes to life in July during the dance and theatre festival and for the *Fête du Costume*, in which local folk groups parade in traditional dress. A resurrected Roman, however, would be appalled at the state of this entertainment venue, with only one pair of columns standing, all the statuary removed and the sides of the stage littered with broken bits of stone. At the river end of rue Hôtel-de-Ville the **Baths of Constantine** are all that remain of the imperial palace that extended along the waterfront. **Place du Forum** is still the centre of life in Arles and you can see the pillars of an ancient temple embedded in the corner of the *Nord-Pinus* hotel.

The Romans had their **burial ground** southwest of the centre, and it was used by well-to-do Arlesians well into the Middle Ages. Now only one alleyway, foreshortened by a railway line, is preserved. To reach **Les Alyscamps**, follow av des Alyscamps from bd des Lices. Sarcophagi still line the shaded walk, whose tree trunks are azure blue in Van Gogh's rendering. Some have an axe engraved on them which is thought to have played the same function as a notice saying "Burglar alarm fitted". There are numerous tragedy masks, too, though any with special decoration have long since been moved – to serve as municipal gifts, as happened often in the seventeenth century, or to reside in the museums. But there is still magic to this walk, which ends at the ruins of a Romanesque church.

The cathedral, museums and medieval Arles

Arles' central square, **place de la République**, fronts the main **gate** of the **Cathédrale St-Trophime**, one of the most famous examples of twelfth-century Provençal stone carving in existence. It depicts the Last Judgement, trumpeted by angels playing with the enthusiasm of jazz musicians while the damned are led naked in chains down to hell and the blessed, all female and draped in long robes, process upwards.

The cathedral itself was started in the ninth century (during the Carolingian period) on the spot where, in AD 597, Saint Augustine was consecrated as the first bishop of the English. It was largely completed by the twelfth century. A font in the north aisle and an altar illustrating the crossing of the Red Sea in the north transept were both originally Gallo-Roman sarcophagi. The high nave is decorated with d'Aubusson tapestries, in which the one depicting Mary Magdalene bathing Christ's feet has a cat jumping from one oil container to another chased by a dog being ridden by a child. The creamy white vaulted galleries above the cloisters are given over to the **Musée Nécropole** which displays, very beautifully, objects of everyday Roman life as well as coffins and urns.

On the other side of the square, a deconsecrated seventeenth-century church holds the collection of the **Musée Lapidaire Paien** (Pagan Art) (summer 9am–12.30pm & 2–7pm; winter 9am–12/12.30pm & 2–4.30/6pm; 11F). This includes wonderful mosaics of Jupiter carrying off Europa and of Orpheus charming the animals, and a bust of Augustus dated after the Christianisation of the Roman Empire, suggesting that the cult of emperor-worship continued secretly.

To see yet more fallen, chipped and time-eroded stones, take the short cut through the ground floor of the classical **Hôtel de Ville** and turn left into rue Balze. The **Musée Lapidaire Chrétien** (summer 9am–12.30pm & 2–7pm; winter 9am–12/12.30pm & 2–4.30/6pm; 11F) is almost all sarcophagi – once the Romans had been converted they gave up their old and much more practical habit of cremating the dead. From a flight of stairs in the museum you can descend to the **Cryptoporticus**, a huge, dark, dank and wonderfully spooky underground gallery, built by the Romans as a granary.

It sometimes seems that life stopped in Arles after the Middle Ages – if not after the Romans. For a corrective, head for the **Muséon Arlaten** (9am–noon & 2–5/7pm; closed Mon in winter; 11F) on rue de la République. The museum was set up in 1896 by **Frédéric Mistral**, the Nobel Prize-winning novelist who was responsible for the turn-of-the-century revival of interest in all things Provençal, whose statue stands in pl du Forum. In the room dedicated to the poet, a cringing notice instructs you to salute piously the great man's cradle. That apart, the collections of costumes, documents, tools, pictures and paraphernalia of Provençal life is alternately tedious and intriguing. The evolution of Arlesian dress is charted in great detail for all social classes from the eighteenth century to World War I and includes a scene of a dressmaking shop. The museum is not included on the global ticket.

Modern art and Van Gogh

In the **Musée Réattu**, (summer 9am–12.30pm & 2–7pm; winter 10am–12.30pm & 2–5/6/7pm; 15F) opposite the Roman baths, you can finally return to the twentieth century, assuming that you ignore the rigid eighteenth-century classicism of works by the museum's founder and his contemporaries. Of the moderns, Picasso is the best represented with the sculpture *Woman with Violin* and fifty-seven ink and crayon sketches from between December 1970 and February 1971 which he donated to the museum. Amongst the split faces, clowns and hilarious Tarasque, is a beautifully simple portrait of his mother. There are works by contemporary artists – an ever-shifting pattern in ball bearings by Pol Bury, Mario Prassinos' black-and-white studies of the Alpilles, Cesar's *Compression 1973* – and, from time to time, exhibitions of photography on the top floor.

If you walk to the back of the sixteenth-century house occupied by the Réattu museum, you'll see its gargoyles jutting over the river. There are lanterns along the river wall (and wonderful sunsets), though much of the river front and its bars and bistros where workers drank and danced away their woes, were destroyed during the war.

Another casualty of the bombing was the "Yellow House" where **Van Gogh** lived before entering the hospital at St-Rémy. He had arrived by train in February 1888 to be greeted by snow and a bitter Mistral wind. But he started painting straight away, and in the period produced such celebrated canvases as *The Sunflowers, Van Gogh's Chair,* *The Red Vines* and *The Sower.* He used to wander along the river bank wearing candles on his hat, watching the light of night-time. *The Starry Night* is the Rhône at Arles; the *Café Evening* is now a shop on pl du Forum; the *Café de Nuit* has been replaced by a *Monoprix* supermarket across the square from where the "Yellow House" once stood.

Van Gogh was desperate for Gauguin to join him, though at the same time worried about his friend's dominating influence. From the daily letters he wrote to his brother Théo, it was clear that the artist found few kindred souls in Arles. Gauguin did eventually come and moved in with Van Gogh. The events of the night of December 23, when Vincent cut off his ear after rushing after Gauguin brandishing a razor blade, were recorded by the older artist fifteen years later. No one knows the exact provocation. Van Gogh was packed off to the *Hôtel-Dieu* hospital where he had the fortune to be treated by a young and sympathetic doctor, Félix Rey. Van Gogh painted Rey's portrait while in the *Hôtel-Dieu* and the hospital itself, in which the inmates are clearly suffering, not from violent frenzy, but from inexpressible unhappiness.

Food and entertainment

Saturday is the big day of the week in Arles, drawing people from all over the Crau region to the north and the Camargue for the **market** that extends the length of bd Georges-Clemenceau, bd des Lices and bd Émile-Combes and many of the adjoining streets. The atmosphere is festive with all the *brasseries* full of friends having their weekly get-together, and the displays of **local produce**, in particular the cheeses and olives, stunning. A smaller food market takes place every Wednesday.

Restaurants

Rather surprisingly perhaps, Arles has a good number of excellent-quality and cheap **restaurants**. If you're looking for quick meals, there's a wide choice of *brasseries* on the main boulevards.

UNDER 100F

Le Van Gogh, 28 rue Voltaire (☎90.93.69.79). Fish soup, stuffed shoulder of lamb, mussels Provençal style – nothing wildly exciting but very good for the price.

Hostellerie des Arènes, 62 rue du Réfuge (☎90.96.13.05; closed Wed and, except summer, Tues evening). The service may be a bit abrupt but the food is real French family cooking. Worth booking.

Le Tambourin, 65 rue Amédée-Pichot (☎90.93.13.32). Fish and seafood in a pleasant atmosphere.

Le Tourne-Broche, 8 rue Balze (☎90.96.16.03). More upmarket, serving salmon and turbot in various guises, and very good pasta.

Le Criquet, 21 rue Porte-de-Laure (☎90.96.82.08). Not very gastronomic but a very cheap *menu fixe* with wine – worth booking.

OVER 150F

Le Vaccarès, 9 rue Favorin (☎90.96.06.17; closed Sun and Mon). Overlooks pl du Forum and serves both new and old dishes in a light, inventive fashion. The fish fritters and the fillet of *sandre* (similar to perch) *à la poutargue* (pressed in millet roe) are exceptional.

Lou Marques, *Hôtel Jules Cesar*, bd des Lices (☎90.93.43.20; closed Nov and Dec). The top gourmet palace in the top grand hotel. The specialities, which include *baudroie* (monkfish soup) and a saffron-flavoured mousse of *rascasse* (scorpion fish), are all served with the utmost pomposity.

Cafés and nightlife

For **café** life, try pl du Forum, which is very much a meeting place. *Bar Le Paris* here is young, noisy, its waiters greeted by each new arrival with kisses on both cheeks; *Le Gallion* on rue de l'Hôtel-de-Ville is also a good old-fashioned friendly *bar-tabac*.

Alternatively, there are the big café-*brasseries* on bd des Lices from which to watch the world go by.

The few cabaret venues are distinctly upscale and exclusive. The city's main disco, *Le Plantation*, on the N570 just outside Arles (☎90.97.11.26), is open Friday and Saturday from 11pm with shows on Fridays.

Listings

Car hire All on bd Victor-Hugo: *Europcar* (☎90.93.23.24); *Avis* (☎90.96.82.42); *Hertz* (☎90.96.75.23).

Car parking *Parking du Jardin d'Hiver*, off bd des Lices and rue Émile-Fassin.

Car repairs The SI can provide a list of concessionaires for most makes of car. Breakdown services: *Rapid'Remorquage*, Balarin (☎90.98.01.82), *Arles Dépannage*, route Caseneuve, quai Gimeaux (☎90.96.08.15).

Change At the SI, bd des Lices (summer 9am–7.30/8pm & Sun 9am–1pm; winter 9am–6pm).

Emergencies Hospital; *Centre Hospitalier J-Imbert*, quartier Fourchon (☎90.49.29.29); ambulance ☎90.96.84.72/☎90.96.87.50/☎90.96.04.27; night chemist, phone police on ☎90.96.02.04 for address.

Launderette *Washmatic*, rue Jouvène.

PTT 5 bd des Lices, 13200 Arles.

Swimming pool *Stade Municipal* off av Maréchal-Foch.

Taxis ☎90.96.90.03; ☎90.96 09.00; ☎90.96.07.94.

Travel agency *Havas Voyages*, 12 bd des Lices (☎90.96.54.40).

The Camargue

The Camargue is one of those geographically enclosed areas that are separate, and unique, in every sense. Its ever-shifting boundaries, the **Petit Rhône**, the **Grand Rhône** and **the sea**, are invisible until you come upon them; its horizons infinite because land, lagoon and sea share the same horizontal plain. And both wild and human life have traits peculiar to this drained and ditched and now protected delta land.

The region is home to the **bulls** and the **white horses** that the Camargue *gardiens* or herdsmen ride. Neither beast is truly wild though both run in semi-liberty. In recent times new strains of bull have been introduced because numbers were getting perilously low. The Camargue horse remains a distinct breed, of origin unknown, that is born dark brown or black, and turns white around its fourth year. It is never stabled, surviving the humid heat of summer and the wind-racked winter cold outdoors. The **gardiens** likewise are a hardy community. Their traditional homes, or *cabanes*, are thatched and windowless one-storey structures, with bulls' horns over the door to ward off evil spirits. They still conform, to some extent, to the popular cowboy myth, and play a major role in guarding Carmarguais traditions. Throughout the summer, with spectacles involving bulls and horses in every village arena, they're kept busy and the work carries local glamour. Winter is a good deal harder, and fewer and fewer Carmarguais property owners can afford the extravagant use of land that bull-rearing requires.

The two towns of the Camargue, LES-STES-MARIES-DE-LA-MER and SALIN-DE-GIRAUD, are as distant and as different as they could possibly be. Such villages as there are hardly qualify to be more than hamlets. The rest of the habitations are farmhouses or *mas*, set well back from the handful of roads, and out of easy walking distance from their neighbours.

For a good general introduction to the area, the **Musée Carmarguais** (daily 9am–5/6/7pm; Oct–March closed Tues; 20F), on the way to STES-MARIES from Arles, halfway between GIMEAUX and ALBARON, documents the traditions and livelihoods of the Camarguais people using self-consciously modern museum techniques.

Practicalities in the Camargue

If you're planning on **staying in the Camargue** rather than using Arles as a base for day trips, there are certain factors to bear in mind. One is an aspect of the wildlife that can be so brutal as to totally destroy a holiday: if you have the sort of skin that attracts **mosquitoes**, then the months from March through to November could be unbearable. Staying right beside the sea will be okay, but otherwise you'll need serious chemical weaponry. It has been known for campers to be so ferociously bitten that they needed hospital treatment. Biting flies are also prevalent and can take away much of the pleasure of this hill-less land for **bicycling**. The other problem is the winds, which in autumn and winter can be strong enough to knock you off your bike (though fortunately you won't have to cope simultaneously with biting insects and high winds). Conversely, in summer the weather can be so hot and humid that the slightest movement is an effort. There's really no ideal time for visiting the area.

Transport

Infrequent buses run between Arles and STES-MARIES and between Arles and SALIN: there's no direct service between the two. Cycling may be your only option. At Stes-Maries you can **hire bikes** at *Camargue Vélos*, 27 av Frédéric-Mistral (☎90.97.94.55), and at *Les Vélocistes*, pl des Remparts (☎90.97.83.26) – the latter also have *vespa* scooters. The SI, on the waterfront at 5 av Van-Gogh, can provide more addresses if these are both booked out. The other means of transport to consider is **riding**. There are around thirty farms that hire out horses, by the hour, half day or whole day. The SI again have a complete list.

For transport as an end in itself, there's the **paddle steamer** *Le Tiki III* which leaves from the mouth of the Petit Rhône (off the route d'Aigues-Mortes 2.5km west of Stes-Maries; ☎90.97.81.68) and operates trips up-river from mid-March to mid-November. Captain Gilbert Valette of Le Braco, 29 rue Frédéric-Mistral (☎90.97.81.86), organises fishing expeditions and boat trips along the Petit Rhone.

For **drivers and cyclists** the main thing to be wary of is taking your car or bike along the dykes. Maps and road signs show which routes are closed to vehicles and which are accessible only at low tide, but they don't warn you about the surface you'll be driving along. The other problem is **theft** from cars. There are well-organised gangs of thieves with a particular penchant, as locals will testify, for British licence plates.

Accommodation

From April to October **rooms** in Stes-Maries should be booked in advance, and for the gypsy festival, several months before. Prices go up considerably during the summer and at any time of the year are more expensive than at Arles. There are some cheap rooms in Salin, and hotels of all prices scattered about the area. A number of outlying *mas* (farmhouses) rent out rooms, and if you have some form of transport, they can be idyllic locations from which to tour the region.

OUTLYING ACCOMMODATION AROUND THE CAMARGUE

Auberge de Jeunesse Pioch-Badet, on the Arles–Stes-Maries bus route, 10km north of Stes-Maries on the Arles road in the hamlet of Pioch-Badet (☎90.97.91.72).

Le Sauvageon, Petite route du Bac – the road linking the D38 and D570 (☎90.97.89.43). Pretty little auberge in its own garden. ④.

Le Flamant Rose, at Albaron between Arles and Stes-Maries (☎90.97.10.18; closed March). *Logis de France* hotel-restaurant with some bargain rooms. ②/③.

Hostellerie du Pont de Gau, route d'Arles, Pont de Gau (☎90.47.81.53; closed Jan–mid-Feb). Old-fashioned Camarguais decor, middle-priced. ④.

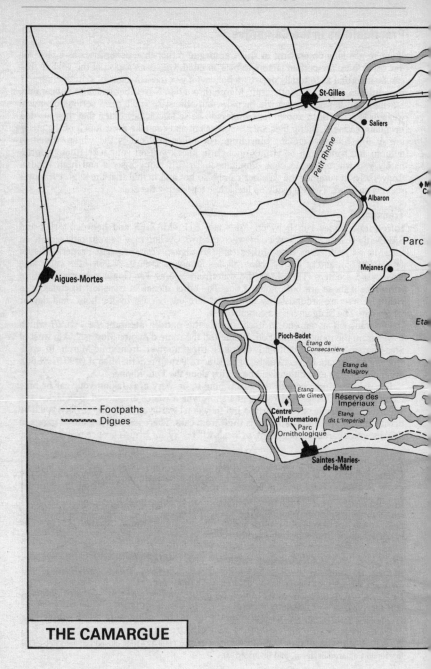

St-Gilles

Saliers

Petit Rhône

Albaron

Parc

Mejanes

Aigues-Mortes

Pioch-Badet

Etang de
Consecanière

Etang de
Malagroy

Etang
de Gines

Réserve des
Imperiaux

Etang
dit L'Impérial

Centre
d'Information
Parc
Ornithologique

Saintes-Maries-
de-la-Mer

- - - - - - Footpaths
vvvvvvvvvvvv Digues

THE CAMARGUE

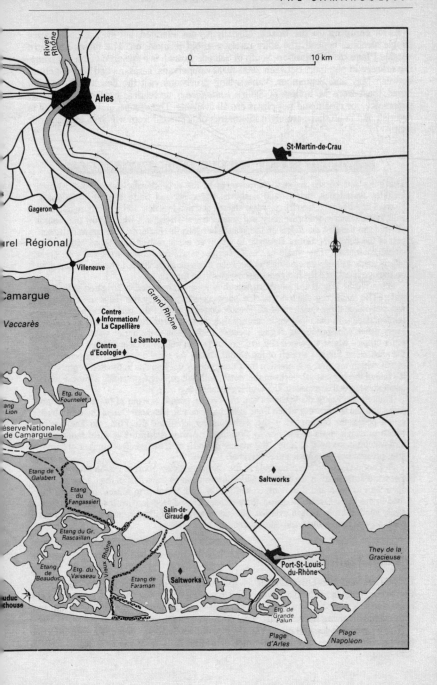

As for **camping on the beach**, officially it's not tolerated, but even at Stes-Maries people sleeping beneath the stars rarely get told to move on. The fifteen-kilometre seaside **Plage de Piemanson**, south of Salin-de-Giraud, is a favoured venue for *camping sauvage* in summer. Between 2000–3000 campervans, caravans and tents pitch up between May and September. Vans selling provisions visit the beach daily – milk, bread (best from M Robert of Salin's *boulangerie*), groceries, fresh fruit and veg, papers, ice, ice cream and hot pizzas are all available. The eastern end of the beach is naturist, and in all there are eight kilometres of firm sand from which to choose your spot.

WILDLIFE, ECOLOGY AND NATURE WATCHING

The bulls and horses are just one element in the exceptionally rich **wildlife**, which includes flamingoes, marsh- and seabirds, waterfowl and birds of prey; wild boars, beavers and badgers; tree frogs, water snakes and pond turtles; and a rich flora of reeds, wild irises, tamaris, wild rosemary and juniper trees. These last, which grow to a height of 6m, form the *Bois des Rièges* on the islands between the *Etang du Vaccarès* and the sea, part of the central **National Reserve** to which access is restricted to those with professional credentials. The whole of the Camargue is a *Parc Naturel Regional* with great efforts made to keep an equilibrium between tourism, agriculture, industry and hunting on the one hand, and the indigenous ecosystems on the other.

After World War II the northern marshes were drained and re-irrigated with fresh water. The main crop planted was rice, so successfully that by the 1960s the Camargue was providing three-quarters of all French consumption of the grain. Vines were also reintroduced – in the nineteenth century they had survived the disease that devastated every other wine-producing region because their stems were under water. There are other crops – wheat, rapeseed and fruit orchards – as well as trees in isolated clumps. To the east, along the last stretch of the Grand Rhône, the chief business is the production of salt, which was first organised in the Camargue by the Romans in the first century AD. It's one of the biggest saltworks in the world, with salt pans and pyramids adding a somehow extra-terrestrial aspect to the Camargue landscape.

Though the Etang du Vaccarès and the central islands are out of bounds, there are paths and sea dykes from which their inhabitants can be watched. One of the best observation points for flamingoes is the path running alongside the Etang du Fangassier, which provides views of the nearby **flamingo nesting ground**. The ideal months for bird-watching are April to June – the mating period – with the greatest number of flamingoes present between April and September.

At Pont de Gau, on the other side of the Camargue, 4km short of Les-Stes-Maries, the **Centre d'Information du Parc** provides information on the whole of the Camargue. It's open 9am to noon and 2 to 6pm; closed Friday from October to March. Just down the road is the **Parc Ornithologique** (8am–sunset; closed Dec–Jan) with some of the less easily spotted birds kept in aviaries, plus trails across a thirty-acre marsh and a longer walk, all with ample signs and information.

Les Stes-Maries-de-la-Mer

LES-STES-MARIES-DE-LA-MER is the town that most people head for in the Camargue, famous as the place where the gypsies gather, every May 24 and 25, to celebrate and ask favours from their patron saint Sarah. The rest of the year is full, too, with events involving horses, bulls, local costume and music.

The **SI** which is located on av Van-Gogh will happily weigh you down with information detailing all these events (summer 9am–1pm & 3–7pm; winter 9.30am–noon & 2.30–6pm).

The town

Stes-Maries is an extremely pretty, if excessively commercialised, town. Its streets of white houses and the grey-gold Romanesque church with its strange outline of battlements and watchtower, have been turned into a one long picture-postcard pose. But apart from peace and quiet you're not going to want for anything. There are miles of **beaches**; a new pleasure port with **boat trips** to the lagoons; **horses** – or **bikes** – to ride; **watersports**; and the **arènes** for bullfights, cavalcades and other entertainment (events are posted on a board outside).

The hundreds of restaurants and bars with informal flamenco-guitarists playing on the terraces, the summer evening buskers in the old town with a crazy variety of instruments, and the carnival atmosphere of **place des Gitans** during each particular festivity, can make Stes-Maries much more fun than any of the larger cities to the north.

As for sights, the fortified **church** of Saintes-Maries allows a look at Sarah's tinselled and sequined statue. It's at the back of the crypt on the right, and always surrounded by candles and abandoned crutches and calipers. The church itself has beautifully pure lines and fabulous acoustics. During the time of the Saracen raids it was where all the villagers took shelter – there is even a fresh water well within it. Between April and mid-November the church tower is open, affording the best view possible over the Camargue.

On rue Victor-Hugo, the local museum, **Musée Baroncelli** (9am–noon & 2–5/6pm; closed Wed and Oct), is named after the man who, in 1935, was responsible, along with various *gardiens*, for initiating the gypsies' procession down to the sea with Sarah. This was motivated by a desire to give a special place in the pilgrimage to the Romanies. The museum covers this event, other Carmarguais traditions and the region's fauna and flora.

Accommodation

As stressed previously, rooms in Stes-Maries need to be booked well in advance at all times of the year, otherwise you may as well stay in Arles or try to find a room elsewhere in the region.

HOTELS

Le Mediterranée, 4 rue Frédéric-Mistral (☎90.97.82.09; March–Nov). Centrally located, wtih some of the cheapest rooms in town. ②.

Le Dauphin Bleu, 31 av G-Leroy (☎90.97.80.21). Overlooking the sea, with a moderately-priced restaurant. ③.

Les Vagues, 12 av T-Aubunal (☎90.97.84.40) Another low-priced option on the road leading out of town towards Aigues-Mortes. ③.

Camille, 13 av de la Plage (☎90.97.80.26; open all year). With a sea view. ④.

Chez Kiki, 13 route de Cacharel (☎90.97.83.27; March–Oct). Nothing very special but serviceable and not expensive. ④.

CAMPSITES

Buses from Arles all visit the *Brises* campsite, and some also run via *Clos du Rhône*. Check with the *Cartreize* booking office.

La Brise, on the Cacharel road just outside the village (☎90.47.84.67). 3* and open all year.

Le Clos du Rhône, at the mouth of the Petit Rhône (☎90.97.85.99). Mid-June to mid-Sept.

Food

The specialities of the Camargue include *tellines*, tiny shiny shellfish served with garlic mayonnaise; *boeuf gardien*, bull's meat; eels from the Vaccarès, rice, asparagus and wild duck from the district, and *poutargue des Stes-Maries*, a mullet roe dish. As you might expect, few of the **restaurants** in Stes-Maries are bargains, though there are any number to choose from, and out of season the quality improves, and the prices come down. The town **market** takes place on pl des Gitans every Monday and Friday.

Le Napoli, 30 rue Victor-Hugo. Simple and satisfying meals from about 100F.

Les Montilles, 9 rue du Capitaine-Fouque. Sometimes has delicious duck mousse on a cheap menu.

Le Brûleur de Loups, av Gilbert-Leroy (closed Tues and Wed). Worth checking out if you're prepared to spend a little more.

THE LEGEND OF SARAH – AND THE GYPSY FESTIVALS

Sarah was the servant of Mary Jacobé, Jesus' aunt, and Mary Salomé, mother of two of the apostles, who, along with Mary Magdalene and various other New Testament characters, were driven out of Palestine by the Jews and put on a boat without sails and oars – or so the story goes.

The boat subsequently drifted effortlessly to the island in the mouth of the Rhône where the Egyptian god Ra was worshipped. Here Mary Jacobé, Mary Salomé and Sarah, who was herself Egyptian, settled to carry out conversion work while the others headed off for other parts of Provence. In 1448 their relics were "discovered" in the fortress church of Stes-Maries on the erstwhile island, around the time that the Romanies were migrating into Western Europe from the Balkans and from Spain. It's thought the two strands may have been reunited in Provence.

Whatever the explanation, the gypsies have been making their **pilgrimage** to Stes-Maries since at least the sixteenth century. It's a time for weddings and baptisms as well as music, dancing and fervent religion. On May 24, after mass, the shrines of the saints are lowered from the high chapel to an altar where the faithful stretch out their arms to touch them. Then the statue of Black Sarah is carried by the gypsies to the sea. On the following day the statues of Mary Jacobé and Mary Salomé, sitting in a wooden boat, follow the same route, accompanied by the mounted *gardiens* in full Camargue cowboy dress, Arlesians in traditional costume, and all and sundry present. The sea, the Camargue, the pilgrims and the gypsies are blessed by the bishop from a fishing boat, before the procession returns to the church with much bell ringing, guitar playing, tambourines and singing. Another ceremony in the afternoon sees the shrines lifted back up to their chapel.

In recent years the authorities have thought the event was getting out of hand and there's now a heavy police presence and the all-night candlelit vigil in the church has been banned. There is a certain amount of hostility between some townspeople and the *gitans* though the municipality has actively countered the racism. It's a wonderful event to be part of, though inevitably finding accommodation in the town is impossible. Another pilgrimage takes place on the Sunday closest to October 22, dedicated solely to Mary Jacobé and Mary Salomé and without the participation of the gypsies.

Salin-de-Giraud

In almost total contrast to Stes-Maries, **SALIN-DE-GIRAUD** is a workers' town, and built as such on a strict grid pattern during the Second Empire. The saltworks company and its related chemical factory dominate the town, which is fiercely Communist. The *bête noir* of its existence is that Salin is not big enough to be its own municipality: they would then have all sorts of public amenities, among which a swimming pool would be top of the list. As it is, the town belongs to right-wing Arles, which sees no electoral advantage in lavishing beneficence on this socialist blackspot. You'll see graffiti declaring *"Salin Commune Libre!"* as well as posters for the *PCF*. The locals are aware of the unique qualities of the region, and they fear plans to replace Salin's ferry boat, *the bac de Bacarin*, with a bridge – which would link Marseille with southwest France and destroy the Camargue forever.

The centre of life in Salin is a huge **bar,** the *Bar des Sports* – next to the *Saladelles* hotel – where *belote* (a card game) championships are held and where the local fan club for Marseille's football team is based. Original paintings by local artists are on the walls, there's a model ship crystallised in salt, pinball, bar football and arcade games, and a clientele that for once is not (as other local bars) exclusively male.

Salin can be an economic place to stay, but it's a good idea to book in advance. There're a couple of modest **hotels:** *Les Saladelles* (☎42.86.83.87; ②) and, rather better, *La Camargue*, 58 bd de la Camargue (☎42.86.82.82; closed mid-Nov–mid-Jan; ③). The cheapest place to stay in summer however is the **Plage de Piemanson** on the seashore to the south (see "Accomodation" under "Practicalities in the Camargue", above. There are three buses daily from Salin to the beach.

Buses to Arles leave from the *Café Station-Bar*.

Salt piles and Port-St-Louis

If you want to take a look at the lunar landscape of the **salt piles**, there's a viewing point with information panels less than 2km south of Salin off the D36 that runs parallel to the Grand Rhône. The Salin saltworks are the world's highest-capacity salt-harvesting site, covering an area of 11,000 hectares, and producing a total of 800,000 tonnes a year for domestic use and export. Across the river and downstream you can see PORT-ST-LOUIS, where the rice and salt of the Camargue are loaded onto ships, and where also, surprisingly, a small fishing fleet still operates.

Eastwards: from Avignon to Apt

From Avignon the roads to the Côte d'Azur and southern Provence head off southeast past CAVAILLON, a major fruit and veg town (Monday market day) distinguished only by its production of *Charentais* melons (in season May–Sept, with a melon festival on Ascension Day). Another 24km along the road is SALON-DE-PROVENCE, training ground for the French Air Force pilots who disturb the air for miles around, and a place to avoid at all costs.

Along the Sorgue and on to the Lubéron

Trains and some buses from Avignon to the Côte, veer east to **L'ÎSLE-SUR-LA-SORGUE**. The same stream that runs alongside rue des Teinturiers in Avignon – the River Sorgue – here splits into five branches which meander their way through this strangely mournful town, turning huge moss-green water-wheels that once powered the town's silk industry. A quick stroll through town should suffice, but if it grabs your interest, you shouldn't have much problem finding a room here (the **SI** is beside the west door of the town's main church); try *Le Vieux Îsle*, 15 rue Danton (☎90.38.00.46; ②). Alternatively, there's a beautiful 3* **campsite** (☎90.38.05.71; March 15–Oct) near the *Pescador* hotel (☎90.38.09.69; ③), at Le Partage-des-Eaux (The Parting of the Waters), 1.5km upstream from the junction of av Général-de-Gaulle and cours Salviati.

The **source of the Sorgue** – one of the most powerful natural springs in the world – is a short bus ride east at **FONTAINE-DE-VAUCLUSE**. At the top of the gorge above the village is a mysterious tapering fissure deeper than the sheer 230-metre cliffs that barricade its opening. This is where the waters of the Sorgue appear, sometimes in spectacular fashion, bursting down the gorge (in March and April normally), other times seeping stealthily through subterranean channels to meet the riverbed further down. Tourists are attracted to Fontaine by the million, with inevitable results. If you're intrigued by the source, and speak French, visit the **Norbert-Casteret Musée de Spéléologie** (10am–noon & 2–6.30pm; closed Mon & Tues Feb–May & Sept–Oct;

closed Nov–Jan) in the underground commercial centre barring the path to the source. At the upper end of the centre you'll find a re-creation of the medieval method of pulping rags to paper – using river power – with a vast array of printed matter on the product for sale. The cheapest and most beautifully situated hotel in Fontaine is the *Hostellerie Le-Château* (☎90.20.31.54; ③), but like everything else it's likely to be booked solid in summer. There's also an IYHF **youth hostel** on chemin de la Vignasse, 1km south on the road to Lagnes (☎90.20.31.65; closed Dec–Jan), and a **campsite** (☎90.20.32.38; open all year), 500m downstream from the village.

Gordes, Roussillon and other villages

Still further east and accessible only by bus from Cavaillon, **GORDES** is *the* picturesque Provençal village par excellence, a favourite spot for the country residences of Parisian media personalities, film directors, establishment artists and the like: reasons enough, perhaps, to skip the place entirely were it not for its castle stronghold. This houses a **Didactic Museum** (10am–noon & 2–6pm; closed Tues except July–Aug; 20F), founded in 1970 by the Hungarian artist that establishment critics deride as the inventor of "op-art", **Victor Vasarely**. The upper floor charts the complex evolution of Vasarely's creative development. It's fascinating to see the training he gave himself in every aspect of visual experience. On the first floor are gorgeous tapestries of cubes turning into spheres and colours chasing their way through squares, circles and diamonds.

Four kilometres north of Gordes, amidst fields of lavender in a hollow of the hills, stands the twelfth-century Cistercian **Abbaye de Sénanque** (Mon–Sat 10am–noon & 2–6pm, Sun 2–6pm; 20F). A community of monks has very recently made a return, after a twenty-year break, to re-establish its former use. It is still open to the public, however, and plays host to various religious exhibitions.

The other stone construction of note in the vicinity of Gordes (3.5km east, off the D2 to Cavaillon) is the **Village des Bories** – strange dry-stone dwellings inhabited, despite their prehistoric appearance, from the Middle Ages right up to the nineteenth century (9am–sunset; 15F).

The best and most surreal detour in the vicinity is to the old **ochre mines** between Gordes and Apt (best approached by bus from Apt). The village of **ROUSSILLON** radiates all the different shades of the seventeen ochre tints once quarried here. There are other quarries, too, in the neighbouring village of GARGAS and, more dramatically, near RUSTREL known as the **Rustrel Colorado**. Difficult to get to – and hence not so inundated with coach parties – Rustrel's cream-, coffee- and vanilla-coloured sands rival Vasarely's works for colour sensation.

If you're looking for somewhere to **stay**, forget Gordes. Instead, try the *Résidence les Ocres* (☎90.05.60.50; ④) in Roussillon, or the *Arc-en-Ciel* campsite (☎90.75.67.17; March 15–Oct) among pine trees on an ochre floor, 2km along the D104 to Goult.

Apt and the Lubéron

After its descent from the Alps, the Durance river makes a wide southern curve before joining the Rhône, skirting the massive rock-fold known as the **Lubéron** that runs for 50km between Cavaillon and Manosque. Despite its isolated position, the Lubéron is becoming increasingly popular with British tourists, mainly due to the unprecedented popularity of Peter Mayle's books, set in and around the village of Ménerbes. Don't be put off though, it's still got a long way to go compared with Gordes and co. (and the Mayles, having succeeded in irritating the local community, have now departed). The Lubéron's northern face is damper, more alpine in character, extremely cold in winter, and dotted with tiny villages which cling stubbornly to the foothills. The southern slopes, by contrast, are Mediterranean in scent and feel. It's almost all wooded, except for the summer sheep pastures at the top, and the there's just one main route across it, through the Combe de Lourmarin.

Apt and the Parc Naturel Régional du Lubéron

The best town base for exploring the Lubéron is **APT**, though in itself it's not much of a town for sightseeing, nor is it renowned for the charm and friendliness of its people. Its large **confectionary factory** spews mucky froth into a concrete-channelled Coulon river and as late as early spring, when mimosa is blossoming down on the coast, the temperature around Apt can drop to well below freezing. It cheers up, however, every Saturday for the weekly **market** when cars are barred from the town centre to allow artisans and cultivators from all the surrounding countryside to set up stalls. As well as featuring every imaginable Provençal edible, the market is accompanied by barrel organ, jazz musicians, stand-up comics, aged hippies and assorted freaks.

Practicalities in Apt

Arriving by bus – Apt's gare SNCF is freight only – you're most likely to be dropped at place de la Bouquerie, the main square lined with cafés and restaurants. The **SI** is at 2 av Philippe-de-Girard just up to your left as you face the river. There's a good choice of **accommodation** in Apt, unlike the more scenic hilltop villages where all rooms are reserved months before the summer season. At the opposite end of the town from pl de la Bouquerie is the hotel *Aptois*, 6–8 cours Lauze de Perret (☎90.74.02.02; ②/④) with some cheap rooms. A *Logis de France* establishment, *Le Ventoux*, 67 av Victor-Hugo (☎90.74.07.58; ③), is flanked by petrol stations, but pleasant once you're inside and with probably the best-value restaurant in town. The cheapest rooms in Apt are bang in the centre at *Le Palais*, 12 pl Gabriel-Péri (☎90.74.23.54; ②), above a rather uninspired pizzeria.

Campers, for once, are treated to a municipal ground within easy walking distance of the town – *Les Cèdres*, on av de Viton (☎90.74.14.61; open all year), northeast of the town centre. Two **gîtes d'étapes**, an easy bike ride from Apt, are the *Bardons* at Castellet to the southeast (☎90.75.20.87) and the *Relais de Roquefure* (☎90.74.22.80) off RN100 in the Avignon direction – very close to the triple-arched Roman bridge dating from the days when Apt was *Apta Julia*. But be warned: most of the local buses are once-daily services.

If you haven't stuffed yourself with chocolates and candied fruit (Apt's speciality), you can **eat** a cheap and extremely edible four-course **meal** at *Le Brémondy* on pl St-Pierre. *La Calèche*, 4 rue Cély, is similarly priced but not quite as *sympa*. Pricey Argentinian specialities and much cheaper pizzas are available at 12 quai Général-Leclerc, with live music weekend nights. Apt's weekend **jazz** venue is *La Tour de l'Ho*, a *crêperie* on bd National.

Lubéron park practicalities

The **Parc Regional du Lubéron** is administered by the *Maison du Parc*, 1 pl Jean-Jaurès in Apt (☎90.74.08.55; Mon–Sat 8.30am–noon & 2–7pm), which houses a small fossil museum designed for kids, and is the place to go for information about every aspect of the Lubéron: the fauna and flora; footpaths; cycle routes; pony-treking; and *gîtes* and campsites.

Given the region's general dearth of public transport, the only practical, and pleasurable, way to explore is by hiking or cycling. Two **bike hire** places are *D. Devoncoux*, 17 quai Général-Leclerc, and *Garage Maretto*, a few doors down. There are special **cycle paths**, courtesy of the *parc*, from Apt to Cavaillon (40km), from Apt to La Bégude (12km) and on to Volx, all signposted in brown.

The Abbaye de Silvacane

If you're heading for Aix-en-Provence from Apt, you'll pass close to another ancient Cistercian abbey contemporary with Sénanque – the **Abbaye de Silvacane**, some 25km south of Apt. On the banks of the Durance and, again, isolated from its surrounding villages, its architecture has hardly changed at all over the last 700 years. The stark pale-stoned splendour of the church, its cloisters and surrounding buildings can be visited 10am to noon and from 2 to 5 or 6pm every day except Tuesday and holidays.

Aix-en-Provence

AIX-EN-PROVENCE is the dominanat city of central Provence – or would be were it not for the great metropolis of Marseille just 25km away on the coast. Historically, culturally and socially, however, they are moons apart. Unlike Marseille, which has all the rough clamour you'd expect from a great port, Aix is complacently conservative, its riches based on land owning and the liberal professions.

Aix was the capital of Provence from the twelfth century until the Revolution. In its days as an independent fiefdom, its most mythically beloved ruler, King Réné of Anjou, held a brilliant court renowned for its popular festivities and patronage of the arts. Réné introduced the muscat grape to the region, and today he stands in stone in picture-book medieval fashion, a bunch of grapes in his left hand, looking down the majestic seventeenth-century replacement to the old southern fortifications, the cours Mirabeau.

Arriving and accommodation

Cours Mirabeau is the main thoroughfare of the town, with the multi-fountained pl Général-de-Gaulle, or *La Rotonde*, at its west end, the main point of arrival. The **gare SNCF** is on av Victor-Hugo, the avenue leading south from the *place* (bus #6, #9, or minibus #1 or #2, to *Rotonde/Jeanne-d'Arc* or *Office de Tourisme*, but easily walkable); the **gare routière** is between the two western avenues, av des Belges and av Bonaparte, on rue Lapierre (minibus #1 or #2 to *Rotonde/Jeanne-d'Arc*; again not very far). The **SI** (daily 9am–10pm) is at 2 pl Général-de-Gaulle between av des Belges and av Victor-Hugo. The principal **post office** is also close by at 2 rue Lapierre.

Accommodation

From mid-July to mid-August (festival time) your chances of getting an unbooked **hotel room** are pretty slim: you need to reserve a couple of months in advance at least. Rents and rates in central Aix are very high and reflected in the prices of hotels, shops and restaurants.

HOTELS

Hôtel Paul, 10 av Pasteur (☎42.23.23.89), and next door, **Hôtel le Pasteur**, 14 av Pasteur (☎42.21.11.76). Though both hotels are outside the boulevard ring, they're within easy reach and comfortable. *Le Pasteur* has its own restaurant. ②/③.

Hôtel Casino, 38 rue Victor-Leydet (☎42.26.06.88). Has a few rooms that are the cheapest to be found in the centre of Aix. ③.

Hôtel des Arts-Sully, 69 bd Carnot (☎42.33.11.77). A bit noisy but very welcoming. You can't book so turn up early. ④.

Hôtel des Quatre Dauphins, 54 rue Roux-Alphéran (☎42.38.16.39). Old-world charm and compulsory breakfast in the Mazarin *quartier*. ⑤ at least.

YOUTH HOSTELS

Auberge de Jeunesse, 3 av Marcel-Pagnol (☎42.20.15.99; bus #8 or #12, direction *Jas de Bouffan*, stop *Vasarely*; reception 7.30–10am & 5.30–10pm; closed Dec 20–Feb 1; no cooking facilities; restaurant April–Oct). Though the building and its position can't be faulted, the forms and regulations are over the top – you can't use your own sleeping bag and you must be an IYHF member. If you're in a group of two or more you'd be better off in a hotel.

CROUS, Cité Universitaire des Gazelles, 38 av Jules-Ferry (☎42.26.33.75; bus #5, direction *Gambetta*, stop *Pierre-Puget*). This student organisation can sometimes find rooms on campus during July and August.

CAMPSITES

Arc-en-Ciel, Pont des Trois Sautets, route de Nice (☎42.26.14.28; bus #3; open all year). 3km southeast of town and like the other Aix campsites not particularly cheap.

Le Félibrige, 5km along the N7 to Puyricard at La Calade (☎42.92.12.11; April–Sept; Puyricard bus from cours Sextius) – a hassle to get to, though you can **hire bikes** once you're there.

The city

As a preliminary introduction to *Aixois* life and life forms, a café-stopping stroll beneath the gigantic plane trees that shade the **cours Mirabeau** is mandatory. The north side is one long line of cafés; the south side banks and offices, all lodging in seventeenth- to eighteenth-century mansions of a uniform hue of weathered stone, with ornate wrought- iron balconies and Baroque decorations. Of the cafés, *Les Deux Garçons* is the intellectuals' haunt, done up in the faded style of the old Orient Express. The other cafés have a shifting hierarchy of snob value, and all are pricey, though very tempting. The youth of Aix are immaculately dressed as if they'd just walked out of a Benetton ad. Immediately striking is the number of Americans, speaking fluent French and acting as if this were home. As indeed it is, for thousands of them, studying at the university.

Vieil Aix: markets and monuments

To explore the heart of Aix, wander north from cours Mirabeau and then anywhere within the ring of cours and boulevards. The layout of **Vieil Aix** is not designed to assist your sense of direction – but what matter when every street is busy with people, bars and shops; the architectural backdrop is of treats from the sixteenth and seventeenth centuries; and every 50m or so, you reach a fountained *place* in which to rest.

Bang in the middle, on **place Richelme**, you'll find a daily morning **market** of fruit and vegetable exotica. The markets of Aix are said to be the best in Provence, and there are plenty of them. Every Tuesday, Thursday and Saturday morning, place des Prêcheurs, and place Richelme become a vast open-air market selling every edible from the region, with fish stalls spreading down rue des Marseillais and flowers filling place de l'Hôtel-de-Ville. **Place de Verdun** has a flea market with bric-à-brac and everything from rabbit hats to plastic earrings, while rues Peyresc, Rifle-Rafle, Bouteilles, Chaudronniers and Monclar – the streets which surround the neo-Classical **Palais de Justice** – sell nothing but clothes.

To turn to the things you can't buy, the **Église de la Madeleine** on pl des Prêcheurs has for decoration paintings by Van Loo, born in Aix in 1684, and Rubens, and a three-panel medieval *Annunciation* in which Gabriel's wings are owl feathers and a monkey is positioned so its head is just below the deity's ray of light. The **Hôtel de Ville**, just north of pl Richelme, displays perfect classical proportions and embroidery in wrought iron above the door. Alongside stands a **clock tower** which you can use to tell the season as well as the time. On the south side of the square, a delicate though fairly massive foot hangs over the architrave of the old corn exchange, now the **post office**. It belongs to the goddess Cybele dallying with the masculine River Rhône.

Rue Gaston-de-Saporta takes you up from pl Hôtel-de-Ville to the **Cathédrale St-Sauveur**, a conglomerate of fifteenth- to sixteenth-century building works, full of medieval art treasures. The best of these is a triptych commissioned by King Réné in 1475, *Le Buisson Ardent*. The two side panels showing the king and his second wife are usually closed over the main picture. A notice in the south nave gives the times (daily except Tues & Sun) when the sacristan will open the picture and talk about it, at length – and very interestingly if you can follow his enthusiastic monologue. If you can't, the essence is this: Mary and babe sit in the burning bush with castles, possibly Tarascon and Avignon, in the receding distance, and Moses surprised by an angel in the fore-ground. Every detail from the Virgin's mirror and the angel's medallion, to the dog's collar and the snail right at the bottom is steeped in theological significance. While you're still hunting for the snail the sacristan will close the painting up again and unlock the panels covering the west doors.

The museums

Just down from the cathedral, through place des Martyrs-de-la-Résistance, is the former **Bishop's Palace**, the setting, each July, for part of the grandiose **music festival**, and housing the **Musée des Tapisseries** (10am–noon & 3–6pm; closed Tues; 20F). The tapestries are superb and not the standard château type, hung to stop the draught. There's also a contemporary section with annual exhibitions, for which the definition of tapestry is broadened to include textiles made of rope, raffia or feathers.

The **Musée du Vieil Aix** at 17 rue Gaston-de-Saporta (10am–noon & 2.30–6/2–5pm; closed Mon; 10F) is worth a look while you're in this part of town. It has a set of religious marionettes, and a huge collection of *santons* (Provençal crib figures) but you won't be losing out that much if you miss it.

Quartier Mazarin and Paul Cézanne

Aix's other central museums are all in the **quartier Mazarin**, south of cours Mirabeau. On pl St-Jean-de-Malte the most substantial of the lot, the **Musée Granet** (10am–noon & 2–6pm; closed Tues; 12F/7F) exhibits the finds from the site of the original settle-ment of Aix, the *Oppidum d'Entremont*, 3km north of the city. Also in the basement, are the remains of the Romans who routed this Celtic-Ligurian township in 90 BC and established their city of *Aquae Sextiae* – which evolved into Aix – around the thermal springs they found in the vicinity and around which there is still a spa.

Upstairs is a very mixed bag of **paintings**: Italian, Dutch, French, mostly seven-teenth- to nineteenth-century, appallingly badly hung and lit. The portraits of Diane de Poiters by Jean Capassin and Marie Mancini by Nicolas Mignard are an interesting contrast, and there is also a self-portrait by Rembrandt. But the rows upon rows of eighteenth- and early nineteenth-century French paintings, including the massive *Jupiter and Thetis* by Ingres, make it only too clear why the country needed its revolu-tions. You do finally reach one wall dedicated to the most famous Aixois painter, **Paul Cézanne,** who studied on the ground floor of the building, at that time the art school. Two of his student drawings are here as well as a handful of minor canvases such as *Bethsabée, Les Baigneuses* and *Portrait de Madame*. If you just want to see the Cézannes, they're to the right at the top of the stairs.

One of Cézanne's many studios in Aix is at what is now 9 av Paul-Cézanne, overlook-ing the city from the north. The **Atélier Cézanne** is exactly as it was at the time of his death in 1906; coat, hat, wine glass and easel, the objects he liked to paint, his pipe, a few letters and drawings. . . everything save the man himself, who would probably have been horrified at the thought of it being public. The *atélier* is open 10am to noon and 2/2.30 to 5/6pm; closed Monday and Tuesday; bus #1, stop *terminus Beisson,* or Coutheron/Puyricard bus, stop *Cézanne*; admission 10F/5F.

Fondation Vaserely

For a totally different experience, both visually and conceptually, you can escape the cloying grandeur of seventeenth-century Aix by visiting the **Fondation Vasarely** (9.30am–12.30pm & 2–5.30pm; closed Tues; 25F) on av Marcel-Pagnol, Jas-de-Bouffan 4km west of the city centre (bus #8 or #12, stop *Fondation Vasarely*). There could be no mistaking the building, itself a Vasarely creation in black-and-white cubes. As at Gordes there are innumerable sliding showcases, showing images related to all the themes of Vasarely's work, including his "plastic alphabet" and designs for apartment buildings. Downstairs, however, the seven high hexagonal spaces, each hung with six huge colour-wonder dimension-doubling designs, is where you'll get the immediate impact of this extraordinary man's work. He believed "creation was, is, and will be collective; without Leonardo da Vinci there would have been no Cézanne, without Cézanne there would have been no Mondrian... and so forth. In short, the aim of any human work – whether its gestation be conscious or unconscious – cannot be other than social."

Eating and entertainment

Aix is not a great gourmet city, despite its wealthy citizenry and brilliant markets. Still, there are plenty of foreign cuisines to choose from, starting with Italian at *Amalfi*, 5 rue d'Entrecasteaux (☎42.38.30.01; closed Sun), Spanish at *La Bodéga*, 8 rue Campra (☎42.96.05.85; closed Sun and Wed noon), with live flamenco and rumba on Friday and Saturday night (reservations required), Egyptian at *Kéop*, 28 rue de la Verrerie (☎42.96.59.05), featuring falafel, stuffed pigeon, and gorgeous milk-based desserts, and Iranian at *Le Jasmin*, 6 rue de la Fonderie (☎42.38.05.89; closed Sun and Wed eve). For **local food**, pl des Cardeurs is a good area to look – *Le Forum* 20 pl des Cardeurs has an excellent midday *menu*, as, too, does *Tarte Julie*, rue Gaston-de-Saporta, near the *Musée du Vieil Aix*, which serves beautiful salads and perfect quiches. **Vegetarians** should also head for *Le Cèdre Bleu*, 4 rue Emeric-David – reasonably priced despite the credit-card stickers in the window.

La Nouvelle Boulangerie on rue Tournefort is open, day and night, including Christmas, selling pizzas, *patisseries*, and other snacks as well as bread, while *La Boulangerie du Coin* on rue Boulégon is arguably Aix's best **bakery**, with over forty varieties. If you're stocking up on picnic fodder, there's a fantastic selection of cheeses at *Gerard Paul* on rue Marseillais, while the region's best chocolates and the local almond paste speciality, *calissons*, made by *Puyricard*, can be bought at 7 rue Rifle-Rafle.

Nightlife

Aix at ten o'clock on a Monday evening the wrong side of summer can do pretty good dormouse impressions. During the annual **Festival of Music** (last three weeks of July), however, the **alternative scene** – of street theatre, rock concerts and impromptu gatherings – livens up the town out of all recognition. The festival's mainstream musical events are extremely expensive: if you want to try to get tickets apply to the *Comité Officiel des Fêtes* at Complexe Forbin, cours Gambetta (☎42.63.06.75). They also deal with bookings for the **Dance Festival** in the first two weeks of July, the **Rock Festival** in June and numerous other expressions of Aix's cultural reputation.

For the rest of the year: the best **jazz club** in Aix – if you can afford the 200F entry charge – is *Hot Brass*, route d'Eguilles-Célony (☎42.21.05.57; 10.30pm onwards); for significantly less, try *Le Scat Club de Jazz*, 11 rue de la Verrerie (☎42.23.00.23), with all kinds of jazz from 10pm onwards; also *Le Cousin Germain*, 15 rue d'Italie (☎42.38.14.05; Thurs–Sat), which offers Brazilian and trad jazz and blues in an otherwise ordinary café.

You can disco in a bowling alley at *Exagone*, 23 bd Charrier, or see a golden oldie (usually undubbed on Thurs & Mon) at *Cinema Studio 24*, 24 cours Sextius. *La Chimère*, montée d'Avignon, on the northern by-pass towards Sisteron (☎42.23.36.28) is a **gay** bar and disco.

Listings

Bike hire *Cycles Nadéo*, montée d'Avignon (☎42.21.06.93).

Hospital *Centre Hospitalier*, chemin de Tamaris (☎42.23.98.00).

Language courses French lang and lit at university during the summer: 29 av Robert-Schuman (☎42.59.22.71); apply to *Comité d'Acceuil*, BP 313, 21, rue St-Fargeau, 75089, Paris CEDEX 20 (☎1.43.58.95.39).

Launderette 60, rue Boulégon.

Political contacts *SOS Racisme*, 27 rue Félibre-Gaut (☎42.26.46.89); *Mouvement Contre Le Racisme, L'Antisémitisme et Pour la Paix*, Bourse du Travail, bd Jean-Jaurès (☎ 42.23.29.76).

Taxis ☎42.26.29.30/42.27.62.12.

Telephones Just about every Aix phone box takes cards, not coins.

Travel agents *Gazelles Voyages Transalpino*, 3 rue Lieutard (☎42.27.93.83); *Nouvelles Frontières*, 13 rue Aumone-Vieille (☎42.26.47.22).

Women Contacts and information from *CIDF Information Femmes*, 24 rue Mignet (☎42.20.69.82).

Mont Ste-Victoire, Cézanne and Picasso

Mont Ste-Victoire, a rough pyramid whose apex has been pulled off centre, lies east of Aix. Ringed at its base by the dark green and orange-brown of pine woods and cultivated soil, the limestone rock reflects light, turning blue, grey, pink or orange. In the last years of his life Cézanne painted and drew Ste-Victoire more than fifty times. As part of his childhood landscape, it came to embody the incarnation of life within nature. Two of his greatest canvases, *Mont Ste-Victoire* and *Paysage d'Aix* are intricately colour-sculpted representations of solid physical nature – not the play of light or tricks of perception of the Impressionists.

You may, however, be more interested in **climbing Mont Ste-Victoire** and in the view from it. The southern face has a sheer 500-metre drop, but from the north the two-hour walk requires nothing more than determination. The path, GR9 or the *Chemin des Venturiers*, leaves from a small car park on the D10 just before **Vauvenargues**, 14km east of Aix (three buses daily). Having reached the 945-metre summit, marked by a monumental cross that doesn't figure in any of Cézanne's pictures, you can follow the path east along the ridge and descend southwards to PUYLOUBIER (about 15km from the summit).

At **VAUVENARGUES**, a perfect weather-beaten, red-shuttered fourteenth-century **château** stands just outside the village with nothing between it and the slopes of Ste-Victoire. **Picasso** bought the château in 1958 and lived there until his death. He is buried in the gardens, his grave adorned with his sculpture *Woman with a vase*. Unfortunately, the château is closed to the public.

EASTERN PROVENCE

Halfway between Valence and Montélimar the River Drôme joins the Rhône – at **Livron-sur-Drôme**. Following the river upstream by rail to **Sisteron** – or by road to Sisteron or **Barcelonette** – is one of the most dramatic ways of entering **eastern Provence**.

In eastern Provence, it is the landscapes not the cities that dominate. The foothills of the Alps gradually close in, eventually reaching heights of over 3000m in the far northeastern corner around **Barcelonnette**. Winter visitors are almost exclusively skiers, while the summer brings a whole variety of dedicated hikers, bird watchers, botanists and climbers. The **Parc National du Mercantour**, stretching 75km from west to east, is the best area for experiencing this mountainous terrain, but the most dramatic geographical feature is the **Gorges du Verdon** – Europe's answer to the Grand Canyon – in the very heart of Provence.

From St-Maximin to Draguignan

From Aix, the main east-bound road and rail routes pass through **St-Maximin-de-la-Ste-Baume**, which claims the relics of Mary Magdalene and the administrative centre of **Draguignan**, only useful for its cheap accommodation. If you're after dramatic scenery, keep going until you reach the Gorges du Verdon or Parc du Mercantour.

St-Maximin and the Chaîne de la Ste-Baume

Thirty-five kilometres east of Aix lies the town of **ST-MAXIMIN-DE-LA-STE-BAUME**. Here, in 1279, the count of Provence claimed to have found the crypt where the relics of Mary Magdalene and Saint Maximin had been hidden by local people during a Saracen raid. The count started the construction of a **basilica** and monastery, both of which were more or less complete by the fifteenth century. Since that time, decoration of stone, wood, gold, silk and oil paint has been lavishly added, particularly during the reign of Louis XIV – one of many French kings to make the pilgrimage to the *grotte* and the crypt. There is therefore plenty to look at in the **chapel**, from the beautifully detailed wood panelling in the choir to the utterly grotesque skull encased in a glass helmet framed by a gold neck and hair in the crypt. The **monastery** itself can only be visited by guided tour (April–Oct 9–11.30am & 2.30–6pm). The buildings are now a cultural centre, hosting classical concerts (for details: ☎94.78.01.93).

The **medieval streets** of St-Maximin, with their uniform tiled roofs at anything but uniform heights, have considerable charm, and there's a reasonable choice of restaurants and shops with local artisanal produce. The **SI** is in the Hôtel de Ville next to the basilica. If you walk west along rue Général-de-Gaulle from the basilica, you'll find St-Maximin's most expensive **hotel**, the *Plaisance*, at 2 pl Malherbe (☎94.78.16.74; ⑤ and above). Continuing in the same direction, there's the marginally cheaper *Hôtel de France* on av Albert I (☎94.78.00.14; ⑤), near the **gare routière**, and, a little further on, the cheapest of the lot, *Le Relais*, route d'Aix (☎94.78.01.79; ③). The local **campsite**, *Provençal* (☎94.78.16.97; April–mid-Oct), is 3km out along the Marseille road, chemin de Mazaguesx. *Chez Nous*, on bd Jean-Jaurès (closed Wed), is *the* place to head for authentic local sustenance.

Chaîne de la Ste-Baume

While Mary Magdalene's *grotte*, where she was left by the angels and spent 33 years before being flown to St-Maximin for last rites, wouldn't really persuade you to suspend disbelief, **the ridge itself** – the Chaîne de la Ste-Baume – and the surrounding countryside is one of the least spoilt in the region. The woods, flowers and wildlife of the northern face have a profusion rare in these hot latitudes, and the distance from the sea is just enough to limit widespread development. The whole area north to St-Maximin and south to Signes is protected. You are not allowed to camp in the woods or light fires, and a royal edict forbids the picking of orchids. The forested plateau running parallel north of the ridge is, once you've got there, excellent **cycling** terrain.

At PLAN D'AUPS, a tiny village 4km west of the *grotte*, you'll find a small **hotel**, *Lou Pèbre d'Ai* (☎94.04.50.42), with some low-priced rooms and a restaurant. The **SI** in the *Maison de Pays* operates in summer.

The Abbaye du Thoronet

Between BRIGNOLES and Draguignan is the last of the three great Cistercian monasteries of Provence. Even more so than Silvacane and Sénanque, the **Abbaye du Thoronet** (10am–noon & 2–4/5/6pm; closed Tues) has been unscathed by the vicissitudes of time, and during the Revolution was kept intact as a "remarkable monument of history and art". It was first restored in the 1850s, and a recent campaign has brought it to clear-cut perfection. As with the other two abbeys, it's the spaces – here delineated by walls of pale rose-coloured stone – that are the essence of the experience.

Unfortunately, the **abbaye** is by no means easy to reach on public transport: there are two buses weekly during school holidays and one daily in term time from LES ARCS on the main road a few kilometres south of Draguignan. Should you wish or need to **stay**, there's just one pricey hotel-restaurant, *Lou Cigaloun*, in the nearby viallge of Le Thoronet(☎94.04.42.67; ⑤).

Draguignan

If you can avoid **DRAGUIGNAN**, 80km east of St-Maximin, so much the better. It is the base for numerous army barracks and artillery schools that use the desolate **Plan de Canjuers** to the north as firing range and mock battleground. It went bankrupt a few years ago after a manic right-wing mayor privatised everything. He resigned, but the Right remained in office. Draguignan does, however, have one really beautifully displayed museum of the old industries of the Var *département* – silk, honey, cork, olive oil, and tile making, along with local customs and festivities. The **Musée des Arts et Traditions Populaire de Moyenne Provence** (9am–noon & 2–6pm; closed Mon & Sun am; 10F) is at 15 rue Roumanille, a couple of streets away from pl du Marché, the old town's main square.

Practicalities

Reasonably priced **rooms** and **restaurants** are not difficult to find in and around the old town. The recently renovated *Dracenois* on rue de Cros (☎94.68.14.57; ②/③) is a reasonable and very central option, while *La Calèche* on bd Gabriel-Peri can provide cheap sustenance. Alternatively, take a stroll down rue de Trans in the old town for *crêperies*, pizzerias and so forth.

If you're exploring the Gorges du Verdon by bus, this is the place to start from. The **gare routière** and **gare SNCF** (connecting Draguignan with the main line at Les Arcs) are at the bottom of bd Gabriel-Péri, south of the town centre. At the top of the boulevard turn left and you'll find yourself on bd Georges-Clemenceau with the **SI** at no. 9 and a place to **hire bikes** at no. 3.

The Gorges du Verdon and region

The vast military terrain of the Camp de Canjuers blocks any approach from the south to the **Gorges** (or **Grand Canyon**) **du Verdon**. The road north from Draguignan to COMPS-SUR-ARTUBY is one of the few public roads through the military terrain. From Comps, the road runs west through 16km of deserted heath and hills with each successive horizon higher than the last. When you reach the canyon, it is as if a silent earthquake had taken place during your journey.

From this vantage point, known as the **Balcons de la Mescla**, you are looking down 250m to the base of the V-shaped, 21-kilometre gorge incised by the River Verdon through piled strata of limestone. Ever changing in its volume and energy, the river falls from Rougon at the top of the gorge, disappearing into tunnels, decelerating for shallow, languid moments and finally exiting in full, steady flow at the Pont de Galetas. West from the Balcons runs the **corniche sublime**, the D71, built expressly to give the most breath-taking and hair-raising views. On the north side, the **Route des Crêtes**, the D952, does the same, at some points looking down a sheer 800-metre drop to the sliver of water below. The entire circuit is 130km long and it's cycling country solely for the preternaturally fit. For drivers it's a must, though the hidden bends and hairpins are hard work, as, too, in July and August, is the traffic. Petrol stations are few and far between.

Public transport around the canyon is less than comprehensive. There's just one bus between Aix, Moustiers, La Palud, Rougon and Castellane on Monday, Wednesday and Saturday from July to mid-September; the rest of the year just Saturday; and another bus, daily except Sunday, between La Palud, Rougon and Castellane in July and August.

HIKING IN THE GRAND CANYON

By far the best way to explore the canyon – if your legs are up to it – is in its depths. To follow the river **from Rougon to Mayreste** on the **Sentier Martel** takes two days; or just the section **between Rougon and Les Malines**, about eight hours. Access to the gorge depends on the French electricity board, which controls the volume of the Verdon. Anyway, it must be done in a guided group (crossing the torrent by rope is no simple matter on your own). Unaccompanied shorter excursions into the canyon include the fairly easy descent from the **Falaise des Cavaliers** (west of the Balcons), crossing via the **Passerelle de l'Estellié** and ascending to the *Chalet de la Maline*, which is run by the *Touring Club* – it's about two hours one way. Another walk of similar length can be done from the **Point Sublime**, passing through the **Couloir Samson**, a 670-metre tunnel with occasional "windows" and a stairway down to the chaotic sculpture of the river banks.

You should get details of the route and advice on **weather conditions** before you set out. You'll need drinking water, a torch (for the tunnels), and a jumper for the cold shadows of the narrow corridors of rock. Always stick to the path and don't cross the river except at the *passerelles* – the electricity board may be opening dams upstream...

La Palud-sur-Verdon: accommodation and information

The best place to **stay** and to get **information** is **LA PALUD-SUR-VERDON** on the north side of the canyon from where the Route des Crêtes loops out. The **youth hostel**, with **camping** in its grounds, is half a kilometre below the village (☎92.74.68.72; March–Nov) and can help fix up guides, horses and canoes (the latter only for the experienced). The most detailed information – maps, books and so forth – is available from the *Cabanon Verdon* on the main street. For **rock-climbers** *Le Perroquet Vert* sells equipment and the *Club Alpin* is based in the *Chalet-Hôtel de la Maline* (☎92.74.68.05) at LES MALINES on the Route des Crêtes to the south of La Palud.

The centre of life in La Palud is *Lou Cafetié*'s bar-restaurant. There are one or two other places to eat, a market on Wednesday morning around the church and a **municipal campsite** just to the west of the village (☎92.74.68.13). As for **hotels** there's *Le Provence* (☎92.77.56.50; ④) and the slightly cheaper *Auberge des Crêtes* 1km east (☎92.77.38.47; ③). The same management runs the *Auberge du Point Sublime* in Rougon (☎92.83.60.35; ③) which lives up to its name and is not wildly expensive.

Other bases around the canyon

While La Palud is little more than a village, there's a handful of larger places which make possible bases for exploring the canyon.

Moustiers-Ste-Marie

Given the choice, **MOUSTIERS-STE-MARIE** is one to avoid, particularly during the high season when the road west out of the gorge through the town is one long traffic jam. There's a glut of hotels, restaurants, souvenir stands and a veritable surfeit of *ateliers* making glazed pottery – Moustiers' traditional speciality. The pottery, like the village itself before its commercial metamorphosis, is pastel and pretty – and on sale in *John Lewis* and *Liberty*'s – but if you want to lug plates home with you, here's your chance.

Castellane

Being the nearest town to the east end of the gorge, **CASTELLANE** has long since stopped behaving as anything else but a tourist camp. Its only distinguishing feature is the abrupt, massive rock to the east of the town, topped by a **chapel**. Since there's little else to do you might as well climb up to it – 30 minutes' worth from behind the modern church. The gorge itself is out of sight, but the view is still worth the trouble.

The **SI**, at the top of rue Nationale, can provide a full list of hotels and campsites, of which there are many. The two cheapest **hotels** – both open all year – are the *Hostellerie du Roc*, pl de l'Église (☎92.83.62.65; ③/④), and *Le Verdon*, bd de la République (☎92.83.62.02; ②/③). The two **campsites** closest to town, are *Frédéric-Mistral* (☎93.82.62.27; open all year) and a little further along, *Notre-Dame* (☎92.83.63.02; April–Oct 20). **Mountain bikes** can be hired on the route de Draguignan opposite the *gendarmerie* – useful for getting out to the campsites and pleasant for riding round the Lac de Castillon, north of Castellane.

Further afield: Riez

A much more pleasant option, though not in the immediate vicinity of the canyon, is **RIEZ**, 15km west of Moustiers. There are pottery workshops here, too, but the main business is derived from the lavender fields that cover this corner of Provence. Just over the river on the road south is a lavender distillery making essence for the perfume industry. At the other end of the town, 1km along the road to Digne, is the **Maison de l'Abeille** (House of the Bee), a research and visitors' centre. Visitors can buy various honeys (including the local speciality, lavender honey) and *hydromel* – the honey alchohol of antiquity made from nectar – and if you show interest, you'll get an enthusiastic tour. It's open daily from 9am to 7pm, and there's no admission charge.

In size, Riez is more village than town but it soon becomes clear that it was once more influential than it is now. Some of the houses on Grande-Rue and rue du Marché – the two streets above the main allées Louis-Gardiol – have rich Renaissance facades, and the Hôtel de Ville on pl Quinquonces is a former episcopal palace. The **cathedral**, which was abandoned 400 years ago, has been excavated just across the river from allées Louis-Gardiol. Beside it is a **baptistery**, restored in the nineteenth century, but originally constructed, like the cathedral, around 600 AD (the key is available from the Hôtel de Ville). If you recross the river and follow it downstream you'll find the even older and much more startling relics of four **Roman columns** standing in a field.

A rather more strenuous walk, heading first for the clock tower above Grande-Rue and then taking the path past the cemetery and on uphill (leaving the cemetery to your left), brings you to a cedar-shaded platform on the hilltop where the pre-Roman

Riezians lived. The only building now occupying the site is the eighteenth-century **Chapelle Ste-Maxime**, with a gaudily patterned interior.

Riez practicalities

Riez is in danger of losing its out-of-the-way charm. Pedestrian precincts have been introduced in the last couple of years and the main **allées Louis-Gardiol**, where most of Riez's limited action takes place, is slowly undergoing a facelift. The musty old *Hôtel des Alpes* on the allées (☎92.77.80.03; ③), once the town's only **hotel**, charges considerably more than it used to. Nevertheless, it's still a better bet than the new *Hôtel Carina*, next door (☎92.77.85.43; ⑤). Alternatively, there's a **campsite** over the river on the D11 before the distillery. There's no **SI** as such; the Hôtel de Ville (☎92.74.51.81) or the *Atelier Sol* at 46 rue du Marché (☎92.74.47.28) can provide information. Hopefully one place that won't have changed is the **restaurant** *Les Abeilles,* again on allées Louis-Gardiol, a peculiar Provençal variation on the greasy spoon, with regional specialities like *aïoli,* served with boiled carrots and potatoes and ketchup on request.

Aups

Further away from the canyon, to the south, **AUPS** is another off-the-beaten-track town which would make a good base for both the gorge and the little villages of central Var – if you have your own transport. Though not swamped by tourists, Aups has several British and American residents and the **Église St-Pancrace**, designed by an English architect 400 years ago, has had its doors restored by two local British carpenters. Aups remains, however, very much an agricultural Provençal town: it specialises in truffles, and, if you're here on a Thursday between November and February you can witness the **truffle market**.

On pl Martin-Bidoué, a **monument** commemorates a period of republican resistance all too rarely honoured. Its inscription reads: "To the memory of citizens who died in 1851 defending the republic and its laws", the year being that of Louis Napoléon's coup d'état. Peasant and artisan resistance was strongest in Provence, and the defeat of the insurgents – who flew the red flag because the tricolour had been appropriated by the usurper – was followed by a bloody massacre of men and women.

One other surprising feature of Aups is a **museum of modern art**, the *Musée Simon Segal et l'École de Paris* in the former chapel of a convent on av Albert I (mid-June to mid-Sept 10.30am–noon & 3–6pm). The best works are those by the Russian-born painter Simon Segal, but there are interesting local scenes in the other paintings, such as the Roman bridge at **Aiguines**, now drowned beneath the artificial lake of Ste-Croix.

Practicalities

Whether you're **arriving** from Brignoles or Draguignan you enter Aups along av Georges-Clemenceau which ends with pl Frédéric-Mistral and pl Martin-Bidoué. The church is to the right, the **SI**, to the left, on pl de la Mairie, and the old town before you. Of the **hotels**, *Le Provençal* on pl Martin-Bidoué (☎94.70.00.24; ③) is the cheapest place to stay. There are two 2* **campsites** close to town: *International Camping,* 500m down av Roziers in the direction of FOX-AMPHOUX (☎94.70.06.80; Easter–Sept), and *Camping Les Prés,* to the right off allée Charles-Boyer towards Tourtour (☎94.70.00.93; open all year).

For **meals**, first choice is the cheap and delicious *Framboise* on pl Maréchal-Foch (closed Mon) followed by the pizzeria/*crêperie* on pl Général-Girard. You can gather provisions at the *Patisserie Canut* on pl du Marché, which sells bread and cakes (try the olive oil *fougasses*) and, close by, at the bottom of rue Maréchal-Foch, you can buy wine in bulk.

Inland along the *Route Napoléon* to Sisteron

North of Castellane the *Route Napoléon* passes through the barren scrubby rocklands of some of the obscurest and emptiest quarters of Provence. Not a lot happens between Castellane and DIGNE except that at **BARRÊME** you can catch one of the great regular **scenic train rides** along the narrow-gauge *Chemin de Fer de Provence* (CFP) that runs from Digne to Nice. There are bus connections between Castellane and ANNOT, four stops down from Barrême (and about 30km to the east as the crow flies), and in summer the stretch between Annot and PUGET-THÉNIERS can be done by **steam-train**. **Timetables** are available from the SI in Castellane, the gare SNCF in Barrême, and Digne SI or gare SNCF.

Digne-les-Bains

DIGNE-LES-BAINS can be a dispiriting place. Despite its status as chief town of the Alpes-de-Haute-Provence *département*, it has nothing going for it unless you need to take the cure for rheumatism and respiratory disorders. The baths, 2km east of the town, and the administrative offices of the *Préfecture* are the only new spa buildings; the rest is peeling into shades of mud and stormcloud. Worse is to come. The **Cathédrale St-Jérôme** is in desperate need of repair, particularly the Gothic stained-glass windows. Death by falling masonry is the closest thought of a spiritual nature that's likely to pass your mind in here. Of the roads and houses of Vieux Digne – which are in just as dire need of repair as the cathedral – there's little to be said, except that on Wednesday and Saturday the local market brings some animation to the quarter.

Arriving from Castellane, the *Route Napoléon* enters Digne along the east bank of the Bléone, arriving at the rond-point du 11-novembre-1918, where the **SI** is situated. The old town lies to the east of this roundabout, the **gare routière** to the north, on av Demontze, and the **gare SNCF** and *Chemin de Fer de Provence* to the west over the river.

Moving on

From Digne, the *Route Napoléon* turns west to MALIJAI before veering north again to follow the Durance upstream to Sisteron. If you have your own transport there are hundreds of miles of roads through the semi-deserted Pré-Alpes de Haute Provence north of Digne, and there are daily buses to BARCELONNETTE.

Sisteron

Sticking to the Route Napoléon, you reach the most important mountain gateway to Provence, **SISTERON**. If you can choose which route you take, follow Bonaparte's footsteps via the D4 on the left bank of the Durance, and you'll appreciate why he was so worried by this city. The site had been fortified since time immemorial and even now, half destroyed by the Anglo-American bombardment of 1944, its citadel stands as a fearsome sentinel over the city and the solitary bridge across the River Durance.

The **Citadelle** (mid-March to mid-Nov daily 9am–7pm) can easily take up half a day. There are no guides, just recordings in French attempting to recreate historic moments, such as Napoléon's march, of course, and the imprisonment in 1639 of Jan Kazimierz, the future king of Poland. Most of the extant defences are Vauban's work, when it was a front-line fort against neighbouring Savoy – the eleventh-century castle was destroyed in the mid-thirteenth century during a pogrom against the local Jewish population.

The best view is from the **Guérite du Diable** look-out post. The outcrop on which the fortress sits abruptly stops here, 500m above the narrow passage of the Durance. In July and August, the **festival** known as *Nuits de la Citadelle* has open-air performances of music, drama and dance in the fortress grounds. There are also art exhibi-

---

THE *ROUTE NAPOLÉON*

In the spring of 1815, after ten months of exile, Napoléon set out in pursuit of the most audacious recapture of power in French history. On March 1, with just 700 soldiers at his side, he landed at the port of Golfe-Juan, unsure as to what kind of reception awaited him. His emissaries to Cannes and Antibes were taken prisoner so the ever-brilliant tactician decided to bypass Grasse and head north through Haute Provence towards Digne-les-Bains and Sisteron along mule paths still deep with winter snow. In just six days, he and his men walked the 350km to Grenoble, and by March 20, he was back in the Tuileries Palace in Paris. One hundred days later, he lost the battle of Waterloo, and was finally and permanently incarcerated on the island of St Helena. In typical French fashion the road known as the **Route Napoléon** was built in the 1930s specifically to commemorate the great leader's journey – though it does also serve as a useful communication link.

---

tions in the vertiginous late medieval chapel, **Notre-Dame-du-Château**, restored to its Gothic glory and given very beautiful subdued stained-glass windows in the 1970s.

Back in Sisteron's old town, you'll see three huge towers built, in 1370, into the ramparts around the expanding town. To their left is the **Cathédrale Notre-Dame-des-Pommiers**, almost as decrepit as Digne's. Behind the altar, various arches and indentations give the appearance of a grotesque ogre's face. From the cathedral, rue Deleuze leads to place de l'Horloge, where the Wednesday and Saturday **market** is held and which, on the second Saturday of every month, hosts a fair.

Practicalities

Arriving by train at Sisteron, turn right out of the **gare SNCF** along av de la Libération until you reach **place de la République**. Here you'll find the **SI**, the **PTT** and the **gare routière**. **Rooms** without a view overlooking the river are not too expensive. The most economical accommodation is the *Centre de Hébergement* (☎92.61.27.49; ①), in the cultural centre on pl du Tivoli, along rue de Provence from the SI. The *Hostellerie Provençal* on av J-Moulin (☎92.61.02.42; ①) is almost as cheap and equally central. Sisteron's 3* **campsite** is across the river and 3km along the D951 (☎92.61.19.69; open all year). A **youth hostel**, 10km to the north in VAUMEILH (☎92.61.43.78; mid-June to mid-Sept) is linked to a **glider school** offering initiation courses at a price.

The food in Sisteron's **restaurants** is nothing special, though the view down the valley from the terrace of the *Hôtel-Restaurant de la Citadelle*, 126 rue Saunerie, certainly is. There are other good places to eat along rue Droite and rue Saunerie. *Le Mondial* **bar** at the top of rue Droite stays open late, as does *Le Primerose* on pl de l'Horloge.

Northeast Provence and the Parc National du Mercantour

Depending on the season, the **northeastern corner of Provence** is two different worlds, but in either case there's no let-up to the mountain barricades that range from 1000m to over 3000m. In **winter** the sheep and shepherds have gone to warmer pastures, leaving the snowy heights to horned mouflons and chamois, and the perfectly camouflaged ermine. The villages, where the shepherds came to summer markets, are battened down for the long, cold haul. Other villages, or rather gatherings of Swiss-style chalets, sports shops and discos, come to life, with a ski lift instead of a church or market place as the focal point. In **spring**, melting waters swell the Vésubie, the Tinée and the Roya, sometimes flooding villages and carrying whole streets away. The fruit trees in the narrow valley orchards blossom. In **summer** and **autumn** the ski resorts

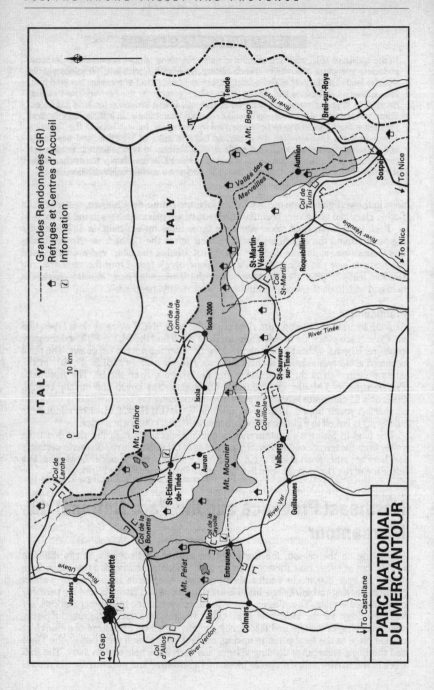

PARC NATIONAL
DU MERCANTOUR

THE PARC NATIONAL DU MERCANTOUR

A long narrow band close to the Italian border, stretching almost down to **Sospel**, has been designated the **Parc National du Mercantour**, with organised walks, mountain shelters and information centres – *Maisons du parc*. The latter can be found in **Barcelonnette** (*La Sapinière*), **St-Étienne-de-Tinée** (*Quartier de l'Ardon*) and **Valberg** (*Maison Valberganne*). The *maisons* can provide maps and accommodation details, and advise on footpaths, weather conditions etc. If you're starting off from **Nice** you can pick up all the information you need at 23 rue d'Italie (☎93.87.86.10).

If you're considering doing some **hiking**, the best guide is no. 13 in the *Footpaths of Europe* series – *Walking the GR5: Larche to Nice* – which covers much of the national park. **Transport** other than by foot is a problem. Apart from the Turin–Nice railway line down the Roya valley close to the Italian border, there are regular **bus** connections going out from Barcelonette or from Sospel but they don't meet, and there are only infrequent buses between villages on market days. **Camping** is not allowed in the park but there are plenty of sites outside its limits, never too far away. There are *gîtes d'étape* in many of the villages, and, in the back country, more basic *refuges* or mountain huts, accessible only by foot and more expensive than a youth hostel. These tend to be on GR5 and 52 (signed red on white) which run through sections of the park.

are ghostly, and from the valleys to the peaks sunlight is filtered through chestnut and olive trees and then pine forests edged with wild raspberries, up to rocks with eagles' nests, moors and sheep pastures where wild rhododendrons and gentians grow.

Barcelonnette

From GAP in the Hautes Alpes, the most direct road into Provence brings you to **BARCELONNETTE**, a place of immaculate charm in which snow-capped mountains are visible at the end of each short boulevard. It is not very big, and a more ideal spot for doing nothing would be hard to find. The central square, **place Manuel**, has café tables from which to gaze at the blue sky and a white clock tower commemorating the centenary of the 1848 revolution. Probably the best **place to stay** in the centre of town is the *Choucas Hôtel* overlooking pl Manuel (☎92.81.15.20; ①–③) – an old-fashioned, homely affair with creaky linoleum and a few cheap rooms at the back. Otherwise try the *Cheval Blanc*, just down the road at 12 rue Grenette (☎92.81.00.19; ③), or the *Provençal*, 30 rue Manuel (☎92.81.03.39; ②). There are two **campsites** on the D902 leading to the Col de la Cayolle, the closest of which is *Le Plan de Barcelonnette*, 500m from town (☎92.81.00.70; June–Sept). For information on the national park, go to the information centre in the local **SI** on pl Manuel.

Basic but beautifully prepared **food** is to be had at *La Mangeoire*, in an old sheep barn, pl des Quatre-Vents (closed Mon). Pizzas and midday *plats du jour* are on sale for very little at the corner of pl St-Pierre and rue Bellon. And, at 6 rue Bellon, *Ubayoglace* serves incredible homemade ices and sorbets made of every imaginable fruit. Wednesday and Saturday are the **market** days, when you'll see all manner of local specialities – jams, game patés and liqueurs flavoured with alpine plants.

The road from Barcelonnette to Sospel

The road across **Cime de la Bonette** – the D2205 from Barcelonnette – claimed to be the highest in Europe, reaching over 2800m, gives a feast of high-altitude views. You may have to brake for a marmot (a two-foot-long furry creature), or for an army truck, as the military are rather fond of this deserted spot, but the green and silent spaces of the approach, circled by barren peaks, are magical.

At **ST-ÉTIENNE-DE-TINÉE**, you can recover from vertigo and maybe see the sheep fairs, held every three weeks or so between March and October. For **accommodation**, the *Hôtel-Restaurant Pinatelle* on route d'Auron (☎93.02.40.36; Jan–Sept; ③) is the cheapest place to stay, and there's a campsite on bd Rouery (☎93.02.41.43; open all year).

From St-Étienne, the **GR5 footpath** heads off into the mountains, past the ski resort of AURON, after which there's nothing but the white quartz and white heather, with only the silvery sound of crickets competing with the waters' roar. The GR5 eventually rejoins the road at ST-SAUVEUR-SUR-TINÉE, another sheep-fair town. From there, roads and paths both go east towards **ST-MARTIN-VÉSUBIE**, a lovely place but with just four expensive **hotels** and an overpriced **campsite** and *gîte*, the *Touron* (☎93.03.21.32; open all year), on the NICE road a short way out. If you can, treat yourself to a terrific pizza at *Chez Vidoni*, 70 rue Cagnoli. The **restaurant** is on the main street of the old village – cobbled and no more than an arm's length wide with a stream of channelled water running down the middle, and overhung by roofs and balconies. The **SI** on pl Félix-Faure provides details on paths and *gîtes/refuges* in the vicinity.

Sospel and north: the Roya Valley

The road from the Vésubie valley joins the Roya valley at **SOSPEL**, a dreamy Italianate town spanning the gentle River Bévéra. You may find it over-tranquil after the excitements of the high mountains or the flashy speed of the Côte d'Azur, but it can make a pleasant break.

From the **gare SNCF** turn left along av A-Borriglione (which becomes av des Martyres-de-la-Résistance) then right past place St-Pierre which is at the east end of the old town. Alternatively, head straight for the *Hôtel de la Gare* (☎93.04.00.73) as it's the only vaguely cheap **hotel**. The *Auberge Provençale*, route de Menton (☎93.04.00.31; ④), is much nicer and not too expensive, but 1.5km uphill from the town. There are four **campsites**, the closest of which is *Le Mas Fleuri* (☎93.04.05.87; open all year), 2km along the D2566 to Moulinet following the river upstream.

If you're not carrying bags by the time you reach pl St-Pierre, wander down rue St-Pierre. It's a gloomy, deeply shadowed street with equally uninviting alleyways running off it until suddenly it opens into **place St-Michel**. Before you is one of the most beautiful series of peaches-and-cream baroque facades in all Provence, made up of the **Cathédrale St-Michel**, two chapels and several arcaded houses. The road behind the cathedral, rue de l'Abbaye, or the steps between the chapels, lead up to an ivy-covered castle ruin from which you get a good view of the town. An even better view can be had from the **Fort St-Roch**, part of the ignominious inter-war Maginot Line, along chemin de St-Roch (9.30am–12.30pm & 4–6pm; closed Mon).

Down below, **place de la Cabrailla** is the liveliest area, with the main **bus stop** and a petrol station. From the *place*, av Aristide-Briand follows the river with various eating places including *Chez Fredy*'s takeaway pizzas. The **SI** is in the tower on the central bridge – a tenth-century structure and kingpin to the picturesque quality of the town. Still on the right bank, just beyond the third bridge, tucked behind the public toilets, is the *Maison des Jeunes* where Sospel's youth occasionally gather for pool games and other low-key entertainment. The town's **restaurant**s are, on the whole, very overpriced – *L'Escargot d'Or*, 3 rue de Verdun, just across the river on the third bridge is probably your best bet.

The Vallée des Merveilles

The first person to stumble upon this high **valley** of lakes and tumbled rocks was a fifteenth-century traveller who had lost his way. He described it as "an infernal place with figures of the devil and thousands of demons scratched on the rocks": a pretty accurate description, except that some of the carvings are of animals, tools, people working, and symbols that could mean anything. There are 100,000 of them, dated to some time in the second millennium BC, and that is about all that's known about them.

The **most direct route** into the valley is the ten-kilometre hike that starts at *Les Mesches Refuge*, 10km west of ST-DALMAS-DE-TENDE (on the D91 and the Turin–Nice railway line). When you're nearly there you'll find the *Refuge des Merveilles* where you can get sustenance, and shelter. Never underestimate these mountains' ability to turn blue skies and sun into violent hailstorms and lightning: the route takes between five and six hours there and back, excluding time spent looking at (and for) the carvings.

La Brigue

LA BRIGUE, one stop up the line from St-Dalmas-de-Tende, is the best place to stay in the **upper Roya valley**; try the *Fleurs des Alpes* on place St-Martin (☎93.04.61.05; ③). At around the same time the waylaid traveller was freaking out about the devils and demons of the *Merveilles*, one Jean Canavéso was carrying out a commission to paint just those things in the sanctuary of **Notre-Dame-des-Fontaines**, 4km east of the village. The frescoes, which cover the entire building, are the sort of thing that wouldn't be shown on television. The goriest detail is a devil extracting Judas' soul from his disembowelled innards. The chapel is open all year: for exact times check with the *mairie* or any of the restaurants in La Brigue.

Tende

If you have no luck finding somewhere to stay in La Brigue, continue north one more stop on the railway line to TENDE, where the French spoken has a distinctly Italian accent. The *Hôtel du Centre*, on pl de la République (☎93.04.62.19; ③), has cheapish rooms, or else try the **youth hostel** *Les Carlines* (☎93.04.62.19; Feb–Sept), down chemin Ste-Catherine, off rue St-Jean past the cathedral.

travel details

Lyon and Rhone valley train and SNCF bus routes

TGV from Lyon: 11–21 daily from Lyon-Perrache to Lyon-Part-Dieu (10min) and Paris (2hr 10min); 3 daily from Lyon-Part-Dieu to Lyon-Perrache (10min) and St-Étienne (47min); 2 or 3 daily from Lyon-Part-Dieu to Grenoble (1hr 15min); 3 daily from Lyon-Part-Dieu to Valence (55min), 2 continuing to Avignon (1hr 50min) and 1 to Marseille (2hr 45min)

From Lyon, north-bound: many late-evening sleeper departures; 3 or 4 trains daily stopping at most stations on the way to Dijon (2hr) and Paris (5hr); 6 or 7 daily to Mâcon (40min), Chalon (1hr 10min) and Dijon (1hr 44min).

From Lyon, east- and west-bound: frequent trains to Roanne (1hr 30min) and St-Étienne (1hr); 8–10 daily to Grenoble (1hr 15min–1hr 45min); 5–6 daily to Bourg-en-Bresse (1hr 50min).

Rhône valley trains: Numerous trains go up and down this line day and night – they don't all stop at all the following places, and some only cover part of the route. From Lyon to Vienne (20min), Valence (55min), Montélimar (1hr 20min–2hr), Orange (1hr 50min–2hr 30min), Avignon (2–3hr) and Arles (2hr 30min–3hr 30min).

Lyon (Perrache or Part-Dieu) to the Côte d'Azur: 9 or 11 daily to Nice (9hr), stopping at Avignon (2hr 30min), Marseille (3hr 40min), Toulon (4hr 25min), Les Arcs (5hr), St-Raphaël (8hr), Cannes (8hr 30min) and Antibes (8hr 40min). *Alpazur*, a *train touristique* (July 1–Sept 9 only) runs from Lyon via Grenoble to Digne; change on to *Chemins de Fer de Provence* to continue to Nice.

Provence trains and SNCF buses

From Avignon 5–8 daily to Nîmes (30 min); 21 daily (7 *TGV*) to Montpellier (50min–1hr), via Orange (20min) and Montélimar (1hr); 36 daily (6 *TGV*) to Valence (1hr 20min/1hr); 14 daily, (9 *TGV*) to Paris (3hr 45min–4hr); 26 daily (9 *TGV*) to Marseille (55min–1hr 12min) via Arles (20–30min); 5 daily to Carpentras (20min).

From Tarascon 7 daily to Arles (by train or SNCF bus: 20–30min); 6 daily to Marseilles (1hr), via Avignon (12min); several daily to Orange (50min), Montélimar (1hr 20min), Valence (2hr) and Vienne (3hr); 10 daily to Lyon (2hr 40min).

From Arles 8 daily to Tarascon (by train or SNCF bus: 20min); 12 daily to Nîmes (20min); 12 daily to Montpellier (1hr); 7 daily to Bordeaux (6hr); 4 daily to La Rochelle (8hr 30min); 3 daily to Nantes (10hr 15min); 4 daily (11 on Sun) to Avignon (20min).

From Aix-en-Provence 6 daily to Briançon (4hr 30min); 6 daily to Manosque (45min) and St-Auban (1hr 10min); otherwise all trains go via Marseille.

From Digne 8 SNCF buses daily to St-Auban (about 35min), continuing by SNCF bus or train to Veynes-Devoluy (another 1hr–1hr 15min), and changing at Veynes for train to Valence (2hr), or Grenoble (2hr). *Chemins de Fer de Provence*, a private rail company, goes 4–5 times daily from Digne via 15 small stations to Nice (3hr 20min)

From Nice 6 daily to Sospel (50min) and Breuil-sur-Roya (1hr 10min); 3 daily to Tende (2hr).

Buses

From Lyon to the Côte d'Azur there's a good town-to-town service all the way along the N7.

Avignon is the focus of a network of local and long-distance buses in Provence.

From St-Rémy 6–9 daily to Avignon (40min); 2 daily to Les Baux (15min); 4 daily to Tarascon (20min).

From Beaucaire 9 daily to Tarascon (10min); 5 daily to Nîmes (40min); 6 daily to Avignon (50min).

From Arles 3–6 daily to Salin-de-Giraud (1hr); 3 daily to Avignon (no service Sun; 45min); 3–8 daily to Stes-Maries-de-la-Mer (1hr).

From Salin-de-Giraud 2–3 daily to Arles (1hr).

From Nice 2 daily to Castellane (3hr), Digne (4hr 15min) and Sisteron (5hr)

From Orange hourly to Avignon (45min–1hr 10min), of which 4 daily stop at Châteauneuf-du-Pape (25min); 5 daily to Sérignan (20min); 5 daily to Carpentras (40min); 4 daily to Vaison-la-Romaine (50min).

From Carpentras frequent to Avignon (45min), 1 stopping at l'Isle-sur-la-Sorgue (15min); 2 daily to Beaumes (15min), Vacqueyras (25min), Gigondas (40min), Sablet (45min); 2 daily to Vaison (45min); 3 weekly during school time to Apt (1hr 5min).

From Draguignan 1–2 daily to Aups (1hr 10min) and Moustiers-Ste-Marie (2hr).

From Digne 1 daily to Riez (1hr 30min); 2 daily to Sisteron (1hr 10min); 1 daily to Barcelonette (1hr 45min).

CHAPTER FIFTEEN

THE COTE D AZUR

The **Côte d'Azur** has to be the most built-up, over-eulogised and expensive stretch of coast anywhere in the world. There are only two industries to speak of – tourism and building, plus the related services of estate agents, yacht traffic wardens and *Rolls Royce* valets. Posters for extreme right-wing politician Le Pen go undefaced, and construction companies pick their labourers from lines of North African immigrants just as galley owners chose their slaves. Meanwhile a hotel serves tender meat morsels to its clients' pets in a restaurant for dogs.

On the other hand, in every gap between the monstrous habitations – in the **Estérel**, the **St-Tropez** peninsula, the **islands** off **Cannes** and **Hyères**, the **Massif des Maures** – the remarkable beauty of the hills and land's edge, the scent of the plant life, the mimosa blossom in February and the strange synthesis of the Mediterranean pollutants that make the water so translucent, devastate the senses. The chance to see the works of innumerable **artists** seduced by the land and light also justifies the trip. See, for example, **Cocteau** in **Menton** and Villefranche, **Matisse** and **Chagall** in Nice, **Picasso** in **Antibes** and Vallauris and collections of **Fauvists** and **Impressionists** at St-Tropez, Nice and Hauts-de-Cagnes. And it must be said that places like **Monaco** and **Cannes**, the star excrescences of the coast, have a twisted entertainment value, just as the seediness of **Marseille** and **Toulon** have a perverse attraction.

The **months to avoid** absolutely are July and August, when all hotels are booked up, the overflowing campsites become health hazards, local people are overworked, and the vegetation is at its most barren.

FROM MARSEILLE TO TOULON

From the vast and wonderful scruffiness of **Marseille** to the rather squalid naval base of **Toulon,** this stretch of the Mediterranean is definitely not what most people think of as the Côte d'Azur: there is no continuous corniche, few villas in the Grand Style, and work is geared to an annual rather than summer cycle. **Cassis** is the exception, but Marseille is the overriding attraction – a city that couldn't be confused with any other, no matter where you were dropped in it.

Marseille

The most renowned and populated city after Paris, **MARSEILLE** has, like the capital, prospered and been ransacked over the centuries. It has lost its privileges to French kings and foreign armies, refound its fortunes, suffered plagues, religious bigotry, republican and royalist Terror and had its own Commune and Bastille-storming. It was

---

HOTEL ROOM PRICES

For a fuller explanation of these price codes, see the box on p.28 of *Basics*.

① Under 100F   ② 100–130F   ③ 130–180F   ④ 180–230F   ⑤ 230–300F

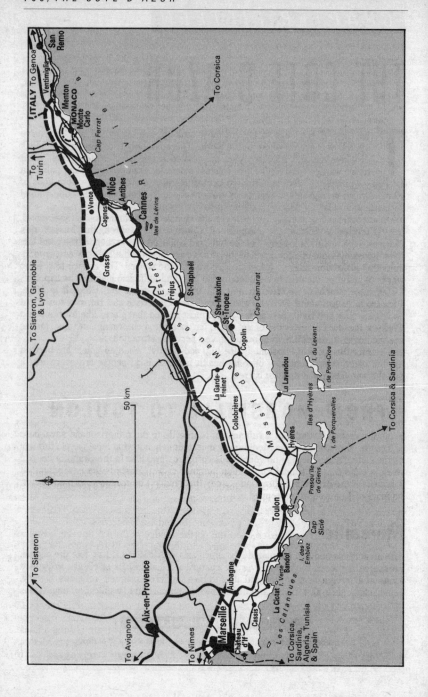

> ### POWER AND POLITICS
>
> In the present state of the *Patrie*, Marseille has every social, economic and political conflict of the country writ large, alongside its notorious protection rackets, bribery, heroin trading and prostitution. Shoot-outs by the **milieu**, as the Marseille mafia is called, or arrests of its leaders provide best-selling headlines for the local papers. What is not so visible is the endemic corruption in the police department and the town hall which, according to some, explains why the lawlessness never explodes.
>
> Politically, through the 1970s and early 1980s, Marseille was the virtual fiefdom of the Socialist minister and mayor, **Gaston Deferre**. His widow has now inherited control of the city's main newspapers, both right and left wing, *Le Meridional* and *Le Provençal*, and it's said that Deferre's successor was her personal choice. He lost the municipal elections in 1989 to an independent socialist. But what has been crucial over the last few years has been the possibility of the *Front National* winning the town hall with Le Pen himself as mayor. The chance of this nightmare becoming a reality has thankfully receded, but that's not to say that Le Pen has lost his massive grassroots following in the city. The dominating fear and violence in Marseille is racial. With the worst housing, lowest paid jobs and highest level of unemployment, the North Africans, mostly Algerian, live with the daily constants of assault, abuse and discrimination from their neighbours and the law. Compared with racism, the activities of the *milieu* pale into insignificance.

the presence of so many **Marseillaise** Revolutionaries marching from the Rhine to Paris in 1792, which gave the name to the *Hymn of the Army of the Rhine* that became the national anthem.

Today, it can't be denied that Marseille is a violent city, that it is neither particularly beautiful nor clean, that it has acres of grim 1960s housing estates. You might not choose to live here, but it's a wonderful place to visit – a real port city with a trading history going back over 2500 years. It's as cosmopolitan as Paris with the advantages of being nearly 800km farther south, having much more down-to-earth, informal inhabitants, and lacking the usual trappings of the rest of the Côte.

Orientation and accommodation

Like Paris, Marseille is divided into *arrondissements* – in this case sixteen – which spiral out from the focal point of the city, the **Vieux Port**. Due north lies the "old town", **Le Panier**, still home to much of Marseille's Algerian population. Several wide boulevards fan out from the Vieux Port, with **La Canebière** by far the most significant, dividing bourgeois Marseille, on the south side, from the North Africans' commercial district, **quartier Belsunce**, to the north. Drifting east past the city's red-light area is a vaguely bohemian, studenty area of bars, restaurants and peculiar shops around **place Jean-Jaurès**. Heading **south** from La Canebière, the city's more glitzy commercial quarter gradually gives way to lush green suburbs and sandy beaches.

The **gare SNCF St-Charles** is on the northern edge of the 1er (the 1st *arrondissement*), just round the corner from the **gare routière** on place Victor-Hugo. To get into town from the train station, take the monumental Art Deco stairway down to the bd d'Athènes, which crosses the main east–west artery from the Vieux Port – **La Canebière**.

Once you're in the city centre, the best way to **get around** is to walk. However, if you need to get across the city fast, the **bus**, **tram** and **métro** network is pretty efficient, though not devastatingly cheap. It's worth knowing that the métro only runs from 5am to 9pm, except when the city's mercurial football team, *OM*, are playing a game. After 9pm, buses run along roughly the same routes until midnight. **Tickets**, which can be bought in *carnets* of six from métro stations or *RTM* kiosks, or singly from bus drivers, must be validated on the bus, on tramway platforms or at métro gates.

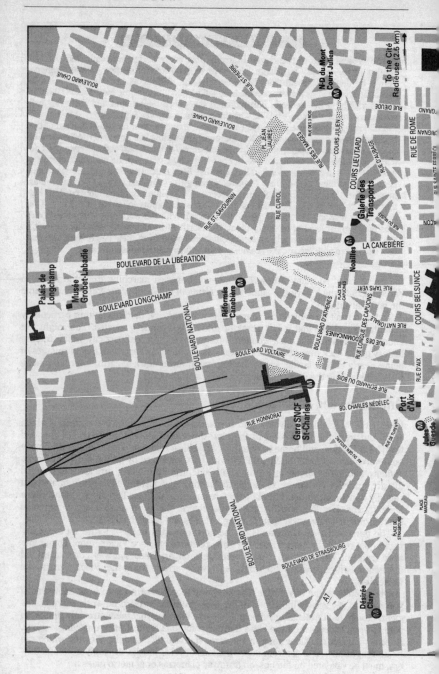

To the Cité
Radieuse (2.5 km)

N-D du Mont
Cours Julien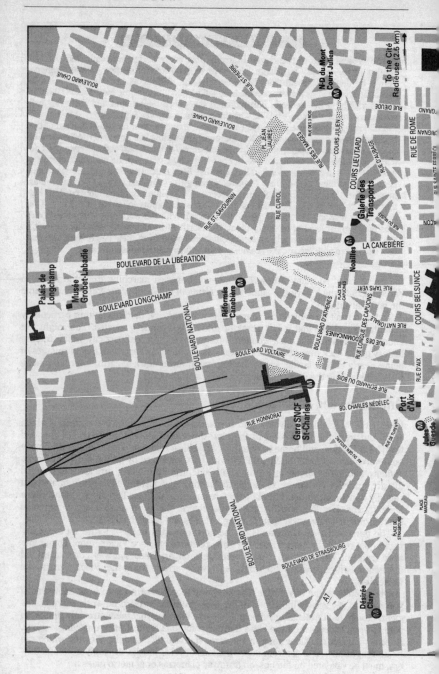

RUE DE ROME

RUE DIEUDÉ

GRAND

RIGNAN

RUE DES 3 MAGES

RUE ST-PIERRE

BOULEVARD CHAVE

RUE DES 3 ROIS

COURS JULIEN

COURS LIEUTARD

RUE D'AUBAGNE

Galerie des
Transports

BOULEVARD CHAVE

PL. JEAN
JAURÈS

RUE CURIOL

RUE ST-SAVOURNIN

LA CANEBIÈRE

Noailles

PLACE DES
CAPUCINS

RUE DU MUSÉE

COURS BELSUNCE

BOULEVARD DE LA LIBÉRATION

Palais de
Longchamp

Musée
Grobet-Labadie

Réformés
Canebière

RUE NATIONALE

RUE LONGUE DES CAPUCINS

RUE DES DOMINICAINES

BOULEVARD D'ATHÈNES

BOULEVARD LONGCHAMP

BOULEVARD NATIONAL

BOULEVARD VOLTAIRE

RUE BERNARD DU BOIS

RUE D'AIX

Port
d'Aix

Gare SNCF
St-Charles

RUE HONNORAT

BD. CHARLES NÉDÉLEC

RUE DE TURENNE

Jules
Guesde

AV. DU GÉN. LECLERC

PLACE DE
STRASBOURG

PLACE
MARCEAU

BOULEVARD NATIONAL

Désirée
Clary

BOULEVARD DE STRASBOURG

A7

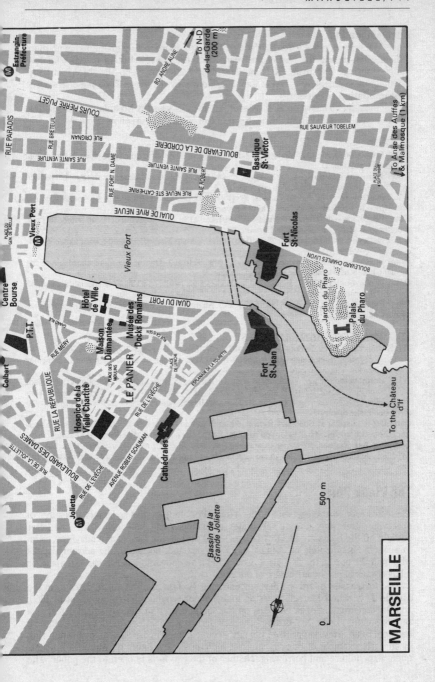

Accommodation

Since Marseille is not a great tourist city, finding a room in July or August is no more difficult than during the rest of the year. But there are few **hotels** catering for low-budget tourists. The main **SI** (June–Aug daily 8am–8pm; Sept–May Mon–Sat 9am–7.30pm, Sun 10am–5pm) is at 4 la Canebière, down by the Vieux Port, and offers a free **acommodation service**.

The most inexpensive options, as ever, are the city's **youth hostels** and **campsites**, all situated quite a way from the centre in one of Marseille's greenest suburbs.

HOTELS

Hôtel Caravelle, 5 rue Guy-Mocquet, 1er (☎91.48.44.99). Friendly, quiet and close to the action, just off bd Garibaldi. ②.

Hôtel Edmond-Rostand, 31 rue Dragon, 6e (☎91.37.74.95). Great charm and atmosphere, and well known, so should be booked in advance. ①/②.

Hôtel le Provençal, 32 rue du Paradis, 1er (☎91.33.11.15). Indifferent rooms, but good balconies from which to watch street life, and a kind *patronne*. ②.

Hôtel Pilote, 9 rue du Théâtre-Français, 1er (☎91.42.02.18). In a street full of cheap hotels, this one is better than some, with a friendly *patronne*. ②.

Hôtel Bellevue, 34 quai du Port, 2e (☎91.91.11.64). Classic Marseille building with fantastic view over the Vieux Port. ③.

Hôtel le Richelieu, 52 corniche Kennedy, 7e (☎91.31.01.92). One of the more affordable of the corniche hotels overlooking the plage des Catalans. ④.

Hôtel Le Corbusier, Cité Radieuse, 280 bd Michelet, 8e (☎91.77.18.15). Very special this one, on the third floor of the architect's prototype tower block – book in advance. ④.

Hôtel Esterel, 124 rue Paradis, 6e (☎91.37.13.90). All mod-cons, expense-account prices and rather smarmy as a result. ⑤.

YOUTH HOSTELS AND CAMPSITES

IYHF Bois Luzy, 76 av de Bois-Luzy, 12^{e} (☎91.49.06.18; reception 7am–10am & 5–10.30pm; bus #8 direction *St-Julien* from Centre Bourse, stop *Bois Luzy*). Cheap, clean youth hostel in a former château. Curfew 11pm. No card needed.

IYHF Bonneveine, 47 av J-Vidal, impasse du Dr-Bonfils, 8e (☎91.73.21.81; reception 7.30–9.30am & 5–11pm; bus #41 or métro *Rond-Point du Prado*, then bus #44 direction *Roy d'Espagne*, stop *Vidal-Collet*). Not so cheap or secure as the *Bois Luzy* hostel, but the lack of curfew and proximity to the beach make up for it.

Camping is possible at Bois Luzy from mid-March to mid-October (☎91.73.26.99; two stops back from the youth hostel on bus #44). You pay dear for the site's somewhat undeserved 4* status.

Camping Les Vagues, 52 av de Bonneveine, 8e (☎91.73.76.30; métro *Castellane* then bus #19 direction *Madrague-de-Montredon* to *Les Gâtons Plage*; June 10–Oct 10). Cheaper and closer to the beach.

The Vieux Port

The cafés around the east end of the **Vieux Port** indulge the sedentary pleasures of observing street life, despite the fumes of exhausts and half-dead fish – the latter straight off the boats on quai des Belges – and despite the lack of any quayfront claim to beauty. The clientele of Cannes and St-Tropez and, no doubt, the ancient Greeks who built the port in the first place, would find it all unbearably tacky. But it remains as it has always been, the life centre of the city.

Two **fortresses** guard the harbour entrance. **St-Jean**, on the north, dates from the Middle Ages when Marseille was an independent republic. Its enlargement in 1660, and the construction of **St-Nicolas**, on the south, represent the city's final defeat as a separate entity. Loius XIV ordered the new fort to keep an eye on the city – after he had sent in an army, suppressed the city's council, fined it, arrested all opposition and, in an early example of rate-capping, set ludicrously low limits on Marseille's subsequent expenditure and borrowing. Neither of the two forts is open to the public. The best view of the Vieux Port is from the **Palais du Pharo** and its surrounding park (small entrance fee) on the headland beyond Fort Nicolas or, for a wider angle, from the **Notre-Dame-de-la-Garde**, the city's Second-Empire landmark which tops the hill south of the harbour (bus #60).

Basilique St-Victor

A short way inland from the Fort St-Nicolas, above the Bassin de Carénage, is Marseille's oldest church, the **Basilique St-Victor**. Originally part of a monastery founded in the fifth century on the burial site of various martyrs, the church was built, enlarged and fortified – a vital requirement given its position outside the city walls – over a perioed of 200 years, from the middle of the tenth century. It looks and feels like a fortress – the walls of the choir are almost 3m thick – and it's no ecclesiastical beauty. For a small fee you can visit (10am–noon & 3–5pm; closed Sun am) and descend to the crypt and catacombs, a warren of chapels and passages where the weight of stone and age, not to mention the photographs of dug-up skeletons, create an appropriate atmosphere in which to recall the horrors of early Christianity. St-Victor himself, a Roman soldier, was slowly ground to death between two millstones.

Le Panier

To the north of the Vieux Port is the oldest part of Marseille, **Le Panier**, where, up until the last war, tiny streets, steep steps and houses of every era irregularly connected, formed a *vieille ville* typical of the Côte. In 1942, however, Marseille came under German occupation and the quarter became an unoffical ghetto for *Untermensch* – of every sort, including Resistance fighters, Communists and Jews. In January 1943, the Nazis gave the 40,000 inhabitants one day's notice to quit and packed them off to the camps. Dynamite was carefully laid, sparing the three old buildings that appealed to the fascist aesthetic: the seventeenth-century **Hôtel de Ville** on the quay, the **Hôtel de Cabre** on the corner of rue Bonneterie and Grande-Rue, and the **Maison Diamantée** on rue de la Prison. The Maison Diamantée now houses the **Musée de Vieux Marseille** (daily 10am–5pm; 10F), which contains a wonderful hotch-potch of mementoes celebrating old Marseille – a modelled street scene of nineteenth-century insurrectional fighting, recipes for plague antidotes, pre-1943 photographs of the area. After the war, archaeologists reaped some benefits from this destruction in the discovery of the remains of the Roman docks equipped with vast food-storage jars, which can be seen *in situ* at the **Musée des Docks Romains** on pl de Vivaux (daily 10am–5pm; 10F).

The Hospice de la Vieille Charité

Along rue Caisserie you'll find steps leading up to place des Moulins. A couple of blocks further north, and almost hidden by the high tenement buildings around it, stands the **Hospice de la Vieille Charité**, a seventeenth-century workhouse with a gorgeous Baroque chapel surrounded by columned arcades in pink stone, all recently restored. Only the tiny grilled exterior windows recall its original use. It's now perhaps the prettiest building in Marseille and a **cultural centre** (Mon–Fri 10am–5pm, Sat & Sun noon–7pm; 25F) hosting major, and usually brilliant, temporary exhibitions and sheltering the city's main archaeological museum . But people in the local cafés will tell you that it was "*beaucoup plus jolie*" when a hundred local families, all with at least ten children, lived in the Hospice before it was done up. They scoff at the gentrification of Le Panier and jokingly ask how the bourgeois are going to get to the concerts and exhibitions without passing through this eighty-percent-Arab quarter. There is little tension here between the working-class French and the immigrants, and none of them want to be moved out to high-rise HLM council estates on the city's perimeter.

The cathedrals

At the western end of Le Panier overlooking the modern docks are Marseille's twin **cathedrals**: the neo-Byzantine **Major**, overshadowing its predecessor, the Romanesque **Mayor Ancienne** (guided tours only) that stands, much diminished, alongside (Tues–Sun May–Sept 9am–noon & 2.30–6pm; Oct–April 9am–noon & 2–5pm).

Around La Canebière

For the local bourgeoisie, **La Canebière** represents an alarmingly central *cordon sanitaire* with the Algerians. The triangular area to the north, known as the **quartier Belsunce** – delineated by La Canebière, bd d'Athènes, bd d'Aix and cours Belsunce – is an extraordinary, dynamic quarter, the main trading ground for Arabs in Europe and from the Arab world. Hi-fis, suits and jeans from France and Germany are traded with spices, cloth and metalware from across the Mediterranean on flattened cardboard boxes on the streets – and not a French middleman in sight.

The Centre Bourse and the Porte d'Aix

One block west and the **Centre Bourse** provides a stark contrast in a fiendish giant hyper-mall of noise, air-conditioning and overlighting – useful, nevertheless, for mainstream shopping. Behind it is the **Jardin des Vestiges**. This was where the ancient port extended to, curving northwards from the present quai des Belges. Excavations have revealed a stretch of the Greek port and bits of the city wall with the base of three square towers and a gateway, dated to the second or third century BC. A museum in the Bourse complex, the **Musée d'Histoire de Marseille** (Mon–Sat noon–7pm; 10F) presents the rest of the finds, including a third-century wreck of a Roman trading vessel.

The expansion of Marseille's present docks started in the first half of the nineteenth century. Like the new cathedral, wide boulevards and Marseille's own *Arc de Triomphe* – the **Porte d'Aix*** at the top of Cours Belsunce/rue d'Aix – the docks were paid for with the profits of military enterprise, most significantly, the conquest of Algeria in 1830. The Third Empire was the next boom time for Marseillais traders with the opening of the Suez Canal in 1869 giving the city a crucial advantage over other French ports.

The Palais Longchamp and Musée des Beaux-Arts

1869 was also the year in which the **Palais Longchamp**, 2km east of the Vieux Port (bus #80 & #41 or métro *Longchamp-Cinq-Avenues*), was completed. The grandiose conclusion of an aqueduct at Roque Favour (no longer in use), it brought water from the Durance to the city. Water is still pumped into the centre of the colonnade connecting the two palatial wings of the building. Below, an enormous statue looks as if it honours some great feminist victory – three muscular women above four bulls wallowing passively in a pool from which a cascade drops four or five stories to ground level.

The palace's north wing is the city's **Musée des Beaux-Arts** (daily 10am–5pm; 10F) – hot, a little stuffy, but with a fair share of delights. Most unusual, and a pleasant visual treat, are three paintings by Françoise Duparc (1726–76), whose first name has consistently found itself masculinised to François in catalogues both French and English. The nineteenth-century satirist from Marseille, Honoré Daumier, has a whole room for his cartoons. Plans for the city, sculptures, and the famous profile of Louis XIV by the Marseillais, Pierre Puget, are on display along with graphic contemporary canvases of the plague that decimated the city in 1720.

---

*Watch the construction site just south of the Porte d'Aix, for the arrival of Marseille's new billion-franc county hall, a typical piece of high-tech French architecture designed by Will Alsop, due for completion in 1994 and likely to be as controversial as the Centre Pompidou in Paris.

The red light district and Musée Cantini

The prime shopping district of Marseille is encompassed by three streets running **south from La Canebière**: rue Paradis, rue St-Ferréol and rue de Rome, a continuation of cours Belsunce/rue d'Aix. A few blocks to the east you'll run into the city's red-light district, where sex is a visible commodity day and night. Marseille's main collection of twentieth-century and contemporary art, the **Musée Cantini**, is situated in these unlikely surroundings at 19 rue Grignan (Mon–Fri 10am–5pm, Sat & Sun noon–7pm; 15F). You'll find works by artists as diverse as Dufy, Léger, Balthus, Bacon, Vasarely and César, but the overdose of recent acquisitions means that the contents have to rotate.

LE CORBUSIER'S CITÉ RADIEUSE

Four kilometres south of La Canebière on bus #21 or #22 is an entirely different kind of architecture from that in the city centre – Le Corbusier's seventeen-storey **Cité Radieuse**, designed in 1946 and completed in 1952. The *Cité* only fails to amaze now because so many architects the world over have tried to imitate Le Corbusier's revolutionary model. Each apartment has two levels and balconies on both sides of the building with unhindered views of mountains and sea. One floor has shops, restaurants and a post office; the third floor is now a hotel (see p.712); and on the top floor you can admire the sculptural and ceramic roof-decoration.

Beaches

The most popular stretch of sand is the **plage des Catalans**, a few blocks south of the Palais du Pharo. This marks the beginning of Marseille's **corniche**, av J-F-Kennedy, which follows the cliffs past the dramatic statue and arch that frames the setting sun of the **Monument aux Morts des Orients**. South of the monument, steps lead down to an inlet, **Anse des Auffes**, and further down the coast, **Anse de Malmousque**, which are the nearest Marseille gets to being picturesque. Small fishing boats are beached on the rocks, the dominant sound is the sea, and narrow stairways and lanes lead nowhere. There's a **coastal path** you can follow here, with steps down to tiny bays and beaches – perfect for swimming when the Mistral wind is not inciting the waves. You can see along the coast as far as Cap Croisette and, out to sea, the abandoned monastery on the Îles d'Endoume and the Château d'If. The end of the corniche is marked by a copy of Michelangelo's *David*, a stone's throw from the artificially constructed **plage du Prado**, best of the local beaches, with remarkably clean water.

CHÂTEAU D'IF

Blacker than the sea, blacker than the sky, rose like a phantom the giant of granite, whose projecting crags seemed like arms extended to seize their prey.

So the **Château d'If** appears to Edmond Dantès, hero of Alexandre Dumas's *The Count of Monte Cristo*, having made his watery escape after five years of incarceration as the innocent victim of treachery. The reality, for most prisoners, was worse: they went insane or died (and sometimes both) before reaching the end of their sentences. Only the nobles living in the less fetid upper-storey cells had much chance of survival – like one de Niozelles who was given six years for failing to take his hat off in the presence of Louis XIV, and Mirabeau, in for debt.

There's nothing else to the *île* apart from the château which is horribly well preserved. Boats leave from the quai des Belges every hour, on the hour, from 7am to 7pm. The château's opening hours fit the the boat timetable, the journey takes 20 minutes and the round trip costs about 40F.

For **buses** along the corniche, #83 runs from the Vieux Port to av du Prado and #80 from the *Estrangin-Préfecture* métro to the Anse du Vallon de l'Oriel. From av du Prado, #19 runs to Madrague, and #20 on out to Cap Croisette.

Eating and shopping

The Marseillais eat just as well, if not better, than the ancient aristos and skin-stretched stars of the Riviera. Fish and seafood are, not surprisingly, the main ingredients, and the superstar of dishes is the city's own expensive invention, **bouillabaisse**, a saffron- and garlic-flavoured fish soup with bits of fish, croutons and *rouille* to throw in and conflicting theories about which fish and where and how they must be caught.

Takeaway food is excellent value in this city. Along the main boulevards, and particularly cours Belsunce, are stands where, for around 10F you can get a half-baguette filled with steak, or kebabs, omelettes, veal and mushrooms, fishcakes, or a hundred other proper dishes, and chips thrown in on top. For picnic fodder, see "Markets", below.

Restaurants

For a wide range of cheap restaurants, **cours Julien**, in the student area around place Jean-Jaurès, is the best place to head for. More upmarket and fishy is the pedestrian precinct around **place Thiars**, behind the south quay of the Vieux Port. Le Panier and the quartier Belsunce are also good for menu-browsing.

CHEAP TO MODERATE

Chez Angèle, 50 rue Caisserie (☎91.90.63.35). Packed Le Panier local with bargain *menu fixe* for basic French food.

Auberge "In", 25 rue du Chevalier-Roze (☎91.90.51.59; closed Sun). In a health-food shop on the edge of Le Panier. Cheap vegetarian *menu fixe* served lunchtimes and early evenings.

Saf Saf, rue V-Scotto. Cheap, noisy and filling Tunisian restaurant just off La Canebière, in the quartier Belsunce. No alcohol.

Ce Cher Arwell, 96 cours Julien (☎91.48.30.41). Small, popular candle-lit outfit serving generous portions of French cuisine – arrive early or book in advance.

Restaurant Le King 12 rue des Trois-Rois (☎91.42.88.47) One of a number of theme restaurants in a lively street, this one is dedicated to the memory of Elvis. The patron even dresses in passable Presley disguise.

Le Balthazar, 8 rue des Trois-Rois. Chic, intimate French place which throws in a carafe of house wine with its very reasonable *menu fixe*.

EXPENSE ACCOUNT

Chez Michel, 6 rue des Catalans, 7ᵉ (☎91.52.64.22; closed Tues, Wed & July). There's no debate about the *bouillabaisse* ingredients here. A basket of the five fishes, including the elusive and most expensive one, the vicious *racasse*, is presented to the customer before the soup is made. Quite simply *the* place to eat this dish. Expect to pay 250F for the *bouillabaisse* alone.

Maurice Brun, 18 quai Rive-Neuve, 7ᵉ (☎91.33.35.38; closed Sun & Mon). Truly authentic Provençal cooking and a view over the Vieux Port for around 350F a head.

Les Arcenaulx, 25 cours d'Estienne-d'Orves, 1ᵉʳ (☎91.54.77.06; closed Sun & Mon). Superb food for 250F a head in this intellectual haunt overlooking the Malmousque plateau.

Markets : food, philately, flea markets

If you're after picnic fare, the local **markets** can supply all you need and more, even if some can be a bit too specialised – like the stalls of white and violet garlic that fill the cours d'Estienne-d'Orves from mid-June to mid-July. Every *arrondissement* has its daily (Mon–Sat) **morning food market**, if not two or three. The main ones are: **pl Sébastopol** near the Palais Longchamp (métro *Cinq-Avenues-Longchamp*), **pl Jean-Jaurès** (métro *Notre-Dame du Mont cours Julien*) and **av du Prado** (métro *Castellane*).

Other more **specialised markets** include: **stamps** on pl Général-de-Gaulle near the Vieux Port on Sunday morning; **old books and records** all day, every day on pl Auguste-Carli (métro *Noailles*); **clothes**, new and old, all day, every day at 16 rue B-Dubois (métro *Colbert/Guesde*); and the main **flea market**, Sunday morning, on rue Frédéric-Sauvage in the 14ᵉ (métro *Bourgainville*, then bus #29, #30 to *Capitaine Geze*).

Nightlife

The *Virgin Megastore*, 75 rue St-Ferréol, is the best place to go for **tickets and information** on gigs, concerts, theatre, free films and whatever cultural events are going on. They also stock a wide selection of English books and run a café on the top floor, open, like the rest of the store, seven days a week until midnight. Other places to head for info are the book and record shop *FNAC* on the top floor of the Centre Bourse, the café and comic shop, *La Passerelle*, on rue des Trois-Mages, and *Thunder Records* next door. At any of these places, you can pick up a copy of *Taktik*, Marseille's independent weekly listings paper which comes out on a Wednesday. For more mainstream events, check the listings of the city's best daily, *La Marseillaise*, or pick up a copy of the free weekly, *Marseille Poche*.

Film, theatre and other events

Cinéma Paris, 31 rue Pavillon, 1ᵉʳ (☎91.33.15.59). The only cinema in Marseille which regularly shows *VO* (*version originale* – undubbed) films.
L'Avant-Scene, 59 cours Julien, 6ᵉ (☎91.42.19.29). Theatre-cum-restaurant-cum-exhibition-space which often puts on special events for children.
Espace Julien, 33 cours Julien, 6ᵉ (☎91.47.09.64). A mixed-bag arts centre, with theatre, jazz, dance and exhibitions.
Théâtre du Merlan, av Raimu, 14ᵉ. Set amid horrific high-rise housing in the north of the city, this cultural centre is remarkable for having a police commissariat on the ground floor. Occasional shows in English.

Live music: cafés and clubs

La Maison Hantée, 10 rue Vian, 6ᵉ (☎91.92.09.40; closed Mon). *Café-théâtre* alternates with country music, R'n'B and rock.
La Cave à Jazz, 24 quai de Rive-Neuve, 7ᵉ. Jazz club and a place for rock, fashion, theatre and dance.
Maison de l'Étranger, 16 rue Antoine-Zattara, 3ᵉ (☎91.95.90.15). A club not far from the gare SNCF St-Charles which puts on regular world music gigs, especially Raï.
Au Moulin, 47 bd Perrin (☎91.06.33.94; métro *St-Just*). An obscure venue in the northwest of the city specialising in weird and wonderful European bands.
May Be Blues, rue Poggioli, 6ᵉ (☎91.42.41.00; closed Mon & Tues). Relaxed blues/jazz club. No entry charge, though drinks go up once the music starts. Open 8pm–2am.
Le Stendhal, 92 rue Jean-de-Bernady, 1ᵉʳ (☎91.84.74.80) Wide selection of malt whiskeys and beers, including *Courage*, and live music Tuesday and Thursdays. Red and black interior, naturally enough.

Mixed clubs and gay bars

Unfortunately, nights out for the young and energetic without much cash are difficult in Marseille. The **clubs** around cours d'Estienne-d'Orves – mainly jazz, some Caribbean – are for trendy kids from the upper-crust *arrondissements*, with prices to match.
Rose Bonbon, 7 rue Venture, 1ᵉʳ. Just off rue Paradis, as good a place as any if you're determined to bop.
Le Boots, 5 rue Haxo, 1ᵉʳ (11pm onwards; closed Sun). Marseille's only remaining gay club.
Le Bateau Ivre, 15 rue Fongate, 6ᵉ (☎91.48.36.19/91.54.09.32; 7pm–midnight; closed Wed & Sun). The main meeting place for gay and lesbian activists, with snacks, full meals on Friday night, and various exhibitions and discussions.

Listings

Airlines *Air France*, 14 La Canebière, 1er (☎91.54.92.92); *Air Inter*, 8 rue des Fabres, 1er (☎91.91.90.90); *British Airways* (☎91.90.77.10) and *TWA* (☎91.91.66.44) both 41 La Canebière, 1er.

Airport *Aéroport de Marignane* (☎42.78.21.00), bus every 15min from gare SNCF St-Charles 6.15am–8pm, and 1hr 20min before each departure time thereafter.

Bike hire *Green Bike*, 135 av Clot Bey, 8e (☎91.25.36.26). Touring bikes and mountain bikes at around 90F a day.

Crêche facilities *SOS Baby-Sitting*, 175 rue Paradis, 6e (☎91.81.81.81). Around 50F a day.

Consulates *Canada*, 24 av du Prado, 6e (☎91.37.19.37); *Eire*, 148 rue Sainte, 1er (☎91.54.92.29); *UK*, 24 av du Prado, 6e (☎91.53.43.32); *USA*, 9 rue Armény, 6e (☎91.54.92.00).

Disabled *Office Municipal pour Handicappés*, 128 av du Prado, 8e (☎91.81.58.80). Information on disabled access and facilities. Also operates a transport service.

Emergencies: Ambulance: *SAMU* (☎91.49.91.91); Hospital: *Hôtel-Dieu* 6 pl Daviel, Le Panier, 2e (☎91.90.61.14); Doctor: *SOS Médecins* (☎91.52.84.85); Dentist: *SOS Dentistes* (☎91.25.84.85); Drug problems: *Accueil* (☎91.50.56.99); Crisis line: *SOS Amitié* (☎91.76.10.10).

Football *Olympique de Marseille* (*OM* to their fans) play at *Stade Vélodrome Municipale*, 3 bd Michelet (☎91.77.07.28; métro *Rond-point du Prado*).

Hitchhiking *Allo-stop*, 1 pl Gabriel-Péri, 1er (☎91.56.50.51; Mon–Fri 3.30–6.30pm, Sat 10am–noon).

Launderettes *Washmatic*, 77 rue d'Aubagne, 1er; *Renov'Express*, 62 rue Breteuil, 6e; *La Savonnière*, rue Rey, 6e.

Money exchange: *Thomas Cook* at gare SNCF St-Charles; Mon–Fri 6am–8pm, weekends & holidays 6am–6pm.

Poste Restante 1 pl de l'Hôtel-des-Postes, 13001, Marseille.

Rape Crisis ☎91.91.38.50.

Showers (and baths) gare SNCF St-Charles *Relais Toilettes* 5.30am–8.30pm.

Students *CROUS*, 38 rue du 141e R I A, 3e (☎91.95.90.06) for information on work, lodgings and travel.

Travel agencies *Nouvelle Frontières*, 83 rue Sainte, 7e (☎91.54.18.48); *Atoll Voyages* for *BIGE* tickets, 103 La Canebière, 1er (☎91.50.53.03).

Women's centre 95 rue Benoît-Malon, 5e, with people around on Tues & Thurs noon–6pm, Fri 9am–noon; *CODIF* runs a library and information centre at 81 rue Senac, 1er (☎91.47.14.05).

Youth information *CIJ*, Stade Vallier, 4 rue de la Visitation, 4e (☎91.49.91.55).

Cassis and La Ciotat

It's difficult to imagine two towns more dissimilar so close to one another on the Côte; **Cassis** would be more at home round the corner from St-Tropez, while **La Ciotat**, still dominated by its now defunct shipbuilding industry, is more akin to the industrial giants of Marseille and Toulon.

Cassis

A lot of people rate **CASSIS** the best resort this side of St-Tropez – its inhabitants most of all. An old Provençal fishing port hemmed in by high white cliffs, its modern development has been limited to a model toytown on steep inclines in which foreign traffic is not encouraged.

The **gare SNCF** is 3km out of town, with precious few buses to take you into town: it's probably simpler to take the bus which drops you at the **gare routière** on place Montmorin in the centre of town. If you're **camping** don't bother going into town – the campsite, *Les Cigales* (☎42.01.07.34; mid-March–mid-Oct), is just off the D559 from Marseille before av de la Marne turns down into Cassis, a gruelling 1km from the port.

The calanques

Port-side posing and drinking aside, there's not much to do except sunbathe and look up at the town's medieval **castle**, refurbished residence of Monsieur Michelin, the authoritarian boss of the family tyres and guides firm.

The favoured lazy pastime, though, is to take a **boat trip** to the **calanques** – long, narrow, deep inlets which have cut into the limestone cliffs. Several companies operate from the port, but check if they let you off or just tour in and out, and be prepared for rough seas. Or, if you're feeling energetic, you can take the well-marked footpath from the route des Calanques behind the western beach. It's about 90 minutes' walk to the furthest and best, **En Vau**, where you climb down rocks to the shore. Intrepid pine trees find root-holds, and sunbathers find ledges on the chaotic white cliffs. The water is deep blue and swimming between the vertical cliffs is an experience not to be missed.

THE COSQUER CAVE

In 1991, a diver, Henri Cosquer, filmed and photographed a series of wall paintings in a cave near Cassis, whose sole entrance has been underwater since the end of the last ice age. The depictions of hundreds of animals, and of human hands, are similar in style to those found as Lascaux in the Dordogne. Despite the culture minister Jack Lang declaring the Cosquer cave a historic monument, there are doubts about the paintings' authenticity. The problem is that few archaeologists specialising in the palaeolithic (old Stone Age) have the necessary diving experience to take a look. It will be some time before a dry entrance can be drilled from above, and even longer – if ever – for public access to be made. If the sceptics are proved right, the cave will still be a fascinating monument – to the lengths, or depths, people will go to perpetrate a fraud.

Accommodation and food

Cheap **rooms** just don't exist in Cassis, the least expensive being the modern *Laurence*, 8 rue de l'Arène (☎42.01.88.78; ③–⑤), or the *Grand Jardin*, 2 rue P-Eydin (☎42.01.70.10; ④/⑤). For a little more – and a view over the port – try *Le Golfe*, quai Calendal, pl du Grand-Carnot (☎42.01.00.21; ⑤). Even so, you can still end up paying well over ⑤ rates for a double, depending on what's available.

There's also a gorgeously scenic but somewhat inaccessible **IYHF youth hostel**, *La Fontasse* in the hills above the *calanques* west of Cassis (☎42.01.02.72; reception 8–10am & 5–11pm; open all year). From the D559 (stop *Les Calanques*) a road leads down towards the Col de la Gardiole. When it becomes a track, take the left fork and after another 2km you'll find the hostel. Rain water, beds and electricity are the only mod cons, but if you want to explore this wild uninhabited stretch of limestone heights the people running it will advise you enthusiastically. To get to Cassis you can descend to the *calanques* and walk along the coast (about 1hr).

Restaurant tables are in abundance along the port-side quai des Baux; prices vary greatly, but if you can afford it your best bet has to be to follow your nose, and seek out the most enticing fish dish smells. The authentic Provençal *ratatouille* at *Chez Gilbert* (no. 19) is hard to beat, though *El Sol* (no. 23) costs less.

La Ciotat

The old shipbuilding town of **LA CIOTAT**, halfway towards Toulon, is – or rather was, until recently – the only town left on the coast where the Left got more votes than Le Pen. In April 1990, after years of cut-backs, and in anticipation of the yard's closure, the *CGT* embarked on an ultimately unsuccessful all-out strike to try to prevent the inevitable. So while the golden-stoned Vieux Port remains charming, the massive cranes and derricks of the shipyards are a depressing reminder of the town's recent demise. On a happier historical note, La Ciotat is the place where the first film sequence was made, in 1895, by the local-born Lumière brothers.

The town

La Ciotat is not a town for keyed-up museum or monument motivation. Neither is it made for quayside lounging; nevertheless, the **old town** differs little from most other Provençal ports and the **beach** is excellent. There are **boat trips** out to the tiny offshore island, the Île Verte (15min), and a number of nearby *calanques*. The strangest sight in La Ciotat itself is the cluster of rock formations on the promontory beyond the shipyards in the **Parc du Mugel** (April–Sept 9am–12.40pm & 2–7pm; Oct–March 10am–noon & 2–6pm; closed Dec; free; bus #3, direction *La Garde*, stop *Mugel*). A path leads up from the entrance through overgrown vegetation and then past scooped vertical hollows to a narrow terrace overlooking the sea. The cliff face looks like the habitat of some gravity-defying, burrowing beast rather than the erosions of wind and sea.

Practicalities

Arriving at the **gare SNCF**, you'll be confronted by a commemorative plaque to the station's star performance in one of the Lumière films. There's no time to linger, however, since a bus, taking you to the Vieux Port some 4km away, meets every train. The old town and port look out across the Baie de la Ciotat, whose inner curve provides the beaches and resort lifestyle of La Ciotat Plage. The town's spanking new **SI** is at the corner of bd Anatole-France and quai Ganteaume in the Vieux Port: if you're here in the second week of July, they can provide details of the **Festival du Cinéma**.

   Hotels are unfortunately at Côte d'Azur prices. *La Marine*, 1 av F-Gassion (☎42.08.35.11; ③), is probably the best bet in the old town and *Beaurivage*, 1 bd Beaurivage (☎42.83.09.68; ④), best for La Ciotat Plage. La Ciotat has seven **campsites**, three of which are by the sea, of which *St-Jean*, 30 av St-Jean (☎42.83.09.68; open April–Oct; bus #4, direction *Gare SNCF*, stop *St-Jean Village*) is the closest to the centre.

   La Ciotat's **restaurants** are not gastronomically renowned, though *Provence-Plage* serves perfectly respectable fish dishes. On quai Stalingrad, *Le Louveteau* and *L'Escalet* both have very cheap *menus fixes*. Rue Fougasse off the old port and bd Beaurivage in La Ciotat Plage are probably the most productive streets for menu-browsing.

Toulon

Viewed from the distant heights of Mont Caume, Notre-Dame-du-Mai or the Fort de Six-Fours, it's clear why **TOULON** had to be a major port. On the whole French coastline only Brest has an equally perfect roadstead: the Breton port is the base for the French Navy's Atlantic fleet, Toulon for the Mediterranean fleet. But despite its climatic advantage, Toulon shares Brest's problems in enticing tourists. It was half destroyed in the last war, and its rebuilt whole is dominated by the military, shipbuilding and armaments industries. The arsenal created by Louis XIV is now one of the major employers of southeast France.

   The shipbuilding suburbs of La Seyne-sur-Mer are, however, being axed, closing the book on a centuries-old and, at times, notorious industry. Until the eighteenth century, slaves and convicts were still powering the king's galleys, and, following the Revolution, convicts were sent to Toulon with iron collars round their necks for sentences of hard labour – their crimes often petty. After 1854, convicts were deported to the colonies, in whose conquest ships from Toulon played a major part. In 1988, as rising unemployment fuelled resentments, the city has earned itself a dark slot in political history for having voted in the one and only *Front National député*.

The town

If you're dependent on public transport for this stretch of the coast, you'll at least have to pass through Toulon. The **gare SNCF** and **gare routière** are on place Albert I. Turning left and down bd de Tessé three blocks brings you to place Mazarin with av Colbert running to the right towards bd de Strasbourg and quai de Stalingrad on the old port. The **SI** is at 8 av Colbert. The main central street is **bd de Strasbourg**, which becomes av Maréchal-Leclerc to the west and av Georges-Clemenceau to the east.

The **Vieille Ville** – now greatly gentrified and crammed in between bd de Strasbourg and quai de Stalingrad on the old port – is pleasant enough during the day. Full of fountains, more often than not of dolphins, it boasts an excellent daily market around rue Landrin and cours Lafayette, as well as a covered fish market on pl de la Poissonerie. Gentrification is gradually transforming parts of the old town, once presided over by the city's considerable North African population, but towards the quays you'll still find every other door leads to a cheap restaurant, bar, jazz dive, night-club or sex shop. As night falls men outnumber women ten to one on the streets – and most of the women are working. This is less true in the **Mourillon quartier** to the east (bus #3), where trendy nightlife glitters down the Littoral Frédéric-Mistral and the beaches face the open sea.

Mont Faron and museums

The best way to pass an afternoon in Toulon is to leave the town 542 metres below you by ascending the summit of **Mont Faron.** Take bus #40, stop *Téléphérique* on bd Amiral-Vence, Super Toulon and you'll find a funicular (9.15am–noon & 2.15–6pm; closed Mon am; all Mon in winter). It's a bit pricey (30F), but a real treat.

At the top there's a **memorial museum** to the Allied landings in Provence of August 1944 (summer 9am–7pm; winter 9–11.30am & 2–5.30pm; 20F) with screenings of original newsreel footage. In the surrounding park are two restaurants, and a little further up to the right, a **zoo** specialising in big cats. Beyond the zoo, you can walk up the hillside to an abandoned fort and revel in the clean air, the smell of the flowers and the distance from the urban sprawl below.

Town museums

Toulon's sea-level **museums** are not particularly intriguing unless you're obsessed with military history and model ships. The **Musée d'Art**, 113 bd Maréchal-Leclerc (10am–noon & 2–6pm) has a very good collection of paintings and sculpture but not the space to show them all at once. The exhibitions are arranged around themes and the artists whose works you may or may not see include Breughel, Carracci, Puget and the Van Loos; amongst the moderns Vlaminck, Friez, Ziem and Rodin; and of contemporaries, Francis Bacon, Christo, Gilbert & George, and Sol Le Witt. The most impressive public artwork in the city is Pierre Puget's **Atlantes** which hold up all that is left of the old town hall on quai de Stalingrad. It's thought that Puget, working in 1657, modelled these immensely strong, tragic figures on galley slaves.

Accommodation and meals

One of the cheapest and nicest **hotels** is *Les Trois Dauphins*, 9 pl des 3 Dauphins near place Puget (☎94.92.65.79; ②) looking out onto the eighteenth-century fountain of three endearing dolphins. Close by is *Little Palace*, 6 rue Berthelot (☎94.92.26.62; ②), also a bargain and pleasant. *Prémar*, 19 and 21 pl Monsenergue (☎94.92.27.42; ①), is on the dockside and a bit seedy, but dead cheap.

The **youth hostel** operates only in July and August: it's on rue Ernst-Renan, Quartier Mourillon (☎94.24.34.96; bus #3 from av Leclerc, direction *Mourillon*, stop *Lamalgue*

BOAT TRIPS AND EXCURSIONS OUT OF TOULON

Several companies offer **boat trips with commentary** around the **Grande et Petit Rade** (Harbour), including *Service Maritime Touristique Varois* and *SNRTM* from quai Stalingrad; and *Vedette Alain* from quai de la Sinse. A much cheaper option, which also spares you the guide, is to take the **public transport boats** from quai Stalingrad to La Seyne, Les Sablettes and St-Mandrier.

La Seyne, a town inseparable from the naval shipyards, had a Communist city council for forty years, and now has a mayor who has busied himself privatising once-public services, firing public employees, and contributing to an unemployment rate of 22 percent.

To the west, by walking, hitching, cycling or the odd bus, you could reach **Six-Fours**, in about 5km. This straggling retirement town pushes up against the hills of the Cap Sicié peninsula. The peninsula has some nice enough walking opportunities through rising heath and woodland – nothing too strenuous or exhilarating unless you make the steep climb up to the riskily positioned chapel, Notre-Dame-du-Mai, on the high cape itself.

St-Mandrier-sur-Mer is sandwiched between the high walls of *terrain militaire* that covers most of the St-Mandrier peninsula to the east of Cap Sicié. Only the bay of Lazaret just before you reach Les Sablettes is free of battleships, with rickety wooden jetties and fishing huts and a surreal Islamic building on the shore past Tamaris.

---

and walk up rue Castel). You could also try the women-only *Foyer de la Jeunesse*, 11–12 pl d'Armes (☎94.93.05.55), which will rent rooms if there's any space.

One of the pleasures of Toulon is **eating**. There are plenty of *brasseries*, cafés and restaurants along the quayside, some selling just sandwiches, while others offer wonderful seafood-based *menus fixes* for under 100F. *La Nautique* is the most popular seafront café for light snacks; *Le Thalassa* and the *Grand Café de la Rade* both serve fishy *plats du jour*, but *La Tartare* is the place to head if they're doing their famous *paella* or mussels. Away from the quayside, *Le Cellier* at 13 rue Jean-Jaurès is good value. Finally, if you're prepared to spend a few more francs, try *Le Ferme*, 6 pl Louis-Blanc (closed Sun and Aug).

THE CENTRAL RESORTS AND ISLANDS

Out of season, the stretch of coastline **between Hyères and Cannes** – the "Côte d'Azur proper" – and its backdrop of wooded hills hold its own against the cynicism engendered by tourist brochure overkill. The magic lies in almost sub-tropical vegetation, silver beaches glimpsed between purple cliffs, secluded islands and medieval hilltop villages. Granted, you're unlikely to tread new ground or make any discoveries of your own, and the seasonal traffic jams and spot-the-square-foot-of-sand beaches are to be avoided, but, out of season, it's still possible to feel very happy to be here.

There are no cities along this stretch: **Hyères**, which preserves a certain air of gentility, and the **St-Raphael-Fréjus** conurbation, are the biggest towns. Of the resorts, **Cavalaire** is probably the least status-conscious; **St-Tropez** is a must, for a day's visit at least; and out to sea, the **Îles d'Or** shelter some of the best fauna and flora in Provence. Inland, the dark wooded hills of the **Massif des Maures** form a backdrop to most of this coast, with the ancient villages of **Collobrières** and **La Grande Freinet** providing contrasting targets – the former as unchanged as you could hope for, the latter still enchanting, but increasingly hemmed in by luxury villas.

Hyères

Lacking a central seafront, **HYÈRES,** the oldest resort on the Côte – listing Queen Victoria and Tolstoy among its early admirers – lost out on snob-appeal when the Côte clientele switched from winter convalescents to quayside strutters. It has the unique distinction on the Côte of not being totally dependent on the summer influx and, while there were fears recently that the declining saltworks would be dispensed with, the land drained and mammoth tourist complexes built, that plan, for the moment, is just a gleam in a speculator's eye, opposed both locally and nationally.

Hyères is consequently very appealing. The old town is neither a tourist trap nor a slum, and the surrounding orchards, nursery gardens, vineyards and fields of early vegetables – taking up land which elsewhere would have been developed into a rash of holiday shelving units – are crucial to Hyères' economy. The town exports **exotic plants**, of which the most important is the date palm, which grace every street in Hyères (and numerous desert palaces in Arabia). The only blight on all this is the presence of an Air Force base, just north of the main port, from which test pilots play up and down the coast with the latest fiendish multi-million franc exports.

Arriving and practicalities

Walled and medieval, old Hyères lies on the slopes of Casteou hill, 5km from the sea and with a ruined **castle** on its summit. From the top of the keep and the ivy-clad towers that outreach the oak and lotus trees, you can see the modern palm-lined expansion of the town and, beyond, the peculiar **Presqu'île de Giens,** leashed to the mainland by an isthmus and a parallel sand bar enclosing salt marshes. The isthmus, known as **La Capte,** is covered by houses and hotels; the much narrower sand bar just carries the route de Sel. Out to sea, east of Giens, the three **Îles d'Or** are visible.

Arriving by air at the Toulon-Hyères airport, you'll either need to take a taxi into town, take a bus from Hyères plage, (a short walk from the airport on the D42) or stay somewhere in the immediate vicinity of the airport. The seaside suburbs of HYÈRES PLAGE and AYGUADE-CEINTURON are both possible options.

Arriving by train you'll find yourself at the end of av Edith-Cavell, 1500m south of the central pl Clemenceau. The **gare routière** is on pl Clemenceau and frequent buses link it with the gare SNCF. From the *place* a medieval gatehouse opens onto rue Massillon and the **Vieille Ville.** Av des Îles-d'Or and its continuation, av Général-de-Gaulle, which runs into pl Clemenceau, form the boundary between the old and new towns. Av Gambetta leads due south towards the port and the Presqu'île de Giens, and there are frequent buses from the gare routière on pl Maréchal-Joffrey to the port (a 15-minute journey).

The **SI** is in the *Rotunde Jean-Salusse* on av de Belgique, two blocks south from pl Clemenceau. **Bikes** and **mopeds**, which you may well need, can be hired at 59 av Alfonse-Denis or 33 av Gambetta, and there's a launderette on traverse Alfonse-Denis.

Accommodation

The one **hotel** in the *vieille ville* is the *Hôtel du Soleil*, rue du Rempart (☎94.65.16.26; ⑤), in a renovated house at the foot of the parc St-Bernard. That apart, the nearest you can stay is at the *Globe*, 10 cours de Strasbourg (☎94.65.05.55; ①/②), a bit dingy but cheap and very close to the gare routière. A short and pleasant walk from the ruins of the ancient château, *Les Orangers*, 64 av des Îles-d'Or (☎94.65.07.01; ③), is extremely comfortable and reasonably priced; and right in the centre of the modern town, the *Hôtel de la Poste*, 7 av Lyautey (☎94.65.02.00; ④), is another option, though overpriced for what it is.

By the sea, *Le Calypso*, Hyères-Plage (☎94.58.02.09; ③), has reasonable rates and a good deal for *demi-pension*. *La Reine Jane* (☎94.66.32.64; ④/⑤) at the Port de l'Ayguade is friendly and run, for once, by a young couple. *La Paella* (☎94.57.42.14; ④) seems overpriced, but it's only 200m from the airport and handy for the beach.

There's no youth hostel near Hyères but plenty of **campsites** on the coast: *Capricorne* (☎94.65.18.55; mid-April–Oct) at LES SALINS; 1* *Bernard* (☎94.66.309.54; Easter–Sept) and 1* *Le Parc* (☎94.66.31.77; July–Aug) at L'AYGUADE-CEINTURON (signed off the D42 just after the airport); the 3* *St-Pierre-des-Horts* (☎94.57.65.31) at L'ALMANARRE; *Campsite La Capte* (☎94.58.00.20; Easter–Oct) on the beach at LA CAPTE; the 3* *Camping Caravaning de la Presqu'île de Giens* (☎94.58.22.86; April–Oct) and a great many more.

Eating and drinking

For **eating and drinking**, there are the terraced café-*brasseries* and **morning market** in pl Massillon; good **fresh produce** to be found in rue Massillon; and, all around this corner of the **Vieille Ville**, a good choice of *crêperies*, pizzerias and little bistros that serve *plats du jour* for around 80F. *Les Templiers*, 2 rue des Écuries off rue Portalet (☎94.65.55.16), has a huge choice of meat, fish, pizzas and crêpes, and further down *La Bergerie*, 16 rue de Limans (☎94.65.57.97), is a friendly and down-to-earth pizzeria, with excellent salads and pizzas that are cooked under your nose in a coal-fired oven. Should you be overcome by a craving for the odd combination of Japanese and American cuisines, you'll find both at *Phil's Grill*, 46 av Gambetta (closed Sun & Sat lunchtime). Spanish food is on offer at *La Parillada del Puerto* on the quayside of the **Port d'Hyères**.

The town and beaches

Entering the **Vieille Ville** at pl Massillon you encounter a perfect Provençal square, animated by a daily market and with terraced cafés overlooking a twelfth-century tower, remnant of a Knights Templar lodge. To the right of the tower a street leads uphill to place St-Paul from which you have a panoramic view over a section of medieval town wall to the Mont des Oiseaux and the Golfe de Giens.

Wide steps fan out from the Renaissance door of the former collegiate church of **St-Paul**. It is only used for special services – the main place of worship is the mid-thirteenth-century former monastery church of **St-Louis** on pl de la République. The belfry of St-Paul is pure Romanesque, as is the choir, though the simplicity of the design is masked by the collection of votive offerings hung inside. The decoration also includes some splendid wrought-iron horror movie candelabras, and a Christmas crib with over-life-size *santons* (visiting 2.30–5pm; in summer 3–6pm).

To the right of the church a Renaissance house bridges rue St-Paul, its turret supported by a pillar rising beside the steps. Through this arch you can head up via rue St-Bernard to the **parc St-Bernard**, full of almost every Mediterranean flower, the Castel St-Clair, and on up to the ruined **citadel**.

Hyères' most original building, the cubist château **Castel St-Clair,** designed by Mallet-Stevens in the 1920s, has now been restored, but only its gardens and terrace, with an excellent view of Hyères and the islands, are open to the public. One wing is given over to the Botanic Conservatory of Porquerolles (Mon–Fri 8am–noon & 2–5pm), and little else can be seen of the interior even by peering in through the windows. To get there, take passage Alain-Samarin from near the *Hôtel Les Orangers* and continue climbing. All the luminaries of Dada and surrealism stayed here, including Man Ray, who used it as the setting for one of his most inarticulate films, *Le Mystère du Château de Dé*.

The modern town and municipal museum

The switch from medieval to eighteenth- and nineteenth-century Hyères is as abrupt as it is radical. Wide boulevards and open spaces, opulent villas, waving palm fronds, whitewashed walls instead of weathered stone, and a strong hint of British colonialism, are the characteristics of the modern town.

If you're keen on the ancient history of this coast, the **municipal museum** (Mon–Fri 10am–noon & 3–6pm; Sat & Sun 10am–noon; closed Tues) on pl Lefèvre may be interesting. It displays the finds of the archaeological digs at **L'Almanarre**, the point where the route de Sel from the Presqu'île de Giens joins the coast. The name derives from the Arabic for "lighthouse", which is what the Saracens built higher up the slope after destroying a Benedictine monastery, leaving only the chapel of St-Pierre-de-la-Manarre.

Out to the coast: beaches around Hyères

Heading down towards the Presqu'île de Giens (*L'Almanarre* or *Hyères-Plage* bus) you pass – on your right, just before the road forks to L'Almanarre and the airport – Costabelle hill, topped by a 1950s edifice, **Notre-Dame-de-Consolation**. A concrete, stone and stained-glass classic of its sorry architectural era, it houses an ancient statue of Our Lady, the object of pilgrimage for almost a millennium.

The **Presqu'île de Giens**, besides the peculiarity of its attachment to the mainland (last broken by storms in 1811), is a fairly nondescript and upmarket resort. It has some fine cliffs facing the sea, and in rough weather you can understand why so many wrecks have been discovered here. **La Tour Fondu**, a Richelieu construction on the eastern side, overlooks the small port that serves the Îles d'Or.

Boats for the islands also leave from the **Port d'Hyères**, beside **Hyères-Plage** back on the mainland. Traffic fumes and the proximity to the airport make the **beaches** here rather undesirable despite the pines and ubiquitous palms. Better to head down **La Capte** – the wider arm of the peninsula – or west of **L'Almanarre**, or up the coast past **Le Centurion Plage** and **Ayguade Plage** to the little fishing port of **Les Salins d'Hyères**. East of Les Salins, where the coastal road finally turns inland, you can follow a path between abandoned saltflats and the sea to a naturist beach.

If you have your own transport, make for the **Cap de Brégançon**, and the beaches along the indented, almost undeveloped coast 15–20km east of Hyères, before LE LAVANDOU. There are three private beaches, all *payant* (about 30F per person), but very pretty, clean and uspoilt, with facilities, and camping possible; the first is the nicest.

The Îles d'Or

A haven from tempests in ancient times, then the peaceful home of monks and farmers, the **Îles d'Or** became, from the Middle Ages onwards, a target for piracy and coastal attacks by an endless succession of assorted aggressors.

The islands are covered in forts, half destroyed, rebuilt or abandoned, dating from the sixteenth century, when François I started a trend of under-funded fort building, to the twentieth century, when the German gun positions on Port-Cros and Levant were put out of action by the Americans. Porquerolles and Levant are still not free of garrisons, thanks to the knack of the French armed forces for getting prime beauty sites for bases. In this case, the army only acquired its *terrain militaire* in 1971, when the French government bought most of the archipelago to save the islands from overdevelopment and to protect their unique fauna and flora. Though controversial, this has prevented the otherwise inevitable Côte build-up, and, in the non-military areas, the government, through the *Parc National de Port-Cros* and the *Conservatoire Botanique de Porquerolles*,

---

FERRIES TO THE ÎLES D'OR

Departures are from:

La Tour Fondue on the Presqu'île de Giens (☎94.58.21.81; bus #66 from the Port d'Hyères). Summer services to all three islands; all year round to Porquerolles.

Toulon (quai Stalingrad; ☎94.92.96.82). June–Sept services to all three islands.

Le Lavandou (15 quai Gabriel-Péri; ☎94.71.01.02). Year-round daily services to Île du Levant and Port Cros, thrice-weekly service to Porquerolles (daily mid-July–Aug).

Cavalaire (☎94.64.08.04). Summer-only services to all three islands.

Port d'Hyeres (☎94.57.44.07). Services to Port-Cros and Levant all year and to all three islands mid-July–August.

---

has taken some sound **environmental initiatives**. On **Porquerolles**, the largest island, water is recycled using the natural means of sun-bred micro-organisms; electricity is generated from gas produced from cane; fertilisers used are compost not chemical; and cars are banned. **Port-Cros** and its small neighbour **Bagaud** are just about uninhabited, so there the main problem is controlling the flower-picking and litter-dropping habits of visitors. On **Levant** the military rule all but a tiny morsel of the island.

Whatever measures are taken to protect them, the Îles d'Or are still a very fragile environment; but their hot, wild, scented greenery, sea and sun constitute the essence of what makes this part of the planet so desirable. **Staying on them**, however, your only cheap option is camping on Levant: accommodation on Porquerolles and Port-Cros is limited to pricey hotels only.

Porquerolles

PORQUEROLLES is the most easily accessible of the Îles d'Or and has a permanent village around the port, with a few hotels and restaurants, plenty of cafés, a market and interminable games of *boules*. In summer its population explodes to over 10,000, but there is some activity year round. This is the only cultivated island and it has its own wine, *appellation Côtes des Îles*.

You can hire **bicycles** from outlets all over the island, but the cheapest option is to pay for the bike with your ferry ticket in Tour Fondue and pick it up as you land in Porquerolles.

The village

The origins of the ancient **Fort Ste-Agathe** which overlooks the village are unknown, but it already existed in 1200, and was refortified by François I, who built a tower with 5-metre thick walls to resist canon fire. The fort has a small **museum** dedicated to wrecks.

The **village** itself dates from a more recent settlement of Napoléon's veterans, whom the emperor felt deserved an island paradise for their retirement. The extent of military influence is evident in the central place d'Armes, named after its original function as a military exercise ground and nowadays thronged with holidaymakers in summer. The village's first non-military notoriety, and a shaping influence on modern developments, came in the 1960s, when Jean-Luc Godard used it – and the calanque de la Treille at the far end of the Plage de Notre-Dame – for the bewildering finale of the film *Pierrot le Fou*.

Around the island

Porquerolles is big enough to get lost in, amid its stunning landscapes. The **lighthouse** due south of the village and the **calanques** to its east make good destinations for an hour or two's walk, though don't even think of swimming on this side of the island. The southern shoreline is all cliffs with scary paths meandering close to the edge through heather and exuberant *maquis* scrub. Gentle sandy **beaches** are to be found on either side of the village. The longest beaches are the **plage de Notre-Dame** and the **plage de la Coutard**, the former 3km northeast of the village just before the *terrain militaire* that takes up the northern tip, and the latter a yachting harbour, with wind-surfers for hire, stretching from the port to the pointe Lequin, where the plage de Notre-Dame starts. The nearest beach to the village, 1km away (continue away from the port past the *Arche de Noë* and take the first, well-signed right) is the **plage d'Argent**, a 500-metre strip of white sand around a curving bay, backed by pine forests and a single restaurant.

Practicalities

Hotels in Porquerolles are generally well over the ⑨ price bracket, and need to be booked months in advance. The most expensive and deluxe is *Le Mas du Langoustier* (☎94.58.30.09; half-board compulsory; mid April–Oct) at the western end of the island. On pl d'Armes in the village, *Auberge de l'Arche de Noé* (☎94.58.30.74; ⑨) with just five attractive rooms, and *Relais de la Poste* (☎94.58.30.26; ⑨) are both well run and good value considering the location. There's no campsite on Porquerolles and *camping sauvage* is strictly forbidden, so it's inadvisable to miss the last ferry to the mainland.

Restaurants in the village are pure tourist fodder. If you've money to burn, you can snack on lobster at the *Mas du Langoustier* (see above), or if you merely feel wealthy, try the grilled fish and paella at the *Auberge de l'Orée du Bois* in the middle of the island on the rue du Phare (the road to the lighthouse). Fortunately, if you arrive in the morning you will be able to buy picnic **provisions**.

Port-Cros

The dense vegetation and mini-mountains of **PORT-CROS** make its exploration much tougher than Porquerolles, even though it is less than half the size. Aside from ruined forts and the handful of buildings around the port, the only intervention on the island's wildlife are the classification labels to some of the plants and the extensive network of paths. You're not supposed to stray from these signposted routes and it would be very difficult to do so given the thickness of the undergrowth. **Staying on Port Cros**, sadly, is not much of an option. The sole island **hotel** is prohibitively expensive, as are the few restaurants around the port, though you can get a sandwich or a slice of pizza. Again, **camping is forbidden**.

The entire island is a protected zone – no smoking outside the port area, no picking of flowers – and, as the only member of the archipelago with natural springs, Port-Cros has the richest **fauna and flora**. Kestrels, eagles and sparrow hawks nest here; there are shrubs that flower and bear fruit at the same time, and more common species like broom, lavender, rosemary and heather flourish in abundance. If you come armed with a botanical dictionary, the leaflet provided by the National Park organisation based at the port will reveal all the species to be seen, watched and smelled. It takes a couple of hours to walk from the port to the nearest beach, **plage de la Palu**; a similar time to cross the island via **Vallon de la Solitude** or **Vallon de la Fausse Monnaie**. You can also follow a 10-kilometre **circuit of the island**.

At the Fort de Lestissac, on the way to the plage de la Palu, there's an exhibition on the island **marine life** which is also protected (July–Sept 10am–6pm). If you have a snorkel and mask the shallow waters between Palu beach and the tiny offshore island are full of diverting fishes. More serious scuba divers explore the underwater world around the **Îlot de la Gabinière** off the southern shore.

Levant: the nudist colony

The ÎLE DE LEVANT – ninety percent military reserve – is almost always humid and sunny. Cultivated plant life goes wild, with the result that giant geraniums and nasturtiums climb three-metre hedges, overhung by gigantic eucalyptus trees and yucca plants. The tiny bit of the island spared by the military is a **nudist colony**, set up in the village of **Heliopolis** in the early 1930s. About sixty people live here all the year round, joined by thousands who come just for the summer, and tens of thousands of day trippers. The residents' preferred street dress, *"les plus petits costumes en Europe"*, is on sale as you get off the boat.

Visitors who come just for a couple of hours tend to be treated as voyeurs. If you stay, even for one night, you'll generally receive a much friendlier reception. Unfortunately, this option is open only to campers or big spenders. There are three **campsites**: *Le Colombero* (☎94.05.90.29; Easter–Oct), *Les Eucalyptes* (☎94.05.91.32) and *La Pinède* (☎94.05.90.47; April–Oct). The **hotels** on Levant, apart from two exceptions, *Le Minimum* (☎94.05.90.03; ④/⑤) and *La Source,* chemin de l'Aygade, close to the port (☎94.05.91.36; Easter–mid-Oct; ④), both with reasonably priced rooms, are even more expensive than those on Porquerolles; all require advance booking and most full- or half-board.

Levant has a better choice of **restaurants** than the other islands, though prices and quality still don't match, even taking into account the cost of transporting supplies. The restaurant of *La Source* (see above) is reasonable, with a good 110F menu.

The Corniche des Maures

The Côte really gets going with the resorts of the **Corniche des Maures**, as multi-million-dollar residences lurk increasingly in the hills, even more luxurious yachts in the bays, and prices – for everything – move into Major League. You can sip the divinest cocktail under the warmest moon, purchase swimwear made of leopard skin, or have your car stereo nicked while you're waiting at the lights. You've arrived at the Côte of Legend, the coast where the rich and famous go to seed: Douglas Fairbanks Jnr (a house in Bormes), the late Grand Duke of Luxembourg, and a host of titled names that *Tatler* readers are assumed to be acquainted with.

The Corniche des Maures includes beaches that shine silver without a filter on the lens; tall dark pines, oaks and eucalyptus to shade them; glittering rocks of purple, green and reddish hue; no trains; no motorways. The resorts themselves might, to an outsider, look similar, but for aficionados each is carefully delineated in terms of money and populace, snobbery and style.

Sheer expense aside, **transport** is the one big problem: this is very much auto-land. Buses are extremely slow, especially in high season, and cycling doesn't get you very far unless you're *Tour de France* material.

Bormes-les-Mimosas

BORMES-LES-MIMOSAS, like all good Provençal villages, is indisputably medieval, with a ruined but restored castle at the summit protected by spiralling lines of pantiled houses backing onto short-cut flights of steps. Attractions include a museum of turn-of-the-century regional painting, a mindlessly ugly pleasure port down by La Favière, flanked by torso-covered beaches; and addresses in the Vieux Village such as "alleyway of lovers", "street of brigands", and "arse-breaker street" (*rue Roumpi-Cuou*). The mimosas here, and all along the Côte d'Azur, are no more indigenous than the people passing in their Porsches: the tree was introduced from Mexico in the 1860s.

The most reasonable **hotels** in the old village are *La Terrasse*, pl Gambetta (☎94.71.15.22; ①/②), with ordinary, clean rooms; *Le Provençal*, rue de la Plaine-des-Anes (☎94.71.15.25; ②), and the *Bellevue*, pl Gambetta (☎ 94.71.15.15; ②). The **campsites** are by the sea off the road to Cap Bénat, closer to Le Lavandou than to Bormes. In high season you should book. Some names and addresses in descending order of price are: *Camp du Domaine*, La Favière (☎94.71.03.12; April–Oct), *La Célinette*, La Favière (☎94.71.07.98; March–mid-Oct), and *Les Cyprès*, av de la Mer, La Favière (☎94.64.86.50; Easter–Oct). For more information, the **SI** in Bormes is at 1 rue J-Aicard.

This being the Côte proper, **restaurants** become rather interesting, though more costly than a hotel room. *Nouvelle cuisine* is served in a tunnel of vines and roses at *La Tonnelle des Délices*, pl Gambetta (☎94.71.34.84; last orders 10pm). *La Cassole*, ruelle du Moulin (☎94.71.14.86; last orders 9.30pm), is a better choice if you're starving, with the most wonderful apple charlotte to plug the last gap. *Le Bonsaï* on pl du Bazaar (☎94.64.85.75) serve a French version of Vietnamese cuisine in chic surroundings. More ordinary dinners can be had at the cheaper hotels listed above and at *La Pastourelle* on rue Carnot.

Le Lavandou

Another Mediterranean fishing village turned characterless pleasure port, **LE LAVANDOU** has little to offer to the yachtless traveller. Ageing photos of old Lavandou festooning the tourist office only serve to remind of the contrast with today's glittering resort, where the sea is hardly visible for yachts, and the remaining beach is continually invaded by the construction of further mooring space. And while tourism has caused the village's population to swell from a few hundred at the turn of the century to around 5,000, the number of boats in the original fishing fleet has dropped from fifty to just twelve, and these are difficult to spot for yachts and schooners.

In summer, if you haven't booked in advance, your chances of finding a **hotel room** are pretty slim. Prices are similar to Bormes with rather less charm at the bottom end of the range. Hotels to try include: *Le Gascogne*, chemin des Douaniers (☎94.71.01.22; ③); *Neptune*, 26 av Général-de-Gaulle (☎94.71.01.01; ④); *L'Oustaou*, 20 av Général-de-Gaulle (☎94.71.12.18; ④); and *Terminus*, pl des Joyeuses-Vacances (☎94.71.00.62; ③).

Sea-view **gourmandise** is pricey chez *L'Algue Bleue*, 62 av du Général-de-Gaulle (☎94.71.01.95; May–Oct; last orders 10.30pm). Rue Patron-Ravello, reached from the seafront up a set of steps near the *Le Château* restaurant, is the best street for menu browsing with some good cheapies such as *La Ramade* at no. 16 and *Zidore* at no. 20.

East to the Baie de Cavalaire

Fishing fleets still bring their catches to the quayside at **St-Clair**, **Cavalière**, **Pramousquier** and **Cavalaire-sur-Mer**, and the odd cove and headland might still be recognisable to someone who tended nets in the early decades of this century. But the massive build-up around the **Baie de Cavalaire** would make them think Marseille or some such metropolis had been shifted to this coast.

Circumventing "private property" signs to explore the rocks and coves between Cap Nègre and Cap Cavalaire, drinking local wine, sunbathing and cooling off in the translucent waters are the usual means of seduction by this alluring coast.

Baie de Cavalaire practicalities

For **places to stay** you'll find the exquisite villages of CAVALIÈRE and PRAMOUSQUIER extremely unamenable. CAVALAIRE-SUR-MER and LA CROIX-VALMER, on the other hand, are bursting with hotels, and out of season can almost certainly accommodate you without a reservation. La Croix-Valmer is a rather more pleasant town than Cavalaire, but its location 3km from the nearest beach – the plage de Gigaro – makes it an impractical base for sun worshippers without their own transport. Both towns are close neighbours to St-Tropez and prices can be very high. The local SIs are at Jardin de la Gare in La Croix-Valmer and on square de Lattre-de-Tassigny by the seafront in Cavalaire.

In Cavalaire cheaper **hotel** options, all in av des Alliés, (a continuation of RN559 as you approach from Le Lavandou), include *Le Marigny* (☎94.64.04.48; ③), *Le Petit Vatel* (☎94.64.11.10, mid-March–Oct; ③) and *Raymond* (☎94.64.07.32, Easter–Sept; ④). The *Pergola* on Promenade du Port (☎94.64.06.86; over ⑤) is an attractive upmarket option.

In La Croix-Valmer, try the simple, badly decorated *Hôtel la Bienvenue*, rue Centrale (☎94.79.60.23; ④), or the rather more pleasant *Ricarde*, 2km from the town centre in the direction of Cavalaire off the RN559, 150m from the plage d'Embarquation (☎94.79.64.07; Easter–Sept; ③). Upmarket options situated in the lush green hills overlooking the plage de Gigaro include the lovely *Château Valmer* (☎94.79.71.46; ⑤) and the *Hôtel la Pinède* (☎94.54.31.23; ⑤).

La Croix-Valmer's **campsite**, *Selection* (☎94.79.61.97; mid-April–Sept), is 2.5km southwest of the town centre on the main road to Le Lavandou. Among the camping options in Cavalaire is the 3-star *Pinède* on chemin des Mannes (☎94.64.11.14; mid-March–Oct) off av des Alliés.

Serious **eating** is to be done at the *Souleias* hotel's restaurant at the plage de Gigaro (☎94.79.61.91) or at *Le Club*, Cavalaire's most expensive watering hole. And there's a reasonably priced Chinese–Vietnamese restaurant, *La Grande Muraille* on promenade du Port in Cavalaire. Cheap eats though – crêpes, pizzas and so forth – are not a problem, and nor is fresh fish if you're self-catering.

The Massif des Maures

The secret of the Côte d'Azur is that, however grossly vulgar the conglomeration of the coast, Provence is still just behind – old, sparsely populated, village-orientated and dependent on the land for produce, not real estate. Between Marseille and Menton, the most bewitching hinterland is the **Massif des Maures** stretching from Hyères to Fréjus. The highest point of these hills stops short of 800m, but the quick succession of ridges, the sudden drops and views and then closure again, and the curling looping roads are pervasively mountainous. Where the lie of the land gives a wide bowl of sunlit slopes, vines are grown. Elsewhere the hills are thickly forested, with aleppo and umbrella pines, holly, cork oaks and sweet chestnut trees.

Much of the Massif is inaccessible even to walkers. However, the **GR9 footpath** follows the highest and most northerly ridge from PIGNANS on the N97 past NOTRE-DAME-DES-ANGES, LA SAUVETTE, LA GARDE-FREINET and down to the head of the Golfe de St-Tropez. The best place for **information about walking** is the *Comité Départemental de Tourism* at St-Raphaël or the Toulon SI. If you're **cycling**, the **D14** that runs 42km through the middle, parallel to the coast, from PIERREFEU-DU-VAR north of Hyères to COGOLIN near St-Tropez, is manageable and stunning, climbing from 150m to 411m above sea level.

Collobrières

At the heart of the Massif is the ancient village of **COLLOBRIÈRES**, reputed to have been the first place in France to learn from the Spanish that a certain tree plugged into bottles allows a wine industry to grow. From the Middle Ages until very recent times **cork** production has been the major business of the village.

The church, the Mairie and the houses don't seem to have been modernised this century. Yet the **Confiserie Azurienne** exudes efficiency and modern business skill in the manufacture of all things chestnut: ice cream, jam, nougat, purée, and *marrons glacées* (shop 9am–noon & 2–6pm).

If you're too overdosed on sticky chestnut to move, or you've fallen in love with the place, there's one **hotel**, *Notre-Dame*, 15 av de la Libération (☎94.48.07.13), which is reasonably priced but has very few rooms. The **camping municipal** (☎94.48.07.01) is open only in July and August. For **food**, other than chestnuts, the *Restaurant de la Petite Fontaine* at 1 pl de la République (☎94.48.00.12; last orders 8.30pm; closed Sun pm) is congenial and affordable but books up fast. If you want to buy some local **wines** there's *Les Vignerons de Collobrières* close to the Hotel *Notre-Dame*.

La Garde-Freinet

LA GARDE-FREINET, originally known as Le Fraxinet, was the Saracens' headquarters in the Maures, and their fortress above the village was the base from which attacks on the interior were made. The foundations, beside the ruins of a fifteenth-century castle, are still visible. Follow the signs to the GR9 at the northern end of the village; a path leads from a car park down to a cross and then up to the fort – about 1km in all, and steep. Today the main occupiers of the village are Oxbridge professors and other anglos with time on their hands. The location is desirable: top notch medieval charm in the **Vieux Village** around the church; tasteful villas hiding behind walls and trees; easy walks to stunning panoramas; **markets** twice a week (Wed & Sun) plus all the modern necessities; and just the right distance – about 25km – from St-Tropez.

For **rooms**, *La Sarrasine* on rue Longue or the D588 after it turns west at the top of the village (☎94.43.67.16; ②) is good value for this part of the world and has an excellent **restaurant**; *Hôtel Fraxinois* on rue François-Pelletier (reception at the *Tabac-Presse*, ②) is also reasonable. There's also a **youth hostel** on route de St-Tropez (☎94.43.60.05, mid-March–mid-Sept) and two **campsites**: the municipal, *Saint-Eloi* (☎94.43.62.40; June–Sept) on the D558 towards GRIMAUD, and *Camping de Bérard* (☎94.43.21.23 or ☎94.43.62.93) at a neighbouring farm.

La Garde's renowned **restaurant** is *La Faucado* at 31 bd de l'Esplanade (☎94.43.60.41; last orders 10pm; closed Tues out of season; booking essential); it's a bit overpriced but serves some beautiful dishes from local produce. Around pl Vieille you'll find other cheaper eateries and on pl du Marché a young, arty café-cum-cocktail bar, *Le Lézard*, with occasional jazz sessions.

Grimaud

GRIMAUD is a film set of a *village perché*, where the cone of houses enclosing the eleventh-century church and culminating in the ruins of a medieval castle appears as a single, perfectly unified entity, decorated by its trees and flowers. The most vaunted street in this ensemble is rue des Templiers which leads up to the pure Romanesque **Église St-Michel** and a house of the Knights Templars. The view from the château ruins are superb. If you're stopping **to eat**, the *Café de France* on pl Neuve (last orders 10pm; closed Tues) serves good local dishes for a reasonable price on a vine-covered terrace. The food at the converted twelfth-century chapel, *Le Coteau Fleuri*, pl des Pénitents (pm only, except Sun; closed Jan–mid-May & Tues except July–Aug; last orders 9.30pm), is a lot more upmarket but not always any tastier.

Cogolin

What makes **COGOLIN** special is the combination of tourism with traditional craft manufacturing – of wind instrument reeds, pipes, cane furniture, silk yarn and knotted wool carpets. They're all serious businesses for the one-off, made-to-order, high-quality and high-cost Côte d'Azur market. One immediate consequence is that Cogolin is alive all the year round, so out of season you might well want to stay here. There's the *Logis de France Hôtel du Golfe*, 13 av Clemenceau (☎94.54.40.34), and the *Coq* on pl de la

Mairie (☎94.54.63.14) and both are reasonable. The **restaurant** at the *Coq* is okay: otherwise take a look around pl Jean-Jaurès and rue Nationale. Alternatively, try the Lebanese specialities at 4 rue Nationale or *aïoli*, opposite, at *La Caverne du Sifleur*.

Visits to Cogolin's **craft factories** are easily arranged. The **SI**, on pl de la République, provide a complete list of addresses and times. Or you can wander down av Georges-Clemenceau and take your pick. For **carpets**, one of the best is the *Manufacture des Tapis de Cogolin* on bd Louis-Blanc (Mon–Fri 8am–noon & 2–6pm; closed third week in Aug). And world-famous **musicians** visit *Prestini Midi*, rue Barbusse (Mon–Fri 8am–noon & 2.30–5.30pm; closed Aug).

The best place to taste at least twelve of the local **wines** is at *Les Maîtres Vignerons de la Presqu'île de St-Tropez* (Mon–Fri 8am–noon & 2–6pm), on the route de Cogolin just off the major roundabout at La Foux, the last town before St-Tropez.

St-Tropez and the St-Tropez peninsula

The origins of **ST-TROPEZ** are unremarkable: a little fishing village that grew up around a port founded by the Greeks of Marseille that was destroyed by the Saracens in 739 and finally fortified in the late Middle Ages. Its sole distinction from the myriad other fishing villages along this coast was its inaccessibility. Stuck out on the southern shores of the Golfe de St-Tropez, away from the main coastal routes on a wide penin-

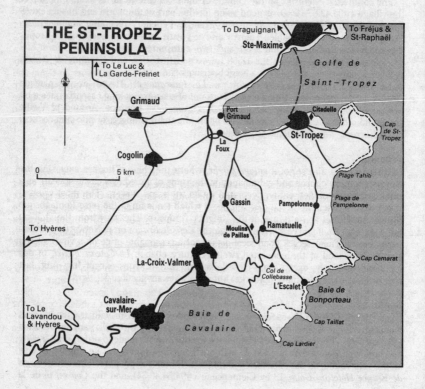

sula that never warranted real roads, St-Tropez could only easily be reached by boat. This held true as late as the 1880s, when the novelist **de Maupassant** sailed his yacht into the port during his final high-living binge before the onset of syphilitic insanity.

Soon after de Maupassant's fleeting visit, the painter and leader of the Neo-Impressionists, **Paul Signac**, was sailing down the coast when bad weather forced him to moor in St-Tropez. Being an anarchist, and rich, he instantly decided to build a house there. **Bonnard**, **Marquet**, **Dufy**, **Dérain**, **Vlaminck**, **Seurat**, **Van Dongen** and others followed. By the eve of World War I, St-Tropez was pretty well established as a hang-out for Bohemians. The 1930s saw a new influx of artists, this time of writers as much as painters. **Anaïs Nin**'s journal records "girls riding bare-breasted in the back of open cars... an intensity of pleasure..." and undressing between bamboo bushes that rustled with concealed lovers. In 1956 Roger Vadim arrived, with crew, to film **Brigitte Bardot** in *Et Dieu Créa la Femme*. The international cult of Tropezian sun, sex and celebrities took off – even the 1960s hippies who flocked to the revamped Mediterranean mecca of liberation managed to look glamorous – and the resort has been big-money mainstream ever since.

St-Tropez: the town

Never come to St-Tropez in high summer, unless by yacht and with limitless credit. The 5.5km of road from LE FOUX (the mainland, as it were) has summer traffic jams as bad as Nice or Marseille; the pedestrian jams to the port are not much better; the hotels and restaurants are full and too expensive; overnighting in vehicles is prohibited; the beaches, as Bardot put it, are covered in turds and condoms and every other sort of rubbish... So save your visit, if you can, for a spring or autumn day and you'll understand why this place has had such history and such hype.

The road into St-Tropez divides as it enters the village into av Général-Leclerc and av du 8-mai-1945, with the **gare routière** between them. On foot, follow av du 8-mai and you'll hit the **Vieux Port**, with the old town rising above the eastern quay. And here you have the classic St-Trop experience: the quayside café clientele *face à face* with the yacht deck martini sippers, and the latest fashions parading in between, defining the French word *frimer* which means to stroll ostentatiously in places like St-Tropez. It's surprising just how entertaining this spectacle can be.

The port, citadel and museum

Up from the port, at the end of quai Jean-Jaurès, rue de la Mairie passes the town hall, with a street to the left leading down to the rocky **Baie de la Glaye**. Further up, along rue de la Ponche, you reach the **fishing port** with its tiny beach. Both these spots are miraculously free from commercialisation. Beyond the fishing port, roads lead up to the sixteenth-century **citadel**. Its maritime museum is not much fun, but the walk round the ramparts on an overgrown path has the best views of the gulf and the back of the town – views that haven't changed since their translations to oil on canvas before the war.

The paintings, suitably, you can see at the **Musée de l'Annonciade** (10am–noon & 2–6pm or 3–7pm; closed Tues & Nov), reason in itself for a visit to St-Tropez. It was originally Signac's idea to have a permanent exhibition space for the Neo-Impressionists and Fauvists who painted here, though it was not until 1955 that the collections of various individuals were put together in the deconsecrated sixteenth-century chapel on pl Georges-Grammont just west of the port. The *Annonciade* features works by Signac, Matisse and most of the other artists who worked here: grey, grim, northern views of Paris, Boulogne and Westminster, and then local, brilliantly sunlit scenes by the same brush: a real delight and unrivalled outside Paris for the 1890–1940 period of French art.

Accommodation

With more and more people wanting to pay homage to St-Trop, **accommodation** is a problem. Between April and September you won't find a room unless you've booked months in advance and are prepared to pay exorbitant prices. If you have your own transport or are prepared to hitch, you may be better off staying in Cavalaire, La Croix-Valmer or La Garde-Freinet (see p.729). The St-Tropez **SI** on quai Jean-Jaurès (summer 9am–8pm; winter 9am–12.30pm & 2–6.30pm) can help with reservations.

Out of season you may be luckier, though in winter few **hotels** stay open. *Les Chimères*, Quartier du Pilon (☎94.97.02.90; Feb–mid-Dec; ③/④), a short way back from the gare routière towards La Foux, on the left, is one of the cheaper options. If they're booked up try *Laetitia*, 52 rue Allard (☎94.97.04.02; April–mid-Oct; ④/⑤), *Lou Cagnard*, rue Paul-Roussel (☎94.97.04.24; ④), or *La Méditerranée*, 21 bd Louis-Blanc (☎94.97.00.44; March–Oct; ④). If you're prepared to pay far in excess of ⑤ rates, try the very comfortable *Hélios*, port du Pilon (☎94.97.00.64) where almost every room has a view of the sea; or, even more expensively, *La Ponche*, pl du Révelin (☎94.97.02.53), an old block of fishermen's houses turned into a luxury hotel with a host of famous arty names in its guest book. The *Auberge des Vieux Moulins* (☎94.97.17.22), on the Ramatuelle road out of St-Tropez, is idyllic but again doubles go from twice ⑤ rates in season. Finally, if you're looking for hand-painted bathrooms, jacuzzis and private gardens you're in the 2000F-a-night league and will gravitate towards the paridisiacal *Bastide de St-Tropez*, route des Carles (☎94.97.58.16).

Returning to earth, **camping** near St-Tropez is also a problem. The best and closest option is *Camping Courban*, route de la Belle-Isnarde (☎94.94.11.84). The next nearest are the two sites on the plage du Pampelonne which charge extortionate rates and, in high summer, resemble an orgy without sex. Otherwise, 6km away off the road to BOURRIAN, near GASSIN the 3* *Camping Parc Montana* (☎94.56.13.03; April–Sept) also has caravans for hire. Within a 3-kilometre radius of Ramatuelle (see   ) are *Les Tournels* on route de Camarat (☎94.79.80.54) and *La Croix du Sud*, route de St-Tropez (☎94.79.80.84; May–Sept).

Restaurants and nightlife

Restaurants in St-Tropez do not come cheap. If you're broke, *La Patate* snack bar on rue Georges-Clemenceau has omelettes, pasta, *pain beignats* and so forth – nothing special but it may save you from starvation. *La Flo* on rue de la Citadelle, *La Frégate* at 52 rue Allard, and the *crêperie* at 12 rue Sibille, will feed you for under 100F. For a little bit more, *Lou Revelen*, near the fishing port at 4 rue des Remparts, serves fresh pasta and seafood dishes in a very friendly atmosphere in which you aren't made to feel like so much more foreign tourist scum. At *L'Echalote*, 35 rue du Allard, you can eat on a terrace garden with the choice of a very expensive gourmet *menu* or a very reasonable four-course *petit formule*.

In season St-Tropez stays up late, as you'd expect. If you get tired of the port-side spectacle, go and see the animation of pl des Lices, where games of *boules* continue until dusk and the old, traditional *Café des Arts* holds sway. If you're mad enough to want to pay to see, and be seen with, the **nightlife** creatures of St-Trop, clubs include the young and boppy *Aphrodisiaque*, 35 rue Allard (every night in summer; Sat in winter); *Le Bal*, a hot and sweaty, gayish club at Résidence du Nouveau-Port (summer nights only); *L'Esquinade* on rue du Four, which stays open latest (but summer only); and the gay disco *Le Pigeonnier*, 13 rue de la Ponche (every night in summer; Sat in winter).

The beaches

The beach within easy walking distance of St-Tropez town is **Les Graniers**, below the citadel just beyond the port des Pêcheurs. From there, a path follows the coast around the **Baie des Canoubiers** (which has a small beach), to Cap St-Pierre, Cap St-Tropez, the very crowded **Les Salins** beach and right round to **Tahiti-Plage** (about 11km).

Tahiti-Plage is the start of the almost straight, five-kilometre north–south **Pampelonne** beach, famous bronzing belt of St-Tropez and world initiator of the topless bathing cult. The water is shallow for 50m or so, and the beach is exposed to the wind, and sometimes scourged by dried sea vegetation, not to mention slicks of industrial pollutants. Though you'll stumble across people in the nude on all stretches of the beach, only some of the bars welcome people carrying wallets and nothing else.

The beach ends with the headland of **Cap Camaret**, beyond which the private residential settlement of **Villa Bergès** grudgingly allows public access to the **plage de l'Escalet**. Another coastal path leads to the next bay, the **Baie de Briande**, where you'll find the least populated beach of the whole peninsula.

To **get to the beaches** from St-Tropez, there's a frequent minibus service from pl des Lices to Salins, Tahiti and Pampelonne, or a bus from the gare routière to Tahiti, Pampelonne and L'Escalet. Or you can **hire bikes and mopeds** from 5 rue Quaranta. If you're driving you'll be forced to pay high parking charges at all the beaches, or to leave your car or motorbike some distance from the sea and easy prey to thieves.

Gassin and Ramatuelle

Though the coast of the St-Tropez peninsula sprouts second residences like a cabbage patch gone to seed, the interior is almost uninhabited, thanks to government intervention, complex ownerships and the value of some local wines. The best view of this richly green and flowering countryside is from the hilltop village of **Gassin**, its lower neighbour **Ramatuelle**, or the tiny road between them, where three ruined windmills could once catch every wind.

GASSIN, the shape and size of a small ship perched on a summit, was once a Moorish stronghold and is now, of course, highly chic. It's an excellent place for a blowout dinner, sitting outside by the village wall with a spectacular panorama east over the peninsula. Of the handful of restaurants, *Bello Visto*, 9 pl des Barrys (☎94.56.17.30), is the least outrageously priced.

RAMATUELLE is bigger than its neighbour, though just as old, and surrounded by some of the best *Côte de Provence* vineyards. The twisting arcaded streets are full of arts and crafts of dubious talent, but it's all very pleasant nonetheless. **Hotels** worth trying are *Chez Tony* on rue Clemenceau (☎94.79.20.46; ③) and *Lou Castellas* on route des Moulins (☎94.79.20.67; ③). The most beautiful French actor ever to have appeared on screen, **Gérard Philippe** (1922–59), is buried in Ramatuelle's **cemetery**. His ivy-covered tomb, shaded by a rose bush, is set against the wall on the right as you look down. In the tiny eighteenth-century chapel close by the cemetery, naive paintings by one André Quellier are exhibited along with the sad documentation of his failed commission to decorate the entire building.

Port Grimaud

Just north of La Foux, the ultimate Côte d'Azur property development half stands and half floats at the head of the Golfe de St-Tropez. **PORT GRIMAUD** was created in the 1960s as a private lagoon pleasure city with waterways for roads and yachts parked at the bottom of every garden. All the houses are in exquisitely tasteful old Provençal style and their owners, Joan Collins for example, more than a little well heeled. In a way it's surprising that the whole enclave isn't wired off and patrolled by Alsatian dogs.

The main visitors' entrance is 800m up the well-signed road off the N98. You don't have to pay to get in but you can't explore all the islands without hiring a boat. Even access to the church is controlled by an automatic paying barrier, though the fee is admittedly nominal. The *brasseries*, English-style pubs, restaurants and cafés, however, are less easily affordable and their ambience, during the day at least, is of patronising benevolence that mere tourists are allowed in at all. It's all a bit like a Côte version of London's Docklands development – though architecturally several cuts above.

The only affordable accommodation in Port Grimaud is a huge campsite, *Les Prairies de la Mer* (☎94.56.25.29), where four-berth caravans are rented out at weekly rates in high season.

Ste-Maxime and around

STE-MAXIME, which faces St-Tropez across its gulf, is the perfect Côte stereotype: palmed corniche and pleasure boat harbour, casino, golden beaches with well-heeled wind-surfers and water-skiers, and an outnumbering of estate agents to any other businesses by something like ten to one. It sprawls a little too much – like many of its neighbours – but the magnetic appeal of the water's edge is hard to deny. To enjoy the resort, however, requires money. If your budget denies you the pleasures of promenade cocktail-sipping and seafood-platter picking (not to mention water-skiing, wet-biking and wind-surfing) you might as well choose somewhere rather prettier to swim, lie on the beach and walk along the shore.

The town

The **SI** on the promenade St-Lozière can give you all the relevant information on trips and pleasures, and advise on hotel vacancies – once again, very rare in summer. Among the cheaper **hotels** is *Le Pourquoi Pas*, 4 av Berthié-Albrecht (☎94.96.12.99; ②). For pleasanter and more expensive surroundings, there's the *Marie-Louise*, 2km south-west in the Hameau de Guerre-Vieille (☎94.96.06.05; closed mid-Oct to mid-Feb; half-board compulsory in summer; ③), which is tucked away in greenery but in sight of the sea.

For the spenders, **Cherry Beach** is the strip of sand to head for. As well as paying for shaded cushioned comfort, you can enter the water on a variety of different vehicles, eat grilled fish, have drinks brought to your mattress, and listen to a piano player as dusk falls. In addition to the beaches, Ste-Maxime has a *vieille ville* to explore and several good **markets**: a daily covered flower and food market on rue Fernand-Bessy; a Thursday morning market in the old town; bric-à-brac every Friday morning on pl Jean-Mermoz; and crafts in the pedestrian streets every Thursday afternoon.

For non-beach **eating** the *Hostellerie de la Belle Aurore*, 4 bd Jean-Moulin (☎94.96.02.45), offers gourmet food on a sea-view terrace; or, for half the price (and a bit of a trek out to Ste-Maxime's industrial zone), there's *Mas des Virgiles*, route de Muy (☎94.96.28.02) which, despite its unpromising location, has excellent fish-orientated menus. Otherwise there are snack bars and *brasseries* along the seafront.

Transport: if you're heading for St-Tropez from Ste-Maxime, an alternative to the bus, at not much greater cost, is to go by **boat**. The service from Ste-Maxime's *gare maritime* runs from July to September with frequent daily crossings of twenty minutes.

St-Donat: the Audio Museum

The **Musée du Phonographe et de la Musique Mécanique** is at parc St-Donat (Easter–mid-Oct 10am–noon & 3–6.30pm), 10km north of Ste-Maxime high up in the Massif des Maures on the road to LE MUY. To reach it you need to take the *Le Muy* bus from Ste-Maxime's **gare routière** on pl J-Mermoz (along av Jean-Jaurès from the seafront). The museum is the the result of one woman's 35-year obsession with collecting audio equipment. She has one of Thomas Edison's "talking machines" of 1878, the first recording machines of the 1890s and an amplified lyre (1903). In addition there's a wide selection of automata, musical boxes and pianolas. Almost half the exhibits still work. If you get a tour from Madame herself you'll find it hard to resist her enthusiasm for the history of this branch of twentieth-century technology.

East to St-Aygulf

The tangle of resorts north to the Argens valley and Fréjus are mostly smaller and lesser clones of Ste-Maxime. Distinguishing VAL D'ESQUIÈRES, LES ISSAMBRES and ST-AYGULF is especially difficult: the overdevelopment of each one-time village spreads into its neighbours, without leaving a single stretch of undeveloped coast between.

For all that, this stretch still has its attractions, revealing traditional white-washed pantiled Provençal architecture amid the filing-cabinet condominiums, and a shoreline of rocky coves and *calanques* rather than golden rules of sand. And if the seaside development gets too much, you can always head up and away into the eastern extremity of the Massif des Maures.

Fréjus and St-Raphaël

The major **Fréjus–St-Raphael** conurbation, on the coast, has a history dating back to Julius Caesar and Augustus. Fréjus, with its centre 3km inland, was originally established as a Roman naval base and St-Raphaël as a resort for its veterans. The ancient port at Fréjus, or *Forum Julii*, had two kilometres of quays and was connected to the sea, which was considerably closer then, by a walled canal – the reopening of which, as a marina, with restaurants, bars and other enterprises alongside, is a cherished local plan. St-Raphaël has recently developed a second pleasure port, now chock-full of yachts.

This is no bad place for a stop-off. Fréjus has Roman, medieval and twentieth-century edifices to take a look at, and St-Raphaël has the Côte *frimeurs*. The towns are connected by fast and frequent trains and have a seaside suburb, **Fréjus-Plage**, where the coastal road from St-Raphaël turns inland towards Fréjus.

Around Fréjus

The population of **FRÉJUS**, remarkably, was greater in the first century BC than it is today. Today's town centre lies within the Roman perimeter; coming from the **gare SNCF** you can still enter the town through the **Porte des Gaules** that leads into pl Agricola. A more direct route is to take rue Général-de-Gaulle just before the Roman archway. After crossing pl de la Liberté, rue Sieyes leads up to **place Formigé**, the marketplace and heart of both contemporary and medieval Fréjus.

The **SI** is just on the other side of the cathedral, on pl Calvini, with an annex at 325 rue Jean-Jaurès.

The Roman remains

Doing a tour of the **Roman remains** gives you a good idea of the extent of Forum Julii, but, scattered at the extremes of the modern town, they're a full day's work to get around. Turning right out of the gare SNCF and then right down bd S-Decuers brings you to the **Butte St-Antoine**, against whose east wall the waters of the port would have lapped. This was one of the port's defences, and one of the ruined towers may have been a lighthouse. A path around the southern wall follows the quayside (odd stretches are visible) to the medieval **Lanterne d'Auguste**, built on the Roman foundations of a structure marking the entrance of the canal into the ancient harbour.

In the other direction from the station, past the Porte des Gaules and along rue H-Vadon, you come to the **amphitheatre**, today used for bullfights and rock concerts. It has recently had its upper tiers reconstructed in the same greenish local stone used by the Romans. The **theatre** is north of the town, along av du Théâtre-Romain, its original seats long gone, though again it is still used for shows in summer. Northeast of it, at the end of av du XVème-Corps-d'Armée, a few arches are visible of the 40-kilometre **aqueduct**. Closer to the centre, where bd Aristide-Briand meets bd Salvarelli, are the arcades of the **Porte d'Orée**, positioned on the harbour's edge alongside what was probably a bath complex.

Medieval Fréjus
Medieval Fréjus is in many ways more interesting than its predecessor, and certainly less tiring to visit. The oldest part of the **cathedral close** on pl Formigé is the **baptistery** – built in the fourth or fifth century and thus contemporary with the decline and fall of the city's Roman founders. Its two doorways are of different heights, signifying the enlarged spiritual stature of the baptised.

Parts of the **Cathedral** itself are tenth century but the most beautiful and engaging component of the close is the **cloisters** (guided tours; tickets from the office on rue de Fleury 9.30am–noon & 2–4.30/6.30pm; closed Tues). Around a small garden of scented bushes focusing on a well, slender marble columns carved in the twelfth century support a fourteenth-century ceiling painted with apocalyptic creatures. Out of the original 1200 pictures, 400 remain, each about the size of this page. The subjects include multi-headed monsters, mermaids, satyrs and scenes of bacchanalian debauchery. Off the upper storey is an **archaeological museum** whose star pieces are a complete Roman mosaic of a leopard and a statue of double-headed Hermes.

Modern Fréjus
Unlikely remnants of the more recent past come in the shape of a **Vietnamese pagoda** and an abandoned **"Soudanese" mosque** – both built by French Colonial troops. The pagoda (June–mid-Sept 3–6pm), still maintained as a Buddhist temple, is on the cross-roads of the RN7 to Cannes and the D100, about 2km out of Fréjus. The mosque is on the left off the D4 to Bagnols, in the middle of an army camp 2km from the RN7 junction. A strange, guava-coloured, fort-like building of typical West African style, it is decorated inside with fading murals of desert journeys gracefully sketched in white on the dark pink walls.

The *Fondation Daniel Templon* is a **modern art gallery** (weekends 10am–6pm weekdays by appointment on ☎94.40.76.30; 25F). Presently located in the *Zone Industrielle du Capitou* off the A8, the collection is to be moved to the Villa Aurélienne at the entrance to the town in 1993. It includes the works of 67 French artists from the period 1945–90, including Picasso, Braque, Matisse and Léger. Take a right off the N7 out of Fréjus, direction Nice /Aix-en-Provence.

Fréjus is a sound bet if you have **kids** to entertain, with a number of activity centres in the vicinity designed specifically for them. One such is a **water amusement park**, *Aquatica* (June–Sept daily 10am–8pm; May–June weekends only 10am–6pm, ; 78F, children 58F) off the RN98. Water scooters, toboggans and pedal boats are the principal forms of transport down chutes into an enchanted river; and there are lakes, and a huge swimming pool with artificial waves and a beach for the less energetic. To get there, take the St-Raphaël–Fréjus bus and get off at the *Géant Casino* stop.

The **Safari Park** off the A8, direction Nice, can be visited either by car or on foot, (June–Sept 9am–6pm, rest of year 10am–5pm; 50F), take the FAYENCE bus from St-Raphaël to the Camps Lecocq stop and it's a ten-minute walk from there. Between Fréjus and St-Aygulf on the RN 98 is a 600-metre **Go-Cart track**, *Azur Karting* (summer 11am–midnight; rest of the year 11am–dusk).

Around St-Raphaël

A large, expensive and characterless resort, **ST-RAPHAËL** became fashionable at the turn of the century, though you wouldn't know it today, the town having lost its Belle Époque mansions and hotels through bombardment in the last war. However there is a tiny **old quarter** around a crumbling Romanesque church by pl Carnot on the other side of the railway line, and fragments of the Roman aqueduct that brought water from Fréjus stand outside the church in a little courtyard off rue des Templiers. Opposite is the **Musée d'Archéologie Sous-Marine** (June–Sept 10am–noon & 3–6pm, closed Tues; Oct–May 11am–noon & 2–4pm, closed Sun). It features underwater archaeology and local finds, as well as local history. If the church is locked you can get a key here.

The **gare SNCF** and **gare routière** in St-Raphaël are side by side in the centre of town. The **SI** is across the *place* from the train station and the more useful **Comité Départmental de Tourism** in the station itself. Some buses leave from the other side of the railway line – there's an underpass just down from pl de la Gare.

Fréjus and St-Raphaël practicalities

Moving between Fréjus and St-Raphaël, you hardly know you've left one or arrived at the other. Fréjus is a preferable place to stay, though St-Raphaël has more choice.

Accommodation

The *Auberge de Jeunesse* in the Domaine de Bellevue, Fréjus, on route de Cannes (☎94.52.18.75), is open all year but needs booking in summer. You can take a bus from either Fréjus or St-Raphaël gare SNCF, to rue Grisole or the hospital and from there it's a well-signed one-kilometre walk. In July and August the hostel picks people up from the stations, so phone when you arrive.

There's a youth hostel by the gare SNCF at BOULOURIS on the coast 5km east of St-Raphaël, the *Centre International du Manoir*, chemin de l'Escale (☎94.95.20.58; mid-June–Oct). It's expensive but luxurious, with a restaurant and the beach a stone's throw away. If you don't want to take a train, there's a bus every half hour during the day from St-Raphaël. Cheap **hotels** in St-Raphaël include *Hôtel des Templiers* over a bar on pl de la République; (☎94.95.38.93; ②) and the *Bellevue* 22 bd Félix-Martin, (☎94.95.07.54; ③). Moving upmarket, try the *Franc*, pl Galliéni (☎94.95.17.03; ③), or the *Provençal*, 197 rue de la Garonne (☎94.95.01.52; ③).

Fréjus lacks budget hotels but for not too much you could lodge at the *Bellevue*, pl Paul-Vernet (☎94.51.42.41; ③), *Le Flore*, 35 rue Grisolle (☎94.51.38.35; ②), or La *Glaciere*, 126 rue Grisolle (☎94.51.56.26; ③). Upmarket hotels include *Auberge du Vieux Four*, 49 rue Grisolle (☎94.51.56.38; ④), which has an excellent **restaurant** and, at Fréjus-Plage, *L'Oasis*, impass J-B-Charcot (☎94.51.50.44; closed Nov–Feb; ④).

Campsites are ubiquitous, with at least eight on the BAGNOLS road out of Fréjus and one close to the Domaine de Bellevue youth hostel. The closest to the sea is the *Camping de l'Aviation* at 250 rue J-Aicard, on the road to the sea (☎94.51.10.13; Easter–Sept). Right on the sea, at Boulouris, is the 4★ *Val Fleury* (☎94.95.21.52; open all year).

Eating: St-Raphaël

St-Raphaël has good **markets**: there are daily food markets on pl de la République and pl Victor-Hugo and a daily fish market on place Ortolan.

Of **St-Raphaël's restaurants**, *La Voile d'Or*, 1 bd de Général-de-Gaulle, (☎94.95.17.04) is a special treat for fish lovers. *Pastorel*, 54 rue de la Liberté, (☎94.95.02.36; closed mid-April–mid-May, Sun evening & Mon) is even better with a highly inventive menu. For something cheaper, try *Les Fines Gueules*, 12 rue de la République (☎94.95.15.60), with cheap *plats du jour* and a fantastic fish paella.

Eating: Fréjus

At Fréjus, **market days** are Wednesday and Saturday. On the second Saturday of June the *Foire de St-François* takes over the town, and on October 6 there's a garlic fair.

One of the best **restaurants** is *Les Potiers*, 135 rue des Potiers (☎94.51.33.74; closed Wed & Sat lunchtime), with menus of fresh seasonal ingredients for very reasonable prices. Cheaper eats can be found on pl Agricola, and at Fréjus-Plage there's a string of eating houses including generous but pricey Italian–Provençal cooking, on bd de la Libértion, *La Romana*, at no. 155, and the basic but good *Cap Sud* at no. 11.

Listings

Bike hire *Dewil Cycles et Loisirs*, av Victor-Hugo, Fréjus-Plage; *Patrick Moto*, 280 av Général-Leclerc, St-Raphaël.

Boats to St-Tropez, Port Grimaud, the Esterel. Tickets and times from *Les Bateaux Bleus*, gare maritime (☎94.95.17.46).

Car hire *Avis*, pl de la Gare, St-Raphaël; *Europcar*, 308 av de Verdun, Fréjus, and pl de la Gare, St-Raphaël; *InteRent*, 275 av de Verdun, Fréjus; *Budget-Milleville*, 40 rue Waldeck-Rousseau, St-Raphaël.

Changing money Gare Maritime, June 20–Sept 30, Mon–Fri 4–10pm, Sat & Sun 9am–10pm; in the *centre commerciale* at the gare SNCF, mid-March to mid-Oct Mon–Sat 9.30am–noon & 3–6pm.

Emergencies Hospital: *Hôpital Intercommunal E-Bonnet*, av André-Léotard, Fréjus (☎94.40.21.21); doctor: *SOS Médecins* (☎94.83.14.14); ambulance; ☎94.40.40.90 or ☎94.95.77.44.

Language courses *France Langue et Culture*, 251 bd des Lions, 83700 St-Raphaël (☎94.95.11.28); June–Aug.

Launderette Pl Victor Hugo, St-Raphaël.

PTT *Caisse Nationale d'Epargne*, av Victor-Hugo, 83702 St-Raphaël; av Aristide-Briand, 83600 Fréjus. **Taxis** ☎94.95.04.25.

Trains Information ☎93.99.50.50; reservations ☎94.95.18.91.

Travel agencies *Havas Voyages*, av Karr, to the right of the gare SNCF in St-Raphaël (☎94.95.33.43); *Beltrame et Fils*, gare routière, St-Raphaël (☎94.95.95.16).

THE RIVIERA: CANNES TO MENTON

The **Riviera** – the seventy-odd kilometres of coast between Cannes and the Italian border – was once an inhospitable shore with few natural harbours, its tiny local communities preferring to cluster round feudal castles high above the sea. It wasn't until the nineteenth century that the first foreign aristocrats began to choose to winter in the region's mild climate. But the real transformation came with the onslaught of 1950s mass tourism. Nowadays, it's an almost uninterrupted promenade, lined by palms and mega-buck hotels, with speeding sports cars on the corniche roads and yachts like ocean liners moored at each resort.

Atrractions, however, still remain, most notably in the legacies of the **artists** who stayed here: Picasso, Léger, Matisse, Renoir and Chagall. **Nice**, too, has real substance as a major city.

Cannes and around

The film industry and all other manner of business junketing represent **CANNES'** main source of income in an ever multiplying calendar of festivals, conferences, tournaments and trade shows. And the spin-offs, of servicing the day and night needs of the jetloads of agents, reps, dealers, buyers and celebrities, are even more profitable than providing the strictly-business facilities. Cannes might be more than its film festival, but it's a grotesquely over-hyped urban blight on this once exquisite coast – a contrast reinforced by the sublime **Îles de Lérins**, a short boat ride offshore.

Orientation and accommodation

The **gare routière** is next to the **gare SNCF** on rue Jean-Jaurès, five blocks north of the **Palais des Festivals**, an orange, concrete mega-bunker on the seafront, and the main venue for Cannes' big events, of which the premier celeb-puller is the **International Film Fesival** in May*. To the west, lies the old town, **Le Suquet**; to the east, the seafront promenade of **La Croisette**. All buses use the main **gare routière** except for the coastal bus, and the seven town buses, which leave from the Hôtel de Ville by the old port. A minibus shuttles along the seafront from square Frédéric-Mistral, west of the old town, to *Palm Beach Casino* on Pointe Croisette at the eastern end of the bay. Alternatively, you can **hire bikes** from *Location Deux-Roues*, 5 rue Allieis near the station; *Cycles Rémy*, 22 av des Hespérides; and from the station itself.

Accommodation

If something or someone compels you to spend a night or more in Cannes, you'll find the best concentration of **hotels** in the centre, between the **gare SNCF** on rue Jean-Jaurès and **La Croisette**, around the central axis of rues Antibes and Félix-Faure. If you can swing limitless credit, doors will open. But if you can't, and you haven't booked one of the cheaper hotels in advance, things may not be easy. There are **SIs** at the gare SNCF (July & Aug daily 8am–midnight; rest of year daily 9am–1pm & 2–7pm) and in the Palais des Festivals (Mon–Sat 9am–7pm), which have a free **reservation service**, but can't guarantee either rooms for late arrivals or rooms at the price you require. With no youth hostel and no chance of sleeping on the beach, it's not a good idea to arrive in Cannes late at night.

HOTELS

Hôtel Azur, 15 rue Jean-de-Riouffe (☎93.39.52.14). Recently renovated and amazing value for this part of town, within spitting distance of the Palais des Festivals. ③/④.

Hôtel Bourgogne, 13 rue de 24-août (☎93.38.36.73). Neither friendly nor very appealing but one of the cheapest and very central. Closed in December. ④.

Hôtel Chanteclair, 12 rue Fortville (☎93.39.67.88). Close to the old town and better than average. ③.

Hôtel les Roches Fleuries, 92 rue Georges-Clemenceau (☎93.39.28.78). Situated just below Le Suquet and luxurious for the price. ③/④.

Hôtel National, 8 rue Maréchal-Joffre (☎93.39.24.82). Clean, adequate and quite close to the station. Unfortunately, a bit depressing. ③.

Hôtel Select, 16 rue Hélène-Vagliano (☎93.99.51.00). A cut above the rest – sound-proofed, air-conditioned roooms with baths. ⑤.

CAMPSITES

Le Grande Saule, 24–26 bd de la Frayère (☎93.47.07.50; April–Sept). 4km west of town, off the D9 towards Pérgomas (bus from the Hôtel de Ville or train to Ranguin) and pretty exorbitant.

Ranch-Camping, chemin St-Joseph (☎93.46.00.11; March–Oct). Same location and price as above.

Camping Bellevue, 67 av Maurice-Chevalier (☎93.47.28.97; Feb–Oct). Slightly cheaper and nearer the sea in Cannes-La Bocca (a western suburb).

Aire Naturelle Clos St-Hubert, quai del Bardie (mid-July–Aug). Same location as *Camping Bellevue* but with fewer facilities.

---

* The mayor is currently trying to shift the film festival to October. If he succeeds, this will happen from 1993.

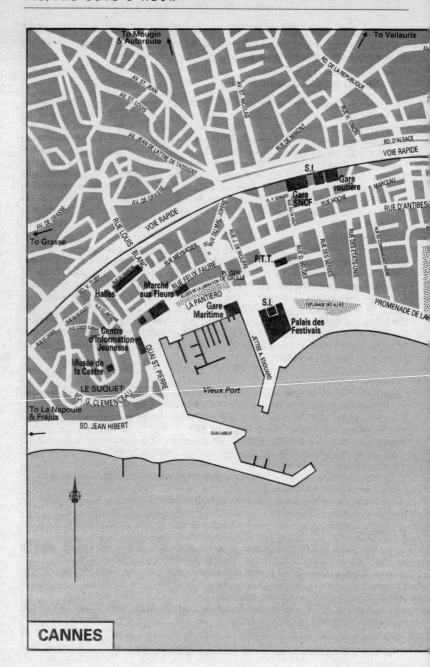

To Mougin
& Autoroute

To Vallauris

AV. ST. JEAN

AV. ST. LOUIS

AV. ST. NICOLAS

RD. DE LA REPUBLIQUE

RUE H. SIMON

AV. JEAN DE LATTRE DE TASSIGNY

BD. D'ALSACE

VOIE RAPIDE

AV. DE GRASSE

S.I.

Gare
routière

R. MARCEAU

AV. DE GRASSE

RUE LOUIS BLANC

VOIE RAPIDE

Gare
SNCF

PL. P. SEMARD

RUE DU 24 AOÛT

RUE HOCHE

RUE D'ANTIBES

AV. DE GRASSE

To Grasse

RUE DU MAL. JOFFRE

RUE J. DE RIOUFFE

RUE DES ETATS-UNIS

RUE DU COMMANDANT ANDRE

RUE MEYNADIER

P.T.T.

RUE D. BELGES

RUE DES SERBES

BD. V. TUBY

RUE DUMANOIR

RUE FELIX FAURE

PL. GEN.
DE GAULLE

ALLÉES DE LA LIBERATION

PROMENADE DE LA

Halles

Marché
aux Fleurs

LA PANTIERO

ESPLANADE DES ALLIÉS

RUE ST. ANTOINE

RUE ST. DIZIER

RUE COSTE CORAIL

Gare
Maritime

S.I.

RUE ST. DIDIER

Centre
d'Information
Jeunesse

Palais des
Festivals

Musée de
la Castre

QUAI ST. PIERRE

JETTÉE A. EDOUARD

LE SUQUET

BD. G. CLEMENCEAU

Vieux Port

To La Napoule
& Fréjus

BD. JEAN HIBERT

QUAI LABEUF

CANNES

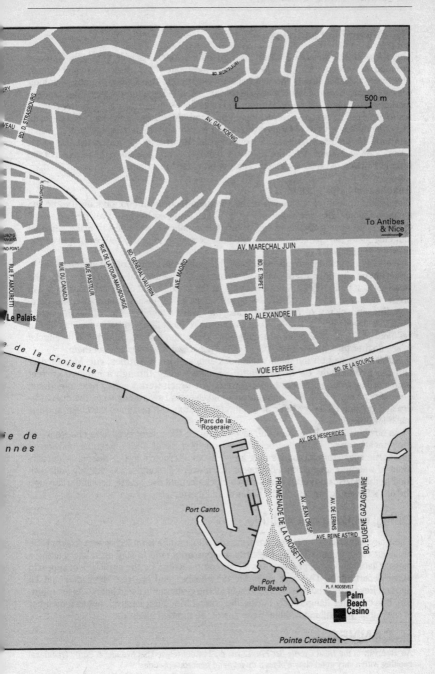

The city and the beaches

The old town, known as **Le Suquet** after the hill on which it stands, is now the home of the kind of residents who benefit little from the modern town's glamorous economy. The twee cosmetic streets that lead you to the summit mask the miserable, stinking passageways where the houses need repair and their lodgers more space. The standard market solution is in operation: do it up and raise the rents and then get a "better class of resident". Still, it remains a refreshing escape from the excess of the La Croisette strip, and one of the few areas of Cannes where you can eat and drink cheaply. Up here, you'll also find the motley ethnographic collection of the **Musée de la Castre** (July–Sept 10am–noon & 3–7pm; Oct–June 10am–noon & 2–5/6pm), housed in the remains of the **fortified priory** of Cannes' eleventh-century monkish inhabitants.

Beaches and star-gazing

Wandering on and off the **beach** in swimming suits or bikini bottoms used to be the norm in Cannes. But now a fine of 75F has been imposed by the mayor for "indecent" dress on the streets. Cannes being Cannes, the police are entitled to make personal judgements on the offensiveness or otherwise of a person's attire. You're all right on the beaches themselves.

West of Le Suquet there are **beaches** which offer the chance of not having to pay to be on them: the only stretch of sand along **La Croisette** that doesn't charge is the small section by the **Palais des Festivals**, at the western end of the promenade. If you prefer to bronze in style, **Martinez** beach offers all the usual watersports plus parascending and plenty of facilities to ease the pain of tanning. The **Majestic** beach, owned by the de-luxe *palais-hôtels*, is where you're most likely to spot a face familiar in celluloid or a topless hopeful, especially during the film festival, though you'll be lucky to see further than the sweating backs of the paparazzi who buzz around them.

Strolling on and off the main streets of Cannes – **rue d'Antibes**, **rue Meynardier** and the **promenade de la Croisette** – is like wading through a hundred current issues of *Vogue*. If you thought the people on the beach were wearing next to nothing, now you can see where they bought the sunglasses and swimming suits, the moisturisers and creams for every hour of the day, the watch, the perfume, the collar and the leash for little FouFou.

As nowhere else along the Côte, save St-Tropez, the millionaires here choose to eat their meals served by white-frocked crew on their yacht decks, feigning oblivion of landborne spectators a crumb's flick away. As an alternative to this dubious entertainment of watching *langoustines* disappear down overfed mouths, you can buy your own food in the *Forville* **covered market** two blocks behind the Mairie, or wander through the day's flower shipments on the allées de la Liberté.

Eating, drinking and nightlife

There are hundreds of eateries, covering the whole range from 75F *menus fixes* to 500F blow-outs and, Cannes being glitter city, **restaurants** tend to stay open late: getting a meal at 4am is no great problem. It's all fair compensation for the city's lack of appeal in other departments. The best areas for the cheaper end are rue Meynardier and Le Suquet. Reserving a table is a good idea at all the restaurants listed below. As for **nightlife**, it accelerates dangerously during the annual May Film Festival, but as a member of the public you will not be able to see any of the **movies** entered.

Cheaper restaurants

Au Bec Fin in the *Hôtel Cybelle-Bec Fin*, 12 rue du 24 Août (closed Sat evening & Sun). Traditional cooking with a very good choice of *plats du jour* and generous portions.

La Croisette, 15 rue du Commandant-André (☎93.39.86.06; closed Tues). Excellent grilled fish.

Le Bouchon, 10 rue de Constantine (☎93.99.21.76; closed Mon). Stubbornly refusing to go upmarket, this fabulous local bistro serves *aïoli*, monkfish terrine, duck with orange and other staple dishes with admirable simplicity. Green tea is on offer as an alternative to wine.

La Grande Brasserie, 81 rue d'Antibes (closed Sun lunch). A good standby for meals and snacks, including gorgeous puddings, in classic Art-Nouveau surroundings.

More upmarket restaurants

Lou Souléou, 16 bd Jean-Hibert (☎93.39.85.55; closed Wed & Tues evening). Fish in all its forms and fine *aïoli* on very reasonably priced menus; plus a view of the sea.

La Mère-Besson, 13 rue des Frères-Pradignac (☎93.39.59.24; closed Sun & lunchtime in Aug). Each day has a different speciality, *estouffade*, *aïoli* and *lottes niçoises* among them.

Bars and clubs

Le Whisky à Gogo, 115 av des Lérins (10pm onwards). The disco where everyone beneath the jetset goes to pound and sweat to mind-numbing music.

La Nouvelle Vague, 17 rue Jean-de-Riouffe (till 3/4am). Piano-bar specialising in guitar playing. A good mix of people and plenty of them dancing.

Le Zanzi-Bar, 85 rue Félix-Faure (5pm–6am). An old favourite amongst Cannois gays; drinks are cheaper before 10pm but the ambience better later.

Le Disco 7, 7 rue Rougières (open 11pm onwards). The admission fee includes your first drink, leaving not enough for many more; transvestite cabaret at 1 and 2.30am.

Îles de Lérins

The **Îles de Lérins** would be lovely anywhere, but at fifteen minutes' ferry ride from Cannes, they're not far short of paradise facing purgatory. **Boats** leave from the *gare maritime* in the old port, 7.30am to 3.30pm in summer (nine crossings daily, reduced to five – last at 2.45pm – out of season). The last boats back leave St-Honorat at 4.45pm and Ste-Marguerite at 6 or 7pm (summer times). Taking a picnic is a good idea as the handful of restaurants have a lucrative monopoly.

St-Honorat

ST-HONORAT, the smaller southern island, has been owned by monks almost continuously since its namesake and patron founded a monastery here in 410 AD. It was a famous bishops' seminary, where St-Patrick trained for seven years before setting out for Ireland. The present **abbey** buildings are mostly nineteenth century, though some vestiges of the medieval and earlier constructions remain in the church and within the cloisters – which only men can visit. But behind them, on the sea's edge, stands an eleventh-century fortress, for use by the monks in times of danger. Of all the protective forts against invaders built along this coast, this is the only one that looks as if it still might serve its original function. At the same time it shows its age without cosmetic reconstruction or picture postcard ruins.

But the forces of this island today are peace and silence within the sound of pine leaves stirring and the sea mapping out its miniscule tide. There are no cars, shops, bars or hotels: just vines, lavender, herbs and olive trees mingled with wild poppies and daisies; and pine and eucalyptus trees shading the paths beside the white rock shore mixing with the scents of rosemary, thyme and wild honeysuckle.

Ste-Marguerite

STE-MARGUERITE can at first be a bit of a let-down after St-Honorat. The water is sludgy round the port, the lagoon at the western end is stagnant and the aleppo pines and woods of evergreen oak are so thick that most of the paths are cast in sepulchral gloom. It is still beautiful, though, and large enough for visitors to find seclusion. The western end is the most accessible, and the best points to swim are the rocky inlets across the island from the port.

The dominating structure and crowd-puller of the island is the **Fort Ste-Marguerite**, a Richelieu commission which failed to prevent the Spanish occupying both Lérin islands between 1635 and 1637. Later, Vauban rounded it off, presumably for Louis XIV's *gloire* – since the strategic value of greatly enlarging a fort facing your own mainland without upgrading the one facing the sea is pretty minimal. There are cells to see, including the one in which Dumas' "Man in the Iron Mask" is supposed to have been held, and a **Musée de la Mer** of local finds, mostly Roman but including remnants of a tenth-century Arab ship.

The fort and museum are open from 9.30/10.30am to noon and from 2pm until the last boat, but access is free to the grassy ramparts of this vast construction.

Mougins

MOUGINS, 8km north of Cannes, is arguably the most exclusive and expensive village on the Riviera. This is due, in no small part, to the fact that Roger Vergé, one of the most famous chefs in France, runs two restaurants here (along with a shop and a school). However, the added attraction of the **Musée des Motos** (April–Sept 10am–7pm; Oct–March 10am–6pm; 30F) makes Mougins worth at least a quick look. No expense has been spared on this indulgent dedication to the automobile and its two-wheeled relations. Inside the hangar-like exhibition space are entire scenes bigger than an average stage-set, including a kitchen in the 1950s (a motorbike in its mass design context), and a creepily realistic Bugatti garage of 1939. If you're feeling fired up after this, the **Buggy Cross à Mougins**, opposite the museum, has a racing track and small but whippy go-carts (July & Aug daily till dusk; rest of the year weekends). If you disapprove entirely of internal combustion engines, they have horses, too.

VALLAURIS: PICASSO

Picasso stayed ten years in **Vallauris**, where he first began to use clay, thereby reviving one of the traditional crafts of this little town in the hills above the Golfe Juan. Today the main street, av Georges-Clemenceau, sells nothing but **pottery** – much of it the garishly glazed bowls and figurines that could feature in souvenir shops anywhere. The **Madoura workshop**, where Picasso worked, is off rue 19 mars 1962, to the right as you come down av Georges-Clemenceau, and still has the sole rights on reproducing Picasso's designs – for sale, at a price, in the shop (open weekdays only).

A bronze **Man with a Sheep**, Picasso's gift to the town, stands in the main square and market-place, place de la Libération, beside the church and castle. The local authorities suggested he should decorate the early medieval deconsecrated **chapel** in the castle courtyard (10am–noon & 2–6pm; closed Tues), which he finally did in 1952. The space is tiny, and, with the painted panels covering the vault, has the architectural simplicity of an air-raid shelter. Picasso's subject is *La Guerre et la Paix*. At first glance it's easy to be unimpressed (as many critics still are). It looks mucky and slapdash with paint runs on the unyielding plywood panel surface. But stay a while and the passion of this violently drawn pacifism slowly emerges. On the War panel, a music score is trampled by hooves and about to be engulfed in flames; a fighter's lance tenuously holds the scales of justice and a shield that bears the outline of a dove. Peace is represented by Pegasus, the winged horse of poetry; people dancing and suckling babies; and the freedom of the spirit to mix up images and concepts with unmalicious mischief.

Vallauris is no place to stay, though it does boast a good cheap **restaurant**, the *Vieux Bourg*, on rue Lascaris in the old town. **Buses** from Cannes and Golfe-Juan run every hour to Vallauris and finish up at the place de la Libération, close to the castle.

Bank-breaking **restaurants** apart, there's at least one place in Mougins – *Le Feu Follet*, on pl de la Mairie (☎93.90.05.36; closed Sun evening & Mon out of season, Nov & March) – where you eat great food for under 100F. To get to Mougins from Cannes, take the **bus** for Grasse and get off at Val de Mougins, a picturesque but long climb from the old town. For the Musée des Autos, get off by the Nice–Cannes autoroute, 3km before the turn-off for Mougins.

Grasse

GRASSE is the world capital of *parfumiers* and has been for almost 300 years. These days it likes to flaunt itself, promoting its perfumed image as a chic eighteenth-century village with a medieval heart surrounded by acres of **scented flowers**. Making perfumes is presented as a mysterious process, an alchemy, turning the soul of the flower into a liquid of luxury and desire. The industry is at pains to keep quiet about modern innovations and techniques – essence might be diluted into perfume, but not its mystery into truth.

Grasse is the official starting point of the Route Napoléon (see p.700), but is equally easy to visit as a day trip from the coast. The town istelf is on a pretty steep incline with some great views over the Côte; the **gare routière** lies to the east of the old town at the *Parking Notre-Dames-des-Fleurs*; a short way uphill is pl de la Foux and the **SI**.

The perfume factories

There are thirty *parfumeries* in and around Grasse, most of them making, not perfume, but the essence which is then sold to Dior, Lancôme, Estée Lauder and the rest. They tell you that one litre of jasmin essence costs 90,000F. Perfume contains 20 percent essence (eau de toilette and eau de Cologne considerably less) and the bottles are extremely small, but the major cost in this multi-billion dollar business is marketing. The grand Parisian couturiers whose clothes, on strictly cost-accounting grounds, serve simply to promote the perfume, go to inordinate lengths to sell their latest fragrance, spending hundreds of millions of francs a year on advertising alone.

A good place to get an overview of the business is the **Parfumerie Fragonard** – actually two venues, one in the centre of town at 20 bd Fragonard, and the other 3km towards Cannes at Les Quatre Chemins. The first shows traditional methods of extracting essence and has a collection of bejewelled flagons. The one outside town is far more informative and admits to modernisation of the processes. A map of the world shows the origins of all the various strange ingredients, which include civet (extract of civet cat's genitals), ambergris (intestinal goo from whales) and musk from Himalayan goats. Other *parfumeries* to tour include *Galimard*, 73 route de Cannes, and *Molinard* at 60 bd Victor-Hugo (closed Sun). These, and all the others, are free; all of them also have shops and give frequent tours in both French and English.

The old town

Vieux Grasse, despite its touristy shops and full range of restaurants, is surprisingly humble, a working-class enclave where lines of washing festoon the high, narrow streets. Rates of pay for the pickers of raw ingredients for perfume essences are notoriously low. The inhabitants say it's like a village where everyone knows each other, and out of season that's certainly the atmosphere that prevails. The rich all live in the neighbouring villages of Mougins and Cabris.

Place des Aires, at the top of the old town, is the main meeting point for all and sundry, and the venue for the daily flower and vegetable market. It is ringed by arcades of different heights and the elegant wrought-iron balcony of the *Hôtel Isnard* at no. 33, and at one time the *place* was the exclusive preserve of the tanning industry. At the opposite end of Vieux Grasse lie the **cathedral** and **bishop's palace**, both built in the twelfth century, the former containing various paintings including three from Rubens and, best by far, a triptych by the sixteenth-century Niçois painter Louis Bréa.

A museum you might like to take a quick flit through is the **Musée d'Art et d'Histoire de Provence**, 2 rue Mirabeau, housed in a luxurious town house, commissioned by Mirabeau's sister for her social entertainment duties (10am–noon & 2–5.30pm/6pm; closed Sat, 2nd & 3rd Sun of the month & Nov). As well as all the gorgeous fittings, and the original eighteenth-century kitchen, the historical collection adds a nice eclectic touch. It includes wonderful eighteenth- to nineteenth-century faïence from Apt and Le Castellet; Mirabeau's death mask; a tin bidet; and six prehistoric bronze leg bracelets.

Practicalities

Three possible **hotels** at the cheaper end of the market are: *Napoléon*, 6 av Thiers (☎93.36.06.37; ③), close to the SI; *Ste-Thérèse*, 39 bd Y.E.-Baudoin (☎93.36.10.29; ③), to the west of the old town and uphill; and *Pension Michèle*, 6 rue du Palais-de-Justice (☎93.36.80.80; ②/③).

Bars and **restaurants** in the old town are good value. *Le Vieux Bistrot*, 5 rue des Moulinets (lunch only; closed Sun) serves great, simple food. The *Crêperie Bretonne* and *La Galerie Gourmand* on rue Fabrières are good stand-bys, and you'll find plenty of other menus to choose from on rue de la Fontette and rue Droite. The bars on pl des Aires give the most opportunity for encounters with the locals – the spit and sawdust *Bar-Tabac L'Ariel* is a good place to start.

For **picnic food**, *La Fromagerie* at 5 rue de l'Oratoire has the best cheese selection. At the *Maison Venturini*, 1 rue Marcel-Journet, you can buy fabulous savoury *fougasses* or sweet *fougassettes*, a sort of five-fingered unleavened bread, flavoured in the Grasse speciality, orange blossom.

Antibes and around

Antibes and its environs is the only place left on the Côte d'Azur – Monaco excepted – where the really, *really* rich and the very, *very* successful still live, or at least have residences. Yet it's not immediately obvious why this area should be so desirable. It's just as built up as the rest of the Riviera, with no open countryside separating **Golfe-Juan** from Antibes, and none on the Cap d'Antibes that isn't surrounded by high electric fences. That said, **Juan-les-Pins** is a great place for night-time animation, while **Antibes** is a quieter but cheaper place to hang out, as are the inland campsites en route to the village of **Biot**, home to the **Fernand Léger museum**.

Antibes

The centre of **ANTIBES** remains predictable pretty, though very little of its medieval stucture is left. The **castle** is a beautifully cool, light space, with hexagonal terracotta floor tiles, windows over the sea and a terrace garden with four sculptures by Germaine Richier.

In 1946, **Picasso** was offered the dusty castle (by then already a museum) as a studio. Several extremely prolific months followed before he moved to Vallauris, leaving all his Antibes output to what is now the **Musée Picasso** (10am–noon & 3–7pm; winter 10am–noon & 2–6pm; closed Tues & Nov; 25F). Although Picasso donated other works later on, the bulk of the collection belongs to this one period. There's an uncomplicated exuberance in the numerous still lifes of sea urchins, the goats and fauns in Cubist non-disguise, and the wonderful *Ulysses et ses Sirènes* – a great round head against a mast around which the ship, sea and sirens swirl; and a whole room full of drawings. Picasso is also the subject here of other painters and photographers, including **Man Ray** and **Bill Brandt**, and there are works by contemporaries, among them the tapestry of construction workers by **Léger**.

Practicalities

Antibes' **gare SNCF**, a block back from the head of the port, lies at the north end of av Robert-Soleau; the **SI** is at the other end on pl Général-de-Gaulle; the **gare routière** is off the adjoining pl Guynemer. The triangular-shaped **old town** lies to the south and east of these points – pick up a free map of Antibes and its environs from the SI – walk down rue de la République to pl Nationale, the heart of old Antibes. **Bicycles** can be hired from *Chenu*, 14 bd Dugommier, and *Wilson*, 43 bd Wilson.

The most economical **hotels** are both close to the gare routière; the *Modern*, 1 rue Fourmillière (☎93.34.03.05; ③), and *Le Nouvel Hôtel*, pl Guynemer (☎93.34.44.07; ③/ ④). There's a **youth hostel** on Cap d'Antibes, the *Relais International de la Jeunesse* on bd de la Garoupe (☎93.61.34.40; June–Sept; closed 10am–5.30pm) which needs booking well in advance. You'll have to get a bus from Antibes and may not be able to get a key to stay out after 11pm. Of the many **campsites** along the coast north of Antibes, *Idéal-Camping*, (☎93.74.27.07), opposite the gare SNCF at LA BRAQUE (one stop north of Antibes), has the advantage of being open all year, but *Le Logis de La Braque* (☎93.3354.72; May–Sept) offers the same prices with many more facilities.

Back in Antibes, rue James-Close, off rue de la République, is jam-packed with good-value **restaurants**: try *La Marmite*, 20 rue de la République. For pizza, there's *Il Giardino*, 21 rue Thuret, though you may have a long wait to be served, and *La Famiglia*, a cheap family-run outfit at the end of rue Vauban (closed Wed). You can get excellent *paella* and *couscous* at *La Calèche*, 25 rue Thuret.

Juan-les Pins

JUAN-LES-PINS, just 1.5km west of Antibes, is another of those overloaded Côte d'Azur names; the summer St-Moritz; the night-time playground for the most expensively outfitted and consistently photographed myths, who retreat at dawn to well-screened cages on Cap d'Antibes. Beyond the image, the place has very little in the way of history. Unlike St-Tropez it was never a fishing village, just a pine grove by the sea, where Napoléon happened to land on his return from exile in 1815. It wasn't until the 1930s that the place began to take off as a full-blown Côte resort.

Practicalities

Cheap **rooms** just don't exist in Juan-les-Pins; the closest you'll get are both close to the gare SNCF – the *Trianon*, 14 av de l'Estérel (☎93.61.18.11; ③/④), and *Parisiana*, 16 av de l'Estérel (☎93.61.27.03; April–Sept; ③). As for **restaurants**, *L'Auberge de l'Estérel*, 21 rue des Îles, is not the cheapest of Juan-les-Pins', but it's very good value considering the excellent food. *Le Cheap*, 21 rue Dautheville (closed Mon out of season), and *Le Provence*, 1 av Maréchal-Joffre, are more economical, though less inspired.

You can get *brasserie* food, crêpes, pizzas and similar snacks, from street stalls till the early hours, and many shops and bars also keep going in summer till 3 or 4am – worth remembering if you arrive mid-morning and wonder why the place is dead. *Le Crystal* on av Georges-Gallice is the **brasserie** at the hub of the milling crowds; its neighbouring **bars**, *Le Pam-Pam* and *Le Festival*, 137 and 146 bd Wilson respectively, compete, both with South American music and glittering cocktails, and are packed in high season. Of the **clubs**, *Les Pêcheurs* on Port Gallice has a hot reputation.

BIOT: FERDINAND LEGER

Seven buses a day cover the 8km from Antibes to the village of **Biot**, where Fernand Léger lived for a few years at the end of his life. A stunning collection of his works can be seen at the **Musée Fernand Léger** (summer 10am–noon & 2.30–6.30pm; rest of year 10am–noon & 2–5pm; closed Tues; 15F), just southeast of Biot.

Léger's art has the capacity for instant pleasure – the pattern of the shapes, the colour – though he can also draw it back to harsh horror as in the charcoal black to brown on off-white paper in *Stalingrad*. It's interesting to compare his life and work with Picasso, his fellow pioneer of Cubism and long-time comrade in the Communist Party. While Léger's commitment to collective working-class life never wavered, Picasso only waved at it when he needed it. Picasso wanted to embrace the whole world and be embraced in return. He chose a complex, dominating, sometimes perverted persona in which to do it while Léger stuck within the reality of himself and the world, an outlook captured by Alexander Calder's wire sculpture portrait of Léger in the museum.

Above the Baie des Anges

Between Antibes and Nice, the **Baie des Anges** laps at twentieth-century resorts with two fine examples of concrete corpulence, the giant petrified sails with viciously pointed corners of the Villeneuve-Loubet-Plage marina, and an apartment complex, 1km long and sixteen storeys high, barricading the stony beach.

The old towns and softer visual stimulation lie inland. **Cagnes** is another artists' town – **Renoir**'s in particular – as is **St-Paul-de-Vence**, which houses the wonderful modern art collection of the **Fondation Maeght**. Even **Vence** itself boasts a small chapel decorated by **Matisse**.

Cagnes

The various parts of **CAGNES** are somewhat confusing: the nondescript coastal zone is known as **Cros-de-Cagnes**; inland above the autoroute is, paradoxically, **Cagnes-sur-Mer**, the town centre, so to speak; while **Hauts-de-Cagnes** is the original medieval village, overlooking the town from the northwest heights.

Arriving and accommodation

The **gare SNCF** (Cagnes-sur-Mer, one stop from the gare SNCF Cros-de-Cagnes) is southwest of the town centre alongside the autoroute. You need to turn right on the northern side of the autoroute along av de la Gare to reach the main square, pl de Gaulle. Close by, you'll find the **SI**, at 6 bd Maréchal-Juin, and a **bicycle hire** place, *Location 2 Roux*, at 3 rue du Logis. From av de la Gare, rue Gén-Bérenger forks left towards **Hauts-de-Cagnes**, becoming montée de la Bourgade and gaining height at an exhausting rate. In summer, a **minibus** service runs from the gare SNCF to Hauts-de-Cagnes via pl de-Gaulle every 45 minutes.

The *Terminus*, 45 av de la Gare (☎93.20.70.53; ③), might have some cheap **rooms** available, but you're better off basing yourself in nearby Nice, or even Antibes. **Camping** is the only other reasonable option: *Panoramer*, chemin des Gros-Buaux (☎93.31.16.15; Feb–Sept), 1km northeast of Cagnes-sur-Mer is well equipped but overpriced; *Le Val de Cagnes* (☎93.73.36.53; open all year) is 4km north of the town but less expensive. If you want to be nearer the sea, try *Orion*, chemin de Vaugrenier (☎93.73.93.73; open all year).

Cagnes-sur-Mer: Renoir

At the top of pl de-Gaulle in **CAGNES-SUR-MER**, av Auguste-Renoir runs right and crosses the road to La Gaude. A short way further on, chemin des Colettes leads off to the left up to **Les Colettes**, the house that **Renoir** had built in 1907 and where he spent the last eleven years of his life. It is now a memorial museum (10am–1pm & 2–5/6pm; closed Tues; 20F), and you're free to wander around the olive and rare orange groves that surround it. One of the three studios in the house, north-facing to catch the late afternoon light, is arranged as if Renoir had just popped out. Apart from Renoir's own works, there are portraits of him by his closest friends – Albert André, Aristide Maillol and others – and several works by occasional visitors such as Dufy and Bonnard. Coming by bus from Antibes, you can get off the Nice bus at the *Béat-Les Colettes* stop.

Hauts-de-Cagnes

HAUTS-DE-CAGNES is a favourite haunt of successes in the contemporary art world, as well as those of decades past, and it lives up to everything dreamed of in a Riviera *village perché*. The ancient village backs up to a crenellated feudal **château** (10am–noon & 2–5pm; closed Tues; 5F), which houses museums of local history, fishing and olive cultivation, along with the **Musée d'Art Moderne Méditerranéen** – with changing exhibitions of the painters who have worked on the coast in the last hundred years. It also contains the **Donation Suzy Solidor**, which consists of wonderfully diverse portraits by all the great twentieth-century painters of the lesbian cabaret star who inspired the music hall song "If you knew Suzy, like I knew Suzy". In addition, if you're here between July and September, you can see the entries from forty-odd countries for Hauts-de-Cagnes' big event of the year, the *Festival International de la Peinture*.

Hauts-de-Cagnes is inevitably an expensive place for rooms and decent **meals**, with only the dubiously named *Le Clap*, off montée de la Bourgade, offering a *menu fixe* for under 100F. However, pl de Notre-Dame, above the castle, is the centre of not just the town's but the whole district's **nightlife**. *Le Jimmy's* is the most famous and the most expensive; *Le Vertigo* on the opposite corner of the *place* charges half the price, but has only a fraction of the kudos; *Le Tourelle*, nearby, is better and only around 70F to get in.

St-Paul-de-Vence

Further into the hills is yet another artistic treat, and one of the best in the whole region, the remarkable **Fondation Maeght** in the village of **ST-PAUL-DE-VENCE**. The Nice–Vence **bus** that stops at pl de-Gaulle in Cagnes-sur-Mer, has two stops in St-Paul: the *Fondation* (July–Sept 10am–7pm; rest of the year 10am–12.30pm & 2.30– 6pm; 35F) is signposted from the second. Admission includes the permanent collections, temporary exhibitions, bookshop, library and cinema, and it's worth every last centime.

Once through the gates, any idea of dutifully seeing the catalogue of priceless museum pieces crumbles. It's you that's seen first anyway – by **Giacometti**'s *Cat* stalking along the edge of the grass. And how can you retain any serious museum etiquette faced with **Miró**'s *Egg* smiling above a pond and his totemed *Fork* outlined against the sky? Or not be bewitched by the **Calder** mobile swinging over watery tiles, by **Léger**'s *Flowers, birds and a bench* on a sun-lit rough stone wall, by **Zadkine**'s and **Arp**'s metallic forms hovering between the pine trunks or the clanking tubular fountain by **Pol Bury**? And that's just outside the building…

There's not much point remaining in St-Paul, despite its *village perché* claims, unless you've got a great deal of spare cash. The best thing to do is head straight on for Vence.

Vence

A few kilometres north, with abundant water and the sheltering Pré-Alpes behind, **VENCE** has always been a significant town. In the 1920s, however, it became yet another haven for painters and writers – André Gide, Dufy, DH Lawrence and Marc Chagall all spent time here, and Lawrence and Chagall died here, in 1930 and 1985 respectively. The old town is blessed with numerous ancient houses, gateways, fountains, chapels and a cathedral which boasts a Chagall mosaic, but the work which people come to Vence to see is that of **Henri Matisse**.

Towards the end of World War II, Matisse moved to Vence to escape the Allied bombing of the coast, and his legacy is the town's most famous and exciting building, the **Chapelle du Rosaire**, at 466 av Henri-Matisse, on the road to La Gaude from the Carrefour Jean-Moulin at the top of av des Poilus (Tues & Thurs 10am–11.30am & 2.30–5.30pm; closed Nov 1–Dec 15; free). The chapel was his last work – consciously so – and not, as some have tried to explain, a religious conversion. "My only religion is the love of the work to be created, the love of creation, and great sincerity" – a statement from 1952 when the five-year project was completed.

The drawings on the **chapel walls** – black outline figures on white tiles – were executed by Matisse with a paintbrush fixed to a six-foot long bamboo stick specifically to remove his own stylistic signature from the lines. He succeeded in this to the extent that many people are bitterly disappointed, not finding the "Matisse" they expect. The only source of colour in the chapel comes from the light diffused through green, blue and yellow stained-glass windows, changing with the day's light. Yet it is a total work – every part of the chapel is Matisse's design – and one that the artist was content with. It was his "ultimate goal, the culmination of an intense, sincere and difficult endeavour".

Practicalities

Vence is a real town with affordable places to **stay** and **eat**. Arriving by bus, you'll be dropped at the **gare routière** on pl du Grand-Jardin, with **bicycle hire** at *Vence Motocycles*, the **SI** nearby and, just beyond, the main gate into the old town. For **hotels**, *La Closerie des Genets*, 4 impasse Maurel (☎93.58.33.25; ③/④), off av M-Maurel to the south of Vieux Vence, and *La Lubiane*, 10 av Joffre (☎93.58.01.10; ③/④), to the west up av Henri-Isnard and av des Poilus, both have low-priced rooms. There's a **campsite** 3km west off the road to TOURETTE-SUR-LOUP, *La Bergerie* (☎93.58.09.36; March–Oct).

For a special **meal**, try *La Farigoule* at 15 av Henri-Isnard, or, on the same street but half the price, *La Vieille Douve* (closed Thurs). Prices tend to be higher in the old town, but there's a wider selection; try the pizzas at *Le Pêcheur*, 1 pl Godeau (closed Fri lunchtime). **Drinking** is a young and noisy affair at *Henry's Bar* on pl du Peyra, and ostentatiously cool at *La Régence* on pl du Grand-Jardin.

Nice

The capital of the Riviera and fifth largest town of France, **NICE** scarcely deserves its glittering reputation. Living off inflated property values and fat business accounts, its ruling class has hardly evolved from the eighteenth-century Russian and English aristocrats who first built their mansions here. Today it's the *rentiers* and retired people of select nationalities whose dividends and pensions give the city its startlingly high ratio of per-capita income to economic activity. And their votes ensured the monopoly of municipal power held for decades by the right-wing dynasty whose corruption was finally exposed in 1990 when the mayor fled to Uruguay.

The traffic is a nightmare, miniature poodles would appear to be mandatory, the phones are always vandalised and the beach isn't even sand. This should be by rights

Details of Nice's calendar are available from the city listings magazines or the *Comité des Fêtes*, 5 promenade des Anglais; (☎93.87.16.28).

February *Mardi Gras Carnival.*

Second and third week of July *Parade du Jazz* in the Parc de Cimiez (☎93.21.22.01).

End of July to beginning of August *Festival de Folklore International* and *Batailles des Fleurs* (unspontaneous flower-throwing bash).

December *Festival du Cinéma Italien.*

one of the most loathsome cities on the Riviera. And yet Nice manages to be delightful. The sun and the sea and the laid-back, affable Niçois cover a multitude of sins. The medieval rabbit-warren of the *vieille ville*, the Italianate facades of modern Nice, and the rich exuberant turn-of-the-century residences that made the city one of Europe's most fashionable winter retreats have all survived intact. Many of the city's museums and sites have, surprisingly, free entry. And the bus and train connections make Nice by far the best base for visiting the rest of the Riviera.

Orientation, arrival and accommodation

It doesn't take long to get a feel for the **layout** of Nice. Shadowed by mountains that curve down to the sea east of its port, it still breaks up more or less into old and new. **Vieux Nice**, the old town, groups about the hill of **Le Château**, its limits, once signalled by the River Paillon, now **bd Jean-Jaurès**, built along its course. Along the seafront, the **promenade des Anglais** runs a cool 5km, until forced to curve inland by the sea-projecting runways of the airport. The central square, **place Masséna**, is at the bottom of the modern city's main street, av Jean-Médecin, while off to the north is the exclusive hillside suburb of **Cimiez**.

Arriving by air, you can get a bus (every 20min) from outside the end door of *Aérogare I* (the terminal for all London flights), to the junction of av Gustav V and the promenade des Anglais, or on to the **gare routière** if you're continuing your journey straight out of town. The gare routière is for once very central, close to the old town beneath the promenade du Paillon on bd Jean-Jaurès; the **gare SNCF** is a little further out, a couple of blocks west of the top end of av Jean-Médecin (bus #12 will take you to pl Masséna).

The main **SI** (☎93.87.07.07; July–Sept 8.45am–7pm, closed Sun lunchtimes; Oct–June Mon–Sat 8.45am–12.30pm & 2–6pm) is beside the gare SNCF on av Thiers. It's one of the most useful and generous of Côte SIs and a lot better than its annexes at 5 av Gustav V and at Nice-Ferber on the road from the airport. Any of these offices can supply you with a free listings magazine, *7 Jours 7 Nuits*, which comes out every Wednesday and covers the whole Riviera.

For **getting around** the city, buses are frequent and run until 12.15 at night. Fares are flat rate and you can buy a single ticket on the bus, or a *carnet* of five tickets. There are also one-day, five-day or weekly passes, all of which can be bought at *tabacs*, kiosks, newsagents and from *TN*, the transport office at 10 av Félix-Faure, where you can also pick up a free route map. **Bicycles**, **mopeds** and **motorbikes** can be hired from *Nicea Location Rent* at 9 av Thiers.

Accommodation

Before you start doing the rounds, it's well worth taking advantage of the **reservation service** offered, for a small fee, by the SI at the train station. The area around the station teems with cheap, seedy **hotels**, but it's perfectly possible to find reasonably

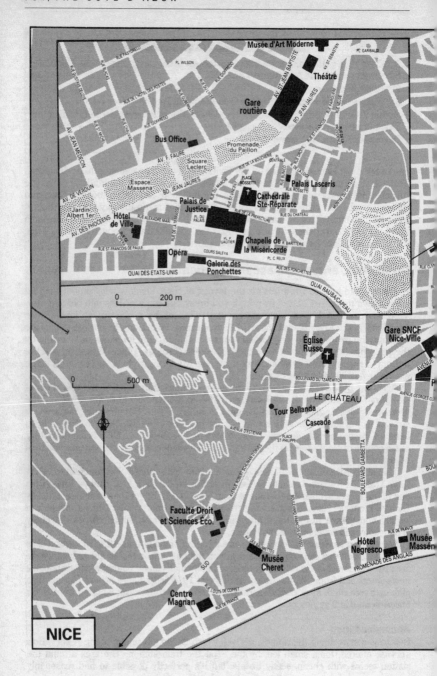

Musée d'Art Moderne
Théâtre
Gare routière
Bus Office
Promenade du Paillon
Square Leclerc
Espace Massena
Jardin Albert 1er
Hôtel de Ville
Palais de Justice
Palais Lascaris
Cathédrale Ste-Réparate
Chapelle de la Miséricorde
Opéra
Galerie des Ponchettes

RUE PASTORELLI
P. WILSON
RUE DE L'HOTEL DES POSTES
AV. JEAN MEDECIN
AV. DE VERDUN
AV. F. FAURE
BD JEAN JAURES
RUE ALEXADRE MARI
RUE ST FRANCOIS DE PAULE
QUAI DES ETATS-UNIS
COURS SALEYA
AV. ST JEAN BAPTISTE
BD JEAN JAURES
PROMENADE DU PAILLON
PLACE ROSSETTI
RUE ROSSETTI
MONTÉE DU CHÂTEAU
QUAI RAUBA CAPEAU
RUE DES PONCHETTES
P. GARIBALDI
AV. ST-SEBASTIEN

0   200 m

Église Russe
Gare SNCF Nice-Ville
BOULEVARD DU TZAREWITCH
LE CHÂTEAU
AVENUE GEORGES CL.
Tour Bellanda
Cascade
AVENUE D'ESTIENNE
PLACE ST-PHILIPPE
BOULEVARD GAMBETTA
Faculté Droit et Sciences Éco.
AV. R. BAUMETTES
Musée Cheret
Hôtel Negresco
Musée Massén
RUE DE FRANCE
PROMENADE DES ANGLAIS
Centre Magnan
RUE DE FRANCE

0   500 m

NICE

priced rooms in Vieux Nice. In summer, there's a fairly good choice of **youth accommodation**, or if you want to pay nothing, this is the one place on the Côte d'Azur where **sleeping on the beach** is tolerated. In fact, so many people do it that it becomes an all-night party throughout the summer.

HOTELS

Hôtel St-François, 3 rue St-François (☎93.85.88.69). On a busy pedestrian thoroughfare in the *vieille ville*, above a restaurant hosting live jazz on Friday nights. An ideal base if you're not bothered by the noise. ②/③.

Hôtel les Orangers, 10bis av Durante (☎93.87.51.41). A cheapie which all American students head for and unfailingly recommend. ③.

Hôtel Central, 10 rue de Suisse (☎93.88.85.08). Very small and not too bad if you can get a room overlooking the courtyard. ③.

Hôtel de la Place du Pin, 10 rue Bonaparte (☎93.56.42.19). Not a bad location between pl Garibaldi and the port. Rooms are reasonable if a little dingy. ③.

Hôtel Excelsior, 19 av Durante (☎93.88.18.05). Unusually light, spacious and clean for somewhere so close to the station. ④.

Hôtel le Capitole, 4 rue de la Tour (☎93.80.08.15). A good if potentially noisy, location in Viuex Nice with a warm atmosphere though not over-generous rooms. ④/⑤.

Hôtel de Lépante, 6 rue de Lépante (☎93.6220.55). Quiet and central, but don't be fooled by the *Belle Epoque* exterior; inside the rooms are plain. ⑤.

YOUTH ACCOMMODATION

International House for Young People, 22 rue Portinax (☎93.62.02.79). Small hippyish hang-out run by a Brit, close to the gare SNCF off av Jean-Médecin to the east.

IYHF Auberge de Jeunesse, route Forestière du Mont-Alban (☎93.89.23.64; reception 7–10am & 6–11pm); bus #14 from pl Masséna, direction *pl du Mont-Boron*, stop *L'Auberge*. 4km out of town and, for two people, not a lot cheaper than sharing a hotel room. The last bus from the centre leaves at 7.30pm and there's a curfew at 11.30pm. No card required.

Clairvallon Relais International de la Jeunesse, 26 av Scuderi (☎93.81.27.63; reception till 6pm); bus #15 or #15A, stop *Scudéri*. Slightly cheaper than the youth hostel but 10km north of the centre and with a 10.30pm curfew. Location apart, it's pleasantly informal and has a swimming pool.

Résidence Les Collinettes, 3 av R-Schuman (☎93.37.24.30; open July & Aug only; women only; reception 4–10pm); bus #17 from gare SNCF or #14 from the centre, direction *Parc Impérial*, stop *Châteauneuf* and walk down av Schuman to Law Faculty complex. Much more central than the *AJ* or *Clairvallon*.

MJC Magnan, 31 rue Louis-de-Coppet (☎93.86.28.75; June to mid-Sept); buses #3, #9, #10, #12, #22 or #24, stop *Magnan*. Not too far from Vieux Nice – and close to the beach.

CAMPING

The only campsite anywhere near Nice is the very small *Camping Terry*, route de Grenoble, LINGOSTIÈRE(☎93.08.11.58), which is 6.5km north of the airport on the N202 and not on any bus route. Unless you have a camper van or caravan to park, it's probably better to have the stars rather than canvas above you and discover the nightlife of the town beach.

Le Château and Vieux Nice

For initial orientation, with brilliant sea and city views, fresh air and the scent of Mediterranean vegetation, the best place to make for is the **Château park** (daily 7am–7pm). It's where Nice began as the ancient Greek city of *Nikea*, hence the mosaics and stone vases in mock Grecian style. There's no château as such, but the real pleasure lies in looking down on the scrambled rooftops and gleaming mosaic of tiles of Vieux Nice and along the sweep of the promenade des Anglais. To reach the park, you can either take the lift by *Tour Bellanda* (the naval museum) at the eastern end of quai des États-Unis, or climb the steps from rue de la Providence or rue du Château in the old town.

Vieux Nice

Only a handful of years ago, any ex-pat or police officer would tell you that **Vieux Nice** was a dangerous place, brimming with drug-pushers, dark-skinned muggers and car thieves. That was always a gross exaggeration, but it still reveals how much the *quartier* has changed of late. In the early 1980s, an upmarket-ing process started with the renovation of low-rent flats, the town hall using every means at its disposal to control who moved in and who got moved out to the high-rises on the city's perimeter. However, gentrification hasn't yet completely taken over, and a fair number of the old residents remain. There are still little hardware stores selling brooms and bottled gas; clothes lines are hung high across the streets; and tiny cafés are full of blue-overalled men. This life co-exists with the expensive boutiques and new restaurants.

The streets of the old town are too narrow for buses – it's an area made for walking. The central square is **place Rosetti**, where the soft-coloured Baroque **Cathédrale de St-Réparate** just manages to be visible in the concatenation of eight narrow streets. There are two cafés to relax in, one sun-lit, one shaded, and a magical ice cream parlour. The real magnet, though, is **cours Saleya** and the adjacent pl Pierre-Gautier and pl Charles-Félix. These are wide-open sun-lit spaces alongside grandiloquent municipal buildings and Italianate chapels and the site of the city's main vegetable and flower **market** (daily 6am–1pm). Over on pl St-François, west of pl Pierre-Gautier, is the **fish market**, its odours persisting till late at night when all the old streets are hosed down with enough water to go paddling.

The River Paillon and the modern town

The **River Paillon**'s covered course is the site of the city's municipal prestige projects. At their worst, up beyond traverse Barla, they take in the form of giant packing crates for high-tech goods, in the multi-media, mega-buck conference centre grotesquely called the **Acropolis**. Though theoretically a public building – with exhibition space, a cinema and bowling alley (open 11am–2am) – international business often limits casual entry. Downstream from the Acropolis, a new and vast marble monument to the ambition of the city's leaders has recently opened, the **Musée d'Art Moderne et d'Art Contemporain – MAMAC** – (daily 11am–6pm except Wed 11am–10pm; closed Tues; free). Neo-Realism and Pop-Art make up most of the gallery's permanent collection, including works by, among others, Andy Warhol, Yves Klein, Roy Lichtenstein and Christo, and plenty of stuff by the pile-of-bricks/crushed-egg-cartons school of art.

Heading north from the Paillon, **av Jean-Médecin** is the city's main shopping street, named after the former mayor whose son also held the post until the courts started examining allegations of massive fraud. The debouchement of the Paillion into the sea marks the beginning of the **promenade des Anglais**, created by nineteenth-century English residents for their afternoon's sea-breeze stroll. Today it's the city's unofficial high-speed racetrack, bordered by some of the most fanciful turn-of-the-century architecture on the Côte d'Azur.

North of the promenade, the chief interest is in the older **bourgeois architecture**: eighteenth–nineteenth-century Italian Baroque and neo-Classical; florid *Belle Epoque*; and unclassifiable exotic aristo-fantasy. The trophy for the most gilded, exotic and elaborate edifice goes to the **Russian Orthodox Cathedral**, off bd Tsarewitch at the end of av Nicolas II (summer 9am–noon & 2.30–6pm; winter 9.30am–noon & 2.30–5pm; 10F; bus #14, #17, stop *Tsarewitch*).

A kilometre or so down the promenade and a couple of blocks inland at 33 av des Baumettes is the **Musée des Beaux-Arts** (Tues–Sun May–Sept 10am–noon & 3–6pm; Oct–April 10am–noon & 2–5pm; free; bus #38, stop *Chéret*). It has too many whimsical canvases by Jules Chéret, who died in Nice in 1932, and far too much of GA Mossa, a recently deceased Nice establishment figure, whose lurid symbolist paintings reek of misogyny. But there are modern works that come as unexpected delights: a Rodin bust of Victor Hugo, a whole room full of **Dufy** and some very amusing **Van Dongens** such as the *Archangel's tango*. Monet, Sisley and Degas also grace the walls.

Cimiez: Romans and Modernists

The northern suburb of **Cimiez** has always been a posh place. Its principal streets – av des Arènes-de-Cimiez and bd de Cimiez – rise between plush, high-walled villas to what was the social centre of the town's elite some 1700 years ago, when the city was capital of the Roman province of *Alpes-Maritimae*. Part of a small amphitheatre still stands, and excavations of the **Roman baths** have revealed enough detail to distinguish the sumptuous and elaborate facilities for the top tax official and his cronies, the plainer public baths and a separate complex for women. The new **Musée d'Archéologie**, 160 av des Arènes – entrance currently from rue Monte-Croce (May–Sept 10am–noon & 2.30–6.30pm; Oct–April 10am–noon & 2–5pm; closed Sun am & Mon) displays all the finds.

The seventeenth-century villa between the excavations and the arena is the **Musée Matisse**, which has been recently expanded and re-opened after a long closure. Matisse spent his winters in Nice from 1916 onwards, staying in hotels on the promenade – from where *A Tempest at Nice* was painted – and then from 1921 to 1938 renting an apartment overlooking pl Charles-Félix. He died in Cimiez in November 1954, aged 85. The collection covers every period and includes the studies for *La Dance*, the huge blue and pink mural in the Palais de Chaillot in Paris, models for the chapel he designed in Vence, and a nearly complete set of the bronze sculptures.

At the foot of Cimiez hill, just off bd Cimiez on av du Docteur-Menard, **Chagall's Biblical Message** is housed in a perfect museum built specially for the work and opened by the artist in 1972. The rooms are light and white and cool, with windows allowing you to see the greenery of the garden beyond the indescribable shades between pink and red of the *Song of Songs* canvases. The seventeen paintings are all based on the Old Testament and complemented with etchings and engravings. To the building itself, Chagall contributed a mosaic and stained-glass windows (July–Sept 10am–7pm; rest of the year 10am–noon & 2–5.30pm; closed Tues; 23F, Wed free).

Buses #15 and #15A from the centre of Nice (place Masséna) run past the Chagall museum and up to bd Arènes. Alternatives for Cimiez, but not for the Chagall, are buses #17, #20 and #22.

Eating and drinking

Nice is a great place for food indulgence, whether you're picnicking on market fare, snacking on Niçois specialities or sampling Jacques Maximin's *nouvelle cuisine*. The Italian influence is strong in all restaurants, with pasta on every menu; seafood is also a staple. For **snacks**, many of the cafés sell *baguette* sandwiches with typically Provençal fillings such as fresh basil, olive oil, goat's cheese and *mesclum*, the unique green salad mix of the region. If you want to buy the best bread, *fougasse* or croissants in town, seek out *Espuno*, 22 rue Vernier, in the old town.

Restaurants

Most areas of Nice reveal excellent restaurants. **Vieux Nice** has a dozen on every street catering for a wide variety of budgets. Another good hunting ground is the **port quaysides** and the area behind.

CHEAPER MEALS

Chez René Socca, 2 rue Miralhéti (closed Mon). The cheapest meal in town: you can buy helpings of *socca* (an egg-pancake), *pissaladière* (onion-tart with anchovies), stuffed peppers, pasta or *cala-*

mares at the counter and eat with your fingers on stools ranged haphazardly across the street; the bar opposite serves the drinks.

Le Moulin Vert, 5 rue du Moulin (☎93.85.50.58). A macrobiotic shop with vegetarian dishes to eat here or take away – pasta and vegetables in various sauces.

Café de Turin, pl Garibaldi (daily 8.30am–11pm). This is the place for oysters, mussels, clams and sea urchins, with a glass or two of wine, either in the tiny sawdust-swept *salle* inside or outside on the pavement. Watch out for costly extras though, and the long queue for tables which forms every night after 8pm.

Pompeii, 16 rue de l'Abbaye (☎93.62.31.42; last orders 10.30pm; closed Mon; *à la carte* only). In an arms-span street of Vieux Nice, this genuine Italian restaurant serves up pasta dishes, gnocchi, zucchini flower and aubergine fritters, all with the freshest ingredients.

MORE UPMARKET

Le Tramway, 11 rue Lamartine (☎93.62.16.74; last orders 10pm; closed Sun). One side of the restaurant is a tram with a mural of pl Masséna circa 1900; the opposite wall gives you the same scene viewed from within the café looking out. Beautifully presented and delicious food – try the *estocaficada*, noodles in pistou or the wonderful *roquefort fondue*.

Le Bistrot de Nice, 2–4 rue S-Guitry (☎93.80.68.00; daily till 11.30pm). The cheaper end of top *nouvelle cuisine* chef Jaques Maximin's latest outfit housed in a converted casino near pl Masséna. The de-luxe restaurant in the same building called simply *Jean Maximin* will set you back over 300F.

L'Ane Rouge, 7 quai des Deux-Emmanuel (☎93.89.49.63; last orders 9.30pm; closed weekends & mid-July–Aug). Lobster is the speciality of this portside gourmets' palace, grilled, baked or stuffed into little cabbages. Sea bass on a bed of fresh asparagus, turbot with salmon eggs, and the creamiest *bourride* are some of the other delights.

La Barale, 39 rue Beaumont (☎93.89.17.94; evenings only until 9pm; closed Sun, Mon & Aug). This cavernous, cluttered comedy-set of a provincial restaurant is more of a social than a gastronomic experience. But feed you it will, with one set six-course menu that includes *pissaladière*, *socca*, ravioli and a sticky delicious tart.

Cafés and wine bars

If, cours Saleya. At the far end of the market place with seats fanning out into the square. Mixed clientele from post-punk to yuppy watch the world go by.

Les 3 Diables, cours Saleya. Smoky, packed poseurs' dive next door to the above. Wall-to-wall leather jackets and classic grooves from the Fifties and Sixties.

Scarlet O'Hara, 22 rue Droite (7pm–12.30am; closed Mon & first half of July). Tiny Irish folk bar on the corner of rue Rosetti. Serves the creamiest and priciest *Guinness* this side of the Irish Sea.

Nightlife

Given the city's staid, affluent population, the luxury hotel bars dominate the late-night scene. Elsewhere, it's the *vieille ville* which offers the most hope, though even here out of season not much goes on beyond midnight. As for Niçois nightclubs, bouncers judging your wallet or exclusive membership lists are the rule.

Chez Wayne, 15 rue de la Préfecture (daily 10am–midnight). Popular bar on the edge of the *vieille ville* run by an ex-pat who shares the French penchant for good old rock'n'roll. Live bands – of greatly varying quality – every night.

Findlater's, 6 rue Lépante (closed Mon). Probably the best of the bouncer clubs – basically a video-bar with a small dance floor, young, trendy clientele, and predictable music.

Le Blue Boy, 9 rue Spinetta (11pm–dawn; entrance charge on Wed & weekends). Women are welcome at this, Nice's best gay venue off bd François-Grosso. There are two bars, two dance floors, DJs who know what's what, and a floorshow every Wednesday night.

Le Munich, 15 rue Cassini (closed Sun). Main live venue for up-and-coming local bands to do their thing – everything from heavy metal to "psyché-noisy".

Jonathan's, 1 rue de la Loge (daily 8.30am–12.30am). Live folk and mellow sounds served up nightly in this old town cellar off rue Centrale.

Listings

Airport information ☎93.72.30.30 ☎93.21.30.12.

Baby Sitting *Association Niçoise de Services*, 1 rue Cavendish (☎93.98.60.98).

Books *The Riviera Bookshop*, 10 rue Chauvain, and *The Cat's Whiskers*, 26 rue Lamartine, both specialise in English books, secondhand and new.

Chemist The *pharmacie* at 7 rue Masséna is open 7.30am–8.30pm.

Emergencies Doctor, *S.O.S Médecins*, ☎93.83.01.01; casualty, *Hôpital St-Roch*, 5 rue Pierre-Dévoluy; ☎93.13.33.00; ambulance ☎93.85.51.15.

Late night shopping *Mobil* station, 123 bd Gambetta, west of the gare SNCF.

Language courses *Alliance Française*, 1 rue Vernier (☎93.87.42.11).

Launderette *Taxi-Lav* (7am–8pm) 24 av St-Augustine, or 22 rue Pertinax.

Newspapers British newspapers and magazines at *L'Espace Sorbonne*, 22 rue Masséna.

Poste restante PTT, pl Wilson, 06000 Nice.

Taxis ☎93.52.32.32.

Youth information *CIJ*, 19 rue Gioffredo (☎93.80.93.93), dispense information on summer jobs, cultural and sporting activities.

The Corniches

Three **corniche roads** run east from Nice to the independent principality of **Monaco** and to **Menton**, the last town of the French Riviera. These bends are the classic location for commercials for three-litre cars – and films where people driving them are killed (it was here Princess Grace met her fate). Napoléon built the **Grande Corniche** on the route of the Romans' *Via Julia Augusta*. The **Moyenne Corniche** dates from the first quarter of the twentieth century, when aristocratic tourism on the Riviera was already causing congestion on the lower, coastal road, the **Corniche Inférieure**.

Buses take all three routes; the **train** follows the lower corniche; and all three are superb means of seeing the most mountainous stretch of the Côte d'Azur. For long-distance panoramas, follow the Grande Corniche; for precipitous views, the Moyenne Corniche; and for close-up encounters with the architectural riot of the continuous coastal resort, take the Corniche Inférieure. Staying in a **hotel** anywhere between Nice and Menton is going to be exorbitant, and it makes more sense to base yourself in Nice and treat these routes as pleasure rides.

The Corniche Inférieure

The characteristic Côte d'Azur mansions that represent the stylistically incompatible fantasies of their original owners parade along the **Corniche Inférieure**. Or they lurk screened from view on the promontories of Cap Ferrat, their gardens infested with man-eating cacti and piranha ponds if the plethora of *"Défense d'entrer – Danger de Mort'"* signs is anything to go by.

Villefranche-sur-Mer: Jean Cocteau

VILLEFRANCHE-SUR-MER, the resort closest to Nice, has been spared architectural eyesores only to be marred by lurking US and French warships attracted by the deep waters of the bay. But as long as your visit doesn't coincide with sailors' shore leave, the old town on the waterfront, with its active fleet of fishing boats and its rue Obscure running beneath the houses, feels almost like the genuine article – an illusion which the quayside restaurants' prices quickly dispel.

The tiny fishing harbour is overlooked by the medieval **Chapelle de St-Pierre**, (9.30am–noon & 2–6pm; closed Fri) decorated by **Jean Cocteau** in 1957 in shades he

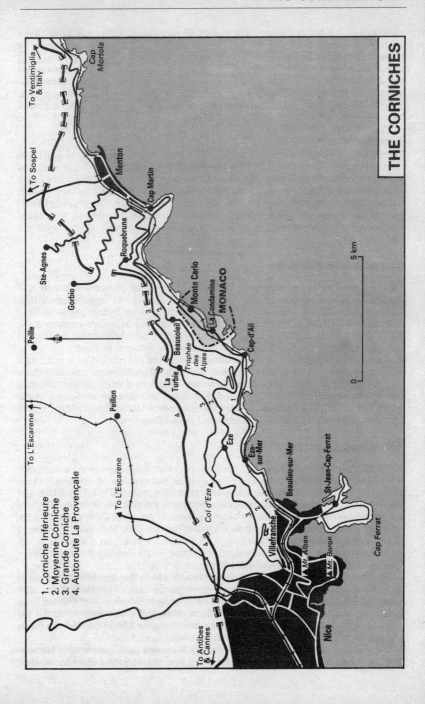

THE CORNICHES

1. Corniche Inférieure
2. Moyenne Corniche
3. Grande Corniche
4. Autoroute La Provençale

To Ventimiglia & Italy

Cap Mortola

To Sospel

Menton

Cap Martin

Roquebrune

Ste-Agnes

Gorbio

Monte Carlo

La Condamine

MONACO

Peille

Beausoleil

Trophée des Alpes

Cap-d'Ail

La Turbie

Peillon

To L'Escarene

Eze

Eze-sur-Mer

Beaulieu-sur-Mer

St-Jean-Cap-Ferrat

Col d'Eze

To L'Escarene

Villefranche

Mt. Alban

Mt. Boron

Cap Ferrat

Nice

To Antibes & Cannes

5 km

0

described as "ghosts of colours". The colours fill drawings in strong and simple lines, portraying scenes from the life of Saint Peter and homages to the women of Villefranche and to the gypsies. Above the altar, Peter walks on water supported by an angel to the outrage of the fishes and the amusement of Christ. The fishermen's eyes are drawn as fishes; the ceramic eyes on either side of the door are the flames of the apocalypse, and the altar candelabras of night-time fishing forks rise above single eyes. On June 29 each year, local fishermen celebrate the feast day of Saint Peter and Saint Paul with a mass, the only time the chapel is used.

Beaulieu

A little further along the coast, at **BEAULIEU**, one of the Côte's more unusual residences is open to the public. The **Villa Kerylos** (2/3–6/7pm; closed Mon & Nov), just east of the casino on av Gustav-Eiffel, is a near-perfect reproduction of an ancient Greek villa. Théodore Reinach, the archaeologist who had it built, lived here for twenty years, eating, dressing and acting like an Athenian citizen, taking baths with his male friends and assigning separate suites to women. However perverse the concept, it's a visual knockout, with faithfully reproduced mosaics and vases, and lavish use of marble and alabaster.

The Moyenne Corniche

Of the three roads, the **Moyenne Corniche** is the most photogenic, a real cliff-hanging, car-chase highway. Eleven kilometres from Nice, the medieval village of **EZE** clings to its rock just below the corniche. There is no other *village perché* in all of Provence so infested with antique dealers, pseudo artisans and other caterers to the touristic rich. It requires a major mental feat to recall that the labyrinth of tiny vaulted passages and stairways was designed not for charm but from fear of attack.

From pl du Centenaire, just outside the old village, you can reach the shore through open countryside, via the **sentier Frédéric-Nietzsche**. The philosopher is said to have conceived part of *Thus Spake Zarathustra*, his shaggy dog story against believing answers to ultimate questions, on this path – which isn't quite as hard-going as the book. You arrive at the Corniche Inférieure at the eastern limit of Eze-sur-Mer (coming upwards, in the other direction, it's signposted to *La Village*).

The Grand Corniche

At every other turn on the **Grande Corniche**, you're invited to park your car and enjoy a *belvédère*. And at certain points, such as Col d'Eze, you can turn off upwards for even higher views. Eighteen stunning kilometres from Nice, you reach **LA TURBIE** and the **Trophée des Alpes**, a sixth-century monument to the power of Rome and the total subjugation of the local peoples. Originally a statue of Augustus Caesar stood on the 45-metre plinth which fell into rack and ruin over the centuries. Painstakingly restored in the 1930s, it now stands statueless, at 35 metres. Viewed from a distance, it still looks impressive, but if you want a closer inspection, you'll have to buy a ticket (May–Sept 9am–noon & 2–7.30pm; Oct–April 9am–noon & 2–5pm).

As the corniche descends towards Cap-Martin, it passes the eleventh-century castle of **ROQUEBRUNE**, and its village nestling round the base of the rock. The **castle** (summer daily 9am–noon & 2–7pm; winter 10am–noon & 2–5pm, closed Fri) has been kitted out enthusiastically in medieval fashion, while the village itself is almost too good to be true. To get to the Vieux Village from the **gare SNCF**, turn east and then right up av de la Côte d'Azur, then first left up escalier Corinthille.

Between the Roquebrune station and the sea, a **coastal path** runs west to **Monaco** and southeast around **Cap Martin**, giving you access to a wonderful shoreline of white rocks and wind-bent pines. The path is named after **Le Corbusier**, who spent several summers in Roquebrune and died, tragically, by drowing off Cap Martin in 1965.

Monaco

Monstrosities are common on the Côte d'Azur, but nowhere, not even Cannes, can outdo **MONACO**. This tiny independent principality, no bigger than London's Hyde Park, has lived off gambling and catering for the desires of the idle international rich for the last 100 years. Meanwhile, it has become one of the greatest property speculation sites in the world – a sort of Manhattan-by-Sea without the saving aesthetic grace of the skyscrapers rising from a single level. Finding out about the workings of the regime is not easy but it is clear that **Prince Rainier** is the one constitutionally autocratic ruler left in Europe. There is a parliament, but it has limited functions and is elected by Monagesque nationals only – about sixteen per cent of the population. A copy of every French law is automatically sent to it, reworded, and put to the prince. If he likes the law it is passed, if not, it isn't. There is no opposition to the ruling family. The citizens and residents pay no income tax and their riches are protected by rigorous security forces – Monaco has more police per square metre than any other country in the world.

Orientation, arrival and practicalities

The three-kilometre-long state consists of the old town of **Monaco-Ville** around the palace on a high promontory, with the new suburb and marina of **Fontvieille** in its western shadow. **La Condamine** is the old port quarter on the other side of the rock; **Larvotto**, the bathing resort with artificial beaches of imported sand reaches to the eastern border, and **Monte-Carlo** is in the middle.

The **gare SNCF** is on av Prince-Pierre in La Condamine, a short walk from the main **gare routière** on place d'Armes. Buses following the middle and lower corniches stop here; other routes have a variety of stations, of which the **SI** at 2a bd des Moulins, near the casino, can give you details (Mon–Sat 9am–7pm; Sun 10am–noon). Local bus #4 runs from the gare SNCF to the *Casino-Tourisme* stop, close to the SI and pl du Casino. One free and very useful public service is the **lifts** linking the lower and higher streets (marked on the SI map), which are incredibly clean and efficient. **Bicycles** can be hired from *Auto-Motos*, 7 rue de la Colle, off av Prince-Pierre.

Accommodation and eating

Monaco has no campsite and caravans are illegal in the state – as are bathing costumes, and bare feet and chests once you step off the beach. If you must stay more than a day, La Condamine is the best area for **hotels**, though don't expect bargains. You could try *Cosmopolite*, 4 rue de la Turbie (☎93.30.16.95; ③) near the station, or its neighbour the *Hôtel de France*, 6 rue de la Turbie (☎93.30.24.64; ④). Another cheapish option is *Helvetia*, 1 rue Grimaldi (☎93.30.21.71; ④). Across the invisible border to the north in **Beausoleil**, you may be able to get a dorm-style bed at the *Centre de Jeunesse Princess Stéphanie*, near the station on av Prince-Pierre (☎93.50.75.05; July–Sept 7–10am & 2pm–1am) – if you arrive early, that is, and hang around long enough.

La Condamine and the old town are replete with **restaurants**, but good food and reasonable prices don't exactly match. **Around the station** you'll find generous pizzas at *Bacchus*, 13 rue de La Turbie, and *Les Deux Guitares*, rue de la Colle (closed Tues). In **Monte-Carlo** itself try *Ramon*, 2 rue du Portier (closed Sat), or the more snackish *Regina*, 13/15 bd des Moulins. It's all standard fare and nothing to write home about, but it simply isn't worth going upmarket unless you're prepared to hit 700F-a-head bills (in which case, dine at *Louis XV* in the *Hôtel de Paris* by the casino).

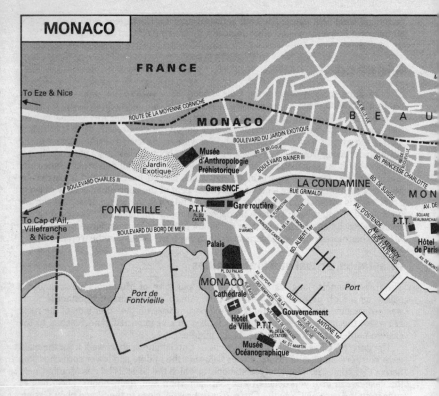

The casino and other activities

The **casino** has to be seen if nothing else. Entrance is restricted to over-21s and you may have to show your passport. Shorts and tee-shirts are frowned upon and for the more interesting sections skirts, jackets, ties and so forth are more or less obligatory. Any coats or large bags involve hefty cloakroom fees.

In the first gambling hall, the **American Room**, slot machines surround the American roulette, craps and blackjack tables, the managers are Vegas-trained, the lights low and and the air oppressively smoky. Above this slice of Nevada, however, the decor is turn-of-the-century Rococo extravagance, while in the adjoining *Pink Salon Bar* female nudes smoking cigarettes adorn the ceilings.

The heart of the place is the **European Gaming Rooms**, through the Salles Touzet. You have to pay to get in (50F) and you must look like a gambler, not a tourist (no cameras). More richly decorated than the American Room and much bigger, the atmosphere, early afternoon or out of season, is that of a cathedral. No clinking coins, just quiet-voiced croupiers and sliding chips. Elderly gamblers pace silently, fingering 500F notes (the maximum unnegotiated stake here is 500,000F), closed-circuit TV cameras above the chandeliers watch the gamblers watching the tables, and no one drinks. On midsummer evenings the place is packed out and the vice loses its sacred and exclusive touch.

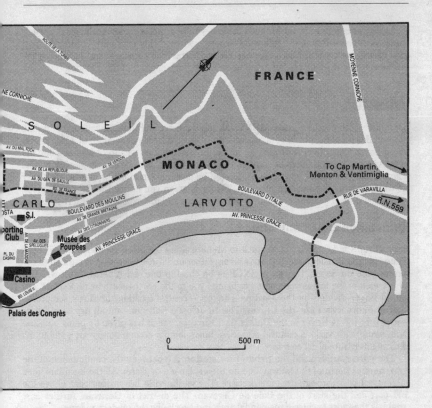

Around the Casino are more casinos and the city's palace-hotels and *grands cafés* – all held by the same monopoly. The *American bar* of the **Hôtel de Paris** is, according to its publicity, the place where "the world's most elite society" meets. As long as you dress up and are ready to be outraged (in English) if asked why you haven't ordered a 200F drink, you can entertain yourself, free of charge, watching tedious humans with fascinating bank accounts against the background of *Belle Epoque* decadence.

Other amusements

Other diversions such as the toy **palace** and the assorted **museums** of the glacé-iced **old town** of Monaco-Ville – where every other shop sells Prince Rainier mugs and similar assorted junk – are less rewarding. The possible exception is the aquarium in the basement of the **Musée Océanographique** (July–Aug 9am–9pm; rest of the year 9.30am–7pm; bus #1 or #2, *Monaco-Ville*; 45F) where the fishy beings outdo the weirdest Kandinsky, Hieronymous Bosch or Zandra Rhodes creations. Less exceptional but still peculiar but cactus equivalents can be viewed in the **Jardin Exotique** high above Fontvieille (May–Sept 9am–7pm ; rest of the year 9am–6pm; 30F).

Remarkably, one highly positive reason for a visit to Monaco could be to see some **football**. The "local" team, *AS Monaco*, have done very well in the French league in recent years under the inspired guidance (and purchasing power) of manager Arsène Wenger. The club play at an impressive stadium in Fontvieille.

Lastly, one time to avoid Monaco (unless you're a motor-racing enthusiast) is early June (Ascension Day to the following Sunday), when racing cars burn around the port and casino for the Formula 1 **Monaco Grand Prix**. Every space in sight of the circuit is inaccessible without a ticket, making casual sightseeing out of the question.

Menton

Of all the Côte d'Azur resorts **MENTON**, the warmest and most Italianate, is the one that retains an atmosphere of aristocratic tourism. Today it's even more of a rich retirement haven than Nice. It doesn't go in for the ostentatious wealth of Monaco nor the creativity cachet of Cannes or some of the hilltop towns. What it chiefly glories in is its climate and year-round lemon crops. Ringed by protective mountains, hardly a whisper of wind disturbs the sun-trap of a city. Winter is when you notice the difference most, when you'd need a change of clothes between here and the exposed central resorts.

Orientation and practicalities

Roquebrune and Cap Martin merge into Menton along the three-kilometre shore of the **Baie du Soleil**. The modern town is arranged around three main streets parallel to the promenade du Soleil. The **gare SNCF** is on the top one, bd Albert-I, from which a short walk to the left as you come out brings you to the north–south av de Verdun and av de Boyer divided by the **Jardins Biovès** – central location for citrus sculptures during February's **Fête du Citron**. The **SI** (closed Sun pm, and all day Sun out of season) is at 8 av Boyer in the **Palais de l'Europe**, which has given up being a casino and, along with various cultural activities, hosts annual contemporary art exhibitions and an international art *biennale*.

The **gare routière** and the **urban bus station** are between the continuation of the two avenues north of the railway line on the esplanade de Carei. All the local bus lines (flat rates) pass through the gare routière. The **vieille ville** lies further east, above the old port and the start of the Baie de Garavan. The district of **Garavan**, further east again, is the most exclusive residential area and overlooks the modern marina.

Accommodation
Accommodation is, as ever, difficult. Menton is no less popular than the other major resorts, so in summer, you should definitely book ahead. The SI won't make reservations for you, though they will tell you where there are rooms free.

HOTELS
Hôtel Mondial, 12 rue Partouneaux (☎93.35.74.18). Not far from the station. The cheapest rooms in Menton and often booked out. ③.

Hôtel Beauregard, 10 rue Albert-1 (☎93.35.74.08; closed Oct–Dec). Classically furnished rooms and no attempt to foist breakfast on you. ④.

Hôtel Belgique, 1 av de la Gare (☎93.35.72.66; closed Dec). More mundane option than the above, but no less clean and conveniently close to the station. ④.

Hôtel Sea Point, 1684 promenade du Soleil (☎93.57.46.33). Overlooking the sea and close to the old town, hence the price. ⑤ and above.

Hôtel le Pin Doré, 1403 promenade du Soleil (☎93.28.31.00; closed mid-Nov to Dec 21). Seafront hotel with its own garden and swimming pool. ⑤ and above.

CHEAP ACCOMMODATION
IYHF Auberge de Jeunesse, plateau St-Michel (☎93.35.93.14; a gruelling flight of steps from behind the gare SNCF or bus #6 from the gare routière, direction *Ciappes de Castellar*, stop

Camping St-Michel; reception closed 9.30am–5pm). No advance booking, no card needed, 11pm curfew and not exactly cheap – camping next door is a better deal.

Camping St-Michel, plateau St-Michel (☎93.35.81.23; open March–Nov). Reasonably priced campsite in the hills above the town with plenty of shade and good views out to sea.

Restaurants

Surprisingly, Menton is not blessed with streets of gorgeous Provençal **restaurants**. If you're not bothered about what you eat as long as it's cheap, the pedestrianised rue St-Michel is promising ground. For a proper **restaurant** meal based on fish, *Chez Gemaine*, 46 promenade Maréchal-Leclerc (☎93.35.66.90; closed Sun evening & Mon), near the gare routière, is the gourmet option; slightly less polished and cheaper is *Le Namouna* in the old port. *Chez Maurice*, 17 promenade de la Mer serves home cooking on a pleasant balcony overlooking the sea.

Menton has a **food market** every day near the gare routière and in the covered *halles* on quai de Monléon below rue St-Michel, with bric-a-brac stalls spreading up to the old town on Friday. For **chocolate** addicts, there's two of the big names – *Godiva*, 8 av Félix-Faure, and *Léonadas*, 17 av de Verdun – to drool over. The town's **lemons** are also celebrated. Have no illusions, however, about cheap local produce: a *citron pressé* served in a Menton bar still costs twice as much as an imported Belgian beer.

Jean Cocteau's Menton

Menton's speciality should be weddings rather than widowers and widows. If you ever need a French marriage certificate, this is the place to get it. The **Salles des Mariages** or registry office in the **Hôtel de Ville** on pl Ardoiono was decorated in inimitable style by **Jean Cocteau** and can be visited without matrimonial intentions by asking the receptionist by the main door (Mon–Fri 8.30am–12.30pm & 1.30–5pm; 5F). On the wall above the official's desk, a couple face each other with strange topological connections between the sun, her headdress and his fisherman's cap. A *Saracen wedding party* on the right-hand wall reveals a disapproving bride's mum, the spurned girlfriend of the groom and her armed, revengeful brother among the cheerful guests. On the left-hand wall is the story of *Orpheus and Eurydice* at the moment when Orpheus has just looked back. Meanwhile, on the ceiling are *Poetry rides Pegasus*, tattered *Science juggles with the Planets* and *Love*, open-eyed, waiting with bow and arrow at the ready. Adding a little extra confusion, the carpet is mock panther-skin.

There are other works by Cocteau in the **museum** he set up himself in the little bastion on quai Napoléon III south of the old port (10am–noon & 3–6pm; closed Tues; free). It contains more Mentonaise lovers in the *Inamorati* series, a collection of delightful *Animaux fantastiques* and the powerful tapestry of *Judith and Holophernes* simultaneously telling the sequence of seduction, assassination and escape. There are also photographs, poems, a portrait by friend Picasso, and ceramics.

The vieille ville and gardens

As the *quai* bends around the western end of the Baie de Garavan from the Cocteau museum, a long flight of black and white pebbled steps leads to the **Parvis St-Michel** and the perfect pink and yellow proportions of **Église St-Michel**. With more steps up to another square, a chapel of apricot-and-white marble, pastel campanales and disappearing stairways between long-lived houses, this is the Italianate and beautiful facade of the **vieille ville**. Just to the south, the winding steps, tunnelled alleys and overhanging houses are the poorest part of the town and likely, soon, to face the speculators' gaze.

On av de la Madone, an impressive collection of paintings from the Middle Ages to the twentieth century can be seen in the **Palais Carnolès** (mid-June to mid-Sept 10am–

noon & 3–6pm; rest of the year 2–5.30pm; closed Mon & Tues; bus #3; free), the old summer residence of the princes of Monaco. Of early works, the *Madonna and Child with St Francis* by Louis Bréa is exceptional. The most recent include winners of Menton's *biennale* and canvases by Graham Sutherland, who spent some of his last years in Menton. Behind the palace you'll find a park with entertainments for kids.

If it's cool enough to be walking outside, the public parks up in the hills and the gardens of **GARAVAN's** villas make a change from shingle beaches. The best of all the Garavan gardens are **Les Colombières**, just north of bd de Garavan (9am–noon & 2–6pm; closed Oct–Dec; bus #7, direction *bd de Garavan*, stop *Colombières*; 15F). Designed by the artist **Ferdinand Bac**, they lead you through every Mediterranean style of garden. There are staircases screened by cypresses; balustrades to lean against for the soaring views through pines and olive trees out to sea; fountains, statues and a frescoed swimming pool.

travel details

Trains

*The **Ventimiglia line** follows the coast more or less all the way from Marseille to Menton, running inland only over the stretch between Toulon and Fréjus. The full journey takes nearly 4 hours.*

Major stops on the Ventimiglia line from Marseille are at Toulon (50min); St-Raphaël (1hr 50min); Cannes (2hr 12min); Nice (3hr); Monaco (3hr 30min); Menton (3hr 40min).

From Marseille 15 daily to Cassis (10–20min); 18 daily to La Ciotat (15–30min); very frequent to Toulon (50min); 4 daily to Hyères (1hr 15min); 9 daily to Paris-Gare de Lyon (5hr–7hr 40min).

From St-Raphaël 15 daily to Paris-Gare de Lyon (9hr 30min–10hr), via Marseille (1hr 30min), Lyon (4hr) & Dijon (7hr 50min).

From Nice 8 daily to Menton (35–40min); 6 daily to St-Raphaël (1hr–1hr 25min); 20 daily to Marseille (2hr 15min–2hr 30min) and 7 daily to Paris-Gare de Lyon (10hr 40min–12hr).

From Cannes 18 daily to Menton (1hr 25min).

Buses

Buses along the coast are slower, more expensive and less frequent than trains

From Hyères 10 daily to Toulon SNCF (30min); 14 daily to Giens (25min); 9 daily to la Tour-Fondue (20min); 14 daily to Le Lavandou (35min), via Bormes (25min); 7 daily to St-Tropez (1hr 35min).

From Hyères/Toulon airport 2 daily to St-Tropez (1hr 30min); 2 daily to Ste-Maxime (1hr 30min) via Le Lavandou (30 min), Cavalaire (1hr), La Croix-Valmer (1hr 20min) and Port Grimaud (1hr 20min).

From Toulon 7 daily to St-Tropez (2hr 10min), stopping at Hyères (35min), Le Lavandou (1hr 10min), Cavalière (1hr 20min) and La Croix-Valmer (1hr 50min).

From St-Tropez 9 daily to St-Raphaël (1hr 20min), stopping at Cogolin (15min), Grimaud (20min), Ste- Maxime (40min), Fréjus (1hr 10min); 3 daily to Ramatuelle (25min); 3 daily to Gassin (20min);1 daily to Bormes-les-Mimosas (45min).

From La Garde-Freinet 1 daily to St-Tropez (45min) via Grimaud (15min) and Cogolin (25min); 1 daily to Le Lavandou (1hr 30min).

From Le Lavandou 1 daily to la Garde-Freinet (1hr 20min), via Bormes-les-Mimosas (10min) and Cogolin (40min).

From St-Raphaël 8 daily to St-Tropez (1hr 30min–2hr 30min); frequent to Draguignan (1hr), via Fréjus (10min); 7 daily to Cannes (1hr 10min), via Boulouris (15 min), le Trayas (40 min) and Miramar (45min); 6 daily to Cannes via N7 (50min); 4 daily to Fayence (45min), via Fréjus and Bagnols-en-Fôret (20min).

From Cannes frequent to Grasse (45min); frequent to Vallauris (15min).

From Nice frequent to Vence (1hr) via Cros-de-Cagnes (20min) and St-Paul (40min); 4 daily along the Grande Corniche to La Turbie (25min); frequent along the Corniche Inférieure to Menton (45min); 5 daily along the Moyenne Corniche to Beausoleil (50min).

From Menton 3 daily to Sospel (50min).

Ferries

For Îles d'Or and Îles de Lérins services see p.726 and p.745

From Marseille (Bassin de la Joliette) to Corsica, Sardinia, Algiers, Tunis and Majorca.

From Nice to Corsica (summer day excursions operated by SNCM, 3 av Gustav V, depart quai de la Commerce; also car ferry service).

From St-Raphaël to St-Tropez, Port Grimaud and the Îles de Lérins (summer excursions operated by MMG, quai Nomy).

From St-Tropez to Ste-Maxime (MMG, quai Jean-Jaurès).

PART THREE

THE

CONTEXTS

HISTORICAL FRAMEWORK

EARLY CIVILISATIONS

Traces of human existence are rare in France until about 50,000 BC. Thereafter, beginning with the "Mousterian civilisation", they become ever more numerous, with an especially heavy concentration of sites in the Périgord region of the Dordogne. It was here, near the village of Les Eyzies, that remains were discovered of a Late Stone Age people, subsequently dubbed "Cro-Magnon". Flourishing from around 25,000 BC, these cave-dwelling hunters seem to have developed quite a sophisticated culture, the evidence of which is preserved in the beautiful paintings and engravings on the walls of the region's caves.

By 10,000 BC human communities had spread out widely across the whole of France. The ice cap receded; the climate became warmer and wetter, and by about 7000 BC **farming and pastoral communities** had begun to develop. By 4500 BC the first **dolmens** (megalithic stone tombs) showed up in **Brittany**; around 2000 BC copper made its appearance; and by 1800 BC the **Bronze Age** had arrived in the east and southeast of the country, and trade links had begun with Spain, central Europe and Wessex in Britain.

Significant populations shifts occurred, too, around this time. Around 1200 BC the **Champs**

d'Urnes people, who buried their dead in sunken urns, began to make incursions from the east. By 900 BC, they had been joined by the **Halstatt people** who worked with iron and settled in Burgundy, Alsace and Franche-Comté near the principal ore **deposits**. At some point around 450 BC, the first Celts made an appearance in the region.

PRE-ROMAN GAUL

There were about 15 million people living in **Gaul**, as the Romans called what we know as France (and parts of Belgium), when Julius Caesar arrived in 58 BC to complete the Roman conquest.

The southern part of this territory – more or less equivalent to modern **Provence** – had been a colony since 118 BC and exposed to the civilising influences of Italy and Greece for much longer. **Greek colonists** had founded *Massalia* (Marseille) as far back as 600 BC. But even the inhabitants of the rest of the country, what the Romans called "long-haired Gaul", were far from shaggy barbarians. Though the economy was basically rural, the **Gauls** had established large **hilltop towns** by 100 BC, notably at Bibracte near Autun, where archaeologists have identified separate merchants' quarters and so on.

The Gauls had also invented the barrel and soap and were skilful manufacturers. By 500 BC they were capable of making metal-wheeled carts, as was proved by the "chariot tombs" of **Vix**, where a young woman was found buried seated in a cart with its wheels pushed against the wall. She was wearing rich gold jewellery and lying next to Greek vases and Black Figure pottery, dating the burial at around 500 BC and revealing the extent of commercial relations. Interestingly, too, the Gauls' money was based on the gold *staters* minted by Philip of Macedon.

ROMANISATION

Gallic **tribal rivalries** made the Romans' job very much easier. And when at last they were able to unite under **Vercingétorix** in 52 BC, the occasion was their total and final defeat by **Julius Caesar** at the battle of **Alésia**.

This event was one of the major turning points in the history of France. **Roman victory** fixed the frontier between Gaul and the

Germanic peoples at the Rhine. It saved Gaul from disintegrating because of internal dissension and made it a Latin province. During the five centuries of peace that followed, the Gauls farmed, manufactured and traded, became urbanised, embourgeoisied and educated – and learned Latin. In other words, Roman victory at Alésia laid the foundations of modern French culture, and laid them firmly enough to survive the centuries of chaos and destruction that followed the collapse of Roman power.

Augustus and **Claudius** were the emperors who set the process of **Romanisation** going. *Lugdunum* (Lyon) was founded as the capital of Roman Gaul as early as 43 BC. Augustus founded numerous other cities, like Autun, Limoges and Bayeux, built roads, settled Roman colonists on the land and reorganised the entire administration. Gauls were incorporated into the Roman army and given citizenship; Claudius made it possible for them to hold high office and become members of the Roman Senate, blurring the distinction and resentment between coloniser and colonised. Vespasian secured the frontiers beyond the Rhine, thus assuring a couple of hundred years of peace and economic expansion.

Serious **disruptions** of the Pax Romana only began in the third century AD. Oppressive aristocratic rule and an economic crisis turned the destitute peasantry into gangs of marauding brigands – precursors of the medieval *jacquerie*. But most devastating of all, there began a series of incursions across the Rhine frontier by various restless **Germanic tribes**, the Alemanni and Franks first, who pushed down as far as Spain, ravaging farmland and destroying towns.

In the fourth century the reforms of the Emperor **Diocletian** secured some decades of respite from both internal and external pressures. Towns were rebuilt and fortified, an interesting development that foreshadowed feudalism and the independent power of the nobles since, due to the uncertainty of the times, big landed estates or *villae* tended to become more and more self-sufficient – economically, administratively and militarily.

By the fifth century, however, the Germanic invaders were back: **Alans**, **Vandals** and **Suevi**, with **Franks** and **Burgundians** in their wake. While the Roman administration assimilated them as far as possible, granting them land in return for military duties, they gradually achieved independence from the empire. Many Gauls, by now thoroughly Latinised, entered the service of the **Burgundian court of Lyon** or of the **Visigoth kings of Toulouse** as skilled administrators and advisors.

THE FRANKS AND CHARLEMAGNE

By 500 AD, the **Franks**, who gave their name to modern France, had become the dominant invading power. Their most celebrated king, **Clovis**, consolidated his hold on northern France and drove the Visigoths out of the southwest into Spain. In 507 he made the until-then insignificant little trading town of Paris his capital and became a Christian, which inevitably hastened the **Christianisation** of Frankish society.

Under the succeeding **Merovingian** – as the dynasty was called – rulers, the kingdom began to disintegrate until in the eighth century the Pepin family, who were the Merovingians' chancellors, began to take effective control. In 732 one of their most dynamic scions, **Charles Martel**, reunited the kingdom and saved western Christendom from the northward expansion of Islam by defeating the Spanish Moors at the **battle of Poitiers**.

In 754 Charles' son, Pepin, had himself crowned king by the pope, thus inaugurating the **Carolingian dynasty** and establishing for the first time the principle of the divine right of kings. His son was **Charlemagne**, who extended Frankish control over the whole of what had been Roman Gaul, and far beyond. On Christmas Day 800 he was crowned emperor of the **Holy Roman Empire**, though again, following his death, the kingdom fell apart in squabbles over who was to inherit various parts of his empire. At the Treaty of Verdun in 843 his grandsons agreed on a division of territory that corresponded roughly with the extent of contemporary France and Germany.

Charlemagne's administrative system had involved the royal appointment of counts and bishops to govern the various provinces of the empire. Under the destabilising attacks of Normans/Norsemen/Vikings during the ninth century, Carolingian kings were obliged to delegate more power and autonomy to these **provincial governors**, whose lands, like **Aquitaine** and **Burgundy**, already had separate regional identities as a result of earlier invasions – the Visigoths in Aquitaine, the Burgundians in Burgundy, for example.

Gradually the power of these princes overshadowed that of the king, whose lands were confined to the Île-de-France. When the last Carolingian died in 987, it was only natural that they should elect one of their own number to take his place. This was Hugues Capet, founder of a dynasty that lasted until 1328.

THE RISE OF THE FRENCH KINGS

The years 1000 to 1500 saw the gradual extension and consolidation of the power of the **French kings**, accompanied by the growth of a centralised administrative system and bureaucracy. These objectives also determined their foreign policy, which was chiefly concerned with restricting papal interference in French affairs and checking the English kings' continuing involvement in French territory. While progress towards these goals was remarkably steady and single minded, there were setbacks, principally in the seesawing fortunes of the conflict with the English.

Surrounded by vassals much stronger than themselves, **Hugues Capet** and his successors remained weak throughout the eleventh century, though they made the most of their feudal rights. As dukes of the French, counts of Paris and anointed kings, they enjoyed a prestige their vassals dared not offend – not least because that would have set a precedent of disobedience for their own lesser vassals.

At the beginning of the twelfth century, having successfully tamed his own vassals in the Île-de-France, Louis VI had a stroke of luck. **Eleanor**, daughter of the powerful duke of Aquitaine, was left in his care on her father's death, so he promptly married her off to his son, the future Louis VII.

Unfortunately, the marriage ended in divorce and Eleanor immediately – in 1152 – remarried, to Henry of Normandy, shortly to become **Henry II** of England. Thus the **English** gained control of a huge chunk of French territory, stretching from the Channel to the Pyrenees. Though their fortunes fluctuated over the ensuing 300 years, the English rulers remained a perpetual thorn in the side of the French kings and a dangerous source of alliances for any rebellious French vassals.

Philippe Auguste (1180–1223) made considerable headway in undermining English rule by exploiting the bitter relations between Henry II and his three sons, one of whom was Richard the Lion Heart. But he fell out with Richard when they took part in the **Third Crusade** together. Luckily, Richard died before he was able to claw back Philippe's gains, and by the end of his reign Philippe had recovered all of Normandy and the English possessions north of the Loire.

For the first time, the royal lands were greater than those of any other French lord. The foundations of a systematic administration and civil service had been established in **Paris**, and Philippe had firmly and quietly marked his independence from the papacy by refusing to take any interest in the crusade against the heretic Cathars of Languedoc. When Languedoc and Poitou came under royal control in the reign of his son Louis VIII, France was by far the greatest power in Western Europe.

THE HUNDRED YEARS' WAR

In 1328 the Capetian monarchy had its first succession crisis, which led directly to the ruinous **Hundred Years' War** with the English. Charles IV, last of the line, had only daughters as heirs, and when it was decided that France could not be ruled by a queen, the English king, **Edward III**, whose mother was Charles' sister, claimed the throne of France for himself.

The French chose **Philippe, Count of Valois**, instead, and Edward acquiesced for a time. But when Philippe began whittling away at his possessions in Aquitaine, Edward renewed his claim and embarked on war. Though, with its population of about twelve million, France was a far richer and more powerful country, its army was no match for the superior organisation and tactics of the English. Edward won an outright victory at **Crécy** in 1346 and seized the port of Calais as a permanent bridgehead. Ten years later, his son, the Black Prince, actually took the French king, Jean le Bon, prisoner at the battle of **Poitiers**.

Although by 1375 French military fortunes had improved to the point where the English had been forced back to Calais and the Gascon coast, the strains of war and administrative abuses, and the madness of Charles VI, caused other kinds of damage. In 1358 there were insurrections among the Picardy peasantry (the *Jacquerie*) and among the townspeople of Paris under the leadership of Étienne Marcel. Both were brutally repressed, as were subsequent risings in Paris in 1382 and 1412.

The consequences of the king's madness led to the formation of two rival factions, in the aftermath of the murder of his brother, the Duke of Orléans, by the Duke of Burgundy. The **Armagnacs** gathered round the young Orléans, and the other faction round the **Burgundys**. Both factions called in the English to help them, and in 1415 Henry V of England inflicted another crushing defeat on the French army at **Agincourt**. The Burgundians seized Paris, took the royal family prisoner and recognised Henry as heir to the French throne. When Charles VI died in 1422, Henry's brother, the Duke of Bedford, took over the government of France north of the Loire, while the young king Charles VII ineffectually governed the south from his refugee capital at Bourges.

At this point **Jeanne d'Arc** (Joan of Arc) arrived on the scene. In 1429 she raised the English siege of the crucial town of Orléans and had Charles crowned at Reims. Although Joan fell into the hands of the Burgundians, who sold her to the English, who tried and burnt her as a heretic, her dynamism and martyrdom raised French morale and tipped the scales against the English. Except for a toehold at Calais, they were finally driven from France altogether in 1453.

By the end of the century, **Dauphiné, Burgundy, Franche-Comté** and **Provence** were under royal control, and an effective standing army had been created. The taxation system had been overhauled, and France had emerged from the Middle Ages a rich, powerful state, firmly under the centralised authority of an absolute monarch.

THE WARS OF RELIGION

After half a century of self-confident but inconclusive seeking after military *gloire* in Italy, brought to an end by the Treaty of Cateau-Cambresis in 1559, France was plunged into another period of devastating internal conflict. The **Protestant** ideas of Luther and Calvin had gained widespread adherence among the poor, artisan, bourgeois and noble classes of society, despite sporadic brutal attempts by François I and Henri II to stamp them out.

When **Catherine de Médicis**, acting as regent for Henri III, implemented a more tolerant policy, she provoked violent reaction from the ultra-Catholic faction led by the **Guise** family. Their massacre of a Protestant congregation coming out of church in March 1562 began a civil **war of religions** that, interspersed with ineffective truces and accords, lasted for the next thirty years.

Well organised and well led by the Prince de Condé and Admiral Coligny, the **Huguenots** – the French Protestants – kept their end up very successfully, until Condé was killed at the battle of Jarnac in 1569. Three years later came one of the blackest events in the memory of French Protestants, even today: the **massacre of St Bartholomew's Day**. Coligny and three thousand Protestants gathered in Paris for the wedding of Marguerite, the king's sister, to the Protestant Henri of Navarre were slaughtered at the instigation of the Guises – a bloodbath was repeated across France, especially in the south and west where the Protestants were strongest.

In 1584 the king's son died, leaving his brother-in-law, **Henri of Navarre,** heir to the throne, to the fury of the Guises and their Catholic league, who seized Paris and drove out the king. In retaliation, Henri III murdered the Duc de Guise, and found himself forced into alliance with Henri of Navarre, whom the pope had excommunicated. In 1589 Henri III was himself assassinated, leaving Henri of Navarre to become Henri IV of France. It took another four years of fighting and the abjuration of his faith for the new king to be recognised. "Paris is worth a mass", he is reputed to have said.

Once on the throne Henri IV set about reconstructing and reconciling the nation. By the **Edict of Nantes** of 1598 the Huguenots were accorded freedom of conscience, freedom of worship in certain places, the right to attend the same schools and hold the same offices as Catholics, their own courts and the possession of a number of fortresses as a guarantee against renewed attack, the most important being La Rochelle and Montpellier.

KINGS, CARDINALS AND ABSOLUTE POWER

The main themes of the seventeenth century, when France was ruled by just two kings, **Louis XIII** (1610–43) and **Louis XIV** (1643–

1715), were, on the domestic front, the strengthening of the centralised state embodied in the person of the king; and in external affairs, the securing of frontiers in the Pyrenees, on the Rhine and in the north, coupled with the attempt to prevent the unification of the territories of the Habsburg kings of Spain and Austria. Both kings had the good fortune to be served by capable, hard-working ministers dedicated to these objectives. Louis XIII had **Cardinal Richelieu** and Louis XIV had **Cardinal Mazarin** and **Colbert**. Both reigns were disturbed in their early years by the inevitable aristocratic attempts at a coup d'état.

Having crushed revolts by Louis XIII's brother Gaston, Duke of Orléans, **Richelieu's** commitment to extending royal absolutism brought him into renewed conflict with the Protestants. Believing that their retention of separate fortresses within the kingdom was a threat to security, he attacked and took La Rochelle in 1627. Although he was unable to extirpate their religion altogether, Protestants were never again to present a military threat.

The other important facet of his domestic policy was the promotion of economic self-sufficiency – **mercantilism**. To this end, he encouraged the growth of the luxury craft industries, especially textiles, in which France was to excel right up to the Revolution. He built up the navy and granted privileges to companies involved in establishing **colonies** in North America, Africa and the West Indies.

In pursuing his foreign policy objectives, Richelieu adroitly kept France out of actual military involvement by paying substantial sums to the great Swedish king and general, Gustavus Adolphus, helping him to fund war against the Habsburgs in Germany. When in 1635 the French were finally obliged to commit their own troops, they made significant gains against the Spanish in the Netherlands, Alsace and Lorraine and won Roussillon for France.

Richelieu died just a few months before Louis XIII in 1642. As Louis XIV was still an infant, his mother, Anne of Austria, acted as regent, served by Richelieu's protégé, **Cardinal Mazarin**, who was hated just as much as his predecessor by the traditional aristocracy and the *parlements*. These unelected bodies, which had the function of high courts and administrative councils, were protective of their privileges and angry that an upstart should receive such preferment. Spurred by these grievances, which were in any case exacerbated by the ruinous cost of the Spanish wars, various groups in French society combined in a series of revolts, known as the **Frondes**.

The first Fronde, in 1648, was led by the *parlement* of Paris, which took up the cause of the hereditary provincial tax-collecting officials – a group that resented the supervisory role of the *intendants*, who had been appointed by the central royal bureaucracy to keep an eye on them. Paris rose in revolt but capitulated at the advance of royal troops. This was quickly followed by an aristocratic Fronde, supported by various peasant risings round the country. These revolts were suppressed easily enough. They were not really revolutionary movements but, rather, the attempts of various groups to preserve their privileges in the face of growing state power.

The economic pressures that contributed to their support were relieved when in 1659 Mazarin successfully brought the Spanish wars to an end with the **Treaty of the Pyrenees**, cemented by the marriage of Louis XIV and the daughter of Philip IV of Spain. On reaching the age of majority in 1661, **Louis XIV** declared that he was going to be his own man and do without a first minister. He proceeded to appoint a number of able ministers, with whose aid he embarked on a long struggle to modernise the administration.

The war ministers, Le Tellier and his son Louvois, provided Louis with a well-equipped and well-trained professional army that could muster some 400,000 men by 1670. But the principal reforms were carried out by **Colbert**, who set about streamlining the state's finances and tackling bureaucratic corruption. Although he was never able to overcome the opposition completely, he did manage to produce a surplus in state revenue. Attempting to compensate for deficiencies in the taxation system by stimulating trade, he set up a free-trade area in northern and central France, continued Richelieu's mercantilist economic policies, established the French East India Company, and built up the navy and merchant fleets with a view to challenging the world commercial supremacy of the Dutch.

These were all policies that the hard-working king was involved in and approved of.

But in addition to his love of an extravagant court life at Versailles, which earned him the title of the **Sun King**, he had another obsession, ruinous to the state: the love of a prestigious military victory. There were sound political reasons for the **campaigns** he embarked on, but they did not help balance the budget.

Using his wife's Spanish connection, Louis demanded the cession of certain Spanish provinces in the Low Countries, and then embarked on a war against the Dutch in 1672. Forced to make peace at the **Treaty of Nijmegen** in 1678 by his arch-enemy, the Protestant William of Orange (later king of England), he nonetheless came out of the war with the annexation to French territory of **Franche-Comté**, plus a number of northern towns. In 1681 he simply grabbed Strasbourg, and got away with it.

In 1685, under the influence of his very Catholic mistress, Madame de Maintenon, the king removed all privileges from the **Huguenots** by revoking the Edict of Nantes. This incensed the Protestant powers, who combined under the auspices of the League of Augsburg. Another long and exhausting war followed, ending, most unfavourably to the French, in the **Peace of Rijswik** (1697).

No sooner was this concluded than Louis became embroiled in the question of who was to succeed the moribund Charles II of Spain. Both Louis and Leopold Habsburg, Holy Roman Emperor, had married sisters of Charles. The prospect of Leopold acquiring the Spanish Habsburgs' possessions in addition to his own vast lands was not welcome to Louis or any other European power. When Charles died and it was discovered that he'd named Louis' grandson, Philippe, as his heir, there again was a shift in the balance of power that the English, Dutch and Austrians were not prepared to tolerate.

William of Orange, now king of England as well as ruler of the Dutch United Provinces, organised a Grand Alliance against Louis. The so-called **War of Spanish Succession** broke out and it went badly for the French, largely thanks to the brilliant generalship of the Duke of Marlborough. A severe winter in 1709 compounded the hardships with famine and bread riots at home, causing Louis to seek negotiations. The terms were too harsh for him and the war dragged on until 1713, leaving the country totally impoverished. The Sun King went out with scarcely a whimper.

LOUIS XV AND THE PARLEMENTS

While France remained in many ways a prosperous and powerful state, largely thanks to colonial trade, the tensions between central government and traditional vested interests proved too great to be reconciled.

The *parlement* of Paris became more and more the focus of opposition to the royal will, bringing the country to a state of virtual ungovernability in the reign of **Louis XVI**. Meanwhile, the diversity of mutually irreconcilable interests sheltering behind that parliamentary umbrella came more and more to the fore, bringing the country to a climax of tension which would only be resolved in the turmoil of **Revolution**.

The next king, Louis XV, was two when his great-grandfather died. During the **Regency**, the traditional aristocracy and the *parlements*, who for different reasons hated Louis XIV's advisors, scrabbled – successfully – to recover a lot of their lost power and prestige. An experiment with government by aristocratic councils failed, and attempts to absorb the immense national debt by selling shares in an overseas trading company ended in a huge collapse. When the prudent and reasonable **Cardinal Fleury** came to prominence upon the regent's death in 1726, the nation's lot began to improve. The Atlantic seaboard towns grew rich on trade with the American and Caribbean colonies, though industrial production did not improve much and the disparity in wealth between the countryside and the growing towns continued to grow.

In the mid-century there followed more disastrous military ventures, the **War of Austrian Succession** and the **Seven Years' War**, both of which were in effect contests with England for control of the colonial territories in America and India, contests that France lost. The need to finance the wars led to the introduction of a new tax, the Twentieth, which was to be levied on everyone. The **parlement**, which had successfully opposed earlier taxation and fought the crown over its religious policies, dug its heels in again. This led to renewed conflict over Louis' pro-Jesuit religious policy. The Paris *parlement* staged a strike, was exiled from Paris, then inevitably reinstated. Disputes about its role continued until the *parlement* of Paris was actually abolished in 1771, to the outrage of the privileged groups in society which considered it the defender of their special interests.

The division between the *parlements* and the king and his ministers continued to sharpen during the reign of Louis XVI, which began in 1774. Attempts by the enlightened finance minister Turgot to co-operate with the *parlements* and introduce reforms to alleviate the tax burden on the poor produced only short-term results. The national debt trebled between 1774 and 1787. Ironically, the one radical attempt to introduce an effective and equitable tax system led directly to the Revolution. Calonne, finance minister in 1786, tried to get his proposed tax approved by an **Assembly of Notables**, a device that had not been employed for more than a hundred years. His purpose was to bypass the *parlement*, which could be relied on to oppose any radical proposal. The attempt backfired. He lost his position, and the *parlement* ended up demanding a meeting of the **Estates-General**, representing the nobles, the clergy and the bourgeoisie, as being the only body competent to discuss such matters. The town responded by exiling and then recalling the *parlement* of Paris several times. As law and order began to break down, it gave in and agreed to summon the Estates-General on May 17, 1789.

REVOLUTION

Against a background of deepening economic crisis and general misery, exacerbated by the catastrophic harvest of 1788, controversy focused on how the **Estates-General** should be constituted. Should they meet separately as on the last occasion – in 1614? This was the solution favoured by the *parlement* of Paris, a measure of its reactionary nature: separate meetings would make it easy for the privileged, namely the clergy and nobility, to outvote the Third Estate, the bourgeoisie. The king ruled that they should hold a joint meeting, with the Third Estate represented by as many deputies as the other two Estates combined, but no decisions were made about the order of voting.

On June 17, 1789, the **Third Estate** seized the initiative and declared itself the National Assembly. Some of the lower clergy and liberal nobility joined them. Louis XVI appeared to accept the situation, and on July 9 the Assembly declared itself the National Constituent Assembly. However, the king then tried to intimidate it by calling in troops, which unleashed the anger of the people of Paris, the *sans-culottes* (literally, 'without trousers').

On July 14 the *sans-culottes* stormed the fortress of **the Bastille**, symbol of the oppressive nature of the *ancien régime*. Similar insurrections occurred throughout the country, accompanied by widespread peasant attacks on landowners' châteaux, and the destruction of records of debt and other symbols of their oppression. On the night of August 4 the Assembly abolished the feudal rights and privileges of the nobility – a momentous shift of gear in the revolutionary process, although in reality it did little to alter the situation. Later that month they adopted the **Declaration of the Rights of Man**. In December church lands were nationalised, and the pope retaliated by declaring the Revolutionary principles impious.

Bourgeois elements in the Assembly tried to bring about a compromise with the nobility, with a view to establishing a constitutional monarchy, but these overtures were rebuffed. Emigré aristocrats were already working to bring about foreign invasion to overthrow the Revolution. In June 1791 the king was arrested trying to escape from Paris. The Assembly, following an initiative of the wealthier bourgeois **Girondin** faction, decided to go to war to protect the Revolution.

On August 10, 1792, the *sans-culottes* set up a **revolutionary Commune** in Paris and imprisoned the king. The Revolution was taking a radical turn. A new National Convention was elected and met on the day the ill-prepared Revolutionary armies finally halted the Prussian invasion at Valmy. A major rift swiftly developed between the **Girondins** and the **Jacobins** and *sans-culottes* over the abolition of the monarchy. The radicals carried the day. In January 1793 Louis XVI was executed. By June the Girondins had been ousted.

Counter-revolutionary forces were gathering in the provinces and abroad. A Committee of Public Safety was set up as chief organ of the government. Left-wing popular pressure brought laws on general conscription and price controls, and a deliberate policy of de-Christianisation. **Robespierre** was pressed onto the Committee as the best man to contain the pressure from the streets.

The Terror began. As well as ordering the death of the hated Marie-Antoinette, Robespierre felt strong enough to guillotine his opponents on both right and left. But the effect of so many rolling heads was to cool people's faith in the Revolution; by mid-1794 Robespierre himself was arrested and executed, and his fall marked the end of radicalism. More conservative forces gained control of the government, decontrolled the economy, repressed popular risings, limited the suffrage, and established a five-man executive Directory (1795).

THE RISE OF NAPOLEON

In 1799 one **General Napoléon Bonaparte**, who had made a name for himself as commander of the Revolutionary armies in Italy and Egypt, returned to France and took power in a coup d'état. He was appointed First Consul, with power to choose officials and initiate legislation. He redesigned the tax system and created the Bank of France, replaced the power of local institutions by a corps of *préfets* answerable to himself, made judges into state functionaries – in short, laid the foundations of the modern French administrative system.

Though Napoléon upheld the fundamental reforms of the Revolution, the retrograde nature of his regime became more and more apparent with the proscription of the Jacobins, granting of amnesty to the emigrés and restoration of their unsold property, reintroduction of slavery in the colonies, recognition of the Church and so on. Although alarmingly revolutionary in the eyes of the rest of Europe, his Civil Code worked essentially to the advantage of the bourgeoisie. In 1804 he crowned himself **emperor** in the presence of the pope.

Decline, however, came only with military failure. After 1808, Spain, then under the rule of Napoléon's brother, rose in revolt, aided by the British. This signalled a turning of the tide in the long series of dazzling military successes. The nation began to grow weary of the burden of unceasing war.

In 1812 Napoléon threw himself into the **Russian campaign**, hoping to complete his European conquests. He reached Moscow but the long retreat in terrible winter conditions annihilated his veteran *Grande Armée*. By 1814 he was forced to abdicate by a coalition of European powers, who installed Louis XVIII, brother of the decapitated Louis XVI, as monarch. In a last effort to recapture power, Napoléon escaped from exile in Elba and reorganised his armies, only to meet final defeat at **Waterloo** on June 18, 1815. Louis XVIII was restored to power.

THE RESTORATION AND 1830 REVOLUTION

The years following Napoléon's downfall were marked by a determined campaign, including the **White Terror**, on the part of those reactionary elements who wanted to wipe out all trace of the Revolution and restore the *ancien régime*. **Louis XVIII** resisted these moves and was able to appoint a moderate royalist minister, Decazes, under whose leadership the liberal faction that wished to preserve the Revolutionary reforms made steady gains. This process, however, was wrecked by the assassination of the Duc de Berry in an attempt to wipe out the Bourbon family. In response to reactionary outrage, the king dismissed Decazes. An attempted liberal insurrection was crushed and the four Sergeants of La Rochelle were shot by firing squad. Censorship became more rigid and education was once more subjected to the authority of the Church.

In 1824 Louis was succeeded by the thoroughly reactionary **Charles X**, who pushed through a law indemnifying emigré aristocrats for property lost during the Revolution. When the opposition won a majority in the elections of 1830, the king dissolved the Chamber and restricted the already narrow suffrage.

Barricades went up in the streets of Paris. Charles X abdicated and parliament was persuaded to accept **Louis-Philippe**, Duc d'Orléans, as king. On the face of it, divine right had been superceded by popular sovereignty as the basis of political legitimacy. The **1814 Charter**, which upheld Revolutionary and Napoleonic reforms, was retained, censorship abolished, the tricolour restored as the national flag, and suffrage widened.

However, the **Citizen King**, as he was called, had somewhat more absolutist notions about being a monarch. In the 1830s his regime survived repeated challenges from both attempted coups by reactionaries and some serious labour unrest in Lyon and Paris. The 1840s were calmer under the ministry of Guizot, the first Protestant to hold high office. It was at this time that **Algeria** was colonised.

Guizot, however, was not popular. He resisted attempts to extend the vote to enfranchise the middle ranks of the bourgeoisie. In 1846 economic crisis brought bankruptcies, unemployment and food shortages. Conditions were appalling for the growing urban working class, whose hopes of a more just future received a theoretical basis in the **socialist writings** and activities of Blanqui, Fourier, Louis Blanc and Proudhon, among others.

When the government banned an opposition "banquet", the only permissible form of political meeting, in February 1848, workers and students took to the streets. When the army fired on a demonstration and killed forty people, civil war appeared imminent. The Citizen King fled to England.

THE SECOND REPUBLIC

A provisional government was set up and a **republic** proclaimed. The government issued a right-to-work declaration and set up national workshops to relieve unemployment. The vote was extended to all adult males – an unprecedented move for its time.

All was not plain sailing, though. By the time elections were held in April a new tax designed to ameliorate the financial crisis had antagonised the countryside. A massive conservative majority was re-elected, to the dismay of the radicals. Three days of bloody street fighting at the barricades followed, when General Cavaignac, who had distinguished himself in the suppression of Algerian resistance, turned the artillery on the workers. More than 1500 were killed and 12,000 arrested and exiled.

A reasonably democratic constitution was drawn up and elections called to choose a president. To everyone's surprise, Louis-Napoléon, nephew of the Emperor, romped home. In spite of his liberal reputation, he restricted the vote again, censored the press and pandered to the Catholic Church. In 1852, following a coup and further street fighting, he had himself proclaimed Emperor Napoléon III.

THE SECOND EMPIRE

Through the 1850s **Napoléon III** ran an authoritarian regime whose most notable achievement was a rapid growth in industrial and economic power. Foreign trade trebled, the railway system grew enormously, and the first investment banks were established. In 1858, in the aftermath of an attempt on his life by an Italian patriot, the emperor suddenly embarked on a policy of **liberalisation**, initially of the economy, which alienated much of the business class. Reforms included the right to form trade unions and to strike, an extension of public education, lifting of censorship, and the granting of ministerial "responsibility" under a government headed by the liberal opposition.

Disaster, however, was approaching on the diplomatic front. Involved in a conflict with Bismarck and the rising power of Germany, Napoléon III declared war. The French army was quickly defeated and the emperor himself taken prisoner in 1870. The result at home was a universal demand for the proclamation of a republic. The German armistice agreement insisted on the election of a national assembly to negotiate a proper peace treaty. France lost Alsace and Lorraine and was obliged to pay hefty war reparations.

Outraged by the monarchist majority re-elected to the new Assembly and by the attempt of its chief minister, Thiers, to disarm the National Guard, the people of Paris created their own municipal government known as **the Commune** (see *Paris* chapter).

THE THIRD REPUBLIC

In 1889 the collapse of a company set up to build the Panama Canal involved several members of the government in a corruption scandal, which was one factor in the dramatic **Socialist gains** in the elections of 1893. More importantly, the urban working class was becoming more class-conscious under the influence of the ideas of Karl Marx. The strength of the movement, however, was undermined by divisions, the chief one being Jules Guesde's Marxian Party. Among the independent Socialists was **Jean Jaurès**, who joined with Guesde in 1905 to found the **Parti Socialiste**. The trade union movement, unified in 1895 as the **Confédération Générale du Travail** (CGT), remained aloof in its anarcho-syndicalist preference for direct action.

In 1894 **Captain Dreyfus**, a Jewish army officer, was convicted by courtmartial of spying for the Germans and shipped off to the penal colony of Devil's Island for life. It soon became clear that he had been framed – by the army itself, yet they refused to reconsider his case.

The affair immediately became an issue between the Catholic right wing and the Republican left, with Jaurès, Émile Zola and Clemenceau coming out in favour of Dreyfus. Charles Maurras, founder of the facist *Action Française* – precursor of Europe's Blackshirts – took the part of the army.

Dreyfus was officially rehabilitated in 1904, his health ruined by penal servitude in the tropics. But in the wake of the affair the more radical element in the Republican movement had begun to dominate the administration, bringing the army under closer civilian control and dissolving most of the religious orders.

Although the country enjoyed a period of renewed prosperity in the years preceding World War I, there remained serious unresolved conflicts in the political fabric of French society. On the right were Maurras's lunatic fringe with its strong-arm *Camelots du Roi*, and on the left, the far bigger constituency of the working class – unrepresented in government. Although most workers now voted for it, the Socialist Party was not permitted to participate in bourgeois governments under the constitution of the Second International, to which it belonged. Several major strikes were brutally suppressed.

WORLD WAR I

With the outbreak of World War I in 1914, France found itself swiftly overrun by Germany and its allies, and defended by its old enemy, Britain. At home, the hitherto anti-militarist trade union and Socialist leaders (Jaurès was assassinated in 1914) rallied to the flag, and to the forces.

The **cost of the war** was even greater for France than for the other participants because it was fought largely on French soil. Over a quarter of the eight million men called up were either killed or crippled; industrial production fell to 60 percent of the pre-war level. This – along with memories of the Franco-Prussian war of 1870 – was the reason that the French were more aggressive than either the British or the Americans in seeking war reparations from the Germans.

In the **post-war struggle for recovery** the interests of the urban working class were again passed over, save for Clemenceau's eight-hour-day legislation in 1919. An attempted general strike in 1920 came to nothing, and the workers' strength was again undermined by the formation of new Catholic and Communist unions, and most of all by the irremediable split in the Socialist Party at the 1920 Congress of Tours. The pro-Lenin majority formed the **French Communist Party**, while the minority faction, under the leadership of Léon Blum, retained the old SFIO title. The bitterness caused by this split has bedevilled the French left ever since. Both parties resolutely stayed away from government.

As the **Depression** deepened in the 1930s and Nazi power across the Rhine became more menacing, fascist thuggery and anti-parliamentary activity increased in France, culminating in a pitched battle outside the Chamber of Deputies in February 1934. The effect of this fascist activism was to unite the left, including the Communists led by the Stalinist Maurice Thorez, in the **Front Populaire**. When they won the 1936 elections with a handsome majority in the Chamber, there followed a wave of strikes and factory sit-ins – a spontaneous expression of working-class determination to get their just desserts after a century and a half of frustration.

Frightened by the apparently revolutionary situation, the major employers signed the Matignon Agreement with Blum, which provided for wage increases, nationalisation of the armaments industry and partial nationalisation of the Bank of France, a forty-hour week, paid annual leave, and collective bargaining on wages. These **reforms** were pushed thorugh parliament, but when Blum tried to introduce exchange controls to check the flight of capital, the Senate threw the proposal out and he resigned. The left remained out of power, with the exception of coalition governments, until 1981. Most of the *Front Populaire*'s reforms were promptly undone.

WORLD WAR II

The agonies of **World War II** were compounded for France by the additional traumas of **occupation, collaboration and Resistance** – in effect, a civil war.

After the 1940 defeat of the Anglo-French forces in France, **Marshal Pétain**, a cautious and conservative veteran of World War I, emerged from retirement to sign an armistice with Hitler and head the collaborationist **Vichy government**, which ostensibly governed the southern part of the country, while the

Germans occupied the strategic north and the Atlantic coast. Pétain's prime minister, Laval, believed it his duty to adapt France to the new authoritarian age heralded by the Nazi conquest of Europe.

There has been endless controversy over who collaborated, how much and how far it was necessary in order to save France from even worse sufferings. One thing at least is clear: Nazi occupation provided a good opportunity for the Maurras breed of out-and-out French fascist to go on the rampage, tracking down Communists, Jews, Resistance fighters, Freemasons – indeed all those who, in their demonology, were considered "alien" bodies in French society.

While some Communists were involved in **the Resistance** right from the start, Hitler's attack on the Soviet Union in 1941 freed the remainder from ideological inhibitions and brought them into the movement on a large scale. Resistance numbers were further increased by young men taking to the hills to escape conscription as labour in Nazi industry. Général de Gaulle's radio appeal from London on June 18, 1940, rallied the French opposed to right-wing defeatism, and resulted in the *Conseil National de la Résistance*, unifying the different Resistance groups in May 1943. The man to whom this task had been entrusted was Jean Moulin, shortly to be captured by the Gestapo and tortured to death by Klaus Barbie, who was convicted in 1987 for his war crimes.

Although British and American governments found him irksome, **de Gaulle** was able to impose himself as the unchallenged spokesman of the Free French, leader of a government in exile, and to insist that the voice of France be heard as an equal in the Allied councils of war. Even the Communists accepted his leadership, though he was far from representing the kind of political interests with which they could sympathise.

Thanks, however, to his persistence, representatives of his provisional government moved into liberated areas of France behind the Allied advance after D-Day, thereby saving the country from what would certainly have been at least localised outbreaks of civil war. It was also thanks to his insistence that Free French units, notably General Leclerc's 2nd Armoured Division, were allowed to perform the psychologically vital role of being the first Allied troops to enter Paris, Strasbourg and other emotionally significant towns in France.

THE AFTERMATH OF WAR

France emerged from the war demoralised, bankrupt and bomb-wrecked. The only possible provisional government in the circumstances was de Gaulle's **Free French** and the *Conseil National de la Résistance*, which meant a coalition of left and right. As an opening move to deal with the shambles, coal mines, air transport and Renault cars were nationalised. But a new constitution was required and **elections**, in which French women voted for the first time, resulted in a large left majority in the new Constituent Assembly – which, however, soon fell to squabbling over the form of the new constitution. De Gaulle resigned in disgust. If he was hoping for a wave of popular sympathy, he didn't get it and retired to the country to sulk.

The constitution finally agreed on, with little enthusiasm in the country, was not much different from the discredited Third Republic. And the new **Fourth Republic** appropriately began its life with a series of short-lived coalitions. In the early days the foundations for welfare were laid, banks nationalised and trade union rights extended. With the exclusion of the Communists from the government in 1947, however, thanks to the Cold War and the carrot of American aid under the Marshall Plan, France found itself once more dominated by the right.

If the post-Liberation desire for political reform was quickly frustrated, the spirit that inspired it did bear fruit in other spheres. From being a rather backward and largely agricultural economy pre-war, France in the 1950s achieved enormous industrial **modernisation and expansion**, its growth rate even rivalling that of West Germany at times. In foreign policy France opted to remain in the US fold, but at the same time took the initiative in promoting closer **European integration**, first through the European Coal and Steel community and then, in 1957, through the creation of the European Economic Community (EC).

COLONIAL WARS

In its **colonial policy**, on the other hand, the Fourth Republic seemed firmly committed to nineteenth-century imperialism, despite the cosmetic reform of renaming the Empire the French Union.

On the surrender of Japan to the Allies in 1945, the north half of the French **Indochina** colony came under the control of Ho Chi Minh and his Communist Vietminh. Attempts to negotiate were bungled and there began an eight-year armed struggle which ended with French defeat at Dien Bien Phu and partition of the country at the Geneva Conference in 1954 – at which point the Americans took over in the south, with well-known consequences.

1954 was also the year in which the government decided to create an **independent nuclear arsenal** and got embroiled in the horrendous **Algerian war of liberation**. If you want to take a charitable view, you can say that the situation was complicated from the French viewpoint by the legal fiction that Algeria was a *département*, an integral part of France, that there were a million or so settlers or *pieds noirs* claiming to be French – and the fact that there was oil in the south. But by 1958 half a million troops, most of them conscripts, had been committed to the war, with all the attendant horrors of torture, massacre of civilian populations and so forth.

When it began to seem in 1958 that the government would take a more liberal line towards Algeria, the hard-line rightists among the settlers and in the army staged a putsch and threatened to declare war on France. Général de Gaulle, waiting in the wings to resume his mission to save France, let it be known that in its hour of need and with certain conditions – ie stronger powers for the president – the country might call upon his help. Thus, on June 1, 1958, the National Assembly voted him full powers for six months and the Fourth Republic came to an end.

DE GAULLE'S PRESIDENCY

As prime minister, then president of the **Fifth Republic** – with powers as much strengthened as he had wished – **de Gaulle** wheeled and dealed with the *pieds noirs* and Algerian rebels, while the war continued. In 1961 a General Salan staged a military revolt and set up the OAS (secret army) organisation to prevent a settlement. When his coup failed, his organisation made several attempts on de Gaulle's life – thereby strengthening the feeling on the mainland that it was time to be done with Algeria.

This feeling was reinforced by an episode in the same year – covered up and censored until the 1990s – when between seventy and two hundred French Algerians were killed by the police in Paris. This "secret massacre" began with a peaceful demonstration in protest against police powers to impose a curfew on any place in France frequented by North Africans. The police it seems went mad – shooting at crowds, batoning protestors and then throwing their bodies into the Seine. For weeks corpses were recovered but the French media remained silent.

Eventually in 1962 a referendum gave an overwhelming yes to **Algerian independence** and *pieds noirs* refugees flooded into France. Most of the rest of the French colonial empire had achieved independence by this time also, and the succeeding years were to see a resurgence of fascist and racist activity, both among the French "returnees" and the usual insular, anti-immigrant sectors.

De Gaulle's leadership was haughty and autocratic in style, more concerned with *gloire* and grandeur than the everyday problems of ordinary lives. His quirky strutting on the world stage greatly irritated France's partners. He blocked British entry to the EC, cultivated the friendship of the Germans, rebuked the US for its imperialist policies in Vietnam, withdrew from NATO, refused to sign a nuclear test ban treaty, and called for a "free Quebec". If this projection of French influence pleased some, the very narrowly won presidential election of 1965 (in which Mitterrand was his opponent) showed that a good half of French voters would not be sorry to see the last of the General.

MAY 1968

Notwithstanding a certain domestic discontent, the sudden explosion of **May 1968** took everyone by surprise. Beginning with protests against the paternalistic nature of the education system by students at the University of Nanterre, the movement of revolt rapidly spread to the Sorbonne and out into factories and offices.

On the night of May 10 barricades went up in the streets of the Quartier Latin in Paris and the CRS (riot police) responded by wading into everyone, including bystanders and Red Cross volunteers, with unbelievable ferocity. A

general strike followed, and within a week more than a million people were out, with numerous factory occupations and professionals joining in with journalists striking for freedom of expression, doctors setting up new radically organised practices and so forth.

Autogestion – workers' participation – was the dominant slogan. More than specific demands for reform, there was a general feeling that all French institutions needed overhauling: they were too rigid, too hierarchical and too elitist.

De Gaulle seemed to lose his nerve and on May 27 he vanished from the scene. It turned out he had gone to assure himself of the support of the commander of the French army of the Rhine. On his return he appealed to the nation to elect him as the only effective barrier against left-wing dictatorship, and dissolved parliament. The frightened silent majority voted massively in his favour.

Although there were few short-term radical changes (except in education), the shockwaves of May 1968 continued to be felt over the next two decades. Women's Liberation, ecology groups, a relaxing of the formality of French society, a lessening of authoritarianism – all these can be traced to the heady days of May.

AFTER DE GAULLE

Having petulantly staked his presidency on the outcome of yet another referendum (on a couple of constitutional amendments) and lost, de Gaulle once more took himself sulkily off to his country estate and retirement. He was succeeded as president by his business-orientated former Prime Minister, **Georges Pompidou**.

The new regime was devotedly capitalist, Pompidou hoping to eradicate the memory of '68 in the creation of wealth, property and competition. His visions, however, had little time to reach reality. Having survived an election in 1972, Pompidou died, suddenly. His successor – and the 1974 presidential election winner by a narrow margin over the socialist François Mitterrand – was the former finance minister **Valéry Giscard d'Estaing**.

Having announced that his aim was to make France "**an advanced liberal society**", Giscard opened his term of office with some spectacular media coups, inviting Parisian trash collectors to breakfast and visiting prisons in Lyon. But aside from reducing the voting age to 18 and liberalising divorce laws, the advanced liberal society did not make a lot of progress. In the wake of the 1974 oil crisis the government introduced economic austerity measures. Giscard fell out with his ambitious prime minister, **Jacques Chirac**, who set out to challenge the leadership with his own RPR Gaullist party. And in addition to his superior, monarchical style, Giscard further compromised his popularity by accepting diamonds from the (literally) child-eating emperor of Central Africa, Bokassa and by involvement in various other scandals.

The left seemed well placed to win the coming 1978 elections, when the fragile union between the Socialists and Communists cracked, the latter fearing their roles as the coalition's junior partners. The result was another right-wing victory, with Giscard able to form a new government, with the grudging support of the RPR. Law and order and immigrant controls were the dominant features of Giscard's second term.

THE POLITICAL PRESENT

In May 1981, people danced in the streets to celebrate the end of 23 years of right-wing rule – and the victory of François Mitterrand's Socialist Party. Five years later, the Socialists conclusively lost their majority in the *Assemblée Nationale* (parliament), while Le Pen's ultra-right *Front National* won a horrifying 35 seats. Mitterrand remained president while the autocratic mayor of Paris, Jacques Chirac, took over the reins of government. But the return of the right was not to last. Mitterrand won a second seven-year term as president in 1988 and his party just scraped through the parliamentary elections that followed.

Since then, as the recession has taken hold, most severely in 1990–91, the Socialists and Mitterrand have become deeply unpopular. The French public, in fact, seem to have lost faith in their rulers as a whole, and lost interest in the old political debates. Amid this political malaise, nationalism seems to be the only potent political force, and one mercilessly exploited by the *Front National* who – at the time of writing, in early-1992 – claim some thirty percent of the electorate.

THE PARTIES IN POWER: 1982–92

The **Socialists** began their first five years in power under the prime ministership of **Pierre Mauroy**. In his cabinet were four Communist ministers: an alliance reflected in the government commitments to expanded state control of industry, high taxation for the rich, support for liberation struggles around the world, and a public spending programme to raise the living standards of the least well-off. By 1984, however, the government had done a complete volte-face with **Laurent Fabius** presiding over a cabinet of centrist to conservative "socialist" ministers, clinging desperately to power.

The commitments had come to little. Attempts to bring private education under state control were defeated by mass protests in the streets; ministers were implicated in cover-ups and corruption; unemployment continued to rise. Any idea of peaceful and pro-ecological intent was dashed, as far as international opinion was concerned, by the French Secret Service's murder of a Greenpeace photographer on the Rainbow Warrior in New Zealand (see overpage).

There were sporadic achievements – in labour laws and women's rights, notably – but no cohesive and consistent socialist line. The Socialists' 1986 election slogan was "Help – the Right is coming back", a bizarrely self-fulfilling tactic that they defended on the grounds of humour. For the unemployed and the low paid, for immigrants and their families, for women wanting the choice of whether to have children, for the young, the old and all those attached to certain civil liberties, the return of the right was no laughing matter.

Throughout 1987 the chances of Mitterrand's winning the presidential election in 1988 seemed very slim. But **Chirac**'s economic policies of privatisation and monetary control failed to deliver the goods. Millions of first-time investors in "popular capitalism" lost all their money on Black Monday. Terrorists planted bombs in Paris and took French hostages in Lebanon. Unemployment steadily rose and Chirac made the fatal mistake of flirting with the extreme right. Several leading politicians of the centre-right, among them Simone Weil, a concentration-camp survivor, denounced Chirac's concessions to Le Pen, and a new alignment of the centre started to emerge. **Mitterrand**, the grand old man of politics, with decades of experience, played off all the groupings of the right in an all-but-flawless campaign, and won another mandate.

His party, however, did not fare so well in the parliamentary elections soon afterwards. The Socialists failed to achieve an absolute majority and Mitterrand's new prime minister, **Michel Rocard**, went for the centrist coalition, causing friction in the party grassroots for whom the Communists were still the natural partners. A bright note, however, was signalled by the FN's loss of all their seats – the consequence of an abandonment of proportional representaton.

Rocard's ensuing **austerity measures** upset traditional Socialist supporters in the

PARTIES AND POLITICIANS

ON THE LEFT

PS (Parti Socialist). The ruling Socialist party of **President François Mitterrand**. The current government is headed by **Edith Cresson**, France's first woman prime minister, a strong nationalist, and on the left of the party. Contenders for her job and the presidency include **Jacques Delors** (president of the European Commission), the social democrat **Michel Rocard** (prime minister 1988–91), and **Laurent Fabius** (leader of the party, opportunist, free of any socialist commitments, and prime minister 1984–86). Other notable figures in the PS include **Pierre Mauroy** (prime minister 1981–84) and **Bernard Tapie** (flamboyant millionaire industrialist, whose power base is in Marseille).

PCF (Parti Communist Français). The unreconstructed Communist party. Veteran leader **George Marchais** remains the general secretary, despite attempts to oust him by a reformist faction led by **Charles Fiterman**.

ON THE RIGHT

UDF (Union pour la Démocratie Française). Union of centre-right parties led by the aloof and aristocratic former president **Valéry Giscard d'Estaing** – who has his eye on the 1995 presidentials. The union includes **Raymond Barre** (prime minister under Giscard) and the current presidential hopeful **François Léotard** (culture minister in Chirac's government).

RPR (Rassemblement pour la République). Gaullist and conservative party, headed by **Jacques Chirac**, populist mayor of Paris and prime minister 1986–88. The party's future rivals to Chirac include **Michel Noir** (mayor of Lyon).

FN (Front National). Extreme right party, led by arch-racist **Jean-Marie Le Pen** and his even more unspeakable deputy, **Bruno Méguet**. FN *députés* in the 1986–88 parliament included members of the Moonies, publishers of Hitler's speeches, and an octogenarian who as Paris councillor in 1943 voted full powers for Pétain's Vichy regime.

---

public-service sector, and nurses, civil servants, teachers and the like were quick to take industrial action. Additionally, though Chirac's programmes were halted, they were not reversed.

The 1980s ended with the most absurd blow-out of public funds ever – the **Bicentennial celebrations of the French Revolution**. They symbolised a culture industry spinning mindlessly around the vacuum at the centre of the French vision for the future. And they highlighted the contrast between the unemployed and homeless begging on the streets and the limitless cash available for prestige projects.

In 1991, Mitterrand sacked Michel Rocard and appointed **Edith Cresson** as prime minister. Initially the French were happy to have their first woman prime minister, who promised to wage economic war against the Germans and the Japanese. The left, including the Communists, were pleased with Cresson's socialist credentials. But she soon began to turn a few heads, with her comments about special charters for illegal immigrants; her dismissal of the stock exchange as a waste of time; her description of the Japanese as yellow ants and British males as homosexual; and by attacks on her own ministers.

Cresson's worst move was to propose a tax on everyone's insurance contributions to pay for compensation to haemophiliacs infected with HIV. This has been one of the biggest scandals of the socialist regime, because three senior health officials – who have since been charged – and possibly some politicians, knew that the transfusion blood was contaminated. Socialists joined the opposition in voting out the bill, and Cresson has become the most unpopular prime minister in the history of the Fifth Republic.

In his eleventh year as president, **Mitterrand** has also hit an all-time low. His reputation for climbing back is formidable but few will bet on his chances in the 1995 presidential election. At the moment, it looks inevitable that the right will win the parliamentary elections of 1993. They will do so, however, on far fewer votes. Abstentionists are the biggest group in the French electorate. The media, that Mitterrand helped gain independence from tight government control, dismisses president and ministers as "the princes ruling over us". The *Bébette Show*, the French satirical-style TV programme, goes off the air for weeks at a time, because according to its creator, there's nothing in French politics worth satirising.

POLITICAL ISSUES

FOREIGN POLICY – AND SCANDAL

Throughout the post-war years, France has maintained an independent and nationalist-orientated **foreign policy**, staying outside NATO, and sustaining its own **nuclear arsenal**. For this, there has long been cross-party consensus, and indeed national pride.

The end of the Cold War looks unlikely to change matters. At the end of the 1980s Mitterrand said that France would finally sign the Nuclear Non-Proliferation Treaty, while giving the go-ahead for a new series of hydrogen warhead tests in the South Pacific. He has hosted international disarmament conferences in Paris while promising the French that their status as a nuclear power will not be threatened. The one concession since the demise of the Soviet Union has been to hint that France might scrap its plans to build new short-range missiles.

Through the late 1980s, however, France seems to have been re-assessing its defence role within Europe. Mitterrand made proposals for a **joint defence force**, first with Germany, then with Western Europe, and now with NATO and the US. These initiatives show France struggling to retain what it sees as its natural leading role in the new world order.

A similar pattern was evident during the **Gulf War**. In the months leading up to conflict, the French made considerable attempts to prevent war – notwithstanding their contribution to arming Saddam Hussain in the first place. But once diplomacy had failed, the small French military force under United States command did little for French prestige.

To the outside world, French international standing had already taken a fall through a series of incidents in the 1980s: most notably, the buying out of **hostages**, and the blocking of investigations into terrorist offences for the sake of trade with Libya and Iran. Mitterrand's failure to denounce the leaders straightaway in the attempted 1991 Soviet coup shocked foreign and domestic opinion alike.

A further scandal – and more questionable political judgement – was in store in January 1992, in the **George Habash** affair. The Palestinian leader was flown into Paris for medical treatment, apparently with government collusion, and then flown out to Tunis. Exactly why was inexplicable, as Habbash was wanted for questioning in France and elsewhere for various terrorist offences. A number of government officials resigned in the wake of the scandal, while Mitterrand, for his part, commented on his colleagues, "they're all mad".

OVERSEAS TERRITORIES

The French have de-colonised to a lesser extent than any of the former powers. They maintain strong links with – and exercise much influence over – most of the former colonies in North and West Africa, as exemplified by recent military forays into Chad and Zaire.

With France's remaining **overseas territories**, governments through the last two decades have said a resounding "No" to independence claims. When the Kanaks of **Nouvelle Calédonie** (New Caledonia, an island near New Zealand) rebelled against the direct, unelected rule by Paris, Mitterrand responded with "autonomy" measures which kept defence, foreign affairs, law and order, control of the television and education in the French governor's hands. Eventually, though, after a massacre by French settlers of indigenous tribe members in 1986, the situation proved too sensitive, and a referendum in 1988 committed France to granting independence in ten years' time.

Both the **New Zealand and Australian governments**, however, were warned to desist from their support for the islands' independence – to stop meddling in French internal affairs as Paris sees it. Both countries have taken strong stands against the nuclear tests at **Muroroa** and suffered from French economic muscle as a result. Meanwhile the subjugation of the Polynesian people to French interests, with slum dwellers surviving on subsistence while imported French goods decimate local economies, goes on and will no doubt continue, whether independence comes or not.

FRANCE AND EUROPE

As a founder member of the **European Community (EC)**, France sees itself very much at the centre – and very much in control – of developments. The single European market, the ERM (currency mechanism) and introduction of a single currency (the *Ecu*), and the future of the European parliament, are not the subject of great debate in France.

THE RAINBOW WARRIOR AFFAIR

For decades the French have been using heavy-arm tactics against Polynesian protesters to hide the human and environmental catastrophe their nuclear tests have been – and are still – causing in the South Pacific. It took a western death, though, to bring the issue to world attention.

This took place in July 1985, when French secret agents blew up the Greenpeace ship, the **Rainbow Warrior**, which was docked in Auckland harbour in preparation for direct action against the French military on Muroroa. A Greenpeace photographer was on board and died in the explosion. Paris attempted a cover-up but two of the agents were arrested by the New Zealand police and sentenced to ten years in jail. The French foreign minister was forced to resign but it was never clear how far up knowledge of the operation went.

Once the controversy died down, the French government procured a UN-sponsored compromise of a three-year confinement to the French island of Hao for the agents. On highly spurious medical grounds, both found their way back to Paris and freedom in 1988. When Auckland objected, France blocked New Zealand's exports to the EC and the UN again stepped in and made France pay £1.2m in compensation.

Then at the end of 1991, another agent in the operation was arrested in Switzerland, thanks to a forgotten Interpol alert still on the Swiss border guards' computers. This coincided with the final round of GATT talks on agricultural trade – in which France could make life very difficult for the embattled New Zealand government. Greenpeace is currently seeking an injunction against New Zealand's decision to drop the extradition demand.

Certainly, nobody seems able to imagine a loss of sovereignty – the issue that obsesses Britain. The thinking goes: the EC is our creation, with any luck the dreadful English will opt out; the technological and creative genius of the French, combined with German industriousness and efficiency will ensure prestige and prosperity for France, and parity with the remaining superpower.

It did not take long for the French to forget their worries of an expanded **Germany**, though Mitterrand tried to slow the pace of reunification. Relations with the Germans have steadily strengthened, precisely because Bonn, now Berlin, was bound to become the powerhouse of Europe. It is interesting that Mitterrand's photo-opportunities with Chancellor Kohl – inspecting troops, inspecting graves, scheming together against Westminster – have no effect whatsoever on the French psychosis about the Second World War. Yet politicians are still questioned about their war activities, and war-crimes trials continue to send tremors through the establishment.

Unlike Chancellor Kohl, Mitterrand has been cautious about recognising the newly emerging **Yugoslav and Soviet states**, and about the possible entry of East European countries to the EC. In this, he is responding to a deeply protectionist impulse in France. Meat imports from Poland, Hungary and Czechoslovakia were banned, after French farmers made their views known with barricades of manure and burning tyres. New immigration laws turned many long-term residents from Eastern Europe into illegal aliens. The close ties France once enjoyed with the countries of the old Soviet bloc have been severely strained.

THE ECONOMY

The ambitious left-wing programme of the 1981–84 Socialist government was scuppered by the massive flight of capital, by bureaucracy and by the opposition of half the country. When **Chirac** subsequently came to power, his **privatisation programme** went much further than reversing the preceding Socialists' nationalisations – banks that de Gaulle took into the public sector after 1945 were sold off along with Dassault, the aircraft manufacturer, and Elf-Aquitaine, the biggest French oil company.

Workers attempting to protect their jobs found themselves being hauled before the law, as Mrs Thatcher has done in Britain. The shock of Chirac's approach to the unions, which in France are mostly organised along political lines rather than by profession, galvanised the usually irreconcilably divided Communist CGT, Socialist CFDT and Catholic FO unions into finding common cause.

The return of the Socialists put an end to further privatisations – and an amnesty for trade unionists who had been prosecuted – but **Rocard** ruled out renationalisation. Public spending was again increased, but not enough to compensate for all the jobs already lost. Rocard's centrist programme provoked a wave of strikes, but lay-offs continued in the mines, shipyards, transport industry and the denationalised industries.

For all this action, **unemployment** never became a key issue in the 1980s. When Chirac came to power in 1986 the official figures stood at 2.4 million. During the election, the comedian Coluche had set up thousands of "*restaurants du coeur*" (restaurants of the heart) to hand out soup and food parcels to those living below the poverty line, many of them the long-term unemployed. But if Coluche hoped to bring a point home rather than simply mock the politicians, he failed.

Official unemployment figures are now approaching three million – ten percent of the workforce. For the first time, the decline of state and private industries, the crisis in agriculture and the numbers of people out of work, have become crucial issues for every politician. The 1991 round of autumn pay demands – always a time for major strikes and demonstrations – reached critical proportions. Days of general strikes brought major cities to a halt, demonstrating nurses received serious injuries from the police, and the farmers had ministers cancelling trips to the provinces for fear of literally getting shit thrown in their faces. On the whole public opinion was sympathetic, and the government caved in several times.

But overall, France has fared well over the last decade, far better than Britain, thanks to keeping rampant monetarism at bay. **Inflation**, down to zero in 1990, has not passed 4 percent. Interest rates and the budget deficit are still comparatively low. **State industries** are still subsidised, much to the disgust of British EC commissioners, and the standard of living is higher than in Britain. French **hospitals** have been offering British NHS patients operations like hip replacements with less than a week's wait. The **education** budget has outstripped defence spending for the first time ever – after successful strikes by lycée students in 1990. And, unlike in Britain, no one has suggested taking water, energy, transport and communications out of state control. These are seen as legitimate national assets, whose subsidy is an assertion of French pride. The railways, in particular, are second to none in Europe.

THE IMMIGRATION ISSUE

From the mid-1950s to the mid-1970s a labour shortage in the French cities led to massive recruitment campaigns for workers in North Africa, Portugal, Spain, Italy and Greece. People were promised housing, free medical care, trips home and well-paid jobs. When they arrived in France, however, these **immigrants** found themselves paid half of what their French co-workers earned, accommodated in prison-style hostels and sometimes poorer than they were at home. They had no vote, no automatic permit renewal, were subject to frequent racial abuse and assault and, until 1981, were forbidden to form their own associations.

The Socialist government lifted this ban, gave a ten-year automatic renewal for permits and even promised voting rights. Able to organise for the first time, immigrant workers staged protests at the racist basis of lay-offs in the major industries. The Front National responded with the age-old bogey of foreigners taking Frenchmen's jobs. The Gaullists joined in with the spectre of falling birth rates (a French obsession since 1945). Both benefited from these declarations in the 1986 elections.

Once in power, Chirac instituted a series of **anti-immigration laws**, so extreme that they sparked unprecedented alliances. The Archbishop of Lyon and the head of the Muslim Institute in Paris together condemned their injustice. Human rights groups, churches and trade unions joined immigrants' groups in saying that France was on its way to becoming a police state. Natality measures and the position of women immigrants brought French feminists into the battle. **SOS Racisme** was born, an anti-racist organisation appealing to young people, in particular to second- and third-generation immigrants.

Since returning to power, the Socialists have played electoral games with the immigration issue, reneged on the vote promise, and failed to tackle the social and economic deprivation of France's immigrant ghettoes.

To do otherwise is seen as a sure vote-loser. Recent polls have shown over two-thirds of the adult French population to be in favour of deporting legal immigrants for any criminal offence, or for being unemployed for over a year. Le Pen's proposals that immigrants have second-class citizenship, segregated education and separate social security, receive forty percent support.

This rampant racism has struck such a chord that politicians of right and left have jumped onto the bandwagon. The Socialist prime minister Edith Cresson said special planes should be chartered to deport illegal immigrants. Kofi Yamgname, the minister for integration and only black member of her cabinet, suggested that immigrants who maintained traditional habits should go home. On the right, Giscard has used the potent word "invasion" and said that citizenship should be based on blood ties, not on place of birth. Chirac has talked of the "noise and smell" of immigrants, and a UDF senator compared the four million immigrants in France to the German occupation.

All of which has boosted the confidence of Jean-Marie Le Pen, who will contest the regional seat of the Provence-Alpes-Côte d'Azur in March 1992. If he wins it, which is possible, then both the RPR and the UDF are likely to enter into electoral pacts. Mitterrand has increased the chances of right-wing deals by ordering a referendum on proportional representation. His Machiavellian motive is to increase the number of FN *députés* in the hope that rather than join forces with Le Pen, the more principled UDF and Gaullist members will help him form a new centrist coalition.

The fate of immigrants and their French descendants has never been so precarious. Fury and frustration at discrimination, assault, abuse and economic deprivation has erupted into battles on the street. At least three young blacks have died at the hands of the police while the right-wing media have revelled in images of violent Arab youths. A Gaullist mayor near Lyon got away with bulldozing a mosque while people were praying in it; refusing a building permit for a new one; cutting off water supplies to the temporary place of worship, then boasting that he'd managed to reduce the Muslim population by ten per cent. Other councils have required that in the building plans for mosques the minarets must be unobtrusive.

Attacking Islam has seemed reasonable to many people, including socialists and feminists, who otherwise are anti-racist. But the inherent contradiction may come to the crunch, if fundamentalists gain power in Algeria. At that point there will be a flood of entry applications from people fleeing the very horrors that have been used in France to justify denying rights to immigrants.

THE ENVIRONMENT

Environmentalists in France are responsible for defending the largest and most diverse country in Western Europe, with the highest number of mammal species (113), and of amphibious species (29); and the second highest number of bird species (342). Most of these amphibians, half the mammals and one-third of the bird species are considered "threatened".

Those threats include agriculture, and especially wetland drainage; acid and other forms of pollution; tourism; and, ultimately, the world's largest nuclear power programme outside of the USA. In 1990, when parliament had its first full debate on environmental issues, it was told that France was fifteen years behind other Western European countries in ecology consciousness.

GREEN POLITICS

Ten years ago, a French **ecology movement** hardly existed. Today green votes count. The Green Parties have a minister in government, and they may well poll more than the PCF at the next elections. They are a far from unified political force, however. On one side are *Les Verts*, a radical wing, led by Euro MP André Waechter, but with elements that are close to the Front National because of shared rural concerns. On the other is Brice Lalonde, minister for the environment, and his *Génération Écologie*.

Brice Lalonde joined Rocard's government in 1988 and his post was upgraded to cabinet level in 1991. He has made enormous compromises – most notably over the nuclear tests in Muroroa – but has also got a great deal done. For the first time, environmental groups around the country have been able to call upon the government, attract media coverage, and succeed in stopping damaging projects. A new local tax on waste has been agreed and further pollution taxes are on the political agenda.

The one area where the greens have been unable to make many inroads is **nuclear power**. The French nuclear industry is the second largest in the world, and the biggest in proportion to domestic energy needs. In fact nuclear-generated electricity is a major French export. Like Britain, France has a nuclear reprocessing plant – on the Cotentin peninsula in Normandy – that brings in a lot of money and discharges waste into the sea.

A halt to nuclear plant construction and increased investment in renewable sources was one of the Socialists' many broken promises from their 1981 manifesto. Things may be moving, however. In 1990, it was revealed that two nuclear waste dumps close to Paris, closed in the 1970s, were thirty times above the acceptable radioactivity levels, and, after initial denials, the Greens' demand for an independent inquiry was met. In 1991 the *Assemblée Nationale* discussed legislation on high-level nuclear waste disposal. This was the first time any aspect of nuclear energy policy had ever been put before parliament.

ENVIRONMENTAL ACTION

Since Brice Lalonde took up his post as environment minister, being green has become respectable and taking action no longer just an idealist gesture. Plans for a **dam** close to the source of the river **Loire**, which threatened wildlife and an outstanding beauty spot, were dropped after a two-year occupation of the site. In the battle against other smaller dams downstream, where the rare wildlife of the floodplains are at risk, one has so far been defeated, despite the powerful pressure of the Loire Development Agency, headed by the mayor of Tours. The mayor's ominous comment, conceding Lalonde's influence in the government, was that he would wait and sign the deal with the next administration.

Other victories have been the cancellation of a secret service project to build a listening station in the protected area of the **Carmargue**; and the halt to construction of a road tunnel through the Pyrenees that threatened one of the few remaining colonies of bears. In both cases Lalonde gave his support to long-standing local campaigns.

Lalonde has not been so effective when the ecological threats have been outside France. Soon after his appointment, on a visit to Australia, he announced that he no longer considered French nuclear tests a danger to the environment. "The situation on the **Muroroa** test site", he told the local press, "has considerably improved". Non-governmental Greens were astonished at the "miracle" of suddenly inoffensive nuclear tests. France has conducted over 160 atomic tests on Muroroa since 1966, fifty of them, prior to 1975, above ground. The Independent Commission on International Humanitarian Issues has reported increases in leukaemia, thyroid cancer and birth defects in the area.

The environment ministry has been silent about another French overseas exercise, well underway in 1991 when Mitterrand hosted a global environment conference in Paris. This is the construction of a giant dam in the rainforest of **French Guiana** to provide electricity for the Ariane rocket launch pad. Some 310 square kilometres of rainforest will be destroyed by flooding, and the rotting trees will poison rivers and produce a host of poisonous gases.

WETLANDS

In its disregard for wetlands, France is no different from any other country, but, at 140,000 hectares a year, the rate of field drainage is the highest in Europe. The World Wide Fund for Nature has been running a public awareness campaign and blames EC grants for the damage.

Wetlands are something of an acquired taste but not only are they often deliciously wild, they are also one of the most productive ecosystems in the world. Their loss would have a serious impact on the food chain and on fisheries and would completely destroy the potential of aquaculture. Almost all European reptiles and amphibians and 47 percent of all endangered and vulnerable European bird species are threatened by their destruction.

By the end of the 1970s France had lost ten percent of its wetlands, including the Marais des Echets near Lyons. The *Office de la Chasse* (Hunters' Organisation) now asseses the total damage at twenty-five wetlands of national importance seriously affected; eighty percent of the Landes marshes and forty percent of the coastal wetlands of Brittany are lost. A further 600,000 hectares are at risk from drainage schemes due for immediate implementation.

At least some of the wetlands now, thankfully, have protection. The remnants near Lyon are in the **Villars Les Dombes Nature Reserve**, a mere 23 hectares created in 1970 but better than nothing. This is a breeding ground for several rare species, including the black-necked grebe, whiskered tern and little egret. Just to the east, the **Marais du Bout du Lac d'Annecy Nature Reserve**, at the southern tip of the lake, is important for corncrake, water rail, garganey, teal, curlew and little bittern. Brittany, meanwhile, has the **Armorique Regional Park**, notable for a small colony of beavers, transported from the Rhône to a tributary of the River Aulne.

Moving south, other important protected wetlands include the **Golfe du Morbihan Nature Reserve**; the **Briere Regional Park** (one of the largest areas of marsh and lagoon in inland France, totalling 7,000 hectares); the **Baie de Bourgneuf**, like Morbihan very important for Brent geese; the **St-Denis-du-Payre**, between Nantes and La Rochelle; the **Pointe d'Arcay**; and the **Baie de l'Aiguillon**, where vast numbers of wildfowl stay over the winter, among them one of Europe's largest concentrations of avocet.

As for the **Camargue**, with over 300 bird species recorded, only the Coto Doñana of Spain and the Danube in Romania can rival it in Europe. Situated between the Petit and Grand Rhône, the marshes and lakes are under increasing threat, not merely from drainage but also from runoff of agricultural land. The Camargue harbours rare birds such as the gorgeous greater flamingo, bee-eaters and great spotted cuckoos; and bitterns, purple herons and egrets on its freshwater marshes. It is also important for the cultivation of rice, corn, wheat, and the rearing of the famous Camargue bulls and semi-wild white horses.

France does not have the protected area that it should in respect of its land area. It may be more than 16,000 square kilometres, as opposed to only 621 square kilometres in 1950, but that comes out to a mere 30 protected hectares per 1000 inhabitants. It's better than some countries, but when you consider that Norway manages 1138.3 hectares per 1000 inhabitants, it's hardly enough. Considering the state of French seawater, and the role wetlands play in filtering out pollutants, conservation is vital.

SEAS AND COASTLINES

The 1975 directive of the European Community requires designated **bathing beaches** to be tested every other week during the bathing season and sets a faecal coliform standard of 2,000 per 100 millilitres of water for 95 percent of samples. (The faecal coliform are a group of bacteria found in the human gastro-intestinal tract and therefore an indicator of the level of sewage pollution.) Many European beaches, including some in France (and the majority in Britain) were still failing this test at the end of the 1980s. To put that into perspective, the US Environmental Protection Agency sets a standard ten times more stringent, and Canada is twenty times more strict. To be within the EC standard is hardly an endorsement for safe bathing and to exceed it is disgusting.

The French situation is, however, improving in at least some respects. Back in 1979, the 930 coastal communes had sewerage for seven million people but a summer population, including six million tourists, almost double that. In 1980, more than a third of seawater samples were failing to reach the EC standard. Since then, increased investment, particularly in tourist sites with preinstalled **sewerage** facilities, had put some 84 percent of samples into the two top EC categories by 1985. The bad news is that many of the holiday developments, though well provided with sewerage facilities, affect the environment in other ways, particularly, once again, by **land drainage**, as with the new resorts of Languedoc-Roussillon.

Pollution in the Mediterranean and the action of too many boats has affected the long **underwater grasses** on which many fish breed. Jacques Cousteau brought public attention to the problem, now far less acute off the French coast than the Spanish,

MOUNTAINS

Parallel to the shameful tourist destruction of the coast, the winter damage in the mountains by skiers and **ski development** has been equally severe. The 1992 Winter Olympics in Albertville has been a monumental environmental disaster from which, scientists are saying, the area will never recover. Elsewhere the ugliness of many "third-generation" ski resorts has repelled even the holidaymakers themselves and created a "fourth-generation" attempt to capture the charm of traditional mountain villages married to the mechanical excellence of high-technology lift systems.

The notion that every French person should be able to enjoy a winter holiday in France has resulted in six million French skiers, all of whom seem to be either on the piste on peak weekends or jamming the roads that lead to them. The planners say that only a crash programme of resort construction could have fed the extensive lift network of the **Tarentaise** that has become the attraction for foreign skiers. Environmentalists argue that over-rapid development has upset the natural water level in lakes and streams, damaged wildlife through noise, pollution and habitat destruction, and — through tree clearance — increased the likelihood of avalanches and mudslides. In 1981, sixty people died as a result of a landslide in Les Arcs.

The *tétras-lyre* or black grouse has been one of the **mountain bird species** most affected, while the larger capercaillie is already extinct in the French Alps. The problem for the black grouse is that, in winter, it favours the same north-facing slopes, at 2000 metres, as the skiers. The black grouse lookouts are also prime locations for mountain restaurants and lift stations, while birds not driven to death through exposure are frequently decapitated in mist by the ski-lift cables. Even breeding is affected, since predators attracted by ski station rubbish often turn their attention to black grouse eggs — as studies at Les Arcs have proved. Jacques Perrier, a *garde-moniteur* in the Parc National de la Vanoise, which the ski terrain of Les Arcs adjoins, describes the tétras-lyre as an indicator. "When the *tétras-lyre* is gone", he says, "people, too, will be finished." If present trends continue, the black grouse does not have long.

A bird that could make a tentative comeback in the Alps is the *gypaéte-barbu* or **lammergeier**. A pair of these magnificent vultures, with their distinctive pinky-gold chest feathers and wedge-shaped tails, was reintroduced in Haute Savoie in 1987. Wiped out by hunting in the Alps, the lammergeier retained a foothold in the Pyrenees where eight pairs are known to breed in and round the Parc National des Pyrénées. The relative remoteness of the Pyrenees has also allowed 45 pairs of *vautours fauves* or **griffon vultures** to survive there.

The **hunting** that wiped out vast numbers of these spectacular but now protected species continues to decimate many smaller, lower-profile species. The hunting lobby in France is well organised and represents around two million people. According to the Royal Society for the Protection of Birds, about one in seven migrant birds passing the Mediterranean are killed every year, by shooting, netting, trapping and bird liming as well as by natural hazards. That amounts to 900 million migrants, and the French play their part with their key passes over the Alps and, as at **Col d'Orgambideska**, in the Pyrenees. It was there that a group of conservationists rented the pass to keep the shooters out. The main victim in the Pyrenees is the pigeon, which crosses the range in October – up to 20,000 of them falling victim to traps each year.

Despite the claims hunters make for their role in preserving species (so that they can continue to hunt them), it was undeniably hunting that severely reduced numbers of chamois, almost caused the extinction of *bouqetin* (ibex), and seriously depleted the brown bear in the Pyrenees.

The creation of the national parks has saved the **chamois**, which became a source of food for the Resistance during World War II, but the appearance of the eye disease *kératoconjonctivite*, especially among the closely related isards of the Pyrenees, is a new source of concern. The much larger **bouquetin**, with its imposing ridged and back-curved horns, was reduced to just 60 individuals through hunting and had to be reintroduced into France, and particularly into the Vanoise, from the Gran Paradiso National Park in Italy. *Bouquetin* now number some 700 in the Vanoise and chamois round 4000. A policy of re-introduction has also helped the **castor** (beaver), down to less than a hundred in the Rhône Valley at the end of the last century, but now numbered in the thousands.

Sadly, re-introduction is unlikely to prove either acceptable or practical in the case of **l'ours brun**. Estimates are that only between fifteen and twenty brown bears survive in the Pyrenees, scarcely a viable population. The French outdoor magazine *AlpiRando* suggests that the distribution could be nine to eleven bears on the slopes of the Aspe and Ossau valleys, three to five round the *cirque* of Lescun, three to five in Haut-Luchonnais near Andorra and perhaps one to three in Ariége and the Pyrénées-Orientales. In 1982 President Mitterrand announced that the bear must be saved, but his funds have been insufficient to hold back logging and ski station construction that is destroying the remaining habitat.

FORESTS

France's upland forests are also taking the brunt of the **acid rain** attack. The country has 13.6 million hectares (33.6 million acres) of forest but remained complacent until 1984, when the realisation that at least one-third of deposition came from foreign sources, and that the damage was real and costly, caused an about face. The monitoring programme set up in 1983 in the Vosges discovered that 35,000 hectares (86,000 acres) were affected, of which 5000 hectares (12,000 acres) were rated serious. By early 1985 one in five conifers were damaged.

Defoliation is now also reported in the forests of Alsace, the Jura, Alps, Massif Central and Pyrenees.

Paul Jenner and Christine Smith

ART

PAINTING

From the Middle Ages to the twentieth century, France has held – with occasional gaps – a leading position in the history of European painting, with Paris, above all, attracting artists from the whole continent. The story of French painting is one of richness and complexity, partly due to this influx of foreign painters and partly due to the capital's stability as an artistic centre.

BEGINNINGS

In the late Middle Ages, the itinerant life of the nobles led them to prefer small and transportable works of art; splendidly **illuminated manuscripts** were much praised and the best painters, usually trained in Paris, continued to work on a small scale until the fifteenth century. In spite of the size of the illuminated image, painters made startling steps towards a realistic interpretation of the world, and in the exploration of new subject matters.

Many of these illuminators were also panel painters, foremost of whom was **Jean Fouquet** (c.1420–c.1481), born in Tours in the Loire valley and the central artistic personality of fifteenth-century France. Court painter to Charles VIII, Fouquet drew from both Flemish and Italian sources, utilising the new fluid oil technique that had been perfected in Flanders, and concerning himself with the problem of representing space convincingly, much like his Italian

contemporaries. Through this he moulded a distinct personal style, combining richness of surface with broad, generalised forms and, in his feeling for volume and ordered geometric shapes, laying down principles that became intrinsic to French art for centuries to come, from Poussin to Seurat and Cézanne.

Two other fifteenth-century French artists deserve brief mention here, principally for the broad range of artistic expression they embody. **Emguerrand Quarton** (c.1410–c.1466) was the most famous Provençal painter of the time; his art, profoundly religious in subject as well as feeling, already shows the impact of the Mediterranean sun in the strong light that pervades his paintings. His *Pietà* in the Louvre is both stark and intensely poignant, while the *Coronation of the Virgin* that hangs at Villeneuve-Lès-Avignon is a vast panoramic vision not only of heaven but also of a very real earth, in what ranks as one of the first city/landscapes in the history of French painting: Avignon itself is faithfully depicted and the Mont Ste-Victoire, later to be made famous by Cézanne, is recognisable in the distance.

The **Master of Moulins**, active in the 1480s and 1490s, was noticeably more northern in temperament, painting both religious altarpieces and portraits commissioned by members of the royal family or the fast-increasing bourgeoisie.

MANNERISM & ITALIAN INFLUENCE

At the end of the fifteenth and the beginning of the sixteenth centuries, the French invasion of Italy brought both artists and patrons into closer contact with the Italian Renaissance.

The most famous of the artists who were lured to France was **Leonardo da Vinci**, spending the last three years of his life (1516–19) at the court of François I. From the Loire valley, which until then had been his favourite residence, the French king moved nearer to Paris, where he had several palaces decorated. Italian artists were once again called upon and two of them, **Rosso** and **Primaticcio**, who arrived in France in 1530 and 1532, were to shape the artistic scene in France for the rest of the sixteenth century.

Both artists introduced to France the latest Italian style, **Mannerism**, a sometimes anarchic derivation of the High Renaissance of Michelangelo and Raphael. Mannerism, with its emphasis on the fantastic, the luxurious and the large-scale decorative was eminently compatible with the taste of the court, and it was first put to the test in the revamping of the old château of Fountainebleau.

There, a horde of French painters headed by the two Italians came to form what was subsequently called the **School of Fontainebleau**. Most French artists worked at Fontainebleau at some point in their career, or were influenced by its homogeneous style, but none stands out as a personality of any stature, and for the most part the painting of the time was dull and fanciful in the extreme.

Antoine Caron (c.1520–c.1600), who often worked for Catherine de Médicis, the widow of Henry II, contrived complicated allegorical paintings in which elongated figures are arranged within wide, theatre-like scenery packed with ancient monuments and Roman statues. Even the Wars of Religion, raging in the 1550s and 1560s, failed to rouse French artists' sense of drama, and representations of the many massacres then going on were detached and fussy in tone.

Portraiture tended to be more inventive. The portraits of **Jean Clouet** (c.1485–1541) and his son **François** (c.1510–72), both official painters to François I, combined sensitivity in the rendering of the sitter's features with a keen sense of abstract design in the arrangement of the figure, conveying with great clarity social status and giving clues to the sitter's profession. Though influenced by sixteenth-century Italian and Flemish portraits, their work remains nonetheless very French in its general sobriety.

THE SEVENTEENTH CENTURY

In the seventeenth century Italy continued to be a source of inspiration for French artists, most of whom were drawn to Rome, at that time the most exciting artistic centre in Europe. There, two Italian artists especially dominated the scene in the first decade of the century: Michelangelo Merisi da Caravaggio and Annibale Carracci.

Caravaggio (d. 1610) often chose low-life subjects and treated them with remarkable realism, a realism that he extended to traditional religious subject matter and that he enhanced by using a strong, harsh lighting technique. Although he had to flee Rome in great haste under sentence of murder in 1606,

Caravaggio had already had a profound effect on the art of the age, both in terms of subjects and in his uncompromising use of realism.

Some French painters like **Moise Valentin** (c.1594–1632) worked in Rome and were directly influenced by Caravaggio; others, such as the great painter from Lorraine, **Georges de la Tour** (1593–1652), benefitted from his innovations at one remove, gaining inspiration from the Utrecht *Caravaggisti* who were active at the time in Holland. Starting with a descriptive realism in which naturalistic detail made for a varied painted surface, La Tour gradually simplified both forms and surfaces, producing deeply felt religious paintings in which figures appear to be carved out of the surrounding gloom by the magical light of a candle. Sadly, his output was very small – just some forty or so works in all.

Low-life subjects and attention to naturalistic detail were also important aspects of the work of the **Le Nain Brothers**, especially **Louis** (1593–1648), who depicted with great sympathy, but never with sentimentality, the condition of the peasantry. He chose moments of inactivity or repose within the lives of the peasants and his paintings achieve timelessness and monumentality by their very stillness.

The other Italian artist of influence, the Bolognese **Annibale Carracci** (d. 1609), impressed French painters not only with his skill as a decorator but, more tellingly, with his ordered, balanced landscapes, which were to prove of prime importance for the development of the classical landscape in general, and in particular for those painted by **Claude Lorrain** (1600–82).

Claude, who started life as a pastry cook, was born in Lorraine, near Nancy. He left France for Italy to practise his trade and worked in the household of a landscape painter in Rome, somehow persuading his master, who painted landscapes in the classical manner of Carracci, to let him abandon pastry for painting. Later he travelled to Naples, where the beauty of the harbour and bay made a lasting impression on him, the golden light of the southern port, and of Rome and its surrounding countryside, providing him with endless subjects of study which he drew, sketched and painted for the rest of his life. Claude's landscapes are airy compositions in which religious or mythological figures are lost within an idealised, Arcadian nature, bathed in a luminous, transparent light that, golden or silvery, lends a tranquil mood.

Landscapes, harsher and even more ordered, but also recalling the Arcadian mood of antiquity, were painted by the other French painter who elected to make Rome his home, **Nicolas Poussin** (1593–1665). Like Claude, Poussin selected his themes from the rich sources of Greek, Roman and Christian myths and stories, but unlike Claude, his figures are not subdued by nature but rather dominate it, in the tradition of the masters of the High Renaissance, such as Raphael and Titian, whom he greatly admired. During the working out of a painting Poussin would make small models, arrange them on an improvised stage and then sketch the puppet scene – which may explain why his figures often have a still, frozen quality. Poussin only briefly returned to Paris, called by the king, Louis XIII, to undertake some large decorative works quite unsuited to his style or character. Back in Rome he refined a style that became increasingly classical and severe.

Many other artists visited Italy but most returned to France, the luckiest to be employed at the court to boost the royal images of Louis XIII and XIV and the egos of their respective ministers, Richelieu and Colbert. **Simon Vouet** (1590–1649), **Charles Le Brun** (1619–90) and **Pierre Mignard** (1612–95) all performed that task with skill, often using ancient history and mythology to suggest flattering comparisons with the reigning monarch.

The official aspect of their works was paralleled by the creation of the new **Academy of Painting and Sculpture** in 1648, an institution that dominated the arts in France for the next few hundred years, if only by the way artists reacted against it. **Philippe de Champaigne** (1602–74), a painter of Flemish origin, alone stands out at the time as remotely different, removed from the intrigues and pleasures of the court and instead strongly influenced by the teaching and moral code of Jansenism, a purist and severe form of the Catholic faith. The apparent simplicity and starkness of his portraits hides an unusually perceptive understanding of his sitters' personalities. But it was the more courtly, fun-loving portraits and paintings by such artists as Mignard which were to influence most of the art of the following century.

THE EARLY EIGHTEENTH CENTURY

The semi-official art encouraged by the foundation of the Academy became more frivolous and lighthearted in the eighteenth century. The court at Versailles lost its attractions, and many patrons now were to be found among the hedonistic bourgeoisie and aristocracy living in Paris. History painting, as opposed to genre scenes or portraiture, retained its position of prestige, but at the same time the various categories began to merge and many artists tried their hands at landscape, genre, history, or decorative works, bringing aspects of one type into another. **Salons**, at which painters exhibited their works, were held with increasing frequency and bred a new phenomenon in the art world – the art critic. The philosopher **Diderot** was one of the first of these arbiters of taste, doers and undoers of reputations.

Possibly the most complex personality of the eighteenth century was **Jean-Antoine Watteau** (1684–1721). Primarily a superb draughtsman, Watteau's use of soft and yet rich, light colours showed how much he was struck by the great seventeenth-century Flemish painter Rubens. The open air scenes of flirtatious love painted by Rubens and by the eighteenth-century Venetian, Giorgione, provided Watteau with precedents for his own subtle depictions of dreamy couples (sometimes depictions from characters from the Italian Comedy) strolling in delicate, mythical landscapes. In some of these *Fêtes Galantes* and in pictures of solitary musicians or actors (*Gilles*), Watteau conveyed a mood of melancholy, loneliness and poignancy that was largely lacking in the works of his many imitators and followers (Nicolas Lancret, J. B. Pater).

The work of **François Boucher** (1703–70) was probably more representative of the eighteenth century: the pleasure-seeking court of Louis XV found the lightness of morals and colours in his paintings immensely congenial. Boucher's virtuosity is seen at its best in his paintings of women, always rosy, young and fantasy-erotic.

Jean-Honoré Fragonard (1732–1806) continued this exploration of licentious themes but with an exuberance, a richness of colour and a vitality (*The Swing*) that was a feast for the eyes and raised the subject to a glorification of love. Far more restrained were the paintings of **Jean-Baptiste-Siméon**

Chardin (1699–1779), who specialised in homely genre scenes and still lifes, painted with a simplicity that belied a complex use of colours, shapes and space to promote a mood of stillness and tranquility. **Jean-Baptiste Greuze** (1725–1805) chose stories that anticipated reaction against the laxity of the times; the moral, at times sentimental, character of his paintings was all-pervasive, reinforced by a stage-like composition well suited to cautionary tales.

NEOCLASSICISM

This new seriousness became more severe with the rise of **neoclassicism**, a movement for which purity and simplicity were essential components of the systematic depiction of edifying stories from the classical authors. Roman history and legends were the most popular subjects, and though **Jacques-Louis David** (1748–1825), a pupil of an earlier exponent of neoclassicism, J. M. Vien, conformed to that to a certain extent, he was different in that he was also keenly sensitive to the changing mood and philosophies of his time, and to the reaction against frivolity and self-indulgence. Many of his paintings are reflections of Republican ideals and of contemporary history, from the *Death of Marat* to events from the life of Napoléon who was his patron. For the emperor and his family, David painted some of his most successful portraits – *Madame Recamier* is not only an exquisite example of David's controlled use of shapes and space and his debt to antique Rome, but can also be seen as a paradigm of neoclassicism.

Two painters, **Jean-Antoine Gros** (1771–1835) and **Baron Gérard** (1770–1837), followed David closely in style and in themes (portraits, Napoleonic history and legend) but often with a touch of softness and heroic poetry that pointed the way to Romanticism.

Jean-August-Dominique Ingres (1780–1867) was a pupil of David; he also studied in Rome before coming back to Paris to develop the purity of line that was the essential and characteristic element of his art. His effective use of it to build up forms and bind compositions can be admired in conjunction with his recurrent theme of female nudes bathing, or in his magnificent and stately portraits that depict the nuances of social status.

ROMANTICISM

Completely opposed to the stress on drawing advocated by Ingres, two artists created, through their emphasis on colour, form and composition, pictures that look forward to the later part of the nineteenth century and the Impressionists. **Théodore Géricault** (1791–1824), whose short life was still dominated by the heroic vision of the Napoleonic era, explored dramatic themes of human suffering in such paintings as *The Raft of Medusa*, while his close contemporary, **Eugène Delacroix** (1798–1863), epitomised the **Romantic movement**, its search for emotions and its love of nature, power and change.

Delacroix was deeply aware of tradition, and his art was influenced, visually and conceptually, by the great masters of the Renaissance and the seventeenth and eighteenth centuries. In many ways he may be regarded as the last great religious and decorative French painter, but through his technical virtuosity, freedom of brushwork and richness of colours, he can also be seen as the essential forerunner of the Impressionists. For Delacroix there was no conflict between colour and design: David and Ingres saw these elements as separate aspects of creation, but Delacroix used colours as the basis and structure of his designs. His technical freedom was partly due to his admiration for two English painters, John Constable and his close friend, Richard Parkes Bonington, with whom he shared a studio for a few months. Bonington especially had a freshness of approach to colour and a free handling of paint, both of which had a strong impact on Delacroix. His numerous themes ranged from intimate female nudes, often with mysterious and erotic Middle Eastern overtones, to studies of animals and hunting scenes. Ancient and contemporary history supplied him with some of his most harrowing and dramatic paintings: *The Massacre at Chios* was based on an event that took place during the Greek War of Independence from the Turks, and *Liberty Guiding the People* was painted to commemorate the Revolution of 1830. Both paintings were his personal response to contemporary events and the human tragedies they entailed.

Other painters working in the Romantic tradition were still haunted by the Napoleonic legends, as well as by North Africa (Algeria) and the Middle East, which had become better known to artists and patrons alike during the Napoleonic wars. These were the subjects of paintings by **Horace Vernet** (1789–1863), **Jean-Louis-Ernest Meissonier** (1815–91) and **Théodore Chassériau** (1819–56).

Among their contemporaries was **Honoré Daumier** (1808–79): very much an isolated figure, influenced by the boldness of approach of caricaturists, he was content to depict everyday subjects such as a laundress or a third-class railway car – caustic commentaries on professions and politics that work as brilliant observations of the times.

THE NINETEENTH CENTURY

Some painters of the first part of the nineteenth century were fascinated by other themes. Nature, in its true state, unadorned by conventions, became a subject for study, and running parallel to this was the realisation that painting could be the visual externalisation of the artist's own emotions and feelings. These two aspects, which until this time had only been very tentatively touched upon, were now more fully explored and led directly to the innovations of the Impressionists and later painters.

Jean-Baptiste-Camille Corot (1796–1875) started to paint landscapes that were fresh, direct and influenced as much by the unpretentious and realistic country scenes of seventeenth-century Holland as by the balanced compositions of Claude. His loving and attentive studies of nature were much admired by later artists, including Monet.

At the same time a whole group of painters developed similar attitudes to landscape and nature. Helped greatly by the practical improvement of being able to buy oil paint in tubes rather than as unmixed pigments, they – known as the **Barbizon School** after the village on the outskirts of Paris round which they painted – soon discovered the joy and excitement of *plein-air* (open-air) painting.

Théodore Rousseau (1812–67) was their nominal leader, his paintings of forest undergrowth and forest clearings displaying an intimacy that came from the immediacy of the image. **Charles-François Daubigny** (1817–78), like Rousseau, often infused a sense of drama into his landscapes.

Jean-François Millet is perhaps the best-known associate of the Barbizon group, though he was more interested in the human figure than simple nature. Landscapes, however, were essential settings for his figures; indeed, his most famous pictures are those exploring the place of people in nature and their struggle to survive. *The Sower*, for instance, was a typical Millet theme, suggesting the heroic working life of the peasant. As is so often the case for painters touching on new themes or on ideas that are uncomfortable to the rich and powerful, Millet enjoyed little success during his lifetime, and his art was only widely recognised after his death.

The moralistic and romantic undertone in Millet's work was something that **Gustave Courbet** (1819–77) strove to avoid. Courbet was a socialist and his frank, outspoken attitude led to his being accused of taking part in the destruction of the column in place Vendôme in Paris after the outbreak of the Commune and, eventually, to his exile. After an initial resounding success in the Salon exhibition of 1849, he endured constant criticism from the academic world and patrons alike: scenes of ordinary life, such as the *Funeral at Orléans*, which he often chose to depict, were regarded as unsavoury and deliberately ugly.

But Courbet had a deep admiration for the old masters, especially for Rembrandt and the Spanish painters of the seventeenth and eighteenth centuries, and his link with tradition was probably one of the underlying themes of his large masterpiece, *The Studio*, which was emphatically rejected by the jury of the 1855 Exposition Universelle, and in which Courbet portrayed himself, surrounded by his model, his friends, colleagues and admirers, among them the poet Baudelaire. Courbet subsequently decided to hold a private exhibition of some forty of his works, writing at the same time a manifesto explaining his intentions of being true to his vision of the world and of creating "living art". Writing the word **Realism** in large letters on the door leading to the exhibition, he stated his intentions and gave a label to his art.

IMPRESSIONISM

Like Courbet, **Edouard Manet** (1832–83) was strongly influenced by Spanish painters, whose works had become more easily accessible to artists when a large collection belonging to the Orléans family was confiscated by the state in 1848. Unlike Courbet, though, he never saw himself as a socialist or indeed as a rebel or avant-garde painter, yet his technique and interpretation of themes was quite new and shocked as many people as it inspired. Manet used bold contrasts of light and very dark colours, giving his paintings a forcefulness that critics often took for a lack of sophistication. And his detractors saw much to decry in his reworking of an old subject originally treated by the sixteenth-century Venetian painter, Giorgione, *Le Déjeuner sur l'herbe*. Manet's version was shocking because he placed naked and dressed figures together, and because the men were dressed in the costume of the day, implying a pleasure party too specifically contemporary to be "respectable".

Manet was not interested in painting moral lessons, however, and some of his most successful pictures are reflections of ordinary life in bars and public places, where respectability, as understood by the late-nineteenth-century bourgeoisie, was certainly lacking. To Manet, painting was to be enjoyed for its own sake and not as a tool for moral instruction – in itself an outlook on the role of art that was quite new, not to say revolutionary, and marked a definite break with the paintings of the past. With Manet the basis of our present expectations and understanding of modern art was set.

Although it is doubtful whether Manet either wanted or expected to assume the role of leader, **Claude Monet** (1840–1926) looked to the older artist as the painter in whose works the principles of **Impressionism** were first formulated. Born in Le Havre, Monet came in contact with **Eugène Boudin** (1824–98) whose colourful beach scenes anticipated the way the Impressionists approached colour. He then went to Paris to study under Charles Gleyre, a respected teacher in whose studio he met many of the people with whom he formulated his ideas. Monet soon discovered that, for him, light and the way in which it builds up forms and creates an infinity of colours was the element that governed all representations. Under the impact of Manet's bright hues and his unconventional attitude, "art for art's sake", Monet soon began using pure colours side by side, blended together to create areas of brightness and shade.

In 1874, a group of some thirty artists exhibited together for the first time. Among them were some of the best-known names of this period of French art: Dégas, Monet, Renoir, Pissarro. One of Monet's paintings was entitled *Impression: Sun Rising*, a title that was singled out by the critics to ridicule the colourful, loose, and unacademic style of these young artists. Overnight they became, derisively, the 'Impressionists'.

Camille Pissarro (1830–1903) was slightly older than most of them and seems to have played the part of an encouraging father-figure, always keenly aware of any new development or new talent. Not a great innovator himself, Pissarro was a very gifted artist whose use of Impressionist technique was supplemented by a lyrical feeling for nature and its seasonal changes. But it was really with **Monet** that Impressionist theory ran its full course: he studied endlessly the impact of light on objects and the way in which it reveals colours. To understand this phenomenon better, Monet painted the same motif again and again under different conditions of light, at different times of the day, and in different seasons, producing whole series of paintings such as *Hay Stacks*, *Poplars* and, much later, his *Waterlilies*. In the late 1870s and the early 1880s many other artists helped formulate the new style, but few remained true to its principles for very long.

Auguste Renoir (1841–1919), who started life as a painter of porcelain, was swept away by Monet's ideas for a while, but soon felt the need to look again at the old masters and to emphasise the importance of drawing to the detriment of colour. Renoir regarded the representation of the female nude as the most taxing and rewarding subject that an artist could tackle. Like Boucher in the eighteenth century, Renoir's nudes are luscious, but they are rarely, if ever, erotic. They have a healthy, uncomplicated quality that was, in his later paintings, to become cloyingly, almost overpoweringly, sickly and sweet. Better were his portraits of women fully clothed, both for their obvious and innate sympathy and for their keen sense of design.

Edgar Degas (1834–1917) was yet another artist who, although he exhibited with the Impressionists, did not follow their precepts very closely. The son of a rich banker, he was trained in the tradition of Ingres: design and drawing were an integral part of his art, and whereas Monet was fascinated mainly by light, Degas wanted to express movement in all its forms. His pictures are vivid expressions of the body in action, usually straining under fairly exacting circumstances – dancers and circus *artistes* were among his favourite subjects, as well as more mundane depictions of laundresses and other working women.

Like so many artists of the day, Degas had his imagination fired by the discovery of **Japanese prints**, which could for the first time be seen in quantity. These provided him with new ideas of composition, not least in their asymmetry of design and the use of large areas of unbroken colour. **Photography**, too, had an impact, if only because it finally liberated artists from the task of producing accurate, exacting descriptions of the world.

Degas's extraordinary gift as a draughtsman was matched only by that of the Provençal aristocrat **Henri de Toulouse-Lautrec** (1864–1901). Toulouse-Lautrec, who had broken both his legs as a child, was unusually small, a physical deformity that made him particularly sensitive to free and vivacious movements. A great admirer of Degas, he chose similar themes: people in cafés and theatres, working women and variety dancers all figured large in his work. But unlike Degas, Toulouse-Lautrec looked at more than the body, and his work is scattered with social comment, sometimes sardonic and bitter. In his portrayal of Paris prostitutes, there is sympathy and kindness, and to study them better he lived in a brothel, revealing in his paintings the weariness and sometimes gentleness of these women.

POST-IMPRESSIONISM

Though a rather vague term, as it's difficult to date exactly when the backlash against Impressionism took place, **Post-Impressionism** represents in many ways a return to more formal concepts of painting – in composition, in attitudes to subject, and in drawing.

Paul Cézanne (1839–1906), for one, associated only very briefly with the Impressionists and spent most of his working life in relative isolation, obsessed with rendering, as objectively as possible, the essence of form. He saw objects as basic shapes – cylinders, cones etc – and tried to give the painting a unity of texture that would force the spectator to view it not so much as representation of the world but rather as an entity in its own right, as an object as real and dense as the objects surrounding it. It was this striving for pictorial unity that led him to cover the entire surface of

the picture with small, equal brushstrokes which made no distinction between the textures of a tree, a house, or the sky.

The detached, unemotional way in which Cézanne painted was not unlike that of the seventeenth-century artist, Poussin, and he found a contemporary parallel in the work of **Georges Seurat**. Seurat (1859–91) was fascinated by current theories of light and colour, and he attempted to apply them in a systematic way, creating different shades and tones by placing tiny spots of pure colour side by side, which the eye could in turn fuse together to see the colours mixed out of their various components. This **pointillist** technique also had the effect of giving monumentality to everyday scenes of contemporary life.

While Cézanne, Seurat and, for that matter, the Impressionists, sought to represent the outside world objectively, several other artists – the **Symbolists** – were seeking a different kind of truth, through the subjective experience of fantasy and dreams. **Gustav Moreau** (1840–98) represented, in complex paintings, the intricate worlds of the romantic fairy tale, his visions expressed in a wealth of naturalistic details. The style of **Puvis de Chavannes** (1824–98) was more restrained and more obviously concerned with design and the decorative. And a third artist, **Odilon Redon** (1840–1916), produced some weird and visionary graphic work that especially intrigued Symbolist writers; his less frequent works in colour belong to the later part of his life.

The subjectivity of the Symbolists was of great importance to the art of **Paul Gauguin** (1843–1903). He started life as a stockbroker who collected Impressionist paintings, a Sunday artist who gave up his job in 1883 to dedicate himself to painting.

During his stay in Pont-Aven in Brittany, Gauguin worked with a number of artists who called themselves **the Nabis, Paul Serusier** and **Émile Bernard** among them; he began exploring ways of expressing concepts and emotions by means of large areas of colour and powerful forms, and developing a unique style that was heavily indebted to his knowledge of Japanese prints and of the tapestries and stained glass of medieval art. His search for the primitive expression of primitive emotions took him eventually to the South Sea islands and Tahiti, where he found some of his most inspiring subjects and painted some of his best-known canvases.

A similar derivation from Symbolist art and a wish to exteriorise emotions and ideas by means of strong colours, lines and shapes underlies the work of **Vincent Van Gogh** (1853–90), a Dutch painter who came to live in France. Like Gauguin, with whom he had an admiring but stormy friendship, Van Gogh started painting relatively late in life, lightening his palette in Paris under the influence of the Impressionists, and then heading south to Arles where, struck by the harshness of the Mediterranean light, he turned out such frantic expressionistic pieces as *The Reaper* and *Wheatfield with Crows*. In all his later pictures the paint is thickly laid on in increasingly abstract patterns that follow the shapes and tortuous paths of his deep inner melancholy.

Both Gauguin and Van Gogh saw objects and colours as means of representing ideas and subjective feelings. **Edouard Vuillard** (1868–1940) and **Pierre Bonnard** (1867–1947) combined this with Cézanne's insistence on unifying the surface and texture of the picture. The result was, in both cases, paintings of often intimate scenes in which figures and objects are blended together in a series of complicated patterns. In some of Vuillard's works, people dressed in checked material, for example, merge into the flowered wallpaper behind them, and in the paintings of Bonnard, the glowing design of the canvas itself is as important as what it's trying to represent.

THE TWENTIETH CENTURY

The twentieth century kicked off to a colourful start with the **Fauvist** exhibition of 1905, an appropriately anarchic beginning to a century which, in France above all, was to see radical changes in attitudes towards painting.

The painters who took part in the exhibition included, most influentially, **Henri Matisse** (1869–1954), **André Derain** (1880–1954), **Georges Rouault** (1871–1958) and **Albert Marquet** (1875–1947), and they were quickly nicknamed the Fauves (Wild Beasts) for their use of bright, wild colours that often bore no relation whatsoever to the reality of the object depicted. Skies were just as likely green as blue since, for the Fauves, colour was a way of composing, of structuring a picture, and not necessarily a reflection of real life.

Fauvism was just the beginning: the first decades of the twentieth century were times of intense excitement and artistic activity in Paris, and painters and sculptors from all over Europe flocked to the capital to take part in the liberation from conventional art that individuals and groups were gradually instigating.

Pablo Picasso (1881–1973) was one of the first, arriving here in 1900 from Spain and soon thereafter starting work on his first *Blue Period* paintings, which describe the sad and squalid life of intinerant actors in tones of blue. Later, while Matisse was experimenting with colours and their decorative potential, Picasso came under the sway of Cézanne and his organisation of forms into geometrical shapes. He also learned from 'primitive', and especially African, sculpture and out of these studies came a painting that heralded a definite new direction, not only for Picasso's own style, but for the whole of modern art – *Les Demoiselles d'Avignon*. Executed in 1907, this painting combined Cézanne's analysis of forms with the visual impact of African masks.

It was from this semi-abstract picture that Picasso went on to develop the theory of **Cubism**, inspiring artists such as **Georges Braque** (1882–1963) and **Juan Gris** (1887–1927), another Spaniard, and formulating a whole new movement. The Cubists' aim was to depict objects not so much as they saw them but rather as they knew them to be: a bottle, a guitar were shown from the front, from the side, and from the back as if the eye could take in all at once every facet and plane of the object. Braque and Picasso first analysed forms into these facets (analytical Cubism), then gradually reduced them to series of colours and shapes (synthetic Cubism), among which a few recognisable symbols such as letters, fragments of newspaper and numbers appeared. The complexity of different planes overlapping one another sometimes made the deciphering of Cubist paintings sometimes difficult, and the very last phase of Cubism tended increasingly towards abstraction.

Spin-offs of Cubism were many: such movements as **Orphism**, headed by **Robert Delaunay** (1885–1941), who experimented not with objects but with the colours of the spectrum; and **Futurism**, which evolved first in Italy, then in Paris, and explored movement and the bright new technology of the industrial age.

Fernand Léger (1881–1955), one of the main exponents of the so-called School of Paris, had also become acquainted with modern machinery during World War I, and he exploited his fascination with its smoothness and power to create geometric and monumental compositions of technical imagery that were indebted to both Cézanne and Cubism.

The war meanwhile had affected many artists: in Switzerland **Dada** was born out of the scorn artists felt for the petty bourgeois and nationalistic values that had led to the bloodshed, a nihilistic movement that sought to knock down all traditionally accepted ideas. It was best exemplified in the work of the Frenchman **Marcel Duchamp** (1887–1968), who selected ready-made, everyday objects and elevated them, without modification, to the rank of works of art by pulling them out of their ordinary context, or defaced such sacred cows as the Mona Lisa by decorating her with a moustache and an obscene caption.

Dada was also a literary movement, and through one of its main poets, André Breton, it led to the inception of **Surrealism**. It was the unconscious and its dark unchartered territories that interested the Surrealists: they derived much of their imagery from Freud and even experimented in words and images with free-association techniques.

Strangely enough, most of the "French" Surrealists were foreigners, primarily the German **Max Ernst** (1891–1976) and the Spaniards **Yves Tanguy** (1900–55) and **Salvador Dali** (1904-89). Mournful landscapes of weird, often terrifying images evoked the landscape of nightmares in often very precise details and with an anguish that went on to influence artists for years to come. Picasso, for instance, shocked by the massacre of the Spanish town of *Guernica* in 1936, drew greatly from Surrealism to produce the disquieting figures of his painting of the same name.

World War II put an end to the prominence of Paris as the artistic melting pot of Europe. Painters had rushed there at the beginning of the twentieth century and after World War I, contributing by their individuality, originality and different nationalities to the richness and constant renewal of artistic endeavour, but at the beginning of World War II they emigrated to the United States. And although many have since drifted back, artistic leadership has remained in New York. Still, desertion of Paris should not obscure the fact that over a span of some six centuries, French painters or painters trained in France produced some of the most significant monuments of European painting.

Ann Rook

ARCHITECTURE

In common with all former provinces of Rome, it is to that city's model of organised authority that France's official architecture has returned most readily. A number of substantial Roman building works survive. In Nîmes you can see the Maison Carrée and the Temple of Diana, one of four vaulted Roman temples in Europe. Gateways remain at Autun and Reims, and amphitheatres can be seen at Nîmes and Arles. The Pont du Gard aqueduct at Nîmes is still a magnificent and ageless monument of civil engineering.

CAROLINGIAN AND ROMANESQUE

The **Carolingian** dynasty of Charlemagne attempted a revival of the symbols of civilised authority by recourse to Roman or 'Romanesque' models. Of this era, practically nothing remains visible, though the motifs of arch and vault are carried on in their simplest forms; and the semicircular apse and the basilican plan of nave and aisles persists as the basis of the succeeding phases of Christian architecture. An interesting anomaly is the plan of the church of **St-Front** at Périgueux, a copy of St Mark's in Venice, brought by trading influence west along the Garonne in the early twelfth century.

Elsewhere development may be divided roughly north–south of the Loire. Southern **Romanesque** is naturally more Roman, with stone barrel vaults, aisleless naves and domes. **St-Trophime at Arles** (1150) has a porch directly derived from Roman models and, with the church at St-Gilles nearby, exhibits a delight in carved ornament peculiar to the south at this time. **Angoulême** Cathedral typifies the use of all these elements.

The south, too, was the readiest route for the introduction of new cultural developments, and it is here that the pointed arch and vault first appear – from Saracen sources – in churches such as **Notre-Dame at Avignon**, **Autun Cathedral**, and **Ste-Madeleine at Vézelay** (1089–1206), which contains the earliest pointed cross vault in France.

In the northern region the nave with aisles is more usual, together with the development of twin western towers to mask the end of the aisles. The **Abbaye-aux-Hommes** at Caen (1066–77) is typical. It contains the elements later developed as "Gothic", in piers, pillars, buttresses, arcades, ribbed vaults and spires. The best examples may be found in Normandy, and it is from here, with the introduction of the pointed arch from the south, that the Gothic style developed.

GOTHIC

The reasons behind the development of the **Gothic style** lie in the pursuit of sensations of the sublime; to achieve great height without apparently great weight would seem to imitate religious ambition. Its development in the north is partly due to the availability of good building stone and soft stone for carving, but perhaps more to the growth of royal aspiration and power based in the Île de France, which, allied with the papacy, stimulated the building of the great **cathedrals** of **Paris**, **Bourges**, **Chartres**, **Laon**, **Le Mans**, **Reims** and **Amiens** in the twelfth and thirteenth centuries.

The Gothic phase began with the building of the choir of the **abbey of St-Denis** near Paris in 1140 to run through to the end of the fifteenth century. Architecturally, it encompasses the development of wider, traceried windows of coloured glass, filling the wall spaces liberated by the refinement of vertical structure; the "rose" or wheel is an early and especially French feature in window tracery. The glass at Chartres shows better than anywhere the concerted architectural effect of these developments. Another distinctive element is the flying buttress outside the walls to resist the outward push of the vaulting.

In the south, as at Albi and Angers, the great churches are generally broader and simpler in plan and external appearance, with aisles often almost as high as the nave. Many secular buildings survive – some of the most notable the work of Viollet-le-Duc, the preeminent nineteenth-century restorer – and even whole towns, for example **Carcassone** and **Aigues Mortes; Avignon** has the **bridge** and the **papal palace.**

Castles, of necessity, lent themselves less to the disappearing walls of the Gothic style. The **Château de Pierre-fonds**, as restored by Viollet, may be taken as typical. The walls of many others disappeared by force, not whim, as gunpowder made them obsolete and a more settled and subjugated order led to the development of château-palaces, such as **Châteaudun** (1441) and **Blois**. The **Château de Josselin** in Brittany is a marvellous example of the smaller fortresses that became common towards the end of the Gothic period. A series of colonial settlements, the *bastides* of the English occupation, remain in the Dordogne region and are a refreshing antidote to triumphal French bombast.

RENAISSANCE

Quite early in the sixteenth century the influence of the new style of the Italian Renaissance began to appear. Coupled with the persistence of Gothic traditions and the necessity of steep roofs and tall chimneys in a French climate, it appears immediately "Frenchified" rather than in its pure imported form. The châteaux of kings and courtiers round Paris and in the Loire valley, such as **Blois, Chambord, Chenonceau and Fontainebleau**, exemplify this style.

There is a wholly un-Italian concentration of interest on the skyline and an elaboration of detail in the facades at the expense of the clear modelling of form. With the passing of time, however, the style became more purely classical.

The Louvre in Paris and the Château de Blois are notable examples of the developing **classicism**. The wing of the **Château de Blois** containing the famous staircase designed for François I in 1515 shows the beginning of an emphasis on horizontal lines and an overlay of Italian motifs on a basically Gothic form. The elevations, designed by **Mansart** in 1635,

though distinctively French, are just as typically classical.

The **Louvre** even more embodies the whole history of the classical style in France, having been worked over by all the grand names of French architecture from Lescot in the early sixteenth century, via François Mansart and Claude Perrault in the seventeenth, to the later years of the nineteenth century. A recent turning point is the controversial work of **I. M. Pei** to break the bonds of Rome with the power of his pyramid extension.

It is unfortunate that the Renaissance style in France is chiefly seen in such structures as the Louvre and Versailles, which because of their scale can scarcely be experienced as buildings. That this is the case is largely due to the developing despotism and concentration of power under Louis XIII and XIV. But there was a lighter side to this. François Mansart, at **Blois** and **Maisons Lafitte** (1640), shows a certain suavity and elegance, which appears again in the eighteenth century in the townhouses of the **Rococo** period, the generally reticent exteriors of which bely the vivacity and charm of the private life within.

On the other hand, **Claude Perrault** (1613–88), who designed the great colonnaded east front of the Louvre, gives an austere face to the official architecture of despotism, magnificent but far too imperial to be much enjoyed by common mortals. The high-pitched roofs, which had been almost universal until then, are replaced here by the classical balustrade and pediment, the style grand but cold and supremely secular. Art and architecture were at the time organised by boards and academies, and in the latter style and employment were strictly controlled by royal direction. Between 1643 and 1774 France was governed by two monarchs, who both ruled by the same maxim – absolute power. With such a limitation of ideas at the source of patronage, it is hardly surprising that there was a certain dullness to the era, at least in the acknowledged monuments of French architecture.

BAROQUE AND ROCOCO

In a similar way to the preceding century, the churches of the **seventeenth and eighteenth centuries** have a coldness quite different from the German and Flemish Baroque or the Italian. When the Renaissance style first appeared in the early sixteenth century there was no great need for new church building, the country being so well endowed from the Gothic centuries. **St-Étienne-du-Mont** (1517–1620) and **St-Eustache** (1532–89), both in Paris, show how old forms persisted with only an overlay of the new style.

It is with the Jesuits in the seventeenth century that the Church embraced the new style to combat the forces of rational disbelief. In Paris the churches of the **Sorbonne** (1653) and **Val-de-Grâce** (1645) exemplify this, as do a good number of other grandiose churches in the **Baroque** style, through **Les Invalides** at the end of the seventeenth century to the **Panthéon** of the late eighteenth century. Here is the Church triumphant rather than the State, but no more beguiling.

The architect of Les Invalides was **Jules Hardouin Mansart**, a product of the academy, who also greatly extended the palace of **Versailles** and so created the cinemascope view of France with that seemingly endless horizon of royalty. As an antidote to this pomposity, the **Petit Trianon** at Versailles is as refreshing now as it was to Louis XV, who had it built in 1762 as a place of escape for his mistress. And even more so is this true of that other pearl formed of the grit of boredom in the enclosed world of Versailles – **La Petite Ferme,** where Marie-Antoinette played at being a milkmaid, which epitomises the Arcadian and "picturesque" fantasy of the painters Boucher and Fragonard.

The lightness and charm that was undermining official grandeur with Arcadian fancies and rococo decoration was, however, snuffed out by the Revolution. There is no real Revolutionary architecture, as the necessity of order and authority soon asserted itself and an autocracy every bit as absolute returned with Napoléon, drawing on the old grand manner but with a stronger trace of the stern old Roman. One architect, **Claude Ledoux**, was highly original and influential, both in England and Germany. And the visionary millennialist **Boullée** could also be said to be a child of revolutionary times, though it is likely that such men were inspired as much by the rediscovered plainness of the Greek Doric order as by radical politics.

In Paris it was not the democratic Doric but the imperial Corinthian order that re-emerged triumphant in the church of the **Madeleine** (1806) and, with the **Arc de Triomphe** like some colossal paperweight, reimposed the authority of academic architecture, in contrast to the fancy dress architecture of contemporary Regency England.

THE NINETEENTH CENTURY

The restoration of legitimate monarchy after the **fall of Napoléon** stimulated a revival of interest in older Gothic and early Renaissance styles, which offered a symbol of dynastic reassurance not only to the state but also to the newly rich. So in the private and commercial architecture of the nineteenth century these earlier styles predominate – in mine-owners' villas and bankers' headquarters.

By the mid-nineteenth century, a neo-Baroque strain had established itself, a style exemplified by Charles Garnier's **Opéra** in Paris (1861–74), which, under the heading of Second Empire and with its associations of voluptuous good living, seductive painting and general "ooh-la-la", provides probably the most persistent image of France among the non-French – though you should avoid being blinded by Puritan distaste to the splendid spatial and decorative sensations that the style can arouse. Nineteenth-century French buildings are due for a reassessment and keener appreciation.

In addition to the correct, official classicism and the robust, exuberant and commercial Baroque, there is a third strand running through the nineteenth century that was ultimately more fruitful. The rational engineering approach, embodied in the official **School of Roads and Bridges** and invigorated by the teaching of Viollet-le-Duc who reinterpreted Gothic style as pure structure, led to the development of new structural techniques out of which "modern" architectural style was born. Iron was the first significant new material, often used in imitation of Gothic forms and destined to be developed as an individual architectural style in America. In the **Eiffel Tower** (1889) France set up a potent symbol of things to come.

A more significantly French development was in the use of reinforced concrete towards the end of the century, most notably by **Auguste Perret** whose 1903 apartment house at 25 rue Franklin, Paris 16^e, turns the concrete structure into a visible virtue and breaks with conventional facades. Changes in the patterns of work and travel were making the need for new urban planning very acute in such cities as Paris. Perret and other **modernists** were all for the high-rise buildings that were going to better the haphazard layouts in America by a rational integration to new street systems. Some of their designs for gigantic skyscraper avenues and suburban rings now look like totalitarian horror movie sets. But it was tradition, not charity, that blocked their projects at the time.

THE TWENTIETH CENTURY

The greatest proponent of the super New York scale, who also had genuine, if mistaken, concern for how people lived, was **Le Corbusier**, the most famous twentieth-century French architect. His stature may now appear diminished by the ascendancy of a blander style in concrete boxing, as well as by the significant technical and social failures of his buildings and his total disregard for historic streets and monuments.

But while his manifesto, *"Vers une architecture moderne"*, sounds like a call to arms for a new and revolutionary movement, Le Corbusier would be perhaps more fairly assessed as the original, inimitable and highly individual artist he undoubtedly was. You should try to see some of his work – there's the **Cité Radieuse** in Marseille and plenty in Paris – to make up your own mind about the man largely responsible for changing the face and form of buildings throughout the world.

One respect in which Paris at the turn of the century lagged behind London, Glasgow, Chicago and New York, was in **underground transport**. First proposed in the 1870s, it took twenty years of furious debate before the Paris *métro* was finally realised in 1900. The design of the entrances was as controversial as every other aspect of the system, but the first commission went to Hector Guimard, renowned for his variations on the then current fashion in style. The whirling metal railings, Art Nouveau lettering and bizarre antennae-like orange lamps were his creation.

Conservatives were less amused when it came to sites such as the Opéra: **Charles Garnier**, architect of that edifice, demanded classical marble and bronze porticoes for every station, and his line was followed, on a less grandiose scale, wherever the métro steps surfaced by a major monument. Thus Guimard was out of a job. Some of the early ones remain (**Place des Abbesses**, 18e, is one), as do some of the white-tiled interiors, replaced after World War II in central stations by bright paint with matching seats and display cases.

Art Nouveau designs also found their way on to buildings – the early department stores in Paris are the best example – but the new materials and simple geometry of the modern or International Style favoured the Art Deco look; again, you're most likely to come across them in the capital.

Skipping the miserable 1950s and 1960s buildings everywhere, France again becomes one of the most exciting patrons of international architecture in **present times**. The **Centre Beaubourg**, by **Renzo Piano and Richard Rogers**, derided, adored and visited by millions, maximises space by putting the service elements usually concealed in walls and floors on the outside. The visible ducts, cables and pipes are painted in accordance with the colour code of architectural plans. You might think the whole thing is a professional "in" joke, but Beaubourg is one of the great contemporary buildings in Western Europe – for its originality, popularity and practicality.

In **housing**, new styles and forms are to be seen in city suburbs and vacation resorts, many of them disastrous and visually unappealing but interesting to look at when you don't have to live there. The latest state-funded projects confirm French seriousness about innovative design – in Paris, the pyramid in the Louvre and the **Porte de la Villette** complex.

The latter also exemplifies a new move away from demolition to clever restoration, in this case nineteenth-century abbatoirs and market halls. Throughout the country you'll see far older period streets, medieval and Renaissance, that look as though they've never been touched. More often than not, the restoration has been carried out by the **Maisons de Compagnonage**, the old craft guilds which have maintained traditional building skills, handing them down as of old from master to apprentice (and never to women), in addition to taking on new industrial skills.

Above all, though, bear in mind the extent and variety of architecture in France and don't feel intimidated by the established sights. If the empty grandeur of the Loire châteaux is oppressive, there are numerous smaller country houses open to the public, and such municipal buildings as the **Hôtels de Ville** tend to offer some charm or amusement, even in the smallest towns.

It is also possible in France to experience whole towns as consistent places of architecture, not only Carcassonne and Aigues Mortes, Dinan and Nancy, but villages off the main roads in which time seems to have stopped long ago. And, besides, from any hotel bedroom, you can simply delight in what Le Corbusier called 'the magnificent play of forms seen in light', in the movement of morning sunlight over ordinary provincial tiles and chimneys.

Robin Salmon

BOOKS

Publishers are detailed below in the form of British Publisher/American Publisher, where both exist. Where books are published in one country only, UK or US follows the publisher's name.

Abbreviations: o/p (out of print); U.P. (University Press).

TRAVEL

Laurence Sterne *A Sentimental Journey Through France and Italy* (Oxford U.P., UK/US). By the author of *Tristram Shandy*, who, despite the title, never gets further than Versailles.

Robert Louis Stevenson *Travels with a Donkey* (Century/Biblio). Mile-by-mile account of Stevenson's twelve-day trek in the Haute Loire and Cévennes uplands with the donkey Modestine. Devotees of Stevenson's footpaths – and there are a surprising amount of both in France – might be interested in his first book, *Inland Voyage*, on the waterways of the north.

Henry James *A Little Tour in France* (Penguin, UK/US). **Tobias Smollett** *Travels through France and Italy* (Oxford U.P., UK/US). **Hilaire Belloc** *The Pyrenees* (o/p). **Stendhal** *Travels in the South of France* (John Calder/Riverrun). Four classics of literary travel in France – though none the most enticing of reads.

Rodney Gallop *A Book of the Basques* (1930, o/p). The classic study of Basque life before the twentieth century destroyed its particularity, by an English clergyman who learned Basque and adopted the country as his own.

Edwin Mullins *The Pilgrimage to Santiago* (Century/Taplinger, o/p). The main medieval pilgrim route to the shrine of Saint James (Santiago/Saint Jacques) began in Paris on rue St-Jacques. Mullins retraces the *Chemin* in this book, details the bizarre pilgrim industry that peaked in the twelfth to fifteenth centuries, and points you to the churches along the way. Fascinating stuff, treating architecture (rightfully) as social history.

Freda White *Three Rivers of France* (Faber, UK/US), *West of the Rhone* (o/p), *Ways of Aquitaine* (o/p). Freda White spent a great deal of time in France in the 1950s – before tourism came along to the backwater communities that were her interest. These are all evocative books, slipping in the history and culture painlessly, if not always too accurately.

Julian More *More about France: A Sentimental Journey* (Cape, UK). Entertaining tales of a lifetime's travel and sporadic residence, from the 1940s to the present, in Paris, Burgundy, Brittany, the Midi and Côte d'Azur.

Julian Green, *Paris* (Marion Boyars, UK). A collection of very personal sketches and impressions of the city, by an American who has lived all his life in Paris, writes in French, and is considered one of the great French writers of the century. Bilingual text.

HISTORY

THE MIDDLE AGES

J. H. Huizinga *The Waning of the Middle Ages* (Penguin/Doubleday). Primarily a study of the culture of the Burgundian and French courts – but a masterpiece that goes far beyond this, building up meticulous detail to recreate the whole life and the mentality of the fourteenth and fifteenth centuries.

Barbara Tuchman *A Distant Mirror* (Ballantine Books, UK/US, o/p). The history of the fourteenth century – plagues, wars, peasant uprisings and crusades – told through the life of a sympathetic French nobleman whose career takes him through England, Italy and Byzantium and finally ends in a Turkish prison.

Emmanuel Le Roy Ladurie *Montaillou* (Penguin/Random House). Village gossip of who's sleeping with whom, tales of trips to Spain and details of work, all extracted by the Inquisition from Cathar peasants of the eastern Pyrenees in the fourteenth century, and stored away until the last decade in the Vatican archives. Though academic and heavygoing in places, most of this book reads like a novel.

Natalie Zemon Davis*The Return of Martin Guerre* (Harvard U.P., UK/US). A vivid account of peasant life in the sixteenth century and a perplexing and titilating hoax in the Pyrenean village of Artigat. Even better than the movie.

REVOLUTIONS

Richard Cobb & Colin Jones (editors) *The French Revolution* (Simon and Schuster, UK/US). One of the best Bicentennial offerings with lots of pictures, texts of the time, and clear explanations by a host of historians.

Alfred Cobban *A History of Modern France* (3 vols: 1715–99, 1799–1871 and 1871–1962, Pelican, UK/US). Complete and very readable account of the main political, social and economic strands in French history from the death of Louis XIV to mid–de Gaulle.

Christopher Hibbert *The French Revolution* (Penguin/Morrow). Good, concise popular history of the period and events.

Karl Marx *On the Paris Commune* (Lawrence and Wishart/Beekman Publications). Rousing prose from Karl, along with a history of the commune by Engels.

Thomas Paine *The Rights of Man* (Penguin, UK/US). Written in 1791 in response to English conservatives' views on the situation in France, this reasoned and passionate tract expresses the ideas of both the American and French revolutions. It was immediately banned on publication, and its author charged with treason, but enough copies had crossed the Channel and been translated for Paine to be elected to the Convention by the people of Calais.

NINETEENTH AND TWENTIETH CENTURIES

Max Bloch *Strange Defeat* (Norton, US). Moving personal study of the reasons for France's defeat and subsequent caving-in to fascism. Found among the papers of this Sorbonne historian after his death at the hands of the Gestapo in 1942.

Alexander Worth *France 1940–55* (Beacon Press, US). Extremely good and emotionally engaged portrayal of the most taboo period in French history – the Occupation, followed by the Cold War and colonial struggle years in which the same political tensions and heart-searchings were at play.

Theodore Zeldin *France 1845–1945: 5 vols* (Oxford U.P., UK/US). Five thematic volumes on all matters French. All good reads.

SOCIETY AND POLITICS

John Ardagh *France Today* (Penguin/Simon & Schuster). Comprehensive overview, covering food, film education and holidays as well as politics and economics – from a social democrat and journalistic position.

Roland Barthes *Mythologies* (Paladin/Hill & Wang). Brilliant analysis of how the ideas, prejudices and contradictions of French thought and behaviour manifest themselves – in food, wine, travel guides and other cultural offerings.

Theodore Zeldin *The French* (Collins/Pantheon). A coffee-table book without the pictures, based on the author's extensive conversations with an extremely wide variety of people about money, sex, phobias, parents and everything else.

Paul Rambali *French Blues* (Heinemann/Trafalgar Square). Contemporary France – Minitel sex, structuralism, May '68, food, television and the rise of the Front National – experienced by a Londoner, already half-French, and gradually becoming a Parisian.

Claire Duchen *Feminism in France: from May '68 to Mitterrand* (Routledge, UK/US). Charts the evolution of the women's movement through to its mid-80s crisis, clarifying the divergent political stances and feminist theory that informs the various groups, and placing them in the wider French political context.

Eugen Weber *My France* (Harvard U.P., US/UK). A collection of essays, fascinating and offbeat, about numerous aspects of French culture and politics. Some prior knowledge of mainstream French history is needed to make the most of them.

ART

Edward Lucie-Smith *A Concise History of French Painting* (Thames & Hudson, UK/US) If you're after an art reference book, this will do as well as any . . . though there are of course hundreds of books on particular French art movements. (Thames and Hudson do useful introductions to Impressionism, Expressionism, Symbolism, etc).

FRANCE IN LITERATURE

Listed below is a highly selective recommendation of works – mostly novels – that are rooted in the various French regions, and which would make good holiday reading.

For an overview of France-inspired authors – both French and foreign – **John Ardagh's** *Writers' France* (Hamish Hamilton, UK) is highly recommended: a knowing, beautifully illustrated guide.

PARIS AND AROUND
Victor Hugo *Les Misérables*
Charles Dickens *A Tale of Two Cities*
Emile Zola *Nana*
Gustave Flaubert *A Sentimental Education*
George Orwell *Down and Out in Paris and London*
Georges Simenon Any *Maigret* thriller.
Henry Miller *Quiet Days in Clichy; Tropic of Cancer; Tropic of Capricorn*
Anais Nin *Journals 1917–1974*

CALAIS TO CHAMPAGNE
Wilfrid Owen, Siegfried Sassoon, Edmund Blunden Various editions of their war poems.
Emile Zola *Germinal*

ALSACE, FRANCHE-COMTÉ AND JURA
Stendhal *Scarlet and Black*
Colette *My Mother's House*
John Berger *Pig Earth*

THE LOIRE
Alain Fournier *Le Grand Meaulnes*
Marcel Proust *Remembrance of Things Past*
Rabelais *Gargantua and Pantagruel*
Zola *The Earth*
Georges Sand *The Devil's Pool*

CÔTE D'AZUR
Alexandre Dumas *The Count of Monte Cristo*
Françoise Sagan *Bonjour Tristesse*
Jean Anouilh *Point of Departure*

Katherine Mansfield *Selected Short Stories*
Colette *Collected Stories*
Graham Greene *Loser Takes All*
F. Scott Fitzgerald *Tender is the Night*

NORMANDY/BRITTANY
Gustave Flaubert *Madame Bovary*
Guy de Maupassant *Selected Short Stories*
Jean-Paul Sartre *La Nausée*
Colette *Ripening Seed*
Honoré de Balzac *Les Chouans*
Pierre Loti *Pêcheur d'Islande*

BURGUNDY
Gabriel Chevallier *Clochemerle*

ATLANTIC COAST
François Mauriac *Thérèse*

THE PYRENEES
Pierre Loti *Ramuntcho*

LANGUEDOC
Hannah Closs *High are the Mountains*

RHÔNE VALLEY AND PROVENCE
Marcel Pagnol *Jean de Florette; Manon des Sources*
Emile Zola *Fortune of the Rougons*
Fréderic Mistral *Mireille*
Alphonse Daudet *Letters from my Windmill; Tartarin de Tarascon and Tartarin of the Alps*
Lawrence Durrell *The Avignon Quintet*

WALKING/HIKING

Footpaths of Europe Series (16 titles; Robertson McCarta, UK). Route guides to most areas of France, covering the system of GR footpaths, and illustrated with 1:50,000 colour survey maps. These are English translations of the *Topo Guides des Sentiers de Grande Randonnée* (CNSGR, Paris), which are widely available in France and themselves not hard to follow with a working knowledge of French.

Cicerone Walking Guides (Cicerone/Hunter). Neat, durable guides, with detailed route descriptions. Titles include *Tour of Mont Blanc; Chamonix-Mont Blanc; Tour of the Oisans (GR54); French Alps (GR5); The Way of Saint James (GR65); Tour of the Queyras; The Pyrenean Trail (GR10); Walks and Climbs in the Pyrenees.* All of these have information for hikers at all levels, though serious climbers should see the same publisher's *Rock Climbs in the Verdon* and *Rock Climbs in the Pyrenees*.

West Col Guides: *Pyrenees West*, *Pyrenees East*, *Pyrenees Central* (West Col, UK). These are more serious guides than the Cicerone ventures – but good stuff if you're committed. They cover both hiking and climbing.

Georges Vernon *Haute Randonnée Pyrénées* (CAF, Paris). East-to-west description of the High Level route across the Pyrenees. Written in easy French.

OTHER SPECIALIST GUIDES

GAY

Gai Guide (Gai Pied, Paris). Dependable listings (in French) of gay and lesbian clubs, saunas, restaurants, places to listen to music, and pick-up spots throughout the country.

GREEN

Mary Davis *The Green Guide to France* (Green Print, UK). Definitely not the Michelin, this is a resource guide to French national parks and wildlife reserves, veggie restaurants, communes, communities and the like.

WORK

Mark Hempshell *Live and Work in France* (Vacation Work, UK). An invaluable guide for anyone considering residence or work in France; packed with ideas and advice on job hunting, bureaucracy, tax, health, etc.

Emplois d'Été en France (published in France; distributed in the UK by Vacation Work). Annual listings (in French) of thousands of summer jobs available in France.

FLOWERS

W. Lippert *Fleurs des Montagnes, Alpages et Forêts* (Miniguide Nathan Tout Terrain, Paris). Best palm-sized, colour guide if you want something to pack away with your gear in the mountains.

LANGUAGE

French can be a deceptively familiar language because of the number of words and structures it shares with English. Despite this it's far from easy, though the bare essentials are not difficult to master and can make all the difference. Even just saying *"Bonjour Madame/Monsieur"* and then gesticulating will usually get you a smile and helpful service.

People working in tourist offices, hotels, and so on, almost always speak English and tend to use it when you're struggling to speak French – be grateful not insulted.

FRENCH PRONUNCIATION

One easy rule to remember is that **consonants** at the ends of words are usually silent. *Pas plus tard* (not later) is thus pronounced pa-plu-tarr. But when the following word begins with a vowel, you run the two together: *pas après* (not after) becomes pazapre.

Vowels are the hardest sounds to get right. Roughly:

a	as in h**a**t	*i*	as in mach**i**ne
e	as in g**e**t	*o*	as in h**o**t
é	between g**e**t and g**a**te	*o, au*	as in **o**ver
è	between g**e**t and g**u**t	*ou*	as in f**oo**d
eu	like the **u** in h**u**rt	*u*	as in a pursed-lip version of **u**se

More awkward are the **combinations** in/im, en/em, an/am, on/om, un/um at the ends of words, or followed by consonants other than n or m. Again, roughly:

in/im	like the **an** in **an**xious	*on/om*	like the **don** in **Don**caster said by
an/am, en/em	like the **don** in **Don**caster when		someone with a heavy cold
	said with a nasal accent	*un/um*	like the **u** in **u**nderstand

Consonants are much as in English, except that: ch is always sh, c is s, h is silent, th is the same as t, ll is like the y in yes, w is v, and r is growled (or rolled).

LEARNING MATERIALS

Harrap's French Phrase Book
(Harrap/Prentice Hall). Good pocket reference – with useful contemporary phrases and a 5000-word dictionary of terms.

Mini French Dictionary (Harrap/Prentice Hall). French–English and English–French, plus a brief grammar and pronunciation guide.

Breakthrough French (Pan; book and two cassettes). Excellent teach-yourself course.

French and English Slang Dictionary
(Harrap); ***Dictionary of Modern Colloquial French*** (Routledge). Both volumes are a bit large to carry, but they are the key to all you ever wanted to understand.

A Vous La France; Franc Extra; Franc-Parler (BBC Publications; each has a book and two cassettes). BBC radio courses, running from beginners' to fairly advanced language.

A BRIEF GUIDE TO SPEAKING FRENCH

BASIC WORDS AND PHRASES

French nouns are divided into masculine and feminine. This causes difficulties with adjectives, whose endings have to change to suit the gender of the nouns they qualify. If you know some grammar, you will know what to do. If not, stick to the masculine form, which is the simplest – it's what we have done in this glossary.

today	aujourd'hui	that one	celà
yesterday	hier	open	ouvert
tomorrow	demain	closed	fermé
in the morning	le matin	big	grand
in the afternoon	l'après-midi	small	petit
in the evening	le soir	more	plus
now	maintenant	less	moins
later	plus tard	a little	un peu
at one o'clock	à une heure	a lot	beaucoup
at three o'clock	à trois heures	cheap	bon marché
at ten-thirty	à dix heures et demie	expensive	cher
at midday	à midi	good	bon
man	un homme	bad	mauvais
woman	une femme	hot	chaud
here	ici	cold	froid
there	là	with	avec
this one	ceci	without	sans

NUMBERS

1	un	11	onze	21	vingt-et-un	95	quatre-vingt-quinze
2	deux	12	douze	22	vingt-deux	100	cent
3	trois	13	treize	30	trente	101	cent-et-un
4	quatre	14	quatorze	40	quarante	200	deux cents
5	cinq	15	quinze	50	cinquante	300	trois cents
6	six	16	seize	60	soixante	500	cinq cents
7	sept	17	dix-sept	70	soixante-dix	1000	mille
8	huit	18	dix-huit	75	soixante-quinze	2000	deux milles
9	neuf	19	dix-neuf	80	quatre-vingts	5000	cinq milles
10	dix	20	vingt	90	quatre-vingt-dix	1,000,000	un million

DAYS AND DATES

January	janvier	November	novembre	August 1	le premier août
February	février	December	décembre	March 2	le deux mars
March	mars			July 14	le quatorze juillet
April	avril	Sunday	dimanche	November 23	le vingt-trois novembre
May	mai	Monday	lundi		
June	juin	Tuesday	mardi		
July	juillet	Wednesday	mercredi	1992	dix-neuf-cent-quatre-vingt-douze
August	août	Thursday	jeudi		
September	septembre	Friday	vendredi	1993	dix-neuf-cent-quatre-vingt-treize
October	octobre	Saturday	samedi		

TALKING TO PEOPLE

When addressing people you should always use *Monsieur* for a man, *Madame* for a woman, *Mademoiselle* for a girl. Plain *bonjour* by itself is not enough. This isn't as formal as it seems, and it has its uses when you've forgotten someone's name or want to attract someone's attention.

Excuse me	*Pardon*
Do you speak English?	*Vous parlez anglais?*
How do you say it in French?	*Comment ça se dit en Français?*
What's your name?	*Comment vous appelez-vous?*
My name is . . .	*Je m'appelle . . .*
I'm English/ Irish/Scottish Welsh/American/ Australian/ Canadian/ a New Zealander	*Je suis anglais[e]/ irlandais[e]/écossais[e]/ gallois[e]/américain[e]/ australien[ne]/ canadien[ne]/ néo-zélandais[e]*
yes	*oui*
no	*non*
I understand	*Je comprends*
I don't understand	*Je ne comprends pas*
Can you speak slower?	*S'il vous plaît, parlez moins vite*
OK/agreed	*d'accord*

please	*s'il vous plaît*
thank you	*merci*
hello	*bonjour*
goodbye	*au revoir*
good morning/ afternoon	*bonjour*
good evening	*bonsoir*
good night	*bonne nuit*
How are you?	*Comment allez-vous? / Ça va?*
Fine, thanks	*Très bien, merci*
I don't know	*Je ne sais pas*
Let's go	*Allons-y*
See you tomorrow	*A demain*
See you soon	*A bientôt*
Sorry	*Pardon, Madame/je m'excuse*
Leave me alone (aggressive)	*Fichez-moi la paix!*
Please help me	*Aidez-moi, s'il vous plaît*

FINDING THE WAY

bus	*autobus, bus, car*
bus station	*gare routière*
bus stop	*arrêt*
car	*voiture*
train/taxi/ferry	*train/taxi/ferry*
boat	*bâteau*
plane	*avion*
railway station	*gare*
platform	*quai*
What time does it leave?	*Il part à quelle heure ?*
What time does it arrive?	*Il arrive à quelle heure ?*
a ticket to . . .	*un billet pour . . .*
single ticket	*aller simple*
return ticket	*aller retour*
validate your ticket	*compostez votre billet*
valid for	*valable pour*
ticket office	*vente de billets*
how many kilometres ?	*combien de kilomètres ?*
how many hours ?	*combien d'heures ?*

hitchhiking	*autostop*
on foot	*à pied*
Where are you going?	*Vous allez où ?*
I'm going to . . .	*Je vais à . . .*
I want to get off at . . .	*Je voudrais descendre à . . .*
the road to . . .	*la route pour . . .*
near	*près/pas loin*
far	*loin*
left	*à gauche*
right	*à droite*
straight on	*tout droit*
on the other side of	*l'autre côté de*
on the corner of	*à l'angle de*
next to	*à côté de*
behind	*derrière*
in front of	*devant*
before	*avant*
after	*après*
under	*sous*
to cross	*traverser*
bridge	*pont*

QUESTIONS AND REQUESTS

The simplest way of asking a question is to start with *s'il vous plaît* (please), then name the thing you want in an interrogative tone of voice. For example:

Where is there a bakery?	*S'il vous plaît, la boulangerie?*
Which way is it to the Eiffel Tower?	*S'il vous plaît, la route pour la tour Eiffel?*

Similarly with requests:

We'd like a room for two	*S'il vous plaît, une chambre pour deux*
Can I have a kilo of oranges	*S'il vous plaît, un kilo d'oranges*

Question words

where?	*où?*	when?	*quand?*
how?	*comment?*	why?	*pourquoi?*
how many/ how much?	*combien?*	at what time?	*à quelle heure?*
		what is/which is?	*quel est?*

ACCOMMODATION

a room for one/two people	*une chambre pour une/deux personnes*	do laundry	*faire la lessive*
a double bed	*un lit double*	sheets	*draps*
a room with a shower	*une chambre avec douche*	blankets	*couvertures*
a room with a bath	*une chambre avec salle de bain*	quiet	*calme*
		noisy	*bruyant*
For one/two/three nights	*Pour une/deux/trois nuits*	hot water	*eau chaude*
Can I see it?	*Je peux la voir?*	cold water	*eau froide*
a room on the courtyard	*une chambre sur la cour*	Is breakfast included?	*Est-ce que le petit déjeuner est compris?*
a room over the street	*une chambre sur la rue*	I would like breakfast	*Je voudrais prendre le petit déjeuner*
first floor	*premier étage*	I don't want breakfast	*Je ne veux pas de petit déjeuner*
second floor	*deuxième étage*	Can we camp here?	*On peut camper ici ?*
with a view	*avec vue*	campsite	*un camping/terrain de camping*
key	*clef*	tent	*une tente*
to iron	*repasser*	tent space	*un emplacement*
		youth hostel	*auberge de jeunesse*

CARS

garage	*garage*	put air in the tyres	*gonfler les pneus*
service	*service*	battery	*batterie*
to park the car	*garer la voiture*	the battery is dead	*la batterie est morte*
car park	*un parking*	plugs	*bougies*
no parking	*défense de stationner/ stationnement interdit*	to break down	*tomber en panne*
		petrol can	*bidon*
petrol station	*poste d'essence*	insurance	*assurance*
petrol	*essence*	green card	*carte verte*
fill it up	*faire le plein*	traffic lights	*feux*
oil	*huile*	red light	*feu rouge*
air line	*ligne à air*	green light	*feu vert*

HEALTH MATTERS

doctor	*médecin*	stomach ache	*mal à l'estomac*
I don't feel well	*Je ne me sens pas bien*	period	*règles*
medicines	*médicaments*	pain	*douleur*
prescription	*ordonnance*	it hurts	*ça fait mal*
I feel sick	*Je suis malade*	chemist	*pharmacie*
I have a headache	*J'ai mal à la tête*	hospital	*hôpital*

OTHER NEEDS

bakery	*boulangerie*	bank	*banque*
food shop	*alimentation*	money	*argent*
supermarket	*supermarché*	toilets	*toilettes*
to eat	*manger*	police	*police*
to drink	*boire*	telephone	*téléphone*
camping gas	*camping gaz*	cinema	*cinéma*
tobacconist	*tabac*	theatre	*théâtre*
stamps	*timbres*	to reserve/book	*réserver*

FRENCH AND ARCHITECTURAL TERMS: A GLOSSARY

These are either terms you'll come across in the guide, or come up against on signs, maps etc, while travelling round. For food items see *Basics*.

ABBAYE abbey

AMBULATORY covered passage round the outer edge of a choir of a church

APSE semi-circular termination at the east end of a church

ASSEMBLÉE NATIONALE the French parliament

ARRONDISSEMENT district of a city

AUBERGE DE JEUNESSE (AJ) youth hostel

BAROQUE High Renaissance period of art and architecture, distinguished by extreme ornateness

BASTIDE medieval military settlement, constructed on a grid plan

BEAUX ARTS fine arts museum (and school)

CAR coach, bus

CAROLINGIAN dynasty (and art, sculpture, etc) named after Charlemagne; mid-eighth to early tenth century

CFDT Socialist trade union

CGT Communist trade union

CHASSE, CHASSE GARDÉE hunting grounds (beware)

CHÂTEAU mansion, country house, or castle

CHÂTEAU FORT castle

CHEMIN DE ST-JACQUES medieval pilgrim route to the shrine of St James at Santiago de Compostela in northwest Spain

CHEVET east end of a church

CIJ (*Centre d'Informations Jeunesse*) youth information centre

CLASSICAL architectural style incorporating Greek and Roman elements – pillars, domes, colonnades etc – at its height in France in the seventeenth century and revived, as **neo-classical**, in the nineteenth century

CLERESTORY upper story of a church, incorporating the windows

CLUNIAC monastic movement and hence its architecture, derived from the Benedictine monastery at Cluny (see p.394)

CODENE French CND

CONSIGNE left luggage

COUVENT convent, monastery

DÉGUSTATION tasting (wine or food)

DÉPARTEMENT county – more or less

DONJON castle keep

ÉGLISE church

ENTRÉE entrance

FERMETURE closing period

FLAMBOYANT florid form of Gothic (see below)

FN (Front National) fascist party led by Jean-Marie Le Pen

FO Catholic trade union

FOUILLES archaeological excavations

FRESCO wall painting – durable through application to wet plaster

GALLO-ROMAIN period of Roman occupation of Gaul (first to fourth century AD)

GARE station; **ROUTIÉRE** – bus station; **SNCF** – train station

GÎTE D'ÉTAPE basic hostel accommodation primarily for walkers

GOBELINS most famous tapestry manufacturers, based in Paris, its most renowned period being in the reign of Louis XIV (seventeenth century).

HALLES covered market

HLM publicly subsidised housing

HÔTEL a hotel, but also an aristocratic townhouse or mansion

HÔTEL DE VILLE town hall

JOURS FÉRIÉS public holidays

MAIRIE town hall

MARCHÉ market

MEROVINGIAN dynasty (and art, etc), ruling France and parts of Germany from sixth to mid-eighth centuries

NARTHEX entrance hall of church

NAVE main body of a church

PCF Communist party of France

PLACE square

PORTE gateway

PRESQU'ÎLE peninsula

PS Socialist party

PTT post office

QUARTIER district of a town

RELAIS ROUTIERS truckstop café-restaurants

RENAISSANCE art-architectural style developed in fifteenth-century Italy and imported to France in the sixteenth century by François I

RETABLE altarpiece

REZ DE CHAUSSÉE (RC) ground floor

RN (*Route Nationale*) main road

ROMANESQUE Early medieval architecture distinguished by squat, rounded forms and naive sculpture

RPR Gaullist party led by Jacques Chirac

SI (*Syndicat d'Initiative*) tourist information office; also known as *OT, OTSI* and *Maison du Tourisme*

SNCF French railways

SORTIE exit

STUCCO plaster used to embellish ceilings, etc.

TABAC bar or shop selling stamps, cigarettes, etc.

TOUR tower

TRANSEPT transverse arms of a church

TYMPANUM sculpted panel above a church door

UDF centre-right party headed by Giscard d'Estaing

VAUBAN Seventeenth-century military architect – his fortresses still stand all over France

VOUSSOIR sculpted rings in arch over church door

ZONE BLEUE restricted parking zone

ZONE PIÉTONNE pedestrian precinct

INDEX